Architecture

FROM PREHISTORY TO POSTMODERNITY

SECOND EDITION

Marvin Trachtenberg

EDITH KITZMILLER PROFESSOR OF FINE ARTS / INSTITUTE OF FINE ARTS
NEW YORK UNIVERSITY

Isabelle Hyman

PROFESSOR OF FINE ARTS / COLLEGE OF ARTS AND SCIENCES
NEW YORK UNIVERSITY

Harry N. Abrams, Inc.

PUBLISHERS

Architecture

FROM PREHISTORY TO POSTMODERNITY

SECOND EDITION

Project Manager: Katherine Rangoon Doyle
Editor: Holly Jennings
Designer: Judith Michael
Photo Editor: John K. Crowley

Endpapers: Bourges Cathedral. France. 1195–mid-13th century
Page 4: Gustave Eiffel. Eiffel Tower. Paris. 1887–89
Page 5: Temple of Apollo. Didyma, Turkey. c. 300 B.C.
Page 6 (top): Choir vaults, Tewksbury Cathedral. England. 14th century
Page 6 (bottom): Choir screen, St.-Étienne du Mont. Paris. 1545
Page 7 (top): August Perret. Interior, Le Raincy. Near Paris. 1922
Page 7 (bottom): Frank Lloyd Wright. The Solomon R. Guggenheim Museum. New York. 1956–59
(Addition built in 1990–92)
Photographs © by Marvin Trachtenberg

Library of Congress Cataloging-in-Publication Data

Trachtenberg, Marvin.
Architecture, from prehistory to postmodernity / Marvin Trachtenberg, Isabelle Hyman.–2nd ed.
p. cm.
Rev. ed. of: Architecture, from prehistory to post-modernism. 1986
Includes bibliographical references and index.
ISBN 0-8109-0607-4 (hc)
1. Architecture–History. I. Hyman, Isabelle. II. Trachtenberg, Marvin. Architecture,
from prehistory to post-modernism. III. Title.

NA200 .T7 2001
720'.9–dc21   2001022388

ISBN 0-13-091841-5 (Prentice Hall/hc)

Printed and bound in Italy
10 9 8 7 6 5 4 3 2 1

Harry N. Abrams, Inc.
100 Fifth Avenue
New York, N.Y. 10011
www.abramsbooks.com

Contents

PART THREE **The Renaissance and the Baroque**

PART FOUR **The Modern World**

Color Portfolio

Colorplate 1   Detail of trabeation, Stonehenge. Salisbury Plain, England. c. 2000 B.C.

OVERLEAF, LEFT:
Colorplate 2   Hypostyle Hall, Valley Temple of Khafre. Giza, Egypt. 2530 B.C.

OVERLEAF, RIGHT:
Colorplate 3   Papyrus half-columns, Funerary Complex of King Zoser. Saqqara, Egypt. c. 2750 B.C.

Colorplate 4
Cyclopean Wall. Tiryns, Greece. 13th century B.C.

Colorplate 5
Ishtar Gate (restored). Babylon. c. 575 B.C.
State Museum, Berlin

Colorplate 6   View from the east, Parthenon. Acropolis, Athens. c. 447–438 B.C.

RIGHT:
Colorplate 7
Detail of corner entablature,
Parthenon. Acropolis, Athens

FAR RIGHT:
Colorplate 8
Detail, Temple of Athena Nike.
Acropolis, Athens. c. 420 B.C.

BELOW:
Colorplate 9
Detail of south wall, Erechtheum.
Acropolis, Athens. c. 420 B.C.

BELOW, RIGHT:
Colorplate 10
Detail, Temple of Zeus Olympius.
Athens. c. 170 B.C.

Colorplate 13   Aqueduct, Pont du Gard. Nimes, France. Early 1st century A.D.

Colorplate 14   Apartment houses. Ostia. 2nd century A.D.

Colorplate 15   Minerva Medica. Rome. 3rd century A.D.

Colorplate 16   Colosseum, detail. Rome. 72–80 A.D.

Colorplate 17   Arch of Septimius Severus, detail.
Forum Romanum. Rome. 203 A.D.

Colorplate 18
S. Apollinare Nuovo.
Ravenna. 490 A.D.

Colorplate 19
Mausoleum of Galla Placidia.
Ravenna. c. 425 A.D.

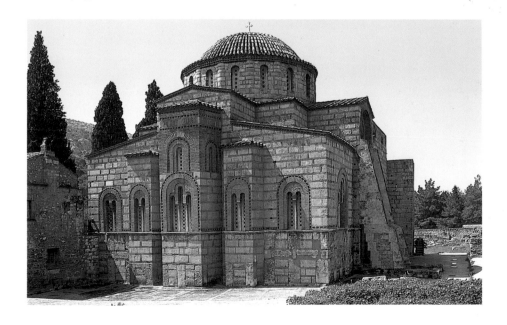

Colorplate 20
Church of the Dormition.
Daphni, Greece. c. 1100

FAR LEFT:
Colorplate 21
View into dome, Hagia Sophia. Istanbul. c. 532–37

LEFT:
Colorplate 22
View into vaults, S. Marco. Venice. 1063–94

FAR LEFT:
Colorplate 23
Church of Hagia Irene. Istanbul. 740

LEFT:
Colorplate 24
Interior, Katholikon, Monastery of Hosios Loukas.
Phocis, Greece. 11th century

FAR LEFT:
Colorplate 25
Detail of facade, Gatehouse (Torhalle) of the Abbey.
Lorsch, Germany. 767–74

LEFT:
Colorplate 26
Detail of apse, Monreale Cathedral. Sicily. 1174

Colorplate 27   Cosmati work, Cloister of S. Paolo fuori le Mura. Rome. Late 12th–early 13th century

Colorplate 28
Nave vaults, St.-Philibert.
Tournus, France. c. 1066–1107

Colorplate 29
Ste.-Madeleine. Vézelay,
France. c. 1104–32

Colorplate 30   Pisa Cathedral. Begun 1063

Colorplate 31   Baptistery of S. Giovanni. Florence. c. 1060–1150

OPPOSITE:
Colorplate 32
S. Nicola. Trani,
Italy. c. 1098

Colorplate 33   West facade, Reims Cathedral. Begun c. 1241   Colorplate 34   Retrofacade, Reims Cathedral. Begun c. 1241

Colorplate 35   Trinity Chapel, Canterbury Cathedral. 1175–84

Colorplate 36   Octagon, Ely Cathedral. Begun 1332

Colorplate 37   Notre-Dame, Paris. 1163–1300

OPPOSITE, ABOVE:
Colorplate 38   S. Domenico (left) and Duomo (distance). Siena. 13th and 14th centuries

OPPOSITE, BELOW:
Colorplate 39   Campo with Duomo in distance. Siena

Colorplate 40   Facade, Orvieto Cathedral. After 1310

Colorplate 41   Campanile. Florence. 1334–60

Colorplate 42   Medieval towers in San Gimignano

OPPOSITE:
Colorplate 43
Filippo Brunelleschi.
Dome, Florence
Cathedral. Begun 1420

Colorplate 44
Michelozzo di Bartolomeo. Palazzo Medici.
Florence. Begun c. 1445

Colorplate 45
Leon Battista Alberti. Facade, Palazzo Rucellai, detail.
Florence. 1460s

Colorplate 46
Leon Battista Alberti. Capital,
S. Francesco. Rimini. c. 1450

Colorplate 47
Filippo Brunelleschi. Capitals, Ospedale
degli Innocenti. Florence. Begun 1419

Colorplate 48   Facade, Certosa. Pavia. 1490s

Colorplate 49   Pazzi Chapel, Sta. Croce, Florence. Built after 1442

OPPOSITE, ABOVE:
**Colorplate 50
Andrea Palladio.
S. Giorgio Maggiore.
Venice. Begun 1566**

OPPOSITE, BELOW:
**Colorplate 51
Jacopo Sansovino.
Loggetta,
Piazza S. Marco.
Venice. 1537–45**

Colorplate 52   Michelangelo. Piazza del Campidoglio. Rome. 1537–61

Colorplate 53
Pietro Lombardo. Sta. Maria dei Miracoli. Venice. 1481–89

Colorplate 54
Andrea Palladio. Loggia del Capitaniato. Vicenza. 1571

**Colorplate 55
St.-Eustache. Paris. Begun 1532**

**Colorplate 56
Jules Hardouin-Mansart. Church of the Invalides. Paris. c. 1680**

Colorplate 57   Johann Lukas von Hildebrandt. Upper Belvedere. Vienna. 1721–24

OPPOSITE, ABOVE:
Colorplate 59   John Vanbrugh with Nicholas Hawksmoor. Blenheim Palace. Woodstock, England. 1705–22

OPPOSITE, BELOW:
Colorplate 60   Salomon de Brosse. Luxembourg Palace. Paris. 1614–24

Colorplate 61   Dominikus Zimmermann. Interior, Die Wies. Bavaria. 1746–54

Colorplate 62
Johann Balthasar Neumann. Staircase, Residence.
Würzburg. 1720–44

Colorplate 63
Egid Quirin Asam and Cosmas Damian Asam.
Interior detail, Sankt Johannes Nepomuk. Munich. 1733–46

OPPOSITE:
Colorplate 64   Jacques-Germain Soufflot. Panthéon (Ste.-Geneviève). Paris. 1756–90

Colorplate 65
William Chambers. Chinese Pagoda, Kew Gardens.
London. 1760s

Colorplate 66
Giuseppe Mengoni. Galleria Vittorio Emanuele.
Milan. 1865–67

Colorplate 67   Richard Boyle (Earl of Burlington). Chiswick House. Near London. 1725

Colorplate 68
Gustave Eiffel. Eiffel Tower. Paris. 1887–89

BELOW, LEFT:
Colorplate 69
George Edmund Street.
St. Paul's American Church. Rome. 1873–76

BELOW, RIGHT:
Colorplate 70
Louis H. Sullivan. Wainwright Building.
St. Louis. 1890–91

Colorplate 71
Henri Labrouste. Facade detail, Bibliothèque
Ste.-Geneviève. Paris. 1842–50

Colorplate 72
Charles Garnier. Facade detail,
The Opera. Paris. 1861–75

Colorplate 73
Jean-Francois-Thérèse Chalgrin and others.
Detail of entablature and attic,
Arc de Triomphe de l'Étoile. Paris. 1806–35

Colorplate 74
Claude-Nicholas Ledoux. Detail, Barrière de Monceau.
Paris. 1785–89

Colorplate 75
Frank Lloyd Wright. Winslow House.
River Forest, Illinois. 1894

Colorplate 76
Le Corbusier. Villa Savoye.
Poissy, France. 1928–29

Colorplate 77
Le Corbusier. Notre-Dame-du-Haut.
Ronchamp, France. 1950–54

Colorplate 78   Edwin Lutyens. Viceroy's Palace. New Delhi. 1920–31

OVERLEAF, LEFT:
Colorplate 79
William Van Alen. Chrysler Building. New York. 1930

OVERLEAF, RIGHT:
Colorplate 80
Gordon Bunshaft (Skidmore, Owings & Merrill).
Lever House from Seagram Building. New York. 1950–52

Colorplate 81   Michael Graves. Model, Portland Public Service Building. 1980–83

Colorplate 82   James Stirling. Neue Staatsgalerie. Stuttgart. 1977–83

Colorplate 83   Jean Nouvel. Galeries Lafayette. Berlin. 1991

Colorplate 84   James Stewart Polshek and Todd H. Schliemann. Rose Planetarium
(in the American Museum of Natural History). New York. 2000

Colorplate 85
Frank Gehry. Condé Nast
Cafeteria, interior. New York.
1996–2000

BELOW:
Colorplate 86
Frank Gehry. Guggenheim Museum
Bilbao, detail of titanium skin.
Bilbao, Spain. 1991–97

Colorplate 87   Christian de Portzamparc. LVMH Building.
New York. 1999–2000

RIGHT:
Colorplate 88   Fox & Fowle. Four Times Square. New York. 1999

OVERLEAF, TOP:
Colorplate 89
Elizabeth Plater-Zyberk and Andres Duany. Seaside, Florida. 1980s

OVERLEAF, BOTTOM LEFT:
Colorplate 90
Rafael Moneo. Museum of Roman Art, view of "nave." Mérida,
Spain. 1980–86

OVERLEAF, BOTTOM RIGHT:
Colorplate 91
Daniel Libeskind. Jewish Museum, detail of exterior. Berlin. 1989–98

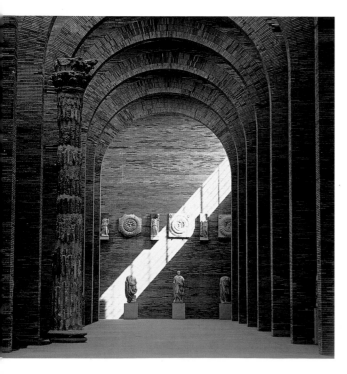

Introduction

Architecture is perhaps the most pervasive of all human things, but what is it?

The art which so disposes and adorns the edifices raised by man, that the sight of them contributes to his mental health, power, and pleasure. —John Ruskin, 1849

You employ stone, wood and concrete, and with these materials you build houses and palaces. That is construction. Ingenuity is at work. But suddenly you touch my heart, you do me good, I am happy and I say "This is beautiful." That is Architecture. Art enters in. —Le Corbusier, 1923

A bicycle shed is a building. Lincoln Cathedral is a piece of architecture. —Nikolaus Pevsner, 1943

The word *architecture* goes back through Latin to the Greek for "master builder." The ancients not only invented the word, they gave it its clearest definition. According to Vitruvius—the Roman writer whose *Ten Books on Architecture* is the only surviving ancient architectural treatise—architecture is the union of "firmness, commodity, and delight." It is, in other words, at once a structural, practical, and visual art. Without solidity, it is dangerous; without usefulness, it is merely large-scale sculpture; and without beauty (as Ruskin, Le Corbusier, and Pevsner emphasize), it is not more than utilitarian construction.

For a given building, all are vital, but in a historical narrative such as this one, the three facets of architecture are not always of equal interest. Some periods, including Roman, Gothic, and the nineteenth and twentieth centuries, were structurally innovative and are fully treated as such by this book. But other periods of equal intrinsic importance, such as Greek and Renaissance, tended to accept inherited structural methods with comparatively little advancement. While the changing function of buildings is certainly an important topic in this book, and a subject that is perhaps more constantly intriguing through history, it too varies in interest. Once the patterns of use of certain long-lived types, such as the Doric temple, the Christian church, or the modern office building, are established, the comparatively minor functional modifications that eventually follow cannot sustain a broad historical discussion such as ours, though they may be significant to specialized literature.

Architecture commands our attention consistently throughout history as a spatiovisual art, for only the monumental forms of buildings constantly evolve with changing times and conditions, and in response to the powers of artistic volition and the needs of society and individual clients. A great building is not a finite entity like a painting or sculpture, which historically have served mostly to decorate architecture. Almost a living being of protean character, architecture is capable of

Forum of Trajan. Rome. Dedicated A.D. 113

S. Marco. Venice. 1063–94

affecting us emotionally and aesthetically as no other art form can. Architecture takes us in, surrounds us, shapes our lives, protects, and sometimes threatens us. It represents who we are and the way we would be seen. It changes with the hours, the weather, and the seasons. It molds its site, makes the city, and may dominate the landscape. Because of its potential size and complexity, a building can accommodate the ambitions of the individual artist in an unparalleled way. Because of its material basis, its cost, its importance in our lives, its high visibility, it captures as no other form the spirit of its times.

While recognizing that architecture may legitimately be considered to include the entire built environment, this book centers on monumental architecture as the spatiovisual art that is the most sensitive, powerful touchstone of the cultural process. This is mainly a history of monumental buildings—works of strong, expertly designed, and highly individual character skillfully built to serve, symbolize, and endure—as well as groups of such buildings and their settings, and the historical

modes in which they were built. Historical study by definition is a process of selection and interpretation. Everywhere in our discussion choices have had to be made as to what to include and to exclude among the vast body of important works—hard choices that have been calculated to convey what we consider most important in devising an intelligible and engaging architectural history. If we imagine the history of architecture as a vast landscape, this book seeks to emphasize the ruggedness of its terrain rather than flattening it.

Many if not most of the works discussed here are highly celebrated in a great range of publications, from erudite scholarly articles and books to tourist pamphlets and advertising copy. In their actual or reconstructed form these well-known buildings provide settings for fiction, movie backdrops, and other scenographies of the public imagination. They are in fact sometimes so familiar that they tend to be taken for granted, treated almost as if they were part of a natural landscape that has always been there and always will be. Forgotten is that these structures were brought into being by a set of exceptional, highly particular, unrepeatable circumstances involving knots of unusually gifted architects, ambitious clients, and specific traits of the society in which they were built. Even more generally overlooked is their exceptional endurance through time—the very fact that so many great historical monuments have continued to exist, to occupy public space in demand for other purposes, often through centuries, sometimes millennia, even as most other aspects of their architectural worlds have decayed, been demolished, or otherwise disappeared, sometimes with scarcely a trace. Part of the motivation for writing this book is to defamiliarize these overexposed works, so that the reader may begin to actually see and understand them historically and aesthetically, and to comprehend how and why they were built and in what special form, thereby suggesting some of the reasons society has valued and maintained them so long (or in the case of many lost works, valued and restored their memory). In the last analysis we know that without these monumental structures, the quality of the environment would be sharply compromised: one must only imagine the planet without them.

Just as this is a book primarily about monumental buildings, so too it is essentially a book about the architecture of the West, not a global account of all cultures and civilizations. Western architectural development was generally more self-contained than not, surprisingly resistant to external influence, even in periods when the relative weakness of the West might have made it more vulnerable than it proved. Its story, in other words, tends to be very much its own. It is, moreover, an immensely rich and complicated story, and an adequate accounting of its fullness, sweep, and texture, even in such a large volume as this one, has proven a far from simple task. We have, however, in addition to a brief discussion of Prehistory, allowed two important exceptions: the Ancient Near East, as a deeply significant part of the formative background of the West; and Islam, treated not in its full scope but regarding its unique parallelism to the Western tradition in its derivation from ancient Roman architecture, which it transformed in ways very different from the West. Moreover, as will be apparent, in the twentieth century the architecture of the West becomes part of global practice.

The fundamental organization of the text by period conforms to the most widely accepted chronological divisions (architects's dates are found in the Index). Although these historical categories and their boundaries are not absolute and are certainly open to discussion, we believe that a chronological account remains most effective for the initial study of architectural history. As such, a primary aim of this book is to provide a comprehensible mapping of Western architecture through its entire existence, from its Prehistory to the most recent developments, which will provide the reader with a basis for further study and thought. In response to the keen and growing interest in the recent past and the many vital issues it raises, the book is purposely weighted toward the present, with the modern age given considerably more than its usual scope in historical surveys. This holds true especially for the eighteenth century—often lost between the Late Baroque and the beginnings of nineteenth-century Romanticism—and most of all for the late twentieth century, which occupies two chapters.

Of these last two, chapter 13 studies the Post-Modernist architectural movement, typified by (but not limited to) neo-

Guarino Guarini. Dome Interior, S. Lorenzo. Turin. 1668–87

historicism and imagistic eclecticism, that ran from the 1960s into the early eighties, when it faded. Chapter 14 (new to this edition) treats the aftereffects of Post-Modernism, yet in wider ways involves the related but distinct phenomenon of Postmodernity, a broader term not limited or specifically referring to architecture but rather signifying the general cultural condition following the collapse in the 1960s and seventies of the cultural and ideological hegemony of the Enlightenment project of Modernity. The condition of Postmodernity has not terminated but continues to evolve, and many of its traits are implicated in themes of the new chapter. These include a radical cultural and ideological fragmentation and pluralism; a deconstructionistic questioning and denial of all universal and idealist claims of value; and a fractured sense of place, time, and identity.

Each chapter in the book is organized differently. Some proceed stylistically, others by building type, still others by strict historical and geographical progression; and some follow conceptual distinctions perceived in the period by historians. This diversity is not arbitrary but reflects differences between periods in their intrinsic character, in what is known as well as disputed about them, in their interest to us, and in what physically remains of them. There is, however, a certain logic to be noted in the discursive progress of the text, whose general trajectory is toward an increasingly complex and nuanced interpretation of architecture. To a degree this progression corresponds very broadly to history itself in two senses. In the great sweep from Prehistory to Postmodernity, architecture itself tends, over the very long run, to become ever more complex. Moreover, the terms of our historical understanding tend to shift in parallel, in the direction of a greater complexity toward works of the present. In any case, the loosely progressive character of our text is pedagogical in motivation, the hope being that its reading will gradually and cumulatively guide the reader to an ever fuller understanding of architecture and its history. Most of all, however, history being the story of unique individuals, developments, events, and acts of creation, we have sought to capture the individuality of historical buildings, their creators, and their times.

ARCHITECTURAL WRITING AND ILLUSTRATIONS

Individual buildings in their three-dimensional form are the core of the book, and their presentation sets an exacting task that demands a certain well-rewarded effort on the part of the reader. Mastery of the specialized vocabulary of architectural writing is facilitated by the explanation of many terms as they are introduced in the text; a glossary is also provided. This commentary includes the discussion of structure, which is not relegated to a separate section, but appears as important developments occur (for example in the Roman and Gothic periods). Many readers will find the visual tools—photographs and the architectural renderings—the most challenging aspect of discussion; to ease the difficulty, a few words about their use and how they work may be of help.

While a painting can be reproduced with a single photograph, and the shape of most sculpture can be grasped through a series of photographs, a monumental building is more elusive. It has an outside and an inside, both usually complicated, as well as intricate detailing. It is strongly affected by its site, and our impressions of it are colored by changing lighting conditions and the presence of furnishings and human activities. Much of its structural detail is invisible, and the proportions of its masses and spaces—often carefully determined, exact mathematical ratios between key dimensions valued for their aesthetic and even philosophical or religious significance—work their effect, seen but inexactly measured by the eye. How do we capture an architectural monument in illustrations?

Photographs are indispensable to reveal the many faces of a building. Straight, overall views from the natural perspective of the observer standing at ground level are generally the most useful shots, but other angles—views up into vaults, down from adjacent structures, aerial photographs—can be immensely revealing. Detail photographs are among the most important, both to the reading public and the architectural historian. Traditionally, architects have been deeply involved in the design and crafting of detail, which was a major means of architectural expression. Certain building types—such as the Greek temple or the Renaissance facade—may even be thought of as giant, intricate sculptures, made entirely of detail. Modern architecture, while generally less personalized and articulate in detail, tends to exhibit the architect's signature in its particulars. Closely related to the photograph is the perspective drawing (figs. 1-42, 3-60). It may show the building from an angle as the building presents itself to the eye. In style, such drawings range from the schematic to the fully detailed. They are useful to historians in reconstructing ruined or destroyed buildings and to architects in visualizing future buildings (figs. 8-39, 12-52).

Such views and photographs have their limitations; they cannot reveal a building's three-dimensional interior-exterior or structural nature. So we use diagrams to represent the structure, space, and proportions of buildings, as well as to reconstruct works that no longer stand. Architectural renderings are necessary both to students of architectural history and builders; such drawings are preserved from the earliest times (fig. 1-44). The most basic—and oldest—type of rendering is the ground plan, which is the representation of a building at a given horizontal plane. This horizontal slice through the fabric usually is made at the base of the building (fig. 3-49); but in complex, multileveled works, plans of higher zones (fig. 12-32) may be made as well, or several zones combined in a single plan (fig. 3-28). Some of the conventions of the plan are obvious: dark shapes represent masses, light ones the voids; walls may be rendered by double lines or solid ink, with interruptions as windows or doors; dots may indicate columns, ringed by their bases. Less obvious are the symbols for features existing above and below the main plane of the plan: the arrow superimposed on stairs pointing the direction up (fig. 4-15); circles for domes (fig. 5-37); an "X" for a cross vault; paired semicircles for barrel vaults (fig. 4-29). All may be further complicated by various shadings, colors, or cross-hatchings to indicate different periods of construction, original versus restored fabric, and so on (fig. 5-17).

An elevation is a drawing of some vertical face of a building. There are two types. The perspective elevation (fig. 8-43) renders the subject in optical perspective, from a single point of view, like a photograph but drawn by hand (or often by computer). The pure elevation instead renders each detail head on from its own level, and while it distorts the way a building looks to the eye, it presents its face with scientific objectivity, and thus is especially useful in archaeological reconstructions and in dealing with measurements and proportions (fig. 10-2).

The cross section is more complex, being a slice through a building, only on a vertical rather than a horizontal plane (fig. 1-23). A cross section reveals both the shape of the structure at the plane of fracture—usually indicated by heavy, solid lines—and the interior beyond that plane, that is, a kind of elevation. It may also include further invisible elements (often indicated by dotted lines). Most buildings have an axial orientation, and the cross section may run along the axis (longitudinal section) or cut across it (transverse section). Precisely where the slice is made is sometimes indicated in the accompanying plan. Cross sections tend to be harder to read than plans, but are extremely useful. Whereas a plan manifests a building's outline, extent, space, patterns of use, the section reveals structure, the coordination of interior-exterior details of the walls, as well as the vertical extent of spatial units.

Through study of plan, section, and elevation, the building is made to reveal itself in its three-dimensional fullness. We need not always combine the several sets of information ourselves, for a still more complex type of diagram exists (invented in the Renaissance) that integrates them: the isometric (and axonometric) projection, which renders the three-dimensional unity of a building in a single drawing (fig. 12-101). Like other diagrams, the isometric projection may be schematic or highly detailed, transparent or opaque. Its difficulty is knowing whether to see it as a worm's-eye or bird's-eye view (usually it is the latter). It tends to stimulate the greatest ingenuity of draftsmanship and often assumes the variant of the cutaway drawing—a detailed, "opaque" isometric with parts of the fabric cut away to reveal interior features (fig. 8-2).

No matter how intricate the diagrams or complete the photographic documentation, we should never confuse such illustrations with the monument itself. As with all art, there is no substitute for the experience of the real thing.

OPPOSITE: **Le Corbusier. Villa Savoye. Poissy, France. 1928–29**

Pages 54–55
Pyramids at
Giza, Egypt.
2750–
2500 B.C.

1-1
Stonehenge.
Salisbury
Plain,
England.
c. 3000 B.C.

Chapter One | Architecture Before Greece

PREHISTORY

The most extraordinary thing about the prehistoric architectural scene is how quickly it rose above the utilitarian level—how readily human imagination and effort were channeled into monumental architecture, whose construction absorbed enormous energies at a time when very survival on a day-to-day basis was so arduous and uncertain. The state of prehistoric archaeology is inherently tenuous and ever-changing, but, paradoxically, nowhere are the underlying motivations, processes, and formulations of architecture laid bare so clearly—or, at least, their issues so dramatically raised.

Things began humbly though. The earliest dwellings of our nomadic Stone Age ancestors in western and southern Europe were multichambered caves and rock shelters, and fragile, tent-like assemblages of poles covered with hides or thatched reeds (fig. 1-2). More permanent structures were impractical for a people constantly on the move to find new sources of food. Of these early efforts to create shelter little remains but post-hole traces visible in aerial photographs and inferred notions based on the living habits of aboriginal peoples who have survived into modern times in remote pockets of the world.

Architecture attains greater substance when we pass one of mankind's turning points into the Neolithic period (or New Stone Age), which began about 9000 B.C. Paleolithic (Early Stone Age) people had been migratory predators, living in small bands that clung to the edge of survival. Neolithic humanity learned to farm as well as to hunt, to domesticate animals and to grow crops, to make pottery for storing produce, and from produce to weave cloth. These new skills and crafts were developed in village communities with complex social structures that marked the beginnings of civilization. Architecture was still mostly in the nature of crude fabrications of organic and impermanent materials such as timber, straw, wattle and daub, and mud. But Neolithic settlements reveal a surprising range, which two examples will illustrate.

On the Anatolian plain near the modern Turkish city of Konya are the remains of an extraordinary community dating to the seventh millennium B.C. Proving a long-held hypothesis that Neolithic culture moved into Europe from the Near East by way of the Anatolian Plateau, Çatal Hüyük, as the site is known, was a highly organized "city" with specialized crafts, an extensive economy partly founded on trade, and elaborate architectural features (including the first known religious shrine). The houses of Çatal and their foundations were made of shaped mud-brick. Roughly rectangular in plan, one story high, and divided into a living space and an attached storeroom, the houses had unusual and revealing features (figs. 1-3, 1-4). The living space was designed with "built-in" benches

along two walls and a floor hearth. The houses were entered through a hole in the roof that was at once chimney and doorway. Movement from house to house took place only over and through the roof. Without windows or doors, and packed into a continuous cellular structure, the houses presented a solid blank wall to the outside. The defensive compactness and structural economy of this architectural program were successful: excavations revealed no destruction by floods from the nearby river, nor were there any signs that the unusual wealth of the city had been plundered.

Equally astonishing was the discovery of an imposing Neolithic town, dating from about 7000–6000 B.C. in Jordan, at the biblical city of Jericho, settled by a people curiously without pottery; but they were skilled in the manufacture of stone vessels, and made portrait heads of ancestors by sensitively modeling plaster over the skulls of the deceased. Their architecture included rectangular, two-room houses with smoothly finished lime-plaster floors and walls. Most notably, the settlement was enclosed by powerful stone walls with defensive towers constructed with surprising technical skill (fig.1-5). The need for fortification against enemies, even greater than for shelter from the unfriendly elements, provoked this first monumental construction. Evidently by the seventh millennium B.C., parts of the ancient Near East, soon to provide the cradle of the first advanced civilizations, had attained sufficient population pressures, territorial ambitions, and technological progress to achieve the dubious advance of full-scale interurban warfare.

The most impressive Neolithic architecture, however, was not built for practical uses. Rather it served—as architecture often would throughout history—less easily definable emotional and spiritual needs, and, above all, the realm of symbolism, ritual, and magic. Paradoxically, Neolithic people's greatest rational efforts were directed at fulfilling their most irrational drives. That these drives were so powerful is easy enough to understand. Although a degree of security had been achieved in the face of nature, the world remained fearsome and perplexing, especially to a humanity with our same basic needs, feelings, and powers of imagination, but dauntingly little knowledge. The nights were haunted by the ominous world of dreams, so easily confused with reality, blurring into the impenetrable mysteries of death and the afterworld. Capricious, awesome forces of nature alternatingly caressed and assaulted the fragile Neolithic communities, and nourished and destroyed their crops. In the heavens, the sun was daily reborn and extinguished, while the moon waxed and waned in a monthly cycle, less mysterious only than the great yearly cycle of the seasons in which all of nature seemed

1-2 Oval hut. Nice. (Drawing by Eric Mose)

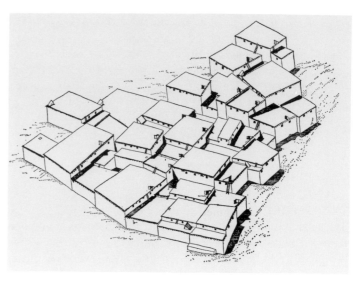

1-3 Houses at Çatal Hüyük, Anatolia. c. 6000 B.C. (Schematic reconstruction of a section of Level VI after J. Mellaart)

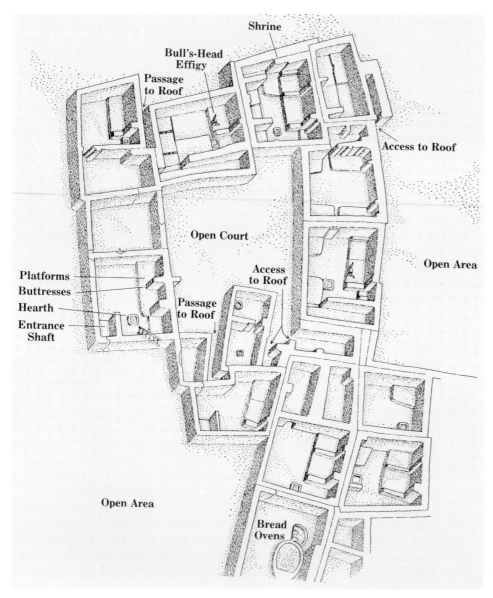

1-4
House interiors, Çatal Hüyük.
(After J. Mellaart)

to pass through a process of rebirth, growth, fruition, and death. With the characteristic animism of the primeval mind, Neolithic people imagined the world in terms of their own bodies, as living creatures of supernatural force and ultimate consequence, inaccessible and unappeased by ordinary means. Their attempts to control natural forces were based on the same fantasy of ritual and magic that had created them. In this activity, monumental architecture played a supreme role.

The principal mode taken by the monumental Neolithic construction is known as megalithic (from the Greek words *megas*=great and *lithos*=stone). Huge stone blocks were assembled without mortar in basic structural arrangements that are still used today. Sometimes the megalithic blocks were set up merely leaning against one another. More significant was post-and-lintel, or trabeated construction, in which vertical uprights support a horizontal beam; this is still the single most important structural device used in architecture. One of the most striking examples of megalithic post-and-lintel construction survives in northern France, in Carnac, Brittany. Believed to have been a single burial tomb, the structure in Carnac was built with two upright slabs of stone supporting a third horizontal capstone and held together by sheer weight (fig. 1-6). The remains of the deceased were placed in the chamber formed by the massive blocks, and the entire structure was covered with a mound of earth materials, called a barrow. In addition to post-and-lintel construction, megalithic builders—who also employed masonry of submegalithic, small-scale blocks—developed the device of corbeling, where successive courses of masonry project forward progressively from the wall plane to bridge a gap. This might provide a solid roof for a space between two parallel walls, or could be worked forward from the sides of a centralized enclosure to form a domelike ceiling.

How did Neolithic society, whose technology was so crude as to lack even the simplest bronze or iron tools, erect such structures? The processes used by megalithic builders were probably not unlike those of the later, more sophisticated Egyptians, whose building blocks were also of colossal scale: quarrying by crudely splitting the lode, transporting by barge and sleds pulled by large crews over rollers, and lifting through leverage over inclined masses of earth materials removed after construction. Sheer abundance of labor, endurance of effort, and a limitless time frame were the real secrets of the megalithic builders.

The terminology of megalithic structures has become a confusing linguistic mixture, but they can be divided into two categories: tombs, such as at Carnac, which are called dolmens (of which some 50,000 stand in Europe); and nonsepulchral forms either of single stones called menhirs, standing alone or in rows, or composed stone groups, often circular in plan, called cromlechs or henge monuments.

Megalithic tombs, apart from underground rock-cut graves, follow three basic arrangements. The simplest is the chamber tomb consisting of a single roofing stone supported by two or more uprights; the passage grave (fig. 1-7) forms a rectangular or polygonal chamber approached through an entranceway and used for collective rather than single burial; the gallery grave was an elongated, rectangular chamber frequently divided into subsidiary units, but without an entrance passage. All three varieties were covered by a barrow of earth materials to produce a rounded, oval, or rectangular mound,

1-5   Neolithic wall of Jericho, Jordan. c. 7000 B.C.

1-6   Megalithic dolmen tomb. Carnac, Brittany. c. 1500 B.C.

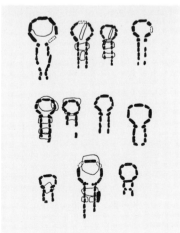

1-7
Megalithic passage graves. Portugal. (Plan after Vergilio Correia)

often fortified by retaining walls and decorated with chunks of stone. One of the finest known examples of such tombs is the passage grave at Quanterness in the Orkney Islands of Great Britain. Covered with a tumulus about 150 feet in diameter and reinforced by concentric retaining walls, its central tomb chamber, surrounded by six side-chambers, all corbel-roofed, accumulated the remains of as many as four hundred members of the tiny community (no more than twenty bodies at any one time) that built it and used it for over five hundred years (see page 589).

With mere survival still such a prime concern, why did Neolithic people devote themselves so much to tombs? Although it has been suggested that they served as socially cohesive foci and to establish territorial rights over surrounding croplands, the deeper answer may lie in the habits of the early human mind. Anthropologists surmise that dreams about the departed may have led to a belief in their continuing existence in material form. In real life, shelter was a prime necessity, and it was natural to imagine the dead in need of it as well. To provide shelter for the dead, to appease their restless and possibly dangerous spirits, and to incarcerate them were ample motives for immense expenditures of energy to create houses in which the dead would not be disturbed, and by which they might be remembered and appeased. Having first lived and buried the dead in hillside caves, people now built artificial caves in artificial mountains for the departed. The first monumental architecture—like so many that followed—thus imitates nature, and provides for deep social, psychological, and symbolic needs.

Even more remarkable than the megalithic tombs are the nonsepulchral monuments. These were of considerable geographic and formal range, and, while they remain enigmatic to us, they all seem to have been connected with some form of worship. Among the most impressive are the remains of temples to unknown gods, still megalithic, but built during the Bronze Age on Malta, Sicily, and Sardinia. These prehistoric structures hint at the intricate types of theistic architecture that eventually appeared in later periods. At Hal Tarxien, Malta, vestiges of the most evolved phase of megalithic temple architecture survive in the enormous stone blocks of a complex of three gigantic structures. Post-and-lintel portals decorated with a pattern of hammered holes, corbeled roofs covering altar-containing apses, carefully dressed limestone slabs lining passages, and altars with carved bas-relief are only some of the features of the grandly scaled structures (fig. 1-8). The unique culture of Neolithic Malta may have descended from the adventurous seafarers of Asia Minor, who settled in the western Mediterranean and brought with them a knowledge of eastern architectural forms and building techniques.

But the most interesting of all megalithic works are the great stone circles—the cromlechs or henge monuments—of the British Isles. The largest prehistoric monument in Europe is the circular sanctuary of Avebury, completely encompassing the old Wiltshire town. There a circular ditch 1,300 feet in diameter enclosed several rings of stones set out with remarkable precision. Avebury is of particular fascination in its connection with nearby Neolithic structures, such as the huge conical earth mound of Silbury, at 500 feet in diameter and 130 feet in height the largest structure in Europe until the Industrial Revolution (in terms of solid mass). Collectively, these works may have formed a "cycle" of monuments used to celebrate the annual life-cycle of the Great Goddess, whose yearly metamorphoses were held responsible for the changes of the seasons so vital to an agrarian society.

1-8 Bronze-Age Temple. Hal Tarxien, Malta

Of all Neolithic monuments, Stonehenge, on the Salisbury Plain not far from Avebury, has commanded the most attention and generated the liveliest controversies. Compact and well-preserved, Stonehenge (figs. 1-1, 1-9, 1-10; colorplate 1) was built in the form of concentric rings. At the center was an altar. Around it, in horseshoe plan, were originally five so-called trilithons, each formed by two uprights weighing about forty tons apiece and supporting a single colossal lintel. Beyond the trilithons was a circle of smaller uprights, made not of the local Wiltshire sandstone that formed the rest of the structure, but of "blue" stone blocks transported, amazingly, 140 miles over water and land, from the Prescelly Mountains of South Wales. The outer, enclosing circle (106 feet in diameter) is the most monumental part of the complex. Huge sandstone monoliths 13½ feet high support what was once a continuous lintel. Beyond this great ring was a circle of small, movable "marker" stones set in fifty-six equally spaced pits, the so-called Aubrey Holes (named for an early archaeologist at the site). The monument was isolated from the surrounding landscape by a trench (foreshadowing the lifting of Greek temples above their sites). A long avenue marked by menhirs pierced the trench and ran to the trilithons. A single, large stone with a pointed top, known as the Heel Stone, still stands on the avenue marking cosmic events.

Everything about Stonehenge is extraordinary. The site evidently was sacred, and so were the "blue" stones brought from so far away. For the period, the construction was highly accurate, with all the uprights plumbed (made exactly vertical) and with mortice-and-tenon joints securing the horizontal beams against the unlikely event of slippage. Each lintel was slightly curved to make part of a circle, and the carefully dressed vertical blocks were shaped to an upward tapering convexity (anticipating the entasis of the Greek column).

In purely formal terms, Stonehenge is subtle and imaginative. Its plan is both centralized—disposed around a vertical axis—and longitudinal, developed along a horizontal axis set into the central plan. The structure was part of the landscape, yet set off from it. It was an enclosure, isolated from the world by successive rings of stone, yet open to it through the stone screens. Indeed, at the very center the participant in the rites of Stonehenge experienced a most profound connection with nature, for the monument seems to have been dominated by a powerful cult of sun worship. From its center, with the awesome trilithons on three sides, one could observe on the fourth side, at the summer solstice (the longest day of the year), the rising sun coming up exactly over the apex of the Heel Stone. The solar orientation of Stonehenge, although rare in its precision, was by no means a singular phenomenon, for major architectural monuments as diverse as Classical temples and Christian churches were oriented to the rising sun.

Solstice worship does not fully explain the complexities of the rings and markers at Stonehenge. And indeed, these complexities have opened the floodgates of archaeological speculation, and interpretations of the irresistible site have poured forth, reaching the limits of intellectual ingenuity and imagination (occasionally offering delirious fantasies that suggest the unfettered Neolithic mind itself at work). Among the more sober researches two basic approaches predominate—the mythic-symbolical and the mathematical-scientific. Thus, it has been suggested that the intricate, circular plan of Stonehenge mirrors the cosmic lunar/solar eye of the Great Goddess; and that the unusually flat upper surface of the outer circle of lintels was for a purpose, namely, that the 3½ foot-wide surface formed an elevated walkway for some ritual, conceivably the First Fruits ceremony of August. Whatever the particulars, the notion that the site was actively used for ritual, rather than being merely an inert solstice marker like some giant sundial, is in keeping with our anthropological knowledge of colorful, dynamic, aboriginal customs: in some way, the site must have been the setting for elaborate ceremony. On the other hand, there are scientists who believe that the construction was meant as a kind of astronomical computer for the prediction of both solar and lunar eclipses. One can well imagine that Neolithic humanity yearned somehow to control by prediction the disturbing phenomenon of the eclipses. Other new surveys suggest that the builders of Neolithic rings had mastered basic units of measurement and elementary geometrical construction. It may be difficult to prove or even to evaluate hypotheses about the intellectual sophistication of a society that has left no written record but only fragments of some of the most unparalleled monuments ever built. Nevertheless, Stone Age architecture though primitive in its rugged gigantism, here established sophisticated principles of planning and construction—axiality, orientation, geometry, statics, transportation, and communal cooperative labor—which later were to characterize much of the most advanced monumental architecture.

Ultimately, the historical significance of megalithic architecture hinges on the difficult problem of its chronology. Until recently, the "diffusionist" theory prevailed, in which megalithic building types and techniques would have originated in the Aegean Bronze Age of Crete and Greece, in the second millennium B.C., and spread westward across the Mediterranean through Spain and thence to the Atlantic coastal region, where the still Neolithic farming communities (without metal tools) took up the "style," which passed through Brittany and the British Isles as far north as Denmark. Based on little hard evidence, the theory fits the picture of the origins of European civilization in the precocious eastern Mediterranean. Recent scientific findings have completely upset this account. Carbon 14 analysis (based on comparative measurements of the radioactive decay of organic matter) of remains from megalithic sites has shown that the northern European monuments in some cases are two thousand years earlier than their Mediterranean "predecessors," with examples in Brittany reaching as far back as 4500 B.C.—the earliest standing stone structures in the world. In this new chronology, the great stone circles of Avebury and Stonehenge date from about 3000 B.C., centuries before their first true competitors—the pyramids of Egypt. And this is as history should "ideally" be (though not always as it is). For Egypt draws on the megalithic traditions of tomb and temple in its main monumental types, and on megalithic construction for its masonry technique, all carried to peaks unimaginable to the Neolithic builders.

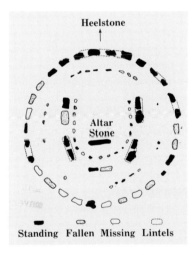

1-9
Stonehenge. Diagram
of original arrangement
of stones. (After F. Hoyle)

1-10   Air view, Stonehenge. Salisbury Plain, England. c. 3000 B.C.

EGYPT

Egypt shares with Mesopotamia the distinction of having produced the first great recorded civilization. As a monumental style its architecture has never been surpassed, arousing wonder from antiquity to the present.

Before architecture was the land. More than any other architecture, that of Egypt cannot be understood without accounting for its setting. The Nile River, its valley, and its delta are the guiding force of Egyptian civilization. The Nile provided not only transportation but the sustenance and plenty of its more than 900 miles of fertile bottom land, enriched annually by the flooding of the beneficent river. The rocky highlands and the Red Sea to the east, and the desert stretching to the west, served to protect the river valley from invasion and disruption. In this valley crucible in the late fourth millennium there emerged a stable political entity and a rich culture whose essential principles and style of life and art would remain intact during some 3,000 years. Protected and secure, Egypt developed a sophisticated culture and an enduring art of great beauty and luxury.

At the core of ancient Egypt was the pharaonic monarchy, whose rulers believed themselves incarnations of divinities and were worshiped in life and even in death. Successive generations of pharaonic family rule defined Egyptian history. This dynastic progression began with the political unification of Upper and Lower Egypt by Menes, the first king of the First Dynasty; it survived some thirty dynasties to a florid ending under the Ptolemys (of whom Cleopatra was the last). Modern historians have grouped these dynasties into broader periods of Old Kingdom (c. 3200–2158 B.C.), Middle Kingdom (2134–1786 B.C.), and New Kingdom (1570–1085 B.C.), with two Intermediate Periods, braced at either extreme by the Archaic Period and Late Dynastic epoch. This lengthy dynastic sequence was complemented by an increasingly powerful priesthood. The pharaoh and the priests headed a centralized society, with a hierarchical structure ultimately based (like most ancient societies, including Greece) on an agrarian economy and dependent on slave labor.

Life in the Nile Valley provided more for architecture than a supportive sociopolitical system. From the cliffs that lined the valley was quarried an extensive range of building stone—from ordinary sandstone to the densest granites and other metamorphic rock, as well as alluvial clay for the less splendid but highly useful brick. Ultimately, however, it was the visual rather than the material character of the valley that mattered. It provided sites that to the Egyptian architects—driven by the limitless building ambitions of monarchy and priesthood—posed a compelling challenge: to create an architecture that would match the scale and grandeur of the river, the mountains, and the desert.

If before the eye of the Egyptian builder there was a challenging set of realities, behind it was a singular manner of regarding the world: Egyptians had at once the most materialistic and the most otherworldly of minds. Their complex religion evolved from elaborate rituals concerning life, death, and afterlife. Even more than Neolithic society, Egyptians were obsessed with the cult of the dead. In their minds, life was a brief, transient passage and the other side of death an eternal extension of the joys of their first existence. Success in afterlife depended on both a final balancing of moral conduct, and on careful provisions for the physical remains of the dead and their comfortable maintenance in the next world.

To ensure immortality elaborate means of preservation were made for the deceased. A person was believed to have a dual being: a material body and a spirit-soul-personality called the ba. The ba survived death but needed the trappings of life; most importantly it needed a body. The intricate Egyptian process of mummification provided a reasonably permanent habitation for the soul and, at the same time, mutilated and rendered harmless the deceased whose potentially malign powers continued to be feared. For extra security the Egyptian duplicated its form, first in the several shells of the mummy case, then in separate sculptural effigies, freestanding as well as in relief incised on the wall of the tomb. Next, the soul in its form as the ba or ka (roughly its double) required those goods and services that the individual needed in life: food, housing, occupation, and entertainment. Hence in the grave of the deceased were deposited abundant goods, and space was provided for continuous prayers and offerings by his or her survivors. As still further insurance, all that the deceased might need was depicted in sculptural figures and in relief and painting on the tomb walls. Thus the tomb was literally the house of the dead.

Archaic and Old Kingdom Tombs. Given the material richness of the land and the divine self-conception of the pharaohs, it is not surprising that Egypt developed a monumental architecture of the tomb. The Egyptian tomb-pyramids are so familiar and their shape so elementary that the layman rarely raises questions as to their origins. However, seemingly simple forms are often more sophisticated than they appear. Certainly this is true of the pyramids, whose form was not given immediately even to the Egyptians with their instinct for the monumental. Their first above-ground tombs, succeeding the earliest burials in sandpits, are those relatively small constructions known as mastabas (fig. 1-11). At Saqqara, the huge necropolis of the ancient capital city of Memphis, about 15 miles southwest of Cairo, important First Dynasty (c. 3200 B.C.) tombs have been excavated to reveal the earliest mastaba constructions. Derived from the Arabic word *mastaba* signifying bench, these tombs were bench-shaped quadratic masses that rose to a height of not less than 30 feet, composed generally of sun-baked mud-brick, with battered (sloping) walls, and a flat top. Although in later examples the exterior walls were faced with stone and articulated by paneled recessions, the brick walls of the earliest royal tombs were decorated with painted geometric designs in brilliant colors. The internal arrangements here—comparatively small hollows in the solid mass—established the fundamental pattern: a subterranean level with the

1-11 Group of mastabas. (Architectural reconstruction after A. Badawy)

burial chamber surrounded by storage rooms for clothing, food, wine, furniture, weapons, games, and even lavatories; at the ground level the rectangular superstructure consisted of similar chambers for the storage of additional goods. Precinct walls surrounding the tomb, chambers for the burial of servants to tend to the king's needs in the afterlife, and stairways were also found in the early Saqqara excavations. Later mastabas included the serdab, or state chamber, with its requisite effigy of the deceased and the so-called false door for the free passage of the ka; also included were an offering chamber appropriately decorated with wall reliefs depicting scenes of offering and ritual prayers. Some of the subterranean crypts were connected to the superstructure by a narrow shaft or stairway. This earliest form of royal Egyptian tomb was an embryonic model for the pyramids, alongside which mastabas continued to be built in large numbers for other members of the royal family.

The transformation of the mastaba into the pyramid is the earliest unfolding of a major architectural idea in which all the steps of change are preserved. The pyramid series, located on the west bank of the Nile, begins at Saqqara. There, in the Third Dynasty, the great King Zoser built in about 2750 B.C. an enormous funerary complex (colorplate 3; figs. 1-12, 1-13) that was a residence for the afterlife, a replica of the royal palace, and a stage for the enactment of the elaborate rituals and festivals of kingship. He was assisted by Imhotep, the first recorded architect in history, who was later deified by the Egyptians. Even Imhotep seems at first to have conceived his patron's tomb as a large example of the traditional mastaba with a difference in building material: instead of the customary sun-baked brick, huge blocks of cut stone were used. No sooner was it complete than it was enlarged, then enlarged again. Still the builders were dissatisfied. At this point a leap of the imagination transpired: the successively enlarged mastaba became the core of a huge superstructure built over an extended rectangular plan 411 by 358 feet, with five sloping setbacks toward the top, now 204 feet high. The first pyramid was thus not the better-known, pure, geometric form, but instead a step pyramid (figs. 1-14, 1-15). It served as a monument to Zoser who, in accordance with the original mastaba convention, was not buried within it but below ground. His tomb chamber, lined with slabs of granite and sealed with a three-ton cylindrical granite plug, rests at the bottom of a 92-foot-deep shaft.

Zoser's step pyramid stands at the center of one of the most ambitious of Egyptian sites. The rectangular funerary complex—1,800 feet by 900 feet in extent—is surrounded by a stone wall 33 feet high (fig. 1-16). The wall does not run in a straight line but follows a breaking pattern of more than 200 evenly spaced projections and recessions, forming sharply defined volumes in the brilliant Egyptian sun. Fourteen of the projections are larger than the others and form bastions. One of these has an actual door, but the other thirteen have false doors through which the deceased pharaoh was meant to pass on his visits to the different realms of his kingdom. Entering through the real door, the visitor passes into a long entrance hall whose most prominent feature is the two rows of half-columns (fig. 1-17) attached to the piers that supported a massive stone ceiling. These half-columns, together with others of different detail at Saqqara (fig. 1-18), are among the first

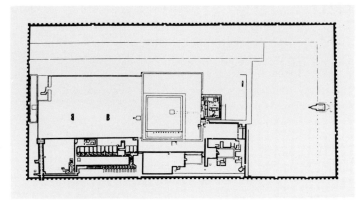

1-12   Plan, Funerary Complex of King Zoser. Saqqara. c. 2750 B.C.

1-13   Model, Funerary Complex of King Zoser.
(M. Hirmer after J. P. Lauer)

monumental columnar forms in the history of architecture. Two aspects of the entrance colonnades are conspicuous: first, the architect did not yet dare to build freestanding columns; second, the engaged half-columns do not take an abstract shape, but imitate the bundles of reeds that had been traditionally used as supports in the perishable residential and commercial constructions of timber-poor Egypt.

Here a leitmotif is announced that will remain central throughout the history of architecture: the imitation of natural forms. The neglect of this crucial element of the art of building is largely a recent phenomenon, the outcome of an age with a generally abstract artistic vision and one in which contact with nature is less direct. But until recently—and clearly from the very beginning of history—the architect invested structures with forms derived from diverse aspects of the natural world. He preserved in stone the organic material of vernacular architecture, as in the entrance hall of Zoser's pyramid (a process repeated later in Greece), and infused it with imitations of multifold levels and aspects of life, nature, and the supernatural. The most impressive of these imitations at Saqqara are the other, famous half-columns, attached to the wall of the courtyard that stood before the building known as the North Palace. Here the half-columns (colorplate 3) imitate not vernacular construction, but an element of nature itself: papyrus plants. The slender grace of the natural model was translated into the elegantly shaped projection of the masonry courses of the wall. The sharply profiled, ovoid stalks reach up to flaring, bell-shaped representations of papyrus flowers that formed the first capitals—the crowning member of a column—in architecture. Whereas the capitals of later epochs generally performed the function of transition between vertical support and horizontal load, here the flower capitals

1-14   Step Pyramid of King Zoser. Saqqara. c. 2750 B.C.
1-15   (inset) Step Pyramid of King Zoser. (Transverse section after H. W. Janson)

1-16   Precinct wall, Funerary Complex of King Zoser. Saqqara

1-17   Entrance hall and colonnade, Funerary Complex of King Zoser. (Reconstruction drawing by J. P. Lauer)

1-18   Facade imitating reed columns. South Building, Funerary Complex of King Zoser

stood free. Their function was boldly decorative. It was also clearly symbolic, for the papyrus was the symbol of Lower Egypt. If the mastaba was a permanent house for the deceased, Zoser's step pyramid was at once a model of his palace, his city, and his kingdom, with symbols such as the papyrus emblematic for parts of his realm.

Monumental architecture tended to be not only functional but also symbolic; the step pyramid embodied Saqqara's deepest symbolism. Its shape was not just a structural or formal device; to the initiate of Egyptian thought it immediately suggested a stairway to the sky which the pharaoh might ascend to join the sun god Amon-Ra, chief divinity of Egypt at this time, in his daily journey across the heavens. It soon became apparent, however, that the symbolism that so strongly permeated the Egyptian consciousness would find even greater expression in the more monumental form of the pure geometric pyramid. This seemingly obvious advance was slow in coming to pass because of the peculiar Egyptian method of building pyramids not as continuous horizontal layers of diminishing size, but rather as vertical, narrow piles abutting each other in ascending steps toward the massive core around which they were erected. The stepped massing could easily be given a pure geometry by adding a final layer of blocks with slanting faces, but structurally the attempt to create a satisfactorily steep pyramid (of 52 degrees from the horizontal) resulted at first in compromises and even structural failure at the Pyramid of Medum (c. 2704–2656 B.C.), whose outer layers were insufficiently supported and gave way to the immense internal pressures of the vast stone piles (fig. 1-19). It was only in the reign of the great pharaoh Khufu (usually known by the Greek name Cheops) during the Fourth Dynasty that the royal architects successfully constructed a pyramid with the designed geometry of an equilateral triangle and a

52-degree incline. (The inclination of the slope is determined by the correspondence of the height of the triangle to the radius of a circle, the circumference of which equals the perimeter of the square plan of the pyramid.)

Khufu's pyramid at Giza (c. 2570 B.C.) is rightly called the Great Pyramid (figs. 1-20, 1-21) for its advanced technology as well as for its size, unmatched by its predecessors or by the smaller (though still enormous) pyramids alongside it that were built by Khufu's successors, Khafre (Chefren) (c. 2530 B.C.) and Menkure (Mycerinus) (c. 2500 B.C.). The Great Pyramid is so immense—originally 482 feet high on a plan 760 feet square (even St. Peter's in Rome or London's Houses of Parliament would fit inside it!)—that the quarrying and lifting of its blocks (fig. 1-22), like all megalithic construction, have continued to puzzle archaeologists. A widely held but unproved hypothesis suggests that, in the absence of lifting tackle, cranes, or pulleys, the stones were hauled upward on an elaborate series of tiered ramps.

Perhaps the most interesting structural details of the Great Pyramid are its internal arrangements (fig. 1-23). At first the traditional subterranean burial chamber was built well below the base of the pyramid, with a passage cutting down to it from an opening in the north face. During construction, the original scheme was abandoned in favor of a burial chamber now incorporated into the mass of the pyramid itself. This in turn was succeeded by a larger chamber higher up, roughly at the pyramid's center, known as the King's Chamber, while the older space was fancifully dubbed by early archaeologists the Queen's Chamber. The King's Chamber formed a space at the heart of the pyramid 34½ feet by 17 feet in plan, and 19 feet high. Its roofing posed extreme difficulties for the builders, who were justifiably concerned about the immense pressure of the hundreds of feet of stone above it. Their solution demonstrates

1-19 Step Pyramid. Medum. c. 2704–2656 B.C.

how Egyptian architecture, the first to develop the technique of carefully fitted, ashlar masonry of relatively small blocks, was still imbued with the more primitive principles of megalithic construction. The Egyptians, in fact, were the greatest of all masters of megalithic architecture and there are few better examples of their mastery than the King's Chamber. There no chances were taken. The multiple ceiling consisted of five separate layers of megalithic slabs laid across the shorter side of the chamber (nine slabs in each layer, adding up to a total weight of 400 tons), while above them was placed a primitive but effective triangular arch to deflect the superincumbent load into the mass of the pyramid. If this relieving arch were to fail, it was expected that the monoliths below it would not all fail, and that the pharaoh's eternal home would remain undisturbed.

Various theories have been proposed concerning the pyramid's inner shaftway. In one version the program of the King's Chamber provided elaborately for communication—and noncommunication—with the world. The intricate route to the burial crypt began at the bank of the Nile in the mortuary temple complex that led from the river to the pyramid. Then, within the pyramid itself, it proceeded along the passage intended for the original subterranean tomb, up along the corridor toward the Queen's Chamber, and into the grandiose passage known as the Grand Gallery (fig. 1-24). Meant to be used only once, for the last stage of the ceremonial transportation of the king's remains to his sepulcher, the Grand Gallery formed an inclined space 153 feet in length and 28 feet in height. The walls, seven feet apart at their base, narrowed gradually toward the ceiling using the device of corbeling that we saw in Neolithic tombs, which reduced the ceiling span from seven feet to a safer four feet. Once the mummified king was laid to rest, the chamber was sealed "forever"; an immense stone portcullis, weighing some 50 tons, was lowered into a recess. This was accomplished not by the toil of immolated workers, as was once thought, but by more humane, ingenious means that might be described as the deployment of self-destructing props—either sacks of sand from which the contents were slowly allowed to empty, or timbers that were set aflame. Though sealed, the crypt remained in communication with the outer world; for mysterious reasons—perhaps for ventilation or for the passage of spirits—two narrow air shafts of 8 by 6 inches led to the faces of the pyramid.

The pyramids at Giza were the supreme Egyptian response to the vast landscape and the pharaonic will to immortality. Nothing that followed could match their immense geometric massings, square in plan, each side a perfect triangle facing one of the cardinal points of the compass, their surface of smooth limestone (long since stripped away) glistening in the sun. The apex of each pyramid was capped with a sheath of gold (the first of its treasures to fall prey to the greed of later times); at the core was the venerated body of the pharaoh, for whom the outer shape provided a "ladder" for his ascent to the sun.

After Khufu, the pyramids at Giza grew successively smaller. The later patrons must have been aware of their sepulchral inferiority to Khufu, and this may have affected the siting of the group. The pyramids are not aligned frontally with respect to one another, but diagonally along the projection of the northeast-southwest diagonal of the Great Pyramid, with some displacement in the case of Menkure's. Were they aligned frontally, their relative sizes would be inescapably apparent. In their actual relationship—most perfectly perceived in the westward approach from the Nile—their relative dimensions are ambiguous due to the visual incommensurability of their distances from one another. And because the pyramids decrease in size as they increase in distance from the observer, the apparent distances are far greater than the actual, making the site seem even vaster than it is. How conscious were the builders of these effects? The architectural eye of the Egyptians was keenly sensitive, and one would like to imagine that the visual interplay among the pyramids was consciously contrived.

Although there were pyramids after the Fourth Dynasty, with Menkure's tomb the pyramid-building impulse passed. This was partly due to the gradual economic and political decline that eventually brought the Old Kingdom to ruin. Pyramids grew smaller, were built of mud-brick, and probably were no longer repositories of kings' remains. One of the most telling causes of this decline was their failure in one critical respect: their impregnability proved illusory and grave robbers soon found their way to the incarcerated treasures. The extent and value of their plunder can be appreciated from the famous treasure of grave goods uncovered in the tomb—much later, and not a pyramid—of the minor ruler Tutankhamen.

Middle and New Kingdom Burial Chambers. The building of exposed tombs above ground was abandoned, and during the Middle Kingdom period the Egyptian tomb returned to earth. This development, which occurred in the cliffs of the Nile where the architecture was mostly not "built" but hollowed out of the living rock, had two phases. The first is illustrated by the

1-20   Pyramids of Mycerinus (Menkure; c. 2500 B.C.), Chefren (Khafre; c. 2530 B.C.), and Cheops (Khufu; c. 2570 B.C.). Giza

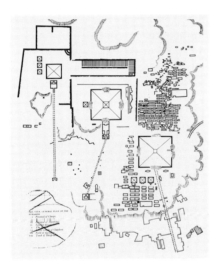

1-21   Plan, Pyramids at Giza

1-22   Detail of blocks, Pyramid of Cheops (Khufu)

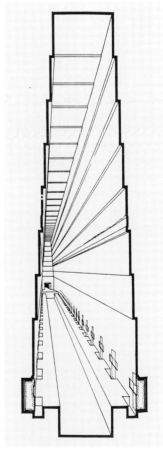

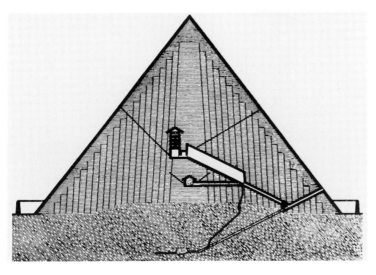

1-23
North-south section,
Pyramid of Cheops (Khufu).
(After L. Borchardt)

1-24   Grand Gallery, Pyramid of Cheops (Khufu). (Reconstruction after I. E. S. Edwards)

1-25 Rock-cut tomb. Beni Hasan. c. 2000 B.C.

so-called grotto or rock-cut tombs of the First Intermediate Period and Middle Kingdom, the sites of which were still marked by small temples at the face of the cliff. The best examples are found at Beni Hasan, 125 miles upstream from Giza on the east bank of the Nile (figs. 1-25, 1-26). Their program comprised three elements: a colonnaded portico for public worship; behind it a combined chapel and effigy chamber usually in the form of a columnar hall; and a sepulchral recess. The pier forms of Beni Hasan have attracted much attention. The interior columns were lotiform—copying lotus plants much as the half-columns at Saqqara copied papyrus—but the facade piers, when not square, were beveled down to 8- or 16-sided prisms, with a short square block remaining at the top as a rudimentary capital. This form is often termed Proto-Doric because of its similarity to the later Greek order, although no positive evidence exists that this resemblance was more than a coincidence. It is hard for many historians to imagine the Greeks going back to the archaic, minor phase of Beni Hasan for their most important architectural form. Yet Proto-Doric forms may have existed in the late Egyptian architecture of the Nile Delta, which would have been accessible to the Greeks. Moreover, Proto-Doric columns appeared prominently at the great New Kingdom Temple of Queen Hatshepsut at Deir el Bahari—the most Classical in spirit of all Egyptian architecture.

The rock-cut tombs of the Middle Kingdom proved no less inviolable to grave robbers than the pyramids. Thus the builders of the New Kingdom decided to sacrifice the monumentality of tombs in favor of increased security. To this end they developed the so-called shaft tomb—a complex series of long underground corridors and chambers hollowed out of the cliffs of the Valley of the Kings on the west bank of the Nile near Thebes. Architecturally these tombs are of minor interest, which is not surprising in light of how they were created.

1-26 Cult chamber, detail, rock-cut tomb

The royal patron would start the tunneling of his sepulchral chambers as early in his reign as possible. How the tomb developed depended on his fortunes and his longevity. When he died, the tunneling stopped wherever it was. After the funeral ceremonies, the artificial cave was sealed up and its point of entrance concealed. An inscription by one of his court officials concerning the tomb of Tuthmosis I reads: "I attended the excavation of the cliff tomb of His Majesty alone, no one seeing, no one hearing."

Mortuary Temples. It is at this juncture, following the decline of the pyramid and the concealment of the burial chambers in the depths of the cliffs, that mortuary temples developed into Egypt's most important monumental form. The most forward-looking prototypes for the great later New Kingdom temples were the funerary temple complexes set before the Old Kingdom pyramids. These normally comprised three interconnected units: a valley temple near the river where the king's body, borne there on a special funerary bark, was embalmed; a mortuary temple at the foot of the pyramid for rituals devoted to the cult of the pharaoh and associated deities; and, connecting these two temple structures, a long, narrow causeway between thick, high walls. At Giza, the temple complex of Khufu's successor, Khafre, is the most impressive preserved example of the form (fig. 1-27). With its creation were crystalized the components of temple architecture: large and open courts, roofed passageways, pillared and colonnaded halls, the axial alignment of spaces, and statue chambers.

The colossal Sphinx (fig. 1-28), immediately to the north of the Valley Temple, represented the god Re-Harakhte on guard

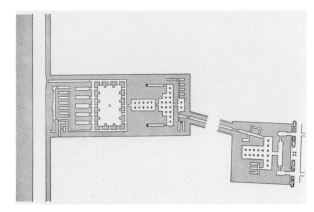

1-27   Plan, valley and pyramid temples of Chefren (Khafre). Giza

over the king's tomb. The temple, slightly off-square in its outer plan, contained an intricately constructed set of interiors (colorplate 2). There were twin entrances leading to a transverse vestibule, off which opened the T-shaped core of the building. This comprised a long antechapel of two aisles plus a triple-aisled main chapel. The structural details of this interior formed the purest of all megalithic architecture. In the Great Hall, square pillars 15 feet high supported lintels of red granite. Colossal statues of Khafre stood between each pair of pillars, illuminated by the light that filtered through the slits in the thick roof.

1-28   The Great Sphinx. Giza. c. 2530 B.C.

1-29   View from northwest, Mortuary temples of Mentuhotep and Hatshepsut. Deir el Bahari.

1-30   Mortuary Complex of Mentuhotep (with Pyramid) and
       Mortuary Temple of Queen Hatshepsut in foreground.
       (Reconstruction drawing after Lange and Hirmer)

1-31   Portico of the Anubis Sanctuary, Mortuary Temple
       of Queen Hatshepsut

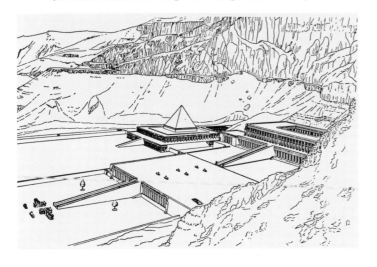

From the Great Hall a covered causeway some 600 yards long ascended northwest to Khafre's Mortuary Temple, still discernible in ruins at the foot of the pyramid. The Mortuary Temple resembled the Valley Temple, but was more spatially complex. From the causeway one reached an intricate set of vestibules laid out along the principal axis of the temple but—recalling the inverted T-shape of the Valley Temple—presenting first a series of transverse aisles of diminishing length leading to a narrow door, in turn leading to a triple-aisled passage leading to a second narrow doorway. Beyond lay a large rectangular cross-axial court, its massive piers decorated with royal sculptures, and surrounded by an aisle leading to the many parallel chapels of the sanctuary proper at the rear of the temple, which was dedicated to a multitude of deities.

Five hundred years later, when the pyramid complex had declined, Middle Kingdom Pharaoh Mentuhotep II chose the base of the cliff at Deir el Bahari for the location of his mortuary temple and for the first time in Egyptian architecture placed a monumental structure against the lofty palisade walls

(figs. 1-29, 1-30). It is not clear whether he retained the pyramid form or whether he constructed a simple flat-roofed superstructure. According to some modern reconstructions of his complex, he may have retained it in a revised role and reduced dimension. The hypothetical pyramid of Mentuhotep II did not dominate the precinct; it was merely one element in an elaborate ensemble of ramps, terraces, courts, and galleries that rose from the flat plane of the valley to the craggy upland heights and into the depths of the cliff. Aligned roughly on an east-west axis, the site began with a broad ramp that led through a ceremonial gateway in the massive outer wall, finally leading into a large courtyard. At the western end of the court an elevated terrace, approached by a ramp, would have been surmounted by the pyramid, beneath which lay a false burial chamber with an empty sarcophagus; the pyramid was framed on all sides by pillared galleries, and these led to a rectangular court carved into the base of the cliffs. Opening off the west side of this court was an aisled hall, and beyond it finally the sacrosanct tomb of Mentuhotep, hidden within the rock.

This novel combination of open architectural elements rhythmically arranged in a dramatic natural setting inspired one of the incomparable monuments of ancient Egypt: the Mortuary Temple of Queen Hatshepsut, one of Egypt's most singular rulers (figs. 1-29, 1-31). Hatshepsut (b. 1479 B.C.), the daughter of the Eighteenth Dynasty pharaoh Tuthmosis I, married her half-brother Tuthmosis II who had previously fathered a son by another alliance. At his death she served as regent to her nephew-stepson, but when the youth came to maturity, she refused to relinquish power and managed to stay on as queen. Since it was so unusual for a woman to rule as king, Queen Hatshepsut assumed the accoutrements of a male ruler; thus many of her official portraits bear a male appearance, including a ceremonial beard. Together with the royal architect, Senmut, she constructed the least typically Egyptian of Egypt's major monuments. Her mortuary temple, dedicated to the sun god Amon-Ra, was laid out below the cliffs at Deir el Bahari beside the monument of Mentuhotep (built 500 years before). The earlier structure served Hatshepsut as a model and, less fortunately, as a quarry. In both works, colonnaded terraces played a predominant architectural role. But their deployment is tellingly different. In Mentuhotep's ensemble, longitudinal axiality was subordinated to centralized terraces around the visually dominant pyramid. In Hatshepsut's temple, there was no such dominating mass, probably because her burial was deliberately separate from her mortuary complex; centralized composition yielded to horizontal axiality. The east-west axis, running perpendicular to the cliffs, was drawn out along an expanded set of three terraces, their retaining walls articulated by double colonnades of square piers (except for the Proto-Doric columns forming a chapel in the northwest corner of the middle level). Hatshepsut's temple was a construction comprised less of stone masses than of the emptiness of terraces, ramps, and a courtyard, the whole playing against the natural terrace below the cliffs. Historically, the monument characterized the shift from the compact geometry of the Old Kingdom pyramids to the linear compositions of the New Kingdom temples: the transposition from the self-contained majesty of the pyramids to temples that required the complementary presence and movement of the worshiper as an active participant.

In its clarity of detail, elegance of proportions, and openness, lightness, and interplay with the landscape, Hatshepsut's monument was the closest that Egypt came to the architecture of the Classical world. This rapprochement is most concretely seen in its preserved colonnades, particularly the Proto-Doric sections, permeated by a sureness of proportions and crispness of line. A salient detail is the trabeation, which comprises two elements: an unadorned lintel slab and the standard Egyptian cornice, composed of a strong torus molding surmounted by a deep gorge, capped by an upright, flat listel band. The gorge, or cavetto, cornice is said to derive from the bending forward of reeds in vernacular civil construction, pushed by roof members. Here its appropriateness to the broad style of the architecture as well as its specific mastery of relief and weight are unsurpassed in Egyptian architecture and nearly equal to the visual sureness of the Greeks.

New Kingdom Temples. In the funerary temples at Giza and Deir el Bahari are found many elements that would appear in the New Kingdom temples at Thebes and elsewhere: long approaches, guardian sphinxes, colonnaded vestibules and inner courts, darkening shrines, and the intricate linear progression of constructed spaces. Essentially the Theban temples projected a controlled series of architectural experiences, passing in stages from exterior openness and light to interior closure and darkness. A psychological awareness of inaccessibility was quite deliberate, for only the select, the pharaoh, and the priests penetrated the sanctuary proper, i.e., the inner sanctum that is often the core of religious architecture. The architects of the Egyptian priesthood developed an intricate, inward-turning world that passed from the earthly to the supernatural realms.

The temples at "the hundred-gated city of Thebes," as Achilles called it in the *Iliad*, were built at two sites on a broad plain on the right bank of the Nile (fig. 1-32); known today as Karnak and Luxor, they were connected by a grand avenue of sphinxes. Although the immense principal temples were begun in the Eighteenth Dynasty, a clearer understanding of their composition can be gained by first studying the smaller temple erected in about 1100 B.C. in the Twentieth Dynasty—the Temple of Khons, son of Amun, within the temple precinct dedicated to his father at Karnak (fig. 1-33). At the Temple of Khons, the essential components and patterns of the great temples were found in elementary form. The worshiper was first met by an imposing facade—the so-called pylon, the ultimate prototype of all the facades of Western architecture—higher and wider than the temple behind it (fig. 1-34). Bilaterally symmetrical, with a stress on the central axis that ran throughout the temple, the pylon comprised two immense, battered walls flanking a lower, single portal at the center. The walls of the pylon were edged with torus moldings, crowned by the characteristic cavetto cornice, and were decorated with complex programs of relief, colossal statues, and masts for royal and religious banners. The facade was thus more than an imposing, if penetrable, barrier to the interior; it also carried a striking set of explicit messages.

Behind the pylon of the Temple of Khons was the peristyle court, a form that, like the pylon, was found in all such temples, and was defined by one or more layers of colonnades on two or more sides. Generally the columns were lotiform in shape, and frequently framed series of monumental statues of the king. Beyond the peristyle court was the most impressive Egyptian interior, the Hypostyle Hall. The term signifies a room whose ceiling is carried by many supports, and such was the case here; indeed, in the greater temples the massive columns overwhelmed the narrow spaces separating them. In plan, the Hypostyle Hall had a double axis. It always formed a rectangle oriented transversally, but the principal axis of the temple cut through the hall in one or more stressed aisles. These aisles led to the sanctuary; but the common worshiper was not allowed to penetrate beyond the Hypostyle Hall. Only the king and priests were ushered through the central door into the inner sanctum.

The precinct wall delimited the temple area from the vastness of nature, while the sphinxes established a channel of movement within that delimitation. The world without was separated from the world within by the pylon. In the peristyle court, huge colonnades surrounded the worshiper. In the Hypostyle Hall, the brilliant Egyptian sky, still seen in the court, vanished and was supplanted by the night sky painted on the ceiling. The space closed in oppressively, dominated by thick rows of columns in dim light. Those finally admitted to

the sanctuary found themselves in semidarkness, in a claustrophobic set of low, confined spaces.

All other late Egyptian temples had the same components, the same sequence of spaces and masses as in the Temple of Khons. Their elaboration involved not a fundamental change of program, but an extension of it, in scale, in enlargement and refinement of various aspects, and in the duplication of one or more of the basic elements. In Thebes, the most stupendous example was the Temple of Amun, at Karnak (fig. 1-32). It measured 1,215 by 376 feet and was set in a vast enclosure together with other, secondary temples (including Khons) and a sacred lake. The building's pretensions were immediately perceived on approaching the immense front pylon—50 feet thick at the base, 146 feet high and 376 feet wide—before which were set two mighty obelisks contributed by Tuthmosis I and Hatshepsut (fig. 1-35). These were placed symmetrically on either side of the main axis but at varying distances from the pylon—the larger nearer to the pylon, that is, farther from the approaching worshiper—perhaps to adjust visually for their varying height (an example of the kind of sophisticated spatial effects we have already witnessed at the Giza pyramids). Both spires, in any

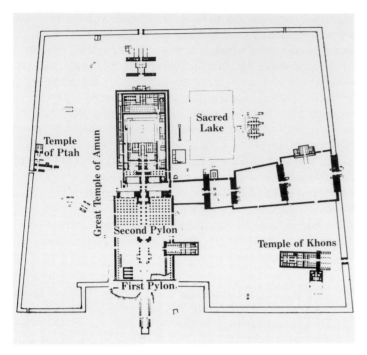

1-32   General plan, Karnak

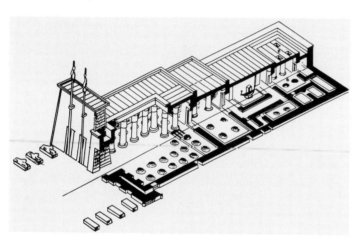

1-33   Temple of Khons. Karnak. c. 1100 B.C.
         (Isometric section after K. Michalowski)

1-34   Pylon, Temple of Khons

1-35   Temple of Amun with obelisks of Tuthmosis I
         and Hatshepsut. Karnak

case, were typical of the obelisks that were set before the great temples. They not only provided strong visual accents but their hieroglyphs usually contained elaborate forms of their patrons' titularies, and their gilded pyramidal apexes symbolized the sacred stone of the sun worshipers. The obelisks tested Egyptian builders to the full, for they were monoliths whose quarrying, transportation, and erection involved the greatest concentration of megalithic technology and expenditure of focused energy.

1-36 Hypostyle Hall, Temple of Amun at Karnak. c. 1290 B.C.

1-37 Model, Hypostyle Hall, Temple of Amun at Karnak. 1305–1205 B.C.

Through the first pylon of Karnak one entered an overpowering architectural realm: a second pylon and later a third; beyond the initial sequence of court and hall there followed a narrower court and hall, then the sanctuary area (resembling a printed electronic circuit in its intricacy of form); and at the far end one reached the Festival Hall of Tuthmosis III, all on an immense scale and with dense sculptural embellishment.

The compounding and elaboration of the basic components of the Karnak temple program must have produced a profound effect on the worshiper. Even today, the beholder is overwhelmed by the scale and richness, staggered by the repetitions, and transported by the architectural fantasies of the priesthood. One aspect in particular was stunningly visionary: the Hypostyle Hall of Seti I and his son Ramesses II (figs. 1-36, 1-37). This largest of all hypostyle halls measured 340 feet in width and 170 feet in depth; its roof of stone slabs was supported by 134 columns standing in sixteen rows—seven rows on each side formed of columns 9 feet thick and 42 feet high, framing two rows of larger columns almost 12 feet in diameter

1-38 Principal forms of Egyptian columns: (a) Palm column; (b) Papyrus-bundle column; (c) Lotus column; (d) "Tent pole" column; (e) Papyrus column with open bud. (Drawing by Enzo di Grazia)

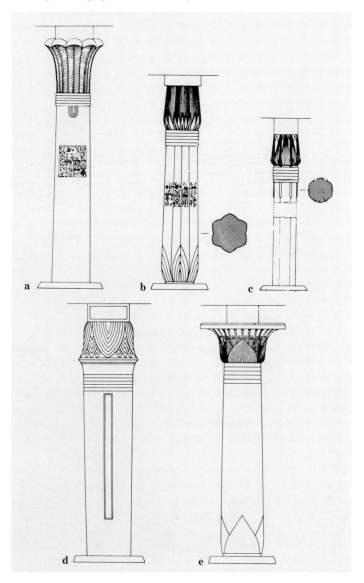

and 69 feet in height that ran through three central processional aisles. The columns and walls were everywhere incised with polychromed figures and hieroglyphs in relief, intensifying the presence of the columnar masses in the narrow interspaces. The columns were of two types: closed papyrus buds on the sides, and open papyrus flowers in the two towering center rows (fig. 1-38). While the roof that the papyrus-bud columns support was closed—the lateral aisles having no lighting of their own—the roof of the three central aisles rose above that of the sides, leaving a vertical gap called a clerestory, which contained slitlike windows. This early clerestory allowed considerable light to fall mainly into the three central aisles, fading off into the side aisles. The effect was that the closed-bud columns of the side aisles appeared to lift toward the light in the central aisles and blossom into the papyrus flowers. The success of this feat of architectural illusionism—achieving the sense of organic growth in columns nearly 12 feet in diameter—was augmented by obscuring the blocks connecting the papyrus flowers with the clerestory ceiling, so that the flowers appeared to rise unencumbered toward the light.

Secular Architecture. The cult of the dead and of the gods dominated Egyptian monumental architecture, but it did not prevent Egyptian life from attaining a richness and vitality that left suggestive, if enigmatic, evidence of itself in secular construction and cities. Egyptian architecture was not all the somberness and gloom of gigantic temples and tombs but, to the contrary, also an affirmation of life busy with trading, farming, administration, crafts, and pleasure. Even the tombs were filled with gay, colorful depictions of Egyptian life, and the temple columns celebrated the vital, living forces of nature. Because the residential buildings of Egypt were usually built of perishable materials, remains of actual structures are lacking. However, the descriptive realism of Egyptian art, especially those surviving small wooden models of everyday life, provide

a useful record. From these sources the appearance of Egyptian country houses—with gardens and outbuildings—and town houses can be reconstructed. Egyptian towns were crowded, with narrow streets of two- and three-story houses like that of the Theban treasurer Tehutynefer (c. 1440 B.C.), the interior of whose home is portrayed in some painted fragments in the Metropolitan Museum of Art in New York (fig. 1-39). The open roof above the three stories of living quarters served as a granary and storeroom, and sometimes as a kitchen. Family suites, servants' quarters, two staircases, and rooms for the preparation of linen, bread, and beer were included in the structure; many latticed windows, set high in the walls, protected the residents from the searing heat and sun; and a variety of columnar supports upheld the ceilings of some of the grander rooms.

Still extant are vestiges of some royal palaces such as the one at Tell el Amarna (fig. 1-40), built around 1370 B.C. by Akhenaten (Amenhotep IV), which has a groundplan of remarkable regularity that parallels developments in the monumental temple structures of the period. At the same time, the arrangement of its interiors—a bilaterally symmetrical design set out on a square plan—forecast the rational and harmonious structures of the Classical world. At the rear of a rectangular annex was a small throne room that was the last in a rhythmic sequence of open courts and colonnaded halls.

Akhenaten's town of Tell el Amarna is an important example of early urban planning (fig. 1-41), although we can do little more than mention it here. Built all at once, about 1370 B.C., as

1-40   Plan, North Palace. Tell el Amarna. c. 1370 B.C.

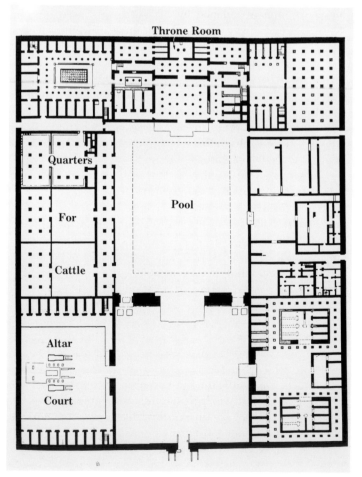

1-39   Wall paintings, Tehutynefer's town house. Thebes.
c. 1440 B.C. (Reconstructed drawing. The Metropolitan
Museum, New York)

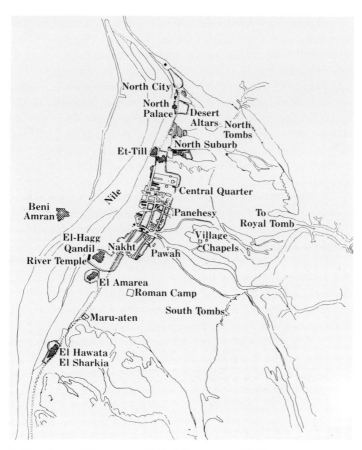

1-41 General town plan. Tell el Amarna. c. 1370 B.C.

a new capital city and residence for the iconoclastic king and his court (and abandoned by his successors soon after his death), it lies midway between Luxor and Cairo on the eastern bank of the Nile. It was composed of large estates for the wealthy, with smaller houses in between, and was well on the way to developing extensive slum areas by the time it was abandoned. It had a military district and a suburb, large and small temples, cemeteries, and shops for sculptors and manufacturers. Brilliant ornamental decoration was common in this unusual city, including foliage sculpted into stone columns once thought to belong to later epochs. Important buildings were given pylons embellished with glazed tiles, as well as polychromed stone relief and abundant wall paintings.

Many varieties of public and domestic architecture are found at Tell el Amarna, from the classically planned apartments of the royal palace to more modest, yet still impressive houses of the court officials, in addition to office buildings and warehouses. Startling in its resemblance to modern architecture is the reconstruction of a block of buildings in the merchant class district of the north suburb (fig. 1-42). Closely grouped on narrow streets to accommodate the commercial thoroughfares and busy traffic, such houses were ample on the interior, comparatively tall, with the roof terraces and loggias common to hot climates that served a variety of functions, including storage and laundry. Few cities of similar antiquity offer as rich an image of Egyptian life, reconstructed from the denuded stones that are the sole architectural testaments of a vigorous and brilliant settlement.

In studying Egypt we have briefly discussed 3,000 years of remarkably consistent architectural history. Egyptian architecture

is generally regarded as manifesting little change. But this is a modern viewpoint, seen through eyes grown accustomed to overnight developments. A more appropriate perspective sets Egypt against the Neolithic age from which it emerged and in which it took early humanity thousands of years to achieve the most rudimentary post-and-lintel dolmens, not to mention the previous tens of thousands of years needed to acquire the simplest tools. From this viewpoint the emergence of Egyptian pyramids in the few generations between the mastabas of the First and Second Dynasties, Zoser's step pyramid, and Khufu's Great Pyramid in the Fourth Dynasty seems a breakthrough of spellbinding potency and speed. The later development of the temple is similarly astonishing in its creative energy and attainment.

Yet for all its power of invention, certain characteristics endure throughout Egyptian architecture. And this leads us back to the character of the land and its influence, perhaps greater in Egypt than in any other architecture. The desert and the Nile River that dominate the landscape are archetypes of both change and eternity; they are always the same, yet always in flux. This seems to be associated with Egypt's creation of an architecture with a special sense of time—and timelessness. One is intended to see the pyramids and the temples not just as forms in space but in the fourth dimension: as enduring through eternity. Thus we can account for their geometric clarity of form, their measure, solidity, and simplicity. The limitless space of the desert, where there are no masses to speak of, was another factor. As if to complement the desert, Egyptian architecture was only minimally concerned with space and maximally with masses. This is not only illustrated in the pyramids but also in the temples, where the forms count so much more than the voids. Unlike the medieval builders, who created voluminous cathedrals as if in compensation for claustrophobic urban crowding, Egyptians, in their monumental architecture on the desert's edge, did not thirst for space. Instead, they experienced a compelling need for definitive blocks of matter to anchor their position in space and time. They were also affected by the linear, fluid image of

**1-42 Houses in the north suburb. Tell el Amarna.
(Reconstruction drawing after H. Frankfort
and J. D. S. Pendlebury)**

the life-giving river. Such an image is connected with the development of increasing linearity and axiality of architectural composition—already seen in the funerary temples of the pyramids, later in the rock-cut tombs and at Hatshepsut's temple, and then definitively in the axial concatenations of the Theban temples. But beyond the desert and the river was the primeval, stone-age past that still lived on, not only in constructions but in the aura of exclusivity and magic with which Egyptian architecture was imbued. Like megalithic works and unlike much of the architecture of the West which attempted to enfold people, the monumental architecture of Egypt excluded all but the king, living or dead, and the priests from the building's innermost parts. There, sealed in the perfect cubiculum of the tomb chamber or sanctuary, the prayers of the priest might become a reality, and the soul of the pharaoh could begin its voyage to eternity.

ANCIENT NEAR EAST

While the architectural development of Egypt was coherent and enduring, the cultures that succeeded each other in ancient Mesopotamia during those same thirty centuries produced a set of more limited, heterogeneous architectural styles. Nevertheless they are of high intrinsic interest, and provide a number of prototypes for the second of the great architectural styles—that of Greece.

In contrast to the clear-cut Nile Valley, the rich valleys of the Tigris and Euphrates rivers or Mesopotamia (the Greek word meaning "between rivers")—had ill-defined edges. To the south and west the area faded into the emptiness of Arabia; to the west and north into the fertile plain of Syria; and to the east its foothills merged with Persian and Armenian highlands—a region strongly influenced by Mesopotamia but never under its control. This unencompassed space presented no natural barrier to invaders and indeed there was continual warfare in the region. The Tigris and Euphrates region, unlike that of the beneficently cyclical Nile, suffered from alternate drought and disastrous floods. From Mesopotamia, therefore, one would not expect the homogeneous, continuous culture of Egypt, nor the same forms of art. Yet tradition assigns to this region the Garden of Eden and the Four Rivers of Genesis, and we know that the transformation from the prehistoric age to historical civilization occurred here even earlier than in Egypt, some five centuries earlier in fact, in about 3500 B.C. At that time small agricultural, pottery-making, cloth-weaving villages were transmuted into societies of cities. Like the Egyptians, the Mesopotamians developed a form of writing, so-called cuneiform or wedge-shaped figures; so many of their historical records are preserved that the resulting confusion of data still has not been unraveled. Their mathematics and science were more advanced than those of Egypt; astrology was their invention; and they are now recognized as the inventors of the wheeled vehicle. They were masters of hydraulics, drainage, and irrigation, and the present bareness of the region betrays little of the ancient cultivated greenness for which it was famous. They were also sophisticated lawmakers: a Babylonian king, Hammurabi (reigned 1792–1750 B.C.), was responsible for codifying and recording the first known extensive body of laws, which included the maxim "an eye for an eye, a tooth for a tooth," and provided equal legal rights for women.

From the fourth millennium to about 500 B.C., the Egyptian dynasties and the centers of power that succeeded each other in the Near East progressed as parallel focal points in the development of civilization. The periodization is ever-changing in the light of new archaeological discoveries, but a basic sequence has been established. Around 4500 B.C., in the lower Mesopotamian valley near the Persian Gulf, Sumerian culture first appeared, reaching its golden age in about 3300 B.C. during the Uruk period (named after biblical Erech or modern Warka where its remains were first found). Overwhelmed in about 2000 B.C. by foreign tribes, the Sumerian civilization—the most original of all the early Near Eastern cultures—was displaced by that of the Babylonians and the Kassites until power shifted in about the fourteenth century B.C. to a bellicose people from the northern highlands—the Assyrians. Their powerful armies helped build the world's first great empire, extending from North Africa to western Persia. However, Assyrian strength could not prevail against the combined invasions of the Scythians, the Medes, and finally the Babylonians who destroyed Nineveh in 612 B.C. The subsequent Neo-Babylonian Revival, with its brilliant hot-house culture, was cut short when in 539 B.C. Babylon was seized by Cyrus, an Achaemenian Persian. The Persians remained in Mesopotamia for two hundred years, and their far-reaching power might eventually have destroyed even ancient Greece had they not succumbed to Alexander the Great in 331 B.C. Thereafter, Mesopotamia was in the hands of the Greeks for a century, the Parthians for over four centuries, and the Sassanian Persians until A.D. 651 and the coming of Islam. The Hittites and associated cultures in Asia Minor and Syria also contributed to the general cultural richness of the region.

Sumer. The Sumerians had neither timber nor stone. For their monumental construction only one material was available, but in unlimited quantities: the mud of the alluvial plain. It was formed into bricks, dried in the sun, and built into massive walls employing earth mortar. If structurally the mud-bricks presented severe limitations, historically their fate was disastrous. The material is highly soluble in water and this meant that the buildings themselves were soluble. They were abandoned upon the collapse of the civilization, and most of them all but disappeared shortly afterward. Needless to say, archaeological research in the region is difficult; in many cases only traces of foundations remain, although we can examine some rare examples of fuller preservation.

The abundance of mud-brick material led Sumerian builders to develop construction methods appropriate to its physical properties. Structurally, such bricks are weak when compared to stone. To compensate, the walls of Sumerian buildings were very thick (serving as thermal insulators as well) and reinforced with the buttresses characteristic of temples throughout Mesopotamian history. Bricks could not be used as lintels to span the distance between walls, and as a result narrow oblong spaces were covered with tunnel vaults; such constricted interiors (with doorways generally placed in the long side) became a primary unit of architecture in the region.

Mud presented other problems: even in the form of carefully shaped bricks it was not very attractive, nor was it resistant to

1-43 Cone mosaics decorating half-columns of Pillared Hall. Uruk

weather. Methods were found to disguise and protect it, first by whitewashing and patterned coloring. The latter method—used only briefly at the end of the fourth millennium—consisted of a "skin" made of thousands of colored cones of clay or stone inserted in patterns into the surface of the structure (fig. 1-43). They transformed the dull and heavy walls into a brilliant polychromed mosaic. Later, instead of the pigmented cones, the Sumerians sometimes used bricks or tempera paint as a wall covering, with the same colors as the cones—red, black, and white—applied to a whitewashed ground or to plain dried mud. A major example of the polychromed cone facing was found at the so-called Pillared Hall at Uruk, where it took the form of diverse reticulated patterns derived from fabric designs.

Sumerian architecture, however, was basically not columnar like that of New Kingdom Egypt. Although the columns and engaged half-columns of the Pillared Hall at Uruk preceded the earliest comparable Egyptian forms at Saqqara by some five hundred years, the column appeared only sporadically and as an unusual decorative feature in Sumer. The characteristic architecture of Sumer was one of heavy walls and great massings, as exemplified in its characteristic monumental building type—the temple. A highly developed cult of

the dead was not part of the Mesopotamian theological system, and tomb architecture was rare in the ancient Near Eastern countries. An important early sanctuary is known as Temple VIII at Eridu, the ancient site near Ur, dated 3500–3000 B.C. Here the characteristic layout of the Sumerian temple was used, similar to the famous plan (fig. 1-44) on the lap of the statue depicting the later King Gudea of Lagash (c. 2150 B.C.). Within an overall rectangular scheme, a central court was bordered by bastions (a carry-over from earlier fortress architecture), and on the long sides were rooms oblong in shape and perhaps vaulted (one of them containing a stair that led to a roof terrace). In the courtyard were set an altar and an offering table. The temple walls were thick and patterned with repeated buttressing. The whole structure was set on a primitive mud-brick platform, with stairs leading up to an entrance on the long side of the temple.

1-45 White Temple. Uruk. c. 3500–3000 B.C.

1-44 Gudea with architectural lap tablet, from Lagash. c. 2150 B.C. (Musée du Louvre, Paris)

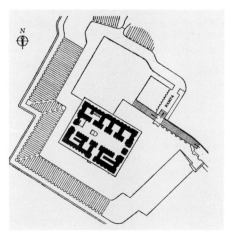

1-46
Plan, White Temple on ziggurat.

The function of the Sumerian temple followed naturally from the Sumerian religion based on the elements; the sky, earth, water, sun and moon, storms and lightning, all were primary forces in it. Essentially it was a religion of an agrarian society dependent on the weather, which ultimately led to the Sumerian invention of astrology as a means by which the priesthood might—so it was believed—predict and control the environment. The principal Sumerian rites were celebrated in the temple; an elaborate ritual was enacted in the courtyard, with offerings set out upon the table and animal sacrifices taking place at the altar. The simplicity of the long court heightened the drama of the ritual.

At the White Temple at Uruk, built in about 3500–3000 B.C., the temple setting had evolved further (figs. 1-45, 1-46). The corner bastions had been eliminated, and the building with its platform had been placed on a huge mound of earth, an artificial mountain called a ziggurat, rising more than 40 feet above the plain. Later, the ziggurat was to achieve remarkable formal sophistication with stepped levels, dramatic staircases, and lines subtly curved, perhaps for optical effects. This last refinement is deduced from the remains of one of the most interesting of all Mesopotamian ziggurats—the Third Dynasty construction at Ur, c. 2150–2050 B.C. (fig. 1-47), where royal architects in the service of King Ur-nammu inventively varied the basic theme: the vertical sides of the platforms sloped sharply inward; the heights of the successive stages were carefully proportioned; the walls curved slightly outward, conceivably to add buoyancy to the weighty structure, thereby anticipating by 1,700 years the infinitely more extensive optical refinements of the Athenian Parthenon. The

ziggurat at Ur had more than the usual single stairway—there were three, and they converged at an impressive gate tower topped perhaps by a dome.

Although ziggurats had been devised as a corrective to adverse terrain—much of Mesopotamia was a region of floods and unhealthy swamps and elevated platforms were highly desirable—more was involved. The form brings to mind the Egyptian pyramid, which indeed it preceded and may have inspired (particularly as the stepped form of many ziggurats approximated that of Zoser's pyramid and the structure of the true pyramids). The Egyptian pyramid was a ladder to the sky, and the symbolic function of the ziggurat was similar—to bridge the gap between human and divine. It not only resembled a mountain but actually was considered a sacred mount, the habitual setting of divine revelation. It was on Mt. Sinai that Moses received the Ten Commandments. Therefore such artificial mountains were built in the cities of the plains to favor the communication between the human and the divine. The shrine, or temple on top, was the hall where the divine manifestation was awaited, the sanctuary of the god served by attendant priests.

Assyria. The principal cities of the Assyrians—Nineveh, Dun Sharrukin (modern Khorsabad), Nimrud, and Assur—are associated with the resounding dramas of the Old Testament. In contrast to the agrarian and commercial south Mesopotamian culture, the Assyrians, who came from the high plateaus of the north, were great warriors and hunters. Their armies swept like a scythe to conquer and control vast portions of southwest Asia. Art produced by the Assyrians was characteristically

1-47 Northeastern facade with restored stairs, Ziggurat at Ur

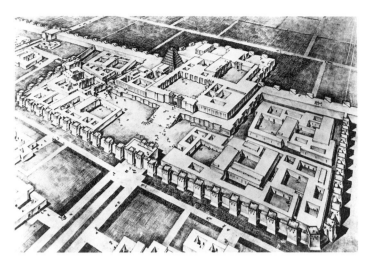

1-48 Citadel of Sargon II. Khorsabad. 742–706 B.C.
(Reconstruction by C. B. Altman)

vigorous, even violent. It exaggerated the muscular stature of its protagonists and dwelled on lion hunts, military campaigns, and the sacking of cities.

The city that most dramatically demonstrated the self-conscious sovereign authority and might of Assyrian kings was Khorsabad, and it is there that the principal remains of Assyrian architecture are found. Dedicated by King Sargon II in 706 B.C., Khorsabad was never completed. It had been his intention to make it a royal capital, but only a part of his ambitious plan, which included palaces, temples, and administrative headquarters, was executed. Built in a flat open field, the city was about a mile square with entrance gates planned for each side. The large barrel vault in one of the Khorsabad gates reveals the Mesopotamian use of vaulting which, however, was not often used because of the preference for flat, beam-supported mud roofs. Although a monumental entrance gate had been planned for the north wall, it was replaced by a bastion-platform on which the royal palace was set (fig. 1-48), protected by man-bull guardian figures flanking the gates to the precinct. The buildings within, in contrast to the outer walls, were characterized by a conspicuous lack of order, crowded together with little consideration for their orientation or aesthetic balance. They were arranged around two major courts about which were grouped smaller courts and a variety of large and small rooms in labyrinthine manner, with public reception halls in one part, private quarters and services in another. The largest room was the throne room, elongated, vast, and preceded on one long side by an antechamber that separated it from a court. One of its short walls contained a shallow niche in front of which was a two-stepped platform on which the royal throne probably stood. Assyrian taste ran to elaborate decoration with relief sculpture, polychromed glazed brick, alabaster revetment, and sculpture in the round; the great halls were embellished with enough of such ornament to satisfy King Sargon's wish for unsurpassed splendor.

Neo-Babylonian Revival. Although the last Assyrian kingdom at Nineveh fell in 612 B.C., the Assyrian kings in Babylon maintained political independence, and they chose to revive the old Babylonian culture rather than continuing Assyrian ways. Monarchs such as Nabopolassar and Nebuchadnezzar ordered temples rebuilt, fortifications restored, and new palaces constructed in the old manner. In contrast to the coarseness of the Assyrian and the vitality of the Sumerian cultures, the Neo-Babylonian Revival was a soft and elegant, if not decadent, age. Architecture was now embellished in lavish style with sumptuous ornaments and brilliantly enameled brick reliefs of sacred animals. The royal citadel was enlarged and, within it, a splendid new palace and a processional avenue were constructed. Babylon itself was surrounded by a new system of thick defensive walls more than eleven miles in circumference, crowned by rhythmically spaced towers (fig. 1-49). One of the wonders of the new Babylon was the highway that ran along the top of the wall, so wide that a chariot drawn by four horses abreast could turn upon it and pass a similar vehicle. The walls were pierced at eight points by city gates dedicated to the principal Babylonian deities; the most famous entrance, the tall Ishtar Gate, was on the heavily trafficked northern side of the city. The Ishtar Gate is the most impressive remnant of the city; it has been reconstructed partly out of its original materials and preserved in the State Museum, Berlin (colorplate 5). In contrast to the ferocity of Assyrian art, here numerous tiers of elegant bulls and Babylonian dragons composed in the low relief of glazed polychrome bricks float against a light blue background. Even the abstract details—friezes, moldings, battlements, the arch—achieve admirable refinement.

1-49 The Babylon of Nebuchadnezzar with the Ishtar Gate
(c. 575 B.C.) and Tower of Babel. (Reconstruction.
The Oriental Institute, University of Chicago)

The Ishtar Gate dominated the wide processional avenue that was bordered by temples and palaces and led to the inner city and to the Tower of Babel—the most famous of all ziggurats of ancient Mesopotamia and many times restored even before the Revival period. Only its groundplan and traces of three broad stairways leading to its summit have been preserved. The city streets were systematically laid out, with some parallel to the river and others crossing at right angles—the result of clear and organized planning.

Of the grandiose palaces constructed at Babylon, the most important was Nebuchadnezzar's, a dense maze approximately 900 by 600 feet, composed of small units disposed in a manner as free as the city streets were orderly. Grouped around five courts, and accessible through narrow passages and alleys, were the administrative offices, the barracks of the garrison, the harem, and the king's private apartments and their service quarters. Among the remaining traces of the palace the throne room has been positively identified. It was a large chamber of approximately 170 by 56 feet with the long walls of the rectangle thicker than those of the shorter ends. This implies the existence of a tunnel vault above, which must have been by far the largest of its time. As in Khorsabad, the throne room of Nebuchadnezzar's palace was entered by a door in the long side. Its facade, however, was not guarded by the demonic creatures customary to Assyrian architecture, but was instead decorated with a surface of glazed bricks and low-relief configurations. Against a deep blue background were reliefs of voluted capitals and graceful floral designs in white, yellow, and blue, and slender masts and palmettes.

The palace was praised by ancient historians for its many splendid features, but none more than its Hanging Gardens whose existence still has not been convincingly separated from legend. If they were not simply a myth, they must have entailed an imaginative transformation of the sacred mountain ziggurat into pleasure palace, for the gardens were raised on stone (not brick) arches as much as 75 feet high—a seemingly sky-suspended green island visible from afar. According to the Greek geographer Strabo, the gardens were irrigated by a screw pump that lifted water from the Euphrates River. One of the many myths about the gardens is that they were built not by Nebuchadnezzar but by a later prince to remind his favorite courtesan of the trees and flowers of her native Persia.

Little else remains of Neo-Babylonian architecture; in fact the literary contribution of the age was more important than the artistic, for it transmitted astrology and other Mesopotamian sciences to the Hellenistic world.

Ancient Israel. It is appropriate, in a discussion of Neo-Babylonian architecture, to include some reference to ancient Hebrew architecture, for the two are historically, if not stylistically, tied together during this period. Monumental landmarks of the earliest Hebrew architecture center around the celebrated temple (fig. 1-50) built by King Solomon in the tenth century B.C. on Mount Moriah in Jerusalem. When ancient Israel was conquered by the armies of Babylonia serving under Nebuchadnezzar in 587–586 B.C., Solomon's temple, foremost symbol of Jewish religion and culture, was destroyed and the Jews exiled.

Descriptions in the Old Testament, as well as archaeological deductions made by comparison with structures unearthed in

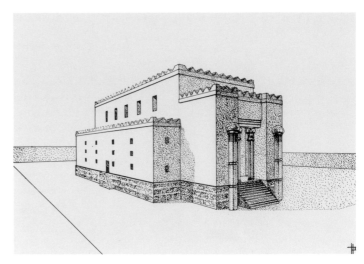

1-50   Solomon's Temple. Jerusalem. 10th century B.C. (Reconstruction after T. A. Busink)

Syria and in other parts of Israel, tell us much about the appearance of Solomon's temple. It was a rectangular structure surrounded by open courtyards; it had an inner sanctum, a forehall with two grand columns of bronze, and between these spaces a larger main room. Typologically it is allied, as we will see shortly, with the Greek temple and its ancestor in Aegean culture, the megaron.

Cyrus, the king of Persia, by proclamation in 539 permitted the Jews to return to Israel from their exile in Babylonia and to bring back the temple treasures sacked by the soldiers of Nebuchadnezzar. The temple was then rebuilt on a more modest scale by Zerubabel and Nehemiah, in 519–515 B.C. Descriptions of this second temple are scarce; the most extensive comes from the Jewish historian Flavius Josephus writing later, in the first century A.D., after the temple had been replaced by still another structure. This final change was brought about under King Herod the Great shortly before the Christian period, and it is this third temple that is associated with events in the life of Mary, Joseph, and Jesus. Herod's temple was destroyed in A.D. 70 by the Romans; its destruction was a severe spiritual blow to the Jews. But still surviving today is the western ("wailing") wall built by Herod around the temple precinct, and because of its history and associations it has become one of the world's most sacred architectural symbols.

Achaemenian and Sassanian Persia. The Persian Empire began sensationally in about 560 B.C. when Cyrus the Great, head of a small aristocracy from the province of Fars (ancient Elam), swept over the region with his powerful cavalry. By the end of the century, Cyrus and his successors, Darius I and Xerxes, had conquered all of the civilized world from the Indus to the Danube rivers, except for Greece which alone held out and stemmed the Persian tide at Marathon in 490 B.C. Although we are thankful that the Greeks survived—for without them there would have been no Western civilization as we know it—the Persians were by no means the "barbarians" that the Greeks considered all foreigners to be. They gained respect even among their archenemies, and from the beginning their art and architecture reflected their highly developed sense of self-esteem. Cyrus styled himself "King of Babylon" (that city being the "Rome" of the pre-Italic world), and his follower Darius called himself "King of the Earth." In keeping with their new imperial posture, the Persians wished to construct buildings of grandeur, but although they had already shown admirable originality in the minor arts, in architecture they were unprepared for their sudden greatness. Their solution was an eclectic synthesis of forms gathered from all parts of their realm—and from Greece besides. Darius's account of the construction of his first palace at Susa tells of mud-bricks supplied by Babylonians, cedar roof beams from Lebanon, precious materials from India and Egypt, gold from Sardis, and stone columns quarried nearby but carved by Ionian Greeks. What is astonishing is that the Persians produced an architecture that was original and coherent despite its eclecticism.

The distinctive Persian style appeared in rudimental form at some of the early sites such as Pasargadae, the Achaemenian capital founded by Cyrus II, but it achieved its monumental flowering at Persepolis. Begun in 518 B.C. by Darius the Great as a new capital, it was continued by Xerxes and completed in 460 B.C. by Ataxerxes in a form close to the original scheme. The complex (figs. 1-51, 1-52) was set along the face of a mountainous spur, leveled and extended to create a large stone platform 1,500 by 900 feet in extent, and surrounded by a fortified wall of mud-brick that at some points reached 60 feet in

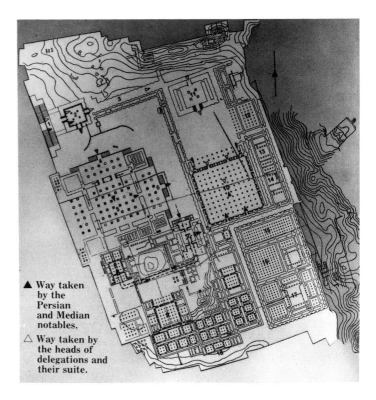

▲ Way taken by the Persian and Median notables.

△ Way taken by the heads of delegations and their suite.

1-51   Plan of terrace, Persepolis. (After the survey by Ali Hakemi)

1-52   Ruins of Persepolis. Iran

height. The site was more than half covered with buildings, but there were no temples; the Persians were Zoroastrians devoted to pure fire and water as embodiments of the Good Principle, and their unpretentious religious buildings were restricted to small towers or platforms for fire worship. Thus entirely secular, the architectural program of Persepolis comprised three principal parts: first, the so-called Palace of Xerxes, the harem, and other living quarters at the south end of the site; second, two great state halls toward the center of the platform; and third, an approach of monumental staircases, gateways, and avenues. Structurally, the builders relied on a hypostyle, many-columned scheme throughout, constructing with it spaces of varying scale, some immense, generally square in plan, enclosed by mud-brick walls (long since lost). Only the monumental stone doorways were left standing together with remnants of the stone columns that were evenly disposed in rows to support the ceilings. It was a systematic, quasi-modular yet elastic architecture with few parallels. The tunnel-vaulted, massive-walled, cramped units of traditional Mesopotamian construction were oppressive when compared to the openness that characterized Persepolis.

Darius's intention when he created Persepolis was to make it the symbol of the empire's sovereignty over its far-flung dominions. The sculptural reliefs on the walls of the stairways and other structures of the complex illustrated gift-bearing ceremonies and ritual processions that took place at Persepolis to honor imperial unity. If the relief decoration, particularly on the stairs, seems on close examination somewhat crude with its abrupt transition between planes (a "cookie-cutter" style), its fine sense of pattern and the crispness of its lines, together with the grand sweep of its movement, produce the desired aura of magnificence. It combines the military and heraldic imagery appropriate to such royal staircases with a gay, festive tone surpassing even that of the Ishtar Gate.

The most impressive aspect of Persepolis was undoubtedly the apadana, the royal audience hall where, it is believed, the ceremony of tribute was consummated (fig. 1-53). It formed a square of 250 feet on each side, and contained thirty-six slender, widely spaced columns soaring 67 feet high with a lower diameter of only 5 feet, their centers spaced 20 feet, or 4 diameters, apart. This hypostyle interior can be compared with its counterpart at Karnak, which was similar in size but contained 134 columns, each twice the diameter of those of Persepolis! The unprecedented airiness of the apadana (lighted through ample windows in the mud-brick walls) was complemented by the extravagant form of the columns. Of all the architectural elements at Persepolis, the columns were the most inventive (fig. 1-54). In the audience hall, their lower halves were of Greek origin: the bell-shaped socle, the pendant leaves decorating it, the torus base cushion, and the taper and fluting of the shaft. Greek columns generally received half the 40–48 flutings of the Persepolis "copies," which, in the latter, emphasized their elongated lightness at the expense of the expression of structural integrity. The capitals were an eclectic assemblage of three components

1-53 Audience Hall of Darius and Xerxes. Persepolis. c. 500 B.C.

1-54 **Types of columns, Persepolis. 6th to 5th century** B.C. **(After R. Ghirshman)**

that seemed precariously balanced one atop the other in an architectural tumbling act. The first component of this extravaganza, immediately over the shaft, was the Persian reminiscence of an Egyptian palm-leaf capital bound by a Greek molding, the ubiquitous bead-and-reel. Above followed eight pairs of crossing volutes of Greek origin but compounded, interleaved, and turned 90 degrees in orientation. Finally, there were the double-headed bulls (sometimes human-headed bulls or griffins). Despite their bizarre appearance they were structurally efficient, for they provided a broad bearing surface and the roof beams were anchored securely

between them. Given the pervasiveness of heraldic beasts in the Near East, their presence was not surprising. Their specific origin, however, is puzzling and may derive from the native metalwork tradition where symmetrical fantasies are dominant. The capital as a whole may have been inspired by the use of forked saplings in Persian vernacular architecture to support lightweight roofs.

There are other aspects of Persepolis that should be noted. One is the throne room, the famous Hall of Hundred Columns (fig. 1-55), built by Xerxes and Ataxerxes alongside the audience hall. In it, the airy dominance of space over mass was even more prevalent than in the apadana, for its stone columns were 37 feet in height but only 3 feet in lower diameter, and spaced 20 feet apart—or almost seven diameters—from axis to axis. When compared to the ponderous Egyptian pillars that ultimately contributed conceptually to the Persian column, the effect is almost of flimsiness, although, curiously, it was the Egyptian column that "copied" nature's fragile plant structure and more truly depicted organic forces. In any case, the visitor to the Hall of Hundred Columns would have been prepared for it by the pools and extensive plantings that were landscaped over the whole site, manifesting a national passion for landscape gardening (the word "paradise" is no more than the Persian word for "ornamental park"). What resulted was a continuity of effect: landscaping, columnar porch, hypostyle interior, and ornamented columnar detail.

With the exception of the pavilions of the Greek conquerors of the Persians—that of Alexander the Great is described as having had columns 30 feet high made of silver and gold—Persepolis and the other Persian palaces (at Susa and Pasargadae) had no successors. They appeared seemingly from nowhere to carry the previous Neo-Babylonian decorative tendency to a fresh and, for the ancient Near East, lighthearted expression that in its eclectic singularity could have no following.

Asia Minor and Syria: The Hittites and Others. The Hittites belonged to a group of partly Aryan peoples who, from their base in northern Syria (Aleppo and Alalakh), overran the Near East

1-55 **Xerxes's Hall of Hundred Columns. Persepolis. (Reconstruction by C. Chipiez)**

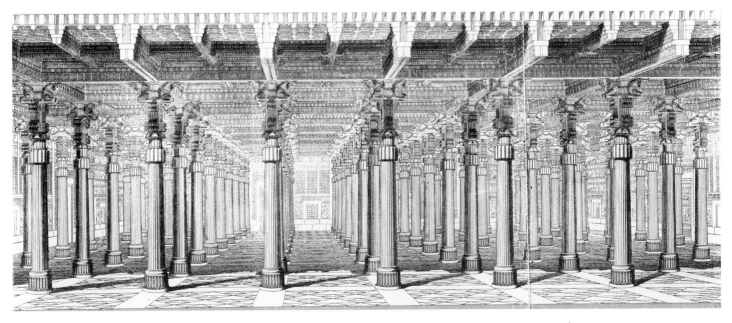

in about 1700 B.C., made their capital at modern Bogazkoy (near Ankara), and established a strong culture. Their best-preserved structures are fortresses; even those of the earliest period (1650–1450 B.C.) demonstrate a sophistication in methods of construction and concepts of powerful military architecture. But more interesting for us was another architectural development, of which only scattered fragments and remnants remain, that ultimately produced, among other novelties, a repertory of decoration that was to influence the Greeks. This significant Hittite contribution centered on an enigmatic architectural type employed generally as a palace, known as the *hilani*, or loggia building. When fully developed, it took the form of a rectangular edifice with a colonnaded loggia in the center of the main side, approached by a broad flight of stairs. On either side of the loggia was a blank wall, while behind it was a long rectangular room running transversely (that is, parallel to the facade). A two-storied variation with higher corner elements may be the ultimate origin of the twin-tower church facade that dominated so much of Christian architecture.

Post-Hittite, north Syrian developments in the early first millennium are best observed in the context of the loggia

1-56   Caryatids at the temple gate at Tell Halaf. 9th century B.C. (Reconstruction. Oriental Collection, State Museum, Berlin)

building. If the Persians created extraordinary capitals, it was the Syrians who concentrated on the bases and shafts of the support system. Under the freestanding loggia columns were stone monsters, either single or in pairs, on whose backs stood an element that was the prototype for the base of the Athenian column: a combination of cushion-shaped forms, often decorated with circles of down-turned leaves. The shafts and capitals of these loggia columns have all vanished, but it is thought that the shafts may have tapered downward. More original was the Syrian substitution of the human figure (usually but not exclusively female) for the shaft. These first stone caryatids—as the genre is called—at Tell Halaf (fig. 1-56), took the form of male figures, with a long columnar garment and tall fez headdress that were later worn by early Greek female caryatids. In some cases the caryatids were nude and wore a crown of downward-curling leaves. A more important variant, usually male, carried the load not on the head but in the upraised arms and was called a telamon or atlas.

Although the Syrians were responsible for other innovations as well, the base forms, and the caryatid and atlas figures suggest the importance of this obscure but inventive region. When the Greeks turned to the area for ideas, it was typical that they took the structurally expressive and human forms with them, but left the monsters behind—where they were to remain until the Middle Ages when, through some mysterious process, they were reborn in the French and particularly the Italian Romanesque.

CRETE AND MYCENAE

Until the late nineteenth century, what was actually the first European civilization was generally considered to belong to the realm of myth. It was in the 1870s that Heinrich Schliemann, who since his school days had dreamed of Troy, astonished the world by discovering that the Troy of Homer had indeed existed as one of no less than nine cities that succeeded each other on a site in Asia Minor. Soon it became clear that Troy was only part of a larger pre-Classical culture—as Homer had indeed recounted. Its first center was the rich but mysterious civilization that appeared on the Aegean island of Crete around 2000 B.C. and flourished there until it was almost totally obliterated during the period from 1400 to 1100 following some natural disaster, possibly seismic. The fall of Crete was paralleled by the rise of a closely related culture on the Peloponnesus, centered at Mycenae, the mythical kingdom of Agamemnon and his tragic dynasty. Following 1100 came a time of invasions and the total eclipse of Aegean civilization. This period is known in Classical history as the Dark Ages (not to be confused with the Dark Ages of medieval history following the fall of Rome), from whose shadows Greece was to emerge.

Although not without sources in the older regions of the East, Crete's culture was unique. Its boundaries and defenses were not deserts or fortresses, but the sea, which yielded great wealth and from which the Cretans created a luxurious, relaxed way of life quite distinct from any other. They reveled in an art of singular spontaneity and fluidity. Their painting—depicting joyous hunts and dances with sacred bulls, and sea creatures such as the fluid octopus—was characterized by lightness, freely shaped forms, and movement in which can be felt the rhythms of the sea on which Cretan culture floated. In architecture, they consciously rejected as unnecessary the axiality, symmetry, and abstraction the East had employed for creating monumentality.

The palace at Knossos in Crete, supposedly of King Minos, was built in 1700–1400 B.C. (figs. 1-57–1-59); it was discovered and excavated by the British archaeologist Sir Arthur Evans early in the twentieth century. Only the ground floor of a sprawling ensemble of several stories gathered about a large court has partially survived. The site is complicated and there is considerable controversy about the functions of its various parts, especially as the upper floors have remained impossible to reconstruct with certainty. Nevertheless, the character as well as certain important features of the palace are clear.

To understand Knossos one must realize that, like the great palaces of Babylon and Khorsabad, it was more than a residence. It was also a religious focal point—the king was Crete's high priest—and an administrative center. But rather than

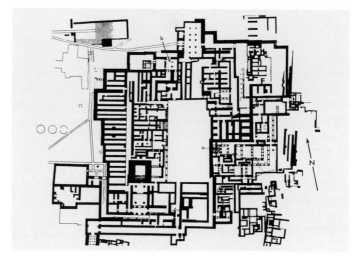

1-57   Plan, Palace at Knossos. Crete. c. 1700–1400 B.C.

1-58   General view, Palace at Knossos

setting these functions in distinct areas, the Cretan monarchy at Knossos gathered together all the functions of kingship in chambers and apartments spread around a single large court. The palace did not embody monumentality or conceptual order; on the contrary, it was picturesque and colorful, its atmosphere one of comfort and informality. There was an ease and richness even in the building materials. Relying heavily on wood and gypsum made it easy to build walls with fine, bright surfaces, and to erect widely spaced columns to support the lightweight wooden roofs. But unfortunately such materials were perishable, and much of the site has disappeared. No columns, for example, survived, and archaeologists have had to rely on luck and ingenuity to reconstruct the forms, principally from their context and from contemporary paintings in which architectural forms were depicted. Both the shaft and

capital of these reconstructed columns are noteworthy. The shaft tapers not upward, but from the top down, producing an unstable, almost floating effect. If the shaft denies architectural weight, a massive disc shoulders the load, and transfers it through a swelling, cushionlike form to the top of the shaft. Later the Greeks would employ a related form of capital in their far more consistent Doric order.

From a terrace running almost 200 feet along the south end of the palace, one reached a complex entrance path to the interior designed with picturesque vistas seen through multiple screens of columns and piers. Lighting—as throughout the palace—came through wells running down from the flat roofs, yielding subtle effects, and there were stairways interwoven with verandahs that in composition would have rivaled the imaginative Late Baroque staircases of Italy and Germany.

The disposition of the state apartments is not known. The ground floor west wing included a storage area and a number of important rooms off the court. These included loggias, an unassuming religious shrine, and the so-called Throne Room (fig. 1-60), with light wells front and back, and graceful and colorful painted decoration. In the royal apartments, to which

1-59   Main staircase, east wing, Palace at Knossos

1-60   Throne Room, Palace at Knossos

1-61   Queen's Megaron, Palace at Knossos. 1500 B.C. (Reconstruction)

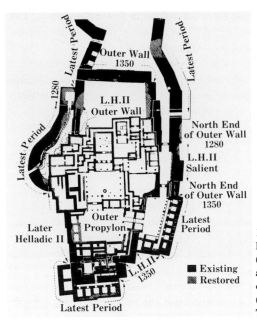

1-62
Plan, Palace
(1250–1200 B.C.)
and south part
of citadel
(1400–1280 B.C.).
Tiryns, Greece

■ Existing
▨ Restored

1-63   Citadel at Tiryns. (Reconstruction after G. Karo)

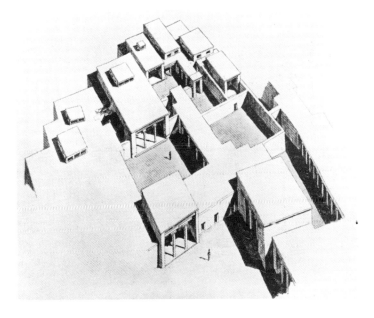

the king and his family would retreat for their private life, ran a staircase with a wonderful play of light over climbing tiers of gaily painted columns—the shafts red, orange, and yellow, the capitals in contrasting dark colors. The most impressive sections of this area were the Hall of the Double Axes and the Queen's Megaron (fig. 1-61) adjacent to the stair at its lower level. Screens of columns or lean rectangular piers diffused light to the interiors, which were subtly back-lit by the light wells. The informal, colorful openness of the Cretan style suited this private portion of the palace well.

After Crete fell around 1400, Mycenaean culture, slowly evolving on the Greek mainland for several hundred years, achieved its zenith. Its character was notably different from that of Crete, for it was neither sustained nor protected by the sea. The Mycenaeans were more a society of warriors than traders. They built citadels rather than pleasure palaces—

tautly organized royal precincts enclosed by huge cyclopean walls of rough-hewn, immense, stone blocks, difficult to access and highly defensible. Of the two main sites, Tiryns is better preserved (figs. 1-62, 1-63), and our knowledge of it can probably be applied to the city of Mycenae. By the end of the thirteenth century B.C., the cyclopean defense walls of the upper city of Tiryns were complete (colorplate 4). They were up to 36 feet thick and lined with galleries with massive corbeled ceilings. Although only royalty resided in the citadel, in times of war it was the refuge for the community living in the city below. The principal residential area was a megaron, in elemental form a rectangular box with a single door, widespread in Aegean architecture. At Tiryns its main space, at the center of which was the hearth, lay behind a double-chambered vestibule.

The monumentality of the Mycenaean citadels was rivaled by that of their tombs. The Cretans never really had a definitive sepulchral type, but instead experimented with various forms. The most important was the so-called beehive or tholos tomb. This was a pointed domical shape, although of corbeled structure. Sunk into the ground, it was frequently given a sloping entrance passage called the dromos. It was this dromos-tholos combination that captured the imagination of the Mycenaeans, and they gradually developed it into a structure of true grandeur. The three greatest extant examples were named by archaeologists (following the ancient Greek author Pausanias) after the Bronze Age protagonists of Greek myth known best in the tragedies of Aeschylus: the Treasuries of Atreus and Minyas and the Tomb of Clytemnestra.

More than the citadels, these noble forms of the late Mycenaean age reflect the powerful minds of the builders. Like the Egyptians, the Mycenaeans recognized that the key to monumentality was geometry and proportions. The clear geometry of the tholos was stressed by proportions in which the diameter equals the height (about 45 feet in the major examples). At the same time its structure was gradually perfected by making the upper levels of corbeling into uninterrupted rings of stone (and thus self-supporting in true domical manner).

Like the tholos buried in the hillside, the dromos leading to it was also aggrandized; it sometimes exceeded 100 feet in length and 30 feet in height at its far end. It, too, was lined with an ashlar stone-facing of huge blocks. Between the tholos and dromos a thick portal-facade structure was built. The portal was surmounted by a lintel of colossal proportions—at the Treasury of Atreus (fig. 1-64) two monoliths weighing some 120 tons. But, recalling the safeguards taken by the builders of the Great Pyramid, even this was not considered enough, and a triangular, relieving corbel arch was constructed above.

The stonework and proportions of these tombs are magnificent; in addition, the surfaces were originally adorned. At the Treasury of Atreus, the interior (fig. 1-65) was studded with a pattern of rosettes, and a frieze of bulls may have decorated the base. At the facade, the red conglomerate stone of the door frame was carved into three fasciae—like later Ionic portals—and to its jambs were attached green alabaster columns similar in form to those at Knossos but here even closer to the Greek Doric order. The lintel of the portal was decorated with imitations of the circular ends of ceiling poles—a forerunner of the Greek dentil molding.

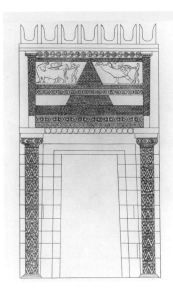

1-64
Facade, Treasury of Atreus.
Mycenae. 13th century B.C.
(After Marinatos)

How these tholos tombs functioned is a puzzle. Apparently the dead were placed in pits below floor level or in the adjoining rectangular chambers which existed in the Treasuries of Atreus and Minyas. After burial, the tomb was permanently sealed, and the dromos blocked by a massive wall. The tholos was thus not used as a funerary chapel but remained curiously empty—a pure, invisible monument to the deceased.

The question of the tomb portals with their forward-looking architectural decoration leads us to the famous Lion Gate (fig. 1-66) at the citadel of Mycenae. Here a massive trabeated portal was built into the wall, with cyclopean jambs and lintel, surmounted by a triangular relief of two heraldic lions standing at a (Minoan) column, the sacred symbol of the earth that they supposedly protected. For all its simplicity, the Lion Gate is of immense historical portent. The powerful sense of structure was an inheritance—ultimately Neolithic—that the Greeks would foster with exceptional refinement. Here, it was combined with the feeling for monumental stone carving in

1-65   View of interior and dome, Treasury of Atreus

1-66 Lion Gate. Mycenae. c. 1250 B.C.

the Lion relief, an element inherited from Egypt but now infused with a new sensitivity to the organic logic and beauty of its subject. And as we will see, the very notion of a triangular relief over a trabeated form was the archetype of the Greek temple front, with its pediment over a colonnade. The Greek successors to the Homeric Bronze Age would fuse the abstraction and organic symbolism, the massiveness and refinement of the structures of Mycenae into an architecture so definitive that it was to be the primary architectural source for the Western world.

2-1
**Temple
of Poseidon.
Paestum,
Italy.**
c. 460 B.C.

Chapter Two | Greece

It is difficult to recapture the brilliance of ancient Greece, and this is particularly true of its buildings. Of all ancient architecture, that of the Greeks is the hardest to appreciate fully. It is at once all too familiar, yet superficially understood, reduced to dry archaeology, or subjected to exaggerated enthusiasm and poetic misinterpretation. The crucial subject of the Greek orders suffers particularly from such treatment. The orders are the key to an architecture that shunned extremes in favor of that just measure to which the Greeks—at least in the exalted period, from the eighth to the fourth centuries B.C.—aspired in all things. Greek architecture does not amaze and overwhelm with mere scale and complexity; it has vigor, harmony, and refinement that thrill the mind as well as the eye.

Who were the ancient Greeks? In the Dark Age that followed the collapse of Minoan-Mycenaean civilization—from the eleventh to the eighth centuries B.C.—their culture took shape in the interaction of two diverse peoples. The Dorians, who invaded from the north about 1100 B.C. and settled in the Peloponnesus, with Sparta as their center, were a militant, disciplined people with a powerful sense of tribal order. In contrast, the Ionians, some of whom had been driven across the Aegean Sea to Asia Minor and the Greek islands, had a mercantile, trading society. By the eighth century B.C., the two groups had mingled and become a single though highly varied culture and they called themselves Hellenes—as opposed to non-Greek-speaking "barbarians." Their political unit was the city-state rather than the kingdom. Greece is a mountainous land of great beauty, but of only pockets of arable land, often along the extensive seacoast. The fragmented geography favored the growth, commonly from Bronze-Age nuclei, of independent, self-sufficient towns of moderate size. Throughout the Archaic (seventh century B.C. to 480) and Classic (480–323) periods, no Greek city succeeded for long in dominating the others. Generally, the main expansive energies of the cities were spent founding colonies outside of Greece: the islands and coastlands of the Aegean, southern Italy and especially Sicily. Many of these distant settlements, great in their times, today offer among the best preserved of Greek archaeological sites.

Despite the political disunity of the cities and the divergent cultural tendencies of Ionic and Doric areas, from the beginning the Greeks strongly sensed their common culture, cherished it, and vigorously celebrated it. The all-important language and the epics of Homer were paramount, and there were the myths and the gods. Typically, although each city considered itself under the protection of a distinct divinity, the gods themselves were considered a large, if not entirely harmonious family. The Greeks, who invented philosophical skepticism, were profoundly religious: in every city, and scattered over the countryside, temples and shrines were built to their gods and goddesses. All Greeks paid close heed to the famous oracles, such as at Delphi; cities vied with each other in erecting treasuries containing their offerings to the oracle. The most famous shrine was the great Pan-Hellenic site at Olympia, with its proud temples to Zeus and Hera, and its Olympic Festival, the athletic games where it was believed that the gods expressed their will in favoring the winners—and, implicitly, the winners' cities.

The Greeks, perhaps more than any other culture, lived at the razor's edge of the historical process. Greek civilization was formed within the matrix of still-active Egyptian and Near Eastern cultures, as well as from the heritage of Crete and Mycenae. The Greeks were the last of the megalithic architects—a late mutation of a group of civilizations that preceded them by several millennia. Yet, from the perspective of Rome and afterward, as the progenitors of Western civilization they seem very "early." Suddenly, in Greece, between the eighth and sixth centuries, philosophy, history, drama, epic literature, democracy, and science appeared; these developments were inspired by a radical new sense of the nature of humanity and its place in the scheme of things: that individuals should strive to shape their own destiny, to exercise their intellect and will—even against the gods. The gods were of a human sort, a product of Greek anthropomorphism which tended to see all things in the human image (including the stars as well as architecture). Humans were gods who lacked perfect beauty, immortality, and power, and the gods were but humans with all their frailties combined with higher qualities. Man became the measure of all things, including the divine, and this new ideal unleashed enormous creative energies.

Greek architecture reflects its makers in its human scale and in its program. Significantly, its typical form was not the tomb; nor did Greeks have much interest in elaborate houses and palaces. They were fascinated by other forms of civic architecture: theaters, council halls, public porticoes, and the planning of the cities themselves. The most important of all Greek architectural forms, however, was the temple. On it the Greeks lavished the finest building materials, the richest decoration, and the most complex architectural form. The temple was not meant to hold worshipers; it stood as the symbolic dwelling of the deity to whom it was dedicated and whose cult statue it usually housed. The prototype of the temple was the Bronze-Age megaron, in particular its use as a royal dwelling. In Greek myth, the god often visits the king—in architectural history, he takes over the dwelling of the king, who himself is displaced from society by the self-ruling body politic. Like the megaron, the early Greek temples comprised a rectangular interior, called the cella (or naos), and an entrance porch with two columns standing between projecting walls. This arrangement was to remain the basis of all temple forms. Interestingly, the earliest known temple had altars and offering tables in the same position as the hearth and serving table of the Bronze-Age megaron. In the later temple arrangement, however, the altar for animal sacrifices is displaced to the exterior by the cult statue: Sacred image rather than ritual now sanctified the building's core.

By the sixth century, the Greek architect could choose among a variety of plans, from simple to complex, each with its distinct nomenclature (figs. 2-2, 2-3). The megaron type is a temple with columns and portico in antis, that is, the columns stand between two antae (pilasters with capital and base) attached to the ends of the projecting walls. If the columns of the porch are not between projecting walls but in front, across the full width of the cella, the temple is termed prostyle, or amphiprostyle if the arrangement obtains at both ends. When the cella is surrounded by a colonnade (pteron), the temple is termed peripteral; this became the principal monumental type (fig. 2-9). The few ambitious examples of a double colonnade are known as dipteral (fig. 2-21). Greek temples are also classified by the numbers of columns across the front and back: two, distyle; four, tetrastyle; six, hexastyle; eight, octastyle; nine (rare), enneastyle; ten (rare), decastyle. Most Greek temples are hexastyle peripteral, but the greatest of all, the Parthenon in Athens, is octastyle. Although restricted to the cella-colonnade combination, the temple could be varied in a number of ways. For instance, the functional front porch might be balanced by a false rear porch (opisthodomos) behind the cella, or the cella could be divided into aisles by interior colonnades.

THE DORIC ORDER

Such variety did not obtain, however, when it came to the elevation of the temple. From the beginning there seem to have been two ideal formal types, known as the orders: the Doric and the Ionic; the third, the Corinthian order, is a sub-style of the Ionic. Order refers not merely to the column, but to the entire set of forms that constitute the principal elevation of the temple. The order determines all aspects of this elevation— the shape, the disposition, and the proportions of all its parts.

At first glance, the scheme of the Doric order (fig. 2-4) appears childishly simple: a trabeated arrangement comprised of a row of columns on high steps; the columns support a lintel, which is surmounted by a triangular crown fronting the saddle roof. Simple and direct indeed, the configuration is one of unveiled comprehensibility of structure and form. Beneath the colonnade is a solid platform, the crepidoma. Whatever the terrain, this platform sets the building off from the landscape, but the abruptness of the transition is softened by three large steps, the top one, on which the temple immediately rests, being the stylobate. The total height of the steps is generally about equal to the lower diameter of the columns. Doric steps were proportioned to the temple, not to the visitor; their steepness and scale made a difficult climb (necessitating the insertion of smaller steps on the front). The shaft of the Doric column—set directly, without base, on the stylobate— tapers upward in a shallow convex curve (entasis). The surface of the shaft is grooved vertically with twenty hollows

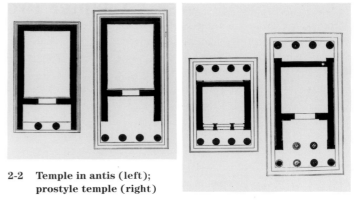

2-2 Temple in antis (left); prostyle temple (right)

2-3 Amphiprostyle temple plans

(flutes) separated by sharp ridges (arrises). In studying the visual meaning of these subtleties, we realize that just as the uncompromising geometry of the temple platform is softened by its steps, so the cylindrical geometry of the column is mitigated by entasis and fluting. They provide an organic resilience, an illusion of response to the weight of the superstructure through graceful muscular effort.

2-4 Diagram of Doric order. (After Grinnell)

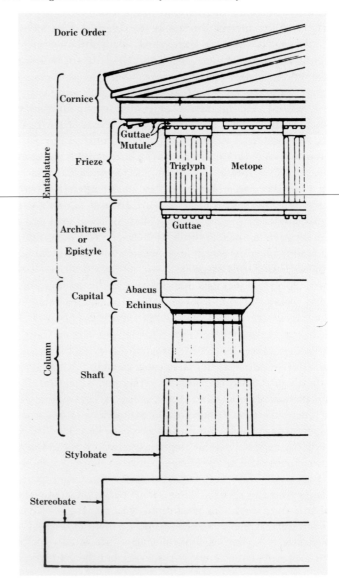

The Doric capital provides a smooth transition from the round shaft to the rectangular superstructure. Carved from one block, the capital is comprised of three elements: necking, echinus, and abacus. The abacus is a square block that takes up the load from the entablature and projects slightly beyond it. The echinus, circular in plan and equal in height to the abacus, passes the load through the necking to the shaft, and it has in the finest examples a subtle hyperbolic profile that creates an impression of organic resilience in the juncture of load and support. The necking, perfecting the transition between capital and shaft, is marked by three raised rings. A few inches down, the shaft is marked by an additional one or more necking grooves (fig. 2-38).

The architrave of the Doric entablature is a simple stone lintel running from the center of one column to the next. The frieze above is the most constant and perhaps most distinctive feature of the order. All other elements of the Doric will be recognizable in the other orders, but the Doric frieze—vertical grooved elements (triglyphs) between nearly square fields (metopes)—is unique (colorplate 7) Below the frieze runs a narrow flat molding, termed a taenia, from which hang strips (regulae) and from them hang conical pegs (guttae). The basic element of the cornice—the crowning part of the entablature—is the horizontal corona that sweeps around the entire temple. Its primary function is to establish a clear line along the upper perimeter of the building. Its effect is of a sharp, strongly projecting upper edge terminating the order with a brilliant line above a deep shadow. It begins with a vertical bed molding from which the Doric corona swings forward. Rectangular slabs (mutules) project under the lower surface of the corona, and from each mutule hang eighteen guttae in three rows of six each—repeating the scale and spacing of the guttae of the frieze. At the ends of the temple, a lighter and simpler raking cornice rises from the horizontal cornice forming an isosceles triangle that frames a deeply recessed tympanum. This triangular superstructure, or pediment, is famous for the sculptural compositions that filled it in temples in Athens, Olympia, Aegina, and elsewhere.

The impression of severity in the best-preserved temples is misleading. Originally, the lines were softened by decoration, now lost. The decorative programs involved more than the figured sculpture of metopes and pediments. There was, first of all, the roof decoration, whose most striking components were the acroteria—large sculptural pieces set above the center and at the corners of the pediment, in the form of floral designs, tripods, monsters, men, and groups of figures. If these ornaments upset our generally false concept of the Greek temple, another aspect of its decoration is even more disturbing to the modern observer, who characteristically projects a puritanical ideal onto the Doric. It has been long known that the temples were painted with bright, almost gaudy, colors. It is difficult for us to accept this archaeological correction of the familiar bleached, bare forms. The triglyphs were painted black and dark blue, the metopes, red; the structural elements were stucco white; gold, purple, green, and other exotic colors were applied to the roof ornamentation; and, finally, the figured sculpture of metopes, pediments, and the acroteria was richly polychromed. As rich as this coloring of the building was, it was never purely decorative; it also served to articulate and balance the forms.

Nestled within the exterior columnar shell of the peripteral Doric temple is the cella; in most examples, little is left but traces of its walls. Because they are so poorly preserved, we tend to neglect cellas in favor of the standing colonnades, but these four-walled, megaron-type houses of the gods were the essential core of the temple. The cella alone was sufficient to constitute a temple, as was the case in many smaller examples.

What did the interior of the cella of a monumental Doric temple look like? Being completely roofed over, it was as dark as the exterior was gleaming. The entrance door was the only source of daylight. The closing of the cella by a roof and a coffered ceiling was not a simple feat for the Greeks, for the pre-Roman architects had difficulty devising monumental roof spans. The Greeks, for all their inventiveness, never developed any structural system other than the trabeated. When, in the Hellenistic era, the arch does appear (and rarely at that), it was employed by the Greeks mainly as a freestanding decorative device. In the Doric temple, the interior of the cella was usually divided into aisles by rows of columns. Clearly, the columns were an aesthetic rather than a structural device. The interior colonnades were usually placed so close to the side walls that they provided little structural support. But without the dividing colonnades, the interior would have been too large and bare in comparison with the density of the exterior, and it would not have formed an appropriate enclosure for the sacred cult image and its treasure, which occupied the cella.

Our eyes are so habituated to the external form of the Doric order that we find the interior manipulation of the same order difficult to accept when, as in the Temple of Poseidon at Paestum (fig. 2-1) the Doric columns were superimposed in two tiers. But the architectural logic for this transgression is inexorable. Within the limited space of the cella, a massive colonnade would have been oppressive. Thus, Doric columns of much smaller diameter were used. Since the proportions of the Doric column were fixed by the relation of diameter to height, these interior columns were shorter than those of the external colonnade. But the interior supports had to rise to a greater height to reach the ceiling. The only solution was to set a second tier of columns above the first, on an intermediate architrave. That this effect was still preferred as late as the fifth century, when the more slender Ionic order was available for just such purposes, emphasizes the unyielding traditionalism of the Doric temple. Yet it may have been thought that for the cella, with its primeval origins and its sacred, mysterious character, the slightly bizarre double tier was quite appropriate.

Doric Temples. Turning from the "ideal" Doric temple to concrete examples, we encounter a deceptively simple pattern: There were surprisingly few deviations from the Doric norm. Development appears to have been not divergent, but convergent, toward the realization of an ideal latent in the earliest Doric designs. It involved not merely a perfecting of the shapes and proportions of the parts of the Doric temple, but also shifts in the innermost meaning of the order.

It is only with the change from timber to the more durable, monumental, stone technique imported from Egypt in the sixth century that we encounter notable standing remains of Greek structures. Perhaps the most remarkable of the Archaic Doric temples is found at Paestum, the Greek colony (Poseidonia) in southern Italy founded around 600 B.C. Today, the city is one of the most impressive of all ancient sites, for directly alongside the Archaic temple—the so-called Basilica (originally, the Temple of Hera I) of about 530 B.C. (figs. 2-5–2-7), the oldest of the temples at Paestum—stands the well-preserved Early Classic Temple of Hera II (commonly called Poseidon), of about 460 B.C. (figs. 2-8, 2-9). The Basilica differs in many ways from our "ideal" Doric temple. These differences are perceived clearly in the plan. The cella is divided into two aisles by a single row of eight massive intermediate supports, equal in thickness to the exterior columns. The plan of the outer colonnades is unique among Doric temples: Not only are the nine columns at each end unusual, but the central column forms a solid mass rather than the customary void on the central axis of the temple. The eighteen lateral columns are more widely spaced than those on the ends, which is also unusual. These anomalous conflicts can be explained by the mathematics of the design, which sacrificed visual harmony of layout to theoretical proportions. However, the physical detail of the Basilica reveals that its singularities were part of a consistent pattern, involving an aesthetic preference for contrast and conflict over serene harmonies.

The number and spacing of the columns are exceptional, but so is their form. The proportions of every feature are extreme and contrasts are exaggerated, resulting in an overpowering sculptural force. The columnar shafts are not excessively thick for the early Doric, but their tapering is extreme—the top diameter is about one-half the lower. The entasis of the column, which appears here for the first time in Greek architecture, is uniquely pronounced. The shafts seem to strain outward from internal stress. This effect is continued in the capital. Its proportions are exaggeratedly broad with respect to the architrave above and the narrow upper end of the shaft, which seems almost to bore into it. Just as the shaft appears to be distended from internal pressures, so the excessive spread of the echinus suggests a cushion flattened by an enormous load. All is dramatic contrast and disjunction rather than the imperturbable euphony of the "ideal" Doric.

We approach much closer to the Doric "norm" when turning to the Basilica's neighbor, the Temple of Hera II (Poseidon). Although built in the provinces with local peculiarities, the

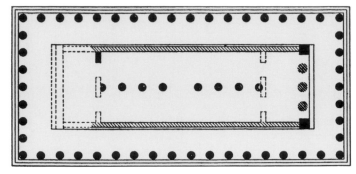

2-5   Plan, Basilica. Paestum. c. 530 B.C.

2-6   Detail of capital, Basilica

Poseidon Temple reflects the totally destroyed but historically important Temple of Zeus at the great shrine of Olympia, built about 465 B.C. The plan of the temple is in the mature pattern of fifth-century-mainland Greece—a cella, divided internally by two double-tiered Doric colonnades, and an exterior colonnade with hexastyle facades and fourteen columns on each side. Its impression is no longer that of the disjunction of elements and the dramatic struggle of structural forces. We now behold a building of a crystalline integrity. The load of the entablature is still heavy, but it no longer seems to crush

2-7   Eastern view, Basilica

2-8   Facade, Temple of Poseidon. Paestum

2-9   Plan, Temple of Poseidon

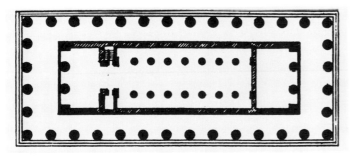

the echinus or distend the shafts into exaggerated entasis. The columns—spaced more closely than at any other Greek temple—rise firmly to meet the entablature. Here we encounter both the general evolution of the Doric order toward the "norm" at the stage called Early Classic and the imagination of an architect with a powerful feeling for plasticity and strength. These factors have converged to produce at Paestum a Doric temple more massively monumental and sculpturally severe than any other example.

The culminating later High Classic stage in the development of the Doric temple is represented by the building known as the Temple of Concord at Agrigento, Sicily, built about 430 B.C. (fig. 2-10). In remarkably good condition, the walls of its undivided cella stand, and on the exterior only parts of the side entablature are missing. Despite its weathered limestone surface, the Temple of Concord presents an architectural image of jewel-like perfection. In part, this is due to its size—only two-thirds that of the Paestum temples—but primarily, the change from the massive strength of Paestum to effortless elegance results from subtle shifts in proportions and in the shaping of details. The columns of the hexastyle peripteral Temple of Concord are more slender—the ratio of their height to the base diameter is 4.61:1 as opposed to 4.20:1 at Paestum—and the interaxial distances are slightly greater: 2.20 times the base diameter instead of 2.12. These changes, which seem so minor on paper, are significant to the eye, particularly in combination with other subtle modifications. The entasis of the shafts has been refined to a barely visible curve. Because the shafts are leaner, more widely spaced, and less distorted into curvature that is not geometrically ideal, they seem neither to suffer from the internal stresses of the Basilica nor to need the stone musculature of Poseidon. They lift effortlessly with structural grace to carry the seemingly buoyant load of the entablature. The capitals contribute to this effect, for their size is smaller than those of the Temple of Poseidon, and the echinus profile has been tightened. Finally, at Agrigento the entablature seems lighter, partly because of the grace of the colonnade, but also because it is flatter and thinner.

2-10   Temple of Concord. Agrigento, Sicily. c. 430 B.C.

The Parthenon. The sublime creation of High Classic Doric architecture was the Parthenon on the Athenian Acropolis, a complex site with a long history. Inhabited from the earliest times, the Acropolis (the word means city-on-the-height) was distinguished by its commanding shape and highly defensible contours. It was surrounded by sheer cliffs on all sides but the west—a crucial fact in its architectural planning. By the fifth century, it had become an exclusively religious and cultural center. The victory of the Greeks at Marathon in 490 B.C., which broke the sweep of the Persian Empire across the Mediterranean, provided the Athenians with the occasion to construct a new temple in marble to replace an older stone structure dedicated to the city's protectress, the virgin goddess Athena Polias, along with a new monumental gateway (Propylaea) to the Acropolis. However, in a temporary reversal, the Persians took Athens in 480 B.C., and they systematically destroyed the city, including every building on the Acropolis. The embittered Athenians vowed to leave it in ruins as a grim reminder of the barbarian invaders.

But by 450 B.C., a new generation, under the leadership of the democratic statesman Pericles, had a different outlook. The independence of the Greeks was so secure—and the hegemony of the Athenians seemed so strong—that Pericles now dared to divert for the reconstruction of the Acropolis the accumulated annual dues contributed by the Greek cities to the defense fund against the Persians. The availability of financial means together with ambition, coming at the height of Greek art, with Athens abounding with great sculptors and architects, produced the extraordinary group of buildings that crown the Acropolis (figs. 2-11–2-14).

The Parthenon, the Temple of Athena Polias (colorplate 6; figs. 2-15, 2-16) dominates the Acropolis from its highest point atop huge substructures that include the temple foundations of 490 B.C. It was designed by the architects Ictinus and Callicrates in collaboration with one of the consummate Greek sculptors, Phidias. The building was erected between 447 and 438 B.C. And in 432 B.C., just before the onset of the Peloponnesian War, which signaled the decline of Athens, the magnificent external sculpture—the high point of Classical art—was

completed. Its centerpieces were the birth of Athena and her struggle with Poseidon, portrayed in the pediments; the metopes depicted legendary battles and the fall of Troy; and around the cella walls was a frieze which represented the annual Panathenaic procession, which wound its way from the city up to the Parthenon. But within a few hundred years the temple's ruin had begun. The interior was "restored" by the Romans; the Byzantines converted it into a church; the Catholics, into a cathedral; the Turks, into a mosque. But a drawing of the mid-seventeenth century shows the building—because of its continual religious employment—still in good condition. However, in 1687 it was used as a gunpowder magazine in a Venetian-Turkish war: The predictable explosion destroyed the entire cella, much of the lateral colonnades, and all of the roofing. The remains deteriorated rapidly thereafter; between 1801 and 1803, most of the sculpture was removed to the British Museum in London. As the building stands today, with its northern colonnade rebuilt, its surfaces spottily bruised, and much of the cornicework gone, it nevertheless retains enough fabric to convey an authentic impression.

The Parthenon is unique in many ways, some obvious, some scarcely visible. Its design was strongly affected by Phidias's gold-and-ivory cult image of Athena. For this 40-foot colossus, an immense cella was needed, over 60 feet in width, with a central aisle some 35 feet wide. The plan of the double-tiered dividing colonnades was an innovation: Instead of merely running directly to the rear wall as was customary, the two colonnades are carried around the end of the naos, behind the statue along a U-shaped path, drawing the framing structure around the goddess.

The expansion of the Parthenon interior is matched by the exterior peristyle and its stylobate, which measures 101 feet 3¾ inches by 228 feet ⅛ inch—not only unusually large but also unusually wide. The width was accommodated by octastyle porches, which were complemented by the seventeen columns of the lateral colonnades. This formula followed the ideal rule whereby the sides of the temple presented twice the number of columns of the ends, plus one. The proportions of the plan of the Parthenon are roughly 4:9, which is repeated in the ratio of the lower column diameter (6 feet 3¼ inches) to the interaxial distance, and the temple's width to its height (45 feet 1 inch). This leads to the length and height of the sides confronting each other in the ratio of $9^2:4^2$ (228 feet: 45 feet). The resulting unity of proportion between such key aspects of the temple contributed to its uncanny harmony. It was undoubtedly from such proportional visions that the famous Greek concept of architecture as "frozen music" was derived—music being a metaphor of cosmic, celestial harmonies.

The design of the Parthenon resulted in almost paradoxical architectural effects. The colonnade is dense and corporeal, yet its columns soar in their slenderness. The huge entablature (colorplate 7) is monumental, yet carried so effortlessly that it seems almost to float. These effects are due, again, to the building's unique proportions: the columns are more slender than any earlier example and, correspondingly, the entablature (especially the architrave) is unusually narrow, hence visually light. What is most remarkable, however, is not the lightness of these components—the development had been in this direction—but rather that the unprecedentedly light solids are complemented *not* by a corresponding increase in

2-11   View from the southwest, Acropolis, Athens.

2-12   Acropolis. (Anonymous 17th-century drawing)

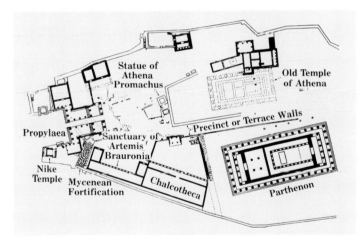

2-13   Restored plan, Acropolis. 400 B.C.

2-14   Model, Acropolis. (By G. P. Stevens)

2-15   View from the northwest, Parthenon

2-16   Cross section, Parthenon. Acropolis, Athens.
        (Drawing after J. J. Coulton)

2-17   Diagram of angle contraction in the
        Temple of Hephaestus, Athens. 449–430 B.C.

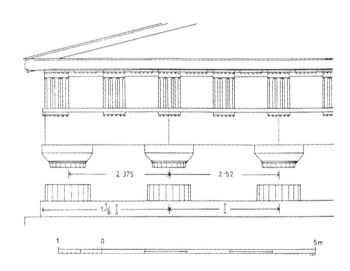

the intercolumnar voids (as was the trend), but by the very opposite: The columns are drawn closer together. The ratio of interaxial distance to lower column diameter is 2.25:1, as compared with the 2.32 of the Temple of Zeus at Olympia and 2.65 of the Temple of Athena Aphaia at Aegina.

The perfection of the Parthenon is expressed in extraordinary ways, and this brings us to two unique aspects of Greek architecture: the Doric angle conflict and the matter of optical refinements. The "angle problem" has to do with the unsightly stretching of the last metope in the frieze of a Doric temple, a solution to the rule that the last triglyph not be placed over the center of the corner column but at the corner itself (fig. 2-17). The problem was solved by "angle-contraction," or simply narrowing the spacing between the corner columns for the required distance, which, as it turned out, contributed to the visual integrity of the temple by lending added solidity to the corner. Thus a virtue was made of necessity. But the Parthenon went further: Its contraction of the corner interaxial distance is *double* the amount necessary to correct the irregularity in the frieze. This introduced a new reverse irregularity in the frieze (the last metope would now be too narrow) which was compensated for by gradually narrowing the metopes from the center bay to the corner.

Perhaps the most remarkable visual developments in the Parthenon are the so-called optical refinements that involve variations from the perpendicular and especially from straight lines (figs. 2-18a, 2-18b). Such variations are found in many Doric buildings, but never to the extent or degree of subtlety found at the Parthenon. Hardly a single true straight line is to be found in the building. The curvatures of entasis and echinus, which began at the Basilica at Paestum as exaggerated muscular shapes, are here reduced almost to the point of disappearance. Yet they are there. The entasis is pared to a barely visible curve, which departs a maximum of $\frac{11}{16}$ inch from a straight, tapering line. This faint curve emphasizes the organic resilience of the column while rendering only a barely perceptible stress, thus reinforcing the buoyant effect of the slender shaft.

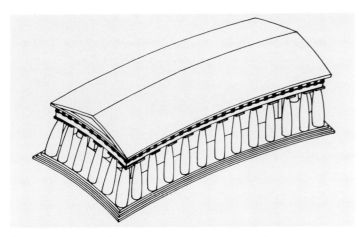

2-18a   Doric temple diagram showing optical refinements exaggerated. (After J. J. Coulton)

2-18b   Parthenon steps showing curvature

The most unusual curvatures of the Parthenon, however, are the result of subtle deviations from geometric regularity. The upward curvature of the stylobate rises 4⅜ inches on the sides, 2⅜ inches at the ends, and the curve is continued in the entablature and the pediment (fig. 2-18b). The entire temple floor rises gently toward the center in the subtlest of domical shapes. Further, nearly all the vertical elements, including the columns, lean inward. The inner faces of the cella walls are vertical, but the outer surfaces taper inward, and the entrance doors to the cella are curved. Finally, the channels of the column flutes deepen gradually toward the top.

The execution of these refinements involved an astonishing degree of craftsmanship and a passion for architectural perfection. But just what was the purpose of these all-but-invisible effects? Today, the preponderant view is that they contribute to the visible grace of the temple and to its vitality. Just as a Doric column without entasis is lifeless, so without the refinements the Parthenon loses the qualities that all the proportioning and crafting of detail alone would never have effected.

THE IONIC ORDER

The Parthenon is the supreme example of the Doric temple. Yet, it is not in any way "typical," for the roof of the false rear cella (the opisthodomos), a room some 60 feet square, was supported not by double-tiered Doric columns but by four single Ionic columns. This leads us to the other structures of the Acropolis, as well as to significant temples elsewhere in Greece.

As the name suggests, the Ionic order (fig. 2-19) was born in the Aegean coastlands of the Ionian Sea. It was there that certain groups of mainlanders, fleeing the invading Dorians, settled about 1000 B.C. and gradually developed a distinct Greek culture. Their cultural character, unlike that of the stolid Dorians, had two opposing tendencies. One was toward the rational—mathematics and philosophy originated among the Ionians. The other tendency was a taste for the rich decorative styles of the East, to which they were exposed geographically and through maritime trade. From the East—Egypt, Syria, and Persia—the Ionians derived a love of monumental architecture, one not of Dorian concentration and toughness, but of the sprawling scale of Egyptian temples and Persian hypostyle halls, with their multitude of columns and decorative forms. But, as they were Greeks and not Easterners, the Ionians developed a Greek architecture that was intermediate between the uncompromising architecture of the Greek mainland and the fantastic worlds of Thebes, Babylon, and Persepolis.

The Ionic order was never as rigid in scheme as the Doric, but it is possible to describe an "ideal" Ionic. In every detail, it is less pure and determinate—softer, richer, and more pictorial than the Doric. At the base of the Ionic temple there is a stylobate, but without the immutable three steps of the Doric. The shaft of the Ionic column, unlike that of the Doric, does not stand directly on the platform; it is set on a cushioning base. Ionic bases have variations, but fundamentally they are comprised of a low, cylindrical (later square) plinth; a spira of two or more concave elements (scotias); and a large upper convex molding (torus), which received various decorations—characteristically, horizontal flutings. As in the Doric order, the Ionic columnar shaft is fluted (the flutes now divided by fillets instead of arrises), and its ratio of height to lower diameter can be 9:1 or 10:1 as opposed to the Doric 4.5:1 or 5.5:1. But the slender, tapered Ionic shaft was rarely given entasis.

2-19   Ionic order of the Temple of Athena Polias. Priene, Turkey. 4th century B.C. (T. Wiegand and H. Schrader)

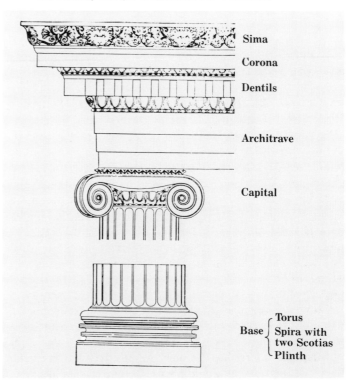

The capital is the most distinctive Ionic feature. Both echinus and abacus are present, but now they are secondary elements dominated by the principal feature of the Ionic capital—the volute, or double scroll. Set between the echinus-topped shaft below and the abacus and entablature above, its form may be thought of as a biomorphic element with a strong, springlike curl. Thus, overhanging ends coil tightly against the column in dense twin, geometrically precise spirals to create the volutes, which suggest the shell form of the nautilus, a familiar species to a seafaring people. The volute is the key to reading the structure. The most obvious quality of the volute is that it seems almost alive in its tendency to curl. Delicate "cushions" above and below the volute imply that it is a fragile organism, an impression enhanced by its detailing. Thus, although the Ionic capital suggests a dynamic relationship between load and support, in its apparent fragility it conveys the lightness of the entablature, an illusion reinforced by the weight-dissolving play of light and shade in its cornicework.

The Greek moldings are important elements of the Ionic entablature. Moldings—continuous sculpted forms, predominantly horizontal, which articulate architectural surfaces—were rare before the Greeks. Even the Egyptians had only two: a torus molding for angles, and the gorge (or cavetto) for cornices. The Greeks combined Egyptian moldings with forms from other sources and with new ones of their own invention to produce an unprecedented system of architectural embellishment that has been in use down to the present (see page 587). Almost all of the moldings exist both in pure and in decorated form, that is, as a continuous, smooth form whose only shaping is its profile, and as that same profile, decorated. The decoration may be either painted or, more commonly, sculpted. A number of forms used for the embellishment of moldings were developed in the sixth century B.C. and refined in the fifth. The forms were not chosen at random, and they provided a complete range of structure, texture, and chiaroscuro. Thus, there are moldings that rise vertically, project horizontally, or lift diagonally. There are elements with bare surfaces, glittering lines, and dense textures; others reflect the sun like a mirror; still others capture deep shadow or move insinuatingly between shadow and sunlight.

The use of the Greek moldings is best seen in the Ionic entablature. The closest approximation to the pure Ionic "ideal" was the destroyed Temple of Athena Polias at Priene (figs. 2-19, 2-20), built about 340 B.C. from the design of the renowned architect Pythius. Its architrave was divided into three fasciae, progressively broader in height, which form three brilliant ribbons of light spanning wide intercolumnar gaps. Because there is no frieze in the true Ionic, the cornice begins immediately above, with the finest of the moldings, the bead-and-reel (astragal), forming a jewel-like line between architrave and cornice. Above follow two progressively larger and stronger forms, the egg-and-dart (ovolo) and the dentils; then, a small cavetto (quarter-round concavity), tiny astragal and ovolo, and, finally, the corona and cyma, decorated with lion heads and the anthemion. We observe not only formal variety and interplay among the moldings, but also the logic of their deployment: Adjacent moldings contrast in shape, scale, and texture, and there is a continuing alternation of sunlit and shaded forms, building up to the strong terminal cyma.

2-20 **Temple of Athena Polias. (Reconstruction after M. Schede, 1934)**

Ionic Temples. Unfortunately nothing stands of the major Ionian shrines beyond bases and a few columns. Our image of the Greek temple is dominated by the Doric, not only because it was the quintessential form, but also because it has survived in many fine examples. The Ionic temple appears in all its splendor by the middle of the sixth century B.C. at Samos and Ephesus. The Temple of Artemis at Ephesus (figs. 2-21, 2-22), which lies in ruins after several rebuildings between the sixth and fourth centuries, was considered one of the Seven Wonders of the Ancient World, and from it we can get an idea of what other Ionic temples were like. At the front end of the dipteral temple (its stylobate 168'9" by 365'9"), the colonnade was tripteral, and at the porch paired columns in antis ran four rows deep. The columns, rising some 60 feet, supported huge lintels. At the center of the temple, as in other major Ionian examples, there was an open courtyard with a large altar and surrounding statues, unlike the roofed-in Doric cella. In all, the visitor to the temple would have sensed the debt to the Orient, but at the same time would have felt part of the Greek world and its ideal of beauty.

The Ionic is known best from the buildings on the Acropolis in Athens, where it not only influenced the Doric (as seen in the elegance of the Parthenon) but was itself subjected to Athenian vigor, clarity, and idealism. The Athenian innovations were thoroughgoing. The complicated base of the Ionic column was reduced to two torus moldings separated by a concave scotia. Known as the Attic base, the form was to dominate all styles of Classical architecture thereafter down to the present. At the top of the column, the Ionic capital was enriched and refined. In keeping with this greater elegance, the columns were widely spaced—as much as four column diameters rather than the typical three diameters used in Ionia. The entablature was made higher to accommodate several changes: Instead of merging the architrave fasciae and the cornice, the entablature was given the lucid tripartite

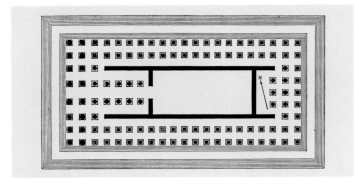

2-21　Plan, Temple of Artemis. Ephesus. Mid-6th century B.C.

2-22　Southwest corner, Temple of Artemis. (Reconstruction by
F. Krischen)

2-23　Temple of Athena Nike. Acropolis, Athens. c. 420 B.C.

division of the Doric, with a frieze that was either blank or embellished with a continuous sculptural relief.

The diminutive Temple of Athena Nike (goddess of Victory), of about 420 B.C., is the earliest Ionic building on the Acropolis (colorplate 8; fig. 2-23). Only about 11 feet high from the stylobate to the apex of the pediment, it has four columns at the projecting porches at each end (tetrastyle amphiprostyle). Its elongated shape and small scale befit its position on a high, narrow substructure. Although jewel-like in detail—including complex, double-faced angle capitals and the first known division of the Ionic architrave into three fasciae—the ratio of the height of the column to its base diameter is low: 7:1 instead of the normal Ionic 9:1 or 10:1. The anomaly is explained by the evident intention to reconcile the Nike temple with the massive 5:1 proportion of its large neighbor, the Doric Propylaea.

The most exceptional Ionic building on the Acropolis is the enigmatic Erechtheum, to the north of the Parthenon (colorplate 9; figs. 2-24–2-27). Built about 420 B.C., the temple was regarded with special veneration. Its site was particularly sacred, for it included the tomb of Cecrops, the legendary founder of Athens, the rock that preserved the mark of Poseidon's trident, and the spring that arose from it. In a walled area just to the west of the temple stood the sacred olive tree of Athena. The building's complexity of plans and levels can be partly understood from this complicated archaeology, as well as from its having housed not only a shrine to Athena Polias, but also altars to Poseidon, god of the sea; Hephaestus, god of fire; Erechtheus, a mythical king of Athens, who had battled unsuccessfully with the sea god; and Butes, brother of Erechtheus and priest to Athena and Poseidon. Moreover, spoils from the Persians were kept in the temple, as well as the famous golden lamp of Callimachus, which burnt for a year without refilling and had a chimney in the form of a palm tree.

The internal outlines of the Erechtheum have been reconstructed, despite its conversion into a church and, later, a Turkish harem. It had a basement and four rooms on the main story, at varying pavement levels. The large eastern room was given to Athena Polias, and the other spaces were divided up among the other figures. The temple exterior reflects this intricacy. No two sides are similar. There are three porches of divergent type, scale, and even level. The only ordinary composition is to the east—the temple facade—a stately hexastyle Ionic porch, mirrored at the west end in a corresponding row of half-columns attached to the cella wall. This became the prototype of endless variations that were to continue through all later periods. But the most unusual compositions are the lateral porches, attached to opposite sides of the west end of the cella. The famous Porch of the Maidens (fig. 2-26) projects toward the south, facing the Parthenon. Here six strong, supple, draped female figures (caryatids) stand on a high parapet, lightly bearing an elegant Ionic entablature. Such caryatids are known in earlier Greek architecture, the best-known example being the Treasury of the Siphnians at

2-24   Erechtheum from the west. c. 420 B.C.

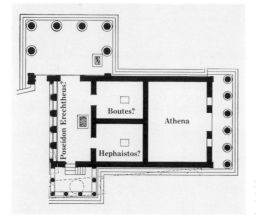

2-25
Plan, Erechtheum.
Acropolis, Athens.

2-26   Porch of the Maidens, Erechtheum

2-27   Detail of east porch, Erechtheum

Delphi (fig. 2-35). At the Erechtheum, they assume the sublime High Classical sculptural style. Because of their context, opposite the Parthenon colonnade and on a building with three other purely columnar arrangements, the Erechtheum caryatids point up the underlying anthropomorphism of the Greek orders:

The presence of the erect human image in the supple organic structure of the Greek column is here explicitly revealed.

This south porch counterbalances the much larger and far more open and airy north porch. Whereas the maidens are lifted above the main grade of the temple (established by the east front), the columnar north porch is set at a lower point on the sloping hillside. This enabled the gifted architect, Mnesicles, to create a soaring colonnade that lifts its entablature to within proximity of the main entablature running along the cella walls. Like its anthropomorphic counterpart, the tetrastyle north porch is two columns deep. But here, the omission of internal columns adds to the airiness of the porch, established not only by the attenuated Ionic columns but also by their unusually wide spacing.

The detailing of the building is extremely refined and is carried to the maximum at the north porch (where, incidentally, the mark of Poseidon's trident was visible through an opening in the pavement, with a corresponding opening in the ceiling). The capitals are considered the most ornate and exquisite ever carved, and the coffered ceiling and the portal, its frame studded with rosettes, are executed with unsurpassed elegance.

The qualities of the Erechtheum and the Parthenon are no less manifest at the grand entrance gateway to the Acropolis, the Propylaea (figs. 2-28–2-32), designed by Mnesicles and constructed between 437 and 432 B.C. but never completed. Like all the Acropolis structures, the gateway was of marble and of great expense. It too had a sad post-Classical history of transformation, partial destruction, and modern salvage. Like the

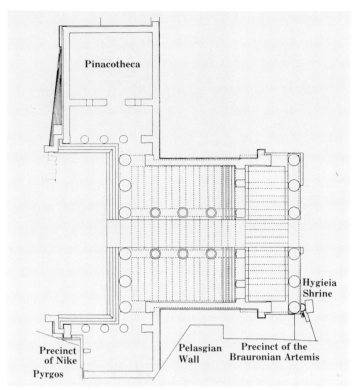

2-31 Propylaea from the east

2-32 Capital, Propylaea

2-28 Plan, Propylaea. Acropolis, Athens. c. 437–432 B.C.

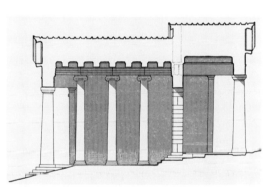

2-29 Longitudinal section, Propylaea

2-30 Propylaea from the southwest

2-33 Acropolis from the east

Parthenon, the Propylaea was externally Doric, but internally employed the Ionic. Like the Erechtheum, it was built on a sloping site and was intended to serve several functions. In its fundamentals, the Propylaea takes the form of a complex screened entranceway. The central part of the structure is a large, open-ended hall with twin hexastyle Doric facades. The architectural problem was how to accommodate within this frame two kinds of traffic—beasts (for sacrifice), vehicles, and processions, as well as the ordinary pedestrian—and to adjust all to the marked slope of the site. The first task was the simpler. Access to the Acropolis was over a zigzag ramp that ran up the west face, leading to the foot of the Propylaea. The main block was divided into three aisles. There was a central ramp for beasts, vehicles, and processions, some 12 feet in width, cutting straight up through the building. On either side were the ways for pedestrians. Mnesicles's great skill is shown in his bridging of different levels along the main axis. The difference between the stylobates of the twin facades is nearly 6 feet. Yet the heights of their orders are almost identical. How was Mnesicles to resolve this difference in a harmonious manner? The interior was cut by a transverse wall into two spaces. In the larger, western room stood two Ionic colonnades separating the central ramp and the lateral paths. These columns (one of which remains standing), although only two-thirds the diameter of the Doric facade shafts, rise some 34 feet, lifting their architrave beams to the level of the east architrave, at the same time aligning with the frieze of the west facade. At the west end of this hall were stairs on each side leading up some 5 feet to doorways, with a corresponding central opening over the ramp. These gave access to the east hall, which, with its ceiling only slightly higher than the coffered west hall version, opened through the Doric porch to the Acropolis.

The central block of the entrance gateway is flanked by two wings. Both are fronted by porches set at right angles to the main Propylaea facade, repeating its Doric order but at a smaller scale and without pediments. This device gave dominance to the center and provided a transition in size to the small Temple of Athena Nike—whose order, reciprocally, was abnormally thick to assimilate it to the Propylaean Doric. Although the south wing of the Propylaea was compromised by its restricted site, so that it was completed only as a facade, the left, or northern, portico fronts a large rectangular hall. This space served as the Pinakotheke, or picture gallery, the first room known to be built especially for this purpose. Light was admitted through the central doorway and the flanking windows; the pictures themselves were displayed on boards fastened to the walls.

SITE PLANNING

The marble structures of the Acropolis were not the icily aloof shapes that they seem to be to the modern observer; rather, each was sited and designed with the others in mind and, moreover, with the observer as part of the visual calculus. Let us, for a moment, try to recapture something of the chain of visual impressions made by the Acropolis when the Periclean program was completed at the end of the fifth century (fig. 2-33). From all sides but the west, it rendered the Olympian impression of majesty atop unapproachable heights. Movement up the west slope was not direct (as the Romans later made it), but along a zigzag path that swept back and forth across the Acropolis axis. As one approached the hillside from the southwest, the first clear form was the Temple of Athena Nike on its high platform.

It disappeared as one moved up the first ramp at its foot, but then it reappeared dramatically at the return of the ramp. At this point, the Propylaea loomed ahead, its twin Doric wings lifting above the Athena Nike structure and framing the monumental hexastyle central portico, whose scale was nearly that of the Parthenon itself. With every step, one was more enveloped by the U-shaped Propylaea, which seemed to reach out and draw the onlooker toward the monumental center. Although the central block of the Propylaea, with its abnormally wide central intercolumniation, invites entrance, one was easily diverted to the Pinakotheke or the Athena Nike precinct. Returning to the main axis, one entered the Propylaea interior. Within, one again confronted the Ionic, lifting the eye to elegant capitals and exquisite coffering detail, all lit by skylight reflected from the marble pavement. Moving through the aisles of the Propylaea, one went up the steps and through one of the doorways to the second level; the space that had just expanded was now compressed by the rise in pavement level. The first Propylaea chamber had presented a series of longitudinal Ionic colonnades and a wall with doorways; now the prospect was the transverse Doric colonnade, the twin of the west front but backlit seen within the porch. And through it, one could glimpse the spacious hilltop and the principal Acropolis buildings. At the Propylaea exit, three forms vied for attention. The closest was Phidias's 30-foot bronze statue of Athena Promachos directly opposite the Propylaea. In the typically Greek way, following an unwritten rule that avoids strictly frontal views of monuments, the statue faced the Propylaea at a slight angle, enough to give a three-quarter perspective toward the Propylaea. This colossal Athena dominated the entrance prospect not only in her size and proximity, but also because neither the Erechtheum nor the Parthenon was yet clearly in view. To bring either temple into full sight one had to move on, possibly to the Erechtheum north porch, but in greater likelihood past the Porch of the Maidens toward the Parthenon, the end of the architectural odyssey, where one would gaze up at the tympanum and other reliefs and peer through the bronze cella door at its east front to catch sight of the other colossal statue, the gold-and-ivory Athena Parthenos.

How distant such an experience seems from those of earlier epochs. To take the most impressive parallel, the New Kingdom temples at Thebes: There too, a variety of architectural forms created a sequence involving anticipation and fulfillment, and the ultimate sight was a form shrouded in darkness and restricted in accessibility. But the exclusion of the public from the Egyptian sanctuary was complete, whereas the Greek cella was at least visible if not penetrable. And in place of the terrifying zoomorphic gods that dwelt in the cavelike Egyptian sanctuary, a goddess conceived in ideal human form, however magnified in scale, stood in the Parthenon. Whereas the path to the Egyptian sanctuary followed an undeviating axis marked by huge obelisks and frontal pylons, the Greeks offered a different formula: a path ultimately leading to the divine mystery but offering variety and freedom on the way, indeed, displaying seemingly endless possibilities of movement and perception.

It is obvious that the differences between Greek and Egyptian architectural complexes involve attitudes toward symmetry and axiality. In Egypt, as later under the Romans, and, indeed, the universal tendency in all centralized or totalitarian states, axiality and bilateral symmetry form the basis of planning. The underlying concern is to limit sharply the

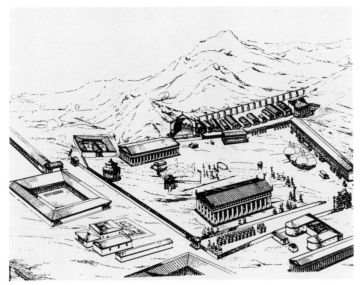

2-34 Panhellenic site. Olympia. c. 470–456 B.C. (Reconstruction after Durm)

2-35 Facade, Treasury of the Siphnians. Delphi. c. 530 B.C. (Partial reconstruction)

2-36 View of the Sanctuary of Apollo. Delphi. (Reconstruction after J. v. Schaubild)

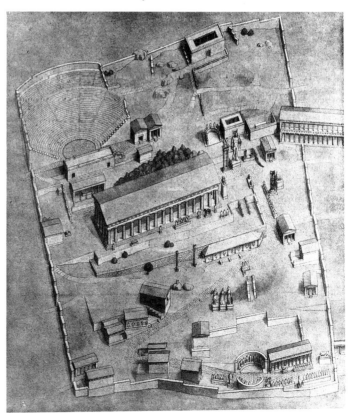

freedom of the human participant in architecture, to control movement and perceptions in much the way life and thought in general are controlled by the state.

Greek architecture does not abandon symmetry. Far from it. But for the Greek architect, strict bilateral symmetry was limited to individual buildings themselves; it was never used in planning a site or a group of structures. Even where it might have been naturally expected, it was pointedly avoided, for a distinction was drawn between the effect on the observer of axiality and symmetry within a single structure and the effect of those principles when applied to the grouping of buildings.

The Greek building—even a gateway, insofar as possible—is conceived as a three-dimensional entity complete on all sides and perfect unto itself. Moreover, care is normally taken so that the viewer perceives it as such. Thus, Greek buildings are not presented frontally, that is, on axis. Rather, whenever possible, the building is first presented from the diagonal, or at least from a position off-center, so that two adjacent sides are seen establishing clearly the three-dimensional integrity of the structure. It is often remarked that the orderly Greeks seemed to strew their buildings around sites in disregard of all principles of orderliness. But this appraisal misses what the Greek architect was after in designing a site. How better to sap the individuality of buildings in a group than to align them in some precise manner—and conversely, how better to emphasize the discreteness of each building than to disalign it from its neighbor. This explains much about the Acropolis plan, and it also lifts a veil of misunderstanding from the Panhellenic sites of Olympia and Delphi. At Olympia, the sanctuaries of Zeus and Hera were not built along the same axis (fig. 2-34). Moreover, the treasuries of the competitive Greek cities avoid alignment of their facades in an assertion of independence; this is particularly true at Delphi, where the Sacred Way winds in a zigzag path up to the Temple of Apollo, between a number of treasuries and monuments scattered alongside as if they were boulders that had fallen from the hillside above (figs. 2-35, 2-36). As seen in groundplans, the various sites seem in disarray, but anyone who visits the important Greek shrines cannot help but be moved by the rightness of the disposition of all elements—which includes the balance between the parts of individual buildings, between the various buildings, and, ultimately, between the buildings and the entire landscape.

2-37 Temple of Hephaestus. Athens. 449–c. 430 B.C.

LATER GREEK ARCHITECTURE

The Acropolis buildings are the embodiment of the Periclean Age. This high point of Greek history ended in 431 B.C. with the outbreak of the Peloponnesian War, in which Athens finally lost to its main military rival, Sparta. The Greek culture that emerged in the fourth century was no longer that of the fifth. It was not only the war. The seeds of cultural change were already present in the fifth century, and beginning with the fourth century a shift took place. Political factors played a major role. The politics of the Greek city-states, Athens in particular, were based on the full participation of the entire body of citizens, whose role in the government was not intermittent and passive but continuous and highly active. At the same time, the Greek political system had depended on a delicate balance between a number of independent city-states, among which Athens and Sparta were the strongest. This system ended in the fourth century B.C. with the rise of Philip of Macedon and the conquest of Greece by his son, Alexander the Great, in 336, followed by Alexander's conquest of the rest of the ancient world before his premature death in 323. Democracy survived this onslaught as a form, but its vitality was gone.

The economic structure also underwent extensive modifications. Earlier, each state was largely self-sufficient. There was much intimacy between city and country. In the fifth century most Athenians still owned farms, but Greece was not an agriculturally rich land. The considerable trade increased in the fourth century, and with it came an increasing specialization of the economic role of individuals and cities. Even the military aspects of Greek life changed. The military service required of all Athenian citizens declined with the rise of cavalry in the fourth century. Because every man could not maintain a

2-38 Capital, Temple of Hephaestus

fighting horse and equip himself as a "knight," mercenaries were increasingly used.

Thus, whereas the Greek citizen of the Classical period was fully involved in every aspect of public life—politically, economically, and militarily—thereafter, this whole man tended to be reduced to a specialized creature, detached from the realities of politics and war, and increasingly limited to private concerns. Culturally, one witnesses parallel phenomena. In the dramatic tragedies of the fifth century, the main concern was with universal human themes. Later, interest in specific personal portrayals and in themes of adventure came to the fore. In the visual arts, there occurred an analogous shift from the representation of universal themes, characteristic of the

2-39   Temple of Apollo. Bassae. c. 420–410 B.C.

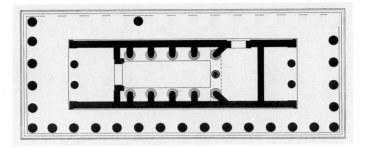

2-40   Plan, Temple of Apollo

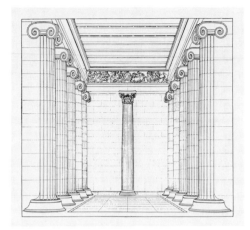

2-41
Interior, Temple
of Apollo.
(Reconstruction
after F. Krischen)

Classical period, to portraiture and the reflection of particularized expressions and emotions of the moment. The breakdown of the well-rounded character of the Classical Greek, the increasing specialization and withdrawal into more private spheres, resulted in an art increasingly individualistic, introspectively moody, and expressionistic.

Change was also manifest in architecture. The Corinthian order, with its richness of ornamentation, was introduced. There was a loosening of the old rules, which gave more freedom to expression. One-of-a-kind monuments appeared. Especially after Alexander, many new cities were founded. However, planned cities were an older tradition in Greece and this subject will be taken up separately.

The shift in architectural style did not occur suddenly with the Peloponnesian War, but began earlier. This is clearly seen in the Doric order. The Temple of Hephaestus, the god of fire, in the Agora at Athens, the best preserved of all Greek temples, is a contemporary of the Parthenon—and may be slightly earlier in design (figs. 2-37, 2-38). It embodies all the refinements of the Acropolis buildings—but to excess. It lacks vitality. The entablature is too high, the columns too slim. Its unstable proportions have been explained by the viewpoint toward the low hillside on which the Hephaesteum sits; and indeed, from below, the foreshortening of the columns and entablature does result in a more balanced effect. Refined optical calculations are, of course, typical of Doric buildings. But here there is a difference. If the "foreshortened" interpretation is correct, it would mean that the entire peripteral structure was principally intended for a single viewpoint, which flouts one of the basic rules of the siting of Classical Greek buildings. Thus, at the very moment that the Parthenon exemplified the culmination of the Doric order, the tendency to go "beyond" the ideal had already emerged. The Parthenon is the final statement of the canonical Doric; beyond it there would be no further advance, only exaggerated invention. Some would even say that the Parthenon, with its paradoxical proportions, interior Ionic, and cella frieze, had itself passed beyond the "true" Doric.

In later Doric temples, the proportions became even leaner. The entablature had shrunk from one-half the columnar height of the sixth century to the visually "ideal" one-third in the fifth century. In the fourth century, it was further reduced to one-fourth the height of the column. The columns became thinner—until by the second century, at Delos, houses were built with Doric columns more than eight diameters in height. Entasis, so crucial to columnar vitality, was abandoned, and the capitals became dry blocks over straight conical sections. As for the entablature, it became the norm to give both Doric and Ionic colonnades the same superstructure: a Doric architrave and frieze, and a dentilated Ionic cornice.

More innovations resulted from combining the Doric with the other two orders. As we have seen in the Ionic-Doric combinations of the Acropolis, the idea of merging the orders began in late-fifth-century Athens. Perhaps the most interesting example of this trend was an unusual temple, probably built by Ictinus, at one of the most beautiful of all Greek sites, high in the mountains of Arcadia. The Temple of Apollo at Bassae (figs. 2-39–2-41), built between 420 and 410 B.C., embodied a number of innovations. Like the Parthenon, it included a continuous figured frieze, but here it was placed around the interior rather than on the exterior of the cella wall. The frieze was part of an interior entablature set over a unique series of spurs that projected from the lateral cella walls and were faced with Ionic half-columns. What was most unusual was that this colonnade (again imitating the Parthenon) was continued with a freestanding column placed at the end of the cella. This single column employed the first known Corinthian capital.

THE CORINTHIAN ORDER

Since the time of the Roman writer Vitruvius, the Corinthian order has been misconstrued as being independent. In origin and character, it was essentially a variant of the Ionic. It did

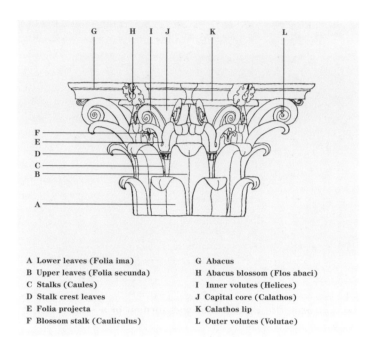

A Lower leaves (Folia ima)
B Upper leaves (Folia secunda)
C Stalks (Caules)
D Stalk crest leaves
E Folia projecta
F Blossom stalk (Cauliculus)

G Abacus
H Abacus blossom (Flos abaci)
I Inner volutes (Helices)
J Capital core (Calathos)
K Calathos lip
L Outer volutes (Volutae)

2-42   Diagram of Corinthian capital. (After Saalman)

2-43
Corinthian capital,
Temple of Athena.
Tegea. c. 350 B.C.

2-44
Old Tholos. Delphi.
(Restoration after
H. Pomtow, *Klio* 12)

not originate in a "third" area of the Greek world, and it is not associated with a distinct temple type or plan. It retained the features of the Ionic order, except for the new type of capital. As opposed to both the Doric and the Ionic capitals, whose components are layered in horizontal strata, the Corinthian capital evolved as a program of two *concentric* layers (figs. 2-42, 2-45). The inner structure of the ideal Corinthian capital is comprised of what are essentially the basic elements of the earlier orders. There is a platelike abacus, which gathers the load from the entablature, and an echinus that expresses the inner structural forces of the column. But the abacus now has a smooth, molded edge and concave sides that curve into sharply projecting corners. The inverted-bell-shape form below, the calathus, is the Corinthian counterpart of the echinus of the other orders. It yields the same firm but springy impression, here formed not by a cushionlike bulge but by a plantlike flare, concave rather than convex and elongated rather than depressed.

The core structure of the Corinthian capital is enveloped (and largely masked) by a complex, vegetative layer, which is not simply naturalistic decoration; it embodies the illusion of organic growth in forms that tectonically interact with the core. Its base is a double ring of acanthus leaves with a high rear leaf placed exactly at each diagonal. From behind the acanthus leaves, eight stalks (cauliculi) spring in pairs at the corners, surmounted by blossomlike calyxes. The cauliculi curve into volutes which reach up, seemingly, to support the tips of the abacus. Pairs of smaller curled elements (helices) also emerge from the stalks, reaching up toward the center of the abacus, where they are surmounted by a floral centerpiece, an anthemion or, more commonly, a rosette.

The features described here represent an ideal to which few Greek capitals actually correspond. In the earliest examples (e.g., at Bassae and Delphi), the acanthus leaves are stubby, the volutes wiry. But soon, as in the Temple of Athena Alea at Tegea (c. 350 B.C.; fig. 2-43) the forms become more luxuriant, the impression riper and fuller, reaching a maximum of

inventiveness in the late fourth century at the Monument to Lysicrates in Athens. It is only in the Late Hellenistic and Roman periods that the "ideal" form became the usual one, for example, at the Temple of Zeus Olympius in Athens, of 170 B.C. (colorplate 10).

None of the early buildings that employed the Corinthian capital are standing, except for Bassae. In any event, the Corinthian was first restricted to the temple interior; it was not used outside until late in the Hellenistic period. Its early use is

2-45   Entablature fragment, Tholos. Epidaurus. 360 B.C.

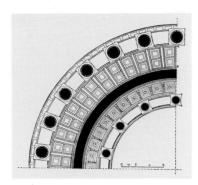

**2-46
Detail of plan, Tholos.
Epidaurus**

2-47   Monument to Lysicrates. Athens. 335 B.C.

at Delphi is comprised of three concentric rings of structure: a circular Doric pteron of twenty columns; a cella wall; and nine interior Corinthian columns. The capitals resemble the one from Bassae. However, the finest example of the type—according to the word of the ancients and the evidence of our own eyes—was the highly developed Tholos of Epidaurus, of about 360 B.C. Not only the capitals but the entire program of ornament—including the marvelous coffered ceiling—were carried to a high pitch of refinement.

The earliest building in which the Corinthian capital is used externally (fig. 2-47) is not a temple, but the monument erected in Athens to support the elaborate bronze trophy won by Lysicrates in 335 B.C. in the choral competition of a Greek festival. The square limestone base, some 9 feet 6 inches on each side, is topped by a course of bluish marble, typical of the increasing colorism of the period. Above stands a white marble cylinder, 7 feet in diameter, like a miniature tholos, only here articulated by six Corinthian columns set beneath the circular entablature. The conical roof was formed of a single marble block carved to resemble roof tiles, supporting a flowing foliate element crowned by Lysicrates's tripod prize. The marble cylinder is hollow, but there is no entrance and it was evidently not intended for any specific purpose. Technically, the monument is significant in that the columns serve to conceal joints between the curved slabs that make up the cylinder; each slab included its section of the entablature. This divergence between real and apparent structure—the columns providing only the *visual* support for the entablature—runs contrary to the more "honest" building methods of the earlier Classical period and is typical of the later epoch, as is the pictorial fantasy of the monument. Here, imaginative individualism emerges as a principal architectural tendency.

HELLENISTIC TRENDS

Although in the Hellenistic period (after Alexander's death in 323 B.C.) there was increased flouting of the hoary architectural traditions, these traditions nevertheless were retained with considerable strength. Thus, it was not until 170 B.C. that the Corinthian appeared as the principal exterior order of a normal peripteral temple: The immense Temple of Zeus Olympius in Athens (colorplate 10; fig. 2-48), with columns 57 feet tall, was set out over a groundplan extending 135 feet

2-48   Temple of Zeus Olympius. Athens. c. 170 B.C.

closely connected with the round temple, an important variant on the standard rectangular type. From early times, the Greeks had built circular structures, first in the form of temporary huts and then as primitive temples. There were also the Mycenaean tholos tombs, such as the so-called Treasury of Atreus, but they were largely underground. The first important round building constructed aboveground was a mid-sixth-century Doric structure at Delphi. (Its lost form has been inferred from parts found reused in another building.) By the early fourth century, the round temple—or tholos—was well established.

The two most important tholoi appear at Delphi and Epidaurus (figs. 2-44–2-46). The early-fourth-century example by 354 feet, dwarfing the Parthenon and rivaling the Doric temples of Sicily and the grand Ionic shrines. A more interesting design than the Athenian giant was the Ionic temple, begun about 300 B.C. (partially completed by the Romans) and dedicated to Apollo, at Didyma on the Ionian coastland (figs. 2-49–2-51). Following the regional tradition, the temple was built as a gigantic decastyle dipteral structure, with a

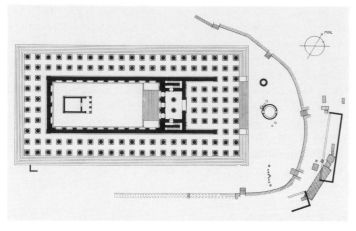

2-49   Plan, Temple of Apollo. Didyma, Turkey. c. 300 B.C.

2-50   Remains of Temple of Apollo

2-51   View of the court, Temple of Apollo

cavernous porch extending—almost like an Egyptian hypostyle hall—five columns deep! The pronaos did not lead to a cella, but ended with a wall, above which was a roofed platform where the rites and pronouncements of the oracle took place. Behind the platform area was a high-walled courtyard, derived from the open-roofed Ionic cella, with a small (28 by 30 feet) prostyle shrine of Apollo near its far end. The courtyard was reached by tunnel-like passages sloping down from the sides of the east porch, and at the east end of the courtyard, a grand flight of steps led up through a columnar screen to the "stage" area of the mysteries of the oracle.

Didyma combines the ancient Ionic temple form with Hellenistic inventiveness, transforming the pronaos from a passage to a deep audience area filled with huge columns. The temple interior has become the precinct for a miniature shrine-within-a-shrine and a theatrical spectacle of stairs and movement, with the Ionian sky visible above the courtyard walls.

Although Didyma was probably the most imaginative of the later Greek shrines, its fame in antiquity was surpassed by a simpler monument of the Ionian coast, the Mausoleum at Halicarnassus (fig. 2-52), one of the canonical Seven Wonders of the Ancient World. Built for King Mausolus by his wife after his death in 353 B.C.—and providing the generic term for later tombs—the Mausoleum was eventually so thoroughly destroyed that no modern reconstruction has proved entirely satisfactory, however painstakingly based on ancient descriptions, representations on coins, and fragments. Nevertheless, its basic outline seems to be established: a tall base 100 feet square; a second story, the tomb chamber proper, fronted by 36 columns in a templelike, peripteral form; a pyramid of 24 steps ending 136 feet above the ground, surmounted by a platform with a quadriga (a chariot pulled by four horses) carrying colossal statues of the royal couple. Typical of the period is not only the freedom to appropriate the temple type for a tomb, setting it on high, surmounted with a fantastic pyramid, but the very idea of dedicating such a monument to the memory of a person. In the Classical period, only simple upright stone

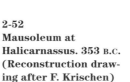

2-52
Mausoleum at Halicarnassus. 353 B.C. (Reconstruction drawing after F. Krischen)

slabs, or stele, frequently with a moving scene carved in relief, were permitted at graves. But, increasingly, in the post-Classical period, the growing cult of the individual encouraged the architect to draw on the ancient Oriental tradition of glorifying illustrious men. The pyramidal crown of the Mausoleum was probably not without a pointed reference to the much admired Old Kingdom pyramids.

Two further structures—in Asia Minor and the Aegean islands—complete our review of late Hellenistic trends. The imposing Altar of Zeus at Pergamum, built between 197 and 159 B.C., is now partly reconstructed in the State Museum, Berlin (figs. 2-53, 2-54). The original structure was sited high on a crest of the terraced upper city. The Altar was set atop a high platform in a large rectangular courtyard, with a flight of stairs leading up to the court between flanking wings. An Ionic order ran over the wings and around the court. The lower zone of the monument was faced with the finest sculptural work of the Hellenistic period—a huge, continuous frieze, charged

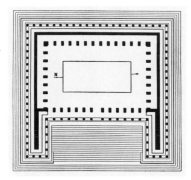

2-53
Plan, Altar of Zeus. Pergamum. 197–159 B.C.

2-54   Altar of Zeus. (Restoration. State Museum, Berlin)

2-55   Sanctuary of Asclepius. Kos. 2nd century B.C. (Restored view after R. Herzog)

with surging movement and intense emotion, depicting the Battle of the Gods and the Giants.

The controlled, axial approach of the Pergamum Altar and the dramatic assault of the monument on the visitor are manifest on a grander scale at the contemporary Sanctuary of Asclepius, the god of medicine, on the island of Kos (fig. 2-55). The sick came here to be healed by the waters of a natural spring and by the ministrations of the priests of Asclepius. Axial flights of stairs led up from an empty lower terrace to a second level; there an altar was framed asymmetrically by two shrines; more stairs led to the top platform, where a temple at dead center was surrounded by a U-shaped portico. In architectural elegance and the scale of the details the shrine is Hellenic, but its overpowering spirit harks back to such Imperial works as Deir el Bahari, and looks forward to the Roman shrines soon to follow. Although in its own right, the Asclepieion is powerful architecture of a high order, it documents a profound change in aesthetic, even ethical, sensibility, and the final abandonment of those unique factors that had gone to make up the definitive works of Greek architecture on the Athenian Acropolis.

CIVIC ARCHITECTURE

Aside from temples, tombs, and altars, Greek architectural energies were directed also at secular architecture, best demonstrated in Athens by the Agora—a combination of marketplace and civic center (fig. 2-56). Although the Acropolis was the oldest area of the city, remains of houses and tombs tell us that from 1000 to 700 B.C. the site to the north of the Acropolis was inhabited. A large area of relatively flat terrain, this site had a number of fresh-water wells. Roads leading from the Athenian port of Piraeus and the hinterlands of Attica converged there. It was the logical place to construct a civic complex. The history of the many archaeological layers of the Agora is long and complicated, and it is best to study its state at the end of the fifth century B.C., when it was more or less complete.

The Agora was located within a roughly rectangular area. Across a diagonal was the Panathenaic Way (or Dromos), leading to the Acropolis, the site of the annual procession, depicted on the Parthenon frieze, venerating the city's protectress. On the west side of the Agora stood a complex group of buildings, including a tholos, and the new and the old Bouleuterion (assembly hall); on a hillock to the rear was the Temple of Hephaestus and the Stoa of Zeus. As a type, the stoa was the most important component of Greek city planning. Giving protection from the elements, yet open, defining both internal and outer sites, the stoa was used for a wide range of public purposes—political, economic, financial, even philosophic. Its makeup was deceptively simple. The most basic version was formed by a rear wall, a front colonnade, and a connecting roof. This fundamental type could be expanded in depth to two aisles and in height to two stories; in plan it could be shaped into an L or even a U (but never a completely closed square—a Roman form of total control over space uncharacteristic of Greek design).

One of Socrates's favorite meeting places was, in fact, the Stoa of Zeus. This stoa was only one of several on the Agora. The grandest—the Stoa of Attalus II, one of three Hellenistic kings of Pergamum—was added in the second century (fig. 2-57). It was built two aisles deep and two stories high, running nearly the whole length of the east side of the Agora but leaving the corners free. It has been reconstructed today (to house the Agora Museum), and in it one can experience the subtleties of light and shade, and recapture the sense of multifunctional use that such forms originally provided.

The Athenian democratic political system was made up of three governing councils: the Ecclesia, the body of all the citizens; the Boule, the council of 500; and the Prytany, the presiding section of the council, 50 of whom were elected each month. The Tholos is believed to have been the clubhouse of the Prytany, where it met for daily lunch. An adaptation of the round temple type, the Tholos was a walled circle, 60 feet in diameter. It had no exterior colonnade, and the interior space was articulated by six columns arranged in two groups of three, set in opposite areas. Next to the Tholos stood the council house, or Bouleuterion. In fact, two of these structures stood in the area, one from the early fifth century turned into the public archives when the second one was built at the end of the century. In the earlier version, seats rose on all four sides of the room, so the speakers always had their backs to one side. This disadvantage was eliminated in the later version, where the benches were placed around three sides, with the speaker's platform at the empty end. Two more notable examples of such council houses are found in Ionia, in the cities of Priene and Miletus (figs. 2-58–2-60). In Athens, intermediate columns supporting the roof formed an obstruction to the view of some participants. At Priene (c. 200 B.C.), the supports were pushed back beyond the rear rows of seats (leaving an aisle for circulation behind them), and the larger space was spanned by a roof whose structure was not of simple beams but of triangular, or trussed, assemblage, allowing unobstructed seating within a beautifully proportioned and articulated space. The Bouleuterion at Miletus, built after 175 B.C.,

2-57   Stoa of Attalus II, the Agora. Athens. 2nd century B.C. (Modern reconstruction)

was similar to the new Bouleuterion in Athens, with circular seating within rectangular perimeter walls, and it left a few seats obstructed by paired intermediate supports. What distinguished it was its great scale—about twice the size of the Athenian example, with seating for over twelve hundred people—its ingenious fitting of stairs into the waste corner space, the half-columnar order on the exterior, and the courtyard into which the altar, normally in the council house, was displaced. This systematic planning is typical of the Hellenistic period of Greek architecture, as is the increasing axiality—the Bouleuterion at Miletus being one of the most axialized of all Greek multiunit buildings.

In Athens, the largest political body, the Ecclesia, met on a hillside called the Pnyx. Originally, the citizens disposed themselves facing down the slope toward the speaker at the bottom. Eventually the arrangement was reversed, with a massive, high structure being built up to support rings of seats facing in the *uphill* direction toward the speaker's podium. This development coincided with the emergence of one of the most important of all Greek architectural forms, the theater.

For the Classical Greek, the theater was not mere entertainment or diversion, but a poetic and musical celebration of the most profound religious and civic beliefs, which all citizens attended. The earliest arrangement was similar to the early

2-56   Plan, Agora. Athens. Late 5th century B.C.

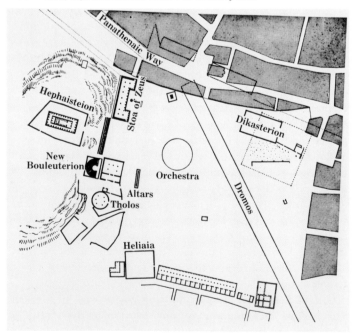

2-58　Bouleuterion. Priene, Turkey. c. 200 B.C.

2-59　Interior, Bouleuterion. (Reconstruction drawing after A. W. Laurence)

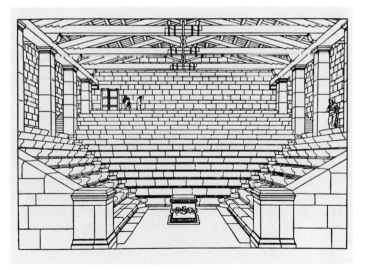

2-60　Bouleuterion. Miletus, Turkey. c. 175 B.C. (Isometric view after J. J. Coulton)

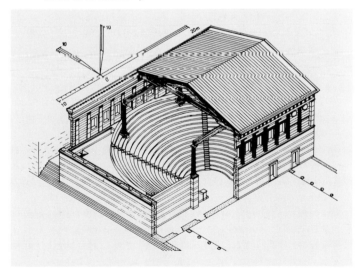

use of the Pnyx, requiring merely a hillside facing the place of performance. The theater took no formal shape until the late fifth century, when the canonical form was evolved. It consisted of four parts: the *skene* (scene), a background structure housing props, etc.; the *proskenion* (proscenium), a low, one-story structure running in front of the skene not as a stage but merely as backdrop facade; the *orchestra*, a circular area for the chorus, dancing, and dramatic action; and, finally, the *auditorium*, rings of seats cut into the hillside for the spectators.

The most famous Greek theater is the fourth-century example at Epidaurus (colorplate 11). Here we have the fully developed circular orchestra (with an altar of Dionysus in the center), the skene and proskenion (in ruins), set within slightly more than a semicircle of seating (387 feet in diameter) climbing the hillside, with conveniently spaced stair-aisles. Epidaurus has uncanny acoustics—with a silent audience, a pin dropped at the center of the orchestra can be heard at the farthest seats. Even more wonderful are the proportions, the scale, and the view out over a majestic landscape. Nowhere was the profound religious

**2-61 Theater. Priene. c. 3rd century B.C.
(Reconstruction drawing after M. Schade)**

feeling of the Greeks for the earth and sky exhibited more than in their theaters. Only the greatest plays and performances could hope to vie with the natural spectacle.

Among the most architecturally evolved Greek theaters is the relatively small third-century example at Priene (fig. 2-61). It looks out over a plain (originally covered by the sea) from just above the main level of one of the most brilliant of all planned cities. Here the proskenion-skene group is moved forward to cut the circle of the orchestra, closely integrating the various parts. Moreover, the acting now took place on the broad roof of the proskenion, and a large section of the skene wall behind was opened up for scenic effects, so that the functional potential of the stage elements was finally brought to fruition.

Other types of Greek architecture beyond those discussed here existed as well. Most prominent were facilities, such as the stadiums at Olympia and Athens, for the athletic games and contests so important to the Greek way of life. In addition to the stadium—prototype of all those down to the present, with a running field set along at least one hillside used for seats, and sometimes two—there was the palaestra, or exercise court, generally in the form of a large open area surrounded by colonnaded porticoes.

Interestingly, the sole important building type not yet mentioned—the house—does not seem to have engaged the Greek architects. Residences were comfortably planned, but of no particular distinction—especially when compared to the public structures. They reflected the general Mediterranean tendency to build around an open courtyard, set near the center of an area defined by an outer wall of simple rectangular shape. Various types of rooms were arranged between the open core and the outer wall. Occasionally, the south wing of the house was lower than the north to admit sun to the interior. In the Hellenistic period, more elaborate schemes were developed, but in general the Greek house was almost exclusively built in an informal, vernacular mode.

CITY PLANNING

It is meaningful that the Greeks did not build great houses or—with the exception of some late, Eastern examples—imposing tombs. Their architectural energies were directed neither toward private life nor the afterlife. It was public life in the

here-and-now that counted (although always in the presence of the gods). For the Greeks, humans were profoundly social creatures, and although this attitude can be found in the writings of Aristotle and others, it is nowhere expressed more explicitly than in their architecture and their city planning.

Greek city planning is based on the idea that the form of cities, the shape of streets and spaces, reflected the people who inhabited them. The first planned Greek city was probably Miletus (fig. 2-62), destroyed in 494 B.C. by fire or earthquake and rebuilt around 460 B.C. Its planner is believed to have been Hippodamus, a Greek intellectual associated with the Pythagoreans. Hippodamus considered himself a philosopher, with his own metaphysical system, from which he derived his principles of city planning. The scheme with which he is credited (although he may have merely intellectualized traditional Greek planning methods) involved five aspects: 1) The city was cut by several main streets crossing at right angles; 2) Most of the resulting rectangles were subdivided into a relatively uniform grid of *insulae* (blocks); 3) The rectangular blocks were further subdivided into house plots; 4) Public buildings were set within the system without interfering with traffic; 5) The plan of the city was adapted to the terrain. But most important was the characteristically inventive way the scheme was actually deployed.

Miletus, today a swampy and deserted spot, was sited on a triple-headed peninsula. As it would have been pointless to attempt unification of all three areas, each was given its own grid system, with port facilities at the edges. A defensive wall ran along the irregular outline of the whole. Space for public buildings was provided toward the city center, between the residential grids. Gradually built up over several centuries, the public facilities came to form an agora—a complex of stoas, council houses, gymnasia, and temples. There were extensions at the western edge of the city—including the theater—jutting out over the water. The disposition of the stoas forming the south part of the Agora is revealing and typical: They are open to the main arteries of traffic at three points, yet form a coherent and functional market space.

The Hippodamian scheme emerged with more clarity at fourth-century Priene (fig. 2-63), a small city, but one of the great examples of urban planning, and comparatively well preserved. Here a unified Hippodamian scheme was constructed on a hillside. Six main streets were established running east-west along the hill contours. These were crossed by sloping or stepped streets running up and down the hillside in a north-south direction. Extensive terracing was employed to keep individual *insulae* flat and to provide large precincts for temples and for the agora, placed toward the center of the town. As at Miletus, although the street pattern was rectilinear, the city wall at Priene followed the contours of the land to the best military advantage, running at the edge of natural ravines that surrounded the city plateau and with an extension to include the acropolis, towering above on the hillside. The disposition of the public structures in the "lower" town was beautifully logical and functional. The agora at the center was shaped by stoas to form a market area. And, as at Miletus, it was arranged to let the traffic flow freely, even on the sloping site. One of the main east-west streets ran directly through the agora, and another was shaped to continue temple to Zeus. Its precinct was not entered directly from the agora but from a point better suited to presenting a three-dimensional image of the modest structure.

In every aspect of Priene, the most classically balanced and composed of Greek urban schemes, there is apparent the Greek sense of practical order, of freedom of movement, of the independence and interdependence of architectural forms, and of the human participant. These ideals are completely different from the severe, abstract schemes of the equally ambitious Roman planners. In Imperial Roman architecture, Greek forms were drawn into a controlled matrix; all relationships were axial and symmetrical, all perceptions predetermined. It was to be an architecture not of independent forms engaging free individuals, but one that created propagandistic images of the power and authority of the state and the gods.

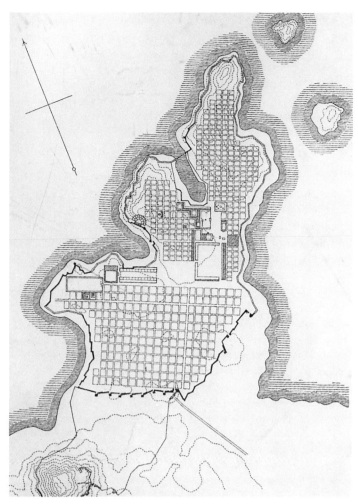

2-62   City plan, Miletus. After 479 B.C.

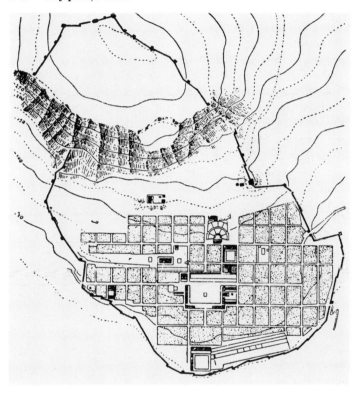

2-63   City plan, Priene

around it to the south, where three separate entrances to the stoa were provided. Beyond the double-aisled north stoa lay the Bouleuterion, with the theater a block farther above. The Temple of Athena (discussed earlier) was set on a terraced precinct that was faced with a magnificent rusticated wall. Theater and temple were about equidistant from the agora, and at a slightly greater distance below were the palaestra and stadium. In a corner area of the agora there was a small

3-1
Porta
Augusta,
Etruscan city
gate. Perugia.
c. 300 B.C.

Chapter Three | Rome

ROMAN PREHISTORY: THE ETRUSCANS

Just as the Minoan Bronze Age led to the emergence of Greece, so Etruscan civilization preceded the Roman. It is not that the Etruscan people were the first settlers on the Italian peninsula (c. 800–700 B.C.), but they were the first to create an important visual culture. The Etruscans did not merely settle, they conquered and ruled the indigenous population with an efficient system of exploitation that established an important precedent for the later Romans. By the sixth century B.C., they controlled all of Tuscany as well as the Po Valley, and finally they seized Campania and what was to become independent Rome. The native Italians had been backward and agrarian; the Etruscans brought with them from Asia Minor a sophisticated Eastern—including Greek—culture. They became prosperous, powerful, and accomplished in warfare, metallurgy, and art. Yet they are a mysterious people. Their language remains largely inaccessible; all traces of their literature have disappeared; their customs and the meaning of their art remain cloudy.

Etruscan architecture was systematically destroyed by the early Romans, who expelled their predecessors from Rome in the late sixth century and drove them from Etruria soon after. What survived were structures that had been hidden, such as tombs, or that were useful or too massive to be conveniently destroyed. Etruscan houses had been built of mud walls or wood, so naturally they disappeared. Except for stone foundations and terra-cotta roof tiles, Etruscan temples were constructed with the same perishable materials. Because of demolition or decay, no Etruscan temples stand, and their scanty remains consist mostly of fragmentary terra-cotta decoration.

Yet this situation is not quite so unfortunate as it might seem. Surviving because of their massive size and utility are the cyclopean city walls (fig. 3-1) built to surround the Etruscan hill settlements at Volterra (Volaterrae), Cortona, and Perugia (Perusia). The walls had massive entrance archways, such as the Porta Augusta at Perugia, built about 300 B.C. These gateways are important on two counts: They reveal early knowledge of the arch and vault, so important for the Romans; and, at Perugia, there is a precocious, if crude, combination of the arch with the Greek orders, which was to become a pervasive Roman motif. Other Etruscan buildings can be reconstructed from small terra-cotta funerary urns made in the forms of houses and temples. Archaeologists have been able to piece together credible reconstructions of a number of temples by relating decorative remains and traces of plans to the written description of the "Templum Etruscum" by Vitruvius, a Roman architect of the time of Augustus, whose treatise, *De architectura*, discusses the key role played by the Etruscans in the venerated architectural past.

The Etruscan temple (figs. 3-2, 3-3) for all its dependence on Greek models did not embody the sculptural idealism of the Hellenic prototypes and certainly none of the refinements of the Doric temple. The Etruscan temple was a slapdash affair of effects; its only visually intricate aspect was luxurious decoration. Its scheme was not modeled on the Greek peripteral form, but on the simpler prostyle arrangement. Although there were Etruscan examples with twin columns standing before a single cella, the more important temples had not one but three cellas, standing side by side as individual chambers for the deities to whom the Etruscans had dedicated the shrine. The cellas occupied about half the plan; usually, they stood behind a spacious tetrastyle porch two or three columns deep. The overall proportion of the very broad scheme was a width-to-length ratio of five to six.

Although the Etruscans adapted variations of the Greek orders for the elevations of their temples, the most significant order was of their own invention. It is known as the Tuscan (or Etruscan) order, and later it was a favorite of the Romans. The Tuscan column was a blend of the Doric and the other Greek orders, greatly simplified. Like the Ionic, the Tuscan column had a base, but it consisted of only a single torus over the plinth. The capital resembled an inverted base; the shaft was unfluted. The proportions of the column were intermediate between the Greek models, the ratio of height to diameter being about seven to one.

These rather plain supports were very widely spaced, only four across a temple front that the Greeks would have provided with six or eight. The viewer's attention thus was not captured by the sculptural splendor of a colonnade, but, rather, it was drawn inward to the interior of the porch and directed upward to the richly decorated roof that constituted the visual centerpiece of the building.

In principle, the Etruscan ridge-roof structure (fig. 3-4) was not different from that of the Greeks, but its proportions were altered, along with certain details. The columns were connected by wooden architraves. Above these, at points over the columns, were set longitudinal beams called mutuli, which, according to Vitruvius, projected forward a distance equal to one-fourth the height of the column. On the lateral mutuli rested the roofing rafters, inclined at the normal Classical pitch but overhanging the temple so that the eaves came down as far as the tops of the columns. This wooden superstructure was covered with a sheathing of intricately molded, gaily decorated terra-cotta acroteria at the front and antefixes along

3-2   Typical Etruscan temple. (Reconstruction model as described by Vitruvius)

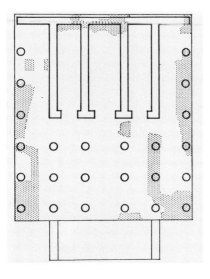

3-3
Plan, Capitoline temple.
Rome. c. 509 B.C.
(Plan by E. Gjerstad
and B. Blomé)

3-4   Etruscan ridge-roof structure, Capitolium. Cosa.
(Reconstruction after A. Boëthius and Ward-Perkins)
1. Architrave; 2. and 3. Mutules; 4. Pediment; 5. Rafters;
6. Purlins; 7. Common rafters; 8. Sheeting of planks;
9. Antefixes; 10. Frieze of the architrave; 11. Sima; 12. Pierced
cresting; 13. Revetment planks below the sima and eaves

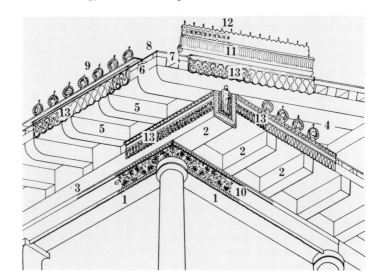

the sides. Sometimes figures, or even groups of figures, stood along the top of the roof, as in the famous example of the Portonaccio Temple at Veii (fig. 3-5).

It has been said that the deep overhang and the terra-cotta revetment of the Etruscan temple were needed to protect the fragile mud-brick walls from rain. But, as always, visual factors were also at work, revealed when we imagine how one actually viewed the temple. The back of the structure was not especially presentable, even in such monumental works as the Temple of Jupiter Capitolinus in Rome, where colonnades were placed along the sides but were not continued around to the rear. Thus it was natural to site the temple directly against a precinct wall. Moreover, from earliest times the Etruscans placed the precinct entrance directly opposite the temple facade, on axis. The temple was not treated as an independent form in space but as a frontal, relieflike image, set on a high podium, with access only by a central flight of stairs. In approaching such a temple, the observer was first caught by the effusive gaiety of the terracotta decoration. The closer he or she came, the more dramatically the overhanging, low-slung roof would loom. At the steps, the roof would reach out to draw the viewer into the cool, shadowed space spread out before the three cellas. The effect was deliberately overpowering. Thus, the impulse to create a monumental architecture of controlled perceptions and calculated pictorial effects and drama appeared early in Italy.

Ample accommodation for temple precincts and the sacred rituals enacted there was provided in the well-organized cities of Etruria. The grid system of laying out a town with wide streets crossed by narrower ones was developed by the later Romans into a sophisticated city-planning program, but its origins were found in Etruscan settlements as early as the sixth century B.C. The town of Marzabotto (fig. 3-6), for example, on a wide plain in the Po Valley near Bologna, was planned with a rectangular outline, within which two main streets crossed each other, forming a small city square at the crossing. Smaller streets cut through the major thoroughfares to create residential blocks. This systematic approach to the problems of organizing community life was characteristic of the practical and efficient Etruscans, whom the Romans also credited with the invention of drainage and sewers.

But so few clues survive to explain the ways of the Etruscans that the closest we can come to any clear image of them is to look not at the scanty remains of their lives but at their houses of the afterlife. Etruscan tombs, famous for their grave goods and uninhibited fresco decoration, survive in surprising quantity in central Italy, in particular at the two major necropolises at Tarquinia and Cerveteri (figs. 3-7, 3-8). Like the Egyptians, the Etruscans filled their tombs with an abundance of material objects needed in the life beyond. Wall paintings suggested life's pleasures for the dead—banquets with dancing, drinking, music; love-making; sporting events and hunting. Terra-cotta effigies of the deceased, some of them full-length and reclining in relaxed poses along the lid of a sarcophagus, seem to defy death with their realism and vitality. The tombs were constructed underground, with chambers and corridors that reflected, in a general way it is thought, the appearance of the terrestrial homes reluctantly left behind.

Structurally, the tombs were divided into two types: corbeled and rock-cut. The former, which included the most lavishly decorated of all, the Regolini-Galassi Tomb (named after its nineteenth-century discoverers) at Cerveteri (c. 650 B.C.), were reminiscent of Mycenaean structures. The horizontal stones of the vaulting, jutting out step-by-step on each side of the narrow passage until they reached the top, were finally covered by large flat stones, which bridged the small gap remaining and created a kind of overhead arch. The Etruscan examples were technically more advanced than those of Mycenae. In one case, the seventh-century B.C. Pietrera Tomb at Vetulonia, the corbeling of the square chamber included spherical triangles, or pendentives, in the corners, the first

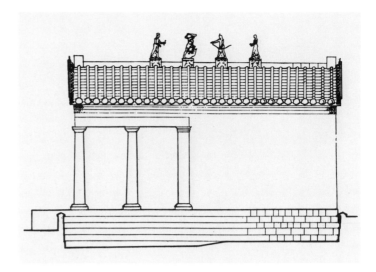

3-5 Portonaccio Temple. Veii. (Reconstruction elevation after A. Boëthius and Ward-Perkins)

3-6 City plan, Marzabotto. c. 6th century B.C.

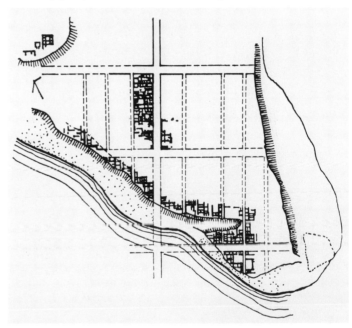

known use in stone of a feature that a millennium later would become the hallmark of Byzantine churches. The corbeled tombs were built of sandstone or travertine; a great mound of earth, or tumulus, surmounted the main chamber, frequently above a cylindrical retaining wall. The rock-cut tombs, common in southern Etruria near Rome and Orvieto, were quarried from the soft volcanic rock indigenous to the region and were also covered by tumulus mounds. Often they were composed, as at Cerveteri, of one or two small antechambers, a large central chamber, and a small inner room beyond. Access to these interiors was through narrow doorways that tapered toward the top. The tombs were much like underground houses, and even the stone roofs included a false beam carved to imitate the appearance of the wooden roof beam of a "real" domicile. Thick slabs of rock were placed around the main chamber; probably, the dead were laid to rest there, along with the tomb treasures of vessels and jewels.

The Etruscans' houses are gone, their literature is lost, none of their temples stand, and their tombs have been

3-7 Tomb of the Reliefs. Cerveteri. 4th century B.C.

3-8 Necropolis of Cerveteri. 7th–6th century B.C.

emptied of their treasures. Although their civilization was, in the words of D. H. Lawrence, "wiped out entirely to make room for Rome with a very big R," an Etruscan legacy has come down to us in architecture through those things the Romans admired and borrowed.

ROMAN CIVILIZATION

With typical precision, the Romans pinpointed April 21, 753 B.C., as the day Rome was founded—centuries before the city would become the center of an empire with its own artistic traditions. Roman architecture developed slowly, emerging from the Hellenistic and Etruscan past only toward the end of the first millennium B.C. By then, Roman ambition, discipline, and ruthlessness had created an Empire that stretched from

the Thames to the Nile rivers, fusing the Hellenistic kingdoms that succeeded Alexander the Great with other states and regions into a vast political realm, transforming the Mediterranean into a Roman lake. A complex society had evolved, which demanded new architectural forms: The Romans became the most prodigious builders of antiquity. Their true genius was not revealed in any particular building or site or even type, but in the brilliant way the Roman architect met the needs of a multifaceted society that endured for a thousand years in a variety of forms, extended over an Empire during most of its history.

What sort of artistic culture did these Romans, in their long and diverse history, create? Early Rome produced citizens of powerful character and great achievement in the realms of politics and war, but its art was meager. The Romans learned first from the Etruscans and then directly from the conquered Greeks. The opening of Rome in the second century B.C. to the influences of the Hellenistic world was of high importance. The native Romans were fine soldiers, devoted to duty, to the gods, state, and family. They were ambitious, disciplined, worldly, but basically coarse, strongly attached to power and the tangible things of the world. Rather than the Greek sense of measure there was constriction of sensibility in early Rome; rather than Greek idealism there was paternalism and superstition. To the modern world, the Romans may seem sublimely self-assured, but they knew better. They recognized their debt to the Greeks, whom they always considered their artistic superiors.

To isolate what the Romans took from the Greeks (and other eastern Mediterranean traditions) is difficult, for they took so much: literature, philosophy, science, and painting styles; and, as the Etruscans had imported Greek vases, so the Romans imported Greek statuary. Indeed, the Romans seemed to have absorbed nearly everything Greek. The cultivation and refinement of the Hellenistic East tempered the raw Roman sensibility. Roman fantasy and imagination were liberated in a manner that pervaded the entire culture. In architecture, this meant not only elements of Greek decorum and proportion applied to the basic Roman sense of structure and space, but also a new appreciation of light, color, and advanced modes of ornamentation. The tension in Roman art and architecture between the underlying indigenous tradition and the infusion of "Oriental" sensibilities lent it pathos and heightened interest where otherwise there might have been only the rather dull presence of unimpeded technical innovation.

Yet, for all that was Greek in Rome, what was intrinsically Roman is more significant. Like the Roman political system, Roman architecture had its highly original aspects: It was new aesthetically, new in materials and techniques, and new in its building programs; it met the needs of the emperor and his court; it provided the surroundings for state-sponsored culture and entertainment in the first cosmopolitan society; it served industry, commerce, and shipping, fulfilling a vast range of practical requirements, with ports, roads, and aqueducts among its most impressive accomplishments.

Building Materials and Aims. Of the many factors that contributed to the success of Roman architecture, the choice of building materials was among the most important. The Egyptians had built largely with sun-dried brick and large stone blocks; the Greeks, with limestone and, occasionally, marble from the Aegean islands. Roman building materials were as diverse as the Empire itself. In the vicinity of Rome, solid building stone was available: buff-colored volcanic tufa, grainy gray peperino, creamy limestone, and rugged travertine. Exotic marbles were imported from the East, and when the quarries at Carrara (Luni), just north of Pisa, were opened by Augustus, unlimited quantities of white marble were close at hand. The Romans perfected brick-making, and their bricklayers were unsurpassed by later craftsmen. Most important, Roman builders perfected a new material, concrete, and developed it into their most characteristic structural medium, without which the grandeur that was Rome would not have been possible.

The Romans employed raw materials, concrete in particular, to erect massive walls and great vaults enclosing vast spaces. It is critical to the understanding of Roman architecture to realize that space was just as important as the mass enclosing it. No earlier architecture involved space as Roman architecture did. Indeed, from the Roman perspective, Egypt and Greece were almost alike in the way their architectural masses greatly overshadowed the voids. Their temples, to be sure, provided interiors, but even at Karnak and in the Parthenon the supports dominate and the space serves as little more than a series of intervals between the masses. In Roman architecture, the use of space was primary; it took on life and became an active element; it expanded to prodigious dimensions and pressed against, and even into, the vaults and walls that enclosed it. But the Roman shaping of space was never a mere exercise in formalism. Not only in the religious sphere, but also in public and even in home-life activity, space in Rome took on prescribed, highly structured patterns. Mature Roman architecture was quintessentially space shaped by vaults, arches, and walls for the purposes of ordered activities.

Factors other than space are also critical to the comprehension of Roman buildings—illusionism, for one, inherent in the basic mix of Roman structure combined with Hellenistic appearance. The Romans had been conditioned by their cultural "betters" of the Greek world to believe that monumental architecture was the architecture of the Greek orders. To the very end, the Romans clung to this notion, and not only did they continue to build in the Greek trabeated tradition, which they extended and developed, but also wherever possible they attached to their new arched-and-vaulted structures some form of the Greek system of orders. Thus, arched structures were made to look, at least in part, trabeated; and massive mural supports were "hidden" behind columns that were made to look as if they supported the whole enterprise.

The importance of appearances in Roman architecture was not restricted to the use of the Greek orders. All the areas of "raw" structure around the visible Hellenic components were masked by sculpted forms and by the artifices of the Roman decorator: travertine and colorful marble overlays (called revetments or incrustations), stucco, frescoes, inlays of multicolored stones, and mosaics of glass and stone fragments. It was not only a question of hiding the raw structure. The Romans, despite their staid origins, were fond of all kinds of extravagance. They were prone to showing off, to pomp and ostentatious display. This propensity, in contrast to the Greek sense of moderation, flourished under the emperors, after the end of the Republic in 23 B.C. Architecture of great lavishness was built by the state in an almost impersonal, bureaucratic way, but also in a more individualistic fashion by the emperors and by private individuals of immense wealth. The results were sumptuous, colorful, even gaudy, certainly nothing like the rough ruins we see now.

The importance of surface appearances—and a tendency to what may be called "facadism" in Roman architecture—brings us to the heart of the relation of architecture to Roman politics and society. In Classical Greek architecture, the building was perceived as a freestanding three-dimensional form by an autonomous, free-moving observer. On the contrary, an architecture of facades, as in Egypt, implied fixed or limited positions from which those facades were to be seen, and the perceptions of the observer were sharply controlled by the approach to the facade. The frontality of a facade, or a building seen two-dimensionally, tended to be complemented by symmetry and by axial approaches. In Rome, the observer was led to confront tendentious architectural images rather than to observe independent three-dimensional entities. Neither autonomous nor free, the viewer was set moving along axial paths, caught up in grandiose schemes, for Roman architecture was characteristically organized in symmetrical, axial, and cross-axial layouts. The message of this architecture was almost invariably state power and majesty, state religion, and state personages. The buildings not only reflected the Roman mentality and political system, but they were also microcosms of the Roman world. Rather than unconstrained beholders, we have participants in the machinery of the Roman state, fitted into well-oiled architectural settings, within which movement and the perception of imagery were predetermined.

THE STRUCTURAL REVOLUTION

The Roman structural program of arch, vault, and concrete was new to the world (figs. 3-9–3-16). None of these individual elements was without precedent: The Egyptians and Mesopotamians had employed primitive arch forms; the Greeks had experimented with the arch and even with concrete. As early as the fourth century B.C., the Etruscans were constructing impressive, if simple, vaulting forms. But the Romans were the first to combine these structural media and fully exploit their inherent potential.

Arches are deceptively simple forms. Structurally, they are far more intricate than the elementary post-and-lintel, or trabeated, system that formed the basis of pre-Roman architecture, in which a rigid slab rests on upright supports. As a rule, an arch also takes upright supports, but the true arch is not rigid. Rather, it is formed of a multitude of small elements that curve over space by resting against each other in delicate balance. A lintel is inert, but an arch forms an organic system. An arch is alive.

The small elements of which an arch is built are called voussoirs. In a stone arch, the voussoirs take the shape of trapezoidal blocks, but in a brick arch it is generally the mortar between the rectilinear bricks that forms trapezoids, which make the curve. The wedge shape not only gives the arch its curve but holds the arch up by keeping the voussoirs from slipping downward. However, each voussoir exerts a downward pressure due to gravity, and this impulse is partly transformed into a lateral pressure, or thrust, because of the wedge shape. The downward load of the arch is not a problem, because it is taken up by the supports in the same manner as in the trabeated system. But the accumulated lateral thrust is the bane of arch builders. Its forces, as they pass from voussoir to voussoir, must be kept within the arch itself. The tendency for the arch to fall inward toward its crown or to break outward at its haunches because of "escaping" thrust must be avoided. And even when the thrust is contained safely along the entirety of the arch, it must once more be accounted for when it emerges from the base of the arch, where it must be absorbed safely by the vertical supports and finally transmitted to the ground. In practice, this means massive supports for the arch, or supports augmented along the direction of the arch in the form of buttresses.

The constructing of an arch is no less painstaking and intricate than its design. Only a complete arch is self-supporting. Therefore, until the arch is complete, the voussoirs must be supported in their proper position as they are laid up. This temporary support is called centering and usually is built of wood (fig. 3-11). It may be built up from the ground or, more economically, from supports at the base of the arch. The critical aspects are that the centering must be strong enough to take the weight of the voussoirs without deformation and, of course, that its outer surface (extrados) precisely follows the intended curve of the inner surface (intrados) of the arch. Once the supports are standing and the centering is in place, the construction of the arch begins. The first pair of voussoirs are set at the springing line, and the rest follow up to the top, where the keystone is finally set, completing the arch. Strictly speaking, the keystone is nothing but the top voussoir. An arch need not even have a keystone; it may simply be completed with a final pair of ordinary voussoirs. When keystones are present, they are frequently accentuated in size and decorated with a sculpted boss. They figure importantly in the visual calculus of the arch design by stressing its axiality, symmetry, and sturdiness. Once the keystone or the top voussoirs are in place and the mortar is set, the centering may be removed. Presumably all has been done correctly and the airborne ring of masonry will stand.

Arches have great potential. The length of a stone lintel is severely limited by its low tensile strength—that is, resistance to stretching forces in the lower part of the slab. Stone lintels of more than 15 feet are rare; more than 20 feet is practically an impossibility because of the necessary thickness and weight of the stone block. But in an arch there are, theoretically, no tensile stresses. All the forces are those of compression, and building stone has very substantial compressive strength, owing to the way it is formed beneath the earth's surface under the high pressures of gravity or deformations in the earth's crust. In fact, the theoretical limit of stone or brick arches has rarely been approached. Clear spans of 60 feet or more were not uncommon in the great ages of arch building (Roman, Gothic, and Renaissance) and there are instances of spans approaching 150 feet. The problem has been that of supports—the temporary one of centering, and the permanent need for the structure to absorb the vertical load as well as the emerging lateral thrusts, a problem that increases with the height of the supporting pier.

The reserve strength of most arches has not gone untapped, however. A stone lintel has "difficulties" supporting itself. Superimposing a load on top of it, such as a wall, further taxes its cohesion and necessitates an increase in its vertical thickness. In an arch, precisely the opposite occurs. The more an arch is loaded—up to a point, of course—the stronger it becomes. The freestanding arch described above is a precariously balanced form. If a wall is set over it, the tendency of the voussoirs to slip out of position is eliminated, and the arch becomes the most solid feature of the entire wall. The capacity of the arch to sustain immense loads is one of its most important and useful aspects, and this was perceived from the very beginning of arch construction. The most notable early instance of exploiting this capacity is seen in the King's Chamber of the Great Pyramid, where a primitive "arch" supports hundreds of feet of overlying limestone. That "arch" is also a prototype for the so-called relieving arch—an arch built *over* a lintel in order to deflect the overlying load from the lintel to the surrounding wall. Relieving arches are ubiquitous in Roman architecture, occurring in practically every wall that has an opening (fig. 3-77). The Romans were extremely inventive in their employment of relieving arches, sometimes building them *into* trabeation to take the weight off the center of the span, elsewhere inventing complex systems of relieving arches running in various directions and levels (figs. 3-51, 3-77). But perhaps the most ingenious of such Roman devices was the flat arch (colorplate 14; figs. 3-9, 3-54). An arch need not take any particular curve. The Romans were satisfied with the semicircle or a segment of it, but in other ages a different geometry was explored. More surprising is that the outer configuration of the arch need not be curved at all. As long as the voussoirs form part of a curve, the structure functions as an arch. A flat arch is nothing but a rectangular piece of a

3-9　Flat arch, Domus Aurea. Rome. A.D. 64–68

3-10　Arch diagram. (After D. M. Robb and J. J. Garrison)

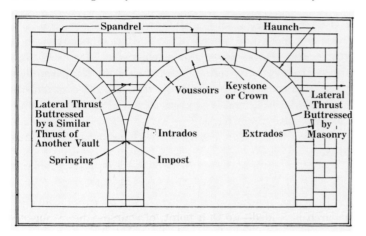

3-11　Centering construction of an arch. (After M. Salvadori)

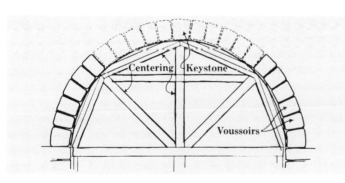

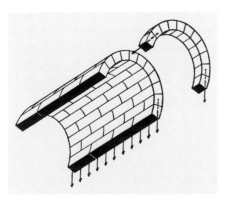

3-12
Arch becomes
a barrel vault.
(After J. Fitchen)

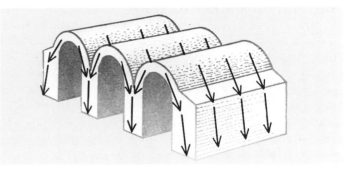

3-13　Barrel vaults. (After Irving Geis)

3-14　Barrel-vault development. (After Rowland Mainstone)

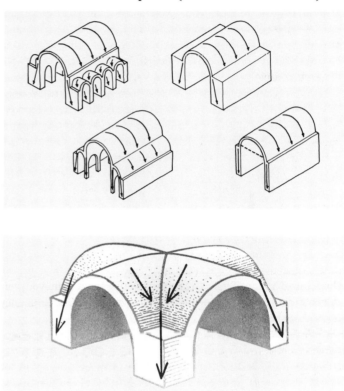

3-15　Cross (groin) vault. (After Irving Geis)

3-16　Groin-vault development. (After J. Fitchen)

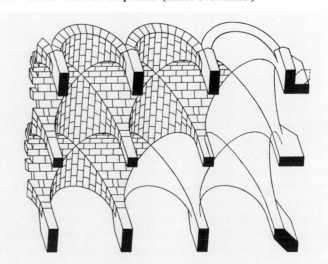

segmental arch. Needless to say, such flat arches are very practical over windows and doorways—obviating the need for a stone lintel and a separate relieving arch—and they exist by the hundreds in the Roman ruins of Pompeii and Ostia.

An arch can thus be extended in scale, varied in form, and piled with great loads. But it has another potential modification of no less consequence. By simply extending it along its axis—that is, in depth—it becomes a vault (figs. 3-12–3-14). There is no structural distinction between an arch and such a vault, but rather a functional difference. Generally, what we mean by an arch supports only itself or, more commonly, a mural structure, whereas a vault may not only support something, but also it roofs over a significant area of a building.

Such simple vaults that extend an arch in depth are called tunnel, or barrel, vaults. They are the earliest form of vault and appear in limited form in Egypt, Mesopotamia, and Hellenistic Greece. But, as with the arch, the Romans were the first to exploit the form and give it widespread use and monumentality. Barrel vaults are relatively simple to build, being merely the direct extension of an arch. They are useful for a number of practical purposes: They can be adapted to varying plans by simple modification; they can be run along a curved axis to form annular vaulting; or the axis can be inclined from the horizontal, forming inclined vaulting over stairways (fig. 3-21).

Useful as the barrel vault is, it has several limitations. It exerts a continuous load, necessitating some form of continuous support. Except at its two ends, it is difficult to light the space beneath it. Although it lends itself to unlimited length, increases in width are achieved only with increased thickness of the vault itself and its support. In any case, regardless of the ratio of length to width, it has only one axis, which contributes to certain desired architectural effects but prohibits others.

The limitations of the barrel vault were overcome by creating a new vaulting type from it—the cross vault (figs. 3-15, 3-16). It is formed by intersecting two barrel vaults at right angles and is often called a groin vault, from the groinlike lines along the intersections. The weight of the cross vault is concentrated at the corners, eliminating the need for continuous supports; it has two axes, and the opening of the space in four directions means ample fenestration as well. Its only limitation is its resistance to plans other than the square, but even this can be solved by manipulating the geometry of the vaulting curvature or by extending vaulting arms in the form of supplementary barrel vaults. One other difficulty is a technical one—keeping the groin lines from veering away from precise paths during construction, for visually the success of the cross vault depends on the crispness of the groins. The ultimate solution to this problem is rib vaulting, which we will investigate later. At this point, it is sufficient to stress the virtues of the cross vault—its economy, openness, and clarity of form—which made it an ever-present aspect of Roman architecture.

The cross vault was employed by the Romans on a great scale and with grandeur in practically all monumental building types. But the grandest type of vault was still another: the dome (fig. 3-53). It is possible to build a domelike structure in the form of a cross vault—by crossing barrel vaults over an octagonal plan, an eight-sided dome results, often called a cloister vault. This form was common in the medieval period (fig. 5-48) but rare in the Roman era. Romans preferred the true dome, or hemisphere, with its fully rounded perfection. Structurally, the hemispheric dome may be thought of in two ways: as an arch rotated 360 degrees or as a set of horizontal arched rings culminating in a single "keystone" at the crown. The dome functions both ways, in fact; its voussoirs are trapezoidal in three dimensions rather than two, as in an arch. Yet, the dome is built up in the latter mode—in complete rings; each ring, when finished, forms a self-supporting component of the final dome, a kind of horizontal circular arch.

The arch was one of history's major discoveries. It enabled architects to span gaps with economy and strength and to enclose vast interiors with assurance. The arch was to architecture what the wheel was to transportation and industry. And just as the wheel reached its heyday in the "machine age" that lasted from the eighteenth to the mid-twentieth century—superseded by a second industrial age of electronics, atomic energy, then genetics, cybernetics and information technology—so the masonry arch dominated a long era that ended only a century ago with the widespread introduction of a new architectural technology of iron, steel, and reinforced concrete (pp. 443–46). Today, it would be difficult for a builder to find a mason anywhere in the industrial world capable of building a sizable masonry arch. The art of arch building, developed and practiced for over two thousand years, has been all but lost. But for centuries, the highest technical skills of the architectural craft were devoted to erecting arches and vaults.

The arch assumed such importance for the Romans because they learned to deal with its disadvantages. So far we have stressed the virtues of the arch, but it also entailed problems: Technically, structurally, financially, and even visually, the arch and its corollaries present massive difficulties especially when the builder passes from the drafting table to the building site. If only the arch could be simplified and made structurally inert like trabeated construction, the perfect building form would be at hand. It was perhaps the highest accomplishment of the Roman engineering genius to combine the arch and all its virtues with the solid structure and unproblematic execution of the inert lintel. This was made possible not by a change in the form of the arch but by the invention of a new building material: concrete.

Roman concrete (significantly different in composition from modern concrete) was a mixture of a mortarlike cement with an aggregate. The cement that had been known from the fourth century B.C. was composed of lime, sand, and water. About the second century B.C., the Romans learned to use pozzolana, a local volcanic ash that yielded a mortar of tremendous strength. In addition, a mortar made with pozzolana rather than sand had the remarkable property of setting on contact with water, making it exceptionally useful for port facilities. This cement was not used between bricks or stone blocks as simple mortar beds; it was mixed with an aggregate—small chunks of solids such as stones, gravel, building debris, and chips from quarries. The mixture of cement and aggregate solidified rapidly into a dense, homogeneous mass that, in effect, constituted artificial stone.

This artificial stone—concrete—had many advantages over natural stone. It did not need to be painstakingly quarried, shaped, or transported. The preparation, mixing, and lifting of the materials needed for concrete required none of the highly skilled labor necessary for stonemasonry. Moreover, concrete could be cast in a form mold of virtually any shape desired and at any scale, far larger than even the largest megalithic blocks of the Neolithic builders or of the Egyptians. With concrete, arches and vaults could be economically fabricated; when complete, these became monoliths (like other forms cast in concrete) and had no voussoirs to malfunction (colorplate 15). Whether they exerted no thrust, as was long believed, is unlikely. A concrete cupola, it has often been said, structurally resembled an inverted porcelain cup: all the loading was vertical, as with a lintel. But recent research has shown that, since concrete has the same negligible tensile strength as stone, arcuated dynamics, including thrust, were at work in it as in other vault structures and had to be dealt with by buttressing. Yet concrete's constructional ease made all the difference to the Romans in building their vast architectural works.

When the semiliquid concrete hardened and its form mold was removed, it did not exhibit a surface that was either weather-resistant or visually presentable. It needed a permanent facing (colorplate 14; figs. 3-17, 3-18). The Romans developed various forms of facing (laid up together with the concrete itself). At first they used random-shaped stones, *opus incertum*, but after about 100 B.C., a more systematized form appeared, *opus reticulatum*, in which four-sided pyramidal spikes were laid edgewise with their three-inch bases facing out, making a reticulated surface pattern. The most commonly encountered type, however, was brick facing, *opus testaceum*, introduced in the early Empire and lasting to the end; it made the concrete wall look as if it were brick. A fourth type of facing was sometimes employed, *opus mixtum*, consisting of beautiful, decorative patterns of tufa, stone, and brick. It always seems strange to the modern observer to be reminded that, except for *opus testaceum*, these elaborate facings were themselves covered, either by plaster or, in monumental interiors, by fresco, stone, or marble veneers, or by abstract and figured stone inlays (also used for floors) known as *opus sectile*.

Several centuries of trial and error were required before the Romans could bring their art of building in concrete to a state of maturity, which they did in the second half of the first century A.D., under the Flavian emperors. Perfection of material and skilled technique of construction were essential to the task. But they were only a means to an end—the realization of new architectural needs and visions. Means and end were highly compatible, and they mutually shaped each other as well. The invention of concrete was largely prompted by the need to enclose space, but the availability and advantages of concrete spurred the spatial imagination of Roman architects. Concrete begged to be shaped into continuous masses around supple, continuously curving voids. However, the interaction of material and architectural vision and the exploitation of concrete's inherent possibilities did not occur immediately upon its invention. Initially, in the late second and first centuries B.C., with rare exceptions, concrete was employed in limited amounts for practical uses in prosaic form. Even after it was generally accepted and exploited, builders continued to use cut-stone masonry on a wide scale, especially in areas of the far-flung Roman world where pozzolana (or its equivalent) was not available and the local craft of stonemasonry was

3-17   **Roman stone facing. Hadrian's Villa. Tivoli.** A.D. **118–34**

3-18   **Public lavatory. Via della Forica, Ostia**

strong (Syria is the prime example). And, obviously, not every Roman building was arched and vaulted. Neither the new technology nor the space aesthetic entirely displaced older ways. Romans continued to apply the orders as a nonstructural veneer for their bold new forms and also to build in trabeated structure, even in monumental Imperial fabrics and particularly in the most traditional building types, such as temples and basilicas. In this respect the story of Roman architecture is tangled and more prone to unexpected twists and surprises than that of any other architecture until the nineteenth century.

Aqueducts, Bridges, Sewers, Warehouses. Roman civilization was primarily a society of cities, and cities need a steady supply of fresh water. The Romans expended huge quantities of it. It has been calculated that at its zenith (population over one million), the city of Rome used some 350,000,000 gallons of water per day for sanitary and industrial purposes and especially for public display. Arcuated structure played a major role in achieving this lavish consumption.

Most Roman cities quickly outgrew their local water supply and came to depend on springs in distant hills. The problem was how to bring the water over those hills down to the city. Pumps were still primitive and were only employed as a last resort. The Romans relied on gravity to move their water supply. But once the water was allowed to fall into a valley, how to get it over the next hill? One way was through piping, but only lead and bronze were available for it, and they were far too expensive and difficult to fabricate and maintain. The alternative was not to let the water fall abruptly, but gradually—to have it run through a roofed-over channel, down a very slight incline, just enough to keep it moving. To create such aqueducts, with a continuous line of descent, sometimes over distances of many miles, it was necessary to tunnel through hills and to bridge deep valleys and broad plains, gradually bringing the water down to the city. Logically enough, the Romans found the arch indispensable in this enterprise, especially in running their aqueducts across valleys, where they frequently had to span rivers as well. It is perhaps not too farfetched to consider the engineering achievements of the Romans with their aqueducts as the equivalents of the Doric optical refinements in Greek temples, so vast, yet precise, were the demands made in surveying, planning, and executing a barely perceptible deviation from the true horizontal, only here for strictly utilitarian, rather than purely aesthetic, ends.

Among the eleven aqueducts that eventually supplied the city of Rome, the finest was perhaps the early-first-century A.D. Aqua Claudia. It brought water from Subiaco—forty-five miles distant—partly over solid masonry, but also over nine and one-half miles of arches, some of them 100 feet in height. At one of the monumental city gates, the Porta Maggiore, over which waterways were carried, the Aqua Claudia was joined by an even longer aqueduct that brought water from a distance of sixty-two miles, the Aqua Anio Novus.

Long stretches of these aqueducts remain as monuments in the Roman countryside. But the most impressive fragmentary remains are found outside Italy, such as the magnificent first-century A.D. span near Nîmes in Provence, the famous Pont du Gard (colorplate 13). It is formed of three tiers of arches, 160 feet in height, 885 feet long, and was part of an aqueduct that brought water to Nîmes from a source twenty-five miles away. On the lower level, the arches are carried by piers buttressed by triangular breakwaters against the force of floods. A corresponding series of arches comprises the second tier, and, as in the level below, the arches that span the riverbed are wider than those on the banks. The conduit through which the water flows is supported by the small arches of the third level. The masonry is not concrete, but ashlar stone, laid dry, without mortar. Aqueducts like this display the Roman architect's ease and assurance in handling proportions and working to great scale with powerful masses of stone.

Aqueducts are very much like bridges (the one at Nîmes is even called one). The technique of arcuated construction was applied by the Romans to both. Bridges, of course, did not have to run level with surrounding hills—the roads could descend to them. Bridges were thus generally lower than aqueducts, and broader, to carry traffic. They were built with great solidity, with admirably smooth roadbeds, and with piers designed to resist the rush of water (as in the Pont du Gard); sometimes there were openings in the piers to alleviate the pressure of flooding. A number of Roman bridges survive and are still in use today. In the city of Rome several stand, including the well-preserved Pons Fabricius and the Pons Milvius (Ponte Molle; fig. 3-19), scene of Maxentius's death at the hands of Constantine in A.D. 312.

3-19   **Pons Milvius (Ponte Molle). Rome**

For all their grandeur, bridges and aqueducts are relatively simple applications of Roman arch construction. But they were not the simplest or the earliest. This distinction is generally accorded to another realm of Roman hydraulic engineering (but one whose invention is credited to the Etruscans). The waters so munificently brought to the cities had to be carried away, together with excess rainwater. These waste fluids were channeled to collecting sewers that discharged into local rivers. Some of the drainage systems were very early examples of arcuated construction on a large scale. The most notable is the Cloaca Maxima, the main sewer of Rome. An open drain in the early centuries, toward the later second century B.C. it was given a powerful barrel vault with three massive rings of voussoirs.

The Romans not only moved water, they used the water to move other things. The city of Rome was a great port, and a port must have warehouses. Among the finest was the so-called

3-20   **Porticus Aemilia. Rome. c. 193 B.C.**
      (Axonometric plan after A. Boëthius and Ward-Perkins)

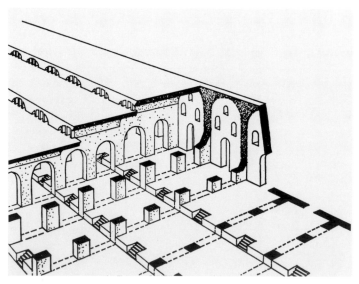

Porticus Aemilia (fig. 3-20), a vast construction built in the early second century B.C. on the east bank of the Tiber; it is an early example of modular planning. The module consisted of a barrel-vaulted unit, and an immense covered area was created by simply multiplying such units in rows, set stepwise at different levels to allow light to reach the interiors. The barrel vaults were supported not by solid walls but by arcades on piers, thus permitting circulation between the rows. The stepped tiers were joined to one another by short flights of steps.

These aspects of Roman civil engineering indicate the virtues of arcuated construction and its immediate and widespread usefulness to the Romans. But as we move from these relatively simple—and mostly early—constructions to grand architectural projects—mostly of later date—the greater significance of the arch emerges, as well as the depth of the Romans' genius in shaping its development. This is best seen in the Roman theater and its close relatives, the amphitheater and the stadium—functionally related types of buildings that not only share a common structural program but, conveniently, form the next step upward in complexity from the aqueduct and warehouse forms.

Theaters, Arenas, Circuses. The theater was not an indigenous Roman form. But when the Romans finally looked beyond their crude native performances to the forms of Greek drama, the Greek theater building, too, was eventually adopted and transformed into something typically Roman. Permanent masonry theaters (in place of the temporary Roman structures of timber) appeared first in southern Italy, near the Greek colonies, and then in the city of Rome and its suburbs. These early buildings formed the basis for the great surviving Imperial theaters.

Basic differences between the closely related Greek and Roman theater forms are shown in a comparison of the plan of the Greek theater at Epidaurus with Roman theater plans, for example, the Theater of Marcellus in Rome (fig. 3-21)—completed in 11 B.C. by Augustus and later transformed into a medieval fortress and a Renaissance palace—and the one at Orange (Arausio) in southern France (first century A.D., fig. 3-22). The Greek theater, we recall, had three disparate elements: the horseshoe-shaped auditorium, the circular orchestra, and the small, rectangular stage building. In the Roman theater, these elements were reshaped and set together in a taut, systematic scheme. Both the public seating area (*cavea*) and the orchestra—no longer used for the performance but for the seating of dignitaries—were reduced to a half circle and were precisely aligned with the much-expanded stage building, where the entire dramatic action took place. Moreover, the entire theater, including the stage building, was contained within a high, unbroken wall.

Visually, the Greek theater included the landscape that it overlooked; architecture and nature were one. The Romans, however, practiced an architecture not of small towns built amid rugged landscapes, but of large cities built on flat, or flattened, terrain. And the Roman theater was an urban form *par excellence*, a closed architectural environment, even when the *cavea* was built (as at Orange, fig. 3-22) into a convenient hillside. Dazzling artifice replaced the spectacle of nature.

The Greeks had used a trabeated backdrop along the top of the stage building, and the Romans uninhibitedly expanded this device by setting beneath the roof an immense facade of superimposed columnar orders framing three symmetrically placed portals. The theater at Sabratha, Libya, dedicated in

3-23 Theater. Sabratha, Libya. A.D. **180**

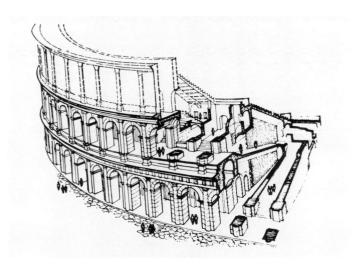

3-21   Theater of Marcellus. Rome. 11 B.C. **(Sectional view after A. Boëthius and Ward-Perkins)**

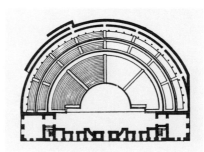

**3-22
Plan, Theater. Orange, France.** A.D. **1st century**

3-24   Theater of Marcellus. Rome. 11 B.C.

A.D. 180, is an example (fig. 3-23). In the Roman East and in North Africa, the composition of these backdrops was particularly imaginative, with strong projections and recessions and sometimes a dramatic alternation of niches, as in the second-century A.D. theater at Aspendos in Turkey.

The exuberance of the theater interior was complemented by an exterior of sobriety and grandeur still visible at the Theater of Marcellus (fig. 3-24). In the late Republican period (late second and early first century B.C.), Roman architects learned to integrate their new structural systems with the Hellenic orders. To the massive structural arcade on piers, a purely cosmetic layer of trabeation was applied; the refined sculptural forms of the rectangular order framing the arch contrasted with, and gave scale to, the bold sustaining structure. With the Theater of Marcellus, where travertine was employed over the whole facade for the first time, the exterior assumed the characteristically Roman plasticity and rhythm of solid and void in the integration of the two systems. Here, too, was exemplified the vertical sequence of the orders recommended by Vitruvius: Doric at the ground floor, then Ionic, and in the lost third level, possibly Corinthian (a recent reconstruction suggests, however, that the third level might have been plain). Behind the elaborate curving facade of this theater, the *cavea* provided seats for about 10,000 spectators. The seats were arranged in three tiers over massive substructures that represent a higher level of engineering than that of the warehouses or the aqueducts. Radially disposed, concrete piers supported inclined, concrete barrel vaulting that, in turn, supported the seating (fig. 3-21). This structure was built in two levels and was intersected by rings of annular vaulting, both near the center and at the perimeter, except at the upper level, where the perimetrical ring consisted of radially disposed barrel vaults set on massive transverse lintels, one for each bay of the facade. These complex interlocking systems of vaulting were mutually reinforcing, and they also provided solid support for the seating, as well as ease of entrance and exit through the numerous stairs and corridors built into the cellular structure.

Such theaters were built, on varying scales, in every Roman city, and along with them were erected the even larger amphitheaters. There were no Greek precedents for these vast arenas, settings for the bloodcurdling gladiatorial games that originated in Campania, the area south of Rome, and spread throughout the Empire (except for Greece, where the barbaric spectacles were resisted to the end). By 80 B.C., the first permanent amphitheater (fig. 3-25) was built in Pompeii (site of the first permanent theater as well). Like those that followed, the Pompeiian arena formed an oval of huge dimensions—350 by 500 feet—and could seat more than 20,000 spectators. The tiers of seats around the arena's central oval were as yet supported by solid earthen embankments, a primitive, if enduring, structural form. These earthworks were contained by a massive *opus incertum* concrete retaining wall that was strengthened by a powerful ring of arches. Access to the seating area took the primitive form of pairs of external staircases leading up over the top of the galleries.

By the first century A.D., the early form of the Pompeiian arena gave way to the mature type, of which there are a number of well-preserved examples in Italy (Verona, for instance) and in southern France (Arles and Nîmes). But the example that stands above all the rest is the titanic Flavian amphitheater in Rome, popularly known as the Colosseum (after the colossal statue of Nero that stood nearby; colorplate 16; figs. 3-26–3-29). Although the building is uniquely famous among amphitheaters, it is by no means singular in form. Rather, it embodies to the highest degree and at the largest scale all those virtues of structure and design seen in lesser examples. Inaugurated in A.D. 80, it was built by the Flavian emperors Vespasian, Titus, and Domitian on the site of an artificial lake that was part of their predecessor Nero's fabled Domus Aurea (Golden House). This was a shrewd political stroke, for Nero's house had been as unpopular a venture as the gladiatorial contests were popular, and Rome, curiously, had no large arena as yet. The site lay near the center of the city and was ready-made for building, having conveniently been excavated to bedrock in order to construct Nero's lake.

At this moment, on an ideal site, one of the world's perfect buildings was erected. Such perfection was attainable because there was nothing, or at least little, that was new about the Colosseum beyond its sheer scale. In function, form, and structure it depended heavily on achievements a century old, the Theater of Marcellus for one, which was not itself a revolutionary work. The great feat of the unknown Colosseum architect was achieved by perfecting earlier ideas, expanding the scale successfully, all within the elliptical form of the amphitheater.

The elliptical plan of the Colosseum measured 616 by 510 feet externally and 280 by 175 feet at the gladiatorial arena. Beneath the arena floor (sand-covered to soak up the spilled blood) was an extensive system of tunnels, chambers, and mechanical devices to facilitate the spectacle. For naval displays and mock battles there was hydraulic provision for artificial flooding of the arena within its fifteen-foot barrier wall. The seating formed a uniform elliptical ring 167 feet wide and 159 feet high at the outer cornice, and it provided for some 50,000 spectators (with boxes for the emperor and other dignitaries at the center of the long "sides"). Its substructures were very much like those at the Theater of Marcellus, with interlocking radial and concentric forms creating a powerful self-buttressing, as well as highly functional, cellular support system.

At the foot of the immense structure was laid a ring of concrete foundations, some 25 feet in thickness. Over this, the ellipse was divided two ways—radially into eighty wedge-shaped sectors, and into five concentric rings of structure. Then a powerful skeleton of travertine piers was erected through the first two stories, with intermediate radial walls of tufa joining the inner rings. The third-floor carrying-walls were concrete. On this dense frame, massive concrete vaulting was run both radially and in concentric rings. This orderly structure provided powerful supports for the massive marble seating (the top level seats being wood) and plentiful means of circulation for the large and potentially unruly crowds of spectators. The Roman mastery, not only of function and structure, but also of materials—concrete, travertine, tufa, brick, marble, and wood—was complete.

Equally masterful was the exterior of the building, which amplified and sharpened the elevation of the Theater of Marcellus. The enormous wall—160 feet high and some 2,000 feet in circumference—reflected the interior and thus comprised three tiers of arcading on piers and a high terminal wall. Once again the canonical sequence of Roman Doric, Ionic, and Corinthian was followed in the applied articulation of half-columns and entablatures. Here, where it is well preserved, can be seen the effectiveness of this gradation of forms, as well as the magnificence and sense of scale it produces. The fourth story was articulated by tall Corinthian pilasters, between which were immense brackets aligned with holes in the uppermost cornice to provide support for a ring of wooden masts from which a huge awning was hung, protecting the spectators from the elements. The pilaster (or flattened column), it should be noted, although of Greek invention flourished in Roman architecture. From a rational standpoint it was more appropriate as an articulation of mural or arcuated facades than the structurally potent column or half-column, and it was, in any case, cheaper.

Competing in popularity with the gladiatorial games were the horse and chariot races (the Roman counterpart of the Greek foot races). The circus, or stadium, was the architectural form developed for these contests of nerve and ruthlessness. Across the straight end were set the stalls (carceres), with brightly painted exits from which the chariots emerged at the beginning of the race. The racecourse was divided down the middle by a low wall (spina) around which the race was run, with conical columns (metae) at its ends to mark the turning points. Often obelisks and other trophies were set up as decorations at intermediate points along the course. Whenever possible, the track was laid out below a hillside or, better still, between two slopes, for the benefit of the spectators. Otherwise, bleachers were constructed, first in wood and then, by the time of Augustus, in masonry.

Almost every city of any importance had at least one circus, along with its theater and amphitheater (and forum, basilica, baths, and other public buildings). Rome itself amassed a number of these stadiums. The oldest and largest was the Circus Maximus (fig. 3-30), which lay in the long valley between the Palatine and the Aventine hills. It was rebuilt and restored a number of times between the first and third centuries A.D., including once by Augustus, in whose day it was also used as an amphitheater (it is said that 3,500 animals were slaughtered there during his reign). It measured about 2,000 feet in length and was 650 feet wide, with seating—we are told—for 250,000 spectators. In structure and form, the seating resembled the cavea of the theater and amphitheaters with trabeated articulation on the exterior, an already old-fashioned formal device that would expire with the Circus of Domitian (late first century A.D.). The best-preserved Roman circus is the one built (A.D. 307–12) by the last pagan emperor, Maxentius, outside the city near his villa and tomb. Enough is preserved of the spina to see how it is set off the main axis and at a slight angle, to produce a wider track at the beginning of the race when the chariots were bunched together, and also to give the outside contenders a fair chance. In such cases, even the Romans would sacrifice symmetry to practicality.

3-25
Amphitheater.
Pompeii.
80 B.C.

Baths. The most spectacular architecture that the Romans devised for the pleasure of their citizenry was neither for races, combat, nor drama. The sensuous needs of the Roman public were not limited to sport or spectacles. Daily life, despite substantial leisure time, was strenuous. Romans, who had grown accustomed to indulging their senses, felt the need for invigorating exercise, bathing, and relaxation. The Greek palaestra provided a model that the Romans adopted in the later Republican period and developed, in their characteristically thorough way, into the complex form of public baths. The procedure at the Roman bath was more than merely swimming or washing; it involved a pattern of exposing the body to various levels of heated air and water, and other stimuli as well. What began as an occasional plunge in a river or pool became a significant part of Roman daily life. During the Empire, the elaborate bathing procedure became a daily practice when possible, and it is said that the Romans took their bathing more seriously than they took their gods.

All baths provided a core program: a common disrobing room, the *apodyterium*; a series of at least two heated rooms—a *tepidarium*, or moderately warm room, and a *caldarium*, or hot room. In well-equipped establishments there was also a steam room or *laconicum*. These chambers not only provided relaxing warmth and provoked salutary perspiration, but they also included warm tub baths for washing (the Romans were, with the Egyptians, the cleanest of the ancients). Besides warmth, the baths offered refreshing coolness on hot summer days, in cold plunges or a swimming pool (*natatio*), or a cool, unheated room (*frigidarium*). Such extensive bathing dried the skin, and so the bath complexes provided rooms where special attendants rubbed the bather with oil, scraped the excess off with a tool known as a *strigil*, and toweled the skin dry.

Because Roman bathing was so pervasive for so long a period, a wide diversity of bath establishments are known to archaeologists (although not all of the 952 baths in the city of Rome noted in a list published in A.D. 354). Rich citizens installed private baths in their homes, and in the villas of the emperors baths were often built with the usual attention to Imperial intricacy and ornamentation. The greatest baths, however, were constructed for the populace. They fall into two categories: the commercial, or communal, baths, and the vast Imperial enterprises.

Among the best preserved of the early standard establishments are the Forum Baths at Pompeii of the early first century B.C. Adjacent to the bath buildings was a peristyle exercise court, clearly derived from the Greek palaestra. But here it was not the court but the bath buildings that predominated. Moreover, whereas Greek heating arrangements in athletic facilities were limited to open charcoal braziers, the Romans developed an elaborate system of heating scarcely equaled until modern times. Furnaces (hypocausts) operated beneath the floors, which were constructed above a pattern of hollow tubes through which the heat was conducted in varying degrees to different chambers. The warmest room, the *caldarium*, was nearest the furnace, often directly above it, and the *tepidarium* was next in proximity. The heat was transmitted to the rooms through tile ducts, which warmed the floors and also the walls. The system, in other words, resembled one of the prouder devices of modern thermal engineering—radiant heating. There were also boilers for hot water and even steam, which was transmitted through piping to outlets in the *caldarium*. The design of these boilers was frequently of a precocious efficiency that has amazed modern engineers. The actual sequence of use of the baths at Pompeii is evident in the plan. One entered the *apodyterium*, either from the street or from the exercise court, through a vestibule. After disrobing, one could either go back through the vestibule to the *frigidarium*, a domed building with corner niches and a pool; or to the *tepidarium* and then to the *caldarium* with its hot bath.

Another example of such direct architectural functionalism is found at the so-called Hunting Baths of the Roman colony at Leptis Magna in North Africa, from about A.D. 200 (figs. 3-31, 3-32). The name is derived from the mosaics, which indicate that the baths were owned by the suppliers of exotic animals for the Roman amphitheaters. At the Hunting Baths, the sequence from cold to hot rooms was even more rigorously structured than at Pompeii. Moreover, the concrete vaulting (itself unusual for North Africa, but showing how the Romans could export their technology) is unusually well preserved. The nearly complete exterior of the building looks amazingly modern, but the bold, suggestive shapes are merely a direct expression of Roman concrete vaulting, franker perhaps than would have been permitted in the capital itself.

3-26   Colosseum. Rome. A.D. 72–80

3-27   Detail, Colosseum

3-28   Plan, Colosseum

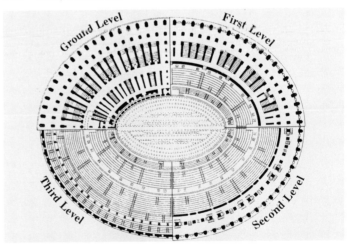

3-29   Colosseum. (Longitudinal section)

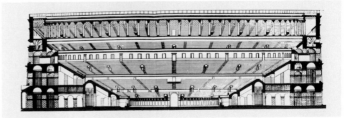

Beginning with Nero, a number of crowd-pleasing emperors built bathing establishments for the Roman populace, which was admitted gratis or for a few pennies. These Imperial baths, or *thermae*, grew to be so immense, dwarfing the usual public bath and even most other monumental buildings, that one Roman writer referred to them as "provinces." The Baths of Titus (known mainly from a Renaissance drawing) appear to have established the overall scheme of the *thermae*, and those of Trajan established their enormous scale. The two largest and best preserved *thermae*, however, are those of Caracalla (dedicated in A.D. 216) and Diocletian (built between A.D. 298 and 306), which remain two of the major architectural presences in Rome.

The plan of Caracalla's structure (figs. 3-33–3-35) reveals at a glance that the difference between the ordinary bath and the Imperial *thermae* is more than one of scale. A scheme of vast complexity and rigorous bilateral symmetry replaced the few simple, barrel-vaulted chambers huddled together informally at Pompeii, nestled within surrounding rows of shops and secondary structures. The bath building of Caracalla was set freestanding within a square precinct comprising some fifty acres enclosed by walls. The precinct contained a capacious reservoir on the south, supplied directly by an aqueduct and located behind the bleachers of a stadium for athletic contests; to the east and west, the walls curved out in giant exedrae containing chambers for cultural amenities—musical performances, philosophical lectures, libraries, etc. The bath building itself, rising in the northern half of the precinct, formed a rectangle measuring 702 by 361 feet. The north-south axis divided it with perfect bilateral symmetry into the two mirror-image halves, while a second, longer cross-axis established a second series of less rigorous symmetries. What is most remarkable about these symmetries is that they order a build-

3-30 Model of the city of Rome with a view of Circus Maximus. (Museo della Civiltà Romana, Rome)

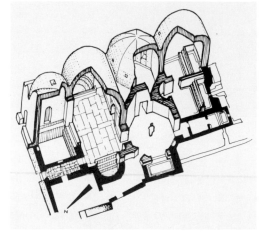

3-32 Hunting Baths. Leptis Magna. (Restored axonometric view by Sheila E. Gibson)

3-31 Hunting Baths. Leptis Magna, Libya. c. A.D. 200

ing so elaborate that a visual grasp of the symmetry of the whole by the bather was improbable. Here, more than anywhere else in Roman architecture, is demonstrated the Roman passion for giving rigorous order to the world, for superimposing on the environment (be it natural or man-made) the standards of Imperial Roman officialdom.

It is fascinating to observe how the Roman planner adapted the long-established program of bathing—so freely realized at Pompeii and Leptis Magna—to such colossal scale and unflinching symmetry. At Pompeii, we noted how the undressing room, the *apodyterium*, was situated, functionally speaking, between the cold plunge and the heated rooms. So, too, at the Baths of Caracalla, the *apodyterium* (frequently mislabeled

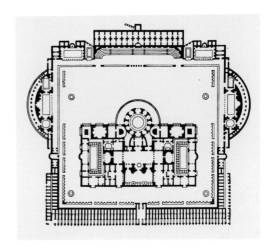

**3-33
Plan, Baths
of Caracalla.
Rome.
c. A.D. 211–17**

**3-34
Baths of Caracalla.
(Reconstruction drawing)**

3-35 Air view, Baths of Caracalla

confusingly as the *frigidarium*) was located at the very center of the bath building. On the main axis, to the north, was the cool swimming pool, while at the sunny south end were the *tepidarium* and the *caldarium*. The spans, covered by the vaulted ceilings, were of visionary scale. The groin-vaulted changing room was 180 feet long and 78 feet wide. The open-air *piscina* was of similar size, and the *caldarium* formed a domed rotunda, 115 feet in diameter, not much smaller than the Pantheon.

In addition to these primary rooms, the main block—which had no less than eight entrances—provided auxiliary facilities, always in twinned, mirror-image form: palaestrae at either end of the east-west axis, surrounded by terraced porticoes; supplementary steam- and hot-rooms along the south flank of the building; various service areas, latrines, and offices filling out the interstices. However, with all this superabundance of facilities, there was one curious omission. At the baths in Pompeii, as at most ordinary bathing establishments, a secondary set of bathing accommodations was provided for women. One would think that planners might easily have included such accommodations in the Imperial *thermae*, their immense size and symmetry almost begging to be used for such a functional division. But in every great Imperial bath there is only one set of accommodations, the bilateral symmetry being not of two independent halves but of a hierarchical pattern with a central "spine" of principal spaces. How did the baths accommodate both sexes? In the earlier history of baths, when separate accommodations did not exist, women visited the baths in the morning, men in the afternoon. This may have been the case during certain periods of the *thermae*, but as time passed, the traditional modesty of the Romans wore thin, and in the later periods of Rome the sexes shared the baths simultaneously (to the distress of the early Christians).

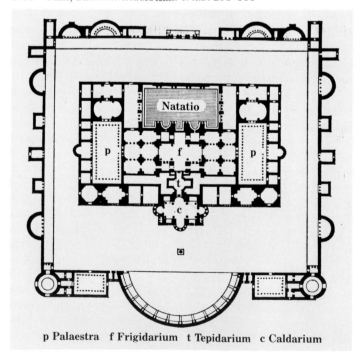

3-36   **Plan, Baths of Diocletian. c. A.D. 298–306**

p Palaestra   f Frigidarium   t Tepidarium   c Caldarium

The Baths of Diocletian (fig. 3-36) resembled those of Caracalla, but they were even larger. The main building was 785 feet by 475 feet and had about 3,200 marble seats for clients, rather than "only" the 1,600 available at the Baths of Caracalla. The disposition of the principal accommodations along the two internal cross-axes was identical in both Imperial establishments, the main innovations at the Baths of Diocletian being the expansion of the swimming pool (*natatio*) and the earlier rotunda. (The apses more conveniently provided areas for hot bathing.) Overall, the spaces of the Baths of Diocletian were more evenly scaled and more tautly disposed, in keeping not so much with "progress" but rather with the general tendencies toward hardening and rigidity evident in later Roman art. Yet, here as nowhere else in the *thermae* were established fathomless axial vistas through room after room, giving an almost aerial quality to a space that was not framed by the rude brick forms we see in the ruins today, but rather by grand Hellenic orders pretending to support the huge vaults and by gleaming walls pierced by screens of columns, arches, and windows. The mural surfaces were dissolved in the color, light, and fantasy of inlays of exotic marble, stucco, and mosaic. Although they teemed with thousands of bathers and attendants, the spaces remained primary and overwhelming. One of them is still preserved, although changed in decoration and in function: The *frigidarium* of Diocletian's *thermae,* with its soaring groin vaults, was after 1,200 years transformed by Michelangelo into the church of Sta. Maria degli Angeli.

Temples. The Romans may have taken their amusements and pleasures more seriously than their gods, but they took their gods seriously enough. If not a people drawn to ecstatic religious experience, the Romans were devout in a sense that involved much superstition. Roman religion functioned most strongly at two levels: the household, where ancestors were worshiped along with the goddess Vesta; and the state, closely bound up with Olympian dogma and rites, dependent on religious sanction and reinforcement. As with the Greeks—and indeed as with all people before the eighteenth century—there was no separation in Rome of church and state. The idea would scarcely have presented itself, for the gods were present in all of life's activities. In particular, all public acts fell under the sanction of the gods; the gods had to be appeased with sacrifice, and their preferences discovered through augur and oracle. Because of the diversity of the Roman Empire, Roman religious beliefs could not be universal. The Romans practiced a wise tolerance of local cults, and religious unity took a political form, expressing the idea that the emperor, the recipient of divine honors, was the head of the international pantheon of deities. It was the duty of all citizens to do a minimum of public worship to this pantheon, particularly after the emperors became themselves divine and religious noncompliance came to be regarded as treason.

Because of the pervasive importance of religion in Roman life, scores of temples were built during every period, often on a great scale and at high expense. They were strongly dependent upon Greek prototypes—the temple was the most Greek of all Roman architectural forms—but none of them embodied the optical refinements, the sculptural brilliance, or the dialectic with the environment that characterized Greek buildings. They tended, moreover, to be functionally debased: the altar shrunk to a small platform on the temple steps, the temple itself used frequently for all sorts of purposes—Senate meetings, displays of art collections, and even as offices for the verification of weights and measures. Nevertheless, the development of the Roman temple is indicative of Roman architecture in general, and Roman architects were eventually to display imaginative variations on the temple type. Among the innumerable Roman temples there are some exceptional structures.

The earliest temples of the Romans were indistinguishable from those of the Etruscans. They shared the axial plan, the broad, frequently triple, cella, the same low silhouette, deep porch, widely spaced columns, and lavish terra-cotta super-structure. Both stood on high podiums, had a frontal flight of steps, and were placed against a rear precinct wall. Unfortunately, no Roman temple from this earliest phase of development is preserved, although many are known to have existed. The greatest was the colossal Temple of Jupiter Capitolinus, built originally in the late sixth century B.C., then rebuilt in 69 B.C. over the old plan, then rebuilt again after A.D. 70. In the late Republican period, a wave of direct Greek influence transformed the Etrusco-Roman temple into something closer to the balanced proportions and the detailing of the original Greek prototype. An example is the small building known as the Temple of Fortuna Virilis, preserved at the Forum Boarium in Rome, dating from the late second century B.C. and built of travertine, tufa, and stucco (fig. 3-37). Under Augustus, who "found a city of brick and left it one of marble," temples were built with marble from the newly opened quarries at Carrara (and more exotic stones imported from the East), which encouraged a greater adherence to the refinements of Greek detail. The most famous example of this period is the so-called Maison Carrée in Nîmes (fig. 3-38), built about 20 B.C. as an official Augustan temple of Corinthian splendor. Both the Temple of Fortuna Virilis and the Maison Carrée shared a feature common to many Roman temples: the expansion of the cella laterally to the very edge of the temple plan. This meant that the cella occupied the entire area of the Greek pteron, leaving only a row of half-columns attached to the side walls, an arrangement known as pseudoperipteral. It is a revealing compromise between Etruscan and Greek sources.

None of the more imposing rectangular-plan temples is preserved as well as these two small buildings, but ruins and reconstructions yield the impression of notable attainments. Augustan richness and refinement were embodied in a number of magnificent structures in the center of Rome. Some are octastyle peripteral works of great height. To achieve this elevation, the temples were set over massive podiums, sometimes even double podiums. The most overpowering was the octastyle Temple of Mars Ultor in the Forum of Augustus. Revealing fragments of two temples in the Forum Romanum are preserved: the Temple of Concord, dedicated in A.D. 10, and the Temple of Castor and Pollux (fig. 3-39), rebuilt between 7 B.C. and A.D. 6. The splendid entablature of the former manifests the high quality of carving that Roman architectural sculptors were capable of in this period, which is also seen in the magnificent order of the Arch of Trajan in Benevento (A.D. 114–17; fig. 3-40) and the arch of Septimius Severus in the Roman

3-37   Temple of Fortuna Virilis. Rome. Late 2nd century B.C.

Forum (203 A.D.; colorplate 17). These display the tendency in entablature design toward a succession of rich motifs rather than the Greek alternation of plain and decorated areas. And they employ one of the favorite elements added by the Romans to the Corinthian cornice, the ornate scroll-console alternating with rosette-filled coffering. The other forum temple, of Castor and Pollux, reached a height above the pavement of 100 feet at the gable and presented some of the finest of Roman Corinthian capitals, with exquisitely intertwined helices and tendrils decorating the abacus, preserved in three standing columns.

As the Empire progressed, the Roman builder still clung to the basic Etruscan-Hellenic program on the one hand, yet on the other, felt ever freer to manipulate its scale, its surroundings, its details, and especially its interior, to achieve novel effects. An outstanding example of this phenomenon is the Temple of Venus and Rome (fig. 3-41), built by the Emperor Hadrian on part of the site of Nero's Domus Aurea (Golden House) and completed in A.D. 135. This unusual building was designed by the emperor himself, overriding the criticism of his former architect, Apollodorus of Damascus, who was not afraid to express his dissatisfaction with the project. In A.D. 283, a fire destroyed the roof, and the temple was rebuilt by Maxentius, who retained the original plan. It called for twin cellas back to back, each cella a 70-foot square with a coffered apse toward the center of the building, and a coffered, barrel-vaulted ceiling. In designing a double cella, it was

3-38   Maison Carrée. Nîmes, France. c. 20 B.C.

3-39   Detail of columns and entablature, Temple of Castor and Pollux. Rome

3-40   Detail, Arch of Trajan. Benevento, Italy. c. A.D. 114–17

evidently Hadrian's intention to allude to the Athenian Parthenon and its opisthodomus. Again following Greek models, Hadrian did not set the sprawling decastyle exterior on the typical high Roman podium, but over a low stylobate. Yet, in a most un-Hellenic way, he placed his temple at the center of a rather confined platform with colonnades of gray Egyptian granite columns running down the long side; the ends were left open. The low-slung building lacked Hellenic grace and it did not rise up dramatically between its dense frame (thus Apollodorus's criticism that it was too low).

Although Apollodorus was Syrian by birth, he had become, in matters of architectural taste, more Roman than the emperor. Surely he would not have had kind words for the unusual temple constructed in his home province. The Temple of Baal at Palmyra (Syria; fig. 3-42), dedicated in A.D. 32, began as a Classical octastyle Corinthian design but incorporated unique features. The entrance was through a massively framed doorway that displaced several columns at a point off-center, on one of the long sides. The building had a Classical entablature, but above it were two stepped terraces, each fronted with parapets of crowstep merlons, which were a

regional tradition. The bizarre roof, used presumably for the local cult's religious rites, was reached by staircases located in three corners of the building. The interior of the cella provided two small shrines. The atypical and idiosyncratic Temple of Venus and Rome and the Temple of Baal suggest the possibilities that had opened up to the architects of the far-flung Empire. In several cases, however, these possibilities resulted not in curiosities but crystallized in Roman temples of great power. This occurred with three widely scattered and differing projects, each a masterpiece of ancient architecture: the sanctuaries at Baalbek and Palestrina, and, in the city of Rome, the temple known as the Pantheon.

The Sanctuary of Jupiter Heliopolitanus (figs. 3-43, 3-44) at Baalbek (in modern Lebanon) was under construction for

3-43   Sanctuary of Jupiter Heliopolitanus. Baalbek, Lebanon. (Reconstruction drawing by B. Schulz)

3-44   Detail of colonnade, Temple of Jupiter Heliopolitanus

3-41   Temple of Venus and Rome. Rome. A.D. 135

3-42   Temple of Baal. Palmyra, Syria. A.D. 32 (Axonometric view after B. Schulz)

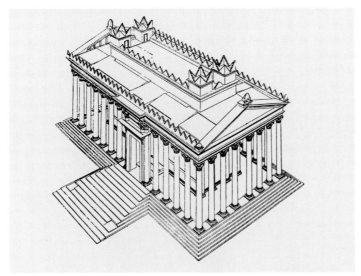

3-45   Sanctuary of Fortuna Primigenia. Palestrina, Italy. c. 80 B.C.

**3-46   Model, Sanctuary of Fortuna Primigenia.
(Museo Archeologico Nazionale, Palestrina)**

3-47
Sanctuary
of Fortuna
Primigenia.
(Restored
axonometric
view by Sheila E.
Gibson)

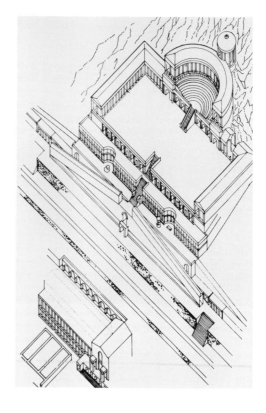

three centuries and never entirely completed; it had three parts: the temple itself (first century A.D.), a forecourt (second century), and a complex entranceway (third century). The buildings are usually noted for their scale and unfairly viewed as major examples of the vulgar Roman penchant for size. They were huge but not exceptionally so for the ancient world. The Temple of Jupiter was immensely high, its vertical dimension unrivaled among temples of the Hellenic type. Set on a podium 44 feet high fronted by an imposing flight of stairs, its columns rose 65 feet, bringing the gable to a point nearly 130 feet above the court and giving the decastyle Corinthian facade an overpowering presence. The visual weight of the building was augmented by the lavish carving of its capitals, moldings, frieze, and brackets. Like Greek temples, it was built without mortar, employing the finest hair joints, yet the podium employed three stone blocks that were probably the largest ever used—each was 60 feet long, 11 feet wide, and 12 feet high, or twice the size of the blocks of any Egyptian structure, exceeded only by some obelisks and colossal statues.

The courtyard and entrance propylon of this temple were of a commensurate grandeur. The temple rose free on one side of the court, while on the other sides there were porticoes of giant red and gray granite columns. At the center of the court stood two towerlike structures; their roofs were used for sacrificial rites. These unusual towers blocked the view of the temple from the central entrance to the court, probably with the intention of inducing surprised awe at the sudden appearance of the great facade as one came around the tower altars. The

architectural expectations of the visitor would already have been subjected to an assault in the propylon. Confronting the nineteen bays and twin flanking towers of its facade, the viewer would have been drawn to the huge flight of steps toward the center, marked by an arch in the lintel (an important Late Antique Imperial motif). Between the facade and the court lay colonnaded passageways on a hexagonal plan, a passage of disorientation, of disconnection with the outside world, preparing the visitor for the phenomenal sight that was ahead.

In its lavish grandeur and sophistication, Baalbek is characteristic of the mature architectural style of Rome and its provinces. It may be seen as a late counterpart of what was surely the preeminent early Roman shrine—the Sanctuary of Fortuna Primigenia (figs. 3-45–3-47), built about 80 B.C. at Palestrina (Praeneste) in the Alban hills, east of the city of Rome. Erected on a steep slope above the three levels of the town, the sanctuary was unusually complex. Three cult objects were involved: a venerated statue of the goddess; a set of miraculously discovered lots (used in the practice of sortilege that largely sustained the intense devotion to the site); and the side of an olive tree from which had flowed honey upon the discovery of the lots. Just how the oracular cult functioned, however, is not known in detail. The reconstruction of the site and the analysis of its building history were made possible only after a World War II bombing raid exposed buried portions of its plan. There was a lower and an upper complex. The lower, of lesser interest, included a grotto, a basilica, and a temple, and may have been simply an ordinary civic center of the town. In the design of the upper sanctuary, the temple itself—a rotunda at the top of the ensemble—was the terminal element of a dazzling sequence of terraces, ramps, and stairways. They climb the steep hillside in one of history's supreme examples of axial planning, exhibiting a precocious mastery of what was at that time the new Roman art of building in concrete.

Of the seven terraces, the first two merely established distance from the lower site. The third was set over a high wall; staircases cut at either end began the drama of the visitor's movement upward; twin ramps ascended to the central, axial stairway, which began at the fourth level. Here, an Ionic portico with shops and two hemicycles swept across the facade. There were provisions for many shops at Palestrina and at similar shrines. Religious festivals were also commercial fairs (as they were in the Middle Ages and still are today). The only note of asymmetry on this level—and, indeed in the whole composition—was a small rotunda on the right side, possibly marking an important sacred aspect of the site. Another row of shops was disposed along the fifth terrace, articulated by an attached, engaged double order. A central stair led to the sixth terrace, a sweeping piazza, enclosed on two sides by Corinthian porticoes that continued to the third side. There, they were interrupted by the framed-arch motif that later was to become so important at the Theater of Marcellus and the Colosseum. Behind this facade ran a vaulted corridor, called a *cryptoporticus*, an escape for the visitors from the heat of summer and the cold blasts of winter to which the open terraces had exposed them. A central stair led to the final level, a semicircular ring of seats capped by a semicircular portico, behind which rose the culminating round temple, whose superstructure had been visible during most of the climb. The miracles and the cult of Fortuna were celebrated at festivals with processions and performances of dance and song in the piazza below the ring of seats. These seats formed a theater, which, in its openness and command of the landscape, was more Greek than Roman and betrayed the dependence of the entire site on Hellenistic terraced, axial shrines. The axiality of Hellenistic sites, however, was never as strict or elaborate as at Palestrina. The whole complex was of an unparalleled grandeur of conception, a Greco-Roman rival to the Temple of Hatshepsut. Looking at Palestrina, we can only agree with a second-century author who wrote that "nowhere is Fortune more fortunate."

If so, then the pantheon of Olympian gods was nowhere more privileged than at the Pantheon in Rome (figs. 3-48–3-53). Unquestionably, it is the greatest structure of antiquity to have survived in a state of near-completeness, and it is one of the most influential buildings of all time. The Pantheon was built by Hadrian between A.D. 118 and 128 on the site of an earlier Pantheon erected by Agrippa, whose reused dedicatory inscription on the facade proved a source of historical confusion in later times. The building has three parts: an immense domed cella; a deep, octastyle Corinthian porch; and a block-like intermediate structure. With its broad cella and deep

pronaos, the Pantheon conforms to the traditional Roman temple in the most basic way. Even the rotunda was not an altogether unfamiliar sight. The Greek tholos form was imitated by the Romans at Palestrina, in the temple probably dedicated to Vesta in Tivoli (Tibur), and elsewhere. But structurally and spatially, Hadrian's rotunda goes back to an uncommon octagonal hall in Nero's Golden House (fig. 3-54). This domed hall (still largely intact), with its central oculus and ring of obliquely lit niches, was one of the first Roman buildings in which the use of space and sophisticated lighting figured prominently. This, as well as the dome, oculus, and niches, made the building an important predecessor of the Pantheon.

Between Nero's octagon and the Pantheon there were other Roman experiments with round building forms, but nothing that approached the Pantheon's scale and consummate command of technology, design, and decoration. At its facade, there was little to prepare the visitor for the interior. Passing through the 85-foot-high porch, the visitor came up to the giant, single doorway, about 20 feet wide and 40 feet high. Entering, he or she found himself—and still does today—in one of the most breathtaking interiors the world of architecture has to offer.

Above a cylindrical base 142 feet in diameter rises a hemispheric dome, reaching a point 142 feet above the pavement. Because the height of the drum is equal to its radius, if the hemispheric dome were extended to a full sphere it would touch the floor. This simple, bold arrangement forms the grandest of proportional harmonies. The elemental shape and proportions realized at giant scale are the basis of the overwhelming character of the Pantheon interior. But its full effect is dependent upon other factors as well—lighting, spatial embellishment, articulation, and decoration.

The primacy of the cylinder and hemisphere is absolute, but these two shapes are not realized as clear surfaces. The perceived number of levels is not two, but at least three, or even five (depending on how one counts), for the cylinder is divided into two tiers and the dome into three zones. Although geometrically, the building has only a single, vertical axis, secondary and even tertiary axes are established by the features of the lowest tier. Here, the wall consists of eight huge, widely separated piers, leaving eight large niches—one serving the entrance, the remaining seven, statues of the gods. Formally, however, the niches serve to introduce the image of an octagon into the cylinder. The associated axial effects are even more subtle. At the entrance, and directly opposite, the hollows push up into the second zone, respectively as a barrel vault and as a half-dome. These two voids create a major horizontal axis at the foot of the building, across which cut three minor cross-axes established by the remaining six niches, which alternate curved and rectangular internal plans to form three opposing pairs. A Corinthian order marches around the lower zone, uniform in detail except for its logical alternation of pilasters and full columns.

The articulation of the second level was altered from the Renaissance through the eighteenth century, but its original form is preserved in drawings and paintings, and a section of it has been reconstructed to the right of the apse. Here, a rhythmic, polychromatic composition runs with the same overall beat as in the lower zone, but with a different meter and at a much smaller scale. The articulating details form a

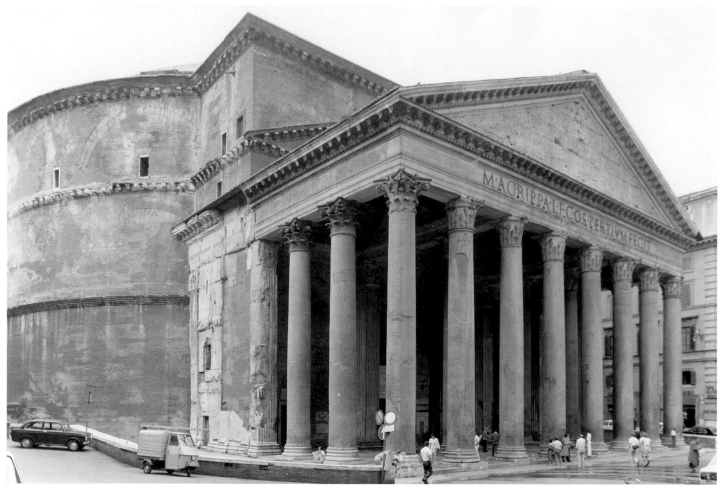

3-48   View from the north, Pantheon. Rome. c. A.D. 118–28

3-49   Plan, Pantheon

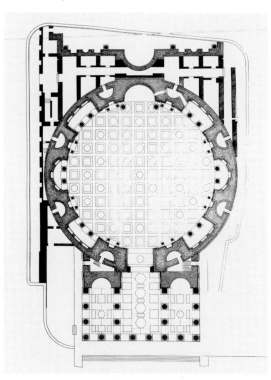

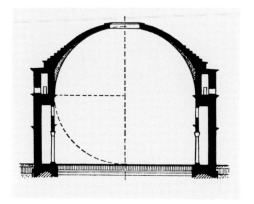

3-50   Section, Pantheon. (After H. W. Janson)

3-51
Pantheon.
(Analytical drawing
of structure after
L. Beltrami)

3-52   Interior, Pantheon

3-53   Dome, Pantheon

3-54   Octagonal room in Nero's Golden House (Domus Aurea). Rome. A.D. 64–68

delicate variation on the motifs of the lower tier, generating a lively interplay of related forms at different scale, proportion, and relief. Together with the spatial and axial elements formed by the niches, they impart vitality to what would otherwise be a monotonous cylinder.

The details of the cupola are no less brilliantly managed. Five rows of coffers, diminishing in size and depth, climb up two-thirds of its height, leaving a ring of pure surface about as broad as the 28-foot diameter of the oculus. This pattern of coffering, with its illusionistic depth, extends the space and blurs the confines of the hemisphere. It also generates sumptuous effects of light and shade with the differing conditions of illumination throughout the day, particularly those of the giant sunbeam that moves across the interior like a cosmic clock evoking the presence of the gods to whom the building was dedicated. Originally, these effects were further enriched by stucco moldings and the glitter of bronze rosettes set at the center of each coffer, and they are still enhanced by light reflected from the gleaming, geometric polychromy of the marble pavement and ground-story wall revetment.

The glowing interior of the Pantheon was made possible by a structural mastery that represents the culmination of Roman architectural technology. The use of materials is even more varied than at the Colosseum. The concrete aggregate ranges from dense basalt in the foundation ring to an airy pumice in the upper level of the tapering shell of the vault. The monolithic concrete of the cupola is flawless and has never given the caretakers of the building serious problems. The most unusual aspect of the structure, however, is found in the drum. The problem was that the hemispheric dome exerted a continuous load around its entire circumference, whereas the cylinder supporting it was continuous only in its upper level. As we have seen, at its base it was not a complete cylinder, but rather a series of eight massive piers connected by a relatively thin outer wall and fragile inner trabeation, leaving eight gaping voids (fig. 3-49). The engineering task was to channel all the weight—or as much as possible—

3-55 Temple of Venus. Baalbek, Lebanon. 3rd century A.D.

of the dome and the upper cylinder away from the voids and bring it to bear on the eight massive piers. This was achieved through a complicated but functionally transparent system of relieving arches and vaulting (fig. 3-51). Two rings of large radial barrel vaults transfer the load of the cupola to the piers; the weight of the filling structure is discharged away from the center of the voids to the periphery, and its load is brought down to the outer wall and the columns. Even the entablature is relieved of any burden by a still further, smaller set of relieving arches.

The Pantheon represents the highest achievement of Roman architecture, both formally and structurally. It combines boldness, scale, and mastery of every architectural art. It is a building that has been valued not only by historians, but also by the Romans themselves, who did it the honor of imitation. It became the model for tombs and temples. Even the unusual third-century A.D. Temple of Venus at Baalbek (fig. 3-55) seems to reflect it. This diminutive architectural gem integrates a tetra-style porch with a domed cella. It was executed not in concrete but with cut-stone voussoirs. The imaginative architect of the late Roman Empire caught the thrusts of the dome with a ring of buttresses in the form of arches on their sides, forming a scalloped circuit that rests on freestanding columns. In its supple curvilinearity the Temple of Venus at Baalbek is as "baroque" a building as was later to be found anywhere in seventeenth-century Europe.

The greatest influence of the Pantheon, however, was to occur during the later European revivals of antiquity: at the Romanesque Baptistery in Florence; in Michelangelo's project for St. Peter's in Rome; in countless creations by Palladio and his followers; and in numerous Baroque and Neoclassical buildings, down to Thomas Jefferson's University of Virginia campus, and beyond.

Basilicas. Among the most important categories of Roman architecture was the basilica, a form that was an indispensable part of any Roman civic center. Like the temple, its history embodied the general development of Roman architecture, and it was probably the most important Roman source for the succeeding period of early Christianity.

There are no pre-Roman basilicas. The genre is clearly Roman, but just what *was* a basilica? The name could be applied to practically any Roman civic building, but it generally meant a roofed hall, rectangular in plan, sometimes with an apse. Colonnades usually divided the interior into central and smaller peripheral aisles. The function of the basilica was reminiscent of the Greek stoa, providing a sheltered area at the main town square for the townspeople to conduct their daily business affairs. Magistrates, who from the earliest time had held court in the open air, moved into "tribunal" areas set aside for them in the basilica, generally in the form of an apse opposite the main entrance, with seating and a sacrificial altar set before it.

We are doubly sure that one of the major early basilicas actually was one, for the word *basilica* is scratched onto a wall of the example that stands partly preserved at Pompeii, dated about 120 B.C. (fig. 3-56). The building, which measures 79 by 196 feet, was divided by large Corinthian columns into a long central space and a continuous surrounding aisle. The interior of the outer wall was articulated in two tiers: engaged Ionic columns below, with pilasters above framing windows that provided ample light. The main entrance was from the forum, through a columnar screen on one of the short sides, and at the opposite end a cagelike columnar structure framed the tribunal of the apseless building. The walls were concrete, the piers and angles tufa, and the columns were of brick. All was stuccoed in coloristic imitation marble, and the whole structure was covered with a single trussed timber roof.

This type of columnar basilica was fully realized in two major examples in the city of Rome. The Basilica Aemilia (figs. 3-57, 3-64) in the Forum Romanum, rebuilt in 14 B.C. by Augustus after a fire destroyed an earlier structure, was a larger example of the type at Pompeii, more elongated in proportions (90 by 295 feet), and lit not by side windows but by a clerestory over the center aisle, a standard basilican feature by then. The main entrance was from the east, although there were three additional entrances between the row of shops (*tabernae*) at the long south side toward the forum. The shops,

3-56 Interior, Basilica. Pompeii. c. 120 B.C. (Reconstruction drawing)

two stories in height, were set behind a two-storied Doric facade added a decade later, compounding the blend of commercial and legal activities with architectural splendor.

The finest example of the columnar basilica was built (A.D. 98–117) by Trajan for his Imperial forum. Called the Basilica Ulpia (from the emperor's family name, Ulpius), it stretched across the forum as a rectangle 182 by 385 feet, with twin tribunes at the ends (fig. 3-58). Two complete circuits of aisle colonnades now enclosed a central space 80 by 260 feet. Above the aisles were galleries, and above them a clerestory stretched up to the ceiling

that was sheathed in gilded bronze. Its glitter was matched by the glow of variegated marbles covering the interior, and this polychromy was complemented by the airiness of the colonnades and the screened view through to the tribunals. The Basilica Ulpia, one of the major public buildings of Rome, was a symbol of Imperial power and patronage, and, as we shall see, an important model for the architecture of the age following.

Considering its date, the Basilica Ulpia was a most conservative building. Except for the roof trusswork there was nothing formally or structurally beyond the range of classic Greek architecture—walls and colonnades supporting a timber roof. Other basilicas were more progressive, although, it should be understood, not more valued by the Romans. Like its sister in the Forum Romanum, the Basilica Aemilia, Caesar's Basilica Julia burned not long after its completion and was reconstructed by Augustus between 12 B.C. and A.D. 12. Its central nave was about the same size as its companion, but it was surrounded by two aisles instead of one. More notably, rather than the antiquated structure of columns and wall, the building consisted of the modern system of piers and vaulting (not unlike the Theater of Marcellus and the Colosseum). Only the central space was covered by a timber roof. The rest formed a massive shell, a fire-resistant cellular construction two stories high around the

3-57 Facade, Basilica Aemilia. Rome. Rebuilt 14 B.C. (Renaissance drawing by Giuliano da Sangallo)

3-58 Basilica Ulpia. Rome. A.D. 98–117 (Reconstruction drawing after Canina)

3-59 Basilica of Maxentius and Constantine. Rome. c. A.D. 307–12

3-60 Basilica of Maxentius. (Reconstructed view of the interior as planned by Maxentius)

central void, open continuously to the forum. The interior was bright and airy, yet, because of the depth of the double aisle, it was insulated from the extremes of the weather.

Augustus had introduced vaulted construction to the basilica, but along the lines of the traditional basilican scheme. He had ruled in an age when the Republic was still a living memory, and its architectural traditions were still intact.

3-61   Basilica. Trier, Germany. Early 4th century

3-62   Interior, Basilica

For Maxentius, three centuries later, no such adherence to the past was necessary, and he all but abandoned tradition with the construction of his new basilica at the edge of the forum (A.D. 307–12, completed by Constantine). The Basilica of Maxentius and Constantine was of a form new to the genre, but not new to Roman architecture, for Maxentius essentially built his basilica in the gigantic form of the central *frigidarium* of the Imperial *thermae* (figs. 3-59, 3-60). Stripped of its context, the *frigidarium* was transformed into a basilica by a few changes. The six lateral areas flanking the three groin-vaulted central bays were expanded in depth and height to form voluminous barrel-vaulted extensions of the central space. This expansion gave the building an impression of basilican amplitude, but its superscaled space, in nakedly affirming Imperial majesty, preserved nothing of human scale or of the spatial variety of the older tradition. Although the structure was in concrete, what was visible were acres of marble veneer and coffering, and eight gigantic marble columns pretending to support the groin vault.

The final basilica—built by Constantine during the early fourth century A.D. at the Imperial capital at Trier (Germany)—was not used for the commercial and legal affairs of the citizenry (figs. 3-61, 3-62). It was essentially an Imperial Audience Hall, and its uncompromising forms express this function. Still intact, it rises as a simple rectangular, unvaulted hall set before a huge semicircular apse. Two rows of immense windows fill the walls, flooding the interior with light even in the dim northern climate. Although the building was flanked on two sides by courtyards and had the luxury of hypocaust heating (warranted by its northern location), the interior of the basilica exhibits an austere grandeur prevalent in Early Christian architecture of the same period: a structurally simple architecture of space, light, and surface. The exterior of the hall is as impressive in its own way as the interior, for the vertical pairs of windows are framed by a row of 90-foot-high blind arches. With the powerful verticalism of this layered mural wall, the basilica at Trier was to serve as an important model for the Romanesque.

THE FORUM AND POLITICAL LIFE

If the basilica was the Roman equivalent of the Greek stoa, the Roman forum was the obvious descendant of the agora. Both began simply as centrally located, open-air marketplaces and developed into elaborate architectural ensembles. But despite superficial resemblances, the differences are profound. The agora always retained something of its informal prearchitectural nature. It tended to be a loosely shaped space framed by stoas, never dominated by a monumental building such as a temple. It was never closed on all sides or disposed with axial symmetry. The Roman forum became all things the Greek agora was not: strictly ordered, generally as a rectangle, surrounded by porticoes, dominated by a large temple at one end. It was as much the temple as anything else that separated the Roman city square from that of the Greeks. The Greeks rarely included a temple in the agora, and when they did, they set it off in a separate precinct. Greek life was permeated with religious feeling, as was Roman life, but the Greeks evidently felt the need to set their shrines apart from the bustle of everyday affairs. Roman life was so dependent on religious sanction,

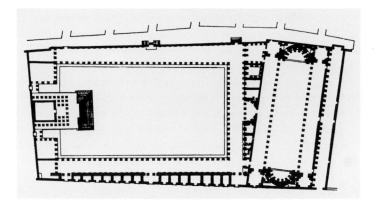

3-63 Plan, Severan Forum and Basilica. Leptis Magna, Libya. Dedicated A.D. 216

and the state so bound up with the gods, that the temple had to be in the civic center.

The aspects of Roman public life were many, and a variety of buildings characterized the forum, either directly on it or just behind the porticoes. The most important of these was the basilica, which housed many activities that, before basilicas, had taken place in the open square. There were rows of shops, and there was the *comitium*, used for political assembly, and the *curia*, for the meeting of the municipal council, or, in the city of Rome, for the Senate. The *macellum*, the meat market, was often a round or polygonal pavilion in a precinct of its own, adjoining the forum. There was a place for the vegetable market, at least one public bath was in the vicinity, and a theater would not be far away. Temples other than the main one were frequently part of the complex.

Despite its tendency toward a common, basic program, the Roman forum assumed a variety of shapes, and no two were alike. Nor did most forums remain the same for very long. Two examples will indicate their normal range, to be followed by a look at their special situation in the city of Rome itself.

The Emperor Septimius Severus took advantage of his long reign (A.D. 193–211) to embellish his native city—wealthy

Leptis Magna in North Africa—with great buildings, among them an imposing new forum to supplement an existing structure that had been built in the first century. The Severan Forum (fig. 3-63) represented the art of forum design in a potent, concentrated form. Two-thirds of the area was taken up by a huge court; porticoes swept uninterruptedly around, except to the west, where they stepped back to frame an octastyle temple of solid marble with red granite columns, rising on a double podium over a grandiose flight of steps. The eastern third of the precinct was occupied by a basilica, with articulated tribunes at both ends. The site of the forum was irregular, but the architect handled it skillfully. He gave the court and the basilica skewed orientations but absolute regularity in plan, and he inserted wedge-shaped rows of shops to fill out the scheme.

The Severan Forum was built by a single patron and his architect; the forum at Pompeii was an accumulation of three centuries. Begun in the pre-Roman period, the building process at Pompeii ended with the destruction of the city by the eruption of Vesuvius in A.D. 79 when, in one of fate's strange caprices, all the inhabitants were destroyed but the flourishing Roman town was preserved for posterity in better condition than any other Roman site. The Pompeiian forum was one of the earliest to have a regular shape—a long rectangle surrounded by porticoes and loggias. The center of the forum remained clear of buildings and was used for festivities, ceremonies, and large assemblies. Beyond the surrounding colonnades was a wide variety of buildings to service the communal life of the city: shops and food markets, temples—dedicated to Jupiter and Apollo—a basilica, warehouses, a *curia*, and a *comitium*. Despite the variety of buildings, the effect of the forum was one of unity and symmetry, with all the structures concealed from view behind the colonnade—the only exception being the Temple of Jupiter, which defined one end of the spacious court.

The Forum Romanum (colorplate 12; fig. 3-64) shared aspects of the forums of Leptis Magna and Pompeii, but it defies definition, having been among the richest of all Roman

3-64 Plan, Forum Romanum. Rome. 1st century B.C.–4th century A.D.

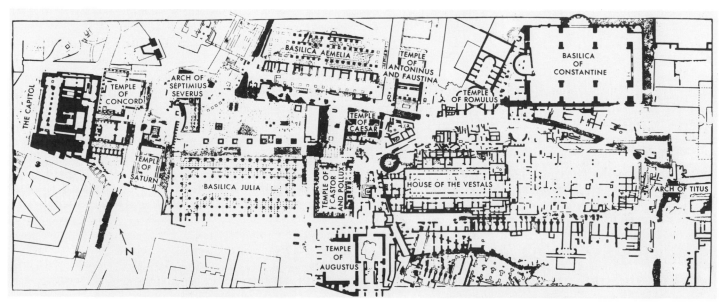

3-65 Arch of Titus in Forum Romanum. Rome. A.D. 90

3-66 Arch of Constantine. Rome. A.D. 315

sites. Beginning in the seventh century B.C. as a small settlement of huts and a burial site, it soon became an important marketplace, lying between several of the more important hills of Rome. By the fifth century B.C., the various functions of the forum began to assume their architectural shapes. Then, somewhat in the manner in which successive Egyptian pharaohs built additions to the great temple at Karnak, successive generations of republicans and, later, emperors added their contributions to the forum. By the fourth century A.D., the area had accumulated no less than ten temples, three basilicas, four triumphal arches, and numerous other monuments and shrines.

Although there was no preordained order for the setting down of these buildings, an order of sorts did prevail because of topography, tradition, and individual planning efforts. Topographically, the forum developed along the edge of the Palatine Hill and ended at the foot of the Capitoline. This natural

contour received an explicit axis in the Via Sacra, the sacred processional way that meandered through the forum to the Capitol. There was always a tendency for the principal buildings of the forum to establish some degree of alignment with the Via Sacra. Near the Capitoline, the forum square opened into an irregular area around which were clustered most of the principal monuments. It was to this main area of the forum that both Julius Caesar and Augustus attempted to give articulate shape. They did so not by drastic measures, but by expanding or rebuilding extant structures (such as the two basilicas discussed earlier), shifting others, and even eliminating some. A well-defined, if slightly V-shaped, square resulted. It must have been imposing, not only because of its own buildings, but also because of others visible beyond, especially the several temples to the east, culminating in the great shrines of Jupiter and Apollo that loomed on the Capitoline.

Just as the main square of the Forum Romanum was aggrandized by a collective, piecemeal reshaping of surrounding buildings, the other principal ordering feature—the Via Sacra—was articulated through a new architectural form: the triumphal arch, a structure bearing statuary and inscriptions to commemorate the feats of successful Roman generals. The earliest examples of the triumphal arch date from the second century B.C., but its origins are obscure. It may have developed from arched town gates or from the Roman disposition to set up decorative arches, not necessarily triumphal. From the time of Augustus on, triumphal arches on the Forum Romanum were found in profusion. Augustus himself built a simple but elegant example at the center of the forum, but its earliest preserved arch is the Arch of Titus (fig. 3-65), erected in A.D. 90 in honor of the conqueror of Palestine. Famous for its sculptural relief depicting the despoliation of the Temple in Jerusalem, it is equally important for the strength of its design and detailing. It conforms to the typical program: a shallow rectangular block with twin facades, punctured by an arched opening, the piers articulated by attached columns carrying a broken entablature, and the whole surmounted by an attic, unadorned except for the dedicatory inscription. The sculptural decoration is uncommonly controlled and the architectural carving, such as the brilliant keystone, is masterful. There are also the splendid capitals, among the first-known examples of the Composite order—a typically Roman invention that joins the Corinthian tiers of acanthus leaves with Ionic volutes.

The classic qualities of the Arch of Titus become clearer in comparison with the famous late arch of the forum, that of Constantine (A.D. 315), opposite the Colosseum. The Arch of Constantine embodies a marked escalation of visual weight: there are three arched openings instead of one, freestanding columns over high pedestals, and the architectural and sculptural ornament has become superabundant (fig. 3-66). This is not merely a "stylistic" change, but one indicative of the changing character of the times, for possibly more than any other type of Roman monument, the triumphal arch is the measure of increasing Imperial pomp, self-advertisement, and rhetorical grandiloquence.

For all that Julius Caesar and his successor did, the Forum Romanum remained something of a clutter—the more that was built even if along rational lines, the more crowded it became. The basilicas gave it magnificent halls for public use, but the main square, for all its hallowed shrines and great sur-

3-67 Model, Imperial Forums. Rome. (Museo della Civiltà Romana, Rome)

3-68 Plan, Imperial Forums. Rome. c. 46 B.C.–A.D. 117

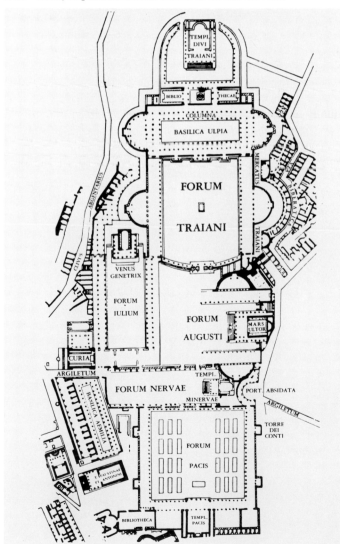

rounding buildings, was not commensurate with the size and greatness of the city. The situation was clear to Julius Caesar. Although he initiated the program of systematizing the forum, the decisive and willful leader must have felt some frustration at the resistance of the old Republican forum to an imposition of rational order. He thus decided to build an entirely new forum, adjacent to, but outside, the confines of the old complex. As politically telling and urbanistically bold as this was, even Caesar could not have visualized what his followers would make of his idea. What he intended as a supplement to the Forum Romanum became a vast ensemble of no less than five new forums, larger than the entire sprawling older site. What was remarkable about the Imperial forums, however, was not merely their collective size, but rather the imagination and discipline evident in their design (figs. 3-67, 3-68). No two were alike; each seemed to comment on the earlier. Wide variety coexisted with high order, forming one of Rome's major symbols of Imperial wealth, culture, and authority.

The qualities that distinguished the Imperial forums were realized to their fullest in the last of the group, the Forum of Trajan (dedicated in A.D. 113), a work so spectacular that even to the jaded sensibilities of a fourth-century emperor it seemed the grandest construction in Rome. In area, Trajan's forum approximated all the earlier forums put together. The

3-69 Column of Trajan in the Forum of Trajan. Rome. c. A.D. 106–13

3-70 Markets of Trajan. Rome. c. A.D. 100–12

3-72 Interior, Markets of Trajan

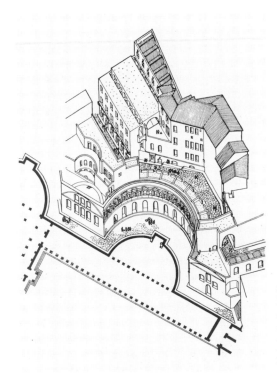

3-71
Markets
of Trajan.
(Axonometric
view after A.
Boëthius and
Ward-Perkins)

emperor's consciousness of the status of his forum in relation to earlier buildings was revealed by obvious formal reflections of them, and by the way in which the main axis and lateral precinct walls of the entire complex were aligned with those of the earlier Forum Pacis—three forums away—a characteristic Roman regularity of form visible only in a groundplan and only dimly, if at all, in actuality. But what this typical kind of Imperial planning lacked in strictly visible qualities, it made up for in visionary character—here, in the image of an architectural composition along a single axis close to one-third of a mile in length with a temple at either end facing the "center." From recalcitrant nature (the terrain presented a major obstacle) and the complexities of history, the Roman emperor created a supremely ordered, majestic world.

Within the Forum of Trajan, the axis held together more than the usual number of components. A monumental entranceway resembling a triumphal arch, carrying a statue of the emperor in a chariot drawn by six horses, was set at the center of the facade. An equestrian statue of Trajan stood in the middle of the main court on the cross-axis created by twin exedrae, while at its far end was not the frontal image of a temple but the immense flank of the Basilica Ulpia, stretching across the line of vision. Triple columnar portals opened to its interior, almost as vast and colorful as the great court just left behind. From the basilica, two minor exits gave on to a small court. At its center rose the Column of Trajan (fig. 3-69), which one had already glimpsed over the roof of the basilica, its 125-foot height proclaiming Trajan's mastery over nature in excavating the adjoining Quirinal Hill to a depth of 125 feet in leveling the site. Its continuous spiral of reliefs, which depict the Dacian wars, proclaimed Trajan's mastery over humanity as well. This small court was bounded laterally by twin libraries, one Greek, one Latin, their walls hollowed with niches to hold the scrolls, adding the presence of culture to that of power. Beyond the column, finally, lay what amounted to a forum-within-the-forum, the colonnaded precinct of the Temple of the Deified Trajan, which, literally, rounded off the whole vast ensemble.

The Romans were as devoted to practicality as they were to grandeur, and this propensity was deeply satisfied by still a further aspect of Trajan's Forum: the attached market facilities set into the adjacent Quirinal Hill. Through his skillful architect, Apollodorus of Damascus, Trajan bestowed on the city no less than 150 shops and offices within his forum, in a pragmatic and technically progressive design. The basic unit of the still-well-preserved Markets of Trajan (figs. 3-70–3-72) was the standard Roman all-purpose *taberna*: a barrel-vaulted cubicle, with a large opening to the street and sometimes a mezzanine lit by a small window. The markets are the finest-known Roman example of modular commercial construction in concrete. The flexibility of the *taberna* unit in size, shape, and proportion permitted Apollodorus to devise a supple scheme arrayed in five levels up to the slopes of the Quirinal Hill, above the monumental parts of the forum. The hemi-cycle facade of the lower levels of the markets, with its weathered *opus testaceum* and row of sophisticated brickwork gables, is today the most prominent aspect of the market structure. In antiquity, however, it was masked behind the curving precinct wall of the forum (with which it is often confused),

and was visible only at close range from the street below. The most impressive part of the markets is the two-storied covered market hall that rises above a "basement" level of shops. There, a spacious, groin-vaulted central promenade has on either side rows of shops opening on to it on the "ground floor" (the fourth level of the markets) as well as on the upper (fifth) level, and the whole space is well provided with light and air.

The Markets and Forum of Trajan are superb representatives of the two sides of Roman architecture—the utilitarian and the monumental—at their height in the early second century A.D.

CITIES AND URBAN LIFE

The evolution of the forums of Rome was symptomatic of Roman city planning. Their history, as we have seen, had three phases. The first was that of the unplanned growth of the Forum Romanum, of the piecemeal accumulation of buildings and monuments erected, destroyed, and rebuilt in a process reflecting the tumultuous history of the city. In the second phase, Caesar and Augustus attempted to bring a semblance of order into this chaotic situation, not by radical, sweeping measures, but through a series of reconstructions, new sitings, and additions. The third phase, which began with the second but outlasted it, involved the construction of a wholly new architectural ensemble (a forum-colony as it were) outside the Forum Romanum—the Imperial forums, each of which was designed with respect to its predecessors so as to create a highly ordered totality.

Roman cities followed patterns analogous to the Roman forums. With rare exceptions, they fell into two broad categories. By far the majority were like the Forum Romanum, growing in an unplanned manner over the centuries to form complex, organic entities into which, from time to time, accents of rational order were injected. Rome itself was the primary example. After the disaster of 386 B.C., when the Gauls sacked and burned the city, it was rebuilt in a helter-skelter manner. Only under the emperors was some order introduced into the overgrown, urbanistic entanglement. New areas were built up, complexes such as the Imperial forums were established, and thoroughfares were cut through the old web. The great fire of A.D. 64 almost resulted in a sweeping reordering, but Nero perished before much of his vision could be implemented, and later emperors contented themselves with inserting tremendous new structures—baths, forums, markets, temples—into the existing urban configuration. A model of the city of Rome was built in the 1930s (located now in the Museo della Civiltà Romana), depicting in detail the city at its architectural maximum; it gives the impression of an overwhelming, disorderly continuum of monumental structures stretching from wall to wall (fig. 3-30).

The opposite category of urbanistic formation was like the Imperial forums—rationally planned configurations set down in "new" terrain. In a general way, this aspect of Roman city planning derived from Greek models. As early as the fifth century B.C., the Hippodamian grid appeared in the Greek colonies of southern Italy, and in the early second century B.C., the first known Roman city along Greek lines, Cosa, was built.

However, a more characteristically Roman form of city planning was the *castrum* type. Possibly following the example of Alexander the Great, the Romans, who were also to conquer the

3-73　Air view, Timgad

3-74　Plan, City of Timgad. Algeria. A.D. 100–17

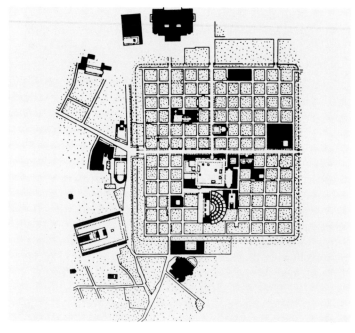

way around in a new campsite no matter where it was in the Empire. The permanent *castrum* fort and *castrum*-planned colonial town, generally established in unruly or frontier regions as anchors of order, were directly derived from the "temporary" military camp. The *castrum* plan is extremely simple: a rectangular—almost square—wall; gates at the center of each side; two main streets connecting the gates, crossing at right angles at the center of town and termed (in modern literature) the *cardo* and *decumanus* for the north-south and the east-west streets, respectively. The four quadrants were divided into *insulae* (housing blocks) by minor streets, and the forum and other public buildings were established at the center (though never *on* center). The virtues of this arrangement in military camps and fortresses were self-evident, and their close adaptation to planned towns reflected the propensity of the Roman mind to geometrically regular and symmetrical design. Here again, the Roman attitude contrasted with the Greek. City planning for the Greeks involved rationality and order but always in a unique, pragmatic arrangement suited to topographical, historical, and practical specifics, and never with the predetermined, bureaucratic stamp of the Roman *castrum* grid.

Examples of the *castrum* town are numerous throughout the Empire, as far from the city of Rome as Silchester, England. A fine example is the exceptionally well-preserved North African city of Timgad (figs. 3-73, 3-74). Laid out by Trajan in A.D. 100 as a colony for military veterans, the town

world and devote much attention to military construction, developed a type of military camp, the *castrum*, notable for its inflexible regularity of shape. This was a virtue in its planners' eyes and also for the soldiers who could always find their

3-75 Porta Appia (A.D. 275–80) and Pyramid of Cestius, Rome.

3-76 Porta Nigra. Trier

formed a square of 1,200 Roman feet. It was divided into twelve blocks in each direction (100 by 100 feet each), within quadrants established by the symmetrically located *cardo* and *decumanus*. The one flaw in the symmetry was the usual one of finding a place for the forum and associated structures. At Timgad, they were set on the line of the *cardo*, just south of the center. Two other features of Timgad were notable. One was the colonnading of the main streets. This design created shaded aisles along the wide thoroughfares, as well as spectacular vistas in the brilliant sunlight, often culminating in a triumphal arch. The second feature was the way Timgad accommodated growth by extension of the major (and sometimes the minor) avenues outward, with further offshoots branching ever more into the distance. This tendency of the city to return to formlessness, or "nonpatterned" growth, was a prevailing phenomenon. Probably the best-known instance of this process was the Roman port of Ostia, founded as a *castrum* fort. The *castrum* form was eventually all but lost in the final sprawl of the city along the waterfront.

Rome and Timgad were examples of the two extremes of Roman city configurations: the all but unplanned and the clear but rigid *castrum* formula. Most cities lay somewhere between, occasionally beginning as planned foundations only to be overgrown by addition and change, but more often starting as ancient sites, later given semblances of order in replanning and extension. However, regardless of the *formal* configuration in plan (which was of boundless variety), most Roman cities—whether large or small, commercial hub or cultural center, port or mountain town—tended to resemble one another in the symbolic and functional aspects of their buildings. This was not a result simply of Roman official policy, but of the coherent fabric of life, particularly public life, once it became fully Romanized. Thus, all cities naturally had a forum, theater, baths, markets, and so forth, generally, but not always, centrally located, and in no fixed arrangement. What is interesting is that they also tended to include structures which were "copies," or local versions, of key monuments of the city of Rome. Therefore, as if to make their city something of a mini-Rome, towns of any ambition would have a *capitolium* (a temple of varied plan but dedicated to the same triad of gods as in the structure on the Roman Capitoline Hill);

another temple dedicated to the Imperial cult; and, among other such structures, a *curia* for meetings of the local assembly.

Roman cities shared other things. The founding of buildings was accompanied by special rites; and another kind of magical force was attached to the *pomerium*, the sacred line around the city within which no one could be interred (except for emperors, who were considered gods). There was nothing magical about the powerful walls that surrounded every Roman city. Their form and construction varied considerably. Early walls—fifth to second century B.C.—were often of the Etruscan type, formed of massive, polygonal limestone blocks set up in high, thick, unbroken circuits. Greeks in southern Italy provided another type, employing squared, ashlar masonry, generally of tufa but adaptable to whatever happened to be the local building stone. The Romans also adopted and developed the twin-towered gate, which provided more protection at the wall's most vulnerable point, particularly when the wall ran behind the towers to form an enclosure in which any enemy who managed to penetrate the gate might be trapped. Rome itself built walls at two critical times in its history. The Servian Wall was built in ashlar tufa only *after* the Gauls destroyed the city in 386 B.C. Later, Rome, at the heart of a secure empire, did not need new defenses until the third century A.D., when the incursions of the barbarians once again became a serious threat. From A.D. 272 to 275, Aurelian built the immense brick-faced concrete wall that provided the basis of the city's defense down to the nineteenth century. Several miles of it still stand, along with many of the twin-towered gates, such as the Porta Appia (now, the Porta San Sebastiano; fig. 3-75). These structures were designed for their visual impressiveness as well as their defensive potency. The most visually elaborate of such gates, however, were not found in the city of Rome but where they were most needed, in distant provinces—the Porte Saint-André in Autun and the massive Porta Nigra at Trier (fig. 3-76).

Houses and Villas. Within the powerful walls of Roman cities there were private dwellings as well as public buildings. These accommodations reflected the rank and wealth of their inhabitants, and since the range of Roman society was so varied, from the lowest to the highest, so were the dwellings. This can be conveniently illustrated by examples from three cities—Ostia, Pompeii, and Rome. At the lowest level of the scale were makeshift quarters above shops or squalid hovels such as those in Ostia on the Via della Foce. Less degrading, but still cramped lower-class quarters were generally available in the multistoried tenement houses, of which there are many remains in Ostia. These so-called *insulae* tended to be built to questionable heights by greedy landlords, sometimes to as much as 100 feet of inadequate construction. After the destructive fire of A.D. 64, Nero established a law limiting the height of this type of building to four or five stories. They were built around central courtyards—relatively narrow shafts for light and air—and the street level was mostly given over to rows of *tabernae* (exactly as in Italy to the present day). Like modern Parisians, the ancient Romans practiced vertical social gradation in their buildings: less desirable, cramped apartments on the upper floors and attic let to members of the lower class, while the lower stories were made into more ample middle-class units, with good ventilation, balconies, and sometimes even running water. This tenement form had the potential for improvements, and before long, enterprising builders transformed these buildings into luxury condominiums for the upper middle class, with spacious apartments, ample courtyards, and gardens. A well-known example in Ostia formed a complex of several such buildings, with its own bathing establishment (fig. 3-77).

But those Romans who could afford it had a house, or *domus*. It varied in size and luxury even more than did apartment buildings. The native Roman form was somewhat restricted in disposition. Like most Mediterranean city houses, it faced inward, a closed rectilinear container well suited to the rectangular blocks of the densely populated city. It had few or no windows (for privacy and security), and, generally, only a single small doorway set between profitable shops on the street front. Inside, the space was arranged in an inflexible sequence of rooms laid out in an axial symmetry that should no longer surprise us—even in domestic architecture. The portal opened to a small entrance room, or *vestibulum*, which led to the *atrium*, the principal space in the house. It was a courtlike area, open to the sky in the center, with a sunken area in the pavement, an *impluvium*, in which rainwater was collected. Around the *atrium*, and illuminated by it, were the living quarters, with a *tablinum* completing the central axis as a receiving room, flanked by the dining area and other accommodations.

In its native Italic form, the *domus* tended to be rather gloomy and restricted. But by the second century B.C., the Romans had learned two methods of improvement from the Hellenistic East. They extended the walls illusionistically with frescoed vistas of architectural and natural prospects (a famous chapter in ancient painting), often of great fantasy, depth, and color. And the space was extended in actuality by the addition of a Hellenistic peristyle courtyard and garden to the rear of the *atrium*. This added nature and light to the *domus*, in which colorful, airy vistas were now created along the main axis.

The rich lived well in such houses, which are preserved in considerable number and variety in Pompeii and Herculaneum (fig. 3-78), but the luxury of even the most elaborate private house paled in comparison with the residence of the emperor. Here there were no restrictions; indeed, the emperor's status demanded architectural extravagance. The only limitations were those of the means to carry out Imperial ambitions. Of all the Imperial residences, Nero's Domus Aurea (Golden House, A.D. 64–68) was the most visionary (fig. 3-79). It was a building that seems to have marked a turning point in Roman architecture, away from rectilinear regularity and enclosure, toward the limitless possibilities of spatial expression latent in Roman structural technology. His scheme transformed a vast area of the inner city into a spectacular, resortlike country villa, complete with a lake fed by artificial streams. A colossal gilt-bronze statue of Nero overlooked his domain, which included—beyond the house itself—scattered fountains, porticoes, small temples, and other picturesque landscape accents. The incomplete *domus* (much of it preserved, to provide one of the most impressive and haunting sights of Rome today) sprawled along a hillside at a spot from which the observer would see only Nero's "country" domain and nothing of the city. The building was comprised of a series of oddly shaped rooms that must have reflected Nero's overheated imagination, among them a dining room with a legendary revolving ceiling depicting the heavens. Other wonders included coffered ivory ceilings from which perfume and flowers were scattered on guests, as well as sea- and sulfur-water baths provided by special aqueducts. Nero's fabulous domain did not long survive his death. It was understandably offensive to the Romans (not for its luxury but for its expropriation of city land). The park was quickly reclaimed for more popular urban structures, and although the house itself remained in use until it became the substructure of Trajan's Baths, within a few decades of Nero's death the Imperial residence was moved back near the political center of the city, to the Palatine Hill, from which the word *palace* derives.

The innovative style and daring scope of the palace of Nero doubtlessly affected the builders of the definitive Imperial residence of the Palatine Hill—that of the Emperor Domitian. Popularly called the Palatium, appearing in scholarly literature as the Flavian Palace (fig. 3-80), the building was composed over the complex topography of the irregular site. The hill sloped steeply in all directions and contained earlier buildings,

3-77   Insula (apartment house). Ostia

3-78   Atrium, House of Menander. Pompeii. c. A.D. 70

some of them sacred and inviolable, and with pre-existing patterns of access. These difficulties were compounded by the functional dualism of the palace: it had to serve the ceremonial and state activities of the emperor as well as the patterns of his private life. The architect's solution was to build two palaces more or less side by side, of roughly the same overall scale and elongated shape, each internally organized with bilateral symmetry along parallel axes, but with interior spaces of different character. Behind the facade of the official wing were three rooms overlooking the forum. There was a large throne room (the Aula Regia) with a shallow apse for the throne opposite the entrance, and massive walls articulated by piers with attached columns. The room to the right was the somewhat smaller basilica with a coffered vault, where the emperor sat in judgment in an elevated apse facing two rows of columns set out about 6 feet from the side walls. To the left was the *lararium*, or palace chapel, a smaller barrel-vaulted room. Beyond the throne room lay a grand peristyle court and beyond the court was the *triclinium*, the state banqueting hall, square in shape with a shallow apse at the far end for the emperor. The residential quarters faced the opposite direction, the southwest, and were disposed around a two-storied courtyard containing a wonderful curvilinear fountain. This portion of the palace comprised an intricate complex of rooms of varying shape and a peristyle court matching, and aligned with, the court of the official wing. These two peristyles formed a strong cross-axis linking the two wings, each courtyard having a double existence, belonging to each other and at the same time adhering separately to the individual palace blocks. Thus, what initially might strike us as rather

un-Roman in an apparent lack of overall order was, in fact, a highly sophisticated conception, diversified between and within the wings, yet unified by a complex play of axes and symmetry.

It is this combination of fluidity, diversity and order, innovation and tradition, that marked Roman architecture during its great age—the late first and early second century A.D.—of supreme architectural accomplishments. It was a style that overwhelmed the senses—particularly if one imagines the richness and glitter of the building materials and decoration—and baffled the mind with its scale and complexity. The sense of the grandiose and majestic was heightened by two further features of the Flavian Palace—a sunken garden playfully designed in the shape of a stadium, and an immense vaulted vestibule that formed the public entrance to the complex, its vaulting springing from a point 60 feet above the pavement. This room was entered through a relatively small, off-center doorway, which must have provided a shock for many visitors when they realized what such an inconspicuous entrance revealed. The Romans were evidently gratified by Domitian's creation, for it continued to serve as the principal Imperial palace down to the end of the empire.

Nero's Golden House had been strongly resented by the Romans not only because it displaced so much public land, but also because it was a country residence within the city; those Romans wealthy enough to afford such a villa had to journey to

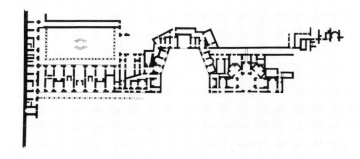

3-79   Plan, Nero's Golden House (Domus Aurea). Rome. A.D. 64–68

3-80   Plan, Flavian Palace (Domus Augustana). Rome c. A.D. 92

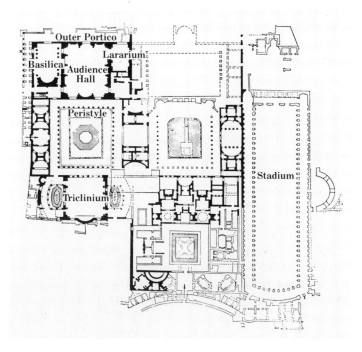

and from the city in order to enjoy it. For all their urban ways, the Romans were lovers of nature, or at least appreciated it deeply as a relief from the hectic confinement of city life. The country houses that gave the Romans so much pleasure were of great variety, not confined by tradition or space as was the city *domus*. However, axial symmetry had become such a reflex element of Roman planning, especially in domestic architecture, that it formed the basis of most private villa plans. The Roman house had already opened itself to nature by including gardens, and the country villa went even further in this direction. In the second-century B.C. example of the Villa of the Mysteries outside Pompeii (named for the subject of its frescoes), we find that, although the principle of axial symmetry was maintained and the building even included the traditional *domus* forms of *atrium*, *tablinum*, and peristyle, the plan did not turn centripetally inward. Instead, it projected outward to the landscape and vistas of the sea through numerous openings and across the high terrace on which the building was set.

If private villas extended themselves toward nature, the country residences of the emperors tended actually to expand over a good deal of the landscape, assimilating into the emperor's domain the natural world that was only visible to the eye from the ordinary citizen's country retreat. The major example of this phenomenon was Hadrian's Villa at Tivoli, built between A.D. 118 and 134 (figs. 3-81–3-84). Sprawling with no discernible pattern over a vast, gently undulating terrain, it formed a loosely gathered ensemble of peristyles, fountains, dining halls, dormitories, baths (two complete sets), libraries, as well as buildings of uncommon, somewhat mysterious, function. Both the whole and the parts reflected the complex personality of Hadrian, a man of inquiring mind, restless imagination, and extensive travels, as well as the limitless means necessary to bring into being any architectural desire or fancy. The villa was, in a sense, Hadrian's version of Nero's Golden House (wisely set in the country, far from Rome).

Three parts of Hadrian's Villa were particularly noteworthy. One was the Canopus—an elongated pool surrounded by a colonnade in which straight lengths of entablature alternate with segmental arched sections framing statuary, a purposeful distortion of the Hellenic orders that was eventually to have wide ramifications. The Canopus also exhibited the rhythmic curvilinear form that was so important in other parts of the villa, in the pavilion of the so-called Piazza d'Oro and the Teatro Marittimo. In the former, the central court was surrounded by an undulating colonnade of alternating concave and convex sections, giving onto the secondary and tertiary screened spaces to form an environment of dazzling openness and fluidity. But the Teatro Marittimo was the most extraordinary creation of the villa, an "island retreat"—a villa within the villa—formed by an outer circular peristyle separated by a moat from the "island." This island was composed of alternating convex and concave columnar screens, arranged in a reflecting concentric form detached from the perfect circle of the peristyle (not to mention from the "real" world beyond).

The free-flowing inventiveness of Tivoli was unique. Nearly two centuries later, the Emperor Maximianus Herculius (Diocletian's co-emperor) competed with Hadrian at Piazza Armerina in Sicily by creating there, in the early fourth century A.D., a villa that preserves a wealth of mosaics, with architectural forms of equal merit (fig. 3-85). At first glance, Piazza Armerina seems to

exhibit something of the picturesque variety and disorderly sprawl of Tivoli, but this is only a superficial impression. It was not only built of fewer elements, but those elements were each of an "impersonal" design with a clear rational purpose, and they were arranged in a logical, if asymmetrical, order. Compared to Tivoli, the layout seemed contrived rather than relaxed and casual. The difference between the two was not merely one of the personalities of the emperors. It was also a reflection of the change from the supreme confidence of Rome in Hadrian's time to the pervasive anxiety of declining Rome from the mid-third century on, when the realm was saved only through the most drastic dictatorial measures. The lateness of Piazza Armerina

3-81 Model, Hadrian's Villa. Tivoli. A.D. 118–34

3-82 Piazza d'Oro, Hadrian's Villa. (Isometric reconstruction drawing by Kähler)

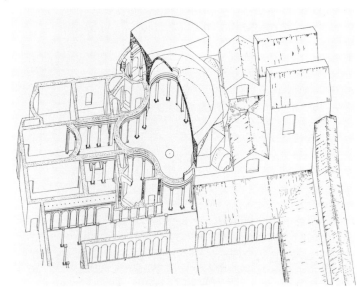

was apparent in its taut logic and in the way it turned inward and away from the landscape—with which Hadrian's Villa had established such an intimate relationship.

It is interesting to compare Maximianus's Piazza Armerina in relatively secure Sicily with the villa built about A.D. 300 by his co-emperor Diocletian at Spalato (Split) on the Dalmatian coast of Yugoslavia (figs. 3-86, 3-87). The former represented a congealing of the earlier planning fluidity, while the villa at Split was a rigidly symmetrical, bristling architectural response to a Roman world threatened by barbarian hordes and crumbling defense lines. It was a true villa, the seaside residence of the emperor-in-retirement, but built in the form of a powerful *castrum* fort. Its massive walls, slightly off-square, with closely spaced defense towers, measured 595 feet (toward the sea) and 575 by 710 feet on the other perimeters. Along the sea ran a magnificent gallery, with only a small portal at the boat landing, but on the other three sides were central twin-towered gates giving onto streets—*cardo* and *decumanus*, as it were—dividing the *castrum*-like villa into quadrants. The two southern quadrants were again divided by an east-west line into monumental precincts near the center—with a large octagonal tomb on the east and a temple and two small rotundas on the west. The residence proper was along the southern extremity with, naturally, the view to the sea. The streets of the villa were colonnaded, and the penetration of the *cardo* into the southern half of the complex, leading to the entrance to the residence, preserves one of the major examples of the treatment of the Hellenic orders in the late Roman period. In this area the

3-83   Canopus, Hadrian's Villa

3-84   Plan, circular casino, Hadrian's Villa

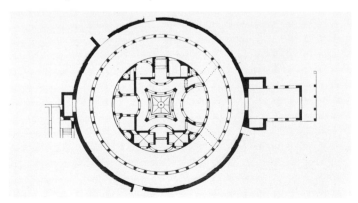

colonnades no longer carry an entablature, but rather a series of arches that normally would have been sustained by piers. This hybrid form of the colonnaded arcade became so universal during the Romanesque and Renaissance periods (and afterward), and is so familiar to our eye, that at first we do not recognize the form for the radical innovation that, in fact, it was. To be sure, this fusion of Greek trabeation and the Roman arch, in place of the earlier layering of one on the other, did not begin at Split. Among the first Roman advocates of the idea was Hadrian, who, we have seen, realized it at Tivoli (in the Canopus) and in his temple at Ephesus in the form of the arched lintel—that is, a lintel that becomes an arch. From Hadrian's time onward, but particularly in the latest phase of the Roman Empire, the radical unit of two straight sections of lintel framing a central arched lintel became an Imperial motif. Nowhere was this image realized more monumentally than at Split, where, on a grand scale and surmounted by a pediment, it marked the entrance to the Imperial residence.

Tombs. It is not surprising that the Romans, preoccupied as they were with self-advertisement and fame, were great builders of tombs. Their grave monuments differed from both the Classical Greeks, who generally required little more than a simple memorial stone, and the Egyptians, for whom the sepulcher was not only a preoccupation but an obsession, yet who contrived only a limited repertory of monumental funeral types. Romans practiced both cremation (like the Greeks) and inhumation (like the Egyptians), and they developed an immense range of tomb structures, from the grandiose Imperial monuments to humble resting places for Everyman, and ranging from the severest forms to the most singular and quirky. Perhaps more than any other architectural form, the tomb reflected the vitality and amplitude of Roman life.

The variety of Roman tombs is demonstrated in three examples. A romantic association with the grandeur of Egypt prompted the Pyramid of Caius Cestius (c. 18–12 B.C.; fig. 3-75) outside the Porta Appia (Porta San Sebastiano) in Rome (tombs tended to be grouped together along the main roads outside cities, the Via Appia Antica in Rome being the primary example). Quite the opposite attempt at immortal fame was taken by M. Vergilius Eurysaces, who made his fortune baking bread for Caesar's legions. How else to enshrine himself but in a massive tomb, right at the Porta Maggiore, built in the form of an oven (fig. 3-88), complete with a frieze demonstrating the manufacture and sale of his product! Entirely unlike these two singular structures, but just as unique, was the mid-second-century A.D. facade of the rock-cut tomb of ed-Deir in Petra in southern Syria (fig. 3-89). Deriving from a local tomb type (ultimately going back to the rock-cut tombs in Egypt's Valley of the Kings), the facade at Petra measured 125 feet in height and 150 feet in width and manipulated the Greek orders with the typical freedom of the Eastern provinces of Rome. But it did so with a brutal force and fantasy that will not be seen again until the Italian Baroque architecture of the seventeenth century.

These examples defy generalization, but many Roman tombs represented an interweaving and development of Etrusco-Italic and Hellenistic traditions. The prototype of the former was the rock-cut chamber tomb with surmounting tumulus, while the latter centered on the classicizing monument, for which the Mausoleum at Halicarnassus was the archetype, with its eclectic stacking of different orders and varying geometric shapes. The definitive aggrandizement of the popular Italic type—which had been inflated by Augustus to a huge, hollow, concrete cylinder, 290 feet in diameter, surmounted by an earthen tumulus planted with evergreen trees around a colossal bronze statue of the emperor—was the Mausoleum of Hadrian (fig. 3-90), completed in A.D. 140. Its 33-foot-high base was 276 feet square and faced with marble. Surmounting it was a cylinder, 69 feet high with a diameter of 210 feet, containing the tomb; above rose a grove of cypresses, as well as a repetition of the cube and cylinder combination on a smaller scale, finally crowned by a figure of Hadrian. Augustus's bid for eternity fell into ruin, but Hadrian's Mausoleum survived as the Castel Sant'Angelo, the major refuge of the popes during the Middle Ages and the Renaissance, when the monument was stripped of its lavish statuary and decoration.

The superimposing of cube and cylinder was the basis not only for this indigenous Italian type, but also, in a geometric sense, for the so-called tower-tomb that originated in the Hellenistic East. As we see in the Julian Monument at Saint-Rémy-de-Provence and the Conocchia Tomb, the proportions were much steeper (figs. 3-91, 3-92). The parts were conceived as discrete classicizing forms dominated by the orders, rather

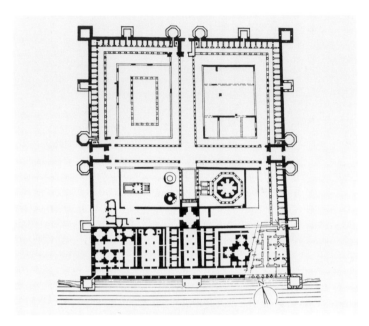

3-87   Plan, Palace of Diocletian

3-88   Tomb of M. Vergilius Eurysaces. Rome

1. Forecourt
2. Vestibule
3. Garden
4. Corridor
5. Audience Hall
6. Private Wing
7. Ceremonial Wing
8. Bath Suite

**3-85   Villa, Piazza Armerina. Early 4th century.
(Axonometric view after A. Boëthius and Ward-Perkins)**

3-86   Entrance, Palace of Diocletian. Split, Yugoslavia. c. A.D. 300

3-89   Rock-cut tomb of ed-Deir. Petra, Syria. 2nd century A.D.

3-90   Hadrian's Tomb (Castel Sant' Angelo). Rome. 15th century view. (Drawing from Codex Escurialensis)

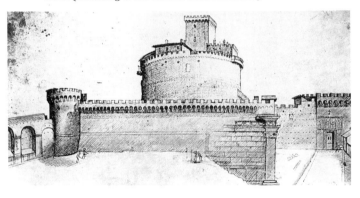

than as an amplification of the old earth hugging Etruscan type. And vigorous articulation, with open upper stories, as well as a surmounting cone, pyramid, or cylinder, were the rule.

The tombs discussed here, regardless of shape, were all extroverted structures designed to impress the passerby rather than envelop the deceased with a monumental space. In later Roman periods, the interior once again became the distinctive feature of a whole range of tomb types. The monumental form of this trend was the domed polygon or cylinder. The Pantheon type became an Imperial favorite and evolved during the fourth century: a high, domed cylinder over a columnar arcade, enveloped by a barrel-vaulted ambulatory, a scheme that plays an important role in the architecture described in the next chapter. Also important for the early Christians were Roman proletarian and subterranean tombs. In a number of instances, associations of freedmen built *columbaria* ("dovecotes"), simple square chambers with the walls hollowed in tiers of niches

for funerary urns. Related phenomena were the catacombs (fig. 3-93), built by the poor to house their remains in mass or clustered burials; and the more elaborate *hypogea*, underground, or partially underground, complexes of chambers for the dead, often decorated in stucco, mosaic, and fresco with a sepulchral imagery charged with the aspirations of the deceased to immortality, aspirations that soon were to call into being a whole new epoch of Western architecture.

3-91   (Left) Julian Monument. Saint-Rémy-de-Provence, France. 40–30 B.C.

3-92   (Right) Mausoleum La Conocchia. Capua

3-93   Catacombs. Rome

Part Two
The Middle Ages

Pages
158–59
Reims
Cathedral,
facade. Begun
c. 1241

4-1
Detail
of arcade
spandrels
and capitals,
Hagia Sophia.
532–37

Chapter Four | Early Christian and Byzantine Architecture

EARLY CHRISTIAN ARCHITECTURE
OF THE WESTERN EMPIRE

The third century was for the Roman Empire a period of political instability, economic decline, and civil war. Dissatisfaction with paganism reached crisis proportions. As a religion, it offered little solace in an age of uncertainty and misery. It was pervaded by uncertainty itself, for its all-too-human gods had to be appeased through sacrifice and superstitious practices which, at best, had only ambiguous results. Paganism never provided a secure promise of salvation, nor did it recognize the worth of a human being. To fill the spiritual needs thus left unsatisfied, a number of new faiths, originating in the East, emerged. At the center of these cults was the idea of a personal identification with a god who dies and is reborn, and in whose rebirth salvation is achieved for all believers.

Christianity was one of several such mystery religions and, at the beginning, not the most prominent. But it offered the magnetic figure of Jesus Christ and his irresistible story; it was otherworldly and mystical, yet personal and comprehensible; and, above all, it promised salvation and eternal life to whomever believed in its doctrine and practiced its rites. In contrast to the pomp and ceremony of the official state cult of paganism, the rites of the Christian religion were relatively simple to practice and accessible to all people. Its leaders were charismatic men such as Saint Paul, who spread The Word throughout the Empire. And it succeeded brilliantly because, in a decaying and uncertain world, it offered not only bright hopes and absolute certainties but also a progressive social program of comfort and caring for the needy in body as well as spirit.

The most crucial period for Christianity was the first three centuries, before it was recognized as the state religion in A.D. 326 by the Roman Emperor Constantine, thereby officially replacing paganism. During that period its dogma, liturgy, and administrative structure evolved. For about a century after the death of the apostles (about A.D. 65), development was slow. Christian congregations were small and scattered, and the religious rites limited mainly to common prayer, baptism, funeral banquets, and ritual meals. But after about A.D. 150, the appeal of the new faith accelerated. By the middle of the third century, Asia Minor was more than half Christian and in Rome there were as many as 50,000 believers.

The picture of the early Church is one of inspired, sustained, yet underground activity. Although in theory illegal, it was in practice tolerated, for its membership was too predominantly proletarian to matter to Roman officialdom. The Romans did not consider the first Christians a sufficient threat to warrant suppression or mass execution, even after the rapid evolution of Christianity and its spread to middle and official classes in the third century. Persecutions, horrible as they were, were less frequent than is customarily believed, and were often short-lived and locally restricted.

Not surprisingly, the first Christian architecture was modest in scope and ambition. The two basic architectural functions—to provide space for the spiritual needs of the living and burial space for the dead—were met in the most pragmatic and unpretentious manner. What we might call Christian community centers or meeting houses were set up, mainly in pre-existing apartments or middle-class houses, where a wall or two might be removed to make a larger meeting hall, or a bath converted into a baptismal font and other rooms used for storage of offerings, or for administration. In Rome such an establishment was called a *titulus*, from the marble title slab affixed to such houses indicating ownership (for example, *titulus Clementis*). Many of these have come down to us as rebuilt, full-scale churches of the later fourth century and afterward (S. Clemente).

Better known than these pre-Constantinian *tituli* are the Early Christian burial places—mass underground grave chambers known as catacombs. These developed as a result of exorbitant land values and the fact that Christian congregations consisted largely of poor people who could afford little more for graves than to excavate the easily dug bedrock around the city. The earliest of these sites, such as the Catacomb of Callixtus in Rome, were laid out in coherent grid plans; but with the centuries came unplanned extensions and multiple levels that resulted in the chaotic mazes that are today so suggestive and terrifying to the visitor. Burial was provided in individual "shelf" tombs or, for better-off individuals or families, within arched *arcosolea* and even private family chambers. The catacombs were intended strictly for burial, funeral rites, and occasional small memorial services for the dead (and especially the martyrs among them). They may have provided a refuge for an occasional Christian during persecutions but scarcely, as myth has it, for thousands of believers who sought safety; and they were much too dark, damp, and confined for regular church services. Indeed, the Christians seem to have preferred open-air cemeteries to catacombs for burial. One such cemetery was on the Vatican Hill—now occupied by the church of St. Peter's. In it, a modest monument of the late second century has been identified, said to have marked the tomb of Saint Peter, who had been crucified nearby. Such monuments to martyrs, and similar pilgrimage shrines, all called martyria, were to play an important role in Early Christian architecture.

It is told that in A.D. 312, during a crucial military campaign, Constantine the Great experienced a vision of a flaming cross bearing the legend "By this sign conquer." Constantine did conquer and thus made the monogram of Christ his symbol; in 313 he issued the Edict of Milan which legitimatized Christianity. As *pontifex maximus*—head of religion, like all emperors—he considered himself to be also the head of the Church and, in fact, to be Christ's vicar on earth (indeed, the thirteenth apostle!). He did everything possible to promote the new faith: filled its coffers, sowed officialdom with its members, supported its establishment against heresy, and ultimately made it *the* official state religion. Paganism was soon reduced to the status of mere superstition. In 330 Constantine moved the seat of the Roman Empire to ancient Byzantium, which he renamed Constantinople, and he dedicated the new capital to the Blessed Virgin. This move had the indirect and long-term effect of dividing the Roman realm into the Eastern (Byzantine) Empire, which survived for more than a thousand years, and the Western Roman Empire, which was gradually broken down into a series of separate kingdoms.

As the state religion in the Western Empire, Christianity assumed an Imperial aura. Church leaders suddenly found themselves elevated to positions of princely state figures. Such a transformation was inevitable since Christianity had developed in the Roman world and, despite itself, was in many ways as Roman a creation as the Empire. Not the least affected by these changes were the style and iconography of the visual arts. Christ, originally the humble shepherdlike preacher, now tended to appear as an enthroned, majestic, and distant personage, like the Emperor. The architecture of the church also underwent changes of the most profound sort. Suddenly the humble shelter that was in use became inadequate and irrelevant. New monumental forms of architecture were demanded by Constantine and the Church. To understand what resulted, it is important to recognize that this architecture of early Christianity was not a radical, independent new style, but still very much Roman architecture. It drew creatively on a long and rich tradition and transposed old forms to new functions.

The most pressing need was for a new house of Christian worship, where the rites of the religion could be celebrated by an increasing number of believers. For such a church, the pagan temple was excluded as a stylistic prototype or for adaptive reuse, for two reasons. Early churchmen, understandably, reacted with phobic recoil to all things overtly pagan. But even if the temple had not been anathema, it would have been ill-suited to Christian purposes. Its interior had never been intended for rites, crowds, or worshipers, and ritual sacrifice had been conducted outdoors on an altar outside the front of the temple. Both extroverted and exclusive, the temple remained principally a shrine for the cult statue. Like the pagan rite, the Christian mass centered on an act of sacrificial character symbolically performed by a priest at an altar, namely the transubstantiation of consecrated wine and bread into the blood and body of Christ, which, when consumed by worshipers, provided for their salvation. But it had evolved as an indoor event, probably the result of the original "secret" nature of Christianity (and also because the Eucharist was in origin a meal). By the fourth century, Christian ritual had become increasingly complex. A building used for worship had to provide a path for the processional entry and exit of the clergy, an altar area where the clergy celebrated mass, a space for the segregation of the clergy from the congregation during the procession and communion, and an area for the separation of the catechumens (those in the process of entering the faith) from the faithful during a portion of the service.

Rome and The Holy Land. These functions explain the plan of the first monumental Christian church. As early as 313, in order to give the Bishop of Rome a worthy residence and seat of worship, Constantine donated an Imperial palace, the Lateran, and built alongside it the church of St. John, or S. Giovanni in Laterano (fig. 4-2). Although the structure has been thoroughly rebuilt, the original project can be reconstructed from the surviving foundations and other historical evidence. A wide central nave was flanked by two narrower aisles on either side and separated from them by a monumental colonnade; the aisles were divided by arcades. The central nave rose above the aisle roofs, and the inner aisle roofs rose above the outer. In this way a clerestory was formed in the nave, with a large window over each bay, and there were minor clerestories above the aisles, as well as smaller windows in the outer aisle walls. Three doors at the west end led into the nave, which terminated in a large semicircular apse. The inner aisles ended simply in a wall, but the outer aisles opened to a pair of rectangular chambers at the far end. Except for the monolithic marble columns, the whole structure was of brick-faced concrete and was covered with simple, truss-timbered roofs.

The functional logic of the building is clear. The processional entrance of the Bishop of Rome (the Pope) and his clergy unrolled grandly down the long nave, with the onlooking congregation gathered off into the aisles. The clergy was then seated in the majestic apse at the end of the nave, separated from the congregation by a silver columnar screen with an arched lintel (a transposition of the Imperial symbolism seen at Split). During the service, the congregation of the faithful gathered close to the altar while the catechumens withdrew to the curtained-off outer aisles, after everyone had presented offerings in the rooms at the ends of these aisles.

This coordination of form and function in S. Giovanni in Laterano is quintessentially Roman and, although the configuration is new, its features—nave, aisles, apse, colonnades,

4-2 **S. Giovanni in Laterano. Rome. As in 320.**
     (Isometric reconstruction after Krautheimer)

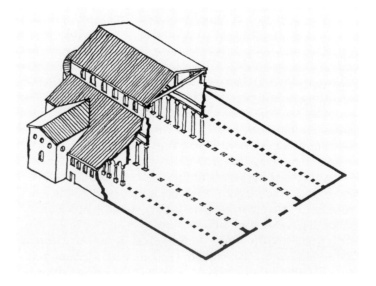

clerestory—are familiar, for they are none other than the components of the traditional Roman basilica reorganized around Christian ritual. Dignified, majestic, associated with Imperial authority yet devoid of overt pagan associations, the basilica, or covered public hall, was the logical traditional form for Constantine's church architects to fall back on. Once transformed, the building became an effective mixture of old and new. The tribune, where the Emperor and courts of law had sat in judgment, became the location of the enthroned Bishop and his clerical entourage. In a Roman basilica, the aisles had circumnavigated the nave, screening it off from the apse; in a church, the returns of the aisles across the nave were eliminated, sharply focusing perspective on the area near the altar at the end of the nave. The Roman basilica had served several purposes, but the Christian basilica served a single, highly ordered ritual. Moreover, the church rendered, principally through its decoration, a richer impression than that of its secular prototype—an impression that was created by columns of marble, chandeliers, candelabra, altars of precious materials, roof beams and the half-dome of the apse shimmering with gold foil, and eventually mosaic and fresco painting covering much of the walls. The exteriors of the buildings were of an unrelieved plainness, and the interior planning and structure were determined by sober functionalism. But because of the lavish interior decoration, what caught the eye in the Constantinian basilica (at least in those buildings favored by Imperial and other extravagant patronage) was a resplendent fusion of color, light, precious materials, and sacred images.

Although S. Giovanni in Laterano was the archetype of the "standard" early Christian basilica in Rome, the most important of the basilican churches built by Constantine was St. Peter's (figs. 4-3, 4-4), begun around 333 but probably planned a decade earlier. It was built on the slope of the Vatican Hill over the second-century martyrium that marked the burial site of Saint Peter, Prince of the Apostles, who had been handed the "keys to heaven" by Christ. St. Peter's originally was not the basilica of the papacy—its future destiny—nor was it ever the Cathedral of Rome; even today that status is retained by the Lateran despite the incomparable scale and grandeur of the new church of St. Peter's that replaced the original in the sixteenth century. Rather, Old St. Peter's was essentially a covered cemetery at the shrine of a great martyr. The huge five-aisled structure was pervaded by the same functional clarity as the Lateran basilica. A triple entrance gate opened to a large atrium for overflow crowds waiting to venerate the saint and for the catechumens during the restricted portions of the memorial services. The far side of the atrium formed a cross-axial porch, or narthex, with five portals opening into the building, one portal for the nave and four for the flanking aisles. The nave did not lead directly to the apse, as in the Lateran, but instead to a vast transverse space, almost as high as the nave, that projected beyond the aisles, and that terminated in small screened-off chambers. This continuous transept—as the form is known—was separated from the aisles by columnar screens, while the nave terminated in a triumphal arch that framed the congruent curve of the large apse in the wall beyond the transept.

A transept is such a ubiquitous feature of the later church buildings that it was long thought to have been a common element in Early Christian basilicas. We now know that the con-

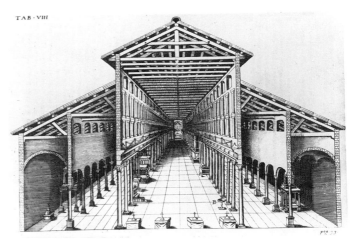

4-3 Old St. Peter's. Rome. Begun c. 333.
(Drawing by J. Ciampini, 1693)

4-4 Plan, Old St. Peter's

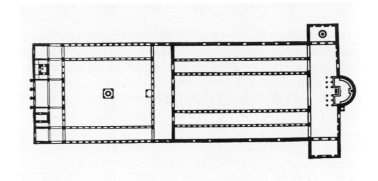

trary was true. Only one major Roman church other than St. Peter's—the late-fourth century basilica of S. Paolo fuori le Mura (St. Paul's Outside the Walls)—employed such a continuous transept; as at St. Peter's, after which it was modeled, the transept served as the martyrium of the saint whose relics were preserved there. Nearby, the nave held hundreds of tombs of those fortunate enough to be buried close to the saint. In the immense transept of St. Peter's, pilgrims might gather to venerate the great apostle, whose relics lay beneath a canopy set on twisted bronze columns before the apse, in an area that at other times might be given over to the mass. The transept-martyrium was thus imperfectly individuated in function, but it proved workable and commodious, somewhat like a huge stage where the setting could be changed for different scenes. This stage analogy is not inappropriate, considering the glitter of the church furnishings and decoration. Moreover, at St. Peter's the lighting was especially dramatic: dark aisles without side windows; nave clerestory windows only every other bay; and a sweep of sixteen double windows to light the transept, where all attention was directed. The superb planning of the building—with its open and closed, axial, cross-axial, and terminal forms not unlike such complexes as the Forum of Trajan—was complemented by this mastery of dramatic lighting.

Constantine also founded great Christian buildings in the Holy Land, where they were almost as famous. He built a shrine at Bethlehem to honor the birthplace of the Savior and at the site of the Holy Sepulcher in Jerusalem, Christ's tomb. These two monuments differed from St. Peter's and from each

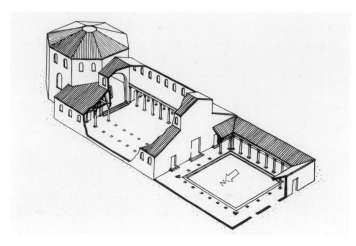

4-5   Church of the Nativity. Bethlehem. As in 333.
       (Isometric reconstruction after Krautheimer)

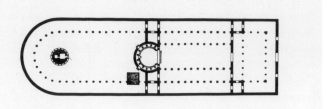

4-6   Plan, Church of the Holy Sepulcher. Jerusalem. c. 335.
       (After Krautheimer)

4-7   Church of the Holy Sepulcher. (Isometric reconstruction
       after Krautheimer)

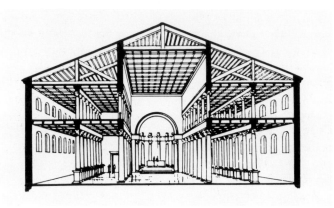

other, but they were essentially variations on the kind of planning seen at St. Peter's. The Church of the Nativity (fig. 4-5) was the simpler of the two. It was founded around 333 and replaced in the sixth century by the present building. Set along a longitudinal axis were a forecourt and an atrium in which the pilgrims could rest and avail themselves of the services of local tradespeople; then came a five-aisled basilica nearly square in plan (93 feet by 95 feet) for memorial services; and finally the martyrium proper—a timber-roofed octagon at the center of which was a circular opening in the rock ceiling of the grotto below, protected by a railing and allowing pilgrims to gaze directly onto the birthplace of Christ. The formal sequence was similar to St. Peter's, but with an octagonal instead of a rectangular martyrium and with all the elements on a smaller scale.

The Church of the Holy Sepulcher in Jerusalem (figs. 4-6, 4-7), constructed about 335, evinced a similar logic but was more elaborate than the Church of the Nativity, for it served a more complicated and even more venerated site. The Emperor had instructed that it be "a basilica more beautiful than any on earth." The completed building had a shortened atrium (due to site limitations) that opened to an interior as compact as that at Bethlehem but programmatically richer. Huge, marble columns with gilded capitals separated the nave from the doubled aisles, which in this case were surmounted by galleries. At the nave end was an apse articulated by twelve columns, symbolizing the apostles. The apse may have enshrined the central symbol of Christ's Passion—what was believed to be the True Cross discovered at the site by Constantine's mother. The outer aisles led to a long peristyle court closing in a curve. This court enframed the Holy Sepulcher, where Christ was buried and resurrected—a rock-cut tomb chamber given conical shape, with a canopy supported by twelve columns.

Central-plan martyria like these two have been traced to several sources, including Roman mausolea and *heroa*, centralized tomb-temples in which the emperors were buried and commemorated in their deified status, much in the manner that Christ was now venerated by the Christians. They probably were inspired as well by Jewish shrines of the prophets, such as the Hellenistic "Tomb of Absalom" outside Jerusalem. Another Constantinian structure in Jerusalem, the Anastasis Rotonda (fig. 4-8), can be understood as a descendant of these traditions. Some years after Constantine's architects had

enshrined Christ's tomb with a canopy, probably around the middle of the fourth century, the emperor (or perhaps his sons) aggrandized the shrine with a round structure, 55 feet in diameter and capped by a conical wooden roof; it was built around the earlier canopied sepulcher to commemorate the Resurrection (Anastasis) of Christ. The conical roof was open to the sky through an oculus, making visible the heavens into which the Savior ascended. The rotunda had an internal ambulatory around a central ring of twenty supports at ground level and a half-circle of galleried ambulatory above. A clerestory augmented the illumination provided by the oculus. Later, in the Middle Ages, the numerous "copies" of Christ's tomb were almost always of the Anastasis Rotonda.

4-8   Anastasis Rotonda. Jerusalem. As in 1609.
       (Engraving by J. Callot)

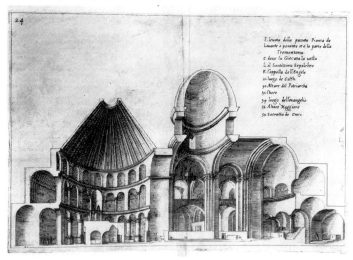

Constantine's buildings in Rome and in the Holy Land were the most prestigious Early Christian structures. He had, after all, a choice of the most sacred sites, as well as an enormous empire and a grand architectural tradition still intact. In Rome, he succeeded so remarkably in creating a Christian architecture that there would be no major innovation in church building in that city for a thousand years. It was only during the Renaissance that Roman ecclesiastical architecture broke out of the Constantinian mold, which had endured in various forms all through the Middle Ages.

A few examples will illustrate the course of post-Constantinian, Early Christian architecture in Rome. More churches were built than at any time before the seventeenth century, when Catholicism mounted an intense campaign of religious art and architecture to combat the Protestant Reformation, but the churches built in Rome presented little originality. S. Paolo fuori le Mura (which burned in 1825 and has since been completely rebuilt) was laid out in 385 to enshrine the relics of Saint Paul who, as the great proselytizer of the faith, was as important to Christianity as Saint Peter. Although details differ, the building is almost an exact copy of Old St. Peter's. This architectural duplication was probably a deliberate device to denote the equal status of the two apostles; it was also indicative of a marked decline in creativity in this final phase of antiquity.

Another major building of the period turned to the past in a different manner. The basilica of Sta. Maria Maggiore (fig. 4-9) did not copy any particular model, but was a revival of a classicistic style. Erected in about 432 by Pope Sixtus III, it was the centerpiece of this revival of earlier architectural modes. Until this time, the Christian community in Rome had shown intense distaste for anything associated with paganism. But after the collapse of Imperial authority in the West, the papacy moved in to fill the vacuum, gathering together what could be saved of the inheritance of antiquity. The trabeated, refined colonnade of Sta. Maria Maggiore, complemented by an elegant pilaster order in the clerestory zone, presented a conscious Christian revival of an archaic architectural style. Shortly before the construction of Sta. Maria Maggiore, a smaller, better preserved church was built, Sta. Sabina (422–32). Distinguished by harmony of proportions and elegance of detail, it embodied a different approach to revival—one of lovingly classicizing design rather than academic effect. Especially notable is the sweeping arcade that springs over twenty-four fluted columns with beautiful Corinthian capitals and bases (fig. 4-11).

To this period of the "Sistine revival," named for the pope under whom it flourished, also belong two important centralized buildings. The octagonal Lateran Baptistery, built by Constantine in 315, was now rebuilt by Pope Sixtus III between 432 and 440. The remodeling was based on Sta. Costanza (fig. 4-10), a church which originally had been the mausoleum of Constantine's daughter. Sta. Costanza was designed, in the tradition of mausolea and *heroa*, as a centralized monument and was lavishly decorated with beautiful mosaics and rich materials. Its domed central space was ringed by an arcade with twelve pairs of composite columns and by a barrel-vaulted ambulatory. At the remodeled Lateran Baptistery, the circular scheme of Sta. Costanza was turned into two stacked octagonal rings of trabeated colonnades rising at the center to support the high central space over the baptismal font. Such octagonal baptisteries were prevalent later, in medieval Italy.

A more imaginative transformation of the Sta. Costanza type was S. Stefano Rotondo (figs. 4-12, 4-13), the second centralized building put up in this same spirit of revival. Built probably as a martyrium between 468 and 483, it comprised three shells of structure: a tall central "nave" over a circular Ionic order; an ambulatory; and four high chapels opening through regularly spaced columnar screens at the outer wall. On the exterior between the chapels were open courtyards with pools and arcaded porticoes. In its detail, lavishness of decor, and especially in the concentric planning employing elaborate groupings of columnar screens, the building harked back to the height of Roman architecture—Hadrian's Villa for example—in the first and second centuries, a forever bygone age.

Milan and Ravenna. The Early Christian architecture of Constantinian and post-Constantinian Rome was, as a last phase of Roman architecture, a generally conservative accomplishment. It had a consistency of structure and design that distinguished it from church building elsewhere in the period, where architectural invention was so varied that it eluded easy classification. A few selected monuments from the most important areas illustrate this situation.

Milan emerged as a major architectural center in the Early Christian period. After Constantine's move to Constantinople in 330, Rome lost the central importance to which it had tenaciously clung despite earlier divisions of the Empire and the establishment of new capitals. After 350, Milan, which had been one of those capital cities, effectively became the residence of the Emperor in Italy and thus the political capital of the West. Then in 373, when it became the See of the great church father, Saint Ambrose, its position as spiritual capital was confirmed and a number of important churches were built there. Two of them (both heavily altered) were of commanding form: the Church of the Holy Apostles (now S. Nazaro), and the Church of S. Lorenzo. It was Saint Ambrose himself who, in 382, laid out the former church as a huge, cross-shaped structure with a single-aisled nave opening through columnar screens into transept arms, each with twin exedrae near the joint with the nave, and each terminating in a rectangular, projecting portal hall (fig. 4-14). The building was a martyrium, for it housed relics of the apostles in a silver casket beneath the altar. The cross shape of this church and others like it alluded to the True Cross.

The bold sweeping volumes of the Church of the Holy Apostles were matched by the spatial and structural sophistication of the central-plan Church of S. Lorenzo (figs. 4-15, 4-16), built around 370 probably as the "chapel" of the Imperial palace. The scheme appears to have derived freely from a Constantinian model—the famous lost Golden Octagon of the provincial capital at Antioch, which, in its double-shell plan, was related to earlier Imperial mausolea and to palace and villa architecture (for example, the Domus Aurea and the villas at Tivoli and Piazza Amerina). At S. Lorenzo, the large central space—78 feet square and originally rising to 90 feet—pushed outward in all four directions in the form of two-storied columnar screens supporting half-domes. Remarkable were the corner structures, not solid masses but L-shaped,

4-9　Nave, Sta. Maria Maggiore. Rome. c. 432

4-11　Interior, Sta. Sabina. Rome. 422–32

4-10　Interior, Sta. Costanza. Rome. c. 350

open-arched pier forms that, in effect, continued the sweep of the exedrae a full 360 degrees around, and yet, because of their cross-braced structure, were firm enough to support the roof. On the exterior of the building, the thick wall took up the imprint of the central quatrefoil by following the curve of the exedrae. At the corners, it formed squares (taking up and buttressing the interior L-shaped piers) that supported towers. These four towers—which still stand—combined with the central dome to create a rich and dynamic silhouette.

Milan's importance as an early architectural center was short-lived, for in 402 Emperor Honorius transferred the Western capital from Milan to Ravenna (on the Adriatic coast in northeastern Italy), where it remained until mid-century. Still later, after various Teutonic groups had swept through Italy, Ravenna became the residence of the Ostrogothic king Theodoric and his followers, who were in close contact with the Byzantine East even though their court was strongly

4-12   Interior, S. Stefano Rotondo. Rome. 468–83

4-13   S. Stefano Rotondo. (Reconstruction by Spencer Corbett)

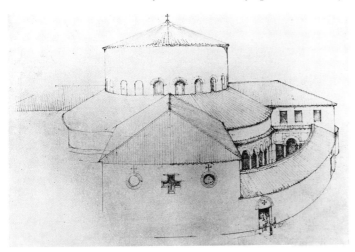

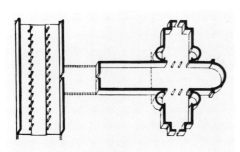

4-14
Church of the Holy
Apostles. Milan.
c. 382. (Isometric
reconstruction
after Villa)

4-15
Plan, S. Lorenzo.
Milan. c. 370

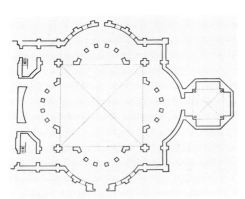

Romanized. In a reign based on Roman legal and political traditions, Theodoric provided Italy with more than thirty years of remarkable prosperity and peace. When he died in 526, the discordant elements in his kingdom that had been suppressed broke out into factional strife, which lasted until the Eastern Emperor Justinian (ruled 527–65) reconquered Italy from the Ostrogoths and annexed it to the Byzantine Empire, making Ravenna the residence of the Byzantine viceroys. Thus, Ravenna (like Venice later) led a complex existence between West and East, and this composite identity was directly reflected in the church buildings of the period—most of which survive not only structurally intact but also with significant remnants of their original decoration.

The Mausoleum of Galla Placidia (colorplate 19), sister of Emperor Honorius, was built about 425 on a cross-shaped plan derived from Milanese martyria. It housed three sarcophagi: that of Galla Placidia, her husband, and her brother. Small though it is, this perfectly preserved structure (originally part of a larger church) presents a compact gathering of volumes on the exterior, strengthened by a continuous arcade of blind niches. The interior, with barrel-vaulted arms and a central pendentive dome, retains its sheathing of gray marble panels and exquisite blue-ground ceiling mosaics depicting saints, a starry heaven, and patterns of slender, coiling tendrils.

4-16   S. Lorenzo, with Renaissance remodeling

4-17 Interior view, Orthodox Baptistery. Ravenna. c. 400–50

4-18 Interior, S. Apollinare in Classe. Ravenna. 534–49

4-19 Tomb of King Theodoric. Ravenna. 526

Even more sumptuous in its interior decor is the Orthodox Baptistery, built about 400–50 (fig. 4-17). On the exterior, its plan is square with rounded corners, but inside the form becomes a niched octagon. Like most buildings in Ravenna, over the centuries its floor has been elevated to accommodate the rising level of the sea. Few early Christian interiors had such a wealth of ornament on the wall surfaces. Exceedingly well preserved are the abstract marble inlays, the stucco sculpture and architectural framing, and the mosaic designs which include ornamental scrolls embellished with leaves, images of saints, and, in the dome overhead, a representation of the Baptism of Christ.

Of the many basilican churches constructed in Ravenna during the Early Christian period, two stand out: S. Apollinare Nuovo of 490, and S. Apollinare in Classe (the original port of Ravenna, long since silted up) of 534–49 (colorplate 18; fig. 4-18). Both buildings were designed on a conservative Latin plan—a nave separated from two aisles by arcaded colonnades, and an apse—yet in proportion, decor, lighting, and special features they reflect eastern influence. Their apses, for example, are polygonal on the exterior; the columns of richly veined marble are widely spaced; and the capitals are carved with Constantinopolitan freedom (those in S. Apollinare Nuovo are from Constantinople), with virtuoso chiaroscuro drillwork to create the effect of lush, wind-blown leaves. The proportions of the buildings emphasize amplitude over length. Whereas the lighting in Roman buildings tends toward dramatic contrasts, in these Ravenna basilicas the aisle windows create an even and diffuse light throughout. In S. Apollinare Nuovo, space is animated by the magnificent row of mosaic saints

line the clerestory walls, and at Classe, the apse is decorated with marble and with gold-ground mosaic to create a shimmering polychrome texture that brings the Eastern world to Italy.

The building that most uniquely reflects the ambivalent political and cultural status of Ravenna is the Tomb of the Ostrogothic king Theodoric, built at his death in 526. The massive, somber structure (fig. 4-19) is constructed in ashlar masonry of large blocks and is surmounted by a monolithic cupola. The two-storied interior—a cruciform chamber below, circular above—corresponds outside to a ring of blind arches surmounted by a narrower cylindrical story. The bizarre structure can be categorized only as an eclectic synthesis. The two-storied form is late Roman but also found precedent in Syria along with the cross-shaped chamber. Moreover, Syria was the only area at this date that could have provided workmen versed in the technique of massive ashlar construction. On the other hand, the enormous dome—truly a megalithic throwback—reflects the tradition of the Germanic stone-covered tombs of Theodoric's ancestors.

Greece, Syria, and the Rhineland. Turning from the Italian peninsula to other regions of the Early Christian world, we find few buildings as free as S. Lorenzo, as unusual as the Tomb of Theodoric, or as conservative as the structures in Rome. However, examples from three regions will demonstrate the vitality and diversity of early church design outside Italy. The late-fifth-century church of Hagios Demetrios, in Salonika, Greece, was the most imposing Early Christian church in the Greek-speaking eastern Mediterranean (figs. 4-20, 4-21). Although it was unsympathetically restored after a fire in 1917, much of the original impression can still be perceived. The groundplan reveals a basilica with a transept, but different from the Latin type. A typical Roman transepted basilica—Old St. Peter's for example—formed a simple perpendicular scheme: a group of parallel aisles intersected by a single transept. At Hagios Demetrios, the relationship between nave, transept, and aisles was different. The transept was not continuous but divided into three sections, with the lateral wings screened off from the much higher central area. In fact, the central part of the transept continued the high space of the nave right to the apse with little interruption. This is best understood on the exterior of the building where we see the nave as the central core of the church, surrounded by secondary layers of space—narthex, double aisles, double transepts, and even a choir beyond the apse (retrochoir). The peripheral zones in turn open outward in a continuous chain of multilevel fenestration. This nestling of the nave within screened layers had its roots in the temples of ancient Greece, where the cella was nestled within the rich texture of one or two columnar screens (as, for example, in a dipteral Ionic temple). In antiquity, these screens were mainly viewed from the outside; at Hagios Demetrios, they are seen from within. But this church pointed to the future, for although the nave was a stretched rectangle, the building embodied a centralized effect. It is exactly this combination of longitudinal and centralized form, shaped by columnar screens into richly layered space, that is a principal theme of Byzantine architecture.

The inland regions of the eastern Mediterranean contrasted with the coastlands in two important ways: the style of their buildings was rooted in archaic local traditions that were resistant, but not impervious, to Hellenism; and many of their churches, probably because of the economic collapse of the area at the end of antiquity, have survived as substantial ruins. The most impressive example was the Syrian martyrium of one of the most curious of holy men, Saint Simeon Stylites, who spent the latter part of his life atop a giant column and was the object of astonishing veneration. His martyrium at Qalat Siman was built around 470 in heavy ashlar masonry. It was grandiose in

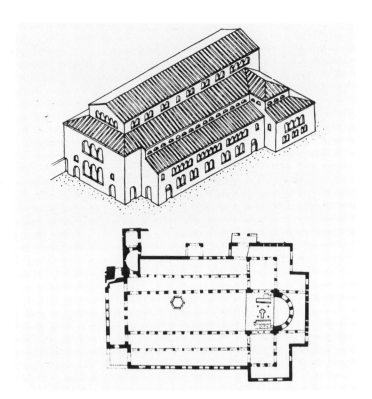

4-20 Hagios Demetrios. Salonika. Late 5th century. (Reconstruction and plan after Krautheimer)

4-21 Nave, Hagios Demetrios

size but simple in scheme (fig. 4-22). A huge, timber-roofed octagon was erected around the pillar of the saint (perhaps originally open to the sky), and four three-aisled naves—each almost a complete basilica in itself—led into the octagon through a ring of massive arches. The Classical detail of the building—predominantly that of heavy, continuous moldings—was elaborate, but rough and unrefined.

A smaller basilican church at Qalb Louzeh, also in Syria, was built in about 500 in the same style (fig. 4-23). This church embodied several interesting features, among them a three-aisled nave divided by a weighty arcade on heavy piers and

4-22   Octagon, St. Simeon Stylites. Qalat Siman, Syria. c. 470

4-23   Church of Qalb Louzeh. Syria. c. 500

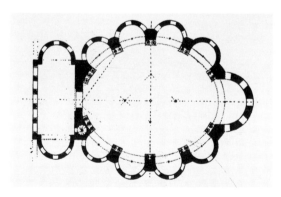

4-24
Plan, St.
Gereon.
Cologne.
c. 380

4-25
North
basilica,
Trier
Cathedral.
c. 380
(Isometric
reconstruc-
tion by Paul
Lampl after
T. Kempf)

roofed by a powerful barrel vault, and also a facade with low twin towers. Qalb Louzeh, and other buildings in the region like it, exhibit a massive style that has suggested to many observers that here may lie the origins of Romanesque architecture. But the famous twin-tower motif was widespread in late antiquity and was by no means restricted to Syria, where the churches lay in areas largely abandoned and inaccessible to the builders of Romanesque churches a thousand miles away and half a millennium later. There could have been intermediate sources, of course, through which the Syrian church style was transmitted to Europe, but the Romanesque forms are by no means as close to Syrian examples as has often been claimed. There is every reason to believe that the basic schemes and massive features of Romanesque buildings were simply reinvented.

The Early Christian buildings of the Rhineland, on the other hand, may have been moving more toward the style of medieval architecture than is commonly imagined. The late-fourth-century (c. 380) martyrium of Saint Gereon in Cologne (fig. 4-24)—an oval space 80 feet long surrounded by nine apses and entered through a double-apsed narthex—was eventually incorporated into a Romanesque church, as was the Cathedral of Trier (fig. 4-25). Originally constructed in the form of a double cathedral—two parallel interconnected basilicas (the design's function unknown)—it underwent a major rebuilding in about 380. The rebuilt north church was particularly important for future developments. It included a propylaeum, an atrium, and a five-aisled nave. Its central-plan east end (later incorporated into the medieval building) was built over a square grid of three by three bays, the central bay rising as a "crossing" tower to which the corner bays responded as secondary turrets. The resulting dynamic skyline was not unlike that of S. Lorenzo in Milan, a city with which the Rhineland maintained close architectural ties, and both pointed toward the bold, thrusting silhouettes of medieval architecture.

BYZANTINE ARCHITECTURE

In the years around 500 the Western Empire was in ruin—Rome twice sacked and Italy in the hands of the Ostrogoths—and the creative impulses of Constantinian architecture and its following were played out. But the Empire lived on in the East. In the course of the next hundred years Constantinople, the capital city that Constantine had rebuilt on the Hellenic site of Byzantium, burst into political and architectural flower. Personally responsible for this phenomenon was the Emperor Justinian, a man of driving ambition who not only reconquered much of the lost Western Empire, but also consciously set out on an unprecedented building campaign that launched a new architectural era. Although the Roman diversity of building types was carried over to the fabled city of Byzantium, so few key sites are preserved or well-documented—the city walls of Theodosius II being a rare exception—that nonecclesiastical Byzantine architecture is a topic best left to specialized studies. Nevertheless, understanding Byzantine church building—often only existing in ruins or remodeled under Islamic rule—is an absorbing and rewarding task.

While it is easy enough to recognize the formal shift from Early Christian to Byzantine architecture in the early sixth century—when the timber-roofed Latin basilican church gave way in the Eastern Empire to domed, central-plan structures—

it is less easy to explain it. This changeover has often been interpreted in functionalist terms: that the domed central-plan type reflects Eastern liturgical practice, in which the central part of the church was dominated by the clergy during much of the service, rather than only the apse and adjacent area as in the West. The dome would have enshrined the liturgical focus. But explaining central-plan churches in Byzantium on the basis of liturgical practices has its limitations. For even though the central plan dominated progressive Byzantine church architecture very early, there is now strong doubt as to whether the clergy so dominated the interior from the outset, or, in fact, if they ever did at all. Moreover, a "form-follows-function" argument at best explains the centralizing tendencies of Byzantine architecture, but tells us little about the specific shapes in which those tendencies were realized. Clearly, other factors are needed to explain more fully the Byzantine architectural novelty.

These factors lead us back to the ideals of early Christianity. It cannot be overemphasized that whereas the value systems in most pre-Christian cultures were rooted in nature and the things of this world, Christianity was otherworldly. The conception of the incarnate God was indeed basic to it, but the new faith denied the value of earthly pleasures, which peoples as diverse as the Egyptians and the Etruscans had perpetuated even in afterlife. The result of this ethereal Christian ethos was a new, specific architectural quest—how to express in the most material of the arts the values and ideals of the most nonmaterialistic of faiths. This was to be a primary source of creative energy in architecture for more than a thousand years. Indeed, the theme was the touchstone of architectural style from the Early Christian period through the Baroque. All the great styles created during the long reign of Christianity grappled with the issue. Two distinct attitudes seemed to alternate in a regular cycle: Early Christian, Romanesque, and Renaissance churches expressed the Christian ethos in a sober and direct manner, while the Byzantine, Gothic, and Baroque styles created dazzling visions and symbols of sacred themes.

This distinction becomes apparent in a reexamination of the Early Christian basilica as a functionalist building, rigorously shaped around the liturgy, yet also Christian in ways that go beyond strict functionalism: its outer plainness, its structural humility and uniformity befit the simplicity and dignity of the ideal Christian; its great scale, the glitter of its ornament, and its luminosity render something of the imagery of Christ, the "light of the world." Yet the inherent symbolic content of the church was comparatively weak. The structural integrity and material solidity of the building remained prominent beneath the decorative glitter: large monolithic piers, solid walls, and powerful roof beams predominated despite the best efforts of the interior decorator to disguise them superficially. The Early Christian basilica was the way of realizing Christian architectural needs within the limitations of the worldly Roman architectural outlook; in it, in any case, functionalism overshadowed symbolism. In the Byzantine style, the priorities were reversed. While serving the liturgy—ultimately in a very coherent pattern—its main emphasis was the creation of a symbolic architectural expression of the innermost significance and ideals of the new faith. This was not merely a question of interior decoration, but of fundamental design.

The Ideal Byzantine Church. Although no two Byzantine churches were identical, we can speak of an "ideal" model of this style. Its attributes include the central plan and the pendentive dome, along with key aspects of structure, lighting, and decoration.

The Plan. Whereas most buildings laid out along a horizontal axis (the Roman basilica, for example) invited visitors to circulate through their space and actively experience their forms, in a central-plan structure the axis ascended away from visitors, leaving no possible active participation except weakly around a central axis. While this tends to be true of any centralized building, its full effect depends on the specific shape taken by the centralizing impulse. In most Byzantine churches, the centralized core of the building was square (or derived from the square). The cubic volume that rose above it provided functional clarity: On one side was the chancel, opposite was the main entrance, and on the other two sides were spaces for the congregation. A circular plan offers no such intrinsic distinctions, and in polygons the sides shrink progressively with the increase in their number, thus restricting the size of the chancel. Perhaps most important is that the cubic form as employed by Byzantine church architects (not, of course, the way an ordinary quadratic room was usually handled) had a self-effacing transparency that was denied the polygon or circular plan. A cube is made of a few planes meeting at right angles to form sharp edges. Not only is it an entity of absolute stereometric simplicity, but also the forms that contain it constitute a series of reductive, two- and even one-dimensional elements: line (or edge) and plane.

The Dome. The central cubic core of the Byzantine church formed an integral part of a larger program that included supporting structure and vaulting as well. In the invariably quadratic volumes of the piers, the central space was echoed to create a perfect harmony of space and structure, which again, in its stark simplicity, attained a self-effacing character. But it was the dome of the church that more ingeniously complemented the cubic spatial core (figs. 4-26, 4-27).

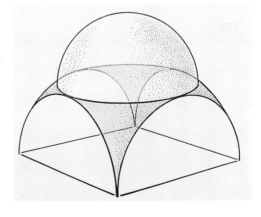

**4-26
Byzantine dome
on pendentives.
(After James H.
Acland)**

**4-27
Pendentive dome.
(After James H.
Acland)**

In the architecture of ancient Rome, the plan of the vaults almost invariably corresponded to the plan of the supporting walls. Thus a building of rectangular plan tended to receive a barrel vault or a square, groin vaulting. Domes were generally placed over cylinders, as at the Pantheon. Occasionally, however, the Romans set domes over polygons or even squares, which created a special structural problem: how to adapt the angular plan of the base to the curved plan of the dome it supported. This could be accomplished in one of three ways. If the walls of the base were thick enough, they might contain the curve of the circle. However, in all but the smallest building this meant enormously thick walls, and thus more practical devices were sought. One was the squinch—a bridge thrown across the corners to support the overhanging part of the cupola. The squinch itself might be arched or simply made in the form of a heavy lintel. The more elegant mode of filling in the support angles was the pendentive—a concave, spherical triangle which emerged gradually from the corner and, unlike the disjunctive squinch, merged perfectly with the base of the cupola.

The pendentive offered the possibility of a more sophisticated solution to the problem of setting a circle on a square. This was to design the pendentives not as unrelated figures but as part of a single hemisphere. The diameter of this theoretical hemisphere was the diagonal of the square. In actual construction, the parts of the hemisphere that extended beyond the square were, of course, not built, but only the spherical triangles that rose within the perimeter. If together with these four pendentives the upper portion of the theoretical dome was also built, the resultant structure was called a pendentive dome (or sometimes, aptly, a "sail vault"). However, here the part perceived as dome was only the upper part of the theoretical hemisphere and thus seemed comparatively shallow, not fully rounded. The solution was to eliminate this "perceived" cupola by lopping off everything of the original (theoretical) hemisphere above the pendentives as well as outside the square, leaving only the pendentives, and topping the decapitated pendentive structure (which formed a complete circle) with a second, smaller, but fully hemispherical cupola whose diameter equaled the side (not the diagonal) of the base square. This type of vaulting is called a dome-on-pendentives.

The Romans, who actually invented pendentive doming, used it very little. But both the pendentive dome and the dome-on-pendentives were favorites of the Byzantine builders and again it is easy to see why: Although in design highly rational, in practice the effect created by the ghostly pendentive structures, which rose with mysterious force from single points and hardly touched one another, was unworldly. Such domes contributed crucial imagery to the interior. If the

4-28 Anthemius of Tralles and Isidorus of Miletus. Hagia Sophia. Constantinople (Istanbul). c. 532–37

Pantheon dome symbolized the worldly cosmos, and even the man-made cosmos, of the Roman Empire, so the ghostly geometry and continuous surfaces of the pendentive types were made to evoke a powerful image of Christian heaven.

Lighting and Decoration. The transcendental effect realized by the Byzantine system of square central core, squared pier forms, and pendentive domical structures, was strengthened by further aspects of the "ideal" Byzantine church design: revetment, articulation, and fenestration. As we shall see from actual examples, the general rule was that no visible surface of the interior be left in a "natural" state—an idea derived from Roman practice but now carried to a new intensity. All was dissolved in color and light—glowing marble pavements, patterned marble revetments of walls, richly veined marble columns, intricately carved capitals, expanses of golden vaulting or extensive mosaic cycles, and, scattered throughout, rhythmic combinations of light formed by fenestration patterns.

Hagia Sophia. If there is one work that realizes the "ideal" Byzantine model, it is the astonishing church of Hagia Sophia built as the new Cathedral of Constantinople (today Istanbul) by the Emperor Justinian in 532–37 (colorplate 21; figs. 4-1, 4-28–4-31). He intended it as the keystone of his vast architectural campaign, and is reported to have exclaimed upon its completion, "Solomon, I have vanquished thee." The building stands as a monument not only to Justinian's ambition but also to his character. The Emperor was a complex and supremely self-confident man. He was determined to restore the breadth of the Roman Empire, and nearly did, if briefly. His sweeping reordering of Roman law—the Justinianic Code—was more enduring. He was deeply religious and convinced that he had a divine mission to reestablish orthodoxy and guide the Church throughout, and even beyond, his dominion. For his new cathedral, rather than relying on local craftsmen he summoned two men from outside the building trade: Anthemius of Tralles, a natural scientist, geometer, and author of a book on conical sections and vaulting, and Isidorus of Miletus, a professor of stereometry and physics at Constantinople. This was an unusual step, but not as radical as we would consider it today, for it is only quite recently that rigid academic requirements have been established for architects. In the past, it was often the case that architects entered the field from other areas. What was important was not any academic diploma or certificate, but rather the ability to conceive fresh and viable architectural ideas. Justinian must have anticipated that only natural philosophers would be able to conceive a building of such visionary effect as he dreamed of and formulate novel structural means to accomplish it. No trade-bound professional would

4-30   Nave, Hagia Sophia

4-29   Plan, Hagia Sophia

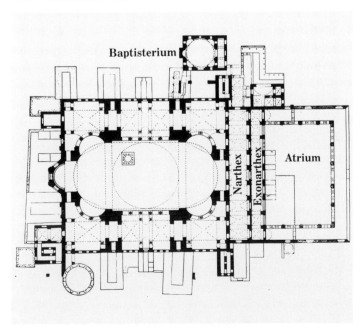

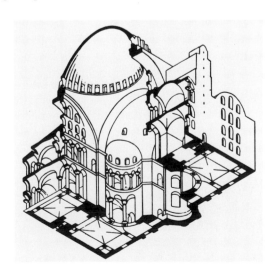

4-31
Hagia Sophia.
(Isometric
view after
W. MacDonald)

have dared to imagine, let alone build the resulting structure, for it was not only unconventional but extremely risky.

Hagia Sophia was built in the amazingly short time of five years. A fortune was spent on its construction, making possible the marshaling of an army of workmen and lavish materials from the farthest shores of the Empire. The daring of the design, and perhaps the speed of the construction, made the structure unstable. Its first dome fell after an earthquake, and its replacement (in 563, with a higher profile than the original) had to be repaired after partial collapses in the ninth and fourteenth centuries. The rest of the church was in repeated need of repair. Yet despite structural flaws, the loss of most of its mosaics and gilded vaulting surfaces, and the Ottoman redecoration as a mosque, the building stands today very much as it did when completed in 537, and it offers an overwhelming, if perplexing, architectural experience. Even the official court historian, Procopius, who watched the building go up, had trouble describing it.

To begin, Anthemius and Isidorus laid out a huge rectangle, almost square, 230 feet by 250 feet. Within the rectangle, a 100-foot square was established, and four huge piers built at its corners. They rise 70 feet, at which point four arches swing across the sides of the square. Above is set a dome on pendentives, the dome itself somewhat less than a full hemisphere and articulated by forty ribs separating a continuous ring of windows at the base. Thus far the building offers no particular distinction apart from the scale of the central domed unit and the extensive fenestration and ribbing of the cupola. Its true greatness comes from the combination of the central unit with the complex figuration of forms that lie between it and the perimeter wall, the most important and adventurous of which are to the east and west. Here, twin half-domes billow out from beneath the high arches of the dome, doubling the extent of the central "nave." Each half-dome rests on three arches supported by the main piers and two smaller piers at the outer edge of the building. Within the outer two of the three arches, in turn, small half-domed apses swing out, internally supported by two levels of arcading. To the east, a short barrel-vaulted forechoir opens to the brilliantly lit main apse; the corresponding bay to the west is occupied by the barrel vault over the main entrance. Thus the nave comprises three levels of vaulting: the dome, the two main half-domes, and the four smaller half-domes (five, if we include the chancel). They define, respectively, the central square, twin half-circles, and triads of smaller half-circles (and a small rectangle) in the plan.

The central unit opens out in billowing tribunes to the east and west, but to the north and south it is confined by two levels of colonnades and above them the clerestory wall. This wall rises to huge arches and is opened in extensive fenestration. Thus, the building does not develop uniformly in all directions, but only with bilateral symmetry. Therefore, even though it has an immense domed core, it also possesses a strong longitudinal axis, a central nave that dominates the interior within a peripheral zone of aisles and galleries that are screened off from the nave by the double levels of arcades mentioned above.

Brilliant in design, Hagia Sophia is not entirely secure structurally. The main piers are of exceptional solidity, built of massive ashlar masonry. The rest of the building, however, was erected of brick in thick mortar beds; this technique had developed in late antiquity in Asia Minor and in its perfected form permitted firm vaulting that was wide-spanned, yet thin and light. But even if comparatively light in weight, the huge dome of Hagia Sophia generates immense thrust. Moreover, the dome is not set solidly on a massive cylindrical base, as at the Pantheon, but is perched high in the air. In the corners the thrust is absorbed by the pendentives, but what of the sides? To the east and west, the half-domes swing up to abut the dome, and the architects calculated—it now seems, correctly—that the half-domes, thin though they were, would absorb the eastwest forces. The unresolved problem lay to the north and south: here the dome tottered freely in the air. Despite the massive buttressing set up at the lower levels, considerable "movement" occurred above the aisles and galleries. The lateral arches, though extraordinarily deep and thick, actually were pushed outward by the immense domical pressures. The stresses set up by these distortions weakened the dome. The wonder is not that the dome, or parts of it, fell several times, but that the building still stands at all.

Our amazement at the endurance of the precarious structure is matched by the aesthetic bewilderment the building has generated among historians and scholars; no two of them agree in their interpretation. Indeed, it is the experience of the building and not its design that is so baffling. This has to do with the complexity and high degree of ambiguity in its every aspect, from its space and structure down to the finest details. Perhaps the most important of these features is the great number of levels of structure that envelop the central space at Hagia Sophia. Three levels of domical structure are built up above arcaded screens, each level larger or more complete than the one below—the small apses, the great half-domes, and the lofty central cupola. The secondary and tertiary levels not only expand the central domed-square of space, but they also create a dazzling buildup of scale from the still human scale of the columnar arcades, through the ever-larger partial domes, to the high central vault. The awesome effect is intensified at the secondary and tertiary levels where the two half-domes form a binary cupola embracing the greater dome, supported by a ringlike chain of smaller half-domes. The space that swells and expands so voluminously upward and along the east-west axis is contained by the columnar screens and arching clerestory walls on the north and south, which seem to be flattened versions of the apsidal screens and vaults to the east and west. The continuities of levels and of the patterns of arcades and fenestration around all sides of the interior create the effect of an immense octagonal space distended but recognizably octagonal, or, more precisely, forming an octagonal polyconch. Thus the building is at once centralized and longitudinal in orientation, square and octagonal in form, and four levels high!

The effect of Hagia Sophia is made still more ambiguous and spellbinding by the nature of the containing forms. Once again, nothing seems simple or defined. Much of the containing frame takes the form of columnar screens through which the central space filters off into the shadowy areas of the peripheral, second "shell" of space that surrounds the "octagonal" core. Elsewhere, levels of fenestration pierce the building's skin in rhythmic groups of three, five, and seven (echoing the rhythms of the colonnades). The base of the dome is pierced by a ring of sizable windows so closely spaced that visually they seem to dissolve the foot of the vault into a continuous ring of light. Below the dome, the pendentives float up mysteriously from points. Like the pendentives, the half-domes seem pure stretched surfaces, for nowhere is the actual thickness of the vaulting allowed to show. The surfaces of the half-domes flow unbroken onto the arches, which meet the pendentives along a line revealing nothing of the thickness of the arches themselves, and similarly with the half-domes below. The lateral arches, to the north and south, are in fact of immense depth, but only a minimal portion of the depth can be seen in the interior. Other massive structural features are similarly masked, including the enormous main piers. The surfaces in the nave are dissolved into color, light, and pattern. In the vaults, this effect of dematerialization is achieved by gold-ground mosaics, gleaming and shimmering surfaces punctuated by only a few images of sacred symbols. The mosaic decoration is largely lost now, but the walls of the nave miraculously preserve what was among the greatest examples of marble incrustation of the ancient world. Disposed in carefully calculated zones framed by delicate moldings, most of the incrustation consists of variegated marble slabs, generally set up in pairs with veining patterns arranged in bilateral, butterfly-like symmetry. But the most elaborate mural decoration occurs in the spandrels of the main arcades—bands, friezes, and in-filling of abstract foliate patterns of extraordinary intricacy and refinement (see fig. 4-1). It is worked with the background so deeply undercut as to give the surface an appearance of lacelike fragility.

This means of denying the solid, structural substance of the building was also applied to the most concentrated foci of decoration—the capitals. Although they nearly all ultimately derive from the Classical Ionic and Corinthian orders, the distance of formal separation is so great as almost to break the thread of connection. Displaying vestigial volutes, the squashed "Ionic" capitals of the galleries, surmounted by huge, lacy impost blocks, and the basketlike voluted forms of the main arcades appear to have little to do with the Classical models beyond the most superficial reminiscences (see fig. 4-1).

While the complexity of conception and detail in Hagia Sophia is spellbinding, the building's unique qualities become even clearer when compared to the Pantheon, its Roman counterpart. Justinian surely had Hadrian, as well as Solomon, in mind as a rival from the past. But whereas the Pantheon presents a monumental Corinthian facade to the world, Hagia Sophia's exterior merely follows the interior volumes (the building was entered through a vast atrium and several cross-narthexes). Within the Pantheon, an elemental clarity and palpability of forms pervade the pure, centralized space. How different Hagia Sophia: At once square and octagonal, centralized and yet longitudinal, these studied ambiguities are made still more uncertain by the screenlike, glittering frame. And where the Pantheon's interior is flooded with a lucid illumination from a single, huge oculus and pierced by a single sunbeam that follows the day's passage, Hagia Sophia's light filters in mysteriously from the aisles and galleries, and everywhere a theatrical configuration of windows creates a luminous dance. In this mysterious light, the vaulting, seemingly without thickness or weight, shimmers and floats magically, in contrast to the visual effect of the Pantheon's hemisphere, whose coffering, if anything, illusionistically extends the perceived thickness and tangibility of the dome. Perhaps most striking is how in the Pantheon one is drawn to stand at the center to experience a profound unity with the vast low-lying rotunda, symbol of the

Imperial Roman world and the Olympian heavens. In Hagia Sophia, the observer's position and perceptions are never clear, the surrounding forms never palpable or referential to mundane reality. The great vault (colorplate 21) does not reach down to enfold one at the center, but floats impossibly high, a distant, symbolic vision of a perfection unattainable in this life—truly, as Procopius wrote, "A golden dome suspended from Heaven."

Other Justinianic Structures. Hagia Sophia was not Justinian's only notable architectural monument, but none of the other buildings approached the grandeur of his great Cathedral. Yet Byzantine architecture continued to evolve over nearly a millennium, and, in many ways, Justinian's lesser buildings provided

4-32 Interior, SS. Sergius and Bacchus

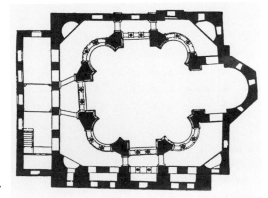

4-33
Plan, SS.
Sergius and
Bacchus.
Constantinople.
527–36

more of a point of departure for subsequent development than did Hagia Sophia. No church of later Byzantine times was much more than half the scale of Hagia Sophia, and later builders looked on it as a kind of architectural miracle.

Two structures form intermediaries between Hagia Sophia, the architecture of late antiquity, and usual Byzantine practice. Both are relatively small and schematically related to Hagia Sophia, but without its visionary scale and intricacies. SS. Sergius and Bacchus (figs. 4-32, 4-33), also in Constantinople, was built as a palace chapel between 527 and 536, so few years before Hagia Sophia that historians tend to regard it as a kind of experimental model for the great cathedral. The execution of the building evidently involved the adaption of a bold, new design to a constricted site, resulting in noticeable deformations. But the building has such a voluptuous spatial character that the distortions hardly matter. SS. Sergius and Bacchus was a further development of the centralized "double-shell" type seen earlier at S. Lorenzo in Milan and its antecedents. Where the Milanese prototype was based on a square, the plan of SS. Sergius and Bacchus formed an octagon, set loosely within a noncongruent square; the double-storied screens of the sides of the octagon were alternatingly flat and apsidial, with a chancel pushing deeply off to the

east—all schematically reminding one of Hagia Sophia. But here the stress was on the rhythmic ebb-and-flow of the octagon, a pulse that was echoed in the vault and the alternatingly flat and rounded sides—the whole soft and organic in feeling.

S. Vitale in Ravenna (figs. 4-34–4-36), begun in about 526 with Italy still under the Ostrogoths but completed later under Byzantine rule, was a much stricter version of a similar scheme. Again the "double-shell" plan comprised a domed octagonal core, with wedge-shaped piers framing two-storied, apsidial columnar screens, with a deep chancel running off to the east. But the plan was more disciplined than that of SS. Sergius and Bacchus. The outer shell as well as the inner were octagonal so that the aisles and galleries comprised a series of uniform trapezoidal spaces in place of the oddly shaped periphery of SS. Sergius and Bacchus, and the sides of the octagonal core were now uniformly apsidial. The feeling of strictness was reinforced by the taller, more "erect" proportions of the interior, and by the regular shape of the cloister-vaulted dome. The exterior, too, embodied precision in design and execution, with a bold buildup of crisply articulated and beautifully proportioned volumes that were surely more than a mere reflection of the interior. Other notable features included the narthex—purposely, it seems, set at an axial slant to heighten the effect of

4-34 S. Vitale. Ravenna. Begun c. 526

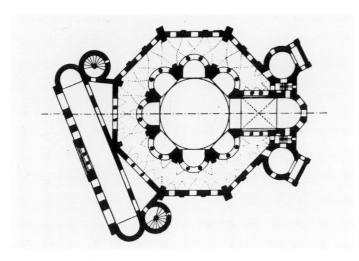

4-35 Plan, S. Vitale

4-36 Interior from ambulatory, S. Vitale

vistas through columnar screens in the aisles—and the decoration, which had marble paneling and capitals closely related to those in Hagia Sophia, and famous mosaic panels of Justinian, Theodora, and their court on the chancel walls.

None of Justinian's other numerous foundations shared the brilliance of Hagia Sophia and its two small relatives. Indeed, the other churches of the period were so sober in conception, so alike one another fundamentally, that they may be said to represent a kind of "standard" design. In terms of Imperial patronage, they represented, perhaps, the more practical side of Justinian's personality. This standard architectural mode was based on two principles: 1. All buildings included at least one unit of the domed-cube module outlined earlier in this chapter, rather than the octagonal form of the examples studied so far (the square core of Hagia Sophia forming part of a more-than-square configuration); this domed cube usually included small, but well-defined, areas beneath each of the four sustaining arches so that in practice the unit might be called a "domed cross." 2. Despite the employment of a power-

ful centralized unit, none of the buildings was purely centralized, for in one way or another centrality was combined with the older longitudinal church form. This adaptation had two modes (with intermediate solutions): either the domed-cube-cross module was repeated along the horizontal axis, or the domed-cross was set into a basilican matrix, forming a "domed basilica."

Logically, the former type was favored for large buildings, the latter for churches of intermediate and small scale. Two fine examples of the multiple-dome form, both famous martyria, were built by Justinian: the Church of the Holy Apostles in Constantinople of 536–50, and the Church of St. John the Evangelist (begun before 548) at his tomb in the Hellenistic city of Ephesus on the coast of Asia Minor. Although neither of these Justinianic churches survives, a relatively good picture of both buildings has been reconstructed. The two churches differed mainly in plans: The Holy Apostles was a pure Greek cross of five domed-cross units; at Ephesus, the western arm included an extra unit, emphasizing the main east-west axis of the church as well as increasing its capacity to hold crowds of pilgrims. In both churches the cross-domed main units were encased within a continuous outer shell of aisles and galleries separated from the nave by columnar screens. A remarkably faithful Romanesque version of the Holy Apostles was the famous church of S. Marco in Venice (1063–94; colorplate 22; figs. 4-37, 4-38). Except for a few Western modifications—the gallery screens omitted and an immense hall-crypt and side chapels added—the Venetian church is so Byzantine in scheme and in the use of precious marbles in revetment and columns (much ornament being in fact Byzantine spoils), and in the sheathing of the vaulting with gold-ground mosaics that it is often included in Byzantine, rather than Romanesque, chapters of architectural history. In S. Marco, as presumably in its lost prototype, the dome on pendentives, the cubic spatial core, the columnar screens, and the coloristic revetment achieve the same dematerialization of structure and dissolving of tangible substance into surface, color, and light as at Hagia Sophia. But in the latter cathedral, the space itself expands fluidly from the central axis into secondary and tertiary zones. In the two major standard Justinianic buildings and S. Marco, the spatial forms are discrete entities. Nave bays, aisles, and galleries are clearly segregated and defined; they stand side by side rather than flowing organically from the center. The combination of centralizing and longitudinal orientation is not one of subtle fusion, but of a simple additive combination of centralized modules arranged along horizontal axes.

The lesser standard churches—more pointedly combining domical and basilican forms—exhibit similar properties and at the same time manifest the flexibility of the common style. At the Church of Hagia Irene (colorplate 23) in Constantinople, in its post-537 form (changed to the present state in 740), a barrel-vaulted, square "nave" bay led to an eastern bay carrying a pendentive vault, the whole terminated by an apse. A variant of this scheme was the so-called Basilica B at Philippi in northern Greece, of which only the foundations remain. Once again, a barrel-vaulted nave was succeeded by a domed central bay, but the latter was flanked by two deep, barrel-vaulted transept arms. A third, simplified version of what we might call the domed-basilica type of Philippi was the basilica at

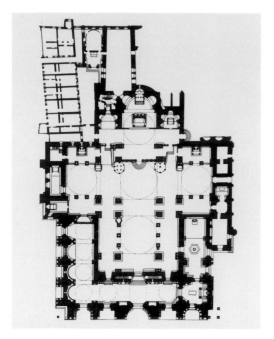

4-37
Plan, S. Marco.
Venice.
1063–94

4-38   Air view. S. Marco

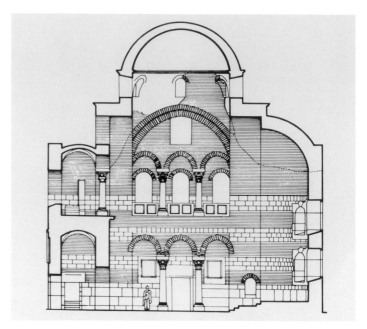

4-39   Basilica at Qasr-ibn-Wardan, longitudinal section. Syria.
c. 564. (Drawing by Enzo di Grazia after H. C. Butler)

the absence of north and south cross-arms—the east-west extension together with the apse providing the vestigial longitudinal emphasis. The church at Qasr-ibn-Wardan, located at a military outpost far from the capital, was built in Roman rubble concrete with imported brick facing and Syrian limestone detail, and it included such peculiar features as squinches and slightly pointed arches; it was very small (43 by 56 feet), a mere corner of Hagia Sophia. Yet in many ways its rather provincial features indicated the future direction of Byzantine architecture.

Medieval Byzantine Architecture (after Justinian). Byzantine architecture after Justinian is usually divided into several phases that follow the political and cultural history of the period: the "Dark Ages" (610–842), a turbulent, architecturally meager time during which Byzantium's energy was sapped in fighting powerful invaders (Arabs, Persians, Bulgars, and others) and in fierce religious controversy that culminated in Iconoclasm (rejection of religious images); the Middle Byzantine Renaissance (842–1204) when the Empire, though much reduced from Justinian's day, was relatively stabilized and seemed to reach a peak in a flowering of the arts; finally, the Late Byzantine phase (c. 1267–1453) during which the Paleologian dynasty ruled over a diminishing Empire which retained a surprising artistic creativity.

The vast and moving spectacle of these long Byzantine centuries—during most of which Byzantium awed Europeans either with its actual greatness or its afterimage—runs as a fascinating, sometimes inverted parallel to the history of the West. There, too, a dark period followed the collapse of Roman Imperial authority, from which at the end of the millennium a new civilization emerged. Medieval Europe artistically reached its high point between the eleventh and thirteenth centuries, lagging slightly behind the Byzantine peak. While the declining Byzantine state was being gradually torn apart in its last two centuries, the European medieval system struggled against internal forces of change. The Late Middle Ages

Qasr-ibn-Wardan in Syria (c. 564; fig. 4-39). Here a single domed-cross unit dominated the few compressed remnants of the basilican form—to the east, an apse and side chambers (contained within a straight outer wall, following Syrian custom); to the north and south, aisles and galleries behind triple arcades, repeated toward the narthex-gallery to the west. The church would have been almost perfectly centralized but for "waned" in Europe with a late artistic blooming not unlike the Paleologian phenomenon, and finally the Renaissance emerged in the same century as the fall of Constantinople.

Although post-Justinianic architecture is usually treated in separate phases, it can legitimately be seen as variations of what might be called medieval Byzantine architecture. This term implies a twofold relationship with Western medieval architecture: the two shared certain formal characteristics, and both differed significantly from the architecture of the ancient world.

It is possible to stress the differences between Hagia Sophia and archetypal Classical structures, such as the Pantheon; it is also possible to see that both buildings share fundamental

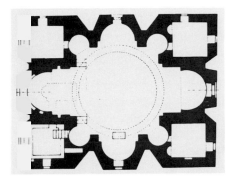

4-40
Plan, St. Hripsime. Vagharshapat, Armenia. 618. (Drawing by Enzo di Grazia after J. Strzygowski)

4-41   St. Hripsime

4-42   Interior, St. Hripsime

properties not found in medieval Byzantine structures—the grandeur, expansiveness, and suppleness of ancient architecture. Hagia Sophia was still within the architectural frame of antiquity. However, despite the amplitude and magnificence of Justinian's great martyria, their spaces no longer flowed and their structures had become hard and sharply defined. In them the organic character of ancient architecture began to disappear. Thus already in Justinian's day, Byzantine architecture had become perceptibly "medievalized." The validity of the distinctions rests on clear formal criteria. Just as Classical Byzantine architecture still embodied the antique architectural "unities," and formal and spatial fluidity, so medieval Byzantine architecture shared with the European medieval movement opposite proclivities: systematic fragmentation of space, abstract prismatic forms, and an inclination to build large buildings of small, fragmented units. These tendencies of medieval Byzantine architecture were strongly recognizable in the bold new style that was created in Armenia in the late sixth and early seventh centuries.

Of the diverse types of known Armenian churches perhaps the one that was most characteristic was St. Hripsime at Vagharshapat, built in 618 (figs. 4-40–4-42). Its scheme embodied an intricate configuration of sharply defined spaces and volumes. From the domed center radiated four apsed cross-arms, separated by cylindrical diagonal niches, forming what is called a cross-octagon. The complex spatial core of the building was encased within a rectangular shell—the corners formed by four identical "sacristies" and the apses flat on the exterior in rectilinear alignment. In plan, the spatiality seems bold and generous, not unlike antique and Byzantine polygonal designs (on which it ultimately depends), but in reality a quite different effect is obtained. Like other Armenian churches, St. Hripsime was built of Roman concrete but faced in massive ashlar masonry, in which the ponderous substance of each block is displayed. This technique was derived from Early Christian Syrian construction. Not only were the components of the wall-facing massive, but the walls themselves were thick and shaped to emphasize unrelieved masonry volume. Much in the manner that we shall later observe in Romanesque architecture, piers and arches were layered to emphasize their thickness; moldings were few and austere; and what decoration there was remained crude, if strong. Space was not active and expansive, but cramped, fragmented, inert, and dominated by the dense stone mass from which it seemed hollowed.

This anticlassical interior style was complemented on the exterior. The rectangular perimeter was broken rhythmically by deep V-shaped niches separating the apses and sacristies, which not only created a bold play of light and shadow, but emphasized the density of the prismatic masonry, an effect reinforced by the austerity of detail. Although in fact the exterior closely reflected the interior, the effect was of dense masonry cubes, prisms, and polygons rather than the earlier one of a masonry skin around voluminous spaces. Moreover, these austere forms were built upward in a powerful massing—low corner cubes, polygonal drum, and pyramidal roof. We have earlier seen a few exceptions to the general abnegation of external monumentality by Early Christian and Byzantine builders in S. Vitale, Trier Cathedral, and Qalat Siman. But in St. Hripsime—even if on a surprisingly small scale (only 56 by 69 feet in plan) as in most Armenian churches—a compact and powerful style was achieved inside and out, exterior massing and internal volumes appearing as if carved from one massive masonry block. With their intricately fragmented spaces within a compact external shell, Armenian buildings such as St. Hripsime suggest much of what is found in later mainstream medieval Byzantine architecture.

Middle Byzantine Renaissance. All of the subsequent phases of Byzantine architecture are still inadequately understood. Much of what was built in the capital has been altered or lost; dating and even the identification of many buildings are uncertain. In the provinces, the picture is frequently still more blurred. The main directions, however, can be securely set out. Nothing truly radical was built. Like the Byzantine state and religion, later Byzantine architecture was conservative. The typical Byzantine church now comprised the same components as a building such as at Qasr-ibn-Wardan: a domed core, a triple sanctuary to the east, and an outer, ancillary shell of space around the other three sides. But the formation of these elements became much more intricate and involved.

Perhaps the main reason that the underlying scheme did not radically change was that liturgical practices remained relatively consistent. From the beginning, Christian architecture was shaped closely around the ritual of the mass, and later Byzantine architecture also conformed to this practice. Ritual and its architectural frame meshed like a well-oiled machine. The elements for the mass were stored and prepared in the two sacristies alongside the chancel—the prothesis (for the Eucharist) and the diaconicon (for the Gospel book). From these chambers departed the two processions that punctuated the service: the Little Entrance, as it was called, when the Gospel book was brought to the altar, and the Great Entrance for the Eucharistic elements. Both processions moved in a circular path—rather than the linear one of the Western church—from the prothesis or diaconicon into and around the domed central area; the priests and attendants carried the holy objects past the congregation and then quickly disappeared into the chancel for the celebration proper. The most monumental area of the small church thus functioned as a kind of stage for the processional display of sacred objects.

The perfected integration of architecture, ritual practices, and doctrine was made possible through a conservative architectural evolution over centuries. It also involved a complex system of symbolism that was projected onto the building. A church was the Lord's Temple; the chancel represented the Seat of Mercy (as well as the Sepulcher and the site of the Last Supper); and the dome symbolized the Realm of Heaven. A canonical system of mosaic and fresco decoration was simultaneously evolved: above the nave, where Christ was revealed both as The Word (the Gospels) and as Flesh Incarnate (the Eucharistic elements), the awesome image of Christ Pantocrator (Judge) looked down from the cupola. Below him, in the curve of the cupola, were arranged the angelic host; in the pendentives and lunettes were scenes of the Life and Passion of Christ; the lower vaulting and walls were covered with figures of apostles, prophets, and martyrs; the Last Judgment took up the entrance wall; and opposite it, the Virgin was visible in the chancel apse. Thus, what the medieval Byzantine church lacked in scale and in dynamic architectural development was compensated by a glittering integration of the architectural program and all levels of function and meaning.

The most common type of medieval Byzantine church is the so-called cross-in-square or quincunx (five-spot) scheme. The main body of the church is laid out in a square grid of nine bays: a domed central core; radiating cross-arms, barrel- or groin-vaulted; and lower, vaulted corner units, which after the eleventh century appear on the exterior as four domed drums that set off the main vault. To the east, this compact form opens to the sanctuary. An outer shell of ancillary space typically envelops these core elements: to the west, almost always a narthex (sometimes a double narthex) with its own vaulting, even domes; and to the north and south, particularly in Constantinople, enclosed aisles or open porticoes, sometimes with secondary apsed chapels of their own.

This compact, efficient plan was clearly announced in Emperor Basil I's imposing church, the Nea Ecclesia of 880, built in the Imperial palace. Long since destroyed, the building is known in its outlines and in reflections in Constantinopolitan churches down through the twelfth century. The best-known extant example is the Bodrum Camii (the Myrelaion), a monastic church built around 920 (figs. 4-43, 4-44). Though poorly preserved, this building embodies the quincunx type in the sophisticated style of the capital. A double-storied building with a smaller cross-in-square configuration at the lower level, the church retains its noble proportions, elegant pumpkin dome, refined details, and strong but restrained exterior articulation of blind arches and unusual semicircular buttressing. Better preserved examples are seen a century later in Greece—at Salonika, where the Constantinopolitan external style is exaggerated at the Panaghia Chalkeon (1028), and at the Church of Theotokos at the Monastery of Hosios Loukas in Phocis, central Greece, where four slender columns stand at the center of the quincunx. The planar exterior of the latter is typical of Byzantine Greece, its surface dissolved with windows and with color and texture (fig. 4-45). The detailing includes intricately carved marble work, dog tooth brick friezes, and a masonry technique known as cloisonné, in which each stone is framed by one or two layers of brickwork. Such buildings seem airy and elegant in contrast to the austere Armenian churches and the more plastically conceived Constantinopolitan structures.

Although the cross-in-square type was prevalent, more elaborate forms appeared contemporaneously. In them, the exterior tended to remain closed and cubic, with the interior volumes manifested only in the apses and domes. But the interiors could be carved into intricate spatial configurations. The two most important of these forms—both of which set octagonal configurations into squares—are the octagon-domed plan and the Greek cross-octagon. The most significant example of the former is the Nea Moni in Chios (fig. 4-46), an Imperial foundation built by Constantinopolitan architects between 1042 and 1056. The entrance formation is particularly elaborate and elegant: a triple-domed, double-apsed outer narthex and an inner narthex with a single dome and barrel-vaulted "aisles." Although the plan of the central space is nominally square, it becomes more complex as it rises: the wall is hollowed into triads of rectangular niches in the lower zone, scooped out into concave forms above, and finally becomes an octagon with huge vaulted squinches over the corners, surmounted by pendentives and a circular dome. The original marble revetment and much of the mosaics remain to

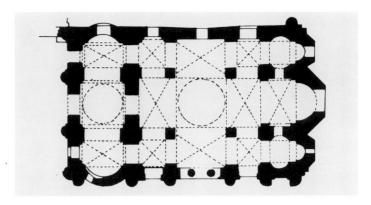

4-43　Plan, Bodrum Camii. Constantinople. c. 920. (Drawing by Enzo di Grazia after A. van Milligen)

4-44　Bodrum Camii from northwest

give a clear idea of the sumptuous impression that the sophisticated building once made.

Perhaps even more impressive is the cross-octagon, which integrates cross-in-square and octagon-domed schemes, as exemplified at the Katholikon Church at the Monastery of Hosios Loukas (1020) and at the Church of the Dormition in Daphni (c. 1100). The former is one of the most brilliant Byzantine designs (colorplate 24). The central core is octagon-domed, square below but transformed through squinches into an octagon above, surmounted by a dome on pendentives. This core is set within a two-storied outer shell into which barrel-vaulted cross-arms penetrate from the core, and the whole is dissolved by openings in the narrow piers and by arches. The space thus begins as a cube, becomes an octagon, a cupola, and a cross, and interpenetrates a secondary belt of structure (though with boundaries and distinctions always clear, unlike Hagia Sophia). The interior is pervaded by light from many sources, and the surfaces are dissolved into the color and pattern of marble revetment and what remains of the once complete cycle of mosaics.

4-45　Katholikon and Theotokos churches, Monastery of Hosios Loukas. Phocis, Greece

4-46　Interior, Nea Moni. Chios, Greece

The church at Daphni, stripped of revetment but with much of the splendid mosaics extant, presents the same scheme in a single-storied version, and the simplification of forms achieves a classic balance and harmony in contrast to the restless excitement of the Katholikon. The sense of elegant proportions is particularly resonant on the exterior (colorplate 20).

These examples of Middle (mid-medieval) Byzantine architecture, diverse as they are, share strong common denomina-tors of concept and style. The ultimate derivation of the vari-ous types from the Classical Byzantine period is perceptible, but the forms are much reduced in scale and, while spatially fragmented, perfectly centralized and integrated. The loose-ness and expansiveness of Justinianic architecture is gone. Here all is tautly disciplined. Space no longer "breathes" but seems almost airless. Architectural gestures are no longer bold and sweeping, but nervous and constrained; what is lacking in sheer power is compensated by concentrated, tense energy. Within simple, cubic, outer forms are created internal geometries of high complexity with perfect functionalism. Although this systematic abstraction has strong medieval par-allels, there remains much that is Byzantine and not medieval in character. We may call the period medieval Byzantine, but not Byzantine medieval. What makes the two churches of Hosios Loukas still very Byzantine is their dependence on the great Classical Byzantine buildings such as Hagia Sophia. Medieval Byzantine art, as well as architecture, derives from earlier models and maintains this connection even when the style becomes dry and abstract. A famous art historian, Adolph Goldschmidt, wrote that Byzantine art preserved and trans-mitted Classical art in desiccated form, like "dehydrated food-stuffs that are inherited from household to household and can be made digestible by the application of moisture and heat" (the Renaissance). Comparing Hagia Sophia with the Nea Moni and the Katholikon, one receives very much the impres-sion of the latter two being essentially "dehydrated" versions of the former.

Late Byzantine Architecture. Nea Moni and the Katholikon appear so fully evolved as to preclude further development. Yet a significant number of examples of Late Byzantine architecture achieved just this feat. Now the possibilities of the medieval Byzantine architectural system were pushed to the limit and, according to some critics, beyond the point where balance and harmony were possible, into excess and mannerism.

Although fine churches continued to be built in the late period in Constantinople, the atmosphere of the past was too strong and the city too conservative to permit the exaggeration of form that now represented stylistic advancement. Only in the provinces were more basic changes possible. At Mistra, for example, one of the last Byzantine outposts in the Peloponnesus, a whole city of churches was preserved. Among them was the Pantanassa, built in 1428, which is literally a domed basilica (fig. 4-47). The lower story was a Western-style, three-apsed, three-aisled basilica (each bay of the aisles, however, pendentive domed), but above, at gallery level, rose a cross-in-square church! With a similar retrospective eclecticism, the fascinating Parigoritissa church at Arta (c. 1283–96) combined the scheme of the Katholikon of Hosios Loukas with the multilayered interior articulation of Nea Moni at Chios, the latter now pushed to extremes of complexity. But the most intriguing developments occurred outside the shrinking Empire itself, in the neighboring kingdom of Serbia, whose importance peaked historically in the fourteenth century; there the spatial imagination of Byzantine architecture was carried to its most intense and exaggerated expression in the

4-48   Church. Gračanica, Yugoslavia. c. 1318–21

church at Gračanica (c. 1318–21; fig. 4-48). The design began innocently as a cross-in-square, but then the scheme was elevated above the "shoulders" of a ground zone of barrel-vaulting that formed the outer parts of a cross-in-square scheme of its own. Thus the whole was built upward with immense complexity, generating a startling effect with this vertiginous ascent, which was intensified by the extreme steepness of the interior bays. Byzantine architecture tended to be steep rather than broad ever since the Nea Ecclesia, but never to the extremes seen here, where the central bay rose to a height six times its diameter, and the domes of the corner bays *eight* times their base. The exterior—unlike the static massings of Middle Byzantine architecture—was built up in wave upon wave as the steep, intricate interiors were exploited for their external volumetric dynamism: corner tympana, domes, lower cross-arms, upper cross-arms, drums, and finally the main dome. In Late Byzantine architecture there was often a mannered preciousness, but examples such as Gračanica showed that Byzantium, just as it managed to hang onto its political life against all odds, remained a living architecture to the end.

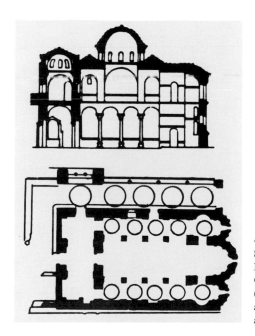

4-47
Section and plan,
Pantanassa. Mistra,
Greece. 1428.
(Drawing by Lampl
after Hatzidakis
and Sotiriou)

5-1
Octagon,
Palatine
Chapel.
Aachen,
Germany.
c. 796–805

Chapter Five | Pre-Romanesque and Romanesque Architecture

CAROLINGIAN PRE-ROMANESQUE

In the year 800 the darkness of the centuries following the collapse of Rome seemed suddenly to recede into past history, for on Christmas day Charlemagne was crowned Holy Roman Emperor by Pope Leo III in Rome. Through military and administrative brilliance, the great king of the Franks had brought a large part of Europe, an area of true Imperial magnitude, under his sway, and with this, the expectations of a renewal of European civilization.

Three hundred years before Charlemagne, the Western Roman Empire had been fragmented into a mosaic of regional and tribal states by waves of barbarian invasions, one of the many blows that destroyed ancient life. The decaying tissue of Classical civilization grew ever weaker, and between the sixth and early eighth centuries, Greco-Roman culture disintegrated. Latin was displaced as the living, common language, and with it expired Classical literary traditions. The body of Roman law gave way, the victim of diverse customs and rules dispensed by local tribes. Along the Mediterranean, trade was brought to a halt following the invasions, resulting in a depressed economy and the virtual cessation of urban life. Classical civilization had been eminently urban, but cities now all but ceased to exist. Rome itself, which had numbered one million inhabitants, shrank to less than fifty thousand. Most settlements were what we would call villages, and in place of the vast social range of Classical antiquity, in the early Middle Ages the population of Europe was mainly peasants, priests, and warriors.

The end of Roman political and social institutions, of cities, wealth, and culture, meant a steep decline in monumental art. From about 500 to after 700 little was built. Large churches with aisles may have existed, but what survived were mostly small, boxlike structures limited to one or two rooms crudely proportioned and constructed. This architectural depression, extending over a half-dozen or more generations, caused the disappearance of the architectural skills that had taken so many centuries to perfect: Roman concrete construction; large-scale vaulting; integrated Hellenic orders; monumental planning; and the sophisticated arts of the Roman decorator—carving, painting, inlay, and mosaic.

Despite these setbacks Europe's lifeline to the antique endured. The traditions of Roman architectural practice were gone, but Roman buildings remained standing throughout Europe—looming physical presences which even in ruin inspired awe, admiration, and often imitation. While there were many areas of the ancient world where Classical ruins exerted little, if any, direct influence on later builders (for example, Greek temples in Byzantium), in the West, a number

of ideas, traditions, and institutions brought builders back to antiquity.

For one thing, the native peoples outside the Italian sphere—including those most destructive—had always been in awe of Rome. They had no monumental architecture of their own beyond some ambitious timber assemblages, and even after they shook off the Roman yoke the sense of Roman architecture as a kind of absolute ideal was transmitted from generation to generation. Of equal, if not greater, importance was the survival of the Church, which emerged in the medieval period as the major force of continuity, stability, and culture. Both the papacy and monasticism had originated in late antiquity. It was natural for the medieval Church to look back to Rome and Roman architecture, and in particular to the splendid monuments of early Christianity, as imitable relics of a Christian age when the Church had been coextensive with the Empire.

The way back to Rome, however, was led not by the Church but by the state. The last Roman emperor in the West had been deposed in 490, but the *idea* of the Empire had not died. The medieval mind perceived no uncrossable distance between itself and Rome. It did not think of itself as a "middle ages" intermediate between Rome and some future high civilization (that concept was invented by the Renaissance). In the medieval mind, in the mind of Charlemagne, the ideas of "kingdom" and "empire" were inextricably bound to Rome. The political entity that he created out of fragments of western Europe had nothing in common with the Roman political system, yet it was meant and perceived as a revival of it, reborn as the Holy Roman Empire, a realm sanctified by a close alliance with the papacy.

If the Roman Empire could be reborn in sanctified Christian form, so could Roman architecture. This rebirth did not happen by chance. Even though Charlemagne spent most of his long reign on one military campaign after another, he had time to establish a strong official policy of reviving "lapsed" Roman culture, especially that of Christian Rome of the age of Constantine, whom Charlemagne considered a model for the ruler of a universal Christian monarchy. Charlemagne's efforts met with such success that we often speak of the Carolingian Renaissance—Carolingian deriving from Carolus Magnus, the Latin for Charles the Great, or Charlemagne. Scholars were summoned to the royal court from all parts of Europe to lead this effort. Their energies were directed primarily at renewing the Latin language and literature, but the arts were not ignored.

Even before 800, a deliberate, energetic campaign to erect imposing buildings was launched by Charlemagne and his political and ecclesiastical associates. The result was an eclectic body of architecture that included not only reactionary copies of Constantinian basilicas and "barbarian" reinterpretations of antiquity, but also forward-looking innovative structures. For all their diversity, however, Carolingian buildings embodied unifying tendencies which justified their status as "PreRomanesque." Most of them looked back to Rome in one way or another, yet, not surprisingly, they never recaptured the organic, sensuous spirit of the antique style. Rather, they exhibited the capacities and sensibilities of their own time, and even the grim determination of still unsophisticated builders to imitate the great creations of the ancient world. Fortunately, Carolingian architecture made up in inventiveness and vitality for what was lacking in sophistication. It exhibited non-Roman qualities of abstraction, fragmentation, and a new volumetric energy—key aspects of later medieval architecture. Although eclectic and without clear direction, it was the first great monumental "style" of post-Classical Europe, unlike the somewhat earlier, interesting but by comparison slight, architectural achievements of the Langobards, Visigoths, Britons, or Merovingians. Even if the Carolingian style did not lead directly to the Romanesque proper, it clearly set the direction toward it.

The Buildings. The Palatine Chapel, built about 796–805 at Charlemagne's palace in Aachen (Aix-la-Chapelle), is the preeminent surviving Carolingian structure (figs. 5-1–5-4). A domed, double-shelled, two-storied octagon, it presents a type reminiscent of Early Christian and Byzantine architecture. Indeed, it is generally accepted that the Palatine Chapel was modeled closely after S. Vitale in Ravenna and was perceived as an antique revival. To the analytical modern eye, however, it is the differences between the chapel and S. Vitale that are of crucial importance. The spatial conception of S. Vitale is one of late antique fluidity: The central space flows upward and around the complex surfaces of the vault and into the swelling, arcaded niches. There is no such fluidity in the chapel, but instead sharp definition everywhere. A heavy cornice separates the ground floor from the upper stories; space is precisely contained by the crisp planes of the octagonal cloister vault and the straight columnar screens of the octagon. In S. Vitale, the octagonal shape of inner and outer shells causes the groin vaults over the ambulatory to take irregular forms. In the Palatine Chapel, the outer wall is built over a sixteen-sided plan, which makes for regular ambulatory patterns: rectangular compartments opposite the sides of the inner octagon and triangular spaces at the corners. These spaces are spanned by a series of barrel vaults tailored to the alternating rectangular and triangular plans.

Differences between Aachen and Ravenna are even greater at the gallery level. The S. Vitale gallery needed only a lightweight timber roof because the central vault was reduced in weight, having been built largely using rings of empty amphorae. But this sophisticated construction technique, a late antique invention, was unknown to Charlemagne's architect. His massive vault needed stabilization in the octagonal wall below. A ring of powerful buttressing was provided by radial, inclined barrel vaulting in the gallery running up over most of the bays to the octagonal core. This vaulting system provides a key to the genesis and meaning of the whole chapel

5-2   Facade, Palatine Chapel

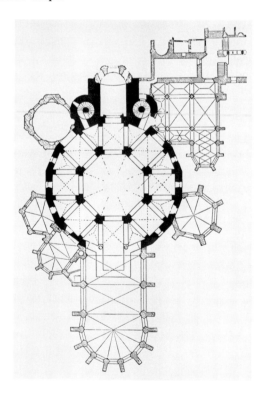

5-3
Plan, Palatine
Chapel (original
in black)

design, for such a ring of vaults derives from Roman theaters and arenas. It was most fully achieved at the Colosseum, a building famous throughout the Middle Ages. ("So long as the Colosseum stands, so shall Rome; when the Colosseum falls, so shall Rome, and with it the world," wrote the Venerable Bede, the eminent eighth-century English theologian and historian, from whose school Charlemagne's court scholar,

5-4 Palatine Chapel, cross section. (After Kubach)

forming the fundamental concept of the basilica. The Early Christian type had low, long, static units of space, mostly running parallel lengthwise, sometimes with one cutting across the others as a transept or narthex, with the apse a semicircular appendage. The exterior had no special character but reflected the interior geometry. At St.-Riquier this dignified but prosaic type became a more complex, dynamic building composed of independent group formations, one at either end of the church, connected by the three-aisled nave. From the traditional transept and apse, the eastern group at St.-Riquier grew into an extension outward and upward: outward by the addition of a rectangular forechoir (for the large community of monks who worshiped there), and upward into a lantern tower that soared above a newly defined crossing area. On the exterior, the tower dominated the transept, apse, and twin stair turrets that climbed up toward it.

This eastern group balanced the form developed at the entrance to the basilica, the so-called westwork. At St.-Riquier, the westwork mirrored the eastern grouping; it comprised a main cross-block, a short projecting entrance arm in place of the apse, stair turrets in the corners, and a lantern tower. Whether the shape and proportions of St.-Riquier's westwork matched the eastern grouping as closely as in the reconstructions is open

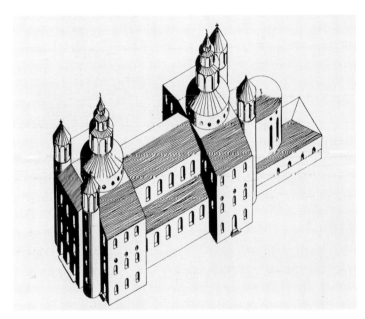

5-5 Church of St.-Riquier. Centula, France. 790–99. (Isometric reconstruction after N. Pevsner)

Alcuin, was drawn.) But Charlemagne's architect imitated the Colosseum structure not so much for the building's fame as for its design and comprehensibility. The Colosseum's rational makeup, its weight and solidity, struck chords of sympathy in an age cut off from antique traditions yet seeking to revive them as part of a new world order.

What Charlemagne and his architects did in the Palatine Chapel at Aachen, then, was to rebuild S. Vitale, one of the most impressive of late antique buildings, in the structural mode of the "classic" Roman architecture of the time of the Colosseum. This architectural synthesis gave a new direction to medieval architectural development. The emphasis on rational, strongly defined spatial units, on chains of modular construction, and on fragmentation were to be among the most distinguishing traits of Romanesque architecture.

The main entrance to the Palatine Chapel is a large structure adjoining the west side. A square mass of stone containing narthex chambers corresponding to the two levels of the chapel rises between twin cylindrical towers and is fronted by a huge entrance niche. This towering entrance structure announces one of the major themes of medieval architecture— the monumental facade—and it connects Charlemagne's chapel with another, but very different, Carolingian building, the monastic church of St.-Riquier (or Centula, 790–99, near Abbeville in northeastern France).

Although St.-Riquier was destroyed in the late Middle Ages, it has been reconstructed on the basis of old views and descriptions (fig. 5-5). Its plan recalls the Early Christian basilica, which enjoyed a new vogue under Charlemagne. This revival was also exemplified by the Abbey Church at Fulda (791–821; fig. 5-6), a lost building that seems to have copied Constantine's St. Peter's in Rome in its immense, continuous transept and unique, terminal, screened chambers. At Fulda, however, as in many Carolingian and later Germanic basilicas, there was a second, western apse at the beginning of the nave. St.-Riquier went much further in its development of the Constantinian prototype, not merely adding a feature or two but also trans-

5-6
Plan, Fulda
Abbey Church.
c. 791–821

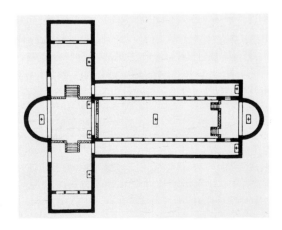

5-7 Gatehouse (Torhalle) of the Abbey. Lorsch, Germany. 767–74

to question, but the development of powerful vertical massings at both ends of the building, their counterbalancing, and their contrast to the low connecting nave, are clear enough.

The theme of the Carolingian westwork leads to another important structure of the period, this time totally intact—the Gatehouse, or Torhalle (767–74) at Lorsch, Germany. The small building, which stood at the entrance to a monastery that has all but disappeared, comprises a saddle-roofed central block flanked by twin cylindrical stair towers (colorplate 25; fig. 5-7). The lower zone of the building forms an open loggia with matching triple arcades to front and rear, while the closed area above was originally a chapel dedicated to Saint Michael. This arrangement—a two-leveled block, the lower level an aisled passage, the upper level a chapel reached by flanking stair towers, the whole forming a monumental facade—was roughly that of the westworks at Aachen and St.-Riquier. But the Torhalle is more than a detached, supplementary westwork. It also bears a telling resemblance to Roman triumphal arches, such as the one in Rome honoring Constantine. Common to both are the two-storied facades, front and back, the lower zone pierced by triple archways framed by Corinthian columns, and the whole richly ornamented. One might say that at Lorsch the westwork formula was restructured as a gatehouse in the form of a Roman triumphal arch, an illustration of the architectural fantasy and ambition for Roman revival so typical of Carolingian architects. The Carolingian imagination is also reflected in the Torhalle's decoration. Even the most Classical of the details—the Corinthian columns and fluted Ionic pilasters—are reduced from antique fullness to dry, decorative schemes. Similarly, the Roman entablature becomes a narrow frieze perched incongruously above the heavy columns, and the antique gable motif appears as a weightless zigzag line. The surface is covered not with relief sculpture in Roman fashion, but with a calculated variety of patterns of white and red stone tiles, with accents in yellow. The final result reflects the tendency toward decorative abstraction of early medieval art—a sensibility that superimposed a flat decorative pattern on the Torhalle walls rather than conceiving the arch as a sculptural organism, as it had been in antiquity.

Not every Carolingian building of significance drew on Classical models. At the time of Charlemagne, the two great world powers were Byzantium and Islam, and there is one Carolingian building that reflects the influence of both. The small church of Germigny-des-Prés (figs. 5-8, 5-9) on the Loire River, consecrated in 806 and overrestored in the nineteenth century, preserves its original plan. It was designed as a Byzantine quincunx, but with all the apses taking the horseshoe shape favored by Islamic architects. The horseshoe shape, which also appears in the supporting arches of Germigny-des-Prés, may be traced to its Islamic sources through the founder of the church, Theodulph, Bishop of Orléans, whom Charlemagne had brought from Spain—at that time the main center of contact between Europe and the culture of Islam. Although the eccentric design of Germigny-des-Prés is often viewed as anomalous, it was no more so than most of the important early medieval structures, which were one-of-a-kind inventions.

Perhaps the most impressive of all Carolingian designs is one that was never built, or even intended to be. About 820, the abbot of the important Swiss monastery at St. Gall received from another highly placed churchman a plan for a monastic complex. The large drawing, in red ink on ivory parchment, is a singular medieval document revealing how the best Carolingian minds conceived the ideal architec-

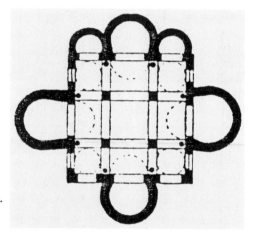

5-8
Plan, Church at Germigny-des-Prés. Near Orléans. c. 799–818

5-9 Interior, Church at Germigny-des-Prés

tural realization of monasticism—their greatest Christian institution. The drawing gives a complete outline for every building in the monastery, its details and its furnishings. The functions, and even the symbolism of certain architectural forms, are clearly spelled out. But to understand the significance of the St. Gall plan, we must first know something about monasticism.

Although the first monasteries were established in early fourth-century Egypt, the impulse on which monasticism is primarily based—the all-absorbing contemplation of God through solitude and austerity—went back to earliest Christianity, to figures such as Saint John the Baptist and Christ himself. The institutionalization of the monastic impulse, with communities of monks organized in religious orders under the control of the Church, developed with the monastic Rule, a complete set of regulations for every thought, action, minute, and hour of a monk's life. The principal religious orders were the Benedictine, founded in southern Italy in the early sixth century; the Cluniac, founded in 910 in Burgundy; the Carthusian; the Cistercian; and a variety of others. In a way reminiscent of the relationship between life and architecture under the Romans, monastic architecture was shaped around the Rule. It made life under the Rule possible, giving it physical form and at the same time symbolizing the monastic ideal.

The typical monastery, where the sequence of prayer, work, eating, and sleeping was regulated, became not only a religious retreat from the world but a center for all sorts of intellectual and manual activities. It was in the Carolingian period that the main aspects of the standard monastery were evolved; they were reflected in the dream of ideal perfection that was the St. Gall plan (figs. 5-10, 5-11). At the center of the rectangular precinct were the core structures—a large double-ended church with altars for the monks and an area for the laity at the west end, where a twin-turreted westwork was designed around a semicircular courtyard; a square cloister on the south was surrounded by arcaded porticoes around which were gathered the most essential monastic service buildings—dormitory, refectory, kitchen, and storage areas. These core buildings provided for life under the Rule. Enveloping the core were structures for the secondary and supportive activities. The library and scriptorium (a copying room for scribes) were immediately behind the church; to the north was the house of the abbot, who served as intermediary between the monastic congregation and the outer world. Near his quarters, along the north edge of the site, were the school (for the laity), the guest house for important visitors, and a coach house. Also provided was a hostelry for ordinary pilgrims to the abbey (which housed a famous relic). The subsidiary aspects of monastic life filled out the rest of the site. To the east, opposite the apse of the church, were twin cloisters serving as a school for the novices, a hospital with nearby physician's quarters, and—conveniently—the cemetery. Agrarian, artisan, and servants' quarters ran in a block along the south, while around to the west were gardens, barnyards, and stables. Artisans and craftsmen were closer to the cloister, with the mill, brewery, and bakery laid out in a rational sequence between the fields and the kitchen. Although the St. Gall plan was meant by its designer to be taken as an ideal model, there is no doubt that it actually could have been built, for it presented no

5-10 Model, Monastery of St. Gall. c. 820. (Reconstruction by Walter Horn)

5-11 Plan for a monastery. c. 820. (Chapter Library, St. Gall, Switzerland, redrawn after Pevsner)

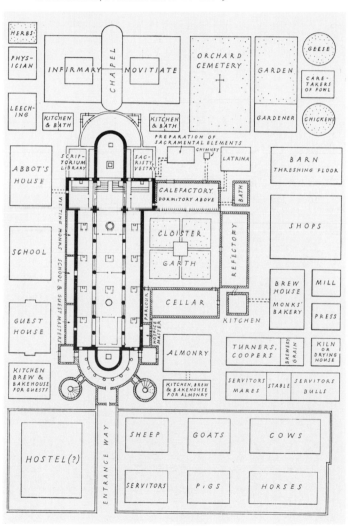

technical problems beyond the capabilities of the period. But the scope of the project obviously embodied powerful religious motivation.

In Christian thought, the blessed life is possible only in an ordered world—Saint Augustine's City of God or Heavenly Jerusalem in the world beyond, and, in the here and now, in some architectural form that reflected divine order and splendor. As we have seen, Hagia Sophia was a visionary embodiment of that concept. In a more prosaic way, and for the first time in the Middle Ages, St. Gall invoked that same vision. It conjured the architectural image of a utopian monastic world in which ideal order and perfection of utility are fused. It also evoked the image of a small but complete city, for in an age without real cities the great monasteries were the closest approximation to them. They included a number of real or counterpart urban features: the abbot's house (or town hall); the cloister (citizens' quarters; fig. 5-12); scriptoria (artists' workshops); a medical center and a cemetery; stables; and hotels. Interestingly, it was in the Carolingian period that monasteries became important cultural centers (historically one of the functions of cities), which they had not been earlier when they had barely the means to survive. It was only in a later phase of medieval civilization, beginning in the twelfth century, that the newly risen cities took over the cultural roles played by the monasteries in their architecture and artists' workshops.

The plan of the church at St. Gall also offered a solution to an important problem in medieval architecture, and one that takes us to the threshold of true Romanesque. Its U-shaped corridor crypt beneath the eastern apse provided an orderly "traffic" pattern for access to the relics of the saints that made the monastery a pilgrimage center. Relics, crypts, and altars received exceptional attention throughout the Middle Ages. Increasing masses of pilgrims and worshipers sought close contact with holy relics, which were usually kept in proximity to an altar. At St. Gall, whose scheme derives from the annular crypt built into the apse of St. Peter's in Rome (in the late sixth century) pilgrims could move along the corridor crypt and view the relics without disturbing the services that might be in progress at the high altar above. But this simple solution alone was inadequate for the problems created by the proliferation of relics, whose worth largely determined the religious importance of a given church. An ideal collection included a relic—bones, hair, splinters of the Cross—of as many important saints as possible. This growing emphasis on the importance and number of relics was reflected in the appearance of multi-aisled crypts (that could accommodate more than one relic). It also resulted in the creation of multiple altars aboveground, which satisfied the need for the growing clergy individually to celebrate mass. The early solution for the disposition of multiple altars was to scatter them around the nave, as we find at St. Gall. But more structured architectural enclosures began to emerge—niches in aisles, multiple chapels, and double-ended churches. Eventually, the annular corridor crypt was transferred aboveground, where it fanned outward into a series of radiating chapels. This innovation belongs to the Romanesque style and period.

ROMANESQUE

Charlemagne's Empire was an unstable entity dependent on his subjects' personal loyalty. His death in 814 was followed by a dark century in Europe—a time characterized not only by political chaos and cultural decline, but also by a wave of violence and terror. Western Europe was pillaged from sea and land by Slavic and Magyar horsemen from the east, Arab pirates from the Mediterranean, and Viking invaders from the north. No place was secure, least of all churches and monasteries which offered the richest plunder.

But despite this apocalyptic climate, Europe survived. The savage energy of its invaders gradually was dissipated: the Vikings settled in Normandy, converted to Christianity, and, in 911, even recognized the French king as their overlord; the Magyars were defeated in 955 and thereafter settled in Hungary; the Caliphate of Córdoba disintegrated in 1033 into a number of weaker states, opening the Iberian peninsula to eventual reconquest by western Europe. The vicious cycle of political instability, invasion, and depression gave way to an upward spiral of rising economic conditions, social and political order, military strength, the renewal of cities, and a new confidence and hope. Commerce was slowly reestablished, and with it came the gradual reappearance of tradesmen, artisans, and the other varied groups of urban life. New prosperity meant a cultural revival, which was infused with a new spirit of religious enthusiasm; this was most vividly manifest in mass pilgrimages to far-flung shrines, a movement that culminated in the Crusades—often misguided military pilgrimages to regain the Holy Land from the Muslims. The new surge of spirituality and energy led to a wave of church-building throughout Europe. Indeed, it seemed to a contemporary monk, Raoul Glaber, "as if the whole earth were putting on a mantle of white churches."

Glaber's metaphor is understandable, but it has led modern historians astray. Romanesque architecture is too often seen as an inchoate phenomenon without any orderly development—a simultaneous springing up, after 1000, of a variety of churches like a vast meadow of flowers suddenly coming into bloom. It is true that the Romanesque was largely a spontaneous, international movement. But it did not appear everywhere all at once, nor did it attain everywhere the same degree of accomplishment and influence. A mainstream

5-12   Example of a Romanesque cloister, St.-Trophime. Arles, France. 12th century

development may credibly be discerned. However, it cannot be understood apart from the complex geopolitical structure of the period.

Today we are so habituated to thinking of political sovereignty in terms of the nation-state that it is hard for us to imagine the medieval situation, in which there coexisted a variety of autonomous, sovereign entities. At the base of this political scaffolding were quasi-independent towns that began to appear in the eleventh and twelfth centuries. At the top was the Imperial sceptre of the Holy Roman Empire in its revived post-Carolingian form. Between them were a plurality of kingdoms—France, England, Burgundy—and many duchies and other aristocratic, feudal domains. In addition there was the Church: the papacy, sovereign politically only over the Papal states, but spiritually—and at times, even militarily—of great authority; powerful bishops; and the major monastic orders.

Kings, emperors, dukes, abbots, popes, and, to a degree, cities—these were the primary patrons of Romanesque (and later, Gothic, and even Renaissance) architecture. Today, advanced architectural trends tend to be uniformly national, even international, in scope. But the stylistic groupings of the Romanesque are of many types—national, regional, sometimes defined not by political boundaries but by natural features such as river basins (the Rhine, the Loire, the Po), or individuated among cities or orders in the Church. Naturally, styles of a progressive area could spread beyond its confines. Normandy is such an example, its architecture exported by the descendants of the Vikings to their new conquests—England after 1066 and, slightly later, southern Italy and Sicily. More than one medieval style, in fact, was not defined by an integral geographic area but by a common function—as in the marking of monumental shrines along the pilgrimage roads to Santiago de Compostela in Spain.

Early Romanesque in Germany, Belgium, and Normandy. Among the earliest contributions to the Romanesque mainstream was that of the reborn Holy Roman Empire, which comprised in the tenth and eleventh centuries most of what is now Germany (and subsequently Italy, whose Romanesque we will discuss later). Like so much of Romanesque architecture, the Imperial Romanesque (often called Ottonian after the founders of the new Empire) was pervaded by two antithetical tendencies, one inventive and progressive, the other conservative and nostalgic. The Imperial Romanesque looked back fondly to the works of Charlemagne, but it also drew on Early Christian, Imperial Roman, and even Byzantine models. Perhaps the most fascinating example of this retrospective tendency was the Münster (Cathedral) at Essen, begun in the late tenth century (and partially rebuilt later). The Münster was of a higher order of complexity than any church yet seen in the West (figs. 5-13, 5-14). Loosely based on the double-ended, Carolingian basilica seen at St.-Riquier and St. Gall, its interior was replete with sophisticated references to Carolingian and Byzantine models. The clerestory wall rested on an alternating file of columns and square piers—a Byzantine motif—and the aisle walls, in Byzantine fashion, were hollowed with a continuous row of niches. The forechoir opened to Byzantine-style side chambers through two tiers of double arcades. But the most intricate aspect of the cathedral lay at the west end of the building: not

5-13 Interior of western apse, Münster. Essen, Germany. Late 10th century.

5-14 Section, Münster (Cathedral). (After Zimmerman)

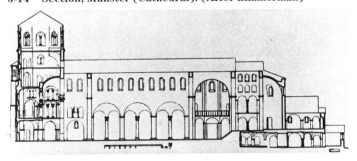

merely a western apse or a westwork, but a highly imaginative combination of both. Viewed from the nave, it presented a half-hexagonal reduction of Charlemagne's Palatine Chapel at Aachen, capped by a pendentive half-dome reminiscent of the semidomes of Hagia Sophia. This screened western apse penetrated halfway into the central bay of the Essen westwork, where an ambulatory was formed between the Carolingian screen and the west wall of the church. Twin stair turrets were set diagonally in correspondence with the sides of the half-hexagon to form internally what was in effect a three-sided, Byzantine, polygonal apse. The three- and four-part groin vaults of the ambulatory supported a gallery, similar to the arrangement at the Palatine Chapel. Above this complex interpenetration of Byzantine and Carolingian forms, the central westwork tower rose as a square, then becoming an octagonal lantern.

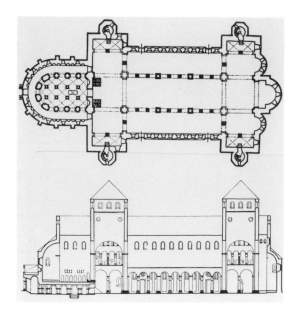

5-15 Plan and section, St. Michael's. Hildesheim, Germany. c. 1001–33. (After Beseler)

At Essen we witness a freedom in design and an energy that contrast sharply with both the perfectionist spirit of the cathedral's Byzantine models and the constricted determination of Charlemagne's architecture. Still, in the context of the larger Romanesque movement, Essen was retrospective. The future lay more with a contemporary church of the Imperial Romanesque, St. Michael's at Hildesheim (fig. 5-15), in north-

5-16 Interior, St. Gertrude. Nivelles, Belgium. 1000–46

ern Germany, built in 1001–33 (severely damaged in World War II and later rebuilt). In certain respects St. Michael's resembles the Münster in Essen—a double-ended basilica with twin transepts, rhythmic alternation of piers and columns, and complex groups of galleries in the transepts. Yet at St. Michael's these elements are developed with a new clarity. The transepts stand lucidly defined against the main longitudinal axis of the church. The square crossings are clearly segregated by powerful diaphragm arches from choir, transept, and nave. The space of the nave is implicitly subdivided into three almost square bays by the alternation of piers (a) and columns (b) in a pattern of abbabbabba. These bays almost match those of the crossings in size, and thus contribute to the rational disposition of the interior spaces, complemented by the balance of volumes on the exterior.

The aspect of St. Michael's that was perhaps most important for the future of the Romanesque was the division of its interior into discrete vertical slabs of space tending to have a square plan. This "square schematism" would eventually be developed into a highly articulated modular bay system. For the moment, however, Romanesque builders were preoccupied with the means of dividing the interior into bays. One way was to extend the use of the diaphragm arch of the crossing to the nave itself. This occurred in the contemporary (1000–46) Church of St. Gertrude at Nivelles, Belgium, an austere building in which all the supports are reduced to bare piers (fig. 5-16). The horizontal slab of space in the nave is cut into two vertically oriented cells of space, but the bays are static and inarticulate.

The turning point in this development was the Imperial Cathedral of Speyer (figs. 5-17–5-19), begun by Emperor Konrad II around 1030 and completed in its first form by 1060. This most monumental of Romanesque churches was remodeled after 1080 to make it even grander. But in the original Speyer, the grandiose east end (choir, crossing, and transepts) was balanced by an immense westwork a hundred feet in height and equally wide that served as a wall between the church and the main street of the town. Underlying the entire east end was a hall crypt that exerted a powerful impression in its mighty columns, its vigorous bays of groin vaulting, and its wall articulation. It is the latter that most interests us here, for it anticipated the articulation of the nave walls, the most remarkable formal aspect of Speyer and the one most crucial for the development of Romanesque architecture. If one compares the reconstructed view of the nave of the original cathedral with St. Gertrude, it is clear that a profound mutation has occurred in the form of the wall. Not only is the wall at Speyer of immense thickness (in relation to its height), but it is shaped into a powerful multilayered configuration. The old form—rectangular piers supporting the arcade from which the clerestory walls rise—is still present, but the arches and wall are set strongly back from the front of the piers, leaving a gap at the top of the piers. This gap is filled by a series of immense pilasters which rise to clerestory level where they support blind arches framing the windows. On this double-layered system is superimposed a third layer—elongated half-columns that rise to support a second layer of blind arcading at the top of the wall.

The nave wall of Speyer was without precedent in medieval architecture; nor was it based on any Byzantine model. Its

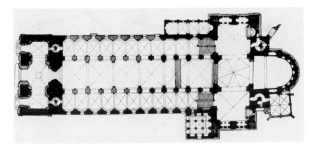

5-17 Plan, Speyer Cathedral. After 1080

5-18 Crypt, Speyer Cathedral

5-19 Nave, Speyer Cathedral. (Reconstruction drawing by Wenzel Hollar, Albertina, Vienna)

prototype was the late antique fourth-century Basilica of Constantine at nearby Trier (fig. 3-61). The massive external arcading of Trier is taken inside at Speyer, where it is further monumentalized by the third columnar layer. The proportions of these columns are distorted far beyond any limits set in antiquity; they are stretched unnaturally, lifting with immense energy to heighten the vertical sensation introduced by the proportions of the nave bays. At the early Speyer we find two factors vital to the Romanesque: the bay system and the powerful, projecting wall system of pier, pilaster, and half-column—an immense layered volume of masonry rising majestically.

To go directly to the later Speyer—a structure that epitomized High Romanesque architecture—would be to jump ahead in the story. Certain important architectural developments roughly contemporary with the original Speyer come first. Architecture in northern France closely paralleled the Imperial School, especially in Normandy where the buildings were crucial not only to the development of the Romanesque in

France, England, and Italy, but eventually also to the origins of Gothic architecture. In the early tenth century, the Vikings had settled in Normandy and adopted the "civilized ways" of Christian France. By the eleventh century their vigor was channeled into the mainstream of European history, but their energies were not yet contained, and the former invaders returned to the sea, conquered England in 1066 and shortly later colonized southern Italy and Sicily where they displaced the Byzantines and Arabs. The force of their character was expressed in their architecture.

Many important buildings of the Norman Romanesque are known, but two will illustrate its early phase. One of the most famous medieval shrines is the stunning site of Mont-Saint-Michel (figs. 5-20, 5-21), where a mid-eleventh-century church crowns a complex monastic construction on a rocky islet separated by water from the Norman coast at high tide. Mont-Saint-Michel can be regarded as a Norman counterpart to Speyer Cathedral. Its nave wall shares the advanced features of the German church: a powerful, layered structure, with sturdy pilasters rising in front of the wall to support a blind arch around the clerestory windows, projecting forward into the nave space with immense half-columns rising from the pavement, dividing the nave sharply into regular bays. But if the similarities between the two churches are obvious, so are the differences. Speyer is austere and unrelieved in its bare, massive forms. At Mont-Saint-Michel, this heaviness, which after Speyer became characteristic of much Germanic medieval architecture, is alleviated by the introduction of elements that in a typically Norman (and eventually French)

5-20 Mont-Saint-Michel. Normandy, France

5-21 Nave, south wall, Church of Mont-Saint-Michel. Mid-11th century

manner visually lighten the structure. Thus, the prismatic piers of Speyer here receive half-columns that disguise their heaviness and define the arcade they support. Similarly, we find in Mont-Saint-Michel not the unrelieved mural expanse of Speyer, but a wall visually lightened by gallery openings that also create a strong horizontal zone contrasting with the vertical lines of the elevation.

Mont-Saint-Michel is the only Norman building of its generation to survive intact. But even in ruins, the Abbey Church of Notre-Dame de Jumièges (c. 1040–67; figs. 5-22, 5-23) gives perhaps a better impression of the power of early Norman Romanesque. Here the organization of the wall is based on the double-bay system, in which alternating major and minor piers are used rather than a uniform series of complex piers. With this system, the major piers establish square (or squarish) double bays in the nave, while the minor piers assist by supporting the arcade and the intermediary wall. The resulting increase in apparent scale and texture caused the scheme to be widely used over the next century and even beyond, not only in Normandy but throughout the Imperial realm. Notre-Dame of Jumièges was especially notable, apart from its influential double bays, for the immense height of its nave and crossing tower. Part of the tower still stands, rising far above the high nave, and from it one perceives the extraordinary impression originally made by the steep shaft of space. The sharply defined energy and verve that typify this building are perhaps best preserved at its facade. Derived from the Carolingian westwork tradition, the central structure is concentrated into a steep volume of brilliant proportion and detail. It is set forward between twin bases of square towers that rise powerfully as octagons above the lines of the nave

5-22
Towers and west-
work, Notre-Dame.
Jumièges, France.
1040–67

5-23   View from the east, Notre-Dame

means to span its central nave with stone vaulting.

The first completely vaulted churches of the Romanesque were not vast structures built by ducal lords and emperors, but modest buildings erected by ordinary, grass-roots patrons in remote areas of the Pyrenees and the western Alps. In these isolated mountain valleys, removed from the mainstream of European culture, a singular architectural tradition thrived for centuries. It was what we might call folk architecture, practiced by generations of local village masons. In the manner of folk artists nearly everywhere these masons built heavily and solidly, using indigenous forms of decoration: combinations of pilaster strips and corbel friezes on external walls, and, on apses, rows of niches just under the roofs. But one of the major aspects of the style, usually heavy and inarticulate in execution, was barrel vaulting.

A particularly interesting example of this suborder of Romanesque—often referred to by the confusing name *premier art roman*, or first Romanesque style—is the Abbey Church of St.-Martin-du-Canigou, built in 1001–26 on a steeply falling site in the French Pyrenees (fig. 5-24). Largely to accommodate both the entrance and the cloister, the church was built in two stories, both three-aisled and barrel-vaulted. The cloister lay at the lower level, while the church itself was reached through its large tower on the high ground. The lower section employed massive piers, while the upper sanctuary used less obtrusive columns at eight points together with a pair of cross-shaped internal buttressing piers at the center of the building, at which point the vault was reinforced by an arch. The nave terminated in three apses. Although small, dark, and very plain, the building nonetheless exhibits considerable skill in handling a difficult site and notable sureness in the fully vaulted construction, albeit on a limited scale.

In the late tenth and eleventh centuries in and around Burgundy—which was located between the two geographical zones that dominated the early phase of Romanesque—the forms used in St.-Martin-du-Canigou and other remote churches were taken up in the mainstream of the Romanesque movement. Here those vaulted but crudely composed forms

roof. This facade was not only one of the high achievements of the Norman school, but was the point of departure for the twin-towered facades that eventually dominated the exteriors of the major French Gothic cathedrals.

Early Vaulted Romanesque in Burgundy and the "Premier Art Roman."   In the Romanesque churches examined thus far, apses, aisles, and sometimes galleries were vaulted, but the wide spans of the nave had only open or closed timber roofs. Thus the buildings were not only easily subject to fire, but were also aesthetically flawed. Timber-roofed interiors can be imposing, but when the articulation of a powerfully sculpted wall passes a certain point, no wooden ceiling or open roof, regardless of how richly it is coffered or how colossal its beams, can quite compete; an imbalance results between massive masonry and relatively fragile, perishable timber. Understandably, Romanesque architects were motivated to envelop the interior of a large church in an integrated stone frame, to find the

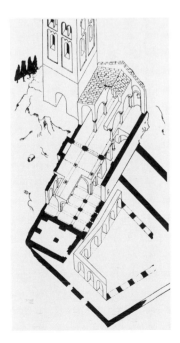

5-24
Abbey Church of St.-Martin-
du-Canigou. France. 1001–26.
(Isometric section after
J. Puig i Cadafalch)

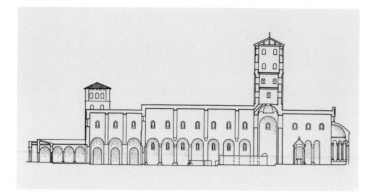

5-25 Second Abbey Church of Cluny, longitudinal section. (Drawing by Kenneth J. Conant)

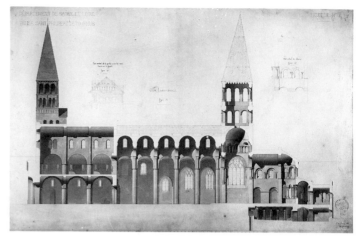

5-26 St.-Philibert, longitudinal section. Tournus, France. c. 960–1120

were fused with the formally sophisticated, but incompletely vaulted, types from northern France and the Empire. Two examples illustrate the stages of this critical development, which was the prelude to High Romanesque.

The Abbey Church of Cluny—the most important of the reforming monastic institutions that spread throughout Europe in the late tenth and eleventh centuries—was originally built in about 910 as a small timber-roofed construction (Cluny I). It was replaced by a larger structure in 955–81 (Cluny II), and then by an immense third church begun in 1088, of which only remnants now stand. It is Cluny II that commands our attention here (fig. 5-25). Its complex program (known from excavations) had five components: an atrium with arcaded porticoes; a three-aisled, three-bayed narthex surmounted by twin towers at the west front; a three-aisled nave of seven bays; a transept with eastern chapels at its extremities and crowned by a large crossing tower; and, finally, an eastern group comprising a large apse at the end of a long forechoir, flanked by two smaller chapels and rectangular side chambers. Almost the entire church was barrel-vaulted. The debt of the building to both northern and southern traditions is obvious: the complex planning, the twin-towered west facade, the balanced interplay of eastern and western towered groups, the pyramidal buildup of levels at the east, indicate the influence of the Norman and Germanic schools, but the vaulting, the interior bareness, and the exterior buttressing and corbel-table friezes, all were features of provincial early Romanesque.

The style of Cluny II was widely disseminated. To name only one influential feature, the plan of its stepped east end appeared in many buildings. The second stage in the emerging High Romanesque was exemplified by a Burgundian building similar to Cluny II in many respects, the Abbey Church of St.-Philibert at Tournus, (c. 960–1120; colorplate 28; fig. 5-26). Except for the lack of an atrium, its twin-towered exterior renders the general impression of Cluny II, with masonry decorated with pilaster strips and corbel friezes and the facade balanced by the pyramidal buildup of the eastern group The earliest part of the church to be erected was the narthex, with two levels, each with three aisles, all vaulted. The body of the church, built in about 1066–1107, is a normal basilican plan. Here the cylindrical piers are stretched to more than twice the height of the narthex columns, and in the center aisle, through intermediate columnar elements, they support a system of

transverse barrel vaults, one per bay. The side aisles are groin-vaulted. While the transverse barrel vaults effect a self-buttressing action (each barrel vault abutting its neighbor with no thrust on the clerestory wall) and thereby provide large clerestory openings, the space below is severely fragmented by this vaulting system. This was frustrating for the architects of mainstream Romanesque, for they were searching for a means of defining bays while still maintaining the spatial unity of the nave.

If the nave of Tournus, however structurally ingenious, represented a dead end, the layout of the choir, begun contemporaneously with the narthex (c. 1000) but completed only in the twelfth century, was forward-looking. Although somewhat earlier examples existed of an apse enveloped by an ambulatory from which a number of chapels radiated outward, Tournus is the earliest preserved example of this important type of choir. Its emergence as a basic architectural form was not simply fortuitous. The proliferation of chapels was in part due to the increasing numbers of clergy and their individual performances of a daily mass. Also, the ambulatory with radiating chapels solved one of the main problems faced by the Romanesque builders—the display of relics at different altars. For relics were no longer relegated, as they had been during the Carolingian period, to the security of crypts, but were housed at the main level of the church where flocks of pilgrims and worshipers eager to see the sacred objects had to be accommodated. With the evolution of this system of ambulatory and radiating chapels—which basically involved nothing more than moving the old type of annular corridor crypt upstairs and opening it outward into chapels—the crowds of relic devotees could flow around the ambulatory from altar to altar, even viewing the high altar from the sides and rear without disturbing the ritual celebration that might be under way in the choir.

High Romanesque in France. Even while the nave and radiating chapels of Tournus were under construction in the second half of the eleventh century, they were already being outmoded by buildings that embodied a full synthesis of northern and southern early Romanesque. One of the clearest examples of this transformation is the church of St.-Étienne in Nevers, 1063–97 (figs. 5-27, 5-28). The nave interior synthesizes the wall eleva-

5-27 Interior, St.-Étienne. Nevers, France. 1063–97

5-28 St.-Étienne

tion of Mont-Saint-Michel or Jumièges (galleries, sharply defined detail, strongly sculpted layers) with the massive barrel vaulting of the upper narthex at Tournus. In the nave, we experience for the first time the seamless, organic mural shell of the Romanesque. It is powerfully structured, clearly organized, and deftly proportioned; it is also strongly sculpted into dense layers of stone that shape and delimit the space, dividing it into steep bays, yet animating and unifying it. The exterior of the east end is developed powerfully and, in comparison with the primitive forms of Tournus, with considerable elegance. The chapels, ambulatory, apse, and transepts generate a rhythmic flow of volumes of stone, punctuated by strong buttresses that contrast with the delicate horizontal lines of the moldings. With great assurance the whole is built up in a pyramidal movement to the crossing tower (not surviving), which served as a visual pivot for the entire building, inside and out.

Although it was not a pilgrimage church, St.-Étienne was one in a group of mainstream High Romanesque buildings—often regarded as the paradigm of Romanesque—that stretched from Nevers through the Auvergne and along the pilgrimage roads that led to the celebrated medieval shrine at Santiago de Compostela on the Atlantic coast of Spain. Five of these pilgrimage churches—St.-Foyes at Conques, St.-Sernin at Toulouse, St.-Martial in Limoges (destroyed), St.-Martin at Tours (destroyed), and Santiago itself—form a stylistically cohesive set that differs from other important Romanesque churches. Begun at various points in the second half of the eleventh century, the buildings expand, enrich, and refine the forms developed at St.-Étienne. If we take St.-Sernin at Toulouse, 1080–1120, as the most evolved example, we find that it differs from St.-Étienne in plan, scale, detail, but not in its fundamental High Romanesque architectural mode (figs. 5-29–5-31). To accommodate crowds of pilgrims, St.-Sernin has five aisles, the outer pair continuing around the transepts to the ambulatory of the apse, forming in effect an unbroken ambulatory around the entire church. This feature is shared to some degree by all five pilgrimage churches, and is the decisive formal link among them. Yet a view of the interior at Toulouse reveals immediately that, despite the additional aisles and the increase in scale, the church can be understood perfectly in terms of St.-Étienne. Because St.-Sernin is a later building, begun in the 1080s as opposed to the 1060s, it is further developed in telling ways. In particular, its proportions are more slender and elegant. This was partly due to the elimination of the clerestory in pilgrimage churches to make the high vault more secure, enabling the designer to increase the relative height of the main arcade and the gallery. But this device also makes the building dark; the only light in the nave filtered in from the aisles and galleries. The resulting obscurity may well have been regarded as a virtue, creating a mysterious atmosphere through most of the building that contrasts dramatically with the well-lit crossing, apse, and chapels. On the exterior, St.-Sernin differs from St.-Étienne in its enriched articulation as well as in the extant crossing tower (which was intended to balance the unbuilt towers of the facade).

A final important feature of the pilgrimage churches concerns the abstract character of their planning. At St.-Sernin, for example, almost the entire building is laid out along the lines of a grid based on the dimensions of the crossing square, of which each nave bay represents half, each aisle bay one-fourth. This modular pattern, often designated as "square schematism," was of vital importance for the High Romanesque.

5-29 Nave and choir, St.-Sernin, 1080–1120

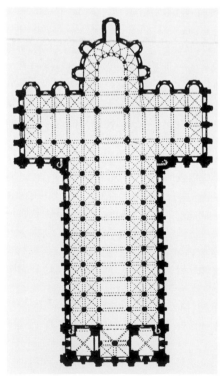

5-30
Plan, St.-Sernin
Toulouse, France,
1080–1120

It gave to the space and its articulation a strongly perceptible geometric rationality.

Square schematism was crucial to the success of the most extravagant of all High Romanesque structures—the third

5-31 Air view, St.-Sernin

Abbey Church of St.-Pierre at Cluny, built in 1088–c. 1121 (figs. 5-32–5-34). For seven centuries this immense structure amazed all who visited it. Regrettably, it was torn down, except for a single transept arm and tower, at the time of the French Revolution. Cluny III had not only five aisles carried along an immense length—the church was about 600 feet at its greatest extent—but two eastern transepts, each with four chapels that supplemented the five principal radiating chapels of the choir. Both crossings were marked by towers, the larger over the main transept to the west, whose ends supported secondary towers. This meant six towers in all, including the twin towers of the facade, counterbalancing each other and, at the east end, dominating the lavish buildup of sprawling masonry volumes. It was an architectural vision that probably conjured up the glittering multitowered image of the Heavenly Jerusalem as it was represented in medieval illustrations and described in Christian literature. No less overwhelming was the interior. Immensely long and wide, it was surpassed in height only by the interior of Speyer and, more than a century afterward, by the largest Gothic cathedrals. There was some justification for the scale and complexity of the building, for it was not just another monastery church, but the heart of the largest monastic institution in Europe. The building was scaled in a visionary way not to its own huge congregation of some 300 monks, but to the entire Cluniac order, which, it is said, could have met for mass within its walls. In a sense Cluny was the monastic counterpart of Imperial Speyer, but we might perhaps more aptly compare it to the Renaissance church of St. Peter's in Rome, also scaled to the idea of the entire community of the Church rather than to a single place or congregation.

5-32 Bird's-eye view, Abbey Church of St.-Pierre (Cluny III). 1088–c. 1121. (Drawing by Kenneth J. Conant)

5-33 Section of the nave and west elevation of transept, Cluny III. (Drawing by Kenneth J. Conant)

5-34 Interior of transept, Cluny III

5-35 Nave, Autun Cathedral. c. 1120–30

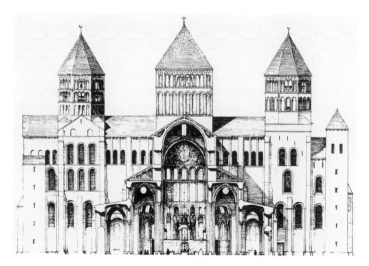

Although Cluny III is, for the most part, irrevocably lost, the wing of the main transept that still stands gives an idea of what had been the vastness and richness of the interior. This fragment and the evidence from excavations, early drawings, and closely related buildings enable us to understand what the church looked like. Structurally it was of a solidity and sophistication unsurpassed in its day; the walls and piers were up to eight feet in thickness, yet the vaulting was relatively light and pointed (a thrust-relieving device borrowed from Islamic architecture). Visually, it made a powerful impact. Particularly telling were the immensely high proportions of the main arcade. Rising to half the interior height, the arcade generated an overpowering verticality not unlike the great Gothic cathedrals a century later. The articulation of the walls was an elaborate and intricately organized design of fluted pilasters, egg-and-dart friezes, scalloped arch moldings, Classical cornice work, and Corinthian capitals, all concentrated in a zone between the nave arcade capitals and the high-vault springing.

Although only graphic evidence of Cluny III remains, we can imagine its original appearance by examining its comparatively modest Burgundian progeny. The Cathedral of Autun (fig. 5-35), built in about 1120–30, was perhaps its most successful follower, although simplified and scaled down. Especially potent at Autun, and suggestive of Cluny III, is the building's intensely detailed classicism. The wall is emphatically layered and almost seems sculpted from a homogeneous mass of stone into deep layers of classicizing forms. The palpable weightiness, almost Roman in feeling, is relieved to some extent by the delicately pointed curvature of the nave vault and the pointed arches of the nave arcade. (This pointed shape heralded the Gothic style, in which the pointed arch was to become not a secondary but a fundamental element.)

Before leaving the Romanesque of Burgundy we should mention another architectural type, best embodied in the important pilgrimage church of Ste-Madeleine at Vézelay (c. 1104–32), particularly known for its sculpture and interior (colorplate 29). To the visitor fresh from Cluny or Autun, the Classical detailing would be familiar; more striking would be the simplification of the nave elevation. Between the nave arcade and the clerestory runs not an elaborate zone, but a broad expanse of plain masonry divided by a single classicizing cornice. As if to compensate for this plainness, Vézelay introduces red-and-white banded arches—another Islamic element—and it is covered not by a severe barrel vault but by a series of large cross vaults.

Regional Romanesque. *Western France, Spain, and Italy (Rome and Venice).* During the Romanesque period, the mainstream movement that we have traced was reflected in one way or another throughout much of Europe. However, certain regional schools paralleled, rather than participated, in the mainstream, some never breaking out of the early Romanesque phase, others (especially in Italy) producing a different Romanesque altogether. In France, two such exceptions were the Romanesque schools of the Poitou and the Périgord, in the western provinces of France, each of which developed an unusual architectural scheme: the former, the hall church, in which the height of the nave and aisles was equal or almost equal; the latter, the domed basilica. The most impressive Poitevin example is the Abbey Church at St.-Savin-sur-Gartempe (fig. 5-36) of the early twelfth century. Here, the groin-vaulted aisles rise almost to the height of the barrel-vaulted nave, which has neither galleries nor clerestory. Even the famous fresco cycle on the ceiling does not distract the eye completely from the dominant interior form—the twin rows of giant, colorful columns. St.-Savin is descended from the earlier development represented by St.-Philibert at Tournus, but whereas St.-Philibert was innovative and heterogeneous in its form, St.-Savin develops the overscaled columnar format with concentration and balance. It remains, however, tied to the earlier phase, for it does not develop the expressive complexity of the High Romanesque mainstream.

The domed churches of the Périgord (south of the Poitou) embody a similar detachment from the High Romanesque mainstream and an adherence to the structural heaviness and formal simplicity of the Early Romanesque. The origins, dating, and development of the Périgord churches are complex topics. Although the type ultimately was based on Byzantine churches or on S. Marco in Venice, it may have evolved—not without their influence—from an early type of single-aisled, rectangular structure, which in about 1100 began to receive domes rather than the usual Romanesque barrel or groin vaulting. When domed crossarms were added to the single line of domes, the Périgord type achieved its maximum program. This occurred at the classic Périgord church, St.-Front in Périgueux (figs. 5-37, 5-38) built largely in the second quarter of the twelfth century (and heavily restored in the nineteenth century). Laid out in a Greek-cross plan, St.-Front employs the archetypal Byzantine dome-on-pendentives in each of the five units—four arms and the crossing. Although schematically close to the Byzantine model, in actual appearance St.-Front is anything but Byzantine. Its structure and space are untouched by Byzantine fluidity and ambiguity. The building is designed with uncompromising stereometric clarity; the lucid volumes of space—hemisphere (dome and pendentive zones), cube, semicylinder (the barrel vaults)—are defined by massive solids deprived of all decoration that might blur their form. No shimmering marbles or mosaics mask the structure, no colonnades ambiguously screen one space from another, and few openings pierce the dense solids. Dome, pendentives, arches, and piers are set off one from another by clear, simple devices—setbacks, stringcourses, masonry contrasts. Whatever is "Byzantine" at St.-Front is reinterpreted through the tradi-

5-36 Nave, Abbey Church of St.-Savin-sur-Gartempe. France. 1095–1115

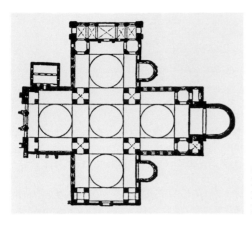

5-37
Plan, St.-Front.
Périgueux, France.
Mid-12th century

5-38 Nave, St.-Front

tions and sensibilities of architects in touch with Romanesque clarity, structure, and rationality.

Turning to the south we find that Romanesque architecture in Spain was largely dependent on France. The most significant example, Santiago de Compostela, is practically indistinguishable stylistically from its sister pilgrimage churches in France. The most interesting Spanish variations, which tend visually to a certain heaviness, are buildings such as León Cathedral, basically French but with Islamic embellishments such as cusped arches. For the sheer variety of its Romanesque styles, Italy was by far the richest architectural area of Mediterranean Europe, perhaps even richer than France. Yet because of this diversity a number of factors must be taken into account in order to understand the Italian Romanesque. For one thing, although the Classical tradition was understandably strong in Italy, the country was open to every kind of influence because of its geographical position. Its continuing political fragmentation played no less a role. France, England, and, for a time, Germany, gradually evolved large, cohesive, political structures, but Italy did not regain the political unity lost at the fall of Rome until the late nineteenth century. The main element of stability and continuity was the papacy, sovereign over Rome and the papal states stretching across central Italy from shore to shore. Another pocket of order was in and around Venice. It was not by mere coincidence

that Venice and Rome were among the most conservative architectural centers of all Europe during the Middle Ages. In medieval Rome the most active building period was the twelfth century, when a series of ambitious popes rebuilt a number of churches in perfect Early Christian style, virtually identical to buildings of the fourth and fifth centuries. The most notable Roman contribution to the Romanesque was the work of a clan of architectural decorators, the Cosmati, who practiced a type of geometric art derived from late antique marble inlay, and whose productions—mostly church pavements and furnishings but also some notable facades and cloisters—are scattered throughout central Italy (colorplate 27). Venice, in its greatest medieval building, the Church of S. Marco (discussed in the chapter on Byzantine architecture), turned not only to the antique past but to faraway Byzantium, with which it was in close contact through maritime commerce. But the rest of Italy, north and south, was to varying degrees politically more fluid and architecturally more adventurous than either Venice or Rome.

Sicily and Southern Italy. Throughout its history Italy south of Rome was open to division, conquest, and reconquest. When the Norman rulers arrived in the mid-eleventh century, for all their ambition, pride, and autocratic ways, they did not seek to purge their new territories of established cultural traditions. They brought their alien Norman ways—and architects—with them and grafted their northern European style of building onto southern architectural stock. When it suited their purposes they not only tolerated but shrewdly promoted the "indigenous" Saracenic and Byzantine architecture. They built pleasure palaces for themselves in pure Islamic manner and even tolerated the building of mosques; in their own new churches they were influenced by the existing Byzantine traditions. Since Saracenic architecture itself was in part derived from Byzantium, these influences became entangled; the resulting designs were even more eclectic when the Normans introduced their northern European traditions. The exotic mixture pervaded the great Norman cathedrals of Cefalù (1131–c. 1240; fig. 5-39) and Monreale (1174–82; fig. 5-40) outside Palermo, both in Sicily. Cefalù embodies a massive east end with a choir flanked by lateral chapels, and a twin-towered facade; these powerful Norman features are connected incongruously by a fragile basilican nave with columnar supports. The interior impression (like that of Monreale) is dominated by the majestic Byzantine mosaic image of Christ in the apse. On the exterior of the eastern parts of Cefalù there is extensive use of the intersecting blind arcade, a Norman motif of Islamic origin. Relatively restrained at Cefalù, this motif was fully developed at Monreale, where it went beyond even the Islamic sources in its colorful exuberance (colorplate 26).

On Italy's southern mainland, the Romanesque fusion was less exotic than in Sicily. Islamic influence was rarified and Byzantine style was restricted to a limited series of domed churches built in westernized form. The characteristic building program was a successful fusion of the traditional Italian basilica with the Norman type as, for example, at Jumièges. The basilica enjoyed renewed popularity following the reconstruction of the highly influential Abbey Church of Montecassino, built around 1075. The designers of the new church at Montecassino rejected Romanesque complexities and turned back to the simple forms of the Early Christian type, including a

5-39   Cefalù Cathedral. Sicily. 1131–c. 1240

5-40   Nave, Monreale Cathedral. Sicily. 1174

5-41   Transept and apse, S. Nicola. Trani, Italy. Begun 1098

porticoed atrium before its columnar, transepted basilica. Only the depth of its transept and the huge triple apses deviate from the Constantinian model.

The Church of S. Nicola in Bari, the first major Norman construction in Apulia, southeastern Italy, was begun in 1085. Here the Early Christian formula was fused with the steep proportions of Norman models, creating a type that can best be seen in S. Nicola's less altered progeny. Of these, S. Nicola at Trani, begun in 1098, is among the most magnificent (color-plate 32; fig. 5-41). Rising directly at the edge of the sea—an Apulian version, as it were, of Mont-Saint-Michel—its towering volumes of white limestone seem to confront the elements defiantly. The Montecassino type of Constantinian eastern end rises majestically in an unbroken line over the crypt that underlies the entire church; the steep proportions of the transept are emphasized by a triad of singularly high, narrow apses. On the interior, these forms exert a sense of spaciousness imbued with a powerful vertical energy, the many windows creating a soaring choreography of luminosity without parallel in Romanesque architecture. In the nave, a false gallery opens over a columnar arcade unusual in its doubling of columns (a device to lighten the visual weight of a given mass of supports). Although strongly "Normanized," the Trani church maintains its southern continuity of space by avoiding wall articulation that was so important in the buildings beyond the Alps.

Northern Italy. Italy north of the papal dominions was generally less conservative than the south. Even where Classical traditions were very strong, there was more openness to the adventurous spirit of the Romanesque. Moreover, because the north was more politically fragmented than the south, Romanesque architecture was more varied and complex. In the eleventh and twelfth centuries Lombard and Tuscan towns successfully challenged Imperial authority and established a constellation of city-states whose autonomy was a source of both cultural individuality and severe political conflict all through the later Middle Ages and the Renaissance. Their political individualism was clearly reflected in the architecture of Lombard and Tuscan towns, whose churches were strongly individuated. In examining the main characteristics of northern Italian Romanesque, we should keep several key factors in mind. Even though the northern towns had struggled free of the Imperial political yoke, Imperial Romanesque architecture, with all its connotations of power and majesty, still exerted strong influence in the region. Interestingly, influence seems also to have flowed in the reverse direction, the Germans being drawn to the south as much culturally as politically. This interchange of ideas, and even workers, across the Alps encompassed a wide range of architectural forms: trefoil plans, double bays, domical vaults, dwarf galleries, and the ubiquitous corbel frieze. All but the first of these features appeared, both at Speyer and Modena. Beyond Imperial Germany, the principal region of northern Europe to influence northern Italy was Normandy. It is significant that the mainstream High Romanesque movement in central France had little effect in Italy. Instead, the already observed affinity of Norman and Imperial architecture—at least during the early eleventh century—appears to have extended down through the Italian peninsula. But the Norman-Imperial influences were diluted by stubborn local tendencies, as if each city felt it could best assert its pride and independence by building unlike any other place.

The reflection of the Norman-Imperial early Romanesque in Lombardy is seen in Sta. Maria Maggiore at Lomello and the Cathedral of Modena. The church in Lomello (fig. 5-42), built around 1040 in the strong red texture of Lombard brickwork, is an Italian version of structures such as St. Gertrude in Nivelles, where the nave is broken into two large bays by wall elements and diaphragm arches. The Cathedral of Modena, built around 1099, is a more sophisticated building. A glance at the interior—from which we must set aside the fifteenth-century rib vaulting and consider only the diaphragm arches and an open timber roof—immediately recalls the great Abbey Church at Jumièges, with its double-bay system, powerful articulation, stepped archivolts, and triple-gallery arcade. Only the Classical capitals, the brick building material, and the broader proportions give away the northern Italian location.

Probably the most characteristic Romanesque building of the region was S. Ambrogio in Milan (figs. 5-43, 5-44). Ambition is the key word to describe this church in its program, structure, and decoration. To the triple apses and barrel-vaulted forechoirs that survived from the church of the tenth century were added a nave of four huge vaulted bays, aisles, and galleries. In front of the basilica is an atrium almost as large as the church, together with a deep facade structure flanked by towers. The new construction probably dates from the early twelfth century. The nave bays of

S. Ambrogio are covered by rib vaults, and while this is not unprecedented in twelfth-century construction, it still makes the Milanese basilica an important monument in the development of medieval vaulting. Rib vaulting (groin vaults in which a sharply raised set of arches runs along and defines the diagonal groin lines) was to become a major feature of Gothic architecture. But rib vaults alone do not make a building Gothic. The massive ribs, of simple, square cross section, do not in Gothic fashion soar lightly through space, but carry into the vault something of the weighty values typical of mainstream Romanesque design. The thickset Romanesque character of S. Ambrogio is more striking in the supporting forms—the massive, compound, alternating piers; the stepped archivolts; and the densely textured, telltale Lombard arched corbel-table-frieze running just below the gallery. Although

5-42 Nave, Sta. Maria Maggiore. Lomello, Italy. c. 1040

5-43 S. Ambrogio. Milan, 12th century

5-44 Nave, S. Ambrogio

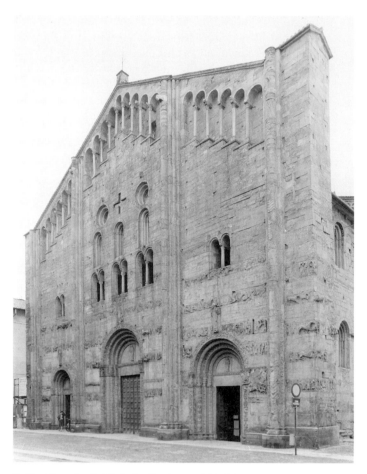

5-45 Facade, S. Michele. Pavia. c. 1100–60

the overall impression is full, strong, and expansive, it is also somewhat gloomy and at times awkward in detail, lacking the poise of the churches in Jumièges, Speyer, and Modena.

The architecture of Lombardy tended toward the ponderous complexities of S. Ambrogio. At the same time, an impressive type of facade (not employed at S. Ambrogio) was developed in this region. It was the so-called Lombard screen facade, whose lines did not reflect the cross section of the basilica it fronted, but rather rose high above the roofs of the basilica to form a simple, broadly gabled wall that "screened" the church behind it from the viewer. The most impressive of the Romanesque examples of this type (which continued into the Gothic period) is found in Pavia, in the Church of S. Michele (fig. 5-45), where the broad expansive planarity is articulated by Romanesque buttressing, windows, dwarf galleries, and relief sculpture.

Tuscany. The final important Italian Romanesque location is Tuscany, whose polished, elegant marble structures could not contrast more strongly with the churches of Lombardy and other Italian regions. We have seen how closely the other Italian regional styles reflected their sources. Tuscany, although indebted to many architectural models, tended to combine them in original syncretistic conceptions in which any stylistic indebtedness was overshadowed by the thoroughness of fusion and transformation. At the same time, Tuscan architecture was classicizing in such a powerful way that its Romanesque is often called the Proto-Renaissance. This is not an unreasonable concept, for Renaissance architects believed many Tuscan

5-46 Facade, S. Miniato al Monte. Florence. Mid-11th–12th century

5-47 Nave, S. Miniato

Romanesque buildings to be authentically antique, and took them as models for their own "revivalist" work.

Tuscan Romanesque divides into two main schools: Pisan (together with Lucchese) and Florentine. Both embodied the same creative, classicizing tendencies, the same elegance and refinement. Tuscany was fortunate in the range and quality of its building materials, which included vast marble quarries. The unusual plenitude of the substance probably reinforced Tuscan classicism, for marble was not only closely associated with ancient architecture, but, as a luminous, fine-grained, easily polished material, it was more adaptable than common stone (not to mention brick) to elaborate, refined detail. The most obvious singularity of Tuscan buildings is their polychromy, achieved through the extensive use of marble revetment on the interior, as was common in antiquity, and with equal splendor on the outer walls. To uninitiated eyes, both Pisan and Florentine Romanesque buildings look much alike in their polychrome elegance, but this initial impression yields to clear distinctions. Florentine Romanesque is characterized by taut, angular volumes, rational, disciplined articulation, and sharp, exquisite Classical detail. In Florentine Romanesque, the two-dimensional form of the rectangle is the decorative leitmotif—rational and abstract—whereas in Pisa it is the arcade, particularly the open arcading that appears so extensively on facades along with sumptuous striped walls.

Florence possesses two jewels of Romanesque architecture—the Baptistery of S. Giovanni (c. 1060–1150) at the heart of the city and the contemporary Church of S. Miniato al Monte (figs. 5-46, 5-47) in the green hills outside the city walls. The latter takes the form of a medium-sized unvaulted basilica, the interior separated into three large bays by four-part piers and diaphragm arches (in the manner of Nivelles, Jumièges, and Modena). Each of these large bays comprises three small bays of arcading over Classical columns (not merely two, as elsewhere). The eastern bay of this harmonious, triadic design is complicated by a split-level arrangement formed by a hall crypt several steps down from the nave, a choir raised grandly above it and centering on the apse, which draws the whole interior to its rich, paneled arcading and half-dome mosaic. Even if it were merely in stone, this interior would be impressive, but it is much more so in its glowing expanse of real and fictive marble incrustation and in the play of the intricate, geometric configurations against the grand, spatial proportions. The facade of S. Miniato prepares the visitor for the interior, not just in its polychrome classicism, but in the specific iteration in the lower facade story of the blind arcading and paneling of the apse. The facade has its own inner logic. The first story stretches out with a bold horizontal sweep, providing a solid base for the whole. The second story lifts buoyantly above the entablature that sweeps across the lower zone, the classicizing relief of the first story now flattened out into shallow paneling and high pilasters. The pilasters are connected in pairs by atectonic stretches of bent architrave, a telltale sign of the Romanesque distance from the true antique. These rectangular twin compositions rise between ingenious diagonal panels that front the side-aisle roof zone, making the difficult transition from aisle wall to clerestory zone, and in turn framing the central motif of the facade—the glittering mosaic of Christ. The third story is completely planar

(except for whimsical little Atlas figures at the corners) in its intricate inlaid patterns, yet capped with a strong, rich cornice that closes the design. Together the two upper stories form the image of a Classical temple front raised on high.

The Florentine Baptistery is even more intensely concentrated and, in fact, is generally felt to be one of the most "perfect" buildings of all time (colorplate 26; fig. 5-48). So classicizing is it that within a few generations after its completion, the Florentines "forgot" its real building history from about 1060 to 1150. By the early fourteenth century, the period of Dante, it had been transformed in their minds into a Roman temple of Mars. Perhaps the main reason for the belief in its antiquity (apart from a desire for it to be Roman) was not so much its Classical detail, but the remarkable resemblance of its interior to the Pantheon. The centralized plan, the series of niches, each comprising corner pilaster-piers framing double freestanding Corinthian columns, the continuous entablature, the apse (originally semicircular as at the Pantheon), all closely reflect the Roman building. The Pantheon is not the only ancient building behind the Baptistery, however, for, like the Palatine Chapel at Aachen two centuries earlier, its galleries also reflect S. Vitale. But in the very eclectic combination of these sources, the Baptistery reveals its medieval date. Moreover, unlike the Pantheon and S. Vitale, where the space is a fluid whole, the interior of the Baptistery forms wedge-shaped prisms of space gathered about the central axis, conforming to the medieval tendency to compose space of modular geometric units. Like S. Miniato, the exterior elevation of

5-48   Interior, Baptistery of S. Giovanni. Florence. c. 1060–1150

5-49 Air view, Baptistery (begun 1153), Cathedral (begun 1063), Campanile (begun 1174), and Campo Santo (begun 1278). Pisa

5-50 Plan, Pisa Cathedral. c. 1063

5-51 Interior, Pisa Cathedral

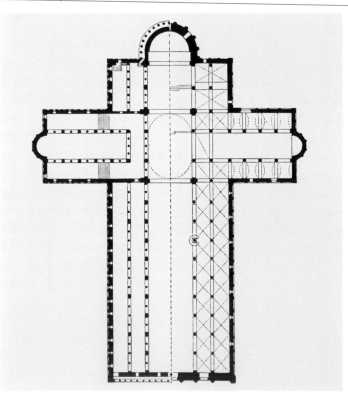

the Baptistery mirrors the interior, providing the observer with an "X-ray" glimpse of what lies within the compact prism of glowing, classicizing form.

Pisa, like Venice, was a great sea power. It was already a major city-state in the eleventh and twelfth centuries when Florence, for all its precocious architectural genius, was little more than a market town. The magnitude of Pisa and its presence on the sea are evident in its Cathedral and its attendant buildings, begun in celebration of the Venetian naval victory over the Saracens in 1062, for they exhibit power and wealth and an almost Oriental splendor. Pisa Cathedral, begun in 1063 and not completed until the thirteenth century, was built on a grand scale in the form of an elaborated Early Christian basilica (colorplate 30; figs. 5-49–5-51). The building has a five-aisled nave, strongly projecting three-aisled transepts, a deep choir, galleries throughout, and an oval dome. The dome rises over a complex crossing area, where the inner nave aisles and galleries continue uninterruptedly across to the choir, screening off the transepts. The monumentality and spatial richness of the interior, with its Classical colonnades and complex vistas through columnar screens (suggesting Byzantine and Islamic influences, evident also in the pointed arches and striping), is no less impressive than the better-known external form of the building. Here, immense volumes expand in all directions: The nave, transepts, and choir push out toward all four points of the compass and at the same time rise around the central axis established by the exotic contours of the onion dome that surmounts the rest. The walls are clad in the Pisan version of polychrome marble revetment used in Florence. This incrustation consists mostly of a mural plane of white marble threaded with narrow, unevenly spaced, dark marble bands, all enveloped in a second multitiered layer of Classical blind arcading. Within the head of each arch, a colorful lozenge panel is sunk into the wall. These elements create the impression of a rich tissue of polychromy defining the volumes almost like stretched Oriental textiles of sumptuous pattern and color. The most elaborate forms were saved for the west facade. Here the lower zone continues the system that envelops the rest of the church, but with richer detail such as the acanthus columns that frame the central portal. Above, the supporting wall steps back, leaving tiers of open arcades spreading across the lower zones and rising through the center along the lines of the basilica. Thus, architectural substance is played upon not only by pattern and color, but also by space and light: the supporting wall is veiled in shadow and the tiers of open arcading appear to rise freestanding in space. Although related in general configuration to the facade of S. Miniato, the contrast between the Pisan and Florentine styles is remarkable. The Florentines shape the polychrome marble into geometric configurations, cerebral and abstract, whereas the Pisan manner is luxuriant and painterly.

The subsidiary buildings at Pisa are scarcely less extraordinary than the basilica itself. Like most Italian bell towers, the Pisan Campanile is not part of the church but is a freestanding monument generating local pride (the Italian term for local chauvinism, "campanilismo," alludes to the bell tower image). Although famed as the Leaning Tower, the structure's principal virtue is not its perilous inclination (due to faulty subsoil). Even if perfectly in plumb, the graceful and harmonious Campanile would be the world's most beautiful bell tower (although it would lose its telling pathos). Structurally, it is no more than a transformation of the flat cathedral facade into cylindrical form, but the ingenious operation was accomplished with aesthetic finesse. The solid base supports six tiers of open arcading, poised lacelike around the shadowed, cylindrical supporting wall.

The Baptistery, built opposite the facade of the basilica, was begun in 1153 and, like the tower, was not fully completed until the fourteenth century. It forms another variant of the cathedral scheme. Here the stretched volumes, decorative skin, and arcading of the cathedral massing are reconfigured. That building's volumetric energy is now concentrated into a domed cylinder pierced by a conical roof, all covering a superb double-shelled interior (that deliberately reflected Constantine's Church of the Holy Sepulcher in Jerusalem).

These Pisan structures are remarkable not only individually but as a group, including the large thirteenth-century covered cemetery, the Campo Santo, situated just north of the basilica. All the buildings embody the same geometric clarity and sense of volume; they utilize the same decorative system and scale, the same color, texture, and materials. The visual rhythms and textures that animate each one also create a deep affinity among them. This sense of harmonious individuality is reinforced by the siting of the buildings, close enough for unity yet with ample individual space, and also their alignments. The basilica is nestled securely between tower and baptistery, which define and extend its presence in their reflection of its form. The whole composition is set against the long, low line of the Campo Santo. Not since antiquity—since the Forums or even the Acropolis—had a group composition of such astonishing power and grace appeared, and few were ever again to equal the architectural vision of the Pisans.

High and Late Romanesque in Germany. In our counterclockwise journey through the various Romanesque styles that evolved around the French Romanesque core, we now return northward over the Alps to the Empire and Normandy, whose architectural development was left in its early phases at the outset of the chapter. Although initially the two regions followed parallel tendencies, sharp divergences emerged after the mid-eleventh century. Norman buildings continued to lead the way in the ongoing development of medieval architecture into the twelfth century; in crucial aspects they provided the point of departure for the Gothic. Quite the opposite was true for Imperial architects. From the outset, under Charlemagne, they were affected by a conservative nostalgia for past tradition, which eventually diminished their ability to keep in touch with the European mainstream centered in France. The Empire was to be the area in which the Romanesque had the longest life or, more precisely, afterlife. Rather than dominating medieval architectural development, as it had done initially, the Empire came to be dominated by the indigenous Romanesque aesthetic. A powerful resistance to progressive French developments was maintained throughout the twelfth and into the thirteenth centuries, akin to the persistent Italian Classicism. Only in about 1220–30, when the prestige of the French monarchy and its new architecture became overwhelming, did the Empire's Romanesque resistance break down. The

5-52　Interior, Speyer Cathedral, as altered in 1080.
(19th-century lithograph, before restoration)

5-53　Speyer Cathedral

hothouse Romanesque growth suddenly wilted with the abrupt exposure to the new architectural climate of French Gothic. But in the nearly two centuries between the original Speyer Cathedral and this point, many impressive buildings were built.

One preeminent example was the first reconstruction of Speyer (figs. 5-52, 5-53). In a campaign beginning in 1080, the ambitious Henry IV aggrandized the cathedral, making it conform to High Romanesque standards. The immense nave was vaulted and its walls remodeled; almost the entire east end was rebuilt. The nave vaults now spanned 45 feet and rose to 107 feet (surpassing the "mere" 40-by-90-foot vaults of the slightly later Cluny III). Yet it was not simply the tremendous vaults that made the new Speyer so impressive, but also the reworking of the nave walls into a double-bay system. The minor piers were left as before, but the major piers received an additional mural layer: massive pilasters enveloped the old half-columns, on which were imposed, as a third layer of articulation, a set of enormous half-columnar vaulting supports. The resulting piers were so colossal that against them the minor piers seemed almost fragile. In terms of sheer massiveness and scale, no Romanesque interior could compare with the Speyer nave. The cathedral's exterior was no less overpowering, particularly the eastern sections: the immense massing built up in boldly juxtaposed, lucid volumes of powerfully articulated masonry; the apse with its strong blind arcading and dwarf gallery; above it the gabled prism of the

forechoir; and the twin towers beyond the crossing tower. Alongside Speyer, Pisa, for all its magnificent glamour, seems fanciful and insubstantial.

High Romanesque in Normandy and England. Norman Romanesque architecture, as already noted, proved to be far more consequential for subsequent development than the Romanesque of Germany. One example of the post-Jumièges generation—the Church of St.-Étienne at Caen—suffices to give a clear understanding of the most critical Norman tendencies (figs. 5-54, 5-55). Its facade, whose towers were completed in the thirteenth century was, together with that of Jumièges, at the head of a long line of twin-towered facades that would dominate the French Gothic. But it is the interior that concerns us most. Originally timber-roofed, St.-Étienne was given rib vaults between 1120 and 1130 and a new choir in the thirteenth century. A comparison with Jumièges reveals the remarkable development that had occurred from one generation to the next. A new concept of the nave wall appeared. The greater portion of the elevation gave way to voids. The arcades pushed up almost to the gallery, and the now undivided gallery openings were expanded to the maximum. The clerestory level was divided into two structural shells (the outer wall and an inner arcade) separated by a passageway, an early example of the so-called "thick-wall" construction invented by the Normans that became very important in future developments.

5-54 West facade, St.-Étienne. Caen, France. Begun c. 1068

5-55 Nave wall, St.-Étienne. 1064–77

The St.-Étienne clerestory presented to the observer a back-lit columnar screen that masked the window-pierced outer wall set at a distance behind it. This undermining of mass extended throughout the interior. Even the piers and arches were fragmented into a multiplicity of columnar details and molded archivolts. The voiding of the wall by openings and hollows, and especially the transformation of the remaining mass into bundles of slender forms were innovative. They looked ahead to the Gothic movement of the mid-twelfth century and after, and thus might fairly be termed Proto-Gothic. Yet the generic Norman character of St.-Étienne must be emphasized. Unmistakably Norman were the logic of its articulation, the clarity of the detail, and the elegance of its deceptively simple forms.

The promise of St.-Étienne was not to be fulfilled in Normandy itself. Although developments in early rib vaulting did occur there in the early twelfth century, Norman architecture lost the dynamism that it had in the eleventh century. This most certainly was connected with the political fragmentation that occurred with the conquest of England, the country to which the ruling house of William and thousands of ambitious Norman subjects were transferred after 1066, leaving Normandy behind and weakening the force of the indigenous Norman school. But it was an event that was directly responsible for the making of the English Romanesque and of later medieval architecture in England.

Unlike their more tolerant kinsmen in the Mediterranean, William the Conqueror and his followers did not have much patience with Anglo-Saxon architectural traditions. The degree to which they attempted a clean sweep of things can be seen at the Cathedral of Winchester (fig. 5-56), begun in 1079, and derived directly from St.-Étienne at Caen. Its transplanted character is visible in the brutal reduction of the continental original (as if the Norman logic had to be stated more forcefully to conquered aliens), the increased heaviness of the proportions, and the plainness of detail. The spirit of the Norman style was not to survive the voyage across the Channel. Other early Anglo-Norman buildings strayed even farther than Winchester from the continental model.

Durham Cathedral, begun in 1093 and completed toward 1130, is the definitive building of the Anglo-Norman Romanesque—indeed, one of the great structures of the period in Europe (figs. 5-57, 5-58). Its scale is enormous, some 400 feet in length, and its forms overpowering. The building carries, moreover, special qualities not easy to fathom. Nominally the interior is based on the system of St.-Étienne, with a reversion to the double-bay scheme of Jumièges with its alternating pier forms and smaller, divided gallery openings. But the structure is far heavier. The huge piers build forward in three layers, while between them stand immense masonry cylinders that form the "minor" supports. The sense of scale is augmented by the increase in the main arcade height (at the expense of the

5-56 North transept, Winchester Cathedral. Begun 1079

5-57 Nave vaults, Durham Cathedral

5-58 Nave, Durham Cathedral

gallery). Yet, within this monumental frame an insistent decoration spreads over key interior forms, with Norman chevron moldings everywhere on the archivolts, and ornamental zig-zag patterns, diaperwork, and fluting incised into the minor piers. These linear decorative accents belong to the art of the Anglo-Saxon world and were seen in the British Isles as early as the seventh and eighth centuries in Irish manuscripts. They contrast sharply with the massiveness of the structure, generating a quality of unresolved tension that may have reflected the difficult world outside, torn by the struggle between the Norman conquerors and the not-fully-submissive inhabitants of Britain.

It is the vaulting of Durham that fully reveals this duality. The choir-aisle vaults, from about 1093, are the earliest of all dated rib vaults; and the vaulting in the choir-transept area (complete by 1110) and in the nave (1128–33) is not far behind. The nave vaults, with their unique double-X pattern of ribs and seven-part filling webs, are particularly advanced, employing even the pointed arch in order to solve geometric difficulties (as well as to grant an unmistakable vertical impulse to the interior). We shall discuss rib vaults later, but here let us simply note their ambiguous character. On the one hand, they can be viewed as continuations of earlier Norman tendencies, for they extend the linear wall articulation of the Norman Romanesque into the vaulting zone. On the other hand, viewed in the context of the Durham interior, the rib vaults form part of a decorative pattern more insular than continental Norman.

Durham was in several ways a turning point in the history of European architecture. Its precocious rib vaulting was to prove crucial for the continental architects, both Norman and French, who originated the Gothic style. At the same time, it

marked the shift in England from Norman rationalism and tectonic discipline to decorative patterning and a stubborn indigenous tendency toward the irrational and eccentric. This complex interweaving of continental and insular traditions would characterize medieval English architecture through the fourteenth century.

The remainder of the story of the Anglo-Norman Romanesque is largely that of the resurgence of local habits and the erosion of the imported Norman style. In mainstream English churches of the twelfth century, such as the nave of Ely Cathedral (colorplate 36; fig. 5-59), the Norman system of disciplined structure gave way to a format stressing an overall linear network and "wall-facing-wall" without vaulting. Ironically, English architects abandoned the medieval structural quest shortly after their precocious creation of rib vaulting at Durham. Later, in the thirteenth and fourteenth centuries, they were to return to the theme of rib vaulting with a vengeance, but for

5-60   Nave, Gloucester Cathedral. Early 12th century

5-59   Nave, Ely Cathedral. 12th century

the remainder of the Romanesque they were content to produce variations on the form of the nave wall.

In twelfth-century English Romanesque, one other important type can be observed in the west-English designs of Tewksbury and Gloucester (fig. 5-60), where a heavy, closed, upper wall is supported by powerful arches set on large high columns that are the hallmark of the school. These massive forms create a typically English architectural mood of indefinable, but somewhat ominous drama. The atmosphere is altogether different from that created by such continental counterparts as St.-Savin-sur-Gartempe and its Burgundian models with their tone of optimistic experimentalism.

6-1
Arcades
of Abder-
Raman I,
Great
Mosque.
Córdoba.
Begun 786

Chapter Six | Islam and the West

The manner in which Christianity dominated the Western world for 1,500 years makes it hard to remember that it was once seriously threatened by a formidable rival—the fervent movement of Islam that, following the death of the Prophet Muhammed in A.D. 632, swept rapidly from Arabia across North Africa into Spain and eastward as far as India and China. From a small band of followers in Arabia, who regarded Muhammed as the last of God's prophets, grew a huge multitude of believers. Guided by the Prophet's injunction to carry the new faith to nonbelievers, the intensely religious Muslims set out on a mission to convert. The countries that succumbed to them were targets primarily because they were filled with potential converts to Islam, but they also possessed material wealth and a brilliant cultural past new to the consciousness of Arabia, an arid, harsh country populated by nomadic tribes. When Arab armies first encountered other civilizations, they saw far more than booty and plunder: They found monumental architectures that met the varied needs of established societies, and that were symbols of prestige, authority, and ideology. The Muslims were understandably eager to produce buildings of their own to rival, if not surpass, those structures that had been left by Hellenistic, Roman, and Sassanian civilizations, or had recently been erected by the Christians. The caliphs, princes of the dynasties related to the Prophet, wanted to be honored, to live, and to worship in monuments that would befit their new status, wealth, and power, and that would symbolize the supremacy of their faith.

ORIGINS OF ISLAMIC ARCHITECTURE

Before their first conquests, the nomadic Arabs had no significant indigenous architectural traditions. It was one of the many miracles of this new civilization that when the Muslims did begin to build in the conquered countries, they almost immediately established a new architecture that would universally be identifiable as Islamic, and that took its place as one of the most brilliant achievements in the history of world architecture. To examine its vast diversity is not our purpose in this survey of Western building; rather it is to study the architecture of Islam as a parallel development to the West. Islamic architecture is unique in the non-Western world in that it alone—not Buddhist, not Hindu, not pre-Columbian— shares many of the forms and structural concerns of Byzantine, medieval, and Renaissance architecture, having grown largely from identical roots in the ancient world. Unlike the Buddhist architecture of fragile walls and sweeping roofs, or the Hindu and pre-Columbian mountainlike, often pyramidal massings—substantially "external" styles, continuing the mode of

the pyramids and ziggurats of the ancient Near East—Islamic architecture, like the Western styles, is primarily an architecture of large interior spaces, of domes and ceilings, arches and columns, walls and vaults, and wall-like facades. But what is important to see here is not only Islam's parallelism to the West, but its divergence: the way, using many of the same forms and materials, it created its unique and different style, or historic panorama of styles, across many cultures and through a thousand years.

The first regions invaded by the Muslim Arabs—and consequently the first regions in which a recognizable Islamic art was created—were modern Syria and Palestine, Iraq and Mesopotamia. By A.D. 635, Damascus had been captured, and before 640 Jerusalem and Caesarea. The "foreign" monuments, therefore, to which the Muslims initially were exposed were the great Constantinian and post-Constantinian Christian foundations that marked the sites sacred to Christ and his martyred followers in the cities of the Holy Land; the churches in Syria; and the imposing remains of the buildings constructed under the Hellenistic and late Roman emperors in both areas. In Iraq and Mesopotamia, they encountered powerful architectural remains that symbolized the imperial might of the Sassanians. Despite the impact all these structures must have made, it took the Muslims only two generations to assimilate the architectural idioms of these cultures and to begin to forge an artistic identity so individual and so authoritative that by the late seventh century they were ready to construct their own monumental houses of worship, tombs, and palaces; these would rival the great structures of earlier conquerors and other faiths. Among the most important results of this process was the Muslim perception of the ritual functions of Roman Imperial architecture and their adaptation to the political ambitions of the increasingly powerful Umayyad Caliphate (661–750), the earliest dynastic rulers of Islam. In the palace-villa at Mshatta in Jordan (c. 744– 750; fig. 6-2), they built clearly defined spaces symmetrically arranged within a regularly laid-out system of turreted precinct walls that suggested military strength. Hypothetical reconstructions of portions of the villa at Khirbat al-Mafjar outside Jericho (739–744; fig. 6-3) reveal a monumental arched portal (like a Roman triumphal arch), a domed and apsed audience hall and assembly space, and the luxury of a vaulted bath complex. By the mid-eighth century, therefore, the massive forms and shaped spaces, the pier-supported barrel vaults and domes on pendentives of late Imperial Roman architecture had been put into the service of the Muslim caliphs, who also appropriated their ceremonial allusions and used them as emblems of Islam's sovereignty and power.

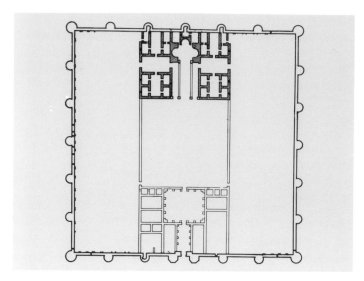

6-2 Plan, Palace. Mshatta, Jordan. c. 744–50.
(From Creswell, 1969)

6-3 The bath, Villa. Khirbat al-Mafjar near Jericho, Jordan.
739–44. (Reconstruction from Ettinghausen, 1972)

6-4 Dome of the Rock. Jerusalem. 691–92

Alongside these impressive rural installations, which are among the earliest examples of Islamic secular architecture and reflect the princely, military, and imperial ambitions of the Muslims, there appeared in Jerusalem a monumental political statement of Muslim ideals for their sacred structures. The central-plan, domed martyria of late antiquity and early Christianity provided the Muslims with a model for the grandiose shrine they built on a site sacred to Judaism and on a scale with which they proclaimed the equality of their religion to those of the Christians and the Jews in the Holy Land. A compact, exterior octagon enclosing a domed cylindrical core, the Dome of the Rock (691–92; fig. 6-4) in its geometry and in its parts—octagonal format, vaulting, columns, piers, arches, ambulatories, rich mosaic decoration, and fenestrated dome of gilded wood (rebuilt in the eleventh century)—represented the Muslims' acquisition of a near-complete Romano-Byzantine architectural program, evoking such ecclesiastical structures as fourth-century Sta. Costanza in Rome (fig. 4-10) and sixth-century S. Vitale in Ravenna

(fig. 4-34), not in a formal sense alone, but (important to the Umayyad Caliphate) for their status as sovereign foundations.

In its isolated shrinelike form, however, the Dome of the Rock is an atypical Islamic religious structure. The more characteristic Near Eastern mosque—an early example being the Umayyad Great Mosque (706–15; fig. 6-5) built within and incorporating the ruins of the walls of a Roman temple precinct in the capital city of Damascus—was developed to function, as had the Roman basilica, as a large assembly place. It was used for prayer, for religious instruction, and sometimes as a royal tribunal. Its most important liturgical feature was the orientation of the plan toward Muhammad's birthplace of Mecca, and a prayer niche (mihrab), adapted from the Roman and then the Christian apse, to articulate the wall facing Mecca (qibla). Quadrangular in outline, the walled precinct of such a mosque included an open court often surrounded by arcaded galleries (at Damascus exceptionally classical in style, fig. 6-6), and, opening from one side of the court, a sanctuary whose flat wooden roof was supported by numerous rows of columns regularly disposed (the so-called hypostyle mosque type).

But the multicolumnar arrangement of a mosque sanctuary such as that at Damascus, related though it may be to aisled structures of the West, represented a marked difference from the antique and Early Christian concept of architectural space: instead of a static, shaped volume formed by an enclosing mass, space is something that moves laterally as well as

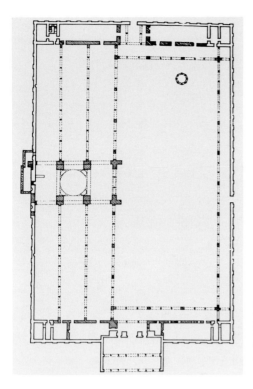

6-5
Plan, Great
Mosque. Damascus,
Syria. c. 706–15.
(From Creswell,
1969)

6-6   Courtyard north side and facade of the sanctuary,
Great Mosque

forward and back, merges, and floats unpredictably out of sight. The Christian basilica, with its three or five aisles longitudinally arranged, formed separate tunnels of clearly directed space to serve its liturgical functions, but the horizontal expansion of the aisles in the hypostyle mosque sanctuary resulted in an entirely different effect; the space floats freely through countless intercolumniations to undefined, invisible reaches, in a manner perhaps suggestive of the metaphysical nature of the Islamic faith. Even the mihrab, owing its shape to the semicylindrical apses of Rome and early Christianity, was used by the Muslims in a fundamentally non-Western and metaphorical way. The Romano-Christian apse was a formal framework for tangible bodies—animate or inanimate; it enclosed Roman judicial courts; it accommodated the chair of a bishop and the seats for his clerical community;

it framed an altar; its orientation was inward, to the nave or chancel that preceded it. The Islamic mihrab, on the other hand, was a metaphor to indicate the direction for prayer (Mecca), a place *outside* the mosque. It was a piece of the physical interior of the building, but, always empty, it was oriented externally and functioned as a symbol recalling the Prophet's leadership of the community in prayer.

Although lending some of its forms to Muslim architecture, the focused, ceremonial nature of Roman architecture did not pertain to the nonhierarchical character of the Islamic religion. Nor did the liturgical priorities of Christian architecture—processions and a place for the Mass—have relevance for Islamic religious structures, which were built around the idea of communal prayer and the direction of Mecca, and served as community centers. Closer to the ideals of Islam was the more "mystical" architecture of Eastern Christianity, those Byzantine structures that as early as the sixth century had departed—by way of their intricate spatial effects and weight-denying shimmer of color and light—from the ritual-based functionalism of the Early Christian basilica. Muslim architects took possession of those inspired effects in Byzantine buildings that best served their own transcendental vision, and then carried them to the greatest possible extremes.

In Mshatta, Khirbat al-Mafjar, Jerusalem, and Damascus, Islamic architecture, less than a hundred years after the conquest of the Near East, had already found a secure syntax of form and structure which corresponded to that of the historical West, but which served all the pragmatic and aesthetic requirements of Muslim secular life and, more important, the spiritual necessities of Islamic religious life.

In contrast to such dynamic building activity in the Islamic East, architecture in western Europe was at something of a standstill, after Justinian and before Charlemagne, with cultural development shifting from the Mediterranean to northern Europe. But the most vigorous European architectural activity during the Carolingian revival and the Ottonian period was Muslim, for in Spain, during the eighth, ninth, and tenth centuries, some of the most splendid of all Muslim architecture was in the process of being realized.

The Arabs, after conquest once more confronting a local culture and using its architecture as a basis for the development of their own monuments, found themselves face to face again with antiquity in Roman Spain. A pier-and-arch system, columns with naturalistic capitals, and the monumentality of Roman architecture became programmatic features of Iberian Muslim architecture. Numerous Roman forms were used to articulate the space of the sanctuary of the finest structure of the early Islamic far West—the Great Mosque in Córdoba, begun in 786 and enlarged in several stages through the tenth century (fig. 6-7). Conforming to the rectangular mosque layout with open courtyard and aisled sanctuary that had been established in the Syrian East and was now transported to the Spanish West, the design of the Great Mosque lent itself easily to the several stages of its expansion through an additive process, bypassing the western concern for preordained regularity.

Among the unique features of the huge sanctuary at Córdoba is its system of double-tiered arches (fig. 6-1), upheld by myriad columns on which rested the original wooden roofs (replaced now by stone vaults). On the first tier, the arches

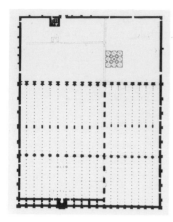

6-7
Plan, as enlarged in 987,
Great Mosque. Córdoba, Spain.
(From Gómez-Moreno, 1951)

6-8   Dome near the mihrab, Great Mosque. 962–66

(supported by columns removed from existing Roman structures) were given the singular horseshoe shape that departed from the Roman round arch and was probably a Visigothic invention adapted by the Muslims from the remains of Visigothic architecture in Spain before the Arab conquest. (The Visigoths were Teutonic invaders who had established a kingdom in Spain, in the fifth century.) From this point forward, the form became a distinguishing feature of Islamic architecture in Spain and North Africa (Moorish architecture). The horseshoe arch at Córdoba was surmounted on the second tier by a smaller round arch borne by piers resting on the lower columns. The two-tier arrangement was an unusual pattern in a religious structure. It may have been an original conception, or possibly it was derived from the design of Roman aqueducts, which were to be seen in Spain. But the straightforward, utilitarian aqueduct design was transformed, in the hands of the Muslims, into an airy cage, which, with its repeated loops and interlacings enriched by materials used decoratively—alternating red brick and white stone—suggested something abstract and not at all practical, something visionary and consonant with the religious spirit of Islam. As it had been in Damascus, space in Córdoba has become mysterious and seemingly limitless, slipping into unseen regions through the proliferating apertures of the polyarched structure. Behind this effect lay the influence of novel features developed in late Hellenistic buildings of the Near East and in the North African provinces of the late Roman Empire: colonnaded screens in front of luminous airy niches generating secondary and tertiary shells of space; the fluid motion of buoyant space along and between a variety of open forms and curving shapes.

The ninth- and tenth-century enlargements at Córdoba added not only more area to the original fabric, but also more elaborate passages to the design, most particularly the remarkable dome above the square bay preceding the mihrab (962–66; fig. 6-8), with its cross bracings, interlacing arches, and rich stucco and mosaic decorative overlay. In the Jerusalem Dome of the Rock, the high dome was an exterior symbol of the power of Islam, and a unique iconic image. The dome near the mihrab at Córdoba is a more representative Muslim feature, wherein the formal and decorative program concentrates on the interior. From the earliest period of Umayyad architecture, Roman, and even more so Byzantine, domical construction had been appropriated by Muslim builders for

both its shape and its symbolism. In Roman prototypes, the dome had served to shape a bubble of space in the interior, to define a volume. For the Muslims, the geometric, decorative, and symbolic potential of the dome led to brilliant inventions that were uniquely Islamic and vastly different from those of the Romans. Most Islamic domes (the Dome of the Rock always an exception), like those of Byzantine structures, rose over square, not circular, plans so that the corners of the square had to be bridged with the squinches or pendentives devised and used expansively by Byzantine architects to create an octagonal or circular base for the dome. At Córdoba, the Muslims devised corner bridges, made of lobed arches, alternating with arches framing clerestory windows and building toward a geometrically intricate, crossed-rib pattern that forms an octagonal base for the petaled dome. The complexity of this abstract design, in combination with its richly ornamented surface, deflects the attention of the observer away from questions of structure and support. What commands notice instead is the dazzling, rotating, multilayered configuration of shapes and patterns.

The mosque at Córdoba is in a strategic historical position. The first monumental religious construction in the Islamic West, it could be viewed as the culminating monument of the early Islamic period. The ninth- and tenth-century extensions of the mosque already belong to medieval Islamic architecture in the West—that of Moorish Spain and North Africa. In fact, the kind of Moorish style announced at Córdoba would mature most powerfully in the thirteenth and fourteenth centuries (just before the end of Islamic rule on the Iberian peninsula in 1492) in the Alhambra Palace at Granada. In the Christian world, this is the age of Gothic architecture; although the Alhambra is primarily a secular structure, it is interesting to weigh the obvious parallels between some of the transcendental aspects of Moorish buildings such as the Alhambra and those of Gothic churches.

On a hill overlooking Granada, the Alhambra—a sprawling palace-citadel that comprised royal residential quarters, court complexes flanked by official chambers, a bath, and a mosque—was begun in the thirteenth century by Ibn al-Ahmar, founder of the Nasrid dynasty, and was continued by his successors in the fourteenth century. Its most celebrated portions—a series of courtyards surrounded by rooms—present a varied repertoire of Moorish arched, columnar, and domical forms. The romantic imagination of centuries of visitors has been captivated by the special combination of the slender columnar arcades, fountains, poetic inscriptions, and light-reflecting water basins found in those courtyards—the Lion Court in particular (fig. 6-9). The morphological, ancestry of these courts can be traced back to ancient Western culture, in particular to the Greek-derived peristyle court of the rear portion of Roman houses, composed of columns, gardens, and fountains, and reserved for private family life. Western also are Gothic engineering devices that, it is often pointed out, provide a structural basis for the support system of the heavy arcades on exceptionally slender shafts. But also found in the Alhambra, and unprecedented in the West, is one of the greatest of all Muslim contributions to the history of architecture, originating in some North African structures of the eleventh century—the *muqarnas* work in the star-shaped vaults of the Alhambra's Hall of the Abencerrajes (fig. 6-10) flanking the Lion Court. A type of three-dimensional architectural decoration formed by stucco, or sometimes wood, into a multiple network of open cells, *muqarnas* resembles the cross section of a honeycomb, with stalactite suspensions. It covers entirely the structural organization beneath the surface of a wall or vault, which appears to have been "scooped out" in the process of forming this uniquely rich cellular overlay.

Muqarnas was another, albeit exceedingly elaborate, aspect of the ubiquitous nonfigural decoration that was one of the features of Islamic architecture, setting it distinctly apart from that of the West. From the earliest structures, the Dome of the Rock, for example, the intense decoration of surfaces became an essential component in the total concept of Muslim building. The Islamic religion did not permit the representa-

6-10   Vault, hall of the Abencerrajes, Alhambra

tion of the human figures on its buildings, but architects more than compensated for this exclusion. Materials used on the interior of buildings were rarely left in a natural state, but, as in Roman, Early Christian, and Byzantine structures, only more so, were enriched with color from mosaic or tile, dissolved by grills or pressed-mold stucco relief, and overlayed with the ornamental calligraphy of Koranic inscriptions, executed in a seemingly infinite variety of plaited, geometrically labyrinthine patterns. In the Jerusalem mosque, and in the many and varied mosques that followed it in the Near East, wall surfaces were carpeted with fields of mosaic, entablatures and cornices were encrusted with relief, capitals were drill-pierced, and Koranic calligraphy was integrated into the stylized ornamental imbrication. Even when, as in eleventh-century Persian Islamic (Seljuk) buildings, the surfaces were common brick, the brick was worked as delicately and exquisitely as stucco and wood by craftsmen of exceptional skill. In the North Dome Chamber of the Great Mosque of Masjid-i-Jami in Isfahan (1088; fig. 6-11), one of the finest examples of Seljuk architecture, workaday brick is magically transformed into something almost gossamer. Squinches are hollowed into billowing concavities, and the drum is articulated by low-relief, ogival, blind arcades with contours so delicate that the cupola above seems to be an air-filled tent of soft fabric anchored by fragile cords. The contrast in the appearance of this chamber and any portion of a contemporary Romanesque structure in the West (Winchester Cathedral, for example, fig. 5-56), is striking. In the Western building, the accent is on monumental physical substance, on the wall as a massive stone shell surrounding an inert hollow of space. At the

6-9   Lion Court, Alhambra. Granada, Spain. 13th–14th century

6-11 Great Mosque of Masjid-i-Jami. Isfahan, Iran. 1088

multiplying, all-enclosing shapes and continuous surfaces a hypnotic trancelike mood of spiritual transport conducive to prayer and to communal meditation. Islamic religious architecture, no less than Christian, especially Eastern Christian (Byzantine) and Gothic, was the dematerialized symbol of a spiritual vision. In both cultures, the worshiper was characteristically (though not always) prompted to "forget" the structure, to disregard evidence of load and support, so that the building fabric could present itself as a seemingly weightless encapsulation by an otherworldly, nonmaterial force. While the flying buttresses and other supports of the Gothic cathedral could be ignored, they were rarely actually hidden; but the joints and underpinnings, the beams and webs behind the deeply recessed, lacelike *muqarnas*, for example, usually worked not only to disguise, but to dissolve and deny, the solid material substance of the interior of a Muslim structure. No matter how dramatically the mass of a Gothic wall might be voided into a network of linear elements, the tectonic system of its verticals and horizontals, the structural logic of its rib vaulting sprouting from columnar supports, the rhythmic sequence of its bays, was always visible, comprehensible, and clearly defined. Intriguingly, a number of elements that helped give Gothic architecture its special linear and even graphic nature, such as the pointed arch, the rib, and elements adopted into its tracery such as lobed arches and some interlace designs, probably came into the West from contact with Islam. But the emphasis on structural logic of Western medieval architecture was alien to the tendencies of Muslim building even though both traditions can be traced to the same ancient formal roots and over the course of time exerted some mutual influence.

The vigor of classic Moorish architecture in Spain was not sustained after the fourteenth century. The Alhambra was the last grand structure in the Islamic far West and coincided with the final phase of Islamic dominance in Spain. European Late Gothic and Renaissance architecture now subsumed the Muslim architectural achievement there. Moorish buildings became increasingly infiltrated by Gothic and Renaissance elements added to already elaborate decorative programs, so that the earlier integrity of the style was destroyed. But roughly contemporary with the Western Islamic golden age (tenth to fourteenth centuries), there had flourished in the Near East—especially in Cairo after its foundation by Caliph al-Muizz in 969—an exceptionally brilliant period of Muslim building, which has some bearing on the relation of Islam and the architecture of the West. Numerous mosques and madrasas (schools for religious instruction), as well as secular buildings such as mausolea, palaces, and citadels, endowed Cairo, first under the Fatimids and then the Mamluks, with what has remained one of the richest concentrations of well-preserved Islamic structures in the world. Not only in Egypt, but in Persia, Syria, and Iraq there proliferated mosques, madrasas, and tombs of a quality of construction and design that have made them milestones of world-architecture.

One of the most impressive of the Cairo structures in terms of size, function, and decoration is the complex of buildings belonging to the mosque-madrasa (begun in 1356) of Mamluk Sultan Hasan al-Nasir, who ruled Egypt from 1347 to 1351 and from 1354 to 1362. The mosque sanctuary with its qibla

Isfahan mosque, the North Dome Chamber is unrelieved by revetment or any material other than its brick; but the wall, even though thick, looks as if it has been peeled back in thin layers, scooped out in small cavities, and dissolved by a variety of ornamental bricklaying so that it finally resembles a supple cloth woven into textile patterns and shaped by the fluid space it encloses.

Roman architecture had also been an architecture of ornament and revetment, but while panels of marble, fields of mosaic, applied orders, rich moldings, and carved friezes covered the brick or concrete surfaces of a Roman building, the structural system rarely was completely hidden. On the contrary, it typically was underscored and displayed. Joints, springing points, space-shaping surfaces, entablatures, vaults, the system of load and support, all were exposed or accented to call attention to the structural armature and definition of the parts of a building. Even the coffering of Roman domes served to extend illusionistically the perceived thickness and solidity of the domical mass rather than to obliterate it as did, for example, the *muqarnas*.

The real or apparent structuralism of the architecture of the antique West was generally rejected by its descendants in the Islamic world (at least in pre-Ottoman Islam). The pervasive ornamental decoration in Muslim buildings tended to obscure such clarity of tectonic organization, and to achieve through the unlimited repetition of interlocking and self-

**6-12   Courtyard, Mosque-Madrasa of Sultan Hasan al-Nasir.
Cairo. c. 1356**

wall is one of four grand vaulted halls (iwans) leading out of an open court through a huge pointed arch in an overall cruciform design (fig. 6-12). The other three chambers functioned as madrasas, and in the corners of the cross were four similar madrasas each with its own complex of student rooms, a courtyard, and iwans. Most majestic of all is the monumental domed mausoleum, flanked by minarets, adjacent to the sanctuary

6-13   Mausoleum of Sultan Hasan al-Nasir. Cairo. 1362

(fig. 6-13). The geometric clarity of the design of this structure and of the entire complex, and the cubic volumes free of columns can be traced back to sources in the West. The centrally planned domed martyria of early Christianity were in the background of the mausoleum structure at Sultan Hasan's mosque; to precedents in medieval Byzantine architecture are owed the sharply defined spaces and austere cubic forms of the Cairo structure, whose stylistic contrast with Moorish Spain underscore the difficulties of generalizations about Islamic design.

MUSLIM BUILDINGS AND THE ARCHITECTURE OF BYZANTIUM

The contribution of Byzantine architecture to Muslim buildings accounts for one of the most significant of the diverse regional styles of the Islamic world and was realized most dramatically in Turkey after the Ottoman conquest of Constantinople, seat of Christendom in the East, in 1453. There the Ottoman architects chose to model their mosques on the churches of Byzantium and primarily, of course, on Hagia Sophia. The Mosque of Suleyman (1550; fig. 6-14) in Constantinople is a paradigm of the type with its huge, domed, central area opening through grand arches to subsidiary spaces vaulted on two sides by buttressing half-domes. Like the principal dome of Hagia Sophia, that of the Mosque of Suleyman—a hemisphere over a cubic space rising from curved pendentives—appears to float above a ring of light formed by closely spaced windows at its base. Like his Byzantine predecessors, Sinan, Suleyman's favorite architect, was able to achieve in his mosque for the sultan the Byzantine effect of weightless surface suspended in an atmosphere made fluid by dappled light and the color of ornament. No less for the Muslim than for the Christian was the suffused light of an interior space a symbol of the celestial, and so the mosques of Ottoman Turkey shared with the churches of Byzantium the rich and glowing embellishments. In a departure from pre-Ottoman mosque tradition, in which the exteriors of the buildings were structurally nonarticulated, the Mosque of Suleyman and other Ottoman structures, once again indebted to the architects of Hagia Sophia, integrated the design and appearance of interior and exterior shapes. The typical profile, therefore, of a sixteenth-century Ottoman mosque, is not dissimilar to contemporary European High Renaissance central-plan buildings where a compact cluster of subsidiary domed units are subordinated to the unifying central dome.

In contrast to this dense massing of arched and domed shapes are the tall tapering minarets at each corner of the mosque precinct. A uniquely Muslim invention, the balconied minaret-tower is recognized, like the spire of a Gothic church, as a religious symbol through its long association with the mosque. Although minarets came to be used as the places from which the faithful were called to prayer, towers in early mosques functioned only as indicators of a sacred site and as symbols of the political power of the caliphs. Minarets are one of the few forms in Muslim architecture to stress the vertical; even with the marked change from the low-ceilinged, early hypostyle mosque that the domed Turkish mosque represents, great height and bold vertical forms were generally not desired as metaphors for the heavenward reach of the spirit, as they were in Gothic architecture.

6-14   Mosque of Sultan Suleyman. Constantinople. 1550

Perhaps nowhere is the relation of piercing minaret to curving dome more poetically realized than in the renowned mausoleum, the Taj Mahal (fig. 6-15), from the last phase of Muslim building. A white marble tomb built in 1631–48 in Agra, seat of the Mughal Empire, by Shah Jehan for his wife, Arjuman Banu Begum, the monument sums up many of the formal themes that have played through Islamic architecture. Its refined elegance is a conspicuous contrast both to the Hindu architecture of pre-Islamic India, with its thick walls, corbeled arches, and heavy lintels, and to the Indo-Islamic styles, in which Hindu elements are combined with an eclectic assortment of motifs from Persian and Turkish sources. The combination of gardens and water as an evocation of the Koranic Paradise one recognizes from the Euro-Islamic Alhambra; the design as a domed cube allies the monument with the preferred Islamic sepulchral type seen in the mausoleum of Sultan Hasan in Cairo; its four iwans, with their long tradition of use in mosques and madrasas, are as much an identifying Muslim feature as the minarets; and the bulbous dome is a reflection of the Persian origins of the Moghul dynasty and the nationality of Shah Jehan's architect. Among the mausoleum's most celebrated features is the ever-present ornament of inlaid stone patterns and Koranic inscriptions; but the ornament is subordinated to the perfect balance of space and mass and to the harmonious proportions that more than in any other Islamic monument command universal admiration.

6-15   Taj Mahal. Agra, India. 1631–48

7-1
West facade,
Laon
Cathedral.
Laon, France.
End of 12th
century

To pass through the portals of Amiens Cathedral (c. 1220–69) and experience its immensity of form and space soaring to precarious heights is to enter a new architectural realm far removed from the Romanesque of only a century earlier (figs. 7-2–7-4). Amiens appears to overcome the limitations of mundane reality with a supernatural leap that denies its existence as mere stone and mortar. The Romanesque church had remained anchored in its monumental physical substance and its classicizing language, weight and proportions; Amiens Cathedral is the physical embodiment of a transcendent, modernist vision.

The visitor from Speyer, Toulouse, or Cluny, after a few unsettling moments, would have recognized the scheme of Amiens. The bay system remains prominent, defined by columnar and vaulting elements visibly descended from the earlier period. Similarly, the basilican scheme of the church, its transept and chapel-encircled apse, are familiar medieval themes. Yet, having recognized the building's link with the past, the visitor would have been struck even more by its originality and modernity. The Romanesque wall, its layers of heavy structure, and the closed surfaces of classicizing Romanesque vaults have given way to modernist skeletal forms. The solid Romanesque columns are drawn out into anticlassically attenuated colonnettes; these powerful shafts take on an almost linear character as they reach upward to the vaulting, which seems to float weightlessly within the skeletal armature of ribs.

This structural skeleton, braced on the exterior by a cage of flying buttresses, opens laterally to high arcades and giant clerestory windows originally filled with brilliant stained-glass panels that gave the interior a glowing luminosity. The elongated proportions (3 to 1) of the central nave cross section reinforce the verticalism of its spectacular height, about 139 feet to the keystone (as against Speyer's "mere" 107 feet). But the space is not only measurably immense. It takes on a distinctly new character. Romanesque space generally seemed an inert hollow within a massive stone shell. By comparison, the space of Amiens seems active and dynamic, an expansive force that lifts the ceiling high, stretching out the skeletal forms to their extreme thinness. Visually important as the stonework, and contained but restless in its energy, the space not only soars upward but drives forward down the nave, restrained finally by the curve of the choir.

THE MEANING OF GOTHIC

Most visitors to Amiens have many misleading preconceptions about the Gothic style, a legacy of confusion that has existed for nearly five hundred years. In the Renaissance it was believed that the Fall of Rome had been followed by a millennium of cultural degradation before art was brought to life again in the fifteenth century. In order to take maximum credit for this achievement, writers of the Renaissance cast medieval art in as gloomy a light as possible: The "Dark Age" came when the invading barbarian tribes of the north "ruined" the ancient arts and substituted their own inferior culture. The Goths, who actually wrought little physical damage when they took Rome in 410, were the tribe held to be chiefly responsible for this catastrophe. Thus, the term *Gothic* was concocted in the Renaissance as a part of its own self-definition.

This etymological muddle was only one of the troubles borne by Gothic architecture. Beginning in the eighteenth century, the style came back in favor and was valued by the Romantic movement for the very qualities the Renaissance had despised—irrational freedom and quintessential Christianity (as opposed to the "rational" and "pagan" architecture of the Renaissance). New buildings were erected in the Gothic style, and architects and scholars researched and pondered its history and meaning. But what were they to make of it? It did not fit the categories and vocabulary that had been developed for Classical and Renaissance architecture—it was strange and different, easier to copy than to understand. The term Gothic was kept, despite its absurdity; no other architectural period carries such an incongruous title. How did this happen? Even to its most brilliant and assiduous students, the style tended to remain elusive. Its mysteriousness, its primal energies seemed to be captured by the term "Gothic," with its overtones of the mysterious origins, fabled wanderings, wild imagination of the barbarian tribes of the north. Eventually "Gothic" came to be a term not that defined its architecture, but that was *defined by* this architecture, and whatever meanings were extracted from or read into it (hence: the "Gothic" novel, crabbed and spooky).

Modern architectural historians have gone to the opposite extreme of the old, simplistic view and have created a bewildering web of interpretations of Gothic architecture. Generally, three approaches tend to dominate: the structural, the visual, and the symbolic. The first emphasizes the skeletal stone structure of Gothic architecture, which is seen as pure engineering logic, as if the builders had little else in mind but the reduction of the massive Romanesque mural bulk to a minimal armature of stone. The nineteenth-century proponents of this viewpoint related the Gothic to their new architectural technology of iron and steel. As schematic, skeletal architecture, Gothic could be viewed conceptually as not that different from the Crystal Palace or the Eiffel Tower.

7-2　Nave, Amiens Cathedral. Begun 1220

7-3　Vaulting, Amiens Cathedral

7-4　Chevet, Amiens Cathedral

The second approach interprets Gothic architecture as part of the visual arts rather than of the science of statics. Some observers emphasize the role of line, which multiplies and takes over the visible interior structure, transforming it from an inert mass into an elegant configuration of lightweight, dynamic form. Others stress the role of light, not only the glow that radiates from the sheets of stained glass, but also the so-called diaphanous effect where Gothic structure is calculated to create visual double shells that optically undercut structural solidity. Alternately the Gothic interior is seen as layers of canopylike forms nestling concentrically one within the other; or the "diagonality" of the orientation of rib vaulting and pier forms (in contrast to Romanesque "frontality") is underscored.

But a building as complex as Amiens, for example, is not erected for structural or visual considerations alone, without emotions that run strong and deep. During the Gothic era, major intellectual and religious currents achieved symbolic expression in the cathedrals. The prevailing intellectual discipline of the period was Scholasticism, and its most famous exponent was Saint Thomas Aquinas (1225–74), whose encyclopedic *Summa Theologica* synthesized the religious and intellectual issues of the time. Important connections between Scholasticism and Gothic architecture have been established, such as the translations of the encyclopedic visions into the stone and glass decorative programs of the cathedrals, or the close correspondence of the rationalistic organization of the cathedrals and the Scholastic treatises.

Scholasticism may be a cultural mirror image of the Gothic cathedral, but this interpretation does not capture the architecture's magic and excitement, which are suggested by a less easily documented, but pervasive, symbolism—that of the cathedral as an image of the Heavenly Jerusalem, the Divine City described by Saint John the Evangelist in the Gospel and Saint Augustine in *The City of God* as the ultimate destination of the elect—those who achieve salvation. As the House of the Lord on earth, the cathedral must attain an otherworldly appearance—in its statuary and stained glass, in its sheer scale and magnificence, and, most crucially, in its inspired and calculated formal transcendence of earthly limitations. It is medieval humanity's visionary conception of transcendental reality, the ultimate architecture of the Age of Faith. Only such an interpretation explains the design of the cathedral and the deep and enduring religious feeling that accompanied its construction. It is this visionary quality, mighty and all-pervasive within the cathedral, that first strikes the visitor.

The visionary primacy of the Gothic cathedral puts the other aspects of the building in proper perspective. The architects began with the symbolic vision as the goal, and—in a true parallel to the hierarchical Scholastic viewpoint—everything else became a means to that end. Thus, the main formal features—space, light, line, geometry—create the transcendent atmosphere of the building; the structural features—rib vaulting, pointed arches, flying buttresses—make possible the visual factors. The flying buttresses, which ring the cathedral, support the forms that shape its visionary interior. To the observer within, who "forgets" the buttressing frame, these forms appear to stand solely on the basis of supernatural force, miracle, and God's Grace, proclaiming the supremacy of faith over reason. As a transcendental style, Gothic shares much with Byzantine. Hagia Sophia is the eastern counterpart to Amiens, not only in concept but also in its statement of the otherwordly values of Christianity. In both buildings, rational, geometric structures create irrational effects.

The Rib Vault. Although we have emphasized the symbolic and visual qualities of the Gothic cathedral rather than the structural aspects, there is no denying the crucial role of the latter, in particular the system of rib vaulting (fig. 7-5). The term is an organic metaphor, alluding to the role of ribs in anatomy as the body's skeletal structure supporting connective tissue.

7-5
Gothic rib vaulting under construction, diagram. (After J. H. Acland)

Actually, the architectural "ribs" are nothing but arches, usually three pairs per rectangular bay, running diagonally, transversely, and longitudinally. It is the diagonal arches that distinguish ribbed from nonribbed vaults, since the surrounding frame of transverse and/or longitudinal arches is not uncommon in Romanesque barrel and groin vaults. This difference is critical, however, not only visually, but also technically and structurally. The cross ribs act together with the outer arcuated frame to create a complete armature of arches along all the edges and main folds of the vault. This has decisive advantages, and to understand them we must go back for a moment to the Roman/Romanesque groin vault, which is formed by the intersection of two barrel vaults at right angles. Although this workhorse of architectural engineering had certain advantages over the barrel vault, it had strong limitations in practice. It is open on all sides to permit the flow of light and space, and its weight is, to a degree, concentrated at the corners, but it is heavy and requires massive centering during construction. Moreover, the groin vault poses a serious technical problem. It fits naturally only over a square plan, and even then the line of intersection of the barrel vaults—the groin lines—forms, theoretically, a warped parabolic curve difficult to construct as a clear, graceful line.

The rib vault overcomes these obstacles. To understand how, we must first realize that the cross-ribbed vault is not merely a traditional groin vault with projecting arches running along its groins. The builder of the groin vault begins conceptually with two tunnels; at their intersection, the parabolic groin lines are formed as a secondary element. But the cross ribs of the ribbed vault are conceived as primary elements, whose curvature is independent of the other arcuated shapes of the vault. Thus, the ribs can be semicircular, segmental, parabolic, stilted, pointed, or any other configuration the builder chooses. Moreover, they can be elevated from point to point over practically every conceivable ground plan—rectangular, triangular, trapezoidal, pentagonal, hexagonal, circular, or whatever. Technically, the ribs also facilitate the construction process. Rib vaults require centering only for the arches of each bay; the arches themselves become a form of permanent centering for the construction of the webs. Structurally, the advantages of this system are enormous; by abandoning the ponderous groin vault for a set of sturdy ribbed arches and relatively thin shells of webbing, the weight of the vault is much reduced.

The Flying Buttress. Ribs act to concentrate the entire weight and thrust at the corners of the bays. The reduced, more concentrated load permits more slender piers and thus larger windows in the nave walls, provided there is sufficient buttressing of the lateral thrust. Since the thrust is gathered and localized at small areas, a counterthrust is needed only at those areas and not, as before, over a great extent. Even if the rib vault springs from a high point—over 100 feet at Amiens—it is necessary only to meet the lateral thrust that emerges from that point and to counteract wind pressures acting on the external surfaces. This is achieved with buttressing, effected by powerful external arches swung above the side aisles and the ambulatory (fig. 7-6). These arches rise from colossal freestanding piers, which absorb the thrust in their immovable inertia and channel the disruptive forces safely to the ground. This

7-6
Flying buttresses, diagram
of forces. (After J. H. Acland)

aptly named system of flying buttresses shifts the required buttressing mass from the nave wall, where it would limit fenestration and require cumbersome supports below, to a location outside the aisle and ambulatory wall, where towering piers can be erected without much affecting the nave or choir interior. This radically freed the planning of the entire building.

The Pointed Arch. Why did the Gothic builders turn from the semicircular, unbroken arch to pointed ones (fig. 7-7)? Two reasons are almost intuitively obvious. Pointed arches look lighter, have an inherent visual buoyancy, pointing upward rather than sinking downward. It is not merely the look, though. A pointed arch actually exerts less thrust than a semicircular arch of the same span. The typical Gothic pointed arch approximates a catenary curve, that is, the natural shape taken by a chain hung between two supporting points. This shape, viewed upright, is the structurally ideal curvature of an arch. This ideal curvature is one in which the lines of force run exactly through the center of its mass, not veering dangerously to either edge as in the round arch (if the forces pass beyond the edges, structural failure results). Thus, a pointed arch can safely be thinner than a comparable round arch, obviously a critical consideration in cathedral construction.

The pointed arch also solves a geometric difficulty inherent in ribbed vaults. The problem comes from the fact that the sides of a square and its diagonal are not the same; and in the case of a rectangle, three separate dimensions (diagonal, width, and length) are involved. To see how the problem arises, consider the common situation of a builder erecting a rib vault over a square bay, with only semicircular ribs and arches throughout. Since the diagonal base of the cross ribs is greater by a factor of $\sqrt{2}$ (or 1.414) to 1 than the base of the framing arches, the former rise proportionately that much higher than the latter. This creates what is called a domical

ribbed vault, typically used in Lombard construction. Generally, a domical vault causes the bay to be deeply shadowed and disjointed from neighboring bays, and it practically nullifies one of the most important structural advantages of rib vaulting: the flow of all the thrust to the corners of the vault. With a domical vault, the ridges of the vaulting webs do not run horizontally; they ascend toward the vaulting center, which is higher (by a factor of 1.414) than the framing arches from which these webs depart. And this means that, much as in a true hemispheric dome, thrust flows down from the top not only along the ribs, but also out in all directions, exerting stress all along the framing arches, which have to be correspondingly massive and provided with considerable support and buttressing. Thus, the domical rib vault usually not only looks clumsy, it is clumsy. The trick is to get the ridges of the vaulting webs horizontal, or nearly so, which means arranging for all of the arches and ribs to rise to a common level (fig. 7-5). It is impossible to do this using exclusively semicircular ribs sprung from the same level, for in such a case only one set of ribs/arches can be a pure semicircle (fig. 7-8). The others must either eliminate part of the curve to form a segmental arch, or add to its height by elevating it on "stilts." With a rectangular bay (typical of Gothic buildings), the builder has three choices. If the cross ribs are semicircular, then the other, shorter, arches must be stilted. If the lateral arches (the shorter ones) are semicircular, then the other, longer, arches/ribs must be segmental. Finally, if the transverse arches are

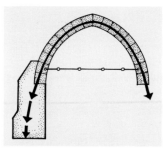

7-7
Pointed arch, diagram of line of
thrust. (After J. H. Acland)

7-8   Four alternative geometric solutions of rib vault over
       rectangular bay A, B, C, D, using differing combinations of
       round and/or pointed arches. (Partly after J. Bilson)

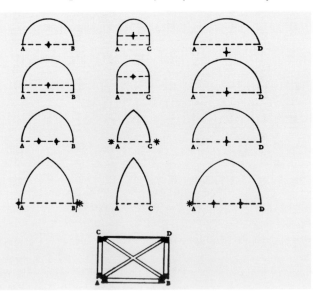

semicircular, then the lateral arches are stilted and the cross ribs are segmental.

These solutions are not merely theoretical; they were actually employed in the early phases of Norman and French rib vaulting. Strange as it may seem, it was only after a number of decades that the builders grasped what would seem to us the obvious step: to abandon the continuous curve of the round arch altogether, to break it at the keystone into a pointed arch, which, by simply varying the degree of "pointing," could be made to rise to practically any height over any base. Thus, the ridges could easily be made level, the only variance between the supporting ribs being their degree of pointing. Visually, this variance creates a lively tension instead of the old unsightly contrast between stilted, segmental, and semicircular shapes. Once the nature and interrelationships of the rib vault, the flying buttress, and the pointed arch are understood, one can follow the complex early history of Gothic architecture.

GOTHIC IN FRANCE

The First Early Gothic Style. The first coherent examples of the Gothic appear in the middle of the twelfth century around Paris, but the roots of the new style go back a century earlier to Normandy and Norman England. It was in Normandy, we recall, at the eleventh-century Abbey Church of St.-Étienne in Caen, that the wall was first changed into mass-dissolving double shells and gathered into linear columnar elements. This treatment was extended to the ceiling at Durham (figs. 5-58, 7-9), first in the choir-aisle vaults (1093) and then over the choir (before 1110), and the nave (1128–33). In the latter vaults— huge double bays with pointed transverse arches and roughly semicircular cross ribs—the desire to carve out enormous cells of space was paramount. At about the same time, this impulse was channeled into even more influential forms in the sexpartite vaults added ex post facto at St.-Étienne. Later in the century, this sexpartite format became standard in the French Gothic.

In the third decade of the twelfth century, the development of Gothic passed southeastward to the Île-de-France. How and why this small region with a minor Romanesque style suddenly gave birth to an architecture that would hold sway over all Europe for centuries is not easy to answer. But the ascendant French monarchy established its seat there, and the dynamic political ambitions of the crown spilled over into other areas. In the twelfth century, Paris became the intellectual capital of Europe, and, within a hundred-and-fifty-mile radius of the city, Gothic art and architecture took form in an extraordinary series of buildings. The earliest examples of French Gothic architecture, small, experimental structures built from about 1120 to 1130, embody a new technique and a new, forward-looking spirit. Cut-stone masonry—rather than the rubble masonry of the Normans—was employed in the vaulting, enabling the architects to build more lightly in actual weight and in appearance. At the same time, arches and ribs were designed with independent curvatures—which the Normans had not done. At first, only the unbroken curve was employed, but soon the pointed arch came into use. The French architects, of course, were concerned not only with novelties of geometry and technique, but also with the visible results. From the beginning, the French vaults were pervaded

7-9   Choir-aisle vaults, Durham Cathedral. 1093

7-10   Rib vaulting, St.-Étienne. Beauvais, France. c. 1125

7-11   Ground plan of chevet, St.-Denis. Paris. 1140–44

7-12   Ambulatory, St.-Denis

with a graceful verve and buoyancy, even in the earliest examples, such as the side aisles of St.-Étienne at Beauvais (c. 1125; fig. 7-10). Here, rib vaulting appears in almost theoremlike purity for the first time. The ribs and arches are stripped clean of the decorative encumbrances of the contemporary Durham vaults, reduced to pure structure and line. The ribs have the typical Early French, unadorned torus profile. The articulate supports, simple and light, are more clearly integrated with the vaulting; the capitals beneath the cross ribs are now set on the diagonal. Although the geometry is not yet at the pointed arch stage, St.-Étienne reveals the new clarity and elegance of the French architects.

The Abbey Church of St.-Denis, just outside Paris, represents the definitive turning point in Early French Gothic. It is the earliest structure that most scholars agree is Gothic in the true sense, for it is the first case in which the hierarchy of the elements of Gothic style is achieved, and where space, light, line, and geometry create a transcendent modernist architectural vision (figs. 7-11–7-15). St.-Denis is a crucial building in other ways as well. Its dedicatory saint was an early Christian martyr who had been confused in the medieval mind with an important philosopher, the Pseudo-Dionysius, whose Neoplatonic writings emphasized the symbolism of light. (Denis is the French equivalent of Dionysius.) The abbey basked in the patronage of the throne, for St.-Denis was the traditional burial site of the kings of France. In the twelfth century, the ambitious Abbot Suger of St.-Denis undertook the reconstruction of the old ninth-century church in the new, emerging architectural style. Suger wrote at length about this experience. He was profoundly affected by the Neoplatonic current of his day, as it was expressed in the writings of the Pseudo-Dionysius. Although he was a religious churchman, Suger was fond of physical splendor. Dionysian Neoplatonism offered a reconciliation of this seeming contradiction. It claimed that through the contemplation of physical beauty we are led anagogically to higher, even divine, realities. Dionysian writings brought Suger close to the Christian theme of God as light. Suger did not have to gloat furtively over his abbey's hoard of precious stone and materials, but could, as he proudly tells us, indulge himself in contemplating them. Gradually, this contemplation induced in him a trancelike state, a form of self-hypnosis that

7-13   Panoramic view from altar, St.-Denis

7-14   Ambulatory vaults, St.-Denis

led to a vision of ideal beauty and, ultimately, to its heavenly source. What is so important is not just that Suger seems to have enthusiastically believed in Neoplatonic exercises, but that he apparently translated his belief into high artistic patronage.

Suger did not live long enough to complete the new church. Most of the interior, in fact, was built in the post–High Gothic style of the 1230s. But the imposing facade (now altered and much restored) is Suger's (c. 1130–40). The crucial structure for the development of Gothic architecture, however, was relatively small scale, scarcely visible from the greater part of the interior: the double ambulatory of Suger's new choir, built between 1140 and 1144.

In Suger's ambulatory, the geometric clarity and skeletal lightness that appear earlier in the vaults of such precocious churches as St.-Étienne at Beauvais were extended to the design as a whole. This is apparent in the plan, which is developed on a strict geometric scheme. From a central point, radial lines intersect with concentric half circles to establish the position of all the upright structural elements of the choir: the hemicycle piers, the intermediate ambulatory supports, and at the outer edge, the buttress piers that divide the seven chapels. Similar layouts in Romanesque ambulatories a half century earlier produced heavy structures with dark and sharply compartmentalized spaces, anything but elegant and transparent. At St.-Denis, however, the massive Romanesque frame is replaced by a skeletal system. The ambulatory supports are reduced to two rings of columns within a concentric

outer frame, itself reduced to a gently scalloped line between relatively slender, though complex, piers clothed in mass-dissolving colonnettes. The outer wall has yielded to two enormous windows per bay, and the walls that in older buildings divided the radiating chapels have all but melted away. The linear mode of design extends to all parts of the structure—supports as well as ceiling. A fluid and transparent space opens in all directions beneath buoyant, graceful rib vaulting and flows along the ambulatory path out to the arching windows. Through this seamless configuration of line and fluid space, light flows uninterruptedly.

At Suger's choir the formal values—space, light, line, geometry—intrinsic to true Gothic create a higher meaning for the architecture and a transcendental, visionary effect. The role of light was particularly important in this respect. Suger himself gave us the clue when he wrote the often-quoted passage describing his new choir as "That elegant and praiseworthy extension, in [the form of] a circular string of chapels, by virtue of which the whole [church] would shine with the wonderful and uninterrupted light of most sacred windows, pervading the interior beauty." The "uninterrupted" transparency of the space, not completely apparent from within the ambulatory, is fully perceived from only one place in the entire choir, but it is the most important spot—from the main altar within the great hemicycle, in other words, from Suger's own privileged viewpoint as celebrant of High Mass (fig. 7-13). Through the uninterrupted line of huge windows, abundant light

7-15   Facade, St.-Denis

7-16　Nave, Sens Cathedral. Begun c. 1130

flowed in toward the abbot. That light, passing through "most sacred windows," became the divine emanation of God; it pervaded the monumental structure and converged on Suger as he performed the miraculous transubstantiation.

For Suger. the facade structure, begun a decade before the choir, was as important as the ambulatory—perhaps more so (fig. 7-15). It was, after all, what the visitor to the abbey first saw, and Suger was concerned that it present as forceful an image as possible. The original facade form is still comprehensible—a twin-towered mass deriving ultimately from the Carolingian westwork and more directly from St.-Étienne at Caen. The type was integrated at St.-Denis with other motifs—the rose window and fortifications, the latter an allusion to the role of the abbey as symbolic defender of the realm and keeper of the regalia of the crown. The novel sculptural program of the three portals is of major importance. In the system begun at St.-Denis, sculpture and architecture are closely integrated; architectural elements take the form of figure sculpture, and vice versa. Just as in the ambulatory, all structural forms are brought into a disciplined, visionary system, so on the facade a complex Christian iconographic program is brought into a coherent, hierarchical configuration.

No traces survive of the choir enfolded by Suger's epoch-making ambulatory. Possibly it was not so radical in design as the ambulatory. To imagine its elevation one can study the contemporary Cathedral of Sens (c. 1130–64). Although portions were rebuilt in the thirteenth century, the Sens nave essentially conserves its mid-twelfth-century appearance (fig. 7-16). Its huge double bays are powerfully defined at the corners by the major piers, and above, by the sexpartite vaulting units. With their five sturdy, attached colonnettes, these piers are even more substantial than their massive Romanesque counterparts at Durham. The pier arrangement at Sens is a logical outcome of the Norman practice of providing every arched or vaulting member with a separate columnar support—one colonnette per pier for the transverse arch, two for the diagonal ribs, and two for the wall arches (formerets, not present in Norman vaults). Eventually, this abundance of forms would be pared down, but at Sens it contributes an almost Romanesque sense of massiveness to the building. Apart from the major piers, the nave elevation at Sens is a departure from the heaviness and the complex decoration of Durham. The "minor" monocylindrical columns are doubled, permitting lighter proportions. The wall above the arches has two thin layers instead of the three dense relief zones of Durham. And running almost playfully up the wall above the intermediate piers is a slender colonnette.

The Second Early Gothic Style. Following St.-Denis and the Cathedral of Sens, a number of impressive structures were built, designed about 1150/60–80/90, to form a second generation of Early French Gothic. One of the problems left unresolved by Suger's generation was that of the main interior elevation—the principal aspect of the church. Sens, and probably St.-Denis, were in this respect still rather heavy, with large areas of Romanesque mural substance remaining. Nor were they very tall. Among the most important second-generation structures to address the problem of the interior elevation is the Cathedral of Noyon (c. 1150/55–65/70; fig. 7-17). Its key innovation, one common to this period, was the addition of a fourth story to the traditional three levels—arcade, gallery, and clerestory. Builders of the time were gradually increasing the overall dimensions of their churches, yet they hesitated to increase proportionally the scale of the individual parts. This conservatism would have meant blank, heavy interior wall areas had the builders not added the new fourth element. In the Noyon choir, a first attempt (c. 1150) took the form of a blind arcade inserted between gallery and clerestory. In the nave of two decades later (c.1170), a striking stylistic transformation has taken place. The form of the supplemental zone is no longer the flat, heavy blind arcade but, instead, a double-layered structure with a closed outer layer and a miniature

7-17   Nave wall, Noyon Cathedral. c. 1170

7-18   South transept, Soissons Cathedral. c. 1180

inner arcade. This form, known as a triforium, derives from Norman usage, such as the original "thick-wall" clerestory of St.-Étienne at Caen. The Noyon triforium had a double function. It was a wall passage, facilitating access to the upper levels for maintenance, and it formed a diaphanous assemblage of space, light, and line. Moreover, it gave a vigorous horizontal accent to the dominantly vertical lines of the interior. For these reasons, the triforium soon became a common device, and it appears henceforth in nearly all French cathedrals.

The triforium was not the only innovation at Noyon. Just as the nave elevation at Sens was pared down, at least in part, from the massive, ornate fabric of Durham, at Noyon, the still-heavy structure of Sens was reduced to a style of linear elegance. The main piers, with the same number of elements, are much lighter, as are the slenderized minor supports. The articulation is crisp and energetic. Because of these details—and the displacement of inert wall by the triforium—the buoyant interior of Noyon seems to be enveloped by a cage of complex skeletal structures. On all sides rise tiers of secondary cells of space forming a diaphanous tissue of screened hollows that play against each other and enrich the central spatial frame.

Noyon was not the last word of this phase of Gothic. The astonishing elegance achieved about a decade later is seen in one of the most exquisite of all medieval interiors, the south transept arm of Soissons Cathedral (c. 1180; fig. 7-18). The four-storied elevation is essentially the same as that of Noyon, but the proportions and details are the result of a process of studied refinement. Nowhere is the idea of a central skeletal cage enveloped by floating tiers of diaphanous screens more effective.

The style of Noyon and Soissons can be seen in a number of buildings, such as St.-Remi at Reims, Notre-Dame-en-Vaux at Châlons-sur-Marne, and, most notably and on a larger scale, at Laon Cathedral (fig. 7-19), where there is a tendency toward greater fullness. The definitive example, however, of the monumental in Early Gothic is Notre-Dame in Paris, which was

7-19 Nave, Laon Cathedral. Begun c. 1160

7-20 Nave and choir, Notre-Dame. Paris. 1163–1250

founded by the archbishop Maurice de Sully (figs. 7-20, 7-21). He did not leave a written account of his architectural patronage, but it is clear that his ambition was the equal of Suger's. Construction began with the choir in 1163. The nave followed after 1178; the facade, 1200–1250. In the early thirteenth century the nave was given a larger, "modern" clerestory along with new buttressing; chapels were built in the peripheral zone of the building, between the buttress piers; flying buttresses were changed and added; and the mid-thirteenth-century transept facades were constructed. The original plan—that is, before the thirteenth century changes and additions—was one of great brilliance, carrying to a higher degree than ever before the geometric and visual clarity of the Suger ambulatory. Looking at the plan, one is struck by its discipline and balance. The five-aisled layout is the same from one end of the church to the other, terminating in a double ambulatory and interrupted only by a transept that does not break the line of the outer aisles. The choir is much deeper than those of earlier examples. Nave, transept, and choir are distinct entities, yet they are formally continuous and harmoniously balanced.

Compared to any other Early Gothic cathedral, the interior of Notre-Dame is overpowering in the effect of its immensity and energy. The building is, in fact, significantly larger than its contemporaries, particularly in height: about 115 feet to the keystone, a dimension that had been only about 90 feet at Laon. Even the most gigantic Romanesque churches, Cluny and Speyer, were now being surpassed by the new style. Looking

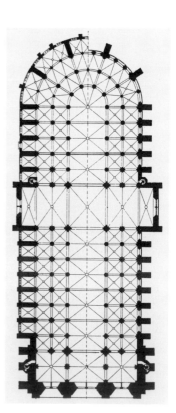

7-21
Plan, Notre-Dame,
showing original building (right)
and 13th-century additions (left)

back from the colossal High Gothic structures, Paris does not seem exceptionally large. But to the visitor from Soissons or Noyon, Sully's new church must have been overwhelming. It was not only the dimensions, but also the shaping of the particulars that created the sense of scale. Not the least of the particulars are the giant monocylindrical nave piers. We have traced the diminution of this component from Durham to Sens to Noyon. But at Laon the form expands again, and at Paris it assumes true grandeur. Paradoxically, the dramatic expansion in the bulk of the piers is accompanied by a radical thinning down of the superstructure. The wall is extremely thin relative to its height, and the detailing emphasizes this thinness. Significantly, rather than a triforium—which would create a

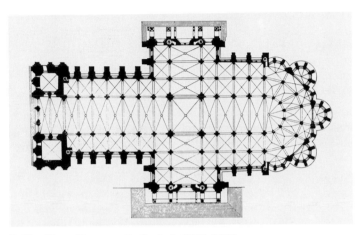

7-22 Plan, Chartres Cathedral. 1194–1220

7-23 Chartres Cathedral

sense of depth in the wall—a series of circular windows originally relieved the area between the gallery and the original, much shorter, lancet clerestory windows. This motif was eliminated in the thirteenth-century enlargement of the clerestory but partly restored in the nineteenth century—in the bays adjacent to the crossing. These oculi, too, emphasized the thin, floating planes of the wall. But the most extreme means devised for the dematerialization of structure were the triplets of radically thin colonnettes that rise uninterruptedly to the vaults. These colonnettes have become so attenuated that for the first time they assume the appearance of pure, fiery, ascending lines of energy. Thus, whereas the cathedrals of Noyon, Soissons, and Laon have harmonious continuities and large central spaces enveloped diaphanously by tiers of smaller ones, the architectural drama of Paris depends strongly on the contrast and exaggeration of effects: Its extremely massive supports boldly uplift a high, thin wall; and the wall is an animated configuration of line, surface, and light patterns that combine to lift the space upward to the grandiose vaults and pull it forward down the immense length of nave and choir.

High Gothic: Chartres. Of all the Gothic buildings prior to 1190, Notre-Dame in Paris most clearly points the way to the High Gothic phase that follows and culminates at Amiens. Yet a great divide separates the two architectural generations. The chasm of separation opens suddenly in a single revolutionary building—the Cathedral of Chartres, begun in 1194, completed (except for the transept facades) in 1220 (figs. 7-22–7-24). No previous building in medieval architecture embodied such a

7-24   Nave from choir, Chartres Cathedral

The changes affected every part of the building. Perhaps the first decision was to abandon the squarish double-bay format with its sexpartite rib vaulting. The quadripartite system that took its place was not in itself new (having been used consistently over side aisles), but its laterally stretched, rectangular proportions were. The old boxy, square bay, with its busy crisscrossing of ribs and intricate three-dimensional vaulting shapes, did not generate a strong lifting impulse; and its rhythmic pace down the nave was leisurely. At Chartres, the simplified vault reads with immediate clarity and caps a strikingly narrowed, soaring spatial unit.

The piers that frame the new bays are, correspondingly, no longer of alternating, disparate form, but uniformly tall and strong. In the twelfth century, architects had been unable to decide between the compound pier, with its many colonnettes rising in unison from the floor to the vault, and the simple, monocylindrical support, so they had included both in an alternating pattern, or had shifted back and forth in preference for one over the other. The Chartres Master resolved this conflict with the invention of a new pier—the so-called *pilier cantonné*—which combined both types in a single form. It incorporated Norman logic and dramatic uplifting all in a single vigorous unit, concentrating architectonic strength just as the new bay format concentrated spatial energy.

Vaulting and pier provided the basic frame for the new Chartres bay. But what of the wall? To create greater monumentality it was necessary to reduce the number of wall elements. Obviously, the arcade and clerestory had to be kept. To

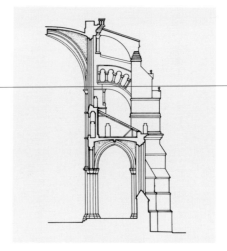

**7-25
Cross section of nave,
Chartres Cathedral.
(After R. Mark)**

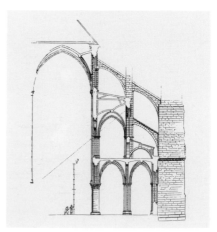

**7-26
Cross section of nave,
Notre-Dame. Paris.
(After Viollet-le-Duc)**

dramatic metamorphosis or such a quantum leap in monumentality. Unfortunately, we do not know the name of the architect of Chartres, but he was one of architecture's supreme masters, endowed with an indomitable will, a powerful intellect, and a bold imagination.

The Chartres Master obviously had studied the monuments of the Early Gothic movement critically and was dissatisfied with the way in which, even at Paris, a multiplicity of relatively small-scale elements were amassed in assemblages of immense visual wealth. He preferred a more austere building of monumental scale, in which the clear dynamic lines of the Gothic style emerged, stripped of distracting detail. But how did he achieve this revolutionary vision? Few of the elements in his architecture were new. He had been well trained in Early Gothic workshops; his rib vaults, skeletal apparatus, and wall articulation were familiar. What the Chartres Master did was to subject these elements to his new set of priorities, thereby discovering a bold new design formula for the Gothic cathedral that is deceptively simple. The process of transformation was one of reduction and synthesis, so that the resulting building was no longer loose and sprawling but was pervaded with a new rigor and energy.

eliminate the narrow triforium would not gain much. The gallery was the logical choice, for it was large and the most distracting element in the entire Early Gothic elevation. Eliminating the gallery and maintaining the relative scale of the triforium allowed for the expansion of arcade and clerestory, particularly the latter, which along with the triforium, could be lowered into the gallery zone. The rigorous Chartres Master elected to increase arcade and clerestory equally and to fill the added clerestory area with a new subdivided window form, called tracery, in the shape of twin lancets surmounted by an oculus. This pattern was to be the basic tracery format throughout the Gothic period.

The visual result of this chain of design events is momentous. Although Chartres, at about 125 feet to the vaulting, is only about 10 feet taller than Notre-Dame in Paris, it seems to be of an altogether higher magnitude of scale and energy (figs. 7-20, 7-24). The soaring proportions of the bay units reinforce the vertical drive of the piers, which is further accentuated by the upward thrust of arcade and window outlines. The vertical lines of energy are cut by strong horizontals, particularly the strong, dark belt of the triforium that sweeps the interior exactly at mid-height. Verticals and horizontals are each so strong and clear that they mutually sharpen and reinforce each other.

Light, too, plays a significant role, for the Chartres Master's reordering of the elevation created vast expanses of fenestration. Of all the Gothic cathedrals, Chartres is the only one where

7-27 Buttresses, Chartres Cathedral

the original stained glass is preserved in its entirety. A subdued, unearthly glow enters through 166 windows resplendent with biblical imagery glowing in deep, saturated primary colors. The magic of Chartres' illumination and the architectonic majesty of the building itself create an extraordinary vision of transcendence. Suger would have felt his architectural and religious desires fulfilled had he been able to behold the miracle of Chartres—a visionary architecture not limited to only a part of the building, as at St.-Denis, but extending throughout the whole church.

The radical transformation of the Chartres interior was possible because it was accompanied by an equally bold innovation in the structure. As we have emphasized, all arched structures generate thrust and usually require extensive bracing to counter it. In Romanesque and Early Gothic churches, the thrusts of the nave vaults are buttressed by galleries and the arches that run between gallery bays. About 1180, it occurred to architects that the arched buttress could be raised above the aisle-gallery roof to a more elevated point of support. Rising in the open above the roofing, such a form well deserves the name flying buttress. Its first known use occurs at the nave of Notre-Dame in Paris (c. 1180) as supplementary bracing set up in addition to the lateral support exerted by the galleries (fig. 7-26). It was typical of the Chartres Master to realize that the flying buttress, if sufficiently developed, made the gallery redundant as lateral bracing. It is the powerful system of flying buttresses at Chartres (figs. 7-25, 7-27) that allows the skeletal nave walls to soar high and free. On the interior, these buttresses are completely hidden (a "secret" of the building's illusionism), but on the outside they form a massing of great bulk. Tremendous exterior piers absorb the ponderous thrust channeled down from the vaults through three tiers of flying quadrant arches, as unforgettable in their power as the interior is in its architectural magic.

High Gothic after Chartres. The Chartres Master, in the judgment of his peers and followers, had overstated his case. Chartres was judged too austere and overbuilt, too massive for the Gothic sense of lightness and elegance. It was the task of the architects who followed to maintain the benefits of the new structural scheme of Chartres and combine this scheme with the established Gothic visual style.

This reaction is evident as early as the new nave and choir at Soissons (succeeding the Early Gothic project preserved in the transept), begun about 1200, before much of Chartres was actually built. (Architects of the period evidently knew each other's plans.) The architect of Soissons drastically simplified the Chartres plan by including only the main attached colonnette of the *pilier cantonné* and by generally thinning the massing. A more ambitious and important development followed at the Cathedral of Reims, the coronation church of the French monarchy and thus the fortunate recipient of lavish royal patronage. One of the major buildings of France, Reims Cathedral (colorplates 33, 34; figs. 7-28–7-30) was begun at the choir in 1211 and was basically completed in the mid-thirteenth century. The building is even larger than Chartres, with vaulting reaching to 131 feet over a stretched nave admirably suited to the spectacle of coronation ceremonies. The lavish sculptural program of Reims is of the highest importance, the culmination

7-28 Capital, Reims Cathedral. Begun 1211

7-29 Ambulatory and chapels, Reims Cathedral

7-30 Nave wall and vaults, Reims Cathedral

of High Gothic sculptural style. The architectural austerity of Chartres is renounced at Reims, where forms multiply and the architectural detailing displays a lavish naturalism, particularly in the interior capitals. At Reims one sees the Chartres scheme reinterpreted in the Early Gothic style of elegance and refinement. The force of this tradition is most evident in those parts of the building least affected by the Chartres innovations: the pre-Chartrian scheme of the ambulatory and radiating chapels. In the Reims chapels, there are graceful central canopy cells set within a diaphanous envelope of screened, secondary cells of space, all in a manner that had been momentarily suppressed—but not eradicated—at Chartres.

However, the nave, at first glance, appears to be a repetition of Chartres: the same four-part vaulting, three-part elevation, and *pilier cantonné*; and many dimensions were even larger. But this first impression is deceptive. Gradually, one perceives how at Reims the model was transformed; the austere forms of Chartres were endowed with the supple, soft elegance seen in purest form in the chapels. The Chartres piers are unique in their juxtaposition of cylindrical and octagonal elements: a cylindrical core set within octagonal colonnettes in one pier, an octagonal core with cylindrical colonnettes in the next, and so on in alternating pairs down the nave. This combination was the single note of fantasy permitted by the stern Chartres Master, but the abruptly contrasting prismatic/cylindrical shapes create lines of disjunction. At Reims, the pier forms are uniformly rounded and subtly graduated in diameter. But more was involved in this transformation than the softening of contrasts. The lancet shapes in all three levels of the elevation are steeper and more pointed in arcuation. There is less unrelieved masonry expanse. The arcade profiles multiply to visually disguise the thickness of the arch and to blend with the nearby colonnettes. In the clerestory, a new, more articulate form of tracery appears, filling the upper nave wall with a linear configuration and completing the extension of the skeletal structural concept throughout the entire elevation. Thus, whatever is hard, bare, and heavy at Chartres becomes soft, fluid, and elegant at Reims; whatever is still massive and mural becomes skeletal and linear.

If Reims is a synthesis of the monumental scheme of Chartres and the elegant style of its predecessors such as Laon and Noyon, what then are we to make of the nave of Amiens (c. 1220; figs. 7-31, 7-32), the paradigmatic building by which Gothic architecture was defined at the beginning of this chapter? In part, Amiens continued the trend away from the massiveness of Chartres. But at Amiens, the primary, pre-Chartrian influence is not the tradition of Laon and Noyon so much as it is the thin, taut style of Notre-Dame in Paris. This style is conspicuous in the thinness of the wall, the extreme attenuation of the columnar elements, and the tensile, wiry energy of the whole. However, Paris served as an inspiration, not as a model. Robert de Luzarches, the architect of the Amiens nave, introduced bold and ingenious modifications.

Amiens Cathedral is significantly larger than Reims, rising almost 139 feet to the vaults and containing the most interior space of any Gothic cathedral. The overall dimensions are immense, but it is the reshuffling of proportional relationships that makes the biggest difference in perceived scale. The cross section of the nave is now steeper than ever; the ratio of width to height is 1 to 3 as opposed to 1 to 2.6 at Chartres. The change in elevation is even more noticeable. A rarely noted fact in the development of High Gothic architecture is that the distance from the top of the arcade zone (marked by a stringcourse) to the top of the wall remains practically constant from Paris to Amiens (c. 60–65 feet). In other words, that part of the building lifted by the arcade remains nearly constant, while the arcade itself grows dramatically—32 feet at Paris, 46 feet at Chartres, 52 feet at Reims, and 65 feet at Amiens, a dimension that finally matches that of the entire upper wall. The steepness of the cross section, the high arcade, and the new thinness of the pier proportions generate a tremendous impression of scale and vertical lift.

Robert de Luzarches did not limit his innovations to proportions. Among his telling changes, the modified pier is particularly important. At both Chartres and Reims, all the vaulting responds rise from bases set above the *pilier cantonné* capitals. But at Amiens, the main colonnettes spring from a base at the pavement, the secondary pair rises from the arcade capitals, and the tertiary colonnettes ascend from the triforium zone. This truly Scholastic rationalization of articulation has a double effect that is more than merely cerebral. The vaulting responds are brought down to the base of the piers, establishing a continuous visual sweep from the pavement to the vaults. Simultaneously, the raising of secondary and tertiary support elements to progressively more elevated springing points pulls the eye higher and higher, to

7-32   Comparative nave elevations. 1. Noyon 2. Laon 3. Paris 4. Chartres 5. Reims 6. Amiens. (After Grodecki)

7-31
Section, Amiens Cathedral.
(After J. H. Acland)

thinner and ever-less-substantial forms. And because the lines of energy depart from the very pavement on which the observer stands, a profound empathy is created between the observer and the dynamically rising stone masses. No other Gothic building achieves this astonishingly bold and sophisticated synthesis of physical, cerebral, and psychological elements.

The High Gothic Exterior: Facades, Towers, Flying Buttresses. The transformation of the calm external volumes of the Early Christian basilica into dynamic vertical massings, which began at the Carolingian St.-Riquier (fig. 5-5) and was continued by the Romanesque to the extravagant silhouette of Cluny III (fig. 5-32), was a development that reached its fulfillment in the Gothic. Although the entire exterior of the cathedral was affected, attention was, quite naturally, paid primarily to the main facade: The twin-towered Norman format of St.-Étienne at Caen was the starting point; its powerfully buttressed lines provided the inspiration for all that followed (fig. 5-54). Beginning with Suger's St.-Denis, new elements and tendencies transformed the severe Norman design (fig. 7-15). The buttresses themselves are stepped and articulated; the windows are larger, more numerous, and are set at staggered levels. And two basic motifs were created: the central rose window and the triad of sculpted portals.

A second leap forward in the Gothic facade occurred toward the end of the twelfth century at Laon (fig. 7-1). The old forms are present, but the replacement of mural substance by skele-

7-33 St.-Nicaise. Reims. c. 1231. (Engraving by N. de Son, 1625)

tal structure and deep spatial forms, to be observed inside the nave of Laon, is reenacted on the exterior. The triple portals are fronted by a deep, vaulted porch, crowned by an exuberant line of gables and pinnacles. Above, the rose motif dominates what has become the principal story of the facade. This zone projects forward again in a triad of deep, vaulted hollows that follow the rhythm established below and mask the buttressed frame. A third, new zone follows, a gallery related to the interior triforium, here serving as an airy terminal line for the facade, masking the juncture with the towers.

The Laon towers are among the most exceptional creations of the period. Solid angle buttresses at their bases change first to an open tabernacle set on the diagonal openwork of ever more slender columns. These convoluted tiers frame high belfry windows and are adorned by life-size sculptures of beasts of burden—poignant portraits, it is thought, of those humble creatures who hauled the stones of the cathedral. These towers captured the imagination of the period as did few other works. They appear in the only architectural sketchbook of the time that has been preserved—by Villard de Honnecourt—and were imitated as far away as Bamberg in Franconia.

There was a compositional reason for the contortions of the Laon tower forms. An octagonal spire was meant to rise over each tower, with airy pinnacles standing at the corners, which together probably would have resembled those built at the church of St.-Nicaise at Reims (fig. 7-33), whose towers obviously derived from Laon and whose destruction during the French Revolution was one of the period's greatest losses. Although, with the exception of Chartres, none of the major French cathedrals have facade spires, practically all were designed to receive them. The fact that the spire later became such a ubiquitous form in Western architecture makes us forget just how novel a part of the Gothic architectural vocabulary it was. A spire is easy enough to recognize, but just what is it? It derives from Romanesque tower caps (fig. 5-32), which took conical or pyramidal form (the latter four- or eight-sided). The difference between these caps and the spire is not one of kind but rather of degree of steepness. When a certain angle is passed—about seventy-five degrees—the effect changes tellingly. The Romanesque cap is stable and contained; the spire embodies a dynamic, upward-reaching gesture that is quintessentially Gothic. All the unresolved complexities of the substructures are resolved in a single, thrusting point. It reaches heavenward with a gesture of purity and concentration that carries the sense of an entire community straining toward the Lord.

If Laon, with its unbuilt spires, was the wave of the future, what are we to make of a facade that seems its very opposite—Notre-Dame in Paris, probably the most famous image in French Gothic art (colorplate 37; fig. 7-34). The Paris facade (1200–50) seems locked into a severe pattern, with restrained formal shifts and restricted movement in depth. Rather than generating strong vertical energy, the portals, windows, and tracery gallery of its main block are gathered into a square, subdivided by a few strong vertical and horizontal elements into a gridlike pattern with the rose window at the center. The monumental strength of the facade is unforgettable, but its progressiveness is less than obvious. Yet, it is present in the intellectual rigor, concentrated sculptural density, and subtle gradation of weight and texture from the lower to the upper parts. Highly

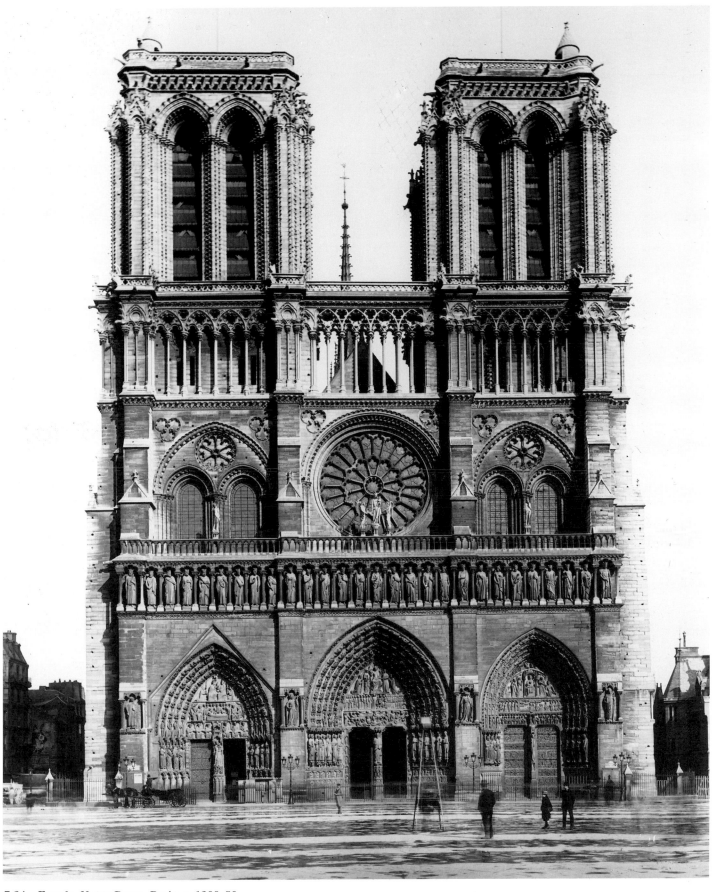

7-34   Facade, Notre-Dame. Paris. c. 1200–50

7-35
Reims Cathedral with
completed towers.
(After Viollet-le-Duc).
13th century

important is the increased prominence of sculpture, particularly the Gallery of Kings, which stretches across the entire width. The kings are not those of France but their Old Testament predecessors, an indirect but forceful icon of the legitimacy of the French throne. (This meaning was so well understood, unfortunately, that the original statuary was destroyed during the French Revolution.) This solid row of monumental sculptures, moreover, acts as a "cornice" to the dense portal zone, just as the openwork gallery crowns the rose-window zone above.

Thus, about 1200, at Laon and Paris two diametrically opposed facade schemes appeared in the Gothic movement. A generation later, these antithetical ideas were fused in the greatest of Gothic facades—at Reims Cathedral (colorplates 33, 34). It was begun after 1241 and completed through the rose window in the thirteenth century; work on the upper levels continued into the fifteenth century but, unfortunately, was stopped before the spires were built. Reims combines the energy and flux of Laon with the discipline and control of Paris. The Laon contribution to Reims is easier to see, in the deep porches, gables, and pinnacles. But these facade elements are now brought into a more coherent form. This advance is most intense in the portal zone. At Laon, the porches create barrel-vaulted hollows that conceal the portal sculpture in deep shadows. At Paris, where the sculptural program had been expanded with the introduction of the Gallery of Kings, the portal sculpture was reexposed by suppressing the porches. At Reims, the dilemma was avoided by casting the porches in the form of enlarged portals, that is, by bringing sculpture forward from the main facade wall, to which it had been previously restricted, and spreading it diagonally over the entire broadly splayed interior of the porches. Indeed, at Reims sculpture spreads far beyond the earlier bounds, tending to appear, in fact, nearly everywhere—flanking the triple porch; over the gables, above, in pinnacles; on the wall over the rose window; and, finally, on the Gallery of Kings, now shifted to a culminating position on the facade and carrying statues of colossal scale. The sculpture adds to the richness of the Christian meaning of the church, and it yields a texture that animates and unifies the whole building. The extension of the sculptural program at Reims was not restricted to the exterior. One of the most moving of all Gothic vistas is that of the interior facade wall (the retrofacade), with its tiers of high-relief sculpture combined with three levels of intricately traceried stained glass. The west facade of Reims was not conceived as a simple wall with sculpture applied superficially; rather, as in perhaps no other comparable monument in Western architecture (only Asian art offers corresponding examples), it forms internally and externally a colossal, organic entity, fusing in the most expressive way all the media available to the Gothic builder.

Architects at Reims and elsewhere devoted enormous energies to their facades, yet Gothic cathedrals were not conceived frontally, but three-dimensionally. Each of the transept arms ended in a wall, and for the exterior of this wall a facade was usually planned. In many cases, these facades competed in grandeur with the west fronts. Moreover, the facades, often only partly completed, were generally meant to carry twin towers. Because so few were built, our impression of the cathedrals is distorted. Six towers were planned at Reims and eight at Chartres. Only Laon came close to completion, with five towers built out of the seven planned. (But their spires are missing.) Reims gives us a good indication of how the completed cathedrals would have looked if we visualize the spires (fig. 7-35). Such a building, with its visionary gatherings of immense forms thrusting up into the heavens, would have seemed to the medieval viewer approaching the tiny cities in which the cathedrals stood no less than a miragelike image of the Celestial Jerusalem.

Most present-day visitors to Gothic cathedrals probably are more fascinated by the ranks of flying buttresses than by the facades. Beyond their structural task, the buttresses play a crucial visual role. Without them, the exterior of a Gothic chevet would seem almost as closed and massive as any Romanesque apse. This is largely owing to of the vast sheets of stained glass, which, paradoxically, seem as opaquely dark and solid on the exterior as they are brilliantly translucent within. It is the flying buttresses that give Gothic attributes to the closed outer walls. Each buttress unit (crowned with its own spirelike pinnacle) seems first to rise with tremendous power and then to leap in sweeping curves up to the clerestory wall, creating a linear cage of Gothic energy that envelops the cathedral.

The flying buttresses are visually so crucial to the cathedral that one could almost imagine Gothic architects inventing them even had they not been structurally so important. Conversely, it seems doubtful that the builders would have included them had they not liked the way they looked, in which case they would have found some other structural solution. A case in point is the

7-36   Buttressing, Beauvais Cathedral, late 13th century

fourteenth-century Cathedral of Florence, whose rib-vaulted nave was built on the scale of an Amiens but without flying buttresses, which violated the Florentines' Classical sensibilities (some buttressing is found beneath the aisle roofs, however). Needless to say, the Florentine nave developed frightening stresses and had to be laced together with unsightly iron tie rods. How different were the French, who quickly exploited the formal importance of the flying buttress, thinning it down to an ever leaner, tauter, more spiky and open appearance. It is a development that reaches its height at Amiens, Le Mans, Cologne, and Beauvais, where the forms are breathtakingly high and thin (fig. 7-36).

Gothic Structural Design Methods: The Workshops. Contrary to modern notions about functionalism and technological progress in the Gothic, French builders learned relatively little about the structural realities of flying buttresses. Recent engineering studies have shown that the most structurally efficient buttress design was one of the earliest—for the Bourges choir (c. 1195). No later buttressing formula ever attained the same degree of perfection. The nave buttressing at Bourges, built a few decades later, was a step backward structurally. Some seemingly advanced designs of the late thirteenth and fourteenth centuries contained serious, even fatal, flaws, as at Beauvais, where the choir collapsed in 1284, a dozen years after its completion. Clearly, Gothic architects knew what they were doing visually, but they were on less certain ground structurally because they had no real engineering knowledge. They did not possess any special science or technology in the modern sense, and we may well wonder how they were able to build the daring structures that have withstood the stresses of time so well.

A principal factor in the enduring stability of the Gothic designs was the tradition of the cathedral workshops. Here, the cumulative experience of generations of medieval builders was lodged in practices, attitudes, relationships, and precepts. Building methods were conservative, and novelties were introduced slowly. All medieval structures were heavily overbuilt, particularly in the Romanesque period, and this allowed the Gothic architects to pare down their fabrics safely and gradually (a century separates St.-Étienne in Caen and Noyon cathedral). Even the most thinned-out fabrics of the thirteenth century and afterward never approached the actual stress limits of arched masonry structures. But if there was no real building science, on what did the Gothic architects rely in creating their innovative designs? Certain conceptual devices were available, in particular geometric and mathematical schemes. There was the equilateral triangle as the basis of a basilican cross section, or a famous series (known as the Roriczer Series after its Late Gothic codifier, Wenzel Roriczer) based on a simple geometric progression for pinnacle and pier designs. Gothic architects had strong faith in such schemes, and even believed that they constituted a science (as did medieval physicists, astrologers, and physicians in their own realms). In the case of one famous dispute, they proclaimed that "*ars sine scientia nihil est*," meaning that the art of building has no validity without the employment of mathematical techniques. In fact, the mathematical rules "worked" only because they were so close to the long-established formulas of rule of thumb.

These nonscientific traditions of the Gothic workshop ensured a safe conservatism; they also made it possible for the

Master to identify, train, and promote architects who were gifted with what can only be called structural intuition. The talent of the modern architectural engineer is expressed by working creatively with abstract, mathematical operations. The Gothic architect, although relying heavily on the compass and square in drafting and on geometric formulae, worked instead in an essentially intuitive manner. Gothic engineering was not a science but an art, and the gifts required for it were closer to those of the visual artist than those of the technologist. Conditioned by the practices of the workshop, Gothic builders were able to perceive, creatively and intuitively, what forms of masonry might best work for new structural ends and stylistic innovations. Today, the roles of architect, engineer, builder, and contractor do not often coincide, but the Gothic architect performed all of these roles, which is one reason why his buildings embody such magnificence and intensity.

The Rayonnant Style. Amiens Cathedral was the purest realization of High Gothic; its attenuated proportions extended the style to its limits. One more step and the building would have become an almost purely linear configuration. Such a drawing out of structural elements into ever thinner proportions is an important theme in the post–High Gothic phase of French medieval architecture, but it is only a part of what happened. Related developments occurred simultaneously. The most

7-37   Crossing, St.-Denis. Begun 1231

7-38 Choir wall, St.-Urbain. Troyes. 1262

significant, perhaps, concerns tracery. What the rib vault was for the Early and High Gothic, tracery is for the succeeding phase.

After Amiens, interest shifted from concern with structural and spatial organization to a preoccupation with patterns of light and line. Tracery was deeply affected by this shift, as well as being its primary agent. Begun in heavy masonry form (called plate tracery) at Chartres, tracery became skeletal at Reims (with bar tracery). Originally designed as a two-dimensional grid to organize the huge new voids in the wall, tracery after Chartres soon developed into intricate shapes, theoretically unlimited in variation and without the structural exigencies of rib vaulting. It tends to spread from the clerestory over much of the interior; it affects the exterior and, eventually, even the vaulting itself, spreading like some relentless tropical vine.

The turn toward linear and two-dimensional form—and the emergence of tracery as a predominant element—appears unmistakably in 1231, when the final building campaign at the Abbey Church of St.-Denis began. Abbot Suger had built the early parts, and now the nave and transept were built, along with a new high choir; significant change is apparent everywhere. The clerestory tracery resembles that of Amiens: In each bay there are twin double lancets, each pair surmounted by an oculus that is framed by a larger lancet—all surmounted by a larger oculus to fill out the whole clerestory. At Amiens, the scheme seems crowded; at St. Denis the same pattern is dramatically opened up (fig. 7-37). The expansion of the "minor" oculi to reach nearly the diameter of the huge main oculus is critical to the amplification of the scale of the clerestory tracery.

7-39 Choir, St.-Urbain

The aggrandizement of tracery is not limited to the clerestory. All the dividing mullions of the clerestory reach down to the base of the triforium, so that clerestory and triforium are fused. Contributing to this fusion is the glazing of the previously solid outer wall of the triforium and the casting of the inner layer as tracery of the same pattern as the clerestory

Gothic Architecture | 243

proper, only on a reduced scale. Thus, clerestory and triforium are conceived not as two superimposed zones of differing character, as before, but as a single complex form; both are assimilated into a single grandiose tracery unit that now dominates the entire elevation, including the piers, whose form is no longer the mighty *pilier cantonné*, but the self-effacing "bundle pier," little more than a gathering of slender colonnettes.

At St.-Denis, the transformation of the formal dynamo of Chartres and Amiens into a pure and rational armature of stone lines spun out and suspended in the air, into a tracery cage of stained glass, is most powerfully realized not in the nave but at the crossing. There one views the rose windows of the transept facades. These openwork wheels are much larger than any previous examples, and they form spidery, radiant patterns, like a geometric sunburst. It is from these and succeeding rose windows that this phase of Gothic takes the French name *Rayonnant*.

St.-Denis represented a relatively conservative transition to the Rayonnant architectural vision. The new ideal emerged more dramatically in other buildings, such as St.-Urbain in Troyes (figs. 7-38, 7-39), whose choir and transept date from 1262. (The nave was completed only in the twentieth century.) St.-Denis had already merged triforium and clerestory *de facto*. Now the pretense of maintaining a triforium was abandoned, leaving only the arcade and clerestory zones. No building is conceived more in the Rayonnant spirit than St.-Urbain, with its walls dissolved into incredibly thin, almost wirelike tracery, making St.-Denis look quite solid by comparison. In this aspect, the choir exterior is even more advanced than the interior in its wiry, spiky—almost prickly—character, resembling not so much traditional stone buildings as shrines created by contemporary goldsmiths.

It is perhaps indicative of the tendencies of the Rayonnant that its definitive monument was not a full-scale church but a chapel, though hardly an ordinary one. The Ste.-Chapelle was built in Paris in 1241–48 by one of the great medieval kings—Louis IX, or Saint Louis—in his palace not far from Notre-Dame (figs. 7-40, 7-41). It served as the royal chapel and as the repository of Holy Land relics, among them fragments of the Crown of Thorns and the True Cross. The building is two-storied. The lower part served as the parish church, while the king and his court worshiped in the upper, or main, chapel, which was directly accessible from the palace. In the upper chapel, the walls, with the exception of the dado zone, are reduced to purest skeletal form (made possible by sophisticated buttressing and encircling iron chains hidden in the tracery). The interior forms a cage of brilliant stained-glass panels; the exquisite stonework is polychromed and gilded; the dado zone is decorated with foliate ornament and relief; and the piers carry statues of the apostles. In a purely stylistic sense, the building is dazzling. Although small by comparison with the cathedrals, its scale would nevertheless have been perceived as monumental, for it is a glittering reliquary built on the scale of a chapel, but at the same time a chapel built on the scale of a full-sized (if comparatively modest) church. Housing Christianity's holiest relics, built by the saint-king (a paragon of medieval virtues), the Ste.-Chapelle was long regarded as the archetype of Gothic architecture, a quintessential statement of the style in its mature Rayonnant phase.

7-40
Cross section,
Ste.-Chapelle. Paris.
1241–48.
(After Viollet-le-Duc)

7-41 Upper church, Ste.-Chapelle

Since the Rayonnant was very much a style of two-dimensional, surface effects, we would expect to see its influence in a number of important facades. This was indeed the

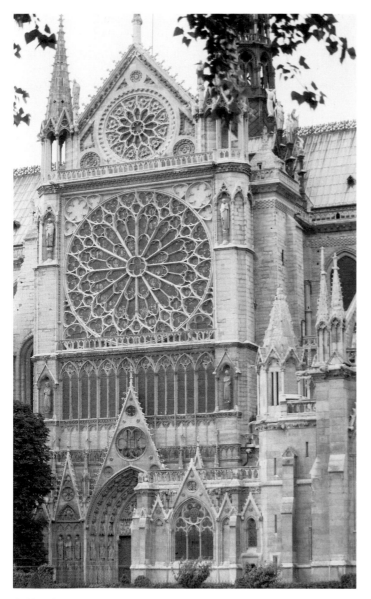

7-42   South transept, Notre-Dame. Paris. Begun 1261

case, and there is no better example than the later portions of Notre-Dame at Paris, where construction along the periphery of the building was under way all through the thirteenth century (fig. 7-21). The imposing transept facades are two classic statements of the Rayonnant. Although the north transept facade (1246–56) by Jean de Chelles is the more energetic design, the facade of 1261 by Pierre de Montreuil, facing the Seine to the south, is the better known and more representative monument (fig. 7-42). There is no clearer illustration of the change from High Gothic to Rayonnant than the comparison of this facade with the west front of Reims. Certain aspects are shared: the zigzag line of the portal zone, the central rose motif, the rich texture. But the movement and animation of Reims no longer obtain at Paris. Here, all is compressed into an almost planar, even rigid, design. The bold gestures of Reims are reduced to an intricate set of nervous, two-dimensional motifs. The facade at Paris marks the beginning of a studied, doctrinaire phase. By 1275, the mainstream development of Gothic had moved from the region that had given it birth.

GOTHIC IN ENGLAND

England was the great rival of France—politically and architecturally. Other regions of Europe produced significant Gothic buildings, but it was only in England that independent Gothic styles of a breadth and grandeur to rival those of France were developed. The two nations were closely related by blood and history. The Norman conquest of 1066 brought to England a French ruling class, and French was the language of the court and the legal system until the fourteenth century. Until 1204, much of France was part of England; the loss of the greater part of this territory did not interfere with English kings' dreams of regaining it. Sporadic continental forays culminated in the Hundred Years' War (1337–1453), the unsuccessful attempt initiated by the chivalric King Edward III to regain the lost dominions. To the modern Englishman, England stops at the Channel, but to his medieval predecessors, the English Channel was an internal body of water separating two parts of the nation.

Little wonder, then, that England was so profoundly affected by continental architecture. Just as the native culture, in particular the Anglo-Saxon tongue, eventually reemerged much affected by the French language, so English medieval architecture bears all the marks of the struggle between indigenous tendencies and imported Norman-French forms. To understand the fate of Gothic in England, we need only be reminded of the Anglo-Norman Romanesque, in which the rigorous Norman harmony of structure and decoration gave way to an expressive style that, paradoxically, combined extreme massiveness with extensive decorative patterning. This disjunctive combination of structural weight and surface complexity was maintained in English architecture throughout most of the Gothic period.

The Gothic in England is usually divided into three phases: Early English, Decorated (or Curvilinear), and Perpendicular. The first took shape in the late twelfth century, when the exhausted Anglo-Norman Romanesque led builders to turn again to France—already on the verge of the High Gothic—for inspiration. Early English is the British Gothic style most directly affected by French models. In England, the indigenous tendencies toward architectural fantasy were inhibited by the rational discipline of the French style. Buildings such as Canterbury Cathedral and Westminster Abbey are, for example, remarkably similar to French prototypes. Yet, even in these structures, native tendencies are evident, and in most Early English cathedrals, such as at Salisbury, Wells, or Lincoln, a purer English Gothic style was achieved.

Early English Gothic lasted for a century; suddenly, the constraints of the French models were lifted, and architecture expressing the highest degree of fantasy in the medieval period—in any country—appeared. Buildings in this style—the Decorated Style, as it is known—produced the most exhilarating effects of space and vaulting, and they were notable for their fluidity of line and variety of copious detail.

The Decorated Style was brought to an abrupt end by the first and most important building of the Perpendicular Style, the choir of Gloucester Cathedral, begun in 1337. With it, the freedom and exuberance of the Decorated Style gave way to a more disciplined architecture, as if all the energy and movement of the earlier style were suddenly frozen. A style of

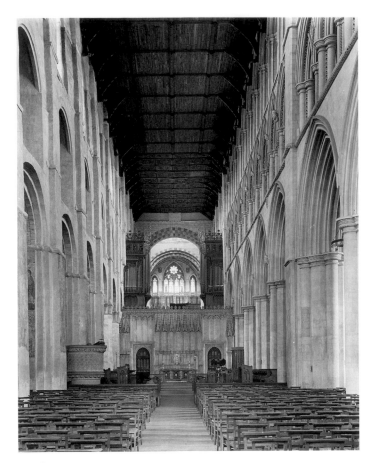

7-43 Nave, St. Albans. Hertfordshire, England. Left wall 1080–90, right wall 13th century

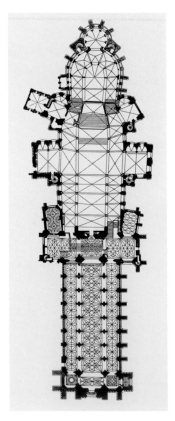

7-44
Plan, Canterbury Cathedral.
Begun c. 1100

dignity and grandeur, the Perpendicular was closely related to the highly disciplined, continental style of the period—the Late Rayonnant—yet it managed to satisfy the English fondness for massiveness and decorative density. The extremes of French and English traditions were definitively fused by the Perpendicular, the longest-lived of all medieval styles, lasting until the sixteenth century essentially unchanged.

English cathedrals differ from the French not only in stylistic character but also in basic aspects of planning. In French tradition, churches tended to be built on single designs. Detailing might change during the long process of construction, but the ground plan, elevation, and scale usually were maintained, or at least not radically altered. If a larger or more modern church was desired, the old building was almost always razed and rebuilt, not merely altered piecemeal or added onto. In England, the situation could not have been more different. There, we almost never find older churches replaced completely by new ones. Instead, an irregular process of change can be observed, whereby individual buildings develop and grow in an almost evolutionary manner. This is particularly true of the way piecemeal accretions were made over centuries along the main axis of a church. Elongated, rambling, composite fabrics resulted, often without any two parts having the same style. The most extreme case is undoubtedly the nave of St. Albans Abbey: its left wall built in a primitive Romanesque style, the right, in a sleek, Early English manner (fig. 7-43). Perhaps the archetype of this tendency is the Cathedral of Canterbury (colorplate 30; fig. 7-44), begun around 1100, and composed of the following: a Perpendicular nave built over early Anglo-Norman foundations; an Early English choir built as a remodeling of a later Anglo-Norman nave; a second eastward extension beyond the High Romanesque apse (which was dismantled) in the form of an Early English, horseshoe-shaped chapel (Trinity Chapel); and finally, the famous Early English circular chapel, known as "Becket's Crown." No greater contrast in church planning can be imagined than that of this sprawling composite of diverse extensions and the unified ground plan of Chartres or Notre-Dame in Paris (the latter despite its many additions). Nor was there less contrast in the ways the churches were perceived by the visitor. One has only to enter the nave or transept of Chartres to grasp its shape and extent, but Canterbury is revealed only gradually, its parts unfolding episodically in all their suspenseful and unpredictable variety of shapes and styles. To the architect of Chartres, the motley variety of Canterbury would have been intolerable. But the English positively favored such architecture. The siting of a cathedral is also connected with its form. French cathedrals were compact masses set tightly into the dense fabric of medieval cities, with houses and shops crowding up against them. But the English cathedral was generally set in an ample close with a vast lawn around it—a situation that encouraged sprawling additions.

Aesthetic attitudes counted most in the development of different cathedral styles. England, although part of the Roman Empire, remained far removed from the Mediterranean core of Classical culture—distant from the traditions of the Greek temples and the great Roman buildings, with their almost compulsive unity and order. In its long history, England was to experience various waves of continental influence, but no matter how diligently architects attempted to assimilate the lessons of the Latinate French and Italians, the unique Englishness of the island's architectural traditions stubbornly persisted.

Early English Gothic. Canterbury was the earliest important example of English builders turning to French Gothic style (colorplate 35). It was a doubly hallowed site. Christianity was established in England in 597, during the reign of Pope Gregory the Great. The first bishopric was at Canterbury, whose archbishop was the Primate of England (and since the Reformation, head of the Church of England). The greatest medieval figure to hold the position of Primate was Saint Thomas à Becket, whose infamous murder in the cathedral in 1170 transformed the church into the greatest of English pilgrimage sites. An architectural shrine for Becket was begun in the years after the rebuilding of the Romanesque choir of the church. The shrine was an extension eastward from the choir in the form of a new horseshoe-shaped apse, the Trinity Chapel, where a tomb was erected in 1220 (unfortunately destroyed by Henry VIII in 1538). An additional chapel, circular in shape—Becket's Crown—was built behind the new ambulatory. Both the new apse and the chapel were completed in 1184. Because a monk who witnessed the events, Gervase of Canterbury, chronicled the construction, we know a good deal about it, including the fact that two successive architects were responsible for the new Gothic structures. The first was a Frenchman, William of Sens, whose design indicates the strong influence of the Early Gothic cathedral of his native city. Crippled in a fall from the scaffolding, he valiantly tried to carry on, but he was replaced by William the Englishman, who adhered closely to the original design.

The resemblance of the Trinity Chapel elevation to that of Sens Cathedral is striking. The three-level scheme, the "false" triforium, and even the motif of doubled arcade columns are shared. Nevertheless, Canterbury differs significantly from its prototype. The French strictness of planning and restraint in detailing are relaxed in a typically English fashion. No French architect would have permitted—on French soil, at least—the horseshoe shape of the chapel. To the smooth French profiles are added typically English dog-tooth moldings nearly everywhere on the heavy, multilayered walls, and the carving of the capitals depicts lush vegetation. Although the builders went to the expense and effort to import Norman limestone for the structure, touches of local Purbeck marble, a dark purplish stone, are scattered throughout the shafts and stringcourses. Thus, in coloration, detailing, proportions, and spatial shaping, the interior remains true to the English tradition.

Canterbury is typical of the ambiguous attitude of English builders toward the French Gothic. They admired and imitated what was clearly the leading European style, yet felt it foreign and inimical to their own deep-rooted traditions. This tension is clear at the Canterbury Trinity Chapel and clearer still at another classic Early English church—Salisbury Cathedral (figs. 7-45–7-47).

Salisbury is exceptional among the major English cathedrals in that it was built on a unified plan in a single campaign (1220–60). Yet, it is the exception that proves the rule, for the plan of Salisbury exhibits traits usually seen in cathedrals built in several stages: extreme length and fragmentation into numerous discrete, square-ended parts. Similarly, the exter-

7-45   Salisbury Cathedral. 1220–60

7-46   Plan, Salisbury Cathedral

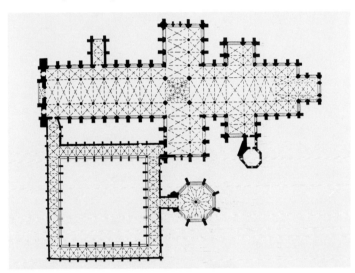

7-47   Nave, Salisbury Cathedral

7-48   Crazy vaults, Lincoln Cathedral. 1192

7-49   Tierceron vaults, Exeter Cathedral. Begun c. 1280

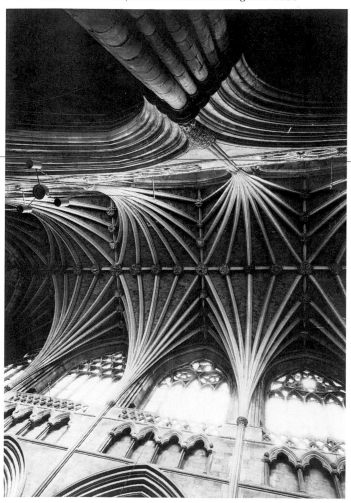

it dissolves into a textilelike series of small bands of niches and arcading for statuary, fluid in proportions and shape, and bearing a resemblance to the Romanesque facades of the French Périgord and Poitou.

The Salisbury interior, however, breathes a more Gothic spirit than the plan and the exterior would suggest. In the nave, a vast spaciousness is created with an uninterrupted sweep in depth, a vertical expansion of height, and a horizontal spreading between the slender piers and the high arcades. Among the important peculiarities of the nave is the stratification of the elevation. Except for the vaulting supports, the walls are composed of disconnected horizontal layers, as if the whole medieval bay system had never happened. And with its thick walls, Salisbury eschews the French skeletal method. Yet, we have defined Gothic not as any particular structural or formal system, but as a transcendental architecture composed of space, light, line, and geometry. In fact, Gothic need not always involve all of these elements, or employ the bay system, or skeletal structure, or even rib vaulting. Buildings devoid of these features may superficially seem at odds with the French buildings in which the Gothic impulse first took shape, but underneath, the spiritual quality is shared: the tendency to transform stone visually into a more elusive substance. Indeed, at Salisbury, a paradox frequently found in the history of art is present: the way in which a seemingly archaic tendency—such as the lack of the bay system—can actually be progressive. The absence of bays, together with the horizontal lines, causes the entire space of the Salisbury nave to be unified. And it is just such effects of spatial unity that are crucial to the later English Gothic and to Late Gothic architecture in general.

Salisbury presents in its main and triforium arcading a profusion of colonnettes and profiles—far different from the bare structural lines of the Romanesque. The architect has exploited the thickness of the English wall to create fibrous bundles of energized stone. It is not only the linear profusion, but also the contained energy that sets the Salisbury wall apart from inert Romanesque prototypes, and it is principally this energy, derived from linear forms, that makes Salisbury Gothic. Yet, it is a new kind of Gothic, in which substance is not denied—as it finally comes to be in France—but strengthened in its palpable presence. This concreteness of substance, pervaded with powerful energy, creates a Gothic style that makes Canterbury, by comparison, look very French.

The tendency to envelop the interior with fibrous bundles of dense linear patterns was taken up uninhibitedly in England in the thirteenth century, at Lincoln Cathedral, for example. Lincoln also marks the beginning of the English elaboration of the rib vault—the so-called crazy vaults of the first choir (1192; fig. 7-48)—where the architect refused to be limited to the usual set of enframing and cross ribs. He added the ridge rib, running along the central fold of the vault, and supplementary cross ribs called tiercerons (here deployed with a unique asymmetry responsible for the nickname).

It is not at Lincoln but at Exeter Cathedral (begun in 1280–90) that the tierceron vault culminates (fig. 7-49). At the corner of each bay spring not three ribs, as in the usual quadripartite vault, or four, as in the crazy vaults, or five, as in some parts of Lincoln, but no less than thirteen ribs and tiercerons. The effect is no longer that of a rational structural skeleton,

nal walls of the buildings are heavy, closed, and dominantly horizontal in line, and the facade has none of the sweeping scale and energy of the twin-towered French models. Instead,

7-50 Angel Choir, Lincoln Cathedral. Begun 1256

but of a jet force erupting in a spray of linear energy. Stalklike bundles of colonnettes sprout upward at arcade level and reach across to join their counterparts from the opposite wall at the ridge rib. In the vaults, a continuous flow of spreading bundles of fibrous stone runs from one end of the building to the other. The effect of these forms on the visitor is new and almost somatic. None of the cerebral abstraction of French Gothic remains. Rather, one is swept along by the dynamism of the arcade and the wavelike flow of linear pattern in the vaults.

The multiplication of line in the vaults and arcading was accompanied by an increase in the decorative weight of the whole elevation. The fullest realization of this phase of English Gothic is the Angel Choir of Lincoln Cathedral (begun 1256; fig. 7-50). The tierceron vaulting and the extensive profiling of the colonnettes of the arcade are familiar, but the zone between them assumes an exceptional richness: Trefoils fill the arcade spandrels; reliefs of angels adorn the triforium spandrels; lushly carved vegetation rings the capitals, appears among the triforium moldings, and emerges from the wall to support colonnettes. Purbeck marble is used unsparingly. The style is ripe, perhaps overripe. Either decline or some radical change seems imminent.

The Decorated (or Curvilinear) Style. Toward 1300, the more daring of English architects realized that adherence to French tracery patterns was not necessary—just as they had earlier

realized that their own vaulting need not be limited to the French schemes, or their piers restricted to French formulas. The powerful English fantasy broke free, and a wonderful variety of tracery forms, almost impossible to categorize, emerged. Although most of these still involved compass-drawn curves and not freehand lines, they looked free, not geometric. The earliest and most pervasive new form was the ogee, an arch of double, reverse curvature reaching up along a sinuous line to a sharp point (fig. 7-56). The ogee was important not only as a symbolic break from French tradition, but also because its dynamic fluidity combined freely with other forms to generate large, free-flowing patterns. Other elements were even "freer" than the ogee, taking outlines classifiable only by the forms that they suggest, such as the "fish bladder," "dagger," or "mouchette," to name some of the more important types. Decorated, or Curvilinear, tracery, as it is often called, could create fantastic assemblages of such novel forms, often in unique combinations. Unlike French tracery, there were no rules (even fantastical arrangements of French motifs were permitted).

Simultaneously with the emergence of Curvilinear tracery, the whole interior of the English cathedral underwent a profound mutation. Salisbury, Lincoln, and even Exeter all still follow the French format. In their piers, wall, and vaulting, the French model is thickened, distorted, piled up with linear and sculptural detail, but it remained effectively French. Suddenly, the foreign scheme lost its hold, and English architects felt free to design their buildings fairly much at will. The deeprooted English tendencies toward fantasy and ornament, drama and movement, which had been suppressed by waves of continental influence, were liberated. For a generation—lasting through the first third of the fourteenth century—England produced a number of dazzling buildings in the Decorated Style that made it, for the moment, the leading architectural power in Europe.

Among the principal works of the Decorated Style is the new choir of Wells Cathedral (1330; figs. 7-51, 7-52). Although the three-part elevation of the original Early English choir is retained, so much is new that any connection with the past is almost imperceptible. The effect of energetic fibrous bundles is realized at Wells with more articulate forms. The vault, which springs from a series of Purbeck marble shafts, forms a netlike pattern, accentuated by intricate boxes of blind Curvilinear tracery. The ribs of the vault are interwoven into a hypnotic pattern that is more radical than the tierceron vaults of Exeter. The latter were derived from the French models simply by adding ribs, but the net vault of Wells is an altogether new conception that animates and unifies the space of the choir beneath it.

Scarcely less remarkable than the vault is the handling of the wall. The clerestory undulates in and out between the piers; the intermediate zone beneath it bears as little resemblance to the classic triforium as the net vault does to classic vaulting forms. The wall surface has been dissolved into a double-shell construction that knows no prototype for the intricacy and detail of its front screen of tracery: interwoven ogee lines and sharp pinnacles that disappear into a line of miniature mock battlements running along the top. Statuary originally intended for the pedestals further complicates the density of Decorated effects. Most important

7-51 Choir, Wells Cathedral. Before 1332

is the way the intricate patterns of line and decoration coalesce into a seamless continuity. Not an inert surface is to be found.

The Decorated Style affected other aspects of Wells Cathedral, often in singular ways. The visitor, passing through the nave, is struck by an astonishing form at its end. Blocking the view to the choir is a gargantuan set of so-called strainer arches (fig. 7-53), built about 1338 to reinforce the crossing piers, which had deteriorated under the load of the crossing tower. The structural function of these internal buttresses is readily grasped, but their scale is overpowering. They produce the eerie zoomorphic impression of a gigantic owl-like creature with scowling brows, yawning beak, and great unblinking eyes. Nothing in medieval architecture prepares one for this apparition, although, in effect, it is an enormous enlargement of those grotesque creatures that haunt Romanesque capitals. Only in the licentious context of the English Decorated Style could such an eccentric architectural event occur.

An exploration of the building eventually brings the visitor to an unassuming doorway in the left transept. A curving stairway (fig. 7-54) leads to a portal in the form of a two-part tracery screen. Through it, one enters one of the most aesthetically liberating rooms of the Middle Ages—the Wells Chapter House (fig. 7-55). A meeting place for the clergy was provided by most important churches, but outside England these rooms were usually minor works. In England, the Chapter House

was developed as an important architectural genre, taking a centralized, polygonal form. The Wells Chapter House, with its umbrellalike tierceron vault and its vast geometric window tracery, is among the most impressive examples. It is a pure expression of the ideals of the English Decorated Style.

Wells Cathedral is one of the most brilliant works in English architecture, yet no single part of the building embodies the awesome force of the French cathedrals. That power is encountered in only one of the Decorated interiors, the octagonal crossing of Ely Cathedral (colorplate 36). The Ely Octagon, as it is generally known, was begun in 1332 at the end of one of the most imposing of Anglo-Norman naves. Unlike most crossings, the Octagon spans all three aisles of the nave. The vault recalls that of the Wells Chapter House, but in place of the central, umbrellalike portion, a gigantic, brilliantly lit octagonal lantern tower soars upward, and at the top is found the "missing" umbrella vault. The Octagon is conceived on the scale of the French cathedrals and is saturated with the same spatial energy and visionary quality. The space within it rises in stages toward a brilliant light. Because of the pivoting orientation of the octagons of its plan, the vault, the lantern, and the space all seem to revolve in spiraling movements upward. The vault appears to hang in space miraculously, as if supported by some invisible force, for it is hard for the observer to imagine how such a stone construction could be supported.

7-52 Choir wall, Wells Cathedral

7-53   Strainer arches, Wells Cathedral. 1338

7-54   Stairway to Chapter House, Wells Cathedral. c. 1285

7-55   Chapter House, Wells Cathedral. Early 14th century

The onlooker fails to realize that the vault is not really stone, but is only painted to look like it. It is an elaborate timber construction, a far lighter, more nimble structure than would be possible in masonry. This illusionistic trick distinguishes the builders of Decorated English from their more structurally "honest" French peers, who never would have permitted such a deceptive affair. The French did hide the buttressing system from the interior view, but the French cathedral is entirely of stone, including the flying buttresses, which are prominently visible on the exterior. Yet both French and English architects were concerned with theatrical effects. The French openly exhibited the sensational flying buttresses that made the interior "theater" possible, relying on the "suspension of disbelief" of the observer once inside to effect the illusion of an unsupported, soaring stone structure. The English architect took no such chances; he was unwilling to depend on individual psychology and aesthetic response. He was more radical, constructing at Ely a vision more spectacular than any French counterpart, but hiding from sight his deceptive architectural devices.

The Lady Chapel (fig. 7-56) of Ely Cathedral (1321), although tiny in comparison to the Octagon, is equally one of the major works of English Decorated Gothic and makes up in intensity of detail for what it lacks in scale. At the dado zone of the walls is a series of seats set in a framework that is astonishing—even for the Decorated Style. Paired, cusped ogees flank

7-56 Pier detail, Lady Chapel, Ely Cathedral. 1321

7-57 Choir, Gloucester Cathedral. Begun 1337

7-58 King's College Chapel. Cambridge. 1508–15

dagger-shaped central tracery; they are, in turn, framed by so-called nodding ogees, which "nod" forward in sinuous three-dimensional curves. The elaborate curvilinearity is accompanied by pinnacles, relief sculpture, and carved vegetation of an extreme density and ripeness. These forms continue in the piers that rise above and are penetrated by fiery shafts that reach to the springing of the vault. In its intricacy of line and detail, and in the fullness of its ornament, the wall even among Decorated monuments is unparalleled in its aura of fantasy.

The Decorated Style was an enchanted moment in the history of architecture. From the beginning, there was something dreamlike and unreal about it. Like all great artistic visions, it could not last. Just as High Gothic quickly succumbed to the Rayonnant of St.-Denis, the Decorated Style, perhaps even more suddenly, gave way at its peak to the new architectural manifesto of Gloucester Cathedral in 1337.

The Perpendicular Style. Gloucester Cathedral (fig. 7-57) is a complex building, and there is much about it (the crossing, for example) that is still strongly Decorated Gothic. But the architectural spirit of its choir is the antithesis of the freedom and fluidity of the Decorated Style. Gloucester gave the name Perpendicular to the Gothic buildings of England that succeeded it. Suddenly, all the details, particularly those related to tracery, were fused into a highly disciplined pattern. At Gloucester Cathedral, every detail of the walls' tracery grid is drawn into a single plane, and every shape within that plane is reduced to a uniform, rectilinear pattern. Although the vault continues the Decorated mood, it has a powerful underlying geometry. In any case, the walls and tracery were the more important influences for the future. Later vaults continued to evolve in sophistication but were pared down to more easily readable patterns. There were to be no more spinning octagons or nodding ogees, but, rather, a vise-like discipline.

The Perpendicular Style was the last English Gothic style. It was dignified, imposing, and looked convincingly international while at the same time embodying a density of linear detail that satisfied the English taste for rich patterning. Almost immediately it appeared at the new naves of Canterbury and Winchester, and it lasted for two centuries in essentially the form of Gloucester, except for greater scale, various refinements, and the virtuoso fan vaults (developed from the tierceron type), which typify the latest phase of Perpendicular. King's College Chapel (fig. 7-58) at Cambridge (1508–15) was essentially a doctrinaire, if mighty, version of a two-centuries-old idea.

LATE GOTHIC IN EUROPE

Gothic architecture was invented and perfected in northern France in the twelfth and thirteenth centuries; we have seen how its story did not stop there. It took root in England in the late twelfth century and was sustained there over the next three centuries. The appeal of the Gothic to the medieval sensibility—and to builders throughout Catholic Europe—was enormous. But only in rare instances was the French style copied closely. Outside the French core, Gothic architecture was affected by local traditions, preferences, and circumstances. Some areas were more receptive to the style than others. The Mediterranean zone, especially Italy with its strong Classical traditions and different sociopolitical, climatic and building conditions, was the least sympathetic to the French style; neighboring England and Germany, whose Romanesque architecture had been more closely related to France than had been, for example, that of Italy, were the areas most strongly influenced.

But there are factors other than geographic to account for the spread of the Gothic. The style was created mainly for a small group of well-born French prelates, mostly bishops and archbishops, and it was strongly supported by the French crown. It was an aristocratic architecture, with attending qualities of grandeur, richness, and refinement. Outside France, the same class of patron, though generally well disposed to the kind of architecture that French Gothic represented, had different ideas about architecture, and there were other classes of patrons, too, both in the church and in the increasingly important secular world.

Gothic is frequently represented as an urban architecture, in contrast to the rural, dominantly monastic Romanesque. This dichotomy presents difficulties, however, when one recalls that Gothic was born at an abbey, St.-Denis; that despite their urban settings, French cathedrals reflect little of the realities of the urban world; and that English cathedrals are, if anything, even more isolated. But this picture changes when we move beyond the Early and High Gothic. Although the renewal of urban life began in the eleventh century, it was

in the late twelfth and thirteenth centuries that cities became important economically, politically, and culturally. Independent towns were especially significant, for it was there that architecture could develop unbound by the tastes and demands of prelates and kings. Free cities flourished where the central governments were weakest. With the erosion of feudalism and imperial authority in the Gothic period, cities tended to thrive in the Holy Roman Empire, but nowhere so strongly as in Italy, where the central authority lost at the Fall of Rome was not reestablished until the late nineteenth century. Cities generated great activity and wealth, and the new social classes included mercantile burghers and guildsmen, as well as the impoverished—though free—proletariat. The architectural response in the new urban centers to the Gothic style was varied and complex. Purely secular architecture was involved—civic and guild halls, fortifications, city-planning schemes—as well as that of religious institutions. The burghers proudly built new cathedrals and parish churches. The urban poor were not forgotten, and a new class of urban monastic churches, built by the new mendicant orders, appeared in response to their needs.

The variety of place, time, and circumstance of Late Gothic architecture produced a stylistic range so wide as almost to defy generalization. But the period is not formless, and some qualified account of its tendencies is useful. Late Gothic architecture rarely embodies the complex formal machinery of High Gothic or of the Decorated Style. But the factors that constitute High Gothic—space, light, line, and geometry—are perpetuated, although in different ways and especially in a different balance. Whereas the classic French cathedrals maintain the early medieval emphasis on the bay system, which fragments the interior into modular spatial units, Late Gothic architecture tends to unify space into a single, fluid totality. Late Gothic architects were fully conscious of the role of light, but rarely did they surround their interiors with sheets of polychrome glass. Rather, fenestration was manipulated to create a strong, even light—as in hall churches (a preferred design scheme of the Late Gothic)—which unified the space. But sometimes uneven lighting was employed for dramatic effects (as in the Ely Octagon).

The use of line developed in two directions in the Late Gothic period. In many areas it became more extreme than ever, but elsewhere it was sharply restricted or almost disappeared as an important element. Line was so crucial an element in the original Gothic formulation—the church interior virtually reduced to a gathering of linear components—that it is hard to imagine Gothic without it. Yet, many Late Gothic buildings employ line in a minimal way. Of course, the buildings had to appear to be constructed of something, and if not of radiant glass and skeletal linear structure, then what? Massive mural substance would have returned Late Gothic to the Romanesque. But if the wall, however thick in reality, could be made to seem extremely thin, the structure would be visually dematerialized. Just as a column could be stretched into a line, so a wall could seem to be stretched into a taut, membranelike surface. Thus, in place of line, or accompanying the much-reduced use of line, one encounters frequently, in the Late Gothic, stretched, floating expanses of surface, which express superbly the period's emphasis on spatial unity.

Bourges, Southern France, and Spain. In the twelfth, thirteenth, and even fourteenth centuries, France was far from being a single political or cultural entity. The great cathedrals of the royal domain—the area around Paris in which Gothic took shape—exerted an incalculable influence on architectural development, but considerable diversity existed. The primary example of this diversity is the Cathedral of Bourges (figs. 7-59, 7-60). Although a contemporary of Chartres—begun in 1195, completed, almost exactly as planned, by the mid-thirteenth century, and in detail deriving from the Early Gothic—Bourges belongs in form and spirit more to the Late Gothic movement, which it seems to have initiated (or anticipated).

The fundamental aim of the architect of Bourges was to create a vast, unified space over a five-aisled plan like that of Paris. The plan included no elements that might detract from the concept. Originally, there were no chapels and there is no transept, either. Yet, the visionary unity of the interior results less from the plan than from the cross section of the building. The inner aisles, rising over tall and slender piers, are much higher than the outer pair. The space seems to explode three-dimensionally in all directions from the center, a movement reinforced by the extreme attenuation of the piers and the fluid character of the articulation.

Great as it was, Bourges had little effect in the Île-de-France, where the preference—even in the Rayonnant period—was for the format and proportions of Paris and Chartres. The followers of Bourges were mainly in southern France and Spain—notably the cathedrals of Burgos, Toledo, and Barcelona—a region where another impressive Late Gothic architectural type was created. The exterior was not the open cage of flying buttresses of northern France; it was closed and massive, usually with powerful buttress walls set perpendicular to the nave and rising to the full height of the building. Between these buttresses, chapels and sometimes galleries were inserted. In contrast to these forbidding exteriors, internally the churches presented an open space, frequently rising in unified hall-church, or near hall-church form rather than as basilicas. Arcade piers were widely spaced, high and slender, producing minimal spatial division. The fragility of these piers was made possible by the solidity of the buttressing, which simultaneously limited the fenestration, so that these interiors, even in the brilliant Mediterranean sun, tend to be dim, mysterious pools of space, especially in Spain.

Several of these buildings are among the most impressive of all Late Gothic designs. Not the least of these is the simplest example, the Cathedral of Albi (fig. 7-61), begun in 1276; it has a single, colossal aisle surrounded by two rows of chapels. Externally, the building is remarkable in its fortified appearance. The exterior of the Church of the Jacobins (Dominicans) in nearby Toulouse (after 1260) is also forbidding, scarcely hinting at the spatial grace and fluidity of the interior. Here we encounter an unusual two-aisled plan, with a single row of piers so high and slender that the space is perceived as a single, unified volume (fig. 7-62).

Still more remarkable is the Cathedral of Palma de Mallorca (fig. 7-63), begun about 1300. Its exterior walls bristle with dense, close-packed buttressing; the interior is a three-aisled basilica of vast and unusual dimensions. The central aisle rises to 145 feet, and the side aisles to 98 feet, behind some of the

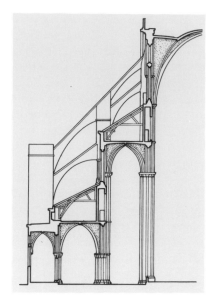

7-59
Cross section, Bourges Cathedral. 1195–mid-13th century. (After R. Mark)

7-60   Choir, Bourges Cathedral

tallest and most slender of Gothic piers. The effect is a combination of the spatial unity of a hall church with the extreme height of a clerestoried basilica. In a sense, Mallorca ultimately derives from Bourges, yet the model was transformed into an authentic, original regional variation.

An advance beyond Mallorca seems unimaginable, yet it happened in the Cathedral of Gerona (fig. 7-64), begun in

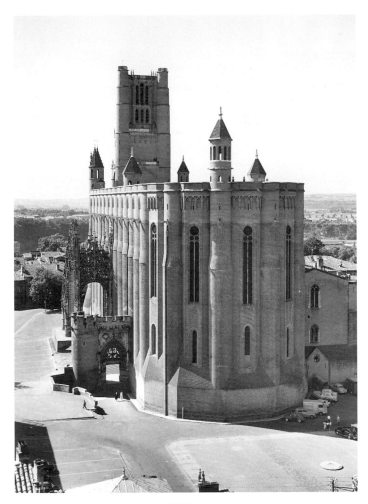

7-61　Albi Cathedral. Begun 1276

7-62　Church of the Jacobins. Toulouse. Begun 1260

1312. When only the choir was complete, in 1416, the architect, Guillaume Boffy, conceived a new plan for the nave that was one of the most audacious of Gothic designs. It was so daring that before allowing him to proceed, an advisory committee of twelve consulting architects was established to evaluate the practicability of the scheme. To the three-aisled, relatively small choir, Boffy appended a nave formed by a single, gargantuan aisle, spanning the entire 75-foot width of all three choir aisles. The nave rose far above the choir to the largest vaults of the period; beneath the vaults is a giant lunette, a triad of immense oculi. The unprepared visitor who enters Gerona Cathedral for the first time is staggered by the blowup of scale, the reduction of the choir, the juxtaposition of diverse forms, and the mighty unity of space. Gerona typifies the Late Gothic at its best, and it is a Catalonian counterpart of such earlier architectural wonders as the Ely Octagon—and even of the great classic cathedrals. Yet, there is a crucial difference between Gerona and Amiens. Gerona depends on shock effects that are strong as initial impressions but become weaker on successive viewings. Amiens is also a building that makes an awesome first impression, but the monument grows in depth and magnificence the longer and more often one sees it. For all its immensity, there is something almost whimsical about Gerona's Cathedral—often a characteristic of "late" cultural forms that find nowhere to go but toward a progressively more sensationalist aesthetic.

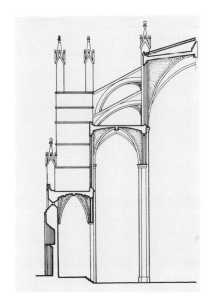

7-63
Cross section, Palma Cathedral. Begun c. 1300. (After R. Mark)

The Cistercians and the Mendicants. Of the southern examples, all are cathedrals except the church at Toulouse, which was an important Dominican foundation, seat of the central administration of the order. It is a rare French survivor among the many churches built by the Mendicant orders in the thirteenth and fourteenth centuries. It is important to distinguish the Mendicants and their architecture from the previous monastic-reform

7-64   Interior, Gerona Cathedral. Spain. Begun 1312

order—the Cistercians, who espoused traditional monasticism and its ideal of withdrawal from the world for the purpose of contemplation and praise of God. Most of the Cistercian monasteries have perished, but the few that remain give us a good idea of Cistercian architecture. The major surviving example is the Abbey Church of Fontenay in Burgundy (1130–47; figs. 7-65, 7-66). Fontenay is essentially a stripped-down version of such local Burgundian Romanesque churches as at Autun or Vézelay. The purposeful building, with its squared-off, no-nonsense plan, purifies the Romanesque of its decorative luxury, just as the Cistercians hoped to achieve a kind of religious purification. The order, especially in its early period, was ascetic but also aristocratic, and the aloof, lucid refinement of interior detail and proportion reflect this patronage. But there is more to Fontenay than a puritanical, aristocratic reserve. The architecture seems to burst with contained force, with a suppressed aesthetic feeling all the more forceful for its restraint—paralleling the literary manner of Saint Bernard of Clairvaux, leader of the order, who in his polemic against artistic fantasy, revealed himself to be profoundly sensitive to artistic form. Stylistically, Fontenay and Cistercian architecture in general are hard to place—neither Romanesque nor Gothic, but rather a puritanical critique of the Romanesque.

The Mendicants and their architecture could not have been more different. The Mendicant orders arose not to combat corruption within the Church, but in response to the spiritual needs of a new constituency. In the cities, freedom, energy, and wealth were accompanied by a troublesome new class, the dispossessed proletarian masses. Their liberation from feudalism

by medieval capitalism was something of an empty gain, for they no longer had even the parcels of land that they had held as serfs. About 1200, several clerical orders arose to help the new poor. Chief among them were the Franciscans and the Dominicans. The latter order (called Black Friars in England, Jacobins in France) was founded in 1215 by a Spaniard, Saint Dominic. The Dominicans were learned (Saint Thomas Aquinas, greatest of medieval philosophers, was a member), but their principal role was to combat the heresies that appealed to the urban poor. They were brilliant preachers who struggled to save their congregations from falling into sin. They were also given charge of the newly founded Inquisition to deal with those who could not be persuaded by more gentle means to abandon their errors. The Franciscans (Gray Friars or Cordeliers) were also effective preachers, but their message was different—less emphasis on sin and more on praise of the Christian virtues of charity, hope, and love. Saint Francis of Assisi, who founded the order in 1209, was the most appealing saint of the Gothic period, a charismatic, mystical man who began his saintly career by casting away his wealth and career to become one of the poor. Saint Francis and his followers, who grew rapidly in number, wandered in the slums, clad (like the Dominicans) only in rough cloth, a rope belt, and sandals, begging for their needs (hence the name Mendicant, from the Latin *mendicare*, to beg), participating in local street life, telling stories, singing, entertaining (as "jugglers of the Lord"), spreading hope and faith and a sense of contact with the Church. The Franciscans became not only what we would call social workers and teachers, but also pawnbrokers (lending at lower than prevailing rates), helping the poor materially as well as spiritually.

At first, the Mendicants possessed no real estate at all. But their tremendous success in the early thirteenth century necessitated permanent quarters, and places to preach, hold Mass, and care for the poor. Soon they were building churches despite themselves—and receiving financial support from the Church-at-large and the bourgeoisie (for reasons of personal salvation as well as charitable sentiment). But one can hardly imagine them building the elaborate and courtly structures of the prevailing monumental style, which had been developed by and for great prelates and kings. A far simpler type of church construction was plainly needed, and the Mendicants tended to reject established church architecture, be it Romanesque or Gothic. What they wanted was not a purified medieval cathedral, but something barely resembling developed ecclesiastical architecture: a simple, barnlike structure, with four walls and a roof, that would hold a large congregation; a self-effacing interior that would not intimidate the poor and in which the preacher could be seen and heard without the intervening, monumental pier forms that were by now an integral part of church construction.

Thus, when the Mendicants began to build, they did not erect churches in the traditional sense, but "preaching barns" that had more in common with simple vernacular construction than with the monumental traditions of European architecture. But as the orders flourished, the Mendicants and their architects responded to their innate aesthetic impulses—an age-old motivation behind monumental religious architecture everywhere: to find formal expression in stone, however minimal, for their beliefs. This had been the desire of Christian architects since the time of Constantine—to give material expression to an otherworldly value system.

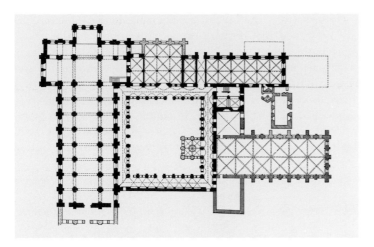

7-65　Plan, Abbey Church of Fontenay. 1130–47

7-66　Nave, Abbey Church of Fontenay

The first attempts of Mendicant architects were tentative and eclectic—such as reviving the "primitive" Early Christian basilican type. But such structural simplicity held little enduring appeal for ambitious patrons and their architects. The Mendicant builders resolved their dilemma rapidly and successfully, for by the mid- and especially the late-thirteenth century they had created an architectural style—actually, a wide range of styles—that constituted an authentic Gothic architectural movement of its own, which paralleled that of the cathedrals. Mendicant churches retained something of the aura of the original preaching barns, but preaching barns transformed into Late Gothic architecture. The boxy space became open and fluid, subtly proportioned, and framed by thin walls with simple Gothic windows. The aisles were divided by high, open arcades over sleek, slender piers (often without capitals) and were covered with a timber roof or simple rib vaults. It was the good fortune of the Mendicant builders that their need for an architecture of openness and simplicity came at the time when a major architectural movement of just these characteristics, the Late Gothic, was in the making.

The Mendicants built wherever there were cities, and nowhere was the urban revival stronger than in Italy. Important Mendicant churches appeared in the central Italian

regions of Umbria and Tuscany—the former the birthplace of Saint Francis, the latter dominated by two of the most artistically dynamic cities of the thirteenth and fourteenth centuries: Siena and Florence. The Basilica of S. Francesco in Assisi (1228–53; figs. 7-67–7-69) is certainly the most famous of all Mendicant churches, less perhaps for its architectural merits than for its tomb of the founder of the order and for the early fourteenth-century frescoes that depict his colorful life. Because it is a monument to Saint Francis, the Assisi basilica is more ornate than the typical Franciscan church. Nevertheless, it does remain true to the Franciscan spirit of simplicity (much of the interior richness comes from the frescoes, which cover the walls and even the ceilings). The main note of architectural complexity is that the building comprises two stories, which, apart from some minor differences, share the same plan: a single-aisled nave of four large, square bays leading to a crossing flanked by a square transept on either side and terminated by an apse (semicircular below, polygonal above). The Lower Church is dark, heavy, and cryptlike, but the celebrated Upper Church is bright, spacious, and elegant. Much about the building is French-derived. The plan seems to have been adopted from the twelfth-century Cathedral of Angers, and the detailing is so decidedly northern French that French masons were probably employed. Yet, the interior resembles neither the massive, heavily layered Angers, nor the skeletal, transparent northern French buildings. Only a minimum of linear form is present: The slender bundles of colonnettes at the bay corners are typically Mendicant in their reticence. The proportions of the nave bays are broad and deep rather than high and steep, creating a buoyant openness rather than the directional energy of the French Gothic. Above, a high wall, which appears extremely thin because of the shallowness of the window jambs, forms a typically Mendicant expanse of taut, stretched surface. Most important in the Upper Church is the harmonious interplay between fluid space, minimal but effective articulation, and an expansive surface envelope that seems as clear and serene as the Umbrian landscape which the church overlooks.

The most striking group of Mendicant churches, not only in Italy but probably in Europe, are the Tuscan basilicas of Florence and Siena. They all share a type of east end derived from the plan of Cistercian churches: a central square choir flanked on either side by rows of smaller square chapels, set along a single, continuous transept. However, in other respects the buildings of the two cities differ. In the Sienese examples, the Cistercian east end is combined with a timber-roofed, barn-like, single-aisled nave of vast dimensions and dignified proportions (colorplate 38; fig. 7-70). The Florentine churches are instead three-aisled basilicas, and each is so distinctive as to demand a separate description.

The Dominican Church of Sta. Maria Novella (fig. 7-71) was begun about 1246 at the choir. The nave, built only after 1279, at first glance seems to be a transformation of S. Francesco of Assisi into a three-aisled basilica, embodying the same combination of slender supports and simple vaults, with continuous, stretched wall surfaces enveloping an expansive and unified space. Yet, on further scrutiny, in addition to obvious differences in detail, there is the evidence of a deeper formal evolution. At Sta. Maria Novella, the lines of the building are cleaner—piers, arches, and ribs set off clearly from the stuccoed

7-67   Apse, S. Francesco, Assisi. 1228–53

Outside Italy, the largest number of Mendicant churches are preserved in Germany. A classic example is the early-fourteenth-century Dominikanerkirche (fig. 7-73) in Colmar (now part of France). Characteristic of German plans, the choir is built as a long, narrow, rib-vaulted area, whereas the spacious nave is enveloped by thin, plain walls and ceiling, subdivided only by twin rows of simple, widely spaced piers, without capitals, that rise to arches just beneath the roof. Plain but generous in proportions, expressive in the Gothic

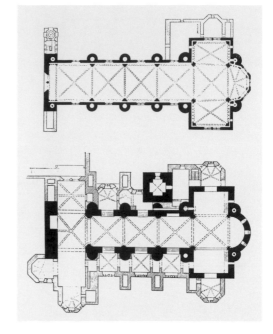

**7-68
Plans of upper and lower churches, S. Francesco**

7-69   Interior, upper church. S. Francesco

white wall and vault surfaces—and at the same time flow into one another with unbroken continuity. The domical vaults have a supple curvature and buoyant lift, while the framing arches and ribs move rhythmically between the bays and aisles. All are bathed in a glowing, uniform light.

Sta. Maria Novella is based on a subtle and harmonious design that slowly reveals its qualities. Its sister church, the Franciscan Basilica of Sta. Croce, begun in about 1296, is a more spectacular, even theatrical work (fig. 7-72). A timber-roofed, rather than vaulted, basilica (except for apse and chapels), the interior exhibits the usual features of Mendicant Late Gothic—simple, slender, widely spaced piers, broad arcades that support thin, expansive clerestory walls and open easily to the aisles to create spatial flow and unity; the structure and detailing are of a minimalist simplicity throughout. Yet, unusual factors are present. The scale of the building is reminiscent of the largest Gothic cathedrals—the nave is about 300 feet long, 64 feet wide, and 100 feet high. In a typical Mendicant building, the space has an omnidirectional fluidity, but at Sta. Croce, strong directional movements are established, as if to revive the spatial dynamism of the High Gothic. In place of round colonnettes, the architect used flat, angular elements, like the lines of pilasters that ascend with high velocity to the roof. The thin catwalk-cornice (*ballatoio*) creates an insistent horizontal that accentuates the forward movement of the huge arches and the compelling march of the pilasters. These forms lead forcefully to the eastern wall of the nave which, like a visual magnet, dominates and draws together the interior. Here a giant interior facade rises, comprising the choir, the inner pair of chapels, the clerestory windows above, and the *ballatoio*, which has climbed upward dramatically over the transept. Together with stained glass and frescoes, these elements create a colossal, shimmering, luminous wall of glowing surfaces and deep shadows, a theatrical apparition in deep sympathy with the diaphanous effects of space and light in the northern cathedrals. The miracle of the building is its paradoxical fusion of such visual magnificence with the Franciscan ideal of poverty, embodied in the gaunt structure and simple, self-effacing details.

7-70 S. Francesco. Siena. Begun 1320

7-72 Nave, Sta. Croce. Florence. Begun 1296

7-73 Nave, Dominikanerkirche. Colmar, France.
Early 14th century

7-71 Nave, Sta. Maria Novella. Florence. Begun c. 1246

stretching of the arcades, and even elegant in detailing (such as the arcade profiles), the church welcomed the throngs who came not only to hear but also to see the charismatic Dominican preachers.

The German Hall Church. Mendicant churches greatly appealed to builders in Germany. Architects in the Germanic area had difficulties in coming to terms with Cathedral Gothic in the thirteenth century. The ambitious churches at Limburg an der Lahn, Freiburg im Breisgau, and Strasbourg reveal

the architects' awkward struggle to absorb the lessons of France. Finally, at Cologne, they achieved a faithful but unoriginal rendering of Parisian types such as Amiens and St.-Denis. The German architects had little feeling for the disciplined design methods of the French school. French architects had found a way to express the irrational with highly rationalistic designs whose spirit proved elusive or unappealing to most builders elsewhere. The Germans had an equally strong predilection for the otherworldly, but it tended more toward a kind of swooning mysticism, at least insofar as it was expressed in architecture. If space could be made to melt and flow, the structure to glide continuously from level to level—without the disciplined fuss of the French—and intense, irrational patterns be suspended from above to fascinate the eye, all might fuse into a transcendental illusion of an otherworldly ambience. Mendicant architecture pointed the way to this aesthetic, but it was not the only basis of the German Late Gothic. Mendicant space and simplicity of supports, combined with imaginative, intricate vaulting design deriving from England, and advanced tracery patterns and other complex details from the Rayonnant as well as from the Decorated Style, formed the mix that became the Late Gothic architecture of Germany. The hall church was the principal format of this German development, which lasted two centuries. The examples given here can only suggest the many variations within the style.

The key building in the transformation of Mendicant hall churches like Colmar into the German Late Gothic type is the Heiligkreuzkirche at Schwäbisch Gmünd (or Gmünd) in Swabia, southwest Germany (figs. 7-74, 7-75). The nave, of hall-church format, was built after 1320 by Heinrich Parler, the progenitor of a dynasty of architects who dominated Germanic architecture of the late fourteenth century. Outstanding among them was Heinrich's son Peter, who was responsible for the great hall choir of Gmünd, begun in 1351. Entering it from the lower, darker nave, the visitor is struck by the assertive dynamism of the interior: Stretched columns stand in the huge light-drenched space, carrying lean but powerful arches and intricate vaulting full of energy. (The vaulting was not completed until the sixteenth century.) The space is encircled by shallow chapels and a clerestory, both with large, tracery-filled windows. Between these two luminous zones, a strong cornice sweeps around, breaking forward boldly over the wall piers, acting to animate and draw together the entire space. Compared to this powerful building, a Mendicant church such as at Colmar seems but a thin, featureless shell, a self-effacing building that carries a plaintive aura of Mendicant impoverishment.

The plan over which Peter Parler's choir rises represents a new type, made complex by its imaginative use of geometry. The inner polygon of round piers is three-sided, but the outer polygon of chapels is seven-sided. The differential, which nowhere resolves into geometric focus or stability, presents to the observer a complex pattern of misalignments and adds an uneasy note to the dynamic flow of the choir. It is instructive to compare Parler's design with Suger's of two centuries earlier (fig. 7-11). Both employ geometry as a fundamental means of organization, yet, Suger's choir results in lucid transparency, while Parler's is tense and restless. This is a clear lesson that, in imaginative hands, geometry was not a passive, predetermined aspect of medieval planning, as is commonly supposed, but a vital tool of expression.

The uses to which geometry was put in the two cases may involve more than the personal preferences of the two builders or the well-known antithesis of "rational" French and "irrational" German art. Suger's choir was born at an optimistic phase of the medieval period, when all aspects of life were in ascendency: the economy and the cities, the Church and the French state, philosophy and the arts. But Peter Parler laid out his choir during one of the most troubled moments in European history. The Black Death, which began to sweep over Europe in 1348, had been a catastrophe of such cataclysmic scope—in

7-74   Choir, Heiligkreuzkirche. Schwäbisch Gmünd, Germany. After 1351

7-75   Plan, Heiligkreuzkirche

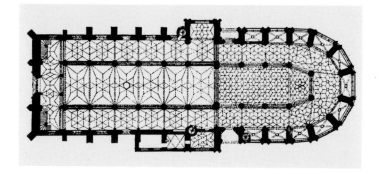

which half of Europe's population perished—that it is hard, even in the modern world, with all its mechanized terror and destructiveness, to comprehend it. The great plague had a chilling effect on the survivors, all the more so because the times were otherwise deeply troubled. The feudal system—with all its colorful trappings, to which men remained romantically attached, even though economic and political realities had rendered it obsolete—was under duress, as was the whole medieval structure of thought and belief. Disturbing change was in the air. Of course, not every contemporary monument reflects the uneasy mood of the mid- and late-fourteenth century, but in Parler's choir at Gmünd, we can readily imagine that the members of the post–Black Death decades found something to echo their romantic attachment to the feudal past and their anxieties of the moment.

Many variations on the hall church were built through the fifteenth century in Germany. Some buildings were simple, others more elaborate in detail. All were sophisticated and imaginative. Perhaps the most fully developed example is the Lorenzkirche in Nuremberg, begun in 1439 by Konrad Heinzelmann and completed later by Konrad Roriczer (fig. 7-76). The format is that of Gmünd, including the plan of three-sided and seven-sided polygons, but every detail is more complex and highly organized. Articulate piers have replaced the simple monocylinders, and they flow uninterruptedly into the vaults. There the multitude of lines cluster into star patterns over the nave, while much looser, contrasting net forms gather over the aisles. The outer wall is more plastic than at Gmünd, the tracery more elaborate, the encircling cornice evolved into a richly decorated balcony.

A decisive advance beyond Gmünd and Nuremberg would seem unlikely, but at the very end of the Gothic period it happened. In the late fifteenth century, Annaberg in Saxony became the center of a silver-mining district, and in 1499 part of its new wealth was invested in the construction of the Annenkirche (fig. 7-77). The hall-type plan is traditional, but the piers and vaults are treated with a new and exciting three-dimensionality. The piers are not the simple octagons that

7-76 Choir, Lorenzkirche. Nuremberg. Begun 1439

7-77 Interior, Annenkirche. Annaberg. Begun 1499

they first seem to be; each face is hollowed into a supple concavity (a Late Gothic equivalent of Greek fluting). Space flows along these piers up to the vaults, which spin in dizzying three-dimensional curves that are of a greater lyrical freedom than the most evolved earlier English and German examples. The space below is unified and thrown into spinning currents by the vaults. In this respect, Annaberg goes beyond the transcendent flight of Amiens and the spatial tension of Gmünd.

Late Gothic Extravagant Design. Outside the Mendicant orders, and especially in northern Europe, the tendency toward elaboration in design and detailing was the prevailing current in Late Gothic architecture. This tendency had its origins in classic buildings in thirteenth-century France—exuberant works such as the facade of Reims and the virtuoso Rayonnant tracery at Troyes. England had picked up these themes enthusiastically; the Decorated Style was, in fact, the first phase of true Late Gothic extravagance. From England, the development passed back to the continent. Beginning in the late fourteenth century, France abandoned the restraint that had limited even the most advanced Rayonnant schemes and plunged headlong into a style embodying many of the characteristic forms of English fourteenth-century architecture. This included curvilinear, "flamelike" tracery patterns, from which the name flamboyant, for the French Late Gothic, was derived. Less well known than the preceding phases of French Gothic architecture, the Flamboyant is nonetheless rich in impressive monuments: rose windows added to the transepts of earlier fabrics, such as at Amiens and Beauvais; new facades, like the extraordinary composite of late forms at Rouen Cathedral; and entire new buildings, such as St.-Maclou at Rouen (fig. 7-78), whose facade sums up the whole movement with its extravagant spatial, structural, and ornamental forms.

Apart from fourteenth-century England and the Spanish Plateresque (see page 324) of the fifteenth century, which was so encrusted with sculptural and vegetative ornament as to seem more Asian than European, the most fantastical works of the Late Gothic appeared in the German Empire. The prototype was the Cathedral of Strasbourg, begun in 1236 (figs. 7-79, 7-80). The nave is a typically heavy-handed Teutonic copy of St.-Denis, but the original facade design is breathtaking. The parchment drawing for this project is still preserved in the Strasbourg Cathedral Museum; it was made by Erwin von Steinbach about 1277 (fig. 7-81). The design calls for a solid structural layer, in front of which is suspended a tracery screen seemingly capable of infinite metamorphosis as it climbs acrobatically up the levels of the facade and into the polygons and spires of the towers. Only the portal zone of Erwin von Steinbach's Strasbourg design was built. Construction on the upper portions of the facade continued through the fourteenth century along modified, more conservative lines, until at last the builders came to the final level. Once again, a spectacular concept came forth from the Late Gothic imagination. It was Ulrich von Ensingen's design of 1399 for the single, asymmetrically placed tower, completed in 1439 by Johann Hülz. Its shaft rises as a tremendous octagon, lit on each side by a high, steep window, with daring, openwork stair turrets standing free at the corners. Dynamic vertical energies flow up into the even more innovative spire, built

7-78   Facade, St.-Maclou. Rouen. c. 1500–14

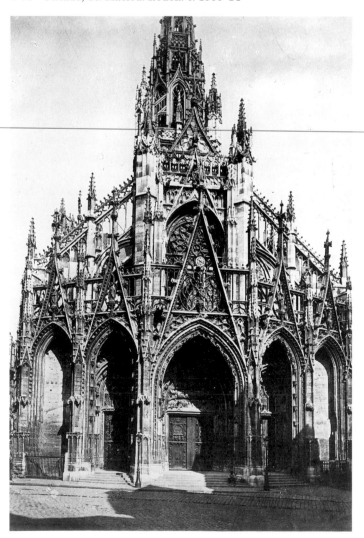

in the form of inverted filigree arches in tier upon tier, like a visionary candelabrum.

The Strasbourg tower was the culmination of the Gothic tradition of spires that began at the south tower of Chartres. Numerous towers of only slightly less extravagance and daring were built (or begun) in the free cities of the Imperial area in the fourteenth and fifteenth centuries. German Late Gothic architects saved their greatest efforts for spectacular, single shafts unlike the clustered tower groups planned for the French cathedrals. Interestingly, many of the single towers stood on the main axis of the church, a Late Gothic return to the early medieval notion of the westwork, now inflated to visionary scale and elaboration. Of these, the most original is the early-fourteenth-century example at Freiburg im Breisgau (the first time the spire itself is conceived as openwork tracery), but the best known stands at the front of Ulm Cathedral (fig. 7-82), the highest of all premodern structures. It rises to some 630 feet and was designed in the late fifteenth century on the model of Strasbourg. Finally, between 1877 and 1890, it was built according to the still-preserved fifteenth-century plan.

An extreme of Late Gothic design liberation is seen in a singular vault over a tiny, irregularly shaped chapel in Sankt Leonhard in Frankfurt am Main (fig. 7-83). Indeed, the nearest comparison to the three-dimensional freedom of this Gothic vault is found in twentieth-century Deconstructivist architecture. Just as the vaulted interiors of the classic cathedrals echoed the cohesion and confidence of the great age of the Catholic Church, so this vault befitted a time when traditional order and ideology were breaking down under a powerful critique and spinning almost out of control. It is not without significance that within a few years of the Frankfurt vault, the breakup of the monolithic Catholic Church began when, in 1517, Martin Luther nailed his revolutionary ninety-five theses to the door of the palace church in Wittenberg.

Fortifications, Towns, and Cities. Castles and fortifications were among the most pervasive and impressive aspects of the medieval scene. Modern warfare has been waged in sporadic eruptions of catastrophic violence, making it hard to imagine the ongoing, violent tenor of medieval life. The basis of social and political organization—at least until feudalism began to wane in the thirteenth and fourteenth centuries—was a system of military contracts, physically embodied in a network of castles extending from one end of Europe to the other. Even as the feudal system declined, castles loomed at every strategic point in the landscape—strongholds of the tenacious feudal nobility and outposts of the growing royal authority.

Although castles were important bases for offensive campaigns, architecturally they were strictly defensive structures. Essentially, a castle was a spot made secure by a ring of barriers. Before the invention of gunpowder in the fifteenth century, these barriers took relatively simple form: stretches of high walls, punctuated at regular intervals by towers, from which the walls could better be defended. To further render siege difficult, the walls were characteristically surrounded by a moat (especially when the castle itself was not perched on inaccessible high ground). From the thirteenth century on, moreover, multiple rings of walls were erected. In the event that the outer perimeter was breached by attackers, the defenders retreated behind the inner walls. Should they in turn prove inadequate,

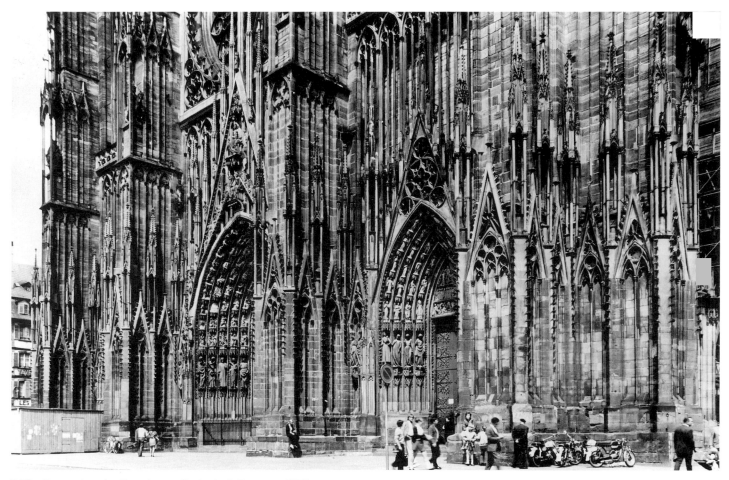

7-79   Lower facade, Strasbourg Cathedral. Begun c. 1277

7-80   Facade, Strasbourg Cathedral

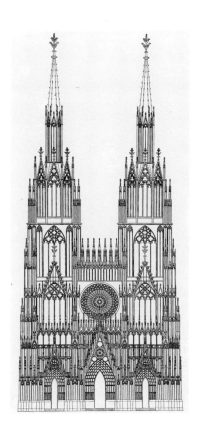

7-81
Facade, Strasbourg
Cathedral. (Facade project
"B," Erwin von Steinbach,
c. 1277. Redrawn after
N. Pevsner)

7-82   Tower, Ulm Cathedral. Designed late 15th century, built 1877–90

7-83   Chapel vault, Sankt Leonhard. Frankfurt. 1507

most castles included an ultimate retreat, the donjon, or keep. It was a massive, amply provisioned tower or towerlike structure, set freestanding in the bailey (inner castle court) or, some-

times, integrated with the walls or gates. The most famous of keeps is the White Tower of the Tower of London, an imposing late-eleventh-century Norman structure surrounded, in the thirteenth century, by several rings of walls. But the greatest was the Donjon of Coucy (fig. 7-84), built between 1225 and 1242 by the highest vassal of the French king. It was in the form of a cylinder 100 feet in diameter and 180 feet high, with foundations going down to bedrock (to prevent mining, a dangerous siege tactic). The walls were over 20 feet thick, and the interior was disposed in a series of three magnificent rib-vaulted central chambers (destroyed in World War I).

The Donjon of Coucy stood within a sprawling complex of fortifications: the castle itself; a larger adjacent precinct where the local farmers took refuge with their livestock; and, across a trench 20 feet wide, the walled town of Coucy—all roughly trapezoidal or rectangular in shape. None (except the donjon) approaches a pure geometric figure. One of the later innovations in thirteenth-century fortifications, seen at Harlech Castle (1286–90), was the development of formalized castle layouts, with buildings that not only were strong, but also looked invincible (fig. 7-85). Such schemes effectively symbolized power and authority. If strength without form was the early castle mode, and formalized strength was the mature solution, then it was also possible to build something that resembled a castle even though it really was not, at least in the full sense. In the fourteenth century, as royal authority became established, castles tended to become more residential, with such amenities as ample fenestration, which took precedence over defense. The classic example of this tendency is the precocious Castel del Monte in Apulia (fig. 7-86), the monumental hunting lodge of Emperor Frederick II, built about 1240–50. It is a superbly proportioned and detailed octagonal structure of white limestone, with octagonal towers at each corner and an astonishingly Classical portal. Set alone atop a hill, it overlooked Frederick's vast game preserves in his southern Italian dominions.

Fortifications were not limited to castles. The concept of a defensive barrier is a flexible one, contractable to a small, towerlike outpost in some lonely countryside, expandable to vast walls that might stand guard over a whole country—Hadrian's Wall in Britain and the Great Wall of China. These are exceptional cases. The common amplification of the castle was the city, whose history is closely related to fortifications. Until modern times, a city was a fortress; walls defined a city. This was as true for the Middle Ages as it had been in Greek and Roman times (we need only recall the similarity of the *castrum* fort and the *castrum* town). City walls were important in three ways—practical, formal, and symbolic. In peacetime, they served to control traffic in and out of the city, ensuring the payments of tolls and duties exacted from those wishing to make use of city markets and opportunities. The walls were also indispensable in defending the city from forces eager to capture, pillage, or destroy it. Understandably, city walls tended to incorporate the defensive features of castles—multiple rings, moats, towers, massive gates, and keeps—on an expanded scale. At the same time, they determined, with incomparable clarity, the shape of the city, where it began and ended; and they marked the sharp division between the urban and the rural spheres of life. Not surprisingly, the walls of a city were commonly its primary image and symbol.

The historical significance of city walls—and the character of the medieval cities within them—is difficult for us to grasp, for modern cities are so different. They tend to have neither clear shape nor positive symbolic value. We think of them as dense, amorphous clusters of humanity and real estate. But historically, cities had form and were highly valued. For the Greeks, cities were the natural context for man, the social animal. The greatest builders of cities were the Romans. The high regard for cities—or, at least, the concept of the city—continued in the Age of Christianity, despite the official devaluation of life in the here and now. One of the supreme visions of Christianity is the City of God, the Heavenly Jerusalem that would be the eternal home of the elect, its image dominated by majestic walls and gates of precious materials. Christian intellectuals spiritualized the concept of the city as they had done with other aspects of existence. At the very nadir of urban life in the early Middle Ages, monasteries provided the closest approximations to cities; we have seen how the plan of St. Gall formed an idealized Christian counterpart of a full, working town. In the High Middle Ages, beginning in the eleventh century, forces of every kind contributed to the rebirth of real cities and civic life. Ostensibly, there was nothing of Christian motivation to this phenomenon, but

only basic, universal human instincts at work. The feudal system had served its purpose of keeping things going in a minimal way during the Dark Ages, but now cities sprang up offering freedom, opportunity, wealth, and culture in place of the oppressive, danger-ridden grayness of rural feudalism. One literally escaped from the countryside into the city, not the other way around. Inevitably, a civic ideology emerged for the new Christian towns, and a variation of the pagan formula evolved. Just as Athena had been the patron goddess

7-84 Donjon of Coucy. France. 1225–42. (After Viollet-le-Duc)

7-85 Air view, Harlech Castle. England. 1286–90

7-86 Castel del Monte. Apulia, Italy. c. 1240–50

7-87   View from Duomo, with Campo and Palazzo Pubblico, Siena

of Athens, so the Virgin Mary or one of the saints became the patron of a city. Each city expressed special affection for, and claimed special protection from, its patron saint, who inspired endless devotion and the creation of monumental art.

But what form did the medieval city actually take? A few, like Paris and London, were large, but most were very small, with populations in the thousands, rarely in the tens of thousands. However, whatever their population, medieval cities possessed a protean energy, reminiscent of the cathedrals that stood within their walls. In form, they were as endlessly varied as the Gothic churches. However, three main types can be discerned. The simplest was a linear configuration: a walled cluster of buildings along a road, with gates at either end. A widening of the road, either at the center or near the gates, provided an area for a marketplace. The second—and most important—type is sometimes called the circular-plan city, but at best it was somewhat rounded, and in reality, usually more amoebalike in the pragmatic route of the wall along a line dictated by topography and real-estate. A third type, rare, but including some very important cities, was square or rectangular, with a gridlike street pattern in contrast to the irregularity of the other schemes. Cities of the third type (such as Lucca and Florence) recall the Roman *castrum* plan, and indeed they should, for many were built over ancient Roman cities. Regardless of their original shape, however, most successful medieval cities tended

to grow in pragmatic fashion. Generally, they expanded beyond the gates, along roads where suburban developments had sprung up. New walls were then built and the developments eventually spread out and linked up in enlarged defensive networks. Unlike our modern cities, though, the shape and image of the medieval city always remained clearly defined by its outermost ring of walls.

The internal disposition of medieval cities was equally fluid, often seemingly formless, yet it reflected a specific historical and economic process. Because of their success, cities became immensely crowded in the thirteenth and fourteenth centuries (one of the conditions contributing to the spread of the Black Death). Streets were narrow and everything was jammed together, especially in the commercially most desirable areas of the center. Only minimum space had been given over to public needs in the early phase of civic development. In the Gothic period, these needs were greater, but so were realestate values. The tenacity of property owners was understandably fierce, but it was counterbalanced by the high feelings of the citizens for their city—an intense loyalty, pride, and love, compared to which modern patriotism seems pallid. Burghers overcame their own private self-interest, which allowed the city centers to be reshaped with expanded arteries, squares, public buildings, and monuments of every sort: churches, bell towers, city halls, loggias, public granaries, fountains, charitable institutions, universities, and hospitals.

7-88 Siena Cathedral. Mid-13th–mid-14th century

In every aspect, external and internal, the cities of the thirteenth and fourteenth centuries were bursting not only with humanity, but also with architectural ambition and activity, which came from a vision of the town as a place worthy of unsparing devotion and effort.

Historical change has not been kind to the medieval city, which was a more delicate organism than its energy suggests. During the Renaissance, cannonproof walls were added, as were larger squares, wider streets, and new buildings, especially palaces, all at the expense of the medieval fabric. The changes were made possible by the new autocratic authorities who replaced medieval local rule, which had often been democratically based. And the modern world, needless to say, has contributed the final touches to the dismemberment of the towns through war, real-estate speculation, industrialism, and the almost universally misguided efforts of ideological "city planners." Fortunately, many exceptions to this lamentable situation exist in Italy, which lagged far behind northern Europe in achieving the modernist ideology and the Industrial Revolution. Although Italy did suffer considerable physical damage in World War II, no Italian city suffered the fate of Dresden, Nuremberg, or Würzburg. Countless medieval urban fabrics survive in Italy, occasionally in near-mint condition. Although these towns are scattered through all regions of the peninsula, the most spectacular group is in Tuscany.

One of the most perfectly preserved Tuscan towns is tiny San Gimignano, long known to connoisseurs but now so famous as to be on the itinerary of tour buses. The town is laid out in linear form along a ridge (type one); a single main street is framed at either end by a gate. At the center, the street opens first to the right, then to the left, into two large piazzas. One is the marketplace (roughly triangular), the other, the civic center (rectangular), with cathedral, town hall, public loggias, and seat of justice all gathered around it. San Gimignano, for all its exceptional clarity, charm, and authenticity, is most famous for the chance preservation of numerous private towers that stand forth proudly from the urban fabric (colorplate 38). Sleek, forbidding, limestone shafts, originally fitted with battlements, they served as urban keeps for the great families of the town during their frequent episodes of feuds and civil warfare. Such gatherings of family towers were by no means exclusive to San Gimignano, but, in fact, were a dominant aspect of urban topography throughout Italy in the twelfth and thirteenth centuries (after which most were dismantled or reduced in height by civic authorities).

San Gimignano was built mainly on a single ridge, but Siena was built on three such hills that meet, and thus it belongs to the second type of medieval city plan, the amorphous, amoebalike configuration. In Siena, the peripheral wall and the magical streets lined with picturesque medieval

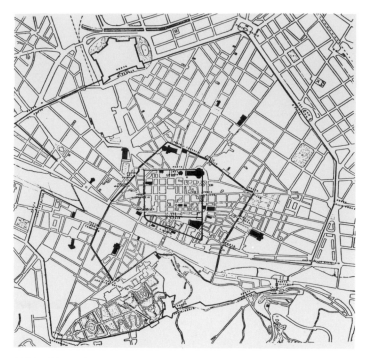

**7-89 Plan with three successive city walls, Florence.
1st century B.C., 1172, 1284**

7-90 Air view, central area of Florence

and palaces on all sides but one, on the "stage" of which rises one of the most impressive of communal palaces, the early-fourteenth-century Palazzo Pubblico (colorplate 39; fig. 7-87). Like nearly everything else in Siena, it is built of red brick and creamy travertine, with lively Gothic windows and an immense high and slender bell tower standing guard to one side. From the *campo*, one can see, glittering on the heights of the town, the upper reaches of the marble Duomo (colorplates 38, 39; fig. 7-88), to which sinuous arteries lead. The cathedral, in its unfinished but densely textured marble forms, is one of the most sumptuous and picturesque of all Gothic cathedrals. It is complemented by the two huge, barnlike Mendicant brick churches perched prominently on other hillside sites (colorplate 38).

Florence has little of Siena's pictorial sweep and color or palpable medieval atmosphere. It may surprise many readers to find Florence mentioned at all in the discussion of medieval urbanism, but, in fact, Florence is not entirely the Renaissance city that it is commonly assumed to be. The city was of supreme importance in the development of all the arts of the Renaissance, but the Renaissance buildings of Florence, on balance, were less important in the urban picture than were those of the Middle Ages. For the Florentines, the Renaissance was merely the icing on the cake. Before Florence became the first Renaissance city, it had been Roman; then it became a medieval city with many layers of development, as well as the home of great medieval cultural heroes, such as the preeminent poet and painter of the Middle Ages, Dante and Giotto. The Renaissance contribution to Florence came mainly in the form of secondary squares and churches, plus a series of imposing private palaces, mostly located outside the core of the city. To this day, Florence remains primarily a creation of the Late Middle Ages, and it is dominated by the monuments of that period.

The core of Florence is Roman in its origins and in its layout, a typical, square *castrum* scheme, which retained its outlines all through the Middle Ages (and is still largely intact; figs. 7-89, 7-90). The forum at the center became the principal marketplace (in the late nineteenth century, when Florence was temporarily the capital of the new Italy, it was enlarged to form the oversized, arid Piazza della Repubblica). The *cardo* and the *decumanus* became two of the main medieval streets; one connected with the Ponte Vecchio, the oldest Florentine bridge, leading across the Arno River to the road to Siena and Rome. During the Gothic period, Florence experienced spectacular growth (becoming one of the principal mercantile and banking centers in Europe), provoking a radical expansion of the city walls in the late twelfth century, and again in the late thirteenth century (fig. 7-89). The final immense circuit of fortifications, still largely intact on the south side of the Arno, marked the demographic peak of medieval Florence (c. 100,000), which it did not achieve again until modern times. Although Florence began with the third—or *castrum*—type of medieval plan, the new areas beyond the Roman core were laid out in a pragmatic, informal manner, both in the lines of the walls and the patterns of the streets.

The development of the inner core of the city (fig. 7-90) was no less spectacular than its outward expansion. In the medieval centuries, the core had become a dense fabric of

houses generate a poetic intensity of life and movement. In the thirteenth century, the town created at its center—a depression where the three hills meet—the most beautiful of medieval squares, the sloping, theater-shaped *campo* (meaning field, referring to its original state), surrounded by houses prized real estate, with a tightly knit pattern of irregular streets (still preserved in the area between the cathedral and the Palazzo Vecchio). Nevertheless, the city managed to carve out of it an exemplary constellation of public architecture. By the end of the fourteenth century two architectural centers had fully evolved, one ecclesiastical, at the Piazza del Duomo, and the other secular, at the Piazza della Signoria. Both were communal enterprises because of the strong link between church and state.

Each center included several monumental buildings sited on an open square. The two squares were connected by a new urban avenue (Via dei Calzaiuoli), which ran parallel to the old Roman north-south axis. Although roughly equivalent in visual "weight," the two centers could not have been more different in form, texture, and even color. The civic buildings—Palazzo Vecchio (city hall) and the immense, triple-arched Loggia dei Lanzi, which complements the closed, fortified bulk of the Palazzo—are foursquared, stone massings (fig. 7-97). The cathedral group—comprising the jewel-like octagonal Romanesque Baptistery, the freestanding bell tower, and the immense multiform cathedral (colorplate 43, figs. 7-91, 7-96)—is never foursquare, but broken and complex in outline (even the bell tower has octagonal corners). Nowhere is it heavy or dark; every surface is covered with an intricate polychromy of glistening marble. The civic buildings rise at the edge of a large L-shaped piazza, but the cathedral precinct is mobile in shape, like the buildings themselves (fig. 7-90). Nevertheless both squares, it recently has been discovered, were ingeniously designed to provide geometrically ordered, ideal views of the major buildings, prefiguring Renaissance perspective.

The city of Florence—which included many other monumental institutional buildings as well—suggests the fullest possible realization of the ideal medieval city, first glimpsed in embryonic form a half millennium earlier in the St. Gall project. But perhaps the most interesting aspect for the modern observer is that the city's form was not due to any single "master plan." It was the collective product of perhaps a dozen generations of Florentine citizens, architects, and masons. Much may be attributed to a mysterious indigenous force that, generation after generation, produced the ambition, the aesthetic standards and planning methods, the architects of genius, and the financing of their visions.

This process is also evident in individual buildings, all of which manifest an expressive intermixing of styles that was characteristic of the inspired eclectic design method at the core of Italian architectural practice, as architects of the period refused any limitation to a purist Gothic. The civic pride of late medieval Florence was most intensely embodied in the Campanile. This reflected the habit of Italians to take special pride in their cathedral bell towers (Italian for local patriotism is *campanilismo*), as well as the exceptional magnificence of the Florentine example. The Campanile (colorplate 41; fig. 7-91) came at a moment of Florentine history when the citizens were unusually sensitive to the symbolism of towers as emblems of autonomy and power. Florentines had spent several generations suppressing the disruptive, violent clans of feudal nobility and tearing down their private, urban defense towers. Although generically related to the bell towers of northern Europe, the Campanile has none of their filigreed

7-91 Campanile, seen from cupola. Florence. 1334–60

7-92 Plan, Florence Cathedral. Facade begun 1296, nave and choir 1357 15th century

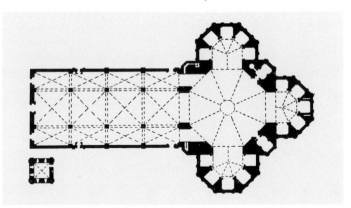

laciness; instead it is imbued with Classical solidity and proportions. Its polychrome marble incrustation harks back to the Romanesque Baptistery, as do many of the building's myriad Classical details that intermingle eclectically with Gothic elements, such as the gabled windows. Compared with the Baptistery, however, the marble skin of the Campanile is more "painterly" in its expansion of the traditional green-and-white bichromy to include elements of pink marble and in its richer and more fluid design. This painterliness is probably connected with the fact that Giotto, or "the world's greatest painter" as he was known, was the first architect of the building. Though he only completed the first story between its founding in 1334 and his death in 1337, and despite the departures of his successors from his design (preserved in a famous drawing), the painterly richness of Giotto's conception pervades the entire building. This does not negate the originality of Giotto's followers at the Campanile workshop, however. The niche zone of the tower exhibits a new sculpturesque plasticity that reveals the hand of the sculptor Andrea Pisano. About 1343, Andrea was succeeded by a "professional" architect, Francesco Talenti, who, paradoxically, returned to the painterliness of Giotto's concept, but in a novel manner, full of eclectic detail. He completed the upper windowed stories by 1360. Despite these changes, the Campanile exhibits an uncanny unity, which was achieved through a design procedure characteristic of period workshops. For all the novelty, each later architect of the tower maintained coherence between his new design and the contributions of his predecessors—in the progressive scale of elements, in the depth and modulation of the surface relief, and in the ingenious extension upward of the lines of Giotto's base, through all the multiform stories.

The Romanesque Baptistery of S. Giovanni was discussed in our previous chapter, and the colossal dome of the Cathedral of Florence, constructed in the Renaissance, will be described in the next chapter. Most of the fabric of the cathedral (fig. 7-92), however, is an eclectic Gothic-cum-Classical design like the neighboring Campanile. We have seen how, by the end of the thirteenth century, an Italian Gothicizing church style of simplicity and openness had evolved from the original Mendicant preaching barns. In churches such as Sta. Croce and Sta. Maria Novella, huge open spaces covered by timber roofs or simple rib vaults were divided by high, wide arcades supported by slender, simple piers. Italian cathedrals of the time tended to be similarly open and mural but, of course, more elaborately articulated and richly adorned. Orvieto Cathedral (colorplate 40; fig. 7-93), for example, built after 1290 under the patronage of the papacy, is a timber-roofed, columnar basilica like Sta. Croce, but with colorful stone striping and sumptuous classicizing capitals and cornicework. Its magnificent polychrome facade (begun 1310) embodies a love of luxurious effects reminiscent of the northern cathedral fronts, but with a typically Italian emphasis on mural surfaces, classically carved detailing, and marble inlays. Even the facade of Orvieto looks restrained when compared with the huge cathedral erected a century later in Milan (begun in 1386), where, since the Romanesque period, architectural taste often had been more lavish than in central Italy. Milan Cathedral (fig. 7-94) was built by the ruling Visconti clan as an immense five-aisled, fully Gothic structure, with Late Gothic choir tracery and elaborate Germanic piers. Compared to most Italian cathedrals, Milan has an intensely northern European look, particularly on the exterior.

The Duomo of Florence (figs. 7-95, 7-96), neither as sober as the Orvieto nave nor as fanciful as Milan, presents the classic example of the Italian late medieval cathedral. It was begun in 1296 by Arnolfo di Cambio, first among all Florentine sculptors. Contrary to the popular misconception of the building as "Arnolfo's Duomo," the structure was built mainly after 1357 on the new design of Francesco Talenti; the nave was com-

7-93   Nave, Orvieto Cathedral. After 1290

pleted in the 1370s, and all but the cupola itself by 1420 (the present facade is from the nineteenth century). Talenti's triple-aisled nave comprises four gigantic bays, each spanning a square of nearly 65 feet on each side. The height of the central aisle rises more than 130 feet to the vaults. Although the Duomo is as immense as Amiens, nowhere does it dissolve into the line, space, and light of the cathedrals of France. Instead, despite its giant rib vaults it retains stately Classical proportions and strong touches of rich classicizing detail, and it carries an aura of the somber, massive grandeur of the monuments of Roman antiquity.

Of even larger scale than the nave of this overpowering building is the centrally planned, trilobed octagon of its eastern end, whose central space rivals the Pantheon in diameter and far surpasses it in height (measuring internally 144 feet between the sides of the octagon, the vault ascending to nearly 300 feet). Externally, it forms a mountain of masonry that towers over the small houses that surround it, with immense polygonal forms building in tiers to the cupola. Its composition suggests both the swelling, ponderous masses of Roman Imperial monuments and the dynamic, staccato ascent of forms in Gothic chevets and towers. The dome was not erected until the fifteenth century, but the heroic conception of its space and massing, its dimensions and curvature, were all fixed in 1367. A model was established by a committee of Florentine painters and sculptors and approved by a vote of

7-94 Apse, Milan Cathedral. Begun 1386

the Florentine citizenry. It was the embodiment of their dream of the greatest possible symbol of civic pride and power.

In the secular, governmental center of the city we confront the fortresslike town hall, the Palazzo Vecchio (fig. 7-97). Its initial builder may have been Arnolfo di Cambio. It was constructed rapidly between 1299 and 1315 according to a series of changing designs. In the first scheme the building was surmounted only by a small tower and ordinary battlements; around 1307 appeared the executed version, with its giant, overscaled superstructure. The colossal, two-level battlements and massive, soaring tower, together with the huge piazza that was gradually opened around two sides of the palace dur-

7-95 Nave, Florence Cathedral (Duomo). Begun 1357

7-96 Florence Cathedral from the east

7-97   Piazza della Signoria with Palazzo Vecchio (1299–c. 1315) and Loggia dei Lanzi (1376–82). Florence

ing the fourteenth century, shifted its visual orientation. Whereas originally the narrow north wall was meant as its main facade, in the final state of monument and site the west front became primary, and as a whole the building was meant to be seen on the oblique from the main entrance to the piazza. Indeed, this view was the most highly developed example of those geometrically ordered ideal perspectives on monumental fourteenth-century buildings mentioned above, in this case comprehending a visual angle of 90 degrees horizontally and 45 degrees vertically to the top of the tower, which served as the visual axis of this carefully constructed urban scenography (fig. 7-98).

Formally, the contrast between the Palazzo Vecchio and equivalent examples north of the Alps—the city halls of Bruges and Ghent, for example—is instructive. Northern city halls, stylistically, are Gothic cathedrals turned secular and toned down slightly in the process. Their silhouettes are made of irregular and slender pointed forms, and their walls are covered with decorative ornament and pierced with tracery. Florence's Palazzo Vecchio assumes a colossal scale (each of its main stories is over 30 feet high), and its rusticated stonework is of antique derivation and civic symbolism (recalling the precinct walls of Rome's Forum of Augustus). Only its gigantic tower, set daringly and dangerously forward over hollow battlements and narrow corbels, embodies Gothic dynamism in its powerful skyward thrust. Its massive columnar belfry perched unexpectedly atop the huge tower projects a maximal expression of civic pride.

To the right of the Palazzo Vecchio stands the Loggia dei Lanzi, built between 1376 and 1382, after a number of houses

had been demolished to make way for it. Its principal architect was Francesco Talenti's son, Simone. Open and arcaded in contrast to the closed block of the Palazzo Vecchio, the Loggia functioned as an enormous outdoor ceremonial space for the town magistrates whose residence and offices were in the palace. A rectangle opened on two sides by huge semicircular arches carried on compound piers (derived, not surprisingly,

7-98   Piazza della Signoria, Florente.
(Scenographic relationship between Palazzo Vecchio and the Piazza della Signoria, angle of view 90 degrees horizontally and 45 degrees vertically)

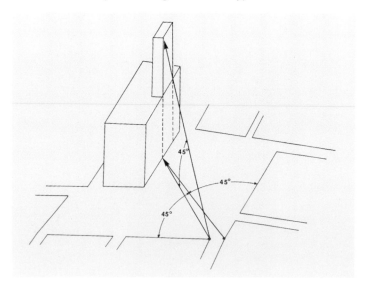

from Francesco Talenti's cathedral piers), it offered comfortable access and easy sight lines for the processions and ceremonies that were an important part of medieval civic life. Beneath the immense vaults of the arcade, the participants were protected from hot or rainy weather. The walls were embellished, on important occasions, with splendid tapestries. Its wide and airy arcade and its gigantic proportions—commensurate with the Duomo as well as the Palazzo Vecchio—are consistent with the self-confident mood of Florence in the last years of the fourteenth century. In its scale and stately proportions, in its clear, rectilinear outline and round arches, it is allied to some of the civic monuments of Imperial Rome.

The city of Florence and the constellation of medieval buildings in its historic center may be visionary, but in the final analysis, unlike the northern Gothic structures, they are not transcendental. The vision is primarily an earthly one. It goes back time and again to antiquity, something the Florentines were fully conscious of, and they often compared their city with ancient Rome. Medieval Florence was thus a two-faced, Janus-like culture. It embodied in the most intense way the spirit of the Middle Ages, yet looked back nostalgically to the antique; more than any other city, it stood with one foot in the Middle Ages and the other in the Classical past. It was only necessary to take a bold, decisive step in the latter direction and antiquity might be visibly reborn. That was the idea of the Renaissance.

Pages 274–75
Jacopo
Sansovino.
Libreria
di S. Marco.
Venice.
Begun 1536

8-1
Facade,
S. Zaccaria.
Venice.
Begun c. 1458

Chapter Eight | The Renaissance

ITALY

We have often heard that the fifteenth-century Renaissance was a dramatic rupture in the fabric of history, marking the end of the displacement of the culture of antiquity by centuries of medieval civilization. This was, ironically, an idea invented by the Renaissance itself. The view of history formulated by Petrarch and his fellow Humanists in fourteenth-century Italy and held through the nineteenth century was that the radiant light of antiquity had been extinguished during the "Dark Ages," and that the yearning to reveal that light signaled a new era in which the Classical past would be reborn. Examples drawn from all fields of human endeavor now demonstrate how almost every portion of that "Middle Age" between the twilight of the ancient world and the so-called dawn of the Renaissance had its own degree of reborn Classicism, its own interpretation of surviving Greco-Roman culture. Thus Classical culture was never totally obscured, and it endured, even if tenuously, in an unbroken continuity.

Intellectuals and writers of the trecento such as Petrarch and Dante fostered the concept of building a whole new culture on the foundations of "lost" Classical learning. Petrarch studied Vergil and Cicero and the syntax of Latin and Greek in the desire not only to retrieve ancient culture but to retrieve it in its original state, stripped of the overlay of medieval "corruptions" of language and ideas. By the early quattrocento the Petrarchan sense of discontinuity with the immediate past—a vast chasm of darkness separating his time from the Classical world for which he and other Humanists felt such strong empathy—and of identification with a remote and distinguished cultural ancestry, had evolved into the new vision of history and the universe that characterized the Renaissance.

The Renaissance vision was based on new concepts of the spiritual and intellectual autonomy of the individual, on the power of human reason, and on freedom from dependence on the supernatural. These concepts had evolved from the early Humanist idea of antiquity as a time when man had been the measure of all things and the faculty of reason his most prized natural gift, when each individual constituted his own authority by virtue of his rational powers. This view was in conflict with the medieval theological system, which taught that ultimate truth was found in the authority of the Bible, other Christian texts, and the Church, and that temporal life was less significant than life in the afterworld. Nevertheless, Humanism was neither atheistic nor heretical. It sought to reconcile ancient literature and philosophy with Christian ideas, without compromising either, and the clergy (the most literate segment of the population) tolerated to a limited extent the rapid spread of new learning and knowledge among a people still devoutly concerned with faith and spirituality.

It was not until the sixteenth century that the perception of a discontinuity with the post-Classical past was explicitly defined by writers as a "Renaissance," and set into a special relationship with art. In 1550, artist and writer Giorgio Vasari, in the preface to his *Lives of the Most Eminent Painters, Sculptors, and Architects*, described the thirteenth century as the beginning of the rebirth or, in his word *rinascità*, of the lost art of the revered Classical past. He saw the fourteenth century as a true proto-Renaissance, and the fifteenth century as the time when Renaissance style was fully realized but still youthful in spirit and expression. He regarded his own century as the period of Renaissance maturity and perfection.

Before Vasari's recounting of the development of Renaissance art, learned fifteenth-century Humanists, notably Leon Battista Alberti, had already written about the growing recognition of antique culture. Alberti described the work of certain progressive fifteenth-century Florentine artists whose Humanistic interests and new skills in technology and science led them to invent linear perspective, study the organic structure of the human body, and devise new theories of proportions based on ancient doctrines of mathematical harmonies. With these powerful tools, painters, sculptors, and architects of the early Renaissance in Florence had succeeded in creating an illusion of reality, of a physical and psychological existence, that differed from and eventually annihilated traditions of medieval art.

In the late Middle Ages, Florence had been one of the most highly developed cities in Europe—economically, intellectually, and artistically. Its prosperity stemmed from its rapid population growth, its success in cloth manufacturing, international banking, the wool trade, and the development of a powerful and effective communal government. Reinforced by strong legislation, this Commune maintained tight control over the projects affecting the appearance and architectural growth of Florence, believing that an orderly, well-planned environment and great architectural monuments bestowed grandeur and importance on a city. In the early 1400s, urbanism and civic pride were transformed into a Humanist ideal, which held that the beauty of Florence would reflect the city's image of itself as an ideal republic inhabited by virtuous citizens. This, together with its great intellectual history springing from Dante and Petrarch, would give Florence a unique opportunity to regenerate the moral, political, and aesthetic values of Classical civilizations. By so doing, the Florentine state would become a "new Athens," belonging to an unbroken continuum from Greece to Rome to its own time.

The matchless skills of Florentine artisans and craftsmen,

the city's wealth, and the involvement of all segments of society in civic projects made the Humanist goals attainable. Around 1420, Florence began to see its first Renaissance buildings, structures based on new, post-medieval modes of rational design and proportional systems that were, generally speaking, believed to have been invented in antiquity. The parts of a building were to be in harmonious correspondence with each other. This harmony, achieved by proportion and by the equality of ratios (a/b = c/d), could be compared to musical harmony with its agreeable, consonant blending of tones. Mathematically based architectural harmony had always required the planning of dimensions and forms so that they corresponded to each other proportionally and visually. In fifteenth-century Florence new systems of scientific rationalism were combined with a new language of form and applied to architectural practice by one man—Filippo Brunelleschi—and he was celebrated forever after as the "father" of Renaissance architecture.

Brunelleschi. Born in Florence, Filippo Brunelleschi began his career as a sculptor and goldsmith; in 1401, he was one of the contestants in the famed sculpture competition for a new bronze door for the Florence Baptistery. For information about his early years we must rely partly on legend and partly on a biography written forty years after his death by an anonymous younger admirer believed to be Antonio de Tuccio Manetti. It is noteworthy that Brunelleschi was the first Renaissance artist to be the subject of a full-scale biography. This was indicative of the Renaissance celebration of personal achievement as well as its transformation of the history of architecture into a history of individual accomplishment instead of a sequence of anonymous monuments. We are told by Manetti that after Brunelleschi failed to win the Baptistery door competition he moved away from sculpture and pursued a career as an architect. He and the great sculptor Donatello may have spent some years in Rome studying Roman sculpture and, more important, the techniques and measurements of Roman architecture.

Brunelleschi, however, was much more than a talented sculptor interested also in architecture and ancient culture. He had a genius for mechanical engineering, statics, hydraulics, mathematics, and other scientific and technological pursuits. Even in his own time he was compared to Daedalus, the legendary inventor and artist of the ancient world, who was renowned for his many skills and his technical ingenuity. With his great intellectual gifts, Brunelleschi, until his death in 1446, designed and built structures in Florence that began to change the appearance of the city and set architecture on a new course from which it did not swerve significantly until the nineteenth century.

We recall that Florence Cathedral (figs. 7-95, 7-96) was begun in 1296 on a design by Arnolfo di Cambio. Little was built, and the project was continued only after 1357 on an enlarged and modified plan by Francesco Talenti, one of the many *capomaestri* in charge of the cathedral's construction. Talenti's design, which assumed definitive shape in 1366–67, called for an enormous octagon at the eastern end of the building to be covered with an eight-sided domical vault of pointed curvature without exterior buttresses. The technical problems of constructing this dome (cupola) over an expanse as immense as the cathedral octagon presented a singular challenge. About 1417, progress on the building had brought it to the cupola stage, and by 1420 a technical solution for the vaulting proposed

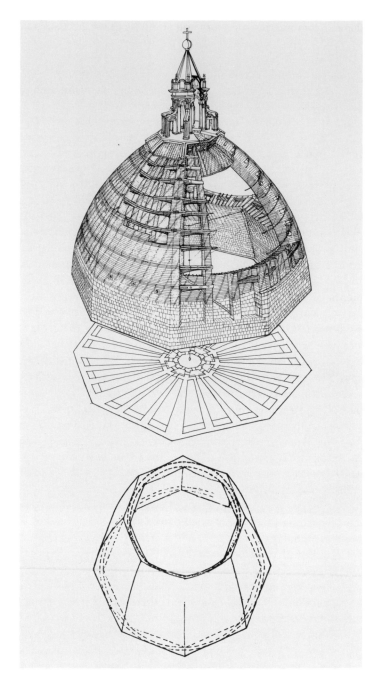

8-2 Cupola, Florence Cathedral. Diagrams: cutaway isometric of complete structure, above (P. A. Rossi); containment of circle in octagon, below (Mainstone)

by Brunelleschi (prepared originally in collaboration with Lorenzo Ghiberti and others) was approved and the difficult construction begun (colorplate 43). Controversy about the hidden parts of its structure, and conflicting intepretations of surviving documents, continue to puzzle scholars and technicians, but certain features about the dome are indisputable. It is constructed with an inner and outer octagonal shell of stone and brick. The two shells rise in parallel and terminate in an octagonal oculus that supports and is covered by a large decorative lantern. The shells are reinforced and connected vertically by a large stone rib in each of the octagon's eight corners, visible on the exterior, and by two smaller stone ribs on the interior on each of the eight sides. Horizontal reinforcements consisting of partially visible tension chains of stone and iron, and one of wood, girdle the vault and contain the tensile forces within the dome. From narrow corridors and stairs in the space between the double shell, the dome can be circumnavigated, inspected, and repaired.

Ingenious and complex geometry, brilliant masonry techniques, and specially designed hoisting machines were among Brunelleschi's spectacular contributions to the successful erection of the dome. However, the most remarkable contribution of all was the concept that led to its construction without the support of centering. This was necessary because the exceptional span and weight of the vault made traditional wooden trusswork centering impractical and dangerous, if not impossible. The only vault that can be built without the additional support of centering is one that is erected on a circular plan (that of the Pantheon, for example), with each completed ring of masonry forming a self-sustaining horizontal arch. Brunelleschi and his team conceived the daring notion to build the octagonal vault as if it were of circular plan in the alignments of its brick construction (as opposed to its overall shape). The complicated geometry and mechanics involved in giving reinforced circularity (or near-circularity—the shape is closer to an ellipse) to the outwardly octagonal vault have been the subject of much technical investigation in recent years. It is enough to recognize that the brilliant circle-within-octagon concept made it possible for Brunelleschi to use the mounting structure of the cupola itself as an armature, containing within the thickness of the octagon circular rings of masonry like those in a true circular dome (fig. 8-2). He raised the huge mass on successive self-supporting pseudo-circular courses of brick until, in the words of Alberti in 1436, the year of its consecration, it rose "above the skies, ample to cover with its shadow all the Tuscan people." In recognition of his technological genius, Brunelleschi was buried in the very cathedral that his cupola surmounted—a rare honor—and was lauded with an epitaph that pays tribute to "Filippo the Architect" for his "Daedalian art."

Brunelleschi had invented a new structural technology that made possible the complex construction of a dome whose form was established in the fourteenth century, and whose scale was equal to the greatest known antique vault—the Pantheon. Florence's self-esteem, reinforced by the stunning achievement, surpassed the city's pride in its kinship with the Classical world. For Alberti—even with his profound Humanist sentiment and veneration of the ancient world—recognized that Brunelleschi's feat of architectural engineering at the cupola was all the more extraordinary because he had not had a precedent in antiquity, that his achievement was "unknown and unthought of among the ancients." He praised Brunelleschi for the new things he was doing: "We [of this era] discover unheard-of and never-before-seen arts and sciences without teachers or without any model whatsoever."

Closely related to the ingenuity of the cupola construction was Brunelleschi's invention (probably c. 1425) of the systematic application of the rules of scientific perspective, which he demonstrated with two panel paintings (now lost) of Florentine buildings and piazzas seen three-dimensionally. From Manetti's description of the panels it seems clear that Brunelleschi's method was based on a single vanishing point toward which all parallel lines drawn on the same plane appear to converge, and the configuration of a visual "pyramid" made by the lines as they connect the eye with the object of vision. Brunelleschi's discovery was not codified until 1435 when Alberti recorded it for the first time in his treatise on painting published that year. But the progressive artists of the early fifteenth century recognized well before Alberti's formulation of the theory how in practice perspective geometry and optics could create the illusion of tangible, three-dimensional objects in a measurable space and in respect to their relative size and distance, a system used down to the present. Brunelleschi himself may have used perspective in order to draw buildings to scale; painters and sculptors applied it to their pictures and reliefs so that the images would appear to be extensions of reality, mirrors held up to nature.

Simultaneously with devising both the cupola construction and linear perspective, Brunelleschi was designing buildings that have become synonymous with the genesis of Renaissance architecture. His Ospedale degli Innocenti (colorplate 47; figs. 8-3, 8-4), an orphanage begun around 1419 on property acquired by the Silk Merchants' Guild, is generally regarded to be the earliest monumental expression of the new style. Tuscan trecento institutions were often designed with arcaded porticoes, and Brunelleschi retained this feature for the Innocenti, but he eliminated the old-fashioned balustrade upon which

8-3 **Filippo Brunelleschi. Ospedale degli Innocenti. Florence. Begun c. 1419**

8-4 **Interior of portico, Ospedale degli Innocenti**

the columns rested, changed the polygonal shafts to cylinders, and transformed stylized "pressed-leaf" capitals into rich Corinthianesque foliage. He translated old forms into a new Classical idiom, which was inspired, however, less by ancient prototypes than by Classicizing details found in Florentine Romanesque structures such as the Baptistery and S. Miniato al Monte, newly varied by Brunelleschi.

The clarity and correspondences of the Ospedale facade, underlined by the friezes, cornices, and bases that framed the individual portions of the ensemble, were remarkable. A nine-step platform (built after Brunelleschi's death) supported a nine-bay arcade with a pedimented window over the center of each bay. Originally the arcade was balanced by a closed bay at each end with framing Corinthian pilasters, an arrangement that emphasized the symmetry of the design just as the pendentive sail vault above each bay stressed the regularity of its square shape. It was not only the clarity of the design and the science behind its proportions that gave the Innocenti its discernible *all'antica* resonance, but also the exquisite carving of its Classicizing details, attributable to Brunelleschi's early skills as sculptor and goldsmith. The step from sculptor to architect was natural and logical; sculptors were trained in designing and carving architectural membering, the architectural framework for sculpture, and church furniture such as pulpits, tabernacles, and choir lofts. It explains the ambidexterity of many sculptor-architects of the early Renaissance, and the sculptural character of much of its architecture.

Soon after the Innocenti was begun, Giovanni di Bicci de' Medici, wealthy patriarch of Florence's most powerful family, recognized Brunelleschi's rising star and commissioned him to build a sacristy (1421–28) for the Medici parish church of S. Lorenzo (figs. 8-5, 8-6). Brunelleschi designed the Sacrestia Vecchia ("Old" Sacristy to distinguish it from the "new" one built in the sixteenth century in the same church by Michelangelo) as a cube surmounted by a hemispherical dome on pendentives, a device he adapted from the Byzantine practice of bridging the corners of the square to provide a circular base for the dome (figs. 4-26, 4-27). Ringed by windows at its base, the dome was partitioned by ribs into twelve segmentally curved webs. A smaller cube, similarly vaulted, formed the altar chapel. The dimensions of the sacristy square became the module for the room's proportional scheme linking plan to elevation, and one of Brunelleschi's most influential contributions to the evolution of Renaissance architectural style was the expression of that scheme by the geometric patterns formed by the dark gray stone, known as *pietra serena*, against the light stucco walls. Equally influential was the sacristy's central plan, whereby Brunelleschi established, as an important new architectural design, concentrically symmetrical forms such as squares, circles, or polygons, with all sides equidistant from the center. The great domed spaces of Renaissance architecture can trace their origins to Brunelleschi's concept. That the Old Sacristy was intended to be the Medici family mausoleum is significant in this respect, since central-plan buildings in antiquity and in the Early Christian period often had been used as burial structures. Four large arches springing from folded corner pilasters articulate the walls above the entablature, in the second of three equal zones into which the height of the sacristy is divided. Each section of wall, horizontal or vertical, and of vault is made separate and complete by its setting

8-5 Filippo Brunelleschi. Old Sacristy, view toward the chancel, S. Lorenzo. Florence. 1421–28

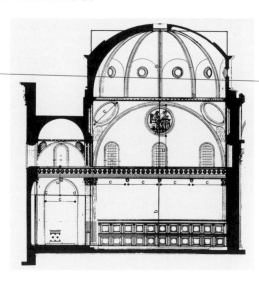

8-6
Old Sacristy,
vertical section,
S. Lorenzo.
(After
G. Fanelli)

within clearly delineated outlines; the result is a coordinated design of incomparable discipline, order, and logic.

The Medici eventually underwrote, in stages, the construction of a large new basilica to supersede the old Romanesque S. Lorenzo built in the eleventh century. In 1421, at about the same time the Old Sacristy was begun, the foundation stone was laid in the first (1421–25) of several campaigns to carry the ambitious project forward. Work halted more than once, and in 1441 Giovanni di Bicci's son, the rich and powerful Cosimo de' Medici financed a new spurt of construction. In plan, Brunelleschi's S. Lorenzo (figs. 8-7–8-9) was not unusual and resembled earlier Latin-cross Florentine basilicas with a

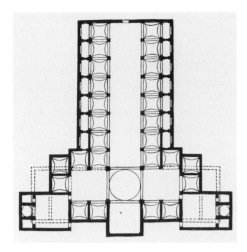

8-7
Plan, S. Lorenzo
(Old Sacristy at
upper left-hand
corner)

8-8   Capital, S. Lorenzo

8-9   Interior, S. Lorenzo, 1421–25, 1441–1460s

flat-roofed colonnaded nave, two aisles, rectangular apse, and transept with a perimeter of private chapels, but its articulation was a new departure. By reinterpreting Tuscan Romanesque formulae and giving new life to medieval planning systems, Brunelleschi transformed the massive polygonal or compound piers, pointed arches, and rib vaulting of Gothic churches such as Sta. Maria Novella and Florence Cathedral into the round-arched, cylindrical-shafted, elegant syntax first expressed in the Ospedale degli Innocenti. In S. Lorenzo, as in all Brunelleschi's interior spaces, walls light in color are divided by the dark *pietra serena* into patterns of rectangles, circles, and segmental arches reflecting geometric schemes of lucid intelligibility.

The cool beauty of Brunelleschi's architecture, apparent in each vista and detail at S. Lorenzo and also, as we will see, at its closely allied sibling S. Spirito, defined early Renaissance style. Lucid, poised, and serene, it was a marked contrast to the dynamics of Gothic architecture: equilibrium replaced soaring movement, and a determinate and concrete system of design supplanted Gothic fluidity and illusion.

If Brunelleschi's authorship of the Old Sacristy, S. Lorenzo, and Sto. Spirito have never been in doubt the same cannot be said of the Pazzi Chapel (colorplate 49, figs. 8-10, 8-11). Until recently the Chapel was almost universally regarded as one of the iconic works in the Brunelleschi canon, even though it was completed long after his death and its building history is riddled with problems. Proposed now as the work of Michelozzo di Bartolomeo — whose career we will survey shortly and who like Brunelleschi was a sculptor as well as an architect—the Pazzi Chapel and the issue of its authorship demonstrate how powerful was the impact of Brunelleschi's formal and typological inventions, of his detailing, and of his new interpretation of architectural language. Immediate and later followers of Brunelleschi often became obsessed with his trademark lucidity and elegance manifested in dark gray against white, and made them the standard for future Florentine buildings. It was a resonant style for the city because it combined a number of traditions held in high esteem by Florentines: intellectualism; craftsmanship of the highest quality; abstract patterns of articulation derived from the dark and light geometric inlay of Tuscan Romanesque buildings. The wish to perpetuate these qualities explains in part why High Renaissance and Baroque modes never took root firmly in Florence although they flourished elsewhere. Few architects (not even Michelangelo when he designed S. Lorenzo's New Sacristy) wanted to displace the civic manner

so powerfully reinforced by Brunelleschi. Nor, in Brunelleschi's own era, did Michelozzo, whose wide-ranging skills included the ability to "appropriate" Brunelleschi's much admired style and, for a certain kind of patron—not as demanding or as involved in architectural projects as Cosimo de' Medici—to provide less rigorous but convincing facsimiles. For example, at the Ospedale di San Paolo, a large hospital complex on a prominent piazza in

8-10　Pazzi Chapel, Sta. Croce, Florence. Built after 1442

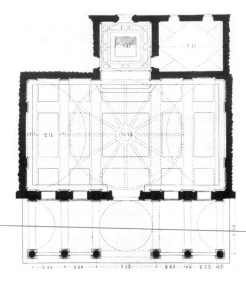

8-11
Plan, Pazzi Chapel

intensifying the decorative quality of the walls. The optical richness of the space is further heightened by the niche-and-oculus motif set into the framework of Corinthian pilasters and entablature, and also by the blue and white glazed terra-cotta reliefs of the apostles, sculptures that are supplemented by the four large polychromed Evangelists that occupy the circular frames in the pendentives. The Chapel has an elaborate porticoed facade supported by six columns and roofed by a central pendentive dome and lateral barrel vaults—analogous to the interior arrangement—all lined with polychromatic glazed terra-cotta.

Florence began to change dramatically under the impact of Brunelleschi's architecture and its counterparts in painting and sculpture. As the new movement unfolded, the work of Brunelleschi himself was affected by the dynamics he had unleashed. During the last decade of his life he significantly modified the vocabulary he perfected at the Old Sacristy and S. Lorenzo. Sta. Maria degli Angeli (fig. 8-12), an oratory built for the Camaldolese monastery in Florence and dedicated to the Virgin and twelve apostles, was begun in 1434 and, for lack of funds, was left incomplete in 1437. The building reached a height of only about 15 feet in the three years of work, and remained in its unfinished state until the 1930s, when it was completed in an unattractive and controversial manner. Unusual in form, Sta. Maria degli Angeli was planned as a domed octagon with a sixteen-sided exterior; semicircular niches were cut into every other facet of the exterior wall. Inside, eight chapels with deeply recessed lateral apses opened off the sides of the octagon, and were linked by a narrow passageway that pierced the apses and served as an ambulatory around the octagon.

In this first perfect central-plan structure of the Renaissance, Brunelleschi emphasized the thick and malleable nature of the wall mass and the plasticity of the forms—particularly the weighty triangular piers between the chapels—rather than the planimetric modes of his other buildings. Many scholars regard it as an example of the most mature phase of his career, a phase dominated by three-dimensional, "space-molding" elements such as deep niches and engaged half-columns. A greater heaviness, more massive forms and powerful profiles can also be found at Brunelleschi's S. Spirito (figs. 8-13, 8-14), designed either in 1428 or 1434 (depending on the interpretation of the

Florence, Michelozzo built a monumental loggia at the behest of the hospital's financial administrator that is a near replica of Brunelleschi's Ospedale degli Innocenti of thirty-five years earlier. That the same course might have been followed at the Pazzi Chapel, albeit in a far more creative way than at the loggia, is a compelling new idea. Designed as a chapter house for the Franciscan monks of Sta. Croce and located on the southern flank of the great Franciscan church (where Michelozzo had been at work in the cloister, on and off, from 1423 through 1452), the Pazzi Chapel was commissioned by Andrea de' Pazzi, head of a Florentine family almost equal in wealth and ambition to the Medici and who desired a family burial chapel similar to the Medici monument, but even more splendid. More complex in plan and articulation than the Old Sacristy, the Pazzi Chapel expands its central domed square into an oblong space with the addition of coffered, barrel-vaulted bays on two of its sides. In keeping with its function as a chapter house, a low bench runs along the walls of the room; opposite the entrance a smaller altar chapel, square and domed, opens from the eastern wall. The double-arched motif of the main wall of the Medicean model is extended to all four sides of the room,

8-12
Filippo
Brunelleschi.
Plan, Sta. Maria
degli Angeli.
Florence.
1434–37.
(Vatican, Rome)

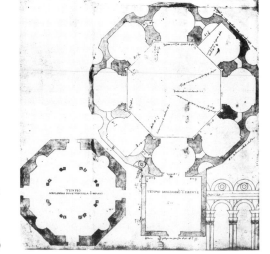

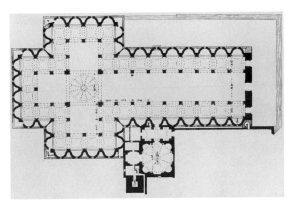

8-13   Filippo Brunelleschi. Plan, S. Spirito. Florence. Begun 1436

8-14   View of chapels, aisle, and nave, S. Spirito

documents) but begun in 1436. A basilican church with a centrally planned eastern end, S. Spirito was ringed by semicircular chapels opening off the domed aisle bays, both arms of the transept, and the apse. These chapels represented the most exceptional feature of Brunelleschi's plan since their shape was reflected on the exterior as an unbroken chain of protruding curves. It was a concept too bold to survive, and after Brunelleschi died the curves were walled over to produce the flat exterior visible today. On the interior, Brunelleschi retained the modular systems and formal correspondences he invented for S. Lorenzo, but the articulation of the later basilica stresses the weight and bulk of the forms. The most obvious illustrations of the change are the bulbous half-columns that flank the chapel entrances, instead of the flat, fluted pilasters of S. Lorenzo. Heavier and more sculptural in effect than its predecessor, S. Spirito is also simpler with regard to ornament and embellishment. The soffits of the arches, for example, and the impost blocks atop the capitals of the nave colonnade, are without carved relief. This emphasis on form without decorative overlay, on the depth of the wall, and on the three-dimensional character of the membering, reflected an escalating Classicism in Brunelleschi's work during the 1430s.

Allied with S. Spirito and Sta. Maria degli Angeli are Brunelleschi's heavily massed, semicircular exedrae (1445–60s) above the tribunes of the eastern end of Florence Cathedral (fig. 8-15). These are formed with deep cavities and thick walls, inflected by paired Corinthian half-columns beneath protruding entablatures. The volumes of the exedrae also represent a departure from the linear-graphic inflections of Brunelleschi's

earlier manner, revealing a closer affinity to Roman architecture than anything that had yet been constructed in Florence. They foreshadowed and probably inspired the strong profiles and grand sonorities of the Classicizing buildings of Alberti and, later, Bramante.

A fellow Humanist wrote of Brunelleschi soon after he died: "The ancient building arts of the Romans were rediscovered by him," although quattrocento Humanists had little idea what those "building arts of the Romans" were all about. The unique surviving first-century B.C. treatise on architecture, written by the Roman architect Vitruvius, prized though it was in the Renaissance for its authenticity and practicality, could not be fully understood. In part this was because of the divergence between ancient and modern needs, typologies and technologies, and in part because the treatise itself lacked clarity. Renaissance Humanists may have believed they knew a great deal about the culture of antiquity but Tuscany, for example, was not particularly rich in Classical remains; indeed, most Roman architecture known to the Renaissance was built in the centuries after Vitruvius and hence not discussed by him. Nor were there critical methods by which to distinguish what we now know as the "periods" of the past and as defining features among historical buildings. Fifteenth-century observers did not realize, for example, that the Baptistery of Florence was an eleventh-century Romanesque structure; it was believed to be an ancient temple dedicated to Mars and later made Christian. They knew nothing about the functions of old buildings; their image of antiquity was, understandably, confused, imprecise, and hypothetical. While Brunelleschi's contemporaries recognized something strikingly new in his buildings, they had little idea of what that freshness owed to antiquity. Indeed, prototypes for Brunelleschi's buildings can be found in the local traditions of Romanesque and late trecento architecture, and in the structures of Early Christianity, Byzantium, and the medieval world of the eastern Mediterranean, as well as in the ruins of ancient Rome. The graceful spring of the Ospedale degli Innocenti's arcade is closer to that of the facade of Romanesque S. Miniato al Monte than to any precursor in antiquity. Moreover, while pendentive domes and domes on pendentives or squinches were rare in Tuscany and in Italy in general, Brunelleschi used them repeatedly. A dome set above a square

8-15   Filippo Brunelleschi. Exedra, Florence Cathedral. Design approved 1439; completed 1445–47

was uncommon in ancient buildings where domes above circles were preferred, but it was a salient feature of Byzantine and Islamic structures. The type of hemispherical "umbrella" dome Brunelleschi favored—with ribs, webs, and oculi piercing the base—was also a non-Tuscan, non-Roman form, deriving instead from Byzantium, where it was most majestically realized at Hagia Sophia. Brunelleschi's new formula in S. Lorenzo's nave arcade of impost blocks with carved relief combined with ornamented soffits also originated in the Christian East and was introduced into Italy in the sixth century in Ravenna, most notably in the church of S. Vitale. Along with the structural system of beveled piers rather than a continuous wall to support the dome at S. Vitale, the octagonal plan of the Ravenna church (fig. 4-34) is one possible model (the octagonal Florence Baptistry with its paired angle pilasters is another) for Brunelleschi's Sta. Maria degli Angeli. That the Angeli appears to be closer to S. Vitale than to any antique source underlines the complexity of the subject of Brunelleschi's Classicism. Powerful Roman echoes reverberate throughout his buildings, but quotations from specific antique structures (other than some from the Pantheon) are hard to identify. Still, an indisputable gap between Brunelleschi and the medieval sources of his style was opened by the authoritative way in which he used the Classical orders, underscored their importance, and through them expressed the proportions and harmonies in his buildings. Moreover, he shaped those orders with consummate sculptural skills learned in his youth, carrying the Florentine craft of carving architectural details to a new high. His profoundly personal style was based on a unique and free interpretation of what he knew of antique architecture and sculpture, and the new language he created was thus born not only of his study of Classical monuments and of the Tuscan Romanesque, but of heterogeneous Byzantine and Islamic modes that had come into Italy by way of the Early Christian and medieval architecture of Venice, Padua, and Ravenna. Out of all these threads Brunelleschi fabricated the first masterpieces of Renaissance architecture. It was left to his followers to produce a more literal, more canonical, and more "archaeological" version of ancient architecture.

Michelozzo and Rossellino. In the flourishing production of Renaissance architecture that followed Brunelleschi's introduction of the movement in the 1420s, two architects stand out. One was the versatile architect-sculptor Michelozzo di Bartolomeo, the first of Brunelleschi's followers, responsible for many notable buildings as well as for the invention of influential new Renaissance architectural typologies—library, monastery, private palace, tabernacle—in Florence and elsewhere. Sustained by the interest and patronage of the Medici family who recognized him as the new "star" of the second generation as they had recognized Brunelleschi in the first, he carried out his most important architectural commissions, the first of which was the rebuilding of the Dominican monastic compound of S. Marco, begun around 1437. He rebuilt the old refectory and the trecento church, made a graceful new cloister framed on four sides by a five-bayed Ionic arcade, and produced the beautiful Library (1442–44; fig. 8-16). Designed with three aisles of equal width, its central aisle barrel-vaulted and slightly higher than the groin-vaulted side aisles, the Library was the most interesting architectural component in the complex. The white walls inflected with gray stone and the slender columns supporting a springy arcade were tes-

8-16 Michelozzo di Bartolomeo. Library, S. Marco. Florence. 1442–44

timony to Michelozzo's understanding of Brunelleschi's new architectural language. He made his own statement, however, with the Ionic capitals (also used in the cloister arcade), whose tightly wound coils and slender scrolls harmonize with the delicate proportions of the columns and the light, airy feeling of the room. But it was the barrel vault that represented Michelozzo's most inspired concept for the Library. (In antiquity, the barrel vault was among the most adaptable and utilitarian of the Roman vaulting systems and never failed to evoke the sensation of a majestic unity of space.) Whereas in the earlier decades of the Florentine quattrocento, Brunelleschi had endeavored to perfect domical vaulting, around mid-century and later, architects turned their attention to the matter of the barrel vault. Painters and sculptors had already responded to its heroic nature and had often reproduced it in two dimensions, but the first monumental architectural barrel vault of the Renaissance was Michelozzo's in the S. Marco Library. It was short in span (though not in length) and was not constructed in legitimate *all'antica* manner, that is, with continuous wall support, but in the more "medieval" form of columnar point support. The S. Marco barrel vault was but one unit in a triple-aisled scheme planned for the functional requirements of a library—light and compartments for desks—which columns fulfilled but a wall did not.

Other buildings by Michelozzo, notably a central-plan tribune for the important church of SS. Annunziata are, like the library at San Marco, crucial to the study of innovative early Renaissance architecture, but it is usually his palace (begun around 1445) for Cosimo de' Medici that is singled out because of its great inventiveness and influence on future secular architecture. During the fourteenth century a synthesis of elements derived from privately owned defensive towers (symbols of power), and from residential (often combined with commerce) palaces of the ruling elite, resulted in the cubic, tri-zoned "fortress" style of official structures in Florence, such as the Palazzo del Podestà or the Palazzo della Signoria. Residential palaces in the "private sector" were generally modest in size (no more than twelve rooms) and appearance, however, for the display of status through private architecture was inhibited by a tradition of sumptuary laws, by Franciscanism and its emphasis on poverty and antimaterialism, and by civic ordinances that controlled the expression of personal individuality in buildings. These restraints were displaced, however, after the mid-fifteenth century, when Michelozzo's palace for Cosimo de' Medici became the first in a line of grandiose palaces commissioned by the Florentine great families—often motivated by intense rivalry—as personal monuments to posterity (colorplate 44; fig. 8-17).

At least twenty small houses were demolished to accommodate Cosimo's new one with its corner site, its more than forty rooms, a colonnaded ceremonial courtyard, garden, loggia, and frescoed chapel with altar. In size and grandeur it rivaled the Palazzo della Signoria—a signal of Cosimo's importance—and it intentionally alluded in its details to Republican Roman buildings. Manifesting the heady, new spirit of individualism that characterized the Renaissance, it brought into the open the ambition of powerful men to use architecture as a metaphor for wealth and influence. Recent studies of Florentine Renaissance

8-17 Michelozzo di Bartolomeo. Courtyard, Palazzo Medici. Florence. Begun c. 1445

palaces have also called attention to the important socio-economic role of these buildings as they supported the city's construction industry and embodied the newly acceptable phenomenon of conspicuous consumption.

The exterior of the Palazzo Medici (enlarged by seven window bays in the seventeenth century by the Riccardi family) gives at first glance an impression not dissimilar to its Tuscan ancestors—cubic, stony, and impenetrable. Even the heavy cornice in its extensive projection recalls the overhanging roofs common to Florentine houses. Yet the style and magnitude of the cornice are unprecedented in secular architecture after Imperial Rome; it was the product of Michelozzo's special affinity for the powerful, weighty forms of antique architecture. And even though the massive rusticated blocks of the ground floor reflect the familiar lithic character of Florentine buildings, they are "archaeological" descendants of such ancient mural constructions as, for example, the Servian Wall that encircled Rome in the fourth century B.C. The choice of this type of rustication was highly suited to a patron who had been compared to celebrated Romans and praised by the Humanists "as if he had been born at Rome or Athens." New studies suggest that the blocks were freshly quarried but worked over to resemble the weather-worn stones of venerable ancient monuments. Two tiers of large windows on a corner site, designed in the most Classical mode possible, are also unusual features in residential architecture, and they allow the passage of an uncommon amount of light and air. Their format—a single arch divided into two lights by a slender mullion—recalls the windows of the Bargello and the Palazzo della Signoria, the two greatest of the civic medieval buildings of Florence, but the arch is segmental and the mullion a Corinthian colonnette.

More than any other feature it is the courtyard of the Palazzo Medici that distinguishes it from its medieval predecessors. It is large, square, at the center of the block, ornamented with an iconographically integrated program of sculpture and framed by a twelve-columned arcuated loggia. Its conspicuous grandeur and display of power, wealth, and intellect were in marked contrast to the small and irregular courtyards in earlier private palaces—primarily utilitarian areas used as shafts for light and air and to house the well and staircase. And because the Palazzo Medici is laid out as an axially organized, centrally planned structure, it is possible for an observer standing at the main portal to look through the courtyard to a garden with a loggia at the rear. Such an arrangement may have been inspired by the Vitruvian description of ancient Roman houses with their axial design, centralized atrium, and colonnaded peristyle garden.

The Palazzo Medici was allied through its sturdy silhouette and general exterior organization to prevailing Florentine palace typologies. With its remarkable innovative elements, however, it also immediately established the model for virtually all of the numerous large private palaces built in quattrocento Florence as well as many comparable structures in other Italian cities. Although the large central courtyard employing Classical arcades was important to this format, the irreducible sign of the new type was its public aspect, the three-storied rusticated facade with lavish windows and heavy Classical cornice. Among the great Florentine examples were the Pitti, Gondi, and Strozzi palaces, designed between the 1450s and 90s.

The most radical variation of this pattern was the Palazzo Rucellai (colorplate 45; fig. 8-18), generally regarded as the

8-18 Leon Battista Alberti. Facade, Palazzo Rucellai. Florence. Begun c. 1457

work of Leon Battista Alberti, one of the most remarkable and influential of Renaissance figures. Unlike the Medici type, here the rustication was flattened, and its presence compensated by three tiers of articulating pilasters framing the windows and portals. Although never repeated in Florence itself, where the Medici model remained compelling, the Rucellai Palace design of about 1460 appears almost simultaneously in a cruder version in the Palazzo Piccolomini in Pienza (1459–62), a work firmly established to be by Bernardo Rossellino, an architect-sculptor comparable to Michelozzo in his versatility and wide-ranging practice, and a close collaborator in the work of Alberti.

Pienza (figs. 8-19, 8-20) is remarkable not only for its Rucellai-like Piccolomini Palace, but as an exceptional example of Renaissance urban planning seen in actual practice rather than speculative theory. Between 1459 and 1462, Pope Pius II, a member of the Sienese Piccolomini family, reconfigured the central area of Corsignano, the small town south of Siena that had been his birthplace, which he now renamed Pienza. Around a regular, trapezoidal space, a set of new monuments was built by Rossellino. At the center rose the grandiose facade of the new cathedral with its triple arcade of giant arches over monumental columns (the first church facade of the Renaissance). To the west stood the Piccolomini Palace, marked by the less grandiose articulation of tiers of pilasters. This papal residence was roughly counterbalanced by the archbishop's palace to the east of the cathedral, its subordinate station (to the papal building) indicated by its smaller size and the absence of all articulation apart from the portal and window frames. Designed as an integrated complex manifesting controlled variety of form around a regular space, the piazza and its buildings were revealed to the observer through several perspectives, the most compelling being the approach through a narrow axial street coming from the marketplace, yielding to the view seen in figure 8-19.

8-19 Bernardo Rossellino. Main piazza, Pienza. 1459–62. (Palazzo Piccolomini on the right)

Alberti. If Brunelleschi, Michelozzo, and Rossellino were practicing architects and men of action but—as far as posterity is concerned—of few words, the opposite must be said of Leon Battista Alberti. He was a brilliant theorist, historian, scientist, Humanist, and, as a writer, left an important body of treatises, essays, plays, poems, and letters. As we have already seen, he was also an architect, although he often distanced himself from the construction of the buildings he designed, leaving their supervision to other architects. Unlike Brunelleschi, who was rooted in Florence and spent most of his life working there, Alberti—born in Genoa in 1404, an illegitimate son in a great Florentine family in exile—was peripatetic, an aristocratic, uprooted, and "stateless" traveler, who received commissions for important buildings in many cities. Brunelleschi probably did not know Latin, or at least not much, whereas Alberti received a full Humanist education at the University of Padua and then studied Canon Law at the University of Bologna. He entered the papal civil service (during the reign of Eugenius IV), a post that gave him the opportunity to travel widely, study, and write. Among his Latin writings were three treatises that formed the theoretical foundations of early Renaissance art, and they were of cardinal importance for the dissemination of Humanist ideals: *De pictura* (1435), in which he formulated the conceptual basis of the art of painting and formalized Brunelleschi's invention of perspective construction into a mathematically and theoretically grounded system of visual representation; *De statua* (c. 1433), a discourse on sculpture and the theory of the proportions of the human body; and *De re aedificatoria, libri X* (conceived in the 1430s, presented to Pope Nicholas V in 1452, published in 1485), a discussion of the theory and a manual for the practice of building, based loosely on Vitruvius's treatise. Alberti's "ten books" were a repository of lofty architectural theory, workaday advice for on-the-site construction, wide-ranging historical discourse, and erudite Classical learning. In addition, they were intended to be the foundation on which architecture's new social status was built—that of a genuine profession rather than a mere artisan's trade. Alberti emphasized the intellectual requirements for the practice of architecture—theoretical as well as practical knowledge, the mastery of geometry, mathematics, philosophy, Classical culture, and so on—through which a craftsman could "promote" himself to architect. As adviser, designer, and consultant on artistic and intellectual matters, Alberti's services were enlisted by perspicacious and ambitious patrons in many cities. It is thought by

many scholars that with the support of the wealthy merchant-patrician Giovanni Rucellai, Alberti endowed Florence with some of its most distinguished early Renaissance structures. The Palazzo Rucellai was a remodeling of several older buildings ("from eight houses I made one," Rucellai's diary records) with a new facade, begun probably around 1457, spreading across the composite structure. The eight-bayed facade remained incomplete at the right end because Rucellai could not purchase the property it was to cover. Although the facade conforms to the three zones of lavish stonework, windows, and heavy cornice of the Palazzo Medici type, its system of articulation, as already mentioned, is strikingly different from other Florentine palace design. Drafted rustication of flat, precisely cut blocks separated by wide spaces are overlaid by a grid formed horizontally by running entablatures and vertically by smooth pilasters nearly level with the wall surface, dividing it into almost equal bays (the portal bay is slightly wider). In the ancient manner, the pilaster orders vary from the first to the third story, with Doric on the first and Corinthian on the third; in place of the Ionic used in the canonical system, the second story pilasters have leafy capitals freely invented from antique motifs. The idiom of pilaster screen over flat masonry was an adaption of the scheme applied to the upper level of the Roman Colosseum.

It bears mentioning here that the existence of Bernardo Rossellino's contemporaneous Rucellai Palace "twin" in Pienza, the Palazzo Piccolomini, has again put the spotlight on intriguing questions of authorship regarding certain major Florentine Renaissance monuments. Like the Pazzi Chapel and the identity of its architect, the Rucellai Palace has been seriously questioned as a work by Alberti; instead, Rossellino has been proposed as its author.

The completion of the facade of Sta. Maria Novella, the Rucellai family parish church (fig. 8-21) is another Rucellai project thought to be the work of Alberti. The facade had been left unfinished above the lower tier in the fourteenth century. From that trecento campaign, Alberti inherited the sepulchral niches with pointed arches, the lateral portals also enclosed by Gothic frames, and the geometrically patterned green and white marble revetment. It was this biochromatism—Tuscan Romanesque in origin and never out of favor in Florence—that Alberti chose as the departure for the revetment system of his new facade (c. 1458–70). Over it, he superimposed a series of tall and narrow arches to accommodate the vertical accent of the Gothic remnants. The arch and the capitals of the engaged order he shaped in a manner not Gothic but Romanesque-antique, thus making possible the introduction of the authoritative Classical language of the entrance, consisting of fluted pilasters framed by noble columns on tall dadoes—this in homage to the Roman Pantheon, a monument exhaustively studied by "archaeologist" Alberti. To mark the separation of the upper and lower stories, Alberti used a tall frieze, and the extremities of the lower story were firmly defined by Classical piers of exceptional purity integrated into the historical mix. Above the frieze, a pedimented temple image, recalling the upper part of Romanesque S. Miniato, diagrammed the height and width of the nave. And in one of the most ingenious and far-reaching adaptions of an antique device (the supporting bracket of an entablature), Alberti concealed the sloping roofs of the side aisles with a scrolled gable, or volute, that was to become an omnipresent feature in architecture until the modern

8-21 Facade. Sta. Maria Novella. Florence. Lower zone 13th century; upper parts Leon Battista Alberti, c. 1458–70

resembles a surviving portion of the fourth century A.D. Basilica of Maxentius, which was, along with the Colosseum and the Pantheon, one of Rome's most awe-inspiring monuments.

At Rimini the project called for a modern enlargement of a fourteenth-century Gothic church. Even in its unfinished state, S. Francesco (called, in the language of Humanism, the Tempio Malatestiano) can be recognized as a turning point in the history of architecture. With this building Alberti moved early Renaissance architecture out of its Brunelleschian idiom into an iconographically explicit referencing of ancient Roman models. During his long periods in Rome, as well as in his travels, Alberti was able to explore systematically a wide range of Roman buildings under conditions not available to Brunelleschi and Michelozzo, thus allowing him to re-create (as they had not been able to do) accurate Roman architectural images—the arcade on piers, triumphal arch, dome, basilica, temple, bath, for example—and to use them in a free but still authoritative manner. He enclosed the Gothic S. Francesco within a Renaissance shell to satisfy the ambitious Malatesta's desire for a glorious memorial structure for himself, his mistress Isotta degli Atti, and members of his court. The lateral tomb arcades have already been described; the lower portion of the facade was designed to evoke the image of a triumphal arch (as a symbol of Malatesta's "triumph" over death through fame and memory, despite a public consignment to hell for his crimes by Pope Pius II). The illusion of a triumphal arch would be even more cogent if the walled-up areas flanking the central arch were left as the concavities they originally had been,

8-22 Leon Battista Alberti. Shrine of the Holy Sepulchre, S. Pancrazio. Florence. c. 1458

age. From these diverse units Alberti fabricated a structure of remarkable consistency and integrity. His method was to relate the parts to one another through simple numerical ratios using as a module the dimensions of the huge square within which the entire facade could be inscribed: two squares half the size of the large square contained the lower facade (to the top of the frieze), and each one was equal to the square outline of the upper-story "temple."

In 1448 Alberti built a chapel dedicated to the Holy Sepulchre in the Rucellai parish church, S. Pancrazio, next to the family palace. Standing in the center is the richly embellished shrine (fig. 8-22) that symbolizes the Holy Sepulchre in Jerusalem and is composed of elements derived from the Florence Baptistry—light and dark patterned stone, and fluted Corinthian pilasters. The entrance to the chapel was defined by columns supporting an architrave, illustrating Alberti's profound comprehension of Classical practice wherein arches (except when they are engaged to a wall) are carried by piers, and architraves are supported by columns. Alberti's wide exposure to Roman architecture, and especially his meditations on theory, led him to interpret the arch-with-column, a favorite device in the Middle Ages, as a "decadent" practice, suitable perhaps for theaters or houses but lacking the dignity required for more serious buildings such as temples (as he called churches). In the churches he designed, he revived the "correct" usage—trabeated at S. Pancrazio, and arcuated at S. Francesco in Rimini (colorplate 46; figs. 8-23, 8-24), built in about 1450 for Sigismondo Malatesta, the predatory Rimini tyrant-prince who, as a Humanist, was one of Alberti's most appreciative patrons. There, on the exterior flanks of the building, deep, arched niches, holding the sarcophagi of Sigismondo's courtiers, are carried by massive piers marked by a strong cornice at the springing line; the whole system closely

8-23 Leon Battista Alberti. Facade and flank, S. Francesco (Tempio Malatestiano). Rimini. c. 1450

8-24 Sigismondo Malatesta and S. Francesco, medal of 1450. (After Matteo dei Pasti)

reaching ground level without the running plinth. Nevertheless, the building's triad of bays, fluted half-columns, and broken entablature were like those found below the attic portion of many surviving Roman arches. Rimini, a notable provincial outpost in the days of the Empire, had (and still has) the distinguished Arch of Augustus, which inspired Alberti to give to S. Francesco its thick, wreath-framed roundel beside the rich capitals of the engaged columns. The dense wall, which was an integral element of Roman building, was restored by Alberti: He thickened the already powerful blocks of masonry on the facade with a superposed order and ornamental relief, and emphasized the wall depth of the lateral arcades with projecting moldings. His plan for the upper zone of the facade (incomplete) above the strong entablature is preserved in a medal of 1450 (fig. 8-24): He envisioned a semicircular pediment upheld by short columns above a three-bayed window (suggesting a Roman bath window) flanked by quadrant arches. Also visible is a gigantic ribbed dome that was to have covered a rotunda beyond the nave extending the full width of the nave plus side chapels. The analogy to the Pantheon (another appropriate image for Malatesta's burial temple) cannot be ignored despite the different character of its dome.

Alberti in about 1470 was provided with an exceptional opportunity to design a church in its entirety—as opposed to designing

additions to an older structure—by Lodovico Gonzaga, Duke of Mantua. S. Andrea (figs. 8-25, 8-26) was never completed, but the portions of it that were finished, both exterior and interior, were to have immense influence on the future of architecture. It is possibly the grandest of all early Renaissance constructions, and it clearly sets Alberti apart—in terms of his comprehension of historical architecture—from all architects preceding him. On the facade, he combined two of his favorite ancient images—the pedimented temple front (pilasters, entablature, trabeation, and triangular pediment) and the triadic triumphal arch (arched central section and lower portals on either side). The height of the facade equals its width, but the barrel vault of the nave reached well above the apex of the pediment, which was also surmounted by a large canopy over the nave window. Alberti therefore disassociated the facade from the body of the church by turning it into an independent narthex one bay deep (which Michelangelo would do in 1516 in his model for the facade of S. Lorenzo) with its own system of coffered barrel vaults and a design combining the image of a triumphal arch with that of a Classical temple front. The giant pilaster order running from dado to entablature to unify the levels of the lateral bays is perhaps Alberti's most prophetic innovation. It gives to the building a sense of colossal scale throughout (it is used also on the interior), and makes Brunelleschi's late architecture seem, by comparison, delicate, fragile, even "Gothic." To look at S. Andrea is to understand the indebtedness of High Renaissance architecture to the breakthroughs made by Alberti. Here are no Gothic echoes, no post-Classical misinterpretations of the heroic spirit of ancient architecture.

The design of S. Andrea's interior was based on the Roman Basilica of Maxentius, with its gigantic nave and wide openings into lateral spaces, and superseded the Early Christian basilica and its Renaissance heirs, basilican churches such as S. Lorenzo and S. Spirito. The conventional system for three-aisled churches composed of columnar screens, separate channels of space, and flat roofs is now supplanted by an enormous barrel-vaulted nave bounded by chapels roofed with buttressing transverse vaults. As in the grandest of Roman monuments, the space of the nave is unified, the vista unimpeded, the scale majestic. To articulate the immense piers between the chapels, Alberti chose the triumphal arch pattern of the facade, thus forging a correspondence between interior and exterior. Framing the chapel arches are pilasters belonging to an entablature running continuously from the entrance to the crossing, and from which the vault springs. This design—so noble in conception—became the model for some of the greatest sixteenth-century longitudinal churches, including St. Peter's and the Gesù.

Alberti died soon after the first stone of S. Andrea had been placed in 1472. Construction was then supervised by Luca Fancelli, chief architect at the Gonzaga court. It was completed to the end of the nave in 1494; the rest followed in the eighteenth century. Alberti probably planned to unite the nave with a domed space bounded by shallow transept arms, but his intentions for the completion of the building are still disputed.

In his *De re aedificatoria*, Alberti discussed almost every aspect of architecture, from commonplace details, such as the distance required between kitchen and dining room to avoid cooking odors but still keep hot food from cooling, to philosophical questions about the five orders, proportions, and the nature of beauty. He described architectural distinctions

8-25 Leon Battista Alberti. Facade, S. Andrea. Mantua. Begun 1472

8-26 Interior, S. Andrea

between houses for farmers and those for gentlemen, between a rich man's country house and his house in town. He explained how the streets of a city should be laid out, and prescribed a hierarchical variety of building types amid which a "temple" (never a church) would be the city's noblest ornament: It should be located in an open wide place, separated from other buildings and therefore visible from all sides, raised on a platform, and shaped either as a circle or as a form deriving from a circle, to which chapels could be added. Perhaps the most far-reaching effect of *De re aedificatoria* can be found in the appearance of some centralized churches built at the end of the fifteenth century and the beginning of the sixteenth according to the Albertian ideal. In addition to outlining a program for the ideal church, he also proposed one for the ideal house and the ideal city, but these descriptions remained strictly theoretical, for he never had the opportunity of realizing them. Still, his theories found their way into the works of others and were of paramount influence in the development of Renaissance architecture, city planning, and future treatises on architecture. The beginnings of Renaissance urbanism, realized in only a few concrete examples in the fifteenth century, can be traced to Alberti. Rossellino's great piazza at Pienza is often thought to have been influenced by Alberti's ideas. Vigevano, a small town near Milan, has a shaped, planned city square (c. 1490), surrounded by loggias, conceived in the spirit of Alberti and Vitruvius, and akin to the ancient forum (fig. 8-27). It served a public function as meeting place, marketplace, and shelter from the elements with its covered

8-27   Piazza Ducale, looking west. Vigevano. 1492–94

arcades. But it also served another purpose: it demonstrated the power of the dukes of Milan, who had a whole quarter of the city demolished in order to produce the new piazza that provided a grandiose foyer to their nearby castle, used to maintain their control of this town.

The Late Fifteenth Century in Tuscany; Giuliano da Sangallo. Giuliano da Sangallo was the most important Florentine architect of the closing years of the fifteenth century. Although many of his buildings embody a reworking of Brunelleschi's style, Giuliano certainly did not lack individuality and creativity. One of his most important buildings, Sta. Maria delle Carceri, in Prato (begun 1485; figs. 8-28, 8-29), marks him as belonging to two worlds—the early Renaissance of Brunelleschi-Michelozzo-Alberti and the emerging High Renaissance with its interest in centrally planned structures and in the monumentalism of ancient buildings.

Sangallo's church at Prato was one of several central-plan churches that sprang up between 1480 and 1510 in central Italy, Tuscany, and Lombardy, as Alberti's theories spread. Centralized churches, particularly those in the preferred shape of the geometrically perfect circle, symbolized the perfection of God. Round forms also reflected the shape of the cosmos and satisfied the Humanist desire to find links between nature and art. Ideas like these were circulated not only through the writings of Alberti but through treatises written by other influential theorists of the period, such as Francesco di Giorgio

Martini (1439–1501) and Antonio Averlino, called Filarete (c. 1400–69), who were themselves indebted to Alberti and Vitruvius. Francesco di Giorgio's *Trattato di architettura ingegneria ed arte militare* (c. 1476–80s) included a lengthy discourse on centralized churches illustrated with numerous plans for the layouts of such buildings, as well as a plan of a basilica drawn around a human figure. This image was based on Vitruvius's famous description of a man with arms and legs outstretched who fit precisely into a square and circle to demonstrate the correspondence between the human body and ideal geometric shapes (fig. 8-30). The highly imaginative untitled treatise on architecture (completed 1465) by Filarete included proposals for a utopian city with some extremely fanciful buildings. The city, named Sforzinda for his princely patron, Francesco Sforza, was shaped as an eight-pointed star; at its center was a main square, its length two times its width, from which all thoroughfares would radiate. Filarete's treatise was accompanied by drawings that included plans for centralized structures; the central plan he preferred above all others was the inscribed cruciform. Until the 1480s, architectural drawings like those by Filarete and Francesco di Giorgio remained experimental—abstract two-dimensional diagrams based on the manipulation of modular grids. Not until Sta. Maria delle Carceri were such designs, together with the theories of Alberti, translated into three-dimensional architectural construction. Earlier in the century, Brunelleschi, Michelozzo, and Alberti designed independent centralized structures, but

8-28 Giuliano da Sangallo. Sta. Maria delle Carceri. Prato. Begun 1485

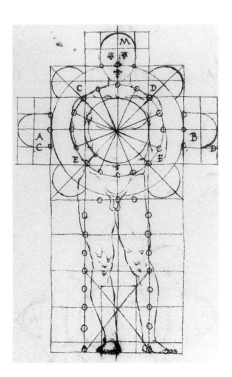

8-30
Francesco di Giorgio.
Drawing, c. 1476
(Il Codice
Magliabecchiano.
Biblioteca Nazionale.
Florence)

until the Carceri was built, keen interest in them was restricted to theoretical literature. Sangallo's church embodied the ideas about symmetry, geometry, and the clear definition of space determined in the quattrocento, combined with the new monumentality of Alberti's buildings. Recent discoveries have associated Lorenzo (Il Magnifico) de' Medici, Humanist, poet, political leader, reader of Alberti's treatises, and greatest of all art patrons in the late fifteenth century, with the design of Sta. Maria delle Carceri.

In the Brunelleschian manner, the interior walls of Sangallo's church are articulated by geometric patterns of *pietra serena* membering applied to a light ground. Although the patterns of rectangles and semicircles are familiar, the fluted pilasters, capitals, entablatures, and cornices that express these patterns are thicker, wider, and richer than those designed by Brunelleschi fifty years earlier. A luxuriously ornamented

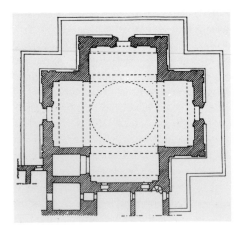

8-29
Plan, Sta. Maria
delle Carceri

frieze of blue and white terra-cotta in high relief marks the separation of upper and lower tiers; above the crossing square floats a twelve-ribbed dome on pendentives with a light-filled ring of oculi at its base; a balustrade separates the dome from the deeply carved cornice of the pendentive field. Shaped as a Greek cross, the church has four equal arms, which on the interior are clad in Sangallo's synthesis of Brunelleschi's plane geometry and, by virtue of the terminal doubled order, Alberti's grand forms. The polychrome marble revetment of the upper stories of the exterior (unfinished on one arm) is mostly nineteenth-century work. In the custom of Tuscan Romanesque buildings, the top zone is a diagram of a small pedimented temple.

Centralized buildings were perceived not only as materializations of abstract concepts relating to the cosmos or Divine perfection, but also as memorial structures commemorating a particular place, person, or event. Such symbolism can be traced back to the small, central-plan, often domed martyria of early Christianity built to mark the site of a martyrdom. Surviving into the Renaissance, the idea of a central-plan building as a monument, a marker, was expanded to include places and events other than those related to martyrial sacrifice. Specifically, the central-plan structure was often adopted to honor miracles associated with the Virgin Mary. This inspired the dedication to the Virgin of Sangallo's Sta. Maria delle Carceri (fig. 8-31; a "miracle-working" image of the Virgin drew worshipers to the site, and a church was needed to accommodate them) and other contemporaneous freestanding, centralized, domed churches. Nevertheless, the original role of such churches as a memorial monument, not linked to the Virgin and constructed to mark the site of a martyrdom, was sustained.

Giuliano da Sangallo was an avid student of ancient architecture, educated in the Albertian tradition of measuring and drawing Roman buildings. He lived for years in Rome and filled sketchbooks with reverential and evocative drawings of

8-31 Interior, Sta. Maria delle Carceri

8-32 Giuliano da Sangallo. Villa Medici at Poggio a Caiano. Near Florence. c. 1485

8-33 Portico, Villa Medici

Roman monuments and architectural ornament. His brand of flexible, rich, freely interpreted Classicism—typical of the quattrocento—is best reflected in the villa at Poggio a Caiano (near Florence) that he built in about 1485 for (and largely under the direction of) Lorenzo de' Medici (figs. 8-32, 8-33). In the facade loggia, Giuliano produced the first "true" ancient temple front in the Renaissance, "true" because it was formed with freestanding columns, as ancient temples had been. By comparison Alberti's Sta. Maria Novella and S. Andrea were images or diagrams, pilastered constructions integrated with the wall. Just beyond the trabeated temple porch at Poggio a Caiano is a vestibule roofed with a rare fifteenth-century barrel vault and decorated originally on one end wall with a fresco (now lost) depicting the story of Laocoön; secular and mythological subjects were appropriate for villas. A gem of early Renaissance architecture, Sangallo's temple-loggia is inserted into the face of what appears to be a conventional cubelike Tuscan villa. But its design is an imaginative innovation: a block with a recess on two flanks forming an "H" turned 90 degrees, open to the landscape through the columns of the loggia, and supported on a balustraded pedestal of piers and arches. (The original double stair was not curved but straight.) Sangallo's temple-facade, barrel-vaulted vestibule, walls decorated with paintings of mythological subjects, and interior grand salon with a monumental barrel vault (constructed in the sixteenth century) to equal the most impressive Roman works, represent a combination of architect and patron who together had come closer than any predecessors to fully realizing the dream of antiquity reborn. Before the Medici Villa at Poggio a Caiano, villas in Tuscany looked "fortified" with their towers and crenellations. But here was the first in a long series of Classicizing villas to evoke ancient Roman villas as they were described in the letters of Pliny. Like those of antiquity, Lorenzo's country retreat was built for repose, study, entertainment, and agricultural activities. To own such a villa became a passionate desire of wealthy Humanists in the sixteenth and seventeenth centuries.

The Late Fifteenth Century in Venice. In a survey of the architecture of a period as rich and complex as the Renaissance, many subjects cannot be dealt with. Patronage, documents and architectural drawings, the socioeconomic context of buildings, all are important for a thorough understanding of the era, but they have been subordinated here to an emphasis on Renaissance style. This is also true of the study of architecture in regional centers such as Urbino and Ferrara. But Venice is one city that cannot be passed by in any discussion of the early Renaissance, even though its greatest achievements in architecture belong to the sixteenth rather than the fifteenth century.

The historic connections of Venice to Eastern cultures, and the unique aquatic topography of the city with its fluid reflections of color and light, had long rendered an uncommon richness to her art and architecture, setting them apart from those of mainland Italy in ways that went beyond usual regional differences. The Early Christian-Byzantine as well as the Gothic buildings of Venice were more colorful, more exotic, more extravagant, and seemingly more fragile than their counterparts on *terra firma*. But even firmly rooted Veneto-Byzantine-Gothic traditions could not withstand the tidal wave of Classical revival that the Renaissance set in motion. It was not until 1460—when the early Renaissance style of Brunelleschi-Alberti was already cresting in Tuscany and in related Humanist centers—that a serious Classicizing tendency first seeped into Venetian architecture, not primarily a Florentine Classicism, but a once-removed version that came by way of Lombardy, northern Italy, and ancient Roman remains on the Istrian coast across the Adriatic.

The first buildings of the Venetian Renaissance were predictably heterogeneous. Lacking the self-assured Classicism of Tuscan architecture they were nevertheless brilliant in the free way they mixed Classicism into the rich Venetian amalgam without concern for rules of architectural "decorum." Two examples will show how their appearance differed from the intellectual and abstract Florentine buildings while being very well integrated into the city's polyglot architectural environment. In craftsmanship and grandeur, if not in canonical application of the grammar of antiquity, they measured up to Florentine and Mantuan monuments, and were far ahead of the earliest Renaissance efforts in other regions.

The most grandiose of these buildings is S. Zaccaria (fig. 8-1), originally a late Gothic church destroyed by fire in the 1450s, rebuilt beginning in 1458 by Antonio di Marco Gambello, and continued by Mauro Coducci who, in about 1490, made a heroic attempt to clothe the Gothic skeleton in Renaissance dress. Gambello's non-Renaissance interior is a telling Venetian commixture of Gothic hall-church height, pointed arches, and tracery; Early Christian pendentive domes; Byzantine double-story pierced wall screens; and, echoing S. Vitale, secondary shells of luminous space beyond the screens. In addition, there were some Classical "suggestions"—more whimsy than serious imitation—in the columns and capitals. But Coducci's contribution to the facade—set above the lower tier because of the vertical rise of the Gothic frame—was like a separate building atop a tall plinth. It consisted of an impressive series of Roman images, most notably the paired, freestanding columns and projecting entablatures of triumphal arches, pier arcades with engaged orders, oculi, round-headed arches, and so forth, with which he almost succeeded in capturing a truly Roman feeling for massing and for the decorative, nonstructural application of the orders to the wall.

While S. Zaccaria is a towering, powerfully articulated monument, the almost contemporaneous Sta. Maria dei Miracoli (colorplate 53), built between 1481 and 1489 by Pietro Lombardo, is small, planimetric, and gemlike—a sculptor's architecture (like that of Brunelleschi) with exquisite craftsmanship, sharply incised lines, and graceful small-scale detailing. If Coducci had been looking to Rome for the new idiom of the Renaissance, perhaps through the intermediary of Albertian buildings in Mantua and Rimini, then Lombardo was finding his sources in Florentine buildings. Here are reflections of the applied trabeation of the Palazzo Rucellai, the engaged fluted pilasters and richly profiled arches of the Pazzi Chapel, the ubiquitous motif of arch-and-oculus, and a number of illusionistic devices that reveal his command of Renaissance perspective systems. On the two stories plus enormous arched front of the curved wooden ceiling, Lombardo worked in flat planes rather than volumes, with applied membering rather than freestanding orders, and with geometric compartmentalizations reminiscent of the Romanesque-derived systems of Tuscany. But what makes Sta. Maria dei Miracoli so brilliant and distinctively indigenous are the inherently Venetian-Byzantine dome, opulent revetment with colored marbles, and the rich ornaments, which mesh comfortably with the Tuscan inflections. Both

buildings were firm expressions of a first Renaissance phase in Venice, a prelude to what fifty years later would be one of the summits of High Renaissance achievement.

Bramante. *The Years before Rome.* In the early sixteenth century, Rome replaced Florence as the center of artistic activity in Italy. Compared to Florence, fifteenth-century Rome had been, artistically, something of a provincial outpost. The shabby appearance of the city, despoiled from waves of invasion and forsaken during the long schism when the papal court had been installed in France, was an affront to the memory of its great past, of which the decaying and pillaged ruins stood as heroic, if melancholic, symbols. Florentine Humanist Poggio Bracciolini compared Rome to a moldering cadaver. A Medici visitor from Florence in the 1440s wrote home, as if he were a civilized traveler in a barbaric land, about the pitiable condition of Rome and its people: "The men who call themselves Romans are very different in bearing and conduct from the ancient inhabitants . . . they all look like cowherds . . . the many splendid [buildings] are in ruin, and what is modern is poor stuff."

Rome's condition wounded the pride of the Church hierarchy because the city was still the center of the Christian world, and worship in its historic basilicas still the goal of legions of devout pilgrims. For a Humanist pope, the indignities were compounded, for not only was the Christian city dilapidated but the great ancient metropolis was barely visible, its ruins overgrown by nature. Of the many complex reasons behind the shift of intense, top-level artistic activity from other regional centers to this unpromising atmosphere, none was more cogent than the ascension to the papal throne in 1503 of the formidable Julius II (Rovere), who had a brilliant vision of a Roman renaissance. It was his ambition to return Rome to its former Imperial majesty, to re-create its lost grandeur and build new monuments even more impressive than the ancient ones. In this mission, he resolved to spare no effort or expense. For the ten years of his reign (1503–13), his extraordinary patronage and energy accounted for the first phase of a campaign for the rebuilding and decoration of Rome; his artists were Bramante, Raphael, Michelangelo, and others. Inspired by what was for many of these artists their first direct, sustained contact with the works of antiquity, they brought about the miracle of transformation the Pope so urgently desired.

The realization of that miracle—the Roman High Renaissance—had its beginnings in the distant provinces of the Marche and Lombardy, birthplace and working environment of Donato Bramante. His career began in his native town of Urbino (the Marche) and matured in Milan (Lombardy). He was born in 1444, but did not arrive in Rome until he was fifty-five years old and had only fifteen years to live. Bramante did not apprentice in the building trades but started as a painter; a sense of design and an understanding of beauty were more highly prized than technical knowledge, which, it was held, could be picked up on the job, left to the masons and woodworkers, or learned through theory. He made his way to Milan by 1481 to work in the court of Ludovico Sforza, son of Francesco Sforza and one of the great Humanist prince-patrons of the Renaissance, who also employed Leonardo da Vinci (by universal consensus the most imaginative artist, inventor, and explorer of nature of the Renaissance and per-

8-34 Donato Bramante. S. Satiro. Milan. 1482

8-35 Donato Bramante. Interior toward choir, Sta. Maria presso S. Satiro. Milan. c. 1485

haps of all time). Leonardo advised Sforza on architecture, sketched plans and elevations of buildings, and wrote about architecture, construction techniques, and machinery for building. Although he himself probably never built anything, his training in Florentine workshops, his knowledge of quattrocento buildings there (he drew Brunelleschi's Sta. Maria degli Angeli), his architectural sketches, and the tectonic compositions of his paintings were translatable into three-dimensional structures by others. Almost without exception Leonardo's designs were for central-plan buildings with dense and heavy forms compactly massed beneath a large dome. That he and Bramante knew each other and exchanged ideas has not been doubted, and the small, circular, ninth-century chapel of S. Satiro (fig. 8-34), which Bramante restored in 1482 with a thick, niched wall, reflects Leonardo's architectural concepts. Simple, powerful, and clear, the building foreshadows Bramante's great Roman works of two decades later; even its tall, high-drummed Lombard dome would be translated into Bramante's special language of antiquity.

S. Satiro was to be joined to a large new basilican church, Sta. Maria presso S. Satiro (fig. 8-35), also a work by Bramante in which, thanks to his early career as a painter of perspective illusion, he was able to perform a remarkable feat. The enormously wide nave and transepts were covered by coffered barrel vaults springing from piers. But at the eastern end, beyond the domed crossing, problems arising from the site boundaries permitted only enough space to construct an extremely shallow extension rather than a conventional full choir. With astonishing ingenuity Bramante met the challenge: Taking a fixed viewpoint inside the entrance, and applying stucco relief and paint to the rear wall of the building and on the sides beyond the truncated structural entrance to the choir area, he created the trompe l'oeil illusion of a three-dimensional continuation of the nave barrel vault complete with coffers, entablature, piers, and the rest. If an observer stands at the proper vantage point, he "sees" a full architectural choir. The stucco lines that represent the verticals of the coffers and the top cornice of the entablature become the orthogonals of the perspective image that provide the illusion of depth. This choir belongs to an important Renaissance tradition of fictive architecture, taking its place with works such as Masaccio's *Trinity*, painted on the wall of the Sta. Maria Novella in Florence, and Andrea Mantegna's illusionistic ceiling of the Camera degli Sposi in Mantua. But of all of them, Bramante's painted choir was the most monumental and the most daring illustration of the "magic" illusion of depth.

The Years in Rome and the High Renaissance. When the French armies invaded Lombardy in 1499 and the Sforzas fell, Bramante left Milan for Rome. Unlike early Renaissance Florence, where most of the artists at work in the city were either native-born or trained there, Rome in the sixteenth century was populated by a community of artists from varied regional centers, who migrated to the city because of opportunities for work provided by the wealthy Holy See and its immediate circle of sophisticated Humanist aristocrats. In Rome, Bramante encountered antique monumentalism for the first time. Its impact is incalculable, and he responded by designing buildings that answered, as closely as possible and in a manner no one else yet thoroughly comprehended, the call to restore to architecture the nobility and might it had in antiquity. His self-assured distillation of antique forms was apparent even in his first Roman building, the cloister of Sta. Maria della Pace (1500–1504; fig. 8-36), where the heavy piers with applied orders in sequence (Corinthian over Ionic) on the two stories, the trabeation of the upper story, and the unadorned, sculpturesque power of the lower story, were derived from systems used in the Colosseum, the Theater of Marcellus, and other eloquent ruins.

8-36 Donato Bramante. Cloister, Sta. Maria della Pace. Rome. 1500–1504

If this was the introduction, then Bramante's next Roman building was the first chapter of a whole new history of architecture. In 1502 (Julius was still a cardinal in exile), Bramante built the Tempietto (little temple) of S. Pietro in Montorio (figs. 8-37, 8-38). The structure, ordered by the king of Spain, was a martyrium built inside a cloister adjacent to the Church of S. Pietro in Montorio to mark the place where, according to legend, Saint Peter had been martyred. Conforming to the Renaissance idea of the appropriateness of such a building as a memorial monument, it was designed as a round, domed structure visible from all sides like a giant reliquary. The original scheme (preserved in illustrations accompanying the treatise and practical design book on architecture written between 1537 and 1551 by Sebastiano Serlio) called for a nobler setting than the infelicitous courtyard in which it is actually set. The small temple was to have been framed like a piece of sculpture, centered in a circular area ringed by columns radially related to the sixteen columns on the round porch of the structure itself, beneath a balustraded architrave. It is the first building since antiquity in which a colonnaded porch encircles the cella, and it is also the building in which, for the first time in the Renaissance, a deep sensibility for Roman *gravitas* was fully expressed in the dense wall and deep niches of the interior and exterior of the cylinder. Unlike the "flat," space-defining walls of the quattrocento, to which orders were applied as relief sculpture, Bramante's walls are conceived three-dimensionally, as sculpture in the round.

They move with space, respond to its force and pressure, appear shapable and pliant. Much of the powerful effect of the small building came from this quality of weight, and from the impact of the unadorned simplicity of the cylindrical cella and its Tuscan Doric peripteros and frieze. The strong Roman sunlight, moving across the columnar shafts and in and out of the niches on the cella wall and the drum, made the volumes even more emphatic—an effect traceable to the influence of Leonardo, who wrote about and illustrated the method of mod-

8-37 Donato Bramante. Tempietto, S. Pietro in Montorio. Rome. 1502

8-38 Plan with projected courtyard, Tempietto. (After Serlio)

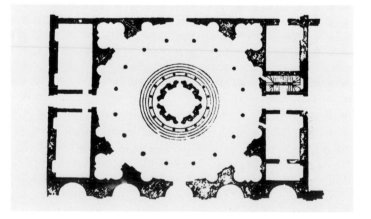

eling with light and shade to achieve three-dimensional form. It is not hard to understand how Julius recognized in Bramante the architect who would realize his vision of a monumental new Rome by looking directly at the scale and virile forms of antique architecture. While Bramante may have been inspired in a general way by the Pantheon and by ancient peripteral temples, the Tempietto was not a replica of any Roman prototype. Its height alone (twice the width) was unique for the type, and the tall drum supporting the dome was purely Bramante's invention, its ancestry lying somewhere in his experience with the high drum of Lombard architecture, which he had already used at S. Satiro. In Rome, the device served a useful function: By elevating and thereby calling attention to the dome, Bramante dramatized the symbolic nature of the Tempietto as a memorial monument. For Bramante, the planning of the Tempietto must have represented the union of illusionistic painting and architecture he had spent his career perfecting. The building, too small on the inside to accommodate a congregation (only 15 feet in diameter), was conceived as a "picture" to be looked at from outside, a "marker," a symbol of Saint Peter's martyrdom.

Bramante's sustained interest in perspective illusionism accounted for the success of the Cortile del Belvedere begun for Julius II in 1505 as part of a papal plan to remodel the Vatican area (figs. 8-39, 8-40). Now drastically altered, it was originally designed as an enormous terraced courtyard that connected, over hilly terrain, the Vatican Palace and a fifteenth-century castle-villa-retreat about 300 yards away. The concept was as grandiose as the construction, and it restored to secular architecture the kind of extravagant self-indulgence that characterized many ancient Imperial projects (Hadrian's villa, for example). It was to function as a garden, a villa, a sculpture court, and a theater, and was in fact known as the *atrio del piacere*, the courtyard of pleasure. Between a pair of corridors, the Cortile rose as a series of axially aligned terraces terminating in a deep semicircular niche set into the precinct wall above a (no longer extant) stair of tapering concentric circles. The terraces were landscaped with elaborately laid-out gardens and fountains, and decorated with sculpture from the papal collection. The whole area served also as a huge outdoor theater, and the complex hydraulic system installed for the fountains might well have been used for flooding the Cortile so that mock naval battles (a form of entertainment known in antiquity) and other aquatic pageants could be staged. The audience was well provided for. From the official *stanze* (rooms that Raphael would later decorate with his renowned fresco cycle) in the papal apartments on the third floor of the Vatican Palace, the Pope and his guests could look out upon Bramante's Cortile complex, which, from that calculated viewpoint, became a coherent synthesis of parts. At ground level, for an audience less elite, there were seats in the form of a huge semicircular bank of steps, resembling an ancient amphitheater.

The Cortile del Belvedere was the first in a long line of works of its kind—where nature became an architectural component—that culminated in Louis XIV's seventeenth-century château at Versailles. Bramante, enjoying the Renaissance "discovery" that reason could bring nature under its control, ordered and regulated nature as if it were a structure made by, and for, man. Greatly admired in his own time and beyond, he was described after his death by Serlio as "a man of such gifts

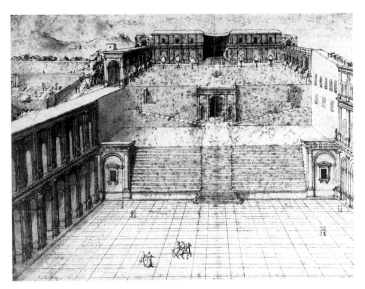

8-39 Cortile del Belvedere, Vatican. Begun 1505 by Bramante. (Perspective view from the Vatican Palace to the north by Sallustio Peruzzi? c. 1560. Phyllis Lambert Collection)

8-40 Cortile del Belvedere. (Bird's-eye perspective to the west, 1579)

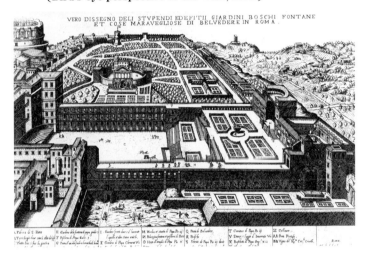

in architecture that, with the aid and authority given him by the Pope, one may say that he revived true architecture, which had been buried from the ancients down to that time." (Almost the same words had been said of Brunelleschi nearly a hundred years earlier.) It was believed in the Renaissance that pleasure complexes such as the Cortile del Belvedere had existed in antiquity; *conoscenti* not only recognized the allusion, but the allusion increased their appreciation of the enterprise. Bramante had incorporated a number of well-known ancient images in the articulation of the Cortile; for example, the facade of the lower tier of the corridors was patterned as a triumphal arch, with paired giant pilasters framing the arch. His most dramatic ancient source was the early-first-century B.C. Sanctuary of Fortuna Primigenia at Palestrina (Praeneste), near Rome, built for the ceremonial rites of the religious cult dedicated to the goddess Fortuna (figs. 3-45–3-47). It comprised an axially controlled complex of stairs and terraces ascending in levels to a large colonnaded niche at the apex. In this methodically arranged outdoor ensemble of architecture and landscape, Bramante, recognizing that the site was comparable to that set aside for the Belvedere Court, found an answer to the problem posed by the graded terrain at the Vatican. Without hesitating to use pagan architecture (if he was even aware of its original function) to indulge the secular hedonism of the Pope, he brilliantly adapted the ancient design to the requirements of his sixteenth-century project.

The Design for St. Peter's. Of the many extraordinary projects fueled by Julius's ambition, none was more audacious than his plan to destroy the venerable fourth-century basilica of St. Peter's and replace it with a huge new church. The enterprise was probably related to an equally grandiose scheme developed around 1505 for the papal tomb (the new church conceived partly as the repository of the tomb), a rich amalgam of monumental sculpture and architecture that was to be the work of Michelangelo. In 1506, Bramante was named chief architect of the new St. Peter's. A bronze medal struck in honor of the undertaking had a portrait of Julius on one face and the image of Bramante's church on the reverse (fig. 8-41). The only record of his concept for the exterior survives in that small relief, for Bramante died soon after the building had been begun and it was not to be completed for another 150 years.

The most remarkable feature of the gigantic project (fig. 8-42) was its central plan (fourth-century St. Peter's was a longitudinal building). Bramante's design called for a Greek cross with apsed arms, inscribed over a square; rising above the tomb of Saint Peter, at the crossing of the arms, was a huge dome supported on four colossal canted piers with deep niches hollowed into each face. Half-domes covered the apses, and smaller, domed, Greek crosses were formed in each intersection of the large arms as part of a buttressing network for the major vault. Tiered quadrangular towers rose in the four corners of the square. Although the central plan was appealing because of its historic symbolism and its "modern" shape, the "equality" of the four arms presented practical problems. There was, for example, no long nave for liturgical processions or one that would cover all the old consecrated ground, nor was there a principal point of focus for the main altar.

The exterior of Bramante's building, known only from the small medal, would have appeared as a gathering of compacted forms beneath a massive hemispherical dome, an arrangement familiar from the architectural sketches for central-plan churches of Leonardo da Vinci. The original dome (understood more fully from illustrations published by Sebastiano Serlio in his architectural treatise in 1537) was daring in its magnitude and was inspired by the shape and size of the dome of the Pantheon. It was to be supported by the four immense piers tied together by arches at the crossing, and buttressed by lesser arches, sturdy walls, and the smaller domes. Cemented masonry, used by the Romans for the construction of their massive vaults, had been revived by Bramante for the dome of the Tempietto and was to be used again for the St. Peter's dome.

Bramante's design for the new church was so impressive that it not only determined the architectural future of the building that was so briefly under his command, but it also influenced church architecture throughout Italy and elsewhere for the rest of the century. Few sixteenth-century churches failed to include at least some of the salient features of Bramante's building: the Greek cross; the gigantic canted piers with their paired pilaster order and deep niches; the wells of space

8-41 Caradosso. Medal showing Bramante's design for St. Peter's. 1506. (British Museum, London)

8-42 Donato Bramante. Plan for St. Peter's. Rome. 1505. (Uffizi, Florence)

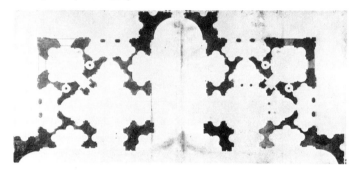

united through arched openings; the barrel vaults; and the fluid shapes of the heavy masonry. Equally effective was the restitution of the heroic scale of the ancient buildings from which Bramante learned so much about the Empire that was lost but could be regained.

The Beginning of the High Renaissance Palace. Palace architecture was as important to patricians in the sixteenth century as it had been in the fifteenth. In Rome, Bramante designed a palace facade system that differed significantly from what had been perfected in quattrocento Florence. His Palazzo Caprini (known also as the House of Raphael because it was acquired by the painter in 1517) dates from around 1510 (fig. 8-43). Now destroyed, it is known only from a mid-sixteenth-century engraving, but its influence was far-reaching and the appearance of the original can be construed from that of its many progeny. Instead of the triadic elevation and rugged, rough-hewn rustication of the Florentine type, Bramante's palace had two stories and was faced with flatter, stippled, precisely cut stone blocks on the ground level. Its most cogent and influential new features were the pier-and-arch arrangement of the lower tier, the pedimented windows, and especially the paired Doric half-columns with frieze on the piano nobile—the first instance of the application of columns (instead of pilasters) to a residential facade. They added body and sculptural dynamics to the wall, and imitated the Roman practice of using engaged columns not for structural support but for density, ornament, and rhythm. The Palazzo Caprini design, or aspects of it,

8-43 Donato Bramante. Palazzo Caprini. Rome. c. 1510. (Engraving by Lafreri, 1549)

became the archetype for some of the most important palaces in Rome, Venice, even Florence, and outside Italy in the sixteenth century.

The effect of Bramante's architecture, by itself and through its dissemination by other architects, was felt all over Italy. After his death, he was followed as *capomaestro* at St. Peter's by Giuliano da Sangallo, Fra Giocondo, and Raphael; in fact, almost every eminent architect of the first half of the sixteenth century and after was trained under Bramante in the Vatican workshop, or succeeded to his position. Apart from those already mentioned, the list included Peruzzi, Antonio da Sangallo the Younger, Giulio Romano, Sansovino, and Sanmicheli. The two great exceptions were Michelangelo and Palladio. Michelangelo became chief architect at St. Peter's from 1546 to 1564 without previously having worked there (or with Bramante). Before discussing the architecture of Michelangelo, however, we must survey briefly the development of the Renaissance villa—an important chapter of sixteenth-century Italian architecture, which grew out of the Bramante circle and the Humanistic environment of High Renaissance Rome.

The Sixteenth-Century Roman Villa; Raphael; Mannerism. It has been observed that the consanguinity of the French word *ville* (city) and the Italian *villa* suggests that a villa bears some relation to a city, that it is not simply a house in the country, but a country house that belongs to a city dweller. It is used as an escape from city life and as a pleasurable retreat for relaxation, entertainment, study, and the appreciation of nature by people of status (with more than one place to live). Pliny the Younger, the great Roman *epistolario*, so described both his own country house at Laurentum and the country retreats of other cultivated Romans in the Empire in the first century A.D. His description, a rare surviving example of Latin literature containing references to houses, was not lost on ambitious Renaissance patrons who, in their enthusiastic pursuit of aspects of life *all'antica*, were inspired to own villas that were Plinian in spirit. As for the form and design of such houses, there was little to go on, for Pliny's letters did not furnish that kind of practical information. In the earliest Renaissance *villa suburbana*, close to, and easily accessible from the city, such as the fifteenth-century Villa Medici at Poggio a Caiano, near Florence, elements of Classical architecture were already strongly emphasized. Furthermore, its striking tetrastyle loggia

opened the building to its natural surroundings, which provided expansive vistas from the elevated site of the villa. By 1515, and probably even earlier, plays were performed there for the entertainment of the Medici and their guests. While Bramante's Cortile del Belvedere was not a true villa but a highly evolved courtyard-garden, it had many features requisite for villa life as described by Pliny and interpreted and expanded in the Renaissance to include gardens and fountains, long vistas, a place for *spettacoli* and for sculpture. The Belvedere concept seems to have fueled the desire among patrons for a sophisticated "suburban" existence, and among the first in a sequence of great Roman suburban villas is the one built in 1509–11 on the bank of the Tiber for Agostino Chigi, luxury-loving Sienese banker and financier to popes, as a retreat for himself and the famous Roman courtesan Imperia. Chigi chose as his architect Baldassare Peruzzi, a Sienese painter-architect who came to Rome in 1503 and was employed by Bramante at St. Peter's. The Villa Farnesina (it has taken the name of its later owners, the Farnese) was a synthesis of a country house and city palace (figs. 8-44–8-46). On its city side, it appears to be a sturdy, closed block, but atop the gentle slope of its open, U-shaped garden side are projecting wings that bracket an arcaded loggia and form a space that served as the "stage" for theatrical entertainments. The interior of the loggia is decorated with frescoes that are among the most beautiful and acclaimed of all High Renaissance paintings. These were the work (1518–19) of Raphael and his pupils; the Classical style and subject (Cupid and Psyche) were in complete harmony with the architecture, the concept of the Farnesina as an antique villa, and with the spirit of pleasure and joyfulness that villa life encouraged. Equally Classical is the rich, fully modeled terra-cotta frieze of garland-bearing putti that is the crowning element of the walls of the garden facade, now bare but once adorned with painted and incised ornament.

A somewhat later villa—begun by Raphael in 1516, continued after his death in 1520 by Antonio da Sangallo the Younger, who worked with Raphael at St. Peter's—is related in spirit to the Farnesina (fig. 8-47). It, too, was built for an enlightened patron (Cardinal Giulio de' Medici, later Pope Clement VII) with antiquarian interests; Raphael may have intentionally tried to re-create for the cardinal the Villa Laurentum described by Pliny. The building eventually came to be called Villa Madama for Margaret of Austria, who acquired it in 1536 through her marriage to Alessandro de' Medici. Its site, mid-way on a hill, offered the panoramic view, fresh air, and communion with nature so important to villa life. The original design of the Villa Madama included a theater, terraced gardens, a great circular courtyard, and, still surviving, a loggia that is one of the finest illustrations of freely interpreted "archaeology" in the Renaissance. At the beginning of the century, ruins of the luxurious Golden House (Domus Aurea) of the first-century A.D. Flavian Emperor Nero were discovered beneath the Baths of Titus. The wall paintings, mosaics, and stucco decoration were greatly admired by Raphael and other connoisseurs of ancient art. Raphael's interest in antiquities was equal to Bramante's (in 1515 he was officially appointed the Pope's Director of Antiquities), and, moreover, he had a unique ability to assimilate Classical forms and images and transform them into his own idiom. The design and color scheme he prepared for the integrated fresco

8-44 Baldassare Peruzzi. Garden facade, Villa Farnesina. Rome. 1509–11

8-45 Garden loggia, Villa Farnesina

patterned fields of ornament, and, above all, the grand cadence of those soaring vaults, the loggia of the Villa Madama must have been the closest approximation in Renaissance Rome of the appearance of Imperial Roman architecture.

After 1520, the majestic poise and the clarity of Roman High Renaissance works were not sustained. The term used to describe changes (subjective, not programmatic) in all the visual arts after the decades of around 1480–1520 is Mannerism, referring to complicated stylistic trends that prevailed from about 1520 until the last years of the sixteenth century. It is an easier concept to apply to painting and sculpture than to architecture, for it is more clearly manifested in stylishly capricious poses, complexities of composition, and ambiguities of space than in the unusual way stone is set upon stone or the language of Vitruvius is spoken. Mannerism in architecture can be discerned, however, when license is taken with the serene harmonies of Classical form. It can often be found in its most whimsical state in villa and palace architecture, where humor and complexity could infiltrate without transgression, and liberties could be taken more easily than in churches or official buildings. The greatest of all Mannerist villas was called a palace—the Palazzo Te (figs. 8-48–8-50) in Mantua—and, like the Villa Farnesina, it was a *villa suburbana*, close to the city and commingling aspects of both palace and villa architecture and function. It was built by Giulio Romano for Federigo Gonzaga, Duke of Mantua and son of Isabella d'Este, one of the most cultivated and erudite of all Renaissance art patrons. Architect and painter, Giulio worked for Bramante and was Raphael's chief assistant. When in 1524 he left Rome for northern Italy as court artist to the Gonzaga, he carried with him the sobriety and *gravitas* of the Bramante-Raphael style, interpolated with his distinctive personal manner. At work on the Gonzaga villa, and free of the weight of the orthodoxy of both old and new Rome, Giulio's "manner" took precedence. His strange, chimerical imagination was most dramatically unleashed in his illusionistic fresco paintings for the interior rooms of the Palazzo Te, but the architecture, too, is filled with complicated and unexpected effects.

The pride of the Gonzaga family were the horses they bred on a small island called Te, close to Mantua. The wish for a place to rest and dine while engaged in equestrian business

8-46 Detail of frieze, Villa Farnesina

and stucco ornament of the loggia of the Villa Madama (executed by Giulio Romano and other artists in Raphael's circle) were adapted from his close study of the architecture and ornament of the Domus Aurea. That architecture also accounted for Raphael's monumental three-bay system for the loggia, in which two huge groin vaulted spaces frame a central domed space, above massive niched piers. Such a program with its unusual rhythmic sequence of domed vault followed by groin vault would have been unusual in a church, had it even been adopted into ecclesiastical architecture of the Renaissance, but a dome used in post-antique residential architecture was unprecedented. With its color scheme and

8-47 Raphael. Interior of loggia, Villa Madama. Rome. Begun 1516

8-48 Giulio Romano. Vestibule, Palazzo Te. Mantua. 1527–34

8-49 Courtyard facade, looking east, Palazzo Te

8-50 Garden loggia, Palazzo Te

was the modest idea from which the villa complex was born. Built and decorated between 1527 and 1534, the Palazzo Te is a low, square structure arranged around a square court beyond which lies an expansive formal garden reached from one of the courtyard wings. An earlier structure on the site was incorporated into the new project. Giulio planned the architecture and interior decorations to be rich and extravagant and to be filled with tricks, surprises, and unexpected delights for the amusement of the Gonzaga and their guests (the social and political purposes of villa entertaining were among its most important functions). To articulate both the outer and inner facades, Giulio used familiar Classical motifs, but he played with them—combining them in inventive and remarkably un-Classical ways—and treated each facade in a different manner. The result was an unsettling absence of Classical consistency and uniformity, and the whole building is characterized by the conjunction of familiar High Renaissance orthodoxy and surprising Mannerist inventions. Blocks, rusticated not by the action of chisel on stone but by the application of a newly invented stippled gesso finish, were combined with highly refined stonework. On the triple-arched north exterior facade, the unusual stucco-rustication (applied also to the giant voussoirs and quoins around the windows) consorts with a thoroughly correct Doric frieze such as the one on the Basilica Aemilia, the most famous and authoritative Doric ruin among the antiquities of Rome. Smooth Doric pilasters march across the facade in a complicated, irregular rhythm: closely paired at the corners, wider in the next bay and framing a niche instead of a window, then three singles framing windows, the last pilaster doubling as one of the pair embracing the arches. These irregularities, however, are not simply the consequences of Giulio's willfulness or his indulgence in complexity for its own sake; they represented the adjustment of his design to accommodate or mask some of the asymmetries and imbalances of the former structure, still a part of the new building. In the vestibule leading from the principal entrance on the west, swollen, grainy columns, which have been described as looking as if for centuries they had been washed by the sea, support a barrel vault overlaid with chains of hexagonal and square coffers. The brilliance of Giulio's concept throughout the villa lay in his allusions to the rules he transgressed. A keystone projects from an architrave, but a keystone is correct only in an arch, not in an architrave. Most entertaining of all, triglyphs "slip" from their place carrying with them pieces of the architecture and arousing what some observers have felt to be the thrilling sensation of a building in the beginning stages of earthquake damage, a sensation of instability in utmost contrast to the architectural repose of Roman buildings of two decades earlier.

Some of Giulio's cleverest *invenzioni* can be found on the garden side of the east facade. Although it is the most "rustic" portion of the villa—closest to nature—he has abandoned the rusticated surfaces of the other sections in favor of a highly polished and formal High Renaissance arcaded loggia borne by clusters of stately columns and piers. Artful rather than rustic, it has been seen as a metaphor for the victory of art— or more precisely Mannerist artifice—over nature.

8-51   Baldassare Peruzzi. Facade, Palazzo Massimo alle Colonne. Rome. 1534

No other building of this period, at least no other villa, can equal the virtuoso Mannerist performance in the Palazzo Te. But the Roman Palazzo Massimo alle Colonne (fig. 8-51), built at about the same time (1534) by Baldassare Peruzzi, is an interesting illustration of a departure from the Bramantesque High Renaissance palace archetype in favor of Mannerist design. The order has descended from the piano nobile, where Bramante first placed it, to the ground floor where it becomes an open porch (its columns giving the palace its name) with irregular rhythmic stresses—a feature that is unique among Roman palaces—leaving the upper portion bereft of articulation. Deprived of the familiar cinquecento density of applied orders, the upper wall of the Palazzo Massimo alle Colonne seems thin and flat, its two levels of small windows floating unanchored on an uninflected screen. Conventional horizontal emphases, indigenous to palace facades since the trecento and supplied by stringcourses stretching from corner to corner, are eschewed. But Peruzzi introduced for the first time in architecture a highly individualized linear design in relief for the window frames, known as strapwork and resembling curled and cut strips of leather, that was later to be exploited as a Mannerist decorative device in the countries of northern Europe.

If the Farnesina and Villa Madama best represented villa style in the decade 1510 to 1520, and the Palazzo Te the most extreme and personally "mannered" of Mannerist villas of the years around 1530, the most important example of mid-century villa architecture in Rome was the country retreat of Pope Julius III—the Villa Giulia (figs. 8-52, 8-53)—built around 1550 on the Via Flaminia by Giacomo Barozzi da Vignola. Vignola's authorship of the villa is not documented, but the most significant portions of its design have always been attributed to him; later additions were made by writer-painter-architect Giorgio Vasari, architect-sculptor Bartolommeo Ammanati, and others.

Vignola was an architect of Mannerist persuasion, but his works were controlled, elegant, and utterly serious, without the eccentricities and extravagances of a Giulio Romano. At the same time, they incorporated richly imaginative and innovative features that had a deep and long-lasting influence on the future of architecture. It was Vignola, for example, who introduced the oval shape into architecture groundplans, breaking the formal and intellectual tyranny of the circle, and sounding the first notes of the dynamic Baroque style that would flourish in the seventeenth century. Like the intellectual theoreticians of the Renaissance before him, Vignola published, in 1562, a book on the five orders (*Regola delli cinque ordini*), and his great esteem for the achievements of Alberti can be seen not only in his wish to produce such a book, but also in his interpretation of Albertian ideas in his Church of the Gesù.

The Villa Giulia, like the Cortile del Belvedere built a half-century earlier, is a long stretch of gardens and terraces, interrupted and organized by units of architecture. There the similarity ends, however, for the villa was planned, in Mannerist fashion, as a sequence of spaces eschewing the principle of one fixed viewpoint, and was arranged on different levels not visible all at once, not even guessed at until they suddenly appeared, more often than not, by way of hidden stairs. The process of illusion begins at the facade of what seems an ample quadrangular block but is instead only one room deep and serves as a kind of foyer, for just beyond lies a curving court that probably was used for theatrical performances (a feature of villa life since at least the

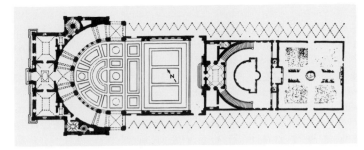

8-52 Giacomo Barozzi da Vignola and others. Plan, Villa Giulia. Rome. Begun c. 1550

8-53 Detail of the nympheum, Villa Giulia

quattrocento). Stairs at the far end of the courtyard lead to an elevated loggia (designed by the Florentine Ammanati) from which the countryside and a lower courtyard, not anticipated, become visible. Hidden stairs lead still further down to a semicircular water basin and sunken grotto with sculptured caryatids, not simply a visual delight but a cool and refreshing deliverance from the heat and sun of summer. The unexpected change of levels through hidden passages, the counterplay of straight and curving shapes, the union of theater, fountains, sculpture, and vistas, all fulfill, indeed, go far beyond, the nostalgic promise inherent in villa design from its earliest expression at the turn of the century, to re-create the ideal Plinian retreat.

There was no single formula that controlled the design of Renaissance villas near Rome; sometimes the gardens, or the fountains, or the sculpture and decoration, would be stressed more than the architecture, and the architecture itself was conceived in any number of ways, as even this sampling has shown. Rome, moreover, was not the only strong center of villa-building activity; in the Veneto region, particularly around Vicenza, there were the villas of Palladio of the mid-sixteenth century, different in style and in function from those of Rome or Florence. The buildings of Palladio, Bramante, and Michelangelo

represented the summit of Renaissance architectural achievement. Of the major architects of the sixteenth century, all but two—Palladio and Michelangelo—had worked under Bramante at St. Peter's.

Michelangelo; Sangallo. Michelangelo Buonarroti was forty years old before he turned to architecture. By that time he had produced statues and paintings that, for their sheer power, expressiveness, and originality, had no equals among Renaissance works—and perhaps no equals thereafter. His creativity seemed infinite, his influence incalculable; and he was to live for almost another fifty years, producing until the end of his life works of poetry, painting, sculpture, and architecture that changed the course of art.

Bramante and Raphael were by all accounts affable and congenial men; Michelangelo, on the other hand, was temperamental and difficult to work with. His patrons, however, particularly the popes, recognized that putting up with his disposition was worth their while since, through the works he made for them, they would be celebrated and immortalized. In 1515, Medici Pope Leo X, successor to Julius II, announced a competition to provide a facade for S. Lorenzo, the Florentine basilica begun almost a hundred years earlier for the Medici by Brunelleschi. Michelangelo was chosen for the S. Lorenzo project from a group of competitors that included Raphael, Antonio da Sangallo the Elder, and Giuliano da Sangallo; although his facade was never executed, written descriptions, drawings, and a wooden model made in 1519 preserve his design (fig. 8-54).

The conventional solution for facing the clearly silhouetted tall nave, lower side aisles, and still lower side chapels of Brunelleschi's church would have been the installation of a decorated screen shaped to conform to those exposed profiles. Michelangelo's solution was to build an independent narthex one bay deep (as Alberti had done at S. Andrea in Mantua) that would be affixed to the front of the fifteenth-century church but would have its own formal and structural autonomy. Even though such a rectangular porch did not mirror the upper contour of S. Lorenzo, it still expressed the cross section of the church interior through projecting and receding planes and a

8-54 Michelangelo. Model for the facade of S. Lorenzo. Florence. 1519

tightly integrated grid system of paired orders and horizontal cornices. They corresponded to the division of nave, aisles, and chapels, and of arcade, frieze, and clerestory. The project called for the incorporation into the architectural scheme of a rich program of relief and freestanding sculpture to be accommodated in the roundels, panels, and niches that appear on the model. It is hardly surprising to observe how sculptural the architecture itself is. There are no fifteenth-century church facades in Florence with which to compare Michelangelo's S. Lorenzo, other than Alberti's brilliantly successful hybrid at Sta. Maria Novella; its flatness and its linear abstractions, representative of quattrocento articulation in general, are transformed by Michelangelo into the dense masses, weighty forms, and varied planes of High Renaissance architecture.

Michelangelo's architecture, with its powerful volumes, its muscularity and expressive force, was conceived as if it were sculpture. In the facade project for S. Lorenzo, in the ill-fated commission for the Tomb of Julius II with which Michelangelo was obsessed for most of his career, and in the New Sacristy he built at S. Lorenzo (fig. 8-55), his sculptural architecture was to be combined with sculpture itself. The basilica of S. Lorenzo had become the Medici family mausoleum: Cosimo il Vecchio (head of the family in the mid-fifteenth century), his wife, his parents, and his sons were all buried there. In 1516, his great-grandson Giuliano, the Duke of Nemours (by marriage) died, followed in 1519 by Lorenzo de' Medici, Duke of Urbino, Cosimo's great-great-grandson. In that year it was decided to establish a separate burial chapel in the church for these recently deceased

8-55 Michelangelo. New Sacristy, Medici Chapel, S. Lorenzo. Begun 1520

members of the family (known as the Capitani), and also for Lorenzo Il Magnifico and his brother Giuliano (known as the Magnifici), who had died earlier and had been provisionally buried in the Old Sacristy. A year after this decision, in 1520, the facade project was halted (never to be resumed), and the less costly tomb chapel got under way. On the north of the building, construction was begun on Michelangelo's New Sacristy to house the new Medici tombs. The architecture of the Sacristy was designed before the program for its tombs was determined, and the first concept was to duplicate the comprehensive system of Brunelleschi's Old Sacristy. Michelangelo did in fact recreate the quattrocento articulation with its dark membering applied to light stucco walls, but in the New Sacristy he changed the height to furnish a mezzanine zone for windows between the first level and the vaulting. He organized the walls into wide bays flanked by narrower ones; in the mezzanine, the narrower bays accommodated windows and framed areas intended as windows, while doors surmounted by marble tabernacles were wedged into the narrow bays below. On opposite walls, the wide bays of the ground level received the elaborate marble architecture-sculpture of the tombs of the Capitani; on the third side, a double tomb planned for the Magnifici was never executed and in its place was installed a simple platform with three sculptured figures. The fourth wall opened to become the smaller square of the altar chapel. The wide bay of the mezzanine zone was defined by an arch that completed a unit begun by pilasters below, and in the uppermost tier a high, coffered dome on pendentives crowned the chapel, a sixteenth-century departure from the umbrella dome of the quattrocento sacristy. The *pietra serena* pilasters of the lower level were monumentalized versions of Brunelleschi's fluted Corinthian pilasters, broadened and made more complex by the addition of a pier and cornice system forming the wall recess behind. Compressed within that recess was the extraordinary marble architecture of the tombs, which, in their sensuous richness and their union of architecture and sculpture, contrasted dramatically with the ordered sobriety of the dark stone enframement of the earlier prototype. Ornamental elements in the tomb niches and tabernacles exemplified Michelangelo's amazing divergences from orthodox Vitruvian rules of Classical architectural design: segmental pediments were broken at the base and stepped forward at the crown; pilasters lacked capitals; in its deeper recess, an aediculated niche was shaped as a "T," its crossbar reversed at the base to project rather than recede; from a door frame hung robust volutes that belonged simultaneously to their own area and to the one above it. Proportions were adjusted as Michelangelo saw fit, friezes and capitals simply omitted if it suited his purpose; he designed architraves, entablatures, pediments, ornaments, consoles, tabernacles, and aediculae that looked Classical but in fact had never been seen before because they were born solely of his imagination and were combined in unfamiliar and unconventional ways. He made his own laws, contrived new rules, and, in the imitation of them by his dazzled contemporaries and followers, a whole new late Renaissance and Baroque style, founded on an illusion of "doctrinal" Classicism, was created.

While the appearance of the structural elements of the Medici Chapel—dark pilasters and architraves in relief on pale walls—conformed generally to the Brunelleschian prototype, Michelangelo's "second architecture," as the white marble tomb niches and tabernacles have been called, had a life of its own, distinct from the *pietra serena* frames. "Wedged" and "squeezed" are words used to describe how the white marble coexisted with the *pietra serena*; they suggest that the marble system had a vitality and force proper to living organisms and not to stone. But Michelangelo perceived life in stone—it was the source of the energy of his figure sculpture. The capacity to extract with hammer and chisel that living quality in the stone—to make inert matter seem organic—was the nature of his genius.

Many of Michelangelo's projects were plagued by problems, and the Medici tomb chapel was no exception. Although the architecture was completed by 1526, work on the sculpture stopped in 1527 and was not resumed until the early thirties. When, in 1534, Michelangelo left Florence to settle permanently in Rome, some of the statues were carved by other hands. Furthermore, he refused to say how he wished the figures to be placed and how the chapel was to be completed.

The High Renaissance Classicism of Michelangelo's model for the S. Lorenzo facade gave way in the Medici Chapel to a highly personal interpretation of Classical form. His new, "organic" language was carried to its greatest extreme in his next Florentine project, another Medici commission for S. Lorenzo—a library to house the Medici collection of manuscripts. It was begun in 1524 (while the Medici tomb chapel was in progress) at the urging of the new Medici pope, Clement VII. The program called for a reading room built above one wing of the monastery buildings around the cloister of S. Lorenzo, a traditional location for a monastery library so that there would be good light and protection of the manuscripts against dampness. Michelozzo's long narrow library for the Medici at S. Marco almost one hundred years earlier was a meaningful forerunner for Michelangelo. Like other Michelangelo projects, this too was halted, begun again, and completed by others while Michelangelo was away from the site. Work on the Laurentian Library went forward from 1524 to 1527; there was another spurt of activity from 1533 to 1534. Finally, when Michelangelo left Florence, the reading room and vestibule (*ricetto*) were completed in 1559 by others, according to models and instructions sent by Michelangelo from Rome.

The long space of the reading room was divided into rectangular bays determined by a series of exterior buttresses, each bay with one smaller over one larger window and a specially designed desk. Vertically, the bays were defined by *pietra serena* pilasters flattened against a white wall and carrying around the room an uninterrupted architrave; horizontally, each bay was marked by bands in the ceiling pattern running from side wall to side wall and repeated in the design of the floor. This additive, repetitive scheme was convenient for the practical requirements of a library, for each bay became an autonomous rectangular box with its own comprehensive system for light, air, and study. The architectural components of the reading room were assembled by Michelangelo in ways that had not been seen before, yet the general impression was not alien to Florentine Renaissance traditions. In deference to the Brunelleschi idiom (the library was, after all, in S. Lorenzo), Michelangelo enlisted the familiar low relief, dark against light, linear abstraction of the quattrocento. In the *ricetto*, however, the tectonic discipline of the reading room broke down: Old forms, familiar language, and Vitruvian rules were put aside and replaced by Michelangelo's new sculptural architecture.

8-56 Michelangelo. Ricetto, Laurentian Library, S. Lorenzo. Begun 1524

8-57 Ricetto stair

The *ricetto* is a tall but not large room; its modest size (about 35 square feet) makes the huge stair that fills it even more spectacular, and the effect of the singular columnar order of the wall even more powerful (figs. 8-56, 8-57). For the middle level of the three-part elevation, Michelangelo designed the most unconventional system of columns, tabernacles, and relief panels in all of Renaissance architecture. Heinrich Wölfflin, the great art historian of the nineteenth century, described the *ricetto* as a "unique manifestation of the Baroque spirit," seeing in its divergence from the architectural norm of the High Renaissance—established by Bramante—the colossal forms and forces of movement that would identify the dynamic architecture of the seventeenth century. It has also been regarded as a cardinal example of Michelangelo's stylistic liberties and of the tensions he created between tradition and innovation. Tall, thick, Doric-like columns with a strange concave abacus above the necking were paired and berthed within rectangular niches as if they were sculpture and not architectural supports (they do in fact support the piers that support the roof). Reversing their traditional function of "holding up," the massive, sculptural brackets beneath the columns are instead "hanging down." The pilasters of the tabernacles belong to no recognizable order and, perversely, narrow toward the bottom. Columns squeezed into the corner niches are overlapped by the tabernacle pediments in defiance of strict Renaissance practice of clear separation of elements.

Into this amazing environment, the immense stair was "poured," its midsection carved as if from some soft, ductile material, while its flanks are made sharp-edged and rigid. There is little space between them and the walls, and in these tight quarters the stair spreads, the pediments push past their boundaries, the niches compress the corner columns. Architecture, in other words, has taken on personality and mood, has been given energy, motion, and tension. As disciplined and controlled as was the reading room, so the *ricetto* was emotional and expressive. In both parts of his Laurentian Library, Michelangelo had anthropomorphized architecture and animated stone.

Michelangelo's Medicean buildings, in spite of their originality, often alluded to the Tuscan early Renaissance idiom of Brunelleschi. Permanently away from Florence after 1534, Michelangelo was free of that compelling presence. A few years after he arrived in Rome, Pope Paul III (Farnese) decided to reshape the Capitoline Hill into a monumental civic piazza; Michelangelo designed the project and his Piazza del Campidoglio (colorplate 52) is one of the most significant contributions ever made in the history of urban planning. The hill's importance as a sacred site in antiquity had been largely forgotten due to its medieval transformation into the seat of the secular government and headquarters for the Roman guilds, and it was in forlorn condition (fig. 8-58) when Michelangelo took charge of reorganizing it as a dynamic new center of Roman political life. The project went forward in slow stages with many interruptions; little was built before his death in 1564. It was begun in 1538 and was not completed until the seventeenth century, but Michelangelo's original design is preserved in engravings from the 1560s by Étienne Dupérac (fig. 8-59).

The first step in reshaping the area was the transfer there of a second-century A.D. bronze equestrian statue of the Roman emperor Marcus Aurelius, symbol of Rome's great past. Two buildings already existed on the trapezoidal site overlooking the Forum Romanum: the twelfth-century Palazzo del Senatore, erected on the ruins of the first-century A.D. Roman Tabularium (record office), and the Palazzo dei Conservatori, an uninspired quattrocento arcaded structure (the loggia

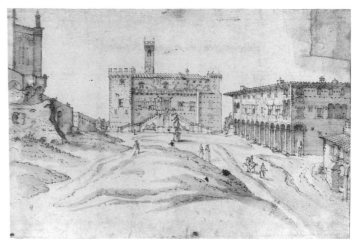

8-58   **Piazza del Campidoglio. Rome.**
(Anonymous drawing, c. 1555. The Louvre, Paris)

8-59   **Michelangelo. Project for Piazza del Campidoglio.**
(Engraving by Étienne Dupérac, 1569)

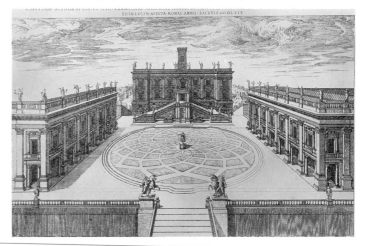

appropriate for public squares) built over an important ancient temple dedicated to Julius Optimus Maximus. To redesign the facade of the Palazzo del Senatore, Michelangelo constructed a monumental double flight of steps at the center of the ground level, installed an order of giant pilasters, and articulated each window bay with a tabernacle surmounted by a rectangular field (a device adapted from the Laurentian Library). Then, by moving the old tower from the side to the center, he reinforced the axis established by the equestrian statue and the new stair. The facade of the Palazzo dei Conservatori was transformed into a grand trabeated scheme with colossal pilasters on huge bases unifying the upper and lower tiers, each loggia bay defined by a smaller columnar order and each window bay by a tabernacular frame of unique sculptural design. A matching building called simply Palazzo Nuovo was built across the piazza to balance the Conservatori and formally to close the space. Although the Palazzo del Senatore is taller than the lateral structures, the disparity is not conspicuous; by articulating the lower palaces with heavy columns, thicker pilasters, and projecting entablatures that stressed the bulk of the building, Michelangelo gave to all three structures equal "weight," or, more precisely, the impression of it. Moreover, the powerful vertical rise of the giant pilasters on the lower buildings made all the palaces seem equally tall. A broad flight of steps at the edge of the piazza lengthened and strengthened the unifying axial force that flowed from the stair through the statue to the central massing of the Senators' Palace and finally to the tower. The balustrade formed a border that made the whole area a defined and finished space. Michelangelo did not substitute the regularity of a square for the Campidoglio's natural trapezoidal shape, and so the lateral buildings appear to converge on the central palace. Coordinated with this dynamic directional pull is his choice of the enormous oval (not circle) of the pavement design that frames the statue and unifies with its sweep all three buildings. Beneath the oval base (Michelangelo's design) of the statue, the ground rises slightly in a metaphoric allusion to the idea of the Capitoline Hill as the *umbilicus mundi*, center of the world.

Coherence and energy are inseparable components of the Campidoglio program. Michelangelo, like Bramante before him at the Cortile del Belvedere, worked with diverse ingredients—buildings, statuary, stairs, an irregular site, the outdoor environment—to form an integrated, rationally organized, and animated entity fundamental to the history of city planning.

Antonio da Sangallo the Younger became chief architect of St. Peter's in 1539. At that time, he inherited from the original Bramante design the four great piers beneath the dome and the huge barrel vaults that tied them together, along with all the alterations in Bramante's plan made by twenty-five years of successive *capomaestri*. Sangallo's own project for the church (preserved in a wooden model) was an ambitious elaboration of the original scheme, and before he died in 1546 a few portions of his design had been built. When in the same year Michelangelo (seventy-one years old) took charge of the project, he ordered those parts demolished. The weaknesses of Sangallo's scheme are apparent in the model. Bramante's colossal integrated fabric had been fragmented into many independent pieces: the original cross-within-a-square was made larger by adding new spaces beyond the apsed arms; the facade was overexpanded to become a semidetached building, connected by a porch to the body of the church and dominated by a pair of multitiered towers as tall as the dome; Bramante's uniform hemispherical dome was separated into two independent colonnades and crowned by a peripteral lantern.

Michelangelo's cure was to amputate (colorplate 58; figs. 8-60, 8-61). He removed the turreted porch and the curving corridors of the apses; he cut away walls flanking the entrance and eliminated the crosses planned in the angle where each apse and square met. The interior spaces were united into one uninterrupted vaulted square and cross. For the exterior, he designed a colonnaded temple front facade, a more dynamic, focused approach than Bramante's serene concept (half a century out of date) of four identical facades. The remaining three sides were integrated by a single pattern of articulation formed by colossal pilasters, linking two stories beneath a narrow attic, and moving smoothly around the outer skin of the basilica. The thrust of the pilasters was carried to the dome; there the order became paired columns in the drum and then ribs soaring toward the lantern. As the vertical elements rose from base to pinnacle, they tied together all the levels of the elevation.

Michelangelo and Sangallo must be discussed together in accounting for the history of another of Rome's most important sixteenth-century buildings. The Palazzo Farnese (figs. 8-62–

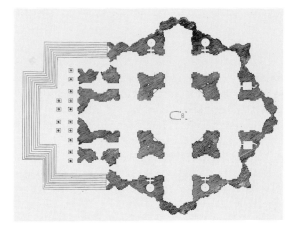

8-60   Michelangelo. Plan, St. Peter's. Rome. 1546. (After Philippo Bonanni)

8-61   St. Peter's from the west

8-64) was begun in 1515 as a remodeling of an older palace for Paul III (Farnese) while he was still a cardinal. Work progressed slowly; by 1541 the Pope (elected 1534) had decided to turn the palace over to his sons, and a new plan for a remodeling and enlargement ensued. Sangallo was the architect, and he brought the facade wing of the palace to the base of the cornice before his death in 1546. Michelangelo then took over, as he had at St. Peter's, and gave it a sculptural potency that the building lacked even though it promised to be one of the heaviest, most massive structures in the history of palace architecture. Sangallo's original design picked up from Bramante's innovative Palazzo Caprini the aediculae windows for its thirteen

8-62 Antonio da Sangallo the Younger. Vestibule, Palazzo Farnese. 1515

8-63 Sangallo and Michelangelo. Facade, Palazzo Farnese. Rome. 1541 and 1546

8-64 Sangallo and Michelangelo. Courtyard, Palazzo Farnese

bays, but instead of adopting the most radical of its effects—the applied orders on the piano nobile of a two-story elevation—he "reverted" to the Florentine quattrocento palace type, devoid of vertical elements separating the bays and with strong horizontal cornices to mark its division into three sto-

ries. Michelangelo gave the facade its most definitive feature—a massive overhanging cornice of Florentine ancestry close in spirit to that on Michelozzo's Palazzo Medici of a century earlier—and he also gave the facade a focal point by stressing the central window above the portal and crowning it with a huge coat of arms. Modifications by Michelangelo in the upper tier of the inner courtyard also added vitality and buoyancy to the dense structure, but Sangallo's genuine feeling for the strength and heft of the huge masonry piers of the arcade, inspired by the Theater of Marcellus and the Colosseum, and for the massive volumes of the barrel-vaulted entrance corridor, is directly in the tradition of Renaissance monumentalism. The broad, deep piazza in front of the palace constitutes an important chapter in the urban history of Rome. Engravings from 1549 depict the pavement of a piazza marked off into squares corresponding to the width of the bays, suggesting that at one stage in the building history there existed an integrated plan relating palace and piazza. This concept, which may have evolved from Michelangelo's interest in urban planning, gives the palace an additional scenographic dimension, making it even more impressive than it already is by virtue of its gigantic size. The sixteenth-century palace-piazza complex must be regarded as another significant contribution of the Renaissance to the history of urban design.

Michelangelo introduced many exciting new concepts and effects into the architecture of the sixteenth century by demonstrating how consonant with the spirit of antiquity were the "living" forms of his own architecture. His work diverged from the mainstream of High Renaissance Classicism, but proved how far the Classical language of architecture could be stretched without being destroyed. It was not until the seventeenth century, however, that the full power of his originality would be felt. Indeed, it was then that many of his inventions became the very features by which the aesthetic of the Baroque would be distinguished from that of the Renaissance.

Sanmicheli; Sansovino. Although Renaissance architecture of the sixteenth century was expressed most comprehensively in Rome, there were notable architects and important buildings elsewhere; indeed, the greatest architect in Italy after Michelangelo, and one of the most consummate and influential architects of all time was Andrea Palladio, who worked in the cities of the Veneto and in Venice. It was not Palladio alone, however, but also architects Michele Sanmicheli and Jacopo Sansovino who gave to this region its first High Renaissance buildings.

Sanmicheli returned to his native Verona in 1527, when Rome was sacked and devastated by the mercenary forces of Emperor Charles V, and opportunities for work and patronage in the capital dried up. He initiated improvements that were to change parts of Verona into a Renaissance city; his programs were based on projects that earlier had been conceived by Bramante and Julius II for redesigning the old streets of Rome. Sanmicheli's ideas about shaping and defining open areas, about laying out broad streets and lining them with impressive palaces, and about redesigning city gates, transformed whole sections of the city. In medieval fashion Verona was ringed by walls; in the sixteenth century, to expand the city and accommodate its growing population, a new ring and entrance gates were put up beyond the old walls. Their principal function was no longer to protect and defend, as in the Middle Ages, but to define boundaries and mark major thoroughfares. In appearance the new program did not suggest an impregnable fortress; the entrance gates became architectural showpieces in Renaissance style, dignified in character and ambitious in design, symbols of a new civic self-esteem. Broad streets were cut through to connect the new walls to the old and they became desirable sites for the construction of new patrician palaces.

Sanmicheli was the driving force behind the construction of the new Verona, and his city gates, palaces, and the urban scheme itself were the means by which he meshed Roman High Renaissance style into the antique and medieval tissue of the city (Verona had been an important Roman settlement). His Porta Palio (fig. 8-65) was built around 1555 as one of the new gates, and while it may recall medieval images of defense by virtue of its placement, its Classical syntax and architectural details link it to stately Renaissance palaces. The face it presents to visitors is dressed with exquisitely cut stone blocks, has three arches framed with paired, fluted Doric columns beneath a frieze, and is richly embellished with carved ornament.

One of the broad new thoroughfares (today Corso Cavour, in the Renaissance Strada Nuova) of sixteenth-century Verona was lined on both sides with grand palaces, conspicuous for their size, elegance, and rich details. Away from Rome and its partiality for simple, virile forms, Sanmicheli was free to express uninhibitedly his own northern Italian preference for refined surfaces. The Palazzo Canossa (begun around 1530; fig. 8-66), among the most sophisticated palaces of the sixteenth century, is one of four built by Sanmicheli for new Verona, and its facade illustrates the skillful way in which he varied Bramante's Roman palace archetype and its system of rusticated ground floor with engaged paired orders on the piano nobile. The stonework is crisp and precise, the rustication flat, the pilasters shallow. An unusual complexity determines the composition of the piano nobile—a horizontal strip

8-65   Michele Sanmicheli. Porta Palio. Verona. c. 1555

8-66   Michele Sanmicheli. Palazzo Canossa. Verona. Begun c. 1530

threaded behind the pilasters to unify the window bays while the coupled order separates them, and the impost molding of the windows cut by the order instead of repeating the continuous run of the ribbon strip above. A vertical extension through the roof cornice is effected with dwarfed coupled panels punctuating a shapely balustrade, and a similarly rich relief in the capitals and in the window arches with brackets is an elegant contrast to the smooth surfaces.

It should be noted that, in addition to the distinctiveness of Sanmicheli's facades, the shapes of Veronese and Venetian palaces built by him and others differed from the sturdy quadratic volumes of Tuscano-Roman buildings. Often they were irregular, for the boundaries of the building site might be controlled by such physical givens as canals. Because Venice's remarkable situation on canals and lagoons afforded it natural protection, it did not require the kind of fortified architecture of the inland. Even in the Middle Ages, in contrast to the crenellations and heavy, rusticated stone blocks used elsewhere to discourage approach and entry, Venetian palaces were made of lacy, light, openwork masonry, perforated whenever possible to admit air and light. Open courtyards were therefore less important in the Veneto than in Tuscany and Rome. Palaces tended to be long, narrow rectangles with a principal facade opening to the canal, and were designed to take into account the need for inner boat docks. A courtyard, ancillary to the overall plan, was fitted in wherever convenient, generally at the rear, where it served as a peristyle garden in the tradition of Oriental houses derived ultimately from Greek, not Roman (central atrium) origins. As one critic has observed, High Renaissance style did not suit Venetian palaces sited on the canals. It made them look too heavy—as if they were about to sink!

High Renaissance architecture was introduced to Venice by Jacopo Sansovino. Born in Florence, Sansovino began his career as a sculptor. He went to Rome in 1505 at the height of Bramante's influence there; in 1527 he left for Venice. In Rome, his skill in copying ancient sculpture led to his employment as a restorer of ancient statues and brought him to the attention of Bramante and Raphael, who were avid antiquarians, and who engaged him to work at St. Peter's. Sansovino had many talents, and, in addition to being an architect, sculptor, and restorer, he was a good architectural technician. It was this skill that first commended him to the Doge of Venice, who was seeking a reliable technical report on the condition of the aging basilica of S. Marco. In 1529, Sansovino was appointed Chief Architect of S. Marco, and he remained in Venice until his death in 1570.

The main square of Venice—one of the most majestic and scenographic public places in the world—is really two squares arranged in an L-shape: the huge piazza in front of the Byzantinizing Romanesque S. Marco, and, stretching away from it to the water, the smaller Piazzetta. As part of a project for the transformation of the Piazzetta, Sansovino built the huge Libreria di S. Marco (pp. 274–75; figs. 8-67, 8-68), one of the most impressive of all Renaissance structures. In its brilliant synthesis of Classical forms and details with the architectural language of the High Renaissance, and with his own genius for stressing the sculptural aspects of architecture, the Libreria is Sansovino's masterpiece. Begun in 1536, it was not originally conceived as a library. Then, in 1537, the building was designated as the repository of an important collection of Greek and Latin manuscripts, given to the Venetian Republic in the fifteenth century and stored in the Palazzo Ducale. From the architecture warehouse that was Rome, filled with the ancient fabrics and the High Renaissance buildings of Bramante and his followers, Sansovino selected forms, systems, details that best suited the sculptural character of his architectural designs. He was especially responsive to theaters and arenas of Roman antiquity—the Colosseum, the Theater of Marcellus—where massive piers were thickened and enriched by applied columns. It was a combination he preferred over the pier with engaged pilaster espoused by Bramante, because it was one of the most volumetric forms in the Classical inventory. Twenty-one arched bays of the two-story Libreria stretched along the Piazzetta, three bays along the canal, serving as the kind of impressive formal enframement of public squares that had by this time become an intrinsic part of Renaissance urban planning. On the lower level, the arcade is carried by piers fronted with the Doric order; Ionic columns are applied to the piers that comprise the Serlian pattern (trabeated lower openings framing a taller arch) of the story above. By using the Serliana with its minor order aside the pier instead of the simple arch-and-pier of the ground level, Sansovino reduced the open spaces and broadened the supporting mass of the upper story as a way of providing additional buttressing for the barrel vault of the reading room behind the arcade. An exceptionally rich garland frieze punctuated by windows runs above the Ionic columns (its origins are in the frieze of Rome's Villa Farnesina) and the whole ensemble is crowned with a balustrade beneath a line of statues.

In urbanistic terms, the Libreria is an extraordinary success, not only as a dramatic backdrop to a dramatic public space but in the way it draws together the individual parts of the Piazzetta. Although its heavy forms and textures could not be more unlike those of the perforated and seemingly weightless facade of the medieval Palazzo Ducale across the Piazzetta, Sansovino conceived the Libreria as an architectural "equivalent" to the Gothic building. He compensated for the gracile delicacy of the older structure with the muscular power of the new one, and for the greater height of the Palazzo Ducale with statues along the crown of the Libreria that stress the vertical

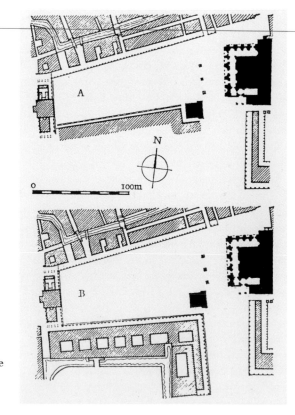

8-67
Plans,
Piazza
S. Marco.
Venice.
Top: before
c. 1530;
bottom:
c. 1600

8-68   Libreria di S. Marco and Doge's Palace. Venice

elements of the building. Visitors sense that they are confronted by buildings that "match"—not in terms of style but of architectural and civic importance.

Atypically, the Campanile of S. Marco was not adjacent to the church, but stood across from it at one point where the piazza met the Piazzetta. On one of its sides, the bell tower was joined to undistinguished buildings; on another, it was abutted by an arcaded loggia used as a meeting place, which was hemmed in by a cluster of small, nondescript structures. Sansovino freed the Campanile from the surrounding structures, and between 1537 and 1545 he built a new loggia at its base. The style of the Loggetta (colorplate 51) was conceived in heroic, Bramantesque terms, but its opulent red and white marble, and its gleaming bronze sculpture, gave it a sensuous aura, in closer harmony with the polychromatism of Venetian architecture than with the unclad masonry monuments of Rome. More than any other source, it was triumphal arches with their integrated programs of sculpture and architecture on a monumental scale that inspired Sansovino in the Loggetta project. Like a triumphal arch, the Loggetta had three portals separated by colossal piers in front of which stood heavy, paired columns framing niches with bronze statues, each column thrust forward beneath a protruding architrave. An attic with panels of relief sculpture surmounted the arcaded story, and the whole complex was completed by a balustrade (the lower balustrade was added later). Although small in size, the

Loggetta, rich with ornament, color, precious materials, and sculpture, makes a powerful impact.

Sansovino's buildings were more elaborate than those of his Roman contemporaries, and they struck the right chord in the Oriental richness of Venice. His combination of robust Classical forms ornamented with high relief sculpture was appreciated for its novelty; Classical severity and muscularity were in refreshing contrast to the fragile linear outlines of Venetian buildings. At the same time, the colored stones and the rich sculpture, which overlay or coexisted with those severe forms, satisfied the Venetian fondness for opulence and embossed surfaces.

Palladio; Vignola. Renaissance architecture spread from its beginnings in fifteenth-century Florence to the dominions of enlightened rulers in other regions of quattrocento Italy, then to Rome, where in the sixteenth century it was furthered by papal patronage, and finally to Venice and the northeast, carried there by artists trained in Rome. The perfectly equilibrated Classical Roman Renaissance style of the first two decades of the sixteenth century expired in Rome after the sack, but it flourished with regional and stylistic variations elsewhere in Italy, in cities such as Mantua, Verona, and Venice. The last of the great Humanist architects—Andrea Palladio—came from that region. He was born in 1508 in Padua, near Venice, and began his career as a stonemason. When he was in his twenties, he was taken up by Gian Giorgio

Trissino, patrician, poet, philosopher, connoisseur, and patron of the arts, who recognized in the young man special intellectual and artistic gifts. Trissino encouraged Palladio to become educated as a Humanist—to study Latin literature, music, mathematics, and the treatise of Vitruvius. Palladio accompanied his patron to Rome, where he studied and sketched ancient architecture. During this process of enlightened exposure to the culture of the past, the young Palladio was transformed from stonemason to architect and antiquarian. Inspired by Vitruvius and the example of Alberti and the treatise writers who followed him, Palladio wrote and illustrated his own architectural treatise, *Quattro libri dell'architettura* (1570)—a document that was, in effect, a manual of Classicizing design, and one that had a profound influence on architecture in many countries for more than two centuries. In the treatise, he set down the plans and elevations of his own buildings, along with theories of architecture derived from his study of antiquity. The *Quattro libri* was not Palladio's only book; he was continually inspired to draw and write as a result of his experience of Roman architecture, and in 1554 he published a guidebook, *Le antichità di Roma*; the same year also saw the publication of *Descrizione delle . . . chiese di Roma*, and in 1556 an important edition of Vitruvius illustrated by Palladio. As an architect in the Veneto, in Vicenza and Venice, he probably had more far-reaching influence with his villas, palaces, churches, and public buildings than any other Renaissance architect.

Palladio's first major commission was for a public building, the Palazzo della Ragione (fig. 8-69), or town hall, of Vicenza. As in the case of Alberti and his Church of S. Francesco in Rimini, Palladio had to construct a new shell around an older structure. The Palazzo della Ragione was a huge two-story hall in which the Vicenza city council met. Built in the mid-fifteenth century on the main square of the town, the core of the building originally had been encompassed by a two-story loggia that collapsed soon after its construction. It was this loggia that Palladio was commissioned to reconstruct in 1548; work was begun by 1549, but the building was not completed until 1617, almost forty years after Palladio's death. The old meeting room on the upper story had been covered by a vast wooden roof, still visible above the balustrade that crowned Palladio's new loggia which was built not only as a new facade

8-69 Andrea Palladio. Loggia, Palazzo della Ragione (Basilica). Vicenza. Begun 1548

for an old-fashioned building, but also to buttress the thrusts of the earlier massive structure. The proportions of Palladio's design—the height of each of the two stories, and the width and number of bays—were determined by those of the older building, but this schematic substructure was overlaid by Palladio with the latest *all'antica* elements imported from Rome and Rome-via-Venice. Sansovino's Libreria was near completion in Venice just before the town hall in Vicenza was begun; because it, too, was on a major public square Palladio may have been inspired to use the Serliana (which, because of this building would subsequently be known as the "Palladian" motif). More significant, perhaps, was that its flexibility served a practical purpose. The bays of the old loggia had been unequal in width; by employing a small order detached from the pier that carried the major engaged order, Palladio was able to adjust the size of the end bay. He made it narrower than the others by reducing the interval between the small column and the pier while maintaining the regularity of the large arched opening. Palladio himself named it the "Basilica," intentionally making the analogy between his building and the ancient Roman halls used for civic functions. It was Vicenza's first Renaissance building.

The success of the Basilica brought Palladio many commissions for private palaces in Vicenza. His palace designs can be traced to four sources: the palaces and villas of the Bramante circle built before 1527, which Palladio knew from his visits to Rome; the richer, regionally transformed works of Sanmicheli and Sansovino in Verona and Venice; the personal variations on Classical Roman formulas carried out by Giulio Romano in Mantua; and the ancient monuments Palladio had studied with great attention and reconstructed. Many of the components of the facade of his Palazzo Thiene (fig. 8-70), from the 1540s—rusticated ground floor, regularly spaced pilasters on the piano nobile, pedimented windows, and projecting keystone and large blocks on the window frames—come from recognizable sources, but they are handled with Palladio's special expressive freedom.

The unusual design of his Palazzo Chiericati (fig. 8-71) of the 1550s was determined by its site. Instead of fronting one of Vicenza's typically narrow streets where a closed facade would have been the norm, it faced a broad park adjacent to a river. To Palladio, the location appears to have suggested both a villa site and a piazza; for the river side he designed a colonnade, a format associated with the openness of a country house as well as with the loggias that shaped Renaissance public squares. The Doric order of the lower story might be perceived as the peripteros of Bramante's Tempietto, unwrapped and stretched across the face of this building. On the piano nobile, the order changed to Ionic; the central bays were not open, as below, but walled; and the wall was pierced by a mezzanine and a window story, rich with sculptured pediments. Palladio accentuated the central pavilion by projecting it forward and by doubling the orders at the corners with a corresponding pattern in the order below.

The greatest sixteenth-century villas were not found in Rome, but in the Veneto; they were the work of Palladio. Although his mastery of architecture led to commissions for many different types of buildings, his villas were the most in demand; in terms of influence, they remain among the most important structures in the entire history of architecture. From them, more than from his other works, was born a whole new style—Palladianism—on

8-70 Andrea Palladio. Palazzo Thiene. Vicenza. 1540s

8-71 Andrea Palladio. Palazzo Chiericati. Vicenza. Begun c. 1547

which eighteenth-century Classical architecture in England, and subsequently in America, was founded.

Palladio's Humanist education, his intellectual kinship to the literary sophisticates of the Trissino circle, and, above all, his zealous study of ancient buildings made him learned about the rules and forms of ancient architecture. But his was not simply theoretical knowledge; unlike the aristocratic Alberti, the quintessential "gentleman architect" who refrained from manual labor, Palladio had been an active professional since his early years as a stonemason, and what he learned from study he put into practice. Based principally on proportions, symmetry, and the image of the temple front, Palladio's Classicism was embodied most vividly in the villas he built in the countryside around Vicenza for wealthy landowners who lived in town but kept a country estate as a pleasurable retreat and an income-producing farm (figs. 8-72–8-74). They were designed with the agrarian activities of their owners in mind. Rectangular blocks were connected to subsidiary wings by a colonnaded portico, sometimes straight, sometimes curved. The main block, usually with porch, contained the family's living quarters, while the supplementary wings serviced the farm; they contained granaries, stables, servants' quarters, or warehouses. The groundplan of each villa was a variation on a theme: a strictly symmetrical arrangement of residential rooms around a central reception hall, the rooms—including two or three *saloni* or bedrooms—on the left corresponding in shape and proportion to those on the right, and staircases or smaller auxiliary rooms inserted in the spaces between the rooms and the hall. Many of the villas were planned more elaborately than they were built; the ideal Palladian villa can be best observed in illustrations in the *Quattro libri*, where he recorded his fully developed schemes for plan and elevation (fig. 8-73).

8-72　Andrea Palladio. Villa Godi. Lonedo. 1538–42

8-73　Andrea Palladio. Villa Godi, plan and elevation.
（from the *Quattro libri*）

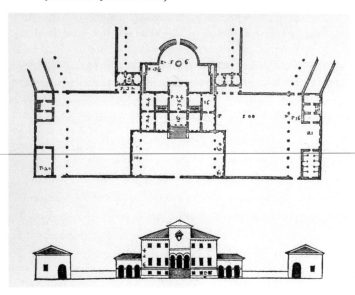

8-74　Andrea Palladio. Villa Foscari. Malcontenta. Before 1560

As the perfect facade for his villas, Palladio adapted the form of the temple front (in this he was preceded by Giuliano da Sangallo at Poggio a Caiano). It was his conviction that ancient temples, with their pedimented, colonnaded facades, duplicated the appearance of earlier dwellings—in other words, that the formula of the sacred temple was determined originally by the vernacular architecture of houses. Palladio thought of the temple as a kind of supreme house, the house of a god but a house nevertheless. And since his villas were intended as re-creations of the villas of antiquity, there was for him no inconsistency in combining sacred and domestic architecture.

Palladio played many variations on the villa theme without sacrificing basics: the side bays of the facade might be emphasized instead of, more commonly, the center; piers rather than columns might support the pediment; a porch might be added as an independent unit rather than being set into the house block. Among all the variants, the Villa Rotonda (begun 1566;

figs. 8-75, 8-76) is regarded as the quintessential realization of his ideas. Its crystal-clear groundplan embodies his principles of villa design: Around a circular central hall, the square of the building is divided into four groups of rooms, absolutely symmetrical. As a treatise writer and well-trained Humanist, Palladio was devoted to the idea of the value of harmonic proportions and to the beauty of mathematics, so that the proportions of the length, width, and height of each room were carefully worked out and every room, according to an exact formula of ratios, related not only to every other room, but to the whole building. A pedimented, hexastyle, Ionic porch, reached in the manner of Roman temples by a majestic stair, precedes each of the four facades, carrying Palladio's ruthless symmetry beyond any notion of practical necessity. But the porches did have a functional as well as a formal role, for the villa was built at the crest of a rise, and the porches provided a commanding view of the countryside in all directions and offered solace from the heat of the day.

As daring as the adoption of a temple form to a house was, vaulting the circular hall of the Villa Rotonda with a dome was even more so. The dome in the Renaissance had always been associated with ecclesiastical architecture (and with the "dome of heaven" image) and had not been used in a domestic building. Although Raphael's dome above the central bay of the loggia of the Villa Madama might be cited as a precedent, it was neither visible from the exterior nor meant to be the dominating feature of the building, as Palladio's dome surely was.

The temple front image, with its evocations of the antique, its harmonious ratios of height and width, and its abstract patterns of geometric shapes, served Palladio well (like Alberti before him) as an inventive answer to the dilemma of how to articulate a facade in the language of Classicism. So versatile a format did it prove to be that he not only transformed it to accommodate a miscellany of country houses, but, later in his

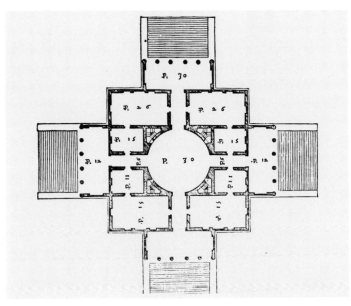

8-75 Plan, Villa Rotonda

8-76 Andrea Palladio. Villa Rotonda. Vicenza. Begun 1566

career, he expanded it to colossal proportions to face two monumental churches in Venice. S. Giorgio Maggiore (begun 1566; colorplate 50; figs. 8-77, 8-78) and Il Redentore (begun 1576) have the same facade pattern: first, a huge, pedimented, tetrastyle temple front placed before the tall nave, its dimensions matched to those of the nave; then, set before the lower and narrower side aisles (but in a plane behind the nave section), a section of pediment on doubled terminal pilasters, stretched on either side to the width of the church, its cornices abutting the columnar order in the forward plane. The result is an ingenious interlocking of two coherent systems—lateral and central—that mirrors the plan and elevation of the church interior without destroying the integrity of the Classical format. In fifteenth-century S. Maria Novella, Alberti solved the problem of the transition between the lower side aisles and the tall nave of a basilican church with volutes; in the sixteenth century, Palladio found a solution with his bisected and interlaced temples, an inventive design that the Romans themselves would have admired.

The light-filled, spacious interior of S. Giorgio Maggiore, a Benedictine monastery church, is functionally arranged to suit the needs of the monastic community and the congregation of lay worshipers. A huge monks' choir, screened by columns, extends beyond a chancel that effectively separates it from the nave. The chancel, itself distinguished from the barrel-vaulted nave by its groin vault on freestanding columns, suggests a semi-independent structure within the program, and has been astutely described as an "altar house." Joined by a domed crossing to the transept, the wide nave opens to side chapels, and the traditional columns of a basilican church have become piers (to support the barrel vault) articulated by giant half-columns and pilasters. Palladio has used a number of vaulting and fenestration systems derived from his close knowledge of the huge bath buildings of Imperial Rome. They are not used

"archaeologically" but with a freedom of interpretation to achieve analogous effects of grandeur and dignity. No visitor has failed to perceive the extraordinary "Venetian" luminosity of the church, the warm light from its many windows reflected on creamy stucco surfaces uninterrupted by paintings or sculp- ture. Palladio's design expresses the organization of the interior spaces of S. Giorgio Maggiore with the same exceptional clarity that he applied to the scheme of the facade.

Palladio's late works were heroic in scale. The unfinished Loggia del Capitaniato in Vicenza (colorplate 54) commemorates the triumph of the Venetians over the Turks at Lepanto in 1571; its side facade is designed as a triumphal arch, and the front is a fenestrated story above a triadic ground floor. Here Palladio is working in his most powerful manner: enormous columns, an entablature with tremendous thrusts above the capitals; a surface rich with relief. Equally colossal is the Palazzo Porto-Breganze (fig. 8-79), also of the 1570s, even with only two bays completed. Gigantic columns on huge plinths are set between the windows, and weighty high relief garland swags hang from the frieze beneath the mezzanine windows. Balconies jut forth to balance the powerful forward push of entablature sections above the capitals. The sculptural force of these late buildings can be compared to Michelangelo's sculptural architecture. In 1554, when Palladio made what was to be his final trip to Rome, he saw Michelangelo's St. Peter's and perhaps drawings of the Capitoline buildings. Although as early as the Vicenza Basilica, Palladio's architecture embodied antique monumentalism, the impression that

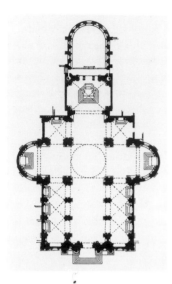

8-77
Andrea Palladio. Plan, S. Giorgio Maggiore. Venice. Begun 1566

8-78   Interior, S. Giorgio Maggiore

8-79 Andrea Palladio. Palazzo Porto-Breganze. Vicenza. 1570s

8-80 Andrea Palladio. Teatro Olimpico. Vicenza. Completed by Silla Palladio and Vincenzo Scamozzi. 1580–85

Michelangelo's titanic structure must have made on the North Italian architect is reflected in the gigantism and exceptional sculptural force of his work following the Roman sojourn.

Shortly before his death in 1580 Palladio saw the near completion of his final work, a theatre (regarded as the first permanent indoor theatre of the Renaissance) that he designed for the Accademia Olimpica of Vicenza, an institution founded and sustained by learned and cultivated Humanists versed in mathematics and the arts and sciences, and of which Palladio was a charter member. Palladio's Teatro Olimpico (fig. 8-80)—with its semi-elliptical auditorium backed by column-framed statues and its stage front in the form of a tri-portal triumphal arch/palace

facade including sculpture in the round and fields of relief—was the architect's attempt to reconstruct an ancient theatre using a richly encrusted language of architectural Classicism, appropriate to the Accademia Olimpica's sponsorship of the production of Classical drama. The Teatro Olimpico is the oldest surviving theatre built since antiquity, and is still used for performances.

Palladio, who was experienced in theatre design and stagecraft, intended the three open portals of the stage front installation to contain changeable painted screens as backdrops. After his death, however, his pupil and assistant, Vincenzo Scamozzi, changed this device to the permanent urban perspectives—sharply receding streets lined with buildings—now in place. (The building was completed by the architect's son, Silla Palladio.) Despite the departures from Palladio's intentions, today's visitor to the Teatro Olimpico can readily experience, through Palladio's brilliant evocation, the Renaissance thrill of believing that the architectural, sculptural, and dramaturgical culture of antiquity had been reanimated in late-sixteenth-century Vicenza.

Perhaps more than any other architect Palladio symbolizes the accomplishment of the Renaissance mission. Antiquity had been discovered, revived, and interpreted. The momentum generated by his interpretations carried Classicism as a style and a philosophy through the nineteenth century.

Renaissance Classicism as a revival style (in distinction to nonreferential styles such as Greek or Gothic) was more analogous than imitative of antiquity. From its origins in early Renaissance Florence, Classicism had worked itself through various degrees of analogy until it "peaked" in the short-lived High Renaissance of about 1480–1520, a brevity typical of "high" phases of art with their fugitive perfection and impermanent equilibrium. After 1520, the delicate balance of Classicism, faith, and rationalism which had existed since the quattrocento, was upset by reverberations from the crisis of the Reformation. One outcome was that church-building activity in Rome and throughout Italy faltered and waned in the second quarter of the sixteenth century. Having lost both a consistency of style and a unity of vision, much of post–High Renaissance architecture became divergent and pluralistic, a mixture of individualism, regionalism, and interpretations of Michelangelism. An architectural crisis had already been forecast with central-plan churches and their seeming lack of concern for the traditional patterns of worship. Ecclesiastical patrons of the later cinquecento, engaged in the fight against Protestantism, wished to see the design of churches return to the forms nostalgically associated with the intense spirituality of the early days of Christianity, long before it became tainted by Humanism. In his *Instructiones* (1577), Cardinal Carlo Borromeo interpreted the decrees of the Counter-Reformation Council of Trent for programs of church architecture. For him, the circular form was pagan, and he recommended a return to the Latin cross. The second half of the sixteenth century witnessed the virtual disappearance of the central-plan church in favor of longitudinal buildings, often with transepts to form a true cross. From time to time a church would be designed as a compromise, but finally the architectural ideals of the Counter-Reformation triumphed.

Amid the intellectual conflicts and artistic diversity of the later sixteenth century, Giacomo Barozzi da Vignola—Rome's leading architect after the death of Michelangelo—pioneered the new direction of Renaissance architecture with his design for the interior of the Church of the Gesù (fig. 8-81), mother

8-81 Giacomo Barozzi da Vignola. Nave, Il Gesù. Rome. Begun 1568

church of the Jesuit Order. In this church he synthesized Renaissance theory with the new spiritual goals that were becoming more and more explicit. The dynamic effort to strengthen the faith among the clergy and the laity by generating powerful emotions associated with Catholic piety had been launched by the wealthy, superbly organized, and intellectual Jesuits. The appearance of their mother church—a part of their enormous Roman monastery—was meant to reflect that power and to express Jesuit convictions about the forms and meaning of worship. Although the building was begun by Vignola in 1568, it was completed posthumously: The nave was vaulted in 1575, the crossing and apse were added in 1580, the facade—designed by another architect and, in style, the beginning of a new era—was constructed from 1575 to 1584. The width of the nave (originally painted white) is exceptional (almost 60 feet), surpassed only by that of St. Peter's. There are no aisles; the nave opens to three chapels on each side and one smaller chapel near the crossing. The side walls are articulated by one great order of doubled giant pilasters, supporting one major entabla-

ture (from Michelangelo's St. Peter's interior), which runs uninterruptedly from facade to crossing. A huge, undecorated (the present decoration is from the seventeenth century) barrel vault covers the whole width of the nave; above the crossing rises a dome, supported by massive piers into which the smaller chapels were cut. There is a transept, but it does not protrude beyond the flanks of the church. The immense space was wonderfully luminous in its sixteenth-century state because of the white surfaces and the large windows that were daringly cut into the curve of the barrel vault on each side. The idea of opening up the clerestory of a barrel-vaulted interior with windows was startlingly new. (Alberti, although ahead of his time with his barrel vault at S. Andrea in Mantua, did not fenestrate that vault.) The barrel vault needed the support of the clerestory walls; to pierce them and thus deprive them of strength meant that additional buttressing would be required, which explains the "Gothic" system of the Gesù's exterior buttresses.

Vignola's knowledge of ancient architecture, his codification of the five orders (published in 1562), and the important buildings he designed and built for important patrons place him in the roster of the great masters of Renaissance architecture. At the same time, the design of the Gesù interior, its spaciousness, the focus of the light from the dome on the high altar, the clearing away of architectural elements that interfere with or distract from spiritual meditation, all conform to the new ideas of worship that came from the Council of Trent and heralded the new style of the Baroque.

FRANCE, SPAIN, AND ENGLAND

No other country could match or even approach Italy's supreme position in the world of art and culture during those two extraordinary centuries of the Renaissance—a position that had been held by France in the twelfth and thirteenth centuries. The creation of the Gothic style in twelfth-century France had been an achievement so immense, and its growth so steady and magnificent, that the Gothic remained firmly rooted there for almost four hundred years. It was politics, not art, that awakened France to the existence of the sweeping new mode of expression that had come into being in fifteenth-century Florence: The invasion by France of various regions of the Italian peninsula (principally those dominated by Naples, Genoa, and Milan) at the end of the fifteenth and beginning of the sixteenth centuries, and the subsequent French occupation of Genoa and Milan, brought the French face to face with the culture of the Renaissance—the new style of art and life—and with the skilled Italian craftsmen who created that style.

The earliest influence of Italian Renaissance modes on art in France can be traced back to the mid-fifteenth century, when they appeared first in painting. Shortly before 1450, Jean Fouquet visited Rome (and possibly Florence) and then included in his miniatures and larger paintings details of architectural forms and decoration that he had seen in Italian Renaissance painting and in the remains of antiquity. Toward the end of the fifteenth century Italian decorative devices derived largely from those of antiquity—swags of fruits and flowers, dancing putti, round-headed shell niches, naturalistic vines and tendrils—became known in France through printing. French publishers and graphic artists acquired Italian engravings and books that were copiously illustrated with these devices and which they soon learned to imitate; their own designs in the Italian style were then printed and widely circulated in France. Three- rather than two-dimensional Italian Renaissance architectural forms were introduced into France for the first time through the enlightened patronage of King René of Anjou, who, during the middle years of the fifteenth century had important ties to the courts of Naples and Milan, and also to the Medici in Florence. The French king brought back to his own court in Provence, in southern France, artists of the caliber of Francesco Laurana (fig. 8-82) who had worked in Humanist courts in Italy, notably in Naples, and who introduced into French architecture the language of Classicism in its Italian early Renaissance translation: shell niches, pilasters, straight entablatures that broke forward over capitals carved with Classical designs, Brunelleschian arcades on columns, and Classical proportions. The Renaissance began to have a wider and more powerful impact when the military campaigns launched against Italy by Kings Charles VIII and Louis XII of France from 1496 to 1515 exposed receptive and cultivated Frenchmen in the kings' armies, and in the French administrative governments in the occupied cities, to the new style. They in turn imported Italian artists and craftsmen to France to satisfy the growing appetite for *la mode italienne* with sculpture (principally tombs) and decorative arts embellished with ornament from the Italian repertoire. It would be almost half a century, however, before Renaissance style was fully assimilated into monumental architecture in France. The first steps in this direction were taken in the châteaux built and remodeled in the first quarter of the sixteenth century by the French kings and members of their courts in the Loire Valley, where the traditional royal passion for the hunt was pursued.

8-82 **Francesco Laurana. Chapel of St.-Lazare, La Major (Cathedral). Marseilles. 1475–81**

8-83 **Antonio Averlino Filarete. Ospedale Maggiore. Milan. Begun 1457**

At first it was not the Renaissance architecture of Florence or Rome that had the greatest appeal for the French, but that of Milan and other cities of northern Italy where Gothic style had not been abandoned. Even though the completed portion of the Ospedale Maggiore (fig. 8-83) in Milan, begun in 1457 by the Florentine architect-sculptor Filarete, owes much (its symmetrical plan and the form of its arcade) to Brunelleschi and fifteenth-century Florentine architecture, it also preserves Gothic elements—pointed arches, slim mullions, towers, rich moldings, and encrusted surfaces—that were esteemed in northern Europe. The facade (1490s) of the church of the Certosa (colorplate 48), a Carthusian monastery in Pavia, near Milan, is so lavishly embroidered with carved relief and polychrome revetment that its Classical outline and structure are almost obscured. Taken individually, however, the elements that make up the dense and fussy ornament of the Certosa and the Ospedale Maggiore are more Classical than Gothic in character; they are stock Renaissance *all'antica* patterns and they include candelabra, garlands and rosettes, grotteschi, heads and busts, pilasters, and slender curling vines. This type of northern Italian decoration appealed to the French because its very existence and its richness were Gothic-based, but its designs were refreshingly new and the craftsmanship admirable. In the early sixteenth century, northern Italian ornament began to appear on the medieval châteaux of the Loire Valley. It was a random borrowing and arbitrary use, and the outcome is usually (and not inaccurately) described as "hybrid." It was these hybrid buildings that first brought a French Renaissance architecture into existence. Then, as Classical concepts and forms based not on northern Italian models but on those of the Roman High Renaissance and of antiquity began to dominate in secular French building in the middle decades of the sixteenth century, French Renaissance architecture found a new monumental mode of expression.

Before 1525, the remodeled medieval châteaux at Azay-le-Rideau (fig. 8-84), at Chenonceau, at Bury, and elsewhere in the Loire Valley, presented an admixture of irregular Gothic contours (derived from the shapes of the roofs, chimneys, and flamboyant pediments) with novel elements such as fluted pilasters, rectangular windows, round-arched portals, columns, cornices supported by pilasters, and, of course, the popular, almost requisite Lombard-Classical ornament including rinceaux friezes, candelabra, and spirally fluted half-columns. These elements were used for their freshness and picturesque richness without much concern for Classical proportions or the rules that, in antiquity, had governed the combination of forms. These hunting lodges, stretching along the edge of rich forest land filled with game and built to service the leisure activities and pleasurable pursuits of their wealthy owners, were grand indeed. But they did not compete in size or in splendor with the royal châteaux at Chambord and at Blois rebuilt by King François I, the first French king who wished to rival the culture of the Italian courts. In his resolve to be a great patron of the arts, François, between 1515 and 1540, brought important Italian painters, sculptors, and architects to France (Leonardo da Vinci was his greatest prize). For the decoration of the interior of his château at Fontainebleau a new style of art was invented by Primaticcio and Il Rosso Fiorentino. Beginning in 1519, one of the king's favorite hunting lodges, at Chambord, was remade into a magnificent moated château (figs. 8-85–8-87). Work was interrupted in 1524, resumed and completed in 1550 after the king's death in 1547. The history of

8-84   Entrance, Château at Azay-le-Rideau. Indre-et-Loire, France. 1518–27

the commission has not survived, but Chambord's design is often attributed to an Italian rather than to a French architect because of the symmetry of the groundplan and the arrangement of the spaces in the quadrangular main block. A Greek cross within a square, the block was divided into four symmetrical apartments by broad corridors forming the cross; the corridors served to isolate the apartments and to lead to and from the four entrances; at the crossing an extraordinary double-spiral stair rose to the top of the block. The regularity of such a layout was unusual in France at this time, although it was already a standard feature of Italian Renaissance architecture. Similarities have been noted between the groundplan of Chambord and that of Giuliano da Sangallo's villa at Poggio a Caiano (fig. 8-32); further, the ingenuity of the parallel spiral stair reflects the intricate inventions found in the drawings of Leonardo da Vinci (who died in France at the court of François I the year Chambord was begun). But the exterior of the full building, with its five-part division into a turreted central pavilion, two lower wings, and corner pavilions to match the center, and with its tall pitched roof carrying

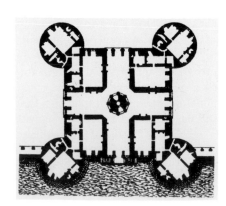

8-85
Plan of center portion, Château at Chambord. Begun 1519. (After du Cerceau)

8-86 North front, Château at Chambord. 1519–50

8-87 Roof, Château at Chambord

windows, lanterns, towers, and chimneys, links it to traditional French medieval castles. Nevertheless, the polychrome revetment lavishly applied to the surfaces of the roof projections copies patterns from the North Italian—especially Milanese—Renaissance buildings that the French admired.

At Chambord Italianate features are subtly intermeshed with the medieval fabric. This was not the case at Blois (fig. 8-88), another of François I's Loire châteaux, where a remodeling was begun a little earlier (1514) than at Chambord. Although the portion of the château at Blois built between 1514 and 1524, known as the wing of François I, still had the verticalism, pitched roof, and irregular contours of Gothic architecture, its Renaissance

elements were conspicuous and sophisticated. The courtyard's monumental spiral stair (traditional in medieval castles) was encased in a pier system with pronounced moldings and powerful balustrades that expressed a genuine realization of the weight and monumentality of Classical buildings. The cross-mullioned windows and the simple pilaster strips defining the wall bays were also established Italian features. If one ignores the steep roof with its dormers and towers on the northwest facade, then the three-story loggia with its balustrade, freestanding columns, arcades, and pilasters is the closest that any French architecture had come to contemporary Bramantesque designs in Rome (the Cortile di S. Damaso at the Vatican, for example).

It is a simpler matter to introduce innovations into secular architecture than into churches, particularly Gothic churches in France. But when between 1528 and 1535 architect Hector Sohier built a new choir with ambulatory and radiating chapels for the fourteenth-century church of St.-Pierre in Caen (fig. 8-89), he produced a structure that expressed the synthesis of decorative Classical forms new to France and the Late Gothic design processes still in use in the first quarter of the sixteenth century. Pointed arches became round; tracery kept its elongated Gothic proportions but assumed Classical form; flying buttresses were pierced by oculi; finials were transformed into northern Italian candelabra; and pier buttresses were cut to resemble pilasters. The structure and the vaulting patterns of the interior were traditionally Gothic, and, apart from a few Italianate ornaments, the choir from the inside had a conventional Late Gothic (flamboyant) appearance. On the outside, however, Sohier could not resist bringing the building up-to-date with his spirited combination of old and new forms and his creative interpretation of Renaissance Classicism.

As there are a number of ways to interpret the coexistence of medieval and Classical tectonic as well as decorative elements in sixteenth-century architecture in France, an attempt to define the character of French Renaissance architecture, especially church architecture, takes us beyond the notion of mere "intermingling" or synthesis. In contrast to the church in Caen, for example, St.-Eustache in Paris was begun in the sixteenth century (1532) and did not need to accommodate itself to an already existing building (colorplate 55). Although its rib vaults

8-88   Staircase, Château at Blois. France. 1514–24

8-89   Hector Sohier. Choir, St.-Pierre. Caen. 1528–35

and flying buttresses, three-tiered elevation, double aisles and double ambulatory were based on French medieval prototypes, the "language" of its style was that of Classicism. Recent research has made clear, however, that the Classicism of St.-Eustache is not solely that of the Italian Renaissance as is typical of secular architecture in France. Instead, the articulation of its piers, its Corinthian capitals, round-headed arches and superimposed antique orders, among other details, also entail deliberate revivals and interpretive reinventions of portions of older, pre-flamboyant French ecclesiastical monuments—for example, those of the Burgundian Romanesque, as well as the High Gothic elevation—that had themselves drawn on surviving local antique structures for their Classical language.

The way deliberate commixtures in architecture in France during the Renaissance were eventually "homogenized" came about partly through the increasing influence of the architecture of cinquecento Rome over that of quattrocento northern Italy, and over Romanesque revivals. Around 1540, significant reverberations from the Roman High Renaissance were felt in France. The Classicism of Bramante and Raphael, the architectural designs of Peruzzi, the systems of the five orders, ancient architecture, and other subjects fundamental to the Renaissance of the cinquecento were transmitted to France through the illustrated treatise on architecture of Sebastiano Serlio and through the presence of Serlio himself in France. The emphasis on illustration over theory in Serlio's treatise, unlike the more abstract writings of Vitruvius, Alberti, and other theoreticians (increasingly studied in France at this time nonetheless), made it a practical tool for French architects and their patrons who could select from it, as from a pattern book, High Renaissance architectural

plans, designs, and devices with Serlio's own fanciful variations and interpolations. François I, impressed by Books Four and Three (first published in 1537 and 1540) of Serlio's seven-book treatise, called him to France to work at Fontainebleau. Little of Serlio's architecture in France survives, but the extant château of Ancy-le-Franc near Tonnerre, Burgundy, which he began in 1546, was an important monument for the transmission of Italian ideas. Milanese ornament had given way to plain surfaces and simple contours; the energy of Gothic linearism was subdued by the serenity that marked Classical structures. Gone too was the pierced openwork characteristic of the earlier phase of the French Renaissance, in favor of the denser massing and stronger volumes of Roman building.

Compared to the vitality of its predecessors, Ancy-le-Franc is a monotonous building. At this moment in the development of French Classicism, architecture in France was in danger of losing the brilliance and vigor bred into it by the complexities and intricacies of Gothic design methods, but it was "saved" by two extraordinary architects. Pierre Lescot and Philibert de l'Orme outdistanced all French predecessors and contemporaries in their comprehension of Classicism. Even more, the buildings they designed fused French and Italian traditions into a new and independent French Classicism that was not merely an imitation of the Italian models they admired but proposed a new national architecture. Lescot's major contribution was his facade in the Louvre's square court (on the south part of the west wing; fig. 8-90), begun in 1546 as part of a royal project to replace the west wing of the medieval palace with a modern building. In collaboration with sculptor Jean Goujon, Lescot produced a new ideal of French architecture that combined the old French tradi-

8-90 Pierre Lescot. Square court, Louvre. Paris. Begun 1546

and shadowy concavities of sixteenth-century Roman buildings. Lescot designed a structure far more buoyant, intricately layered, and opulently detailed than its muscular counterparts in Rome.

More than any other French architect of the Renaissance, Philibert de l'Orme, Lescot's contemporary, came closest to realizing the Italianate Classical ideal. For one thing, de l'Orme had actually studied in Italy; in Rome in the 1530s, following the Humanist example, he examined and measured the ancient buildings and wrote treatises on architecture which contained theory, practical information about building (de l'Orme came from a family of masons), and a proposal for a new French order to be added to the canonical Greco-Roman five. Those sections that remain of the Château d'Anet (figs. 8-91, 8-92) built by de l'Orme for the brilliant and powerful Diane de Poitiers, mistress of King Henri II, reveal it to be the herald of the great future of French Classicism. Neither the frontispiece (before 1550, now in the École des Beaux-Arts in Paris) with its extreme verticalism, nor the Entrance Gate (c. 1552, in situ) with its fanciful contours, could be mistaken for Italian, rather than French, architecture, but in both de l'Orme handled the orders with Italianate severity and simplicity. In the three tiers of the frontispiece, the Doric, Ionic, and Corinthian orders were superimposed in correct sequence, and the triumphal arch of the upper tier, with its high pedestals and huge prominent moldings, easily matched the grandeur of antique prototypes. The Entrance Gate also preserved Gothic height; it was put together with an imaginative combination of forms without reference to any previous program of architecture, but there was a new monumentality in the powerful volumes and in the severely plain surfaces that established the building's kinship with the forceful structures that Bramante introduced into early-sixteenth-century Rome. It was with the Chapel of Anet (1549–52), however, that de l'Orme really entered the full tide of Renaissance architecture. It was centrally planned and surmounted by a dome, the first circular church in France. In concept it owed much to the Italian Humanist theorists who had promoted the central-plan church as the ideal building of the Renaissance. The dome (to become a dominant aspect of seventeenth-century French architecture) appeared in France for the first time in the Chapel at Anet, its Pantheonic coffering and hemispherical form offering further testimony of de l'Orme's respect for the great exemplars of antique architecture. The interior of the Chapel is of particular interest, for it dramatically reflects the impact of de l'Orme's Roman sojourn: The canted corners, colossal order of fluted Corinthian pilasters framing two-tiered wall bays, and flanking barrel vaults between the piers were direct descendants of Bramante's system for the crossing piers at St. Peter's. In this small building all vestiges of the Gothic have been suppressed, displaced by a fully re-created Renaissance style. For better or worse, France found itself in the 1550s in possession of a national Renaissance architecture that replaced the much-cherished but now extinguished Gothic.

In Spain and in England, the story of a deeply ingrained but spent medieval style succumbing to a new Classicism followed much the same line as it did in France: first the coexistence of Gothic structure and Renaissance ornament, and eventually the formation of a new national Renaissance style. The Renaissance architecture of Spain, however, was a brief and seemingly unnatural interruption of a preferred building style

tions of château architecture with the new spirit of Classicism and, at the same time, satisfied the longing of the French to maintain the marriage of sculpture and architecture.

The familiar five-part facade of French châteaux is preserved by Lescot at the Louvre, but he has expressed it in the idiom of the Italian palace of the cinquecento. The central and end bays are singled out from the rest of the fabric by their forward projection and their extension above the upper cornice of the top story, but these units bear little resemblance to the massive cylindrical and pinnacled turrets of their medieval ancestors. They do not protrude above the top of the roof, are quadrangular in shape, and are clad in the mantle of antiquity—stately pairs of fluted half-columns with Corinthian capitals on two stories and curved pediments on the upper tier (an attic story that replaces the customary dormer windows cut into the roofs of French buildings). The two sections of the building, joined in the second plane of the three "pavilions," are articulated by standard Roman High Renaissance features: on the ground floor, an arcade with Corinthian pilasters; on the piano nobile, windows with consecutive segmental and triangular pediments. They are executed, however, with emphases that are particularly French. The proportions of the orders are not Classical; the narrowness and elongation of the windows attest to their Gothic ancestry. Vertical elements prevail, but because of the prominent stringcourses Lescot's Louvre was certainly more "horizontal" than any contemporary French building. He kept the French pitched roof, but modified its height. Above all, his facade is unmistakably French because of its avoidance of the heavy volumes, unadorned orders,

8-91 Philibert de l'Orme. Entrance Gate, Château d'Anet. Eure-et-Loir. c. 1552

8-92 Chapel interior, Château d'Anet. 1549–52. (After du Cerceau)

that, largely because of its Islamic heritage, favored surfaces completely overlaid with energetic and elaborate ornamental interlacings. That style was best expressed not by the ordered intellectualism of the Renaissance but by the tension and emotionalism of Gothic and Baroque.

Spanish Renaissance architecture was launched in the early sixteenth century with a style known as Plateresque—a word that refers to the opulent and intricately carved designs of silversmiths. In keeping with Spanish taste for rich ornament, it prevailed until about 1550. Large-scale stone buildings were lavishly covered by clusters of carved ornament made of an eclectic mixture of interlaces, arabesques, and motifs taken from Gothic, Moorish, and Italian Renaissance sources. Italian Renaissance motifs had been transmitted into Spain primarily through sculpture, in the work of Italian sculptors who were imported to carve tombs and altars, and through the tombs carved in Italy for wealthy Spanish patrons and then sent to Spain. Plateresque was uniquely Spanish, yet even while it flourished during the 1520s its supremacy was challenged by a few brilliant examples of a very different kind of architecture, one that was closely allied to the majestic, but simple, forms of the Italian High Renaissance. The unfinished palace of Charles V (fig. 8-93) at Granada, begun by Pedro Machuca in 1526, was designed with the architecture of Bramante and Raphael in mind. Its round courtyard, which evokes the circular vestibule designed by Raphael for the Villa Madama, has

8-93 Pedro Machuca. Courtyard, Palace of Charles V. Granada. 1526–68

8-94   Juan Bautista de Toledo and Juan de Herrera. Escorial. Madrid. 1563–82

superposed, unadorned Doric and Ionic columns carrying simple entablatures. Compared to Plateresque examples, it has a purity and chasteness bordering on austerity. Machuca had been in Italy as late as 1520 and could therefore translate with relative ease the grand forms of the Renaissance into a clear and direct Spanish architecture, which contrasted sharply with the tortuous complexities of the Plateresque.

The starkness that Machuca, along with his contemporary Diego de Siloe, introduced into Spanish architecture was the dominant feature of the Escorial (fig. 8-94)—the extraordinary building that epitomized Spain's architecture after mid-century and was Philip II's monument to posterity. Philip's architects were Juan Bautista de Toledo and, after Toledo's death in 1567, Juan de Herrera. Both architects knew Italy, and Toledo had practiced architecture there. He designed the Escorial, thirty miles northwest of Madrid, as an enormous rectangular precinct enclosing a royal palace, a monastery, and a church. The cornerstone was laid in 1563, and the complex finished in 1584. The period of its construction corresponded to the years of the Catholic Reform after the Council of Trent, and the building's astonishing severity and sobriety were indicative of both the religious spirit of Spain and of Philip II's own fervent Catholicism. His was a strict, ascetic faith, reflected in the Escorial's unadorned facades, rigid rectangular layout of

spaces, and square towers marking each of the four corners of the building. The major responsibility for the church design was Herrera's, and it reflected the earlier plans of Toledo and Italian Renaissance prototypes. Neither the Renaissance character of the Escorial, nor its stark austerity were enduring; the Spanish temperament was too remote from Classicism and rationalism, its aesthetic penchant for Plateresque too powerful to support a mature Classical style. The severe style of the Escorial reverted, in the Baroque period, to the freedom and ornamental exuberance of Plateresque. From then on, Spanish architecture found its most brilliant expression not in the cultural centers of the homeland, but far away in the American colonies.

In sixteenth-century England, as in Spain, Renaissance style was not comfortably accommodated. The history of Classicism in English architecture begins in the seventeenth century with Inigo Jones, who created the English Renaissance through his love of Palladio. There are a few sixteenth-century examples of great country houses of the landed gentry, which, like the châteaux of the Loire Valley, absorbed aspects of Italian design. Once Classicism did take firm hold in England, however, it dominated architecture for centuries. Although they started late, English architects led the field with their skill—indeed, genius—in creating the most universal translations of the Classical language of architecture.

9-1
Gianlorenzo
Bernini.
Cathedra
Petri,
St. Peter's.
Rome.
1657–66

Chapter Nine | The Baroque

In the seventeenth century Renaissance architecture was propelled toward a brilliant new and international phase—the Baroque (with a Rococo sequel in the eighteenth century)—by the spiritual, political, and cultural upheavals promulgated by the Counter-Reformation and the Council of Trent (1545–63). Unlike that of the predominantly Italian sixteenth century, the architecture of the new era materialized not just in Italy but in France, Germany, Austria and central Europe, Russia, England, and Spain, and even stretched as far as the New World.

In Catholic Europe it reflected an optimism arising from the victory over the Protestant Reformation. A strong defensive fight on the part of the Church and, in the decades at Trent, a dynamic effort to establish its own programmatic reform of the abuses that had been developing since the thirteenth century resulted in a reconstructed clergy and a reaffirmation of Catholic piety. The rift with powerful countries that had embraced Protestantism—Holland, England, and most of Germany—remained permanent, but centralized papal power was restored by the early part of the seventeenth century. In the remaining Catholic countries a powerful national Church, at least nominally supported by the state, was established. Spiritual values that supposedly existed before the decline of the Church (a decline widely believed to have begun with Renaissance Humanism and its interest in "pagan" culture) were reinforced. Not the least of the Church's weapons in sustaining a spiritual renewal were paintings, statues, buildings, and oratories that stirred worshipers and moved them to seek the rewards of faith. It is no coincidence that not only the visual arts but also drama and music reached new heights in the intensified spiritual climate of the period.

If it was a time of spiritual resurgence, it was also a time of great physical splendor. Works of art were often vast in size and lavish in nature. Artists were asked to satisfy a burgeoning taste for magnificence by creating complex and spectacular programs in which architecture, sculpture, painting, decoration, and urbanism were fused. In politics, ambitions were equally grandiose; it was in the seventeenth century—especially in the France of Louis XIV—that art became the instrument of monarchical absolutism and was created almost exclusively for the goals and the extravagant tastes and pleasures of the religious and political aristocracy.

Yet for all the success of its reform activities in the face of Protestant rebellion and of its restoration of Catholic piety, the Church in the seventeenth century found itself confronted not only by a shrinking of its authority in relation to the expanding ambitions of the governments of secular states, but also by a new threat just as grave as those of the Reformation and of nationalism, and one which it was even less equipped to combat: the growth of science. This was the century of Galileo, Newton, and Kepler—the "century of genius" as it is often called—when a new rational world was being born, no longer dependent on metaphysical, Scholastic thought, or on the mysteries of the supernatural. We have seen how this process had begun in the Renaissance with its concentration on mathematical science and the revelation of God through the ordered geometry of the universe. But just as Christian doctrine and the idea of divinity had not been abandoned during the Renaissance despite its rational and Humanist views of man and nature, neither were they abandoned during the Scientific Revolution of the seventeenth century. They had to contend, however, with increased inquiries, new theories about the heavenly bodies (now seen through a telescope), and a strong interest in the control of nature through humankind's scientific knowledge. Galileo's investigations were repudiated by the Church because they confuted traditional Scholastic thought about the structure of the universe on which Church doctrine was founded. The seventeenth century learned that the earth was no longer the center of the universe but just one of the celestial bodies made up of particles of matter in motion, and it was Kepler's discovery that heavenly bodies moved not in circular paths, as had always been believed, but in elliptical orbits. While the influence of the Catholic Church on the art of the period was profound, so was the influence of the theories of the new science, often in conflict with religion. The theory of motion, it has been said, was the keystone to seventeenth-century science; it was both exuberant motion and exalted spirituality that gave to much of Baroque art its distinctive nature.

BAROQUE IN ITALY

It is fitting to begin our examination of the international character of seventeenth-century Baroque architecture with buildings of late-sixteenth-century Italy for two reasons: First, it was in Rome that commissions for buildings from the papacy and from high officials of the Church were plentiful, intended not only to bestow enduring glory upon the patron, but also to draw attention to Rome as the center of revitalized Catholicism and as the most richly endowed and historically important city in Christendom; and second, Baroque as a style in architecture evolved from two diverse aspects of Roman sixteenth-century architecture—the High Renaissance translations of antiquity by Bramante and Raphael before 1520 and, more directly, the Roman buildings of Michelangelo and Vignola of the 1550s and sixties and the interpretation of those works by younger architects such as Giacomo della Porta. Michelangelo's

9-2 Giacomo della Porta. Facade, Il Gesù. Rome. 1575–84

radical, sculptor's concept of architecture as something living was the stepping stone to the dynamic, expressive aspects of Baroque buildings; and it was Vignola whose oval forms first gave Renaissance architecture a fluid, directional character and whose Church of the Gesù, designed to conform to new doctrines about worship, became the foundation of Counter-Reformation church style.

At the peak of its development (1630–60s), Roman Baroque architecture was dramatic in effect and majestic in form, but its beginnings were subtle. Buildings that forecast the change are difficult to distinguish from their predecessors. In few places is this clearer than in the facade (1575–84) designed by Giacomo della Porta for Vignola's Gesù (fig. 9-2). Vignola had built a longitudinal church with an open, aisleless, barrel-vaulted interior, free of the columns, aisles, chancel, and other units that cluttered or fragmented the space of the nave, distracting worshipers and separating them from pulpit and altar. Even though he produced several facade plans, his patron, Cardinal Alessandro Farnese, found none of them satisfactory. While the cardinal had strongly supported, in 1568, Vignola's plan for the interior, he astutely recognized that the facade projects submitted several years later by the aging architect did not reflect a new dynamic spirit. He chose instead the facade design by the younger and more progressive Giacomo della Porta, an architect whose reputation was based on his successful completion of several of Michelangelo's architectural projects after the death of the master in 1564. The wisdom of the cardinal's decision in each instance was attested by the far-reaching impact of both the facade and the interior on church design in Italy and elsewhere in the wake of Counter-Reformational zeal.

Della Porta's facade had some novel effects compared to two-story Renaissance churches in Rome with their regular intervals and bays of equal "weight": The entrance bay became a strong visual center because the volume of the orders increased as they "moved" from the corners toward the center. On the lower tier, the terminal paired pilasters were transformed into two and a half pilasters (the "half" is a pilaster strip) in the next bay, and the cornice was pushed forward to contribute to the increased "emphasis." In the next stepped-forward bay the order became a pilaster and a half-column frame for the entrance portal, set into a bay projecting even farther forward. Above the portal rose a semicircular pediment, a richly sculptured coat of arms, a double pediment, an aedicula window with still another pediment, and finally a second coat of arms. The rhythmically built, formally accented facade "informs" the worshiper that the entrance to the sanctuary, the first step toward the union with God at the altar, is the building's most important exterior attribute.

By stressing one direction, by concentrating on the middle axis and its vertical ascent, by affirming the sculptural drama of the columnar forms, della Porta broke the hold that sublime Renaissance equilibrium and parity had on architecture. Along with the compelling forward movement of the nave, the facade represented a new "psychology" of architecture in which the church was oriented to the worshiper. In the fifteenth century, buildings by and large were abstract and self-contained; they had their own inner logic, and their quadratic walls enclosed motionless compartments of space. Bramante, in the early sixteenth century, turned inert masses of masonry into organic forms by the action of space, but it was only with Michelangelo's radical architecture, which took on aspects of human anatomy and human emotional forces, that some kind of psychological response was elicited from the observer. It was the combination of Michelangelo's dynamic forms and the forceful designs of the worship-oriented Gesù that formed the strongest bridge from Renaissance to Baroque architectural style as the sixteenth century drew to a close.

The Meaning of Baroque. The term "Baroque," like "Gothic," was first used disparagingly to describe, from a later point of view, a style of art and architecture that departed from a Classical norm. There is some argument about the etymological origin of the word—perhaps from the Portuguese *barocco*, describing pearls of irregular shape—but it is clear that it referred to aspects of seventeenth-century Italian art that, in relation to Classicism, seemed bizarre, grotesque, and irregular. Eventually it served as a convenient umbrella under which to gather a variety of international styles that flourished in Europe from around 1600 to the middle of the eighteenth century. It included not only chronological subdivisions such as Early, High, and Late Baroque, but also the special French variant referred to as Classical Baroque or Baroque Classicism, and the new style of Rococo that arose in France around 1700 partly in opposition to the Baroque style that preceded it. In this chapter the term is used primarily to refer to the art and architecture of the seventeenth century. It is also used, for convenience, as an adjective to describe the art of Italy in that period, in distinction to seventeenth-century French Classicism. Rococo, also originally a hostile term coined after the fact (thought to be a combination of *rocaille*, referring to shellwork and stonework decoration used in grottoes, and *barocco*), refers to the new style created in France at the beginning of the eighteenth century and that was displaced by the next style-era—Neoclassicism.

The history of Baroque architecture, like that of the Renaissance, can be recounted as a history of individual personalities.

Carlo Maderno. It was often the case that the distinctive character of Roman Baroque architecture was most effectively realized in church facades that were added to older buildings. Certainly one of the most expressive examples of the vitality of early Baroque architecture in Rome is Carlo Maderno's facade of Sta. Susanna (1597–1603; fig. 9-3). Founded in the eighth or ninth century, Sta. Susanna had been enlarged and rebuilt in the thirteenth; it was this church that Maderno was commissioned by Cardinal Girolamo Rusticucci, titular cardinal of the church, to remodel once again, and he did so by using as a point of departure della Porta's Gesù. Kindred features are the two levels separated by a narrow mezzanine, an upper pedimented story flanked by volutes, the crowning units of the central portal contained within the mezzanine, and the entrance as an accented feature in a boldly inflected lower story. Sta. Susanna, however, is taller and narrower than the Gesù and its vertical thrust is more compressed and therefore more forceful than that of its model: The steps are narrowed, the central bay is squeezed forward on both tiers, the volutes are contracted, and there is a high-relief emphasis on the center. More often, and with more energy than in the Gesù, the planes of Sta. Susanna move forward; the entrance portal fills the center bay completely. Columns protrude almost far enough to stand free, their capitals tied together by the high-relief decoration of the wall surfaces. The kind of movement created by the cavities and excurvations of Sta. Susanna's vigorous surface displaced the cool equipoise of Renaissance buildings; furthermore, the clarity of Maderno's composition supplanted the ambiguities and complexities of late-sixteenth-century architecture.

Maderno was born in northern Italy, near Lake Lugano, far from the remains of ancient Roman architecture and their powerful impact, and he was schooled in the regional preference for decorated surfaces and sculpturally enriched architecture. Once in Rome, exposed to the potent effect of the ruined monuments, he synthesized both traditions so successfully that he satisfied the hopes of his patrons for an architecture that would be sumptuous and exciting but, at the same time, would remain undisputedly Roman and discernibly Classical, clearly identified with the Christian and ancient history of the city. He dominated the first generation of Baroque architects in Rome. In the same year (1603) that Sta. Susanna was completed, Maderno was named chief architect at St. Peter's. In 1606, the nave of the fourth-century Constantinian St. Peter's—still standing over consecrated ground—was finally destroyed, and in 1607 Maderno began the construction of a long processional nave with majestic facade where the old nave had been.

The project constituted a crucial revision of the Bramante-Michelangelo Greek cross plan for the great basilica in which the four arms were of equal length. Construction of St. Peter's had been under way for exactly a century. In 1506, Julius II and Bramante had launched their project for a church that would

9-3   Carlo Maderno. Facade, Sta. Susanna. Rome. 1597–1603

symbolize a new Rome; a hundred years later this monumental structure had survived the many architectural campaigns to which it had been subjected as a fabric of astonishing unity, though still incomplete. Michelangelo, during the middle decades of the sixteenth century (beginning in 1546), had given the church a new cohesiveness by demolishing the decentralizing and complicated additions of his predecessor, Antonio da Sangallo. In the late 1580s and early 1590s, the huge dome of St. Peter's, and its minor domes, were completed by Giacomo della Porta in a way that translated Michelangelo's language into the Baroque idiom already initiated by him with the vigor of his own architecture and of his painting and sculpture as well. At the beginning of the seventeenth century, when Renaissance conflicts about architectural form and liturgical function, about central and longitudinal plans, had been resolved, it fell to Maderno as "architect to St. Peter's" to lengthen the eastern arm of the church, and to design a facade (colorplate 58) that would include a balcony for papal benedictions.

Respecting the facade scheme that Michelangelo had originally designed, Maderno began with a pedimented columnar porch—the temple front esteemed by Renaissance architects—as a center, and in the new way first devised by della Porta for the Jesuits and developed by himself at Sta. Susanna, he built up hierarchically toward that center from the extremities by increasing the volume and rhythm of the gigantic membering with each step. A bell tower was proposed for each end of the facade. Much of St. Peter's dome is hidden by the facade—an insoluble problem caused by the length of the nave. Maderno extended the already immense width of the church front by one more bay at each side to support the towers, and made this massing appear less dense by cutting arched openings into the lower tier of the bays. The tower plan did not survive (although later, under Bernini, it was revived), but Maderno's lateral substructures remained.

Maderno's work on the nave and facade of St. Peter's was carried out from 1607 to 1615. At the time of his death in 1629, he was the most authoritative exponent of the new, dynamic architectural style of the early Baroque. In the generation that followed, three master architects—Gianlorenzo Bernini, Francesco Borromini, and Pietro da Cortona—brought (each in his own highly idiosyncratic way) Baroque architecture in Rome to its "High" phase, comprising roughly the 1630s through the 1660s, when Roman building reached a level of sophistication, boldness, and inventiveness that has marked that era as one of the supreme moments in the history of architecture. But it was not only in architecture that this zenith was reached; it occurred in all the visual arts, and in music. Frequently the various arts were combined to create splendid ensembles and to share and play off against each other's special qualities. The separate ideological compartments for each art built on the foundations of Renaissance theory were now dissolved by a thirst for the dazzling effects that a fusion of the arts could produce. Pictorial elements such as light and shade were transferred to sculpture and architecture; rich color was imparted to architecture and to music, musical resonance to painting, sculptural form to architecture, and so forth. The results were spectacular and theatrical: Artists did not hesitate to use the devices of stagecraft—concealed lighting, curtains painted or even carved from richly chromatic marble—and to use illusionism to heighten the dramatic impact of their works. For the spectator, religious emotion was enhanced or even generated by art, and churches and chapels became theaters where dramas of miraculous visions, heroic martyrdoms, and the history of Christianity were enacted. Art was made to serve the Church, as it had during the Middle Ages, by encouraging the faithful to cling to the promise of salvation that the Catholic Church claimed it alone could offer. More religious buildings were built than ever before in Christian history. It was an assertion of the confidence of the Catholic Church in the endurance of its restored strength. By the third decade of the seventeenth century, a period of immense creative accomplishment was under way, and no artist exemplified so perfectly the plentiful talent and emotional excitement manifested in all the arts in that period as did Gianlorenzo Bernini.

Gianlorenzo Bernini. Bernini, whose artistic genius revealed itself in early childhood, was born in Naples in 1598, the son of a Florentine sculptor. He was equally brilliant as a sculptor, architect, and theatrical designer; his work gave to Rome much of the dynamic quality that still characterizes the city, and it is powerful enough to stand side by side with the great ancient monuments without being diminished. Just as Maderno best represented the early phase of Baroque architecture in Rome, the High Roman Baroque owes its spirit to Bernini. In harmony with his abundant gifts, his versatility, and his culture were Bernini's ebullient personality, his easy grace, and his ability to get along with the powerful papal aristocrats who were his patrons. Baroque Rome was a joint creation: the urbanistic-political-dynastic ambitions of Urban VIII Barberini or Alexander VII Chigi to create a new world capital of culture were given shape by Bernini's art. Almost all his working life was spent in Rome carrying out grandiose papal programs, but his fame was so widespread that he was summoned to Paris by Louis XIV to transform the Louvre into a palace appropriate for the Sun King (one of the few ill-fated commissions of Bernini's career).

Bernini and Architecture as Theater. Bernini's talent was so multifaceted that he was capable of creating works of art that varied immensely in both form and expressive content. When producing sculpture, for example, or some of his decorative ensembles such as the interior of St. Peter's, he could be exuberant, even flamboyant. When designing architecture alone he could create works of austere grandeur. At least two strains were reflected in this versatility—Classicism and "architecture as theater"—and they both became important components of Roman Baroque style. In the facade of the small church of Sta. Bibiana (fig. 9-4), a commission given to Bernini in 1624 by Pope Urban VIII, his Classical side predominates. His transformation of the exterior of the old church (first built in the fifth century and restored in the thirteenth) is so sober and traditionally Classical that at first the results appear not substantially different from the High Renaissance designs of Bramante and Raphael of the early sixteenth century. Despite the fact that the building follows by two decades the construction of the facades of Maderno's Sta. Susanna and St. Peter's, it is devoid of rich capitals, columns, sculpture, and the rhythmic movements and rippling volumes that gave to the great structures of the early years of the century the excitement of a new language. The architectural vocabulary is one of extreme

9-4   Gianlorenzo Bernini. Facade, Sta. Bibiana. Rome. 1624

clarity and simplicity (even austerity), with its straight moldings, rectilinear shapes, and perfectly balanced upper and lower stories with bays of equal dimensions. Yet with all this, the effect of Sta. Bibiana is markedly different from that of a Renaissance church because its very austerity is highly dramatic. Similarly, Bernini framed his Classicizing circular, domed church of Sta. Maria dell'Assunzione in Ariccia (near Rome) of 1662—his homage to the Pantheon—with curving facades of exceptional severity, yet the effect of the setting alone was nothing if not theatrical. His instinct for "architecture as theater" determined the appearance of S. Andrea al Quirinale (1658–70; figs. 9-5, 9-6), an elliptical church with the short axis stressed by the entrance with altar opposite. Across this space the visitor is confronted by a compelling vision of a marble figure of cloudborne Saint Andrew ascending to heaven through the altar's split pediment. Colored marbles, gilding, and rays of light accompany the exciting vision and enhance the tonal richness of the interior of the building, but the architectural membering is disciplined and noble. The Classical restraint of the interior architecture is carried outside to S. Andrea's novel facade. This facade is among the most prophetic architectural conceptions of the period, with its colonnaded porch swinging away in a vigorous convex arc above a platform of shallow steps that repeat the curve in a series of widening arcs. Above the

9-6   Facade, S. Andrea al Quirinale

9-5   Gianlorenzo Bernini. Interior, S. Andrea al Quirinale. Rome. 1658–70

frieze, a segmental pediment, intensely sculptural in nature, breaks in the center to frame a giant coat of arms. The fluid forms of this pediment offer a rich contrast to the disciplined articulation of the facade and anticipate the design of the interior altar niche with which it is aligned.

Despite its Classical vocabulary, the scenographic facade of S. Andrea is absolutely new in conception and original in design. Compared with it, the facades of the Gesù, Sta. Susanna, and even St. Peter's can all be perceived as part of a phenomenon that belongs to the Renaissance of the sixteenth century. They may represent the final manifestation of that phenomenon, but they are still conceptually late Renaissance facades—architectonic and thoroughly integrated with the mass of the wall behind. Bernini's bold concept of the protruding curve, sculptured pediment, and scenographic wings for S. Andrea was a giant leap forward into a new Baroque world of "effects," of "interpenetrations," of "movement," and of "showmanship," all of which were held in light harness by the conventions of Renaissance Classicism. Controlling the way a monument should be viewed—majestically framed and set apart from its surroundings—was for Bernini an integral part of the planning process (his design for S. Andrea a telling example), and in this respect he is indebted to the ideas of Alberti, Bramante, and other Renaissance forerunners, who proposed as theory or carried out in practice various systems—platforms, spacious piazzas, framing colonnades, shaped precincts—to emphasize or dramatize the singular character of a building.

Bernini's consummate performance as a visionary, "theatrical" artist (he was also a playwright and a stage designer) is the chapel he designed in Sta. Maria della Vittoria (1645–52) for the Cornaro family (fig. 9-7) in which he depicted a mystical vision experienced by the great Counter-Reformation saint Theresa of Avila. The Cornaro Chapel is one of the most dynamic multimedia complexes in Roman Baroque art, and represents a powerful fusion of sculpture, architecture, painting, and stagecraft. Against the richly chromatic marble wall above the altar of the shallow chapel, Bernini built an oval aedicula niche crowned by a curved, broken pediment and framed by paired columns set obliquely (to improve the sight lines). The niche, through its convex curve projecting into the observer's space like the porch of S. Andrea al Quirinale, serves as a stage on which the ecstatic moment when the heart of Saint Theresa is to be pierced by the arrow of divine love is illusionistically revealed by the carved marble figures of saint and angel. On the lateral walls of the chapel as if in boxes at a theater, marble relief figures of an "audience," the cardinals of the Cornaro family, discuss and meditate on the miraculous revelation they confront. Bernini painted the upper walls and the ceiling of the chapel above the forceful entabla-

9-7 Gianlorenzo Bernini. The Cornaro Chapel, Sta. Maria della Vittoria. Rome. (18th-century painting. Museum, Schwerin)

ture to represent a radiant heaven; he conjured billowing clouds out of stucco, and he even used sunlight, which enters from a window above the entablature, to enhance the illusion of celestial light.

Bernini at St. Peter's. If there is one monument in which both the theatrical and the Classical sides of Bernini come together on the grandest possible scale, it is the basilica of St. Peter's. Bernini had begun work on the St. Peter's Baldacchino (fig. 9-8), the colossal canopy that marked the tomb of the Prince of Apostles at the crossing of the church, in 1624, just in the same years that the austere Sta. Bibiana was under construction. It marked the beginning of Bernini's almost sixty-year association with the church that symbolized the spiritual heart of the Western Christian world. He was appointed architect of St. Peter's following Maderno's death in 1629, but from 1623 until his death in 1680 Bernini was at work in one way or another on planning the interior, adding to the exterior, and creating sculptural and architectural ensembles for the basilica. Although they stretch over a period of six decades, Bernini's varied works for St. Peter's can be discussed together, for they were conceived as parts of a unified design in which he amalgamated the visual arts in all media to create one gigantic, focused, theatrical tableau in which the Baroque drama of inspired religion could be acted out with magnificent effect.

At the exterior precinct of St. Peter's we confront Bernini at once at his most dramatic and most grandly austere. When Maderno's facade was completed in 1615, the area in front of the church remained an amorphous stretch of ground. Adjacent to the church was an aggregate of papal buildings—palace, library, administrative offices—serving different functions and lacking order and unity. The accession to the papal throne of Alexander VII Chigi (reigned 1655–67) was the impetus for a series of ambitious urban projects to renovate the tangled core of the old city, which had not been affected by the first modernization of Rome undertaken by Pope Sixtus V in the sixteenth century and restricted to areas outside the center. Enlisting the talents of his favored architects, Bernini and Pietro da Cortona, Alexander attacked several key locations, the improvement of which, he postulated, would not only solve the hopeless congestion (pedestrian and coach) of Roman traffic but would also bring the credit for their new openness and beauty, their regularity and convenience, to the Pope himself. He was determined to make a coherent system out of the Vatican area, to join together in a rational manner the church and the auxiliary buildings, and to relate them to the area in front of the church. In 1656, Bernini devised the immense oval enclosure, its axis running transversally, parallel to the expansive facade of the building, and formed by a stone forest of simple but gigantic columns four rows deep (figs. 9-9, 9-10). (In scale and sweep its only rivals were the great Imperial Fora.) The Colonnade was joined to the area immediately before the facade by two long corridors running from the outer edges of the facade to the piazza, forming a trapezoidal space that "tightened" the expanse of the facade and directed the pilgrim to the main portal.

Aside from shaping and organizing a vast expanse of space, Bernini's piazza served as a stage for ceremonial papal processions and as an "auditorium" for the multitudes who came to witness those ceremonies, to worship in the church, and to be present for the papal benediction delivered at Easter and on

9-8
Gianlorenzo
Bernini.
Baldacchino,
St. Peter's.
Rome. 1624

other special days from Maderno's Benediction Loggia above the entrance to the basilica. It was also a place from which to observe papal appearances on the balcony of the Vatican Palace apartments. Ingeniously, the transversal orientation of the oval took in with its sweep the miscellany of Vatican buildings fringing the basilica on the north and integrated them with the piazza and the church, while the three aisles of the colonnade served as roadways for carriages and sidewalks for pedestrians and protected visitors from sun or inclement weather. The piazza had one significant antecedent: the first-century A.D. Colosseum was also an oval amphitheater, and it, too, had been a place for spectacles and crowds.

9-9 Air view, St. Peter's and piazza. Rome

Bernini's choice of the oval form was of paramount importance. The circle was the preferred geometric shape for the early and High Renaissance because in its ideal form and completeness, in its purity and equipoise, it was believed to refer to divine perfection and to correspond to a universal order. In the seventeenth century, however, the dynamic and kinesthetic qualities of the oval form (already realized in a number of sixteenth-century church plans) were preferred to the stasis of the circle. Movement, accent, and energy replaced Renaissance balance because they corresponded to the emotional currents with which Baroque art was charged. It is not irrelevant that in 1609 one of the many remarkable scientific discoveries of the century was made—Kepler's first law of planetary motion—

proving the shape of each planet's orbit to be an ellipse, with the sun at one focus. That the piazza should be given an elliptical form while the Church vigorously opposed the astronomer's threat to the traditional picture of a fixed universe is one of the ironies of the history of this period. Just as the longitudinal church with its directed axial focus had won out over the imperturbable centralized church of the Renaissance, so the ellipse with its dominant axis and inherent motion suitably supplanted the nonaxial equilibrium of circular forms. Nowhere is this more dramatically realized than at Bernini's piazza for St. Peter's.

The two corridors that lead away from the edges of the church facade follow the incline of the terrain to join the curve of the elliptical colonnade and create the "keyhole" figuration of the piazza, making the area one of the world's most astounding architectural sites. Its size alone accounts for much of its impressiveness. Four rows of simple and majestic Doric columns—300 all together—carved from Roman travertine form an oval 650 feet across the long axis, marked by three monuments: laterally by fountains propelling tall jets of water and in the center by an Egyptian obelisk that had served as a turning post in the chariot races at the ancient Circus of Nero. As they enter the piazza, the faithful are embraced by "the motherly arms of the church," Bernini's own description of his Colonnade. The Colonnade becomes simultaneously a dramatic frame for the church, a nurturing enclosure for the crowds of faithful, and a stage for the processions and other sacred spectacles on which, at this particular period, the Catholic Church so strongly depended for its appeal.

Effective though it may be in eliciting an emotional response from the spectator, the architectural language of the Colonnade is restrained, even sober, and illustrates the most reserved side of Bernini—Bernini as Classicist. Inside St. Peter's, however, it is Bernini as impresario, as grand decorator of Baroque ensembles, and as visual and theatrical interpreter of Christian history and papal doctrine that dominates. His talent for coordinating architecture and sculpture, illusion and reality, imagery and iconography, for conceiving remarkable combinations of color and material, and for the carving of vibrant, impassioned marble figures yielded potent theatrical and spiritual effects. The crossing of the church is a huge volume of space articulated by the dome and the four renowned piers surviving from the Bramante design. In the center of the crossing, above the tomb of St. Peter and the high altar, stands Bernini's spectacular gilt and bronze Baldacchino (fig. 9-8) of 1624 (his interpretation of the original Early Christian monument, with four spiral columns of marble that marked the shrine). Bernini planned the area of the crossing in 1627–29 as one grand visual and conceptual unity to be focused on the four most important relics in the church. In the upper niche of each of the four piers is a reliquary, designed by Bernini and executed between 1633 and 1641, composed of spiral columns and a curved entablature with segmental arch above; between the columns is a relief of the relic. Each lower niche holds a huge statue of the saint appropriate to the relic (the figure of Saint Longinus, for example, and the relic of the Lance with which he pierced the side of Christ), and the four statues are

9-10 Gianlorenzo Bernini. Colonnade, Piazza of St. Peter's. Rome. 1656

united through pose, gesture, and style. Thematically and stylistically they tighten the already integrated program of the crossing. And as the focus of this vast but cohesive sculptural-architectural-spatial entity stands the Baldacchino.

Bernini planned the decoration of the crossing during the reign (1623–44) of Pope Urban VIII Barberini, and so the Baldacchino is embellished with emblems of the Barberini family; and it was Urban VIII who made possible (partly by out-and-out theft from ancient monuments such as the portico of the Pantheon) the immense amount of bronze needed for the construction of the gigantic canopy. Spiral columns, entwined by vines of laurel (a Barberini emblem), support a deep entablature from which a simulated tasseled canopy appears to be suspended, and above which rises an open superstructure of S-curved diagonal ribs joined at the top to form a base for the crowning Orb and Cross. So completely, and in a fashion so original, has Bernini synthesized Baroque artistic ideals that sculpture and architecture have fused, and the Baldacchino defies classification as one or the other, its hard bronze material appearing to be transformed variously into cloth, wood, vines, leaves, and flesh. With its vigorous outlines, the richness of its surface, and the massiveness of its dimensions (appropriate to the scale of the church) the Baldacchino stands as a quintessential Baroque monument. All the overwhelming impressions of the interior of the basilica are anchored by its authoritative presence.

Prodigious as it is, the Baldacchino cannot—nor for that matter can the piazza or the crossing of St. Peter's—justly be considered as a thing apart. Like the rest, it is but one unit in a spectacular series of interlocking shapes, materials, spaces, and icons, forged by Bernini into a carefully orchestrated program, intended to provide the visitor with the opportunity not only to observe and meditate on images of Christianity, but to experience physically and to participate in an extraordinary process through which the concept of the Church Triumphant is revealed step by step.

The scheme begins a good distance from the basilica, at Ponte S. Angelo (fig. 9-11), in the seventeenth century the only bridge across the Tiber to lead to St. Peter's and for which Bernini designed (and assistants carved in 1667–71) ten huge figures of angels carrying the symbols of Christ's Passion. The expressions, the postures, and especially the dynamic patterns of the drapery of these figures encouraged the pilgrim as he crossed the bridge and helped guide him toward the church. Between the bridge and St. Peter's lay a maze of narrow streets that at one turn impeded and at another gave access to what would be the startling first view of the expanse of the piazza. Bernini's original plan (never executed) included a third colonnaded arm across the entrance to the piazza, creating yet another suspense-building obstacle between the viewer and the immense space. Even so, it was a dazzling experience for the traveler emerging from the dark labyrinth of surrounding streets to confront at last the openness of the piazza, the gigantic enframing colonnades with their larger-than-life-size statues above the balustrade of the roof, and ultimately St. Peter's facade. (The experience can be had even today, if the visitor approaches not from the center but from the streets to the side.)

Baroque planning was perfected by Bernini in his St. Peter's scheme: The visitor was beckoned forward by the angels on the bridge, embraced by the arms of the oval, directed to the facade by the trapezoidal shape of the space before it, drawn to the main portal by its emphatic centrality. Inside the building, the dynamic sequences increased in intensity: the awesome nave, the gigantic canopy marking the saint's tomb and the papal altar, the message of the reliquary program of the crossing, and—visible all along the great length of the nave through the spiral columns of the Baldacchino—a shining object fixed against the farthest apse. This gilt-bronze reliquary enclosing

9-11 Ponte S. Angelo and Tiber. Rome

9-12 Gianlorenzo Bernini. Scala Regia, Vatican Palace, Rome, 1663–66

the original Bishop's Chair of St. Peter—the Cathedra Petri carried by the Fathers of the Church—was the visual and the spiritual climax of the pilgrim's journey. Like his Baldacchino and Cornaro Chapel, Bernini's Cathedra Petri (1657–66) is architecture, sculpture, and painting fused into an amazing vision (fig. 9-1). As the visitor approached from the nave, the great dome opened above him, the crossing statues enfolded him, and the whole dynamic sequence of spatial and visual sensations culminated before the apparition of a cloud-supported relic of Christ's first bishop. From the point of view of art history, the Cathedra Petri, with its explosive contours framed by the spiral outlines of the Baldacchino, is one of the most effective images created by Bernini. It had a powerful influence on architecture, sculpture, and decoration in countries outside of Italy, especially Germany.

Bernini's program for piazza and church extended to integrating them with the adjacent Vatican Palace, location of the papal apartments and receptions halls, by means of a newly designed grand staircase known as the Scala Regia (fig. 9-12). Narrow, dark, and dangerous to navigate until refashioned by Bernini between 1663 and 1666, the Scala Regia as the principal link between St. Peter's and the palace required an architectural importance and grandeur commensurate with its function. Bernini made the landing at the bottom of the main flight of steps a continuation of the vestibule of the church and

dramatically accented this connection with his equestrian statue (1671) of Constantine's Vision of the Cross. He defined the entrance to the stair with the image of a triumphal arch made by two rows of Ionic columns flanking a tunnel vault, and then, ingeniously employing a system of perspective illusion, diminished in height the columns and side walls, narrowed both the space between the columns and the width of the stair, and lowered the height of the vault to give the visitor the impression of greater length and monumentality than in reality were there. Windows at the half-landing and top produced islands of light in the dark vault; a 180-degree turn led the visitor to the upper flight and the entrance to the palace.

Bernini and Palace Architecture. Finally, because Bernini understood so well the ambitions and tastes of seventeenth-century Roman aristocrats, he reinvented palace design in a way that reflected contemporary standards of magnificence. Beginning in 1664 he built for Cardinal Flavio Chigi a palace facade (fig. 9-13) of regal and commanding character, inspired by his simultaneous planning of Louis XIV's Louvre. (It was enlarged in the eighteenth century when it became the property of the Odescalchi family and is known today as the Palazzo Chigi-Odescalchi.) Bernini coupled the upper two stories with a grand march of giant pilasters that trace their origins to Michelangelo's Capitoline palaces. The emphatic central section, with its framed portal, balconied window, and coat of arms, was by this time a familiar sequence in palace architecture, originally devised in the sixteenth century by Michelangelo for the facade of the Palazzo Farnese. The Palazzo Farnese system of an uninterrupted run of pedimented windows had prevailed in Roman palace building for more than a century until Bernini displaced it with the radical articulation of the Palazzo Chigi.

Francesco Borromini. During all the stages of his long and brilliant life Bernini managed to accommodate easily both the vibrancy of his theatrical side and the stateliness of his Classical side. It is not as simple to categorize Francesco Borromini, Bernini's contemporary, who was no less important to the development and diffusion of Baroque style, but whose temperament and career were very different. He was reclusive, neurotic, and tragically ended his life with suicide. Borromini

9-13 Gianlorenzo Bernini. Palazzo Chigi-Odescalchi. Rome. Begun 1664

had come to Rome in 1619 from northern Italy, like della Porta and Maderno (his uncle) before him. He was a highly skilled stonecarver and architectural draftsman, and he worked in the St. Peter's shop first for Maderno and then for Bernini. Eventually he became one of Bernini's chief assistants (many of the details of the Baldacchino have been attributed to him). In 1634, Borromini's opportunity to demonstrate his own extraordinary talent came with his first independent architectural commission: to build for the new Spanish order of the Discalced Trinitarians the church of S. Carlo alle Quattro Fontane (called S. Carlino because of its small size; figs. 9-14–9-17). The interior was constructed in 1638–39, the facade begun more than twenty years later, in 1665; by 1667, the year of his death, Borromini had completed (without its sculpture) the lower story and had only just begun the upper tier.

S. Carlino's interior conformed to the growing penchant in the seventeenth century for oval designs and to Borromini's fascination with intricate geometrical exercises; besides, an oval plan was well suited to the church's small and narrow building site. Borromini oriented his S. Carlino oval longitudinally, that is, with the entrance at one tip and the high altar at the other (at S. Andrea, Bernini had arranged entrance and altar across the short axis of the oval) and, eschewing a uniform outline, except in the dome's base, between entrance and altar he squeezed the upper and lower extremities of the oval so that it took on an undulating contour, which he then extended to the elevation. He designed the walls to weave in and out as if they were formed not of stone but of a pliant substance set in motion by an energetic space, carrying with them the deep entablature, the cornices, moldings, and pediments. The novelty of the effect of this animated architecture is perhaps best appreciated when compared to the motionless space and stable walls of a Renaissance structure, or even to the buildings of Bernini (S. Andrea for one) where it is still the walls that shape the space and not vice versa. The transformation by Borromini of architectural space into an active rather than a passive entity (already anticipated in the Renaissance by Bramante and Michelangelo) was to become one of the most salient features of later seventeenth- and eighteenth-century architectural design.

Borromini's expressive new manner was in striking contrast to Bernini's majestic, controlled Classicism. But it was not simply their different temperaments that accounted for a dissimilarity in the architectural vision of the two men; it was also the difference in their response to ancient and Renaissance sources. Although much of seventeenth-century Roman building had more to do with Michelangelo as a source than with

antiquity, Bernini and Borromini continued to find inspiration in the ancient monuments. But the archetypes preferred by Bernini were the great Roman "classics" among the Classical monuments—the staid, dense fabrics (exemplified by the Pantheon) studied and interpreted before him by Alberti and Palladio, Bramante and Raphael, and then by Bernini himself. Borromini, on the other hand, had an affinity for the more "baroque" structures of late Imperial architecture—the fluid forms and shapes of Hadrian's Villa (fig. 3-82), the play of curves in the small Temple of Venus at Baalbek (fig. 3-55), and

9-15   Interior, S. Carlo alle Quattro Fontane

9-16   Facade, S. Carlo alle Quattro Fontane. Begun 1665

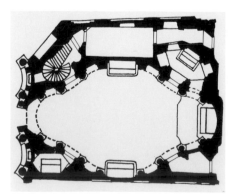

9-14
Francesco Borromini.
Plan, S. Carlo alle
Quattro Fontane.
Rome. 1638–39

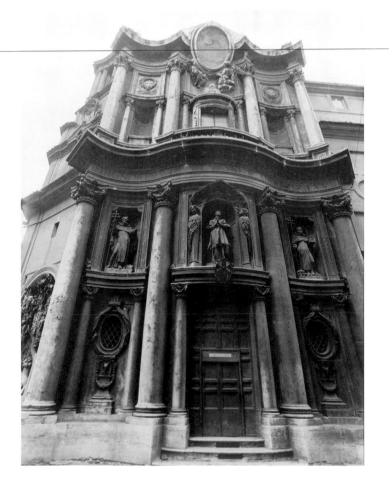

9-17 Dome interior, S. Carlo alle Quattro Fontane

Borromini's S. Carlino facade was a "showpiece"—architecture turned into theater—but unlike the theatricalism of Bernini, which was based on a fusion of all the arts, Borromini's bravura effects were achieved by means of the architecture alone. Undulating walls and complex geometric shapes are also characteristic of his other works, such as S. Ivo della Sapienza (figs. 9-18–9-20), built on an extraordinary plan—a star made by a pair of intersecting triangles—between 1643 and 1648 (consecrated in 1660) at the northern end of the long Renaissance courtyard of the old university of Rome. The wide two-story concavity of the lower facade was built between 1594 and 1597 not by Borromini but by Giacomo della Porta as the front of a church of his own. Rising above it are the lobules of Borromini's drum supporting the singular lantern that is described as "being of almost oriental exoticism." Illuminated by six large windows set above a simple, wide entablature that reproduces the intricate shape of the groundplan, the interior is one space, its plan a six-pointed star with three points terminating in convex forms and the other three in semicircular lobes. Beyond the entablature lies the smaller circular ring of the lantern base, and uniting these perimeters are radiating spokes formed by the angles of the dome wall that carry to a climax the vertical impulse begun by the colossal folded pilasters below.

9-18 Francesco Borromini. Detail of dome exterior, S. Ivo della Sapienza. Rome. 1643–48

the exaggerated movements and ungrammatical combinations in the architecture of far-flung regions such as North Africa and Asia Minor. It is known that Borromini had reconstruction drawings of late Roman architecture in distant places, and these help to explain the uncommon shapes of his buildings.

Due to a lack of funds, the facade of S. Carlino was begun more than two decades after the interior was completed. Borromini carried the flexuous motion of the interior walls to the facade, creating as unorthodox a church exterior as Rome had seen. Three bays separated by engaged columns billow in and out in a concave-convex-concave pattern on the lower level; a cornice that swings with the rhythm of the lower bays divides the first and second stories; in the center bay of the upper story is a bulging aedicule that has been likened to a sentry-box; and at the crest, a double-curved pediment (an alteration of Borromini's design by his nephew, who finished the work) is transformed into a flamelike fantasy of its former conventional triangular shape. Like Michelangelo, whom he admired, Borromini allowed himself unprecedented freedom in dealing with the orders, manipulating them as if they were pieces of sculpture; indeed, the articulation on the S. Carlino facade is an idiosyncratic transposition of Michelangelo's Capitoline system, with its trabeated bays edged with lower columns beneath a closed upper story, flanked by a colossal order.

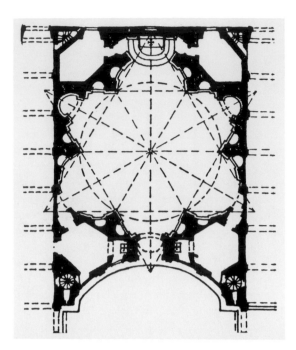

9-20 Dome interior, S. Ivo

9-21 Francesco Borromini. Interior, Oratory of S. Filippo Neri. Rome. 1637–40

(1637–40; fig. 9-21) Borromini designed large windows for the greatest possible luminosity, and he arranged loggias and galleries either to perforate or be visible beyond the defining walls of the room. He constructed, for the spaces past the twin porticoes, false ceilings pierced by ovals with hidden windows beyond so that a diffused radiance was visible through the openings. The overall effect was one of openness and light, of pierced walls and dissolving boundaries.

Guarino Guarini. While Borromini's inventions were crucial for Baroque and Rococo architecture in northern Italy, and even more so for the architecture in countries north of the Alps such as Austria and Germany where they were embraced with great enthusiasm, in Rome they were not taken up. The architects of the next generations in Rome looked more to Bernini and to conventional Classical systems of the Renaissance and Baroque than to Borromini. In the north, however, those aspects of Borromini's style—the openness, the light to emphasize space, the dematerialized mass, the intricate geometrical schemes, and the verticalism—were adopted with alacrity probably because they were reminiscent of the breathtaking effects of Gothic architecture. It was the very absence of "correctness," of respect for the canons of Classicism, that commended the architecture of Borromini to regions where the Classical tradition had a tenuous rather than a resolute hold. This was the case in the Piedmont, in the city of Turin, where the first regional translations of Borromini's architectural formulae were made by Guarino Guarini. He was not only an architect but a mathematician, philosopher, and priest (of the

Borromini's ingenious moving surfaces, flexible forms, and intricate geometry had a far-reaching impact on the future of architecture, and so did the spatial fluidity and the luminosity of his church interiors. His was a light, bright, open architecture that was a vivid contrast to the heavy, closed forms of contemporary Roman buildings, which recalled the monumental nature of ancient structures. For the Oratory of S. Filippo Neri

9-22   Guarino Guarini. Dome interior, S. Lorenzo. Turin. 1668–87

9-23   Guarino Guarini. Dome exterior, Cappella SS. Sindone. Turin. 1667–90

9-24   Dome interior, Cappella SS. Sindone

Theatine Order). He shared Borromini's passion for intricate geometric calculations, which Guarini applied with great ingenuity to the design of church domes, designs that effectively altered the traditional idea of a dome as a clearly defined bubble of space enclosed within a solid wall. A Guarini dome, such as the one in his Church of S. Lorenzo (fig. 9-22) in Turin (1668–87), becomes a luminous cage of slender intersecting ribs over which floats the light-filled space of the lantern visible through the complex rib network; the base of the dome is a circle, and the base of the buoyant lantern is formed by eight semicircular lobes, each framed by a pair of splayed ribs. This extraordinary configuration of space, light, and mass has been described by a Guarini scholar as "a great work of hallucinatory engineering."

Built almost simultaneously with S. Lorenzo, Guarini's other Torinese church, Cappella SS. Sindone (1667–90; figs. 9-23, 9-24) with its famous relic of the Holy Shroud, is also crowned by an exceptional cupola of pointed profile. The complexity of its structure is mirrored in the three levels of the exterior: First, immense windows in the drum (source of the interior brightness) terminate in a Guarinesque version of Borromini's serpentine cornice at S. Carlino; next, between finialed buttresses zigzag moldings reflect the interlocking hexagonal ribs of the interior surface; finally, windows for additional light, surmounted by a pagodalike lantern with oval windows on each of its narrowing layers. The view into the dome from below reveals a realm of soaring height and brilliant luminescence in which float kaleidoscopic images of circles, semicir-

cles, and diminishing hexagons that cut across corners as they rise to the star-shaped base of the lantern. This concept makes clear that it was more than mathematics and the designs of Borromini that inspired Guarini's geometrically complex vaulting systems; here, too, is the influence of Moorish buildings of Sicily (which he knew because he had worked in Messina), with their dazzling interplay of intersecting ribs derived from Islamic architecture.

Baldassare Longhena. Islam, Sicily, and Borromini were a heady combination for seventeenth-century Turin, and Guarini's visionary structures introduced a welcome note of exoticism to a city architecturally drab but receptive to the excitement of the theatrical side of Baroque art. Exoticism was hardly alien to Venice, however, and the boldness and drama of Baroque buildings were not destined to have significant reverberations in a city that already had its share of rich architecture. But Venice did produce one Baroque church by a native Venetian architect, Baldassare Longhena, which belongs unequivocally in the canon of great Italian buildings of the seventeenth century. Sta. Maria della Salute (fig. 9-25) was designed in 1631–32 (not completed until 1682) as an ex-voto to the Virgin for her deliverance of Venice from an outbreak of plague in 1630. It is situated majestically at the entrance to the Grand Canal and is one of the most distinctive silhouettes of the Venetian skyline. Longhena drew upon two powerful architectural traditions of the Venice region in designing the church. For the plan, he looked to the Byzantine octagon with ambulatory of S. Vitale in Ravenna (fig. 4-35) and, for the elevation, to Palladio's giant orders and semicircular triadic Roman bath windows. It is a compact, central-plan, high-domed structure, its main entrance raised on a stepped, hexagonal platform at the edge of the canal. The exterior is richly articulated by statuary, huge buttressing

9-25 Baldassare Longhena. Sta. Maria della Salute. Venice. Designed 1631–32

volutes, and a series of seven facades. Inside, six rectangular chapels, each with its own pedimented facade, open at the ends of the cross-axes of the octagon; opposite the entrance is a separate space, formed as a domed square with two flanking semicircular lobes, where the main altar and its sculptured tableau of the Blessed Virgin driving the plague from Venice are seen immediately and dramatically from the entrance.

From the outside, Sta. Maria della Salute looks its most "baroque," and it is often described as resembling a gigantic sculptured lantern. Yet Longhena had a specific symbol in mind for the powerful contour of his church: The dedication of the building to the Virgin suggested to him the image of a crown for the Virgin as the Queen of Heaven. The voluptuous curves of the building (the "crown") are held in check by the straight lines, right angles, and geometry of the Classical pedimented facades and by the simple mass of the dome.

By following Borromini's influence on Guarini in Turin, and in looking briefly at Venice, we have been temporarily distracted from following the developments in mainstream Baroque architecture in Rome. There the fluid, virtuosic fantasies of Borromini remained unique, while the more conservative (with respect to ancient and Renaissance traditions) manner of Bernini, and his contemporary Pietro da Cortona, dominated.

Pietro da Cortona. Pietro da Cortona, like Bernini, was multitalented, equally gifted as architect, painter-decorator, and sculpture designer. A stonemason's son, he was born in Cortona (Tuscany) in 1596 and first apprenticed as a painter in Florence. In Rome he attracted the high-level patronage of the circle of Cardinal Francesco Barberini, nephew of Pope Urban VIII, and eventually of the Pope himself. Cortona's first important building was SS. Luca e Martina (begun 1635; figs. 9-26, 9-27), which in the Rome of the 1630s and forties (before the impact of Borromini) was exceptional for the curve of the center section of wall on both stories of its facade—a curve that reflected the apsed end of the arm of the Greek cross plan behind it—and for the rich forms of the escutcheon, borne by paired figures, instead of a traditional pediment. The swelling wall between the lateral piers was a marked departure from the sober facades of Maderno's St. Peter's or Bernini's Sta. Bibiana. As a painter and decorator, Cortona was interested in creating impressive effects in architecture; furthermore, he was indebted to Michelangelo for the vitality of the facade of SS. Luca e Martina. In Baroque fashion, the highly sculptural columns and pilasters are spread across the whole extent of the building; they are aggressive and muscular, moving in upon and squeezing the oval frames of the upper reliefs, the niches below, and the portal, so that pediments, like those of Michelangelo in the Laurentian Library, overlap the framing members.

Along with Bernini, Cortona was a favorite architect of Pope Alexander VII. The role of the popes in reshaping Rome through architecture and urban planning to regain its status as the political and cultural capital of the world is one of the most important chapters in the history of the era that began with Julius II in the early sixteenth century. It was a wish ultimately associated with papal ambitions for self-glorification, for the continual reinforcement of the idea of the sovereign authority of the Church above all, and, in the seventeenth century, for the need to challenge the new national capitals that were threatening to rival the supremacy of Rome. Alexander VII

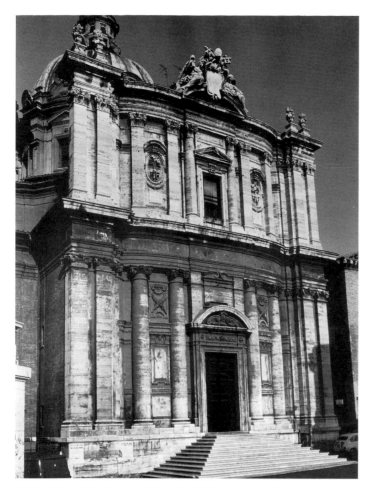

9-26   Pietro da Cortona. Facade, SS. Luca e Martina, Rome. Begun 1635

9-27   Interior, SS. Luca e Martina

was one of the most active of the papal "urbanists," and at his behest Cortona designed in 1656–57 a facade for the church of Sta. Maria della Pace (fig. 9-28) as one of the Pope's ambitious projects for redesigning Rome. Often cited as the paradigm of Roman Baroque style at mid-century, the facade was made for an older, undistinguished church located in one of the densest sections of Rome. Alexander was eager to turn this project into

an opportunity to modernize the city—to convert a narrow, ordinary street into a spacious, shaped piazza that would accommodate the cumbersome coach traffic that was choking Rome's thoroughfares. Such a piazza would also scenographically set off the new facade of the church. To realize his ambition, he had the approaching street broadened and a wide polygonal piazza formed. Intruding houses that fringed the area were reduced in size, refaced, and turned into the articulated lateral wings—a concave nest, in effect—that framed the upper facade of the church at the same time that they emphasized the extraordinary forward thrust of the lower narthex. The most striking impact of Sta. Maria della Pace, however, came as much from the grandeur of its forms as from its theatrical setting. Few buildings could match the power of those four pairs of severe Tuscan columns resting on a curved stylobate, recalling the noble image of Bramante's Tempietto. The wall surface devoid of sculpture and the crisp, rectilinear shapes of the upper story suggest that Cortona had curbed his earlier bent for rich ornament. In the two decades since he designed SS. Luca e Martina, the preferred mode of expression had become a Berninian theatricalism under the tight control of Classicism, the latter reinforced by Alexander VII's enthusiasm for the antiquities of Rome. The increasing austerity of Cortona's style (continuing in his works of the 1660s) was true of the drift of Roman architecture in general in the 1650s and sixties, but it was not the direction followed by the ever unconventional Borromini.

Carlo Rainaldi, Carlo Fontana, and Classicism in the Later Seventeenth Century. From the beginning of the century through the 1660s Roman building had been dominated by four great architects—Maderno, Bernini, Borromini, and Pietro da Cortona. In the decades that followed, some of the early vitality that had brought Baroque architecture into being and sustained it ebbed away. Replacing it was a severe and authoritative approach to building, such as that expressed in the impressive church of Sta. Maria in Campitelli (designed 1658; built in 1663–67) by Carlo Rainaldi. Like Sta. Maria della Salute in Venice, it too was an ex-voto to the Virgin for halting

9-29 Facade designed by Maderno and Rainaldi, S. Andrea della Valle. Rome. 1661–65

a fierce epidemic of plague. The grandeur of the aedicular facade is created by the combined effect of its pronounced vertical extension through two equally developed stories, reaching to a powerful compound pediment above the upper story, and its constraints on any horizontal expansion. The volutes, for example, are reduced to mere slender ribbons. The facade is devoid of niches, sculptured figures, and ornamental relief; the wall is plain, and the dominant elements are the huge scale and severe, monumental quality of the freestanding columnar order.

The facade of S. Andrea della Valle (fig. 9-29) exemplifies the High Baroque Classicism of Rainaldi in the 1660s—a ponderous sculptural style founded on powerful forms, plentiful columns, pronounced verticalism, and massive proportions. Designed originally by Maderno, the church front had reached only as far as the pedestals of the lower order at the time of his death in 1629. Between 1661 and 1665 Rainaldi, probably with the assistance of Carlo Fontana, brought to completion an imposing facade of immense height crowned by a massive pediment in layered planes with sharp edges. The columns are arranged in pairs, each set framing a tabernacle niche, the entrance portal, and the large upper window. Although it lacks the magisterial severity of some of his other works, S. Andrea della Valle bears the mark of Rainaldi's authoritative manner and is one of the major Roman church facades of the second half of the seventeenth century.

From this survey of monuments it is evident that seventeenth-century Roman architecture was replete with "approaches" to Classicism, from the reverent but vivacious reinterpretations of Bernini to the imperious monumentalism of Rainaldi. Even Borromini's wanton nonconformity constitutes an attitude toward Classicism in the sense that it underscored his

emancipation from rules and from determined formalism. The academic, late Baroque Classicism of Carlo Fontana was still another interpretation. Born in northern Italy, near Como, Fontana came to Rome before 1655 and worked at the core of High Baroque style in his role as assistant draftsman to Bernini, Cortona, and Rainaldi, before embarking on an independent and highly successful career as architect and engineer. In his church of S. Marcello al Corso (1682–83; fig. 9-30), Fontana employs the language of established Baroque practice with a new exactitude, discipline, and fidelity to rules of correspondence and proportion based not only on the antique but also on antecedents in the High Renaissance. Although the orders cluster around the aedicula of the central bay, they lack vitality because of the precision with which they correspond to the pilasters behind and above, and because of the rigorously determined dimensions of the wall projections that they articulate. Fontana was an extremely influential architect, with a large following among the next generation in Rome and with important students such as James Gibbs and Fischer von Erlach, who were later to make significant contributions to the development of Baroque architecture in their own countries, in England and in Austria. It was not in the seventeenth-century Italy of Fontana, however, that academic Classicism, purism, and discipline were given their most serious expression, but in seventeenth-century France.

9-30 Carlo Fontana. Facade, S. Marcello al Corso. Rome. 1682–83

Eighteenth-Century Architecture in Rome. Many architects other than those singled out here were kept busy in Rome during the seventeenth century, building great numbers of churches ("they sprang up like mushrooms," it was said), oratories, chapels, palaces, villas, to say nothing of their involvement in vast projects of urban restructuring. Not all the monuments they produced are noteworthy, but their sheer number and generally impressive size have given Rome its overwhelmingly Baroque character. By the eighteenth century, new architecture in Rome tended to follow either extreme Classicism on the one hand, or extreme theatricalism on the other. Alessandro Galilei's facade of S. Giovanni in Laterano (1732–36; fig. 9-31) is an example of eighteenth-century late Baroque Classicism. A competition for the facade had been announced by Pope Clement XII; it is easy to see how the commission was given to Galilei, for his noble design accords with the conservatism in architecture espoused by the Church in this period. He drew from the finest achievements of the sixteenth and seventeenth centuries, synthesizing Maderno's St. Peter's facade, Michelangelo's palaces on the Campidoglio, and Palladio's churches into a severe, highly disciplined facade of colossal scale that was meant to symbolize the international authority and power of the Church.

Among Rome's most appealing sites are two eighteenth-

9-32   Francesco de Sanctis. Spanish Steps. Rome. 1723–25

century city planning monuments famous for their exceptional theatricalism. The Spanish Steps (1723–25; fig. 9-32), designed by Francesco de Sanctis, link the Church of Trinità dei Monti with the Piazza di Spagna below (taking its name from the palace which housed the Spanish Embassy). One of the most effective plans for the expansion of Rome during the late Renaissance, and one that is often regarded as the beginning of modern city planning, was devised in 1585–90 by the powerful and visionary Pope Sixtus V. He cut through the pastures, fields, and thickets surrounding the core of the old city with a star pattern of wide, straight streets that linked the city's seven main churches. This scheme provided pilgrims with easy access to the shrines that had to be visited in one day, repopulated deserted areas, and imposed an orderly, rational system of circulation on the formless hilly terrain above the helter-skelter of the medieval city. (In the process, the Pope and his architect, Domenico Fontana, also restored the ancient columns of Trajan and Marcus Aurelius, but "Christianized" them by adding to their summits full standing figures of Saint Peter and Saint Paul respectively.) The hills of Rome had defeated Sixtus's ambition to join the churches in the upper and lower parts of the city, but in the eighteenth century they finally were connected, not by a Sistine street but by the colossal outdoor stairway that constitutes one of the most theatrical designs in the history of city planning. It conforms to the undulations of the natural terrain over which it is built and repeats them in a series of swinging curves. The Spanish Steps and balustrades move in and out with a dynamic energy that directly influences the movements of the visitor-participant. The design is based on a complex pattern of elliptical curves anchored at regular intervals by rectangular

9-31   Alessandro Galilei. Facade, S. Giovanni in Laterano. Rome. 1732–36

9-33　Nicola Salvi. Trevi Fountain. Rome. 1732–62

9-34　Filippo Juvarra. Air view, Stupinigi. Turin. 1729–33

9-35　Interior, Stupinigi

and trapezoidal forms. Few Baroque monuments can offer a more effective interaction of spectator and architecture than this stair, which serves not only as a tie between the upper and lower city, but also as a park and a villa garden, a place for strolling, resting, and viewing Rome.

Equally famous is the Fountain of Trevi (1732–62; fig. 9-33), designed by Nicola Salvi about a decade after the construction of the Spanish Steps. It is an extraordinary late Baroque synthesis of Classicism (an ancient triumphal arch set into the facade of a palace articulated by a giant order of pilasters), illusionism (stone cut to simulate layers of natural rock), and technology (hydraulic engineering to create the fountains, cascades, and pool). Titanic in size, it is also an extravagant Baroque fusion of architecture, sculpture, the painterly effects of light moving over water, and the sound of flowing water.

Eighteenth-Century Piedmont. Although eighteenth-century architecture in Rome was impressive, the true "golden age" of Roman Baroque had been the seventeenth century. After 1700, the center of the world of art and architecture shifted from Rome to Paris. Within Italy, the most remarkable feats in eighteenth-century building also took place far from Rome, in the regions of the north, particularly Piedmont and the city of Turin. Lacking significant artistic traditions of its own, Piedmont was forced to rely on artists from other places imported by the Savoy dukes to create a Piedmontese genre and style. We have already observed the exceptional buildings given to

seventeenth-century Turin by Guarino Guarini. Thirty years after Guarini's death, Vittorio Amedeo II, Duke of Savoy and King of Sicily, brought Sicilian Filippo Juvarra to Turin, then the capital city of the Kingdom of Piedmont. Juvarra, probably the most skillful and virtuosic architect of his time, was expected to provide—and did—an extraordinary number of palaces and royal residences, churches and chapels, appropriate

9-36　Filippo Juvarra. Superga. Turin. 1719–31

to the new wealth and splendor of the House of Savoy and its territory. From his earliest work for the king in 1716 it was clear that Juvarra had a masterful command of formal Classical and academic resources, acquired from his years of study in Rome in the workshop of Carlo Fontana. His great originality, however, lay in his ability to give to his architecture a remarkable quality of light and openness, a singular richness of decoration, and special theatrical effects. By using screening columns and large open areas of diffused luminosity he transformed traditional structures into unconventional, airy cages—pierced and filled with light—where the solid walls of the Renaissance appear to have been wondrously dissolved. Effects such as these prevailed at this period; they were the result of architectural cross-currents moving through Italy, France, Germany, and Austria that in the early eighteenth century provided Italy with a Rococo style of which Juvarra was the most skillful practitioner. The lodge at Stupinigi (1729–33; figs. 9-34, 9-35) for the royal family's hunting parties and *fêtes* is a remarkable example of Juvarra's inventive combining of academic Classicism with Rococo scenography. Four two-storied wings of immense scale, each containing two great rooms, are arranged in an X-pattern and open from a three-tiered oval salon. One long, curving side of the oval opens through tall glazed doors onto a stepped terrace; the other side, where the wings were extended to join additional pavilions that form the boundaries of a huge hexagonal garden court, also opens onto steps and a broad terrace. All around the palace are sweeping lawns and wooded fields. The splendor of the richly decorated interior walls, the aristocratic character of the whole ensemble, and the grand fusion of nature and architecture reflect the architectural message that Louis XIV's Versailles was spreading to all the royal courts of Europe. The theatrical spirit of Stupinigi—indeed, the drama of all of Juvarra's architecture— can be attributed to his early training as a stage designer and his understanding of the Piedmontese appreciation of the flourishes and fanfares that are part of courtly life.

In his ecclesiastical architecture, Juvarra worked with the same feeling for grandeur, theater, and nature. On a hill overlooking Turin stands his dramatic monastery complex constructed between 1719 and 1731. The Superga (fig. 9-36), the monastery church, was partially enclosed within the structure

of the sanctuary. The plan is an almost complete circle joined on one side to a rectangular choir area and on the other to a square colonnaded porch. Transept arms open where the circle and rectangle meet. Above the circle rises a majestic dome and lantern supported by a tall, windowed drum. The articulation of the exterior is an artful composite of seventeenth-century Roman themes derived from Michelangelo and Bernini, while the colonnaded pedimented porch recalls the Pantheon. Sober, Classical, academic, and Roman, the Superga is an illustration of Juvarra's thorough grasp of the essential features of seventeenth-century Roman Classical Baroque design. At the same time he has enriched them by his theatrical use of scale and light, and by his adoption of the most advanced concepts of architecture north of the Alps.

When Juvarra died in Spain in 1736, he left behind a talented pupil, Bernardo Vittone, the first native Piedmontese to become an important master of architecture in his own region. Vittone studied in Rome in 1731–32 before entering Juvarra's shop in Turin. Together, Juvarra and Vittone solidified the achievements of eighteenth-century Piedmontese architecture.

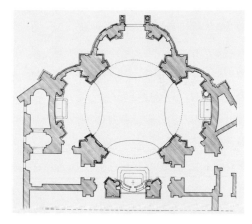

9-37
Bernardo Vittone.
Plan, Sta. Chiara.
Bra near Turin.
1742

9-38　Interior, Sta. Chiara

But Vittone, while absorbing much from the buildings of Juvarra, also studied with great care the work of Guarino Guarini, the earlier genius of Torinese architecture, and unified both styles in his own work, for example in his acclaimed church of Sta. Chiara in Bra, near Turin, of 1742 (figs. 9-37, 9-38). Vittone planned Sta. Chiara as a quadrilobe made by a circle intersected at four points by oval chapels, with four curved piers to support the dome. The reverse curve contour of the archivolt above each chapel entrance penetrates, with its heraldic crown, the balustrade of the bright and wide gallery at the second level. Above the central space stretches a dome perforated with rhythmically outlined openings, beyond which are glimpsed painted visions and a radiant luminosity. Adding to the height and light of the inside space, a fenestrated lantern rises over the central dome.

Vittone's brilliance at Sta. Chiara brought Italian Rococo architecture to the level of the Rococo structures of France, Germany, and Austria. He handled Rococo formulae with no less confidence than his counterparts to the north. He, too, could dissolve solid enclosures and replace them with fragile, open cages; he could design complex geometric figures and fluid interpenetrating shapes, and could ornament surfaces with stucco and paint in pastel shades and bathe them with direct and indirect light.

The Rococo came into being in France in the eighteenth century partly as a reaction to the weighty formality of seventeenth-century French Classical Baroque. In whatever country it appeared, at the core of Rococo architecture were the pliant surfaces, shaped spaces, and hidden light sources of Borromini, the theatrical illusionism of Bernini, and the visionary geometry of Guarini. But by the eighteenth century, Italian supremacy in architecture—indeed, in all the arts—having sustained itself for 500 years, had to give way to the vitality and creativity that emanated from France and central Europe. The emphasis shifted away from Italy as France became the world center of art and culture.

THE SEVENTEENTH CENTURY IN FRANCE

The Italian response to antiquity left a great deal of room for individuality and freedom of interpretation in architecture. In the Renaissance, even Vitruvian rules served as a guideline rather than as dogma. Italian Renaissance buildings were lively, independent reinterpretations of the past, based less on theory, archaeology, and history than on a sense of good design combined with Humanist ideas, and Italian Baroque architecture by and large continued this pragmatic tradition.

In France the approach was different. The seventeenth century is accurately described as the French national golden age of Classical architecture, but it was a Classicism of a formal purity, austerity, and discipline somewhat remote from the comparatively rugged and expressive versions of Italian Classicism. The explanation for the contrast goes back into the traditions of French architecture, to the structural logic on which the Gothic cathedrals were founded and to the rational processes that made possible the irrational effects of those buildings. This rational tradition, the theoretical underpinnings of the Gothic systems, became an integral part of the French attitude to architecture. It accounts for the receptivity of the French in the sixteenth century to Italian architectural treatises as, above all, a welcome source of theoretical knowledge, and as a codification of rules for the use of the orders—the most important rational system by which the proportions, harmonies, and correspondences of architecture were fixed.

In the seventeenth century, as French national culture began to develop along the same absolutist lines as the government, the inherent French affinity for logic and discipline was formalized into a coherent body of rules by which the arts and literature were governed in accordance with the spirit of the state. Academies for literature, for painting and sculpture, and for architecture were founded and guidelines for a genuine French Classicism, distinct from its seventeenth-century Italian Baroque counterpart, were established. The academies promoted the expression of a noble artistic style in which the dominant characteristics would be clarity, formal beauty, and dignity. Artistic production was controlled by rules and formulae, and the rules applied to literature and painting as well as to architecture. Just as it is possible to observe a particular proportional relation between the elements of an architectural order, so can we find, for example, a definite ratio between the number of scenes and the number of acts in the dramas of Corneille and Racine, leading Classical playwrights of the period. In architecture, it was a style that was especially suited to the formality and splendor of the period not only because the monuments were of a prescribed nobility and dignity, but also because they were enlarged to heroic size.

The formal, powerful effect of seventeenth-century French buildings can be attributed to the respect for reason and discipline codified in the academies. But a clear direction toward this goal was set long before the first academy was officially founded, when at the beginning of the century France was transforming itself from a country with a medieval, feudal form of government into a nation-state with its king as supreme royal power. Protestantism had found enough of a foothold in France during the sixteenth century through the reforming teaching and writing of Jean Calvin, one of Martin Luther's disciples, to plunge the country into a series of devastating civil wars of religion that began in the 1560s and dragged on for three decades. In 1589, Henry IV, a Bourbon (the royal family) and a Protestant, succeeded to the throne; in 1593, to secure the approval and loyalty of his people, he became a Catholic ("Paris is worth a mass"). With the help of his brilliant minister, Maximilien Sully, the king established a comparatively firm and authoritative government until his reign ended in 1610 with his assassination. His son and heir, Louis XIII, was only nine years old at the time of his father's death; administrative affairs were handled by the regent Queen Marie de' Medici; the country was set once again on a disastrous course. The political brilliance of Cardinal de Richelieu, one of the most illustrious statesmen in the history of France and Louis XIII's prime minister beginning in 1624, reversed the tide. The hundreds of small fiefdoms into which the country had been fragmented were consolidated into one nation. He saw to it that the king took over all the rights that formerly had belonged to the feudal nobility, and with those rights he built up a powerful central administration. Before his death in 1642, Richelieu saw his efforts succeed: The state had become sovereign, and France was on its way toward becoming the most important country in Europe. Louis XIII died a year after his minister and was followed on the throne by Louis XIV, whose long reign as the *grand monarque* was the consummation of the process by which the power of the state and the crown had become absolute.

Henry IV and City Planning. In matters of art, Italy's position remained unchallenged at the beginning of the seventeenth century while France was pursuing the policies that would after 1665 usurp even that position. During the first half of the sixteenth century French architecture had undergone a spirited development; it had consolidated various strains—its own national medieval tradition, new tastes that reflected an enthusiasm for Italian art, Italian craftsmanship, and Italian theoretical writing about architecture—into an integrated Renaissance style that was not a "transitional" composite but a wholly French concept of monumental building. After mid-century the expensive and debilitating religious wars inhibited any strong surge of architectural activity, and with a few exceptions (de l'Orme's Chapel at Anet, for example) little architecture of significance was produced in France during the last third of the sixteenth century. In the early seventeenth century, however, following the 1598 Edict of Nantes issued by Henry IV (granting Protestant privileges and officially supporting religious toleration) during his comparatively stable and well-organized reign, there were signs of change. Peace brought with it a revitalized enthusiasm for religion, church architecture was consequently sparked into life once again, and several urbanistic projects were undertaken, most of them continuations of plans unfulfilled during the troubles of the previous century.

To strengthen royal authority, it was the king's intention to develop Paris into an illustrious royal capital. He inaugurated a number of projects that included the widening of streets and the building of bridges and residential squares marked with symbols of royal patronage. The large, shaped city squares of Italy (with their reference to the ancient fora of Rome) were not known in France where the heavily populated cities were made of intersecting chains of narrow streets without the intervals provided by open spaces. The town square programs of Henry IV bestowed a completely new look on certain quarters of Paris, and they immediately acquired a special cachet because of their link to royalty and the court.

The Place des Vosges (fig. 9-39), Henry IV's most important contribution to the history of French architecture, was one of three "royal" squares planned during his reign as special settings for sculptured monuments of the monarch and as housing for the bourgeoisie. The earlier Place Dauphine (c. 1605), on the Île de la Cité, was triangular in shape to conform to the contour of the island in the Seine and was framed on its three sides by contiguous, identical, three-story private *hôtels* with uniform facades. Built soon after was Place des Vosges (1606–12). Known originally as Place Royale, the square furnished still-medieval Paris with a new spatial breadth and grandeur. Its regularity, large size (almost 500 feet square), and self-containment symbolized the serenity and organization that characterized the reign of Henry IV and distinguished it from the chaos of those that preceded it. The sides of the square were defined by uniform houses two stories above a ground-floor arcade, made of brick with stone quoins and with dormer windows beneath the tall, sloped, slate-covered roofs. Precisely opposite each other on the north and south sides, a pair of tall pavilions were built—one for the king and one for the queen—architecturally accenting the square and at the same time denoting it as a royal precinct. Place des Vosges served as a site for royal ceremonial displays and, in 1629, an equestrian statue of Louis XIII was placed in the center. Not only were the

9-39 **Place des Vosges. Paris. 1606–12. (17th-century engraving. Bibliothèque Nationale, Paris)**

geometric regularity of the plan and the uniformity of the framing facades in harmony with Classical principles of design, but the arch-and-pier system of the ground-floor loggie were also derived from the most Classical passages in Italian High Renaissance architecture. Already in the first decade of the seventeenth century, Henry IV's Place des Vosges forecast what would become a major theme of the century: a Classicism born of Italian Renaissance theory and practice but treated with the special discipline and rigor indigenous to French architecture since the Gothic period and expressed in majestic dimensions that symbolized the power of the monarch.

Salomon de Brosse. The Place des Vosges was not an isolated example of a new direction in French architecture in the first quarter of the seventeenth century; there were churches, palaces, and public buildings, principally works by Salomon de Brosse, who came from a family of distinguished architects and was the outstanding builder of the period. The power of his work temporarily swept away the lingering taste for the scattered, small-scale ornamental elements of French Renaissance architecture, which he replaced with heavy, unadorned, large-scale structures based on ordered systems. The most important church built in Paris at the time was de Brosse's St.-Gervais (1616), or more accurately his facade for St.-Gervais (fig. 9-40), for it was a late Gothic building to which he appended a new front. The forceful verticalism of his design was largely dictated by the building's Gothic origins, but de Brosse repudiated its medieval provenance by using strong Classical language and a highly visible rational organization. The articulation of the first story is a majestic series of paired Doric columns (the most "virile" of the orders) and a triangular pediment over a Doric frieze; above, three bays of a "triumphal arch" with the entablature pushed forward over each pair of Ionic columns correspond to the divisions of the lower level; the full third story is an independent aedicula of Corinthian columns beneath a segmental pediment with rectangular inset. Apart from two simple niches for life-size statues, there is no ornament. In its place de Brosse has stressed the sculpturesque strength of the columns and the clarity of the organization, important foundations for the architectural future of France.

9-40 Salomon de Brosse. Facade, St.-Gervais. Paris. 1616

The Luxembourg Palace (begun c. 1614), probably de Brosse's most renowned work, was built for Marie de' Medici, second wife of Henry IV, who came to Paris from Florence (her father was Francesco I, grand duke of Tuscany) with an enormous dowry. Unhappy with the French royal residence, the Palais du Louvre, and homesick for the Florentine ducal residence (Palazzo Pitti) in which she had grown up, she "ordered" a new palace. In plan, the Luxembourg Palace (colorplate 60) is conservative; it conforms to the standard French château type: a central block (*corps de logis*) joined by two wings to lateral pavilions (doubled here) with long corridors projecting from the pavilions to form the sides of a large court (*cour d'honneur*). The antecedent enclosed courtyard and five-part scheme were unexceptional, as were the steep roofs and tall chimneys; but the stonework and articulation were unusual in France and were derived from the vigorous rustication on the garden facade of the Florentine Palazzo Pitti. Engaged Doric columns were "stapled" to the wall with closely stacked tiers of masonry recalling the dense massing and monumental forms of the Italian Renaissance prototype, enlarged to seventeenth-century proportions.

French Classicism. In the decades of the 1640s and fifties, and beginning even earlier in the 1630s, the powerful Italianate cadences of de Brosse, and the more direct Roman High Baroque influences in France emanating from the celebrity of Bernini and Pietro da Cortona underwent a gradual process of transformation.

French architecture began to be refined in the direction of the severe academic anti-Baroque formalism it was to exemplify after 1665, in the works of three architects who designed for sophisticated patrons from the highest circles of the royal and ecclesiastical courts and for the king himself. Because the great architectural ensembles of the seventeenth century in both Italy and France were made almost exclusively for patrons at this level, they were monuments of heroic dimension and unrestrained luxury. All three architects—Jacques Lemercier, François Mansart, and Louis Le Vau—came from families in the building trades. Lemercier, the oldest, had studied architecture in Rome in the early part of the century when della Porta's facade of the Gesù and his dome for St. Peter's, and Maderno's facades for the great basilica and for Sta. Susanna, were vivid recent impressions. In France, he came to the attention of Richelieu and carried out a number of commissions for his distinguished patron, including the Palais Richelieu (today Palais Royal) and the Sorbonne (now the seat of several faculties of the University of Paris, then the seat of the theology faculty).

The church Lemercier designed for the Sorbonne (figs. 9-41, 9-42) is his most celebrated work. It was begun in 1635, more than twenty-five years after the architect's return from Rome, and in a climate of intense religiosity that stimulated the building and remodeling of many churches. The Gesù and St. Peter's, the most cogent symbols of the supremacy of the Church, were primary architectural exemplars for the French. Lemercier's Church of the Sorbonne reflects both of them: The west facade is in two stories joined by volutes placed above the side chapels in the manner of the Gesù. Heavy, muscular Corinthian columns, like Maderno's at St. Peter's, define the central section, and pilasters mark the receding lateral planes that represent the side chapel walls. The height of the nave is expressed in the upper story, crowned by a pediment across its full width. Rising high above the pediment is the graceful, narrow dome; it symbolizes the resolution of a natural conflict that arose when the French adopted architectural Classicism and its stress of the horizontal while sustaining their devotion to the soaring Gothic profiles of their architectural past. The compromise was to retain the vertical energy of the Gothic with uncommonly tall and slender domes while articulating the structure with Classical forms of exceptional purity and nobility. Because of its unusual height, the dome can be seen to advantage from both the east and the west; but it is most spectacular on the north where a temple portico, surmounted by a rectangular attic and hipped roof, level with the roof of the transept and much lower than the nave, reveals the tall drum and the bold thrust of the narrow cupola.

The founding of the first of the academies (this one primarily for literature) in 1635 coincided with the construction of the purest example of François Mansart's elegant classicism. For the château at Blois (fig. 9-43) belonging to the Duc d'Orléans, brother of Louis XIII, Mansart built a new central block (the Orléans wing). The clarity of its composition and its refined, "academic" restraint established a standard against which subsequent Classicizing styles would be measured. The building is given its dignity and precision by the regularity and even rhythm of the doubled orders on the three levels of the facade. Relief ornament is kept to a minimum, the surfaces are smooth, and the edges of the forms, which protrude from the wall with the greatest discretion, are crisp and sharp.

9-41　Jacques Lemercier. North facade, Church of the Sorbonne. Paris. Begun 1635

9-42　West facade, Church of the Sorbonne

9-43　Cross section of Grand Staircase, Château at Blois

A continuous pitched roof made with a double slope on all sides, the lower slope steeper and longer, known as a mansard roof (taking its name from the architect), unifies the upper portion of the block. With this monument, French classicism had taken its own clear and firm direction: It had moved away from the robust muscularity of Italian Baroque forms (made to seem even more three-dimensional in Italy when strong Mediterranean sun and shadow played over the surfaces) toward severe and simple massings, precision and elegance of detailing, and a cool intellectual character more suited to the "gray" tonalities of northern Europe.

More dramatic and "Baroque" than the reserved facade is the interior of Mansart's wing at Blois, where the salient feature is the grand staircase enclosure in the central pavilion. Encapsulated within the high slope of the mansard roof is a beautiful dome and lantern, revealed through an opening in the coved ceiling on the first floor. The stairs rise to the first floor only; above are the open ceiling, the gallery, and then the dome. Mansart's ingenious arrangement here recalls certain optical effects in the contemporary work of Borromini in Rome (in such buildings as the Oratory of S. Filippo Neri of the 1630s; fig. 9-21) where open galleries and luminous bodies of space were visible through perforated walls. Although Mansart's eloquent architectural language differed from that of the architects working in Italy in the first half of the seventeenth century, he shared their dramatic sense of space and light.

In 1632, three years before he began work at Blois, Mansart designed one of his most remarkable structures, the Church of Ste.-Marie de la Visitation (fig. 9-44) on the Rue St. Antoine in Paris. Before the seventeenth century, domed structures were uncommon in French architecture, but as soon as the dome had been "discovered" in the buildings of Italy (particularly the dome of St. Peter's), the French made it their own with amazing tenacity. It was not reposeful hemispherical Pantheonic domes that they adopted, but the soaring forms that rose and tapered into elaborate lanterns. Mansart's Church of the Visitation is nothing other than a dome from top to bottom. In plan, it is a large circle with a series of oval chapels elevated and reached by stairs that open off the central space. On the outside, the dramatic interior space is matched by heavy masses of stone and the exaggerated emphasis of each of the forms—the immense semicircular arch of the entrance portico with the sloping roof behind it, the weighty buttresses classically austere, the protruberant broken cornice, and the bulging cupola with its high window-pierced lantern. Unlike Lemercier, Mansart had never trained in Italy, but he knew Italian architecture and architectural books and treatises thoroughly, and admired the published illustrations of works by Palladio, Michelangelo, and Vignola. During the 1630s, Italian Baroque currents, although held in check, continued to have their effect on his work. His circular scheme for the Church of the Visitation was an attempt to construct in France a building referring to the centrally planned

churches of the Italian Renaissance but made more complex by the introduction of the oval shape.

Châteaux before Versailles. For political as well as artistic reasons, the most illustrious structure of seventeenth-century France was Louis XIV's Château at Versailles of the 1660s; indeed, the evolution of French château architecture can be plotted in relation to it, with earlier examples perceived as forerunners in the sense that their formal arrangements of pavilions, wings, gardens, terraces, and courtyards, and their rich interior decoration, were steps in the increasing stateliness and magnificence of aristocratic residences. Already at the Orléans wing at Blois, Mansart had forecast the commanding dignity of Versailles; almost a decade later, at his more complex Château of Maisons, begun in 1642 (figs. 9-45, 9-46), he perfected the symmetry of planning and clarity of articulation that would keep a structure as enormous as Versailles under control. The self-contained "town square" plan of earlier châteaux has been changed at Maisons. Formerly, a large central square courtyard would be framed by the main building block on one side and projecting wings joined by a balancing corridor on the other three. Mansart has set aside the *cour d'honneur* concept, freed the building from ancillary units, and made it an independent block—a monument in itself—open on all sides to its surroundings. In the block, the old French five-part scheme stressing center and farthest points has been retained, but Mansart has integrated the sections with a brilliant system of horizontal and vertical interpenetrations—for example, the entablature below the roof in the end pavilions has been stepped back to make the pilaster order of the second floor appear to rise to the aedicula of the dormer windows above. The balanced, prismatic masses of the entire structure are defined by crisp edges and sharp angles and are discreetly ornamented by precise and elegant detailing. The receding and projecting planes are under tight control, and the mansard roof of the upper story forms a neutral background against which the cubic geometry of pedimented windows is offset. The sculpturesque strength of the orders, characteristic of buildings where Italian Baroque influence is pronounced, has been suppressed here in favor of a refined articulation of the wall surface and the powerful volumes of the building masses. Large and complex though it is, Maisons is held in perfect equilibrium by the clarity and logic of its systems. Mansart's interest in the Baroque persisted, however, despite the stringent rectilinearity of the exterior of Maisons; hidden within the quadratic blocks of the wings are large rooms of oval shape.

If there is one building that can be regarded as a direct forerunner of Versailles (less for its architecture than for the circumstances surrounding its existence), it is the château of Vaux-le-Vicomte (1657–61; fig. 9-47), built for the king's Surintendant des Finances, Nicholas Fouquet. One of the wealthiest, most ambitious, and most extravagant patrons in France, Fouquet wanted his château to be second to none. To achieve his ambition, he hired a team of artists—painter and decorator Charles Le Brun, André Le Nôtre as landscape gardener, and architect Louis Le Vau, working together for the first time. Like Maisons, Vaux-le-Vicomte stood as a grand, independent monument unattached to secondary structures and not part of a courtyard enclosure. It was a curious combination of the traditional five-part design with an astonishing and novel shape for the central section—a huge oval covered

9-44   François Mansart. Ste.-Marie de la Visitation. Paris. 1632

9-45 François Mansart. Château of Maisons. 1642–46

9-46 Vestibule, Château of Maisons

by a dome and fronted, on the garden side, by a two-storied pedimented "temple," the main entrance to the château. A readjustment of the relationship of the sections of the block was necessary at Vaux, for the lateral pavilions needed extra weight and volume to balance the extraordinary protuberance of the domed oval. Compared to Lemercier and especially to Mansart, and the Classical restraint of the vocabulary and discreet overlapping of planes in their buildings, the work of Le Vau had exhibited worrisome "baroque" tendencies. He was susceptible to the extravagant curves, moving walls, and shaped spaces of the Italian High Baroque that were regarded

with disapproval by French academicians. But Le Vau recognized that only a facade charged with all the drama of the Baroque could match the gardens designed for Vaux by Le Nôtre, gardens so spectacular that they incited the envy of Louis XIV, who was determined to outdo them at Versailles. On the interior, Le Brun, even more attuned than Le Vau to Roman High Baroque currents, designed the vaults of the oval salon with a system of stucco-framed paintings (never executed) as animated and richly conceived as the decorative ensembles of Pictro da Cortona for the great palaces of Italy.

The French Garden. In the seventeenth century, the garden in France became a work of art almost equal in importance to architecture. Its origins go back to the late fifteenth century when the French fascination with Italian art, architecture, decoration, and other of life's embellishments led to the importation into France of Italian objects and skilled craftsmen. Included were gardeners, who were asked to re-create for the aristocratic châteaux the geometric formalities of the Italian garden. The new gardens in France retained the basic Italian system of a square format divided into smaller squares, but in the course of the sixteenth century they underwent a significant transformation in size—increasing so that they might have covered an area five or six times larger than the château itself. There were also revisions in design: Flower beds with co-ordinated color patterns became ever more important and were set out in intricate configurations derived from embroidery work (*parterres de broderie*); small squares became large; and, most significant, the organizing principle was no longer simply squares within a square but a total composition—including the house—unified by a symmetrical axial network binding the parts together.

It was in the seventeenth century that the formal grandeur of the French garden was given its greatest expression by André Le Nôtre. His design for Vaux was based on a system of disciplined and elegant geometric patterns that had high intellectual appeal; here, the spirit of the Academy was being methodically applied to nature. The result was one of the most famous of the French "gardens of intelligence," strictly controlled like all the other arts in France by the application of Classical rules of order. Now nature was shaped according to man-made laws, its varied elements governed by the principle of axial symmetry—sometimes a Herculean task involving the destruction of small villages and the transporting of countless tons of earth.

9-47 Louis Le Vau and André Le Nôtre. Garden facade, Château of Vaux-le-Vicomte. 1657–61

The garden at Vaux was vast, the grandeur of its scheme consonant with that of the château and equal to any architectural undertaking. It featured a great central vista bordered laterally by masses of forest, the open expanse in the center carpeted with embroidery-patterned flower beds with wide paths crossing at right angles, symmetrically laid out pools of water, varied levels, and carefully placed statues and urns. Controlled, rigorous, and intellectual, the gardens at Vaux and others by Le Nôtre were a part of the Classical character of the seventeenth century. But they also belonged to the "baroque" theatrical spirit of the period for they served as outdoor stages where the extravagant, formal "dramas" of courtly life were enacted, and spectacular parties were held, and they became actual stages for the performance of plays, by Molière, for example. The gardens were of unprecedented scale, and even though they were calm and tranquil in mood, their expansive space, limitless vistas, and dramatic contrasts of light and shade (dark forests, open stretches of flower beds) can be convincingly compared to similar expressive qualities in Italian Baroque painting. The Renaissance gardens of Italy, which preceded them, were walled spaces of regular geometric shape with a limited range of distance, reflecting the principles of perspective vision that determined the spatial concepts of Renaissance art. The limitless expanse of French seventeenth-century gardens, on the other hand, conformed to what Giedion has described as the "infinity of nature," the "indefinitely extended perspective" of Baroque painting and architecture.

Versailles. Louis XIV had visited Vaux-le-Vicomte, and he envied both the house and the gardens. When he decided to remodel his father's château at Versailles into the largest and most splendid palace in Europe (figs. 9-48–9-50), it was Vaux and its team of artists that provided the initial inspiration. The history of Versailles is complicated but the main lines can be sorted out. In 1624 Louis XIII built the first Versailles, a small rectangular building with two small wings, to be used as a hunting lodge. It was a modest structure whose architect is unknown (although Salomon de Brosse has been proposed), and it was not renowned in its time. In 1631 it was decided by the king that a more important building was called for; without demolishing the 1624 structure, the king's architect and engineer Philibert le Roy built the "second" Versailles of Louis XIII, consisting of three buildings of brick and stone framing a square court, with the front closed by an arcade, and surrounded by beautiful gardens. It was this structure (visible today in some of its original form at the end of the "Cour de Marbre") that young Louis XIV visited; he retained a sentimental attachment to it throughout his life.

Louis XIII had succeeded to the throne in 1610 at the age of nine; because of the young king's minority, Cardinal Richelieu as prime minister held the supreme power until his death in 1642, which was followed six months later by Louis XIII's own demise. Once again the successor was a child—five-year-old Louis XIV—and the state once again was run during a long minority by a brilliant prime minister, this time the Italian Cardinal Jules Mazarin. In 1661, when Mazarin died, the twenty-three-year-old Louis XIV assumed full control, not only of the state, but of matters of art and architecture, deciding in the next year to remodel his father's "second" château at Versailles without demolishing the building. For this project

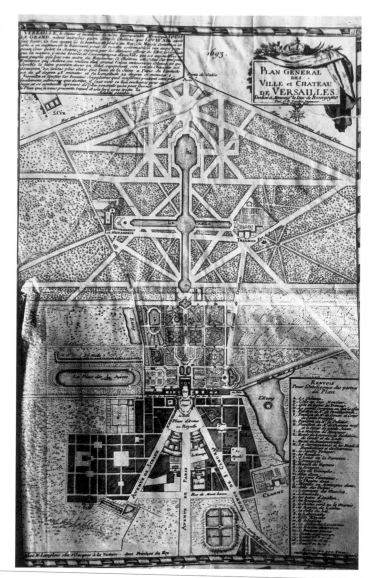

9-48   Plan, Versailles. (After engraving by Blondel)

9-49   Garden facade, Versailles. (17th-century engraving by Israel Sylvestre)

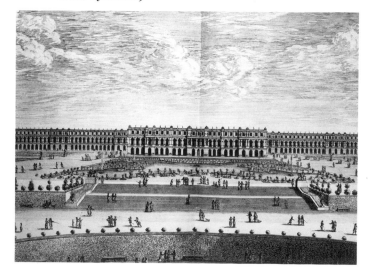

the team of Le Vau, Le Nôtre, and Le Brun—all from Fouquet's Vaux-le-Vicomte—was engaged. Only a few of the architectural and decorative features of the older structure were changed; the major remodeling was reserved for the gardens,

9-50   Jules Hardouin-Mansart and Charles Le Brun. Galerie des Glaces, Versailles. Begun 1678

where Le Nôtre—once again imperiously subjecting nature to his authority—created a huge, symmetrically arranged expanse of flower beds, lawns, and statuary (there were also an orangerie and a rare-animal menagerie). It was in this setting that the comedies of Molière and the operas of Lully were performed for the court, and gorgeous *fêtes* lasting two and three days were given in honor of Mademoiselle de la Vallière, the king's mistress. Remodeling the gardens was of paramount importance to the king for it was his ambition to offer *fêtes* and banquets more magnificent and elaborate than the celebrated parties given at Vaux by Fouquet, and the gardens were to be the setting for these extravagant diversions.

By 1668 the reign of Louis XIV was marching steadily toward its apogee as a regime based on the concept of the "divine right of kings," with his ministers subjected unequivocally to his will, and his power absolute. For a king and court of such increasing authority, the Versailles of Louis XIII was no longer sufficient; Louis XIV wanted it appropriately enlarged as a setting for his ceremonial and personal life, but, again, without demolishing any of the old building for which he had such strong affection. To satisfy the king's wishes, this time architect Le Vau designed the famous Versailles "envelope" (1668–71), whereby the old château of Louis XIII was enveloped on three sides by new buildings. Versailles had two "faces": one toward the town and the major roads linking it to Paris, the other looking out to the seeming infinity of the immense gardens and park, a pastoral, nonurban vista. Le Vau's "envelope" kept the city-oriented facade intact, but he added to the garden side a magnificent new rectangular block, vast in size, and in design a marked departure from previous palace architecture in France: It had an Italianate flat roof, a rusticated ground floor arcade, and an Ionic order of pilasters and columns articulating the first floor, the center section of which formed an open terrace. The splendor of this enlargement was matched by Le Nôtre's garden which, in its ordered symmetry and formal perfection, reflected the balanced Classicism of the building.

The greatest sumptuousness of the ensemble, however, was reserved for the palace interiors designed by Le Brun, whose extravagant Baroque decorative schemes had already helped make Vaux-le-Vicomte the most important building in France at mid-century. His furnishings for the rooms for Versailles have not survived, but their appearance has been reconstructed well enough from remaining fragments, and from records and sketches, to indicate the luxurious appointments, lavish scale, and iconographic program which, with glorious effrontery was centered on the identification of Louis XIV with the sun god Apollo. Ceilings were decorated with stucco, paint, and illusionistic panels; walls were either covered with velvet and hung with paintings from the king's collection, or paneled with marble (with which the floors also were paved) in varied colors. In some of the rooms the furniture and embellishments were made of gilt bronze and solid silver (later melted down to meet the needs of the state treasury); there were fresco paintings, sculpture, illusionistic tapestries, painted architecture, and a dramatic and magnificently decorated staircase (staircases could function very well as the theaters for official ceremonies) known as the Escalier des Ambassadeurs (destroyed in the eighteenth century) that led to the opulent state apartments. No opportunity was lost to reinforce the impression of a court of matchless wealth and power, expressed through formal ceremonies and lavish *fêtes*, and at the center of which stood the radiant Sun King himself.

Despite the brilliant success of Le Vau's majestic design for this "second" phase of Louis XIV's Versailles, the king's ambition was still not sated. In 1678, eight years after the death of Le Vau, the palace underwent still another enlargement and redecoration; this time the architect was Jules Hardouin-Mansart, nephew of François Mansart. Hardouin-Mansart had become "Premier Architecte" to the crown; the Versailles that he created with his extensions to the already existing structures, and that he decorated in collaboration with Le Brun even more lavishly than before, is by and large the building we see today. To Le Vau's Classical rectangular block he added two vast wings to provide accommodations for the entire court along the garden, one on each side, set back from the center and articulated on the three levels of the elevation with the same system used by Le Vau in the central block. The result is a colossal horizontal sweep, monotonous perhaps in its extensive repetition, but nonetheless overwhelming because of its amplitude and equilibrium. The most dramatic change in this, the "third" Versailles of Louis XIV, came with the transformation of Le Vau's terrace (in the central bays of the first floor) into the famous royal reception room, the Galerie des Glaces (fig. 9-50), where huge windows inserted into arches separated by pilasters correspond to an equal number of Venetian mirrors on the opposite wall; above the corridor thus formed runs a huge and elaborately decorated barrel vault. The mirrors reflect the light that enters through the windows and also reflect, in infinite succession, the glazed arcade so that the illusionary effect is a dazzling tour de force. Although the architectural language of the Galerie des Glaces is generally Classical, the special features that stand for the Classical Baroque of seventeenth-century France are the grandeur of the effect, the monumental scale, and the richness of the materials. Without compromising the dignity of Classical forms, the design of the Galerie des Glaces provided the perfect setting as well as the perfect symbol for the absolutism of the monarchy, and for the magnificence and pomposity of the court rituals at Versailles.

Jules Hardouin-Mansart. Hardouin-Mansart understood perfectly the monumental architectural ambitions of king and state (one and the same), and especially at Versailles succeeded in expressing the royal will in language that left no doubt about the artistic and political triumph of French academic discipline over Baroque license and extravagance. Versailles was the most spectacular secular symbol of the reign of Louis XIV; Hardouin-Mansart's work there followed soon after the founding, in 1671, of the Academy of Architecture, the institutional addition to the already established academies for literature, painting, and sculpture, and its doctrines controlled the principles of building design for the rest of the century—but not completely. About 1680, Hardouin-Mansart planned the Church of the Invalides (colorplate 56), part of a military hospital, and it represents the remarkable persistence of the Baroque idiom in France even at a period of the most intense Classicism. Its plan is geometrically rigorous—a Greek cross in a square with circular chapels in its corners, linked by an ambulatory forming an inner square. A dome rises at the crossing, and it is in the dome (and in the facade) that rhythmic and illusionistic Baroque effects are—albeit in constrained fashion—once again in evidence. From the interior, the view into the double-shelled dome is not unlike that in Italian examples inspired by Borromini and Guarini—through a round opening to a painted surface illuminated by a concealed window, a dynamic spatial effect that is uniquely Baroque. On the facade, the orders build up hierarchically toward the center; above, the tapered dome lifts with "Gothic" energy to become the ecclesiastical equivalent of Versailles as a symbol of royalty.

City planning projects belonged to the architectural programs of Louis XIV's reign; the tradition of creating royal squares in Paris as monuments to the greatness of the ruling monarch had its origins in the reign of Henry IV. To honor Louis XIV at the end of the seventeenth century, Hardouin-Mansart designed two impressive squares: the Place des Victoires (1685, of which little of the original character remains), and the more famous Place Vendôme of 1698 (fig. 9-51). Both were designed as monumental settings for statues of the monarch placed in the center of the square. The Place des Victoires was circular (flattened on one side), the Place Vendôme rectangular with beveled corners. The surrounding buildings were not the rather modest houses of Henry IV's Place des Vosges, but grand and impressive palaces animated by the colossal order of Michelangelo, Palladio, and Bernini. The Place Vendôme was originally an enclosed space with only one street crossing it; Place des Victoires was intersected by three streets, and in both places torches, symbols of victory, burned day and night before the royal statue.

The Louvre. Although the king and his court were ultimately to reside at Versailles, with the country's politics and diplomacy carried out from there, the capital of France was still Paris. The king's city palace, the Louvre, was at least nominally regarded as the seat of Europe's greatest power. The series of buildings and courts that comprised the Louvre complex had been put together in piecemeal fashion. In the sixteenth century, Pierre Lescot's southwest facade on the Square Court was the first completely successful architectural expression of French traditions and Italian High Renaissance vocabulary. At the beginning of the seventeenth century, the royal residence was transferred from the Louvre to the newly built Luxembourg Palace because Henry IV's queen, Marie de' Medici, found the old apartments cramped and uncomfortable. Through the 1660s, the Louvre was to be revitalized with new buildings to close the remaining side of the Square Court and with the important exterior facades. For the most impressive location—the facade to the east—the king's powerful Superintendent of Construction, Colbert, asked for designs not only from the architects of Paris but from the most important architects of Rome, at that moment still the architectural center of the world. When Gianlorenzo Bernini responded with two designs, in 1664 and 1665, he was called to Paris (his "royal entrance" into France is legendary), but he failed to anticipate the resistance to his proposals from

9-51   Jules Hardouin-Mansart. Place Vendôme. Paris. 1698

factions upholding inveterate traditions of French architecture, and from xenophobic French architects who resented his presence. His first design called for a curved central unit against which a jutting convex pavilion was set off. The aggressive movement and lack of the stable rectilinearity that had been so thoroughly developed by French Classicizing architects were shocking. The second scheme was an appreciably toned-down version of the first, with the convex unit eliminated. A third project, although more conventionally Classical and more closely related to Roman palace architecture of the Renaissance than the two earlier designs, still did not suit the French. They thought that it was too tall and overwhelmingly massive, that it dwarfed the other buildings in the complex, and that the interior apartments were inconveniently arranged. Out of deference to the great Italian architect, they began to work on the foundation for the third proposal, but when Bernini left Paris in 1665 to return to Rome they abandoned his design.

The responsibility for a design was finally given to a collaborative team composed of Le Vau, Le Brun, and Claude Perrault, a learned scholar and scientist who was to produce, in 1673, an important edition of Vitruvius. Between 1667 and 1670, their famous and often imitated design for the east facade (fig. 9-52) was completed, its authoritative, dignified, and lofty character supremely representative of the king's reign and the victory of French Classicism. The overall composition reasserts the persistence of the five-part scheme for French palace design. Between a tall, fenestrated base and a flat Italianate roof, whose line is broken only by the pediment of the central section, runs a stately colonnade of doubled, freestanding, fluted Corinthian columns, in the manner of Roman peristyle buildings. On the end pavilions, the columns are transmuted into flat and precisely cut pilasters. The rhythm of the coupled columns, the patterns of light and shade produced by the contrast between the surface of the columns and the recesses of the corridor between them and the rear wall, and the magnitude of the scale, are now familiar components of the grand manner of the seventeenth-century Classical Baroque in France. But the elements are more strictly Classical than ever before; they are almost archaeological in nature—probably the result of Perrault's erudite studies of ancient architectural theory and practice—and have a controlled elegance unprecedented

in architecture of the Baroque era. So successful was this design that all the other facades around the exterior of the Square Court (including the one built by Le Vau on the south in 1643) were made to conform to this great model of the cool and commanding countenance of the state.

Despite Colbert's efforts to make the Louvre the primary seat of the government and Paris the venue of the court, the king's interest was in Versailles (connected directly to the Louvre by a road across the countryside). Before the east facade of the Louvre was completed, he had established the court and the nobility at the suburban château and its adjacent town, and he had begun the great enlargement and enrichment of the building. For three decades, life at Versailles was pursued with such a prescribed formality in such sumptuous surroundings that in time the rituals became empty of meaning. By the end of the century everyone, including the king, needed a change. And so the stage was set for the appearance of the new and refreshing style that would be known as the Rococo.

Rococo in France. The change from the grand scale of life and art at Versailles coincided with the genesis of a new style in decoration and architecture. It was initiated by a designer of interiors, Pierre Lepautre, just at the turn of the century, in designs for painted surface ornament, based on flowing lines and arabesques, contained within a panel. These contours were soon transferred into relief and became the outline of the panel itself. Near the end of the seventeenth century, two buildings (now destroyed) were constructed on the grounds of Versailles, both relatively small in size and one, the Château de la Menagerie, was embellished on the interior with the new delicate and amusing design patterns. The novel decoration was so pleasing to everyone, including the king, that in the first years of the eighteenth century, when several apartments in the large château were to be remodeled, they were made in the refreshing new manner that came to be called Rococo.

After the death of the king in 1715, the focus of court life under the regent, the duc d'Orléans (the new king, Louis XV, was a child of five at the time his grandfather, Louis XIV, died), was transferred from Versailles to Paris. As a welcome relief from the public pomposities that had characterized life at Versailles, the aristocracy in Paris sought to create a different setting. They

9-52   Louis Le Vau, Charles Le Brun, and Claude Perrault. East facade, Louvre. Paris. 1667–70

9-53 Germain Boffrand. Salon de la Princesse, Hôtel de Soubise. Paris. 1735–40

9-54 Pierre-Alexis Delamair. Hôtel de Soubise. 1705–9

built private houses with smaller rooms conveniently and comfortably arranged, more intimate in form and function, and decorated in an elegant and sophisticated manner markedly dissimilar to the heavy formality of the Louis XIV style. During the period of the Regency (1717–23), the Rococo style was perfected in the *hôtels* (private town houses) of Paris for the new generation of urban sophisticates who inhabited them. Although in composition the decorative schemes ornamenting the walls of their salons may still have been symmetrical and arranged within rectilinear panels, several new elements appeared that were to become standard features of the fully developed Rococo: large mirrors above S-curved mantles, a white and gold color scheme, painted panels over the doorways, and wall panels decorated with medallions and linear arabesques. The grammar of Classical architecture and ornament has been replaced by motifs abstracted from natural forms—plants and shells and vines—or from the "grotesques" (because they were found in grottoes) of ancient Roman ornament. The colossal pilasters, Corinthian capitals, high-relief entablatures, and heavily painted vaulted ceilings of the seventeenth century were swept away by a light eighteenth-century breeze.

One of the more evolved examples of a French Rococo interior is the oval Salon de la Princesse in the Hôtel de Soubise (fig. 9-53), in Paris, built around 1735–40 by Germain Boffrand

for the Prince de Soubise. The rectilinearity of the earlier Hôtel de Bouvallais has given way to lines that dip and curve and sway. The wall panels, window recesses, and cornices are outlined with gilded moldings that contrast with the creamy white walls and pale blue ceiling. Large windows allow a brilliant light to enter; its reflection in the equally large mirrors increases the luminosity of the space. There is a low and curving mantle, and the upper wall has paintings above the panels that alternate with mirrors, windows, and doors. The whole system is overlaid with a linear network of ornament based on ribbons, scrolls, shells, tendrils, and similar pliant forms. In contrast to the interior, the exterior of the Hôtel de Soubise, built by Pierre-Alexis Delamair (fig. 9-54)—and in general the exterior of many Regency *hôtels*—is restrained and chaste in appearance. Although the large, numerous windows denote a luminous interior, there is nothing that would suggest the undulating forms, pastel colors, and exuberance of the decor found inside. In Italy, the moving walls of Borromini—a distant ancestor of Rococo style—had been employed without inhibition on the facades of Borrominesque buildings, but in France such movement, redolent of "baroque," was restricted by and large to interiors. The end of the Rococo in France was signaled by just such a chaste and pure structure. Ange-Jacques Gabriel's Petit Trianon (built in 1762–68 for Louis XV) is delicate and buoyant when compared to the large scale and massive appearance of traditional French aristocratic residences, and is thus recognized as a product of the Rococo spirit. At the same time its straight lines, unadorned surfaces, and Classical discipline foretell the new movement of Neoclassicism, which was to replace both the Baroque and Rococo and was to be the first step in the creation of the architecture of the modern world.

BAROQUE AND ROCOCO IN GERMANY AND AUSTRIA

Although it could hardly have been foreseen in the fervent origins of the Counter-Reformation, the seventeenth century, with its restoration of a faith that generated the construction of even more church buildings than during the heyday of Romanesque and Gothic architecture, was also the beginning of the end of the great period of Christian architecture. From the disintegration of the Roman Empire until the later years of the eighteenth century, church buildings were the principal architectural monuments of Europe. After the middle of the eighteenth century, a new secular spirit, founded on rationalism and scientific thinking, challenged the religious orthodoxy and faith that in one form or another had survived since the fourth century. A series of revolutions—political and economic—eventually led to the decline of the influence of the Church. Religious structures became less important, less necessary. New modes—public buildings, private residences, commercial structures—would replace them in the modern era. Before its expiration, however, religious architecture achieved one more extraordinary crescendo in the late Baroque and Rococo churches of Catholic Germany and Austria.

We have observed thus far a Baroque style in architecture that put roots down in Rome and grew outward. It developed two branches: one, adhering to the Classicism of the Roman High Renaissance and antiquity, and perpetuated in Italy by the Bernini of the St. Peter's colonnades, spread into the congenial soil of France, where it was transmuted into a distinctively Gallic mode of severe Baroque Classicism; the other, a combination of Bernini's theatrical side and the pure architectural expressionism of Borromini, spread from Rome into Piedmont and then across the Alpine border into Austria and Germany, countries that were receptive in the late seventeenth century to a new style of architecture. The national architectural style of Germany's past was the Gothic: The monumental tradition of Italian High Renaissance architecture had a minor impact in a country torn apart during the sixteenth century by the conflicts of the Reformation, and with little of its architectural history based on the language of Classical form. By the end of the sixteenth century, the Counter Reformation had its effect, and in the Catholic (southern) parts of Germany, and in Austria, the renewal of religious confidence was the impetus for the beginning of a long and rich period of church construction. Throughout the seventeenth century, a new national style was formulated with a lineage that could be traced as far back as thirteenth-century German Gothic architecture with its special affinity for the mystical effects of spatial and structural fluidity, and for complex decorative detail. Just as the disciplined and rationalist methods of French Gothic cathedral construction endured and, in the seventeenth century, became the foundation of French Classicism, so the dynamic emotionalism of German Gothic was easily transmuted into the impassioned and spectacular buildings of the German Baroque. Aspects of Italian Baroque art—the drama of Bernini, the fluidity of Borromini, the decorative ensembles and visionary ceiling paintings—predictably played an influential role in the formation of German Baroque style, and they began to appear in the Northern buildings soon after the middle of the seventeenth century.

Eighteenth-Century Austria. The late-seventeenth-, early-eighteenth-century buildings of Johann Fischer von Erlach, among the finest monuments of Austrian Baroque architecture, have their share of quotations from Italian sources—pilasters framing round-headed niches filled with sculpture, massive arches, heavy, sculptural architraves, but at the same time their creamy color and scrolled stucco framing reveal as another source of inspiration the new decorative style of the French Rococo.

The great period of German and Austrian late Baroque and Rococo architecture runs from about 1710 to 1750, corresponding roughly to the peak of the Rococo in France. Fischer von Erlach's earliest training was as a sculptor and stucco worker, followed by an architectural apprenticeship in Rome under Carlo Fontana from 1682 to 1685. His Karlskirche (fig. 9-55), begun in 1715, in Vienna, is dedicated to Carlo Borromeo, the Italian cardinal and saint of the Counter-Reformation. What is most extraordinary about this structure is the successful coherence of its design despite a seemingly irreconcilable eclecticism. In front of a longitudinally placed oval nave stands an unusually wide facade composed of a bizarre combination of elements. A Corinthian hexastyle temple portico on top of a stepped podium, archaeological in its fidelity to Roman temple fronts, represents the entrance to the church. Above the colonnade is a triangular pediment, rectangular attic, and dome, in the same sequence found in the Pantheon but in Baroque translation. The high dome on a tall drum over the narrow groundplan comes from seventeenth-century French churches in which this particular combination was employed, but the round windows in the base of the dome are framed with the richly carved moldings and sculptural embellishments characteristic of Austrian

Baroque ornament. The portico is flanked by two gigantic replicas of the Column of Trajan, which neatly lock into the cavities created by the curve of the facade on either side (a device appropriated from Borromini's S. Agnese, in Rome). The facade terminates with two arched pavilions, themselves a peculiar combination of Italian, French, and, at the gable level, Austrian Baroque forms. On the interior, the oval space opens horizontally across the short axis into rectangular chapels that function like a compressed transept; oval chapels open on the diagonals; the high altar is placed in the center of a long, narrow extension of the longitudinal axis that terminates, in a Palladian manner, behind a screen of columns arranged in a semicircle.

The eclecticism of the Karlskirche is so uninhibited that it produces a unique, original architectural vision carried out with admirable self-confidence and as the natural outgrowth of the architect's intellectual curiosity. A gifted scholar as well as sculptor and architect, Fischer von Erlach was the author of an influential treatise on the history of architecture (*Entwurf einer historischen Architektur*) published in 1721, which included descriptions and illustrations of architecture in exotic places such as Egypt and China.

Another Austrian structure of the early eighteenth century, different in genre and style from the Karlskirche but equally dramatic and impressive, is the Benedictine Abbey at Melk (figs. 9-56, 9-57), in lower Austria, rebuilt in 1702–6 by the architect Jakob Prandtauer. The site of the monastery is a rocky precipice majestically rising along the bank of the Danube, and Prandtauer fully realized the theatrical potentialities of the location by placing the church at the end of a long courtyard formed by two rows of monastic buildings that stretch to the end of the promontory. Tall and white, the building lifts out of the rock into a soaring dome and pinnacled towers, its facade dynamically flexed into motion through a series of undulating curves. Viewed from the river below, the ensemble is one of the most exciting in all of Baroque architecture, but the interior (completed by others) is rather heavy and solemn. Its articulation—a Corinthian order of double pilasters—comes from the Gesù and St. Peter's. But the walls and entablature borrow Borromini's "swell and ebb" device that was universally adopted and dramatically exploited in German and Austrian architecture.

9-55   Johann Fischer von Erlach. Karlskirche. Vienna. Begun 1715

9-56　Jakob Prandtauer. Benedictine Abbey. Melk, Austria.
1702–6

9-57　Interior, Abbey Church. Melk

Eighteenth-century Austrian architecture is also noted for secular buildings of exceptional beauty, such as the summer palace of Upper Belvedere (colorplate 57) built for Prince Eugene of Savoy, in Vienna, in 1721–24. Johann Lukas von Hildebrandt was the architect; he, Fischer von Erlach, and Jakob Prandtauer were the three great masters of the Austrian

Baroque whose buildings rivaled those of their contemporaries in Italy and France. Hildebrandt had both physical and sentimental ties to Italy. He was born in Genoa (his German father was a captain in the Genoese army), and before settling in Vienna he studied architecture in Rome with Carlo Fontana. Not surprisingly, the Upper Belvedere is a sophisticated blend of Italian, French, and Austrian components freely interpreted by the architect to create a formal but still charming royal summer villa. On its garden side, the building is composed of massed forms with a central section against which are huddled two flanking blocks of three stories, a pair of lower blocks, and finally a pair of terminal pavilions, octagonal in shape and covered by hemispherical domes that contrast with the sloping, peaked roofs of the other sections. The entrance facade has a light and open central pavilion beneath a gaily curving pediment. Beyond its arcaded portico, an airy staircase leads to the upper levels or down to the gardens. The surface of the building is embellished with ornamental relief and curved window moldings, and the roofs and domes terminate in cheerful finials. These details create the "atmosphere" of a pleasurable retreat and lighten the heavy massing of the structure.

Bavaria. It was in Bavaria in the second quarter of the eighteenth century that German Rococo architecture reached its zenith. The medieval German penchant for fluid structure and space was revived in flexible eighteenth-century walls that moved in reverse curves and carried with them cornices, architraves, and entablatures. The oval form, preferred because of its emphatic directional pull, was employed with an intricacy and complexity far beyond that of Italian prototypes. Theatrical illusionism—the fusion of painting, sculpture, architecture, and stucco to depict miraculous events close to the church altar (stage) or on ceilings—corresponded to the mystical bent of German Gothic art. Church interiors were designed to emphasize the sight lines to these "stages": Transepts were shallow or did not exist at all to eliminate a competing directional force; corners were bevelled, and supports for galleries and vaults arranged obliquely so that the gaze could "slide" easily along walls or piers to the point of dramatic focus, which was lighted through large, clear-glass windows. The complex decorative detailing of German Gothic architecture was expressed in eighteenth-century Bavaria through the medium of French Rococo ornament. Rich encrustations of bravura stucco work were a specialty of the region, learned originally in the sixteenth century from imported Italian craftsmen, then becoming a highly developed native skill; in exaggerated French linear contours, stucco ornament was displayed against stretches of creamy white background. In general, the decoration of German and Austrian church interiors at this period was extremely rich in density, color, and design. The surface of the ceiling would be "painted away" to simulate heaven revealed, the church interior becoming part of the celestial kingdom made radiant with pastel colors and gilded surfaces. Such extension of space through illusionistic painting and open architecture—walls pierced by galleries, windows, and shaped openings—was typical of Baroque practice.

The Benedictine Abbey Church at Ottobeuren (1744–67; fig. 9-58), for example, is the work of one of the most important eighteenth-century Bavarian architects, Johann Michael Fischer. With the assistance of Simpert Kramer, Fischer designed a church based on a conventional basilican plan with

9-58 Johann Michael Fischer. Interior, Abbey Church. Ottobeuren. Germany. 1744–67

ment; surfaces are garnished with elaborate stucco relief, and rich colors glow and shimmer dramatically in the diffused light. The lighting is particularly theatrical; the Asams, by adapting themes from Bernini's dramatic ensembles, silhouetted, in the upper tier, an ethereal image of the Trinity against a background of light radiating from the hidden windows beyond the cornice. This effective sculptured illusion of the supernatural is integrated with the architecture and the lighting to create an atmosphere that heightens the religious experience. It is here, in the visionary atmosphere of Sankt Johannes Nepomuk that we can see how in Germany two strains of Roman Baroque—the architectural expressionism of Borromini and the theatrical visions of Bernini—become the central, if somewhat exaggerated, components of Bavarian style.

The church that is generally regarded as the model of south German Rococo ideals stands alone in the center of a rural Bavarian meadow. It is the small pilgrimage shrine known as Die Wies (colorplate 61; fig. 9-60), built in 1746–54 by architect Dominikus Zimmermann and his brother, Johann Baptist Zimmermann, a painter and stucco worker. The building is remarkable for its lightness, both of color and weight. It is constructed of wood, and therefore the freestanding double piers carrying the vault, relieved of the function of supporting

9-59 Egid Quirin Asam and Cosmas Damian Asam. Sankt Johannes Nepomuk. Munich. 1733–46

a nave, transept, and choir. On the exterior, it is quiet and controlled, its affiliation with the Baroque signaled only by the bulging convexity of the entrance and by the dramatic flanking towers. In contrast to the sobriety of the outside, however, the church interior is a rich symphony of color, light, sculpture, architecture, and stucco, all of which conceal the outlines of the building's structure.

Fischer was an architect and not, as were many of his contemporaries, an architect-decorator, equally skilled at building, fresco painting, sculpture, and stucco work, designing and executing the amalgamations of which many Bavarian interiors were composed. A pair of such architect-decorators were the famous Asam brothers, Egid Quirin and Cosmas Damian, who worked for architects in their capacity as decorators and craftsmen but who, at other times, were entirely responsible for the decoration and the architecture of their own projects. Like many German artists of the period, they put in some years of study in Rome (with Carlo Fontana) and returned to Bavaria with an appreciation for the majestic forms of Roman Baroque architecture and for Bernini's exciting tableaux of miraculous events. In Munich, they were the architects and also the decorators of the small Church of Sankt Johannes Nepomuk (colorplate 63; fig. 9-59), built in 1733–46 adjacent to their house and used as their private chapel. It exemplifies the brothers' most scenographic style. The interior of the tall, narrow church has two levels separated by a gallery that weaves along the wall in shallow curves; the frescoed ceiling is illuminated by light entering from windows concealed behind the upper cornice. The building is replete with quotations from Borromini and Bernini, picked up during the Asams's fruitful Roman sojourn, but intensified and stretched to the fullest extent of Bavarian Baroque style. The architectural forms are charged with move-

9-60 **Dominikus Zimmermann. Die Wies. Bavaria. 1746–54**

9-61
Johann Balthasar Neumann.
Plan, Vierzehnheiligen.
Near Staffelstein. Begun 1743

9-62   Interior, Vierzehnheiligen

a heavy load, are slender, with wide spaces between each pair. The oval nave is surrounded by a broad ambulatory (essential in a pilgrimage church); abundant windows on two levels illuminate the pastel and gold color scheme. (The exterior, which has a convex facade, is painted white and yellow.) The structural armature of the nave is so veiled by sculpture, painting, stucco relief, gilding, and brilliant color that it becomes functionally invisible. More important than the sense of mass and support is the absence of it; instead, the open space, bright light, flashes of gold, and visionary world overhead enchanted the pilgrims and lifted their hearts.

Among the most eminent South German architects of this era was Johann Balthasar Neumann, designer of buildings noted for ingenuity of plan and structure. At the pilgrimage church of Vierzehnheiligen (figs. 9-61, 9-62), begun in 1743, near Staffelstein, in the Main River valley, Neumann's ingenuity was put to the test in order to solve a difficult problem: how to construct, over a foundation already built by an earlier architect who laid out the building as a longitudinal basilica, a church in which an important sculptured shrine (of Christ's Fourteen Helpers to whom the church was dedicated) was to become the focal point of the nave. This would have been a simple matter in a centralized building, but was an awkward arrangement for a conventional basilica. Neumann's solution was to retain the general configuration of the basilican plan while inserting within it a novel geometric system whereby the nave and transept were formed from a series of circles and ovals—circles for the arms of the transept, and ovals of different sizes (and axial orientation) for the nave, apse, and side chapels. These overlap each other with a contrapuntal interplay that recalls the music of the period. By suppressing all conventional signs of a basilican nave-transept crossing—the logical site for a shrine—and by expanding the boundaries of the nave through the colonnades that followed the billowing curves of the largest oval, Neumann provided a spacious enclosure for the shrine in the center of the church. The illusion of spatial expansiveness in the interior is heightened by light pouring in from huge windows.

An effective device used by Neumann in the Vierzehnheiligen was the bringing in of light through an invisible aperture that lay beyond the nearest open surface, making it appear as a diffused radiance. The technique originated in the architecture of

Borromini and was developed by Guarini, but it was Neumann who carried it to its most breathtaking effect in his Residence (fig. 9-63) of the prince bishops in Würzburg, built between 1720 and 1744. The most remarkable sections are the staircase, the Kaisersaal (reception room; fig. 9-64), and the church. Neumann, gifted with a sense of the spectacular, promoted the idea of a stair from an often humble and merely functional appurtenance into something wondrous. Leading to the Kaisersaal is a ceremonial stair (colorplate 62) constructed with the kind of engineering ingenuity for which Neumann is celebrated: Contained within a wide shell of articulated walls and windows, the stair is ascended first on a single, central flight and then, in the reverse direction, on one of two wings that double back and flank the center. The ascent is into an ever-widening, increasingly luminous, and seemingly infinite expansion of space that culminates in a great ceiling fresco by the painter Giovanni Battista Tiepolo, filled with illusionistic devices that simulate a great breadth of cloud-filled sky, crowds of people, buildings, landscape, and birds. Climbing the stair, the visitor participates in the exhilarating experience of interaction with the architecture that is often the calculated effect of Baroque buildings. Neumann's stair—for the intensity with which its inanimate components stimulate this kind of response—is one of the most successful of Baroque kinesthetic works. The purpose of the stair was to provide access to the imperial reception halls, notably the huge Kaisersaal, which was reached after first passing through the Weissesaal. Almost as large as the Kaisersaal, the Weissesaal, with its white and gray color scheme and delicate stucco work, served as an intermediate station, a kind of rhythmic pause between the extravagance of the staircase and the overwhelming scale and polychromy of the Kaisersaal. Neumann designed the Kaisersaal so it would be of a magnificence that would neither compromise the grandeur of the stair, nor be a disappointment after the elation of the ascent. It is an immense oval, almost excessively rich in decor: Pastel colors, veined marble, and opulent gilding are set off against a brilliant white. Its most spectacular feature is Tiepolo's painted vault (1751), which appears to billow out like a gorgeous silken canopy above the room's entablature. Below the vault, the wall articulation, although exceptionally rich in polychromy and material, is still recognizable as a Classically based system of

9-63   Johann Balthasar Neumann. Church, Residence. Würzburg. Designed 1732

9-64   Kaisersaal, Residence

column, arch, and entablature. The surface of the vault, however, is covered by a lacy net of gilded relief in flowing, asymmetrical designs, slender, and scroll-like, derived from the French Rococo decoration of the Parisian *hôtels* of the 1720s and thirties.

The architecture, landscaping, and decoration of princely residences in the eighteenth century as symbols of pleasure and celebrity became ever more opulent, such as the combination of open arcades and confectionary sculpture at one of the pavilions of the Zwinger, the royal palace in Dresden built from 1705 to 1722 for Augustus the Strong (fig. 9-65). Another German example is the Amalienburg (figs. 9-66, 9-67), the small hunting pavilion built for the Electress Maria Amalia, wife of the Elector Karl VII Albrecht of Bavaria. Situated in the park of the Nymphenburg Palace near Munich, the little pavilion was built between 1734 and 1739 by François Cuvilliés the Elder. Cuvilliés, who was responsible for some of the most brilliant Rococo buildings of eighteenth-century Munich, was a Walloon who began his career at the age of eight as court dwarf in the service of the Elector Maximilian II Emanuel of Bavaria. Sent by his patron (who astutely recognized his talent) to study art and architecture in Paris, Cuvilliés returned to Munich in 1724 and became court architect in 1725. From Paris he brought with him the repertoire of Rococo decoration that was currently enchanting the French aristocracy, and these he employed with great agility in the interior of the Amalienburg. A "retreat" within the park of the large and formal palace (the Nymphenburg), the pavilion is small and charming, light and gay, decorated in the fashion of the Parisian *hôtels* (it is exactly contemporary with Boffrand's Hôtel de Soubise). The main salon of the single-story building is circular, its walls pierced by a series of doorways and large windows reflected (in the manner of Versailles) by large mirrors. The pale blue surface of the walls is frosted with delicately executed, silvered stucco relief in patterns of entwined branches with fluttering leaves. The dancing cornice that divides the skylike domed ceiling (with

9-65   Matthäus Daniel Pöppelman and Balthasar Permoser. Zwinger Pavilion. Dresden. 1705/8–22

9-66 François Cuvilliés the Elder. Amalienburg. Near Munich.
1734–39

9-67 Interior, Amalienburg

stucco birds illusionistically fluttering about) from the window level is less architectural than organic, appearing to be soft turf sending up clusters of feathery shoots. The simpler exterior (with a curving facade that repeats the circular shape of the salon) has much of the sobriety that characterized seventeenth-century French Classicism, and bears the same relation of exterior reserve to interior opulence that we observed in the French Rococo *hôtel*. In the end, however, the Amalienburg demonstrated how, in Germany, the French-born Rococo style, released from the restraints of French tradition and made more plastic, more architectural than decorative, reached the

crest of its expressive potential. Such a Franco-Germanic adaptation was not new; it had occurred almost four centuries earlier when the greatly admired Gothic architecture of France was imported into Germany. There its emotional potential was exploited, and it was transformed into a German Gothic of exceptional expressiveness. In the eighteenth century as in the fourteenth, the French style became Germanic, with complexity replacing orderliness, "hard" forms softening, and tectonic boundaries becoming blurred.

In the second half of the eighteenth century, the freedom and gaiety of the Rococo, and the pomp and drama of the Baroque—both French and German—were finished. A new style, based on a strictly interpreted Classicism, replaced them.

BAROQUE AND ROCOCO IN SPAIN AND ELSEWHERE

As an international phenomenon, Baroque architecture had a rich development in many more regions than those we have been considering here. But Italy was the center of its creation, and France, with its Classicism, contributed to it a wholly new dimension. It was again in France that the new style of the Rococo was born, by and large as a reaction to the Baroque, and it flourished there primarily as a decorative, ornamental art. In Germany and Austria, the Rococo was monumentalized, transformed into architecture while continuing to serve as decoration. This singular translation of Baroque and Rococo into a German language constituted an independent national style powerful enough to match the achievements of Italy and France. The abundant Baroque and Rococo architecture of Bohemia also has a character of its own, formed primarily out of Italian sources by the Dientzenhofer family of architects who settled in Prague in the seventeenth century. In the Mala Strana section of the city Christoph Dientzenhofer began a large monastic church for the Jesuits dedicated to St. Nicholas in 1703 (fig. 9-68). The first campaign was completed in 1711 with the vaulting of the nave; the later domed choir and sanctuary are the work of Christoph's son Kilian Ignaz, who took up the project in 1737. A basilican church with a wide nave of three bays flanked by three chapels on each side above which ride serpentine galleries, St. Nicholas—facade and interior—is indebted above all to the powerful inspiration of Guarini and Borromini in its curvacious rhythms and undulations, and in its sculptural architecture. The original intersecting ovals of the ceiling are now covered by a huge fresco; to the concave-convex pattern of the wall pillars are applied obliquely set pilasters rising through two stories to the light-piercing apertures of the gallery level.

The Baroque architecture of western Europe became important to Russia during the reign of Peter the Great (1682–1725), and artists and architects from Italy, Germany, and France came to Russia to work under his patronage. The style of building and decoration they produced is known as Petrine Baroque, but it was only during the reign of Empress Elizabeth two decades later (1741–62) that a vast, rich, full-blown Baroque style unabashedly inspired by Versailles and by later European developments was carried out in the royal palaces around St. Petersburg by her court architect, Bartolomeo Rastrelli. Born to an Italian family of sculptors and architects who had established themselves in St. Petersburg, Rastrelli specialized in exuberantly decorated palatial buildings but also was the author of a number of brilliantly conceived late Baroque church buildings, particularly the small church of St. Andrew in Kiev (fig. 9-69). Begun in 1748

9-68 Christoph Dientzenhofer. Nave, St. Nicholas, Prague, Mala Strana, 1703–11

9-69 Bartolomeo Rastrelli with Ivan Michurin. St. Andrew, Kiev. Begun 1748

on Rastrelli's design but carried out by Moscow architect Ivan Michurin, the slender, rich, and elegant St. Andrew is based on the traditional Russian pentacupolar plan, with four elements around a central dome. Here the central dome with its undulating cornice is set above a tall windowed drum and is crowned by a flask-shaped lantern that identifies it as Russian. In place of four minor domes are four slender colonnaded towers whose finials repeat the shape of the central lantern. St. Andrew is replete with Baroque elements, but Baroque soon would be displaced in Russia by the Neoclassicism favored by Catherine the Great.

In Spain, however, Baroque and Rococo styles assumed a unique national character that did not conform closely to its sources. Moreover, as a result of the Spanish Conquest, that unique vision of the Baroque and Rococo was transferred to the New World.

Baroque architecture in Spain through the first quarter of the seventeenth century was dominated by the sober, unadorned style of Juan de Herrera and Juan Bautista de Toledo, architects of Philip II's "severe" Escorial complex. This "court style" was perpetuated by masters such as J. B. Monegro and Jorge Manuel Theotocópuli (son of El Greco) in important buildings in the northern part of the country, but its austerity could not be sustained and was overtaken by the national predilection for lavish surface ornament—the Plateresque of the fifteenth and early sixteenth centuries. By the eighteenth century, Renaissance Plateresque had become Rococo Churrigueresque—an ornamental style taking its name from a family (Churriguera) of architects

9-70 Pedro de Ribera. Hospice of San Fernando (now Municipal Museum). Madrid. 1722

and sculptors, whose buildings were distinguished by an especially luxuriant heaping of elaborate surface ornament. Among the most notable Churrigueresque masters was Pedro de Ribera, whose portal for the Hospice of San Fernando (fig. 9-70) in Madrid, constructed in 1722 of coarse sandstone, reveals in its contours the influence of the curving open forms of French Rococo, but is encrusted with knotted chunks of florid ornament in a manner practiced in no country other than Spain. These barnacled, crustaceous forms suggest, ironically, that perhaps the appearance of Spanish Rococo truly evoked the scaly grottoes whose worked surfaces of shell and rock (*rocaille*) gave to the new style the first part of its name.

While the Churrigueresque style pervaded the architecture of Madrid and the north of Spain, the Andalusian architects of the south, traditionally receptive to Italian influence, developed (in the second half of the seventeenth and the first half of the eighteenth centuries) a manner that combined inspiration from Borromini, Bernini, and others with a distinctive form of painted and gilded stucco interior and exterior decoration. Florid though the ornament was, it did not obscure (as Churrigueresque did) the shape and structure of the monumental, often Classicizing forms beneath it. In the Sacristy (1732–45; fig. 9-71) of the Cartuja of Granada, for example, designed by Francisco Hurtado Izquierdo with Luis de Arévalo and José de Bada, the basic Renaissance (Il Gesù) plan of wide nave, side chapels separated by piers articulated with giant pilasters, absent transept, and domed crossing asserts itself majestically beneath the layers of thick stucco embroidery, manifesting the clarity and full monumentality of the Italian prototypes. It was this Andalusian merging of Italian church

models and Classicizing forms with ornate polychrome stucco overlay that was exported to the New World. It can be seen most clearly in the *sagrario* of the Cathedral of Mexico (1749) by Lorenzo Rodriguez, and the interior (finished by 1750) and facade (finished 1760–65) of the church of La Companía in Quito, designed by Leonhard Deubler, whose plans were strongly influenced by Italian examples.

THE SEVENTEENTH CENTURY IN ENGLAND

The direct transfer of ideas and forms from Italy to England during the centuries of the Renaissance was inhibited by several factors. One was the physical distance of the two cultures, and another was the absence of active patronage emanating from either the English royal court or the Church to inspire the migration of continental craftsmen in search of wider opportunities for work. In the sixteenth century, the feudal castle-fortress and the perpendicular Gothic church still accounted for the general "look" of monumental English architecture. What little was known, and superficially used, of Italian or Classical style had come to England indirectly. It consisted by and large of the imitation of French and Flemish interpretations of Italian Renaissance designs. Some awareness of the illustrations in Serlio's treatise giving schematic patterns for roofs, cornices, entablatures, decorations, and the correct use of the orders accounted for other minor infiltrations of Renaissance style. A dramatic change in this situation, however, came about in the seventeenth century. At that time English architecture was totally revised by two remarkable men—Inigo Jones and Christopher Wren. Insofar as one meaning of the term "Renaissance" in art has come to be the idea of a separation from the medieval world, then we must say that what was chronologically called the Baroque in England became, stylistically, the beginning of English Renaissance.

9-71 Francisco Hurtado Izquierdo with Luis de Arévalo and José de Bada. Sacristy of the Cartuja. Granada. 1732–45

Inigo Jones. Inigo Jones was a stage designer and painter as well as an architect, and it may have been his interest in stagecraft that took him to Italy at the end of the sixteenth century to learn about the renowned costumes and set designs invented for Italian theater productions. His love for things Italian was immediate; in the course of time he made numerous trips there, learned the language, traveled to many cities, studied the remains of Classical antiquity and the new

9-72 Inigo Jones. Queen's House. Greenwich, England. 1616–35

buildings of the Renaissance, and, most significant, read and studied the treatises written by Italian Renaissance architects and Humanists.

Of all the treatises, it was Palladio's *Quattro libri dell'architettura* that most influenced his development as an architect and was responsible for the introduction by Jones of Palladian architectural modes into England. Jones also examined, at first hand and with great attention, Palladio's buildings in the Veneto, the mathematically proportioned, geometrically lucid structures he designed in part as his interpretations of ancient architecture. The *Quattro libri* contained plans and elevations of many of Palladio's buildings, particularly the villas for the landed gentry around Vicenza. Along with examining the structures themselves, Jones studied the treatise thoroughly (his own annotated copy still exists). In England, in his position as Royal Surveyor from 1615 to 1642, Jones designed buildings that were an homage to his idol; by so doing, he brought

true Italian Renaissance architecture, hence Classicism, into England for the first time.

Only a handful of Jones's buildings survive, although it is believed he built more than forty. From Palladio he adopted the rectangular block form, the ratio among parts, the Classical vocabulary and use of the orders, and the bright interiors of

9-73   Inigo Jones. Banqueting House. London. 1619–22

9-74   Interior, Banqueting House

9-75   Inigo Jones. Queen's Chapel, St. James Palace. London. 1623–27

9-76   Inigo Jones. Gateway for Chiswick House. Near London. 1621

northeastern Italy (as opposed to the comparatively tenebrous Roman Renaissance buildings). We can imagine the extraordinary impact his buildings made when, with their innate Classicism, poise, and sense of order, they were seen against the standard Gothic, Tudor, and Jacobean profiles of which English architecture in the early seventeenth century was composed. Yet with all their novelties they were wonderfully harmonious in the urban and rural landscape of England; their broad, low massing, inherent elegance, and human scale made them seem perfectly appropriate to their new setting.

Inigo Jones's earliest surviving royal architectural commission is the Queen's House (fig. 9-72), in Greenwich, begun in 1616 for Anne of Denmark, wife of King James I. Work was halted in 1618 and was not resumed until 1630, this time for a new queen, Henrietta Maria, wife of Charles I. It was completed in 1635. During the hiatus in construction, Jones built a new Banqueting House (1619–22; figs. 9-73, 9-74) at Whitehall Palace for James I, to replace a previous one destroyed by fire. When the Banqueting House in London was completed (before much could be seen of the Queen's House), it bore no resemblance to anything ever built in England before. Although it relied heavily on Palladio's architecture, it was not a reproduction of any one building. It was a completely self-assured structure, built by an architect who was not a slavish imitator but who comprehended and thoroughly assimilated the ideals of Palladio's Classicism. It consists of one great cubic room that served for royal receptions, ceremonies, and the performance of masques. The exterior elevation has three levels: a rusticated base; a first story with a series of windows crowned by alternating segmental and triangular pediments on brackets separated by engaged Ionic columns, and pilasters that are doubled at the ends of the building; and a second story with Corinthian columns and pilasters that correspond to those below, as do the windows (but with straight cornices), and with a garland swag tying the capitals together beneath the flat balustraded roof.

To our eyes the idiom is familiar—a crisp Palladian version of Bramante's Roman High Renaissance palaces—but in England not only was it excitingly new, it was, with its noble lines and dignified mien, remarkably suited as the architecture of royalty. The same holds true for the Queen's House, where the serenity, elegance of proportion, and formal symmetry were especially apt for its sovereign patron. The house is formed like an H (a design that harks back to Sangallo's late quattrocento villa at Poggio a Caiano for Lorenzo de' Medici), the two longer sections joined by a bridge that crossed the road running between the palace grounds and an adjoining park. (The open sides of the H were filled in by a pupil after Jones's death.) From a distance the building appears to be a bright, single cube, set like a piece of geometric sculpture in an expansive green landscape. The south facade consists of an open colonnaded loggia between two closed blocks, a motif reminiscent of Palladio's Palazzo Chiericati. In the north section the central hall is a 40-foot cube (the interior of the Banqueting House is a double cube) balanced by a symmetrical series of rooms to the right and left. The plan reflects the theoretical ideals of the Renaissance Humanists and their interest in ideal forms and harmonious proportions.

Inigo Jones's sure feeling for Classicism can be found in the drawings and sketches that are attributed to him, and in all his surviving works. His Queen's Chapel (fig. 9-75) at St. James Palace (1623–27) is an example of a Classical church with a

monumental triangular pediment on the exterior, a double cube interior covered by a coffered barrel vault, with a Serliana (Palladian) window above the altar. The Gateway (now in Chiswick Park; fig. 9-76) that remains from Chiswick House in Chelsea (1621) is Jones's version of a Roman arch, with Tuscan columns set against massive rusticated voussoirs. The facade of St. Paul's Church at Covent Garden (built in 1631 but restored in the eighteenth century) reveals Jones to be a student of archaeology and the history of ancient architecture as Palladio had been before him. Its deep porch, Tuscan order, and heavy, low pediment represent his attempt to recreate the appearance of an Etruscan temple of the sixth century B.C.

From the point of view of the perpetuation of Classical architecture, Inigo Jones is the most important architect ever to have worked in England. The language of architecture he brought to that country was responsible for the most significant direction English architecture (and indirectly the architecture of the New World) was to take, for it was believed to have sprung from Vitruvius, and thus became the foundation of the Neoclassicism of the eighteenth century. It was also relevant, by its evocation of lost historical modes, to the historicism of nineteenth-century English architecture.

Christopher Wren. Just as Inigo Jones introduced the Renaissance to England, Christopher Wren, the dominating figure on the architectural scene in England in the second half of the seventeenth century, established there the forms and spirit of continental Baroque architecture. Like Jones, Wren was a person of many parts. He was a renowned man of science at the peak of the Scientific Revolution of the second half of the seventeenth century, and was described by Isaac Newton as one of "the greatest Geometers of our times." In his youth he was interested in mathematics and mechanical instruments, and he became Pro-

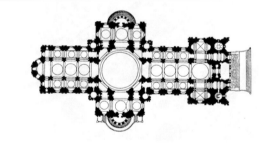

9-77
Plan, St. Paul's Cathedral

9-78   Interior, St. Paul's Cathedral

9-79   Christopher Wren. Facade, St. Paul's Cathedral. London. 1675–1709

fessor of Astronomy at Oxford in 1661. In 1669 he was appointed Surveyor General of the King's works (Charles II), the same court position held by Jones earlier in the century. Jones's consuming interest in the architecture of Palladio, antiquity, and the Roman Renaissance was the result of his travels in Italy; more than half a century later, Wren's single trip abroad to France (where he met Mansart, Le Vau, and Bernini who was in Paris for the Louvre project) opened his eyes to the grandeur of French Classical Baroque. He seems to have known Italian Baroque and Renaissance architecture from treatises and drawings.

It was out of a calamity that Wren's great architectural talent emerged. Following the disastrous London fire of 1666,

he developed a farsighted and ingenious plan to rebuild the city (in a completely new form) from the ashes. But because his scheme uprooted established real estate interests and did not preserve property boundaries as they had been, it was rejected by the king under pressure from special interest groups. However, Wren was still able to carry out part of his plan—to rebuild the heavily damaged Gothic Cathedral of St. Paul's and fifty-two small parish churches.

St. Paul's, the largest cathedral in England, is Wren's masterpiece (figs. 9-77–9-79). With it, he brought a repertoire of new forms (the dome, for example) and architectural combinations into English architecture. The building (1675–1709) is something of an encyclopedia of Wren's impressions of the architecture of the continent, but he has been criticized for not applying his scientific knowledge of mechanics and materials to its construction. Clearly remembered from his months in Paris (1665–66) studying architecture were various projects for the east facade of the Louvre (completed five years before the English church was begun), and also the special élan with which the great domes of French seventeenth-century churches, particularly the dome of Lemercier's Church of the Sorbonne, soar above the stories of masonry below. Wren fashioned the facade of St. Paul's with two tiers of paired Corinthian columns like those of the Louvre and framed them between towers inspired by those of Borromini's Roman church of S. Agnese. Above the two-story base rises a tremendous peripteral dome that reinterprets Bramante's Tempietto of 1502. Pietro da Cortona's projecting curved porches of Sta. Maria della Pace have become St. Paul's transept porches.

Other Italian models, notably St. Peter's, were important for Wren in the conception of the English cathedral. Bramante's original Greek cross scheme was adapted by Wren in the first plan (1672) for the new St. Paul's, a daring domed Greek cross within an octagon combined with Borrominesque curving walls linking four colonnaded porches on the exterior. The central plan design set off in England the same clerical controversy that had arisen in Italy, since the conservative preference was to repeat the traditional cruciform plan of old St. Paul's. Wren's second project was a compromise, similar to the solution at St. Peter's, where the east-west arm of the Greek cross was extended into a long nave; the third and final plan returned to the wide-bodied longitudinal nave with aisles and transept of the Gothic original, with the shortness of the transept arms a vestige of the Greek cross.

Controversy surrounds Wren's engineering method for the Cathedral since the perimeter walls, articulated by pilasters and windows, are not structural but serve to screen an interior system of flying buttresses that support clerestory walls. The scientific ingenuity of the striking, wide dome that rises from its two-story base to dominate the city is beyond question, however, and can compare to Brunelleschi's solution for the octagon of Florence Cathedral two and a half centuries earlier. Wren devised a triple-dome scheme whereby the outer dome is a light shell made of lead-sheathed timber, the middle dome is a cone of brick and metal that supports the outer dome and its lantern and rests on the drum, and the inner dome is a low hemispherical vault above the crossing.

In terms of the history of English architecture, the eclecticism of St. Paul's, the very diversity of its "foreign" sources and the ways they are assimilated, makes St. Paul's all the more English, for eclecticism and borrowing have been characteristic of English buildings since the Gothic period. Even Inigo Jones engaged in the wholesale "borrowing" of Italian models, which then became, through pragmatic adjustments of scale, site, and function, suitably English. Wren, too, selected his models carefully, and with St. Paul's he was able to fashion an English Baroque by making the building's eclectic elements conform to the historical English affection for massiveness and width in building (derived from Anglo-Norman Romanesque), the dignity and grandeur that had adhered to English architecture since the time of Perpendicular Gothic, and the indigenous English tendency toward spatial complexity, formal variety, and architectural fantasy, present in

earlier structures such as the Cathedral of Canterbury and the portions in Decorated Style at Ely and Wells. Wren produced in St. Paul's a pragmatic assimilated composite that, in its grand scale and majestic self-confidence, was as Baroque in spirit as contemporary monuments in France and Italy.

A few years before St. Paul's, Wren built St. Stephen's, Walbrook (1672–79; figs. 9-80, 9-81), his own parish church on the street where he lived, as one of the churches to replace those destroyed in the 1666 conflagration. Here it is Wren as geometrician who dominates, for the design of the building is based on a series of abstract figures that in the complexity of their formal interaction recall the structures of Byzantium. Within a rectangular outline is nested a square space defined by twelve columns and covered by a huge dome. The circular base of the dome is not carried, in the conventional way, by pendentives

9-80 Christopher Wren. Interior, St. Stephen's, Walbrook. London. 1672–79

9-81 Plan, St. Stephen's, Walbrook

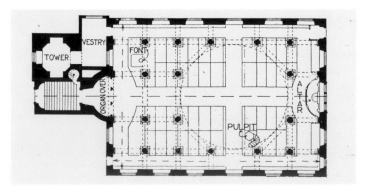

formed above the arches of the square, but on a circle formed by eight arches that spring from eight of the twelve columns, cutting across each corner in the manner of the Byzantine squinch. Inscribed within the circle of the dome is a Greek cross formed by the nave and an aisle that crosses it. The space moves fluidly through the columnar screen (the only walls are on the perimeter) to create a unified room filled with light (an immense clearglazed window backs the altar, and there are windows framed by each arch beneath the dome). If there is an "English Baroque" that can be likened to that of the continent, it is not only in the grandeur of St. Paul's but in this smaller building with its dynamic flow of unconfined space, its expressive light, and its richness of gilded relief in the coffers and pendentives of the dome, entablature, and capitals. But here the drama of the Baroque is made to serve the Protestant liturgy. Wren imagined the parish churches as auditoriums where the entire congregation could comfortably see and hear the preacher, where the laity and clergy would not be architecturally separated, and where a unifying dome, a compact interior, unencumbered space, and clear light would foster spiritual assembly.

Gibbs and Vanbrugh. If the Classical and rational traditions that were at the foundation of the architecture of Wren and particularly of Jones presaged the Neoclassicism of eighteenth-century England, it was James Gibbs and Sir John Vanbrugh who were the forces behind the Romantic historicism that was to become the other significant eighteenth-century trend in English art. Gibbs trained in Rome under Carlo Fontana in the first decade of the century. His finest work is London's St. Martin-in-the-Fields (1722–26; fig. 9-82), a celebrated building that spawned countless offspring in England and the New World. It was the remarkable combination of the wide, colonnaded temple front with lofty spire rising behind the pediment that was to be so fervidly taken up. The temple front and the architectural elements of each tier of the steeple reflect Gibbs's Roman experience and his familiarity with Italian Renaissance, Mannerist, and Baroque forms, as well as those of Roman antiquity. The idea of a steeple, however, comes out of the very different tradition of the Gothic cathedral. The inclusion of this steeple at St. Martin-in-the-Fields heralds the Romantic interest in reviving the forms of medieval architecture.

English Romanticism was also fueled by the architectural creations of Sir John Vanbrugh, whose career was as flamboyant as the buildings he designed. He was a soldier, arrested and imprisoned in France in 1690 for spying; he was a playwright who wrote popular and successful comedies; and almost by chance he began to work as an architect in 1699. A man of creative gifts, imagination, and daring, Vanbrugh, without any formal training, had an intuitive sense for designing buildings, which he did for members of the English aristocracy he frequented. (Characteristically, he designed no churches.) He acquired the necessary technical knowledge for construction on the job, and left the details to assistants.

Vanbrugh's major work (probably done with some collaboration from Nicholas Hawksmoor, one of Wren's assistants), and the best example of his imposing brand of English "baroque Baroque," is Blenheim Palace (1705–22; colorplate 59). The building was given to the duke of Marlborough in honor of his great military victory over the French at Blenheim in Louis

9-82   James Gibbs. St. Martin-in-the-Fields. London. 1722–26

XIV's war for the succession to the Spanish throne. Vanbrugh designed a prestigious palace of such titanic scale that it became (and has continued to be) more a national symbol of England's prestige and power than a ducal residence. A colossal pile of masonry, it follows no particular stylistic current, but is a freewheeling amalgam of oversized forms plucked with abandon from the history of architecture.

An ancient temple porch is set before a High Renaissance palace, the two unified by a colossal order. A pair of colonnaded wings (a version of Bernini's St. Peter's colonnade) curve away from the ends of the central block, form a screen for a cluster of rectangular blocks behind, and butt against two huge lateral pavilions. On top of these pavilions, and indeed atop most of the building including the entrance porch pediment, is a heavy superstructure made of piers and finials. These portions of the palace are fronted by an enormous courtyard, from which two immense symmetrical wings, actually minor palaces with independent entrances, open to either side. Although its gigantic spread is in the tradition of Versailles, the architectural elements of Blenheim are heavy and bombastic and have none of the elegance and harmony of proportions that distinguish the French monument. But Vanbrugh was seeking to create the impression of something not only heroic but also romantic in its evocation of medieval castle-fortresses with their heavy massings and irregular profiles. Working intuitively, and with only superficial references to the Classical tradition, Vanbrugh produced an imposing melange that had the power to overwhelm in the same way as all the great monuments of Baroque architecture.

Pages 372–73
James
Stirling.
Neue
Staatsgalerie,
Stuttgart.
1977–83

10-1
James Wyatt.
The Octagon,
Fonthill
Abbey.
1795–1807.
(Engraving
from J.
Britton)

Chapter Ten | The Eighteenth Century

THE HISTORICAL SETTING

In our minds there exists for every age an ideal architectural image, often represented by a single monument—the Parthenon for ancient Greece, Old St. Peter's for early Christianity, the Tempietto for the High Renaissance. No period is more architecturally diverse than our own, yet the phrase "Modern Architecture" also conjures up an image—that of a large, multistoried building of pure geometric massing, constructed of a steel frame and a glass envelope, devoid of ornament, and used as a corporate headquarters, a structure, in other words, such as the Lever House (colorplate 80). Such buildings can be traced back to the early twentieth century, but no farther. Although the nineteenth century was, in nearly every sociocultural aspect, unequivocally "modern" or rapidly becoming so, it was also the period of buildings such as the Paris Opera or London's Houses of Parliament, which were disconcertingly similar to works of previous centuries. Nor was the eighteenth century any different. Indeed, just as history turned then to march bravely into the future, architecture seemed to retreat into the distant past, beginning with monuments such as Chiswick House (colorplate 67), built outside London in 1725 as a "copy" of Palladio's Villa Rotonda of almost two centuries earlier. The architecture of historicism—the revival of earlier styles, as opposed to the Modernist affirmation of the "new"—coincides with the momentous changes that transformed the old order of Europe into the modern world of the eighteenth and nineteenth centuries. Why historicism has proved so important in the architecture of modern times, and, conversely, how the roots of architectural Modernism were formed, are questions to be explored against a broader historical background.

Architecture and the Industrial Revolution. Few would dispute the fact that the greatest historical event to occur in this volatile "modern" period was the Industrial Revolution. So profoundly did it alter human life that it has been compared to the agrarian revolution of the Neolithic period, when the nomadic hunter became a village-dwelling farmer (and the first architecture appeared). Despite the diversity of premodern history, certain material aspects of life had remained basically unchanged. The majority of people were subsistence-level, village-dwelling farmers, and the same limited sources of energy were employed, the same simple materials and means of transportation were used, with labor and production organized in the same primitive way. The Industrial Revolution broke this pattern, and the old manner of life and work was swept away in an astonishing series of technological breakthroughs. In place of human and animal muscle power, the coal-burning steam engine offered seemingly unlimited amounts of energy; to replace the laborious, piecemeal production of individual craftsmen, machines were devised to turn out goods in quantity; and in place of natural materials, iron, then steel, and eventually many other metals and synthetic substances were used. Factories grew rapidly, and with them came an increase in the populations of towns and cities. Improvements in agricultural productivity, sanitation, and average income level contributed strongly to the growth and physical well-being of a population increasingly concentrated in cities. In a more mobile economy, traditional social distinctions began to erode, hastening the end of the old way of life.

Before the Industrial Revolution, the imaginative energies of European architects had been channeled principally into the evolution of ever-more-elaborate versions of a few restricted forms: the church, the palace, and the fortress (along with variations, such as the villa and the town hall). Now a much broader functional base for architecture presented itself. There were the industrial constructions themselves—factories, warehouses, railroad stations (later airports), and bridges—and buildings for related commercial and service industries such as banks, exchanges, department stores, markets, and office buildings. A second group of building types developed in response to the expanded population in cities. Thus, beginning in the late eighteenth century, palaces of justice, seats of parliament, large theaters, hospitals, hotels, resorts, public parks, and libraries were built in abundance and at great expense. Mass housing was an increasing preoccupation of architectural planners, and the single-family middle-class house (in place of the aristocratic residence) became one of the forms most intensely developed. Traditional forms of construction were adequate for certain of these new building types, but others stimulated the invention of new constructional means, provided by the very technology that fostered the Industrial Revolution. Traditional building materials had been those either taken directly from nature—stone and wood—or gained through simple processing of natural materials—mortar and brick. Material requiring a higher level of technology and energy input—iron and glass in particular—had been used sparingly, but the Industrial Revolution was able to provide these in larger quantities at lower cost and higher quality. "Industrial" building materials made it possible for engineers to devise structures of tremendous height, span, and strength, and the new technology provided the means that ensured the materials' full exploitation. This involved the use of new design methods and powerful machinery in construction. Guesswork was replaced by precise, mathematical means of assessing the strength of materials and of structural configurations.

In terms of the millennia of human history, the Industrial Revolution occurred with traumatic swiftness, but compared with political revolutions, it was a slow-motion event beginning in England in the second half of the eighteenth century and spreading to France after 1830, to Germany after 1850, to the United States after the Civil War. Even in England, the most advanced and prosperous nation of the nineteenth century, it took several generations before industrialization spread from its origins in weaving, mining, and a few railroad lines to become a pervasive economic and social fact, reaching its full extent only in the early twentieth century. The Industrial Revolution's overwhelming effect on architecture was also gradual, following a step-by-step pattern of evolution: first, its program; later, its construction; and only at the end, its monumental appearance.

The Intellectual Revolution and the Enlightenment. With minor exceptions, these steps all occurred well after 1800, but what of architecture in the eighteenth century? Industrialism was not the only "revolution" to contribute fundamentally to the formation of the modern world. Indeed, the economic transformations were a result of developments in the intellectual sphere. These developments, often termed the Intellectual Revolution, originated in Renaissance Italy where a set of new attitudes had taken form. It was in the Renaissance that the radical concept of the spiritual and intellectual autonomy of the individual was introduced, especially the importance of personal experience of the natural world, and the powers of reason to understand that experience. The effects of this transformation of human consciousness were gradual, but, over the generations, its cumulative force snowballed and, ultimately, its impact was shattering. Beginning with Copernicus's theory that a spinning earth and other planets revolved around the sun (rather than the earth being the center of the universe), many stunning discoveries in mathematics and physics were made by brilliant scientists of the seventeenth century, culminating with the towering figure of Isaac Newton. With the turn of the eighteenth century, the intellectual and scientific movement was warmly embraced by society-at-large, and when Newton was buried in 1727—two years after the Chiswick House design—it was with royal honors.

Concomitant with the new ideas about the physical world there appeared an equally radical reformulation of the nature of the humanity that inhabits it, continuing the direction set by Renaissance philosophers. The key figure was John Locke, a contemporary of Newton's. He proved, at least to the satisfaction of the advanced thinkers of the age, that, far from being a fallen creature cursed hereditarily by Original Sin, man was born innocent and as pure potential—in Locke's famous phrase, as a *tabula rasa* (blank sheet) on which experience "wrote" afresh, forming every person's character and abilities. A half century later, Jean-Jacques Rousseau insisted that early man—a kind of "noble savage" still supposedly found in primitive cultures—had been good and pure before being enslaved and corrupted by civilization.

It is hard to overestimate the revolutionary potential of such ideas, not only in the elevated spheres of philosophy and science, but also for society and culture at large. The Renaissance had emphasized individual thought, action, and achievement; the Enlightenment—as the eighteenth-century phase of the Intellectual Revolution is known—advanced theories about humanity as a group of potentially innocent and rational beings. Intoxicated by the discoveries of Newton and the other scientists, men and women of the Enlightenment believed fervently in the power of reason to discover and conquer all. Rationalize society, its institutions, laws, educational system, it was thought during the Enlightenment, and humanity will be restored to something resembling the pure and blissful state described by Rousseau, a notion that took political form in the American and French revolutions.

Romanticism and the Cult of Sensibility. If the eighteenth century was the Age of Reason, as it is often called, it was also an age of antithetical trends. The Renaissance individualism that ultimately led to the Enlightenment inevitably called forth a parallel emphasis on individual feelings and imagination. In the eighteenth century, reason was worshiped, and simultaneously the subjective—and secular—emotional experience was cultivated to an unprecedented degree. In this respect, the period is also the Age of Sensibility, which blurs into the somewhat later Romantic movement. The cultivation of the subjective and the irrational took many forms. With the stress on the unfettered uniqueness of the individual, the artist became the Romantic cultural hero who struggled to break the rules (including the dictates of reason) in order to achieve his personal "genius." The Romantic temper tended to reject the present state of things; indeed, it tended to reject the present altogether. Toward the mid-eighteenth century, dissatisfaction with nearly every aspect of the status quo swept through the enlightened circles of Europe. In part, this was a recoil from the cultural and social decadence of the *ancien régime*, but it was also rooted in the intolerance of rationalism for the "decadent" art and architecture of Rococo society. One reaction was to alter things radically, through reform and revolution; another was to escape into a Romantic fantasy world, into an idealized vision of distant times and places.

Eighteenth-Century Historicism. Historicism was a perfect architectural medium for this Romantic Age of Reason and Sensibility. To the rationalist, it offered an ever more purified Neoclassicism to replace "Barocco" decadence, while the cultivation of feeling and fantasy resulted in architectural gratification in the escapist world of re-created styles, ranging from the exotic East and the mysterious "Gothick" to a Neoclassicism exploited not for its rationalism but for its evocative potential for poetic reverie and associations. It is important to realize, however, that historicism as such was nothing new, being, in fact, nearly as old as architecture itself. The Romans were adept at it, Romanesque was founded on it, and it was the point of departure for the Renaissance. Old St. Peter's, the cathedrals of Aachen and Speyer, and S. Lorenzo are all historicist buildings. Indeed, beneath all the stylistic development through the Renaissance and the Baroque there was a constant exploration of diverse aspects of antiquity, as well as a recycling of previous Renaissance and Baroque forms themselves. However, prior to the eighteenth century, historicism had been limited by a number of factors. In monolithic societies ruled by the idea of authority, historicism had served essentially as raw material for ongoing, self-propelled, monolithic stylistic development. But in an increasingly pluralistic age, with authoritarianism giving way to individualism and cultural relativism, historicism cast a far wider net and, in doing so, filled a vacuum and was elevated from a secondary to a central architectural role. As all historical styles became available to satisfy an infinity of moods, tastes, and needs, it was not as a parade of styles, as historicism is often called disparagingly, but as a protean, dynamic style itself (like Renaissance or Baroque). It was a style that expressed the complex nature of modern society, no longer stable and monolithic as it had been for centuries, but volatile, pluralistic, and in constant need of ever-new and varied architectural forms.

The rise of historicism was dependent on still another factor: the birth and development of modern architectural scholarship. The re-creation of styles obviously depends on relatively accurate knowledge of them. Prior to the eighteenth century, knowledge of the architectural past, other than of the masterpieces of the Renaissance and selected Classical monuments, was vague and confused. Architectural scholarship began in earnest as part of the Enlightenment's extension of scientific methods to the cultural realm, and led to an increasing sophistication of knowledge, precision in dating, and conception of historical styles. Such scholarship was not merely an academic matter. Beginning in the mid-eighteenth century with the discovery of Pompeii and Herculaneum and the shocking reality of the true Greek Doric order, and lasting until far into the nineteenth century, architectural scholarship offered revelation after basic revelation, startling images of the past that became compelling new models for practicing architects, many of whom led double lives as architect-scholars. Not only did they seek to recapture the past in theory, but they also created designs and invented architectural concepts that played a major role in the Romantic architectural movement.

THE AGE OF REASON AND ROMANTICISM IN ENGLAND
The Palladian Revival. Even though architectural historicism seems to materialize suddenly at scattered places across Europe in the eighteenth century, a pattern of events can be discerned. For one thing, Classical and Classically derived styles dominate, although the revival of other architectures, particularly medieval styles, is a factor from early in the period. The earliest example of Neoclassicism, however, was a revival of antiquity through a Renaissance intermediary, Andrea Palladio.

English Palladianism of the early eighteenth century clearly shows the interaction between politics, ideas, and art. In the political background is the struggle between the Tories and the Whigs in the late seventeenth and early eighteenth centuries. Liberal, mercantile, and rationalist in outlook, the Whigs looked with disfavor on visible manifestations of their opponents' ways, and they developed an intense hostility to the Baroque buildings of Vanbrugh and Hawksmoor, whose bombastic excesses, such as the "false and counterfeit . . . magnificence" of Blenheim Palace, were identified with Tory causes. Whig critics detested the Baroque for its political connotations and for its unnaturalness, and they turned back to the serene rationality of Palladio as an antidote. (Conveniently, they forgot that the Palladian manner had first been imported to England by Inigo Jones as a vehicle of absolutist Stuart pretensions.) In 1715, a year after the inauguration of George I, Inigo Jones was hailed as a British Vitruvius in the influential publication of Colen Campbell, *Vitruvius Britannicus*; his style

was the proposed model of a Classical, noble, English style, the antithesis of the continental Baroque of the absolutist Catholic powers. Jones's model, Palladio, was now revalued principally for his great series of villas, in which Vitruvian architecture had been adapted to the needs of a mercantile aristocracy closely bound to the land, a historically ennobled class in which the Whig aristocracy saw itself mirrored, and whose way of life echoed that of the Roman patricians themselves—commuting between the Senate and their country villas—familiar to the English from Pliny and other ancient sources.

The most important of the several protagonists of the Palladian revival was Richard Boyle, the third Earl of Burlington. Although not quite among its earliest pioneers, Lord Burlington was the individual with the social status, financial means, and intellectual fiber to make it a significant and enduring movement that dominated English architecture from about 1720 to 1760. One would not easily confuse the best-known building of the Palladians—Burlington's Chiswick House of 1725 (colorplate 67)—with its model, Palladio's Villa Rotonda of the 1550s in Vicenza (fig. 8-75). The dominant element of Palladio's massing is a grand cubic central block. Into it is set a cylindrical core, appearing on the exterior as a Pantheon-like, stepped, hemispherical dome. And from each side, an identical hexastyle Ionic porch, set above a noble flight of stairs, opens out to the landscape. Lord Burlington's translation from sixteenth-century Italian to eighteenth-century English language nowhere achieves the bold, organic clarity of Palladio. There is no sense of a central cube at Chiswick House, but rather one of four papery walls rising on a square plan. Floating above the chimney-cluttered roof is an octagonal dome with Roman *thermae* windows (a favorite device of the Palladians) cut into its thin walls. Only one side of the building receives a templo front entrance (smaller than Palladio's counterpart, leaving more blank surface at the corners), set above a complicated stair arrangement and a distracting row of openings into the basement. Whereas Palladio's design represented the epitome of Italian Renaissance three-dimensional, integral wholeness and clarity, Burlington's creation seems almost like a stage-set pastiche of insubstantial forms. To our eyes, Chiswick House embodies an intricacy that stems from the difficulty of even such a forceful personage as Burlington to fully escape the deep current of English anti-Classicism and its fanciful tendencies. But such qualities were invisible to Burlington's eighteenth-century English admirers. To them, the restraint, simplicity, and discipline of the Classical masters were the building's strongest qualities. Chiswick House stood forth as the first manifesto of a new, rationalist architectural order.

Burlington's mastery of his architectural ambitions evolved rapidly in the 1720s, and in 1730 he produced his most mature design, the Assembly Rooms at York (figs. 10-2, 10-3), which represented a radical advance beyond Chiswick House, both in visual properties and in the realization of Burlington's resolve to reestablish the eternal rules of architecture. Burlington's point of departure in accomplishing this task had first been the direct imitation of Palladio's buildings. Now it was Palladio's descriptions, drawings, and reconstructions of antiquity that guided the Englishman. This shift in perspective—occasioned in part by Burlington's acquisition of a collection of Palladian drawings of ancient buildings in the late 1720s—is grasped

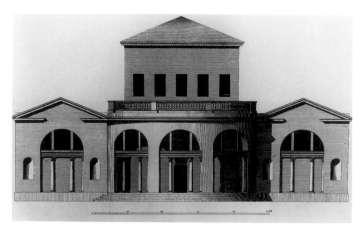

10-2 Richard Boyle, Lord Burlington. Facade, Assembly Rooms. York. 1730. (Engraving from C. Campbell, *Vitruvius Britannicus*)

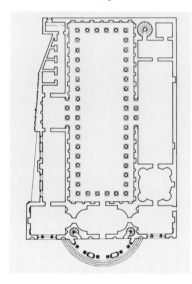

10-3
Plan, Assembly Rooms

to the accomplishments of eighteenth-century science. In Renaissance theory, Classical art was considered to have distilled near-perfection of form from the raw phenomena of experience. Thus Renaissance architecture, in its abstraction and idealism, its correspondence to eternal Platonic ideas and proportional harmonies, was now viewed as a close approximation to the new concepts of science and philosophy, and Palladio was seen as its purest embodiment.

The facade of the Assembly Rooms—replaced in 1828—was as remarkable as the interior. Palladio provided Burlington with no hint of a facade for the Egyptian Hall but this was not insurmountable, for what he was building was not an Egyptian hall but an assembly room for the York gentry in the form of an appropriate ancient model. If the Egyptian Hall provided the principal interior, another ancient building type could serve for the facade. While he was planning the building in 1730, Burlington published his collection of Palladio's drawings for the restoration of Imperial Roman *thermae*. Roman baths were, after all, monumental palaces of public entertainment. Burlington's transformation of the *thermae* into the York facade was iconographically ingenious and formally brilliant. He extracted eclectically from Palladio's drawings the features essential to the image of the Roman baths, reduced to diagrammatic but recognizable form based on the most reductive Palladian style. The telltale motif is the so-called *thermae* window type—a twin-columned trabeation surmounted by twin mullions, taken by Palladio from the Baths of Diocletian—which Burlington superimposed on the five round-headed openings that run across the austere facade. The main external elevation of the Baths of Caracalla was dominated by a huge, projecting *caldarium* rotunda, which Burlington schematized into a segmental porch. His triple vestibule—three apsidal rooms of contrasting but symmetrical geometry—is also a paradigm of the vast mirror symmetries of the Imperial Roman models. All the devices used by Burlington at York—the schematic geometry of massing; the discrete independence of the units; their direct interfacing without traditional cushioning modulations; and the repetitive employment of a few strong Neoclassical motifs (such as the *thermae* window)—were to be fundamental to Neoclassical architecture, especially in its ultimate form in late-eighteenth-century France.

William Kent, Burlington's great protégé, was in every way the opposite of his teacher. Of humble extraction, a house painter's apprentice, Kent was first discovered by a group of wealthy patrons who sent him to Rome for nearly a decade of serious study of art. There he was recruited by Burlington and brought to Burlington House in London as one among several artistic retainers, for at the time Burlington saw himself as a Medici-like patron at the center of a budding renaissance movement. His circle included Colen Campbell, who had converted him to Palladian ways, the poet Alexander Pope, and others. At first, Kent was to be Burlington's painter, but when his painterly talent proved to be less than that of genius, Burlington directed him to architectural decoration—in the mid-twenties Kent provided Chiswick House with its lavish interior detail—and, after 1730, to architecture. Together, they dominated the English architectural scene until Kent's death in 1748.

Kent's appeal to Burlington was an attraction of opposites. Burlington was taciturn and reserved; Kent, gregarious.

most easily in the interior of the Assembly Rooms. His commission was to build "a large Dancing room, not less than 90 feet long." His rationalist reaction was to research Palladio to find an ancient counterpart to an assembly hall and then actually build it as Palladio and his sources described it, irrespective of the practical requirements of an eighteenth-century dancing hall. Burlington discovered what he was looking for in Palladio's interpretation of Vitruvius's description of a spacious hall built in the "manner of the Egyptians," according to Palladio "very suitable for festivals and entertainments." Burlington's Assembly Rooms follow Palladio's reconstruction of the Egyptian Hall to the letter—a long rectangular central space, enveloped by a dense Corinthian colonnade and a narrow, continuous aisle. The dimension of the length of the Egyptian Hall was missing in Palladio's partial plan, but he wrote that the Egyptian Hall "resembles Basilicas very much," so Burlington gave the hall of the Assembly Rooms the eighteen-column length of Palladio's reconstruction of ancient basilicas. All details follow Palladio scrupulously, including the intercolumniation and aisle width of only twice the diameter of the columns—a narrowness that severely hampered dancing. Such practical deficiencies never diverted Burlington from his resolve to reestablish an architecture of absolute Classical standards as revealed by Palladio. Nor did they prevent him from seeking in Palladio an architectural counterpart

10-4　William Kent and Lord Burlington. Main facade, Holkham Hall. Norfolk, 1734

10-5　Plan, Holkham Hall

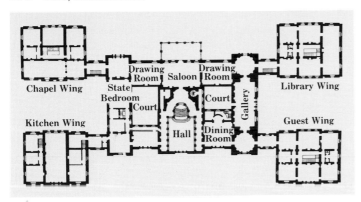

10-6　Entrance hall, Holkham Hall

Burlington was too cerebral to be entirely comfortable with the arts, and he concentrated on his pedantic ideal of reestablishing values in rigid Classical form. Kent was a born artist. His lack of the narrow, formal education of the day left his fertile imagination free to explore novel areas. He was fluent in many design media—fashion, festival decoration, furniture, book illustration, architecture and its decoration. He could work in the severely Classical Burlington manner or create whimsical "Gothick" novelties—and was among the originators of the Gothic Revival. Kent was also a master of landscape design, and it was he who practically invented the English garden, regarded by some as England's most significant contribution to eighteenth-century architecture.

Holkham Hall (figs. 10-4–10-6), the immense country house in Norfolk designed in 1734 for a Whig magnate, Thomas Coke, Earl of Leicester (and his great art collection), was Kent's grandest architectural production. The building, however, depends heavily on Burlington's style, and it is usually assumed that he played a strong role in its conception. The plan immediately reveals his dogmatic rationalism in its foursquare uniformity and symmetry and in its division into discrete parts. The central block of staterooms is flanked at the angles by quasi-independent secondary units for the chapel, kitchen, library, and guests. The same analytic fragmentation is apparent in the sweep of the main facade, which is deeply indebted to Burlington's earlier work. Each of the

three vertical units that front the corner pavilions is self-contained, and each pavilion, in turn, is independent of the central block, where, again, every detail is autonomous. How old-fashioned Vanbrugh's Baroque masterpiece of Blenheim, only three decades older, seems in its rhetorical extravagance, intricate texture, and variety of elements. One appreciates the satisfaction that a modern man of "taste," such as the Earl of Leicester, derived from his new estate—so lucid and rationalist in plan, chastely restrained in detail, and completely purged of all Baroque traits. But most of all, Leicester would have been proud of the masterstroke of the building—the entrance hall—one of the major interiors of eighteenth-century Europe. It has a daring expansiveness and sweep that Burlington himself would have been incapable of. Its point of departure was Burlington's Egyptian Hall at York. But here, narrow intercolumniation and the return of the aisle along the facade are combined with several additional forms. One is the Palladian "basilica"—which has an apse with stairs leading up into it. At Holkham Hall, stairs lead through it, for the apse takes the screened form of Palladio's Venetian churches. The colonnade, moreover, is lifted above a marble base and is surmounted by a rich coffered vault. In all of this, we witness the breakdown of Burlington's puritanical language; his rule of functional Classicism no longer holds. But it no longer mattered—not even to Burlington, for the aura of Roman magnificence gained by all the transgressions was far more important. Kent's freedom of design and luxuriant flair at interior decor were winning out. Palladianism here is at the edge of becoming something else.

Archaeological Neoclassicism. Enthusiastically received as a liberation from the extravagance of the Baroque, Palladianism dominated England until about 1760. It remained an active force in English building practice until the early nineteenth century (known as "Georgian"), spreading, moreover, to northern Europe (Germany, Russia) and to the American colonies, where Thomas Jefferson was an enthusiastic Palladian in his early work. However, in progressive mid-eighteenth-century English circles, a reaction to Burlington set in. Patrons grew tired of Palladian pomposity. The style was too severe and restricted, too airless and bookish. An aura of clarity and simplicity was still desired, but, as one leading patron put it, "simplicity improved by art and care"—code words for a less cerebral, more palpably sensuous, manner.

Scientific research had shown that the Renaissance was something fundamentally different and distinct from antiquity itself, and a new generation of architects experienced an insatiable hunger for the architecture of the ancient world, not as filtered through Renaissance architecture and treatises, but the real thing, which had been found through archaeological studies. English architects were the first to evolve a Neoclassical style that evoked the richness of antiquity, not merely its theoretical shadow. But this new archaeological Neoclassicism was far more than an isolated English phenomenon. It flourished not only in London, but also in Paris and in Rome, and each of the three centers played a distinct and vital role.

By the eighteenth century, Rome, the goal of religious pilgrimage, had also become the goal of artistic pilgrimage. The grandiose architectural relics of antiquity once again seized the imagination (as they had during the Renaissance) and inspired fresh study, not only of the antiquities of Rome itself but also of those that might be studied elsewhere, using Rome as a base. Among the latter, the most spectacular were the cities of Herculaneum and Pompeii, buried by the eruption of Mount Vesuvius in A.D. 79 and discovered nearly intact in 1738 and 1748, a sensational event that perhaps contributed more to Neoclassicism than anything else. But Rome was also where those personages devoted to the new Classical archaeology assembled—English gentlemen on the Grand Tour, French students on Grand Prix fellowships, students of all backgrounds connected with the various academies, and brilliant individuals such as Robert Adam, Piranesi, and Winckelmann.

If Rome was the material and emotional center of Neoclassicism, Paris was its cerebral counterpart. The tradition of French Classicism had been so thoroughly established in the seventeenth century through monumental buildings, theoretical writings, and the powerful Académie Royale d'Architecture that it had hardly been interrupted by the Rococo. French architecture had a thrilling affair with the stunning, curvaceous novelty, but it did not last long, and even while it lasted, French architects tended to remain faithful to the grand tradition in their more monumental work. This continuity was vital to the brilliant success of French Neoclassicism. It was in France that the greatest number of imposing Neoclassical monuments were constructed and there too that the most influential Neoclassical theories were advanced—all held together by the weight of French Classicism.

London had neither Classical ruins, nor—compared with the continent—much Classical architectural tradition. But eighteenth-century England had compensating qualifications for its leadership role in Neoclassicism: the absence of a strong Renaissance Classicism, which freed England, enabling it to turn back that much more quickly to antiquity itself. Burlington and his circle represented a precocious revival of interest in things antique and gave England, in effect, a head start. In 1732, the eminent Society of Dilettanti was formed, an association of gentlemen with firm archaeological interests, which they furthered as patrons, architects, or archaeologists. The English were the most adventurous and painstaking exponents of early "field" (as opposed to library) archaeology. They were the first to survey scientifically the Acropolis (1751), Palmyra (1753), Baalbek (1757), Split (Spalato; 1757), and Ionia (1764–69). Their work reached as far as China. In 1757, William Chambers published *Designs of Chinese Buildings*, the first concrete Western architectural glimpse of that land.

Archaeological publications played an important role in the Neoclassical movement by bringing the splendor of distant ruins into architectural reach. Two of the most important archaeologists of the period, however, were neither French nor English, but Italian and German, and their importance was not so much in the novelty of their discoveries as in their extraordinary style of presentation.

Giambattista Piranesi, a Venetian engineer and architect, was one of those who haunted Rome. He built little, but from 1743 to the 1760s he published views and reconstructions of real and imaginary Roman ruins that were presented with unparalleled drama: exaggerated scale, theatrical angles and lighting effects, a mood of decaying grandeur, and elaborate detail (figs. 10-7, 10-8). No one had ever seen or portrayed ancient architecture this way. The visual force of his etchings was decisive in winning many to the cause of Roman architecture.

But not everyone agreed with Piranesi's vision of its supremacy, especially with his nationalistic claim of the superiority of Rome to Greece. Together with the Piranesian obsession with Rome there appeared a parallel cult of Greek art. This constituted more of a novelty than we might at first imagine, for in the Renaissance and Baroque periods Greek art was little known and less imitated. Even the great German archaeologist J. J. Winckelmann, who almost single-handedly

10-7 Giambattista Piranesi. *Baths of Diocletian*. (Etching. The Metropolitan Museum of Art, New York)

10-8 Giambattista Piranesi. *The Prisons*. (Etching, Plate III, first state. The Metropolitan Museum of Art, New York)

created the "Grecian" movement, never was in Greece (despite several opportunities) and knew its art largely through Roman copies. Nevertheless, his knowledge of the subject— gained through years spent in Rome and Naples—was phenomenal. More importantly, his aesthetic response to the works themselves, particularly sculpture, was unparalleled, and his publications, culminating in his *History of Ancient Art* of 1763, were what mattered. Winckelmann's writings on Greek art were as crucial to its revival as Piranesi's etchings were for Roman architecture, and this influence depended on a literary flair that matched Piranesi's graphic genius, for

Winckelmann's writings are saturated with visual sensitivity and vivid expression.

Perhaps the most surprising forms to be retrieved from the Greek past were those of the architecture, not in the softened lines of their Roman interpretations, but in all their elemental severity and lucidity. It was the Doric order that especially startled the European architectural community. The squat columns, the absence of bases, the austere entablature—all the more austere in the engravings of the time—shocked the mid-eighteenth-century sensibility, which was still somewhat attached to the Rococo, although rebelling against it. Seen as rude and primitive, the Doric was at first rarely imitated; but gradually, in the final quarter of the century, it came to be appreciated for its archaic qualities, and eventually it was widely used along with other Greek forms in the Greek Revival movement of the early nineteenth century.

Although the first of the new Doric structures appeared in England—a diminutive structure built at Hagley Park in 1758 by James ("Athenian") Stuart—at first, as elsewhere in Europe, the Roman mode was the one most widely welcomed as an alternative to the strictures of Burlington and the other Palladians. But in the mid-eighteenth century, Rome meant something quite different from what it had meant for Bramante or Bernini. A case in point is the outstanding English architect of the post-Palladian period, Robert Adam.

Adam studied the remains of antiquity in the company of a French master, Charles-Louis Clérisseau—also the mentor of Thomas Jefferson—whom he met during a lengthy sojourn in Paris before arriving in Rome. This is an important detail because French Classical architecture was notable for its comprehensive planning, its precise handling of detail, and for its polish and elegance—qualities of Adam's work that indicate he learned to see antiquity, at least in part, through French eyes. From Imperial Roman architecture, Adam derived a number of characteristic features. Among them were plans that set together a series of rooms of contrasting geometric shapes, like those in Roman *thermae*, and a tendency to deploy freestanding, interior columnar screens. Also, he made much use of Roman interior ornamentation, especially stucco moldings and paneling.

Adam's use of such forms—along with Etruscan motifs and numerous aspects of sixteenth-century Italian Renaissance architecture, whose highly evolved detailing and intricacy of effect he much admired—was governed by several factors. From the beginning, he seems to have set out consciously to create a personal antique style, and this intent was reinforced by his friendship with Piranesi, who advocated employing antique sources with originality and imagination. Adam's work, however, must be seen not only in terms of his continental and antique sources, but also within the context of mid-eighteenth-century England. His clients were not Roman emperors or Renaissance princes but refined and cultivated English gentlemen who, like Adam himself, were steeped in the current ideology of "taste" and favored the exquisite in all things.

Although Adam did execute a number of major exterior designs, his fame rests on his interior work, which often involved the remodeling of pre-existing houses. A celebrated example of the Adam style is Syon House (figs. 10-9–10-12), Middlesex, where in 1762 he was commissioned to redo the entire interior of what had been a large Jacobean mansion.

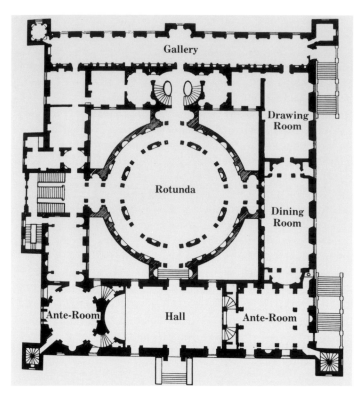

10-9   Robert Adam. Plan, Syon House. Middlesex, England.
1762–63

Adam's scheme to bring the inert, ancient walls to life was bold and comprehensive. A vast, intricately formed rotunda—unfortunately never executed—was intended for the bleak central court. The unpromising old quadrangular shell around the court was filled with a series of splendid new rooms. The entrance hall, on the south, is on the building's main axis but is oriented laterally across it in a single-apsed basilican form. Twin columns screen the hall from an even more imposing anteroom whose rectangular shape is ingeniously reduced to a square by the row of detached columns that dominates the interior. Next follows the dining room, again a rectangle, this time elaborated in antique fashion by a favorite Adam motif, twin screened apses.

The manner in which Adam transformed the building's medieval plan into a recollection of Imperial Roman schemes was complemented by the imaginative decorative treatment of the new interiors, involving a variety of forms culled by Adam from his vast knowledge of the Classical past. His idea was to re-create an "authentic" Roman style of interior decoration, and this aspect of his work is seen at its finest in three of the interiors of Syon House—the entrance hall, the anteroom, and the gallery. The entrance hall, lined with antique statuary and exquisite Neoclassical Adam furniture, immediately informed the visitor of its day of the new Classical language. The proportions of the room are airy and resonant. The principal embellishment of its walls takes the form of a restrained, crisply delineated Roman Doric order, in which every detail is carried out with the refinement that characterizes all of Adam's work. The short axis of the room is the major axis of the building and thus receives the maximum development of the order in the form of a pair of facing miniature triumphal arches, complete with little coffered barrel vaults and spandrel roundels. A sec-

ondary, bracketed pilaster order (sixteenth-century in origin) frames the clerestory windows, connecting the main order with the beamed ceiling, whose double-X pattern is precisely reflected in the Greek-fret inlay of the pavement, firmly unifying the room vertically as the main order does horizontally.

The Doric sobriety of the entrance hall is succeeded by the Ionic ornateness of the adjacent anteroom (fig. 10-11). In terms of color alone, the shift of mode is striking: Monochromatic chastity yields to sumptuous polychromy—glittering gilded details and twelve richly veined green columns, some of which had been excavated from the Tiber River and shipped to Syon in 1765. Using them on three sides of the room as engaged columns with a broken entablature, and freestanding on the fourth, Adam again suggested the Roman triumphal arch theme by surmounting the columns with gilded statues. The luxuriant marble shafts demanded appropriately ornate capitals. Because he never slavishly copied antique models but adapted and combined them to his own ends, the capitals are those of the Erechtheum, but their necking detail was replaced by a type Adam would have known from the Roman baths. The nearby gilded Roman trophies were adapted, via Piranesi, from examples on the Capitol, whereas the coffered ceiling was taken from the first of the Palladians, Colen Campbell. Adam's aim was never to enforce any particular antique canon, but to please in a way that suggested a palpable connection with Rome, no matter what the actual sources were.

The Jacobean Long Gallery (fig. 10-12) at Syon House was so long and narrow that it precluded Adam's reforming the space *all'antica* as he had elsewhere in the building. He was limited to redecorating the surfaces, and the intense life he bestowed upon the unpromising room is a true measure of his genius. As in the entrance hall, Adam's method was first to use a principal order to organize and animate the inert walls, and then to include a secondary order to articulate secondary features. In the entrance hall, these are stratified in two horizontal zones, whereas in the gallery the second is set within the first. On the outer wall, the main order is established in a row of Corinthian pilasters spaced with a regular rhythm following the window/wall alternation. On the opposite inner wall, these pilasters appear in groups of four, articulating the bookshelf bays between the several doorways, which are framed with an expanded version of the same pilaster order in the form of aediculae. On both walls, the secondary order, set within the first, takes the form of diminutive, attenuated Ionic pilasters. The ceiling is as intricate as the walls, with which Adam managed to link it at regular points. Nowhere in this scheme is the eye allowed to rest, for everywhere the panels are filled with spirited stucco enrichments—S-fluting, festoons, medallions, and rinceau arabesques.

Adam characterized the gallery at Syon as being "in a style to afford a great variety of amusement," and elsewhere he made explicit his predilection for a "variety of light mouldings" and especially for "movement," by which he meant "the rise and fall, the advance and recess, with other diversity of form." Diversity, lightness, and intricate movement are all aspects of Adam's art, beyond whatever Classical sources he may have employed. England had not experienced the continental Rococo—Lord Burlington saw to that—but in the mid-eighteenth century it appeared, it is often said, in masked form in the work of Adam and his school as a kind of Neoclassical Rococo. There is much

10-10 Entrance hall, Syon House

to be said for this viewpoint, for an interior such as the Syon House gallery seems at odds with such Neoclassical ideals as Winckelmann's "noble tranquility and quiet grandeur," and shares with the Rococo its interwoven, mobile linear patterns, its delicacy of touch, and its lighthearted spirit and gaiety. Yet there is more to Adam than that. Architecture has often been called "frozen music" and there is much about Adam's work that is reminiscent of that art, particularly the musical traditions of the eighteenth century. Something of a J. S. Bach is experienced in the fuguelike intricacy of a room such as the Syon House

10-11
Anteroom,
Syon
House

10-12　Gallery, Syon House

gallery, but there are also intimations of a Mozart in its lucid grace and lightness, its etched Classical vocabulary, and the pathos hidden in its lighthearted air.

The Sublime, the Picturesque, and Associationism. The most radical new architectural phenomenon to appear in eighteenth-century England was neither the rationalism of the Palladians nor the glittering Neoclassicism of Robert Adam. It was something less startlingly novel, yet all the more influential. It was in fact not a stylistic movement per se, but a new aesthetic syndrome that reflected an emphasis on the subjective and on emotion that was the reverse side of the Enlightenment, and it centered on three concepts: the Sublime, the Picturesque, and what we will call Associationism.

Architecture, to some degree, has always tended to evoke associations, but in the eighteenth century this tendency was heightened; it became far more explicit and even programmatic. The origins of this development are connected with the far-reaching implications of Neoclassicism and historicism in general. Greece turned out to be different from Rome. Each had its authentic character and its unique value. And if this was true of Greek and Roman architecture, so it also proved true of other practices as their shapes gradually emerged from the shadows—medieval, Chinese, Hindu, Islamic, even primitive. But long before much was really known about these architectural styles, a good deal was known and a lot more believed about the societies that had produced them, so that when the architectures themselves came into focus, they did so with strongly established overlays of thought and feeling. What is more, these notions were not "scientifically" dispelled by eighteenth-century rationalism but, on the contrary, they were cherished for the emotional and aesthetic pleasure they rendered and the way they seemed to give meaning to the otherwise meaningless new architectural shapes. The way in which the period reveled in associative responses can be seen in two quotes, one from the beginning of the Associationist movement, a second from its point of full development. Sir John Vanbrugh, in addition to being one of the masters of the English Baroque, was also a builder of such things as a castellated "Gothic" mansion for himself. Arguing chiefly on the ground of Associationism, he said that buildings of the distant past should be conserved because they inspire "more lively and pleasing Reflections on the Persons who have inhabited them; on the remarkable things which have been transacted in them, or the extraordinary occasions of erecting them." A hundred years later, this valuation of architecture for such associational effects was fully expanded by John Claudius Loudon, who in 1806 claimed that a Greek or Gothic structure could evoke "Sublimity; Beauty; Deformity; Picturesque Beauty; Sculpturesque Beauty; Antique Beauty; Romantic Beauty; Wildness; Tranquility; Melancholy; Age and Ruin; Elegance; Gaiety; Novelty; Ridicule." In the eighteenth century, two categories mentioned at the head of Loudon's list were chiefly seized upon—the "Sublime" and the "Picturesque"—for explicitly Associationist theorizing and design. These terms may seem quaint and innocent to us, but for the period they had far-reaching implications.

To grasp the significance of the Sublime in the eighteenth century, we must first of all realize that it was not synonymous with beauty. Rather, its emphasis was on the subjective reaction to aesthetic stimuli; as one writer put it in 1762, "Great and elevated objects considered with relation to the emotions produced by them, are termed grand and sublime." Characteristically, the principal effect of the Sublime was terror. This is explicitly clear in Alexander Gerard's *Essays of Taste* of 1759, in which he proclaimed that "Objects exciting terror are . . . in general sublime; for terror always implies astonishment, occupies the whole soul, and suspends all its motions." It was as if the Enlightenment turned on itself to produce the blotting out of reason by the most primal of emotions.

The "terror" of the Sublime was not that of a traumatic nightmare but, as the principal analyst of the phenomenon, Edmund Burke, called it in his famous book of 1757, *A Philosophical Enquiry into the Origin of Our Ideas of the Sublime and Beautiful*, "that delightful horror, which is the most genuine effect, and truest test of the sublime." Sublime horror, or the horrific Sublime, was a controlled, mock terror experienced nowadays in the likes of horror films and amusement-park rides. In the eighteenth century, it was a central cultural phenomenon, and architecture could provoke a sense of the sublime with the right style. Again, Burke made it explicit: "All edifices calculated to produce an idea of the sublime ought to be dark and gloomy." For England this tended to mean Gothic, and later, for France, an advanced, visionary Neoclassicism.

The Picturesque was perhaps an even more influential concept than the Sublime. The term first appeared innocently as *alla pittoresca* in sixteenth-century Italy to distinguish drawings painted with a brush from those drawn with crayon. Like the Sublime, the Picturesque was an expression of that powerful current of nonrationalism that accompanied the Enlightenment. In the course of the eighteenth century, it assumed two distinct meanings. One was connected with seventeenth-century Italian landscape paintings and the development of the English garden. Its other aspect was a general aesthetic ideal, expressed in the literature of the period, in which Picturesque beauty was what appealed to the eye of the painter for pictorial representation: "rough" forms that in their irregularity and asymmetry offered rich effects of chiaroscuro, colorism, and dramatic compositional arrangements.

We may well wonder what was behind all of this, when in the final analysis what was actually involved was the use of irregular, asymmetric architectural composition. Since the nineteenth century, we have more or less taken for granted this compositional mode, but before the advent of the Picturesque, only regular, symmetrical design was officially recognized in the canon of architectural beauty. In the eighteenth century, antirational design concepts required justification on some defensible grounds. Analogy to established pictorial modes was thus offered to sanction the use of irregular—Picturesque—architectural composition. Similarly, analogy to the sublime phenomena of nature—howling winds, roaring seas—was advanced in support of the irrational, emotionalist inclination toward "terror" and "gloom" in art. Paradoxically, the justification for these anti-Classical aesthetic categories rested on the oldest of all aesthetic doctrines, that art imitates nature—in the latter case directly, in the former, through established styles of painting.

The Gothic Revival. The new concepts of the Picturesque, the Sublime, and Associationism fused into a potent aesthetic that greatly contributed to several architectural movements, of which the Gothic Revival was perhaps the most telling. The Gothic Revival—which experienced several eighteenth-century Georgian phases before its transformation into the Victorian Gothic of the mid-nineteenth century—was not unheralded in England. Strictly speaking, it was not really a revival, since the Gothic had never completely expired. By 1612, when Inigo Jones's Classical movement was launched, England had the accumulation of over six centuries of medieval architecture. Every building was medieval, and every experience, every ritual of life was colored by this overwhelming architectural inheritance. There remained in England a bedrock of deep-seated religious, national, and emotional attachment to its medieval buildings, underlying the waves of Classical and rationalist rejection of the Middle Ages. It was not only a matter of grass-roots feeling, but also of continuous architectural practice. All through the period of English Renaissance and Baroque architecture, the Gothic style continued to be used, especially for ecclesiastical and collegiate structures.

In the eighteenth century, it was soon realized that the Gothic was full of "sublime" features. Gothic buildings were dark and gloomy; their vast height, pointed windows, and broken lines all contributed to that delicious sensation of terror so crucial to the Sublime. Gothic was also eminently Picturesque. It was full of asymmetry and irregularity, particularly in cathedrals such as Canterbury or Wells, and if preserved cathedrals were inherently Picturesque, the numerous ruined medieval hulks that dotted the countryside were doubly Picturesque and pervaded with Sublime echoes as well.

The expression of these themes constitutes one of the major chapters of eighteenth- and early-nineteenth-century literature. The association of Gothic—especially Gothic ruins—with melancholy, death, and horror occurs in a stream of melodramatic sentiment in eighteenth-century English literature, from poetry to prose essays and the "Gothic novel." Writers considered the Gothic a kind of movable scenery for escapist worlds of legend and dream, evoking gloomy and often ghoulish allusions to the transitoriness of life. The Gothic novel was the most popular literary vehicle of emotional medievalism. The genre began in 1764 with *The Castle of Otranto: A Gothic Story* by Horace Walpole, a literary and cultural personage who also figured prominently in the architecture of the early Gothic Revival. Walpole's novel, with its setting in a haunted castle, signaled a turning from the more restrained melancholy of the earlier Gothic poets to a new violence of passion and horror. Walpole was among the first to write of Gothic architecture as a serious style, comparable to the Greek. He called the Gothic Picturesque, but he was also instrumental in allying it with the aesthetic of the Sublime. His *Otranto* spawned a succession of Gothic novels in England and on the continent. In France, François-René Chateaubriand described a cathedral as a building one could not possibly enter without a "shudder," and the movement culminated in Victor Hugo's great novel, *Notre-Dame de Paris*, where the cathedral sets the whole mood of the "Gothick" story of the hunchback Quasimodo.

An important aspect of the Gothic Revival was the archaeological rediscovery of the Middle Ages. England's medieval architecture was the subject of near-total confusion concerning its history and even its actual appearance. A hint of the ignorance that obtained in the early eighteenth century, for example, was that Westminster Abbey (mid-thirteenth century) was believed to have been built by Edward the Confessor (eleventh century). Toward the middle of the eighteenth century, the scientific and archaeological spirit of the times came into action. But the architectural material was dauntingly vast and entangled, progress was slow at first, and even the most basic descriptive concepts and vocabulary were lacking, for the architectural literature had previously been almost exclusively monopolized by Classical material. What to do with all of the disorderly Gothic paraphernalia of structure, articulation, and decoration? In a primitive attempt to rectify this situation, one of the pioneer Gothic revivalists, Batty Langley, published a tract in 1747 outlining his notion of five Gothic orders as a parallel to the Classical Vitruvian model. Many of the best archaeologists were also poets (or vice versa), drawn to the material emotionally. Among them was Thomas Warton, who loved moonlit ruins and in 1763 published original sketches depicting the origin and development of Gothic architecture. His contemporary, Thomas Gray, made considerable strides and already knew, for example, the dates of the Ely Cathedral's Octagon and Lady Chapel and appreciated their importance. Such pioneer efforts continued, and in the early nineteenth century everything seemed to come finally into clear focus. In 1813, William Gunn described the differences between the Gothic and the Romanesque, and in 1817, Thomas Rickman established the architectural divisions for England still in use today—Anglo-Norman, Early English, Decorated, and Perpendicular. On the continent, parallel efforts were under way, which soon isolated the principal structural features of Gothic (flying buttresses, pointed arches, etc.) and—to nearly everyone's surprise—discovered by the 1830s that it was neither

the Germanic Goths nor the English Saxons who had invented Gothic architecture, but the French architects of the twelfth century. In Franz Theodor Kugler's *Handbuch der Architektur* of 1842, the historical picture of the Gothic was practically the same as it is today.

The significance of the scholarly and literary side of the Gothic Revival was enormous. It was as important for medieval architecture as the Renaissance had been for antiquity, for it reclaimed half of the architecture of Europe by giving it value and understanding and endowing it with new intellectual and spiritual life. It also shaped the architectural side of the Gothic Revival—historicist reconstruction, which, by the 1750s, acquired a new architectural accuracy, imaginative depth, and ambition. The man chiefly responsible for this development was Horace Walpole. It was not, however, an architecture of Sublime horror that Walpole was after at Strawberry Hill (figs. 10-13–10-15), a small house overlooking the Thames that he purchased as a seat of retirement in 1748. At first, the enlargements, as can be seen in the exterior of the southern wing, were unexceptional for the time. But in 1754, Walpole gathered about him a "Committee" of several close associates, mostly literati who, like himself, dabbled in architecture, and it is their successive additions, lasting into the 1770s, to the house that accounted for its renown. The most prominent of the group, Richard Bentley, illustrator of Gray's *Elegies*, was responsible for the screen and chimneypiece of Strawberry Hill's famous Holbein Chamber. Its first impression is one of lavish delicacy and dense but lighthearted curvilinearity of

10-13   Horace Walpole, Robert Adam, and others. Strawberry Hill. Twickenham. 1749–77

10-14 **Holbein Chamber, Strawberry Hill. Screen and chimney piece by Richard Bentley. After 1754**

10-15 **Library designed by John Chute, Strawberry Hill. 1754**

repetitive motifs. This and other interiors of Strawberry Hill—such as the Library by John Chute—have been called Rococo Gothic. Even Walpole termed the house "pretty and gay." But what most contemporary observers saw in it was the new accuracy of Gothic details. The screen of the Holbein Chamber was copied after a gate in Rouen; its chimneypiece was based on a tomb in Canterbury Cathedral. Sources for Chute's Library were seventeenth-century engravings of Old Saint Paul's Cathedral (destroyed in the London fire of 1666) and a tomb in Westminster Abbey. This new realism affirmed

the Gothic as something to be taken seriously, rather than merely being reflected casually and superficially. Yet there was more to it. The illustrator of Gray's melancholy *Elegies* and the author of *Otranto* knew that intimate domestic interiors dominated by accurate reproductions of Gothic tombs, bits of a cathedral destroyed by fire, and a gate from the city where Joan of Arc was burned at the stake were not merely "pretty and gay" but conveyed the distinct tenor of the "delicious" funereal pathos of the Sublime.

On the exterior of Strawberry Hill, the new note struck was not Gothic accuracy or pathos but the Picturesque. Walpole had declared himself in favor of "Chinese" asymmetry in 1750, and his building obliged by following an L-shaped path in its gradual accretion of ever-new, old-looking parts. Interestingly, it was Robert Adam—the only complete architectural genius associated with the fabric—who, beginning in 1759, gave Strawberry Hill its definitive mark of asymmetry in his round tower at the southwest corner. The Picturesque quality of the exterior also lay in its misleading air of natural growth through the centuries—resembling pictures of quaint old villages and manors. This accretionism, as we may call it, was not intended at the outset by Walpole, but emerged in the diverse contributions of its authors. The end result was full of potential for later builders in Picturesque modes.

Strawberry Hill was remarkable for the 1760s, but within a few decades it was being called a "Gothic mouse-trap." The author of this abuse was William Beckford, the enigmatic millionaire who at the end of the century outdid Walpole in his own Gothic villa, Fonthill Abbey (figs. 10-1, 10-16). Beckford's architect was James Wyatt, who began as a gifted follower of Robert Adam but ended as the greatest Gothic Revival master of his time.

Beckford first commissioned Wyatt, in 1795, to build a ruined abbey with a few habitable rooms in which to spend an occasional day or two in the romantic seclusion for which the patron was well known. But within five years, a vast, new, full-time dwelling was under way, its construction driven day and night by the impatient Beckford. Complete within a few years, it was an astonishing sight even from outside the forbidding eight-mile circuit of 12-foot walls that surrounded the property. Observers knew, of course, that it was Beckford's house, but what they saw was a miragelike version of a full-scale Gothic cathedral, composed, like the typical English medieval church, of a complicated accretion of multiform parts, gathered about a huge, Ely-like crossing tower 276 feet high. The proportions of this monument to Picturesque accretionism were—as one immediately sees in the crossing tower—extreme in their attenuation. Of the four cross-arms that extended with eccentric symmetry from the base of the tower, the pair running north-south were barely 25 feet wide, but 300 feet in length. On the interior, the central octagonal hall rose 120 feet to open into the vertiginous shaft of the lantern, and gloomy tunnel-like corridors of space stretched horizontally into seemingly endless depths, offering a powerful encounter with that delectably terrifying experience of the "Infinite Sublime." Looking at the interior, with its stunning spatial effects and newly heightened realism of Gothic detail, it is hard to imagine Wyatt's creation as a domestic setting—until one notices the two quite ordinary parlor sofas. At Strawberry Hill, Walpole had dared put a tomb in a living room; but at Fonthill, the

10-16   James Wyatt. Fonthill Abbey. 1795–1807. (Engraving
         from J. Britton)

entire living room is transformed into what is, first, a Gothic cathedral with all that implied, and second, a cathedral stretched to terrifying proportions. The tower was so high and narrow as to look structurally precarious. And indeed it actually was, for corrupt contractors had taken advantage of Beckford's obsessive haste and skimped on the foundations. One night in 1825, the tower collapsed, taking much of the outlying fabric with it. The abbey lay in ruins, eventually to disappear with scarcely a trace. But for a short period, had Beckford not already sold the building, he would have had the ruined Gothic abbey that was all he originally wanted.

The English Landscape Garden. One may at first wonder what is so remarkable about the English Landscape Garden. It looks so obvious and innocent in its gentle contours, sweeping lawns, clumps of trees, little serpentine lakes, and artful scattering of pavilions. Such parks, which seem not much more than nature itself slightly rearranged and replanted, proliferated everywhere in the nineteenth and twentieth centuries. Most public gardens in most cities were variants of the English type, be it the Englischer Garten in Munich, Central Park in New York, the Parc des Buttes-Chaumont in Paris, or the famous parks of London. We tend to forget that when the type was created in the eighteenth century, it was remarkable indeed not only in its novelty but also in the range of its sources and meanings.

First the Italians of the Renaissance and then the French in their seventeenth-century villas and châteaux had led Europe in reviving the antique traditions of elaborate landscape settings for architecture. The most striking aspects of the continental gardens were their artificiality and formality. Their design was a sophisticated art of intricate geometric plans, elaborate terracing, stairs and ramps, and carefully shaped plantings.

English builders of the eighteenth century were repelled by the continental "garden" for political, philosophical, and aesthetic reasons. The gardens at Versailles—a vast domain reshaped by André Le Nôtre for Louis XIV as a symbol of his absolute rule, in a sense over nature itself—were resented by France's liberty-loving enemy across the Channel. The philosophical objections centered on one of the pet themes of eighteenth-century rationalism—the concept of the Natural, that is, the "natural" forms of things before they have been misshapen by historical forces of unreason. The universe had revealed itself through science as something supremely ordered and rational. Architecture, a synthetic creation of the intellect, came under this rubric. But hills, lakes, trees, and flowers take their own free and varied forms. Freedom and random variety, not preordained rational order, formed the natural state of the outdoors. Hence, the continental garden was viewed as the hatefully artificial antithesis of the natural.

English garden designs that followed from this idea were not simply fenced-off parcels of natural landscape similar to modern forest preserves. Far from it. In their own way, they were as artificial and sophisticated in design as their French and Italian counterparts. For the English garden was not only a rejection of the formal garden and an affirmation of the natural landscape, but it was also a response to specific sources that combined painting, poetry, myth, travel, and even art collecting and other forms of personal aggrandizement. The deepest roots were literary. Just as the Gothic Revival was rooted in "Gothic" literature, so the eighteenth-century English Landscape Garden was bound up with the Arcadian mode of Vergil and Ovid, evocations of a lost golden world of myth and pastoral solitude, an escapist vision of antiquity first revived by the Renaissance. The literary expression of the Arcadian was paralleled by its pictorial realization in the celebrated seventeenth-century Roman school of landscape painters— Claude Lorrain chief among them—who depicted Arcadian Greece in the topographic language of the landscape around Rome, rich in Picturesque incident and dotted with rustic houses and melancholy ancient ruins. Englishmen on the Grand Tour collected such paintings and saw the Italian landscape through them and through the poetic and mythological traditions behind them. When they returned to England, they sought to re-create such settings, with all their associations, in their country homes.

Translating the visions of the Roman Baroque painters and the ancient poets into the gardens of English estates involved considerable genius, for the native materials were very different. English landscape architects did not attempt to transplant the idealized shapes of the Roman countryside literally, but rather to evoke the Picturesque effects of the Italian vision, to re-create its nostalgic and idyllic moods. The first to do this was William Kent, who, as Walpole put it, "First leaped the fence and saw that all of nature was a garden." In the 1730s and forties, Kent turned his imagination loose on the outdoors and created the English Landscape Garden in its fullest dimensions, which involved not only natural materials but architecture (including built mock ruins), sculpture, and a syndrome of allusions to the worlds of painting, poetry, and mythology.

The most remarkable example of the Kentian garden, which was later popular on the continent as the *jardin anglais*, was Stourhead (fig. 10-17). It was not designed by Kent himself but by another follower of Burlington, Henry Flitcroft, working closely in the 1740s and fifties with his patron, Henry Hoare, a culturally ambitious banker. Stourhead was the perfect realization of the eighteenth-century yearning for a Vergilian and Claudian Arcady. The Stourhead park was created in a luxuriant valley, which Flitcroft made into a lake with a path around it that provided a sequence of Picturesque views and encounters with temples, statuary, springs, and a grotto, all involving layers of visual, literary, and even personal allusion. One of the principal Picturesque views at Stourhead is known to reflect Claude Lorrain's *Coast View of Delos with Aeneas* (fig. 10-18) and the passage from Vergil on which it was based, relating Aeneas's account of his experience in the Temple of Apollo at Delos. Going further into the work of ancient legend, the circuit around the Stourhead lake entails an allegory of Aeneas's journey through the underworld—the grotto, for example, represents the descent into Avernus, to behold there the statues of the inspirational Nymph and the fruitful River God. The architectural set-pieces, each in a Picturesque location, include a Temple of Apollo, a Temple of Flora, a Pantheon (from the Claude painting), and a Palladian bridge. Furthermore, the Middle Ages are mixed in. From the

10-17   Henry Flitcroft and Henry Hoare. Stourhead Park. 1744–65

10-18   Claude Lorrain. *Coast View of Delos with Aeneas*. (National Gallery, London)

entrance to the grotto is revealed a vista of the local medieval village with its parish church and a fourteenth-century decorated stone cross, moved to Stourhead from Bristol. Even more remarkable is the three-sided Alfred's Tower built by Flitcroft on Kingsnettle Hill, where Alfred the Great, who represented the idea of enlightened kingship, had raised his battle standard against the Danes in 870.

The medieval "furniture" of Stourhead emphasizes the point that the Picturesque and Associationist aspects of the English Landscape Garden were by no means limited to the Classical world, but could involve almost anything. To borrow and to assimilate elements from remote, non-European sources were among the delightful indulgences of the eighteenth-century artistic imagination. Chinese forms—the popular chinoiserie mode of eighteenth-century decoration—were especially appealing, and in the "natural" English Landscape Garden they struck exotic chords that set up an evocative "Oriental" resonance. The most extreme example of this direction, foreshadowing the general architectural eclecticism of the late nineteenth century, was London's Kew Gardens, as originally set up in the 1760s by William Chambers to include: Temples of Bellona, Pan, Aeolus, Solitude, the Sun, and Victory; a Chinese Pagoda (colorplate 65); a House of Confucius; an Alhambra; a Roman theater, a mosque, a ruined gate, and—not to be omitted from such "follies"—a Gothic cathedral.

Such gardens, of course, were at a great remove from the typical English countryside, which was agrarian and gentle in its rolling hills, lakes, and hedgerows. In the estates created after 1750 by landscape architect Lancelot ("Capability") Brown, such as Blenheim, Longleat, or Chatsworth, the countryside was gently reshaped to look, to eighteenth-century eyes, more "natural" than nature itself, forming the perfect setting for the villas at their centers. Typically, these estates offered vistas of sweeping lawns running right up to the house, serpentine ponds artfully disposed, and varied clumps of trees (a Brown speciality, evoking forests) and screens of greenery to mask the boundaries of the site. There were no rules for their designs, no set geometries or symmetries, no clearly defined paths of movement for the visitor; it was all a matter of atmosphere, sensibility, and mood.

Capability Brown's style of landscape design was tremendously successful and justly renowned. Many estates were converted from older, formal styles by his heroic efforts. Brown, a forceful individual by whom, reputedly, even the king was intimidated, when asked why he had not worked in Ireland, replied, "I haven't yet finished with England."

The High Picturesque Style. The Picturesque was one of the most important aesthetic ideals to emerge in eighteenth-century England. Its early phase, as we observed in the Gothic Revival and the Landscape Garden, was chiefly engaged with Associationist values and thus implied a conception of architecture as largely an expression of literary ideas, images, and values—in other words, as subservient to nonvisual, and especially to nonarchitectural, media. By the end of the eighteenth century, the Picturesque had evolved from the spontaneous movement it had been through most of the century into a self-conscious, well-analyzed aesthetic program—from what might be called the early Picturesque to the High Picturesque phase. Associationism still continued, but the theorists now emphasized things like irregularity and variety for their own sake, and the manner in which these characteristics give the impression of the work having been built, in the words of one of the writers of the 1790s, "piece-meal, during many successive ages, and by several different nations." Most of all, theorists stressed the way in which such designs contribute to the "principal features of [such] a place," its blending "picture-esquely" into its "natural" setting, whose accidental features were to be exploited rather than concealed. These newly emphasized criteria, though still bound up with literary sources, were at least more visual and, in effect, returned the Picturesque to the mainstream of the visual arts. No longer was it to be merely the plaything of an occasional Walpole or Beckford; it could be absorbed into the mainstream of architecture and be put to much wider use.

Many artistic movements produce a dominant figure; for the High Picturesque it was John Nash. Although his career ended in scandal at the death of his patron, George IV, in 1830, during the previous three decades, the period of the High Picturesque, Nash led the movement with a series of glittering successes. Never an artisan concerned with painstaking detail, Nash had a conceptual boldness and agility, a breathtaking ability to improvise, all in perfect harmony with the spirit of the Picturesque. His enormous range and his command of styles are best observed in country houses, in which he excelled. In 1802 appeared his Italianate Cronkhill (fig. 10-19), whose compact, asymmetrical massing, Italian vernacular loggia, and round tower reflected a building in Claude Lorrain's painting, *Landscape with the Ponte Molle*. In 1811, Nash began his extraordinary Blaise Hamlet, based conceptually on an English pictorial tradition best represented by Gainsborough's depiction of quaint old villages. The cottages of Nash's Hamlet, which reflect a contemporary vogue seen in numerous publications for rustic cottage designs, create an inspired illusion of the vernacular: artfully disposed cottages that in a varied and energetic manner combine thatch roofs, dormers, gables, brick and half-timber construction. Finally, in 1815, Nash took up the then-fashionable exoticism of "Oriental" modes at the Royal Pavilion at Brighton (fig. 10-20). Inaccurate in the details of its imaginative combination of Gothic, Chinese, and Indian forms, it is nevertheless unsurpassingly effective in its exotic image of the state tent of an Indian potentate. Nash used

10-20   **John Nash. Royal Pavilion, as remodeled 1815–23. Brighton**

cast-iron onion domes and minarets to achieve a lacy Picturesque luxuriance and movement of silhouette, which mask the underlying symmetry of the partly completed Palladian building with which he started.

Nash's major achievement was his spectacular example of urban planning—the Regent's Park and Regent Street scheme in London. It cannot be approached, however, without some consideration of earlier English urbanism. The English mentality, which favored in architecture the particular over the general and the individual entity rather than comprehensive schemes, was not particularly conducive to city planning, and significant examples of its practice do not abound. The most notable example prior to the eighteenth century was Christopher Wren's unexecuted plan for the rebuilding of London after the Great Fire of 1666, which, with its intersecting avenues, squares, and monuments, was dependent on French and Italian precedents. Wren's plan was summarily rejected, and the type it represented never caught on in England (although it continued elsewhere until the end of the eighteenth century, for example, in Pierre-Charles L'Enfant's plan for Washington, D.C., of 1791).

It was, perhaps, only in the heyday of the Picturesque that anything notable in the way of urbanism could occur in England, and the fact remains that Nash's London project was the most inspired example of city planning in English history—with one exception, Bath, without which Nash's urbanism cannot be understood. Just as eighteenth-century Englishmen created, in the Landscape Garden, a successor to the formal garden type of the continent, so they also developed a radically new concept of urban design, in which Palladian, Neoclassical, and Picturesque ideas all participate. This event occurred in mid-eighteenth-century Bath (figs. 10-21, 10-22), a sleepy country town of Roman origin whose healing waters had suddenly

10-19   **John Nash. Cronkhill. Shropshire. 1802**

10-21   John Wood the Younger. Royal Crescent. Bath

10-22   John Wood the Elder and John Wood the Younger.
Bath, air view including the Circus, 1764, and the Royal
Crescent, 1767

10-23   John Nash. Plan, Regent Street and Regent's Park.
London. 1812–27

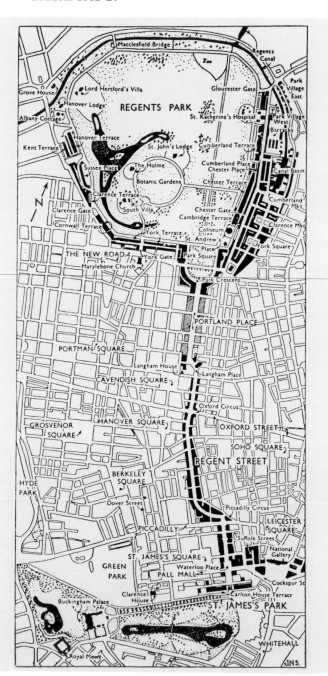

made it again an extremely fashionable spa. Two local architects, father and son, were responsible—John Wood the Elder
and John Wood the Younger. The development, which mainly
involved speculative row-housing built on the land of a huge
estate, began innocently with the elder architect's Queen
Square (1729–36), a large rectangle dominated by a pedimented
Palladian block of houses on one side. It was not much more
than a competent reflection of contemporary London schemes
(which, in turn, went back to French prototypes such as the
Place des Vosges). But in the 1740s and fifties, responding to
Neoclassical currents, John Wood conceived the inspired, if
quixotic, idea of recreating some of the monuments of Roman
Bath, which were to include an Imperial gymnasium, a forum,
and a circus. The first went unrealized, the second was disap-
pointing, but the third was a stunning success. The Bath
Circus disposes some thirty-three houses around a circle (which
Wood thought might be used "for the exhibition of sports"),
interrupted only by three radiating streets. The scheme combined the French *rond-point* format with the ingenious idea of
using the Colosseum turned outside in, its three successive
orders much reduced in scale, without arches but with cinque-
centesque doubled columns. At the end of one of the three
streets of the Circus, John Wood the Younger in 1767 took his
father's idea a sensational step further in the thirty houses of

the Royal Crescent. Built over an elliptical curve with a massive Palladian Ionic order, the whole grand facade looks out over the countryside across the expanse of gently sloping lawn.

Appearing a generation later, Nash's London project took up the ideas of Bath and the whole Picturesque tradition. His plan expanded and evolved through nearly two decades following its inception in 1811. First came Regent's Park (fig. 10-23), a vast English garden that was to accommodate some fifty villas, a lake, a royal pleasure palace, a church, a "national Valhalla," all surrounded with a belt of terraces in mixed Palladian and Neoclassical styles (fig. 10-24). The second phase, initiated in 1813, was Regent Street (fig. 10-25), which ran from the park crescent to Carlton House, the now-destroyed princely residence. With its variety of facades and monumental colonnades, Regent Street ran in a crooked and curving path along a line dictated by practical and visual needs. A third stage expanded the scheme still further to the southwest to include Saint James's Park, a rebuilt Buckingham Palace (whose problems caused Nash's downfall), and numerous other features. Finally, behind the park terraces Nash devised enclaves of urbanized "cottages." Not only did the project as a whole have the dimensions of a city-within-the-city, but it accommodated numerous functional necessities such as access, services, and marketing. Although few of the villas and other buildings intended for the park were built, and the whole northern segment of the belt of terrace-fronted houses was never executed,

10-24   John Nash. Cumberland Terrace. Regent's Park. 1827

10-25   John Nash. Regent Street. (Engraving by T. H. Shepherd)

enough of Nash's High Picturesque scheme was built so that the king, prior to his death in 1830, could well have felt justified in having exclaimed in 1811 at the outset, "It will quite eclipse Napoleon."

By "Napoleon," George probably meant not only the Corsican's current architectural projects, but the French achievements of the previous century. In fact, the reason we have ignored up to now one of the most imaginative of English Neoclassical architects, Sir John Soane, is that his ideas cannot be realistically understood without some notion of eighteenth-century France, which responded to and complemented so much of what we have observed in England.

THE EIGHTEENTH CENTURY IN FRANCE

Compared with England, architecture in France has always had an apparent uniformity, and this was also true in the eighteenth century. English architecture of the period spun outward into a panorama of Classical, medieval, and exotic revivals, Landscape Garden types, and the aesthetics of the Picturesque and the Sublime. French architecture trod a much narrower path, for it spoke only one language, a virile but subtle Classical language carried forward from the sixteenth and seventeenth centuries.

Although the Rococo was a somewhat superficial phenomenon in France, in the early eighteenth century it was a strong enough fashion that the Neoclassicism that followed is often viewed as a reaction to a style of flippant decadence and effeminacy. A project that documents this change in taste is the facade of St.-Sulpice in Paris. In 1726, at the height of the Rococo, Juste-Aurèle Meissonier proposed a facade design that, had it been executed, would have been in its sinuous grace one of the masterpieces of the style. But few Rococo exteriors were built in France, and this was the case at St.-Sulpice. Beginning in 1732 with the first project of Giovanni Niccolò Servandoni and continuing through a series of modifications by himself and others, notably his pupil Jean-François Thérèse Chalgrin, a remarkable facade took shape that was, when completed in 1777, the quintessence of French Neoclassicism, most of whose major themes the work embodies (fig. 10-26).

The St.-Sulpice facade slams the door rudely in the pretty face of the Rococo, putting up in place of its delicate curvilinear patterns a monumental structure of bold clarity and austere solidity. Its sculpturesque strength, its visual firmness, its ease with Classical forms—all reflect the centuries-old tradition of Classicism in France. Knowledgeable contemporary observers, however, would have been struck by something more—that the facade of St.-Sulpice was a radical departure from the conventional French Classical type. This type, which derived from the Roman Baroque formula of the Gesù and Sta. Susanna, was based on a concatenation of high-relief sculptural forms built up hierarchically toward the facade center. St.-Sulpice defied all aspects of the Baroque formula. The monumental forms of its main block were conceived not as sculptural high relief, but as freestanding, trabeated structure, the lower Doric order carrying not only itself but also the second, Ionic order above. Moreover, there is no emphasis on the center, but in fact a de-emphasis (often the case in Neoclassicism). The entablatures are unbroken; the colonnade runs straight across, acknowledging no hierarchies except for

10-26   G. N. Servandoni and J.-F.-T. Chalgrin. Facade,
St.-Sulpice. Paris. 1732–77

the structural doubling of columns at the tower bases; the facade wall, rather than stepping forward at the center, disappears there entirely.

These innovations at St.-Sulpice were a conscious rejection of certain Baroque concepts, and they advanced a complex new syndrome of historicist affirmation. The 1740s and fifties, when the executed St.-Sulpice project evolved from Servandoni's initial design, were crucial years in the rediscovery of antiquity. Architects turned back to the virile ruins of Rome and journeyed even further into the past. In ancient Rome, the primary architectural means had been walls and arches, to which the Greek orders were applied as sculptural embellishment; for the Greeks, the orders themselves had been primary, serving as the embodiment of post-and-lintel structure and as a freestanding sculptural medium. It was just this directness and integrity, this rationality and structural honesty, that were so in tune with the French Neoclassical temper, which had a close affinity to the rationalist mainstream of earlier French architectural theory.

Structural Neoclassicism. As in the case of the English Palladians, it was characteristic of the early architects of Neoclassicism to quench their thirst for the antique through historical intermediaries; and the French were no different. The seventeenth-century model for the unbroken, double-columned, trabeated porticoes of St.-Sulpice was the east facade of the Louvre, and it is no accident that the probable chief author of that facade was Claude Perrault, the most important theorist of French architectural rationalism of the seventeenth century. Perrault not only advocated trabeated columnar architecture as the only lucid and honest style, but he also defended his

position with references to ancient Greek temples and, surprisingly, to Gothic cathedrals. This combining of such different, and essentially antithetical, styles as Greek and Gothic was not so eccentric as one might suppose. What a rationalist like Perrault saw in them was not their visible presence but certain underlying structural aspects. He defended the paired shafts of his Louvre colonnade by reference to the clustered shafts on the piers of Notre-Dame of Paris. Such ideas were not limited to Perrault's day, for an appreciation of the Gothic ran as an undercurrent through the French Classical period. The rationalist spirit that had first produced the Gothic cathedrals now inspired a renewed fascination with the structural principles of those monuments, a return to the skeletal concept of their masonry frames, which, with an extraordinary twist of the rationalist imagination, could be brought together with the newly appreciated architecture of the Greeks.

In the intense climate of eighteenth-century rationalism, the Greco-Gothic structural idealism of Perrault intensified. The climax of what was a movement, rather than an undercurrent, came around mid-century in the complementary forms of architectural projects and publications. The most influential theorist was the Abbé Marc-Antoine Laugier, whose radical manifesto of structural rationalism, *Essai sur l'architecture*, appeared in 1753. Laugier went much further than Perrault in his search for the rational sources of architecture. His ultimate model was neither the Gothic frame nor the Greek orders; it derived from a historical fiction invented by Vitruvius: the notion of the first architecture as a primitive hut, a rudimentary trabeated structure of nothing more than four trees, serving as uprights, supporting an open superstructure of lintels and a pitched roof of logs and branches. What Vitruvius and his Renaissance followers had seen merely as architecture's embryonic beginnings, Laugier now held up as an absolute ideal. His image of the primitive hut was as compelling as Locke's *tabula rasa* and Rousseau's noble savage.

Another writer went even further. The Venetian friar Carlo Lodoli dispensed altogether with "historical" models, claiming that architecture should derive entirely from the nature of its materials and the laws of statics. For him, all the architecture of the Renaissance and of Rome was false, being based on the "dishonest" Greek orders, which had mistakenly employed in stone the forms originally developed for timber construction. The only masonry architecture true to the nature of its materials, Lodoli held, was that of Egypt—and of Stonehenge.

The radical rationalism of Laugier and Lodoli had a vogue among architectural enthusiasts of the time, and ultimately it provided a theoretical basis for later Modernists. But, practically speaking, in the Neoclassical period, their notions served mainly to redefine and to purify the manner in which the Classical architectural language was used, rather than causing it to be completely abandoned, as the two theorists urged. In this respect, Laugier was particularly influential. Following his urging, pedestals, pilasters, engaged orders, broken entablatures, and entablatures over arches were shunned; the more a building consisted of freestanding columns rising directly from the pavement, the more perfect it was. And indeed, one major building—which Laugier himself enthusiastically acclaimed the "premier model of perfect architecture, the true masterpiece of the architecture of France"—is usually seen as the closest architectural counterpart of his ideas: the church of the patron saint of Paris, Ste.-Geneviève, known as the Panthéon since the Revolution (figs. 10-27, 10-28). Its gifted architect, Jacques-Germain Soufflot, accomplished little else of distinction, pouring most of his talent into the single great structure that took decades to complete (1756–90). Soufflot's principal aim in the church, he claimed, was to unite "the structural lightness of Gothic churches with the purity and magnificence of Greek architecture." The extreme structural economy of the building and its French rationalist bias for columnar structure is apparent in the plan. Built on a Greek-cross scheme of Renaissance roots, its five domes—schematically not unlike S. Marco in Venice or St.-Front in Périgueux—are supported by ranks of widely spaced, slender columns and light, triangular crossing piers. The interior (colorplate 64) reveals the Classical "magnificence" of form that Soufflot preferred (despite Laugier) in the shape of an elegant Corinthian order, fully detailed yet extremely crisp and pure, that supports slender arches. Much of the vaulting is cut away in late Baroque manner, although in their near-skeletal lightness, these upper parts were also inspired by the Gothic. The complex transitional position of Soufflot is clearly evidenced in the exterior of the Panthéon, which is so much more massive and austere than the interior that one would not naturally link them as two aspects of a single building. Even in its original state, when opened by triads of large, now-walled-up windows (which made the interior still more buoyant), the exterior approximated the nascent Neoclassical ideal of discrete, austere, geometric blocks.

The Panthéon was thus far more than the mere realization of Laugier's theory. It represented a watershed in the history of French Neoclassicism. A preoccupation with form rather than structure, an obsession for increasingly bold, austere compositions now overtook French architects. Much like the Gothic, the French Neoclassical style developed progressively and dramatically, decade by decade. Although a great deal of overlapping occurred, three phases beyond Structural Neoclassicism can be discerned in the period (making four in all). The first of these, which overlapped the structural-rationalist vogue, occupied the 1750s and sixties and might be called Archaeological Neoclassicism (stimulated by the excitement of the archaeological expeditions of those decades). Yet it continued to look back to the grandiose projects and powerful style of the seventeenth century, to the golden age of French Classical architecture. So extensive was this backward glance that to the untrained eye many of the Neoclassical buildings of this eighteenth-century phase seem to resemble closely their seventeenth-century predecessors.

The next step of Neoclassicism was less, rather than more, archaeological. The architects of the 1760s and early 1770s were bolder and freer in their handling of Classical form. They were less concerned with a realistic re-creation of the antique—or of the seventeenth century—and were more caught up in their own formal vision. If this phase of the development is given the name Radical Neoclassicism (often termed Le Style Louis XVI), then the final phase of the eighteenth century, which carried imaginative freedom to its limits and abandoned any pretense of fidelity to the letter of antique architecture, might be called Revolutionary, or Visionary, Neoclassicism. Running from the mid-1770s to the end of the century, it was part of the political and cultural climate of the French Revolution.

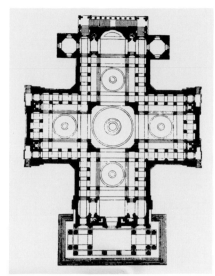

10-27
Jacques-Germain
Soufflot. Plan, Panthéon
(Ste.-Geneviève). Paris.
1756–90

10-28   Panthéon (Ste.-Geneviève)

Archaeological Neoclassicism. The goal of Archaeological Neoclassicism was the integration of the magnificence, solidity, and clarity of antique models with the traditions of French Classicism. The architect who most successfully and convincingly revived seventeenth-century French Classicism in the 1750s and sixties was Ange-Jacques Gabriel. Like his father, Gabriel was Premier Architecte du Roi from 1742 until 1774. His best-known structure, the Petit Trianon—designed for Mme de Pompadour in 1761 and considered among the most perfect buildings in France—is one of several modest works he erected for the court (fig. 10-29). At the Petit Trianon, the handling of the order, the window frames, balustrades, and other features derive closely from the French Classical tradition. Gabriel's debt to the past is equally apparent in the building's noble aura of imperturbable dignity, its harmonious proportions, and the precision and elegance of its detailing. But the deceptively modest structure exemplifies Neoclassical taste, for it is severe in its cubic geometry, restrained in articulation, and barren of the accents of relief sculpture typical of seventeenth-century French design. In evidence here is that aura of architectural chastity so characteristic of the new style, which by comparison makes the most sober buildings of the French Classical past look muscular and heavily textured. In its

10-29   Ange-Jacques Gabriel. Garden facade, Petit Trianon. Versailles. 1762–68

restrained architectural language, the Petit Trianon was making the same statement about the purification of architecture as did Lord Burlington's Chiswick House.

Gabriel also produced large-scale works. His most ambitious project was a Parisian square, originally designed in 1753 as a commemorative monument to Louis XV, carried out from 1755 to 1775, later compromised in form and renamed the Place de la Concorde (fig. 10-30). Gabriel's scheme was a radical departure from the squares of the Baroque period—such as

St. Peter's in Rome or the Place Vendôme nearby in Paris—which were conceived as enormous ceilingless rooms, dominated by massive walls that were horizontal extensions of the powerful sculptural designs of church and palace facades. The Place Louis XV does include such a facade, but only along one side of its rectangular space. The other sides are bounded only by dry moats—which are nearly invisible to the visitor—balustrade walls, and little statue-topped pavilions at the canted corners; the central fountain is the strongest visual complement to the facade. Even at that, the facade, which reflects Perrault's at the Louvre, does not build toward its center in hierarchic Baroque fashion, but has a Neoclassical void in the form of an avenue leading to the planned Church of the Madeleine. The resulting serene, unobtrusive air of open expanse, largely defined in an almost conceptual way by low balustrades and nearly invisible moats, reflected the rationalist spirit of mid-century Neoclassicism. However, Gabriel's sensitivity to the peculiarities of the site also played a strong role in the design. Place Louis XV was not situated in the heart of the city but rather at what was its edge, being bounded on two sides by gardens—the Tuileries to the east and, to the west, the parklike Champs-Elysées—and on a third by the Seine. Adjacent on these three sides to the "natural" environment of greenery and water, the square was left virtually open, with only the most subtle means to establish its boundaries, thus appearing to expand visually far beyond its theoretical confines.

The aesthetic singularities of Place Louis XV mirrored important tendencies in urbanistic design of the period. Large-scale city squares were no longer simply walled spaces of regular geometric shape, but complex assemblages involving the functional

10-30   Ange-Jacques Gabriel. Place Louis XV (now Place de la Concorde). Paris. 1755–75. (Engraving by G. L. le Rouge)

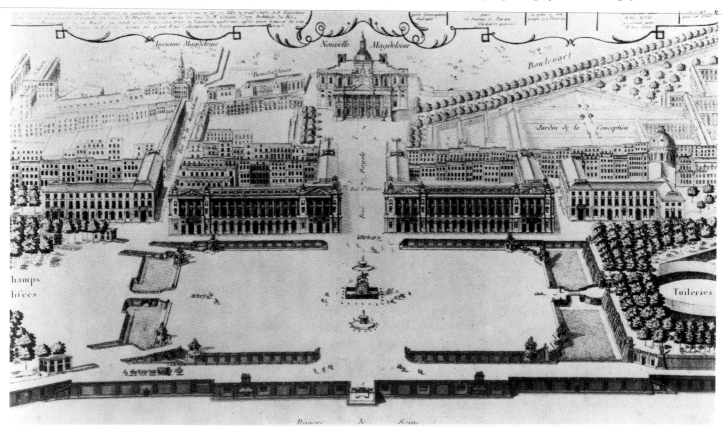

10-31   Emmanuel Héré de Corny. Air view, Place de la Carrière. Nancy. 1751–59

interpenetration of all imaginable media—not only walls with orders, but sculpture, stairs, theatrical sets, water (fountains, ponds, and even rivers), and the landscape in general, artificially planned or in its natural state. This trend grew out of one of the major themes of the Baroque—Bernini's fusion of the arts. Late Baroque Rome was one of the advanced centers of such urbanistic design, as seen in the Fountain of Trevi (1732–62) with its palace-facade-cum-fountain, the theatrical Spanish Steps (1723–25), or the Piazza S. Ignazio (1727–28), where theater design moved out into the city streets. In England, there was the parallel development of Picturesque urbanism, with its contextual emphasis on architecture in a "natural" environment, and the urban planning of the Woods and Nash. In the case of Place Louis XV, Gabriel fused the two major French palatial images of the age of Louis XIV into a brilliant new configuration. His *place* is not only a reflection of the Louvre facade, but also of the garden aspect of Versailles. The facade wall seeks to dominate the space before it in the same way, and the balustrades, moats, and pavilions are a translation into urban terms of the parterres, hedges, and trees of Versailles. A city square at the edge of a river between two parks, Place Louis XV was a Louvre-like Versailles in the city streets.

Rivaling Gabriel's project was an equally ambitious French urban scheme in the city of Nancy (fig. 10-31). Begun two years earlier, in 1751, and exhibiting certain Neoclassical features, it really belongs in an earlier historical position and may be fairly considered the major example of Rococo urbanism. Designed by the architect Emmanuel Héré de Corny largely between 1751 and 1759, the complex comprised an intricate sequence of spaces laid out on a single, elongated axis. Proceeding from the monumental Place Stanislas through a short, narrow street ending in a triumphal arch, one enters the long, tree-lined residential Place de la Carrière (originally a tournament grounds), which ends in a cross-axial double hemicycle, separated from the terminal apsed garden by a palatial administrative building. The triumphal arch is, true enough, Neoclassical in intent; the canted corners of Place Stanislas do open through elegant ironwork screens to streets and gardens in an eighteenth-century contextual gesture. The whole design is symmetrical, linear, and firmly balanced in the French Classical tradition. But where Place Louis XV is

lucid and idealizing, permeated with the rationalist temper of Neoclassicism, the Nancy scheme is playful, sensuous, and digressive, embodying Rococo ease and mobility. It begins with a scaled-down Place Vendôme that bleeds out its corners and feeds its spatial energy through a narrow street and a triumphal arch. The space then runs along freely between trees and house fronts, only to bounce back and forth between double hemicycle screens; finally it moves through a palace and into a garden. Despite its dynamism and occasional glimpses outward, the whole is still turned inward in the manner of the seventeenth century—self-contained and fundamentally set off from the environment. That two urbanistic ideas as different as Gabriel's and Héré de Corny's could appear simultaneously serves to emphasize the architectural vitality of mid-eighteenth-century France.

Radical Neoclassicism. In the 1760s, stimulated by the resurgence of building activity after the Peace of Paris of 1763, there emerged a new architectural generation. Of the principal members of this group, two—Étienne-Louis Boullée and Claude-Nicolas Ledoux—would go on to do their great work in the later 1770s and the 1780s. Three others—Marie-Joseph Peyre, Charles de Wailly, and Jacques Gondoin—produced, around 1770, the major monuments of Radical Neoclassicism.

The point of departure for these architects was neither the antique nor the seventeenth century, but rather the new fusion of these sources in Archaeological Neoclassicism. Their work cannot be understood without also taking cognizance of the increasing influence of Piranesi. Gondoin, the most advanced of the Radical Neoclassicists, was a close friend of the Venetian visionary. The most crucial element of all, however, was the passionate idealism that was in the air. It compelled architects toward an uncompromising purism and the favoring of forms more severe and even larger-scaled than those of antiquity itself.

The architectural production of both Peyre and de Wailly was rich and varied and is not conveniently reduced to any formula. Their most significant contribution to the Neoclassical style can be seen in a collaborative Parisian work, designed between 1767 and 1770, that is their best-known building—the Théâtre-Français (later Théâtre de l'Odéon, now Théâtre de France; fig. 10-32). Piranesi's hold over their imagination is immediately apparent in de Wailly's rendering of the foyer, through whose gloomy illumination and stark, columnar frame appear vistas reminiscent of the hallucinatory images in Piranesi's etchings of imaginary—and nightmarish—prisons, the *Carceri d'invenzione*, which Piranesi had based, interestingly, on earlier projects for opera scenery. The foyer, together with the rest of the complex interior program of the theater—auditorium, stage, etc.—is set into a rectangular block of uncompromising severity. Uniformly rusticated masonry is drawn around all four sides, which are punctured by stark, regularly spaced openings—an arcade on the ground floor, rectangular and circular windows above, all devoid of frames. The usual massive terminal cornice does not appear; there is only a minor one near the top, the principal horizontal being the extension of the entablature from the projecting Tuscan Doric porch on the facade. The coursing joints of the columnar masonry of the porch uniformly continue the lines of the rustication of the main block, thus emphasizing the underlying geometric unity of the whole.

10-32 Marie-Joseph Peyre and Charles de Wailly. Théâtre-Français (now Théâtre de France). Paris. 1767–70

By comparison, the Petit Trianon of less than a decade earlier seems almost fussy and permeated with the traditional reflexes of French Classicism: openings are still surrounded with elegant frames; intermediate elements still create gradual transitions; distinction in the sculptural treatment of the facade is hierarchical. But in de Wailly and Peyre's theater, almost nothing is embellished, blurred, or graduated. Nearly everything stands on its own, as a discrete entity, and is directly juxtaposed with its neighbor without a cushioning intermediary (as in Burlington's work three decades earlier). The uncompromising rationalist temper of the age seems to direct every aesthetic choice.

The reputation of Jacques Gondoin, the most daring and brilliant of the three main exponents of Radical Neoclassicism, rests on a single building, but one so remarkable that even during Gondoin's lifetime it was called the masterpiece of eighteenth-century architecture. Designed in 1769 and completed in 1775, the École de Chirurgie (School of Surgery, now the École de Médecine) in Paris draws into a single structure the most progressive tendencies of the time. Gondoin's most inspired notion was to build the principal interior of the school, the Anatomy Theater (fig. 10-33), in the form of an ancient theater covered with a Pantheon-like half-dome. The adaptation of this vault to the needs of the building—and to contemporary taste—could not have been more effective. The architectural ideals are evident in the blank expanse of wall, the strongly coffered ceiling, and the oversized half-oculus that opens a flood of light on the anatomical drama—all achieved with sensitive proportional balance and refinement of the minimal detailing. The plan of the complex (fig. 10-34) reveals how Gondoin smoothly incorporated all the necessary accommodations of such an institution—a small hospital, classrooms, laboratories, library, etc.—in a cramped and irregular site. It also displays the brilliant design of the monumental courtyard and the facade wing, where the basic element is an unvarying Ionic order attached to walls or piers except toward the street, where there are four freestanding Ionic colonnades. Functionally ingenious, the latter not only support a needed street-level wing of the upper story, but they are spaced to create a central aisle giving access to the lateral wings of the building.

Aware of possible criticism of his proliferation of columns,

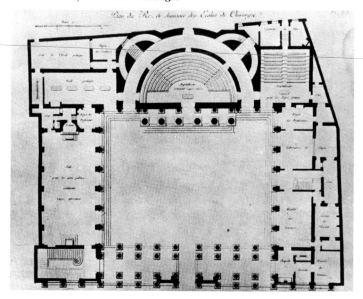

10-33 Jacques Gondoin. Anatomy Theater, École de Chirurgie (now École de Médecine). Paris. 1769–75

10-34 Plan, École de Chirurgie

Gondoin emphasized their magnificence of effect as appropriate to such a royal scientific foundation, and he also stressed the screened vista of the court offered by the facade (figs. 10-35, 10-36). He claimed that "a school whose fame attracts a great concourse of pupils from all nations should appear open and easy of access." But what contemporaries found most remarkable—indeed, shocking and delightful—about his treatment of the colonnaded street facade was its aesthetic novelty. As sympathetic critics put it, Gondoin defied the entire French

10-35 Street facade, École de Chirurgie

10-36 Court facade, École de Chirurgie

tradition—e.g., the Louvre. He neither divided the massing into pavilions, nor broke the line of the colonnade in a sculptural buildup at ends and center. The whole facade, in its entire height and from one end to the other, runs in a ruthlessly straight line, its columns and windows marching with unflinching rhythm beneath undeviating, continuous trabeation.

Gondoin's facade, and the courtyard walls behind it, would have been so rationally pure as to be pedantically dull had the Ionic colonnade not been used as a matrix for a set of livelier forms that were quotations of ancient architectural types. Encased within the street facade, Gondoin set a vestigial triumphal arch, with inset reliefs referring to royal patronage and Classical allegory. Opposite, in the courtyard and fronting the Anatomy Theater, was a Corinthian porch (again with appropriate allegorical relief). Finally, behind the Ionic wall, was the Pantheon-theater itself. Triumphal arch, Pantheon-porch, Pantheon-theater—these Roman images follow in sequence on the main axis, set lucidly within the Ionic frame of facade and court. The experience of visitors, physicians, and students catching a screened glimpse of the interior from the street, passing through the triumphal arch, court, and temple facade to enter the Pantheon-like scientific shrine itself, was breathtaking, and it need not puzzle us that the building

was so greatly admired. Gondoin, in contemporary eyes, had achieved his idea of creating a temple enshrining medical science—a Temple of Asclepius.

Revolutionary/Visionary Neoclassicism. The trajectory of French Neoclassicism grew steeper in the years after 1770 as events led to the Revolution. A symptomatic building of these decades was Claude-Nicolas Ledoux's prison (fig. 10-37) for the new municipal center of Aix-en-Provence, designed in 1784 (begun shortly thereafter, but abandoned incomplete in 1790). For this grim architectural form, Ledoux chose not a Classicizing image but a medieval fortress, with massive, closed walls, corner towers, slit windows, and machicolations. Even in the Middle Ages, this type had tended toward geometric regularity, an effect which Ledoux heightened by building in bare masonry deprived of all decoration except the most basic horizontal cornices. It was crucial to Ledoux that his buildings be recognizable for what they were. As such, they were examples of *architecture parlante* where the forms of the buildings expressively displayed and communicated their function. Thus, it was necessary that a prison be immediately recognized as such and not confused with a fortress. This Ledoux accomplished by several iconographic means. The slit windows do not run vertically—as in the "arrow loops" of fortifications—but horizontally, to guardedly admit light and air. There are corbels so widely spaced as to resemble the patterns of machicolations—but no battlements above, instead prismatic, claustrophobic roofed forms. The entrances, multiple rather than single, project in the form of columnar porches and not as castle gates. Although obviously Classical, the porches are reduced to squat, closely spaced columns carrying a half cylinder of inarticulate masonry that suggests the lines of a Classical pediment. Thus resembling a cyclopean stone block from which the elegant forms of a true Classical porch might be carved, this form in its forbidding primitivism can only be called sub-Doric. It strongly contributes to the identity of the prison and asserts its grim purpose, yet also symbolizes a state that endows even such a sinister institution with touches of civilized, however authoritarian rule. Significantly, the planned internal features of the prison were unusually humanitarian, with spacious cells and tree-planted courtyards reflecting the concern of the period for prison reform.

An image that reveals the yet more extreme tendencies of the period is Ledoux's project for an Inspector's House at the Source of the Loue (fig. 10-38). Part of Ledoux's project of the ideal city of Chaux, the Inspector's House was intended to serve and to symbolize state control over the use of the nearby river by literally running it through the house and providing the tunnel with windows for a direct view of the torrent. Devoid of decoration, the Inspector's House is entirely geometric in form. It is composed of cubic and cylindrical masses: a rectangular central building, flanked by two sets of double stairs to fill out a square overall plan, scooped out to serve as a "base" for a hollow cylinder through which the river passes. Remarkable here are not only the powerful scale of the building and its interplay of pure forms, but its relationship to the environment. The river exists in the most intimate connection with the building, and laterally, the building looks out through Palladian windows to the landscape. The first impression of Ledoux's rendering is of a building profoundly connected to its

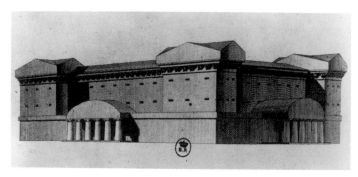

10-37 Claude-Nicolas Ledoux. Prison of Aix-en-Provence. Designed in 1784. (Engraving from his *L'Architecture*)

10-38 Claude-Nicolas Ledoux. Inspector's House at the Source of the Loue. (Engraving from his *L'Architecture*)

setting, dynamically asserting its power over nature and yet peacefully coexisting with its cliffs and waterfalls, and even its Picturesque old mills (through which the stream also flowed).

Clearly, such designs as Ledoux's Prison and River Inspector's House achieve a definitive mutation of Neoclassicism. We call it "Revolutionary" because it has sharply severed ties with the past, and "Visionary" because of its goals and methods. Its sources tend not to be historical models but to come directly from realms of the intellect and the imagination situated in eighteenth-century concepts of nature, both in the raw and in the ideal form of "eternal" geometric verities that give shape to the world. Ledoux also incorporates imagined, fictive constructs, be they primeval, sub-Classical orders, or futuristic, hyper-Classical fantasies. Whatever the imaginary sources, the final design projects the light of the architect's inner vision in inspired bursts of architectural form-making, as witnessed in Ledoux's two works.

The achievement of this culminating phase of Neoclassicism involved several important factors. Not the least of these was the role of the architectural fantast Piranesi, who was taking an ever-greater hold over architects' minds; and his own Neoclassical vision evolved dynamically. He conjured up a stupefying architecture of his own invention in the nightmare images of the *Carceri* (Prisons); in the *Parere sull'architettura* of 1765, he stressed further the freedom of the modern architect from allegiance to ancient rules or models; finally, in 1778, were published his studies of the Greek temples of Paestum, a series of plates unsurpassed in their evocation of the somber power of the Early Doric. In Piranesi's rendering, the impression of the order almost approaches Ledoux's sub-Doric.

In the literature and politics of France, disturbing forces of change were at work. In 1774, Louis XVI succeeded his indolent, pleasure-loving predecessor. Determined at first to rescue the French economy from the disarray into which it had fallen, the new king appointed as his minister a man of force and vision, Anne-Robert-Jacques Turgot, who set in motion a series of drastic reforms. But the king dismissed Turgot after only two years of an administration that might have spared France the Revolution. Reform could be suppressed, but not intense dissatisfaction and unrest, which grew luxuriantly in the fertile soil of corruption and exploitation.

In literature, the key to the mood of the pre-Revolutionary decades was the growing influence of Jean-Jacques Rousseau. In the *Social Contract* (1762), Rousseau heatedly insisted that sovereignty resided in the will of the people, not in the divine right of kings. This idea was in tune with the liberal-rationalist thought of the times, and its political effect was incalculable. Furthermore, in their own realms, his nonpolitical publications were of tremendous vogue in the final decades of the century. Rousseau's great theme was the life of the sentiment, and he stressed the profound effect of nature on feelings and the effect of feelings on the perception of nature. To the optimistic faith in reason and progress of the earlier part of the century, Rousseau counterposed a darker, Romantic vision. His ideas reinforced the mood induced by Piranesi, and they represent a crucial factor in Revolutionary/Visionary Neoclassicism. Ledoux's Inspector's House and the Prison can hardly be imagined without them.

Behind Rousseau's Romantic experience of nature was the cultural drift of England in the eighteenth century. French architecture in the 1770s experienced a powerful wave of direct English influence essential to Revolutionary/Visionary Neoclassicism. It comprised the whole complex of the Picturesque and the Sublime, the English Landscape Garden, and the melancholy fondness for ruins. France was suddenly filled with publications on gardening and also with architectural works in the English fashion. A veritable epidemic of the *jardin anglais* swept the country, with remarkable examples such as the gardens at Ermenonville, which, with their dreamlike setting, served as a retreat for Rousseau who is buried there, or the Jardin de Monceau (fig. 10-39), built in Paris by Louis Carrogis de Carmontelle for the king's brother, the Duc de Chartres. Monceau reveals how the French landscape architects adapted the English concept to their own taste. To accommodate the French love of the commodious and the comfortable, the new gardens were laid out to provide a maximum of Picturesque incident and stimulation for Rousseau-like thought and conversation—with a minimum of fatigue. No English-built ruin was quite so extraordinary as the country house at the Désert de Retz (fig. 10-40), near Chambourcy, erected between 1774 and 1784 for Racine de Monville by François Barbier; its Picturesque setting was designed by the famous painter of Roman ruins, Hubert Robert. As the English loved the crumbling Gothic, so the French adapted the concept of ruins to their own Classical tradition—here in the form of a gigantic fluted column in decay. The most famous of all these French examples of English taste is the imaginative Hameau of 1778 (fig. 10-41), a rustic "hamlet" built by Richard Mique on the grounds of Versailles for Marie-Antoinette and her ladies-in-waiting to amuse themselves at playing shepherdesses and milkmaids.

External factors were important, but the transformation from Radical Neoclassicism to the grand Visionary manner, in terms of individual architects, was ultimately dependent on

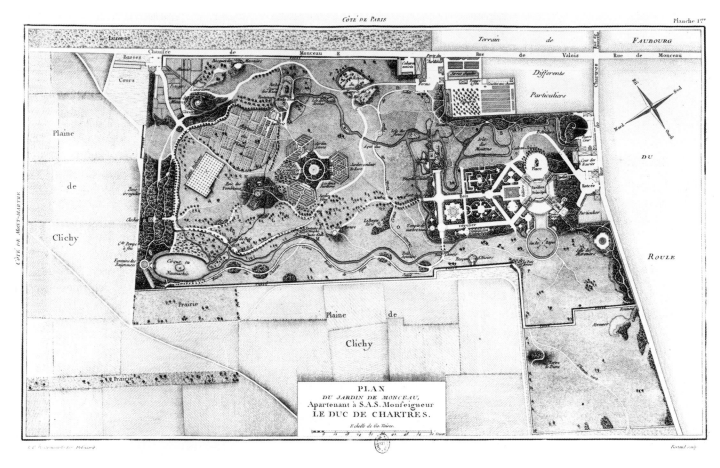

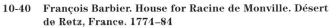

10-39 Louis Carrogis de Carmontelle. Plan, Jardin de Monceau. Paris. 1773–89. (Bibliothèque Nationale, Paris)

10-40 François Barbier. House for Racine de Monville. Désert de Retz, France. 1774–84

10-41 Richard Mique. Hameau, Versailles. 1778

the drive and genius of the movement's two leaders, Ledoux and Boullée, who were endowed with more fertile imaginations than others of their generation and with a greater willingness to take risks. Neither Boullée nor Ledoux was ever in Italy; they knew antiquity and the Italian Renaissance entirely through publications—mainly those of Piranesi, by whom they were powerfully affected. For them, consequently, antiquity was something fluid in concept, not restricted to the actual forms and buildings of the ancient world. They understood buildings such as the Colosseum and the Pantheon not as tangible, fixed realities, but as unconfining images of the imagination.

Ledoux. Ledoux did not begin as a designer of visionary schemes. Although he is held in high esteem by Modernists partly because of his willingness to strip buildings of ornament, he is first known to us as a highly accomplished interior decorator. His aptitude for ornamentation was, in fact, so dazzling that it is astonishing how he was able later in his career to suppress this talent and puritanically deny his buildings the lush embellishments that he had loved.

A series of elegant Parisian homes of the late 1760s established Ledoux as a leader among the rising architectural generation, and they brought him increasingly influential patrons, among them Mme du Barry, mistress of Louis XV and cultural arbiter at the court. In 1773, Ledoux became a member of the Académie Royale d'Architecture and Architecte du Roi. While continuing to design imaginative houses, he expanded his activities to the public domain; the new commissions were crucial for Ledoux's development. In the mid-1770s, he undertook a series of remarkable projects, some successful, others remaining on paper. His most ambitious work of this period was the famous Saltworks (fig. 10-42) at Arc-et-Senans, near Besançon (1775–79), built on the design approved in 1773 and still standing. Today's reader might wonder how such a seemingly mundane commission could have even interested Ledoux. In eighteenth-century France, however, salt production had a touch of drama: It was a fiercely guarded monopoly of the state, and the high tax on salt was an important source of royal revenue. Smuggling and illegal production of salt were punishable by death or the galleys. A saltworks was thus a strongly secured paramilitary institution, closed to encroachments of the outside world and ruled with stern authority within. Such, in any case, is the image of the Saltworks of Ledoux, whose enthusiasm for the job one can easily imagine after his years of creating mainly polite and polished domestic settings.

Ledoux disposed the various buildings making up the factory along the edge of a huge half-circle. At the center of its diameter line is situated, with clear logic, the Director's House (fig. 10-43), flanked by the twin buildings used for the evaporation process; opposite, on the main axis, is the entrance to the compound, and to either side along the circumference are the storage halls, which formed part of the wall enclosing the site. The whole is an undisguised embodiment of eighteenth-century rationalism and a symbol of the rigid, ordered system of salt production and taxation. The architectural forms that rise over this scheme, however, suggest anything but a lucid rationalism. Instead, they silently convey the darkly poetic drama of salt production, with its Dantesque clouds of steam and smoke, in an ominous vision of primitive strength and forbidding authority—the Piranesian mood so strongly achieved by Ledoux later in the Aix prison.

The massive entrance gate (fig. 10-44) to the Saltworks rises over the roofs of the adjoining storage buildings; it is a masonry block of huge Tuscan columns, a heavy entablature, a bare attic. The powerful rustication of its rear wall is interrupted by an arch, through which spills an avalanche of carved boulders all but burying the small central doorway. Once past this grotto—which suggests the underground source of the salt-laden waters—the visitor confronts the Director's House, grim in its projection of authority, though tempered with a certain civilizing Classical restraint. As originally planned, it rose as a closed mass with bare chimneys projecting from its roof and frameless windows restricted to the shadows of the immense pedimented porch, where colossal Tuscan columns stand like a row of totalitarian guards.

Of Ledoux's works of the mid-1770s, the Saltworks was crucial in the liberation of his visionary energies. What was still lacking was a more personal interpretation of Renaissance and ancient vocabulary, and a more uninhibited disregard for, and dislocation of, traditional massing. This divide appears to have been crossed by Ledoux toward 1780 in several rural projects, including a prodigious, stripped-down, but claustrophobic Hunting Lodge and a Caretaker's Hut in the form of a perfect sphere.

10-42   Claude-Nicolas Ledoux. Air view, Saltworks within the Ideal City of Chaux. Arc-et-Senans. 1780–c. 1800. (From his *L'Architecture*)

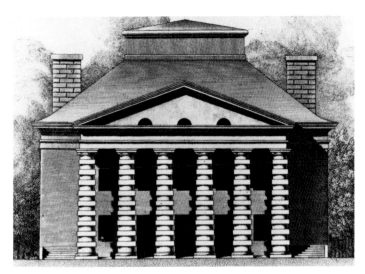

10-43　Claude-Nicolas Ledoux. House of the Director of the Saltworks, elevation. (From his *L'Architecture*)

10-44　Claude-Nicolas Ledoux. Main entrance, Saltworks. Arc-et-Senans. 1775–79

By the mid-1780s, he was at the height of his powers. It was then that he received the commission for the Aix prison, conceived the idea of expanding the Saltworks into the Ideal City of Chaux, and built the innovative tollhouses of Paris.

When it was decided, in 1783, to construct a new set of walls for Paris, Ledoux was awarded the staggering commission for the more than fifty tollgates—or *barrières*—to be sited at the entrances of the various roads into the city (fig. 10-45). In 1787, because of cost overruns typical of Ledoux's extravagant practice, he was removed from the job; but work continued under a sympathetic follower, and by 1790, when progress was again halted, Ledoux's conception had been largely realized. Most of the *barrières* survived the Revolution—remained, in fact, until the 1860s, when all but four were torn down during Haussmann's replanning of Paris. All, however, were published by Ledoux, and several were photographed before destruction. This evidence, together with the four gates that remain, which are representative and among the best, give a good picture of what was collectively one of the most impressive architectural works of the eighteenth century.

The *barrières*—and Ledoux's notions about them—manifest many of the themes that preoccupied the architect and his generation. In Ledoux's mind, the gates were to be the Parisian equivalent of the Propylaea of Athens—a noble sentiment char-

acteristic of "enlightened" Neoclassicism. The Picturesque ideal of variation enters as well, for no two *barrières* were alike; all were strongly individuated, to a degree defying categorization. Restricting ourselves to only those *barrières* still extant or preserved accurately in photographs, one example which is easy to perceive as a development of the earlier Ledoux is the Barrière de l'Étoile (fig. 10-46). It was essentially an extension of the Arc-et-Senans Director's House, but with the massive porch extended around all four sides, which adds to the authoritarian aura of the building. It is, however, in the Barrière des Bonshommes (fig. 10-47) that for the first time we see those dislocations of massing and detail, those perverse combinations of form that shocked Ledoux's contemporaries and that distinguish the Revolutionary from the Radical stage of Neoclassicism.

But the *barrières* were varied indeed, and often involved subtlety as well as shock value. The Barrière de Monceau (colorplate 74; fig. 10-48), which still stands at the edge of the *jardin anglais* of the same name, is a Neoclassical updating of Bramante's Tempietto, with Greek Doric columns, and it looks like a garden pavilion of the period. In part it was just that; the upper story was reserved exclusively for the owner of the park. Just as subtle and even more impressive is the Barrière de la Villette (fig. 10-49). Its unusual form was functional, for the cylindrical superstructure opened all around with views commanding the outlying harbor of the Ourcq Canal. But obviously far more than functionalism was involved. With this building Ledoux sought no less than to rival—on his own terms—a set of great historical works and to make the final statement of a type that begins with Hadrian's Pantheon and Mausoleum, runs through Bramante's St. Peter's, Wren's St. Paul's, and Hardouin-Mansart's Invalides down to Soufflot's Panthéon, which was just nearing completion. Ledoux was dismayed at the dilution of the formal purity of the ancient models in their "modern" descendants. For that matter, the ancient examples themselves were insufficiently pure for Ledoux's revolutionary, rationalist temper. He was able to reduce the whole tradition to the crystalline perfection of three lucid and harmonious forms, with a porch of sub-Doric purity, square prismatic piers, and clean, reductive moldings.

Following the *barrières*, Ledoux's practice declined, and during the 1790s it ceased. The Revolution was a period of hard times for architects, especially difficult for Ledoux. During the Terror, he was imprisoned for over a year. The final decade and a half of his life was occupied mainly with his architectural treatise. Its first volume was published in 1804, and the rest was brought out only in the posthumous edition of 1847. The work carries the characteristically descriptive Enlightenment title, *Architecture considered in its relationship with art, custom and the law*. The text that accompanies the remarkable illustrations of Ledoux's works and projects reveals that he was neither much of a writer nor a systematic thinker. Far more consequential was the book's graphic presentation of Ledoux's late style—his projects for the ideal city of Chaux, now truly approaching the realm of the futuristic.

Reexamination of the River Inspector's House of Chaux reveals its progress beyond even the most progressive works of Ledoux's earlier phase, such as the Barrière de la Villette. Interestingly, both works, which function as gateways and symbols of authority, comprise a cylindrical superstructure set over a squared base. But whereas the Villette in the final

10-45   Claude-Nicolas Ledoux. Projects for *barrières*. Paris. 1785–89. (From his *L'Architecture*)

analysis is an assemblage of diverse structural and sculptural components—colonnade, pediment, arcade, rusticated masonry, etc.—along geometric lines, the River Inspector's House is conceived and realized intrinsically in geometric form, as a pure geometric envelope. The ranges of windows in its flanks seem to be cut into its otherwise inviolate, continuous volume. Moreover, where the Villette reduced the Pantheon dome to a cylinder, now Ledoux not only purifies the cylinder but turns it ninety degrees on its side. Rather than merely "looking out," the cylinder now actively, physically engages nature.

Bold as the River Inspector's House is, the limits of Ledoux's reach toward the futuristic were attained in another of the Chaux projects—his conception of a Cooper's Workshop (fig. 10-50). Both designs share the geometry of the horizontal cylinder and the squared base, but in the Cooper's Workshop these are fragmented into almost cubistic form. Two cylinders with hollow cores, resting on freestanding segmental walls, now interpenetrate to face symmetrically in all four directions. Ledoux himself admitted how iconographically "bizarre" this project was, depicting the barrels that the cooper made, complete with symbolic hoops. Yet a veiled architectural model was nevertheless at work, namely the Roman quadrifrons arch (such

as the Arco di Giano in Rome) which faced four ways at an intersection, exactly as the Cooper's Workshop ("*au centre de quatre routes*"). Thus the crossing of views through the cores of Ledoux's cylinders involved a learned Classicism as well as an imaginative twist of the Picturesque.

Ledoux's play with architectural symbolism at Chaux is still more extreme in the Oikema—euphemistically, the Temple Dedicated to Love, the House of Sexual Instruction, in other words the town brothel (fig. 10-51). Through some vague, paradoxical process, virtue would ultimately be rekindled by vice in this paternalistic institution. Its underlying architectural scheme was as arcane as its program, for the groundplan took the outline of the male sexual organs. In a curious, and, probably for Ledoux, conscious way, this bizarre notion reflects one of the oldest patterns of Western architecture—being an inversion, some would say a perversion, of the way in which so many churches were built in the form of a Latin cross, a form, like Ledoux's, more plainly visible in a groundplan than in reality. But the actual appearance of Ledoux's sleek building was anything but odd. Like most of the public buildings of the city, the Oikema comprises a terraced base with symmetrical pairs of stairs; a geometric superstructure; and sub-Classical porticoes

10-46 Claude-Nicolas Ledoux. Barrière de l'Étoile (before demolition). Paris. 1785–89

10-47 Claude-Nicolas Ledoux. Barrière des Bonshommes (before demolition). Paris

10-48 Claude-Nicolas Ledoux. Barrière de Monceau. Paris

and windows, to which Ledoux added here a set of full-blown Classical porches. These components are, by virtue of the phallic metaphor of the Oikema, stretched into an elongated massing, whose uncluttered lines sweep from one end to the other and off into the landscape. Ledoux's Neoclassical language here is so advanced that the image of such abstract forms driving toward the horizon will not be seen again until the twentieth-century Modernism of a Frank Lloyd Wright or a Mies van der Rohe.

The Oikema, the Cooper's Workshop, and the River Inspector's House are among the most haunting examples of Ledoux's late style. But what of the city of Chaux as a whole (fig. 10-42)? Not surprisingly, Ledoux's urbanistic ideas were as advanced as his individual buildings. The most striking impression of Ledoux's general view of the city is its dualism, which counterposes geometric idealism and the Picturesque. The center remains rationally pure in plan, but toward the edge, the symmetry loosens, and the whole bleeds imperceptibly into the wooded countryside. The eighteenth-century English estate combined a Palladian

10-49 Claude-Nicolas Ledoux. Barrière de la Villette (after restoration). Paris

manor with a Capability Brown wooded lawn, and now Ledoux extends this concept of an architectural core in intimate relationship with "natural" surroundings to a whole city. Completely absent is the *sine qua non* of the traditional city—its wall!

Even more remarkably, apart from the Saltworks, there is no need in Chaux for a state bureaucracy and a massive apparatus of law and order, for in this ideal city morality and virtue reign supreme. The Panarèthéon is dedicated to all the virtues, depicted in a continuous frieze of statues around its central cubic mass. The Temple of Memory presents virtue-inscribed minarets at its corners. The House of Union is "devoted to the 'moral virtues' . . . agriculture, commerce, and to literature." In the Palace of Concord, family quarrels, a primary source of violence, will be peacefully healed within walls "adorned with the maxims of the great moralists, ancient and modern, and the names of Socrates, Plato, and Marcus Aurelius will be inscribed in letters of gold." And in the Oikema, even vice would be transformed into virtue.

Like many liberals of his day, Ledoux was a Freemason and was deeply affected by the social and moral Utopianism of the Enlightenment. But he was unique in the degree to which he infused this romanticism into an architectural program. Nowhere is this more evident than in the profound egalitarianism of the domestic buildings of Chaux. The workingman's dwelling is simpler than the house of the stockbroker with its rotunda, but both are of the same purist architectural vocabulary and stylistic cut. Ledoux defied the hallowed tradition of social distinctions in architecture, in which there was no common denominator between a merchant's Classical palace and the vernacular proletarian hovel. Everyone is not reduced to the same rank at Chaux, obviously, but the impression is not of intrinsic social hierarchies, either—rather, it is of what might be called stratified egalitarianism. Ultimately, the secret of Chaux was the singular identity that Ledoux achieved between the romantic idealism of his social beliefs and the elevated, idealistic purism of his later manner of design.

Boullée. Boullée and Ledoux are often paired as if they were the interchangeable partners of an architectural firm. Both, to

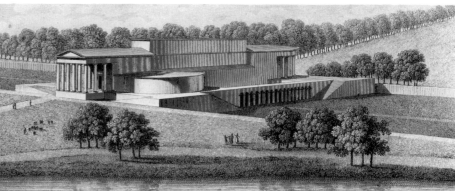

10-50   Claude-Nicolas Ledoux. Project
        for a Cooper's Workshop. (From his
        L'Architecture)

10-51   Claude-Nicolas Ledoux. Project for Oikema or Temple Dedicated to Love. (From
        his *L'Architecture*)

be sure, were members of the same generation, whose careers for some time traced parallel paths, and both ended as visionaries drawn to austere geometric compositions of high symbolic energy. Yet in talent and temperament, ambition and achievement, they could not have been more different.

Ledoux was a builder; even without his unrealized works on paper, he would rank among the great Neoclassical architects. Boullée, however, would today be considered a minor figure without his visionary drawings. It is not that his career was otherwise undistinguished. As an architect, he had, by the early 1760s, a flourishing practice in the kind of domestic work that simultaneously established Ledoux. Around 1780, Boullée finally appeared set for a fine career in public construction, having received several appointments as the architect of large-scale state enterprises. But in 1782, for no apparent reason, he gave them up and, apart from some remodelings, thereafter abandoned architectural practice altogether.

The self-imposed collapse of Boullée's career is perhaps not so inexplicable as it first seems. To begin with, he never wanted to become an architect. His great love was painting, which he studied with a prominent artist until he was coerced by his architect father into following in his footsteps. For over thirty years, he tried his best to be a dutiful son, but in the early 1780s, experiencing what today might be called a belated midlife crisis, he abandoned the pursuit of a strictly architectural career. In its place he followed a new one, which was neither that of architect nor painter, but something of both. He became an architectural visionary.

The model for the resolution of Boullée's conflict was Piranesi and his impracticable but unforgettable architectural images. One might even say that Boullée, consciously or not, became the French Piranesi, an artist who built comparatively little, but whose unbuildable architectural visions were of immense influence. Ultimately, Piranesi's melancholy vision of antiquity found reverberant, indeed amplified, echoes in the gloomy shadows and silhouettes of Boullée's Neoclassical style.

Like Piranesi, Boullée wrote as well as drew. His famous drawings were initially meant as illustrations for the architectural treatise he began in 1780, *Architecture, Essai sur l'art.* For Boullée, who was drawn to the theories of the Picturesque and the Sublime, the primary purpose of architecture was to produce an "expressive picture." Architecture to him was not a matter of three-dimensional structures, but two-dimensional images—visual poetry—eliciting sensations in our bodies, our feelings, our minds. Specific forms give rise to specific sensations, which Boullée "scientifically" catalogued. The most potent shapes are the elementary ones: pyramid, cube, cylinder, cone, and, especially, the sphere. The most powerful effects are created by the shadows thrown by these simple forms and received by their immense surface planes, stripped of all but the most crucial decorations. Claiming to have been the inventor of the "architecture of shadows," he finally insisted that it is not three-dimensional forms, nor even their two-dimensional primary images, but the illusory forms of darkness they create that are architecture's most effective means.

Boullée's drawings exemplify his fusion of English Picturesque/Sublime theories with French Neoclassical geometric purism. His visionary projects followed the reductive path of Ledoux to its limits, simultaneously reducing architecture to simple geometric schemes and extravagantly inflating the scale of its components. The visionary aura of these compositions depends heavily on Boullée's novel mode of presentation; he sets his buildings beneath cloud-filled heavens and in strong side-lighting, producing dramatic chiaroscuro effects, and he often generates powerful melodramatic moods with teeming crowds or lonely figures dwarfed by the buildings whose very scale they indicate.

Among the few visionary drawings of Boullée remotely connected with an actual project is the plan for a Metropolitan Cathedral (fig. 10-52) that evolved in 1781 from a scheme for the church of the Madeleine in Paris. Using as a model Soufflot's Panthéon, Boullée transformed it into a structure of unattainable majesty by the techniques outlined above. He combined colossal geometric masses in a centralized scheme: hemispherical dome; cylindrical drum; and identical, cubiform, colonnaded cross-arms with Corinthian porches. The dramatically side-lit forms rise starkly into cloud-filled heavens; the scale is indicated by the stairs and the crowds, as well as by the use of atmospheric perspective that makes palpable the distance from the viewer. Against this sweeping vision, Soufflot's church, which in its day seemed so uncompromising in its reform of the late Baroque, now looks almost Baroque itself (fig. 10-28). Although Boullée's formal purism is paramount, few of his schemes are so absolutely pure as not to include telling forms of elaboration—cornicework, inscriptions, sculpted accents, rustication, but, above all, the orders. He had little feeling for the tectonic and sculptural spirit of the orders as conceived by the Greeks; he saw them rather as an essentially pictorial device to create sensations of the Sublime. His Cathedral

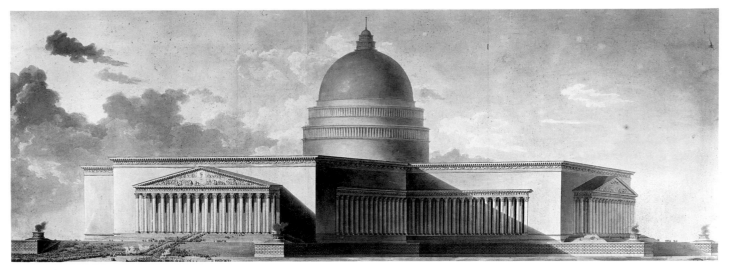

10-52 Étienne-Louis Boullée. Metropolitan Cathedral project. 1781. (Bibliothèque Nationale, Paris)

employs columns by the thousands for the interior, in the hundreds for the drum, and, most pointedly flouting antique usage, spread in double rows of sixteen in the porches.

Boullée's visionary ambition was limitless, as is seen in his project of 1783 for a Cenotaph to Newton (figs. 10-53, 10-54). It combines the fascination of the period with the new cosmology and Boullée's passion for the sphere as the perfect form of the Picturesque/Sublime. Conceived as a gigantic hollow sphere

10-53 Étienne-Louis Boullée. Project for Newton's Cenotaph. 1783. (Bibliothèque Nationale, Paris)

10-54 Étienne-Louis Boullée. Project for Newton's Cenotaph, cross section. (Bibliothèque Nationale, Paris)

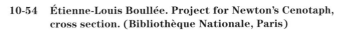

resting on a terraced and landscaped cylindrical base (recalling the Imperial Roman tumulus tombs), the vault of the interior— empty except for a raised catafalque at the bottom—was pierced by tiny openings so as to create by day an illusion of the star-filled heavens (a planetarium, in other words). Boullée loved all elementary geometry, but most of all the sphere, not only for its absolute purity and perfection, but also for its surprisingly painterly qualities. He exclaimed that "of all bodies, it offers the largest surface to the eye, and this lends it majesty. It has the utmost simplicity because that surface is flawless and endless" and it has "an outline that is as soft and as flowing as it is possible to imagine." And in Boullée's rendering, the magnificence of its shadow effects is unsurpassed. What prompted him to employ the form for the Newton memorial was his notion of Newton's discoveries (which he may have confused with Galileo's). Normally restrained in literary expression, Boullée was led to a passionate outburst: "Sublime mind! Vast and profound genius! Divine being! Newton! Accept the homage of my

10-55 Étienne-Louis Boullée. Project for Egyptian-Style Cenotaph. (Bibliothèque Nationale, Paris)

10-56 Étienne-Louis Boullée. Project for "Sunken" Pyramid. (Bibliothèque Nationale, Paris)

weak talents. . . . Newton! . . . If by the . . . sublimity of your genius you have determined the shape of the world, I have conceived the project of enveloping you with your discovery!"

Although Boullée conceived any number of visionary projects in the style of geometric Neoclassicism, he was, it seems, predisposed to the funebrial gloom of sepulchral monuments. His drawings of warriors' tombs, cemeteries, chapels of the dead, and the like are varied in concept, but he achieved his most revolutionary inventions in his series of pyramidal cenotaphs. In these he was inspired by the Egyptian pyramids, which he knew from illustrations and admired as "conjuring up a melancholy picture of arid mountains and of immutability." They were the very "image of grandeur." Earlier post-Egyptian architects had sporadically used the pyramid form for tombs, but, like the Pyramid of Cestius in Rome, all were minuscule reproductions of the Egyptian models. Boullée dared not only to rival the Egyptians, but also to surpass them in the imagined scale of his Egyptian-Style Cenotaph (fig. 10-55). Its histrionic dimensions were rendered by Boullée's usual means—antlike human figures crawling up endless stairs and tier upon tier of (un-Egyptian) pedimented colonnades climbing into the clouds. In two further drawings, he used the pyramid to carry his funebrial sensitivity to its peak by formal means that are unsettlingly futuristic. One version offers a pyramid of such purism that it anticipates the abstract architectural language of the twentieth century. The other pyramid variant is even more remarkable, foreseeing a model of conceptual architecture/sculpture that even now seems advanced (fig. 10-56). Boullée writes, "An idea, as new as it was daring, came to me . . . to create buildings that gave the illusion of being buried." Here a pyramidal structure of low lines seems to disappear into the earth the way an iceberg slips into the sea, suggesting an immense hidden mass far greater in size than its revealed tip.

In these drawings, the imagination of Boullée is unfettered by the constraints of the "buildable" or by any implicit conceptual limitations of architectural tradition. Like Ledoux, Boullée draws together with deceptive simplicity the diverse strands of Neoclassicism, stretches them to the limit, and goes beyond the farthest theoretical reaches of the Classical world. The work of these two men embodies a freedom of the imagination rarely matched in the history of architecture. But Boullée was a creature of the dark side of the Romantic movement. His mood is so far from Utopian as to be practically apocalyptic, but disguised in the deceptive lucidity of geometric Neoclassicism, just as the dark mood that took possession of France at the time found expression in rationalist jargon. His megalomaniac visions of the Neoclassical Sublime, in watered-down form, became the architectural norm of totalitarian regimes. It is no mere coincidence that the closest approximations of Boullée's dreams were projected (some begun) in the political horror of the Third Reich and the architectural ideals of Hitler and his protégé Albert Speer. This merely emphasizes the uncanny manner in which Boullée served as a springboard for what is best and worst in the architecture of the modern world.

RADICAL AND VISIONARY NEOCLASSICISM IN ENGLAND

Neoclassicism began in England with Palladian rationalism and ended there in the irrational extravagance of Sir John Soane. The progression from the former to the latter involved the same four Neoclassical modes followed in France: Rationalist, Archaeological, Radical, and Visionary. The first two brought us from Burlington through Robert Adam. But discussion of the subsequent phases was postponed until now because of their strong dependence on France, where Neoclassicism moved ahead of England after the 1760s. The 1770s and eighties in France saw a sensational fusion of the most advanced English and continental currents—the Picturesque and the Sublime, Piranesi and the sophisticated new archaeology, all within the matrix of an evolving Neoclassical formalism. The advanced phases of English Neoclassicism also mixed such heterogeneous materials, but, unlike the creations of Ledoux and Boullée, Neoclassical architecture in England passed into the Visionary stage by becoming more eclectic, ultimately with a strong tinge of medievalism. The spirit that took hold of English Neoclassicism in the decades leading up to 1800 and afterward was not one of lucidity and Classical formalism, but a primitivist spirit bathed in the mysterious waters of the ever-powerful English medieval past.

George Dance II. Radical Neoclassicism in England began, as in France, with a sharp reform of purely Classical modes—a shift from the lighthearted Adam style of the 1760s to the severe manner of George Dance II in his Newgate Prison (fig. 10-57), designed 1768–69. Its rational scheme comprised three large quadrangles, one each for male and female felons, and one for debtors (all male, as women were still deprived of financial responsibilities). The center unit was set back to allow space for a Keeper's House and twin flanking Entrance Lodges within the street line of the facade. The interior accommodations were surprisingly humane for the date, but the facade that loomed over the London streets until its destruction in 1902 was the signal event of the building. Dance had studied in Italy, where he was a close colleague of Piranesi, and this experience is plainly evident at Newgate. Many writers have been struck by its Piranesian aura, its imaginative exploitation of rusticated masonry to realize a powerful dramatization of incarceration and retribution. Dance created a forceful architectural "prison" language made up of an imaginative diversity of models, and he used it to give the Keeper's House, the Entrance Lodges, and the Quadrangle walls distinctive forms that symbolize their functions. The Quadrangle walls were windowless for absolute security, but Dance avoided monotony by breaking their corners slightly forward and by relieving the resulting end bays with blind arches containing rusticated aediculae. Paradoxically, the latter features emphasized the confining character of the wall, for they give the impression of walled-up openings that seal off forever the incarcerated souls behind them. They looked all the more claustrophobic in their juxtaposition with the Keeper's House, which seems self-righteously open everywhere, with rows of arched windows reaching down even to the basement. The Entrance Lodges strike an intermediate attitude, open, but seemingly only "one way," as Charles Dickens observed sixty years later, "looking as if they were made for the express purpose of letting people in, and never letting them out again." The Piranesian festooned chains displayed above the doorways, the rugged entrance rustication, and the gloomy grate beneath the overlying arch all contributed to Dickens's grim impression.

For all its strong visual distinctions, the facade of Newgate embodied a sense of unity. This was achieved by the overall rus-

10-57   George Dance II. Newgate Prison. London. 1768–69. (Sir John Soane's Museum, London)

10-58   George Dance II. Common Council Chamber, Guildhall. London. 1777–79. (British Architectural Library)

ticated texture, the repetition of motifs, and the two-level, triadic composition of all the divisions of the facade. Interestingly, the tripartite formula reflects numerous Palladian schemes. This move toward the Renaissance tradition is not isolated in Dance's design, for the basic pattern of rustication comes from Palladio's

Palazzo Thiene; the voussoir detailing of the aediculae goes back to Giulio Romano's Palazzo Te; and the "palazzo style" itself seems to reflect the Palazzo Pitti. Dance skips back over the fussy, "Rococo" Neoclassicism of Adam to the Burlington approach, in which the Renaissance rather than Rome is his source, but the Renaissance seen through the eyes of Piranesi.

The Renaissance proved to be an intermediate step for Dance, who continued to explore the past for a fresh Neoclassical formula. It was found at his Guildhall in the City of London, a complex judicial and administrative building that occupied much of the architect's energy in the 1770s and eighties. The most important contribution to the Guildhall was the Common Council Chamber (fig. 10-58), designed in 1777 (unfortunately, later destroyed). Its deceptively simple forms paradoxically combined advanced continental Neoclassical ideas and a freewheeling medievalism, ultimately the decisive combination for English Visionary Neoclassicism. The central space of the Chamber was covered by a pendentive dome over simple piers and arches detailed only by a medievalizing stringcourse. But what was most "medieval" was the Byzantinizing vault, which had, however, a Roman oculus and Roman fluting treated to produce the very un-Classical effect of a parachute, or tentlike, ceiling. The resulting primitivist impression was intensified by moody, dramatic lighting, which was evocative of Piranesi. But the basis of the design is reductionist structure, and this derived from the rationalist French ideal of skeletal construction championed by Laugier, embodied in Soufflot's Panthéon, and thereafter largely disregarded in France until the nineteenth century.

John Soane. Although John Soane collected no fewer than eleven copies of Laugier's treatise and was an outspoken devotee of French Neoclassical architecture, it is important to remember that in England, eclecticism, under the banner of the Picturesque, had become a force of increasing consequence, and had found its greatest proponent in Nash, with his command of everything from rustic hamlets to Moghul palaces. Soane was Nash's almost exact contemporary, and although he remained aloof from all the "movements," he practiced a range of styles as remarkable as those of Nash. This side of Soane is often overshadowed by a fascination with his more personal Neoclassical manner, and it is not generally realized how much of an eclectic architect he was.

Soane's masterpiece was the remodeled Bank of England, and it played so large a role for him that it would be difficult to imagine his career without it. Before being appointed Surveyor to the bank in 1788, Soane, who had been a favored student of Dance, had achieved little distinction. His task as Surveyor, a position which lasted from 1788 until his resignation a few years before his death in 1837, was to remodel and add to the work of his predecessor, Sir Robert Taylor. At the beginning, there was little thought that the outcome of Soane's appointment would be a vastly expanded complex. The bank evolved piecemeal, almost like a small city, or the typical English cathedral, whose contrasts emerged as each successive age added heterogeneous stylistic elements to the earlier structure. In Soane's case, of course, these contrasts were a deliberate, dramatic realization of the Picturesque ideals of variation and accretionism. Just how Picturesque was Soane's conception of his bank is revealed by a view he had made of it in 1830, showing it completed, but in a state of ruin much resembling a Roman bath or an Imperial palace (fig. 10-59). Each of the subdued entrances in its Neoclassical facade walls opened to stylistically different interiors— the Greek Revival Doric vestibule to the west, Lothbury Court (fig. 10-60) to the north with its monumental columnar screens in the style of Adam, while to the east, an oval vestibule opened to the most important interiors of the bank, which were grouped symmetrically around the Rotunda. The axes of these separate units led inward, to the seemingly chaotic jumble of the innermost parts of the bank, where the axes "met." And yet even here,

Soane accommodated these anomalies with subtle craft. Before its destruction, the whole of the bank, with its labyrinthine, Picturesque complexity, was a spellbinding experience.

The unique Soanic style was developed in the Rotunda and the surrounding offices, where Soane began his work on the bank in earnest in 1792 with the Bank Stock Office (fig. 10-61). The architect was proud of the vaulting, which employed the lightweight medium of hollow, amphoralike terra-cotta tubes that had been rediscovered in the Byzantine buildings of Ravenna. But his formal innovations were more consequential. Soane's point of departure was the pendentive vaulting of Dance's Guildhall interior, with its reductionist vocabulary and top-lighting effects, all now carried to a far fuller realization. The space expands into a reflection of Imperial Roman schemes such as the Baths of Diocletian or the Basilica of Maxentius, with its high central bays and barrel-vaulted aisle units. In the end bays, the light enters through segmental *thermae* windows, while in the center a saucerlike disk, through which a circle of indirect light enters the space below, floats over a ring of slender piers. The articulation is equally remarkable; there are none of Dance's fussy scallops or carved flutes, hardly any plastic elements at all, only minimal incised detailing. So forceful is the handling of the forms that only gradually is it evident how unconventional Soane's design is. The pilasters lack capitals and the windows lack frames; the vaults are segmentally flattened; and the movement of the pendentives of the central unit is broken off, and instead of a full vault, a saucerlike dome suddenly hovers disconnectedly above. Three-dimensional substance, the natural fullness, roundness, and density of form, are everywhere denied rather than realized in the assertive Classical architectural tradition.

10-59   Sir John Soane. Bird's-eye view showing principal features of the interior, Bank of England. 1830. (Modified from the original watercolor. Sir John Soane's Museum, London)

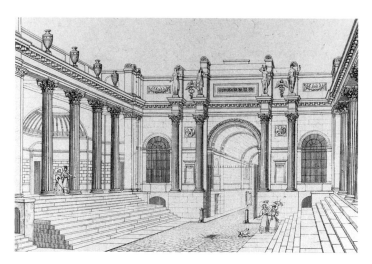

10-60   Sir John Soane. Lothbury Court, Bank of England. London. 1797. (Sir John Soane's Museum, London)

Interiors similar in format to the Bank Stock Office were built by Soane, several of them after a turning point in his career. In 1806, he was appointed Professor of Architecture at the Royal Academy, and with characteristic thoroughness, he spent the next three years preparing his lectures on the whole history of architecture. The result of his reappraisal of historical styles can be observed in the Old Colonial Office of 1818 (fig. 10-62). In the 1792 Bank Stock Office, the suspended saucer-dome above a ring of fenestration was an important element. In the Old Colonial Office, this device is repeated in the more monumental form of a ring of Ionic columns that reveals the influence of the rising Greek Revival fashion. But the most crucial innovation is the form of the supporting arches below. The fluting has now been extended over the entire run of the arch (accompanied by narrow panels in the barrel vaulting). A Classical form of articulation has been treated in medieval fashion, specifically in the Late Gothic manner of a building such as King's College Chapel at Cambridge.

Soane's architecture, it has been said, lacks "self-assurance" and a "definite unity of impression"; it "never commands," and it betrays an "element of malaise." Such gratuitous negativism, although responsive to Soane's peculiarities, does not lead to an understanding of Soane historically, for his manner was very much in tune with the artistic currents of his time. This is implicit in his enormous success. He was not only the builder of the Bank of England, one of the great structures of the age of Neoclassicism, but the designer of numerous other public enterprises, including an uncompleted (and destroyed) series of projects for Parliament and the London law courts, Masonic halls, and the extant Dulwich Art Gallery. The Soanic style, although not without some sharp criticism from his contemporaries, touched the sensibility of the age. It was part of English Romanticism, the world of Walpole and the Gothic novel, and poets and artists such as Coleridge, Blake, and Fuseli. It was a world in which Soane's Bank of England would have been an appropriate stage for dreamlike, even nightmarish, "Gothick" events.

Yet to confine Soane's style to the Romantic world of cultivated disorder is to deny the importance of his architectural position in the mainstream of the international movement that we have followed as an exchange between Parisian-Roman Neoclassicism and the English Picturesque, Sublime, and Gothic Revival. Soane was deeply affected by France; yet he was able to transform its example into a manner that was both intrinsically English and Romantically his own. This transformation of continental phenomena involved something quite specific, namely the medievalizing tendencies mentioned earlier. The Soanic style may legitimately be called "Gothic" in its medievalist detailing and its spectral aura. Soane integrated the tradition of the English cathedrals and Fonthill Abbey with continental Neoclassicism. He created, in other words, a Neoclassical version of the Gothic Revival, or, paradoxically, what might well be called a Gothic Neoclassical style.

In the most eccentric and personal of all his works, his own London house, Soane went even further. This extraordinary building resulted from Soane's reconstruction of three small row dwellings at 12–14 Lincoln's Inn Fields, an intermittent process that lasted from 1792 to 1824. The intricacy of its interior, a rabbit warren of claustrophobic planning and unpredictably shifting levels, resulted not so much from piecemeal construction as from Soane's cultivation of Picturesque complexities. The house is an urban version of Walpole's Strawberry Hill, and it leaves an unforgettable impression on all who visit it. Soane gave the building to the English nation as a museum, which it remains, with its teeming collections of drawings, paintings, sculptures, ancient and medieval spoils, and artifacts of every kind. In the so-called Dome (fig. 10-63) of the Museum, Soane's collection of ancient architectural fragments was originally arranged in a manner suggestive of Piranesi—a piling up of antiquities on multilevel arches and vaults resembling

10-61   Sir John Soane. Bank Stock Office, Bank of England. 1792. (After Stroud)

10-62   Sir John Soane. Old Colonial Office, Bank of England. 1818. (After Stroud)

10-63
Sir John Soane. The Dome.
Sir John Soane's Museum,
interior as arranged in
1813. London. (From a
drawing by J. M. Gandy.
Sir John Soane's Museum,
London)

10-64 Sir John Soane. Breakfast Parlour, Sir John Soane's Museum. 1812

subterranean Roman sepulchral ruins. The house was characterized by a variety of Gothic Neoclassical styles, and one example in particular—the Breakfast Parlour (fig. 10-64)—serves to anchor the architect in the cultural cross-currents of his age and also to prophesy a later era.

The room is tiny, its details unassuming, but the effect of the whole is brilliant. It is built on a rectangular plan, with "mysteriously" top-lit spaces at either end and a square, vaulted unit in the center, formed by a pendentive structure with a lantern over simple corner supports. Refined and buoyant, the Breakfast Parlour is recognized as another example of Soane's synthesis of diverse English and French sources already observed in the bank offices. But there is more to this seemingly innocent interior. Convex mirrors appear throughout, and they are a key to the room's effects. The solidity of the forms dissolves into line and plane, and these in turn diffuse into shifting, intangible reflections. There are no sure boundaries, only interpenetrating, reflecting planes and edges that offer no resting point for the eye. Soane was especially proud of his Breakfast Parlour, but had trouble describing its revolutionary effects, writing that "the views from this room . . . the mirrors

in the ceiling, and the looking-glasses, combined with the variety of outline and general arrangement in the design and decoration of the limited space, present a succession of those fanciful effects which constitute the poetry of architecture." What Soane seems to be suggesting is that the interior was not conceived as a concentrated Classical unity, but as a "succession" of fragmented "fanciful effects," a Picturesque dissolving of Classical forms into a series of "poetically" evocative optical phenomena. This clearly derives from the Picturesque, but it transcends its sources just as the contemporary painter J. M. W. Turner, in dissolving the traditional determinate form of painting into a style of color, space, and light, transcends his "picturesque" sources. And just as Turner looks forward to the Impressionists and to the Modernist movement, the Soanic style of the Breakfast Parlour is also prophetic. In monumental architecture, there was to be nothing quite like Soane until the abstract architectural style of the early twentieth century. Like his French counterparts, Soane, in destroying canonical Classical tradition, realized the culmination of the Picturesque and the Neoclassical movements and prepared the architectural soil for a future harvest.

11-1
Jean-
François-
Thérèse
Chalgrin.
Arc de
Triomphe.
Paris.
Begun 1806

Chapter Eleven | The Nineteenth Century

The decades that saw the final realization of the spirit of the Enlightenment and eighteenth-century Romanticism in the visions of Boullée and Ledoux, and in the work of Nash and Soane, also witnessed the birth of a new, and very different, architectural spirit. Strangely, it carries no name other than that of its century. Yet it was an age hardly as colorless as this label suggests. On the contrary, architecturally, as in everything else, the nineteenth century was unprecedentedly complex, even bewildering in its variety and detail, and panoramic in range. Historicism continued as the primary stylistic medium, reaching its peak expansion as every known architectural age was revived. But it no longer spoke with the spontaneity, the authority, or the aura of liberation of eighteenth-century historicism. Rather, the spirit of poetic release was transmuted by the nineteenth century into a more prosaic mood pervaded by a sense of entrapment in the past, of anxious self-limitation and conflict in the obsessive reenactment of historical styles.

The direction taken by the nineteenth century was initially a profound reaction to the excesses of the previous period. The very ideas that moved men to peaks of expression in the realm of the imagination plunged them into a quarter-century nightmare of turmoil and bloodshed in the "real" world.

The trauma experienced by Europe between 1789 and the final defeat of Napoleon in 1815—regicide, terror, toppled thrones, middle-class usurpers, a desecrated church, ghastly wars of "liberation"—can only be compared in its devastating effect on the consciousness of Europe with the terrible period in the last century between 1914 and 1945, with its world wars, revolutions, great depression, death camps, and the atomic bomb. And just as more than a half-century later we still have not assimilated those events, the recoil from the French Revolution persisted well into the nineteenth century.

The reaction to the French Revolution was swift and severe. The Congress of Vienna in 1815 restored the French monarchy and attempted everywhere to turn back the clock to the days of the *ancien régime*. It was agreed by the establishment that the cause of mankind's recent sorrows had been not the intolerable conditions that had provoked the revolutionary fury of rationalism but mainly rationalism itself, particularly its political form of liberalism, a creed to which not only revolutionaries but monarchs nearly everywhere had enthusiastically subscribed. Louis XVI, it was believed, had lost his head because he had encouraged liberalism. The new conservatives of the nineteenth century espoused a passionate belief in the past in place of a blind faith in reason, and they made a firm commitment to history in every form. Belief in the primacy of the past was not merely a cynical apologism for the restored

establishment, or an agent against progressive change, but became a deeply pervasive cultural phenomenon.

In the last analysis, however, what is so characteristic of the nineteenth century is the conflict between conservatism and the mounting forces of change. The struggle between tradition and innovation is present everywhere in history, but not with the unrelenting upheaval and intensity of the nineteenth century. The revolutionary fervor of the eighteenth century had been driven largely by the Intellectual Revolution, but now it was the thundering engine of the Industrial Revolution and all its consequences that was accelerating like a locomotive running downhill out of control, unleashing a continuing avalanche of change that eventually was to bury practically every living vestige of the old ways. A major manifestation of this process was the intensified class struggle. The centuries-old class structure, which had been accepted by virtually everyone because (repression aside) it had meant a secure position and defined role in society, now was coming undone. In a world of unparalleled social and economic flux, the anxious status of the middle class was intensified and spread to society as a whole. The position of the aristocracy was increasingly shaky, and that of the uprooted lower classes was a quicksand of exploitation and unemployment.

This free-floating social relativism was a major reason why the nineteenth century in virtually every realm—sociopolitical, cultural, and intellectual—became obsessively preoccupied with history. The past became a tangible, fixed anchor in a world in flux, serving as the "roots," the foundation for a world in a process of disruptive change and pervasive conflict. The primary philosophical spokesman for the new outlook was Georg Wilhelm Friedrich Hegel, who believed that reality was historical, a stage by stage unfolding of truth through the dialectic. For Hegel and his era, reality and truth were not found in the revelations of reason, but were rather a matter of process, history, and conflict. It is not generally realized just how pervasive Hegelianism was outside the philosophical realm, or how its perspective was shared by the three intellectual giants of the period, whose revelations were so radical, consequential, and brilliantly presented that the human consciousness still vibrates from their shock waves.

In 1859, Charles Darwin demonstrated that the species evolved over millions of years and that the process of evolution was one of a "universal struggle for existence." The contemporary economist Karl Marx boasted of having "stood Hegel on his head" with his socialist theory of dialectical materialism, in which economic realities move ideas rather than vice versa (as in Hegel), a theory in which Marx insisted that "the whole history of mankind . . . has been a class struggle." If Darwin saw life as a process of everlasting conflict between all creatures, and Marx envisioned human history as a dialectical conflict between the economic classes of mankind, then Sigmund Freud completed this new picture with his portrait of the human individual as a creature profoundly in conflict with himself. In Freud's view, the individual is not a *tabula rasa* on which experience "writes," but one who undergoes a complex personal history beginning at birth, a struggle between rational and irrational, conscious and subconscious, life-giving and death-seeking inner forces.

THE ARCHITECTURAL PREDICAMENT

Conditions in architecture closely paralleled those in society-at-large. These connections are easiest to perceive through the pervasive theme of conflict, which was particularly strong and many-sided in the architectural realm. The "battle of the styles," the tumultuous competition between historical revivals that persisted through most of the century, involved not only the contest between Classical and medieval partisans but also embittered infighting within the two camps. Beneath these surface battles, however, were far deeper and more pervasive conflicts. On the one hand, new scientific scholarship produced a new clarity in the picture of historical styles, making them irresistible models for architects; technology, on the other hand, provided iron, steel, glass, and other industrial materials in overwhelming abundance, along with new techniques of design and construction. But the forms of historicism had been developed for preindustrial architectural techniques and thus tended to be inimical to the new technology. Furthermore, the new needs of nineteenth-century industrial society were inherently at odds with historicist building types and styles. Yet the new materials and structural methods tended toward an unprecedented economy and lightness that collided with the bourgeoisie's predisposition to heavy, ornate, traditional styles.

The purpose of this chapter is not to mystify the reader with overlapping images of wheels-within-wheels, but rather to demonstrate just how the nineteenth century, with its upheavals and unleashing of explosive new forces in every realm, tended to have conflict and contradiction built into its very being, and how, inevitably, these discords appeared in manifold form in architecture. But perhaps they appeared most vividly in the personal predicament of the practicing architect. Historicism was in conflict with the workings of the architect's imagination, which was now plagued by an acute retrospective consciousness. That casual, personal, and intuitive connection with the architectural past that had been the way of the Greeks (toward Egypt), the Romans (toward Greece), the Middle Ages and Renaissance (toward antiquity) had begun to dissolve in the eighteenth century, and in the nineteenth it had changed. In its place was a new relationship, forged by historical and intellectual forces—in particular Hegelian-Darwinian—and the propensity to see reality in terms of historical process, to *believe* in the architectural past. This historicist orthodoxy was reinforced by a radical new architectural knowledge, a broad and deep erudition in which architectural history as a field of "scientific" learning was almost as highly organized and detailed as physical and life sciences.

If we imagine an architect being not merely erudite and scholarly but actually having to *build* in the past styles now known and "worshiped," we find unavoidable inner conflicts. Exact copies of historical models were rarely produced (for various reasons, among them the irrepressible human drive toward originality); and when imaginative novelties were introduced, an immediate tension arose between what was known to be the authentic original and its variation. Architects of earlier historicizing periods, such as the Renaissance, had also experienced such tensions. But because their knowledge of the past and their bond with it were comparatively loose and fluid, the tension served mainly to heighten the impact of the new work, to enrich this new work rather than to inhibit the architectural process with an often crippling self-consciousness and even guilt at the "betrayal" of the past, as we find in the nineteenth century.

But there was a still deeper process of conflict at work here. Although nineteenth-century architects consciously believed in the styles they knew so well, their commitment was not a matter of gut feeling, but of comparatively superficial cerebration. For a Brunelleschi, a Bramante, even for a Ledoux, a deep imaginative affinity with the past was still possible; their intuitive sympathy for it pervaded every detail of their work. But in the nineteenth century, the new conditions of life and art had become so radically different from those of the pre–Industrial Age as to sever those deep bonds between present and past that had always existed. It was as if the emotional distance between the nineteenth century and the past was increased in proportion to its acute knowledge and conscious worship of it: as architects came to know more and more about the past, their feeling for it progressively weakened. But there was little in the background of nineteenth-century architects, or in the realities of their lives, that had much intrinsic connection with the historical styles in which they had to build. Thus, far more than an outer conflict between the new material basis of architecture and the historical styles was at issue. The inner voices of the architect spoke a different language than those heard before the Industrial Revolution, and, correspondingly, his feeling for outline and weight, sense of scale and proportion, sensitivity to color and texture, and response to image and symbol tended to be of a radical new departure, which was severed from the past by an uncrossable void. It is the presence of this invisible conflict that we recognize in every work of the period—not merely the heaviness of taste, vulgar display, excessive complexity, utilitarian bias, and other obvious qualities, not only that cast iron was inimical to forms developed for stone, or that the orders resisted adaptation to a building of ten or twenty stories, but the fact that architects had to build in the "styles" that they were not really moved by, styles whose intrinsic qualities were antithetical to the architects' own, new aesthetic feelings. This syndrome was realized in the mechanical, cold treatment of the orders, in their mishandled shapes, proportions, and scale, and in the harsh and distended transformations of the graceful Gothic styles.

The extraordinary thing is that the architecture of the period could also be brilliant. A number of gifted and determined architects transcended the century's conflicts and transformed the inchoate substance of the period into an effective architectural style, sublimating the convolutions of an industrialized, urban, predominantly bourgeois, but highly pluralistic, form of living into their art. But in an age of explosive change and unparalleled complexity, architecture would not have the refined, harmonious beauty of the past. It would be instead worldly and spectacular in works such as the Brooklyn Bridge and the Paris Opera. But above all it would be achieved in terms of historicism and eclecticism.

Evolutionism and Historicism. Until recently, nineteenth-century architecture has been explained by categorizing and chronicling its multifarious revivals and taking them at face value, thereby dismissing and rejecting historicism. "It was a grave symptom of a diseased century that architects were satisfied to be storytellers instead of artists," wrote Nikolaus Pevsner, one of the most important historians of Modernism. To a degree it is all true. The ostentatious, sometimes indigestible, decorative quality that typifies nineteenth-century architectural production cannot be disguised; and that spectacle of styles passing one after another, some disappearing and suddenly reappearing, nearly all borrowing bits and pieces of each other's costumes, does resemble some "fancy dress ball." The steep decline in "taste" from Louix XV to Napoleon I and Napoleon III cannot be denied. But to imply seriously that the Victorians were vain or fickle is an irresponsible misreading of the age. Anyone familiar with its major architectural writers such as A. W. N. Pugin, John Ruskin, and E.-E. Viollet-le-Duc knows that the aesthetic atmosphere was hardly frivolous.

Beginning in the 1820s, the question was put over and over by architectural writers: "In what style should we build?" (Valdenaire A. Hubsch, 1828); "The great question is, are we to have an architecture of our period, a distinct, individual, palpable style of the 19th century?" (Thomas Leverton Donaldson, 1847); "Every age but the present has had, in some degree, at least, a style of its own" (George Gilbert Scott, 1850). The nineteenth century produced enough imaginative architects to have bridged the gap between historicism and a new style had there not been some powerful, invisible force blocking the way. The presence of this block emerges in such apodictic statements as Scott's "no age has ever deliberately invented a new style . . . something morally impossible." This sense of futility was expressed vividly in the definitive scholarly statement of the nineteenth century, in the eleventh edition of the *Encyclopaedia Britannica* (1910): "And as to the theory of the new school that we should throw overboard all precedent in architectural detail, that is intellectually impossible. We are not made so that we can invent everything *de novo* . . . the attempt can only lead to baldness or eccentricity. Every great style of architecture of the past has, in fact, been evolved from the detail of preceding styles." This superannuated defense of historicism lays bare the strongest obstacle to radical architectural originality—the doctrine, articulated by Hegel and especially by Darwin, of evolutionism. If nothing is created *de novo* (except once at the beginning of time, even Darwin had to admit), and everything evolves from something else, spontaneous generation of the forms and images of architecture is thus "morally" and "intellectually" impossible.

The anticreationist doctrine of architectural evolutionism thereby denied imaginative freedom to the nineteenth-century designer, and it condemned him—like Dr. Frankenstein in Mary Shelley's contemporary horror story—to creating a living art out of bits of the dead past. But the haunted mansion to which the architect was confined had many, many rooms. Moreover, if forbidden the outdoors, he was at liberty not only to use the rooms as he pleased, but to do a great deal of interior remodeling and rebuilding. The doctrine of architectural evolutionism was two-sided: on the one hand, it entailed a claustrophobic proscription; but on the other, it gave the architect powerful new means to work within the confines of the past, for the new doctrine implied

that the styles were not fixed but evolutionarily mobile and fluid. Above all, they were adaptable to the challenging new circumstances in which architecture found itself.

Eclecticism and Technology: The Brooklyn Bridge. When something really new was built in the nineteenth century, it was thought to be "engineering" and not "architecture," a notion that includes the two most sensational structures of the period—the Crystal Palace in London and the Eiffel Tower in Paris. The forces behind such spectacular works were the new technology and materials, and they affected not only engineering constructions but architecture in general. Although the new technology may have been in many ways opposed to the architectural mainstream, it became very much part of the nineteenth-century architectural whole. Thus, eclecticism was a characteristic condition of the employment of new materials for new structures. New York's Brooklyn Bridge (1867–83), with its Egypto-Roman-Gothic masonry piers combined with a double system of steel suspension cables, superbly exemplifies the eclecticism of materials and structure as well as of historical styles.

The great suspension bridge (fig. 11-2), designed by John Roebling and completed by his son, Washington, is formed of a roadbed hanging from cables, which, in turn, hang from towers. Several systems of movement across the bridge were provided: two outer lanes for carriages, a pair of inner lanes for a cable train, and an elevated central boardwalk intended as a "promenade over the Bridge on fine days to enjoy the beautiful views and the pure air." To sustain the enormous weight, two systems of suspension were employed: the usual vertical cables hung from drooping parabolic curves; and cables stretched directly between the pier tops and regularly spaced points on the roadbed, forming triangular structural units that Roebling called wire trusses.

To architectural historians, perhaps the most interesting of the bridge components are the granite towers that rise almost 300 feet above the water. Engineering calculation determined their overall bulk but not their formal detail, for which Roebling evolved a design less appreciated than it might be. Anyone can see that the towers are basically Gothic, looking like revisions of cathedral buttress towers. But they are not

11-2 John and Washington Roebling. Brooklyn Bridge. New York. 1867–83

purely Gothic. One of Roebling's early projects for the bridge towers had been in the Egyptian style, and the gorge molding from that project reappears in stiffened form atop the executed versions. This stylistic eclecticism is obvious, but what is not usually noticed is the way Roebling has manipulated Egyptian and Gothic detail to form an image that can only be meant as a Gothic-Egyptoid version of a Roman triumphal arch. The towers are pier structures with connecting walls and arches, but they have been made to look like high, solid walls—complete with attic zone—with arches cut through them and buttresses attached as Gothic versions of the columnar detailing on Roman arches. The Egyptian gorge molding of the attic even corresponds to Corinthian trabeation.

The creation of a Classical image out of Gothic and Egyptian forms was not mere eclecticism for its own sake. It expressed Gothic spiritual grace and Egyptian strength with an air of Roman civic magnificence. In the dedication ceremonies of 1883, reference to the last appeared in statements about the bridge as "America's Arch of Triumph" and "New York's Brandenburg Gate." By "arch of triumph" was meant not only the towers themselves but the even greater arch of the bridge as a whole. The bridge realized a visionary leap from shore to shore (not only of the East River, but metaphorically the oceans and the American continent) that captured the expansive American ethos of the period. It was, as John Roebling saw it, the final link in the chain of the movement from east to west.

Considering the success of the bridge, it is strange that architectural critics have rarely ceased to criticize the "impurity" of Roebling's design. They thrill at its scale and flight over city roofs and water, and they delight in the effects of the complex patterns of overlap among its cables. But its towers are seen as an unfortunate lapse of taste on the part of Roebling, who should have had the good sense to build them in stripped, "straight," engineering form. In this view, the bridge would then have been harmonious and not "schizophrenically" divided between forward-looking science and eclectic, backward-looking art. But it is precisely the ambivalence and formal conflicts of the Brooklyn Bridge, its multileveled eclecticism of diverse historical styles and unalloyed technological forms, that is so characteristic of nineteenth-century architecture. With the Brooklyn Bridge, the picture of the period's intrinsic qualities begins to take clearer shape.

Conventional Architecture. Although in the final analysis it is our belief that nineteenth-century architecture will be remembered mainly for its exceptional high-technology constructions, the renewed admiration of scholars for more conventional buildings of the period is surely justified by their consistently high level of design, fine craftsmanship, and responsiveness to human needs. By and large, most of the important, conventional monumental buildings were either part of, or related to, three stylistic currents: International Neoclassicism, the work of the École des Beaux-Arts, and the Victorian Gothic. These phenomena differ not only in style, but in their geography. Neoclassicism, the reader will recall, was in the eighteenth century a geographically contained interaction of a relatively small group of personalities working mainly in London, Paris, and Rome. After 1800, this confined, dialectical movement became an international current that spread throughout the world. By about 1840, however, France again assumed leadership with

the École des Beaux-Arts, while Victorian England, although continuing to produce works of Classicism, produced the most important Gothic revival styles of the century.

INTERNATIONAL NEOCLASSICISM

Germany. One of the greatest architects working in the first half of the century was the Prussian genius Karl Friedrich Schinkel. His career was so closely connected with the rising Prussian state that the royal family walked behind his funeral bier at his relatively early death. Schinkel was fortunate to work in Prussia not only because of its tremendous support of building activity in the 1820s and thirties, but because of its ambition to surpass its rivals. In architectural terms, this competitiveness meant an eager receptivity to the two major architectural powers, France and England, whose respectively Neoclassical and Picturesque traditions Schinkel took up with a vengeance, and pushed to extreme architectural statements. He possessed a truly protean imagination and intellect, practicing all the styles including Grecian, Romanesque, Gothic, *Rundbogen* (Italianate vernacular construction), Renaissance, and Functionalist, and he synthesized a number of experimental eclectic manners of his own. Moreover, he not only worked in seemingly every architectural type—tiny houses and small parish churches, bridges, military barracks, monuments, theaters, museums, villas, and palaces—but in many artistic forms. He devised the decorative detail of his interiors, often as ornate as the exteriors were austere, and he was a notable designer of furniture. He published his own architectural works in lavish volumes. And as a talented painter, he worked first as a producer of dioramas, then of Romantic canvases of landscapes and cathedrals in the manner of Caspar David Friedrich, and, finally, of stage sets for forty-two of the most important theatrical and operatic productions of the period.

Schinkel's painterly activity, with its predominantly architectural subject matter, was crucial for his future career in several respects. Through it he sharpened and expanded his architectural imagination by creating illusory works impossible actually to build, yet more realistic than in sketches or even elaborately drafted renderings. The experience, moreover, heightened his sensitivity to the integration of buildings and their environment. Few architects fused building and site more creatively than Schinkel. Finally, the rendering of architecture in dioramas and in stage sets gave him a mastery of architectural illusionistic effects and devices.

The first building to win Schinkel international fame was his Berlin Schauspielhaus (National Theater) built in 1819–21 (fig. 11-3). It involved a complex functional program that Schinkel disposed in a decisive manner: The theater proper occupies the high, deep, central block, while the lower, shallower wings left and right contain respectively concert and rehearsal halls, together with a royal reception lounge, administrative offices, and storage facilities. He insisted that the post-and-lintel mode of his theater walls was Greek. In his own words, he "tried to emulate Greek form and methods of construction insofar as possible in this complex work." At the height of the Greek Revival, it was natural for him to view the trabeated tectonics of the theater as Greek. However, the interlocking pilaster orders that make up the exterior of Schinkel's building are not Greek but unmistakably Michelangelesque—the Michelangelo of the Capitoline Palace facades with their skeletal framework of a giant pilaster order, within which

11-3 Karl Friedrich Schinkel. Schauspielhaus. Berlin. 1819–21

several secondary levels are set in strong relief layers. But just as no one today would take the chilly forms of the Greek Revival for the Greek original, so no one would mistake Schinkel's elevations for Michelangelo's. Their differences are revealing. Michelangelo's Capitoline forms an "organic" architecture that, like his sculpture, gives the illusion of living forces at work in the stone. Schinkel reinterpreted Michelangelo through functional-ist nineteenth-century eyes, almost reducing the illusion of mus-cular stresses to an abstract grid of inert stereometric forms.

Almost, but not quite. Schinkel, for all his geometric lucidity, was nevertheless an artist preoccupied with architecture as illusion. If we look at the theater again, we find that the build-ing's massing is not uniformly proportioned and static, but builds forward and upward with shrewdly calculated projectile energies, gathered into asymmetrically balanced movement. He plays with the temple front image so that the real hexastyle Ionic entrance porch is repeated in relief on the other three sides of the building, creating the effect of a centralized struc-ture, when in fact it is merely bilaterally symmetrical.

Schinkel was, we have observed, deeply concerned with the integration of architecture into its setting. The theater fronts a square flanked by two large eighteenth-century churches, each centralized in plan, capped by a high dome, and with hexastyle porches on at least three sides. His raised central block, illusionistic fronts, and illusory centrality mirror the architectural program of the theater's neighbors, creating fas-cinating reflections among the three buildings. To make sure that all of this was not lost on his audience, he acted as stage designer: the stage backdrop for the opening of the theater on May 26, 1821 (at which a Greek play by Goethe, *Iphigenie auf Tauris*, was performed), was a view of the theater complete in its whole setting between the two flanking churches.

Schinkel's next major building, the Altes Museum (1824–28; figs. 11-4–11-7) in Berlin is usually considered his greatest work, superior in its concentrated serenity to the agitated vir-tuosity of the theater. But this differentiation may be largely a matter of the two building types. There is truly something intrinsically theatrical in the architectural "performance" of the Berlin theater; but the museum was meant to suggest a shrine of cultural treasures, a place for calm and deep com-munion with the great works of art of the past ages. Even the siting and the approach to the museum contribute to this effect. The building faces the Royal Palace across Schinkel's refurbished, formal garden square of restrained patterns of parterres, shrubbery, and a fountain, laterally framed by rows of trees, which on one side screen off a canal and on the other hide a clutter of architecture, parting only for Schinkel's Ionic portico of the ungainly Berlin Cathedral. The museum is set in the monumental heart of Berlin, yet because of Schinkel's imaginative urbanistic touches it presents to the beholder a serenely orchestrated panorama into which the museum blends with utmost grace. And just as the site is made to contribute to the "noble tranquility and calm grandeur" of the museum— the famous eighteenth-century phrase of Winckelmann which summed up the ethos of the Greek Revival—the museum con-tributes powerfully to the site's majesty. No more monumental image was created in the nineteenth century than Schinkel's majestic Ionic colonnade rising into clear view above a high podium and a central flight of steps, its success a matter of those refinements of scale, proportion, and detail that give all such deceptively simple works their grandeur.

Far more than a facade, Schinkel's Altes Museum has always been considered a model of planning and utility. The layout is emphatically Francophile in its elaborate symmetry

11-4   Karl Friedrich Schinkel. Altes Museum. Berlin. 1824–28

11-5   Altes Museum in setting, with Berlin Cathedral. (After Schinkel)

11-7   Balcony, Altes Museum. (After Schinkel)

11-6   Plan, Altes Museum. (After Schinkel)

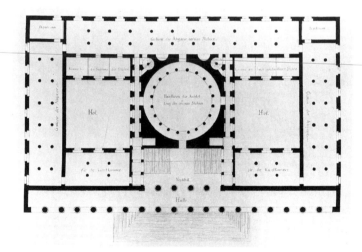

and axiality, its processional entrance through columnar screens and stairways, and its dominant central feature. But his imaginative artistry carried him beyond any simple reproduction of models. Halfway along the museum's axial sequence of spaces he did something no French architect would have done, providing a Picturesque view from a balconylike landing out through the facade screens to the square, a view integrated with the entrance interior. At the same time, the building is utilitarian in the handling of the well-lit galleries along the outer walls, with flexible spaces and wall panels running perpendicular to the windows for glare-free lighting of paintings.

Schinkel's Grecian Neoclassical buildings were his most significant works. But the stimulus of an 1826 excursion to

England dissolved his Classical style and set him off on new paths. His late buildings from about 1826 to 1840 demonstrate his experimentalism and his eagerness to follow novel directions as far as they would go. For utilitarian works—especially commercial and military buildings such as warehouses and barracks—walls were reduced to stripped post-and-lintel frames (partly inspired by factory buildings in England). But for structures of a higher order, eclectic solutions were devised. The tectonic skeleton was either cast in historicist form—as in the giant Romanesque arcades of his 1853 library project—or combined with historicist detailing, most notably in his famous Bauakademie (architectural school; fig. 11-8) of 1836 in Berlin, with its powerful framework of piers built in polychrome brickwork, the wall and window detailing extracted from the North Italian Renaissance. Such designs looked forward to the development of commercial buildings of the later nineteenth century, which would culminate in the United States in works of Richardson, Sullivan, and the Chicago School.

Picturesque tendencies were always present in Schinkel's work, but after 1826 they became central concerns. His most extreme Picturesque adventures were extravagant, unbuilt villa projects. What he actually built in the Picturesque mode (mainly estates for Prussian royalty) was tame by comparison, but nevertheless brilliant. The main villa at Charlottenhof (fig. 11-9), outside Potsdam, of 1826–27, with its Doric porch,

11-8 Karl Friedrich Schinkel. Bauakademie. Berlin. 1836

would be almost Palladian were it not for its asymmetrical siting on steeply sloping terrain. The basement emerges on one side, and its asymmetrical loggia and garden are integrated with the landscape in the manner of contemporary English estates. Between 1829 and 1836, together with his talented follower, Ludwig Persius, Schinkel expanded the Picturesque charms of Charlottenhof with an intricate water-garden complex provided with the Tea House, the so-called Roman Bath, and, most delightful of all, the Court Gardener's House (fig. 11-10). Together they make a deceptively simple grouping of bare forms that subtly blends with nature. The high quality of this work emerges when its taut, asymmetrical massing of Italianate vernacular construction (*Rundbogen*) is seen against loosely ordered and casually detailed earlier English counterparts.

Schinkel did not necessarily produce the single greatest work of nineteenth-century architecture, but in terms of the quality, range, and influence of his total output he may fairly be considered the finest representative of International Neoclassicism. He did not work alone in Germany. His most important near-competitor was another Prussian, Leo von Klenze, whose long career was mostly spent in the service of the rival German state, Bavaria. Superficially, their careers were similar: both men were launched in the 1810s with official appointments—von Klenze being made Director of Court Building in Munich in 1814—and their most distinguished buildings were Grecian. However, within the limits of International Neoclassicism, their buildings could not have differed more. Klenze was endowed with none of Schinkel's fiery intellect; his works share none of the Berliner's tectonic depth and polished brilliance of detailing. In comparison with Schinkel, von Klenze's work is shallow, at times almost naive, but in comparison with most of his other peers, he stands out.

Von Klenze produced the most evolved versions of two of the most characteristic International Neoclassical building types—the Doric Temple-on-High and the Propylaea gate. His Walhalla (fig. 11-11), or monument to German worthies (its interior lined with their portrait busts), conceived around 1820 and built in 1831–42, sets a Doric temple into a hillside overlooking a serene panorama outside of Regensburg. The siting is sensitively Romantic, the forms of the Parthenon-like temple sure and lucid, although typically hard and cold, with the tremendous stairs providing a highly dramatic if intimidating

approach. His Propylaea in Munich (fig. 11-12), designed in 1817, executed as late as 1846–50, is freely eclectic in setting the Doric central portico between twin pylonlike towers, which, with their Egyptoid gorge cornices, produce a novel combination of Athens and Luxor. The Propylaea works well in its context, marking the axial entrance to the Königsplatz, which is fronted on the sides by near-twin museums. The earlier of these stark Neoclassical blocks is von Klenze's Glyptothek, built in 1816–34 as a public sculpture gallery.

If the Königsplatz makes Munich something of a New Athens, von Klenze's larger urbanistic contribution to the city, the Ludwigstrasse (fig. 11-13; done partly in collaboration with Friedrich von Gärtner), was intended to give it an Italianate aura. The broad, straight avenue runs out from the core of the city, cutting numerous cross-streets, opening left and right at intervals into a square or a forecourt. At its inner end, between the two streets that fork into the city, the Ludwigstrasse is marked by the Feldherrnhalle (by Gärtner, 1841–44), a slightly fussy copy of the fourteenth-century Loggia dei Lanzi in Florence, while the street's outer terminus is defined by the Siegestor (by Gärtner, 1843–40), a massive Imperial Roman triumphal arch. The side "walls" of the avenue are a variety of Italian quattrocento styles and, to a lesser extent, cinquecento palatial facades. Superficially, many of the buildings are unde-

11-9 Karl Friedrich Schinkel. Schloss Charlottenhof. Potsdam. 1826–27

11-10 Court Gardener's House, Schloss Charlottenhof. 1829–36

11-11   Leo von Klenze. Walhalla. Near Regensburg. 1831–42

11-12   Leo von Klenze. Propylaea. Munich. 1846–50

niably authentic in detail, being based on recent, detailed French publications of Italian Renaissance architecture. Yet the Ludwigstrasse exhibits none of the plastic vitality of the originals, which appear to have been dehydrated onto paper but not fully rehydrated into buildings. The architects were unable, or unwilling, to translate linear engravings into convincing three-dimensional structures. The whole entity looks rather like a wide central-European street that has been superficially redecorated to give the Hollywood-like impression of "Main Street Italy." In its unbridgeable distance between the

11-13   Leo von Klenze with Friedrich von Gärtner.
Ludwigstrasse. Munich. 1840s

historical models and their historicist revival, the Ludwigstrasse was a perfect representation of nineteenth-century tendencies; yet in its coherence, precision, and controlled variety, it was perhaps the highest realization of European urbanism of its time.

Great Britain. Britain was the most distinguished of Germany's Neoclassical competitors, and it is not coincidental that the two exhibit so many architectural affinities in this period. Germany shared a deep archaeological spirit with England, a nostalgic attraction to the remains of antiquity and of Italy as opposed to the more idealizing, formalistic approach of France. Schinkel, we have seen, was keen on England, especially the Picturesque; the British reciprocated, many of their Grecians being strongly influenced by Schinkel and by his powerful stylized mode of handling Greek forms. But such affinities should not obscure the differences in International Neoclassicism between the two countries. Apart from Schinkel, German Neoclassicism was characterized by a tendency to stylistic uniformity. In England, to be sure, there was a Grecian "center" formed by Robert Smirke, William Inwood, William Wilkins, and others, whose conservative works tended to resemble one another (and too often our picture of the British Greek Revival is limited to a narrow choice of their buildings). But English architecture had always been at its best in eccentric deviations from normative aesthetic positions. Even in the generally repressive mood of the International Neoclassical period, British architecture allowed for a wide range of individualism.

The leader of the centrist Greeks was Robert Smirke, whose stylistic authority is exhibited at its best in his British Museum facade (fig. 11-14), of 1824–47 in London. In its rigid, disciplined march of not less than forty-four identical Ionic columns around a U-shaped portico broken only by the central pedimented porch, the facade was a rejoinder to Nash's contemporary slapdash Picturesque Regent's Park structures (such as Cumberland Terrace, 1826–28; fig. 10-24). It was also a response to Schinkel's Berlin museum facade, begun in exactly the same year, but a weak response, for it lacked Schinkel's vitality, movement, and poise. Smirke evidently could not decide between an eighteenth-century massing of discrete wings and center blocks and early-nineteenth-century rigid uniformity and continuity. This unresolved ambiguity limits the facade, which does not move beyond a suave dignity, characteristic of the centrist British Grecians.

The more individualistic British architects, particularly Charles Robert Cockerell and Alexander Thomson, produced eccentric, compelling works far removed from the centrists. Robert Cockerell was an important figure in many ways. He made significant archaeological discoveries in Greece on his Grand Tour; inherited from his father the surveyorship of St. Paul's Cathedral; acquired John Soane's position as Surveyor to the Bank of England (1833); and was an influential lecturer as professor at the Royal Academy from 1841 to 1856. Instinctively he was drawn less to Greek architecture than to individualistic Renaissance and Baroque personalities, to Giulio Romano, to the mannerist side of Palladio, to the intricacies of Wren, and to the inventive sophistication of Ledoux. But his work is more convoluted than that of the Renaissance and Baroque masters, for Cockerell tended to carry the complexities of buildings to extremes. His most characteristic work was a series of insurance offfices and Bank of England branches, mostly variations

11-14   Robert Smirke. British Museum. London. 1824–47

closed relief, the unified gabled massing of the temple distorted and fragmented, and Palladio's bold, clear strokes of chiaroscuro and giant scale suffocated by the integration with the Doric. Further historicist complications were eclectically added: the arch in the pediment, and, most unsettling for an insurance company, the cut-off basement ambiguously rising into or sinking from view (adopted from Giulio Romano's house in Mantua). Cockerell was thus a perfect example of the nineteenth-century architect and his inner aesthetic conflicts. The discords in his buildings had nothing to do with materials, methods, or programs, but involved the unbridgeable aesthetic distance between the architect and his sources. Even as he took it upon himself so fastidiously to quote them, he devastated their intrinsic formal qualities through stylistic transformations and especially through eclectic convolutions.

on the theme established in one of his first innovative designs, the Westminster Life and British Fire Office of 1831 in London (destroyed in 1908; fig. 11-15). The external shell of the building fused two models—the peripteral Doric temple and Palladio's Loggia del Capitanato in Vicenza. The former realized the main order, whereas the latter supplied the complex filling wall and the attic story that, as it were, raised and carried the pediment of the Greek order on intermediate stilts. Rather than reinforcing each other, the two historicist forms tended to cancel each other out—the lucid, freestanding Doric colonnade reduced to

11-16   Alexander Thomson. Queen's Park Church. Glasgow. 1867

11-17   Alexander Thomson. Caledonia Road Free Church. Glasgow. 1856

11-15   Charles Cockerell. Westminster Life and British Fire Office (destroyed). London. 1831

11-18 Charles Barry. Travelers' Club (at left, 1829–31) and Reform Club (center, 1837–41). London

The works of Alexander "Greek" Thomson were equally idiosyncratic. He was one of several Scottish architects for whom the Greek Revival was not merely a matter of urban embellishment, as in England, but the style in which the monumental character of their chief cities would be cast. William Playfair and others made Edinburgh into the "Athens of the North," and Thomson created much the same effect with his numerous buildings for Glasgow. The last of the Grecians, his career only began in 1847 when most architects had long since abandoned the style; and he acquired his nickname because he so staunchly upheld the antique tradition against the rising tide of the Victorian Gothic. Within the Classical realm, however, he was far from a purist. Greek meant not only the canonical Doric and Ionic forms, but especially their reductive interpretation by Schinkel, by whom Thomson was strongly influenced. Yet the antique was for the Scotsman not only a Schinkelesque Greece, for it ultimately extended to the Greece of Alexander the Great (his real namesake), stretching as far as the Nile and Ganges Rivers. Thus, his works range from the long, low Schinkelesque U-shaped Moray Place of 1859 to conceptions of "fearsome" originality, as it has been termed. The most notable among the latter is the Queen's Park Church (fig. 11-16) of 1867. Into its sweeping portico, an Egyptian in antis portal is asymmetrically set, behind which rises the massive pedimented church with a clerestory of squat lotus-form columns, the whole surmounted by a towering Indian stupa! Seen in historical context, the church carries a certain pathos, for it embodies a desperate effort on Thomson's part to rival in his own "ancient" terms the colorful eclecticism of the High Victorian Gothic and Second Empire styles currently in vogue. However, Thomson was at his best in another of his Glasgow churches—the Caledonia Road Free Church (fig. 11-17) of 1856 (a Protestant institution like the others). The asymmetrical design simultaneously recalls the Erechtheum, the Picturesque, and the later Schinkel. Its volume is concentrated in subtly textured masses so dense and solid that the whole seems carved from a huge block of ice, which just might survive the chilly Scottish summers.

A final key figure of British Neoclassicism was Charles Barry, the fashionable eclectic who, together with Pugin, built the Gothic Houses of Parliament in London. Shortly before the Parliament structures, he led England around another stylistic corner with his Renaissance Revival Travelers' Club (1829–31) and the Reform Club (1837–41; fig. 11-18). In those years a rising dissatisfaction with the Grecian mode was expressed by a turn to the more vivid Classicism of the Renaissance. Barry's Travelers' Club closely resembles Raphael's Palazzo Pandolfini, while the Reform Club recalls the Palazzo Farnese. Although in both works the scale of the originals is reduced along with much of their vitality and authority, enough of their presence is retained to achieve what was considered a very realistic Renaissance effect.

Russia, Scandinavia, Italy. On the continent, no true competitor either to Germany or to the British Isles can be found, although not for any lack of profusion of Neoclassical buildings. The sensibilities of northern lands tended to be the most receptive to the Grecian manner, and both Russia and Scandinavia took up Neoclassicism enthusiastically. Russia—a westward-looking, but still half-Asian, repressive autocracy—produced a vast amount of monumental masonry in the style. St. Petersburg is perhaps a more Neoclassical city than Glasgow or Edinburgh. Much of it was built by foreigners, English, French, and Italians, who willingly exaggerated the monumental potential of Neoclassicism; hand-in-hand went the characteristically Russian grandiosity of effect of such native builders as Adrian Sakharov. Although often overscaled, Russian Neoclassicism occasionally rivals

11-19 Thomas de Thomon. Exchange. St. Petersburg. 1804–16

11-20 M. G. B. Bindesbøll. Interior, Thorvaldsen Museum. Copenhagen. 1837–48

the best of western Europe, the finest example being perhaps Thomas de Thomon's Exchange (fig. 11-19) of 1804–16, in St. Petersburg, a building far superior to its Paris counterpart.

Scandinavia produced less in sheer quantity, but two of its leading architects, C. F. Hansen and M. G. B. Bindesbøll, both Danes, were exceptionally able, maintaining into the nineteenth century something of the fine, bold formal keenness of the French late eighteenth century, not slavishly but inventively. Their manner is perhaps best embodied in the courtyard of Bindesbøll's Thorvaldsen Museum (fig. 11-20) of 1837–48, in Copenhagen, whose hard-as-granite, razor-sharp Grecian detailing and taut proportions contrast effectively with the refined naturalism of its murals.

Italy, a native land of Neoclassical sources, produced little of high distinction in this period. If anything, it was too close to the sources of the style, too pervaded by antique remains, which were commonplace parts of everyday life. Neoclassicism, after all, was a romantic style predicated on an unbridgeable distance between a design and its ancient sources. In Italy, the culture of the Renaissance, even of pagan antiquity, was in many aspects still alive. Typically, Italian attempts at being Grecian achieved an uneasy compromise between the animation and color of the Renaissance and antiquity and the chilly aestheticism of authentic International Neoclassicism. This ambiguity is seen in such Neapolitan examples as the warm, bottom-heavy Teatro S. Carlo (1810–11), and the church and square of S. Francesco di Paola, which familiarly combines the Pantheon and Bernini's Piazza of St. Peter's. But exceptions do occur, such as the charming contrasts of massing and proportions in the twin-porched Caffè Pedrocchi in Padua, of 1826–31, by Giuseppe Jappelli and Antonio Gradenigo.

United States. Sharply contrasting to Italy was the rising country devoid of a Classical past and monumental tradition altogether—the United States. To be sure, the colonies had at various times adopted European styles from their mother countries, but for the most part little more was built than competent provincial copies and passable derivations. At the time of the Revolution, the Georgian style reigned—in America called Colonial—a conservative blend of Neo-Palladianism seasoned with a mild Neoclassicism. With the Revolution, however, a non-English alternative was essential to assert architectural independence along with everything else. Full-blooded Greco-Roman Neoclassicism (called in America the Federalist style, so closely did it become identified with the new state) was the clear choice for a number of reasons. It was at the time in ascendancy throughout Europe, especially in France, which was the source of radical American political ideology. It was visibly different from the Georgian manner, but not so different as to be unpalatable to the American sensibility, which in any event would have favored the vigorous directness and austerity of Neoclassicism (at least for its official buildings). Then, too, the former colony was painfully conscious of a cultural inferiority to Europe, and it was natural to seize upon the most prestigious of historical models. But the most positive attraction of Neoclassicism was its symbolic potential. This involved not only the democratic overtones of anything Grecian, but Roman Neoclassicism as well, which Americans—who chose to be governed by a Senate from the Capitol and to use such symbols as the Roman Eagle and the Tribunal Fasces—saw as an evocation of the Roman Republic.

Americans adopted Neoclassicism wholesale, and quickly became adept in its practice. By the middle of the nineteenth century, they succeeded in giving not only Washington but the growing nation a substantially Neoclassical architectural self-image embodied in federal office buildings and state capitols, banks and exchanges, prisons and hospitals, and hotels and universities. This did not mean, however, that the Federalist style ever became a force internationally. It retained a provincial cast, a certain self-conscious ungainliness, never attaining the self-assurance of, let us say, the British Museum facade (not to speak of a Schinkel or a Cockerell). It was only after 1865, when H. H. Richardson returned from Paris, that the United States became an active, rather than a passive, participant in world architectural history.

The two exceptions to this generalization in the final analysis are the exceptions that prove the rule, for neither the great American patriot Thomas Jefferson, nor the English immigrant Benjamin Henry Latrobe were the Olympian architects that they are often made out to be. In reality, Latrobe was hardly the equal of his models—Soane and Ledoux—and Jefferson remained, for all his inventiveness, an amateur whose buildings lack cohesiveness and finesse. Nevertheless, their careers, which were intertwined, are significant in other terms. Indirectly responsible as Secretary of State and later as President for much of Latrobe's contribution to the capital, Jefferson's own architectural production was a sensitive barometer of changing political and architectural conditions. His works documented and were instrumental in the shift from the Colonial to the Federal style. The former is found at Monticello (fig. 11-21), Jefferson's own estate in the hills outside Charlottesville, Virginia, built in 1771–82 (with some later changes). Full of personal touches and pervaded with Jefferson's eccentric detailing, the house is quintessentially Georgian, combining a plan adopted from Robert Morris's *Select Architecture* of 1755, with a facade from Palladio's *Quattro libri* (of which Jefferson reputedly owned the only copy in the colonies).

Jefferson's post-Revolutionary architectural turn occurred abruptly. When abroad in France in 1785 he was commissioned to design the Virginia State Capitol (fig. 11-22) at Richmond. Together with his architectural tutor, Clérisseau, who had earlier been the companion-mentor of Robert Adam, he conceived the bold, Neoclassical idea to model it after the Roman temple that had so strongly impressed him on his travels—the Maison Carrée in Nîmes. Despite Clérisseau's assistance, Jefferson treated his model in a contrary manner to what a French architect might have done. Even though he shifted from Corinthian to Ionic, and reduced the flanking half-columns to pilasters, Jefferson's State Capitol is really as insubstantial in appearance as his own, earlier Neo-Palladian house. In his hands, even a Roman temple is given a shaky, cardboard quality reminiscent of an earlier enthusiast architect who also had relied heavily on publications of foreign styles—Lord Burlington.

No building type exposes an architect's inadequacies more mercilessly than the Greco-Roman temple. As eighteenth-century English garden planners realized, gentlemen architects are wiser to work with projects less demanding of solid professionalism. Thus Jefferson's last major work—the University of Virginia campus at Charlottesville (fig. 11-23)—was more suited to his talents. Although it still exhibits the quirky infirmities of his earlier work, these do not matter much for here the effect of the whole and its picturesque variety and charm are important. The basic scheme he evolved between 1804 and 1817 for his "academical village" is simple: two rows of five Palladian pavilions connected by colonnades, facing each other across a lawn that sweeps up to the Rotunda (serving as library), added at Latrobe's suggestion in 1823–37. The scheme derives, ironically, from one of the monuments of French absolutism, Louis XIV's Château de Marly, which Jefferson had admiringly visited. In adapting it to an American university, Jefferson scaled down the French program, transposed it into his personal Neo-Palladian style, and deformalized its natural setting. He made his ten pavilions—each containing professorial living quarters and a lecture room—slightly different, each contributing to an eclectic collection of learned allusions: one refers to the Ionic order of the Temple of Fortuna Virilis, another to the Doric of the Baths of Diocletian, a third contains a central exedra from Ledoux's Hôtel de Guimard, and so

on. Such variations, which were consonant with the spirit of the university's Classical curriculum, constituted more than a learned hodgepodge, for they asserted the individuality of the ten professors, their subjects, and even their students. By fusing the absolutist French scheme of Marly with the tradition of the Picturesque English garden and its scattering of historicizing pavilions, Jefferson found a convincing architectural metaphor of the governing ideal of the young republic, namely, the harmonious coexistence of the individual and the state, as well as the parallel federal system of semiautonomous states within a national union proudly proclaimed in the Neoclassical American motto, *E Pluribus Unum*.

If Jefferson transcended his provincial location by turning his attention to publications, travel, and often distant contacts, Latrobe did the opposite. By leaving the European soil, from which he had drawn his architectural formation and ideals, and by migrating to a distant, backward land, he deprived himself of that daily contact with his peers and their stimulating new ideas and critical standards, becoming in the process something of a provincial himself. Indeed, what is to be admired most about him is the force of character that enabled him to accomplish as much as he did in such an architecturally bleak and unformed environment. His buildings began to rise in Richmond, Philadelphia, Baltimore, and Washington shortly after his arrival in the United States from England (where he had studied with Robert Cockerell's father and had much admired Soane and Ledoux). They were of considerable variety in type and style, and all novel on the American scene. In 1798, he built the first Greek Revival structure in the United States—the austere Bank of Pennsylvania in Philadelphia; a year later it was Sedgeley, the first Gothic Revival house; and a year after that the Philadelphia Waterworks pumping station, based on Ledoux's Barrière de la Villette. The building widely considered his most important work is his Baltimore Cathedral (designed in 1804–8; fig. 11-24). While its exterior, even without the onion tops of the towers added later, is rather ungainly, the interior does form an impressive sequential buildup of vaulted spaces: barrel-vaulted entrance, saucer-domed forechurch, Pantheonic central rotunda (65 feet in diameter), and finally the column-lined apse (now behind a forechoir inserted later in the century). But whether it forms a Neoclassical masterpiece is open to question, for the interior exhibits a certain jumpiness, a feeling of incomplete integration of eclectic effects. Looking at the rotunda, we find that in

11-21 Thomas Jefferson. Monticello. Charlottesville. 1771–82

11-22 Thomas Jefferson. Virginia State Capitol (wings post-Jefferson addition). Richmond. 1785

11-23 Thomas Jefferson. University of Virginia, Charlottesville. 1804–17

11-24 Benjamin H. Latrobe. Interior, Baltimore Cathedral. Designed 1804–8

combining the depressed segmental arches and stripped detailing of the Soane-like lower zone with Adam-like coffered vaulting, Latrobe achieved a novel juxtaposition, to be sure, but one that has neither Adam's buoyant grace nor Soane's somber mood. The two tend to cancel each other out in a chilly, forbidding impression that is typical indeed of the early nineteenth century in its vein of eclectic correctness.

How closely Latrobe approached the level of his European models is not important, for what America wanted from him was a stolid, conservative, and easy brand of Neoclassicism, and this he gave his adopted land, especially through his pupils Robert Mills and William Strickland. Their generally severe and massive, inflated Palladian blocks dominated monumental construction in the United States until the 1840s and even after through Strickland's pupils Thomas U. Walter and Alexander Jackson Davis. The many works of these architects, their contemporaries and followers, contributed little to the historical development of architecture. But beginning with the Washington White House and Capitol, they established Neoclassicism as the official American image, resulting in a seemingly unshakable Neoclassical dominance of monumental architectural practice. It was a dominance only sporadically interrupted, a tradition to which Americans would instinctively return from occasional flights into more imaginative architectural realms. The return occurred in different forms, however, and the point of departure for the later phases of Neoclassicism in America would be the École des Beaux-Arts in Paris.

THE ÉCOLE DES BEAUX-ARTS

The twists of architectural history are often ironic. Reviled throughout the heyday of Modernism and moribund for decades, the architectural section of the École des Beaux-Arts in Paris had to be terminated by the student revolution of 1968 before it was rediscovered. The turning point in its revindication occurred with startling expediency in 1975 with a spectacular

exhibition of École drawings at the Museum of Modern Art in New York City. What was revealed in the exhibition, its catalogue, and subsequent publications was a unique nineteenth-century phenomenon.

The École des Beaux-Arts was many things, none of them simple. It was a group of buildings on the Seine's Left Bank; it was a powerful state institution; it championed certain aesthetic traditions and ideals; it pursued a method of instruction, a means of selecting and promoting talent; it promulgated an overlapping series of styles; above all, it was the most powerful cultural entity that ever existed for the training of highly skilled architects. Although the École des Beaux-Arts was established only in 1819, it was not an entirely new institution. State-sponsored study of architecture in France goes back to 1671, when the Académie Royale d'Architecture was created by Louis XIV's minister, Colbert, as one of a group of scientific and cultural institutions of learning. Abolished during the Revolution, Colbert's academy underwent several transformations until it emerged in 1819 as the École des Beaux-Arts (for painting, sculpture, and architecture), a section of the new Académie des Beaux-Arts, which was itself a division of the newly created Institut de France, the ultimate arbiter of cultural authority.

The goals of the École were clear: to establish universal architectural ideals through study of the five orders, their highest actual embodiment in Roman and Renaissance buildings and writings (hence the vital importance of the Prix de Rome and study in Italy), and their noble adoption by seventeenth-century French Classicism. Antiquity, the Renaissance, and the French seventeenth century were to remain the formal ideal of the École, but in practice the planning and design of École buildings were founded on two principles: one, abstract and conceptual—the building's ordered scheme; the other, functional and experiential—the movement of the human participant through the building, thus architecture experienced aesthetically.

École planning took its point of departure from a well-known structure—Jacques-Germain Soufflot's church of Ste.-Geneviève (fig. 10-27). With the exception of the dominant central volume, the church's entire plan is built up of rectangles and squares, consistently disposed in several ways. A crossing of two giant rectangles is exploited for a nearly complete biaxial symmetry, disturbed only at the entrance. Within the scheme, rectangle is set within rectangle, square within square within square, most clearly in the arms of the church. Inner squares (or rectangles) are in places "omitted" to expand the spatial volume, for example, the center of the building. Outer squares overlap, not only laterally, but diagonally, and these overlapping spaces tend to form pairs of secondary axes—narrow, continuous corridors creating deep vistas and providing for channels of circulation separate from the main features, unifying the building functionally as well as schematically. Last, but not least, a modular grid underlies the spacing of nearly every element.

These planning characteristics were so consistently present in the École's competition schemes and real buildings (always inflected to contingencies) that they were clearly a matter of self-conscious cultivation, indeed, so much so, that by the early nineteenth century a specialized vocabulary existed for the Beaux-Arts planning system. The *parti* (from *prendre parti*, to take a stand) was the basic scheme of the building, its fundamental solution of the functional program. *Composition* concerned the detailing of the *parti*, which involved both the *distribution* and the *disposition* of the elements, their articulation and linking together into a cohesive whole. The *point* was its principal volume; its *circulations* the network of access and movement. Even the grid (as realized in pavement squares) had a name—the *mosaïque*. But perhaps the most suggestive term was the *marche* of the building, a word that concerns the second basic aspect of Beaux-Arts planning referred to above, that is, architecture as used and experienced aesthetically. The *marche*—a term used figuratively for the sequence of images in a poem, the action of a play, the moves in chess, or the fictive layers of space in a painting—was the imaginary experience of walking through a plan in the mind's eye and ultimately the experience of the building itself. It was the building perceived as a sequence of architectural images, a highly ordered series of tableaux.

The special architectural system of the École des Beaux-Arts was difficult to acquire. Those who sought to imitate it from afar, through study, publications, and even actual buildings, were never entirely successful. Only through study at the École itself could its complex, ambiguous, paradoxical architecture be mastered, and only then because of a remarkable pedagogical system that imprinted its aesthetic and methods on the aspiring student. The École was not like most programs of study, which involve chiefly a set curriculum of classroom courses, test-passing, and, in the arts, satisfaction of certain set levels of proficiency. Such passive aspects were part of the École system, but they were not its core. The École had a more powerful engine. Although merely completing requirements of the first level—a two- to four-year study of everything from mathematics and perspective to all manners of construction (including wood, stone, and iron)—was considered qualifications for ordinary architectural practice, for the more talented students success at the École only came in the form of the Prix de Rome. Unlike most institutions, where the fixed numbers allowed to enter are also allowed to graduate, the structure of study at the École—normally taking as long as 12 to 15 years to complete—was pyramidal. At the bottom, it was in theory completely open and democratic; anyone, French or foreign, between fifteen and thirty years of age, could take and pass the entrance exam. But the top of the pyramid narrowed to an elitist point, for only one person per year could win the all-important Prix de Rome through a grueling series of competitions, thereby securing the completion of education in Italy, and thereafter an assured career building the monumental public works to which all École architects aspired. The pyramid was thus not merely a passive ladder of progress, but a funnel-like dynamo which generated the most driving incentives—graspable ambition, and fortune and fame for a few.

The Prix de Rome was essential to the Beaux-Arts system for a more intrinsically architectural reason. The student acquired architectural theory in the École classrooms, and design technique in the competitions and *ateliers* of master-architects. His training was highly conceptual even with the emphasis on draftsmanship. This was the exaggerated outcome of the process begun in the Renaissance of elevating the artist to high intellectual status, and this bias was not only deeply ingrained in the architect, but bound up with the strong conceptual side of the Beaux-Arts aesthetic. For the Prix de Rome winner, the five-year stint in Italy was thus a crucial complement, even an antidote, to those years of immersion in various forms of theory

and conceptualism. At the French Academy in Rome, the task of the first three years was to produce analytic studies of ancient buildings, of the fourth year, a complete reconstruction of one of them. The student was still drawing rather than building, but he had at least to confront the concrete substance of architecture itself. Here was achieved that mastery of sculptural form that was so important in the Beaux-Arts system. It was typical of the system, and, indeed, of the period as a whole, that only in the final Roman year was the student required for the first time to create an architectural concept entirely of his own. But it was almost inevitable, given the years of indoctrination, that this final effort resulted in designs hardly "free" at all, but rendered precisely along those Beaux-Arts Neoclassical lines that gratified the Academy in Paris, to which the student's work was sent for criticism.

The complex pedagogical system of the École is a subject of study in itself; indeed, in many ways it is more interesting than the majority of the actual buildings it produced. But its best works were exceptional, as were the novel stylistic concepts they embodied. Nineteenth-century architecture in France is highly complex in its evolution, but on its principal, Classical side (as opposed to Neo-Gothic) it basically falls into five phases: the Napoleonic and post-Napoleonic episodes of the first third of the century; the movements led by Henri Labrouste, then by Charles Garnier in the middle third; and, finally, the late work of the École which runs into the twentieth century, alongside the modern movement. The first two of these phases were, in effect, France's contribution to the international chapter of Neoclassicism, a contribution that, as noted earlier, was a weak effort in comparison to Germany and England and to what French architecture had been in the eighteenth century. The point of departure for France was its own late-eighteenth-century style, which was now transformed into a typically nineteenth-century phenomenon. Napoleon's urbanistic ambitions, which later inspired his great-nephew Napoleon III, were largely unrealized, but he was responsible for several of the most imposing monuments of Paris—imposing, that is, more for their size, lavishness, and prominent siting than their intrinsic quality. Napoleon was affected by the grandiose visions of Boullée, but his taste was far less austere, tending toward pomp and ostentation recalling Imperial Rome and, to a lesser degree, Louis XIV. His principal Parisian centerpieces were the huge Trajanic Colonne Vendôme; the gigantic, templelike, Corinthian Church of the Madeleine (fig. 11-25) with its ornate, domed interior; and, of course, the prodigious Arc de Triomphe de l'Étoile (colorplate 73; fig. 11-1), which dilutes the authoritative austerity of Boullée with bombastic displays of colossal relief sculpture and zones of rich architectural decoration.

Immediately following Napoleon's inflated pomposity, French architecture experienced near-total collapse. In the 1810s and twenties, virtually nothing of consequence was built in France, this being an extreme expression of the reactionary atmosphere of the period. But everywhere in Europe about 1830 there was a recovery of aesthetic nerve, a more daring and expansive mood. France also participated in this revival of architectural spirits. Although influenced perhaps by the English and German architects, whose work in the twenties was in advance of Paris, and extra-architectural currents such as Positivism, the renewal of vitality at the École largely came

11-25   Alexandre-Pierre Vignon. Church of the Madeleine. Paris. 1807–45

11-26   J. I. Hittorff. Interior, St.-Vincent-de-Paul. Paris. 1830–46

from within, from the archaeological work that climaxed the École's program of study. For students in Rome, the depth and variety of ancient architecture offered new sources for the imagination. French architecture found its way out of the doldrums through students thirsting for a more individually expressive, more immediate and "relevant," architectural direction, and finding it in their archaeological activity.

A transitional figure in this process was J. I. Hittorff, a German immigrant who, after studying at the École, in 1822 went to Italy (on his own, the Prix de Rome being closed to foreigners) where he pursued a tantalizing notion that was in the air—that Greek temples had been originally painted in bright colors. In Sicily, Hittorff found evidence for the theory, which he developed into the thesis that Greek temples were given an overall coating of yellow paint and their details highlighted in vivid shades of red, blue, green, and gold! This shocking theory of polychromy—based on real but fragile evidence—produced a controversy that went on for decades, during which time Hittorff himself was building a great deal of often undistinguished architecture. His Church of St.-Vincent-de-Paul in Paris (1830–46; fig. 11-26) is a large, tautly planned, formally chilly Early Christian revival structure with many Beaux-Arts traits, as well as extensive polychromatic decoration.

Hittorff was followed to Italy by a group of similarly minded French students in the late twenties, chief among them Henri Labrouste, who won the Grand Prix in 1824. In 1829–30, he sent from Rome to the Paris Academy a shocking series of "reconstruction" studies of the temples of Paestum. A bitter and intense controversy ensued, for Labrouste had included vivid polychromy; more than that, his work conjured a vision of Greek architecture not as the unvarying embodiment of an absolute architectural ideal, but as limited solutions for concrete programs. He saw Greek architecture as a kind of elevated vernacular that the ancients developed for specific needs. It was valid for the Greeks, but not necessarily for nineteenth-century France, and it offered not a definitive ideal, but a relativistic model: just as the Greeks developed an architecture for their needs with their means, so must also the nineteenth cen-

tury. And that is exactly what Labrouste was to attempt in his renowned Bibliothèque Ste.-Geneviève, of the 1840s.

Labrouste was severely punished for his heresy: The Academy saw to it that he built nothing for a decade and that none of his students won the Grand Prix. When he did finally build the Bibliothèque, it was a building that in many ways was as shocking as his archaeology. Yet the system of the École was indelibly imprinted on Labrouste's life and imagination, and his library is a great achievement not only for its novelty, but also for its creative fusion of École traditions with Labrouste's radical innovations.

The Paris Opera and Haussmann's Replanning of Paris. The most grandiose realization of the École's ideals was Charles Garnier's Opera House built in Paris in 1861–75, a heady period of material prosperity when a new taste set in for lavish architectural eclecticism, heavily depending on a conflation of French and Italianate Renaissance-Baroque sources. It was an affirmation of the grand manner of the École, but in a new mode of sensuous exuberance and unrestrained plasticity. Garnier's Opera at first seems un-Labroustian, but paradoxically the extravagant Neo-Baroque of the Opera was a formulation that depended on the advances of Labrouste's generation. For Labrouste had insisted that an archaeological site be given a full explanation of its particulars; that a library take the specific form of a library in the widest sense; and that the functional ends of a project justify the stylistic means. For Garnier, given the spirit of his times, this meant building an opera house as theatrical in essence as Labrouste's library was bookish, using whatever stylistic means necessary. Garnier, in fact, defended his sensational building against critics on just such functionalist grounds—that its style suited an opera house that was intended as total theater, with the audience participating as actors in the complex sociocultural event it housed. He went even further, insisting that the polychromatic accents were as fitting to such a building as rouge and lipstick were to a lady's gala array. But finally he left behind the rationalism of Labrouste and of the Beaux-Arts doctrine, perceiving that for his decorative style "there is no guide other than the inspiration and will of the one designing the building." He even dared to write the following self-intoxicated statement: "The style I employ is my own . . . it is the style of my times that I produce and affirm; it is my personality that I lay bare . . . feelings alone, and nothing else, guide my eyes, my hand, and my thoughts."

Garnier's Opera House needs also to be seen in the context of the remarkable contemporary urbanistic developments in Paris. The exploding population of the city entailed correspondingly greater needs of the most basic things such as housing, water supply, markets, circulation, transportation, and sewers. Some classes were able to express their demands more effectively, especially the new dominant economic and political power—the middle and upper-middle classes. For them, not only hospitals, schools, and parks, but libraries and other cultural facilities, as well as the right sort of environment in which to reside, shop, and socialize, were becoming obligatory.

Napoleon III (1808–1873) was not a charismatic leader like his great-uncle, but he was similarly ambitious and single-minded. He wanted to rebuild Paris into a modern city to answer just those needs outlined above. Even as autocrat, he could not have done this alone. But he had the genius, or good fortune, to choose as a collaborator in conceiving and executing his dream Baron Georges-Eugène Haussmann, a lawyer-administrator as self-confident as his superior. His contribution to the project was so enormous that the nineteenth-century city is often called Haussmann's Paris.

Just as the problems Paris faced are not difficult to understand, so their solutions are conceptually not of great subtlety. Water was needed: a system of aqueducts, rivaling those of ancient Rome, was erected. Paris was plagued by inadequate drainage: a vast network of sewers was built leading the water to exit into the Seine below the city. At night the streets were dark and dangerous: gas lighting was installed. There was no adequate central market: the iron construction of Les Halles Centrales was built. There were few parks for recreation: a system of miniparks was sprinkled throughout the city, and no fewer than five large parks were planted around the periphery. New hospitals, asylums, and schools were created wholesale, along with new prisons and administrative centers. The Louvre was significantly expanded; the École des Beaux-Arts enlarged; the Bibliothèque Nationale fully realized; and a monumental new Opera brought into being.

Perhaps the most challenging single problem mastered by Haussmann was the heart of all city planning, the system of streets (figs. 11-27, 11-28). In the Paris of 1850, the glitter of brilliant individual architectural works sharply contrasted with the city's disordered tangle of streets and twisting medieval alleys. Haussmann's solution was not restricted to any of the formalist plans that had sufficed in earlier periods, such as the Roman grid, the Renaissance star, or the Baroque avenue. In a manner typical of the nineteenth century, it is pragmatic and formalist,

11-27   Baron Georges-Eugène Haussmann. Project for modernizing the street plan of Paris. 1853. (Plan after Armand)

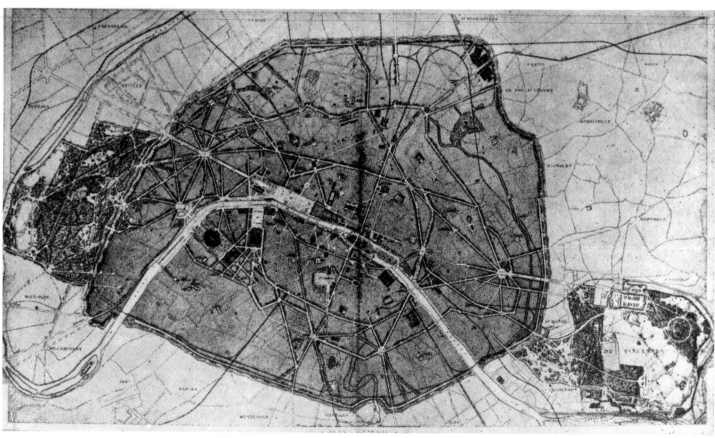

utilitarian and monumentalizing, and finally extremely eclectic. Basically three integrated modes of street planning were used. First, there was a crossing of main, axial streets. Second, two concentric rings left by the old circuits of city walls were fully exploited, and between the rings an important supplementary "bypass," the Boulevard Haussmann and the Boulevard Voltaire, was run. These principal arteries were supplemented by a third kind of avenue—pragmatic extensions between important points, such as the Rue Turbigo, which ran between the northern railroad stations and the central markets.

This extraordinary network, which simultaneously freed the circulation of the city and endowed it with a new formal order, fulfilled other needs as well. The eastern part of Paris was the working-class quarter, which had been the hotbed of revolution. The wide new avenues in that zone served simultaneously to discourage mobs fighting from behind barricades and to facilitate troop movements from military barracks set up at strategic points throughout the area. In the western part of Paris, the wide Haussmannian streets performed an altogether different function, for this was the quarter of the middle and upper-middle classes. Commodious new apartment buildings erected along these boulevards served their residential needs, while the streets themselves functioned as principal places to promenade, shop, and socialize.

The glittering centerpiece of the new Paris was the Opera House (colorplate 72; figs. 11-28–11-32). It is an overpowering building, as overwhelming a presence in the Paris streets as its ancient counterpart, the Colosseum, was in Rome. Its monumentality is not only a matter of scale, but iconography, style, and—finally—quality. Although the building for a long time was regarded as pompous, ostentatious, and vulgar, recent revaluation of the nineteenth century has reversed the Opera's critical fortunes. The Opera was intended to be far more than a theater in the ordinary sense. For Charles Garnier it was the setting for a ritual in which the spectators were also actors, participants in a rite of social encounter, seeing and being seen. The architect wrote of the "magic effect" of the "animated and smiling faces" of the "varied and elegant crowd," the "air of festivity and pleasure" in the use of the building. What Garnier is telling us is that the Opera had absorbed much of the role formerly assumed by the Church and the court in their ritualistic and social functions. The bourgeoisie, not the clergy or aristocracy, was now the dominant class; the Opera was the chief ceremonial gathering place for this new "society" which sought to absorb the symbols and customs of the classes it had displaced.

The sociology of Garnier's building explains many of the extraordinary aspects that endow it with the grandeur and iconography formerly given to the cathedral and the royal residence. Its site was paramount. The Opera was so centrally located, so perfectly given access from virtually all important parts of Paris, that the replanning of the street system might almost have been done mainly with the Opera in mind (figs. 11-27, 11-28). Notre-Dame Cathedral had been the former center of the city, but now that position was undeniably taken by the Opera.

Anyone arriving at the foot of the Opera not knowing what it is might imagine that it is something more important than a musical theater. Certainly the building does not look like the temple-fronted block of most theaters, and at first an observer might wonder if it was not an important ecclesiastical structure. Not only are its dimensions those of the largest of churches—almost 600 feet long, 300 feet wide, in places 200 feet high—but its form is suggestive of a composite cathedral image: a sprawling, multiform massing, with a tall chevetlike form behind a dome, transept facades, and, most critically, a "west" facade with end pavilions like twin towers. Moreover, the building is covered with sculptures reminiscent of medieval cathedrals, but here the saints and narratives are replaced by busts of composers—the saints of music—and by personifications and allegories of choreography, lyric poetry, and so forth.

The new Opera was not only the "new cathedral" of bourgeois Paris, but also its new palatial court, for the cathedral image is overlaid by a second image, that of Perrault's east facade of the Louvre with its sweeping, end-pavilioned, double colonnade (figs. 9-52, 11-29). Yet this eclectic iconography is even more complicated, for within the second image resides a third, that of Michelangelo's Capitoline Palace facades in Rome—a two-storied elevation, whose mural upper zone rests uneasily on a trabeation that is supported by columns pushed out to the ends of the bays, both stories contained in a giant order (colorplate 52). Even more than the Imperial eagles at his private entrance to the Opera, this image proclaimed Napoleon III's intention that his Paris be the "New Rome," its Opera the new capitol. It was an ironic twist of fate that when the building was actually opened in 1875, the Third French Republic was on the verge of being established, and the Opera became, in effect, a de facto celebration of that event. But Napoleonic or not, the new Paris was the New Rome of Europe, and the Opera was symbolically its capitol, palace, and cathedral rolled into one.

Such external posturing does not fully explain why the building is so large. In size, the auditorium is unpretentious, its seating capacity restricted for visual and acoustic qualities to 2,158 (compared with 3,600 in the smaller La Scala Theater in Milan). But the stage is colossal, especially the invisible wings and stage structure, and behind it are not merely the usual dressing rooms but a large extension containing rehearsal and practice facilities and administrative quarters, exhibiting the typical nineteenth-century mixture of the utilitarian and the grandiose. One might say that the Opera is so large because it contains not one but three diverse "theaters": the usual stage theater in the middle; the "invisible" theater academy behind it; and toward the front and sides and below the auditorium, the third "theater" for the audience.

From all parts of Paris operagoers converged on the building through Haussmann's boulevards, some by foot, others by carriage. The carriage-borne came in through the entrance pavilion (porte cochère) at the right of the building, proceeded straight ahead to a large circular vestibule beneath the auditorium, and turned left toward twin flights of stairs leading to the foot of the main staircase (fig. 11-33). Here they met the rest of the spectators coming from the opposite direction, the pedestrians who had entered through the main facade. Together all ascended the Grand Stair, the more privileged to the first landing and entrance to the orchestra and first boxes, the rest up the branching flights to the main level and upper tiers. The building provided lounges and a Grand Foyer, and such amenities as a library, a doctor's surgery, a flower shop, a smoking-room for men, and an ice-cream parlor for women.

11-28   Charles Garnier. Air view, The Opera. Paris. 1861–75

11-29   Facade, The Opera

11-30   Plan, The Opera

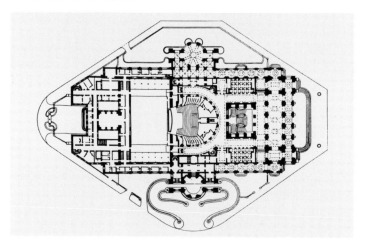

All of the well-oiled Beaux-Arts circulatory machinery, which articulated socioeconomic distinctions among the audience yet at one dramatic moment brought all society together, was explained at length by Garnier. He wrote about his pragmatic methods in designing the building, observing, for example, that at the opera people tend to walk in pairs, determining certain circulatory dimensions; and since it was mostly women who arrived by coach, the circular vestibule was given a "feminine" style and copious mirrors. He confessed his pride in such advanced utilitarian features as the ventilation system and the elevator. But it was the sumptuous theatrical effect, and not the means, that mattered.

11-31 Lateral view, The Opera

11-32 Section, The Opera. (After Garnier)

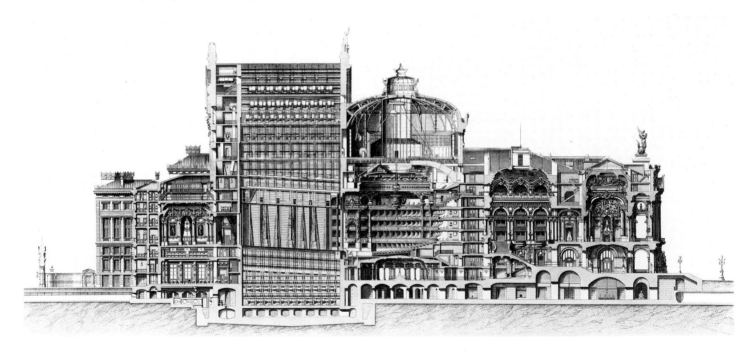

The kinesthetic and visual sensations of moving through the low-ceilinged spaces of the approach paths, the explosion of space in the Grand Stair Hall, the social encounter of *tout Paris* at the stair, the ascent before the "audience" of onlookers, many of them gazing down from the four tiers of balconies ringing the staircase, all of this constituted a vibrant social drama. But what raised it to the level of high art was Garnier's eclectic architectural language, especially in the Grand Stair Hall.

Garnier openly admitted the debt of this interior to Victor Louis's eighteenth-century Neoclassical theater in Bordeaux (fig. 11-34), notable for the lucid rationalism of its cubiform spatial organization, with a stairwell three stories high and a T-shaped stair occupying four of nine theoretical bays of the modular plan. But Garnier subjected the Bordeaux scheme to a series of formal modifications antithetical to his model's chaste rationalism. The rustication of the base of the eighteenth-century interior became in Garnier's hands a heavily molded pier cluster. The elegant colonnade of single Ionic shafts expanded into a powerful arcade over double (and sometimes quadruple) columns backed by heavy piers. The lucid extension of space beyond the Bordeaux stair hall dissolved into indeterminacy in Paris. And the monochromatic French Classical limestone detailing yielded to polychromatic Italianate plasticity. The most crucial transformations were realized in the stair itself. Here Louis's crystalline structure became an elaborated configuration of sensuous curves, a freestanding entity that leaps through space, with the floor dropping away beneath it to a shadowy, cavernous zone. This hollowed, bridged aspect

11-33   Staircase, The Opera

11-34   Victor Louis. Theater. Bordeaux. 1773–80

of the Paris stair is derived from a favored Baroque type, the Imperial stair (as in Würzburg; colorplate 62), in which, however, the bridged upper flights doubled back rather than merely branching left and right. By combining the T-plan of Bordeaux with the Imperial bridge, Garnier retained the "theatrical," stagelike effect of the former while capturing the dynamic spatial excitement of the latter. A third source further heightened Garnier's architectural drama. The combination of twin flights dropping downward to tenebrous depths with flights rising to an upper zone revived the ecclesiastical image of stairs descending to a crypt beneath a raised choir (e.g., as in San Miniato in Florence, a city in which Garnier spent almost three years of his Grand Prix because of a civil war raging in Rome). Fittingly, the "crypt" in the Opera took the secularized form of a "grotto of the dance" directly beneath the central flight.

Yet the allusive layers of the staircase are still richer. In addition to everything else, Garnier's interior is a blow-up of Michelangelo's famous *ricetto* of the Laurentian Library (fig. 8-57)—of its steep, top-lit space, its giant, doubled columns, but most of all its revolutionary stair that aggressively fills most of the floor space; even its lavalike flow of steps is seen in Paris. Garnier's inversion, distortion, and magnification of this and other forms impart to his interior an eerie, dreamlike quality inspired by the eighteenth-century *Carceri* etchings of Piranesi, whose aura haunts the Grand Stair Hall, with its giant intimidating columns, its mysterious candelabra figures threatening to spring to life, its dense, nonstop decoration filled with relief and dripping with gilt, the row of giant sunburst heads in the vault, and the queasy ambiguity of levels.

The Second Empire Style and the Late École. Other architects of the time were less flamboyant than Garnier, but several abided by similar stylistic rules. The most notable of these in France were L.-T.-J. Visconti and Hector-Martin Lefuel, who began to build the new extension wings to the Louvre in 1852 (fig. 11-35). These new pavilions prominently exhibit the stigmata of what came to be known as the Second Empire style—the mansard roof (often with dormers or dormerlike excrescences) and an extremely vigorous articulation of the wall. At the New Louvre, as at the Opera, this plasticity is more than simply "Baroque"; instead, it combines a French sixteenth-century emphasis on relief sculpture, Italian sixteenth-century modes of rustication, seventeenth-century French-Italianate grand manner displays of columns, and even accents of austere eighteenth-century detail.

The style of the New Louvre and the Opera was in tune with the expansionist mood of the times. As a result of its few prestigious examples, the Second Empire style was perceived internationally as the most recent creation of the most culturally esteemed capital in Europe. Not surprisingly, it was taken up enthusiastically in numerous countries. England, for one, was highly receptive; Leeds's Town Hall, with its huge mansarded tower, is the most impressive British example. America (still influenced by England) followed suit with the Old State, War, and Navy Building in Washington and the exaggerated French manner of Philadelphia's City Hall (fig. 11-36). In Germany, a lust for architecture was part of the madness of Ludwig II of Bavaria, who built a number of historicist extravaganzas, among them the Neo-Baroque Schloss Linderhof. But one building that genuinely rivaled those in Paris was the Palais

11-35　L. T. J. Visconti and Hector-Martin Lefuel. New Louvre. Paris. 1852–57

11-36　John McArthur, Jr. City Hall. Philadelphia. Begun 1874.
(1897 engraving after an 1881 rendering)

de Justice (fig. 11-37) in Brussels by Joseph Poelaert, who was trained at the École. The building was erected over a labyrinthine Beaux-Arts plan. Its facade embodies dislocations of proportions and unrestrained exaggerations of scale, which center on an overwhelming aedicular entrance that evokes the grave powers of retribution of the halls of justice.

The Second Empire style was the last forward-looking creation of the École. After reaching a peak of energy from 1840 to 1870, a hundred-year decline set in from which it never fully recovered. To understand why the École was unable to maintain its leadership in the mainstream of architectural progress after the 1860s is not a simple task, but the main grounds are clear enough. In its successful period, the École had been capable of self-renewal

and of accommodating reform. But even as the École was struggling in the 1860s with the Second Empire manner, it was challenged by a radicalism from outside the system in the person of Eugène-Emmanuel Viollet-le-Duc, a formidable architect who had refused to study at the École in his youth and had developed a forward-looking structural aesthetic alien to the Beaux-Arts system and everything it stood for. In 1864, he attempted a reform of the methods and aesthetics of the École, but failed miserably. The École cut itself off from the new direction he represented and consequently from what was to be the mainstream of architectural Modernism, whose forces were just beginning to gather. Without the nourishment of new ideas, the École declined after 1870 into archaism, decadence, and the empty formalism for which it became so well known toward the end.

The extraordinary thing is that the École did endure for another century, and that, ironically, its greatest superficial success came in the period from about 1870 to World War I. In these decades, it became something of an architectural basic-training school to the world. Logically, the country that availed itself most fruitfully of this unique opportunity was the United States, which earlier had grafted itself onto International Neoclassicism and now stood in need of the more advanced styles that the École offered. Richard Morris Hunt, the first American at the École, set a standard of success for his countrymen: from 1846 to 1852 he did so well in the École and in the *atelier* of Lefuel that when the latter took over the construction of the New Louvre from Visconti, Hunt soon followed him and was actually given responsibility for the Pavillon de la Bibliothèque (1854–55). Although lacking a driving architectural vision, Hunt was an important figure in raising the professional standards and standing of American architecture. Thanks to his training, he was a virtuoso practitioner of eclecticism, working convincingly in every current style including Gothic, the "Neo Grec," the Shingle Style, the François I mode, Grand Manner French Classicism, and North Italian Renaissance, the last being the mode of one of his most

11-37   Joseph Poelaert. Palais de Justice. Brussels. 1866–83

spectacular projects, the Breakers at Newport, a house built for Cornelius Vanderbilt (fig. 11-38). After Hunt, a steady stream of Americans found their way to Paris, returning with a mastery of École methods of planning, siting, composition, and detailing that was put to good use in the large-scale structures they were given charge of. The highly formalist, classicizing École training of this period gave American architects a basis for creating a kind of Grand Manner, Classical "packaging"—an independently conceived formal envelope that could give the exterior of a large, complicated building its scale, rhythm, and coherence. Hardly a better example of this exists than New York's Grand Central Station, whose simple monumental dignity of external appearance belies the complexity within (fig. 11-70).

No American architect—or architect of any origin in this period—was more proficient at designing in the Renaissance Re-Revival, blurring into French Grand Manner Roman Revival that was the prevailing American style after 1880, than the architectural firm led by McKim, Mead and White. Charles Follen McKim had studied architecture at the École before setting up a partnership, first with William Rutherford Mead and soon after with the flamboyant Stanford White. Their hundreds of buildings are exemplars of competent and polished Beaux-Arts Classicism. The range in quality, however, was considerable, and the best example is probably not the famous Boston Public Library of 1887, which is a ponderous reworking of Labrouste, but the structure that is considered the manifesto of the Renaissance Re-Revival—the Villard Houses (fig. 11-39) in New York of 1882. The U-shaped massing of the building is untroubled, yet powerful; the detailing of its dark brownstone is superb, as is the scale and spacing of the windows in their concentration toward the center, and the way the wings of the building turn the corner and take up part of the central block. The joint with the central "corps de logis" section is marked by quoins running down the middle of the wall, with all details, including the cornicework, following the slight setback of the center. The finesse of the design is such that one tends to overlook the cool, almost mechanical nine-

11-38   Richard Morris Hunt. Interior court, The Breakers. Newport, Rhode Island. 1892–95

11-39   McKim, Mead and White. Villard Houses. New York. 1882

teenth-century austerity of execution that sharply distinguishes it from the true Renaissance architecture. In the final analysis, in terms of historical significance rather than quantity of output, it was not McKim, Mead and White and the other Beaux-Arts firms that were the most significant American products of the École. Rather, it was two architects whose work superficially hardly looks Beaux-Arts at all, yet whose Beaux-Arts training was basic to their great contribution to the Modernist movement then in the making: H. H. Richardson and Louis Sullivan, discussed in the next chapter.

VICTORIAN GOTHIC

Victorian Gothic was the most successful of all nineteenth-century medieval revivals and was England's major contribution to the period. Its uniqueness must be seen against a special set of circumstances, which could not have been more different from those surrounding the École des Beaux-Arts. Whereas the École was as systematized and centralized as the French state itself, in training, patronage, and even stylistic variation Victorian architecture remained in such matters fragmented and individualistic, as architecture always had been in England. The training of architects persisted as a haphazard affair of personal tutelage and apprenticeship. As a result, the conceptual mastery of even the best English architects rarely equaled that of the common run of their French contemporaries. But the English advantage was the accommodation of every sort of architectural talent and sensibility. Moreover, such various talents found an extraordinary degree of building patronage, not only state, civic, and church support, but also private means. The variety of the interests and taste of both the aristocracy and the new men of wealth was such that it was a rare architect who could not find backing for his practice somewhere in the unprecedented prosperity of Victorian England between the 1830s and 1870. Whereas in France, the typical Grand-Prix winner would build only a handful of works of consequence—perhaps even pouring himself into a single, major commission—Victorian architects erected hundreds. Sir George Gilbert Scott was responsible for almost 1,000 buildings in his lifetime; George Edmund Street built 263 buildings by age fifty-seven (plus 360 restorations); William Butterfield and Augustus Pugin were each involved with over 100 works; and even the crankiest of Victorian Gothic architects, Edward Buckton Lamb, put up some 30 to 40 churches. This architectural profligacy involved not only the quantity of works, but their quality. Victorian architects were given the means to explore and refine their ideas in actual practice rather than merely at the drafting board. Morever, because of the seemingly limitless financial means, the practice was often one in which architectural fantasy was given free rein.

These material conditions do not explain how and why the Gothic became so immensely popular in the Victorian period. To understand the "Gothic" situation at the outset of the Victorian era in the 1830s, we must first briefly review the Gothic Revival to that point. In the previous chapter, we saw that in all the phases of Georgian Gothic an increasing "realism" of Gothic detail was invested with strong elements of Associationism, with historicist form and romantic feeling interwoven. After 1800, however, form and feeling split. Drained of romanticism, the Gothic of the period—in a manner typical of the repressive dryness in most styles of the time—tended toward thin, wiry, decorative effects devoid of conviction. Yet it was precisely in these early decades of the nineteenth century that decisive strides in Gothic scholarship were made, the knowledge of Gothic history, structure, and detailing forming a virtually com-

plete picture by the 1830s. A double gap opened in the world of the Gothic Revival: first, between inaccurate standards of practice and the new body of accurate knowledge; and second, between Gothic as dry, formalist revival and Gothic in its potential as a carrier of meaning and emotion.

The Early Victorian Gothic of Pugin. In the late 1830s, these gaps suddenly were bridged in the twin form of a major building and the emergence of a great architectural figure. The building was the new Houses of Parliament in London (figs. 11-40–11-42); the man, Augustus Welby Northmore Pugin. In 1834, a fire destroyed the old parliamentary setting of the Palace of Westminster, opposite Westminster Abbey. The competition for the new building held the following year admitted designs only of the two "British" styles: the Gothic and the Elizabethan. Of the ninety-seven entries, all but six were Gothic, including the winning project by Sir Charles Barry, who had the good sense to commission the lavish detailing of the building from the brilliant young Pugin. The resulting building is as contradictory as its two authors, neither of whom was happy with the results. Barry would have much preferred a Classical structure and gave the building, wherever he could, symmetry and regularity. In plan, Commons and Lords Chambers are attached left and right to a core of entranceways and lobbies, and all these spaces are encased in a huge, rectangular frame of committee rooms, libraries, and offices as symmetrically disposed as possible. In the building's main facade, on the Thames River, the asymmetries of the turrets contribute picturesque "Gothic" accents to what remains essentially a tight, symmetrical massing with a regular fenestration and silhouette (even if this regularity meant on occasion stairs cutting across a window). It was this aspect of the building that fully justified Pugin's famous remark about it to a friend: "All Grecian, Sir: Tudor details on a classic body." Although Pugin was no happier with the ambivalent building than was Barry, his detailing of it was so authentic and at the same time so bold, colorful, and imaginative—whether in the two grand towers or the polychromatic interiors, such as the throne end of the House of Lords—that in the public eye the Houses of Parliament clearly represented a victory for the Gothic in the ongoing battle of the styles. As a focal national monument, the building lent to the style a legitimacy and an appeal that contributed heavily to its Victorian resurgence.

Pugin was far more than a master of authentic Gothic detailing. A tragic figure, twice a widower who lost his mind a year before his suicide in 1852 at age forty, Pugin combined in himself architectural mastery and wild-eyed romanticism, a positive zealotry for the past, and a revulsion toward the present. Several important singularities of Pugin were inherited from his father. A French emigré who had fled to England in 1792, Augustus Charles Pugin worked briefly in the office of John Nash. In the 1820s, caught up in the rising tide of Gothic scholarship, he turned to publishing detailed technical drawings of Gothic detail for the use of builders and craftsmen, works in which the young Pugin assisted, acquiring thereby that precocious mastery of Gothic form so important for his career. In his own influential publications (*Contrasts*, 1836, and *The True Principles of Pointed or Christian Architecture*, 1843), the young Pugin set forth a synthesis of the new Gothic archaeology, rationalist theory inherited from his French father, and a personal, nostalgic escapism which he found in

11-40　Sir Charles Barry and A. W. N. Pugin. Houses of Parliament. London. 1836–c. 1860

11-41　Plan, Houses of Parliament

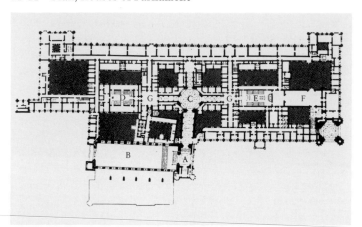

11-42　House of Lords, throne end. Houses of Parliament

concrete form in Roman Catholicism, to which he had converted in 1835. Pugin organized these themes around a central criterion of aesthetic value which was, simply, "truth." Architecture was either an embodiment of truth, or it was falsehood. In this severe, fundamentalist view, only one architecture was possible for England—the Gothic—which was the expression of the true genius of the English people, the architectural embodiment of the one true religion, and the only true form of construction in masonry (the pointed arch being the most efficient form). Moreover, within the English Gothic basic distinctions were to be made. The Perpendicular (Tudor), which Pugin himself brought to a high point of revival in the Houses of Parliament, was a "false" Gothic of the time of the Reformation and the decline of the Church. Only the pre-Perpendicular was true Gothic, and truest of all was the "Second Pointed" style of the period of Westminster Abbey and soon after, from the mid-thirteenth to the early fourteenth century, when medieval Catholic culture was at its high point. Intent on re-creating the illusion of the lost golden age of "truth," he wrote: "We can never successfully deviate one tithe from the spirit and the principles of pointed architecture."

But in actually designing a new church, Pugin did not make literal copies of historical models; it was the convincing illusion of historical models reborn, not merely replicated, that he instinctively grasped as the only possible aim. Essentially what he advocated, and what was widely accepted, was a form of radical functionalism. Pugin's rule was that each functional part of the building, usually a nave, chancel, entrance porch, or tower, must assume its necessary plan and volume, and that these components must be set together in an orderly way. Although there was a hierarchy of importance of interior decoration (the liturgically dominant chancel receiving the richest ornamentation), in the basic architecture of the building no part was intrinsically more important than another. Neither symmetrical regularity nor picturesque asymmetry existed in organization. The building had a front, sides, and a rear, but there could be no traditional facade. The Puginesque building thus took shape directly from function to plan, from plan to interior volumes, from interior volumes directly to external massing. Paradoxically, the irregular outlines of his buildings, which followed naturally from his method, made them *look* as if planned for Picturesque effects. Undoubtedly, it was this pseudo-Picturesque impression that made Pugin's buildings so visually appealing in a period in which the Picturesque sensibility was very strong.

11-43   A. W. N. Pugin. St. Wilfred's. Hulme, Manchester. 1839–42. (After Pugin)

11-44   Interior, St. Wilfred's

Of Pugin's numerous churches no two are alike, and the Church of St. Wilfred's (1839–42), Hulme, Manchester, is as typical as any (figs. 11-43, 11-44). The forms that rise over its compact, slightly asymmetrical plan create an external massing that is low, heavy, and severe. The tower is of massive masonry, with simple, rugged details, and the whole structure is true to Pugin's functionalist principles. Similarly, on the interior, strongly profiled arches rise over short, heavy columns; the windows of both the side walls and the clerestory are deeply splayed to emphasize the rude thickness of the walls; the proportions of the nave are low, and the wooden roof is simple and bare. Only in the choir, cleanly separated from the nave by an arch, is there a greater elaboration—a rose window, a triad of stained-glass lancets, an ornate altar screen, and seats for the clergy. Especially compared to pre–Pugin Gothic, St. Wilfred's creates the impression of a medieval parish church of undeniable authenticity, at least to nineteenth-century eyes.

The High Victorian Gothic of Ruskin, Butterfield, and Others. Pugin's doctrines, which in their radical functionalism foreshadowed important tenets of Modernism, formed the theoretical basis of both the early and High Victorian Gothic. However, the High Victorian period, whose onset coincided with Pugin's death, brought new ideas and a different spirit, favoring a dynamic, open eclecticism whereby to an English Gothic stylistic core were added French, German, and particularly Italianate elements. The last of these entailed an intense colorism of materials that was the main architectural attraction of Italy to the High Victorians, who wove a heterogeneity of materials, patterns, and masonry into strongly plastic forms, creating a vivid new style that differed sharply from the restrained works of the Pugin years. In its restless energy and its dynamic effects, indeed in its very aesthetic permissiveness, the High Victorian Gothic offered an English parallel to the Parisian Second Empire style.

Just as Early Victorian Gothic owed nearly everything to Pugin, High Victorian Gothic can scarcely be imagined without the writings of John Ruskin and the buildings of William Butterfield. Ruskin was a peculiar man and a peculiar writer even for a Victorian. His writing style was not one of argumentation, but rather of thundering assertions and oratorical techniques of hyperbole, repetition, furious declamation, and exaggeration. He praised what he liked, and vice versa, without regard to reasoned consistency. Yet the verbal brilliance and energy of his "pulpit style" was of such poetic force and vision that its influence was incalculable. Although he devoted only a few years to writing about architecture, Ruskin is said to have been the main critical force behind the survival of historicism in later nineteenth-century England.

Ruskin's principal architectural writings, *The Seven Lamps of Architecture* (1849) and *The Stones of Venice* (1851–53), are a vivid hodgepodge of ideas from everywhere, and acute, often biased, observations about particular architectural works. Like Pugin, Ruskin raged bitterly against the modern age—against its worship of money, its factory system and machine production, against iron itself ("the most fruitful source of corruption . . . in modern times") and all it implied. He sang the praises of ancient buildings, erected by craftsmen who loved their work. Pugin had believed that true architecture could only emerge from a religious, Catholic context, a notion that Ruskin secularized, broadening its appeal. His doctrine was that good architecture could result only from the efforts of good men working in the context of a healthy society (such as the Middle Ages). In practice, since it was easier to reform architectural design than society itself (not to speak of human nature), the concept was somehow reversed: the creation of a good building could both confirm and contribute to the goodness of its creators and their society. This vision spurred the building efforts of the Victorians, and later it became a mainspring of energy for Modernist architects who also imagined they could change the world through good design.

Ruskin's architectural aesthetic departed radically from Pugin's, for his position was as antifunctionalist as possible. The essence of architecture for Ruskin involved not the necessary aspects of a building, but to the contrary, precisely those features that were unnecessary; as he elaborated, "if to the stone facing of that bastion be added an unnecessary feature, as a cable moulding, that is Architecture." Ornament, in other words, was what distinguished architecture from mere construction. What sort of ornament? Ruskin was above all after color and visual energy, and what he loved were large, flat surfaces endowed with as much color as possible. He favored alternating bands of stone and brick, which he reasoned would stress the horizontal layering of masonry and, metaphorically,

11-46   Interior, All Saints'

represent the strata of the earth from which all architectural materials derive. He advocated "permanent" or "constructional" polychromy, that is, not mere paint or loosely applied sculpture, but a solid layer of revetment and accents of color built into the wall.

Ruskin's aesthetic was essentially a revival of the eighteenth-century Picturesque in disguise. Architecture to him was essentially a matter of vivid, two-dimensional, visual impressions. Given this attitude, his short list of specifically permitted styles (all others being little short of abominations) becomes comprehensible. With one exception—the English "Middle Pointed" as a basic framework to which polychromy could be applied—they are all Italian, and all strongly emphasize colorful, irrational surface effects: Pisan Romanesque, Venetian Gothic, and, in Florence, "Giotto's Tower." The last is his favorite building, being purely a painter's and sculptor's architecture, exquisitely carrying "constructional" polychromy to its maximum.

During the years when Ruskin's ideas were being formulated, the architect William Butterfield was erecting in London the Church of All Saints', Margaret Street (1849–59; figs. 11-45, 11-46), which was the counterpart in brick and stone (and numerous other materials) to the eminent critic's books, constituting more than in words the definitive manifesto of High Victorian Gothic. This remarkable building cannot be understood, however, without some knowledge of the intermediary institution between Pugin and Butterfield, the Ecclesiological Society and its liturgical building campaign.

Hundreds of churches were built in the Victorian period. Although a number of them, including all of Pugin's, naturally, were Catholic, reflecting the Anglo-Catholic revival of the middle third of the century, by far the vast majority were Church

11-45   William Butterfield. All Saints'. Margaret Street, London. 1849–59

of England. In the eighteenth and nineteenth centuries, the Anglican Church had been weakened by liberalism, science, and industrialization. Reform drives were begun, and the deepest response was found in movements born at Oxford and Cambridge. The threat to the Church was combated by a new emphasis on spirituality, on the sacraments, and on the liturgy, with a heightened attention to decorative elements that accompany church ceremonies—altars, vestments, music, and the like. The question of ritual and especially of its sensuous elaboration and architectural framework became the chief concern of a movement founded by a group of Cambridge undergraduates in 1836 as the Cambridge Camden Society, which, by 1845, had become the influential institution known as the Ecclesiological Society. In its publications, specific prescriptions for the form of Anglican church buildings were promulgated. Through the 1840s they essentially reflected Pugin's ideas, but by 1850 they sought a more assertive style which would vividly embody the new spiritualism and provide an expressive, colorful setting for the liturgy. Such shifts in style and sensibility were, in any case, in the air—in the Second Empire style of Paris and the writings of Ruskin—and the Ecclesiologists succumbed to these various factors when they commissioned Butterfield to design the Church of All Saints'.

As the building rose (its walls were up by 1852, and its design soon published), it became startlingly clear that here was a church the likes of which had not been seen before. The building cost £70,000, whereas Pugin's most expensive church had required less than £40,000. Yet the first thing that would have struck the observer was its fabrication in brick, lowly brick that no early-nineteenth-century architect would have used in such a lavish monument because of its ignobility and over-assertive coloration. But it was precisely the vivid color and texture of brick that Butterfield was after. Inspired by Siena, and independently paralleling Ruskin if not influenced by him, he threaded double stripes of black brick through the red main material, and at the top of the wall complicated the pattern with zigzag and interlace motifs. The massing of the church assaults one's architectural sensibilities, for the program of All Saints' is unusually complete: a large church and tower, entrance porch, entrance court, choir school (to the left), and clergy house (to the right). Ordinarily, these forms would be spread out comfortably over a site several times the area of the small city lot on Margaret Street, into which Butterfield squeezed everything with unnaturally steep, vertical proportions. All of the large masonry surfaces and volumes crowd and press against one another, threatening to annihilate the already shrunken courtyard. Only the lean lines of the tower rise triumphantly above the architectural crush. The excitement is intensified by the brickwork itself.

The church's exterior prepares one for the interior, which bristles with the same brutal energies. From the geometric inlay of the floor to the densely polychromed, gilded timber ceiling, the surfaces assault the eye ceaselessly with a heterogeneity of materials, patterns, and shapes. Polished red granite columnar shafts support unpolished capitals of luxuriant leafwork; the nave spandrels are crammed with inlaid patterns in polychromatic brick, stone, and marble that jar one another; aisle walls are decorated in bands of glazed brick and Minton tiles; and jamb stones have inlaid mastic patterns. The decorative intensity of the nave is surpassed by the even more Italianate chancel with its marble altar screen and tiers of blind arches and tracery, paintings, stained glass, and furnishings (all designed by Butterfield or under his direction).

Butterfield's startling and influential style was controversial in its day, and debate about it continues. Was it a naive reaction to the blandness of current practice or did it offer something more sophisticated and purposeful? A strong case can be made for the latter because of the Ecclesiologists' patronage of Butterfield. They supported him because they welcomed his revolutionary new mode as an expression of their desire for a bold architectural affirmation of their ritualism, the need for a unique style of their own. Pugin's purpose was to create the illusion of a medieval parish church reborn in the nineteenth century and thus to transport the worshiper back to the Age of Faith. In contrast, with Butterfield there was no shred of nostalgia, certainly no possibility that his compound of English, German, and Italian elements might yield any illusion of romantic transport to the past. The strategy of the Ecclesiologists (not unlike the Roman Baroque) was to capture the devotion of the churchgoer through calculated action on the senses and the imagination, and Butterfield's style literally leaves no stone unturned to celebrate the liturgy and at the same time to engage the worshiper.

Even though it was the building that initiated and defined an epoch, All Saints' was only one of Butterfield's nearly one hundred churches. None of the others equalled the total impact of All Saints', but several extended the intensity of its interior decoration to a new, even higher pitch, notably the chancel of

11-47   J. L. Pearson. St. Augustine. Kilburn, London. 1870–80

the Church of All Saints', Babbacombe, Devon (1865–74), and the chapel of Keble College, Oxford (1867–83).

Had we space, the work of many other architects would find their place here, notably Butterfield's nearest rival, George Edmund Street (colorplate 69), but also including those who eventually led the turn away from the polychromatic eclecticism of the High Victorian Gothic to a sober, post-1870, Late Victorian trend, exemplified in works such as J. L. Pearson's St. Augustine's (fig. 11-47), Kilburn, London (1870–80), an austere, though dignified and spacious church. With relatively dispirited buildings like this one, however, the heyday of the Victorian Gothic was clearly past.

Before leaving High Victorian Gothic, some mention must be made of the secular work of the movement. The Gothic style that was created as something intensely spiritual quickly became a visual fashion. It was employed for practically every building type as a medieval alternative to the flamboyant Classicism of the Second Empire style so popular in England. Any list of secular High Victorian Gothic construction would include the Gothic interior of the Crossness Sewage Works (fig. 11-48) in London by Joseph Bazalgette (1865); the Oxford University Museum by Deane and Woodward (1855–60); G. G. Scott's Midland Grand Hotel fronting St. Pancras Station, and his Albert Memorial (1863–72; fig. 11-49), both in London. The last was among the most extravagant of nineteenth-century monuments, and it took the form of a huge Gothic canopy

11-48   Joseph Bazalgette. Crossness Sewage Works. London. 1865

11-49   G. G. Scott. Albert Memorial. London. 1863–72

11-50   Alfred Waterhouse. Town Hall. Manchester. 1867–77

11-51   Alfred Waterhouse. Interior, Town Hall

(inspired by the Scaliger Tombs in Verona) of great decorative lavishness and sanctimonious ostentation.

The most impressive of all secular works of the High Victorian Gothic is Alfred Waterhouse's Manchester Town Hall (1867–77), a building equally brilliant in its functional and visual solutions (figs. 11-50, 11-51). The site of the enormous building was an acute-angled block in the shape of a near-isoceles triangle. Although Waterhouse marked the main entrance with a tower, the building has no facade as such, or rather, is all facade, animated with changing rhythms, bristling with bay windows, turrets, gables, and chimneys, and encrusted with rich, polychromatic cornicework and sculpture. Yet the whole structure is unified by continuous horizontal levels and carefully controlled silhouettes and relief. Particularly successful is the handling of the acute-angled corners, softened by polygonal faceting and by bay windows. The interior of the building is laid out with a sureness that would have gained admiration in Paris—the Assembly Hall set almost freestanding in the center, the offices filling the three wings around it. The circulation arrangements are both effective and imaginative: a corridor runs around all three sides linking the offices, with spiral stairs at each angle. The two stairs near the main "facade" interpenetrate a secondary set of stairs flanking the entrance to the Great Hall, generating Gothic columnar vistas. At its best, the High Victorian Gothic in sweep and vision, if not in harmony and refinement, could almost rival the great structures of the English Middle Ages.

THE ARCHITECTURE OF TECHNOLOGY

It is difficult to exaggerate the radical change that the new industrial world of the nineteenth century brought to architectural materials. Since the beginning of architectural history, the same basic substances had been employed. They were provided directly by nature and used in their natural or near-natural state, only cut, shaped, and dried into the functional forms of timbers, stone blocks, and clay bricks. The exceptions were lime mortar and Roman concrete. Metals, which had the tensile strength that masonry materials lacked, were employed in minor and supplementary ways. Bronze was expensive as well as brittle. Iron, the structurally more important metal, was available in limited quantities and uneven quality, and was too easily converted to rust by the elements. It was, therefore, restricted in use to things such as tie rods and chains, and, along with bronze, to masonry cramps and decoration. Prior to the nineteenth century, the structural presence of iron in architecture was scarcely noticed.

The Industrial Revolution changed all that. Ferrous materials became available in such large quantities that they could play far more than a minor architectural role. In 1800, the world production of iron stood at 825,000 tons; by 1830 it was 1,825,000 tons, and nearly 40,000,000 in 1900—almost a fifty-fold increase over the century. The growth was not only in quantity, but quality as well. Iron, found bountifully in the earth's crust as an oxide, is a material of almost protean variability. It is not simply pure or impure, but can be made hard or soft, brittle or ductile, strong or weak. These qualities depend on carbon content, freedom from impurities (slag), and heating and cooling treatments of the refined metal. Traditionally, three versions existed: cast iron, wrought iron, and steel. Cast iron is the crudest form, containing the most impurities and thus extremely brittle. Wrought iron, because it includes almost no carbon, is highly malleable (hence its name), but also comparatively soft. The optimum material is steel, which incorporates a restricted amount of carbon for hardness but is otherwise free of impurities, giving great strength and, as a result of tempering treatments, is also malleable.

Cast and wrought iron came into prodigious manufacture in the early and mid-nineteenth century as a result of rapid growth in demand, new means to transport materials, and more efficient iron-founding techniques. But the mass production of steel required further technological advances to rid the metal of weakening impurities and to control more perfectly the degree of carburization. Such advances were made with the Bessemer process (put into use in 1860) and the open-hearth process of 1864; scientific iron metallurgy in the last third of the century perfected these techniques.

A significant but little-known fact is that the main form of increased steel production was technically not steel but a kind of wrought iron. It lacked a crucial property of true steel—its hardening power—yet it differed from the older forms of wrought iron because it was free from the weakening presence of slag, at the same time being malleable (unlike cast iron). It was called steel only because the name carried the status of a high-quality and high-priced product, illustrating once again how pervasive the habits observed in architecture were in the nineteenth-century mentality. Instead of inventing a new name for a fundamental new product, a historical name (hence a historical image associated in the public mind with superiority) was misappropriated for it.

That the new structural materials were touched by nineteenth-century mental habits is also seen in the alternative new building substance—concrete, composed of an aggregate of broken stone, gravel, or other small chunks of hard matter embedded in a matrix of lime, sand, and water. In use since Roman times, its modern revival depended on the invention of Portland Cement in 1824, a substance of many times greater strength, durability, and fire-resistance than the age-old lime cement. Mass concrete began to come into widespread use in the 1850s and sixties, in the construction of the sewers of Paris, for example. However, even with Portland Cement, the use of concrete was still severely restricted by its low tensile strength, but the remedy was at hand in the newly available iron and steel; their properties complemented those of concrete. Whereas the latter material was cheap, easily molded into large structural forms with great compressive but little tensile strength, iron and steel were expensive, difficult to shape, yet endowed with extreme tensile strength and easily procurable in the simple form of long, thin bars. Furthermore, whereas iron rusted and was disposed to failure in fires, concrete was both fire- and weather-resistant. The solution was another typical nineteenth-century synthesis of opposites—an "ideal" structural material, ferroconcrete, in which iron bars (steel in its simplest, cheapest form) were embedded in concrete at its weak point to make up for its missing tensile strength, while the concrete, conversely, protected the iron elements from fire and rusting (fig. 11-52). Concrete reinforced by iron was adaptable not only to the obvious use of long beams, but also could form columns, walls, arches, and vaults, all of surprising thinness, strength, and virtually unlimited shape.

In the case of cast iron, it is not an exaggeration to say that the early nineteenth century fell in love with the substance (believed God-given, being so useful and plentiful) and used it for everything imaginable. Bridges, conservatories, factories, commercial buildings, markets, museums, churches, and libraries in which cast iron was used (often in combination with glass now available in unlimited quantities) proliferated in the first half of the century and flourished so richly in the middle decades to about 1870–80 that the period has been called the Cast Iron Age (figs. 11-73–11-78). After it was discovered that the exposed iron members typical of cast-iron architecture were highly susceptible to the ravages of fire, a prolific phase of construction with steel, now fireproofed, followed from 1880 into the twentieth century. The steel structures took the form of gargantuan engineering works and important skyscrapers in Chicago and New York. Ferroconcrete was the last material to appear (in the 1890s) and the last to affect architecture, as it became the European Modernist structural material par excellence (figs. 12-58, 12-78).

New Methods: Engineering and Materials. Before the nineteenth century, structural forces were understood only in approximate empirical terms. It was not until the late eighteenth century that exact knowledge began to replace guesswork, and structural design was first put on a scientific basis. Only in the later nineteenth century did the science of statics—an aspect of physics ultimately dependent on Newton's Laws of Motion—finally become architecturally viable. The invented techniques depended on abstract procedures in which structural components represented calculable forces that could be measured precisely and directed through structural devices—arches, slabs, beams, piers, trusses—as through a complex plumbing system. Such a method was intrinsic to the employment of ferrous skeletal construction, which was the main form of technically advanced work in the period.

The new methods of structural design were created and put into practice by members of a new profession, that of the civil engineer. Before the eighteenth century, to be an "engineer" meant to be a builder of "engines" of warfare, a master of its mechanical and constructional arts (which included road and bridge building as well as weaponry). In the great upsurge of public works—canals, harbors, docks, lighthouses—during the eighteenth-century Enlightenment, and the outpouring of constructive and mechanical activity in the Industrial Revolution, the men who applied to civilian needs the arts that had previously been the domain of the military engineer set themselves apart, adopting the name "civil" (i.e., civilian) engineer for their métier. In this fast growing profession, structural expertise was removed from the domain of the architect where it had always been. Earlier, most of the great architects had dealt with structure as an integral part of the design. But in the mid- and later nineteenth century, the most spectacular advances in structure were made by those who understood the rapidly evolving new science sufficiently to work creatively within it—the professional civil engineers. These were figures such as the Roeblings, who built the Brooklyn Bridge; Gustave Eiffel, whose spectacular iron railway bridges developed pylons that culminated in the Eiffel Tower; and William Le Baron Jenney, who created the steel-framed skyscraper in Chicago—all of whom were products of new technological schools. Many of their structures, especially pure engineering works such as the Eiffel Tower, shocked and bewildered the more aesthetically sensitive of the contemporary audience (although the masses loved them). The typical engineer's lack of training in the visual traditions of architecture predisposed him callously to disregard niceties of scale, proportion, and

11-52 Beams of reinforced masonry, reinforced concrete, and prestressed concrete: a. Pope, 1811; b. Wilkinson, 1854 patent; c. Hennebique, 1897 patent; d, e, f. modern reinforced concrete; g. modern prestressed concrete. (After Mainstone)

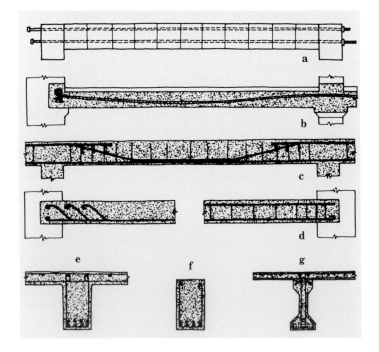

detail, and the adaptation of raw structures to human sensibilities. Yet, one must not magnify the dichotomy between engineers and architects. Just as certain engineers were able successfully to deal with architectural form, so a number of gifted nineteenth-century architects assimilated structural advances and architecturally exploited their potential. These figures—outstanding among them the Frenchman Henri Labrouste—were precursors of the Modernist builders who exercised dazzling talents in employing fully the new architectural technology.

The new methods depended not only on new architects and engineers, but on the revolutionary qualities of the new materials. With the qualified exception of Roman concrete, it can be said of preindustrial materials that they were extracted from the earth, made into pieces, and heaped up in piles. Energy and imagination flowed into the aesthetic shaping of these heaps of matter, achieved through proportion, articulation, and elaboration; particular emphasis was directed to the load-support, or tectonic relationships between the individual piled-up pieces. What resulted were the varied forms of bases, shafts, capitals, architraves, cornices, impost blocks, keystones, ribs, that is, the components of load and support. Except for the tensile forces contained in the lower strata of lintels, the stresses involved were essentially compressive ones, whether in pyramids, walls, trabeated frames, or arches and vaults.

The new industrial materials are conspicuously different. First, every industrial material is of a uniform and determinate quality, something rare in traditional materials. Stone varies unpredictably between quarries and even within the same quarry from bed to bed, with grain and vein structures assuming all the variety of nature, no two blocks, in fact, being the same. Timber varies similarly from tree to tree, and bricks, especially in early production, from batch to batch. But a given grade of industrial steel is of predictable uniformity, a feature crucial to engineering calculations. Further, all the new materials are distinguished by a much greater tensile strength that permitted a radical new thinness to any component of a structure, as well as allowing a greater scale for any such structural whole.

Such tensile strength is associated with another aspect of the new substances. Whereas older materials were shaped by a cutting action into small units, the structural forms of the new materials are created from inchoate, liquid masses that are poured, molded, extruded, or beaten into almost limitless shapes. In the case of ferroconcrete, an entire building can literally be cast as a single, monolithic unit. In iron and steel-frame structures, the individual members, rather than receiving the feeble mortar bond of traditional construction, are permitted by their high tensile strength to be so firmly and completely bolted, riveted, or welded together as to form a structural unity, as functionally seamless and integral as the monolithic ferroconcrete counterpart (figs. 11-53, 11-54). No matter which modern technique is employed, the resulting integrated building could not be more different from the loosely adhering piles of small, discrete elements of traditional practice.

The final contrast between the old and new materials concerns their visual surface qualities. Here we find modern materials at a disadvantage, at least initially. By and large, traditional substances were chosen not only for their structural properties, but because of their aesthetic qualities, the visual richness provided by their color, texture, and pattern. Precisely cut ashlar limestone blocks; columns and cornices of glowing, polished marble; piers of weathered travertine; and sunlit brick arches were all of high intrinsic appeal. But few materials are visually deader than iron. Concrete is no better, being equally dull

11-53 Nineteenth-century cast-iron building structure being demolished in 1984. New York

11-54 James Bogardus. Factory design showing tenuous strength of cast iron even with parts of structure missing. 1856. (After Giedion)

compared to traditional masonry. The monotony and lifelessness of modern materials are inherent in the very uniformity that makes them such perfect structural media.

If we pull together these observations about the new substances with a view to their larger architectural implications, we find ourselves confronting the problem that faced the architects of the Industrial Age: the Greek-derived formal system that had been the basis of all Western architecture was invalidated by the new materials. The old architectonic system developed to articulate load and support had no real meaning in the new integral equilibrium of seamless parts. Such differentiation was foreign to structures of iron, steel, and ferroconcrete. Moreover, the thinness of the new structures, permitted by the strength of the new materials, was inimical to the sculptural detailing of traditional forms of articulation. Details created for limestone and marble, and even for brick and wood, tend to be drained of vitality in iron or concrete.

The invalidation by the new industrial materials of the historic forms of Western architecture presupposes the idea that form and structure should follow the dictates of the nature of materials employed. This thesis—which goes back to the eighteenth-century theorist Lodoli—was to become a touchstone of architectural Modernism, but in the nineteenth century the imaginative leap to a new tectonic system was impossible for architects to make: the gap between the old familiar ways and the strange new materials was simply too great to cross. However, the fact that architects could not completely surrender to the new technology does not mean that they did not respond to it. Quite the contrary. Few, if any, wanted to be left behind. In fact, it is just the unpredictable variations of their response that make nineteenth-century architectural history so rich and convoluted—a succession of talented, well-meaning figures struggling imaginatively with forces that they only vaguely comprehended.

Modes of High-Technology Architecture. Nineteenth-century architects accommodated the new technology in three basic modes: 1. simple substitution of materials while leaving forms essentially intact; 2. modification of older forms while exploiting the greater strength of the new substances; and 3. creation of essentially new structural forms altogether. Thus, a Corinthian column could simply be cast in iron; it could be much attenuated to exploit the iron's strength; or a completely new form of iron pier could take its place.

The first mode, substitution, was particularly popular in the Cast-Iron Age because materials that are poured, molded, or pressed into form serve not only the creation of integral structures but also the process of mass production, in this case the manufacture of architectural components. The temptation to duplicate traditional architectural forms in cast iron was irresistible (figs. 11-54, 11-73).

The latent conflict that such a process involved, however, was dramatized in the second case—the distortion of traditional forms to exploit the new strength of materials. It is revealing to compare the attenuated cast-iron columns of nineteenth-century interiors (fig. 11-78) with the visually similar attenuation of supports in the Gothic period. In the medieval instance, a meaningful illusion of weightlessness was achieved. But everyone understood that iron was so strong that even the thinnest iron columns were physically capable of bearing immense weight. Dematerialization was thus obviated, or, if realized,

only to the extent that the observer was led to forget that the supports were iron and not masonry. But since the cast-iron Gothic churches of the mid-century were objects of bitter criticism, such suspension of disbelief would have been difficult. The role of architect as a kind of structural magician was for the moment lost and would only be regained when antitectonic sorcery could be effectively applied to the inherent powers of the new materials. In any case, the compromise of adapting old forms to new materials was an uneasy one, full of the conflict and ambiguity characteristic of the period.

The third category, the creation of new forms, is particularly complex. New structures could appear either as pure engineering forms (which needs no explanation here), as self-conscious formalist inventions (a Modernist topic), or in eclectic combinations with historical styles (the most interesting and varied nineteenth-century mode). In some of these combinations, a new structure could be entirely hidden from view. The best illustration is found not in a strictly architectural work but in the greatest sculptural monument of the period, the Statue of Liberty, completed in 1886, in New York Harbor (figs. 11-55, 11-56). To the onlooker, the monument, some 300 feet in height, presents nothing unusual apart from the scale and the site: an eclectic granite pedestal surmounted by a Neoclassical colossus fabricated of hammered copper. Completely hidden within is the extraordinary structural program that supports the visible forms. The foundation block constitutes the largest concrete mass of its day. The concrete core of the pedestal walls is reinforced by ferrous elements that are run along the inner surface in the form of heavy iron straps bolted to massive cross-yokes of steel girders anchored in the masonry at the top and bottom. But the armature of the statue itself—connected by huge bolts to the above-mentioned cross-girders—is the most remarkable of the monument's

11-55 Statue of Liberty, cross section. 1875–86. (After S. Horace Pickering)

11-56 Gustave Eiffel. Statue of Liberty, steel armature. 1879–84

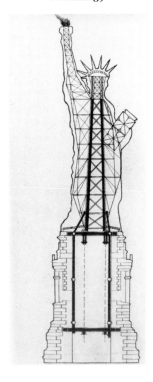

supports, and well it should be, for it was designed by the preeminent French engineer of the period, Gustave Eiffel himself. The core of his wrought-iron structure is a tapering pylon of massive angle-girders cross-laced into a rigid unit, from which secondary, much lighter trusswork reaches toward the interior skin of the statue. The actual connection to the skin is effected by a system of flexible, springlike iron bars (that allow for thermal expansion of the statue), while a powerful, cantilevered beam rises to carry the asymmetrical load of the torch arm. The copper shell of Fréderic Auguste Bartholdi's statue is entirely hung from this multilayered skeleton, like a modern curtain wall, being nowhere self-supporting at only 2.5 millimeters in thickness.

Hidden structure, such as that of the Statue of Liberty, was used extensively in nineteenth-century architecture, but new structural forms were also openly set side-by-side with traditional fabric. The railway stations of the period were the most widespread examples of such combinations. The passenger terminal usually took historicizing form, but the train shed was built in the purist engineering manner of the fire-breathing machines that inhabited it (fig. 11-65).

The most progressive scheme generally used in the period was the combination of new and traditional structure in the same unit—a masonry shell with a visible internal structure entirely or partly of iron. This mode was employed in a variety of new building types, including early factories, commercial buildings, markets, galleries, and stores. It was used by the architect Henri Labrouste in his great library building in Paris, the Bibliothèque Ste.-Geneviève, probably the finest work of the mid-century; and it was a medium through which the most forward-looking and influential architectural thinker of the period, Viollet-le-Duc, depicted a way to the future (fig. 12-3).

High-Technology Constructions. *The Iron Bridge.* Before the era of iron, stone reigned supreme in bridge construction. Developed by the Romans in innumerable river spans and aqueducts, the form

11-58   Jean-Rodolphe Perronet. Seine River Bridge. Neuilly. 1772. (Engraving by J. F. Germain. Bibliothèque Nationale)

endured into the modern period. Although its four constituent elements—piers, arches, spandrels, and roadbed—remained unchanged, a number of significant modifications were realized by later builders for reasons of stability, economy, utility, and sometimes aesthetics. In the Middle Ages, for instance, at the Ponte Vecchio in Florence (1345), flattened, segmental arches were substituted for the Roman full semicircular arches, with the obvious advantages of a greater span to height ratio, permitting a flatter roadbed in conjunction with fewer arches over the bridge length. It was characteristic of the Renaissance visually to refine this feature in the adjacent Florentine bridge of 1567, the Ponte Santa Trinita (fig. 11-57), where the arches followed a sinuous, elliptical curvature. But the perfection of the arched stone bridge—many think aesthetically as well as structurally—was attained in the period of early civil engineering, the late eighteenth century. In 1772, Jean-Rodolphe Perronet (director of the first civil engineering school, the École des Ponts et Chaussées) built his famous bridge over the Seine River at Neuilly (fig. 11-58), a structure that despite its traditional materials and format clearly manifested the rising new technical spirit. Because of the several years

11-57   Ponte Santa Trinita. Florence. 1567

11-59   Abraham Darby. Severn River Bridge. Coalbrookdale, England. 1779. (Science Museum, London)

required to build a multiarched bridge, it had been necessary since Roman times to construct each arch as a self-supporting unit, that is, with piers thick enough to support the arches of the incomplete bridge through the winter months. Perronet realized that when the bridge was complete the thickness of the piers was superfluous because the thrust, rather than having to be resolved in each pier, could be transferred from pier to pier to the riverbanks. The piers could thus be made thinner without any loss in stability, indeed, with a gain in the factors of endurance for the bridge would present less of a blockage to the river flow. Before Perronet, the minimal ratio of pier thickness to span had been around 1 to 5; in his bridge, with its 120-foot-spans between piers only 13 feet thick, it was 1 to 9. There was one catch, however; all the arches had to be erected in a single year. This was accomplished with generous state patronage, which permitted at one time a crew of as many as 772 men and 167 horses. Perronet's contemporaries doubted the viability of his daring concept, but the bridge survived until 1956, when it was wantonly dismantled.

Just at the moment when Perronet brought the arched stone bridge to perfection, an irresistible competitive form made its first appearance: the arched bridge of iron. It is no coincidence that several of its potential advantages had been sought by Perronet—economy, utility, and scale. Even in his reformulation, the stone arches remained ponderous in dead weight and thrust, necessitating piers that were still immense compared to most construction. Only with iron could any significant gains be achieved. Whereas the compressive strength of limestone is 20 tons per square foot, that of cast iron is 10 tons per square *inch* (or 72 times more!). This elevated compressive strength of cast iron is by far its greatest virtue, being four times its tensile strength. Arches are entirely a matter of compressive force, and thus the obvious way to exploit cast iron in a bridge was to substitute iron voussoirs for those of stone. So great was this comparative advantage that its characteristic visual appearance was realized in one of the first iron bridges, the one over the Severn River (fig. 11-59) at Coalbrookdale, England, completed in 1779 by Abraham Darby, a member of the prominent English pioneering iron-founding family. Here the old massive substance of bridges has melted away. The five sets of paired cast-iron ribs, each 70 feet long, seem but the skeletal ghost of bridges past, with quirky, eighteenth-century forms that include Gothic Revival ogee arches.

The Coalbrookdale Bridge was the embryonic phase of iron bridge construction. A decisive advance was to fabricate arches not merely of two attenuated, comparatively unstable, skeletal units, but of a great many cast-iron voussoirs (like a typical stone arch). Easily founded and extremely rigid, such a bridge could be built to vast dimensions. This concept was first promoted in 1783 by the American inventor Thomas Paine; in 1801, the future English bridge builder Thomas Telford proposed a colossal new London bridge of such a structure (fig. 11-60), a single arch leaping 600 feet across the Thames River, with a rise of only 65 feet. This visionary project, although probably technically unattainable at the time, was based on the success of the famous Sunderland Bridge of 1793–96, a stunning 236-foot realization of Paine's stone-into-iron voussoir notion, a sober, clear-headed advance beyond the primitive Severn structure.

Although many such spans were erected in the early nineteenth century, the solution was a transitional one, for it exploited only the compressive strength of iron, and nothing of the tensile strength that even cast iron was endowed with, not to mention the increasingly available wrought iron. Moreover, bridge development was accelerated by the sudden need for vast numbers of new spans with the coming of the railroad after 1830, whose Achilles' heel was the inability to climb any but the slightest grades, necessitating the construction of innumerable tunnels and bridges (a modern parallel to the Roman aqueduct system with its slight, even, *downward* incline). In England alone, the number of bridges rose from 30,000 in 1830 to 50,000 in 1850 (mostly for the railway). But not only numbers were involved. No earlier bridges had to accommodate the enormous weight and the kinetic shocks of the rapidly moving train; and few earlier bridges had to cross such valleys, rivers, and waterways as was commonly required of the railway bridge. The inventiveness of bridge builders was channeled into realizing the most efficient and expansive exploitation of ferrous materials, in both their tensile and compressive strengths. This resulted in not only the reformulation of the arched bridge, but also the invention, or reinvention, of other forms: the girder, the truss, the cantilever, and the suspension bridge.

The simplest employment of the double strength of iron was the girder. Even a cast-iron girder could withstand high tensile stresses, thereby permitting far longer spans than stone lintels.

11-60　Thomas Telford. Thames River project. London. 1801. (Science Museum, London)

Hundreds, even thousands, of simple cast-iron bridges, 20 feet to 60 feet long, were built in the nineteenth century using such beams. Given the correct cross section and sufficient depth, solid iron girders of enormous length could also be fabricated, as Robert Stephenson proved in 1850 in his famous tubular Britannia Bridge (fig. 11-61)—or pair of railway bridges—over the Menai Strait (an arm of the Irish Sea), constructed with a system of "shorter" beams 230 feet in length and longer ones twice that.

More efficient, and with far more potential than either the simple iron girder or the voussoired cast-iron arch, was the truss, a structural form that was to prove among the most ubiquitous of all in modern engineering (fig. 11-62). Known in timber to the Romans and thereafter to all roof and bridge builders, the truss is based on the unique indeformability of the triangle. Under load, its components may eventually break, but the triangular figure itself will not otherwise distort (unlike a rectangle or any other shape). A truss is a structure built up of two or more triangles, sharing sides. The simplest of truss forms is the so-called king post of two right-angled triangles with a common vertical side (used widely in roof structures). In a truss, depending on the direction of loading, some members are subjected to compressive stress, others to tensile ones. If the truss is inverted, so are most of the stresses. The king-post formula is so simple that the word truss was generally not applied to it, being reserved for longer chains of triangles, beginning with the so-called multiple king-post type (known to Gothic builders and Palladio). As such, a truss if further extended forms a kind of girder, and may even be thought of as a solid girder with the unnecessary parts removed. Trusses can easily be fabricated to far greater depth and correspondingly longer spans than girders, with less expense and technical difficulty.

The advantage of the truss is compelling, and what seemed an almost limitless variety of truss formulae appeared in the course of the century to satisfy the growing need for bridges of increasing span and height as the railway system expanded throughout the world. Toward mid-century, the mathematical, analytical basis of truss design, that is, true modern truss engineering, came into being; and the fact that the truss could be applied to practically every other structural element of bridges as well, including towers and even arches, increased its use. The first engineer to utilize fully this potential was the brilliant figure we

have encountered before, Gustave Eiffel. In a series of magnificent wrought-iron railway bridges over deep river valleys, Eiffel perfected a system that combined spidery trusswork pylons (models for the Statue of Liberty armature), crescent-shaped trusswork arches (hinged at the joints for thermodynamic flexibility and design precision), and long, continuous trusswork girders. The finest realization of Eiffel's system was his Garabit Viaduct (fig. 11-63) in southern France (1880–85), with its para-

11-61　Robert Stephenson. Britannia Bridge. Menai Strait. 1850

11-62　Bridge trusses of the first half of the 19th century.
　　　a. Burr, 1804; b. Town, 1820; c. Howe, 1841; d. Pratt, 1844;
　　　e. Whipple, 1846; f. Warren, 1848. (After Mainstone)

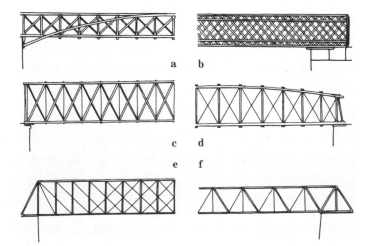

11-63 Gustave Eiffel. Garabit Viaduct. France. 1880–85

bolic arch rising 231 feet over a 541-foot span (with trusswork 33 feet deep at the crown), its total length 1,715 feet, and the whole a matter of quintessentially French economy and visual elegance.

Nevertheless, Eiffel's formula was not the ultimate realization of the potential of the truss. Another variant, almost always of ungainly visual appearance, but of strong structural advantage, was the cantilever. Ultimately of ancient Chinese origin, the cantilever consists of a beam projected from a supporting tower with a counterbalancing beam behind it, joining up with a similar cantilevered unit projecting symmetrically from the opposite shore. There can, of course, be more than two such cantilevered units in a bridge, and their span can be (and commonly is) extended by hanging a supplementary girder between the two cantilevered arms. The American and German engineers who pioneered the trussed cantilever in the 1860s, seventies, and eighties quickly realized that if the bridge towers are treated not as discrete supports on which the other trusswork is merely hung additively (as in Eiffel), but are conceived in an integral manner, the whole cantilevered unit, including the towers, becomes a *single* truss of potentially tremendous depth (that of the tower height) and corresponding length and strength.

The definitive example of this concept was an awesome modern construction—the Forth Bridge (fig. 11-64) in Scotland, built in 1882–89 on the design of Sir Benjamin Baker, who was knighted for his achievement. The main part of the Forth

Bridge consists of three gargantuan cantilevered units, each cantilever arm projecting 680 feet from towers 350 feet high, the whole bridge 5,330 feet long, weighing some 38,000 tons. Like many of the visionary engineering works of the period, it met with an instant popular fame which was diluted only by isolated cries from the aesthetic establishment. Ironically, one of the forefathers of Modernism, William Morris, seems to have hated it most, declaring that "every improvement in machinery (was) uglier and uglier until they reached the supremest specimen of all ugliness, the Forth Bridge."

The nineteenth-century eye had no such problems with the suspension bridge, a form endowed with great visual comprehensibility and beauty of line. In the definitive example, the Brooklyn Bridge (fig. 11-2), the main structural forces—unlike the visually entangled structural pattern of the Forth span— are dramatically divided between massive stone towers, all dense compression, and the spidery steel cables, whose tensile forces draw them out into stretched curves, rays, and harplike plumb-lines. To these, the suspension bridge's third element adds its visionary magic—the roadbed that soars in a single, gliding curve from shore to shore, expressing neither tensile nor compressive force, but simply floating in midair. It is this dramatic interplay of structural modes and sweeping visual lines, all rendered on a heroic scale, that makes the suspension bridge so compelling.

Interestingly, unlike other nineteenth-century bridge forms, the suspension bridge changed little in its basic contours throughout its development, which begins with Telford's 580-foot bridge of 1826 over the Menai Strait, and by the mid-twentieth century reaches the 4,200-foot Golden Gate Bridge in San Francisco (1937), and the competitive, 4,260-foot Verrazano-Narrows Bridge (1963) in New York.

The Brooklyn Bridge was the greatest of nineteenth-century bridges. Its leap of scale beyond its predecessors was not just another step in the continuing series of such advances, but was the first leap into that world of heroic scale that revealed the power of the Industrial Revolution, and it was the first permanent, gargantuan high-technology structure to be brought into an urban setting, where it formed a crucial part of the circulation system of a metropolis. Although the skyscrapers of the Chicago School are usually heralded as the beginning of American

11-64 Sir Benjamin Baker. Forth Bridge. Scotland. 1882–89

architecture, from nearly every point of view the Brooklyn Bridge was a more potent symbol of the rising new world power.

Nineteenth-century bridges represented the cutting edge of high-technology architecture. Apart from the Eiffel Tower, which was an extrapolation of Eiffel's bridge pylons, there is nothing else that approaches them. Writings on the period tend to extol the 200- to 400-foot spans of train sheds and exposition halls. But what is a 400-foot span built comfortably on solid city ground compared to one erected in a remote mountain valley, over a torrential river, or over an ocean inlet? This is not to mention that iron bridges of more than four hundred feet were achieved in the first third of the century, and that within the next fifty years that length was quadrupled. What is significant about railroad stations, exhibition buildings, and the like is not the progress of their ferrous or ferrovitreous technology, which for the most part is based on bridge design, but the way ferrous structural techniques were adapted to numerous purposes in a variety of eclectic combinations, together with one other factor—the industrial productivity that made it all possible.

The Stable of the Iron Horse. It is hard today, with jet air travel commonplace everywhere, to recapture the excitement of the railroad experience when this first means of mechanized transport exploded into European life in the decades after 1830. Only a trip into space might now provide a sensation comparable to what the railroad journey meant to a humanity whose movement over land had always been restricted to the fitful pace of animal power. A challenging architectural gap opened between the city streets and the iron rails, and the nineteenth century responded with the creation of an altogether new building type—a stable for the thundering iron monster, a place to arrange passage, to dispose of luggage, await departure or arrival, and in general make the jolting transition between the familiar urban world and the realm of steam and speed. The railroad station involved every significant factor of high-technology construction: utilitarian planning for masses of travelers, every manner of historical styles and modes of eclecticism, and all the tensions and conflicts attending such combinations. It was the most unprecedented of building types, yet more than 100,000 examples were constructed in the century following 1830. With so vast a range it is possible to sketch only the outlines of the nineteenth-century train station and the tasks its builders faced.

The railroad station combined two architectural forms that were inherently antithetical: the train shed and the passenger building. The former, although providing for the passengers' comfort by sheltering them from the elements, had to be scaled in overall dimensions to the trains—wide enough to accommodate a number of parallel tracks and platforms, and high enough to diffuse the noxious clouds of steam and smoke. The technology that produced the railroad also provided the technique to house it, in the form of metal-and-glass roofs. These were taken up as the fitting architectural environment for the iron leviathan. The passenger building could not have been more different in function and form. It was not an industrial construction housing

11-65   St. Pancras Station. London. 1863–76. (Science Museum, London)

11-66   Railroad Station. New Haven. 1848–49. (Beinecke Library, Yale University)

machinery, but an urban building exclusively for human use. It was urban in scale, materials, and style—a new kind of city gate—and often it outwardly reflected historicizing city-gate formulae. Whereas engineers were generally given the job of designing the train shed, the passenger building was the responsibility of an architect, and it usually was the last on the list of priorities, after rails and the train shed.

The structural problem of the train shed, like that of the bridge, was mainly a matter of free span. From bridge technology, a number of alternatives made themselves available—trusswork, the cantilever, and, most commonly in large stations, the trusswork arch. Here the essential task of the engineer, like that of his Roman ancestors who had extended the arch into the depth of the barrel vault, was to make the iron arch into an iron vault, converting pure structure into a spatial envelope. This was accomplished by building a series of identical arches (or cantilevers, etc.), one behind the other, connecting them with longitudinal ribs, and covering the whole, or most of it, with iron-framed glass panels. Niceties of design came into play in this operation to be sure, but the essence of it was simply repetition—as typical a manifestation of the age of limitless mass production as one might find. Yet the spatial effect of the

train shed was in inverse proportion to its simplistic conceptual basis: it came to be overwhelming. Beginning with the 40-foot truss roof of London's Euston Station (1835–39), the sheds, in the form of the trusswork arch, rapidly grew toward the greatest single shed of all, St. Pancras Station in London (1863–76; fig. 11-65). Its 243-foot span was not an exceptional dimension for bridges, as we know, but for an interior it was extraordinary, especially extended in depth to form the widest and largest undivided space ever enclosed. The skeletal transparency of the ferrovitreous vault added a futuristic, magic dimension to the stunning space, especially as the vault was made to spring from the platform level where the passenger stood. The shed thus achieved in three-dimensional terms the same forward leap that the bridge accomplished in pure structural daring. Nor was St. Pancras the last word. Its single span was never surpassed by more than a few feet, but larger total volumes were enclosed by running several enormous sheds side by side; this German speciality was seen in its most spectacular form at the Leipzig Station (1907–15) with eight sheds and a total width of 984 feet.

The passenger buildings grew along with the train sheds, indeed eventually outreaching them in extremes of scale, monumentality, and sophistication, especially in buildings planned by architects trained in the French school. The station, like nearly every other building type, tended to follow nineteenth-century fashions of historicism and eclecticism. Everything was possible, and seemingly every possibility was explored in the nineteenth century. Stations were fitted into Egyptian and Greek temples, medieval cathedrals and fortresses, Renaissance palaces, and they even blossomed into exotic Xanadu-like oriental fantasies (New Haven, 1848; fig. 11-66). Often the choice was simply a matter of prevailing stylistic fashion. Since the railroad station was born in the heyday of the Greek Revival, it is not surprising to find the passenger building of London's Euston Station taking the form of a Doric propylaea (fig. 11-67). The next decade saw passenger buildings in other guises, for example that of a medieval fortification, reflecting the Romanesque revival and the resurgence of castellated-fortress traditions (in Salem, Massachusetts, 1847). Not only styles and historical types, but also basic architectural forms figured in this process; two in particular were the arch and the clock

11-67   Euston Railroad Station. London. 1830s. (National Railway Museum, York)

11-68   Lewis Cubitt. King's Cross Station. London. 1851–52. (Museum of British Transport, London)

11-69   F.-A. Duquesney. Gare de l'Est. Paris. 1847–52

tower, which appeared ubiquitously in station facades. The former was a veiled reference to the Roman triumphal arch, in any case symbolizing the event of passage from one place to another and, in many instances, explicitly reflecting the shape of the train shed. The tower was a symbol of centrality and power; with its iconic clock, it drew on the tradition of bell towers and their signaling the momentous events in urban life as well as the passage of time—now referring to the comings and goings of the trains. Although there never appeared a definitive formula, architects were by and large remarkably successful in this patchwork game: We generally recognize a nineteenth-century railroad station for what it is.

A major issue for architects was the extent to which the train shed might be incorporated in the station facade. There were three basic solutions: completely hide the shed, reveal it directly, or play with its form. These alternatives are exemplified in three classic, mid-nineteenth-century stations. At St. Pancras Station, the shed is hidden behind a florid, High Victorian Gothic railway hotel by G. G. Scott. Conversely, the twin vaults of the train shed of King's Cross Station (1851–52) in London, by Lewis Cubitt, are boldly revealed in its uncompromisingly functionalist facade (fig. 11-68). The third alternative is represented by the Gare de l'Est (1847–52; fig. 11-69) in Paris by F.-A. Duquesney, where the shed image is integrated

in a particularly sophisticated and effective manner. Working in the fashionable Italian Renaissance style, Duquesney set twin, cinquecento palaces into a U-shape reminiscent of Italian villas, yet also reflecting the classic French château design of end pavilions connected by a lower *corps de logis*. Another glance reveals a cathedral image: the central window suggests the rose window of the Gothic facade, not only in its shape and position, but also in its (ironwork) rayonnant tracery. Although we know that the building is neither Renaissance palace nor medieval cathedral, its iconography suggests both the opulence of the former and the transcendental experience of the latter. Since it could not be both cathedral and palace, the building must be "something else," and the nature of that "something else" was indicated by its openness at ground level (for the vast crowds in transit) and, most crucially, by the half-rose window (not the whole one of cathedrals), perceived as the two-dimensional projection of the only part of the building unique to the railroad station—the barrel-vaulted iron shed.

Our three examples can only suggest some of the more important mid-century solutions of the station "problem." Perhaps a better idea of the progress made in answering the challenges posed by the type can be gained if we extend our survey to the late phase (1890–1920) of the railroad station. New York's Grand Central Station (1903–13) by Reed and

11-70   Reed and Stem, Warren and Wetmore. Grand Central Station in 1914. New York. 1903–13

11-71   Grand Central Station, diagram. New York. (Drawing by Ed Novak)

Stem, Warren and Wetmore (figs. 11-70, 11-71) is contained within a Tuscan Doric shell; while it does not have the serene harmony of a Doric temple, it is endowed with the grand scale and dignity of the French Beaux-Arts tradition in which its designers were trained. It signals clearly to us that it is indeed a railroad station with its two station icons: the prominently displayed, sculpturally celebrated clock towering above the main facade, and the triad of vast arches below. But it is the interior of Grand Central that represents the *nec plus ultra* in station planning: two levels of tracks (divided between commuter and long-distance lines), a barrel-vaulted, monumental concourse (one of the great interiors of the period), and a more-than-complete set of easily reached services, all connected by an ingenious system of ramps and stairs that are integrated on several levels with the surrounding streets, sidewalks, and subway system. Stations were built after Grand Central, but none approached its adroitness in planning, which represents a fusion of French design methods, American pragmatism, and the powerful urban forces in wealthy New York.

The Iron Workplace and Marketplace. It was natural that the factories and marketplaces that came into being during the Industrial Revolution—a whole range of buildings housing the production and exchange of goods and services—should be transformed by the use of industrial materials. The first of these building types to be affected was the textile factory. For its simple brick-walled structure, which ran as high as seven and eight stories, the substitution of iron for timber and brick proved irresistible, given the modular system of supports that employed mass-produced, standardized components (i.e., dozens of identical columns and beams). By 1796–97 the first textile mill with a complete internal skeleton of iron appeared in Shrewsbury, England. The one that followed in 1799–1801 at Salford—built by the Boulton and Watt team famed for their steam engine—is better known (fig. 11-72). As recorded in its original drawings, this cotton mill was 140 feet by 42 feet in plan and seven stories in height (unusual for its day). Each floor was divided by two ranges of cast-iron columns carrying a grid of cast-iron ceiling beams running to the walls. They supported segmental brick vaults that were leveled to the above-lying floor level with an infill of rough concrete.

In the first half of the nineteenth century, innumerable examples of such iron workplaces (in reality sweatshops filled with iron machinery) were built in England and elsewhere. By 1850, wrought-iron beams were substituted for the comparatively brittle cast iron in frameworks, sometimes supporting concrete-over-iron vaults; this had spread more generally through high-grade construction in Britain and diffused to a lesser degree elsewhere. The principal type in this diffusion was an all-purpose commercial building nearly identical in its scheme to the early factories. The main difference was that whereas the factories were generally sited in outlying or rural locations, the commercial buildings were distinctly urban. Factories were generally freestanding and hence could be opened all around with windows; the city buildings were typically row buildings, their fenestration restricted to facade and rear (except for corner locations). Maximum window area on the two facades was thus a priority for these deep, narrow, commercial "loft" spaces, but at the same time a more formal manner of facade was required than for the rural, utilitarian factory sheds. The cast iron that had earlier been so desirable for the internal structure offered the builder of about 1850 an equally irresistible solution to the requirements of the commercial facade. This idea was simply to project the skeletal iron structure of the interior directly onto the facade in the form of properly historicizing cast-iron articulation. Both advantages of iron could thus be exploited: its reproducibility of any desired shape by the casting process, and its strength, permitting these shapes to be attenuated and thus minimally

11-73   John Gaynor. Haughwout Building. New York. 1856

11-72   Boulton and Watt. Working drawings for a textile mill. Salford, England. 1801. (After Giedion)

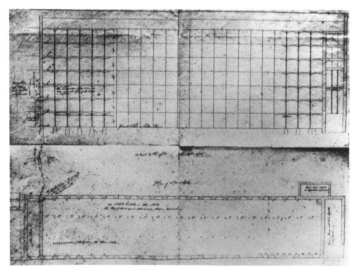

11-74 Peter Ellis. Oriel Chambers. Liverpool. 1864–65

obstructive of fenestration. Cast-iron facades were more common in the America of the 1850s, sixties, and seventies than anywhere else. It was a New York entrepreneur named James Bogardus who claimed to have first invented the idea, and scores of striking examples are still preserved in New York's Soho district. The earliest examples realize the potential of cast iron in a simple trabeated format of surprising elegance. But a post-1850 passion for more sculptural architectural effects resulted in elaborated facade schemes, often of arch-and-lintel Renaissance modes, which somewhat compromised the openness and structural directness of the simpler type. Perhaps the classic realization of these tendencies was the Haughwout Building (fig. 11-73) in New York (1856), built by John Gaynor of prefabricated cast-iron sections produced for him by Bogardus's competitor, Daniel Badger. Based on the sixteenth-century Venetian style of Jacopo Sansovino, the building, rather than mindlessly extrapolating the two magnificent marble stories of Sansovino's Libreria into five clumsy zones, as one might have expected, creates instead an unmistakable aura of authenticity. This quality is due mainly to the building's proportions, wherein the mural massiveness of the Venetian original has been pared down, leaving a skeleton of columns and an airy, yet firm, texture entirely appropriate to the myriad-columned iron fabric.

Such cast-iron fronts were not the whole story of commercial facades of the period. Medieval, and even Islamic, fashions proliferated along with Classical modes. A tendency appeared, moreover, to mitigate the layer-cake effect of identical floors with the employment of the giant order, not only in Classical guise, but also powerful Romanesque and slender Gothicizing

forms, as well as wildly eclectic combinations. Nor were such facades limited to cast iron. Just as fronts looking like masonry were often of cast iron, conversely, those employing elements that looked as though they were, or should be, cast iron were not infrequently of stone. And often materials were mixed. Perhaps the most fascinating and forward-looking example of such entangled, yet progressive, tendencies is the well-known Oriel Chambers (fig. 11-74) of 1864–65 in Liverpool by Peter Ellis. The cantilevered, bay-windowed oriels are all plate glass and slender iron frames, but the Gothicizing columnar elements (a form of giant order) that gather the facade into high, narrow bays are of stone. Nevertheless, it was from such experimental commercial works of the third quarter of the century that the crucial Modernist development of the Chicago School would draw its resources in the following decades.

Such commercial buildings were not only places of work, but also of exchange. Many, like the Haughwout Building, served as department stores, offering under one roof the goods previously sold separately in specialty shops. Many-storied sales emporia were a particularly American phenomenon, growing in the late nineteenth century to buildings of prodigious scale. But in Europe, especially in France, a different architectural solution for department stores had already begun to take shape in the early nineteenth century. French architects did not simply stack characterless utilitarian slabs of space one above the other, but designed more architecturally ambitious interiors. As realized in such classic, late-nineteenth-century examples as the Magasins

11-75 Gustave Eiffel and Louis-Charles Boileau. Magasins du Bon Marché. Paris. 1876

11-76 Victor Baltard. Les Halles Centrales. Paris. 1853. (Engraving by V. Baltard and F. Callet. Bibliothèque Nationale, Paris)

11-77 J. B. Bunning. Coal Exchange. London. 1846–49. (After Hitchcock)

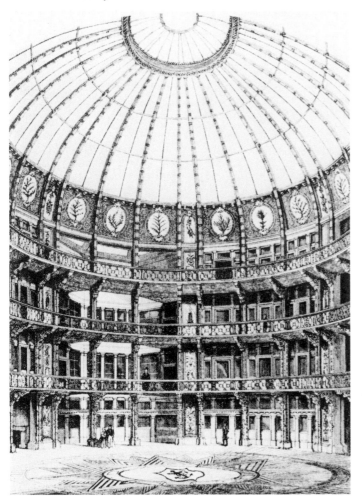

du Bon Marché (fig. 11-75) of 1876, in Paris, by Eiffel and the architect Louis-Charles Boileau, the shopper was engulfed by large wells of space roofed by ferrovitreous skylights, surrounded by tiers of balconylike sales areas, and crossed by aerial iron bridges. The result was a glittering, light-flooded shrine of consumerism meant to lure the masses of customers from competitors offering virtually identical merchandise.

Other forums of exchange were also given high-technology architectural surroundings. The most basic consumer marketplace was, of course, the produce and meat market. In earlier centuries such market areas had been sheltered, at least in part, with open, loggialike structures. In the nineteenth cen-

tury, this practice was adapted to the new building technology, which was perfectly suited to market needs. Required was not any monumental form of wall, but simply canopies of roofing that could be quickly and cheaply supplied in ferrovitreous form. The most impressive of the early iron marketplaces were the Halles Centrales (fig. 11-76) in Paris, begun in 1853 as part of Haussmann's grand urban scheme. He had rejected the original design of the architect Victor Baltard, which called for an expensive masonry pile, insisting "Du fer! Du fer! Rien que du fer!" Baltard's spectacular rows of iron sheds (destroyed in the 1970s) demonstrated the potential of the new technology even in the hands of an unenthusiastic builder.

Of the many nineteenth-century mercantile exchanges, the most notable high-technology example was J. B. Bunning's Coal Exchange (fig. 11-77) of 1846–49, in London. Here one saw almost nothing of the masonry walls, but rather a richly polychromed interweaving of a circle of iron ribs reaching from the floor up through the ferrovitreous vault. Meshed through these verticals were three tiers of balconies supported by classicizing iron consoles.

Still more elevated as a place of "exchange" was the gallery, where public interaction of a more general sort was encouraged beneath iron-and-glass vaults, often framed by fashionable shops and high-class commercial enterprises. The most famous specimen of this eminently urban institution is the Galleria Vittorio Emanuele of 1865–67, in Milan, by Giuseppe Mengoni (colorplate 66). It is a building that, as much as any other, puts to rest misapprehensions about the validity of nineteenth-century architectural eclecticism, for here is revealed just how majestic can be the often maligned, "compromised" combination of floating ferrovitreous vaults over elaborate street facades. The Milan Galleria is one of the few buildings whose effect on even casual visitors lives ever after in their sunniest dreams.

Cast-Iron Cultural and Religious Buildings. The use of high-technology materials and methods in nineteenth-century architecture took the form of one of those "pyramids of distribution" so familiar to us from the social sciences. The new technology was most widespread in utilitarian building types—factories, bridges, train sheds, markets, which provided for what were usually considered the "lower" economic forms of human activity. As one moved up the pyramid through department stores, exchanges, galleries, and beyond, the new materials tended to be used in a restricted way, camouflaged by historicizing forms, or even hidden entirely from view. These tendencies were strongest at the top of the pyramid, in the realm of culture and religion, from which the visible fabric of the new architectural technology was generally excluded. However, there were some notable exceptions; and because such high-level works often received the most monumental and creative architectural treatment, these examples are distinguished buildings indeed.

It was a long-standing French tradition to view the Gothic as a historical embodiment of architectural rationalism. In the mid-nineteenth century, this current was revived and was manifested in the construction of a number of cast-iron Gothic churches. The main practitioner of cast-iron Gothic was Louis-Auguste Boileau (father of Eiffel's collaborator in the Bon Marché store), and his approach was essentially to retain a Gothic formal vocabulary and scheme, but to exploit the elevated strength of iron to reduce further structural mass. St.-Eugène in Paris (1854–55; fig. 11-78), the first of Boileau's several iron Gothic churches, was coherent

11-78 Louis-Auguste Boileau. St.-Eugène. Paris. 1854–55

and even moving in the extreme attenuation of its cast-iron columns, the thinness of its clerestory walls and arches, and the lightness of its vaults, whose webs were made up of so many iron sheets. But neither St.-Eugène, nor the later St.-Paul in Montluçon (1863–66), nor any of his other cast-iron works realized the vision of his more ambitious unexecuted schemes. A project of 1854, for example, called for a chapel at St.-Denis in which the vaults were built up over columns of extreme attenuation to a Mooresque pyramid of webs and window lunettes. The hostile reactions provoked by Boileau's iron architecture were symptomatic of the times, for he was caught in a typical nineteenth-century crossfire of contradictory objections: Some critics felt that no iron structure should look so overtly Gothic as Boileau's, but rather more like a railway shed; yet such purely utilitarian forms were considered inadequate to the spiritual demands of a church.

One of the greatest cultural buildings of the nineteenth century to use iron in a prominent, visible way was unquestionably the Bibliothèque Ste.-Geneviève in Paris, designed by Henri Labrouste and built in 1842–50 (colorplate 71; figs. 11-79–11-81). The large (278 by 69 feet) two-storied structure filling a wide, shallow site is deceptively simple in scheme: the lower floor is occupied by stacks to the left, rare-book storage and office space to the right, with a central vestibule and stairway leading to the reading room which fills the entire upper story. The ferrous structure of this reading room—a spine of slender, cast-iron Ionic columns dividing the space into twin aisles and supporting open-work iron arches that carry barrel vaults of plaster reinforced by

iron mesh—has always been revered by Modernists for its introduction of high technology into a monumental building. But their admiration of Labrouste's masterpiece was limited to its ironwork. The masonry shell, even if elegantly proportioned and finely detailed, was much lamented as an imprisoning, moribund hulk. Fortunately, recent scholarship has exposed the blindness of this approach to the true character of the building. The edifice is in fact important not because it uses iron, but for the way it is used, and the work is great as a complex and meaningful whole. In other words, in the Bibliothèque Ste.-Geneviève we are at the very top of our pyramid of high-technology architecture. At this pinnacle, things were quite different from the bottom, for unlike a railway bridge, a train shed, or a factory, in Labrouste's library there was no clear need for iron. The width of the reading room could easily have been vaulted with traditional techniques, and the use of iron entailed no significant economies. Certainly no advancement of engineering was involved (although the plaster-over-iron vault was ingenious). In using iron, Labrouste was making a purposeful statement that can only be understood in the context of the whole building, a work that turns out to be a paradigm of the sophisticated eclecticism of the period.

The system by which Labrouste endowed his structure with meaning was brilliant. His fundamental idea was to identify the building as a library by giving it the appearance of a book. Such an idea, of course, was one that Ledoux would have loved. One can even imagine how Ledoux, who we recall had designed a brothel in phallus form and a cooper's workshop as a hooped barrel, might have conceived such a library. But in Labrouste's day, such spontaneous, romantic enthusiasms were no longer permitted. The solution had to be more structurally reasonable, functionally responsible, and historically allusive. Labrouste's principal iconographic device was one of architecture's oldest means—the inscription. He inscribed his building with the names of 810 of the authors whose books were to be contained in it. The names were engraved on the stone panels that back the wall-shelving inside, and they run chronologically from left to right around the three public faces of the building, thus making the building resemble a book since we read the names in sequence like words on bound pages.

The device of the extended inscription was one key to the image of the building as a library; another was created by means of architectural allusion. The earlier libraries on which Labrouste drew were the two most prominent solutions to the problem of constructing a freestanding, two-storied library on a long, narrow site: Christopher Wren's Trinity College Library at Cambridge (1676) and the more famous Libreria di S. Marco in Venice by Jacopo Sansovino (1536). What Labrouste took from them was their arch-on-pier structure. But he rejected their columnar, trabeated articulation as structurally nonessential forms that did not convey the function of the building. To take their place he found other sources. One was the Medici Bank in Milan of the 1460s (recorded in a drawing by the Renaissance architect and treatise writer Filarete). The Paris library presents an uncannily close approximation to this building in its long, low proportions, its closed lower and opened upper stories, the small sharply silled windows of the lower zone, its frieze of festoons, and even the spandrel decoration over the main windows. The major disparity between Labrouste and his model is the form of the upper story, where the Milanese windows are replaced by a row of arches over piers. This transforms the upper

11-79 Henri Labrouste. Bibliothèque Ste.-Geneviève. Paris. 1842–50

11-80 Foyer, Bibliothèque Ste.-Geneviève

story into a reflection of the flanks of Alberti's famous Tempio Malatestiano in Rimini. But again there is a discrepancy: apart from some tombs of the Malatesta dynasty, Alberti's arches are completely empty. For a facade whose openings are half-filled with screen walls Labrouste turned to an ancient source, the Ptolemaic Egyptian temple. One such example is the shrine of Hathor at Dendera, a building that suggests a closed box covered with inscribed literary symbols, remarkably suggestive of the library. The meaning of these overlapping models is not hard to find. If a bank is a treasury of material wealth, a library is a storehouse of the more precious riches of the world's great literature. The other models—pagan and Christian temples—reinforce this reinterpretation of the "library," for they convey the idea that its contents are not only precious but sacred.

The architecture of the reading room appears to have its own overlapping levels of signification. The arcade of the outer wall represents antiquity; the structural scheme within is basically medieval—a two-aisled space with light vaults over a central spine of slender columns, similar to a Gothic refectory; the iron material and iron arches present the modern age. Perhaps the most trenchant aspect of this ancient-medieval-modern symbolism is the last layer. It was not the mere presence of iron that signaled the reading room's Modernism, but iron in the form of a railway shed, since parallel, iron-arched barrel vaults were nearly exclusive to stations at the time. Nothing symbolized the modern

world better than a train station. Yet library-as-train shed could carry still another meaning: the library as a place of journey into the historical world of the intellect and the imagination.

Labrouste was prevented by the site from having the garden forecourt to the library that he had wanted as a transition from the street, so he created one illusionistically with fresco. On both sides of the vestibule a garden seems to rise behind low "walls," in Labrouste's words "from the fertile soil of the imagination." Here, too, the historical theme of the building asserts itself, in the busts of French cultural luminaries lining the walls, and above all in the architecture: The piers, with their rigid lines and prominent impost blocks, create the impression of an Egyptian hypostyle hall; the fluting of the piers renders them Classical; and the ironwork arches connecting them represent modernity. Just as the ironwork of the reading room renders the iconography of the railroad shed, so the ironwork of the vestibule creates miniature renderings of one of the other prominent high-technology novelties—the cast-iron bridge. Again this was not a symbol of mere contemporaneity, for the idea of a journey into the realms of the imagination appears to have been a leitmotif of the library.

But what of Labrouste's library in its relation to Beaux-Arts architectural ideals? To anyone seeing with École-trained eyes, the building looked very strange. Everything about it seemed antithetical to tradition. Its proportions were long and narrow, its two stories cleft apart; the orders were reduced to half-enclosed arch-carrying piers, visually subordinate to the inscriptions; the bays seemed repetitive, without distinction of facade and sides, indeed, with not much of an entrance; the extensive ironwork, moreover, was shamelessly exposed. An acute observer, however, would have seen Labrouste's distortions of tradition not as perverse but as a necessary part of the library's new logic and symbolism. The building, in fact, is impossible to imagine *apart* from the École, whose aesthetic system Labrouste heroically bent to his own purposes. This was not only a matter of the polish of the design and its details. The plan is a typical, cross-axial Beaux-Arts scheme ingeniously realized in two congruent stories—the long main axis of the upper floor crossing the short main axis of the lower zone—rather than the usual single level. Other signs of Beaux-Arts planning are the modular spacing, the precise *distribution* and *disposition* of the various elements, and above all in the *marche*, the processional sequence of strong, resonant images from the exterior, through the entrance, to the reading room. The stamp of the École is everywhere, and it gives to what might have been a hodgepodge of functional space and symbolic images a dynamic and architectural order.

It is vital to see French architectural radicalism of Labrouste's generation not as extraneous to the École, but rather for what it really was—a reform movement from within, conceived and practiced within the parameters of the École system. Labrouste was the most gifted of his circle, and his Bibliothèque Ste.-Geneviève pushed the Beaux-Arts system to its limits. He never again attained the same level, but a decade later (1858–68) he did build one other important high-technology building—the Bibliothèque Nationale in Paris. For Modernists, its stack room has always been the high point of Labrouste's career (fig. 11-82). In order to provide for 900,000 volumes, he built five stories of stacks alongside a central well. The ceiling is entirely ferrovitreous, and the stack floors are a transparent grid of cast-iron plates, allowing light to filter through (a device that Labrouste probably derived

11-81   Reading room, Bibliothèque Ste.-Geneviève

from the engine rooms of steamships). The transparent impression of this dazzling space with overlapping screenlike forms is intensified by the balconies and the bridges, which presage the

Bon Marché department store of the following decade.

Although the stack room was ostensibly one of those strictly utilitarian, high-technology constructions of the period, with

11-82   Henri Labrouste. Stacks, Bibliothèque Nationale, Paris. 1858–68

almost no decoration or historicizing embellishment, it was not pure engineering. Labrouste was incapable of designing anything without transforming it into art (even the patterns of rivets). No matter what he built, it was architecture with a capital A, determined visually and not merely by engineering calculations. Intentionally or not, Labrouste could not help but create in the Bibliothèque Nationale's stack room what was among the first, if not *the* first, significant Modernist architectural design. Yet he remained a man of the mid-nineteenth century. An extraordinary glass partition gave a full, distant view of the stacks to the reader, but Labrouste hid them behind heavy velvet curtains.

The Iron Exhibition Building. Despite their often stunning success, these examples of high technology, from the simplest iron bridge to Labrouste's libraries, in one way or another have their limitations as embodiments of the industrial civilization that was increasingly a central fact of life in the nineteenth century. Factories, markets, railroad stations, and exchanges were, after all, grimy affairs, and even though many of the aspirations of the age were brilliantly realized in iron architecture, the structures were only fully appreciated by an elite audience. Nowhere have we encountered an Industrial Age counterpart of what Amiens Cathedral was for the Age of Faith, Brunelleschi's dome for Renaissance Florence, and St. Peter's for the High Renaissance and Baroque. Yet the nineteenth century did produce an iron "cathedral"—not a lasting monument in the traditional sense but ambitious, temporary structures erected in the half-century when the Industrial Age was reaching its maximum crescendo: the international expositions that began in London in 1851 and climaxed in Paris in 1889.

To understand the architecture of the exhibitions, one must know their purpose. The idea was to bring together in one place the products of all the nations, to facilitate their study, improvement, and sale in a world of increasing free trade. Of course nationalistic pride played a big role—England flaunting its advanced industrial prowess to the world in 1851, France showing in 1878 how it had recovered from the Franco-Prussian War, and America in 1876 celebrating its 100-year rise to power. The exhibitions were not merely trade fairs, but displayed every manner of invention and production including industrial machines, means of transport, agricultural implements, household wares, as well as the applied and fine arts. The fairs were, in effect, celebrations of industrial civilization itself, not only its material reality but its highest ideals. The fair buildings can deservedly be called iron "cathedrals" because ultimately the exhibitions were an expression of faith, of a blind yet understandable belief that the Industry of Nations would in its accelerating progress solve the needs of mankind.

Still another dimension to the celebrative character of the exhibitions was their role as an industrial version of traditional popular festivals—Fasching, Carneval, Mardi Gras, Oktoberfest, and so on. This is an important factor in understanding why high-technology architecture was permitted for such notable public events. To be sure, modular ironwork facilitated rapid assembly and easy dismantling, vital economic considerations. As a typical industrial product, straightforward iron construction was also considered appropriate for industrial display. But the degree to which ironwork was exploited and displayed in exposition constructions of great scale, inventiveness, and extravagance can only be understood in terms of the spirit of popular festivals. Traditionally, they were events in which everyday limits of dress, speech, behavior, even sexuality were disregarded in a heady atmosphere of often drunken permissiveness. For the moment everything was possible—including a structural extravagance, normally proscribed, that celebrated the energy of the event.

Although the international fairs were held in many cities throughout the world, none created more of a sensation than London's Exposition of 1851 with its Crystal Palace (figs. 11-83, 11-84). Its designer was a prominent garden architect, Joseph Paxton, who, in conjunction with the engineer-contractors Fox and Henderson, created what amounted to a giant greenhouse, which was fabricated of little more than panes of glass and iron-and-wood framework. Their contemporary, Charles Dickens, in *Household Words*, captured the audacity of the scheme in the following breathless description:

Two parties in London, relying on the accuracy and good faith of certain iron-masters, glass workers in the provinces, and of one master-carpenter in London, bound themselves for a certain sum, to cover 18 acres of ground, with a building upwards of a third of a mile long (1851 ft., the exact date of the year) and some 450 broad. In order to do this, the glass-maker promised to supply in the required time nine hundred thousand square feet of glass (weighing more than 400 tons) in separate panes, and these the largest that were ever made in sheet-glass, each being 49 inches long. The iron-master gave his word in a like manner, to cast in due time 3,300 iron columns, varying from 14 1/2 ft. to 20 ft. in length; 34 miles of guttering tube, to join every individual column together, under the ground; 2,224 girders; besides 1,128 bearers for supporting galleries. The carpenter undertook to get ready within the specified period 205 miles of sash bar; flooring for an area of 33 millions of cubic feet; besides enormous quantities of wooden paling, louvre work, and partition.

11-83   Joseph Paxton. Crystal Palace. London. 1851. (As enlarged and reerected at Sydenham, 1852–54)

The description vividly conveys the most telling aspects of Paxton's Crystal Palace: the vast scale of the whole, the small scale of its parts, the tremendous quantities necessary, the capacity of manufacturers to turn out such forms in virtually limitless amounts, and the entrepreneurial willingness to accept such production demands, deadlines, and risks. Indeed, without even being erected, this visionary building, to be assembled of utilitarian forms that dissolve into transparency and shrink into themselves, offered a poignant symbol of the Industrial Age.

In form, the Crystal Palace could not have been more simple or direct, yet its historicizing overtones are inescapable: its modular layout and structure were a reflection of the medieval bay system; and in expanding a greenhouse to visionary dimensions, the builders appear to have turned to the format of the English cathedral—a long, low, squared-off, multi-aisled, stepped massing, into which a somewhat higher barrel-vaulted transept was inserted to incorporate a huge, living elm tree. When the building was reerected at Sydenham in 1852 (where it stood until burning in 1936), a second transept was incorporated, giving it even more the appearance of a transparent Lincoln or Salisbury Cathedral.

The familiar outline of the building, its structural simplicity and directness, and the small scale of the parts put visitors immediately at ease. It also thrilled them with futuristic effects such as the transparency of the walls and ceiling, the dematerialization of the structure, and the limitless repetition of identical forms into the seemingly endless 1,851 feet of its length. But they would not have been so charmed by the building without one factor more—color. In order to give the industrial construction a properly "architectural" effect, an architect and writer, Owen Jones, was appointed Superintendent of the Works. He devised a scheme of colored decoration derived from recent advances in color theory, which was to paint the entire interior with alternating stripes of red, yellow, and blue, separated by white. Over the repetition and overlap of transparent structure was now superimposed repetition and over-

11-84   Interior, Crystal Palace.
(Royal Institute of British Architects)

lap of bands of accents of color, which dissolved the whole into a Turneresque play of light and air. One contemporary described the dazzling effect with wonder, noting the way "all materiality blends into the atmosphere" in the building, which gives "no idea of the actual size or distance involved," concluding that the "incomprehensible and fairylike" spectacle seemed "*A Midsummer Night's Dream* seen in the clear light of midday."

The tendency to fall back on convention even when working with high-technology construction was evident in the second Paris Exposition Internationale in 1867, which was influenced by the traditions of French Neoclassicism (rather than English Medievalism). The scheme of the exhibition building (fig. 11-85) was essentially that of the Colosseum—a huge oval (1,607 by 1,266 feet) integrating both concentric and radial planning. Seven concentric galleries were each given over and scaled appropriately to a given industry. The Galerie des Machines, twice the scale of the others, was logically arranged at the perimeter with its immense industrial machinery, followed inward by the galleries exhibiting clothing, furniture, raw materials, and the fine arts. But the cleverest device, taken over from the Colosseum, was the radial plan, whereby each wedgelike sector of the building was restricted to the seven industries of a particular nation. Thus, in this *colisée du travail*, order was brought into the chaotic output

11-85 Exhibition Building. Paris. 1867. (After Giedion)

of the Industrial Age by translating the geometry of a Classical model into a rational exhibition layout (a feat the Romans themselves would have admired). One could proceed either by product, comparing the output of one country to the next, or move from product to product of a given country. For a moment, the torrent of material change was frozen into a seemingly coherent pattern.

At the climactic Exposition Universelle of 1889 in Paris, the Utopian idea of gathering every product of civilization under one roof was abandoned. Instead, it was the possibilities latent in high-technology construction that now absorbed the builders—the prospect of creating some futuristic design that, like a true cathedral, would in its intrinsic character and not its mere size transcend the usual limitations of architecture. Structurally the earlier fair buildings had been fabricated in simple trabeated or vaulted modes that did not depart from traditional solutions; and they presented what the observer was already familiar with in greenhouses, railway sheds, and other common high-technology works. But in the 1889 exhibition, two constructions assaulted the visitors not only with titanic scale but with radically advanced structural solutions alien to the traditional formal language of architecture. The historicist veil that lay over the new technology was now pulled away, and what was revealed in 1889 at the Galerie des Machines and the Eiffel Tower was disturbing and deeply moving.

The Galerie des Machines (fig. 11-86), designed by the architect C.-L.-F. Dutert in collaboration with Contamin and several other leading engineers, was one of the most astonishing space-enclosing high-technology creations of the nineteenth century. The scale of its unbroken, central space was tremendous—1,378 feet in length, 148 feet in height, and, above all, 377 feet in width—half again that of St. Pancras' railway shed. Like the train shed, the Galerie des Machines was nothing but a series of bridge arches, twenty of them to be exact, connected by longitudinal girders that supported the ferrovitreous grid envelope. Two decades earlier, Eiffel had already erected wrought-iron bridge arches of considerably greater span (541 feet) under more arduous conditions. But scale and construction that seemed natural in a bridge became overwhelming when brought into the city. By 1889, people had become used to such enclosures for railway stations and fairs, but Dutert's building was peculiar in its structure. The arches were not of the usual arched-truss configuration that had always given the reassuring illusion of being iron versions of traditional vaults. Everything about them was perplexing. They seemed impossibly thin in section, which measured 11 feet in height, but only 29 inches in thickness (a lightness permitted by the use of steel). They did not follow any usual curvature. In fact, they hardly looked like arches, but rather like twin cantilever arms curving up and then reaching diagonally across to be joined by pins where they met at the apex. Most upsetting were their connections with the ground: the girders came down to a point, which rested in a little hinged slot in the pavement. Such hinged joints, which prevent thermodynamic expansion and contraction from creating stresses, had been common since 1870 in the bridges of Eiffel and other advanced engineers. But nakedly displayed at the foot of a gigantic architectural interior made it all the more disturbing. Finally, nothing was what it should be and even professional builders were dismayed: "This lack of proportion produces a bad effect; the girder is not balanced; it has no base. . . . it starts too low. . . . The eye is not reassured. . . . The supports are too empty." But of course a Romanesque builder would have had similar words for Amiens Cathedral—one can imagine them: "too thin, too high, no apparent buttressing, the eye is not reassured." As at Amiens, the effect of the Galerie des Machines was unearthly. It seemed to tear the visitors from their familiar world and transport them into a strange yet wonderful domain.

In the Galerie des Machines, the grimy train shed was transformed into a bright futuristic image of industrial promise. This vision was achieved not only by the form of the building but also by its contents. The interior was jammed so full of machinery of every sort that an elevated trainlike contraption was devised to carry the bewildered visitor through, accommodating as many as 100,000 spectators a day. Years after having this experience as a child, the Modernist sculptor Raymond Duchamp-Villon remembered it as "a hallucinatory passage through the brightness of the nave in a travelling bridge, above whirlpools of twisting reptilean belts, creakings, sirens, and black caverns containing circles, pyramids, and cubes." The Galerie des Machines was essentially an interior, its disturbing effects restricted to those who were temporarily enclosed by it. The Eiffel Tower (colorplate 68), set up in 1887–89 on the banks of the Seine River at the entrance to the fair, was even more troubling, not only in its weird, unprecedented configuration and its supermonumental scale—at 300 meters being nearly twice the height of any previous construction—but because it could be seen from all over the ancient city. We are so familiar with its form that we can hardly recapture its original effect. Modernists have scorned the outcry against it, especially the famous letter of protest by leading cultural figures: "We, the writers, painters, sculptors, and architects come in the name of French good taste and of this menace to French history to express our deep indignation that there should stand in the heart of our Capital this unnecessary and monstrous Tour Eiffel." But the letter was justified, for the tower was the greatest affront not only to the architecture of Paris, but also to the eye of the Parisian, for whom its structural logic and revolutionary aesthetic language were incomprehensible.

Essentially, the structure of the Eiffel Tower—which was a far-ranging extrapolation of Eiffel's spidery, wrought-iron bridge pylons—could not have been more simple: four immense, tapering, curved, lattice-girder piers that meet asymptotically. These piers rise from an immensely broad square base—125 meters on a side—and are laced together at two levels by connecting girders to form an integral unity of great stability. But the structure *looked* unstable in the disquieting manner that the arches of the Galerie des Machines looked unstable. (The lightness of the tower is legendary: so airily spun out is the metal that a true scale model one foot high would weigh one-fourth of an ounce!) Although it did not rise mysteriously from points, it was mysterious enough and far more threatening, for if it should fall! . . . To quell such dire misgivings, visually stabilizing, decorative ironwork was added—the proto–Art Nouveau frillwork of the platforms (removed in the 1930s) and the nonfunctional arches at the base.

These elements, in particular the arches, served to dissuade the public from its fears about the building's structural solidity and also managed to give it a desperately needed iconographic content to which one could somehow relate. The Eiffel Tower stood at the entrance to the fairgrounds, where an arch traditionally belonged: The four arches around its base, together with the first platform as "trabeation," were seen to form a titanic "triumphal arch as striking as those which earlier generations have raised to honor conquerors" (a reference to Napoleon's

11-86   C.-L.-F. Dutert. Galerie des Machines. Paris. 1889

Neoclassical arch across the Seine). But most revealing about the mentality of the period was the way not only the base but also the *whole tower* was seen as a visionary arch (not unlike the shore-to-shore "arched" leap of the Brooklyn Bridge). It was noted that "the Eiffel Tower rising from its four iron piers forms the arch of the triumph of science and industry." This arch image did not present the usual curvature, yet still it formed an arch, like the top of an ogee. Everyone knew the work was a tower—*La Tour Eiffel, La Tour de Trois Cent Mètres*—but no tower had ever looked remotely like it, nor did a tower belong in that place. Thus, in an almost surrealist manner, the eye of the period, acting in desperation, transformed the building into an arch-in-the-form-of-a-tower. Even as the frontiers of high-technology construction were forcing architecture to move beyond the limits of the eclectic vision, eclecticism managed in a desperate gesture to stop, for another instant, the wheels of aesthetic change.

That the cultural establishment had wanted to stop the whole project altogether may have reflected one further aspect of the Tower, a dark aspect that constituted an even deeper threat than the one to visual traditions and urbanistic harmony. Eiffel's Tower rose impudently far above all the religious and dynastic buildings whose iconographies and styles had been adopted by the ruling bourgeoisie; worse, its advanced system of elevators carried daily tens of thousands of ordinary working-class Parisians to a viewpoint high above everything. For the duration of their excursion, Paris, so recently ravaged by socialist revolution, lay at their feet. The futuristic specter of this symbolic social triumph—the Tower as a reminder of the explosive forces of change and social pressures from "below"—may have been the ultimate cause of the panicky indignation of the establishment: the Tower was the new iron "cathedral" of *le peuple* of nineteenth-century Paris.

12-1
Hugh
Stubbins
Associates.
Citicorp
Center.
New York.
1974–77

Chapter Twelve | Modern Architecture

THE BIRTH OF MODERN ARCHITECTURE

The birth of modern architecture—like the Renaissance—hinged on the recognition of a deep historical discontinuity. One of the great obstacles in the nineteenth century to Modernism had been the rigid insistence on the continuity with the past. About 1900, however, the architectural avant-garde severed this bond. The immense spectrum of historical styles, which had been so passionately researched and churned by the nineteenth century in its troubled pursuit of architectural relevance, was now recognized as antithetical or, at best, irrelevant to architectural Modernism. The way to the future, it was suddenly realized, was not through the past. The past was over—an almost unbridgeable void had opened between it and the present.

This new view of history is now so ingrained that it is difficult to imagine how revolutionary it was. The sudden liberation from historicism was exhilarating. If the nineteenth century was a period trapped in irresolvable conflicts of its own making, the Modernist movement was, by contrast, one of high spirits and intoxicating new vistas as a torrent of freed energies poured forth in an array of avant-garde developments.

Among the factors that fueled this burst of creativity was Evolutionism. The nineteenth-century version might well be called Historicist Evolutionism, for it emphasized the unbroken chain of evolving forms. Modernist Evolutionism stressed instead two quite different aspects. The turn-of-the-century philosopher Henri Bergson crystallized one of these new thought-currents in his concept of the *élan vital* and of the evolutionary process not as struggle but as novelty—a great energy pouring forth in endless fecundity. The other side of Modernist Evolutionism stressed adaptation—new forms appearing in active, vital response to the ever-changing environment. For architects who needed the creative authority to build a revolutionary architecture, the new evolutionist viewpoint provided crucial support (thus, for example, the argument of the Chicago architect John Wellborn Root, in 1890, to the effect that past architectural forms had been made *extinct* by the new basis of modern life, which was evolving its mutant species of architecture). Many forces acted in concert in fostering the new architecture, including Modernist individualism. The Victorian constraints were broken, and the cult of the sovereign individual and the glorification of the free, creative life appeared, taking extreme form in Nietzsche's doctrine of the superman. Ibsen, Bergson, and Shaw all espoused anarchical "life forces" and untrammeled self-realization.

The contemporary forces acting on the architect were not only intellectual; the real world, in which architecture operates, had changed. The industrial machine age had matured. It not only permeated life as an overwhelming economic fact; the machine itself had been tamed and it penetrated daily living, especially that of the taste-making, affluent classes, who could afford the telephone, domestic appliances, and above all the motor car. On a grander scale there were the sleek, new steamships, and an eternal dream of mankind was fulfilled in the wondrous airplane. In its overpowering presence and thrilling beauty, the world of the machine not only engulfed people's lives—it swept over their imagination. The early twentieth century was a period so under its spell that intellectuals as brilliant as H. G. Wells and Julian Huxley could flatly state that "all animals (including mice and men) are combustion engines of an intricate and curious kind" and that "the human body is a machine . . . which does its own repairs, sees to its own fueling and lubrication . . . and has the capacity of making new machines to replace itself." Architecture was under the imperative to "adapt" to the machine age and was inspired to do so in the near-worship of the machine (fig. 12-2).

This adaptation would have been impossible had not architecture's new material means also undergone a process of maturation. The previous chapter emphasized the gradual emergence in the nineteenth century of new building materials: cast iron at the beginning, then wrought iron, with steel and perfected engineering techniques, along with reinforced concrete widely available only at the century's end. But now the new technology was ready for a new architecture—and vice versa. Earlier, architects had been unwilling to confront those drastic aesthetic implications of the new architectural technology, which entailed abandoning traditional architectual principles. These ramifications now became instead doubly appealing on account of their novelty and the vision they offered of a new architecture created (by the God-like Modernist architect) in the image of the machine. This aspiration would be most directly expressed in Le Corbusier's famous dictum, "The house is a machine for living in."

Machine-style architecture became the core of architectural Modernism, but machine-style buildings only resembled "machines" in a loose, metaphoric way. It was imagined that buildings were being made to function analogously to machines—that is, in a tightly planned, rational manner, such as we have admired among the Egyptians, the Romans, and the Beaux-Arts. Visually, it was never the functioning guts of machines that were reflected by the new architectural mode, but rather their housings and their external hardware—the hulls, railings, gangways, and smokestacks of ships, the shells of cars and turbines, the openwork frame of early aircraft, and, of course, the new structural "machinery" of steel and ferroconcrete. Typically, the imitated shapes tended toward elementary geometries, simple

12-2   Le Corbusier. Comparison of cars and temples, emphasizing their formal resemblances and parallel evolutions. (From his *Vers une architecture*, 1923)

forms that were the touchstone of the ingrained Classical taste of most architects of this mechanomorphic persuasion.

Modernist doctrine of the early twentieth century had great propagandistic success in promoting the development and spread of the movement, proclaiming that technological, mechanomorphic architecture was humanity's social and moral salvation and could make people better through a purer, more "rational" and "functional" architectural environment. But looking back historically, it is crucial to realize that there are many modern architectures, not merely one. Modern architecture is not just machine-style architecture, but a far more complicated phenomenon. Modern architecture is many-sided and ever-changing because modern life is many-sided and ever-changing. The early twentieth century, for all its mechanology, was a period of immense vitality, evoked by such names as Freud and Einstein, Bergson and Wittgenstein, Joyce and Kafka, Picasso and Duchamp. It was an epoch shaken in every sphere by revolutionary phenomena—Cubism, the Relativity Theory, the Oedipus Complex, the Russian Revolution, the "Great War"—a long list that includes antihistoricist architecture, whose radical iconoclasm is unthinkable in any less revolutionary times. The new architecture was part of the larger revolutionary picture; and like that picture, it was far from crystallized into a clear, uniform configuration, but was fluid and fragmented. Thus, alongside the dominant mechanomorphism appeared strong biomorphic and even geomorphic tendencies—the imitation of "natural" nature in all its variety and unpredictability of forms. Architectural models for a modern architecture seemed limitless and included the world of

art—architecture-as-sculpture and architecture-as-painting—and even so-called primitive and exotic architectures. Only the explicit revival of the European past was forbidden.

NINETEENTH-CENTURY FORERUNNERS IN THEORY AND PRACTICE: VIOLLET-LE-DUC AND WILLIAM MORRIS

Of the several mid-nineteenth-century theorists who attempted the difficult passage from historicism to Modernism, only one writer, Viollet-le-Duc, came close enough to be of crucial importance; his writings later became a bible for some of the early Modernists, such as Frank Lloyd Wright. Although many of Viollet-le-Duc's notions now appear tendentious and his designs ungainly, these flaws were the result mainly of his daring originality. He arrived at his novel ideas through epic perseverance over several decades of work and thought, largely as a unique participant in the Gothic Revival. Swept along in the Romanticism of Victor Hugo's novel *Notre-Dame de Paris*, he was soon caught up in the movement to save the cathedrals. He became the most active of restorers (including of Notre-Dame itself, in 1844) and also the greatest connoisseur of his time of French medieval architecture while simultaneously employing his erudition and artistic talents to produce a number of Neo-Gothic buildings. Yet, Viollet had always been a rebel—fighting on the barricades of the 1830 Revolution, refusing to take the route of the Académie des Beaux-Arts—and soon he rebelled against historicism itself, including the Gothic branch that he had vitally nourished. His rebellion hinged on his idea that the Gothic was not to be an end in itself but a means to a new end: the creation of an authentic "style of our own times," a style employing the new ferrous materials. Whereas others insisted on evolving a new style out of the old, Viollet advocated only the extraction of Gothic principles, not the regeneration of its forms, writing that "the principles and methods introduced by the lay architecture of the late twelfth century adapt themselves, without effort, to the use of these new materials."

But why the Gothic, which, after all, was an architecture of stone par excellence? The main structural problem of all architecture is stability. In Greek-derived architecture, it is attained through the immovable inertia of its massive forms. But, according to Viollet, in both the Gothic and in ferrous construction, stability is achieved through tenuous "organic" configurations of interdependent parts. Modern designers, according to Viollet, could profit immensely by studying how Gothic architects had achieved their "organic" solutions with stone, and then transferring the lessons gained into solutions in iron, of which Viollet offered a number of ingeniously contrived examples (fig. 12-3). If these designs looked strange to the historically conditioned eye, no matter: They were "rational," that is, functional, in every detail, and it was only through a new, pure "rationalism" that a new architecture of iron and steel would be created.

Viollet-le-Duc's break with historicism amounted to the revival of a dormant tradition of French architectural theory that interpreted the Gothic cathedrals not formally or symbolically, but in terms of their structural rationalism. In the view of Perrault, Laugier, and Soufflot, they stood not as fabrics to be directly imitated, but as models to be analyzed, their principles of organization to be adopted into contemporary building. Not only did Viollet daringly extend this idea, he took an even greater leap. He proposed a method of abstracting "principles" from nature itself—the microgeometry of the universe and the equilateral triangle (and derivative polyhedra) that underlie the crystalline structure of matter. As an example of how he would give architectural form to this idea, Viollet proposed (in his *Entretiens sur l'architecture*, 1863–72) a vast public hall for 3,000 people (a manifestly modern program), its walls in stone (which he valued for its properties of stability, endurance, and insulation), but vaulted with an extraordinary polyhedral, skeletal iron structure rising from huge iron diagonal struts (fig. 12-4). This was Modernist "architecture of the future," so futuristic that only the purest Modernist of the mid-twentieth century, Buckminster Fuller, actually followed Viollet's polyhedral concept in his geodesic domes. The liberating effect of this famous design and other aspects of Viollet's doctrine was incalculable.

Yet more than the intellectual courage and artistic vision of Viollet-le-Duc were needed to make Modernism into the movement that ultimately swept the world. Moral passion was required, the passionate belief that a new architecture was the means to a better world, and the primary force here was England. The first country to be heavily industrialized, it not only reaped the benefits but experienced the evils of industrialization first and most sharply: the worker uprooted from the crafts and made a factory slave; cities blighted by industrial construction; and the avalanche of consumer goods spewed forth by the factories, tainted by vulgarity of design and shoddiness of fabrication. For some reformist leaders (Pugin and Ruskin for example), the response was to turn their backs on the modern world completely. For Pugin, we will recall, the way

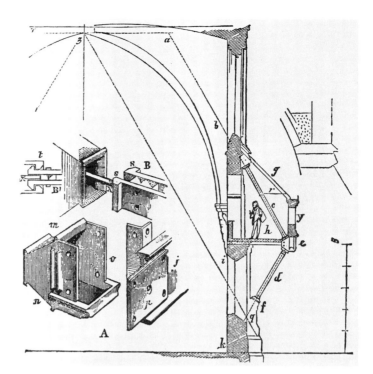

12-3 E.-E. Viollet-le-Duc. Example of modern structure, using iron, based on "Gothic" principles. (From his *Discourses on Architecture*, Vol. II, 1863–72)

out was an escape into a Catholic, Gothic world. Ruskin was not a Catholic, but he was a moralizing medievalist and a historicist. The beauty of medieval buildings was, for him, not so much their embodiment of a religious spirit as the joy of the medieval craftsman shining through his work. For this reason he was opposed to all restoration—to him the defacement of those precious surfaces that were the bearers of that joy of the craftsman.

Pugin of the 1830s and forties, and Ruskin of the 1850s were followed in the 1860s and seventies by William Morris, who made this reformist tradition so important for Modernism. While fiercely remaining anti-industrial ("production by machinery is altogether an evil"), he became also antihistoricist in important respects. It was the medieval process of handcraftsmanship that he emphasized, not the medieval styles. Art, for Morris, was simply "the expression by man of his pleasure in labor," and had nothing to do with those "dreams of Greece and Italy . . . which only a very few people pretend to understand or be moved by." Rather than escaping into the past, Morris faced up to the world. He was an important early figure in English socialism, and he called for an art "by the people and for the people." In other words, he not only advocated restoring to the laborer the dignity and beauty of the crafts, but enfranchising the whole community with the works produced. His was a passionate commitment to finely designed, well-wrought, nonhistoricist surroundings for the entire community. Morris's vision of human salvation through a new mode of architecture, and the applied and fine arts, was advocated not only by words—Morris's famous series of thirty-five lectures of 1877–94—but through deeds: the exquisitely furnished Red House built for him by Philip Webb in 1859, and, most importantly, the firm he founded in 1861—Morris, Marshall and Faulkner, Fine Art Workmen in Painting, Carving, Furniture, and the Metals—which was the turning point in the English Arts and Crafts movement.

12-4   E.-E. Viollet-le-Duc. Concert hall for 3,000 with new method of vaulting. (From his *Discourses on Architecture*, Vol. II, 1863–72)

But there was a glaring contradiction in Morris's theory. For all his progressiveness, he remained with one foot stubbornly planted in a past process of production. As he himself painfully realized, hand-production was expensive, so expensive, in fact, that his exquisitely wrought articles were in practice destined mainly for "the swinish luxury of the rich," as he put it. Morris was too committed to his hatred of the industrial world to take the obvious final step: accept the machine, learn its ways, and teach it to produce works not shoddy or vulgar but in their modern manner well-designed, well-wrought, of solid materials, and just as beautiful as traditional handcrafted articles. Yet even if Morris could not himself take this step—which occurred in Germany after the turn of the century—his example made it possible, just as his moral passion and his socialist vision of the arts as the means to a better world were to be touchstones of the modern art movement.

The Domestic Revival: Old English, Queen Anne, and Shingle Styles. The nineteenth-century theories we have just surveyed have a parallel branch in Late Victorian architectural practice, expressed for the most part in relatively modest, middle-class houses. The so-called English Domestic Revival of the

last third of the nineteenth century was based on a variety of post-medieval, pre-Palladian architectural sources other than churches, monumental castles, and "great houses" of England—mainly smaller manor houses, cottages, yeomen's dwellings, and agrarian and modest monastic buildings. It was as English as English can be: informal, asymmetrical, anticlassical, solid, spacious, unpretentious, and exuding comfortable domestic virtues. It was strong on charm, and close to nature in its unassertive, irregular forms and rhythms. The attraction to this tradition was not a question of simple aesthetic perversity. The generation of the 1870s and eighties was after something not easily definable, but which is communicated in letters written by a member of the circle that created the new style. "You don't want any style, you want something English in character," he wrote, "something sweet picturesque homely farmyardish Japanese social domestic." Whatever it was, it would be "delicate [and] tender"—as opposed to the "fire and energy" and "muscularity" of the High Victorian styles—and definitely not "French . . . aspiring, grand, straining after the extraordinary."

Behind these tangled aspirations were clearly certain emotional factors; nationalism, obviously, as well as a generational reaction against the harsh High Victorian Gothic; and a powerful escapism from the real and imagined evils of the modern world that Pugin had preached in spiritual terms, Ruskin in moralizing terms, and Morris in his secular glorification of the medieval craftsman. The peculiar style of the Domestic Revival was powered by a complementary vision—the longing on the part of the inheritors of the new industrial wealth to return (with their wealth) to the imagined ease and simplicity of preindustrial life. But not just any preindustrial architectural framework for this lifestyle would do. Gothic was too shrouded in religion; anything truly Classical was too stiff and foreign. By a process of elimination as well as inbred sympathies, the one domestic "period" tolerable to this otherwise permissive generation was spread over two centuries—from the Tudor period roughly down to the reign of Queen Anne (1702–14). Not only was this range of formal sources enormous, but eclectic architects now felt free to pick and choose and combine details as never before, with each design an individualistic case. Nevertheless, as created in the late 1860s and 1870s by a trio of architects in the Arts and Crafts circles—Philip Webb, William Eden Nesfield, and the dominant Richard Norman Shaw—the Domestic Revival may be divided into two main branches: the Old English and the Queen Anne.

The transformation of a near-vernacular, "low" source into what must be recognized as a "high" style is clearest in Shaw's Old English mode (fig. 12-5). He took up the asymmetrical half-timbered vernacular of the sixteenth and seventeenth centuries—rudely picturesque fabrics with saddle roofs, multiple chimney stacks, dormers, weather boarding, and large bay windows subdivided into numerous panes by mullions and transoms. Whereas the originals tended to be charmingly chaotic in their incessant variety and helter-skelter display of these elements, in Shaw these same elements were gathered into studied, sophisticated compositions of elegant proportions, complex rhythms, and vigorous asymmetries.

Similar transformations and stylistic qualities were exhibited by the best-known examples of the less rustic, more formal Queen Anne mode, notably Shaw's own brick house in Hampstead (fig. 12-6), London, 1874–76. The sloping site was

12-5　Norman Shaw. Leyswood. Sussex, England. 1868–69. (*Building News*, 1871)

12-6　Norman Shaw. Shaw's house. Hampstead. 1874–76. (From *A Portfolio of Drawings of Artists's Homes* by Maurice B. Adams, 1883)

the occasion for the effective play of symmetry versus asymmetry in the multitiered bay window on the left and the oriel to the right, both of which display the telltale double-hung, high and narrow, small-paned windows of the mainstream Queen Anne, with their white trim playing against the red brick. Also prominent are the quasi-Palladian window motif of the bays, and the tile-hung gables. But Shaw's house represented only one stylistic position among the several possibilities of this mode, which could be far simpler, or far more elaborate, in the piling up of decoration and even minor *japonais*

decorative accents, and with elaborate "Flemish" gables, or, at the seaside, with verandahs (derived from India via the eighteenth century).

By the end of the 1880s, the Queen Anne style was over, and the Domestic Revival entered its final phase, essentially limited to the 1890s, in which a single figure dominated, Charles Voysey. His modest country houses seem stylistically plain and unassuming, but it is just this "plainness" that was Voysey's great contribution, for his houses were among the very first buildings anywhere to be free of overt historicist imitation.

If we look at one of his key designs—the house at Shackleford, Surrey, of 1897 (fig. 12-7)—and compare it with the works of the previous generation, it becomes clear that Voysey's plainness was a far from simple quality. The building maintains the traditional English domestic look, revealing the degree to which Voysey was steeped in the same domestic traditions of the sixteenth and seventeenth centuries that had shaped the Old English and Queen Anne modes. But where Shaw transformed their picturesque detail into sophisticated new eclectic formulae, Voysey radically reformed the domestic tradition by abstracting its general lines and functional particulars, and by omitting decorative detail altogether. Thus we see prominent gables, but without tile-hanging; the easy spread of Old English massing, but no half-timbering; chimney stacks, but without paneling; small-paned sash windows and bays, but in the simplest possible form. The windows are especially calm, of uniform shape, and—a most important detail for Modernism—consistently disposed in near-continuous horizontal bands. Voysey's distillation of English Domestic roots brought him to the edge of Modernism, but he did not pass its threshold. The aesthetic nerve of England—a gradualist country of historical compromise rather than revolution—failed just as Modernism was being born.

At the turn of the century, the Domestic Revival was carried no further in England, but fortunately it had been transplanted to the fertile soil of anglophile America in the 1870s, and it emerged there with new vitality in the 1880s as the so-called Shingle Style. This was not only a notable development on its own merits, but was an important point of departure in the 1890s for the young Frank Lloyd Wright. Americans took up the English Domestic Revival not merely because it was fashionable, but because they felt similar urgings in post–Civil War industrialization to retreat to a more natural setting—in America typically the seaside—and to a premodern architectural environment, especially early Colonial. That the American Colonial period overlapped the age of English pre-Palladianism made the styles based on the latter just that much more appealing. But American blurring and transformation of the two distinct English sources, Queen Anne and Old English, was so extensive that despite the profuse bay windows, small-paned sashes, turrets, and other important details, an Englishman would barely have recognized anything familiar in many Shingle Style houses.

The most superficial change was the cladding of external walls with wooden shingles—traditional American material dating from the early Colonial period—in imitation of English tile-hanging. But the use of wood involved the structure as well as the surface. American wood-framing, in place of solid English brickwork, meant freedom in planning, massing, and even decorative flourishes. Space assumed freer shapes and became less compartmentalized, tending to flow through wide

12-7　Charles Voysey. House at Shackleford. Surrey. 1897.

12-8　McKim, Mead and White. Interior, H. Victor Newcomb
House. Elberon, New Jersey. 1880–81

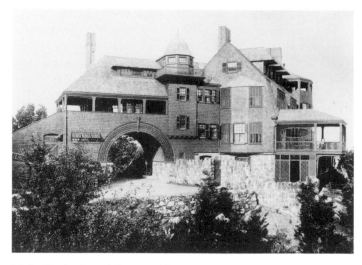

12-9　Peabody and Stearns. Kragsyde. Manchester-by-the-Sea,
Massachusetts. 1882–84

12-10　McKim, Mead and White. William G. Low House. Bristol,
Rhode Island. 1887

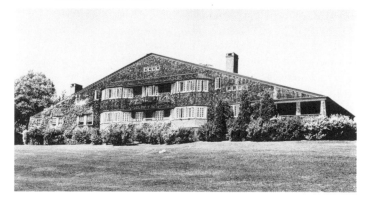

openings from room to room and through French doors out
onto wide verandahs to the outdoors. A good example of a
Shingle Style interior was the living hall of the Newcomb
House in Elberon, New Jersey, of 1880–81, by the firm of McKim,
Mead and White (fig. 12-8). Its spatial configuration is defined
by the ceiling beams, the abstract floor patterns, and the continuous, friezelike element below the ceiling—Japanese in
inspiration—that becomes open grillwork where the hall flows
out into surrounding rooms, bays, and nooks. And often in
such houses, the elaborate main staircase would move boldly
down into the living room, fusing levels as well as areas.

Such spatial fluidity expressed peculiarities of American customs and climate. Where the English tended to segregate men
from women, adults from children, and all from the servants,
Americans were more democratically open and tolerant, not
needing a closed room for every social hierarchy and function. An
open plan facilitated through-ventilation, an important factor in
the hot American summers, and since America was far ahead of
England in the use of central heating, it did not matter if individual rooms could not be closed for heating in the cold winters.
But the peculiarities of the Shingle Style were more than a
matter of sociology or climatology. Post–Civil War America was
one of unprecedented, newly gained, industrial wealth, whose
owners were characteristically prone to confidence, boldness,
and even brashness. This spirit seems reflected in the flurry
of effects in the Newcomb House hall, a room that one could

easily imagine up the Atlantic coast within the walls of the
astounding contemporary house, Kragsyde, at Manchester-by-
the-Sea, Massachusetts, by Peabody and Stearns (fig. 12-9) of
1882–84. Perched on a promontory that grows out of the seacoast rock, Kragsyde freely pivots with the panoramic sweep,
opening in every direction, at every level, in a variety of bays,
turrets, porches, and verandahs that reach out to nature. In
such works, Americans were not only responding to their lively
impulses but also to the dramatic physical environment. Compared to this exotic seaside creature, even the most adventuresome designs of Richard Norman Shaw—from which many of
Kragsyde's individual features derive—seem staid and quaint.

Kragsyde represents one tendency of Shingle Style design—
openness, fluidity, and movement. The other main current often
showed the same bold assertiveness, but in different guise. At
the famous William G. Low House (fig. 12-10) by McKim, Mead
and White in Bristol, Rhode Island, of 1887 (destroyed in 1952),
in place of asymmetric abandon and complication we find a
studied concentration of effects—a huge asymmetrical porch
within a symmetrically ordered whole, Queen Anne bay windows gathered under an overhang, the whole under a single
saddleback roof which grants the facade unusual scale. The
structure is endowed with an important American historical
reference to seventeenth- and eighteenth-century Colonial farm-
houses that still dot the East Coast—simple, boxlike, shingled
or clapboarded constructions with the roof sweeping down

almost to the ground (often asymmetrically as in the "saltbox" type). Perhaps only architects with the Beaux-Arts sophistication of McKim, Mead and White could have so successfully fused the Queen Anne style with such an unassuming, bygone vernacular on such a grand scale and with such smooth handling of detail. The bold vision behind the Low House was something uniquely American at that almost modern moment.

Henry Hobson Richardson. In the eyes of many modernists, the masterpiece of the Shingle Style was neither Kragsyde nor the Low House but an unassertive, unassuming house in Cambridge, Massachusetts, by Henry Hobson Richardson. The Stoughton House of 1882–83 (fig. 12-11) reminds us of Voysey's houses of the 1890s, and well it should, for it represents the same purist distillation of native and imported traditions. The outlines of the past are here—asymmetric massing, small panes, the bay, turret, and dormer—but transformed into natural, functional form without exaggeration, superficial play of effects, or decorative historicist flourishes. The constituent elements are so reduced to their essence, and Richardson's handling of them is so sure and convincing, that we seem to see them in their true form for the first time. The uniform shingles are used in a simple, natural way—to cover, not to decorate—and are allowed to flow unbroken over the surface. They form a wooden skin stretched over the building's serene volumes, to whose sense of composure the drawn-in corner turret adds rather than detracts disruptively. The window panes are comfortably small, not preciously itsy-bitsy, and the windows themselves of easy proportions (compare the narrowed shapes and complicated bays of the Low House). The two wings of the L-shaped massing are in graceful balance, the swelling, vertical volume of the turret contrasting the adjacent, horizontal hollow of the porch. The left front, with its ascending triangle of triple, double, and single windows is answered at the right end of the building with its three ground floor windows, two above, and the single dormer light. The entire building, including the fluid interior plan, is deceptively plain, and is informed with post-historicist intelligence, subtle wit, and dignity.

Richardson, although he has been called "the last great traditional architect," was the first American architect of world-class stature, not only considered a genius by his countrymen but with real influence abroad. He was a famous bon vivant, and his zest for life found artistic expression in his love for fine materials. He could make brick seem to glow like marble, and even cheap perishable shingles came to life in his hands. But his consuming passion was for stone. This attraction was nourished in his early training in Paris, in 1859–62 at the École (the second American, after Hunt, to matriculate) and in the ateliers of French architects, where he absorbed the ancient French tradition of stone construction. But Richardson soon dared to do things in stone no nineteenth-century Frenchman would have dreamed of, and the most spectacular example of this is the Ames Gate Lodge in North Easton, Massachusetts, of 1880–81 (fig. 12-12).

The walls of the Lodge—which actually comprises a two-storied guest wing and a one-storied orangerie—are not simply made in the rugged, quarry-faced style for which Richardson became famous; they are actually built of the kind of boulders found in the dry walls enclosing New England fields. The building forms a superbly balanced, Picturesque massing, with brilliant details such as the monolithic window frames and the

12-11   **Henry Hobson Richardson. M. F. Stoughton House. Cambridge, Massachusetts. 1882–83**

12-12   **Henry Hobson Richardson. Ames Gate Lodge. North Easton, Massachusetts. 1880–81**

mysterious "eyelid" dormers. But its impression is of "a great glacial moraine roofed and made habitable," for it is not merely built of natural materials, but seems to be a feature of the earth's natural geology in material, form, and spirit, an impression strongly reinforced by the ground-hugging sweep of the continuous roof. The Lodge's other remarkable feature is the gaping archway, whose rusticated voussoirs push clear up into the roofline. Nominally the arch functions as the entrance to the rest of the estate, but, whether intentionally or not, it reminds one of nothing so much as a railway tunnel cut through a mountainside. Such a reference would hardly have been lost on the owners, for the Ames family was the promoter of the Union Pacific Transcontinental Railroad, whose completion had been celebrated by Richardson himself in the Ames Monument of 1879 in Sherman, Wyoming, near the site of the "golden spike."

The architect's most prevalent and influential manner was neither the "geological" mode nor the Shingle Style, but the Richardsonian Romanesque, as it was contemporaneously dubbed already in his day by a following that tended to copy its most superficial features (namely its rustication, round arches, and colonnettes). It was a fusion of all that Richardson had

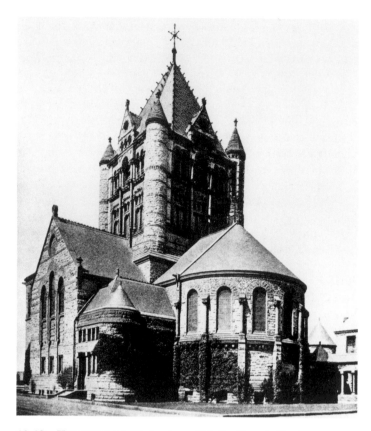

12-13 Henry Hobson Richardson. Trinity Church. Boston. 1873–77

learned in his Paris studies, his European (especially English) travels, and his American experience. The most "Richardsonian" of his buildings, in the sense that the style was commonly understood, was Trinity Church in Boston (fig. 12-13), built in 1873–77, a powerful work that immediately established his national reputation. The aisleless, unified space of the interior, which comprises a short nave, deep chancel and transepts, and a vast crossing, differs from true Romanesque interiors usually divided into aisles and bays, and it glows with a subdued polychromy, polished wood, and rich stained glass, all Richardson's own, late-nineteenth-century creation (although executed by many collaborators, including Edward Burne-Jones and John LaFarge). But, as in most of his work, the exterior is the main event. Here the Romanesque references are explicit, for the facade is modeled (largely by followers) after St.-Gilles-du-Gard in France; the tower is closely copied (by Stanford White, his brilliant young assistant) after Salamanca Cathedral in Spain; and the polychrome decoration of the apse and transept is inspired by the Romanesque of the French Auvergne. Yet the whole, especially seen from the east, has a concentrated force rare to the period in any style. How has Richardson managed this? The interior spaces speak directly as bold exterior masses. A few simple volumes of almost equal size are built up with elemental power—the steep transepts, the swelling apse, and the majestic crossing tower. These contrasting forms are integrated by the uniform density and texture of the pinkish quarry-faced granite with brown sandstone trim and by the carefully orchestrated play of colonnettes and round-headed "Romanesque" windows. Each volume receives its due embellishment, especially the tower with its powerful buttresses, the dormers, and the crocketed low spire.

Just what are we to make of this Richardsonian Romanesque? Its overt sources are continental, and the bold simplicity and logical integration of plan and massing are French. But its energy and the richly textured polychromy decidedly recall the High Victorian English Gothic of Ruskin. By the time Richardson died in 1886, in his prime at age forty-eight, he had transformed the High Victorian style of Trinity Church into something far beyond its European sources. His mature style of the 1880s took form in diverse building types—houses, libraries, railroad stations, court houses, even a vast Piranesian prison in Pittsburgh. But most critics agree that the Marshall Field Wholesale Store in Chicago, of 1885, sadly destroyed for a parking lot in 1931, was his most compelling building (fig. 12-14).

The store filled an entire block with its oblong, quadratic bulk. Because it rose to only seven stories of uniform floors around a central court, it was easily buildable in masonry rather than the still-problematic steel construction used in the taller, early skyscrapers of the time. Only its internal framework was metal. Richardson's main idea for the solid stone external walls was to reduce them to a series of uniform piers rising from the foundations to the cornice, connected only by three tiers of arches and a fourth tier of trabeated work. Because the spandrel areas were limited and the windows consistently set back, the walls approximated a gigantic stone armature. The building was almost, but not quite, skeletal in appearance; Richardson purposely left too much surface area for that and, moreover, avoided unnecessary interruption of the surface, whose massive stone blocks seemed to flow as continuously as the Stoughton House shingles.

The tension between murality and skeletonization was but one aspect of the complex interplay of formal elements in the Field Store. The rhythms of the arches doubled, and then redoubled in the trabeation. The massed solids of the stone played subtly against the dark hollows of the openings (and

12-14 Henry Hobson Richardson. Marshall Field Store. Chicago. 1885–87

vice versa). The whole was drawn together with an overlay of ultimately Classical formulae. The canonic triadic structure of stylobate-column-entablature, so emphasized in Beaux-Arts instruction, was realized with subtle means: the low segmental arches of the basement floor, the upright arches of the two main stories, and the horizontal sweep of the trabeation. The massive framework of the top story, including windows and cornicework, drew the whole together into a cohesive image. Standard elements of Richardsonian Romanesque were reductively transformed. The polychromy of Trinity Church was reduced to the subtle play between red granite in the basement and red sandstone above. The quarry-faced rustication looked almost uniform, being subtly graded upward in the size of the blocks along with a shrinkage of the piers themselves. The Richardsonian colonnettes were gone, except at the corner of the building at its intermediate levels. Carved decoration was restricted to rudimentary capitals in the arcade screens and to the crocket cornice at the top of the building.

There was little novelty in the Field Store as a type of commercial structure. The giant arcaded order used in the organization of the external walls can be traced to commercial facades in iron and/or stone of the 1850s and sixties in England and America and even further back to Schinkel's utilitarian buildings. By the 1870s, New York was the leader of the arcaded facade, and by 1881 the architect George B. Post—prominent also in early skyscraper design—had taken the New York arcaded school about as far as it would go in his Produce Exchange (fig. 12–15), a prestigious building that Richardson would have known and evidently used as a model for the Field Store.

Typologically, the Field Store may have depended on Post, but stylistically Richardson had leaped ahead. The Produce Exchange, to be sure, was of exceptional quality compared to most contemporary New York work, but compared to the Field Store it appears jumpy and confused. Its basement and main arcade are blurred into one horizontal unit, surmounted by an arcaded order that is neither part of the "shaft" of the building nor of the cornice. The proportions seem random, and barren brick surfaces harshly contrast with dense Renaissance terracotta ornament. Obviously all of this is the antithesis to the discipline, integration, and lucidity of the Field Store. But more important, the essentially neo-Renaissance Produce Exchange remains within the confines of historicism. The Field Store

recalls a number of historical precedents, such as the Pont du Gard, Speyer Cathedral, and the quattrocento Florentine palazzo type, yet it resembles none of them, or even all of them combined, in the eclectic sense. Like the Stoughton House, which copies none of the colonial houses whence it derived its shingles, the Field Store was a true post-historicist work. In its electrifying play of abstraction, it was almost modern.

Richardson was no Modernist, yet he was of crucial importance for the following generation of American architects, who took him as their role model. He had been the first American to create a personal, monumental style, a forceful individualistic American style. The man from New Orleans and Harvard had succeeded where most, if not all, Europeans had failed (what nineteenth-century European had a style named after him?). And if one American could do it, others could follow.

EARLY MODERNISM

The Chicago School. Richardson's masterpiece did not fall on barren ground. Chicago in 1885 was the scene of a vast building boom precipitated by a cataclysmic fire in 1871 that destroyed most of the ramshackle early city. But the new construction activity was more than a rebuilding in more permanent materials. It was driven by explosive demographic and economic growth as the city rapidly became the commodities and railroad center of an undeveloped continent suddenly opened to exploitation. As the price of land skyrocketed, the maximum use of each building lot became imperative in the relatively small downtown area being developed (the Loop). Piling up stories to structures of eight, twelve, sixteen or more floors—accessible by the elevator that had been developed in the 1850s and sixties (mainly in New York)—was the obvious solution. Structurally, however, the means of efficiently erecting such lofty buildings was far from simple, not to speak of the formal challenge.

That the first modern architectural movement was generated in this cauldron is due to several factors, not the least of which was the prevailing cultural climate. From its very beginning in the 1830s, Chicago had strong cultural aspirations, which found expression in a large market for books and the early foundation of a symphony orchestra, a museum, and an art academy. By the last two decades of the century, the city had a thriving intellectual life centered at the University of Chicago with its luminaries such as Thorstein Veblen and John Dewey, and it had a caring architectural public, at least among educated ranks, of increasing discrimination and expectations.

Material and cultural circumstances made the new architecture possible, but, as always, architects made it happen. None of the architects of the so-called Chicago School came from Chicago. They were typical rootless Americans willing to shake off the past and follow where the future seemed to beckon. They spanned three generations. But apart from the founding figure, William Le Baron Jenney, born in 1832 and most successful for engineering innovations, and Frank Lloyd Wright, born in 1869 and mainly a designer of houses, the Chicago architects were born around 1850, coming to architectural maturity at the age of about forty around 1890. By then the six leading architects of this generation had paired off into three teams, each a set of complementary talents: Burnham and Root, Holabird and Roche, and Adler and Sullivan. For some reason probably connected with the demanding tasks being confronted, the Chicago movement was mainly a doubles game.

12-15   George B. Post. Produce Exchange. New York. 1881

One of the major works of the Chicago School is the Monadnock Building of 1889–91 (fig. 12-16). The client demanded an extremely "simplified" appearance, and John Wellborn Root, who did most of the designing in his partnership with the entrepreneurial Daniel Burnham (the force behind the 1893 Chicago World's Fair) delivered it, being himself of the firm opinion that "these buildings, standing in the midst of hurrying, busy thousands of men, do not appeal to them through the more subtle means of architectural expression. . . . To lavish upon them profusion of delicate ornament is worse than useless. . . . Rather should they by their mass and proportion convey in some large elemental sense an idea of the great, stable, conserving forces of modern civilization." To convey these forces, Root gave his tall, elongated building a flared base and parapet suggesting the lines of an Egyptian pylon, but even more remarkable is the total absence of any ornamental elaboration. The building rises as sixteen stories of sheer brickwork, as square, uniform piers, rectangular windows, and thirteen-story bay windows that serve as space-extending, rhythmic accents. There is no rustication, no carved detail, only the simplest windowsills projecting from the plane of the wall. Apart from its Egyptianesque silhouette, the Monadnock Building is a work of pure structure, form, and directness.

12-16 Burnham and Root. Monadnock Building. Chicago. 1889–91

The Monadnock Building shared with Richardson's Field Store its conservative structure—internal iron framing with exterior walls of solid, load-bearing masonry. In such masonry construction, the thickness of the walls grows in proportion to the height of the building. In the seven-story Field Store this was not a big problem, but in Root's sixteen-story building it meant piers 72 inches in thickness at their base, which consumed valuable floorspace, restricted fenestration, and imposed a prodigious load on Chicago's notoriously infirm, mudlike soil. The Monadnock Building pushed masonry framing as far as it would go, and the building was the last of its kind. Although formally advanced, it was, in fact, technically outmoded since masonry construction had been made obsolete by the obvious solution: complete metal framing.

Why was such framing a novelty in the Chicago of the late 1880s? After all, cast-iron framing had been developed to a state of near-completeness by the mid-nineteenth century, most prolifically in the New York commercial buildings of Bogardus and Badger with their historicizing cast-iron facades. Although such structures continued to rise to the end of the century, cast-iron framing had meanwhile revealed a hidden, and often fatal, flaw: its susceptibility to fire. Burning buildings can generate such intense heat that exposed iron will warp, buckle, collapse, or melt down altogether. This weakness became clear in numerous tragic instances of the 1860s, climaxing in the Chicago fire, which reduced to a slag heap many a "fireproof" cast-iron structure.

The obvious solution was to fireproof the iron members by encasing them in heat-resistant materials such as hollow tiles, brickwork, or concrete. The bulky piers and beams that resulted could be incorporated in partition walls or the floor structures. But the facade, with its articulate, expressive form, was much more difficult to fireproof. Not surprisingly, most facades, especially those of "high quality" buildings, returned temporarily from cast-iron to masonry. The pressure, however, to evolve a fireproof, iron-structured facade was enormous, given the advantage of ferrous construction particularly at facades, where the relative thinness of structure meant maximum openness and fenestration. The solution was found with the inspiration to separate the carrying, fireproofed ferrous structure from the carried visible elements. Such a nonsupportive wall is called a curtain wall, being a masonry (or later, metal) screen "hung" (actually built on a series of little shelves) story by story on the fireproofed iron frame, each story of curtain wall only supporting its own fabric. Free from carrying any real load, the curtain wall could take almost any shape, and it is easy to understand why it was to be one of the protean conceptions of the modern building art.

The evolution of fireproofed iron framing and of the curtain-wall facade between the 1850s and the 1890s is indicated by recent studies to have been a more complicated story than once was believed. Not only Chicago, but New York and other cities (including Paris) played a role, and nowhere was the development other than a quasi-scientific process of piecemeal advances. In Chicago, however, not only was this technical progress of extreme vigor, but it was accompanied by unparalleled architectural innovation.

The pivotal Chicago figure was William Le Baron Jenney, the French-trained engineer-architect, whose Home Insurance Building of 1884–85 was the first of the curtain-wall structures.

12-17 William Le Baron Jenney. Fair Store under construction. Chicago. 1890–91. (After Condit)

However, it only employed the curtain wall in its upper stories, and it must be regarded less a solution and more a point of departure for a series of innovations by Jenney himself and the other leading Chicago builders over the next decade that finally added up to what we often call "skyscraper" construction: riveted, all-steel fireproofed framework, internal wind bracing, and full curtain-wall facades. A contemporary view of Jenney's Fair Store of 1890–91 under construction (fig. 12-17) gives a good idea of such a steel skeleton, which has become so familiar a sight in the twentieth century that we rarely recognize it for the radical novelty it represented. Unlike the cast-iron facades, which mimicked traditional construction, Jenney's steel skeleton is absolutely uninflected. Its members are made of I-beams of practically identical form. There is no inherent distinction between the corner and the center, the bottom or the top, or even between vertical and horizontal elements, nor among the spatial modules these elements make up. For the builders, this meant an unprecedented ease of construction, and for interior designers, matchless flexibility in partitioning and repartitioning commercial space. But it also posed a new and challenging situation in facade design, for the uninflected new structure—without the variations that result from orchestrating the several distinctive parts, the sides as against the middle, the bottom, the top—confounded all historical precedent. Whether Greek or Roman, medieval or Renaissance, the underlying basis of facade design was just such inflection, but such designs had never accommodated so many stories. What were the Chicago architects to do? Even apart from deciding if and how to adapt some historical style to the skyscraper, there was a more basic question of formal interpretation. The skyscraper consisted of many identical stories, therefore it might be exhibited in its many horizontal layers; but these layers made it a very tall building, and thus its verticality might equally well be expressed. Or the facade could be—like the steel skeleton—left neutral; it could be a direct projection of the skeleton into masonry cladding, whose image was neither vertical, horizontal, nor historicist but simply an imitation of the supportive structural machinery: that is, mechanomorphic. But even mechanomorphism was not a simple matter, since it could be

carried to various interpretive levels, even to surprising heights of architectural poetry.

Jenney was not the one to lead the way out of this maze; the younger members of the Chicago architect teams provided the formal vision that gave the Chicago School its historical stature. No building better demonstrates their formal mastery of Jenney's steel-framed curtain-wall technique than the 14-story Reliance Building of 1894–95 (fig. 12-18). Built by Daniel Burnham and Company in the years immediately following Root's early death, the work was designed by another member of the firm, Charles B. Atwood. Not the least remarkable fact about the Reliance Building was the erection of the framework of its top ten stories in only fifteen days (July 16–August 1, 1895). The seemingly effortless fact of construction was paralleled by the buoyant grace of the finished exterior. The contrast between the massive masonry bulk of the Monadnock Building of five years earlier, with its smallish windows punched through the thick

12-18 Daniel Burnham and Company. Reliance Building. Chicago. 1894–95

brickwork, and the skeletal transparency of the pure curtain-wall envelope of the Reliance Building could not be greater. Although the detailing of the tile-facing takes the historic form of delicate Gothic shafts and stringcourses, the net effect is not a recognizably medievalizing image but rather of a gigantic weightless envelope of linear and planar elements. The continuous spandrels, the rhythmic bands of "Chicago" windows (central fixed panes, flanking double-hung sashes), and the slender vertical elements give clear dominance to the stratified horizontalism of the steel frame, yet the main impression is of a soaring buoyancy of the whole. In other words, the Reliance Building facade not only realizes the mechanical, layered character of the steel frame and its lightness (one-third the weight of an equivalent structure in stone), but exposes its aesthetic potential.

A very different, and more typical, Chicago interpretation of the steel frame was presented in a type created by Holabird and Roche in their Marquette Building of 1893–94 (fig. 12-19). Here it is not the lightness of the structure that is revealed in the curtain wall, but its brute strength. As in both the Monadnock Building and the Reliance Building, this interpretation was realized in an overlay of historicizing detail (as always in Chicago of the 1890s), in this case neither the ponderous Egyptian nor the fragile Gothic but the solid Classical—appearing in the drafted rustication of the base, quoinlike corner bays, and the paneling and cornicework of the top. Yet beneath it all, the powerful image of the rectilinear, modular frame dominates, an image of strong, continuous piers that support massive lintels recessed in the center bays. In the later work of Holabird and Roche, such as their 325 West Jackson Boulevard Building of 1904 (fig.12-20), the mechanomorphic interpretation of the

12-20   Holabird and Roche. 325 West Jackson Boulevard Building. Chicago. 1904

frame increasingly dominates the curtain wall as the Classicism recedes into minimal inflection and detail. This purist solution projected less visual presence than the prototype Marquette Building, but it was of high portent for the future: a generation later, Mies van der Rohe was to base his influential late style on the progeny of the Marquette design.

Louis Sullivan. The Reliance and Marquette buildings and their descendants were a forceful response to the challenge of the skyscraper; yet they seem almost simplistic compared with the works of the third team of Chicago designers, Adler and Sullivan. Perhaps even more than in the other Chicago workshops, their division of labor was sharp. Louis H. Sullivan was a self-indulgent poetic visionary, whose career leaned heavily on the presence of Adler, a tough-minded engineer, planner, and builder. But too much should not be made of Adler's support: even after their break in 1895, Sullivan continued to produce (although in shrinking volume) and created his most daring work, the Schlesinger and Meyer Store.

Sullivan, whose background included study at M.I.T. and the École des Beaux-Arts, is one of many architects of modern times who wrote a great deal, rarely illuminating his work and often clouding the issues, but his key ideas are possible to reconstruct. His famous dictum was "form follows function," by which he meant not mere functionalism, for which the phrase was unfortunately often taken, but something more complex. If Sullivan was a rationalist he was even more an evolutionist. One of his favorite words was "organic." "Function" was to lead to "form" not mechanically, but "organically" and "evolutionistically." The social and material environment, whose needs were so pressing, posed an evolutionist challenge to architecture, to which it responded organically, evolving new forms to meet those needs.

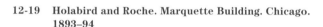

12-19   Holabird and Roche. Marquette Building. Chicago. 1893–94

The architect, for Sullivan, was to become a sort of natural force—a doctrine fully in keeping with the heady atmosphere of creative individualism of the early Modernist period. Free from allegiance to historical styles, the designer might generate mechanomorphic solutions to technical challenges and also biomorphic invention to satisfy the need for a living ornament and vital presence in architecture. Sullivan's biomorphic ornament was extraordinary, for it was intended to depict not any particular species but the process of botanical evolution itself. A building was thus a portrait of both the mechanomorphic and the biomorphic forces of evolution at work.

Of the many complex factors influencing Sullivan's style, a single building—Richardson's Marshall Field Store—was of paramount importance. The powerful structure had an effect on many architects of the Chicago School, but on Sullivan, whose Beaux-Arts training enabled him to appreciate its brilliance more fully, its impact was enduring. It was not only a model to emulate but a challenge to compete with Richardson on his own terms. Sullivan's style changed immediately upon the erection of the Field Store from a flimsy manner full of quirky detailing to massive Richardsonian effects. The fullest instance of this influence was his Auditorium Building of 1887–89, a huge, ten-story revision of the Field Store that was a theater, a hotel, and an office building in one. It was planned masterfully by Adler and detailed on the interior by Sullivan in his "evolutionistic" botanical style. But architectonically, the smaller, simpler Walker Warehouse that followed in 1888–89 (fig. 12-21) is more interesting to us, for it grappled with Richardson more boldly. Sullivan stripped the prototype of "Romanesque" rhythms, rustication, and carved ornament, and what remains is the essence of Richardson's conception, its strongly articulated and cohesive form. Sullivan intensified its inflection, the differentiation and interaction of its parts, giving it twin, arched Richardsonian entrances between trabeated flanking bays separated cleanly from the four-story arcade above. Now given a double rhythm, the arcade was succeeded by the quadruple rhythm of the trabeated final story that reflected the basement and that was drawn together by two simple stringcourses

12-21   Adler and Sullivan. Walker Warehouse. Chicago. 1888–89

12-22   Louis H. Sullivan. Schlesinger and Meyer Store. (Now Carson-Pirie-Scott Store). Chicago. 1899–1904

and nothing more. In its taut abstraction, the Walker Warehouse updated Richardson's scheme, bringing it closer to the Modernist ideal that Sullivan was seeking.

The Walker Warehouse is the "missing link" between Richardson and the first of Sullivan's masterpieces—the Wainwright

Building in St. Louis of 1890–91. The Auditorium Building and the Walker Warehouse still had old-fashioned masonry facades, for which massive Richardsonian arcading was appropriate. But the Wainwright Building was a ten-story edifice of rectilinear "skyscraper" construction (colorplate 70). Having mastered

Richardson's scheme in purified form, Sullivan was free to use it as a point of departure. Whereas the other Chicago architects exhibited the steel frame as a curtain wall with a superficial overlay of historicist detail, Sullivan refused to practice either such superficial historicism or mechanistic schematism. Behind the Marshall Field Store lay the grand Western tradition of the orders, which both Richardson and Sullivan had indelibly absorbed at the École. Sullivan now returned directly to that tradition and conflated it with what he had developed from Richardson. Thus, the Wainwright Building had the two-storied trabeated base of the Walker Warehouse—now extended uniformly across the front without arched entrances—above which rose the massive Richardsonian corners, his strong recessed spandrels, and finally the definitive horizontal form. However, these features no longer followed a Roman-medievalizing scheme of arches, but rather were gathered into a gigantic trabeated order. For this, Sullivan doubled the number of piers—only every other vertical corresponded to a real structural member behind it—giving the curtain wall a sculptural presence so reminiscent of Classical effects that the building has often been called a "fluted" skyscraper. The Classical image of the verticals was completed by the huge horizontal form they appear to support, a powerful story-high cornice scaled to the size of the whole building (and especially to the massive corners). The sumptuous terra-cotta detail of the cornice and the spandrels was Sullivan's creation, inspired by numerous sources (including the antique rinceau motif), but developed into altogether unique configurations.

In the Wainwright Building, Sullivan brilliantly met the immediate challenge of the skyscraper: the fitting of a strong visual organization on its multistoried, repetitive structure. He repeated the Wainwright formula in 1894–95 in the Guaranty Building in Buffalo, for whose thirteen-story curtain wall lighter proportions, more effusive detailing, terminal arches, and a row of oculi in place of the massive Wainwright cornice produced Sullivan's vision of the skyscraper as a "proud and soaring thing." Yet both buildings—the Wainwright more forcefully—retained traditional tectonic inflections, the main part of the structure appearing to weigh heavily on the massive two-storied base. Even though in 1894–95 such effects were old-fashioned, given the Modernist outlook already expressed in the Reliance Building, Sullivan refused to yield these traditions of the grand manner of European architecture. It was several years before he satisfied both voices—the grand manner and the mechanomorphic Modernism that spoke ever more insistently in the Chicago School toward 1900—in the building that is a *summa* of the Chicago skyscraper movement as well as his own career.

Sullivan's Schlesinger and Meyer Store (the Carson-Pirie-Scott Department Store after 1904) began in 1899 as a modest nine-story, three-bay addition to the booming retail establishment at the southeast corner of Madison and State Streets (figs. 12-22, 12-23). In 1903–4, the whole older store was replaced by an enlargement of the nine-story Madison Street addition, now extended in twelve-story form to the "world's busiest corner" and around it for seven bays along State Street. Although two post-Sullivan extensions of 1904 and 1960–61, of five and three bays respectively, continued the basic scheme, it is Sullivan's composite building of 1899–1904 that concerns us.

Its extraordinary design did not take shape all at once, as it

12-23 Louis H. Sullivan. Cast-iron ornament, Schlesinger and Meyer Store.

is often assumed, but in two phases. Perhaps because the addition of 1899 was such a modest affair in the middle of the block, Sullivan was satisfied to give it a simple facade of purist "Chicago" windows in a mechanomorphic grid. More remarkably, when he came to enlarge his building in 1903–4, he used this scheme as the basis for its much expanded elevation. Even if Sullivan had added nothing else to the design, the horizontals, given continuity and stretched out over the extensive facades, would have effectively rendered much of the "floating" Modernist effect seen in the Reliance Building. But Sullivan insisted on retaining in his buildings the traditional interaction of inflected parts—the play of middle against bottom and top, of the center against the sides. The Chicago window grid was the middle; but in place of an earlier massive entablature, Sullivan hollowed the top story into a balcony, with only a thin, sharply projecting cornice above it (sadly replaced in 1948). Even more imaginative, the base was a two-story, cast-iron screen of brilliantly inventive "evolutionistic" foliage that masked the connection of the building with the ground so that its piers seem to float up from nowhere.

But the interaction of parts was incomplete. What of the play of the sides against the middle, the adjustment of emphasis in the verticals that might give a focus to the sweeping horizontal lines? Again, Sullivan inverted the traditional configuration of Richardson, the École, and his own earlier skyscrapers: Rather than aggrandizing the outer corners of the building, he made the outer piers identical to the intermediate ones; only the central corner was accentuated, with a curved gathering of attenuated colonnettes, which generated a powerful but weightless jet of vertical energy, acting as a focal hub and emphasizing, by contrast, the floating lines of the horizontals.

The owners evidently requested a turretlike corner to recall the pavilion that had been attached to the original store (and also, as originally, to advertise the main entrance), and such picturesque massings were common in the Chicago of the nineties. But the true significance of Sullivan's corner pavilion is its role in an unprecedented composition, one in which Sullivan disassembled, inverted, and reassembled the form and meaning of the traditional facade, paradoxically creating a design that was rooted in the grand manner of Europe, and yet was uncompromisingly Modernist. The Carson-Pirie-Scott Store was thus among the first great works of the modern movement.

Early Frank Lloyd Wright. In 1904, the year that Sullivan completed his store, Frank Lloyd Wright, the youngest member of the Chicago movement, constructed an edifice in Buffalo, New York, that made an even more radical leap forward into Modernism. In his Larkin Building (figs. 12-24, 12-25), the concept of the office building was exploded and its fragments recrystallized into pure geometric form. Formally, the structure was almost totally abstract, yet it was also completely functional in its gathering of space around the office routine of a mail-order company. A rectangular, skylit atrium was surrounded by two circuits of slender piers—one at the court, the other at the building exterior—supporting the deep galleries that provided most of the work space, well-lit from the court skylight and from bands of Chicago-window fenestration. Several secondary elements were added to this core, including an extension to the north that provided reception facilities, lavatories, lockers, etc. Formally more important were the giant corner piers, to which were appended at the ends of the building slightly lower, similar piers containing stairways and the ductwork of an innovative ventilation system. Although in plan and in function these piers were secondary, on the exterior they acted as primary form-giving elements, appearing to support colossal lintels formed by the upper story of galleries. This megastructure framed and was partially supported by the smaller-scale pier-and-gallery armature. New and particularly characteristic of Wright were the highly integrated form and function of the building, and the interpenetration of its geometric blocks of space and structure. Wright really meant what he said in 1901 when he wrote: "The tall modern office building is the machine pure and simple." The Larkin Building was not that "tall," but its industrial-looking structure seemed huge and powerful in a machinelike way.

Although its gallery and pier armature derived from the Chicago skyscraper, the concept of the Larkin Building as a whole did not. Rather, it was the transposition into an office building of Wright's personal style, which had taken shape not where the bourgeoisie worked, but where it lived: the domestic architecture of the affluent. But so complex is the evolution of Wright's extraordinary series of houses built during the early phase of his long career, that we can only begin to give an idea of it here.

Wright's flamboyant personality and sense of prophetic mission were nourished by his pioneer mother, who hung engravings of cathedrals over his crib in her determination that her son become an architect. Such real and mythical biographical factors fed Wright's unique style and the development of an ineradicable personal cult among his students and public. He was the most futuristic of all the Modernists, especially in his

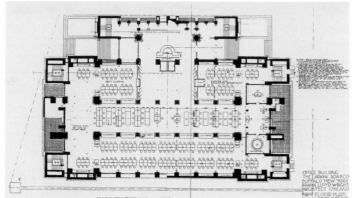

12-24 Larkin Building and plan

early work, which leaped so far ahead of its time that it took the rest of the world nearly a generation to catch up.

Less than two years of engineering study at the University of Wisconsin convinced Wright that he did not want to be an engineer. But the time was not wasted: only a trained engineer could have invented the structure (for example, in the Larkin Building) necessary to create his three-dimensional new forms. Although his apprenticeship in the architectural studio of Joseph Lyman Silsbee lasted less than a year (1887), Silsbee was a skilled practitioner of the latest Anglo-American domestic styles, which were to be Wright's own point of departure. It is harder to define what Wright took from his most important student phase, five years in the office of Adler and Sullivan (1888–93). Sullivan's mannerisms appeared superficially in Wright's earliest work, but were quickly shed. Sullivan's metier was the commercial building of the Chicago School mainstream; Wright began with houses and they remained his bread-and-butter. Sullivan's contribution was all facade; Wright worked radically in three dimensions almost from the beginning. Like Sullivan, Wright's imagination was liberated by the notion of the "organic" in architecture, but he meant by it the evolutionist concept of architecture responding to new materials and needs (and not evolutionist ornament in Sullivan's botanical sense). Wright's best-known "organic" notion—that houses should open toward and conform to the lines of the landscape—had little meaning for Sullivan and his self-contained structures. Wright always

12-25   Frank Lloyd Wright. Interior, Larkin Building. Buffalo. 1904

called Sullivan his *lieber Meister* (beloved master), but he was his student not in terms of stylistic allegiance, but as the heir to Sullivan's former preeminence.

Wright claimed another unusual source in his early career: a childhood experience with a pedagogical toy, a set of Froebel Blocks that his ambitious mother had bought for the architect-to-be at the 1876 World's Fair. Their possibilities of geometric interplay may lie behind such works as the Larkin Building, for they would have had a profound effect, according to a passage of Wright's later writings: "That early kindergarten expe-

12-26   Japanese temple at the Chicago World's Fair. 1893

**12-27   Frank Lloyd Wright. Rear view, Winslow House.
River Forest, Illinois. 1893**

rience with the straight line; the flat plane; the square; the triangle; the circle! If I wanted more, the square modified by the triangle gave the hexagon—the circle modified by the straight line would give the octagon . . . adding thickness . . . the square became the cube, the triangle the tetrahedron, the circle the sphere. These primary forms and figures were the secret of all effects . . . which were ever got into the architecture of the world. . . . All are in my fingers to this day."

A further early inspiration, played down by Wright although its crucial importance to him is obvious, was Japan. He was an avid collector of Japanese prints, and in 1893 he had the opportunity to see the small temple exhibited at the Chicago World's Fair (fig. 12-26). (In 1905, he made the first of several visits to Japan itself.) The temple appealed to him as a poignant contrast to the bombastic Neoclassicism of the fairgrounds. More intrinsically, he was drawn to its extended "floating" roofs, its absence of "walls" in the Western sense, in their place only a skeletal framework of slender wooden supports as the only barrier subdividing the free-flowing interior and dividing it from the outdoors. Its feeling for materials, especially for wood used in the simplest possible way, was close to Wright's own love for this medium.

Against the background of these varied but overlapping factors, we can trace the unfolding of Wright's early style by examining three of his houses. The Winslow House in River Forest, Illinois (colorplate 75) was a study in contrasts, revealing the

many directions in which Wright was being pulled in 1893. The front of the house was all geometric severity, rigidly quadratic and symmetrical, opening only in a few widely spaced, squarish plate-glass windows punched through the wall. In its post-historicist coolness and simplicity, the facade paralleled the work of Richardson and Voysey; yet where they were casually informal, Wright was austerely formal, reducing all to uniform abstraction and taut control, sharpening the contrasts of material and relief.

The rear garden facade of the Winslow House (fig. 12-27) was so different from the front that it was hardly recognizable as part of the same building. It shattered the front's boxlike order with its splintered, aggressive forms thrusting every which way—a dining porch jutting forth, a *porte cochère* springing sideways, a wrought-iron screen lunging forward, and a polygonal stairtower pushing through the roof, which itself was fragmented into many directions. A dark band of Sullivanesque interlaced ornament on the second story undercut the solidity of the roof, which, with its deeply extended eaves, seemed almost to float.

The Winslow House was a lesson in Wright's avowed aim of "breaking the box," but it was only a beginning. The heterogeneity of form on the rear facade still carried the signs of Anglo-American domestic currents, and the whole lacked integration. By the end of the decade Wright found his way out of the jumble-vs.-order dilemma of the Winslow House, and his solution had no better example than the Ward Willits House in Highland Park (another Chicago suburb) of 1902, often considered the first of his Prairie House masterpieces (figs. 12-28, 12-29). Abstraction was the main key to the transformation of style; heterogeneity of form and detail had given way to a uniform vocabulary of pure line, surface, and volumes, which permitted configurations that were dynamic and open, yet tautly unified because of the abstract design basis. This abstraction affected the plan, space, and massing, as well as the structural shapes, so that we confront not a box on one side and picturesque fragmentation on the other, but a house conceived from its central fireplace core out to its edges as an integral, cross-shaped configuration. Its free-flowing interiors opened through the near-continuous bands of windows to the outdoors, whose space interpenetrates the deep porches beneath long, low hip roofs that carry the eye in every direction out into the low-lying "Prairie" landscape.

Comparing the Winslow and Ward Willits houses reveals that Wright had found a new method of breaking the box. By "box" Wright meant walls, which in the Winslow House were retained, only punctured, bent, or folded in a variety of ways. But now murality itself was under attack, and Japan had become Wright's ally in this assault. To his elevation, he freely applied the Japanese model of a wooden skeleton framing geometric panels, latticework, and openings, transposing it into Western terms, into a thicker structural armature of piers and slabs. Superimposed over this armature were window-bands and a network of stucco panels in dark frames that mimicked Japanese latticework.

In the Ward Willits House, the breaking of the box was still incomplete—much wall, however disguised, remained—and the abstract effect depended on a Japanese overlay. Within a few years, Wright took the final step, and in his great Robie House of 1909 (figs. 12-30, 12-32) there were neither walls nor overt traces of Japan, but as abstract a conception as was possible in

12-28   Frank Lloyd Wright. Ward Willits House. Highland Park, Illinois. 1902

12-29   Main floor plan, Ward Willits House

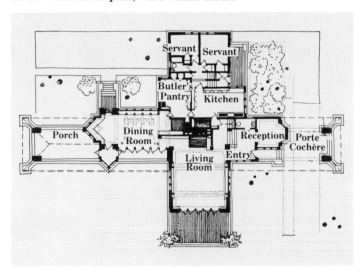

the terms of the Prairie House. The box of the Winslow facade had vanished. In its place was a three-dimensional interweaving of space and geometric blocks (not unlike what Wright had possibly made out of his childhood toys), diverse levels of parapets, balconies, and low-slung cantilevered roofs (with internal steel supports) hung on rows of short, narrow piers around a powerful central chimney. Wright had already exaggerated the extended horizontals in earlier houses, but in the Robie House this stretching of proportions not only leads the eye out to the landscape but energizes the whole building. The elongation, vector-shaped "prow," rows of windows, and decklike terraces suggest an ocean liner (and such Wright houses were often dubbed "Dampferstil," or "steamship style," by the admiring and much influenced Germans). But the lifting eaves of the main roof and its intersection with the cross-arm and upper roof suggest the complex, openwork image of the just-invented airplane. And even today one feels that, if a large propeller were attached to the facade near the chimney and started up, the "airplane house" would slowly but surely take off!

The tension between the dynamic openness and protective enclosure in the Winslow House was more integrated in the Robie House: for all its transparency and space/mass interpene-

tration, the building was closed to the street viewer. The entrance was hidden off to the right, and the house was secure behind clifflike tiers of unbroken parapets, like some medieval city wall, so that it formed a fortress as well as a plane and a (battle)ship.

Such dualism also pervaded Wright's interiors. On the one hand, they were given a radical degree of openness, with space flowing (as in the Robie House) from room to room without conventional walls and doors, and to the outdoors through ribbons of windows, balconies, and terraces. Yet this centrifugal freedom was countered by powerful centripetal impulses. The fireplace, from which the house radiated, was also the hub to which it gravitated—a huge masonry "hearth" that for Wright was equivalent to a kind of domestic altar of worship dedicated to the "gods of shelter." The surroundings tended to complement the hearth, especially in the low-ceilinged, heavily paneled living rooms of many of his houses. Paradoxically, Wright's preoccupation with shelter is also seen in rooms of overtly opposite features, such as the living room of the Francis W. Little House of 1913 (fig. 12-31), the grandest of all his early domestic interiors (and now installed in the Metropolitan Museum of Art in New York). This spectacular room formed a typically Wrightian transformation of the open, two-leveled Japanese-influenced interior elevation observed earlier in the Shingle Style. The friezelike element below the ceiling became a continuous band of lateral windows; the heavy, beamed ceiling was covered with graceful windowlike linear patterns around low-relief grillwork (in effect not unlike the Newcomb House floor inlay); and the clutter of Victorian furniture was replaced by Wright's own designs inspired by Morris's Arts and Crafts movement, each piece an example of his architectural style in miniature, to create the total environment to which Wright, like Morris, was passionately devoted. But what gave this open and spacious room its sense of protective enclosure was a gathering of effects: dark wood, the twin cage of surrounding heavy beams, and especially the ceiling, which strongly delimited the space within it and the area within the rings of beams beneath it. With such interiors, and the exteriors that complemented them, Wright's early style reached a level of achievement he would not gain again until the mid-1930s.

12-30   Frank Lloyd Wright. Robie House. Chicago. 1909

12-31   Frank Lloyd Wright. Living room, Francis W. Little House. 1913. (The Metropolitan Museum of Art, New York)

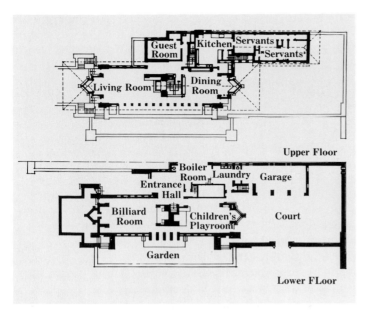

12-32 Plan, Robie House

Fantasy and Expressionism in Europe. During the early modern period in Europe, no movement was comparable in power to the Chicago School, but it made up for this in experimental vitality and diversity in the search for new forms. In the broadest sense, European developments can be divided into two parallel formal currents. Although practically all architects at the time supported a "return to nature" for inspiration, some meant this more literally than others and turned to the biomorphic, and sometimes geomorphic, world as the central source for their work, which often spilled over into exoticism, irrationality, and ultimately the intense exaggeration of effects called Expressionism. The countercurrent also found inspiration in the real world (as opposed to the past), but in the man-made world of the machine, along with the abstract realm of geometry. In practice, the two theoretically antithetical currents were rarely pure and are to be seen as broad trends with much fluidity and overlapping. Our distinctions are possible because one direction or the other generally predominated in a given body of work.

Art Nouveau was one of the terms used to describe the international vogue for biomorphic fantasy in design that had originated in the decorative arts of the 1880s and appeared in architecture by the early nineties. The movement took its name from the Paris shop established in 1895 specializing in the sensational new style, which received similarly revealing names elsewhere—Stile Liberty in Italy (after the famous London shop), Jugendstil (youth style) in Germany, and Modernismo in Barcelona. The names given to the new mode expressed well its initial impression in the ponderous, late Victorian environment in which it was born—a springlike naturalism full of youth, freedom, novelty, and modernity. The blossom faded as quickly as it had bloomed, however, for like every sensational style, Art Nouveau consumed itself in the need for ever more extravagant forms. By 1900, reaction had set in most everywhere (with the notable exception of Barcelona). Although by 1905–10 Art Nouveau was dead, it had a successor in what is usually called Expressionism.

In architecture, the Art Nouveau phase of biomorphic fantasy had three main centers: Brussels, Paris and Nancy, and Barcelona, through which the style spread and developed in more or less that order. It is generally agreed that Victor Horta, working in Brussels from 1892, was the first architect to take up the fashion in a significant way. As seen in the entrance hall of Horta's most important work, the Tassel House at No. 6, rue Paul-Emile Janson (formerly 12, rue de Turin) of 1892–93 (fig. 12-33), wrought iron was his principal means of translating into the three dimensions of architecture what had originated in the decorative arts as two-dimensional patterns of ink, dye, or paint on paper and fabric. The early- and mid-nineteenth-century rage for cast iron exploited its capacity to reproduce historicist facade detail, but it was the ductility of wrought iron that attracted Horta—its capacity to be drawn out into long, sinuous, biomorphic curves of springlike strength and vitality. Interestingly, it was Viollet-le-Duc who appeared to have inadvertently stimulated the Art Nouveau use of iron. Several of his plates illustrate how medieval stone foliage designs could be converted into ferrous decoration.

In the Tassel House, the ironwork served as the primary means of organizing and animating space. Around it, floor mosaics and painted walls and ceilings took up the whiplash patterns, which, together with the curving surfaces of walls, stairs, and ceiling, gave the interior the typical flowing impression of Art Nouveau. The curvilinearity of the style may at first recall eighteenth-century Rococo interiors; but whereas the Classically-based Rococo was intricate, gilded, and bounded artifice, the Brussels interior had openness, transparency, and asymmetrical flux. Moreover, although Rococo lines were full of vitality, Horta's whiplash curves were far more naturalistic and looked like real tendrils, which have sprouted from the supercharged soil of a miraculous springtime.

Horta transformed architecture into a semblance of natural life and growth and dissolved the "box" into a mellifluous configuration. But however much Horta's walls may be warped, overrun with decoration, and pierced with curvilinear openings, they remain walls. The "box," in other words, was twisted or melted into a novel, biomorphic shape, but it remained intact; indeed, much of the power of Horta's architecture arose from this struggle between traditional geometric stasis and the life forces that were brought to move it.

Yet the Art Nouveau quality of the Tassel House and of many of its descendants in Belgium and France remained essentially one of effects, not of fundamentals. Rarely, if ever, did the style take over the *whole* structure of traditional or monumental building types. Rather, this occurred in "submonumental" forms such as temporary exhibition buildings and new, utilitarian structures. The year 1900 saw the opening of the Paris subway system (*métro*), for which the prominent Parisian architect Hector Guimard designed the entrance pavilions, a good number of which survive as the most prominent and purest works of the French Art Nouveau (fig. 12-34). Comprising three types—open and closed entrances and ticket offices—Guimard's cast-and wrought-iron pavilionlike structures were halfway between furniture and the adventurous ferrovitreous construction of the nineteenth century (such as the Eiffel Tower and the Galerie des Machines). Guimard's handling of iron at first glance recalled Horta's, but it was actually quite different. Ultimately inspired by the intricately molded stucco work of the Rococo, Guimard exploited not only the ductility of wrought iron but the sculptural potential of cast iron to create a unique Art Nouveau idiom.

If Horta's designs were all whiplash tendrils, Guimard's sinuous, intricately sculpted and molded forms suggested (as in Sullivan's ornament) the evolution of some strange new form of life, partly veined stalks and tendrils, partly zoomorphic creatures at once bonelike and insectlike. His subway entrance looked as if a bizarre future species had sprouted from the earth to hold signs and to light the way down to the underworld, to its futuristic means of transportation.

Guimard's *métro* pavilions are among the most intense realizations of French Art Nouveau, yet they look restrained against the sensational work in Barcelona of Antoni Gaudí. In his Casa Batlló of 1905–7, the lower parts of the facade are literally skeletal, with the stone masonry shaped into an undulating framework so unmistakably resembling a concatenation of dinosaur-sized bones that it can only be called "osteomorphic" (fig. 12-35). Although the wall reasserts itself, the facade above it gently moves beneath a reptilian skin of variegated tiles and inlaid plates, and it rises to a multicolored roof whose spiny crest sweeps up and down like a dinosaur's spine. But the tiers of balconies are the most haunting aspect of the upper facade: wrought-iron forms more skull-like than masklike, macabre, as in the dreams of a demented amateur naturalist returning from a visit to a paleontology museum.

Gaudí's Casa Milá of 1905–10 was an even more extreme transformation of the "box," for, unlike the Casa Batlló which was a remodeling of a pre-existing structure, it was entirely built by Gaudí and occupied a large corner site (figs. 12-36, 12-37). In defending his luxury apartment house against its

12-33 Victor Horta. Interior stair, Tassel House. Brussels. 1892–93

12-34 Hector Guimard. Métro station. Paris. 1900

12-35 Antoni Gaudí. Facade, Casa Batlló. Barcelona. 1905–7

12-36　Antoni Gaudí. Facade, Casa Milá. Barcelona. 1905–10

12-37　**Plan of typical floor, Casa Milá**

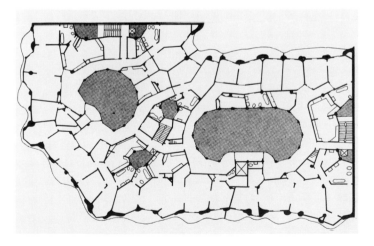

critics, Gaudí insisted that there was no such thing as a straight line in nature; whether or not this is true of nature, it is certainly true of his building, including its amorphous plan. The facade—built of massive stone blocks although looking like concrete—reflects Gaudí's geomorphic vision, for the hollowed stone masses suggest, as Gaudí indicated, both the waves of the sea and the cliffs and mountains that rise above it, with seaweedlike clumps of wrought iron that form the balustrades. Gaudí's naturalistic dreams for architecture usually entailed

some truly fantastic touch, and the Casa Milá does not disappoint us, for standing above the surflike roof are strange chimney forms that suggest monstrous, helmeted guardian figures.

Gaudí can be understood partly in terms of the northern European Art Nouveau that he knew through publications and its eager reception in the progressive cultural atmosphere of *fin de siècle* Barcelona. But he was also caught up in the intense nationalism of the time, which for him involved an attachment to wider Iberian, Mediterranean architectural traditions—to the rich encrustations of the Plateresque, the extravagant Spanish Baroque, the exotic Moorish edifices of southern Spain, and the even more exotic vernacular modes of North Africa (not to mention the giant anthills he saw there). To this tradition Gaudí brought not only his individualism and visionary passion, but a surprising factor: his personal interpretation, or rather misinterpretation, of Viollet-le-Duc. Thus, when the French theorist advocated "organic rationalism" and compared it metaphorically to the organic functionalism of the parts of a tree or an animal skeleton, Gaudí built a structure that literally looked like a tree, a skeleton, or whatever. Or, when Viollet-le-Duc illustrated in the *Entretiens sur l'architecture* the inward-leaning corner columns of Greek Doric architecture, and for clarity exaggerated this leaning, Gaudí built his columns leaning strongly inward (as in the facade of the Casa Milá), theoretically to absorb the vaulting thrust and do away with buttresses, but in reality for the visually shocking

12-38　Detail of spires, Church of the Sagrada Familia

the same story, whose fundamental theme, despite national variants, was the preoccupation with biomorphic and geomorphic fantasy. But just as Gaudí's Mediterranean context set him off from the cooler northern atmosphere of Art Nouveau, so did a number of factors distinguish Expressionism.

One factor may well have been place. That Expressionism was essentially a German movement was probably not accidental. Repeatedly, Germany had at times exhibited a tendency toward mysticism and emotional extremes in its art—the Late Gothic, the Late Baroque, the "Sturm und Drang" phase of Romanticism. Nor was the timing of the Expressionist outbreak fortuitous: it was bound up with the traumas of World

12-39　Antoni Gaudí. Church of the Sagrada Familia. Barcelona. Begun 1884

effects that resulted. For Gaudí's unbridled genius, the doctrine of rationalism was, paradoxically, an essential factor in generating the flights of irrationalism that were at the center of his art.

Gaudí was a devout Catholic, and, although he poured his fantasy into many forms, he saved his greatest flights of imagination for religious architecture. He worked on his Church of the Sagrada Familia (figs. 12-38, 12-39) from 1884 until his death, but was never able to complete more than a fragment of it. Thus, the famous south transept facade does not front any interior but rises as an immense freestanding monument to Gaudí, and includes work from most phases of his career. The inner facade wall reveals the hard-edged effects of his pre–Art Nouveau years; the portals, which from a distance look like a melted-down Reims, in fact present a kind of naturalistic rendering of the Grotto of the Nativity in Bethlehem; while above rise four extraordinary towers, begun after 1910, only one completed by Gaudí's death. These spires are formed of slender ribs separated by irregularly spaced blocks, terminating in surrealist, wheel-like finials erupting with spherical globules. Natural processes of growth and change appear to have escaped natural limits.

Gaudí's bizarre architectural world had such affinities to the movement known as Expressionism that it can be seen as an early Catalan parallel to the movement as much as an outgrowth of Franco-Flemish Art Nouveau. In reality, Art Nouveau, Gaudí, and Expressionism were three overlapping chapters of

War I and associated events, and the movement peaked in the years 1918–21. The severe economic deprivations experienced in Germany during these years and immediately following not only made for a grim atmosphere but meant that almost nothing was built. Barred from the realities of construction sites, architects were free to build castles in the air. The situation was reminiscent of Revolutionary France in the late eighteenth century, when the unemployed Boullée and Ledoux created their most extravagant fantasies. And as in France, the specter of revolution in postwar Germany affected the mostly left-wing architects, who were steeped in German political socialism as well as in the nineteenth-century Arts and Crafts socialist dream of a better world through good architecture and design. That such expectations bore so little connection with the dire material and political realities of postwar Germany made the fires of architectural utopianism burn all the brighter.

In this emotionally charged atmosphere, the irrational became the norm. In place of Sullivan's "form follows function," we find the pronouncement of a leading architect, Hans Poelzig, "form rises out of the mystic abyss," and the words of the leading Expressionist theorist, Bruno Taut, "architecture . . . consists exclusively of powerful emotions and addresses itself exclusively to the emotions." Architects drew on the philosophers Nietzsche and Bergson and saw themselves as spiritual mediums who submitted themselves to the forces of life as well as to the *Zeitgeist*; this inspired utopian architectural visions that were meant to have a profound psychological and spiritual effect on the quality of life.

These architectural condensations of "emotions" and "life forces" mostly took the form of polemics, tracts, exhibitions, models, and especially drawings; several Expressionist architects found work designing movie sets (among them the famous, still shocking *Cabinet of Dr. Caligari*). Expressionist architecture, however, whether fantasized or built, tended to coalesce around several key biomorphic and geomorphic motifs, the most important being The Creature, The Cave (and Mountain), and The Crystal. These images were already present in Art Nouveau, but in Germany they tended to assume an aggressive, often charmless, visionary intensity unlike Art Nouveau's springtime efflorescence.

The most important surviving structure realized in the manner of German Expressionism was one of the many creaturelike designs projected by Erich Mendelsohn—the Einstein Tower outside Potsdam, Germany (fig. 12-40). Built in 1920–21 as an observatory where research was carried out by an associate of Albert Einstein, the structure embodied an eerie combination of

12-41   Hans Poelzig. Entrance foyer, Schauspielhaus. Berlin, 1919

12-42   Auditorium, Schauspielhaus

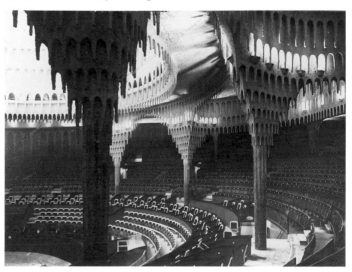

12-40   Erich Mendelsohn. Einstein Tower. Near Potsdam, Germany. 1920–21

zoomorphic form with the world of technology. Intended as a concrete structure, but built in brick covered with a sculptural layer of concrete, it makes an unmistakably feline impression. It seems a powerfully muscled, crouching beast with extended forepaws, ribs, and torso, its head the observatory half-dome with its farseeing nocturnal eyes—all as if Egypt's Sphinx had been reborn in the twentieth century as an Einsteinian Sphinx that asks and answers ultimate questions.

Internally, the Einstein Tower is disappointingly conventional. The foremost Expressionist interior—or set of interiors—was Poelzig's Grosses Schauspielhaus of 1919 in Berlin. At the time, theater in general was regarded as an essential experience in the liberation of the human spirit, and it was Poelzig's intent

12-43   Bruno Taut. Glass Pavilion. Cologne. 1914

12-44   Staircase, Glass Pavilion

12-45   Ludwig Mies van der Rohe. Project for Office Building for Friedrichstrasse. Berlin. 1921

to create in his theater (actually a drastic remodeling of a circus building) an intense psychological atmosphere that would heighten such an experience. The entrance foyer (fig. 12-41) was a circular room around a central column in the form of a palm tree, whose lines extended across the ceiling and down the walls, all painted a vivid shade of green. The main event was the theater itself (fig. 12-42), made to resemble a cave by the thick tiers of stalactites hung from the ceiling, painted blood-red, and illuminated by hundreds of multicolored lights hidden in their depths to suggest the gleaming iridescence of minerals. It perhaps suggested the cave in which lived Nietzsche's Zarathustra (a literary role model for the Expressionists), the primitive cave in which religion and art were born.

The form that fascinated Expressionists most, however, was the crystal. This was not as strange a preoccupation as one might at first think, for the veneration of crystals had a long tradition. It runs from Saint John the Evangelist's description of the New Jerusalem being "clear as glass" and the River of Life "bright as crystal," to Boullée's crystalline pyramids, London's Crystal Palace, and Viollet-le-Duc's rationalist ideal of the crystal as nature's perfect structural model. The Expressionists' immediate prophet was Paul Scheerbart, whose visionary book *Glas Architektur*, of 1914, was filled with visions of diamond castles, emerald domes, sapphire towers, and futurist dreams of a complete new glass culture. Crystal was magical, concealing nothing; it was a bridge to the supernatural and had the capacity to capture, fragment, and multiply the light of the cosmos. So potent were its transcendental powers that, according to Scheerbart, "a person who daily sets eyes on the splendor of glass cannot do wicked deeds."

In the crystal, the escapist Expressionist cult of irrationality found its symbolic medium. Theorist Bruno Taut was so affected by Scheerbart that his Glass Pavilion (figs. 12-43, 12-44) at the Werkbund Exhibition in Cologne, in 1914, was dedicated to the author. Taut's most significant crystalline creation, however, was not a building but an imaginary world of *Alpine Architektur*, depicted in his 1919 book of that title. There he had an apocalyptic vision in which all continents were carpeted with glass and precious stones in the form of "ray domes" and "sparkling palaces," a world extended into the cosmos in a "stellar architecture."

Beyond Taut's temporary Glass Pavilion, little was actually built to express such utopian crystallography. One architect, however, Mies van der Rohe, later a major figure, in 1919–21 produced a series of projects for glass-walled skyscrapers that are Expressionist and more. The most important of these was a sheer, prismatic, star-shaped massing calculated to reflect light like a crystal (fig. 12-45). It was not implausible, but buildable, and foreshadowed the epidemic of glass-walled structures of the mid- and late twentieth century, most of them immense in scale but devoid of the soul and feeling of the Expressionists's radiant dream.

The European Mainstream. Art Nouveau and Expressionism touched deep chords of the human spirit, but another side of early European Modernism was in closer touch with the realities of the modern age. The mechanomorphic world, with an overlay of geometric abstraction and Classicism, played an increasingly dominant role. Prior to the 1920s, the situation was very fluid, and alternative currents ran back and forth between schools and often within the work of individual architects. Nowhere is this complex situation better illustrated than in the trend that, improbable as it may seem, spanned Glasgow and Vienna. In both cities, the new current was associated with a reaction to Art Nouveau's unstructured amorphousness. In Glasgow, Charles Rennie Mackintosh was the brilliant leader of a small Arts and Crafts coterie; like many early European Modernists, he realized his formal vision more in the decorative arts than in architecture. He is often pictured as an Art Nouveau designer, which is true to the extent that he began in that camp; but while never completely renouncing Art Nouveau, he transmuted its convolutions into a sparser idiom, which he often combined with severe geometric abstractions.

Mackintosh's most important building is the Glasgow School of Art, of 1897–1909 (fig. 12-46). Most of the expanse of the main facade is opened up with fenestration that gives north light to studios lining this side of the structure. These large, severe rectangular windows descend from the Tudor tradition via the Queen Anne revival, here subdivided by plain, unmolded transoms and mullions. Because they are so inflated in size and set in enframing masonry of such rectilinear severity, the wall assumes a functionalist, abstract, modern look. In contrast, the monumental entrance bay of the facade is eccentric and eclectic. In it are set together a Queen Anne oriel, a Baroque aedicula, and a Scottish baronial tower, creating an

12-46   Charles Rennie Mackintosh. Facade, Glasgow School of Art. 1897–1909

12-47   Josef Maria Olbrich. Secession Building. Vienna. 1898–99

asymmetric, yet coherent whole. Not the least effective of the elements contributing to the facade's vitality is the overlay of Mackintosh's sinuous Art Nouveau ironwork. Thin screens of fencework and railings with their ball-flowers and curligigs, a taut arch carrying the lantern over the steps, and weird brackets for window cleaners's scaffolds add an elusive dimension.

In the late 1890s, Mackintosh became a sensation on the continent through a number of publications and exhibitions. His work was received with much enthusiasm in Vienna, where a group of gifted architects was searching for an alternative to the florid local brand of Art Nouveau. The first architectural work of Viennese Modernism served also as its manifesto: the quarters of the Vienna Secession (fig. 12-47), the movement founded in 1897 among whose leaders was the building's architect, Josef Maria Olbrich. Designed for exhibitions, the building has a skylighted interior framed by closed outer walls that Olbrich formed into a geometric massing enlivened with both historicist allusion and nonhistoricist decoration. The facade of this Temple of Art is reminiscent of an Egyptian pylon. On it appear the three Muses (over the doorway) and laurel leaves, which form the gilded metal openwork of the building's most unusual feature—a spherical "dome" resting lightly in a vaguely Egyptian cradle of truncated piers. The facade was consciously intended as a witty response to Fischer von Erlach's domed eighteenth-century Baroque Karlskirche facing it across the square (fig. 9-55). Like the church, the Secession building housed "sacred" rites; its dome was meant as a spherical laurel tree embodying an occult symbolism related to the tree-of-life tradition, here connected with the visitor's initiation into the "sacred mysteries of art." Evocative of *fin de siècle* Vienna, this symbolism, as well as its historicist overlay, distinguished the Secession House from the contemporary work of Frank Lloyd Wright that at first looks so similar. But Wright was far more radical in his analysis of buildings into pure, geometric solids and interpenetrating spaces—a step never fully taken by the Viennese School.

A close associate of Olbrich was Josef Hoffmann, the principal founder in 1903 of the Wiener Werkstätte, the Viennese parallel of the Arts and Crafts movement. He was the most brilliant of the Viennese decorative-arts Modernists, and his post–Art Nouveau architecture was so marked by its obsessively cubiform vocabulary that he was given the nickname of Quadratl-Hoffmann. His Purkersdorf Sanitarium of 1903 (fig. 12-48) embodied this geometricizing tendency at its severest. But his most splendid building was a lavish residence, the Palais Stoclet in Brussels (fig. 12-49) of 1905–11, built for one

12-48   Josef Hoffmann. Purkersdorf Sanitarium. 1903. (After Sekler)

12-49   Josef Hoffmann. Palais Stoclet. Brussels. 1905–11

of his wealthy private clients. It is made almost exclusively of a variety of rectilinear forms and fragments, shaped into a complex, picturesque exterior with a dazzling array of interiors. Although devoid of ornament of the usual sort, it was encrusted inside and out with luxurious materials, notably bronze-framed marble, looking like a blow-up of one of Hoffmann's more elaborate decorative objects.

If the Modernism of Hoffmann and Olbrich was essentially geometric, that of their teacher, Otto Wagner, in his Vienna Postal Savings Bank, 1904–6, was one of functionalist, high-technology mechanomorphism. Wagner, born in 1841, was a generation older than most of his pupils. Although he had moved in the 1890s from historicism to Art Nouveau and the ostensibly functionalist position that "nothing that is not practical can be beautiful," none of his other Modernist works attained the level of the Postal Savings Bank (fig. 12-50). Its interior clearly came from the nineteenth-century ferrovitreous tradition of the railway station and the Crystal Palace and its followers. Wagner's Postal Savings Bank was the first major example of the nonhistoricist reshaping of engineering vocabulary into monumental form. The architectural refinement of proportion and detail was seen in the cross section with its post–Art Nouveau juxtaposition of flat and sweeping curves in the delicate aluminum (not iron) vault framework, and in the even illumination. Slender piers tapered downward with a subtle elegance, their rivetheads formed into decorative patterns. Not the least in this imaginative interior were the extraordinary furnishings—lamps, desks, stools, and above all the robotlike, cylindrical air ducts lining the walls.

For Adolf Loos, the fourth major figure of Vienna's architectural avant-garde, the Modernist directions pursued by his colleagues were not taken far enough, for he aspired to an extreme, geometric purism. The closest he came to realizing his idea was in two modest houses: the terraced, flat-roofed "Algerian" Scheu House of 1912, and the better-known Steiner House (fig. 12-51) of 1910, both in Vienna. His point of departure in the latter was Hoffmann's Purkersdorf Sanitarium design—a stripped, stuccoed, cubiform box, slightly U-shaped, opened by simple, rectangular windows, and articulated only by a thin, flat cornice. In Loos's House, however, the geometry was bolder, especially the curved roof rising from the street facade; the massing was more compact and assertive; the windows appeared more "functionalist," especially the horizontal units; and the cornice was thinner. Whereas Hoffmann's design looked like a Palladian villa stripped, geometricized, and made to look modern, Loos's house seemed inherently a radical exercise in functionalist, geometric purism.

The Steiner House was bold and forceful, but it would never have acquired its reputation had it not been connected with Loos's sensational theoretical ideas dealing with the question of ornament. Until Loos, nobody was against it in principle, only against its unnecessary or inappropriate use. This was a dilemma for Modernists, since they had to decide where and how to create a new ornamental vocabulary. Loos's drastic solution was to eliminate ornament altogether. What eventually gave this simple, if radical, notion currency was his essay of 1908 entitled *Ornament and Crime*, in which ornament was associated with scatological graffiti, as in public lavatory scrawlings—infantile, primitive, erotic, criminal, and irrelevant. For Loos, an ornamented building was like a tattooed

12-50   Otto Wagner. Interior, Postal Savings Bank. Vienna. 1904–6

12-51   Adolf Loos. Steiner House. Vienna. 1910

man. Although tattooing was permitted among Papuan cannibals, a "modern man who tattooes himself is either a criminal or a degenerate," and so is "a man of our times who smudges erotic symbols on walls"—all ornament being, in Loos's mind, of erotic origin. The underlying sexual hysteria conveyed by this argument might have given Sigmund Freud, had he chanced upon the article, cause for amused confirmation of his interpretation of late-nineteenth-century Viennese emotional pathology. But for Loos, the upshot was inescapable: "The evolution of culture marches with the elimination of ornament from useful objects."

In postwar Paris, to which Loos migrated in 1923 and where his article was translated and republished, his doctrine was enthusiastically received. For the architects in the process of creating High Modernism, anti-ornamentalism was a key factor, and Loos's Steiner House was seen as an important precedent. But anti-ornamentalism was not the only new architectural idea celebrated in postwar Paris; among the ideological complements to Loos's puritanical extremism was Futurism.

As the enthusiastic reaction by a handful of young Milanese radicals to the arrival of the Industrial Revolution in northern Italy around 1900, Futurism was the most extreme of all Modernist positions. The Futurists called for architecture to be totally absorbed by the Industrial Revolution. Loos's buildings were stark, but they were still in the monumental tradition of the West, built as enduring Platonic solids. For the Futurists, that tradition was dead: the Machine lived, splendid in its speed and power. A roaring racing car, proclaimed the Futurist Manifesto of 1909 that launched the movement, is more beautiful than the *Victory of Samothrace*, that paragon of ancient statuary. And "just as the ancients drew their inspiration . . . from the natural world, so we . . . must find our inspiration in the new mechanical world," wrote the architect Antonio Sant'Elia in 1914, in what was to become the Manifesto of Futurist Architecture. Thus, the new buildings can no longer resemble anything of the architectural past, but rather must follow a "definitive Futurist aesthetic of giant locomotives, spiral tunnels, ironclads, torpedo boats, Antoinette monoplanes, and racing cars." The Futurists also insisted that architecture of whatever form no longer be monumental and enduring but, like boats, trains, and cars, be part of the transitory and expendable equipment of the Industrial Age. But what to do with the architecture of the past? As one might guess, not only were the Futurists against all "preservation, reconstruction, and reproduction of ancient monuments," but they urged "blowing sky-high, for a start, all those monuments . . . arcades and flights of steps . . . digging out our streets and piazzas . . . raising the level of the city . . . reordering the earth's crust and reducing it to be the servant of our every need." The passage's vehement iconoclasm fed the ever-widening current of intolerant antihistoricism, which would accompany Modernism like a dark shadow in all its later phases.

Although not a single structure accompanied the Futurist polemics, drawings produced in 1912–14 by Antonio Sant'Elia revealed what the Futurists had in mind. The essence of the machine being power and speed, a Futurist architecture would be one of movement, and buildings could be imbued with kinetic energy. This dynamism was seen in Sant'Elia's project for a dramatically freestanding apartment tower with widening tiers of bridges, continuous setbacks, and illuminated advertising at the summit (fig. 12-52). The whole structure arched backward over a maze of service features and was precariously balanced above a hollow, through which urban arteries were intended to pass, all, of course, completely bare of any ornament. The sense of architecture in machinelike motion was conveyed even more dramatically in Sant'Elia's project for a new Central Station in Milan (fig. 12-53). Not a "building" in the usual sense, the new station formed the transport hub of a city intersected by a network of movement—roads, bridges, rails, pedestrians—with the suicidal idea of an airplane runway integrated into the scheme. City planning since ancient Greece had always involved movement within and around the solids and spaces of architecture. Yet even in Haussmann's Paris, the purpose of movement was to and from such monuments as the Opera. Sant'Elia's project had no place for monuments, squares, facades, or repose of any sort, but, as in the contemporary Futurist paintings of Umberto Boccioni and Carlo Carrà, only relentless movement in and for itself. Most of Sant'Elia's drawings were lucidly realized. But the Futurist concept was impracticably visionary and ended abruptly in 1916 with the deaths in battle of Sant'Elia and Boccioni.

The problem of the industrial city was an important theme in the modern tradition, provoking a wide range of solutions as in Ledoux's utopian city of Chaux, Haussmann's pragmatic reshaping of Paris, and Shaw's escapist garden suburbs. The difficulties involved not only the question of circulation that preoccupied the Futurists, but also the accommodation of factories, commercial buildings, residences, public facilities, as well as mass housing for a swelling population. The closest that any of the early Modernists came to theoretically resolving

12-52 Antonio Sant'Elia. Apartment tower project. 1914.
(After Banham)

12-53 Antonio Sant'Elia. Central Station project for Milan.
1914. (After Banham)

these factors was the Cité Industrielle (figs. 12-54, 12-55) of
the Frenchman Tony Garnier, who in 1917 published his plan,
conceived in 1899–1904, for an ideal modern city of 35,000

12-54 Tony Garnier. Transport center, Cité Industrielle. 1917

12-55 Residential quarter, Cité Industrielle

inhabitants. The city was zoned into separate areas for industry, residence and services, and health facilities, each laid out
on a flexible grid pattern, with fluid, natural contours (not
unlike the tripartite ancient Greek city of Miletus) and ample
means of circulation. As seen in the view of an industrial transport hub (with factories and a dam for hydroelectric power in
the background), everything was kept, wherever possible, at a
human scale. Industry's brute power was not allowed to dis-
rupt the tissue of civilization in this modestly scaled, rationally
disposed, urban world. Garnier had been deeply affected by
Émile Zola's depiction of nineteenth-century urban evils, and
so the awesome forces of industry, magnified by Sant'Elia, were
here tamed and made to coexist with humanity. Even with
mass housing, Garnier's urbanistic instinct led him to create
varied neighborhoods of plain, yet charming, small, flat-roofed
houses scattered along tree-lined streets.

Garnier's Cité Industrielle was exemplary in still another
respect: it was planned entirely in reinforced concrete. The
virtues of the new material (discussed in the previous chapter)
were its alliance of the tensile strength of steel with the compressive resistance of concrete, its cheapness, adaptability, ease
of fabrication, and durability. Despite these obvious advantages, it was only in the 1890s that ferroconcrete became technically viable as an aboveground building material, and only
after 1900 that it was generally made an architectural, and not
merely a structural, medium. In the 1890s, engineer François
Hennebique erected the first building entirely made of the
new material, and he developed the basis for slab-and-beam

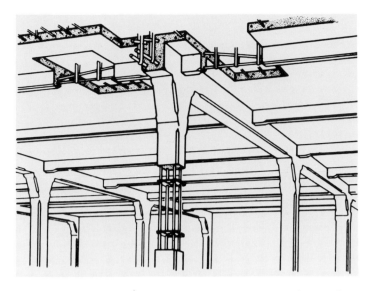

12-56 François Hennebique. Trabeated system for reinforced concrete. 1892. (After Curtis)

12-57 Auguste Perret. Ponthieu garage. Paris. 1905

12-59 Max Berg. Interior, Jahrhunderthalle. Breslau. 1912–13

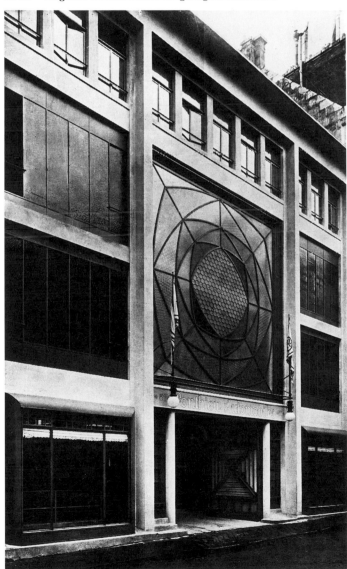

construction so important to the twentieth century, in which the slab floor/ceilings were not carried passively but actively contributed to the ferroconcrete frame (fig. 12-56). Just as the

Chicago School translated Jenney's steel skeleton into a viable skyscraper aesthetic in the 1890s, Auguste Perret a decade later made Hennebique's medium aesthetically valid. The classic example was Perret's garage of 1905 (fig. 12-57) in the rue Ponthieu, Paris. The facade reflected the concrete post-and-beam construction behind it and formed an integral part of that structure, while concomitantly presenting a forceful visual composition. Stripped of detail—no bases, no capitals, no entablature—it nevertheless exhibited the formal harmony of the French Classical tradition. At the same time, its overall scheme carried the echo of the most famous medieval facade in France— Notre-Dame of Paris: its subdivided square format, triadic verticals, terminal gallery, and even its central rose window (fig. 7-34). Some years later, in 1922, Perret reached the height of his powers in the church at Le Raincy, outside Paris (fig. 12-58). The scheme was obviously medieval: the combination of longitudinal and transverse barrel vaults, lightness, and stained-glass walls. But here it was translated into the modern ferroconcrete idiom: slender supports, thin segmental vaults, and prefabricated, latticework curtain walls. The effect, Gothic reborn, would have delighted Viollet-le-Duc.

Despite its success, the Hennebique-Perret system represented only an inhibited step in the exploitation of ferroconcrete, employing it almost as a substitute for timber or steel framing rather than exploiting its intrinsic potential (even the vaults of the church in Le Raincy being so flat as to resemble slabs). The only early Modernist structure to reveal the architectural promise of ferroconcrete was the Jahrhunderthalle, the huge public hall erected in Breslau in 1912–13 as a centennial monument to Germany's liberation from Napoleon (fig. 12-59). The work was designed by Max Berg, an architect who gave up his profession in 1925 for Christian mysticism. What was astonishing about it was not merely its scale, covering some 21,000 square feet, or the strength of its curving concrete members, but its haunting echoes of the past. Its elliptically arched base resembled a Roman or Renaissance bridge bent into a circle, while the ribs above suggested a skeletal Pantheon. The most telling inversion of historical allusions, however, was the lighting. The lower parts of the dome were completely lit, but what would normally be the bright oculus was dark—a negative ghost of the Pantheon. This dark circle surrounded by a hemisphere of lightness suggested the iris of a huge inverted eye—the eye of the cosmos, or, as one contemporary later put it, "the cosmos opened to reveal the courses of the stars and the empyrean." Although entirely geometric in form, the building is closely bound up in spirit with German Expressionism, then in the process of formation.

Expressionism represented only one side of Germany's contribution to early Modernism. In general, the modern movement was from the beginning actively supported by the German state and by industry until the Nazi takeover in 1933. A key figure was Hermann Muthesius, a government official who transplanted the English Arts and Crafts movement to Germany, with a crucial modification of its doctrine. He advocated the acceptance of the machine as a legitimate tool, the adoption of mass production of consumer goods, and the necessity of creating a *Maschinenstil* (machine style) for that purpose. In 1907, Muthesius founded the Deutsche Werkbund, an association of forward-looking manufacturers, artists, writers, and architects, aimed at "selecting the best representatives of art, industry, crafts, and trades, of combining all efforts toward high quality in industrial work." In architecture, he believed that it was the destiny of Germany "to restore to the world and our age the benefits of an architectonic culture," a sober, new style distilled from Schinkelesque Classicism to succeed the nineteenth-century saga of architectural "decay."

Not the least important of Muthesius's acts was his appointment of several leading Modernist architects to head existing academies of art. Among them was the pivotal figure Peter Behrens, who attracted to his office as assistants three of the great architects of the twentieth century—Walter Gropius, Mies van der Rohe, and Le Corbusier. Behrens also acquired an extraordinary position as design consultant of the AEG, or General Electric Company of Germany, designing or overseeing the design of everything built, used, or manufactured by the corporation. This included factory and office buildings and their furnishings, industrial and household products, and even the official AEG stationery. Of the numerous works done for the giant firm—which represented the first important alliance between the architect-designer and modern industry—the outstanding structure was the Turbinenfabrik (turbine factory) of 1909 in Berlin (figs. 12-60, 12-61). It was the first industrial building brought successfully into the mainstream of European architecture (a counterpart of Wright's Larkin Building in

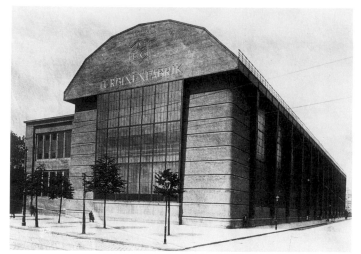

12-60   Peter Behrens. Turbinenfabrik. Berlin. 1909

12-61   Turbinenfabrik, cross section. (After F. Hoeber)

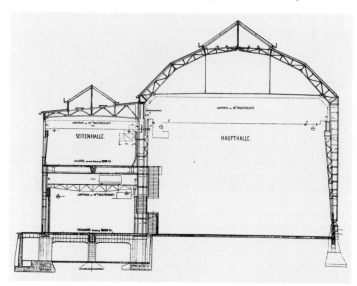

12-62   Walter Gropius. Fagus Factory. Alfeld-an-der-Leine. 1911–13

America). Structurally, the main hall of the building was a row of three-hinged steel arches, a nineteenth-century type used in bridges, railway stations, and exhibition halls. But whereas in the nineteenth century the building would have been a simple ferrovitreous cage or, conversely, covered with a historicist blanket, Behrens converted the factory shed into a noble architectural monument full of historical resonance with more than the hint of a Classical temple transmuted into "modern" form. Because the glass of the flanks was recessed, the lower members of the three-hinged arches stood forward like a giant colonnade (approx. 680 feet in length), and the thin corner walls appeared to be massive rusticated pylons ostensibly supporting a pseudo-pediment closing the vaulted ceiling. Behrens's most brilliant touch was glazing the vast facade by hanging in front of it a fragile, transparent ferrovitreous curtain wall. Where the rest of the building evokes past architectural glories, this floating, glistening curtain wall proclaims the present and promises the future.

The most precocious of Behrens's pupils was Walter Gropius. More than any other works of early Modernism, his designs established the divide between the older generation of architects and his own, which reached adulthood in the twentieth century. Soon after setting out independently in 1910, Gropius conceived as a brilliant Modernist critique of the Turbinenfabrik his Fagus Factory (a shoe-last manufactory), of 1911–13, in Alfeld (fig. 12-62), not just to be different but to teach his master a lesson in Modernism. Whereas the Turbinenfabrik was an arched industrial shed pretending to be a Classicist, pedimented monument, the Fagus Factory was true to its structural self: a post-and-slab construction with a row of slender, brick-faced supports carrying a simple, brick-faced parapet. Where Behrens solidified the corners of the facade and left its center open, Gropius planted a solid entrance block at the center of the facade, but left the corners open, bending the curtain wall around without even a thickening of its slender steel mullions. The treatment of the glazing was crucial: Taking his cue from Behrens's facade, Gropius hung the glass curtain wall in front of the skeleton, thereby creating a floating effect and emphasizing its transparency. But the treatment of the glazing panels differed: Behrens's were small and traditionally vertical; Gropius's were larger and horizontal, typical of the twentieth century, and they subtly revealed the three-storied interior by fronting the floors with bands of opaque panels.

The Fagus Factory, which dramatically realized the *Maschinenstil* ideal of Muthesius and his associates, was the prototype of so much that followed in this century that it is only through such close comparative analysis that we recognize how it represents the definitive turning point in transforming the new high-technology iron structures of the nineteenth century into a fully architectural medium. The collective work of the early Modernists of Europe was impressive in exploring the intrinsic aesthetic potential of the new technology. Apart from the brilliance and quality of these buildings, they were important as a springboard to the High Modernist phase soon to follow. But that transformation entailed more than simply a maturing of the ideas of early modern Europe.

HIGH MODERNISM

The Bauhaus. Where Early Modernism experimented freely in its search for a viable new architectural style, High Modernism gave the firm impression of having found one. This transformation was plainly revealed in Walter Gropius's workshop wing of his Bauhaus (figs. 12-63–12-65) of 1925–26 in Dessau, Germany, where the glazing is drawn without interruption around the entire block. Of the supporting structure, only the parapet and socle remain visible, functioning as the upper and lower armatures of suspended ferrovitreous sheets. And where the Fagus Factory rests firmly on the ground, the Bauhaus unit, lifted above a setback half-basement zone, appears as a pure, quadratic volume of glass, suspended weightlessly in midair.

This ideal, machine-age vision extends through the whole Bauhaus complex. But just what was the Bauhaus? Essentially it was the embodiment of Muthesius's Werkbund, which combined the ideals of William Morris with machine-age aesthetics and methods of production. The Bauhaus originated in 1919 as Gropius's fusion of the old Weimar Academy of Fine Arts with the Decorative Arts School, which had been established by Muthesius (and the Art Nouveau designer van de Velde) in 1903. It was set up as a state school in which fine arts, crafts, industrial design, and architecture were taught as parts of an all-embracing aesthetic discipline, bridging the gap between the artistic and industrial realms in pursuit of an ideal machine-age environment. The abstract style that came to characterize Bauhaus work first took shape when the Hungarian Modernist László Moholy-Nagy arrived in 1923 as second in command, and then definitively with the move from old-world Weimar to industrial Dessau in 1925.

The Bauhaus building in Dessau was a direct translation into physical terms of the complex organization of the school and a projection of its spirit into the new architectural language it was instrumental in creating. Its unique plan consisted of three arms radiating from the center, each arm bent into an "L." Each part of these L-shaped arms was given over to a distinct purpose: the three large outer wings housed the workshops, the classrooms, and, in the balconied, five-storied block, the studio/dormitories. Connecting them to the center were, respectively, a short, three-storied entrance (next to the workshops); an elevated, two-storied arm (bridging a road) for administration and architecture; and, sliding beneath one end of this "bridge," the one-storied unit containing the auditorium and the dining room.

Despite the formal diversity assumed by these components, the impression of the whole was of strong uniformity. All forms were rectilinear and quadratic; levels and proportions were consistent throughout. Of crucial importance, the stretched, weightless volumes so striking in the workshop wing were extended nearly everywhere with the use of setback half-basements and with ribbon windows (and most other openings) brought flush to the stuccoed, undecorated wall surfaces. Thus, the blocks were transformed into hovering volumes contained by thin, stretched skins of transparent glass and opaque plaster membranes.

But there was more to the Bauhaus than abstract form and a functional plan; these fused into a High Modernist image suggestive of an airplane, that most futuristic of all modern machines. The building's conceptual axis was a hub around which (as seen in an air view) the L-shaped arms seemed to rotate like a gigantic, three-bladed propeller. Gropius wrote that the air view was a principal perspective of the Bauhaus, and he used aerial photographs in his first publications of his masterpiece. As he was well aware, Dessau was the home of the Junkers aircraft factory, whose test planes often flew overhead. Thus it seemed that the machinelike building slowly revolving on the ground was a counterpart of the machine pulled through the sky by its rapidly revolving propellers.

Like most "High" phases of artistic movements, High Modernism as represented by the Bauhaus was a visionary ideal shared for a brief time by leading artists and reflecting a transient convergence of ideological, socioeconomic, and artistic tendencies. The "lost generation" of World War I, its inherited system of values shattered, was not in the mood for the *laissez-faire* experimentalism of Early Modernism, and in the 1920s it worked to fuse previously divergent, disorganized tendencies into a compelling new architectural ideal. The Russian Revolution, European economic recovery, and the seeming rise of representative governments made a new set of values and hopes for a better world seem possible. The improved tools and powers of technology needed only to be seized and redirected toward high ideals. So attainable seemed this utopian vision that people across Europe were caught up in a tide of communal belief and action (which had a dark undertow in Fascism). If ever a period had a *Zeitgeist*, this was the one. The Bauhaus was a central symbol of this spirit, in its doctrine, style, methods, and building, but most of all in the way such keenly individualistic artists as Paul Klee, Wassily Kandinsky, Oskar Schlemmer, Josef Albers, Lázló Moholy-Nagy, and others submitted themselves to a common ideal of one universal style valid for all the arts and products of modern life.

Elementarism and de Stijl. At the Bauhaus, Gropius created one of the definitive buildings of the period, but of course he was not single-handedly responsible for the creation of High Modernism itself. As its often used (and abused) name, International Style, indicates, it was an international phenomenon involving many individuals and groups across Europe. Also at work was an important extra-architectural agent: nonrepresentational art. Before the 1920s, while architecture was still groping through its early modern phase, the other arts had already gone through a revolutionary development; in the

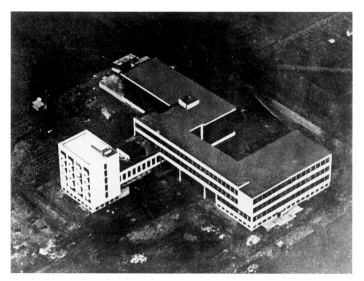

12-65   Air view, Bauhaus

12-66   El Lissitzky. *Proun 1 D*. 1919. (Kunstmuseum, Basel)

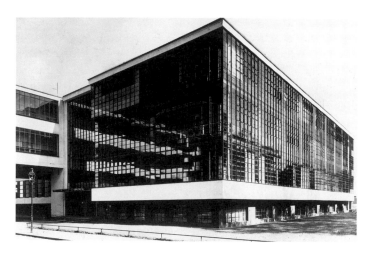

12-63   Walter Gropius. Workshop wing, Bauhaus. Dessau. 1925–26

12-64   Plan, Bauhaus

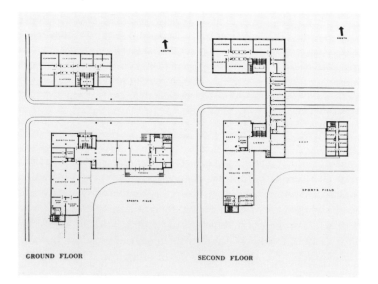

GROUND FLOOR   SECOND FLOOR

twenties, these arts provided the aesthetic principles by which architecture was transmuted into its High Modernist mode. Of the intricate story of abstract art, what concerns us here is a particular post-Cubist phase of nonobjective abstraction known as Elementarism. In painting, it was based on the concept of autonomous, geometrical units floating in a gravityless space, which extended infinitely beyond the picture. Conversely, Elementarist space was imagined as a continuous grid and a work of art as the structure that made its rectilinearity visible by giving body to its lines, planes, and the spaces between them. A work of art might show only one of these elementary planes or solids, but paintings and sculpture generally involved a number of "elements" in free, three-dimensional relationships.

Elementarist art had both a Western and an Eastern front (similar to World War I). Beginning in 1914–15, Russia led with the Suprematist and Constructivist movements, which were fused toward 1920 by El Lissitzky and his Proun ("for the new art") paintings. They were intended, as he wrote, to suggest "a world of crystalline organisms floating in a visually infinite space." Lissitzky had traveled and was widely known in Western art capitals, including at the Bauhaus. One can imagine, for example, his *Proun 1 D* (1919; fig. 12-66) as an air view of a group of buildings and so arrive at the formal concept of the Bauhaus and the basis of its aesthetic language—floating planes and hovering volumes, intersecting and overlapping in rectilinear configurations. Here, too, were the means by which Elementarist art accommodated the Futurist image of the machine world and also touched another chord of the Modernist spirit—the love of the Platonic solids that formed the basis of Classical architecture. Abstract art bridged the gap between the energy of the Futurist machine and the repose of the Classical past, to which most early-twentieth-century architects, for all their radical slogans, still remained very much attached.

The Bauhaus—and High Modernism everywhere—was strongly influenced also by the Elementarist front in Holland, where the country's neutrality during World War I had permitted an unusually full artistic development. Unlike Russia, where Elementarist concepts were not translated into completed buildings until the late 1920s, in Holland there was a vigorous interchange from 1915 to 1925 between philosophy, art, and architecture that gave Dutch Elementarism an intense spiritual dimension. Between 1910 and 1920, the great abstract painter Piet Mondrian worked his way from Parisian Cubism to the pure, rectilinear abstraction of his famous paintings composed of nothing but an asymmetrical grid of rectangles of black, white, and the three primary colors, blue, red, and yellow, separated by lines. The forms are sensed as pure, floating planes, and the grid lines extend, in theory, beyond the painting to infinity. The painting made visible the order of the universe and was meant to symbolize the basic principles of life. Following the ideas of the mystical Dutch philosopher M. H. J. Schoenmaekers, Mondrian believed that vertical elements represented the active principle; horizontals, tranquility and repose; and their perpendicular conjunction, a vital tension and balance. Such intellectual iconography was crucial to High Modernist architecture nearly everywhere.

Although Mondrian extended his paintings into three-dimensional interior decoration, more important was the fusion of his aesthetic with a purely architectural tradition: the work of Frank Lloyd Wright in Chicago. Wright's work came to Holland in three forms: the German publisher Wasmuth's publication of Wright's major buildings, in 1911, which circulated throughout Europe; the visit to Chicago and subsequent propaganda of H. P. Berlage, a Dutch leader of Early Modernism; and the Wright imitation villas, of 1916, of Robert van't Hoff, who had also been to America. As of 1916, Wright's style was an astonishing, revolutionary phenomenon. He had indeed dynamited the "box" into abstract fragments (just as Picasso and Braque simultaneously dynamited the representational object of painting), and reassembled them in a dynamic way. Wright's forms appeared to rise and hover, and his claim to a "machine style" was convincing. But as the Elementarist art of Mondrian and others came into focus toward 1920, Wright's manner of abstraction no longer seemed so ideational. The problem was that his fragments remained dense, solid, material forms—massive chimney piles and piers, and long, powerful slabs of textured masonry. The aesthetic outlook that caused this problem also provided the means to its solution: the American Early Modernism of Wright was "purified" by European intellectualism. By retaining Wright's free planning and open structure, but transforming his massive slabs of matter into Mondrianesque floating planes, one of the most significant High Modernist architectural conceptions was brought into being.

The conjunction of Wright and Mondrian occurred in the context of de Stijl (the style), a movement founded in 1917 by Mondrian, Theo van Doesburg, van't Hoff, Oud, Gerrit Thomas Rietveld, and other artists and writers. De Stijl was founded on the principle of a universal modern style, applicable to all the arts (though less concerned with industrialism than the Bauhaus group). It was committed to an architectural and functional ideal of satisfying "all physical and spiritual needs," but aesthetic concerns tended to take precedence over structural and functional ones; this bias was apparent in the first de Stijl product, Rietveld's stunning but non ergonomic wooden chair of 1917. De Stijl statements about the visual implications of High Modernist architecture were unusually articulate. For example, in 1921 Oud wrote that "reinforced concrete offers a homogenous coherence of supporting and supported parts . . . horizontal spreads of considerable dimensions, and the possibility of coordinating pure planes and masses . . . on a constructive basis, the fundamentals for an art of building of an optically immaterial, almost hovering appearance."

Van Doesburg, in a manifesto of 1923, went further: "The new architecture is anticubic; that is, it does not seek to fix the various functional space cells together within a closed cube, but throws them . . . away from the center of the cube toward the outside, whereby height, width, depth, and time tend toward a wholly new expression in open space." This centrifugal theory of architectural composition—which derived from the "dynamited" buildings of Wright—was most fully realized at the Bauhaus, where van Doesburg lectured in 1922, and which "throws its space cells" away from the center so completely as to leave practically nothing there. Van Doesburg himself illustrated his theory in several studies done in 1923 in collaboration with Cornelis van Eesteren, which boldly realized the fusion of Mondrian and Wright (fig. 12-67).

The final stage in Holland is represented by Rietveld's Schroeder House, of 1924, in Utrecht (figs. 12-68–12-70). Through the inspired treatment of simple architectural features—walls, balconies, railings, struts, windows, transoms—a

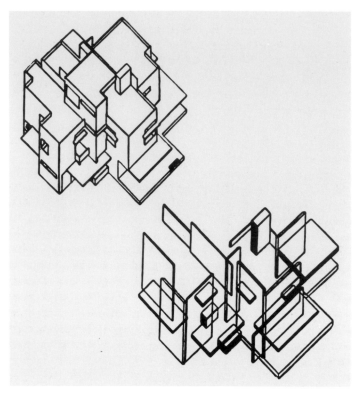

12-67   Theo van Doesburg and Cornelis van Eesteren. Studies for houses. 1923

12-68   Gerrit Thomas Rietveld. Schroeder House. Utrecht. 1924

12-69   Interior, second story, Schroeder House

12-70   Second-story plan, with partitions extended, Schroeder House

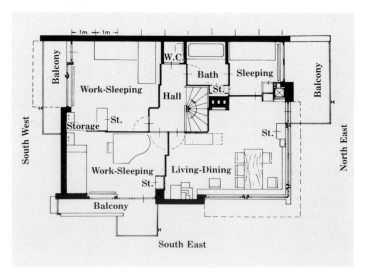

small suburban house becomes a pure de Stijl composition of lines, planes, volumes, transparency, and color. A careful analysis is revealing. At the center of the main facade stands a white, uninterrupted, vertical plane, projecting just beyond the roofline. This central element appears to overlap a light gray, L-shaped plane to the upper left, from whose surface an L-shaped balcony knifes forward around a white parapet floating up from the ground story; the extreme right-hand corner of the balcony is supported by a black, steel I-beam standing against the white background of the central vertical plane; additional iron elements appear as thin tubular industrial railings encircling the balcony. To the right, a collection of forms asymmetrically balances the left grouping: a roof that floats forward over the corner window, whose transom is bright red, its other components black; a white rectangular plane running behind the central element at the level of the balcony parapet; and at the lower right, a ribbon window behind a gray wall along the ground (balancing the gray area of the upper left).

This inspired, precise interplay of abstract Elementarist–de Stijl forms is carried three-dimensionally not only around the sides but through the interior of the house, particularly the upper story. Here the outer wall planes and window grids realize de Stijl effects that continue in Rietveld's wooden fittings and furnishings—stair railings, lamps, chairs, tables—all designed and laid out in a rectilinear configuration that mirrors the style of the exterior. The most imaginative internal devices are the floor-to-ceiling sliding panels tucked away neatly in odd corners, which, when extended along tracks, divide the unbroken space into separate compartments for work, sleep, dining, bathing, etc. Rietveld was neither an artist nor an architect, but a gifted avant-garde furniture designer who took up architecture. At the Schroeder House we observe how much the cabinetmaker he remained, not only in the integral importance of furniture to the architectural design, but also in the way the interior was conceived as a large cabinet full of folding/sliding panels and doors. In fact, Rietveld's métier determined the construction methods of the entire house: surprisingly, its only concrete elements are the footings and the balconies, the rest being brick and timber. These traditional Dutch domestic materials were used not only because Rietveld was insecure with ferroconcrete, but because he thought it would be too heavy for linear and planar de Stijl effects. He fooled everyone, including Gropius (who published the house as an exemplary construction of "steel, glass, and concrete"). Important is not Rietveld's illusionism, but that materials could be adapted to the High Modernist vision of form rather than vice versa.

Looking back from the high point of de Stijl design at the Schroeder House to its American source, the distance gained by Rietveld on Wright, in the fifteen years during which abstract art worked its effect on architecture, is extraordinary. Compared to the pre-Wrightian architecture, Wright's Robie House seemed poised for flight, but compared with the weightless gathering of lines, planes, and volumes of the Schroeder House, it appears an earthbound display of dense masonry textures and muscular weight. The power of the Schroeder House derives not from mass and energy, but from the intricate purity of its proportions and relationships.

For all its professing of impersonality and functionalism, High Modernism was a style infused with humanistic values and idealism. Its restraint was a defense against the self-indulgent individuality of the prewar and Expressionist period, and against the monumentalism that was still part of Early Modernism. No High Modernist building displays the aggressive scale and overpowering effects of the Turbinenfabrik, the Jahrhunderthalle, the Sagrada Familia, or Mies's glass skyscraper projects. Even the largest works refrain from monumentalism, as seen in the Bauhaus and in the large de Stijl buildings, such as the town hall of Hilversum, of 1926–30 by Willem Marinus Dudok, with its closely gathered, interlocking quadratic volumes (fig. 12-71). In the Dutch context, this design mode leads once more back to early Wright (the Larkin Building). But where Wright's building rises up against its brutal industrial environment with aggres-

sive scale and monumentality, the Hilversum town hall stands serenely on a lake amidst greenery; none of its sizable forms have exaggerated scale or effect, even the soaring tower is broken into perpendicular volumes to undercut its weight; and all is carefully woven into an ever-changing tension, precise sense of balance, and studied harmony of vertical and horizontal, large and small, far and near, open and closed elements.

Early Le Corbusier. The trail of High Modernism that links Russia, Germany, and Holland leads also to France, where Paris in the 1920s was still the artistic capital of the West. High Modernism there was dominated by a towering figure, the architectural counterpart of Picasso—Le Corbusier (born Charles-Edouard Jeanneret in French Switzerland), whose stature among early- and mid-twentieth-century architects was rivaled only by Frank Lloyd Wright and Mies van der Rohe. Born in 1887, he was a child prodigy, whose talents, ever complicated and full of surprises, survived into vigorous old age. Like many others in the movement, Le Corbusier's High Modernist theory and practice combined Classical idealism of form, Futuristic mechanomorphism, and abstract art, but to him they were not of equal importance. The foundation of his High Modernism was Classical idealism, and beneath it was an even deeper layer of architectural belief, namely in the primacy of emotional response. As he openly stated: "You employ stone, wood, concrete, and with these materials you build houses and palaces. This is construction. Ingenuity is at work. But suddenly you touch my heart, you do me good. I am happy and I say 'This is beautiful.' That is Architecture. Art enters in." Architecture, in other words, was not an absolute, but was humanly oriented; its effect on the human condition was its *raison d'être*. But with what forms? Again Le Corbusier was explicit: "Architecture is the masterly, correct, and magnificent play of masses brought together in the light. . . . Cubes, cones, cylinders, and pyramids are the primary forms which light reveals to advantage. . . . These are beautiful forms, the most beautiful forms." This romantic, Neoclassical belief (echoing the doctrine of Boullée) that architecture involves the emotions created by the play of light on geometric masses profoundly affected his machine-age streak.

Perhaps Le Corbusier's most famous dictum was "a house is a machine for living in." He was wrongly castigated for this statement as an advocacy of an inhuman functionalism, for he meant nothing of the sort. All progressive architects at the time advocated some form of mechanomorphism. If anything, Le Corbusier's statement was a humanizing critique of the original Futurist dogma that "a house is a gigantic machine." For Le Corbusier, the house was not threateningly "gigantic," but rather it was "for living in," and it was the creation of a mechanomorphic house furthering life-enhancing feelings that counted uppermost to him during High Modernism.

Although the stress of the "machine-house" statement was thus not on the "machine," the machine aspect nevertheless was crucial to Le Corbusier's approach. For him, the new architecture was machinelike in several ways: its machine-age materials and methods of construction; its machinelike efficiency in serving physical and psychological needs; and its resemblance to the actual look of machines. His infatuation with contemporary machinery was almost as strong as his love for Classical forms. This was possible because the contemporary machines that he most admired—ships, cars, planes—tended

12-71   Willem Marinus Dudok. Town Hall. Hilversum, Holland. 1926–30

superficially to resemble the simple geometric forms of Classicism. By 1923, in any case, when he published *Vers une architecture* (wrongly translated as *Towards a New* [sic] *Architecture*), his brilliant and influential statement of High Modernism, he envisioned a virtual identity of Classical architecture, Platonic forms, and mechanical products, each seen through the other (fig. 12-2). He described a steamship in terms usually reserved for Classical buildings: "an important manifestation of tenacity, of discipline, of harmony, of beauty that is calm, vital, and strong"; while he wrote about the Parthenon as if it were a steamship: "All this plastic machinery is realised in marble with the rigour we have learned to apply to the machine. The impression is of naked, polished steel."

For Le Corbusier, as for every High Modernist, abstract art was a key to the formal resolution of the tension between the machine and the Classical norm of beauty. His buildings, like those of his international colleagues, displayed the floating volumes and hovering planes of Elementarist art, and the vogue for thin, weightless skins of masonry and glass drawn around taut massings. However, unlike the centrifugal fragmentation of the Bauhaus or the complicated open formwork of the Schroeder House, Le Corbusier's classic designs, especially in his residential buildings, tended to present, externally, a single, quadratic, boxlike structure. This format reflected Le Corbusier's espousal of Classical form and the whitewashed, cubiform, vernacular structures that lined the shores of his beloved Mediterranean. His house design was also connected with post-Cubist Parisian art, in which he played a role about 1920 as a painter in a movement called Purism. Le Corbusier's Purist paintings (fig. 12-72), invariably still lifes of common household objects—bottles, glasses, carafes on a tabletop—employed Cubist multiview techniques while retaining the geometric integrity of the objects, and they spilled over into his architectural conceptions: large volumes; groundplans resembling his paintings of curved/angular forms within a rectangular frame; and standing forms sometimes appearing three-dimensionally on rooftops, suggesting sculptural blow-ups of his canvases.

Beginning in 1914, Le Corbusier produced several new structural formats for houses, of which the most important was his so-called Domino type (fig. 12-73). It derived from the ferroconcrete work of Hennebique and Perret, but whereas Perret's point of departure was the post-and-lintel frame, which he filled in with floor slabs, Le Corbusier began with the floor slabs as primary, dominolike units floating on six freestanding posts (placed at the positions of the six dots on a domino playing piece). The structure was thus freed of trabeated rigidity, not only in the openness of the interior but in the cantilever of the floor beyond the line of supports, from whose presence the periphery of the building was liberated. Over the next decade, Le Corbusier explored the implications of this structure and in 1926 published his ideas as the "Five Points of a New Architecture" (fig. 12-74), a reference to the five Classical orders: 1) the elimination of the ground story with the elevation of the house above *pilotis*—freestanding ferroconcrete posts; given the domino format, this amounted merely to omitting the ground-floor walls; 2) a flat roof, used as a garden terrace; 3) free interior planning by means of partition walls slotted between the supports; 4) free composition of the external curtain walls; 5) a preference for ribbon windows. No part of this scheme was itself new, but Le Corbusier saw that the whole of his program was more than the sum of its parts. In one respect it could be justified by Modernist determinism (the use of concrete "predetermined" such a scheme) and by functionalism (liberating the house from the dark, humid ground story, letting in salutary light and air, efficiently exploiting space, including the roof, and thus promoting a vigorous life-style). But what ultimately mattered most to Le Corbusier was not structure or function, but the scheme's potential for space and volume, for attaining the High Modernist image of a masonry and glass membrane stretched around a geometric form, literally hovering in the air on slender stilts, and, like a Greek temple, set clearly against nature and infused with light and air from all around.

Among the earliest projects to conform to this new architectural order was Le Corbusier's 1920–22 Citrohan House (fig. 12-75). The name was an intentional pun on Citroën, the French car manufacturer, with the idea that the house was to be a mass-producible "machine for living" to alleviate the severe postwar housing shortage. It was functionally impeccable: above the ground-floor carport-loggia was a double-height living room lit by a large industrial window; to the rear, bedrooms, kitchen, bathroom; and two levels of terraces. The model pro-

12-72   Le Corbusier. *Still Life*. 1920. (Museum of Modern Art, New York)

12-73   Le Corbusier. Domino House, construction system. 1914

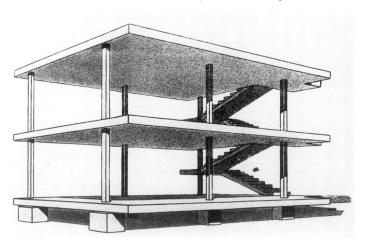

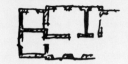

Jusqu'au béton armé et au fer, pour bâtir une maison de pierre, on creusait de larges rigoles dans la terre et l'on allait chercher le bon sol pour établir la fondation.

On constituait ainsi les caves, locaux médiocres, humides généralement.

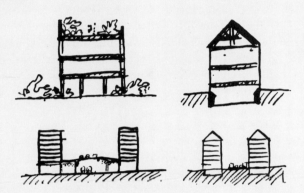

Puis on montait les murs de pierre. On établissait un premier plancher posé sur les murs, puis un second, un troisième; on ouvrait des fenêtres.

Avec le béton armé on supprime entièrement les murs. On porte les planchers sur de minces poteaux disposés à de grandes distances les uns des autres.

Le sol est libre sous la maison, le toit est reconquis, la façade est entièrement libre. On n'est plus paralysé.

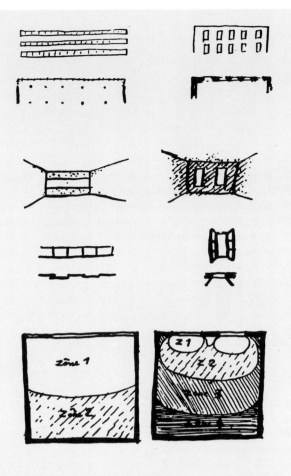

La tabelle dit ceci: à surface de verre égale, une pièce éclairée par une fenêtre en longueur qui touche aux deux murs contigus comporte deux zones d'éclairement: une zone, très éclairée; une zone 2, bien éclairée.

D'autre part, une pièce éclairée par deux fenêtres verticales déterminant des trumeaux, comporte quatre zones d'éclairement: la zone 1, très éclairée, la zone 2, bien éclairée, la zone 3, mal éclairée, la zone 4, obscure.

12-74   Le Corbusier. "Five Points of a New Architecture." 1926. (From *Oeuvre complète*, 1910–29)

jected an aura of salutary efficiency and vitality. What is more, it was named the Citrohan House not only by analogy, for if one steps back and looks at the 1922 model, it has the generalized shape of a 1920s Citroën sedan.

By 1928–29, Le Corbusier's Citrohan House had evolved, through year-by-year model changes, into the "Parthenon" of his High Modernist period: the Villa Savoye at Poissy outside Paris (colorplate 76; figs. 12-76–12-79). Although its site is now compromised by an adjacent school (the building itself having been nearly ruined by occupying soldiers during World War II, and thereafter almost demolished for a school swimming pool), the villa originally looked out from a half-circle of trees across a gently rolling, idyllic landscape below it. Unlike the confined urban locations of most of Le Corbusier's earlier houses, the openness of the Poissy site permitted a freestanding building and the full realization of his five-point program. Essentially the house comprises two contrasting, sharply defined, yet interpenetrating external aspects. The dominant element is the square single-storied box, a pure, sleek, geometric envelope lifted buoyantly above slender *pilotis*, its taut skin

12-75   Le Corbusier. Citrohan House. 1920–22.
(From *Oeuvre complète*, 1910–29)

slit for narrow ribbon windows that run unbroken from corner to corner (but not over them, thus preserving the integrity of the sides of the square). The secondary element is fragmented and is composed of incomplete circular forms—the tubular

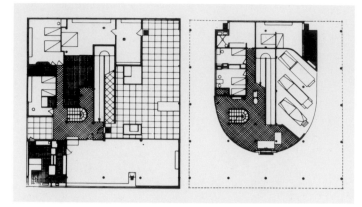

12-76 Le Corbusier. Ground floor and second-floor plans, Villa Savoye. Poissy. 1928–29

12-77 Entrance, Villa Savoye

12-78 Upper story, Villa Savoye

12-79 Ramp, upper story, Villa Savoye

lighthearted play that is his signature. These contrasts at the Villa Savoye are everywhere one looks and include structure and space, repose and movement, interior and exterior, and the clash of details. Entering the foyer, one is struck at once by several of these oppositions: as throughout most of the building, the Domino grid of supports is deliberately left exposed and kept distinct from partition and curtain walls, so that structure and volume are seen as separate elements. The truly dramatic gesture in the foyer, however, is the juxtaposition of the steep spiral stair—threaded through the height of the building like a corkscrew—against the leisurely ramp that ascends in an effortless glide. Although the stair nominally is for servants, it is not tucked away but stands boldly like an abstract sculpture, challenging one to choose between the means of ascent.

The upper levels of the building further expose the human orientation of Le Corbusier's concept of the machine for living in. On the *piano nobile*, the interiors are gathered around a large, open garden court, with the closed, secluded private quarters to the left and rear, and common areas to the front and right. The *grand salon* opens to the court through sheets of glass, while above it the solarium, closed to the exterior, also opens toward the center. The area is pervaded with subtle tensions, elisions, and oppositions, as where to the rear of the garden court a closed cubic volume counterposes the adjacent cube of space that bleeds through the ribbon windows to the landscape (fig. 12-75). The detailing frequently involves playful compositions (the nautically trimmed stairway to the solarium) as part of the villa's ever-changing architectural discourse.

The Villa Savoye is not only a superb fusion of functionalism and dazzling formal invention, it is also alive with historical and contemporary allusion. Its exterior leads in one direction back through Palladio and the Doric temple to Neolithic lakeside dwellings on stilts, and in another to the machine age of racetracks and steamship funnels. The interior ramps evoke, it has been said, the great entrance ramps of ancient Tiryns and Mycenae. And what is the whole *piano nobile* but the Mediterranean house gathered around a court, becoming a "jardin suspendu" in Le Corbusier's words, a hanging garden with echoes of Babylonian luxury?

The Villa Savoye is among the major icons of twentieth-century architecture, but it is often overshadowed in the public eye by the urban planning schemes of Le Corbusier, especially his 1922 vision of a "Contemporary City for Three Million

windscreens of the roof solarium and the half-oval enclosure recessed behind the *pilotis* within a semicircular driveway (containing a glass-walled foyer, servants' quarters, and three garage spaces). But most of all, the stunning exterior realizes fully Le Corbusier's ideal of "the masterly, correct, and magnificent play of masses brought together in the light."

Like the exterior, the rest of the villa also has formal oppositions, which create effects ranging from somber drama to the

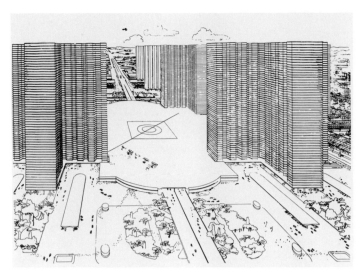

12-80 Le Corbusier. "Contemporary City for Three Million Inhabitants." 1922. (From *Oeuvre complète*, 1910–29)

Inhabitants" (fig. 12-80). He loathed the traditional city with its dependence on the street, filled, as he saw it, not with the vitality of urban life but rather a life-threatening chaos of traffic, noise, and fumes. His new urban concept was based on a combination of opposites: nature and the machine. The center of his ideal city obviously derived from Sant'Elia's multilevel Milan Central Station down to the landing strip folly. Machine-age techniques allowed high-rise construction, and the machine provided the transportation linkage between the resulting high-density population clusters. But rather than filling the interstices between building groups with dense Futuristic complications, Le Corbusier separated his buildings widely, connected them with multilevel highways, and left the rest in greenery. Automobile trafffic passed beneath multilevel residential quarters that were elevated above it on pilotis and looked out over nature. The result was a vast urban park punctuated by interconnected architectural islands of limited population clusters set into the landscape. Although built of "industrial" products, Le Corbusier's "contemporary city" was not mired in grimy industrial chaos, but was filled with light, air, greenery, cleanliness, and efficiency.

In both his ideal city and the villa at Poissy, Le Corbusier's machine-age logic seemed impeccable. But unfortunately, the conception that worked to create a humanly oriented individual house tended to achieve the opposite on a large scale. Although his imagined urban vistas looked serene and ordered, the individual within them was totally subjugated to the automobile for mobility, overwhelmed by vast highways and immense towers of a deadly uniformity, which the empty sea of green (in summers) poorly compensated. This was the dispiriting, brave new urban world that, as practiced widely in the later twentieth century, we know only too well. It was a world that resulted from the dark side of High Modernism, where its insistence on rational efficiency and fidelity to the machine age got out of hand. Le Corbusier's personal responsibility for this "madness of reason" is not to be denied—he even seriously advocated the gutting of vast amounts of ancient Paris for such "ideal" schemes. But the idea was in the air: he merely crystallized the machine-age urban drift, for better or worse, into its most lucid and influential form.

Early Mies van der Rohe. Closely rivaling Le Corbusier and Wright as form-givers of twentieth-century architecture was Mies van der Rohe, leader of the Berlin School, which in the 1920s was the major center of the architectural avant-garde. Mies, who was first a devotee of Schinkel and a student of Behrens, then for a few years a visionary Expressionist, could not have been more different from his Parisian and American counterparts. He disdained self-promotion, and wrote little. But two famous remarks give him away: "I don't want to be interesting. I want to be good," and an aphorism that might be inscribed on his every building, "Less is more." He had none of the new-idea-a-minute inventiveness of Le Corbusier and Wright. His buildings embody little extraneous iconography of the kind Le Corbusier delighted in; they tend to refer only to themselves, and as such are the purest of modern architecture, if not at first glance the most striking. But Mies's mature work brought to white-hot focus high powers of concentration, resulting in a diamondlike radiance of conception and execution. His passion was the perfection of structure, proportions, and detail. Wherever possible, he employed sumptuous architectural materials—travertine, richly veined marbles, tinted glass, bronze, and water—with acute sensitivity and finesse. Nor was space itself, that most basic of architectural materials, neglected. His best work is never tentative, but always rings with finality.

Nowhere could Mies's qualities be better observed than in the German Pavilion for the Barcelona Exposition of 1929, a showpiece of High Modernism (figs. 12-81–12-83). Nothing about it was original in the usual sense. Basically, it derived from the de Stijl–Elementarist open-form aesthetic of overlapping planes floating in space; however, these tendencies were fused with the Domino principle of Le Corbusier: floor/ceiling slabs supported by a grid system of slender piers, between which partition walls were slotted. Mies's starting point in the plan was the large rectangle of the travertine podium that was raised about a meter above the surroundings; to it, a small rectangle was extended to the upper left, and a medium-sized one to the right. These pavement rectangles were overlapped and conjoined by the roof slabs, respectively square and rectangular; the latter was supported by a Domino of slender, cross-shaped, chrome-plated steel piers, the former by wall structures. Two areas remained unroofed, and these were either fully or partly inset with black-glass-lined pools, which contrasted with the travertine pavement, defining still another "layer" of rectangular subplanes within the whole. To these horizontal planes, vertical slabs of matter were added: first, U-shaped outer walls of travertine and green Tinian marble at either end, and one straight length along the larger pool to close the space (next to the stairs, the wall became glass for a view to the interior); and then, under the main roof, five partition walls within the Domino of supports, two of onyx, the others of glass (clear, obscure, or bottle-green), set in chrome-plated mullions. With a few simple forms—albeit a sumptuous variety of masterfully used materials—Mies conjured up a rich visual experience. The spatial diversity and flow created by the overlapping and intersecting planes were heightened by the contrasting colors and textures of the materials and by the transparency and reflections of water, glass, and polished marble. This ever-shifting flux was anchored in space by the plan's basic geometry and the Domino grid of gleaming columns, which stood out sharply against the panels. No detail was left unperfected, least of all the furniture

12-81　Ludwig Mies van der Rohe. Interior, Barcelona Pavilion. International Exposition, Barcelona. 1929

12-82　Plan, Barcelona Pavilion

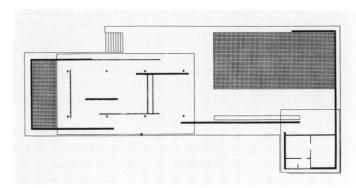

12-83　Barcelona Pavilion

designed for the Pavilion—especially the celebrated Barcelona chairs of steel and leather that in their sleekness and luxurious functionalism crystallized the aura of the whole building.

The Weimar Republic was notable for its efforts to build mass housing and even more notable for assigning much of this construction to the avant-garde. All the major German architects, including Gropius, Behrens, Mendelsohn, Poelzig, Taut, and Mies, participated in projects for suburban housing settlements, a typical such *Siedlung* being formed of groups of low-rise, three- to five-story apartment blocks or row houses. Stringent economic limitations meant modest scale, simple materials (typically brick or cinder block faced with stucco), small windows, and absence of decoration. Aesthetic considerations were reduced to what Modernists were best at: abstract handling of massing,

proportions, rhythm, and space. Supreme at extracting the most from the least, Mies produced in 1927 the most distinguished building of the German mass-housing movement for the Weissenhof Siedlung in Stuttgart—a sleek, narrow block with fine proportioning, a dynamic roof line, and an internal steel skeleton containing twenty-four diversely planned apartments.

If Mies's apartment building was exceptional, the Weissenhof Siedlung as a whole was unique (fig. 12-84). It was not the usual development project but a model display of modern domestic architecture sponsored by the German Werkbund. Le Corbusier was granted two buildings at the "front" of the site; Mies had the largest building situated at the highest point, and he was

12-84　Ludwig Mies van der Rohe and others. Weissenhof Siedlung. Stuttgart. 1927

12-85　Raymond M. Hood. McGraw-Hill Building. New York. 1931

also made master-planner of the whole *Siedlung*. He laid out the scheme not with the typical grid of streets but in rectangular blocks with connecting terraces, making the hillside into a flowing terrain-sculpture. But most important was the conspicuous harmony among the many divergent housing types and diverse architectural personalities. Here, for all the world to see, was the evidence of a truly modern architectural movement nearing the height of its powers.

LATE MODERNISM

High Modernism was never simply a "style" in the ordinary sense but a utopian movement created by diverse forceful personalities who for the moment shared the ideals of nineteenth-century rationalism and socialism and were inspired by twentieth-century abstract art and Futurism. They were driven by a revolutionary calling to raise the human condition through

12-86　Richard Neutra. Lovell House. Los Angeles. 1929

a newly designed environment of pure, functional machine-age forms. But no sooner was the movement formed than it began to disintegrate; and even without the Hitlers and the Stalins and deep worldwide economic depression, High Modernism by the early thirties had been demystified, reduced to a formalist doctrine (regular volumes, stripped surfaces, flush openings, etc.)—converted to an International Style by Henry-Russell Hitchcock and Philip Johnson in their influential Museum of Modern Art exhibition and catalogue of 1932. Le Corbusier himself turned his back on High Modernism in 1930.

The Late Modernism that followed was led by the leaders of High, and in one case Early, Modernism (Wright). Without exception, they survived into vigorous old age and continued to dominate the scene well into the 1960s. In addition, a true Late Modernist generation of architects, many of distinction, emerged in the post–World War II era. What the young built was strongly influenced by their elders, for the collapse of the High Modernist movement did not end High Modernist formal tendencies: as in most "Late" phases, they were refined and exaggerated, as well as being complicated by the resurgent forces of Early Modernism, especially Futurism and Expressionism. The "melting pot" of Late Modernism, appropriately enough, was dominated by postwar America (apart from Le Corbusier). Mies, Gropius, and other leading European architects had fled there in the 1930s, and it was natural that, with the rest of the world in ruins, America's postwar monopoly of power, wealth, and self-confidence would find its architectural outlet.

Modernism had begun simultaneously in the 1890s on both sides of the Atlantic, but Europe was the first to benefit from a European-American dialectic. About 1930, it was America's turn to take up the Modernist torch. The transfer involved both the Americanization of Modernist architecture and the shift from the "High" to the "Late" phase, for the new American structures typically lacked the utopian, idealizing discipline and inner spirit of Europe in the 1920s. Many important American examples differ in telling ways from their European models. Raymond M. Hood's magnificent, sleek, green-tiled McGraw-Hill Building (1931; fig. 12-85) in New York carries a heavy ornamental crown that "compromises" it; in the same way, the massive, curved granite base of the contemporaneous Philadelphia Savings Fund Society Building of George Howe and William Lescaze undermines the functionalist purity of the shaft rising above it (see page 582). Whereas even a luxurious, private villa by Le Corbusier, such as at Poissy, was able to project the utopian social ideals of High Modernism, the sprawling, opulent Lovell House (1929; fig. 12-86) in Los Angeles, by the Austrian immigrant Richard Neutra, lacks such idealism and the taut formal discipline of its European counterparts.

Later Frank Lloyd Wright. This current in the United States was the setting of the late career of Frank Lloyd Wright. That he had a late career at all was surprising, for after 1914 he was beset by personal tragedy, financial reverses, and stylistic malaise. Although Wright's reception of European Modernism roughly paralleled the American examples just mentioned, there was a vital difference: in the hands of lesser architects, provincial effects of dilution often resulted from the transplanting, but not with Wright. By fusing the chaste European abstraction of the 1920s with his own nineteenth-century

American individualism and passion for organic contextualism, he produced a unique, powerful Late Modernist idiom.

Although Wright worked prolifically until his death in 1959, the three most important works of his later career were conceived between 1936 and 1943: the Fallingwater House, the Johnson Wax complex, in Racine, Wisconsin (1936–39), and the Guggenheim Museum in New York City (not built until the 1950s). Fallingwater—a house built in Bear Run, Pennsylvania, in 1937, for the Pittsburgh millionaire Edgar J. Kaufmann—is the most universally loved of all Wright's works, especially as seen in the famous architectural photograph that views the structure dramatically from the stream below (fig. 12-87). Although objectively speaking this viewpoint exaggerates the cantilevered projection and ascent of the massing, it captures well the feeling of this extraordinary house. The stream at Fallingwater runs alongside and under the house; terraces seem to draw it into the orbit of the structure, from which a flight of steps descends mysteriously down to the water. The building derives its unique spirit from this intimate connection with the stream and the setting. The rusticated chimneys and piers spring from rugged outcroppings of the rock of which they are built; while from the piers, huge ferroconcrete terraces reach out into the space of the gorge and the thickly planted trees in an embrace of architecture and nature. The house's advance in purity and lucidity beyond its obvious point of departure in Wright's early style (e.g., the Robie House) was made possible by the European influence of Elementarist High Modernism. Although Wright understood the taut, white, ferroconcrete planes of the European prototypes, at Fallingwater he treats ferroconcrete in his own manner as if it were poured stone with soft, rounded edges, not Le Corbusier's sharp-edged membranes. But more than any other elements, the site and scheme distinguish Fallingwater from European High Modernist houses. Whereas the Villa Savoye stands guard nobly over an open, settled countryside, and the Schroeder House acts out its de Stijl choreography with formal, clipped gestures, Fallingwater explodes with the sweep of the nineteenth-century American "frontier." And although both the Villa Savoye and Fallingwater were built for millionaires, the former rises like a temple to the machine age, whereas Fallingwater openly celebrates a self-indulgent, however aesthetically sensitive, capitalist individualism retreating into its private natural domain.

The Guggenheim Museum (1956–59), which sits opposite New York's Central Park like an architectural spaceship amid terrified, straightlaced Fifth Avenue neighbors, is also a symbol of American industrialist individualism directed here to the public good rather than to private enjoyment (figs. 12-88–12-90). The celebrated main exhibition space is uniquely simple—an expanding spiral ramp hung on thin, radial piers. Pictures are displayed mostly on the outer wall of the ramp, lit by a combination of natural light from an enormous skylight and artificial illumination (originally also from slits in the spiral outer wall). The spiral rises at one end of a block-long, rounded slab (containing more exhibition space), under which the visitor passes to enter the museum. A counterbalancing massing of contrasting square and circular forms, containing administrative offices, rises at the other end of the slab. (The interior and especially the exterior were compromised by the ill-considered additions of 1992.)

Just as Fallingwater is a Late Modernist "remake" of the Robie House, so the Guggenheim Museum derives from Wright's

12-87 Frank Lloyd Wright. Fallingwater House. Bear Run, Pennsylvania. 1937

other early masterpiece, the Larkin Building. But where the Larkin interior is stiff and right-angled, within the Guggenheim all is liquid continuity and flux. The diameter of the central space slightly narrows upward, while the ramps themselves broaden so that the space appears to breathe; a strong, convex countercurve creates a rhythmic pulse in the flow of the spiral, and the spiral itself invokes the forces of natural growth. The height of the parapets equals the gap between them, while the whole well of space is bathed in light from a giant *oculus* in the top, creating a luminosity comparable to that of the Pantheon.

At the Guggenheim Museum, Wright transformed the underlying scheme of the Larkin Building into one of the most magical spatial experiences, but the building was attacked for not presenting the neutral, right-angled spaces of most museums, and for the inevitable clash between rectangular paintings and slanted walls. Some even claimed that Wright, the architect, intended a put-down of art. Wright felt otherwise: "It is not to subjugate the paintings to the building that I conceived this plan. On the contrary, it was to make the building and the painting an uninterrupted, beautiful symphony such

as never existed in the World of Art before." He insisted that the visual detachment of the paintings from the slanted wall would avoid their looking "as though painted on the wall behind them"; that the viewer's progress, after riding the elevator to the top, was an effortless descent down the ramp, "drifting from alcove to alcove" (between the radial piers); and that the atmosphere of "harmonious fluid quiet" was more favorable to the new abstract art than "the incongruous rooms of the old static architecture." Wright's museum did what few other museums even attempted: to become more than a passive frame for the curatorial arts of exhibition and actively to heighten, in an architectural way, the viewer's experience of the art shown within it. At every moment, one simultaneously is in intimate proximity to a small group of works yet in the presence of the entire exhibition, large "strips" of which are visible across the room. But perhaps most important is the fact that art exhibitions typically are chronological in structure, and so is the Guggenheim Museum as its spiral path projects the presence of the fourth dimension—time—and shows works of art in an imaginary stream of time past, which physically draws the viewer through it.

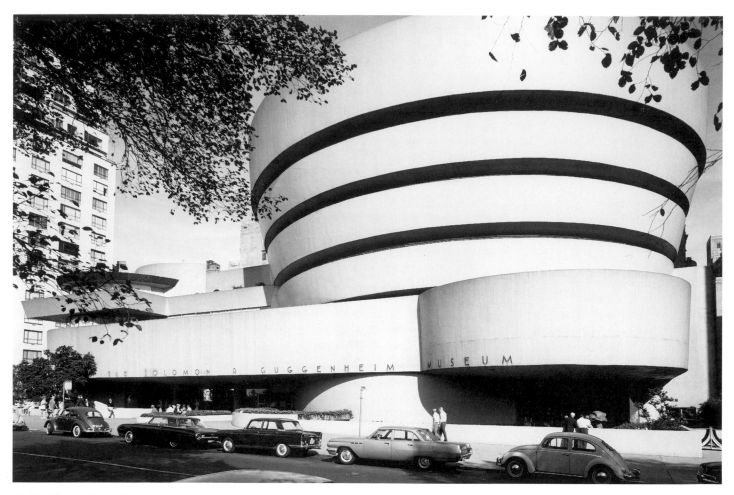

12-88 Frank Lloyd Wright. The Solomon R. Guggenheim Museum. New York. 1956–59

12-89 Interior, The Solomon R. Guggenheim Museum

12-90 Ramp galleries, The Solomon R. Guggenheim Museum

Later Mies van der Rohe. Whereas Frank Lloyd Wright absorbed European High Modernist ideas, Mies van der Rohe in person came to America in 1938—not to California (like Neutra), nor to Cambridge (where Gropius became an influential professor at the Harvard Graduate School of Design), but to Chicago where he was called to teach at the Illinois Institute of Technology. Chicago in the 1930s was no longer a vital architectural center, but it had a great past. Although Mies's new career involved a number of building types, his most influential contribution was to the skyscraper. Just as the development of Wright's early style was revived by the effects of European Modernism, now the Chicago skyscraper, dead since the turn of the century, sprang to life again, transformed in the hands of Mies van der Rohe (figs. 12-91–12-96).

The union of Mies and the Chicago skyscraper was an attraction of deep affinities. Mies wrote: "The most important idea in modern architecture is the skeletal idea developed right here in Chicago." It was not only the "skeletal idea" but the rigor and boldness of its realization that attracted him. Yet its revival posed a dilemma: Mies could not, of course, return to the gravitational historicist masonry of the Chicago School curtain walls, nor could he altogether revoke the High Modernist abstraction of the facade and the concept of the building as volume as opposed to mass. He searched for a synthesis, one realizable in machine-age form.

Mies believed that "structure is spiritual" and, not surprisingly, he found what he was searching for in the steel skeleton that he admired so much. The principal component of the "Chicago" frame is the I-beam, which is not seen in a completed building, where it is buried within a thick fireproof casing. Mies's genius was to realize that the invisible I-beam was exactly the form he wanted. Reduced in scale, refined in shape, it could be applied externally to the curtain wall as closely spaced mullions framing the window bays and running over the entire facade from edge to edge and top to bottom (fig. 12-92). To dress up a skyscraper facade with a raw nineteenth-century structural element was a daring gesture at the time of its conception in the late 1940s, but Mies was a firm believer in the nineteenth-century dogma of architectural "truth," at least metaphorically. Just as the column had been used from antiquity to the nineteenth century to express gravitational forces within structure, the structural I-beam would be visually omnipresent in small scale as a truth symbol of the new structural reality. Not resting on the ground or basement stories like a column, but hung on the facade above the *pilotis*, the miniature I-beams stress the vertical, yet together with the spandrels form a narrow metal grid stretched over the surface. Such a program at once symbolizes the broader structural grid behind it, and gives the building the sculptural presence of the Chicago School, yet the buoyant impression of a Modernist facade is maintained. Further, the I-beams have no beginning or end and thus reach to infinity (like Constructivist–de Stijl elements). Viewed from below, their potential endlessness evokes the image of a yard of railroad tracks (tracks are also I-beams molded to receive wheels), a concept not inappropriate to Chicago, the "railway hub of America."

Mies's skyscraper style—the most influential Modernist formula of the postwar period, with worldwide imitations and derivatives—took shape in the decade between his Promontory Apartments in Chicago, of 1946–48 (where the I-beam was first projected but not used), and the Seagram Building in New York, of 1954–58, designed in collaboration with Philip Johnson (mainly responsible for interiors), where the I-beam, as well as every other element, was developed to perfection.

Few leading Modernists had the opportunity to build so luxuriously as at the Seagram Building, which is clad in solid bronze and tinted glass and lavishly uses an even more expensive material—New York midtown land. The 38-story, 520-foot tower occupies only 25 percent of the building lot (fig. 12-93). Although this is the maximum allowed a tower by the New York setback law of 1917 (created to counteract the tendency to line Manhattan's narrow streets with sheer shafts), the code also permits stepped volumes around the tower out to the sidewalk. This potential is only fractionally realized at the Seagram Building, in relatively low 4- and 10-story steps to the rear (providing additional space and originally masking unsightly buildings to the east). These low volumes are connected only to the three central bays of the five-bayed tower that extends to the rear as a "spine," with the result that from Park Avenue the tower looks perfectly rectangular and freestanding, with a block-long plaza spreading out before and around it.

But Mies's mastery of planning involves more than mere space. The Seagram plaza presents the building on an honorific platform, raised like a Greek stylobate three steps above the sidewalk on Park Avenue and progressively more toward the east where the terrain falls off sharply, emphasizing the isolation of the tower. Bounded laterally by twin pools with fountains, groves of beech trees, and bench-high precinct walls of massive serpentine marble, and thus isolated from the turmoil of the streets as if by architectural magic, the plaza enfolds the visitors on its pink granite pavement and gently directs them over it toward the tower, from which a canopy slides out in protective welcome. From this perspective (fig. 12-94) the front line of piers stands like a majestic hexastyle Doric porch, within which the gleaming bronze-and-glass wall of the lobby opens in triple revolving doors that lead to four massive travertine-clad banks of elevators.

Throughout the building, one is reminded of Mies's earlier work (the Barcelona Pavilion) in its supple proportions, interaction of form and structure, solid and void, pools and pavement, but especially its dialectic of order and freedom, stasis and movement. The imposition of order on the Seagram site is absolute. The lot is subdivided into bays 27'9" square, 10 of them from front to rear, 7 side to side, determining the placement of all the piers. Each bay comprises 6 by 6 smaller modules (4'7 1/2" square) defining the spacing of the paving stones, the bronze mullions, and almost all other elements. Paradoxically, the result of this method is not the rigidity of the typical "modular" building, but dazzling lucidity, a consequence of the ingenuity with which the major and minor grids are exploited, and of the harmonies generated among the squares of the plan, and the double-square (windows) and square-and-a-half (spandrel panels) proportions within the facade.

Materials and detailing are as crucial to the Seagram Building as composition. Like the Barcelona Pavilion, the materials are sumptuous: travertine, pink granite, pink-gray tinted glass subtly consistent with the bronze work—materials that endure and with time acquire a noble patina of age. Each detail—including elevators, light fixtures, door handles, even the bronze mail chutes—is designed with crispness and care. The greatest efforts were directed to the curtain wall, especially at the corners (fig. 12-95). First, the wall is not carried over the corner but stops a few inches short of it, exposing a substantial angle of the corner pier. This device gives the corner of the building visually a traditionalist strength, and, by implication, reveals the hidden presence of the intermediate piers behind the curtain wall (seen only in the ground

12-93   Plan, Seagram Building

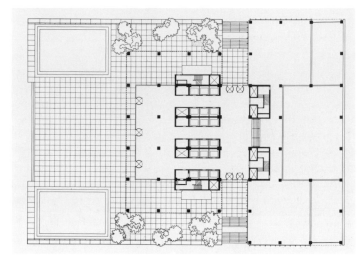

12-91   **Ludwig Mies van der Rohe. Seagram Building. New York. 1954–58**

story). Secondly, the curtain wall is given an implied thickness at the corner (of two of the eight "flutings" on the piers), to which the I-beams add a second "layer," thereby creating the sculptural relief. Thirdly, there is the high refinement of the relief—the double-stepped spandrel panels and window frames, the firm profile of the I-beams—and the integration and spacing of all these elements.

A detail plan of the corner of the building reveals the secret of how Mies achieved his facade (fig. 12-96). The actual pier, with its I-beam embedded in a fireproof casing, stands at a remove from the *apparent* corner pier, which is completely fake, while the curtain wall is only as thick as the slender window frames and not as substantial as the two-flute reveal suggests. Mies has been attacked for such "falsity," but this critique overlooks

the symbolic character of architecture. There is hardly a notable historical building that does not "misrepresent" its structural nature for the purposes of art: the Greek temple, whose columnar drums only touch at their circumferences, being slightly hollowed in the middle; the Gothic cathedral with its flying buttresses; "rusticated" Renaissance palaces, and so forth. Mies is "true" to structure in the sense of the historical types cited. The appearance of the Seagram Building symbolizes accurately the essence of its structure and transmutes it into the powerful visual language of twentieth-century art.

The real problem with the building, and with Mies's work in general, is its inimitability. Within a five-block radius of the Seagram Building stand at least a dozen derivatives, which constitute a sobering, if sometimes unintentionally comic, lesson in how many ways a great design can be misinterpreted and abused; this was repeated worldwide in the 1960s and seventies. Mies's style is a paradigm for the machine age, but despite his belief that he had invented a "universal" style for all purposes, it is, like the Greek orders, at its best in grand public works. Unlike the ancient orders, however, which were imitated for millennia in an endless range of building types, Miesian "orders," like most abstract forms of modern art, only come to life in the hands of their creator. Mies's work looks impersonal—and that was his intention—but it embodies as personal a style as any created in the twentieth century.

12-94　Lobby entrance, Seagram Building

12-95　Corner detail, Seagram Building

12-96　Plan of mullions and corner pier, Seagram Building. (Courtesy Seagram Building)

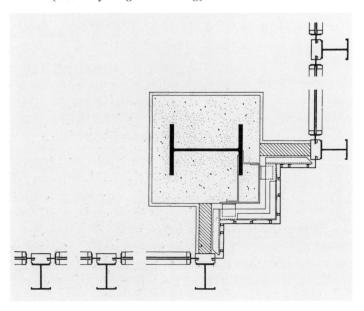

Later Le Corbusier. In contrast with the late works of Mies and Wright, which relate easily to their earlier production despite strong development, the late career of Le Corbusier is startling. His medium still is ferroconcrete, now used, however, not to draw thin planes around geometric volumes but to create bold sculptural effects with rugged textures, and imposing scale and weight. At first it is hard to believe that the late works are by the same architect who designed the Villa Savoye. But such an impression oversimplifies Le Corbusier's personality, and overlooks the connections between his early and late careers. Beneath Le Corbusier's High Modernist facade was a man of extremes and inner conflicts; he could drive rationalism to irrational excess. His early city-planning concepts called for the virtual destruction of established patterns of life and great cities such as Paris. His *Modulor* system of proportions, developed in the 1940s, was so complicated and arbitrary that few critics or architects actually understood it. Le Corbusier developed a Nietzschean view of his calling, a ruthless will to impose his artistic authority on the world. Nothing was sacred to him but the current phase of his art. "Burn what you loved, love what you burned," he wrote around 1910, and he meant it. As a High Modernist, he became so ashamed of his youthful works that in his eight-volume *Oeuvre complète* he suppressed the seven substantial, precocious buildings erected between 1904 and 1916, alluding only to one house of 1906 as having been "probably dreadful." He even lied outright: "During the war I gave up all architectural work," neglecting the culminating building of his early career, the Villa Schwob of 1916, in La Chaux-de-Fonds, Switzerland, in which his previous Jugendstil manner gave way to a quasi-Expressionist, exaggerated plasticity of volumes. After the High Modernist ideal collapsed around 1930, he again eagerly "burned" what he had loved, and returned to the emotionally charged, Expressionist streak of his youth but in such new form that its connection with his work of decades earlier was scarcely perceived.

Le Corbusier's Expressionist late style (and the work of other architects influenced by it) is often called Brutalism after its aggressive, roughly finished forms and its characteristic

12-97 Le Corbusier. Unité d'Habitation, section. Marseilles. 1947–52. (From *Oeuvre complète*, 1946–52)

12-98 Unité d'Habitation

12-99 Roof, Unité d'Habitation

material—*béton brut* or raw concrete. However, the Brutalist concept was not new to Le Corbusier, who in 1923 wrote: "The business of Architecture is to establish emotional relationships by means of brutal materials." In the 1920s, whitewashed, rendered-over ferroconcrete and painted steel was a "brutal" affront to tradition; by the 1940s, however, the wide acceptance of the International Style had raised the threshold of what was considered "brutal." The perfect medium now was raw concrete, especially when cast in wooden formwork that left its roughly textured imprint on the concrete surface—a mode at first dictated by postwar economies, later by fashion. More than materials, though, was affected by Le Corbusier's escalation of the shocking and sensational in the 1940s. In the 1920s, abstract art and flat-roofed architecture were the height of avant-garde radicalism; two decades later, a significant Modernist statement required much stronger language.

The years after 1930, with worldwide economic depression and World War II, were hard times for practicing architects, especially in Europe. Le Corbusier built practically nothing between 1933 and 1945. In his dazzling works around 1950, he displayed his new antitechnological, antirationalist ideas in a reassertion of primal feelings, sensual shapes, and raw textures—a Brutalist revindication of the human spirit in a brutal new world.

Le Corbusier's most influential late work was his first significant postwar structure—the Unité d'Habitation in Marseilles of 1947–52 (figs. 12-97–12-99). The giant, twelve-story apartment block for 1,600 people is the late modern counterpart of the mass housing schemes of the 1920s, similarly built to alleviate a severe postwar housing shortage. Although the pro-

gram of the building is elaborate, structurally it is simple: a rectilinear ferroconcrete grid, into which are slotted precast individual apartment units, like "bottles into a wine rack" as

12-100   Le Corbusier. Front view, Notre-Dame-du-Haut. Ronchamp, France. 1950–54

12-101   Notre-Dame-du-Haut, axonometric projection. (From *Oeuvre complète*, 1946–52)

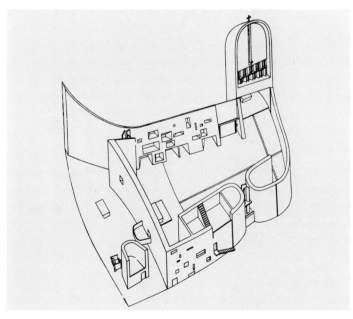

12-102   Rear view, Notre-Dame-du-Haut

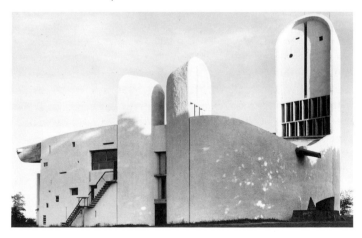

form the major external feature. At the center, "interior streets" run through the grid, which on the seventh and eighth floors are developed into communal facilities that include shops, a restaurant, and even a small hotel, while on the roof of this "temple of family life" are found athletic facilities and play areas for children.

As a building type, the Marseilles block derives from Le Corbusier's 1922 project that stacks up many Citrohan-type modules alongside deep individual terraces. Here this scheme is streamlined and combined with the architect's five-point

the architect put it. Through ingenious planning, twenty-three different apartment configurations were provided to accommodate single persons and families as large as ten, nearly all with double-height living rooms and the deep balconies that program for individual houses. Strictly schematically, it recalls the Villa Savoye—an amply fenestrated, quadratic volume elevated on *pilotis* and carrying a roof garden—only transformed from top to bottom into the potent heavy imagery of Le Corbusier's late style. The slender *pilotis* have become massive concrete "legs." ("The columns of a building should be like the strong curvaceous thighs of a woman," he wrote in the 1930s.) The earlier, thin, membranelike wall and ribbon windows are replaced by the deep openwork of the concrete *brise soleil*, or sun break, invented by Le Corbusier in the late 1930s, arranged here in subtly varied rhythms and with surfaces painted red, blue, or yellow in random patterns. The roof garden has become a landscape of *béton brut* forms dominated by chimneys that resemble smokestack funnels. If the Villa Savoye suggests some fragile raftlike vessel, the Unité d'Habitation gives the impression of a massive ship of humanity, carrying an entire village safely across the suburban greenery of Marseilles.

This impression was not a gratuitous formal gesture, for, as its name suggests, the Unité was meant as more than just rationally planned housing. It embodied Le Corbusier's ideal of the individual's integration within the collective, with privacy ensured by lead sound-insulation sheets between apartments. It was an ideal inspired by monastic communities in Greece and Italy; by nineteenth-century utopian projects for minisocieties; and, in a more practical way, by ocean liners, such as the one whose cross section he published in 1933, praising its interior streets, shops, services, and social and spatial integration. In a world that had become perilous, the Unité secured the privacy and safety of the individual, within a communal structure that was itself a forbidding, shiplike fortress, self-sufficient and distanced from a hostile world. Yet the building is pervaded by an unsettling aura: its base is anthropomorphic (a woman's "strong curvaceous thighs"); its crown is nautical; its body is a geometric abstraction. It is, in other words, the architectural equivalent of the dreamlike displacements and incongruous combinations of Surrealist artists such as Salvador Dali, Joan Miró, and especially Victor Brauner. They were representatives of a movement in which Le Corbusier himself had been caught up as a painter in the 1930s with images of tumultuous nudes and biomorphic monsters called Ubus.

Surrealism is a key to other late works of Le Corbusier, most notably the church at Ronchamp, France, of 1950–54. Although designed only three years after the Unité, Notre-Dame-du-Haut was a more extreme statement of Le Corbusier's late style (colorplate 77; figs. 12-100–12-102). Programmatically, as seen in the isometric view, the church is simple—an oblong nave, two side entrances, an axial main altar, and three chapels beneath towers—as is its structure, mainly rough masonry walls faced with whitewashed Gunite (sprayed concrete) and a roof of contrasting *béton brut*. Formally and symbolically, however, this small building, which is sited atop a hillside with access from the south, is immensely powerful and complex. Although its interior is a roughly four-square space along a longitudinal east-west axis, the exterior walls and roof are organized diagonally into sharply contrasting group formations. Toward the "front," the *concave* south and east walls are pulled into one unit jutting out beneath an enormous overhanging roof, whereas to the "rear," the north and west walls are shaped into an undulating, *convex* continuum with no visible roof, flowing up into

towers, interrupted only by an entrance. Serving as a visual anchor, and as pivot to both groups, is the bell tower, its convex, closed side turned toward the concave front, and vice versa. Some of these external features may be considered functional: the overhanging roofs shelter the principal entrance and the external apse, formed by the east wall, which has an altar and pulpit for outdoor services. However, such functions could be satisfied with far less extravagant means. What counted more to Le Corbusier was the visual impact of the sculpted, restless configuration, angular and upward driving on one side, rounded and earthbound on the other.

At Ronchamp, as in the other works of Le Corbusier examined here, the forms may be expressive in a purely abstract way, but they are not without the images and associations that enabled him to create a multileveled symbolism for the church. His patron, Father Courturier, believed that the most effective expression of the religious consciousness would result from allowing the architect all possible imaginative freedom. It was a freedom Le Corbusier took. In the huge roof slabs (actually hollow) and in the rugged cleft walls of the main facade are seen the dolmens of Carnac, an echo of Ronchamp's pre-Christian shrine. Christian images leap forth: a nun's cowl, a monk's hood, praying hands, a church spire. But there is still another image, for looming over us at the angle of the walls is the jutting prow of a ship, with lifeboats (the roof) hanging over its sides (the concrete imitating their wooden planks). Here Le Corbusier has transformed his love of nautical imagery into Christian iconography, for, among Christian symbols, the ship is the Church itself, St. Peter's ship, saved from sinking by the Lord, and also the ship that is Noah's Ark, mankind's salvation from the Flood, finally at rest on Mount Ararat. A shiplike Notre-Dame-du-Haut has come to rest on its sacred hillside in the Vosges mountains, a memorial to the survivors of the recent war that had destroyed the pre-existing church on the site.

The rear of the building again fuses the mythic and the Christian. In its undulating forms can be seen a giant reclining female, her face turned plainly toward us in the hooded tower, surely the mythical Mother Earth. The twin towers at the entrance are the traditional twin towers of church facades, but also a cleft in the rocks through which we enter the extraordinary grottolike interior of Notre-Dame, a Christian grotto pervaded with signs of fear and hope. The ceiling drops ominously toward the center (from a maximum height of about 32 feet over the altar to about 16 feet), yet it seems to float above the south and east walls, allowing a blazing slit of light to come through. The walls are subterranean in feeling to the north and west, fortresslike to the south, where deeply splayed "fortress" windows are glazed with brilliant abstract stained glass, whose light pervades the interior with a magical glow recalling the great cathedrals. All visitors to this powerful and mysterious environment, irrespective of religion, are drawn back to the primeval sources of faith. Few modern buildings have equaled Ronchamp in its concentrated formal, structural, and symbolic power, and Le Corbusier, whose late career blazed most brightly in the five to ten years immediately following the war, never again would gather his forces as brilliantly.

Our brief survey of the late styles of modern architecture's giants has concentrated on only a few works. Each of these prolific figures built (or projected) numerous other important structures in the period. Le Corbusier designed an enormous range typologically as well as geographically, from small rustic houses outside Paris to a visionary new governmental city at Chandigarh in India, as well as museums, college buildings, exhibition halls, and other works in Europe, Japan, and America. Mies, his fluted skyscraper perfected at the Seagram Building, simultaneously pursued several other forms, notably the giant open-span hall, which reached its apotheosis at the Berlin Neue Nationalgalerie (1962–68). Wright, a generation older than the others, continued to produce a stream of works well after his eightieth year. The buildings of these preeminent modern masters rightfully dominated the architectural scene through the 1950s and into the sixties. However, it was in this period that Modernism truly became the International Style that it had been prematurely acclaimed in 1932; it was no longer just the property of a small, radical avant-garde but, for good or ill, the dominant architectural mode nearly everywhere throughout the world. The new generation of its practitioners had not participated in making the revolution, but inherited it as a *fait accompli*. Numerous bright and energetic talents endeavored to carry the Modernist enterprise forward, but few succeeded in breaking from the pack. The latecomers generally took their cues from the giants, either in direct derivation or by exploring, updating, and recombining the strategies of Early and High Modernism. Buildings that at first seemed unprecedentedly new in this period, upon reflection turned out to derive in one way or another from the heroic period of modern architecture. But in many cases, retrospective dependency was offset by the vitality of the early ideas' potential.

After World War II: Corporate Headquarters and Other Works. In this period of unprecedented urban reconstruction and economic expansion, the multistory building was the single most important type, whether as residential blocks or serving the tremendous growth of institutions, bureaucracy, and business. Many of them were erected by giant corporations as prestige headquarters. They were scattered over the globe from Hong Kong to Düsseldorf, but largely concentrated in the American cities where the skyscraper movement had begun, in Chicago and especially New York, which after World War II rose to be the cultural, financial, and corporate capital of the world. For example, from the corner of Park Avenue and 53rd Street, one has within view the following major works of the period: diagonally facing each other, Lever House and the Seagram Building of the 1950s; a few blocks south, Union Carbide and the Pan Am Building of the 1960s; a block to the east, the Citicorp Tower of the 1970s; while just out of sight, a few blocks to the northwest (on Madison Avenue) is the Post-Modernist AT&T Building, completed in 1984. The diversity and impact of these buildings—and of lesser, more diffuse gatherings of towers in Chicago, Houston, and elsewhere—is enormous, but it should not blind us to the fact that in plan and structure the Late Modernist skyscraper tended to be little changed from the pioneer works in Chicago of the 1880s and nineties. Their construction technology and patterns of use, in fact, developed relatively little: steel frame, a core of elevators and services, office space around the perimeter. The diversity and evolution of the tall building is, in this sense, superficial, restricted to the treatment of the curtain wall. But such skin-deep variations,

12-103   Skidmore, Owings & Merrill. John Hancock Center. Chicago. 1965

together with siting and supplementary features such as atriums and galleries, can make all the difference between numbing eyesores and life-enhancing works of art.

The point of departure for the Late Modernist skyscraper was the aesthetic program of High Modernism, filtered through International Style doctrine and reinterpreted by Gordon Bunshaft (of the firm Skidmore, Owings & Merrill) in the Lever House of 1950–52 (colorplate 80). Although, in 1947, the Corbusier-inspired Secretariat Building of the United Nations had already appeared in New York City as a thirty-nine-story slab with its two main faces entirely in glass, Lever House was a more decisive turning point, especially in the eyes of corporate patronage. It was not the working quarters of a nonprofit international organization on the river boundary of Manhattan but the Park Avenue headquarters of a leading American manufacturer of hygienic products such as toothpaste and soap. Thus began the still unresolved love-hate relationship between impersonal, profit-oriented, bureaucratic patronage and an architectural style rooted in 1920s radicalism and humanistic idealism. In its initial phases, however, the postwar style's intrinsic qualities represented a masterful synthesis and expansion of the High Modernist 1920s—the glass-walled Bauhaus machine shop and Le Corbusier's five-point scheme. Lever House counterposes two rectangular volumes, sheathed in a thin curtain wall of stainless steel and glass, floating on *pilotis*, the lower volume carrying a roof garden and enclosing a garden-atrium retreat. Its thin, twenty-story tower was small by New York standards (trading space and potential profit for beauty, urban values, and prestige), but for an International Style building it was unusually large. The mastery of proportions and of detailing was and remains exceptional, a harbinger of the technological excellence of the metal-glass curtain wall that was to become the special province of Late Modernist American builders.

The spell of the 1920s, which inspired Lever House and other refined and graceful designs, did not survive into the 1960s, a decade ruled by an atmosphere of explosive American wealth, power, and ambition, and, in general, the abandonment of traditional limits of behavior and sensibility. Two aspects of Mies's skyscraper style were seized upon and exaggerated: the sculptural weight of the fluting and the "visible" display of structure. Also not to be overlooked as an influence was the Brutalism coming from Le Corbusier's late style. Skyscrapers grew immensely in size—to as many as 110 stories, outreaching the 102 stories of the Empire State Building that had held the record for over thirty years; and their relative visual weight was oppressive and overwhelming. The taut and buoyant curtain wall became an aggressive scaffolding of steel or masonry members, a real or symbolic exhibitionism of skeletal structure. The new monumentalist spirit engaged nearly every architect. Walter Gropius, who in thirty years had hardly inched beyond the Bauhaus, in 1963 loaded Grand Central Station, a Beaux-Arts landmark, with the Brutalist sixty-story, masonry-faced Pan Am Building, and, at the last moment, turned it 90 degrees so that it blocks forever the sight lines of Park Avenue. Skidmore, Owings & Merrill moved from designing small-scaled refined structures, such as Lever House, to progressively heavier, even overpowering towers: the Union Carbide Building of 1963, the massive Chicago Civic Center of 1965, and the leviathan of 1960s skyscrapers—the tapered ninety-five-story John Hancock Center in Chicago (fig. 12-103), which superimposes on its dense, brawny frame a series of disruptive X-braces, subverting what was left of the spirit of Mies.

In the 1970s, the pendulum appeared to swing back. On the surface, the monumentalism of 1960s architecture was transmuted into a more subtle language, but, underneath, the socioeconomic forces behind skyscraper construction intensified as land and rental values exploded and corporate patronage became more impersonal and removed from the urban context. The shift can be seen by the late 1960s, when a second John Hancock Tower was planned for Boston by I. M. Pei and his chief designer, Henry N. Cobb, and completed in 1977 (fig. 12-104). At first glance, the sixty-story building appears to have returned to the thin-skinned International Style sleekness of the Lever House. In reality, however, the revival was deceptive. Lever House retained the High Modernist program of simple geometric solids floating in a space that penetrates through a largely transparent skin. In the John Hancock Tower, ideal geometry has given way to a "sculpted" parallelogram with V-grooves in the short sides; and the building's skin has become a frameless grid of identical, opaque, mirror-glass panels that mask the structure and all the internal features of the building as effectively as a blank stone wall. It is true that mirror glass, first developed around 1960, assists air conditioning by reflecting heat and is economical and efficient to design and construct by hiding windows and everything else behind it. But such a cool, mirror-glass building of the 1970s is as forbidding, antisocial, and hostile as a person wearing mirror sunglasses. Ask it what it is or where to enter, and it tells you that the sky is blue and that you are on the sidewalk.

But simultaneously steps were taken to counteract the antisocial qualities of the skyscraper in the form of supplementary features that project the image and sometimes realize the substance of civic responsibility and public responsiveness. A number of factors conspired in this development. New zoning laws and tax incentives generally compensated the builders in one way or another for public amenities provided, so that good architectural public relations now made good economic sense. The question was how to manage these public relations architecturally. What was provided for the public had to seem part of the building—pulled inside, set underneath, or made contiguous. Interestingly, the prime model of these solutions was the popular series of Neo-Futuristic hotel lobbies created by John Portman beginning in the late 1960s. They are spectacular, balcony-hung, pool- and greenery-filled spaces, notably in the Hyatt Regency Hotels in Atlanta and San Francisco (fig. 12-105). A toned-down version of this idea first migrated into corporate commercial structures in Philip Johnson and

12-104   I. M. Pei and Henry N. Cobb. John Hancock Tower. Boston. 1977

John Burgee's IDS Center in Minneapolis of 1973: between a large mirror-glass office building and a smaller hotel and shops, a large greenhouse atrium was inserted with retail space, cafés, and other amenities. Although such contiguous fer-rovitreous atria were perhaps the most popular solution—they did not disturb the integrity of the tower, take up its valuable lower floors, or cost much to build—more architecturally ambitious solutions were also attempted. Of these, one of the most successful—and symptomatic of the whole period—is the Citicorp Center in New York of 1974–77 by Hugh Stubbins Associates (fig. 12-1). The tower itself is an unremarkable synthesis of the 1950s, sixties, and seventies. Its top is sliced off at 45 degrees (like Johnson and Burgee's earlier Pennzoil Place in Houston), with the original intention of providing for solar energy panels, and with the result of a distinctive profile recognizable miles away. Its skin is not mirror glass, but sleek, white aluminum with narrow continuous ribbon windows almost as closed in effect as mirror glass. But what really opens an impenetrable void between the huge tower and the observer is its elevation on gigantic piers (outdoing even Le Corbusier's Marseilles block). They are more suggestive of the towering supports of some giant bridge or elevated highway than of the underpinnings of a building. Their impact is all the more powerful because they are placed not firmly at the corners, but at the center of each side. Such a specter of precarious instability—curious in a bank—had not been seen in architecture since the Galerie des Machines of 1889 in Paris. The immense tower seems to blast off skyward like a gigantic rocketship leaving the launching pad of public services huddled in the dust beneath it. The drama of this architectural spectacle did not hamper the popular success of its shops, restaurants, even a church and a subway entrance, gathered around an atrium at its base. The public relations aspects of the double-function building, like so many of its kind, are ambiguous, but as a large-scale urban structure, the Citicorp can be counted as a success. It is true to the nature of corporate patronage, yet responsive to the inhabitants of the city, and it is visually stunning.

More amenable than the skyscraper to structural and formal experimentation were buildings in other categories. Toward 1960, under the pressure of Le Corbusier's late works and impatience with the International Style, these designs became increasingly adventuresome, not only imitating Le Corbusier's buildings directly, but following his lead back to early-twentieth-century Modernism. As an antidote to the slick, impersonal International Style of plate-glass sheets and skinny steel and aluminum members, the Brutalists offered an aggressive style of rough, chunky concrete forms. The key work of the American most closely identified with the style is Paul Rudolph's School of Art and Architecture Building, of 1959–63, at Yale University (fig. 12-106), where the oppressively proportioned, balcony-hung interior turned out to be nearly unusable (an "antidote" more lethal than the Miesian "poison"). The shaggy exterior in corrugated concrete is a visually potent conflation of Wright's Larkin Building, of the Marseilles block and other proto-Brutalist late works by Le Corbusier (notably the monastery of La Tourette), and of de Stijl aesthetics. Few works of the movement were to adhere so defiantly to the literal meaning of "Brutalism," and in retrospect the Yale building has acquired a certain poignancy in its innocent intensity and purity of affect and conviction.

12-105   John Portman. Lobby, Hyatt Regency Hotel. San Francisco. 1972

Rudoph's building may have been on the mind of the Hungarian-born, Bauhaus-educated emigré American architect Marcel Breuer when he designed the Whitney Museum in New York, completed in 1966 (fig. 12-107). He also was surely thinking (along with his client) of Wright's sensational Guggenheim Museum, finished only in 1959 a dozen blocks away. The Whitney was an inspired critique of both recent monuments and one of the most skillfully designed works of the period. A cuboid version of Wright's conoid-rotonda, functionally it was impeccable by

12-106   Paul Rudolph. School of Art and Architecture Building, Yale University. New Haven. 1959–63

12-107　Marcel Breuer. Whitney Museum of American Art. New York. 1966

anyone's standards, with its three main exhibition floors of varying height, each an open gallery adaptable through movable partitioning to a wide range of exhibition needs. A sunken court
provided a sculpture gallery and extended the museum down to
a glazed basement story, while a beautifully proportioned staircase detailed with bronze, teak, and granite offered an alternative access to the museum's huge, originally "Breuer-blue"
elevator. Total exhibition space amounted to several times that
of the Guggenheim, all on a building lot half its size. Although
monumentality was certainly sacrificed to functionalism here—
offering nothing comparable to Wright's breathtaking central
void despite exterior similarities—Breuer nevertheless ingeniously arranged for a dramatic entrance over a concrete-
canopied bridge across the sculpture court. In the context of the
cantilevered, cubo-projective closed massing of the exterior, the
entrance span seems almost a drawbridge over a moat, giving
privileged access to a cultural stronghold. The fortified imagery
is heightened by the small, slanted windows with protective
hoods scattered sparsely on the upper walls, uncannily reminiscent of the arrowloops and other small openings for observation
and firepower in medieval castles. The exterior thus lent the current idea of Brutalism a specific and relevant iconography.

Far more than being just another exercise in Brutalism,
Breuer's tautly shaped exterior is reveted in beautifully crafted
granite slabs rather than presenting raw concrete, toning
down its Neo-Corbusian aggressiveness. It is finally a model
of civic responsibility and plain old architectural good manners
in its restricted height, maintenance of street alignments, proportioning of its stories relative to neighboring buildings, and
absence of intrusive, staring windows. Perhaps only a talented
architect who had first become aware of modern architecture in
the cubic volumes of Adolf Loos in post–World War I Vienna,
had learned to design at the Bauhaus, and spent nearly a half-
century planning and constructing hundreds of projects, could
have devised and articulated such an intricately simple,
urbanely expressive, and uncompromisingly usable building.

Brutalism spanned a broad gamut of style as well as location
of practice. As a concept, the mode originated in England, where
it was widely practiced not only in the concrete medium, but in
steel and glass, at first by Peter and Alison Smithson, then most
consummately by James Stirling. Stirling's Hi-Tech Brutalism of
the Engineering School at the University of Leicester (1959–63)
exhibits the three-dimensional energy and sharp juxtapositions
of Rudolph, but it derives from the "factory aesthetic" of

12-108 James Stirling. Engineering School, University of Leicester. England. 1959–63

Futurism and Constructivism rather than from Wright and Le Corbusier (fig. 12-108). Certain of its prominent features are functional—the two cantilevered auditoriums, the skylights in the low laboratory wing pivoted to the north; others, like the off-set columns of the office tower, are purely aesthetic. All are sensitively handled in their materials, detailing, and proportions, with a control and integration of forms and effects that distinguish Stirling's output in general (another example is the library of the history faculty at Cambridge University).

A strong revival of Expressionism, not unrelated to Brutalism in its agressive form-making, characterized many non-skyscraper buildings of the 1960s. In Germany, one of the original Expressionists, Hans Scharoun, had the opportunity to build what he had earlier only dreamed of—notably his wavelike Berlin Philharmonic Concert Hall (1956–63). Gottfried Böhm's concrete, crystal-growth pilgrimage church at Neviges (fig. 12-109) is perhaps a more intensely emotive and formally concentrated work. Two Scandinavians were also prominent Neo-Expressionists: Jørn Utzon, with his sail-form Opera House that juts out into the harbor of Sydney, Australia (1956–73), and Finnish-born, American-educated Eero Saarinen, whose Trans World Airlines Terminal at Kennedy Inter-national Airport in New York City is perhaps the most successfully "expressive" and functional work of the group. It is not coincidental that the Neo-Expressionist examples cited are churches and music halls—buildings in which the emotions and spirit take flight. The TWA terminal (fig. 12-110), which convincingly suggests some giant prehistoric bird about to take wing, conveys the essence of flight itself, externally as well as within the gracefully fluid interior.

In these Late Modernist revivals, an accurate process of selection was at work. In each of the examples cited, form is symbolic of function, not only in the various instances of "flight," but in Stirling's "factory aesthetic" technology school and in Rudolph's artistically willful school of design. In a Late Modernist house or villa, the revival strategy was even more obvious, for it was based on unambiguous allusion to the domestic mode of the Schroeder House and the Villa Savoye. But while the iconography was much the same, the forms, fifty years later, were different. Closed volumes with ribbon windows and one or two balconies were replaced by elaborate, openwork abstractions with double- and triple-height interiors and huge panels of glass. More intricate spatial complications now prevailed. Three New York architects (of the group known

12-109 Gottfried Böhm. Pilgrimage church. Neviges, Germany. 1962

12-110 Eero Saarinen. Trans World Airlines Terminal, John F. Kennedy Airport. New York. Completed 1962

as the New York Five) led this development: Michael Graves, Peter Eisenman, and Richard Meier. The first two tended to push composition to nonfunctional, even antifunctional, extremes of daring experimentation in built theory. Graves created complex, open scaffolding for mysterious houses as yet unbuilt; Eisenman produced dense, compact designs in which, for example, a single house might comprise two sets of de Stijl framework, one rotated 45 degrees within the other, with predictably unpredictable, mazelike results. Richard Meier struck a classic balance between these extremes with a series of beautiful and exciting, yet restful, works begun in the early 1960s and continuing unabated to the end of the century (not always with such poise). But in the final analysis, his Smith House (fig. 12-111) in Darien, Connecticut, of 1965–67, presented a dehydrated version of Rudolph's Art and Architecture Building. In spirit, it was a witty play of de Stijl formalism that carried little trace of the noble idealism of the Villa Savoye and its mistaken hopes of a bright tomorrow. With such works, Modernism had become a predictable new conservatism.

12-111 Richard Meier. Smith House. Darien, Connecticut. 1965–67

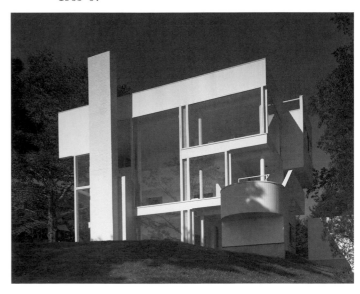

13-1
Charles Moore
with U.I.G.
and Perez
Associates,
Inc. Piazza
d'Italia.
New Orleans.
1975–80

Chapter Thirteen | Second Modernism (through Post-Modernism)

In the 1960s and seventies, it seemed to many that the first cycle of architectural Modernism, which had begun in the 1890s, encompassed three generations, and passed through three phases, was finished as a living movement capable of further growth. Modernism was pronounced dead. Obituaries were read over its unburied, or imaginary corpse by proponents of a new architectural wave that embraced overt historicism, garish symbolism, vivid ornamentation, and humble vernacular models. After the mid-1970s, this new avant-garde tended to call itself, or to be called, Post-Modernism (or PoMo).

It was in retrospect that the true nature of this surprising turn of events was understood. Indeed only after Post-Modernism peaked and architecture had moved decisively to different paths in the 1980s was it realized that although destined to be short-lived, PoMo was not an isolated, chance event but a late phase of a long-term development lasting most of the twentieth century. This recognition came about through the ideology of Post-Modernism itself, which engaged a new historical perspective that regarded Modernism as a specific historical movement of limited possibilities and duration, rather than being seen, as previously, as an absolute imperative ideal for modern life. It was now realized that another broad architectural current had run alongside the "mainstream" of Modernism (charted in Chapter 12)—a succession of developments not always neatly separated from the "central" activity yet distinctive and important, indeed crucial to the full and continuing story of modernity. Its events have long been known and studied but not until recently was it possible to perceive them as constituting a linked series basic to twentieth-century architecture. Indeed so important was this alternative stream of architectural production that it deserves the name that will be used here, Second Modernism (which does not necessarily imply a secondary status).

The story of Second Modernism starts with the modernist degree zero of traditionalism and leads through stages newly defined here, which include Art Deco and such individualistic figures as Alvar Aalto and Louis Kahn, to the developments associated with the term Post-Modernism. In this perspective Post-Modernism, which during its heyday had seemed to many of its proponents an "escape" from architectural modernity, becomes an integral phase of a more complex and complete accounting of the architecture of the twentieth century.

TRADITIONALISM

Ultimately Second Modernism is rooted in the massive resistance to Modernism in the first half of this century, in particular the first three decades. Simply because a score of progressive architects repudiated historicism at the turn of the century

should not mislead us into thinking that the rest of the world followed. Far from it. The bulk of early-twentieth-century architecture, particularly of a monumental, official, or commercial character, took the form of what can be called Traditionalism, which accommodated new building types within old-fashioned covers. Although superficially resembling for this reason the nineteenth-century revivals, Traditionalism had a markedly different character. Nineteenth-century historicism was not only the agent of reaction; it was a living organism full of high spirits, impossible hopes, and unresolved conflicts. But in the early twentieth century, the vital, proto-Modernist juices of historicism were absorbed by the Modernist movement, leaving Traditionalism high and dry, a great, hulking shell of the past, concerned not with being "of our time," but with bloodless "good taste" and "correctness." And indeed, few architectural styles were ever more suavely "correct" in everything from decorative detail to site planning. Compared with the flimsiness of much of Modernist output, its solid, self-assured, lavish, yet dignified works have much appeal to the late twentieth century, and the nostalgic pull of its window to the past is understandable. This is especially true of monumental Classical structures such as Henry Bacon's Lincoln Memorial in Washington, D.C. (1911–22)—a massive, colonnaded block that combines cenotaph and temple, grandly sited on a reflecting pool, in style virtually indistinguishable from the early nineteenth century of Schinkel and Smirke. Not all Neoclassical Traditionalism was so cold-blooded. The most forceful exception was the work of Sir Edwin Lutyens (a Post-Modernist favorite). An adept master of Queen Anne, Palladian, and Georgian styles, he left his great work in the new capital in New Delhi. The sweeping Viceroy's Palace (1920–31; colorplate 78) forms a majestic Palladian massing, executed in a bold Neoclassical style, which combines Boullée and Schinkel with ancient Indian traditions—rich Moghul materials and sharply cut profiling, and a dome that alludes to the famous early Hindu stupa at Sanchi.

If there was one particular building type that brought out the best in early-twentieth-century Traditionalism, it was the skyscraper in New York City. From the beginning, the New York skyscraper movement was distinguished by its unrestrained scale and its high-spirited, theatrical style. The New York buildings, the antithesis of the boxlike slabs of sober Midwestern Chicago, were exuberant, free-form massings with lavish detail and flamboyant crowns, such as mansards, domes, and steeples. After 1900, when New York regained the leadership in skyscraper construction it had temporarily lost to Chicago, that flamboyance was modified by the new spirit of Traditionalism into something generally more "correct" and "tasteful" than the garish modes of late-nineteenth-century eclecticism. The was the acclaimed masterpiece of the group. (Others were the triangular Flatiron Building, 280 feet, 1902; the Singer Building, 600 feet, 1908, destroyed 1968; and the Metropolitan Life Tower, 700 feet, 1909.) Through shrewd control of proportions, setbacks, window grouping, and vertical articulation, Gilbert produced a building that is both a 29-story office block and a huge, 50-story, stepped tower that rises through the block. Of particular note in achieving this effect is the way the narrow-wide-narrow spacing of the tower articulation is extended down through the substructure. The verticalism is reinforced by the lavish, but delicate, white terra-cotta Gothic detail, which clothes the building with fine vertical lines; these are overspun at intervals by crisp stringcourses and fluid runs of suspended Gothic canopies, with subtle decorative accents gathering in richness toward the top. The various Gothic formulae were exploited, Gilbert explained, to make what was dubbed the "Cathedral of Commerce" ever more "spiritual."

TRADITIONALIST MODERN (AND ART DECO)

In the period between the wars some Traditionalist architects responded to the new stylistic modes of the twentieth century, eventually even going over completely to "straight" Modernism. At first, however, they kept Modernism at arm's length, filtering it through their still Traditionalist vision, often in combination with sources neither Traditionalist nor Modern. The eclectic results offended both hardline Traditionalists and hard-core Modernists, yet the popular success of this amalgamated style, which can be called Traditionalist Modern, was enormous. Its principal medium was again the New York skyscraper, thriving as never before in the period between the two world wars. Paradoxically, just as America was plunged into the Great Depression, dragging most of the world down with it, the most glittering of its towers went up—the spectacular, 77-story Chrysler Building of 1930 and the Empire State Building of the following year, even bigger (102 stories) and sculpturally more assertive. The designer of the Chrysler Building was William Van Alen, a comparatively obscure architect who rose to the occasion. Part of his effort was due to the ambition of the building's patron, the automobile magnate Walter Chrysler, who was determined to have the world's highest building and a unique, personal variant of the latest skyscraper fashion. The Chrysler Building (colorplate 79) is the quintessential example of the Traditionalist Modern mode generally called Art Deco, after its first clear manifestation at the Exposition Internationale des Arts Décoratifs et Industriels Modernes in Paris, in 1925. Art Deco is a style mostly used in the decorative arts: an amalgam of Cubist-inspired European Modernism, with streamlined, rhythmic machine forms, exotic Pre-Columbian and Navajo zigzag imagery, and a love of gaudy colors and shiny materials such as plastic, aluminum, and stainless steel along with sumptuous wood and stone. Although derived in part from Art Nouveau, it was angular, staccato, boldly sculptural, and synthetic in feeling. The Chrysler Building used Art Deco to the fullest, from the deep red African marble and exotic wood inlay in its lobby, and the gargoyles that copy the 1929 Chrysler hood ornament, to the triangle-punched stainless steel spire (added at the last moment to the design during construction to outdistance a rival building). The gray-trimmed, white brickwork of its shaft combines Traditionalist vertical lines with Modernist horizontality and ribbon windows running to corners, where a

13-2 Cass Gilbert. Woolworth Building. New York. 1913

drive for height elicited progressively taller office towers of superb formal quality from Traditionalist skyscraper designers. Cass Gilbert's 792-foot Woolworth Building of 1913 (fig. 13-2)

13-3   Raymond M. Hood, Wallace K. Harrison, and others. Air view, Rockefeller Center. New York. 1931–39

staccato Art Deco accent is created by the quoinlike patches. Similar combinations pervade the crown of the building, where a series of narrowing arches resolves the shaft into the Gothic ogee curve of the spire. The building violates rules of "good taste" and "correctness" upheld by Traditionalists, and it mocks the idealist puritanism of the Modernists, yet it comes away triumphant. There is something touching in its courageousness and its quirky eccentricities, a poignant spirit rarely seen in monumental works.

The most ambitious of the New York skyscraper projects of the time was Rockefeller Center (1931–39; fig. 13-3). There the philanthropic inheritors of great wealth permitted no egocentric displays, no questionable taste, creating instead one of the most complex and socially responsive of all twentieth-century urbanistic designs. Its program is exceptionally well-ordered and perfectly integrated into the Manhattan grid. It includes low, medium, and high buildings; the two centerpieces are Raymond M. Hood's sleek 70-story RCA Building and Donald Deskey's magical Art Deco shrine—Radio City Music Hall (fig. 13-4). (Both involved the collaboration of other architects as well.) As part of Rockefeller Center's admirable urbanistic ideals, there is a mall, a sunken skating rink, roof gardens, an underground circulation network, shops, theaters, and a glittering nightclub-in-the-sky. Stylistically, at Rockefeller Center,

13-4   Donald Deskey and others. Interior, Radio City Music Hall, Rockefeller Center. New York

13-5   Gunnar Asplund. City Library. Stockholm. 1920–28

apart from its theaters and nightclub, Traditionalism and Modernism are blended to produce an image of quiet self-assurance, enduring solidity, and restrained power. On the one hand, there are traditional elements such as verticalism, monumental limestone cladding, and axiality; on the other, modern starkness of detail (except around entrances and public areas), Art Deco Cubist sculpting of mass, flat roofs (without spires), and asymmetric displacements.

Traditionalist Modernism was by no means restricted to New York or to the skyscraper, but was a strategy with endless variations. One further example illustrates the range and potential of the approach. Just before he became one of Scandinavia's leading High Modernists, the Swedish architect Gunnar Asplund built the Stockholm City Library (1920–28; fig. 13-5), a building which, with its cubic base plus cylinder design, is strongly dependent on the traditions of Neoclassicism. Asplund provides a huge, Classical doorframe broken into the wall, creating a welcoming, public entrance; small ground-story windows signify stacks with services above; and the cylinder is, of course, the reading room. Yet for all its inspired Neoclassicism, the library has a Modernist aura, which is realized by its expansive volumes enveloped by thin mural planes and by the absence of detail (except to separate stories and mark the entrance).

ALTERNATIVE- OR COUNTER-MODERNISM

In searching out the roots of Post-Modernism, which is so involved with historicist content, we have so far accounted for the continuation of historicism (twentieth-century Traditionalism) and the accommodation of Modernist ideas within a Traditional format (Traditionalist Modern). We now arrive at a third phase, in which extra-Modernist ideas are accommodated within a Modernist format, a phase we describe as Alternative- or Counter-Modernism. Two unique architects, whom historians have never quite known how to place, stand out in this development: Alvar Aalto and Louis Kahn.

Alvar Aalto. Like his Swedish colleague Asplund, the Finnish architect Alvar Aalto began in the early 1920s in the style of Neoclassical Traditionalist Modernism, then absorbed in the late twenties the High Modernism of Gropius, Le Corbusier, and others, which he transformed into his own distinctive mode of Counter-Modernism. Aalto's buildings are easy to look at but difficult to understand, that is, to know what commands such worldwide respect, especially from the architectural profession. Although they present interesting compositions, they lack the gripping visual impact of other modern works. If we compare, for example, Aalto's finest residential building, his Villa Mairea of 1938–39, with the Villa Savoye or Fallingwater, we may wonder what the shouting is about. In this loose, informal sprawl there is no sign of the compelling form that was the Modernist ideal, no exceptionally photogenic, graphic images. In fact, the virtues of Aalto's work come across poorly in photographs. Far more than other major builders of our time, Aalto created an architecture not merely to quench the thirst for high art or pure structure, but in response to the more direct needs of women and men as active, sensate beings. Whereas other Modernists tended to use functionalism as a front, Aalto really meant it.

Aalto was a realist. Rather than designing utopian architecture for machine-age mankind-to-be, he accepted flesh and blood humanity for what it was and built accordingly. Aalto's buildings exist for no purpose other than human use. He carefully provides for human needs in buildings that are oriented toward what we would call "creature comforts," not, however, in sybaritic excess, but in a restrained, high-minded manner. His clients were socialist-oriented inhabitants of a war-torn, thinly populated, Arctic land. The hostile physical environment of Arctic cold and long dark winters was a factor in explaining Aalto's avoidance of assertive formalism and his obsession with warming comforts: the environment was challenging enough without architecture adding to the stress. Aalto's idea was that the built environment should provide the nourishing surroundings denied by nature during most of the year. Ultimately his work was an architectural extension of the "cradle-to-grave" security that was typically Scandinavian in its sensitivity to basic human needs and in its socialist phobia of ostentatious luxury.

Aalto's genius in translating experiential factors into a contemporary architectural idiom was revealed in a group of buildings he designed in 1927–28, none more striking than the Municipal Library in Viipuri (built 1930–35). The building (figs. 13-6, 13-7) consists of two white-stuccoed rectangular volumes of unequal size, set partly overlapping side by side. The larger is taken up mainly with the reading room, the smaller with the lecture hall; stacks are provided at a lower level, along with a children's library, and all is linked by an ingenious cross-axial entrance system. The reading room is one of the most lucid interiors of the twentieth century. Its crisply geometric, whitewashed severity makes it visually as High Modernist in spirit as the building's exterior. But first impressions can be deceiving, and there are diverse features, unseen as well as plainly visible, that extend the room beyond the usual High Modernist conceptions. The main stairway balustrade is a freeflowing frame for the entrance part of the stairs; and its railing, while visually crisp, is shaped not for the eye but for the hand, just as the treads and risers of the stair are shaped for the feet. Rows of conical skylights are modernistically elegant, yet are designed to provide the strong, even light so important for a library. Similarly, the small fixtures projecting from the ceiling are not for direct artificial lighting, but for washing the walls with a soft illumination. The walls are completely windowless (side windows mean harsh lighting); even more anomalous in a High Modernist interior, they are built of solid masonry, thirty inches thick, for acoustic insulation from exterior street noise. Aalto completed these creature comforts with a filtered air system and radiant heating. Thus, while the reading room looks High Modernist, it is geared not only to visual, aesthetic sensibility, but to our hearing, sense of touch, heat and cold, even breathing.

The lecture hall of the library is predominantly Counter-Modernist. One long side wall, admittedly, is open to the adjacent garden through High Modernist fenestration, but the wooden end-walls and the ceiling are dramatically shaped into a wavelike continuum that dominated the interior. It was for acoustical excellence and not for some arbitrary formalism that these wood-paneled surfaces were designed. After the library at Viipuri, the undulating curve crops up constantly in Aalto's work, always superbly combining utility and strong visual appeal. It appears, for example, in the multistoried display walls of his famous Finnish Pavilion for the 1939 New York

13-6   Alvar Aalto. Reading room, Municipal Library. Viipuri, Finland. 1930–35

13-7   Lecture hall, Municipal Library

World's Fair; in both the walls and the ceilings, whitewashed for a spiritual effect, of his church in Vuoksenniska of 1957; as the plan of the M.I.T. dormitory in Cambridge of 1949; even in his city planning, furniture, and in his glass vases, which are among the finest pieces in twentieth-century decorative arts.

By the late 1930s, the personal, Counter-Modernist aspects of the library permeate Aalto's style. This is best seen in the Villa Mairea (named after the artist-wife of Aalto's most important patron; figs. 13-8–13-10). To be sure, High Modernist influence is present in the villa's flat roofing (in a land of massive snowfall), in its crisp, simple volumes and plain surfaces, but other elements enter in. The base of the villa is faced with gray granite, and much of the rest with narrow strips of teak and other woods, with resulting textures that appeal to the sense of touch. The windows are disposed strictly for views and illumination, and they are hung on the *exterior* with teakwood venetian blinds. Although the influence of Wright is apparent in the horizontally stretched lines, nowhere is there Wright's explosion of cantilevered forms reaching toward the landscape. Instead, the building is molded in a pragmatic, functional way: to the rear is an L-shaped portico, roofed with sod, containing the sauna and half-enclosing the pool area (a scene more Japanese in its sensitivity to natural materials and forms than Western); to the front is a free-form entrance, and to the side a free-form loggia set concentrically beneath

13-8 Alvar Aalto. Villa Mairea. Noormarkku, Finland. 1938–39

13-9 Plan, Villa Mairea

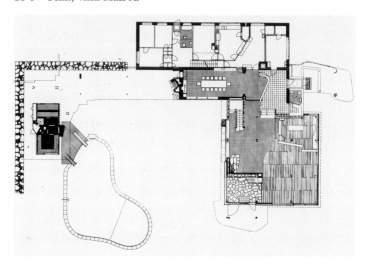

13-10 Pool and sauna, Villa Mairea

the second-story studio. The villa's dominant external feature is this studio, which partly rests on slender supports. It might well be taken as Aalto's rejoinder to the superstructure of the Villa Savoye: at the Villa Mairea, we have not a "Classicizing," geometric sun screen, but an enclosed, wood-paneled studio, looking like the stump of some primeval tree in the Finnish forest that is the building's setting. This naturalistic imagery, sensory richness, and fluidity extend through the interior of the villa, where a range of similar Counter-Modernist features play against the simple, rectilinear plan. These include the wood-paneled ceiling and the flooring, which is casually divided, sometimes diagonally, between various wood and masonry materials. Groups of slender wooden poles screen the commodiously shaped stair; most revealingly, the steel columns, although set out on a Corbusian Domino grid in the living room area, are wrapped in leather, but only to the height that one can actually reach. When Aalto wrote, a year after the Villa Mairea, that the purpose of architecture is "to bring the material world into harmony with human life," he was clearly not mouthing empty words.

Aalto continued to expand and refine his style until his death in 1976, reaching peak output during the 1950s and sixties. In this period he came to the fore as a master of group design and urban planning. His obsession with "psychophysical" considerations and his mastery of what makes for architectural intimacy limited his effectiveness in large-scale planning, but no contemporary architect was more successful in medium- and small-scale projects. Perhaps his finest urbanistic achievement is the Civic Center (1949–52) of Säynätsalo (fig. 13-11), a town of 3,000 inhabitants on a small island in an inland sea. A small town-council chamber and a few local government offices were needed originally, but Aalto was able to enlarge the project to include a library, apartments, and shops. These are grouped on several stories around a squarish court, which is partly filled with the earth dug from foundation work to raise it one story above the surrounding area. This provides for ceremonial emphasis as well as a quiet, intimate character. It also gave Aalto three levels to work with—shops and some apartments at the street zone;

13-11 Alvar Aalto. Civic Center. Säynätsalo, Finland. 1949–52

further apartments, the library, and town offices in wings around the raised court; and lifted symbolically above the town offices, the cubiform town-council chamber with its single-pitched roof (a favorite Aalto formula). Two corners of the court are left open (as in Greek agoras) for stairways, one a normal straight flight leading up from the commercial area below the town offices, the other a deliberately irregular flight with treads left in grass-planted sod, leading away from the town center. It is typical of Aalto's imagination that, while these stairs form an ingenious contextual device linking the city and the forest, the view up them is reminiscent of the scenography of Italian hill towns, understandably one of the two Mediterranean sources to which Aalto was drawn, the other being the Greek theater, the most site-integrated of all Hellenic forms. Other architects of the postwar period were also drawn to Italian hill towns, but none was more successful than Aalto in recapturing their spirit. The secret of this urbanistic gem is that it did not directly imitate; instead, Aalto abstracted and translated from hill-town components, making them into his own urbanistic language and using richly textured, local red brick and the wood natural to the setting.

Louis Kahn. Louis Kahn's vision of an Italian hill town at the Richards Medical Research Building (1957–61; fig. 13-12) of the University of Pennsylvania in Philadelphia—the building that made his worldwide reputation—could not have been more different from Säynätsalo. Where Aalto's was an idyllic village street scene, Kahn created with brick-walled shafts, which form the exhaust chimneys for the glass-walled laboratories, the image of a medieval city bristling with menacing defense towers. We have emphasized how Aalto's work differs from Modernist buildings—like Braille differs from print—in its preoccupation with human use and its responsiveness to the senses. Kahn's style, too, was different in a way that made him another major Counter-Modernist. His point of departure was nominally the same as Aalto's—the idea of function. But rather than analyzing function into its minute "psychophysical" components, Kahn philosophically explored the essence of the building's intended use, which then served as a springboard for his creation of an answering architectural form. He

was consumed by an almost mystical vision of architecture. Buildings for him were not inert configurations of form and space but living organic entities, created by the architect for human use. Thus Kahn asked himself not how to accommodate economically or beautifully this or that space requirement, but "What does the building want to be?" The vitality and animism of his designs, however, did not depend on the freeform, biomorphic shapes of Expressionism but on something intrinsically tectonic. That Kahn's greatest admirers have been builders is not coincidental, for he was an architect's architect.

One of Kahn's principal ideas was the distinction between "served" and "servant" spaces: at the Richards Laboratories, for example, the glass-walled workrooms are "served" by separate, freestanding brick chimneys. They are not, as in Modernism generally, combined into one package, nor, as in Brutalism, left as exposed ductwork. To realize its potential organic wholeness, each "served" space has its independent structural frame with a complete set of supports, just as living creatures have a complete set of legs. And since for Kahn it is light that brings architecture to life, each "served" space also has its own source of natural illumination (artificial light having an unvarying "dead" quality in contrast to ever-changing daylight). Openings in the walls are not for views or for continuity with nature, but to admit light to the interior space; walls, by deflecting it, shelter the space from an illumination too powerful and intense. The resulting pavilion system of discrete, served/serving architectural units with enveloping light screens tends to fuse into multilayered architectural gatherings. This potential was realized in the few years between Kahn's Richards Laboratories,

13-12 Louis Kahn. Richards Medical Research Building, University of Pennsylvania. Philadelphia. 1957–61

13-13   Louis Kahn. Air view, National Assembly Building. Dacca, Bangladesh. 1962

13-14   Plan, National Assembly Building

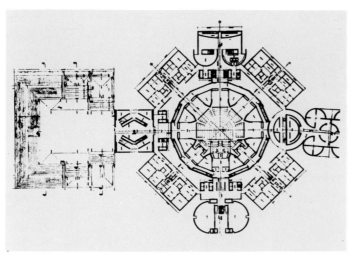

where the layers are only beginning to gather, and his National Assembly Building in Dacca, Bangladesh (figs. 13-13, 13-14), designed in 1962 as a dense, seemingly impenetrable, concentric agglomeration of walled spaces clustered around the central Assembly Chamber: press offices, secondary meeting halls, and a mosque (slightly off-axis to face Mecca). The minor units are themselves multilayered, admitting light through geometric cutouts in their solid, forbidding walls, which suggest not a medieval Italian hill town, but an austere, overpowering image of a fortress enclosed by rings of walls and towers.

These qualities depend on Kahn's near-exclusive use of masonry and especially of reinforced concrete in his mature work (as opposed to steel and glass, which he had mastered earlier). These he deployed not in thin High Modernist skins, but in solid, muscular, structural armatures and shells, which derived from the rugged primitivism of the late style of Le Corbusier, about whom Kahn exaggeratedly said, "He was my teacher, although he didn't know it." Le Corbusier's input came late in Kahn's life, during the 1950s. This was a secondary layer of influence over the deeper core of Kahn's Beaux-Arts training at the University of Pennsylvania in the early 1920s under the distinguished American Beaux-Arts master Paul P. Cret, in whose office Kahn worked in 1929–30. Kahn's vision of architecture, rooted in the Beaux-Arts tradition, was one of space-defining masonry masses and lucid structure, laid out in geometric, formal schemes dominated by the complex play of symmetrical axes and cross-axes, with a strong processional character of space and images.

But the sources of Kahn's Classicism, which was such a key to his work, were not limited to the classroom learning of the École. So often in the history of European architecture, the sources of renewal had been found directly at the well of antiquity itself, and so it was with Kahn. The turning point in his career was a year's residency at the American Academy in Rome, in 1950–51. He had been abroad in the 1920s with little effect, but later his receptivity and sensitivity to the underlying character of ancient architecture was very great. What

532 | THE MODERN WORLD

13-15   Louis Kahn. North gallery, Kimbell Art Museum. Fort Worth. 1966–72

13-16   Kimbell Art Museum

he saw in the Mediterranean world—the pyramids, Thebes, Mycenae, the Acropolis, Tivoli, aqueducts, arenas, baths, and the Pantheon—was the translation of function into bold forms, clear planning, pure geometry, and simple vital structure. It was not the richly decorative weight or rhetorical magnificence of the antique beloved in the nineteenth century, nor the sculptural play of its forms in sunlight, as with Le Corbusier, but its conceptual and structural vitality and accountability that Kahn was moved by and was able to recreate in modern form language.

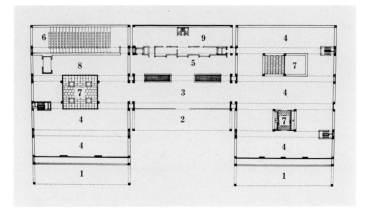

13-17   Plan, Kimbell Art Museum. (After M. D. Meyers) Gallery Level Plan: 1. Porch; 2. Entrance Porch; 3. Entrance Hall; 4. Gallery; 5. Book Sale; 6. Auditorium; 7. Open Court; 8. Kitchen; 9. Library

Kahn's architecture also projects a strong emotional quality, a brooding nostalgia for the lost ancient world. For the most part, this mood is elusive, mysteriously infused into his severe masonry. Its most self-conscious realization is in the layering of the perimeter of buildings. About 1959–60, Kahn translated the *brise-soleil* idea of Le Corbusier into freestanding perimetric screens, developed to the maximum at the building in Dacca, a device about which Kahn wrote: "I thought of the beauty of ruins . . . of things which nothing lives behind . . . and so I thought of wrapping ruins around buildings." The vast mural layers at Dacca, which Kahn also called "an offering to the sun," cut by huge, mysterious circles, squares, and triangles, are thus meant not only to control the blinding sun of the Indian subcontinent but to give the building the aura of ancientness by evoking the image of ancient ruins, crumbling Roman walls punched with empty openings, and "useless" structures "which nothing lives behind." This visionary iconographic leap was to prove Kahn's most significant influence in contemporary architecture.

But Kahn was able to achieve the same power and ancient aura in a less flamboyant manner. Many of his mature projects from 1951 to 1976 are divided between two approaches to planning: centralized structures with concentrically layered spaces aligned on rotating axes (as at Dacca); and additive assemblages of modular units. Among the latter is his much admired work, the Kimbell Art Museum in Fort Worth, Texas, of 1966–72 (figs. 13-15–13-18). The principal floor of the museum, set over a basement story that evens out the sloping site, consists mainly of a repeated structural unit, an enormous barrel-vaulted bay 20 by 100 feet, laid out in six parallel

13-18   Kimbell Art Museum, cross section. (After M. D. Meyers)

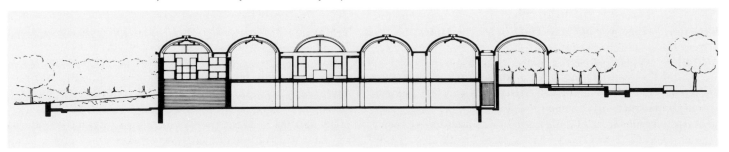

rows, each row three units deep end-to-end. The idea for such a barrel-vaulted scheme is not new. It derives from Le Corbusier, who used it as an alternative to the Domino model in some of his late works; but on the scale and in the spirit that Kahn used the form, we can trace it back to second-century B.C. Roman warehouses such as the Porticus Aemilia (fig. 3-20). What is remarkable about Kahn's treatment of the ancient design is that he recaptures its archaic power by transforming it into modern structural terms. Whereas with both the Porticus Aemilia and Le Corbusier, the traditional barrel vaulting must spring from a continuous support surface of walling, trabeation, or arcades, in the Kimbell Museum the 100-foot-long vaulting unit is supported only at its corners by narrow piers (two feet square), eliminating the support walls and thereby freeing the interior space—a crucial functional virtue for a museum. This span is possible because Kahn's vault is a single unit of reinforced concrete, forming, in effect, a concrete beam of semicircular profile. Visually, however, the vault does not seem to be the self-supporting unit that it is, but a traditional vault supported continuously by lintels posed on the corner piers, lintels so slender that they appear hardly capable of supporting themselves, let alone a barrel vault.

To bring light into the museum's interior, Kahn transformed the structure even further. He slit open the apex of each vault from end to end, leaving only minimal structural bridges every 10 feet. To avoid the glaring light that the 2½-foot-wide slot would have created, Kahn invented a high-technology, interior version of his usual external masonry sun screens—a "natural lighting fixture." Hanging below the vault are curved aluminum panels perforated with tiny holes that allow a small portion of light to penetrate directly, while the rest is reflected from the highly polished upper surface of the aluminum onto the vault and thence down to the interior. The resulting mixture of "silver light," as Kahn called it, combined with a gentle "green light" diffused through the interior from strategically placed sculpture-garden courts, creates a luminous atmosphere tinged with the coloration of both earth and sky. Kahn's treatment of the ceiling, however, was aimed at more than just the light it shed on the space below, for the appearance of the vault itself was a crucial consideration. As a type, the barrel vault offered Roman grandeur and nobility, but it also carried drawbacks—a heavy, gloomy appearance appropriate in a warehouse or Romanesque church but antithetical to a museum. Kahn found a way to preserve the former characteristics while avoiding the latter. We have observed how the illusionistic lintels dematerialize the vault; the slice through its crown further reduces its sense of ponderous solidity; the computer-designed curve of the "natural lighting fixture" lights up the vaulting surface (normally dark and heavy); and that same curve visually combines with the vault to form an ogeelike effect, thereby inverting the usual sinking tendency of the vault into a pseudo-Gothic lifting toward the light. Thus, Kahn created for his museum a serene, yet dynamic, atmosphere combining Roman *gravitas* and Gothic buoyancy.

Kahn's organization of the museum's whole is as powerful as that of its basic parts. The barrel-vaulted bays are separated by narrow "servant" spaces with flat ceilings containing air-conditioning ductwork and the like. Since the only permanent walls are around the perimeter, the "servant" spaces add to the flexibility of interior features: the stairs, for example, are all contained within "servant" spaces; garden courts are either 20 feet square (spanning only the "served" space) or 36 feet (including both adjoining "servant" spaces). The museum's principal function as an exhibition space is accommodated with movable partition walls.

If flexibility was one virtue of Kahn's plan, the other was its lucid Beaux-Arts order: the cross-axial alignment of the bays; the creation of a U-shaped garden facade by omitting two middle bays to form an entrance court; the making of wall-less loggias at the ends of the U, fronted by fountains. All this serves to position the entering visitor at the center of the huge comfortable building. Throughout the museum there is a masterfully crisp, minimalist detailing of every joint, edge, and transition which only an architect steeped in the Classical tradition could have created. In its totality, the Kimbell Museum is one of the few contemporary structures in the world of a stature to hold its own against the great historical lineup of the centuries; this was Kahn's own measure for himself.

POST-MODERNISM

Robert Venturi. No architect admired Louis Kahn more than did Robert Venturi, yet Venturi's architecture took a completely different direction, which ultimately carried him across the threshold of Post-Modernism. Where Kahn spoke in poetic aphorism and built lucid visions, Venturi played the role of a Princetonian academic and *enfant terrible*. His few modest early structures had a powerful effect on contemporary architecture, but his theoretical writings were even more influential. After several apprenticeships (including a stint with Kahn himself), Venturi in 1954–56 received a fellowship to the American Academy in Rome. He was drawn to a different Rome, a different Mediterranean, a different layer of architectural history than the ancient realm of geometric starkness and lucidity that had cast its spell on Kahn. During Venturi's stay at the Academy, the unconventional buildings of sixteenth-century Mannerist architects such as Giulio Romano, Vignola, and Michelangelo were hot scholarly topics. By temperament as well as intellect, Venturi was drawn to ideas about "Complexity and Contradiction in Architecture," which became the title of his first book, written in 1962 and published in 1966 by the Museum of Modern Art.

The argument of the book is learned and complex, but its main thesis is simple. Venturi, writing in the rebellious spirit of the 1960s, was fed up with "the puritanically moral language of orthodox Modern architecture." Less is not more, as in Mies's equation; instead he claimed, "Less is a bore." According to Venturi, architecture should not be based on exclusion and restriction, but be permissive, accommodating the complexities and contradictions inherent in construction, in history, in life itself. In Venturi's words, architecture should be hybrid, not pure; perverse, not impersonal; redundant, not simple; inconsistent, not clear; conventional, not designed; of messy vitality and richness of meaning rather than unity and clarity of meaning; and so forth.

Venturi explained his architecture of Complexity and Contradiction with theoretical arguments, lists of antidotes to Modernist toxins, and examples from a vast range of historical practice, illustrated in full-page displays of postage-stamp sized illustrations (fig. 13-19). He revealed how architectural history is filled with buildings that, far from being "organically"

13-19 **Robert Venturi. A page from his book *Complexity and Contradiction in Architecture*, 1966 (enlarged):**
94. Michelangelo, Rear Facade, Palazzo Farnese, Rome; 95. Michelangelo, Medici Chapel, S. Lorenzo, Florence;
96. Jefferson, University of Virginia, Charlottesville; 97. Granada Cathedral; 98. Foligno Cathedral;
99. Vanbrugh, Eastbury, Dorset (elevation); 100. Johns, *Three Flags*, 1958; 101. Church of the Holy Sepulchre,
Jerusalem (plan); 102. Peabody and Stearns, Black House (Kragsyde), Manchester-by-the-Sea, Massachusetts

integrated, are pervaded with contradictions between exterior and interior, corners and center, top and bottom. He shows an architecture filled with fragmented forms, with axes that shift suddenly, with diagonals that brutally skew through the fabric—effects to which he gives names such as "superadjacencies," "double-functioning" elements, "multi-functioning" rooms, etc. Although he finds these occurrences particularly common in Mannerist and Baroque architecture, his examples embrace styles as disparate as Hellenistic and Shingle, and architects as varied as Soane, Ledoux, Butterfield, Furness, and Lutyens; and Le Corbusier, Kahn and other Modernists play a vital role. He eventually included virtually all the Western world's important architecture in his sweep so that his countercurrent turned out to be the mainstream itself. What he offered in effect is a revision of the way we see architecture.

Although veiled historical allusion and "unhistorical Classicism" had meant much to Modernists, Venturi felt that their basic outlook was deeply antihistorical. A half-century of Modernism had produced a kind of historical amnesia in architecture. As a "cure" he wanted, in T. S. Eliot's words, a "perception not only of the pastness of the past, but of its presence." The "presence of the past" was something mysteriously felt in the work of Kahn, but Venturi openly proclaimed it as articulate doctrine. Reopening the door to the past, not only its Mannerist side but more generally, and welcoming its open participation in contemporary architecture were among Venturi's greatest gifts to Second Modernism.

In 1972, Venturi, together with his wife, Denise Scott Brown, an architect and planner, and the architect Steven Izenour, published a second assault on Modernism. *Learning from Las Vegas* chronicles the architectural slumming of an undaunted group of sociologically oriented architectural researchers in the honky-tonk wasteland of the American roadside "strip"—not merely vernacular or industrial construction, not Miami Beach or Levittown suburbia, but the Modernist architectural nightmare in Las Vegas in the Nevada desert (before its beautification of the 1980s and after). Venturi's purpose was to demonstrate how visually potent and stimulating this architecture was, particularly to an automobilized audience and its highway sensibility of billboards, signs, and symbols. He praised its garish interior settings and poolside oases that combined everything from blazing electronics to cheesecake sexuality and garish Classical statuary. In Las Vegas Venturi claimed to rediscover "the forgotten symbolism of architectural form" (the book's subtitle in its second edition of 1977) that had been submerged by Modern architecture. He correctly calculated that his readers would be drawn to the worse-than-banal imagery of Las Vegas and accept its lessons through the same influences that he and his collaborators had felt, especially the Pop Art movement of the 1960s and its celebration of commercial, mass-media iconography.

For all its openness to nonarchitectural currents, *Learning from Las Vegas* remains essentially a book about architecture and one in which Venturi's position has radically shifted. By the late 1960s, when he was writing *Learning from Las Vegas*, he felt that any architecture concerned mainly with space, form, and structure was irrelevant, socially coercive, inappropriate, and out of touch with the new electronic technology and with the automobilized, electronicized, and suburbanized sensibility

of its users. Repeatedly, Venturi claimed: "This is not the time and ours not the environment for heroic communication via pure architecture"; in general, he is fed up with "too much architecture." His polemic comes to a focus in his now-famous distinction between the architectural "duck"—a building that formally tries to symbolize its function (such as a roadside stand in the shape of a duck selling ducks)—and the "decorated shed"—a structurally and formally trivial, utilitarian construction given a superficial layer of explicit symbolism and applied ornament. He insists that we must abandon the "architectural soap opera" of "dead ducks" and concentrate on the "decorated shed." Not only is the latter a "people's architecture as the people want it," Venturi writes, continuing the '60s rhetoric, it is what the people *need*, that is, architecture as a "system of communications within society" to satisfy "the need for explicit and heightened symbolism." Reinterpreting architectural history in this new light, Venturi now emphasized the Parthenon's symbol-laden sculpture, claimed that the Arch of Constantine was a proto-billboard, and that "Amiens Cathedral is a billboard with a building behind it." He concluded that if we learn our lessons correctly from the strip—and from suburbia—"the archetypal Los Angeles will be our Rome and Las Vegas our Florence; and like the archetypal grain elevators some generations ago, the [Hotel] Flamingo sign will be the model to shock our sensibilities towards a new architecture."

Of course the last four words of this quotation are the English title of what previously had been the most influential architectural book of the twentieth century—Le Corbusier's *Vers une architecture*. Venturi's *Learning from Las Vegas* and *Complexity and Contradiction* are also impassioned, polemical works informed with a revolutionary vision of architecture, brilliant in their aphoristic phrases, historical juxtapositions, and photographic montages. The books' influence cannot be overestimated: they are the essential texts for "reading" Post-Modernism, every important architect of the time having been deeply affected by them. It is important to emphasize, however, that in developing his position Venturi treated the Modernists as blindly and unsympathetically as they had treated nineteenth-century architects in their day.

So crucial were Venturi's ideas to contemporary architecture that he might well be called the Viollet-le-Duc of Post-Modernism. And like Viollet-le-Duc, Venturi's theories have overshadowed his executed works, which were often regarded as being cramped by his intellectualism. It is true that Venturi's designs, especially the important works of the early 1960s such as the Guild House in Philadelphia and his mother's house in Chestnut Hill outside that city, are tense, nervous, even jumpy. These qualities were to become inherent to most Post-Modernist buildings by virtue of their foundation on the ideas formulated in Venturi's work.

The Vanna Venturi House in Chestnut Hill is clearly a house; that is, it does not pretend to be a ship, an airplane, or an organic device to commune with nature (fig. 13-20). Yet it is not just any house. It is a conventional American suburban, stuccoed, wood-frame crackerbox with all its stigmata—pitched roof, front porch, back porch, central chimney, and the rest. These conventions are presented as deadpan as the imagery of a contemporary Andy Warhol Brillo Box or a Roy Lichtenstein cartoon painting. Critics called the house "ugly and ordinary,"

13-20   Robert Venturi. Chestnut Hill House. Philadelphia. 1962

a phrase that Venturi adopted gleefully for the Pop archi-tecture he was pitting against the prevailing style of soap-opera "ducks." This house was as shocking an affront to Modernists as Loos's Steiner House and Le Corbusier's Citrohan had been to traditionalists in their day. It was ordi-nary only in its overt iconography, and ugly only in the emo-tions it provoked in its critics, who were really saying that it was ugly *because* it seemed so ordinary. This Venturi house did indeed parody the conventional house so completely that at first one did not realize how completely Venturi had trans-formed it, enriching it with wit, irony, and allusion. The process of transformation began with inflating the scale of the cracker-box by stretching the facade several feet above the roof and giv-ing the heightened roofline a sweeping symmetry. Venturi then cleft the partly freestanding, gabled facade so deeply down the center and cut the gaping front porch so high into the wall that the shape is made ambiguous: are we seeing two half-facades in the process of merging, or a complete facade that has been split in two? The strip of "lintel" that dubiously joins the two halves looks precariously narrow even for the crackerbox con-struction. Venturi's solution to this imaginary structural weak-ness is the symbolic arch above, a mere molding, and, at that, interrupted in the center. Yet visually it effectively deflects the "weight" from the hollow. The enigmatic configuration of the facade's central area is not altogether original: it derives from Kahn's contemporary "ruin wrappings," where slotted parapets and stretched lintels are encountered in solid masonry. These Venturi transformed into a Cubist surface abstraction much in the way two centuries earlier Burlington had rendered the solid forms of Palladio into a papery Neo-Palladianism. Histori-cist allusions are found in the binary cleavage of the facade, where we can recognize the split pediment of Blenheim Palace, and even the pylon of an Egyptian temple complete with its linteled, gaping doorway. Such allusions did not obliterate the

"houseness" of the Venturi House, which remained primary, enhanced by formal vitality and witty historical resonances along with a curious illusion of scale.

That the house in Chestnut Hill is the work of a highly accomplished architect, and not only a theorist, is borne out by the details found throughout the house. The facade, for exam-ple, consists not only of clearly visible planar elements but extends sharply into the deep hollow of the porch, through the cleft above it, to the broad mass of the clerestory of the second story which suggests a large central chimney mass until one sees the small actual chimney projecting above it! Among all the intricate ambiguities a strong unity is felt: the porch and clerestory wall are precisely the same width and size; the width of the cleft matches the height of the ribbon window; and the size and number (five) of window panels is identical on each side. The diverse elements are held together in a precar-ious tension that grips the observer and involves him or her actively in its formal and symbolic dynamics. The work of Venturi is incomplete without an intense dialogue with the human participants; this consideration extends throughout the house—to its contrasting sides and rear (with a balcony and lunette window); and especially to the interior, where the axis shifts at entrance, diagonals skew through, and stairs run in reverse perspective and in one case to nowhere at all, in a manner full of the refreshing vitality, irony, and lighthearted wit so typical of Venturi's Pop-architecture style.

Venturi's block of ninety-one apartments for the elderly, sponsored by the Society of Friends, proclaimed itself GUILD HOUSE in a shockingly bold, commercial sign at the door (fig. 13-21). It was, of course, not a house but housing, and Venturi did not hesitate to give it the look of conventional housing, with grimly utilitarian, cheap, dark brown brick walling and sparse windows resembling postwar urban renewal projects as well as, according to Venturi, the "tenement-like

13-21 Robert Venturi. Guild House. Philadelphia. 1960–63. (Symbolic golden TV antenna removed)

backs of Edwardian apartment houses." This housing type is, if anything, even more banal than the crackerbox house, and Venturi does nothing to spare us its unfortunate connotations. On the contrary, his point is to assert its conventionality, because only thus can he express those ironic tensions and transformations created by the intervention of nonconventional, historicist imagery. The Philadelphia housing project, while materially and iconographically remaining true to itself, reflects the dignity of a Baroque church or princely residence. Like a Baroque church facade, the symmetrical massing is made to break forward in three strong steps toward the center, where the visual weight is concentrated in a variety of pseudo-Baroque effects. The entrance zone is faced to the second story with white glazed bricks, and curved inward below the sign to the recessed doorway set behind a pseudo-column of polished black granite. Above, the perforated steel-plate parapets of the balconies are painted white to create a continuity of surface and are framed between columns of windows. All these elements are gathered beneath a Neo-Palladian lunette that fronts the common room. Finally, the emphatic axial line, which runs from the entrance cylinder through the balcony divider, originally erupted above the roof (in another pseudo-Baroque effect) as a gold anodized, fake TV antenna (later removed). In perhaps his most extreme *enfant terrible* moment, Venturi described it as "a symbol of the aged, who spend so much time looking at T.V."

This roguish affront to the elderly was only half of the Venturi equation. The other side was his ennoblement of old age by endowing its otherwise banal housing with architectural dignity. Such conflict and irony are at the heart of his style, a juxtaposition of low vernacular and high art, of ignoble present and noble past, of statement and denial. A crackerbox house becomes also its own antithesis—Blenheim Palace or an Egyptian pylon; a predestined slum forms a Baroque facade.

Venturi's assaults on Modernism eventually were successful, especially after he was joined by numerous fellow rebels, but his belief that he was creating a people's architecture was misguided. For years few clients sought him out. His witty style was lost on the masses, and to the wealthy patrons of the architectural vanguard he was not ostentatious enough to make the kind of media impact on which so much post-1960s architectural patronage increasingly depended. But Venturi's ideas created a hunger for "difficult" architecture. His ideas were taken up by the avant-garde and carried into ever freer practices, moving from an ironic play with historicist allusion to a world of historicizing extravagance.

Charles Moore. Our emphasis on Venturi's central role in the formation of Post-Modernism should not give the mistaken impression that he worked in a vacuum. Among the others who in various ways complemented him, none was more important than Charles Moore. The two men were exact contemporaries (born in 1925), and between the mid-1950s and the early 1970s their careers ran along parallel lines (Moore died in 1993). So strongly were both Moore and Venturi influenced by Kahn that they may be said to have formed the Kahn School. Both were affected by Kahn's feeling for the architectural past, by his predilection toward building in layers, and by his involvement with symbolic meaning. Like Venturi, Moore was committed to the Post-Modernist notion that a building should openly proclaim its function. Similarly, Moore was deeply involved with reestablishing Venturi's "presence of the past," but he used historicist language that was more explicit and more Roman-Mediterranean than Venturi's, in a freer, more extroverted style leading directly into full-blown Post-Modernism.

The core of Moore's involvement with historicism was his preoccupation with, as he called it, "the making of places." By

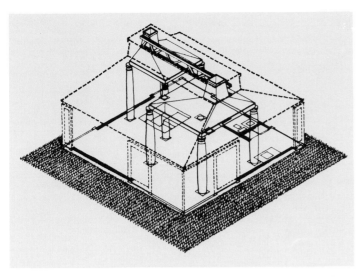

13-22 Charles Moore. The architect's house, isometric projection. Orinda, California. 1962. (After C. Jencks)

the 1960s, particularly in America, and most particularly in suburbanized car cultures as found in California, where Moore taught and practiced, places had begun to look disturbingly alike: this street like that, this shopping mall, urban sprawl, or modernized downtown like that one, Berlin like Cleveland, and so on. Moreover, as one traveled increasingly by air or by superhighway, even the usual sense of distance traversed was confounded. The result was a spatial and topographical disorientation perhaps only intuitively felt by most people, yet nevertheless an increasing ill of contemporary civilization. Moore's aim was to recapture, if only piecemeal and metaphorically, the lost "sense of place."

Three examples illustrate Moore's development of this theme between the early 1960s and the mid-1970s. His small 1962 house in Orinda, California, establishes a "sense of place" by layering small, individualized spaces within a larger, neutral frame that separates the spatial arena from the outer world (fig. 13-22). Within a darkened, barnlike, hip-roofed shell, Moore sets two trabeated classical baldacchinos, constructed of slender, ten-foot-high, wooden Tuscan columns salvaged from a demolition site, their superstructures askew

13-23 Charles Moore. Dormitory complex, Kresge College. Santa Cruz, California. 1965–74

so that they shape a single skylight. His historical sources for the canopies include everything from four-poster beds and the famous breakfast parlor at Soane's house in London to altar baldacchinos (like Bernini's at St. Peter's) and small aedicules that enframe statues of medieval saints. Here they enshrine a sunken bath/shower and living room area; the irony is created by the gap between sacred and profane, the sublime and near-ridiculous, recalling Venturi's contrasting of banal and noble form.

At his dormitory complex for Kresge College in Santa Cruz, California, of 1965–74, Moore moves his placemaking design outdoors (fig. 13-23). The L-shaped layout rambles through a redwood forest, widening, narrowing, twisting along its central "street" in his version of the "Italian hill town." Paradoxically, Moore vividly evokes the picturesque vitality of the hill town by fronting the street facades with a varied series of stuccoed, trabeated screens, stairs, and "arches." These flimsy-looking, Pop-Hollywoodish forms are accented with bright, primary colors at strategic places, marking with 1960s irony as "monuments" such functional banalities as a public telephone and laundromat.

Moore's obsession with the "sense of place" took its most vivid form in a work of pure urbanistic scenography—the Piazza d'Italia (figs. 13-1, 13-24, 13-25) in New Orleans, built in 1975–80 (in collaboration with a Los Angeles group, U.I.G., and a local firm, Perez Associates, Inc.). The idea was to provide the small Italian-American population of New Orleans with an architectural focus of ethnic identity, a piazza where its annual feast of St. Joseph could be celebrated. The Italian tradition of colorful display, together with the imagery inherent in the concept "Italy" and the classicizing trends of the accelerating Post-Modernist movement, set off Moore's imagination on a wild, yet brilliantly controlled, run. The site was an off-square block already occupied in one corner by a nondescript office tower amidst rather bleak surroundings, but these difficulties merely heightened the scenographic intensity necessary for an effective Italianate "sense of place." Moore's prototypes for his circular piazza included the circular Place des Victoires in Paris, Hadrian's circular Maritime Theater at his villa near Tivoli, and, most importantly, Nicola Salvi's Trevi Fountain in Rome, a spectacular combination of Classical facade, allegorical earth sculpture, and water. Moore's earth sculpture is not allegorical, but realistic—the map of Italy, built up diagonally from the circle's center to its circumference, a cascade of steplike forms, making a rough contour model of Italy's "boot." This rises in height toward the "Alps," contains small fountains representing Italy's major rivers, and is flanked by a pool marking the Adriatic and Tyrrhenian seas. New Orleans's Italians being mostly of Sicilian descent, "Italy" is set in the circular precinct so that Sicily falls at its center, surrounded by concentric rings in the pavement that evoke not only radiating waves of water but also a solar-system image with Sicily as the sun. Gathered around "Italy," over asymmetrically staggered segments of the outer five pavement rings, stand a variety of trabeated screens. They represent the five orders and progress in richness and scale outward and upward toward the "Alps," where a layered Serliana gateway, the lines of its superstructure ablaze with neon, culminates the stenography between prominent Latin dedicatory inscriptions. In addition, in the fanlike corridors connecting the circular piazza with the

13-24   **Charles Moore with U.I.G. and Perez Associates, Inc. Piazza d'Italia. New Orleans. 1975–80**

13-25   **View from above, Piazza d'Italia**

New Orleans street grid stand various Classical and sub-Classical pergolas and triumphal arches that visually anticipate the central piazza itself. Moore's five orders are executed mainly in a vibrant mixture of Pompeian colors and stainless steel; the detailing is a startling blend of historical accuracy and aquatic and luminescent invention—water cascading down sectioned columns as transparent illusory "fluting," water jets in place of Corinthian leaves, stainless steel Ionic volutes, neon necking, and spandrel waterspout heads (depicting the architect!). The Piazza d'Italia was at once archaeological, Modernist, commercial, and high camp. There was something

13-26   Strada Nuova, Venice Biennale. 1980

in it for everyone, yet it projected an inner logic and conviction that saved it from being the throwaway *pasticcio* that it easily might have been.

Moore's Neoclassical extravaganza was realized in the climactic years of Post-Modernism as a movement that overtook the international world of progressive architecture. The half-decade was punctuated by two important Post-Modernist events. The 1975 exhibition of the École des Beaux-Arts at the stronghold of Modernism, New York's Museum of Modern Art, gave official sanction to Venturi's idea of the validity of historicism for contemporary life. The spectacular array of École drawings emphasized the potential of historicism for individualistic, and even eccentric, architectural expression and the authenticity of drawing as an architectural medium in its own right. In 1980, the centerpiece of the prestigious Venice Biennale international art exhibition was the Strada Nuova (fig. 13-26), a Hollywood-like street of sham facades erected in the huge, cinquecento arsenal, each of the twenty facades (and the exhibition booths behind them) by a different Post-Modernist architect, among them Venturi and Moore. The Strada Nuova provided a shocking revelation to the public—as well as to the architects themselves—of a dynamic, self-confident, new international "style" of surprising breadth and depth. Although the world had now caught up to them, Venturi and Moore were the guiding spirits of the show. The "official" theme of the exhibit, which later traveled to Paris and Los Angeles, was "The Presence of the Past."

Post-Modernism burst forth not only with exhibitions but with real buildings, including some imposing monumental projects that far overleaped the tentative early work of Moore and Venturi. This wave seemed to peak about 1977–78, when the most grandiose works of Post-Modernism were begun (all completed by 1983–84). As we explore the colorful results, it should be kept in mind that our few representative examples can only suggest the great range of the new architectural scene. Although the continuing importance of Venturi's ideas can hardly be overestimated, it was, more than anything else, the flamboyant classicizing work of Charles Moore that set the tone for full-blown Post-Modernism, as well as giving it certain directions, which may be observed in three varied projects.

O. M. Ungers. Few commissions could have been more characteristic of Post-Modernism than the new Museum of Architecture, founded by the late German art historian Heinrich Klotz in Frankfurt-am-Main, nor could a more fitting solution have been found for the project than the building erected in 1981–84 by O. M. Ungers (fig. 13-27). In it, Moore's layered "house-in-a-house" prototype was fused with Kahn's "wrapped ruins." To create the Museum, Ungers gutted a nineteenth-century sandstone, urban villa, whose walls became the preserved "ruins," within which a much narrower new "house" was built at the center beneath a skylight ceiling, with an intermediate new third "shell" near the old walls. The three shells engage a variety of floors, balconies, and partition walls to create a configuration of exhibition and service spaces, nearly everywhere the new "house" being fragmentarily visible. This vivid interplay of the architectural present and past is completed by the

13-27   O. M. Ungers. Museum of Architecture, axonometric
section. Frankfurt-am-Main. 1981–84.
(Courtesy the Museum)

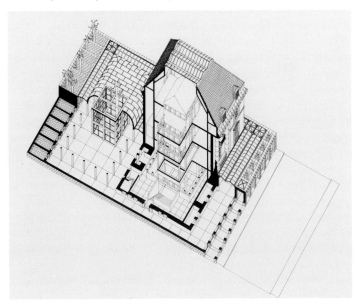

13-28   Hans Hollein. Austrian Travel Bureau. Vienna. 1978

13-29   Robert Stern. Project for a storefront for Best Products, Inc., detail. 1980 (From *Architectural Design*)

"wrapping" of the nineteenth-century "ruins" themselves at street level by glass-roofed gallery corridors and an elaborate garden court to the rear. At the back of this court, a row of discrete cubicles enshrines a line of ancient trees, so that the concept "architecture" encompassed by the museum is broadened to include its natural setting.

Hans Hollein. In his Austrian Travel Bureau of 1978 in Vienna (fig. 13-28), the designer Hans Hollein took up the underlying topographic theme and scenographic methods of Moore's Piazza d'Italia, but with a new twist. Hollein transformed a pre-existing hall with "a scenario of iconographical, metaphorical, and associative elements" that suggest not one place, but many places worth traveling to in space, time, and imagination: in other words, the idea of travel itself. The three-dimensional collage of allusive forms and images includes a grove of brass palms modeled after those in Nash's Brighton Pavilion, suggesting travel to the nineteenth century, to England, and to paradisical tropical islands. Among the palms is placed a broken "Grecian" column; nearby, pyramids emerge from a wall; a flock of birds and a model of the Wright Brothers' biplane hang in the air; and there are rivers, mountains, and a ship's railing. Of the more than thirty motifs, the most prominent are those on the central axis of the room—an Oriental pavilion, a chessboard seating area, and a sales booth for theater tickets, backed by a woodcut of Sebastiano Serlio's *Comic Scene*, overhung by a metal "theater curtain," and furnished with a cash register in the form of a Rolls Royce hood. Completing this artful collage and heightening its infectious mood of travel and adventure is the hall itself, made to resemble Otto Wagner's Postal Savings Bank of 1904–6. Although the overt connotation is, of course, travel to turn-of-the-century, early Modernist Vienna, the architectural reference ironically mocks the whole purpose of the Travel Bureau, which is not to encourage savings, but to promote free-spending, late-twentieth-century consumerism.

Robert Stern. Our third example of Moore-related work, which also entailed socioeconomic comment, again pursued the di-

rection taken at the Piazza d'Italia. The particular obsession of the New York architect Robert Stern at the time was the ancient orders, which he subjected to transformations saturated with wit, invention, and insight. In his unexecuted project for a storefront for Best Products, Inc. (a catalogue retailer of household goods), Stern's ingenuity is seen at its extreme (fig. 13-29). His method is based on Labrouste's famous cross-sectional drawings of Doric columns from Paestum (included in the 1975 Beaux-Arts exhibition) and on the actual layering of flat columnar elements by virtuoso architects such as Borromini. In the detail of the Best Products facade, showing the entrance and one of the smaller, flanking portico units, Stern projects in actual construction Labrouste's drawn sectioned image—the reverse side of the standard half-column—hollowed out with a space in the shape of a column. The result of this process of reversal, fragmentation, and superimposition is a three-in-one set of images: the whole sectioned outer column; the pair of asymmetrical, Egyptianesque columns formed by its two halves, supporting the "lintel"; and the contained, negative column-shaped hollow (about which Stern said, regarding a related project, "Since the void columns are the means by which one enters . . . it is as if one is in fact walking through history into the past"). In the small side unit a fourth image takes over: of a "fat woman" whose head is formed by the TV-shaped "metope" above, its hollow core destined for the display of the Best products, inescapably suggesting that the "idiot box" has taken control of and replaced the consumer's brain. With his slapstick humor, Stern escalated Venturi's earlier affront to the elderly. Venturi's notorious golden TV antenna now seemed a mild satire compared to Stern's mocking of society-at-large, so witty and playful (and so close to the undeniable truth) that no one could really take offense.

Michael Graves. Stern's reformulations of the order seem facile, however, when compared to the complex transformations of Classical syntax and historicist allusion in the work of Michael Graves. Few contemporary architects penetrated as deeply as Graves into the Classical form language of both the arcuated and trabeated modes, or created with them such suggestive new images. Graves said that he designs as if he were a child; and when we see the model of his Portland Public Service Building of 1980–83 (colorplate 81), it resembles at first glance nothing so much as a child's colorful construction (simplified in execution because of cost). It suggests not the abstract geometry of Wright's Froebel Blocks, but what a well-traveled child might produce if asked to draw what he recalled from Athens or Rome: a structure made of simple, stepped, toylike blocks and a few oversimplified Classical forms, with the usual scale relationships thrown to the winds. While Graves enters a Neoclassical, mock infantile fairyland, his design is hardly the ingenuous scratchings of a child but a sophisticated vision.

Analysis of the Portland Building model reveals a layered interweave of mural, trabeated, and arcuated structure, the play of depth and surface illusion, abstraction and figured image, the present and the past. It begins as a child's construction, its three-storied stepped base surmounted by a near-cube of twelve stories. The scale of the cube is established and exaggerated by the grid of small windows (three feet square in the model, four feet as executed), and the face of the cube is opened with a huge, mirror-glass window to the front. This window (and its counterparts on the flanks) is so large that a second "reading" of the building is suggested, trabeated rather than mural—a huge aedicular unit framing the window. Superimposed on the cream-colored main facade is a "secondary" maroon-colored set of forms—twin, giant pilasters with bracket capitals and a colossal keystone. Seen by itself, the keystone makes the whole building a square flat-arched unit, but when seen with the pilasters, the broad keystone paradoxically forms a supported lintel. However, where a keystone is inherently a form in depth, the pilasters are indicated as thin surface elements by the way the window transom appears to run straight behind them just beyond the front plane of the building. This play of surface versus depth permeates the whole structure, which may be seen as a solid, massive cube or as a thin, Modernist curtain wall (which it became in execution, spun over a steel frame). Even more jolting is the play of figured iconography: the pilaster-keystone group forms a double anthropomorphic image: a huge face with the capitals as eyes and a standing figure—a broad-shouldered, Atlas-like "strong man." Finally, the upper bracket and rooftop structures (omitted in execution) that form the head of the giant yield still another level of image and scale—a set of little Classical pavilions, a flourish balanced on the building's flanks by enormous festoons (of fiberglass, again omitted). Yet, apart from the roof, this central part of the building threatens to dissolve before one's eyes at the realization that the fluting of the pilasters and the "mortar joints" of the keystone are nothing but vertical and horizontal ribbon windows.

Graves did not conjure this dynamo of "Complexity and Contradiction" out of thin air, but out of historicist allusion. The overscaled pilasters are Soanic; the isolated keystone runs in a tradition from the Italian Mannerists to Ledoux, on whom the concept of the cubiform massing (even its little windows) is closely modeled. But the Portland Building as a whole suggests one of the icons of Early Modernism seen earlier in this book: Behrens's great Turbinenfabrik with its grand pediment, its corner piers, and above all its giant central window (fig. 12-60). Originally the harbinger of the future, the window is transformed by Graves into a remnant of the "defeated" Modernist past, imprisoned behind his Classical Atlas.

Graves's monument to Post-Modernism was intended to serve its immediate public. Beginning with Venturi, Post-Modernists harped on the potential of historicist conventions for meaningful public rhetoric and symbolic display. The Portland Building model projected a civic building: one of dignity, scale, color, and vitality, with layers of ancient civic archetypes of Greek temple and Roman arch, and even with an explicit image of humanity itself. The Atlas figure and giant face would embody all the people of Portland, Oregon, who have symbolically taken the reins of the future in hand with this very building. The double image alludes to their deepest past, to the totemic communal art of the Northwest Indians, the oldest inhabitants of the Portland region.

Philip Johnson. The most powerful figure of American Post-Modernism was Philip Johnson, the reigning dean of American architecture. To appreciate his power in the American cultural and economic establishment, one must remember that his

13-30 Philip Johnson and John Burgee. Model, AT&T Building. New York. 1978 (now Sony Building)

13-31 AT&T Building

13-32 Lobby, AT&T Building

influence in 1980 led the Portland competition jury to award Graves their project; in addition, that stolid symbol of American corporate enterprise, AT&T, let Johnson (together with his partner John Burgee) build its new headquarters (figs. 13-30–13-32) on Madison Avenue in New York City in Post-Modernist form for an unprecedented sum (reputedly more than 200 million dollars; the building was later sold to Sony). This project was revealed in 1978 to the howls of the critics, who regarded it as a bad joke, a monster replay of Venturi's "T.V. antenna." Undeniably, the building—all 647 granite-clad feet of its 36 oversize stories, the height of a standard 60-story tower—looked like a colossal Chippendale highboy cabinet (with the faint overlay of a pay phone coin slot at the top, coin return at the bottom!). The critics' outrage blinded them to the qualities of the building and to the range of its wit and irony. Ingenious was Johnson's perception, first, that an unusually flat skyscraper rising over an open lobby contained the latent image of a chest of drawers, and, second, that this image might be brought out clearly in the recognizable form of the Chippendale highboy.

A highboy was not just any old chest of drawers with a scrolled top. Highboy was the American term for the concept, derived from England in the late seventeenth century, of setting a chest on a stand, for convenience. Even in refined, late-eighteenth-century versions (like the Chippendale style), the two-part basic elevation is retained: a stand on legs (normally now with its own drawers) carrying the main chest, usually set back a little, with its scrolled "bonnet." Johnson's treatment of the bottom of his building was as crucial as the top and obviously more difficult, given its complex structural and functional contingencies. Rejecting for formal and economic reasons the "easy" solution of a setback to suggest the chest-on-stand image (it would have been too literal), Johnson instead conjured it by abstracting and exaggerating its features, as we have seen in Graves. Thus, the main aspect of the "chest" is its many levels of drawers—here forming the 28-story shaft, revealing behind the mullions and pilasters its 28 "drawers" of office space. The essential iconography of a highboy stand, however, is not its drawers but its legs, often high, spindly, and as numerous as six, with four across the front, and its closed "skirt" typically embellished with a central, arched cut. These are precisely the features, blown up to 10-story scale, that form Johnson's "stand," with its many spindly legs and its enormous mural "skirt" cut into by a high central arch. Together they form a 100-foot-high unit clearly distinct from the windowed "chest" above. Compared with this inventiveness, the scrolled pediment, although crucial to the Chippendale effect, was child's play.

Johnson, like Graves, did not stop with this single level of iconic transformation. The "highboy stand," which dominates the view of the building from the surrounding streets, contains (at least) three "secondary" historicist images: its main facade is the recollection of the Pazzi Chapel (with a few extra loggia bays), including its telltale coffering and oculus-over-arch motif, blown up to become the giant window fronting the lobby; inside is not the expected Renaissance interior, but a Romanesque confabulation that includes decorative touches of Roman *opus reticulatum*; and the surrounding loggia (glassed-in by Sony) carries one off in the opposite historical direction to a French eighteenth-century, coffered hypostyle hall.

It seems futile, and perhaps irrelevant, to ask if there was any purpose to all of this besides heady public entertainment. Johnson was inscrutable about it, admitting to the desire for a "sense of monumentality" out of his huge granite machinery, a "passion for greatness" undermined, however, by his self-mocking, ironical stance. Like Venturi's only more so, Johnson's "method" was a matter of pervasive statement-and-denial, of giving with one hand and taking back with the other, all along poking satirical fun at his clients, his public, his profession, and himself. Thus, "the world's greatest skyscraper" is spiritually deflated by the very Chippendale effect that distinguishes it. (The half-gallery to the rear seems to prop up the tottering, freestanding cabinet that belongs against a wall.) The highboy image that makes it so "American" (like an architectural flag) also makes the American pedestrians into Lilliputians scurrying around its feet. Above, in the closed and barred "drawers," are thousands of workers, and in the airy quarters at the top are the executives. Johnson uplifts, debases, then ennobles, for within this provincial, subarchitectural Chippendale is encapsulated the pure Early Renaissance, fronting the grandiose Middle Ages, enveloped by lucid Neoclassicism. But the building as originally completed saved its strongest ironic stroke for last. At the center of the lobby stood the notorious *Golden Boy*, the gilded Beaux-Arts colossus, moved to the new building from AT&T's old headquarters as an enduring corporate symbol (now removed). This garish mediocrity was the focus of an image of such extravagant wit that it seemed to roll Venturi, Stern, Hollein, and Graves into one: the image of a winged *Golden Boy* under the "skirts" of Ma Bell, who takes the form of a highboy wearing a scrolled "bonnet." This punning chain of irony may well have been entirely fortuitous, but such combinations were almost the inevitable outcome of the complex allusive collage methods of Post-Modernism.

On purely visual terms, it is not surprising that the AT&T Building projects an impression so brittle and jittery that Graves's Portland design seems by comparison smooth and integrated. Partly, the jumpiness resulted from the disjunctive form of its highboy model, which Johnson shrewdly realized was appropriate to a skyscraper so hemmed in on every side by towers that in reality we rarely see its whole elevation comfortably. The building instead emphasizes the parts we do see clearly: the 10-story base, which works its tendentious effects on the nearby pedestrian, and the scrolled pediment, a corporate symbol visible miles away.

James Stirling. The expansion of the Staatsgalerie and the new chamber theater in Stuttgart, 1977–83, by James Stirling (with Michael Wilford), is another key work of Post-Modernism that was strongly affected by its difficult site (colorplate 82). The complex shouts "theater and museum" from a hillside setting to the motorist speeding by along the eight-lane highway at its feet (figs. 13-33, 13-34). Its message needs no inscription, the building being, in Stirling's deceptively mild words, "a collage of old and new elements . . . to evoke an association with museum." Its three main wings (housing the beautifully lit and proportioned painting galleries) repeat the U-shaped plan of the old Renaissance Revival museum next door but present to the eye a powerful Egyptianesque massing. Its closed walls are cleft, pylonlike at the center, topped with a gorge cornice, and faced with solid masonry, whose sandstone and travertine stripes, carried across the whole complex, convey not Egypt but medieval Italy. (This historical point is underscored by a prominent Tuscan Romanesque window.) The court framed by the U-shaped wings overflows with an ordered cascade of powerful forms, spilling forward beyond the "U" toward the edge of the terrace over which the museum rises. Sweeping ramps, trimmed with pink and blue tubular railings, recall the ancient world of Egypt and Palestrina, Tiryns, and Mycenae, even the Acropolis (with the first known picture gallery in its U-shaped Propylaea), and at the same time the famous switchback ramps of Le Corbusier's Villa Savoye. An open rotunda, the sculpture court, again cuts two ways historically—to the world of Hadrian as well as to Schinkel, whose great museum in Berlin centered on a rotunda for sculpture. The museum entrance is a free-form shape: its undulating glazed front with bright green framework simultaneously evokes Paxton, Gropius, and Aalto, while unmistakably suggesting the presence of a grand piano and the performing-arts function of the complex. Stirling's Post-Modernist intermix of "old and new" images achieves poignancy at the entrance to the complex. The blue-columned, red-linteled, glass-roofed Hi-Tech taxi stand is a Futurist version of Laugier's "primitive hut," carrying us back beyond Egypt and Mycenae to mythical prehistory. Among all the great styles in Stirling's historical rainbow only the Renaissance seems missing, but there it is in the old binary museum next door. Although most Post-Modernists, as we have seen, employ historicist collage to create metaphors of place and other meanings, Stirling's style was unique in its range and integration of references from the history of architecture.

Stirling's grand historical collage provides the visitor with a rich variety of visual experiences (quite apart from the objects housed in it); two among them are crucial. One is the principal view of the museum, either from the roadway or from the sidewalks dominated by the presence of traffic. In either case the building competes successfully against its wheeled enemy with bold forms that climb the hill and sweep along in a blur of flowing stripes. Another view of the building involves a more dramatic experience leading away from the car world into the challenging depths of history. The project required Stirling to provide a mid-block pedestrian link between the highway and the terraced street behind the museum. He turned this constraint to advantage with a zigzag pathway that leads up into the rotunda, where a steep, circumferential ramp swings clockwise through a half-circle, permitting a full view of the sculpture exhibit—but not access to it—before it turns to exit to the upper street through a tunnel in the cleft walls.

A masterstroke of urbanism, the Stuttgart circuit, which leads the pedestrian in a mnemonic path through its collage of architectural history and into the heart of the art museum

13-33   James Stirling. Neue Staatsgalerie, Stuttgart. 1977–83

13-34   Model, Neue Staatsgalerie

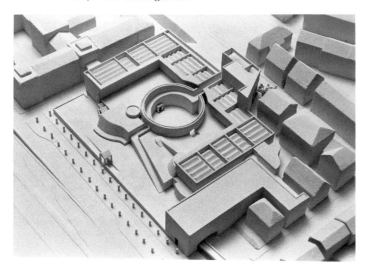

itself, suggests something that was close at hand to Stirling: the eighteenth-century circuit of streets and squares at Bath in England, in particular the Circus and Royal Crescent, where the climbing path pirouettes along circles and half-circles with spectacular views. Just as Bath was a quintessentially English creation, Stirling was a quintessentially British architect. Venturi wrote about designing with the architecture of Europe in one's bones; Stirling re-created the architecture of Europe with the buildings of England in his bones, even when working in Germany. The Stuttgart museum, with its blazing Italianate polychromy and its jostling of masses, looks like Butterfield all over again, and Stirling was called the Butterfield of Post-

Modernism, as well as its Hawksmoor and Norman Shaw, a list that could be expanded. The Stuttgart museum forms a sensuous architectural narrative almost as full of dramatic transformations and surprises as Wells Cathedral or Soane's Bank of England. Even in his early work, Stirling's Brutalist handling of Futurist and Constructivist forms suggested a 1960s Butterfield, but his will-to-the-picturesque was only fulfilled after his breakout of Modernist strategies in the early 1970s into the new Post-Modernist world of explicit historicism and the doctrine of "Complexity and Contradiction," which, as it were, now gave Stirling, like Secret Agent 007, "license to kill." Many Post-Modernists employed the technique of historicist collage to create metaphors of place and other meanings, but no other Post-Modernist building can compare with the magisterial sweep and urbanistic depth of the Stuttgart Museum. Stirling's late style was unique in its extreme range of references and their integration, and it distinguished him in England and worldwide. It was not without justification that Stirling was affectionately and reverently called "Big Jim," alluding not only to his physical bulk, but also to his status among architects in the years before his death in 1992.

Difficult as architects such as Stirling, Johnson, and Graves were for the public, they were in fact centrist figures in a movement that extended to extremist fringes. Three final, internationally diverse examples further illustrate the kind of Pandora's Box that Venturi and his friends had opened.

Aldo Rossi. The Milanese architect Aldo Rossi (d. 1997) enjoyed cult-figure status as the leader of a poorly understood, though widely admired, Italian group called the Neo-Rationalists, and which optimistically called itself Tendenza (Tendency). The group represented a kind of architectural parallel to political extremes in Italy, with their calls to a new "order" for a society that since the fall of Mussolini failed to achieve any sense of permanence. The specific disorders that provoked Neo-Rationalism were the chaotic suburban communities that sprang up after World War II around big cities such as Rome and Milan. The way to architectural salvation, in the eyes of Tendenza, was a return to an extreme form of architectural order.

Rossi concerned himself with the analysis of "typologies." He believed that "The Architecture of the City" (the title of his 1966 book) is reducible to a limited number of types, and that each type is reducible to a simplified form of Platonic idealism (or rationalism as the Platonic view is known). Thus, for example, every dwelling from palace to hovel becomes a single type—"house"—which is reduced to severely simplified, geometric form, the timeless condensation of all existing "houses" into a single formula. Rossi's reductionist vision derives from a variety of models: the familiar Post-Modernist aim of symbolic and historicist allusion; Laugier's idea of returning architecture to the scheme of the "primitive hut"; Boullée and Ledoux's geometric massing; and, most visibly, the severe reinterpretation of High Modernist ideas by architects of Fascist Italy in the 1920s and thirties. This last was a far from innocent revival on the part of Tendenza, the reappearance of Fascist Modern being an open affront to most Italians, a calculated shock effect that paralleled Venturi's use of low vernacular and lurid Las Vegas.

Rossi's strategy was thus the inverse of the "collage" method of Stirling, Hollein, and others. Rather than building a metaphor of "museum" or "travel bureau" with a barrage of diverse images, he evokes a diversity of meaning from a simple, reductive form: a condensed dream image, as it were, rather than a dream sequence. Not surprisingly, his designs, especially for his favorite types such as the monument, the cemetery, and the asylum, often had haunting, eerie overtones. Here Rossi relied heavily on what were in effect Surrealist devices, often recalling the paintings of Giorgio de Chirico: exaggerated scale and proportions, closed, forbidding walls, obsessive repetition, and abnormal juxtapositions. The last mentioned is perhaps the key to his work's visual success: the jolting contrasts in color, scale, and shape between his puristic buildings and their usually chaotic surroundings.

Among Rossi's best-known work was an exception that proved the rule—his Teatro del Mondo of 1979 (fig. 13-35), a temporary, gaily colored, wooden construction set afloat on a barge in the canals of Venice for the 1980 Biennale. The building was a re-creation of the Theatrum Mundi, a sixteenth-century floating festival theater, and Rossi formed it as a distillation of the spirit of Venetian architecture: central cube, surmounting octagon, pyramidal roof, and flanking, slablike twin towers. Its surface of wooden planking is devoid of detail except for a few windows. At first glance, the stark, hard-edged, weightless form seems as alien a presence amid the luxurious architecture of Venice as it would be in a suburb of Milan. But Rossi's point was that even though seemingly alien, the building really *belongs*. Whereas other Venetian buildings seem to float on the water's edge, the Teatro *really* floats; and where most Venetian buildings are given color accents or are atmospheri-

13-35   Aldo Rossi. Teatro del Mondo. Venice. 1979

cally dissolved with coloristic effects, the Teatro is literally all color. The ever-changing imagery of Rossi's theater reaches far beyond Venice. It can appear to be a twin-towered westwork of a medieval church, and a moment later a medieval castle or city gate. Its crown is like the Baptistery of Florence, but that octagon, extended imaginarily down through the building, becomes a pyramid-topped campanile like the bell tower of San Marco. Its form even has an anthropomorphic overlay—head, shoulders, chest, eyes—that elides into Rossi's reference

13-36   Arata Isozaki. Fujimi Country Club. Oita, Japan. 1973–74

to the lighthouses of Maine: "marvelous, high wooden structures . . . houses of light that observe and are observed."

Arata Isozaki. The metaphorical emphasis of Post-Modernism was at the heart of its reception in Japan, where the movement was taken up with fervor. The resulting diversity took the form of an ever-varied synthesis of national traditions and Western ideas, techniques, and references. Nowhere is this process seen more clearly than in Arata Isozaki's Fujimi Country Club of 1973–74 (fig. 13-36). The form of the building is almost as deceptively simple as Rossi's: a continuous barrel vault over a sinuous plan, resembling a question mark, with terminal facades derived from Palladio. What could be more Western than a golf clubhouse, a concrete barrel vault, and Palladio? Yet one look at the building and we intuitively sense its strong Japanese aura. But in what?

In Isozaki's book of 1976, *The Rhetoric of Cylinders*, the architect reveals unwittingly his Japanese bias. The design, he writes, "began with the image of a building that was a semicylinder undulating and skimming across the ridge of a line of hills . . . a symbol that would be clear enough to hold its own against the expanse of hilly terrain." Although he recognizes that the resulting form has "the sense of movement of oil squeezed from a tube" and "unavoidably" suggests a "giant whale," its primary image is the question mark. Why a question mark? Isozaki explains: "It is only natural that pursuing a fluid form on a flat surface should resemble the traces of movement of the hand or the pen. But when asked why, in this particular case, those traces became a question mark, I have no answer. Probably the form approached the question mark without my

being aware of it." For a Western audience, this sounds like fuzzy-minded dissembling, but its appeal to Japanese culture is clear and direct: to the acceptance and cultivation of the enigmatic in art, to the creation of metaphorical images that arise from the hand's spontaneous movement in the art of calligraphy so central to Japanese tradition. The Fujimi Club, in other words, is a calligraphic building—the spontaneous response of the drafting pen to the commission and the site. Yet the "calligraphic" plan of the building is not its only Japanese attribute, or even the most important. Its barrel vault may be as Western as the Colosseum's and St. Peter's, but no Western architect would allow it to dominate the building's external aspect as it does in the Fujimi Club. It dominates the exterior in the way Japanese roofs traditionally have dominated their substructures. To Palladio, Isozaki accords the inverse treatment: solid Renaissance fronts are reduced to abstract, membranelike screens approximating the traditional Japanese wall.

SITE. The spirit of wit and irony that ran through most Post-Modernism informed the entire strategy of our final example, the so-called Tilt Showroom of Best Products, Inc. of 1976–78, in Towson, Maryland. The startling building (fig. 13-37; now demolished) was one of several such projects designed for Best Products, Inc. by SITE (Sculpture in the Environment), a design collaborative formed in 1970 by Alison Sky, Michelle Stone, and James Wines, whose work attracted wide public attention. Like SITE's Peeling Project of 1971–72 in Richmond, Virginia, where the brick veneer of the showroom facade seemed to be "peeling off," and its Notch Project of 1976–77 in Sacramento, California, whose lower corner formed the

13-37 SITE (Sculpture in the Environment). Tilt Showroom of Best Products, Inc. Towson, Maryland. 1976–78 (destroyed)

entrance by being broken off raggedly, the Tilt Showroom was a Venturian "decorated shed" in the act of self-destruction. This "event" paradoxically transformed the structure into a decorated "duck" connoting its meaning through its "sculptural" shape more than by its nominal ornamentation. Such "de-architecture," as SITE called it, was created as a daring and effective response to a daunting problem. What was needed was a way of attracting the motorized consumer to a drab warehouse-salesroom for bargain-price household goods, situated in a shopping mall at the edge of parking lots, amid a chaotic variety of competing commercial establishments. In this environment the Tilt Showroom stood out unforgettably. Even more crucially, it was wonderfully effective in attracting customers who were lured by its novelty in a wasteland of banality and delighted by its amusement park spirit. Indeed, they were compelled toward its mock-disaster image much as a highway accident compels every car to slow down.

It has been said that Post-Modernism was "double-coded," with its colorful historicism for the public, and its Modernist abstraction for the connoisseur. In fact, it was usually the other way around—the public being now at home with Modernism but for the most part illiterate about historical architecture. In the most important buildings of the movement, such levels are interwoven in a complex manner and involve a fluid spectrum of response. The Tilt Showroom, for example, was not merely a still from a disaster movie; it reverberated with connotations, not personal or erudite as in many, if not most, Post-Modernist buildings, but close to public experience. The facade was tilted in a calculatedly ambiguous way so that one could never be sure whether it was lifting away or falling shut. It became an open sesame entrance to a magic cave of consumer goods; or an escape from an Alice in Wonderland paper cutter, with its specter of painful notches heightening the thrill; or a suburban garage door tilting open (or closed) at the touch of a button. Again changing, it anticipated the act of ripping open a cardboard box containing some desired object purchased in this very store. Finally, something was left to the architectural connoisseur: the delight in its formal play, its ambiguity and wit, and in the subtle details that carry off the illusion. But perhaps most of all it was the historical recall that was so haunting—the eighteenth-century landscape garden and its built ruins. If we think of them as a group, the numerous SITE showrooms for Best Products formed a kind of coast-to-coast scattering of follies—a corporate landscape garden of the late twentieth century.

Although the public was enchanted by SITE's work, few critics took it seriously, certainly not as seriously as "high" art works such as the AT&T and Portland buildings, or the Stuttgart museum, which understandably aroused indignation. Yet Venturi was on the right track. Perhaps we should learn to value not only architectural sermons and high-wire acts, but also the inspired flash of wit and irony that brightens the skies of our architectural landscape.

14-1
Norman
Foster.
Hongkong
and Shanghai
Bank. Hong
Kong, China.
1979–86

Chapter 14 | Modernisms: Renewal and Hyper-Diversity in Recent Decades

From its beginnings the modern movement has been shaped by protean creative energies and fierce critical thought. Throughout the twentieth century these deep forces have always proven themselves vital. While modern architecture has often been seen as unified (as in the "International Style" formula), it has in fact always been a diverse and unruly phenomenon. In the closing decades of the twentieth century its high-intensity creativity, self-critical reflection, and entangled diversity reemerged with a stunning force.

Given the direction of prior events, this resurgence demands some explanation. As we saw in Chapter 12, the "primary" line of Modernism—running from around 1900 in Chicago, Vienna, and Barcelona to the post–World War II works of Wright, Le Corbusier, Mies and their followers—seemed drained of vitality by the 1970s. Concurrently, a parallel architectural current, the "Second Modernism" of Chapter 13, was nourished and brought to maturity by a series of powerful architects from Aalto and Kahn through Venturi, Moore, Rossi, Stirling, and others. In the late 1970s out of this current emerged a wave of historicism newly concerned with imbuing modern architecture with the "presence of the past." This revisionist wave seemed to many the key to the architectural future.

Events soon proved this picture false. The return to the premodern past was hardly universal. Even in the heyday of Post-Modernist classicism, as the AT&T Building and Stuttgart Neue Staatsgalerie were rising with their blatant historicist imagery, massive masonry, and ornamental flourishes, modernist outrage at these "transgressions" was never extinguished. Resistance to the new historicism was continuous, and by the late 1980s the historicist (and related) currents of the 1970s mostly seemed to have blown way like some weather anomaly. The earlier, mainstream modern movement had regrouped, and its vital forces emerged as if newly empowered by its very survival.

Yet the changed climate of the two decades closing the twentieth century should not be misconstrued as an innocent return to primary Modernism or picking up where it had left off in the third quarter of the century. A Pandora's Box of radical critique and ideas had been opened by the impact of what we have termed Second Modernism and its latest phase, Post-Modernism. New ideas, methods, and attitudes had emerged that would not be suppressed.

A key to understanding the new scene was that, in reality, the use of premodern typologies, images, ornament, and materials, despite fierce and often successful opposition, continued in certain important architectural areas. But there was another aspect to the historicist outlook, which affected virtually all new architecture. The new historicism of Post-Modernism involved not merely the problematic return to the premodern past: more importantly, the entire modern movement itself came to be historicized. This distancing effect was reinforced by the quickening recession into the past of the "primary" modern masters—Wright, Le Corbusier, Mies, Gropius—who all had died between 1959 and 1969 (also Kahn in 1974), and who by the 1980s were no longer present as compelling forces. Certainly it now would be problematic for Modernist architects of any persuasion—most of the new leaders having come to adulthood well after World War II and as late as the 1960s—to imagine themselves as spontaneously evolving an unbroken movement reaching back to 1900. Architects no longer needed to labor under a genealogical burden of having to be the true and loyal sons and daughters of the great modern masters, an inhibition ironically comparable to the evolutionism of nineteenth-century historicism from which modernity thought it had escaped. Architects were empowered by a new freedom of architectural choice and invention. One could work absolved of the historical imperative to conform or to contribute to any evolutionary line of formal descent. The energies released by this newfound critical freedom meant that, given the range of talent, training, interests, experience, and possibilities of individual architects, together with the ever-changing, mercurial demands of clients, one might almost have predicted that a high diversity of invention would characterize the architecture of the final phase of the twentieth century.

Thus the century ended much as it began, with an explosive multiplicity and complexity, only now carried to a higher magnitude. Whereas the early twentieth century shed the nineteenth-century burden of historicism only soon to be saddled with the exclusionary imperative to be modern in certain defined ways, the closing twentieth century showed no signs of adherence to the claims of any single architectural vision. Although certain critics regarded this fragmentation negatively, radical and virtually limitless freedom was as crucial to the general vitality of the period as it was to the creativity of every major individual architect. Because so much of this energy and diversity hinged on the enduring liberation from the ideological confines of Modernism, yet also tended to avoid the historicist literalism and facadism of Post-Modernism, these decades may have entered an age of what might be termed a true Postmodernity—critically Modernist but with a reborn spirit and energy, unconfined by Modernist dogma, a merging and transformation, even, of "classic" and "Second" Modernist ideas and other, ever new currents of thought.

What may have stood apart most from earlier Modernist tendencies, however, was the cutting loose from self-imposed limits. Late-twentieth-century architecture—epitomized by Frank Gehry's dazzling Guggenheim Museum in Bilbao and

Norman Foster's staggering Hongkong and Shanghai Bank—tended toward a radical complexity of form, limitless growth of scale, luxury of materials, extravagance of structure, intricacy of detail, and brilliance of finish. In all of these, architecture engaged an uninhibited pursuit of self-indulgent visual pleasure and delight, as contrasted with the self-limiting tendencies of the puritanically restrained modern movement of the early- and mid-twentieth century, and went far beyond what had seemed extravagant in the 1960s and seventies. In its new power to dazzle and delight vast segments of the public (rather than instruct and improve a select group)—something that it had also tasted in Post-Modernism—architecture seemed to return with a vengeance to the uninhibited scale, material splendor, and popular support in the nineteenth century of the railroad stations and bridges, department stores and exhibition halls, libraries and museums, houses and villas (with echoes, perhaps, of the deeper past). Indeed, what the closing decades of the twentieth century may have revealed to those still unaware of the fact, is that the "classic" Modern movement never produced models for a viable or sustainable architecture for modern living as it claimed. Far from being the destination of some inevitable architectural journey, the movement appears to have been an idiosyncratic exception, a remarkable aberration in the larger pattern of humanity's search for shelter, meaning, and pleasure in the built environment of the modern world.

The exuberant tendencies and hyper-diversity of so much of the new architecture were driven by powerful external factors. Perhaps the key determinant was the "architectural wealth effect." The 1980s and nineties witnessed explosive economic growth on a global scale. Unprecedented wealth was created, which invariably produces the demand for ambitious architecture. Those into whose hands the concentration of wealth flowed included multinational corporations; their executives and large shareholders; entrepreneurs and "tycoons"; cultural, educational, and other institutions with vast income and endowments; extravagantly paid celebrities of the overlapping worlds of sports and entertainment; in general, the monied class of countless new multimillionaires and billionaires (and further enriched members of older wealth); and in a trickle-down effect, the newly affluent upper-middle classes. Among these groups were many who wanted and could build for a range of purposes. They wanted architecture to generate more money, hence bigger and better stores, malls, offices, factories, airports and other commercial and industrial typologies. They wanted architecture to improve the physical environment in which they worked and lived, played and traveled, learned, and were entertained and culturally uplifted: houses, apartments, and villas; transportation and communication centers; sports and art centers. These desires hardly stopped at the utilitarian level of space: above all, the representational and visual dimensions of architecture were pursued aggressively in these decades, to increase productivity, consumption, attendance, corporate value, and institutional and individual prestige. That wealth was behind so much of the new is apparent also in the virtual absence of two of the major traditional movers of monumental architecture: with rare exceptions neither the state nor the church were much of a visible presence in significant architectural events. Even in regions where public financing was important, the state itself was rarely directly represented in significant architecture. In the world of late capitalism, economic interests and individual desires were coming more than ever to deeply overshadow the traditional forces of political and religious authority and aspirations.

NEOMODERNIST EXTREMES: HIGH-TECH

The late twentieth century, despite its new perspective on the past, continued in important sectors the modern preoccupation with architectural essentialism. Time and again from the eighteenth century to the present, the question was earnestly asked, "What is architecture?" The predominant answer might be called Primal Modernism. Laugier, Lodoli, Pugin, Viollet-le-Duc, and other theorists shared an impassioned belief in an ideal architecture rooted in hard criteria centered on architecture-as-truth-to function, materials, and structure. This ideological package was uncritically absorbed and promoted by Modernists beginning with Sullivan and Wright. It again played a major role in the closing decades of the twentieth century, although now considered but one among many possible legitimate architectural paths.

Central to Primal Modernism was the mechanomorphic idea that architecture should be relentlessly machinelike in its open expression of structure. In practice, this amounted to the exhibitionistic display of the new structural realities of the modern age: iron, steel, concrete, glass, and other industrially produced architectural materials; and the new engineering formulas in which they were employed, including reinforced slabs and beams, trusswork, cantilevers, and curtainwalls. The Crystal Palace, St. Pancras Station, the Eiffel Tower, the ideal Gothic and rationalist projects of Viollet-le-Duc, the Futurist city, and Russian Constructivism were all variations on the extreme idea that monumental architecture should be a direct expression of the new structural realities unmediated by traditional surface forms. Buildings were meant to be and, above all, meant to *look* as if they emerged directly from engineering technology (the "factory" look).

Although industrial-strength mechanomorphism was manifest between the 1950s and the seventies—in Brutalism, for example, or the technomorphic sci-fi fantasies of urban life in vast "megastructures" published at the time in journals like *Archigram*—toward 1980 it burst forth anew in a series of vastly ambitious works, some of them of unprecedented scale and expense in modern architecture. The center of this practice, commonly termed High-Tech, is generally seen in a trio of architects: Norman Foster, Richard Rogers, and Renzo Piano (the latter two already responsible for the Centre Pompidou in Paris of the 1970s, a major earlier manifestation of this trend, see page 590).

If any building can be regarded as the manifesto of the High-Tech movement, it is Foster's Hongkong and Shanghai Bank (HKSB; figs. 14-1–14-3). Built 1979–86 in what was still the British colony of Hong Kong (part of China since 1997) as the headquarters of the dominant financial institution of one of the world's most energetic and successful economic capitals, decades later this staggering building has not lost its capacity to shock and delight. Foster rejected the standard format of the office tower, a typology central to modern life and the identity of core economic institutions and world cities. Rather than employ the usual closely spaced grid of framing members (going back to Chicago of the 1880s and used in every office

14-2 Norman Foster. Hongkong and Shanghai Bank, interior. 1979–86

tower that we have discussed), the HKSB instead employs a novel structure of large-span components. Giant cylindrical masts are gathered into groups of four to form huge, ladder-like pylons. These are in turn grouped in four pairs, each unit pushed toward the ends of the rectangular plan. The entire building is carried by these colossal piers: giant trusswork units cantilever from them, and from these mighty supports the rest is literally suspended, with six to nine stories hung from each set of cantilevers. Simultaneously, Foster inverted the distribution of the high-rise interior. Instead of the standard elevator and service core surrounded by a belt of space, the services were displaced to the exterior, housed in discrete shafts also supported by the colossal megastructure, leaving the center open and the space free edge to edge.

All of these moves were fully exploited by Foster in the building's space and appearance. Towering above a forest of smaller banal office buildings and the neoclassical domed courthouse, the HKSB boldly displays its megastructural machinery. The main facades each comprise only five multistoried units, producing enormous scale. The whole recalls bridge construction, the cantilevered trusswork of the gargantuan late-nineteenth-century Forth Bridge and suspension structures like the Brooklyn Bridge (figs. 11-64, 11-2), here brought into the heart of the city, reformulated and multiplied vertically five times. Adding to its brute power are the many sleek service shafts that ascend the building's full height with dizzying visual speed. Topping out the tower is a pair of huge maintenance cranes that give the whole a calculated unfinished look. Seen against its neighbors, the Bank looks more like an engineering or machine assemblage than architecture, and is undeniably saturated with all the techno-macho spirit of such works.

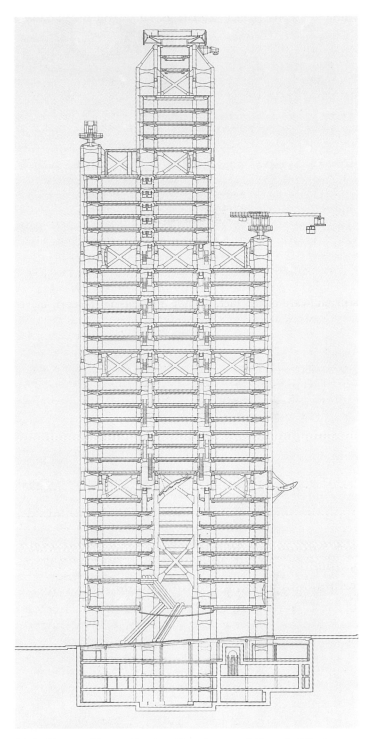

14-3 Norman Foster. Section, Hongkong and Shanghai Bank

Not immediately perceived is Foster's refinement of detailing and subtle accommodations of architecture culture that make the whole far more than a brute piece of huge machinery. This is seen in the proportions of the ladderlike pylons and the intricate joins and overlaps of the trusswork and suspension features, and also in the exquisite curtain wall. What is not revealed is the way visible forms are only a surface skin hiding the invisible structure beneath, which is not massively rounded and sculpted but rather of thin-membered H-beams and lacy latticework trusses and struts closely resembling, for example, the openwork fabric of the Eiffel Tower.

The interior of the HKSB is more articulated and spectacular than any previous office tower. Rather than stack up identical stories over a lobby, Foster exploits the wide-span megastructural frame to produce maximum spatial drama and functional diversity. This begins at the bottom by throwing the building open to important streets, accommodating their different levels by sloping the floor, which reinforces the intended effect of an internal piazza. In the huge central bay of the building, this urbanistically integrated entrance is given a curved glass ceiling, which a bank of escalators penetrates at skewed angles. As one ascends, a spectacular space comes into view: a huge central atrium rising 170 feet through 10 stories of the building disposed on the deep balconied "shelves" of vast surrounding floors. In the ceiling of the atrium is nestled a unique device: a huge set of angled mirrors, which gather sunbeams reflected to it from a second set of mirrors hung on brackets on the south wall of the building (computer-driven to follow the sun), and then directs this sunlight directly down through the atrium and into the piazza through its glass ceiling. The magical effect of this "sun scoop" is that those walking in the piazza feel sunlight on their bodies and see cast shadows on the floor, as if they were in an actual piazza.

Above atrium level, the floors run through the center in vast spaces extending from edge to edge of the building. These upper stories are gathered into five groups for data processing, international operations, senior executive offices, CEO quarters, and VIP conference and dining rooms. Separating the sectors are double-height stories corresponding to the giant cantilevers, intended for "communal" use. Foster described the sectors as "villages," and village identity was emphasized by elevators that stop only on the "communal" floors, with prominent escalators providing intra-"village" communication. Thus from the "piazza" through the atrium to the "villages" with their "communal" spaces, Foster's tower had an urbanistic dimension that made it more than just another inventive office building. It evoked the spirit of Alberti's idea six centuries earlier that

14-4 Richard Rogers. Lloyds Building. London. 1978–86

"The atrium, salon and so on should relate in the same way to the house as do the forum and public square to the city. . . ." One need only change "house" to "office tower."

The HKSB was nothing if not deeply responsive to contemporary architecture. Certain imposing and controversial recent skyscrapers were clearly in Foster's sights. His deeply megatrussed, superscaled building easily overpowered the superficially crossbraced leviathan of skyscrapers of the 1960s, the John Hancock Center in Chicago (fig. 12-103). Similarly, the shadowy public zone of the Citicorp Building of 1974–77 (fig. 12-1) was shamed by Foster's integral piazza-cum-atrium; and his sun scoop far outshined the facile (if iconically effective) slanted sun-gathering top of the New York bank. Yet the high rise to which Foster was most reactive was Philip Johnson's notorious AT&T Building announced and begun in 1978 (figs. 13-30, 13-31), just a year before the Hongkong bank. Foster's design was fiercely opposed to the historicist flippancy of the Chippendale-cum-Pazzi Chapel stone-coated New York skyscraper, which epitomized everything hated by the opponents of classicist Post-Modernism, especially the High-Tech crowd of core Primal Modernists. At its very moment of triumph, Post-Modernism thus came under a deadly assault of more than words. Against inauthentic pastiche, Foster seemed to offer instead a deeply reasoned, formally integrated, brilliantly progressive work truly of its time.

Yet if the building seemed more "honest" than its New York contemporary, such principles came at a steep price: almost a billion dollars, making it easily then the most expensive building of the modern world, against the mere $200 million with which the AT&T Building had shocked the public. Nor was the Hong Kong colossus even that "honest," for its structure was intricately masked by a thin aluminum skin no less formalistically determined than Johnson's heavy cut-stone revetment. Indeed, there was certainly no logical necessity, let alone technical inevitability, to the novel structural formula used by the HKSB, particularly given its cost. The overall, supposedly structure-determined shape of the HKSB was in fact no less arbitrary, no more faithful to any true logic of architectural ethics than the overtly iconographical and historicist shaping of the AT&T. Both buildings were clearly aimed at the same goal: the display of the wealth and power of the founding corporate institution through an architecture of overpowering cost, visual weight and shock value. In one case this was achieved through sensationally "reactionary" stonework and historicist iconography, in the other through dazzlingly "progressive" megastructural complexity and scale, or hyper-Modernist iconography. If one work was superficially historicist, the other was falsely integral. Both were deeply ideological constructs, in the sense of pretending to be what they were not. In any case, if the New York building was on the cusp of entering the closing phase of twentieth-century architecture, the Hong Kong monument was a full-blown example of the Neomodernist extreme at the center of this globally dispersed and financially superendowed period of architecture.

A High-Tech design often paired with the HKSB is Richard Rogers's Lloyds Building of 1978–86 in the City, or financial district of central London (figs.14-4–14-6). Foster and Rogers were partners earlier in their careers, and the interior of Lloyds resembles the atrium zone of the Hong Kong bank, with a rectangular central well of space surrounded by open office floors

14-5   Richard Rogers. Interior, Lloyds Building. 1978–86

14-6   Cross section, Lloyds Building

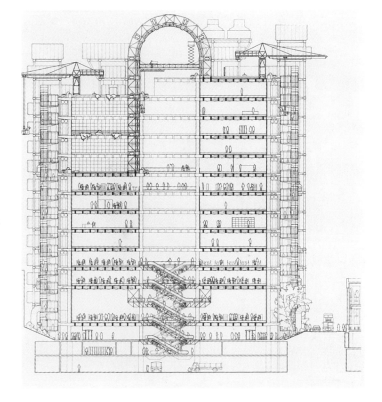

supported by cylindrical piers. In both buildings services are dispersed to towers at the edge. With this the similarities fade. The Lloyds Building is not about megastructural organicism; nor does it have complicated layers above the atrium zone. Instead it terminates with a glazed barrel vault. The Lloyds's interior forms a unitary multistoried space, a vast market called the Room, for the frenetic trading activity of the world's best-known insurance underwriting company, willing to insure anything, from ships to film stars' legs. The Room's centerpiece is a relic from Lloyds's previous headquarters—the classically framed, two-centuries-old Lutine Bell that was rung when an insured ship sank. A notable mid-nineteenth-century ancestor of this interior is the Coal Exchange of the same city (fig. 11-77).

The exterior of the Lloyds Building is soaked in contradiction and a complexity made to look as complex as possible. Dispersed unevenly around the building (exploiting the irregular site) are service towers of tubes, ducts, shafts, glass and metal boxes and other mechanomorphic forms containing elevators, stairs, lavatories, and HVAC (heating, ventilation, air-conditioning) equipment, not to mention the nearby service cranes and hanging devices for window cleaning. The cantilevered expansion of the various service towers as they rise

14-7   Renzo Piano. Air view, Kansai Airport. Japan. 1988–94

14-8   Renzo Piano. View of roof, Kansai Airport

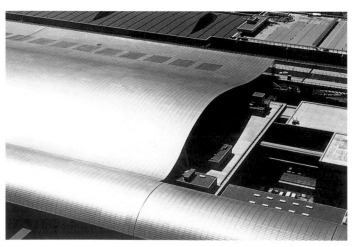

inflates them to enormous scale near the top, producing the unmistakable look of medieval fortifications, like the watchtowers with battlements and oriels scattered throughout Britain; by comparison the HKSB service towers seem strict and restrained. These architectural supplements dominate the exterior, especially from the south (fig. 14-4), where the main building is deeply set back at the eighth floor, visually splintering into fragments. This setback displays the cross section of the barrel-vaulted atrium, projecting an explicit historical reference, to the central nave of Joseph Paxton's 1851 Crystal Palace (figs. 11-83, 11-84), a work important to the genealogy of extreme mechanomorphic architecture.

Only superlatives describe the epic scope of Renzo Piano's Kansai Airport in Japan of 1988–94 (done in collaboration with architect Noriaki Okabe and engineer Peter Rice). Intended to revitalize Japan's second most populous region, the airport was set on the largest artificial island ever built, five kilometers off the coast near Osaka (fig. 14-7), and is reputedly the only artifact, apart from the Great Wall of China, that can be seen with the naked eye from space. The island solved the problem of land availability and allowed twenty-four-hour service without disturbing any sleeping population. Construction of the 4.37-by-1.25-kilometer platform necessitated more than a million caissons in the soft ocean bed and the demolition of three mountains to make enough crushed rock for the fill. Alongside the single runway the air terminal took shape as a single structure stretching 1.7 kilometers, making it the world's longest building. Its 900 supporting piers were designed to constantly adjust to the uneven settling of the landfill. Access is by car and train through causeway and tunnel, as well as by hydrofoil. As many as 10,000 workmen were employed at a time, and the cost was in the billions of dollars.

The sheer scale and difficulty of construction was not Piano's only great challenge. Whereas its sister typology, the railroad station, had rapidly evolved efficient and experientially coherent solutions, the airport remained generally problematic. Functionally, many spatially flawed airports have imposed a nightmare on passengers, being disorienting and unpleasant in layout and sequencing. Formally, rare is the airport that is more than an exercise in banality if not worse.

In the Kansai air terminal a bold attempt was made to solve the deep-rooted problems of both function and form (figs. 14-7–14-10). Piano sought a radical simplification and clarification of layout and distribution of functions. Entrance is through the multistoried base of the gigantic T-shaped plan. Access to the planes is along the 1.7-kilometer top of the T, with domestic gates in the central section and international gates in the flanking extensions, to which computerized shuttles speed passengers. Throughout, the emphasis is on ease of circulation, and on legibility and transparency: entering passengers can see through several layers the ferrovitreous departure zone in the distance, and everywhere the architecture itself indicates one's position, orientation, and goal, without signs (as in few modern buildings).

This efficient and experientially salutary system is contained by a visionary architectural envelope. The entire terminal was made to suggest a vast airplane wing. The cross section of the terminal, especially the leading edge, has an unmistakable winglike shape (although its actual curves are determined by a subtle geometry using arcs of circles up to 17 kilometers in radius), so that passengers already feel they've entered their aircraft, smoothing the transition. Perceived externally, especially from the air, the building seems literally winglike, with its subtle taper toward the ends and the flaplike central entrance extension of the curve. From the air, the shimmering fluid roof also suggests the waves of the sea. If Piano's design is in some ways reminiscent of Saarinen's TWA terminal of 1962 (fig. 12-110), Saarinen's design seen a generation later seems almost ingenuous in its flying-dinosaur shape so directly inspired by early-twentieth-century Expressionism, and almost quaint in its modest scale. Kansai instead was not only relentlessly mechanomorphic and technologically inspired in the advanced manner of its time, but embodied a more convincing aviomorphic visual poetry as well as being closely adapted to the real needs of late-twentieth-century travelers.

If Piano cultivated the look of logical inevitability in his visionary airport, no such illusion was possible at the International Forum in Tokyo by the Argentinean architect Rafael Viñoly (figs. 14-11–14-13). Built in 1990–96 on the site of the old City Hall and overlooking the tracks of the Bullet Train, the Forum was conceived in response to the perceived lack of a monumental public space in the city. Whatever its intent, however, even in its siting the huge project fit another broad typology, that of the convention center mushrooming in every major city, in which conference rooms and lecture and display halls are clustered around vast, overlit, and subfunctional spaces generally done up in low-budget High-Tech style, and often on a marginal site near railway tracks or highways. In Tokyo Viñoly gave this genre a new monumentality and polish, the look of limitless ambition and inexhaustible funding (in fact, it cost more than $1.5 billion). It was intricately planned to accommodate many public functions in the gargantuan quadratic wing containing several large auditoria ("Great Halls," with up to 5,000 seats), conference and meeting rooms, and a vast underground hall for exhibitions beneath the adjacent tree-lined garden space. But architecturally the distinguishing feature of the complex is the colossal "Glass Hall" across the garden. Over a pointed ovoid plan, a vast cage of extravagantly structured metal and glass rises vertiginously to an immense height (over 200 feet) where the openwork ceiling is carried dramatically by immense hanging beams. The main organizational entry and break-out space for events, it architecturally astounds the few visitors who can occupy it at any given time. The Glass Hall was meant to architecturally symbolize the new Tokyo. Yet in the final analysis its immoderation wears thin, its Piranesian impression flattens and merges in the viewer's mind with previously experienced bland and unconvincing, agoraphobic, glassed spaces of the generic "convention-center" type, and the huge building becomes a telling, and somewhat chilling, example of the gratuitous monumentalism characteristic of the financially bloated and eager-to-impress period.

The metal-and-glass High-Tech architectural medium was deployed with widely differing results, as two final examples further illustrate. One of the works to grace the Freidrichstrasse commercial avenue of Berlin, which promoted a citywide rebuilding campaign after the demolition of the Wall in 1989, was the new branch of the biggest Parisian department store, the Galeries Lafayette. Designed by French architect Jean

14-9   Renzo Piano. Interior, Kansai Airport

14-10   Section of passenger flow, Kansai Airport

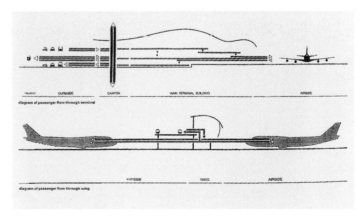

Nouvel in 1991, its dazzling central space recalls the multistoried glazed rotunda of the Parisian store (and ultimately such nineteenth-century predecessors as the Bon Marché store; fig. 11-75). But instead of a domed cylinder, the core of the Berlin building is formed by two huge metal-and-glass cones joined along their entire base, one disappearing into the earth, the other open to the sky (colorplate 83). The double cone intersects and is visible from all floors in mesmerizing vertiginous vistas. Geometry is used here not to produce any ideal harmony, but instead to dazzle, disorient, and seduce the observer

14-11 Rafael Viñoly. International Forum. Tokyo. 1990–96

14-12 Rafael Viñoly. Interior, International Forum. Tokyo. 1990–96

into the mindless world of consumerism in a highly imaginative version of the glittering spectacle encountered in most department stores.

In New York City, geometry was used in a more rationally comprehensible manner by James Stewart Polshek and Todd H. Schliemann in the Rose Planetarium at the American Museum of Natural History, which opened in 2000 (colorplate 84). The jewel-like building was directly inspired by Boullée's 1783 Cenotaph project for a monument to Newton (figs. 10-53, 10-54). In New York we find a High-Tech updating of Boullée's solid masonry: an 87-foot metal sphere seems to float within a transparent cube structured by a refined trusswork armature so precise that the costly water-white glass (purified of the iron that makes ordinary glass greenish) remains virtually undistorted. In Boullée's somber sphere the heavens were to be statically represented by daylight entering a cosmographic pattern of small holes in the vault. In New York, the upper half of the sphere is the site of the Space Theater—the Planetarium proper—where spectacular information-packed programs are displayed using a projector driven by a supercomputer that can simulate millions of stars as well as clouds of cosmic gas and dust, black holes, supernovas and other heavenly phenomena. The sphere is encircled by informational walkways: the 360-foot Cosmic Pathway, explaining the 13-billion-year history of the universe (in which the duration of *Homo sapiens* is represented by the width of a human hair); and the Scaling Walk, which uses the sphere itself as a proportional reference in charting the sizes of all things, from the largest galactic clusters to neutrons and electrons, an ingenious extrapolation of the traditional relationship between architecture, numbers, proportion, and the world. The informative and irresistible displays (designed by Ralph Appelbaum Associates) continue below the sphere (supported by a tripod of massive struts) in the Hall of the Universe, where the fifteen-ton Williamette Meteorite gives a strong touch of reality to the imagistic atmosphere. But beyond its compelling, architecturally integrated pedagogical program, the Rose Planetarium demonstrates how sleek mechanomorphic design can be far more than a fetishistic, hollow promotional gesture of High-Tech. If in Boullée's visionary scheme Newton's catafalque was to be placed within his cosmos, here the cosmos itself was placed within a glass cube that symbolizes modern society's expanding mastery of nature's secrets. Urbanistically this image presents a compelling visual counterpoint to adjacent Central Park, and at night it glows magically against New York's justly fabled, glittering skyline.

14-13 Plan, International Forum

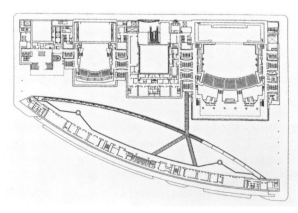

NEOMODERNIST OPPOSITIONS:
AROUND DECONSTRUCTIVISM

These diverse examples of the High-Tech movement shared the ideals of formal perfection and integration of form and function. But the late decades of the twentieth century also experienced a powerful oppositional current. The perfectionist ideal of monumental architecture since antiquity—epitomized by the Renaissance theorist Alberti's assertion that perfection was possible in a design to which "nothing may be added, taken away, or altered, but for the worse"—was now put to aggressive critical questioning.

To be sure, mainstream Modernism had claimed that it sought not perfect form or style but rather to express function in formal terms, puritanically renouncing aestheticism and its quest for pure visual pleasure. The central Modernist doctrine that "form follows function" was, however, very deceptive. Any definition of the "function" of a building was bound to be arbitrary in its inclusion/exclusion of diverse needs. "Follows" could mean anything from prosaic formal translation to deliriously imaginative expressions of "function" as we have observed in tracing the complex histories of Modernism. Thus the core Modernist doctrine of functionalism turned out in practice to be little more than a mask. Modern architecture hated the idea of the arbitrary, but could not escape it.

In the late twentieth century architects came to recognize and creatively engage these stubborn facts. That a building could never be perfect meant, in effect, that one need not strive to make it look perfect, either formally or in terms of satisfying function or other criteria. One was now freed not only from history, teleology, typology, functionalism, and other Modernist doctrines, but also from the ancient and seemingly eternal doctrine of perfectibility itself that had continued at the heart of Modernist practice. The very look of imperfection, of disfigured perfection, of architecture not achieved but incomplete, coming into being with difficulty, complexity, and internal contradictions became a new ideal among many critics and architects. That this inverted, antinormative ideal would contribute strongly to the new hyper-diversity of architecture was almost predictable. There are infinitely more ways to achieve imperfection than its opposite, or to express the capricious rather than the predetermined.

Such an architecture of course was not a novelty of the 1980s. Antinormative waves go far back in history. We need only recall the Renaissance Mannerism of the Palazzo Te (figs. 8-48–8-50), or later the Romantic fetishizing of ruins, decay, the fragment, and all manner of irregularities in the Picturesque. Nor had the twentieth century been lacking in such shocking departures. At the very heart of Modernism was a rebellious, anarchic spirit: Wright's campaign to "break the box" of the traditional house and other types, the Futurists' intention to uproot, smash, and bury all traces of the historical city and set in its place a vast architectural machinery, Le Corbusier's resolve to "burn" the past, including his own earlier work, all act out the same dream. This vision also drove the other arts, as in the shattering of pictorial space by Cubism, the denial of rationality and conscious control of form in Dadaism, and the destruction of narrative in literature. More recently, Robert Venturi argued influentially for an architecture of "Complexity and Contradiction." This influence turned out to be lasting, and it could be maintained that

the new spirit was essentially Venturism (the latest episode of modern iconoclasm) taken to the extreme.

The rebellious wave of the 1980s, however, sought to distance itself from past architectural discourse by instead apparently moving laterally toward other disciplines and media, including cinema, psychoanalysis, philosophy, and literary theory, for inspiration. It was strongly drawn to Parisian intellectual currents, notably the work of the eminent philosopher Jacques Derrida. Certain architects and theorists recognized in Derrida's critical method, which he called Deconstruction, ideas parallel or relevant to their own architectural concerns, thinking, and practice. Although few among them actually understood Derrida's difficult writings or depended directly on his ideas, some knew his work (at least retrospectively) and most of the others involved did not vociferously object to being associated with him, especially the architects chosen for "Deconstructivist Architecture," the important exhibition held at the Museum of Modern Art in New York in 1988.

It was there that the New New Thing of the 1980s was christened as "Deconstructivism" (superseding the old New Thing, Post-Modernism, launched by MoMA's own 1975 exhibition of Beaux-Arts drawings, itself a reversal of the Modernist orthodoxy that the same institution had solidified in its 1931 International Style show). This event gave apparent coherence to disparate threads of the trend, yet ultimately limited its life through codification (which made it, in turn, something to be superseded: by the millennium, "DeCon" had pretty much gone the way of "PoMo"). The term Deconstructivism was critical, for it suggested that the new avant-garde somehow fused the Derridean method of Deconstruction with the Constructivist architecture (mostly ideal or unbuilt projects) of the years following the Russian Revolution, which simultaneously also informed High-Tech. Although numerous formal parallels suggest that Neoconstructivism would have been a sufficient term (to the limited extent that the new wave actually was based on the Russian work), Deconstructivism stressed that the new movement was not revolutionary in the politically engaged sense of the early Russians, but was instead more anarchical, even apolitical, pervaded with Derridean—and hyper-Venturian—ironical distancing, (self) contradiction, and (limitless) complexity. Constructivism had aimed toward the construction of a new political realm. Deconstructivism tended instead toward the self-absorbed practice of a whole string of D-words—disjunction, displacement, dislocation, deviation, distortion, decentering, destabilizing—applied to basic architectural concepts such as typology, function, and context, as well as to composition and formal language. All of this was eventually seen as related to the Derridean project of demonstrating through relentless analysis how all philosophical (read: "architectural") ideas and statements are undermined through the very foundations of their own thought.

Among the protagonists of this movement were Wolf Prix and Helmut Swiczinsky, a.k.a. the Viennese architecture firm Coop Himmelblau. Impassioned critics of Modernist rationalism, especially as represented by High-Tech, in 1980 they wrote, "We want architecture that bleeds, that exhausts, that whirls and even breaks . . . cavernous, fiery, smooth, hard, angular, brutal, round, delicate, colorful, obscene, voluptuous, dreamy, alluring, repelling, wet, dry throbbing . . ." "Our architecture is not domesticated," they proclaimed, "it moves

14-14   Coop Himmelblau. Rooftop Office. Vienna. 1983–88

around in urban areas like a panther in the jungle [and resembles] a wall of nerves from which all the layers of urban skin have been peeled away."

Even such macabre, apocalyptic statements, intended to make Venturi seem tame, did not quite prepare one for the defining work of Coop Himmelblau, the Rooftop Office in Vienna of 1983–88 (figs. 14-14–14-16). Le Corbusier had shocked the public with his hyper-functionalist, mechanomorphic houses; and Venturi scandalized architecture with a house that mockingly exaggerated vernacular house typology. But such gestures seemed restrained compared to Coop Himmelblau's Deconstructivist jewel, which undermined everything (except of course the central status of the architect, never questioned by the movement). It blatantly repudiated the context of the nineteenth-century apartment block atop which it sat in an ancient bourgeois neighborhood. It ridiculed its function as the office of a small law firm, especially the conference room with its Modernist Eames furniture. It took the Modernist idea of exploding the box to warp speed, reducing the chilling mechanistic perfection of High-Tech to an obscene and threatening shambles, for a moment making the idea of formal perfection itself a virtually unthinkable thought. As Deconstructivism in action it could not have been more perfect.

14-15   Coop Himmelblau. Interior, Rooftop Office. Vienna. 1983–88

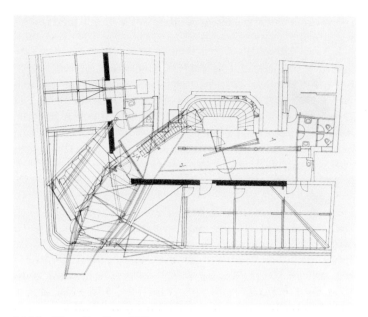

14-16   Plan, Rooftop Office

It baffled the critics, who could not agree as they groped for a basic description of it. While certain writers saw it as an "eagle" that had "landed" on the roof—and flight was indeed a recurrent image in Coop Himmelblau's writings—to another it seemed "as if an insect has settled on a roof made of leaves, eaten all but the stalks and veins leaving gossamer spider's webs between them." Alternatively, it was a robotic android; "a writhing, disruptive animal breaking through the corner . . . a skeletal monster"; or (according to the same critic) a roof that "splits, shears, buckles" from its own latent pressures, released by the architect yet still present as the building itself. The building seemed the result of a violent, relentless "interrogation" combining the techniques of psychoanalysis and physical torture, drawing "impurities" to the surface much—it was imagined—as Derrida deconstructed language from within. Regarding the effect on the observer, one critic responded, "We are contorted, racked, cut, wounded, dissected, intestinally revealed, impaled, immolated . . . thrust into a confusion between belief and perception," while another wrote, "It is disquieting, because it challenges one's sense of stability, coherence and identity which we associate with pure form." Thereby the final agenda might be to produce a keen, heightened awareness of the problematic existence of late-

14-17   Taiwan, 1999. Collapsed buildings after earthquake

twentieth-century atomized and alienated bodies and selves in a world of blind, overpowering forces of capital, commodification, and consumerism.

The Deconstructivist method was easily confused with superficially related strategies and processes, and certain distinctions needed to be stressed. The catalogue of the MoMA show addressed this issue head on, stating that Deconstruction is "an architecture of disruption, dislocation, deviation, and distortion rather than one of demolition, dismantling, decay, decomposition or disintegration. It displaces structure rather than destroys it." Thus the movement sought to distance itself from the Romantically rooted aesthetic of the ruin and decay. Deconstructivist buildings often exhibit tilted, thrusting, colliding and fragmented, cut, stripped, slashed and bent prisms, bars, and shards of form, and thus often bear an uncanny resemblance to the architectural results of demolition, bombing, or natural disasters such as the massive earthquakes that rocked Taiwan in September 1999 (fig. 14-17). Such resemblances are deceptive, for Deconstructivism was *not* the destruction or dismantling of structure, especially not by apparently external forces. Indeed it was not essentially about structure itself, or even de-structuring (as in the 1960s and seventies work of SITE; fig. 13-37), but rather chiefly concerned the internal questioning of the ideological constructs that inform the designing, making, and use of architecture (including structure). Deconstructivism, as in Coop Himmelblau's work, sought through the very design of its buildings to identify and challenge all such ideological preconceptions including, as already noted, the idea of "function," "typology," "structural integrity," and "ideal form."

These distinctions allow us to discern essential differences between authentic Deconstructivist works and others that bear a false resemblance to them, such as the following example. At first glance Coop Himmelblau's 1980s law office would seem to

14-18   Günther Domenig. Offices in Völkermarkt. Austria. 1995

find a Deconstructivist variation in a work of 1995 by the fellow Austrian architect Günther Domenig (fig. 14-18). His entrance pavilion built as the initiatory structure at a state-sponsored industrial park near Völkermarkt explosively cantilevers an openwork ferrovitreous structure asymmetrically into space from an orthogonal five-storied office structure that grows into it. Whereas the Vienna rooftop performs an infolding choreography of vitalistic self-contradictory, antifunctionalist, disquieting images, Domenig's pavilion projects a fully resolved gesture of welcome to the yet-to-be-developed park, "the swirling curve of a powerful living, glossy bird's wing . . . a signal of strength, virility, generosity and hope." Nothing contradicts its double function of space-container and rhetorical gesture, which are smoothly integrated rather than disturbingly problematized. Domenig's pavilion so closely draws on Russian Constructivism that it begs to be called Neoconstructivist.

The architect who appeared most consistently in contemporary discussion of Deconstructivism is the Iraqi-born, London-based Zaha Hadid. This identification informs us of the often rather fuzzy nature of Deconstructivism, for Hadid professed little interest in Derrida ("I've gone to two lectures of his . . . nothing curious about them"), and she claimed her work to be intuitive rather than theoretical. Her architecture was inspired by the Russians, only not the mechanomorphic Constructivists but the more formalist Suprematists (such as El Lissitsky; fig. 12-66). For a time she followed them also in producing not buildings but unbuilt and often virtually unbuildable architectural fantasies and research. Like any number of admired contemporary figures—including the late John Hejduk, Lebbeus Woods, and Daniel Libeskind (the last eventually an important builder)—Hadid became known for her architectural renderings, which manifested a dazzling formal originality and seductive representational skills. Through a set of these designs which won the 1982 international competition for the "Peak" project in Hong Kong (never built), she became a global celebrity in the architectural world (figs. 14-19–14-21).

Hadid's "intuitive" method produced spectacular results with a Suprematist-derived strategy. Architectural form was rigorously purist and geometrical, tending toward thin, sharp shapes including bars and "plates." Right angles and orthogonality were avoided. Planes met at acute or oblique angles. Spatiostructural axes overlapped in layers of nonalignment. Abstract volumes tended toward extreme, prismatic elongation and stretching. Maximum angular intersection and collision were cultivated throughout. That these measures would be realized with boldness and panache one might almost have expected from her statement that "the point for me about the Suprematists was that it's like looking at the Galaxy through a microscope: Cosmic." The Peak project was a luxurious residential club for the economic elite of the city (no Modernist social idealism here). Hadid's vision called for first reshaping the mountain itself: "The hillside was rock; the idea was you excavate the rock and replace the old geology with a new one. Therefore each layer was slightly different and it was seen like a 'plate'; geological plates stacked up on one another." The club itself was to thrust out of the upper slopes of the mountain into space (or be speared into it), as fast-moving story-height slabs and bars stacked in vertical layers: at the bottom, two glass-fronted, residential levels, then common facilities (including bar, squash courts, health club), four penthouses, and on top the promoter's quarters. In plan the layers were disaligned at various angles (each retraced internal features of the adjacent layers) to form a startling, jagged composition that seems, with the minimal vertical supports obscured, impossibly self-supporting.

Hadid characterized her "hedonistic resort" as "a Suprematist geology," its architecture like "a knife cutting through butter, devastating traditional principles and establishing new ones, defying nature but not destroying it." For the public, however, it was not Hadid's rare statements but her compelling Neosuprematist formal language, her brilliantly tilted, skewed, skewered, colliding bars and plates, that quickly was identified as the prototypical Deconstructivist "look." Her manner was

14-19   Zaha Hadid. Peak Project. Architect's drawing. 1982

14-20　Zaha Hadid. Peak Project. Architect's drawing, detail. 1982

less threatening and challenging than Coop Himmelblau's and certainly did not require the mastery of any intellectual key to be appreciated at least superficially. Such could not be said about certain other Deconstructivist architects, whose designs were heavily text-based and theory-dependent for even basic comprehension.

The most prolific of this cerebral group was the American, Peter Eisenman. Just as Coop Himmelblau's rooftop office challenged the concepts of function and structure, in much of his most important work Eisenman interrogated the nature of site. This critique engaged the late-twentieth-century preoccupation with context, the way a new building may be inflected in its alignment, materials, scale, and form to the existing architectural environment. Whereas Contextualism usually involved what is present at the site, Eisenman became chiefly concerned with mapping what is absent. Drawing on a term used by Derrida, Eisenman reconceptualized the site as a palimpsest—a sheet of parchment on which writing is erased for a new text, leaving the original text's traces. He pictured the architectural site as a palimpsestlike repository of various layered traces of the past, the idea being that a new building there should restore the erasure as an imaginative reinscription in its design. Eisenman conceptually excavated down to earlier layers, to ancient foundations, urban axes, buried and effaced streets, and then ingeniously displayed some of these at the surface on the site itself. The building thereby became a spectacle of its site history, of what was there before it. At times a history of what ought to have occurred there was inserted in this dialogue with the past.

At the Wexner Center for the Arts, built at The Ohio State University in 1982–89, Eisenman's palimpsest method is used in all its arbitrary rigor, together with his usual denial of functionalist norms and refusal to make architecture easily readable, for the scheme can be understood only in the knowledge

of both Eisenman's logic and the prehistory of the site itself (figs. 14-22, 14-23). The campus planning grid deviated 12.5 degrees from the town grid, so Eisenman restored the town grid to the campus in the form of the slanting "spine" of the new art center, a long glazed passage between two extant large, campus-oriented auditoriums. The roof of the spine sloped and collided with service "bars" lying in its path at various levels, while an adjacent remnant triangle provided assorted oddly shaped, glazed new exhibition spaces. A "frontispiece" for the complex was produced by the partial "restoration" of a destroyed armory on the site, a cluster of fragmentary brick towers and walls also serving as a "hinge" between the campus grid and Eisenman's renewed town grid, and extending deeper into the complex as a reinscribed sign of its lost origins.

Eisenman is often paired with Bernard Tschumi in his pursuit of Derridean theory and conjuring of abstruse philosophy in

14-21
Peak Project,
site plan

14-22 Peter Eisenman. Wexner Center for the Arts. Air view. Columbus, Ohio. 1982–89

14-23 Isometric drawing, Wexner Center for the Arts

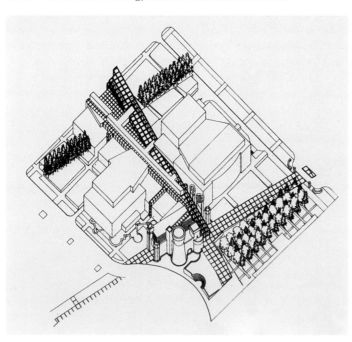

architectural design. In his winning entry of 1982 for the international competition for the new Parc de la Villette in Paris (executed to a state of near completion over the following decade), Tschumi aspires to repudiate all past models and ideals of architectural theory and practice. He suppresses not only the idea of design perfection, but seemingly the idea of design itself as a technique by which an architect composes a scheme at all, especially one marked with signs of architectural individuality. He refuses all origination including specifically the model of the big-city park, the type developed in the nineteenth century out of the English landscape garden (e.g., the Parc des Buttes-Chaumont in Paris, Central Park in New York City). Through such techniques of Deconstruction of the architectural program, Tschumi intended to challenge the ideology on which the program itself (the official brief for the Parc) was based.

Tschumi's scheme superimposed three independently conceived, highly "impersonal" conceptual layers (fig. 14-24). First, a grid of points at 120-meter intervals provided locations for the thirty Neoconstructivist pavilions, or "follies"; each used a 20-meter cubic module that could be contracted, expanded, closed, or opened with ramps, wheels, stairs, and openwork cages in forming the varied series (figs. 14-25, 14-26). Second

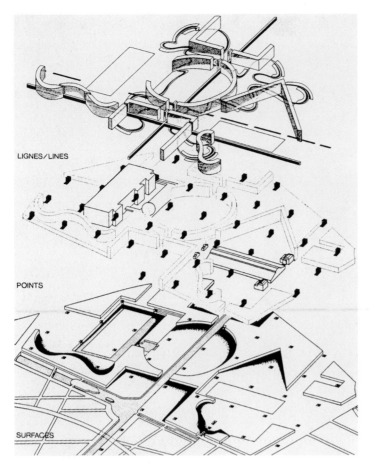

14-24 Bernard Tschumi. Parc de la Villette, project diagram of layers. Paris. 1982

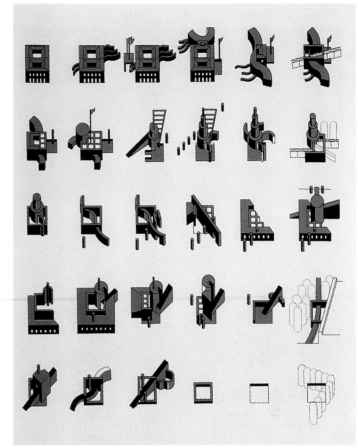

14-25 Bernard Tschumi. Parc de la Villette, scheme for the pavilions. Paris. 1982

came a system of lines, cross-axial and curvilinear, forming routes and marking boundaries. Third was a system of surfaces, providing spaces for large open-air activities. Because each layer was devised autonomously, when brought into a single plane a complex, unpredictable interaction between the three systems resulted, of distancing and coincidence, collision and conflict, emphasizing Tschumi's desired role of chance in the architectural process. Similarly, none of the revolutionary-red pavilions was specifically designed for any of the uses intended for them as a set—restaurants, bars, gymnasia, shops, workshops, day-care centers, multimedia displays, and so on—but could be adapted interchangeably for these and other purposes, undermining the notion of functionalism.

Tschumi did not develop his noncontingent scheme out of thin air. Despite his desire to suppress all origination and to be as impersonal as possible, he had to begin somewhere. Among the numerous precedents that inform the Parc de la Villette are the English garden and its follies; the Bauhaus pedagogical method using the point, the line, and the plane; the *Bürolandschaft*, or generic bureaucratic office environment of power outlets (Tschumi's impersonally designated points), partitions and corridors (his lines), and carpets (his planes); the 1960s automatic, aleatoric music composition techniques of John Cage (Tschumi's systematic programming); the program of the Situationists, a politically engaged movement of the 1950s and sixties that explored how events unfold in space, in particular the sensory experience of moving around the city (which was to be heightened in the Parc). Despite the ideas that inform Villette and its undeniable

Deconstructivist allure, the feeling the Parc produces even in the knowledgeable visitor can easily be, not creative engagement with unfolding spatial experience, but impatience with a maze of radical-chic irony spread far and worn thin, a space-devouring realm of soul-numbing agoraphobia.

Such would assuredly not have been the case with the runner-up entry in the Parc de la Villette competition by Rem Koolhaas (in collaboration with members of his Rotterdam-based Office for Metropolitan Architecture, or OMA). Although sharing the layering technique and the aim to reinvent the city park, Koolhaas's layers were denser and more imaginative than Tschumi's, generating a compelling experience almost to the point of overload (figs. 14-27, 14-28). Koolhaas's fundamental layer (a) was composed of forty-three narrow, parallel strips, randomly and repeatedly dedicated to various uses including ordinary gardens, discovery gardens, play-prairies, and so on. Repetition and extensive contact area between the activities made their interfacing and interaction very dense. This experiential intensity was heightened by the other layers. There were grid-scattered "confetti" (layer b) of kiosks, play-grounds, and picnic areas, while circulation paths (layer c) included a neon-lit north-south Boulevard and a meandering Promenade. Plazas and other major areas of the fourth layer (d) comprised a museum, *grande halle,* "music" city, two forests, baths, and an "astronomy garden" with a Saturn-model and a real satellite rocket (fig. 14-29), and much more. All was integrated with the surrounding urban fabric by a final layer (e). Through this "provisional enumeration of desirable ingredients . . . [and] implantation of activities in the most efficient

14-26   One of the pavilions. Parc de la Villette. Paris

and explosive manner" the desired result was to have been "the most dynamic coexistence of activities x, y and z to generate through mutual interference a chain reaction of unprecedented events." Koolhaas's Parc was to have functioned, as the architect put it, like a Russian Constructivist "Social Condenser" through the essential strategy of "horizontal congestion."

That such a park might have produced an experiential euphoria will not surprise the reader of Koolhaas's sensational 1978 book, *Delirious New York*, which established him as an innovative architectural force. Koolhaas pushed Venturi's critique of Modernism to another level (without mentioning him), with an emphasis on urbanism. Venturi had demanded that architecture become permissive, hybrid, perverse, redundant, and possess a messy vitality. Koolhaas, who would not have denied such aims, now added a second pair of "C-words" to Venturi's "Complexity and Contradiction" formula, advocating an anti-Modernist "Culture of Congestion." Among Venturi's iconoclastic models were the small town "Main Street" and the highway strip culture epitomized by Las Vegas. Koolhaas instead now revisited New York's Coney Island of around 1900 (mostly destroyed by the rampaging Modernist city planner Robert Moses in the 1950s). The centerpiece of this fabulous theme/amusement park had been the Dreamland complex that included Lilliputia, Fall of Pompeii, Creation, Canals of Venice, and Japanese Teahouse (soaked in an atmosphere of permissiveness and eroticism rigorously suppressed in the late-twentieth-century counterparts produced worldwide by Disney, Inc.). Such close juxtapositions of wildly disparate architectures and activities resurfaced in Koolhaas's Villette program, but his book's central paradigm was

Manhattan, which he opposed to the sterile, tragically influential Ville Radieuse model of Le Corbusier (whose tripartite scheme, itself opposed to Le Corbusier's negative reading of Manhattan, was in reality the disguised model for Tschumi's point-line-plane scheme for the Villette park, accounting for its agoraphobic properties). Koolhaas's radical urbanism should also be seen against the Neo-Rationalist program of the 1970s led by Aldo Rossi, which reduced the city to neatly defined typologies soaked in an overpowering nostalgia for a lost cohesion and legibility of urban life.

For Koolhaas, Manhattan's inflexible grid plan of 1811 made "the history of architecture and all previous lessons of urbanism irrelevant." That no building could be bigger than a block "immunized" the city against "totalitarian intervention" and encouraged developers to build densely upward, into the twentieth-century skyscrapers for which the island is famous. Each block tended toward a single structure, housing a discrete lifestyle, indeed devolving further, with the resulting Culture of Congestion "arranging" in each floor "new and exhilarating human activities in unprecedented combinations." Against Modernism's insistence on conformity between interior and exterior, Koolhaas (in characteristically psychoanalytic terms) praised the "Great Lobotomy" of the New York skyscraper, its radical dissociation of facade and interior that produced "unprecedented freedom" and spared "the outside world the agonies of the continuous change raging within it." Modernism had wanted to promote a single utopian lifestyle through a rational, uniform new architecture that thoroughly displaced the old; in "Manhattanism" Koolhaas saw instead how high

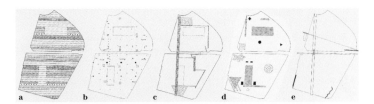

14-27 Rem Koolhaas. Parc de la Villette, five-part scheme. Paris. 1982

14-28 Rem Koolhaas. Parc de la Villette, all layers superimposed. Paris. 1982

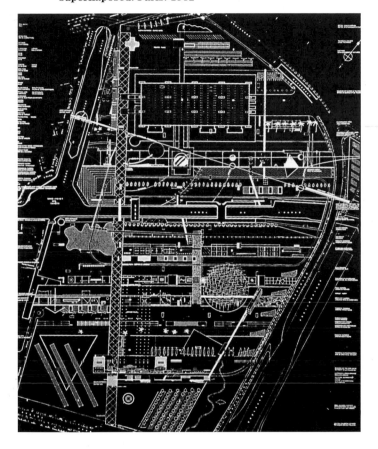

population densities and unplanned juxtapositions of varied activities might spontaneously generate ever new, more exciting activities and modes of human interaction in a world of radical pluralism. Rather than Modernism's wholesale demolitions and rebuilding, shrewd and limited interventions might instead reequip the city with facilities needed for society to function within current real conditions and contingencies. Yet the excitement of Koolhaas's idea cannot be leveled to such pragmatism. A single sentence conveys his visionary reading of Manhattan: "a mythical island where the invention and testing of a metropolitan lifestyle and its attendant architecture could be pursued as a collective experiment in which the entire city became a factory of man-made experience, where the real and the natural ceased to exist" and that has "consistently inspired in its beholder ecstasy about architecture."

Architectural ecstasy was the direction toward which the work of Frank Gehry, arguably the most important architect to emerge in the closing decades of the twentieth century, tended as well. With his practice rooted in the least traditionally urban of cities, Los Angeles, Gehry's sensuous, exuberant work is often as space-devouring as freeway interchanges. Yet more than one

European, Asian, and North American historical city found a prominent place for his work, and thereby often found itself transformed. Through an extensive series of increasingly original and masterful buildings that began in the 1970s—each pervaded with a rigor of function, structure, and detailing, thoroughly convinced of its own exuberant newness and spatiovisual splendor, at once superb, playful, witty, and utterly free of the dark burden of heavy irony common to much contemporary design—Gehry produced an unheralded new vision of what architecture can be. The least polemical or theoretical and most intuitive of modern masters, using built form exclusively he has redefined the meaning of "genius" as it applies to architecture at a moment when it was believed by many that such individual creativity was no longer sustainable by the modern world. He accomplished his extraordinary breakthroughs with an unassuming yet charismatic personal manner. In a time increasingly dominated by the devouring powers of communications and media technology, an age that felt betrayed architecturally by Modernism, Gehry has for many millions of people restored belief in the legitimacy of modernity and architecture itself.

The remodeling in 1977–78 of his modest two-story 1920s bungalow in Santa Monica remains a major turn in the history of the modern house (figs. 14-30, 14-31). With typical low-key candor he later explained that he had not been happy initially with either the house he had purchased or its context: "There's a smugness about middle-class neighborhoods that bothered me, I guess. I thought it was a kind of dinky little cutesy-pie house. We had to do *something* to it. I couldn't live in it." For Gehry, life was, as he put it, not a "chocolate sundae"—"people bite each other." With this house, not only the neighborhood but the very definition of an "ordinary" house felt the bite that resulted from Gehry's admitted "intense need somehow to change things and to transform them." Even in Los Angeles, a city long habituated to flamboyant domestic architecture, Gehry's remodeled house registered a seismic shock, especially in its middle-class neighborhood. Its new facade alone was perhaps enough to have inspired the unknown sniper who reportedly fired a shot into it. From the front the original house is all but masked by an architectural assault on the conservative streetscape, a seemingly helter-skelter screenlike assemblage of low-end, down-and-out, commercial and "junk"

14-29 Model of "astronomy garden." Parc de la Villette. Paris

14-30 Frank Gehry. The architect's house. Santa Monica, California. 1977–78

14-31 Frank Gehry. Isometric view, the architect's house

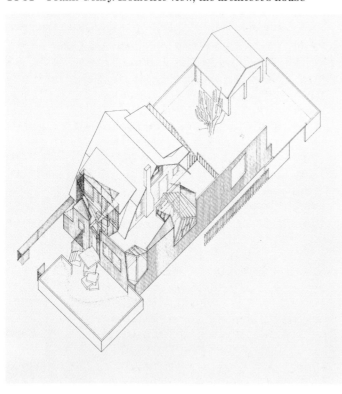

materials: slanted walls and tilted roofing of corrugated iron; scattered stairs and rudimentary entrance of rough ordinary plywood, partly unpainted; and perhaps offering the greatest offense, a cagelike screen of chain-link fencing prominently extended beyond the top of the house (resembling a baseball cage or prison rooftop). Only the fenestration explicitly signals that the assemblage is not accidental or a shantytown apparition but is intricately and purposely designed. This is especially true of the large angled plate glass window at the right corner, which Gehry said was inspired by Marcel Duchamp's famous cubist painting *Nude Descending a Staircase* so that "as you walk around it, it would rotate"—just as another such window on the side wall represented "the ghost of Cubism trying to crawl out," according to Gehry in one his most Deconstructivist moments. Inspiration by art—rather than architecture—was often claimed by Gehry, who counted among his close friends and clients numerous painters and sculptors; in his office hung reproductions of works by Claus Sluter, Gentile Bellini, and Brancusi. But like many highly creative figures, including other Deconstructivists who played down architectural inspiration and foregrounded literary and philosophical sources, his own accounting of influences masked key forces, for Gehry's work was densely interwoven with numerous important strands of Modernist architecture from Wright through Aalto, Kahn, Venturi, and others. In fact, repudiating the "arty" slot in which many critics wanted to put him, he demanded to be called an architect, not an "artist." "My intention is to make architecture," he repeatedly insisted, rejecting the value even of his own sketches. "That's what I concentrate on—the final building, not the drawings."

When Gehry claimed to be just a commentator on the beauty of the common streetscape and that "this other thing called 'design' is a sort of forced attitude," he was reacting to the puritanical "good design" ethos promoted relentlessly by Modernism as an architectural commandment. Gehry took up in a verbally muted but architecturally aggressive manner Venturi's 1960s iconoclastic renovation of Modernism in word and deed. Venturi, we recall, had devastatingly attacked the "puritanically moral language of orthodox Modernism" and promoted a "messy vitality" that would be hybrid, perverse, inconsistent, and conventional rather than pure, impersonal, clear and "designed." In practical terms, this had translated into Venturi's hyper-designed Chestnut Hill House and its naughty sophisticated play with stereotypical American house typology, exaggerating and parodying all its features (fig. 13-20). These moves had enabled Venturi to reinvent the shock generated by the houses of Wright, Rietveld, and Le Corbusier in their day (the house being a central typology in Modernism's development). In so doing Gehry had redefined what might be called the electrostatic house: the kind of a house that at a given historical moment shocks the architectural world and advances the avant-garde frontier. In his own house Gehry of course could not repeat Venturi's strategy, so he went a step further— indeed, several steps—raising the lessons of "Complexity and Contradiction" to another power, as it were. He started not with a house typology but with a real "cutesy-pie" old house and gave it a kind of radical L.A. plastic surgery, only in reverse. Almost doubling its size, he wrapped it with a second spatial shell on three sides (including the facade), whose envelope of "junk" was formally sophisticated in its near-chaos look, going just beyond radical-chic in its material slumming. Like Venturi's house—which it knowingly reflected in the facade clefting and combination of square and rectangular windows left and right—it was a masterpiece of formal invention and finesse, ugly only in the emotions it produced in its critics.

The treatment of the old house contained by the industrial materials was as stunning as its wrapping (regardless of other factors, the old house had to be kept for the manic new assemblage to register as "house"). No partitions were moved or totally eliminated, but the plaster was stripped from walls and ceilings, so that the interior was surgically peeled back to its bare structure of studs, joints, and siding. In strategic places the siding was also removed, opening screened vistas through the outer shell. Conversely, from the peripheral zone, the outside wall of the old house became an interior wall, whose windows revealed the depths of the space. Gehry liked to say that "Buildings under construction look nicer than buildings finished," in fact, "Buildings look like hell when they're finished—but when they're under construction they look great." That the aesthetic of the "unfinished" has precedent in antiquity, the Renaissance, and Romanticism did not compromise the novelty of Gehry's idea of returning his house effectively to its state of becoming, making it look like it was under construction both inside and out, with its facade resembling also the sheds and makeshift enclosures often seen in building sites. The net effect was to deconstruct, reconstitute, and intensify one's perception not only of architectural space but time, as was Gehry's intention: "I wanted to blur the edges . . . between the old and new . . . you're not sure what you're looking at. I guess that's the game I'm about in the house, to try and blur those edges—real and surreal." That Gehry's project would be later seen as a primal event of Deconstructivism was inevitable, for its facade seems to hover between Venturi's 1962 house and Coop Himmelblau's 1988 rooftop (the next step beyond Gehry in shock-voltage), while the interior was regarded as a Deconstructivist critique of the idea of structural and formal closure, marked by sharp Deconstructivist accents like its "escaping-ghost" window. Yet from the perspective of his later work, what is most striking is Gehry's astonishing mastery of common materials used in unprecedented, dazzlingly original and dynamic ways to produce not Deconstructivist angst and bewilderment but deep aesthetic pleasure in the taut, crisply textured planes of corrugated iron, the veiled, shimmering transparency of the chain-link fencing of the facade, and in the seductive, highly functional spaces aglow with the newly exposed redwood with which Gehry discovered the old house had been built.

Early in their careers it is often only in their own houses or studios that architects are able to pursue their most advanced ideas, which later spread to their other work. By the late 1980s Gehry's architectural capacity and charisma were such that clients lined up to build his architectural dreams, spare no effort or expense, secure in the knowledge that the result would be as functionally gratifying as it was devastatingly beautiful. Among the most dazzling examples of this phenomenal practice was the cafeteria (colorplate 85; figs. 14-32, 14-33), begun in 1996 and completed in 2000, for the New York offices of the magazine publishing empire Condé Nast (publishers of *Vogue*, *The New Yorker*, *Vanity Fair*, to name a few). Unlike the celebrated Modernist house typology, cafeterias are a low-end architectural genre. Gehry's high-low strategy at Condé Nast maintained a recognizable cafeteria look—glossy, undecorated surfaces, plain wood floors, widely spaced tables, industrial-style chairs, leatherette booths (all designed by Gehry), and an absence of art, mirrors, fancy lamps, or other typical restaurant embellishments. This traditional iconography was, however, radically transformed by a retro-futuristic use of extravagantly costly curved plate-glass panels and blue titanium-lined walls and ceiling. Although confined within the rectangular lines of an office building, the plan of the cafeteria's internal features undulates in a pattern reminiscent of Gaudí's Casa Milá (fig. 12-37). Similarly Gaudíesque are the sinuous, tilted piers dividing the booths and the astonishing huge, frameless, overlapping plate-glass panels that subdivide and mold the central area, each a different shape, their flowing lines taken up by the cloudlike suspended ductwork. One is not jarred but charmed by the three diverse impressions that the resulting space magically conjures: a typical cafeteria (say, of the 1950s); a landscape, from the earthy tones of the rock-colored benches and the wooden tables with yolk-yellow tops, the sinuous contours of the glass moving like (according to Gehry) "reeds swaying in the breeze," and the dreamy "clouds"; and a pool, created by the blue-tinted waves of titanium and the flowing glass panels that swim with reflections and refractions of people, space, light, and objects constantly in easy motion. The

14-32   Frank Gehry. Condé Nast Cafeteria. Model. New York. 1996–2000

space is energizing, yet it is also seductive and even soothing, perhaps most of all in its astonishing acoustics so unlike what one anticipates from all the shiny metal and glass surfaces: by perforating and backing the titanium wall and ceiling panels with sound-absorbing material, Gehry produced an uncanny underwater quiet, sense of ease and illusion of privacy virtually everywhere in the cafeteria.

At the turn of the millennium the most celebrated work of Frank Gehry—and of late-twentieth-century architecture—was his Guggenheim Museum in Bilbao near the Atlantic coast of Spain, of 1991–97 (colorplate 86; figs. 14-34, 14-35). Many fac-

14-33   Frank Gehry. Plan, Condé Nast Cafeteria

tors conspired to bring into being this remarkable building, which like its New York "parent" seemed to change the face of architecture—certainly museums—forever. The initial impulse came from the Basque regional government, which envisioned a new museum in Bilbao as part of a program to regenerate the economically depressed region. At the time, New York's Guggenheim was just embarking on a program of establishing satellite museums globally. When approached by Basque officials, the museum's director, Thomas Krens, rejected their idea of converting an abandoned riverside warehouse and proposed instead a huge new building on the site. There ensued a global competition among Gehry and two other invited architects, Arata Isozaki and Coop Himmelblau, respectively representing America, Asia, and Europe. There was no limit to Krens's ambition for his new building. It should have a grandiose central entrance space like Wright's New York museum, he told Gehry. The "dominant model for the atrium should be a cathedral such as Chartres," he hubristically urged, which would provide "fun and surprise." In any case he wanted to "make it better than Wright"—daring words that empowered and inspired the architect to push his medium to its limits.

The astonishing result, developed in a design process of many stages, was as complex a building as has ever been built. The plan reveals two rectilinear volumes, perpendicular to

each other, that intersect, collide, and fuse with a billowing cluster of numerous curvilinear spaces of various shapes and sizes, all gathered about the central atrium (figs. 14-36, 14-37). Functional differentiation deeply informs the scheme. Like the New York museum, Bilbao was intended for the exhibition of twentieth-century (and later) art, but was to spatially separate contemporary from classic modern art, Krens directed, with "galleries for living artists different from galleries for dead artists," as Gehry put it. He arranged that everything from giant sculptures by Richard Serra and environmental electronic LED displays by Jenny Holzer to traditional framed paintings and photographs find their true place. The stacked, interpenetrating zones of what Gehry called his six "stodgy" rectilinear galleries glow with finely tuned proportions and diffused luminosity. Supple curvature and masterful lighting make the gargantuan 450-foot "boat" gallery (one of seven nonlinear galleries) a living and breathing architectural environment for its appropriately scaled contemporary artworks (fig. 14-38). Not even the unrivaled sweep of this gallery could outshine the magical spatial realm of the atrium (fig. 14-39). Wright's great rotunda rotates within a repetitive rhythmic geometry, and Chartres Cathedral soars within taut linear cells, but Gehry's even higher, 164-foot atrium skyrockets in a leaping spiral of plaster-faced piers that swirl upward like unfurling sails past vertiginous elevator cages and distant catwalks

14-34　Frank Gehry. Guggenheim Museum Bilbao. Air view. Bilbao, Spain. 1991–97

14-35　Frank Gehry. Guggenheim Museum Bilbao. Bilbao, Spain. 1991–97

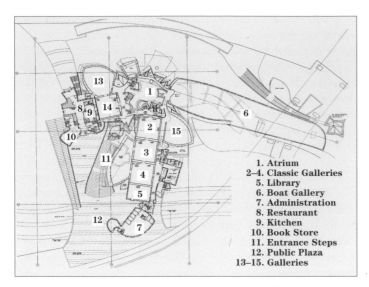

14-36 Frank Gehry. Plan, Guggenheim Museum Bilbao

1. Atrium
2–4. Classic Galleries
5. Library
6. Boat Gallery
7. Administration
8. Restaurant
9. Kitchen
10. Book Store
11. Entrance Steps
12. Public Plaza
13–15. Galleries

14-37 Frank Gehry. Section, Guggenheim Museum Bilbao

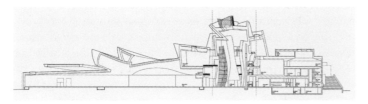

toward waves of vast windows and skylights. Gehry notes that his atrium was loosely inspired by the Expressionist sets of Fritz Lang's 1926 film, *Metropolis*, which would take it back to the Futurists and their dreams of elevators that "swarm up the facades like serpents of glass and iron." Gehry has translated the Futurists' sinister, apocalyptic images into a bright and shining, joyful spatial vision. Designated for the orientation of the visitor, the atrium in reality produces a disorientation and then reorientation from the ordinary world into Gehry's spectacular realm of cathedral-like "fun and surprise" and a reborn Art Nouveau raised to a higher magnitude.

One of Gehry's most astonishing achievements at Bilbao is the way the building's highly functional spaces translate almost directly on the exterior as a cluster of sweeping, explosive, yet lucid forms visually ravishing from almost every angle. Its sculptural force and beauty were rivaled in its century only by a few works of Wright, Le Corbusier, Mies van der Rohe, and Kahn. Its metal skin recalls the period of Gehry's house, but at Bilbao cheap corrugated iron has been transformed into luxurious titanium covering the entire building except for the blue-tinted stonefaced rectilinear spaces. Applied in thousands of small shingles, the lustrous reflective skin, although only one-third of a millimeter thick, is more durable than stone, yet because of its membrane-thinness, it ripples like leaves in the wind. Adding further subtlety, its coloration changes with the sun and sky from silver to white to gold. Immense in scale (longer than the entire Metropolitan Museum of Art in New York), the Bilbao's form language is steeped in history and pervaded with multiple layers of personal and public imagery. While under construction, its swirling latticework steel skeleton evoked the most famous of Russian Constructivist projects, Tatlin's visionary Monument to the Third International. Complete, it bears a strong resemblance to certain undulating

Expressionist projects by Hermann Finsterlin of 1919. As seen from the dramatic main perspectives of the opposite riverbank or the bridge that cuts through its colliding forms—which mostly seem like ideal geometries warped, stretched, twisted, and otherwise reshaped under the pressure of a giant sculptor's hand—the museum generates image upon image: a ship in its own reflecting pool above the river; a huge scaly fish with fins, surging through the elements; at the center, a giant roselike "flower" (Gehry's term). Nautical imagery was frequent in Le Corbusier and early Modernism; the "flower" indirectly recalls the giant rose windows of Gothic cathedrals like Chartres; and the fish was a favorite theme of Gehry, a Pisces whose favorite childhood memory was the live carp his grandmother bought for dinner every week, kept in the bathtub where he watched it swim with endless fascination, later to become, he said, "a symbol for a certain kind of perfection that I couldn't achieve with my buildings." All of these motifs masked an under-image (as seen from the river): the New York Guggenheim, with its low-slung horizontal volume sweeping from the left into the high rotunda at the right, here exploded into a Cubist-Deconstructivist assemblage of colliding, shimmering fragments.

In many ways the Bilbao Guggenheim fuses and obliterates distinctions between the Deconstructivist and High-Tech currents. Indeed, it was more advanced materially and technologically than most works of key High-Tech architects like Foster and Piano. Neither its structure nor its titanium skin could have come into being without advanced computer technology (fig. 14-40). During the last three decades of the twentieth century, CAD (computer-aided design) became an increasingly

14-38 Frank Gehry. "Boat" gallery, Guggenheim Museum Bilbao

14-39   Frank Gehry. Atrium, Guggenheim Museum Bilbao

common design tool indispensable for many applications. By the 1990s some architects, such as Hani Rashid and Greg Lynn (pioneers of the "paperless studio"), were experimenting with designs produced entirely by computer. However, this extreme application of computers remained highly controversial: for most architects and architecture schools it was an abuse of method, interrupting the direct, intuitive connection with the

14-40   Computer diagram, Guggenheim Museum Bilbao

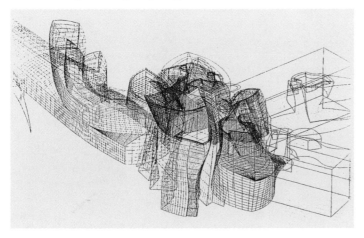

imagination sustained by traditional methods of drawing and modeling, although for others the computer was instead an unlimited tool that empowered all human faculties. While always remaining in the former camp, using sketches, traditional drafting, and extensive modeling in wood, cardboard, and other standard materials, Gehry nevertheless pioneered the use of computer techniques in an extremely important way: not to design form, but to facilitate its fabrication. In the early 1990s, Gehry and his associate Jim Glymph realized that CATIA, a system devised by Dessault Systems for French Aerospace to digitize complex three-dimensional products such as an airplane wing or fuselage, could be similarly used for complex architectural forms. CATIA, as transformed by Gehry and Glymph, permitted designs and models made in traditional ways to be digitized by scanning and developed into three-dimensional computer images of high flexibility and precision, which in turn could be exactly analyzed into buildable components; the computer files could be transmitted to fabricators, in fact directly to computer-robotic manufacturing devices for structural support details, window frames, glass or titanium panels, and so on. The result was that every detail in a building could be different (every window or titanium panel, for example), be produced cheaply, and, above all, be priced exactly, so that true cost estimates and a realistic budget were feasible (crucial for client and contractor alike). These were all factors that previously had severely limited the realization of the highly complex formal language that Gehry developed in the 1980s. Bilbao was the first structure in which Gehry realized his variation of the CATIA computer technique (the Condé Nast cafeteria was another), effectively a technological answer to the much-lamented demise of traditional craftsmen and crafting techniques. Gehry has said, "When I drew the plan of Bilbao I was so happy, because I realized that it was a beautiful thing. I'd never seen anything like it." If the world agrees, it was because Gehry, like so many of history's greatest architects, proved himself not only a formal genius but a supreme master of the demanding art of the buildable and of getting it built.

ALTERNATIVE STRATEGIES: PLACE, TIME, AND MEMORY

For all their divergences, High-Tech and Deconstructivism share a common universalism. They tend to be about Architecture with a capital "A," and not about the possibility of numerous different architectures shaped by factors of difference rather than some uniform set of values. For the most part both High-Tech and DeCon resist the stubborn fact that every building is situated in a singular place in nature and the built environment; that it occupies a particular point in a collective time-consciousness inherent to the site; that the site tends to be inhabited by localized memories of lived human experience; that buildings can revive, reaffirm, and redirect such memory traces in ways beneficial to the cultural and psychological well-being of the inhabitants.

Few of the buildings discussed in the two previous sections of this chapter involve active engagement with the concreteness of place, time, and memory. Many deny this dimension altogether. Most could have been built with a few alterations on numerous interchangeable sites around the globe. Architects of the Modernist genealogy often remain uncomfortable with contextualism, experiencing it as a limitation on their creative sovereignty and a subtraction from their work rather than added layers of experiential reality.

Among the strategic alternatives to this anticontextual knot of Modernist practice is a range of engagement by new work with various dimensions of the architectural environment: with *place* in its many senses. More than a nominal or secondary contextual inflection, explicit and plainly visible rather than theoretical (like Eisenman), and generally differing from Charles Moore's "making" of new places (although sometimes extending it), such engagement becomes here a dominant theme of architectural design. Two stunning buildings in Manhattan, both completed in 1999, propose alternative modes of this trend.

Few buildings interact more effectively with their immediate surroundings than the LVMH Building of 1999–2000 (colorplate 87) by the French architect Christian de Portzamparc, who has said, "There is no universal key anymore" to architecture. Sited in one of the world's major concentrations of luxury commerce, on 57th Street near Madison Avenue, the New York quarters of Moët Hennessy Louis Vuitton promotes corporate prestige with its uniquely folded and faceted, jewel-like glazed curtain wall floating in front of its 24 stories (using three types of glass framed by green, red, and white fluorescent tubing along the folds). The alluring presence of the finely crafted facade of this relatively modest building (for Manhattan), which effortlessly compensates for its mere 60-foot width, depends critically on contextualism. One of Portzamparc's main reasons for the fragmentation of planes involved an inverse contextualism: to thwart reflections of the mammoth granite IBM Building facing across the street. "I didn't want it to be just a mirror," he explained about his design. The precise way the facade is folded and scaled, however, relates to its closer neighbors, the Modernist Chanel Building to the west and a 14-story prewar brick structure to the east. A compelling narrative was made to shuttle between the three buildings. In the lower part of the LVMH facade, the folded form at the left seems to be sliding or emerging from behind the larger folded form on the right, itself either peeling back or moving forward over the left part. This ambiguous movement spreads as the LVMH gently plays with its neighbors, compressed but also pressing against them. This interactive flow together with certain similarities in scale and pattern of fenestration between LVMH and its neighbors produce a three-part collaged unity of old, older, and new buildings, dominated by the glowing center where all is resolved in the faceted, flowerlike upper stories. In its conversational display of urbane architectural wit the LVMH Building vindicates not only contextualism but the idea that good architectural manners need not preclude self-assertion, and that relatively modest buildings can be a beneficial presence in the modern cityscape, where blockbusters (like Bilbao or the Hongkong and Shanghai bank) are not necessarily required.

Nevertheless, sometimes really large, high-energy buildings are demanded by the setting. Times Square is one of Manhattan's anomalous spaces where the street grid is intersected and opened up by the diagonal avenue of Broadway. Here teeming streets shape a dynamic area drenched in the riotous imagery of acres of brilliant electric advertising signage intensified in the rebuilding of the entire zone in the 1990s. If Portzamparc's jewel would have been lost in this most frenzied and challenging of modern city spaces, its contemporary, Four Times Square (4TS, which houses a big law firm and Condé Nast, including Gehry's Cafeteria), responds masterfully to it (colorplate 88; fig. 14-41). In this powerful 49-story building completed in 1999, freestanding above the fifth floor, the New York architectural firm Fox & Fowle imaginatively extended contextualism into three dimensions, and beyond. The building fractures in its lower stories into restrained corporate entrances on the Forty-second and Forty-third Street fronts, versus the flamboyant curves and stepping along Broadway, where the building's razzle-dazzle signage is most startling in an 8-story corner cylinder whose surfaces glow in a vast array of LEDs flashing the latest stock quotes and other news of NASDAQ, at the time the world's hottest stock market (see figs. 12-22, 12-23 for an early-twentieth-century counterpart). As 4TS rises, its fragmented facades compete for spectators in the wildly diverse surrounding visual field, with complex layered and peeled zones of stone cladding and glass curtain walls at different levels and on different sides of the building, which is set back in subtle steps dictated not by zoning requirements, but by aesthetics. Up through these zones 4TS gives the illusion of being many buildings, each targeted to a different viewpoint. In the top stories, however, the inflection to immediate surroundings yields to a second contextualist mode. Here we find uniformity of all four sides of 4TS, together with great scale and iconicity in its Neoconstructivist crown (containing the mechanical systems), whose context is all Manhattan and its identity-conferring iconic skyscrapers (e.g., the Chrysler Building and Empire State). Finally, 4TS incorporates a strong contextualism with respect to the natural environment. An imposing range of energy-saving and environmentally friendly features make it an extremely "green" building. Yet 4TS is exemplary in another important

14-41   Fox & Fowle. Four Times Square. New York. 1999

way. It demonstrates that innovative, high-quality commercial architecture does not preclude profit, for it was built not as a prestigious corporate symbol (like LVMH) but on spec as a rental project. The difference here was an enlightened commitment of the developer, the Durst Corporation, to architectural and civic values.

It would be hard to imagine a contemporary architecture more different from the hyper-Modernist, acutely urban contextualism of 4TS than the New Urbanism movement that spread through the United States in the same period. Ultimately deriving from the "place-making" ideas of Charles Moore but far more conservative in tone, its initial adumbration was Seaside, a Florida beachfront community conceived in 1978 by the architects Elizabeth Plater-Zyberk and Andres Duany and the developer Robert Davis, and built mostly over the following decade (colorplate 89). It rejected modern architectural styles, turned away from the modern city, and repudiated suburbia as a radical experiment in modern living, condemned for its faceless, isolated, car-dependent, consumerist, TV- and pop-culture-dominated lifestyle deprived of civic, community, and family values in an endless land-devouring sprawl. In their place, Seaside embodied principles set out in a building code called "Traditional Neighborhood Development," which stressed the public over the private realm, the town as a whole over its parts, and the "human" over everything else. In architectural terms this meant a small vacation community for about 2,000 inhabitants, gathered closely around the public institutions and facilities of the central area (including the town hall, open market, tennis courts, offices, shops, and park), with closely spaced variously sized homes on small lots helping define straight streets lined with wide sidewalks. No residence was more than a short stroll from the center (to discourage driving and encourage neighborly encounters). Picket fences, elaborate porches, and gabled roofs were everywhere in pastel-colored construction that permitted wide formal variety so long as it was all in a vernacular, nonmodern mode (even when illustrious outside architects participated).

The attempt of Seaside to reconstitute a lost sense of place, to revivify the small-town atmosphere of another time, conjuring up memories of a bygone way of life, has been wildly successful in inspiring numerous similar, highly popular developments. Yet the movement—guided by the newly formed "Congress of the New Architecture"—has been sharply criticized as sentimental nostalgia, socially reactionary in the quasi-gated exclusivity of many examples, and conformist and controlling in its tendency to regulate personal behavior as well as the community's architectural look (especially at Celebration, Florida, developed by Disney, Inc.). Not at all urban but rather little more than a New Suburbia masked by a tendentious theoretical spin, New Urbanism was, in other words, just another of those periodic escapist reactions to modernity seen, for example, a century earlier in the English Domestic Revival (pp. 468–71). Indeed, Seaside was used for the set of the 1997 movie *The Truman Show* to convey the simulacrum of a town where a real man lives in a totally false world without knowing it.

Other architectural currents in this period demonstrated that place, time, and memory could be invoked in a more open and progressive manner. Architects found ways to avoid the nostalgic escapism, cultural claustrophobia, and flight from modernity seen not only in the New Urbanism but widely around the world in a variety of purist, dead-end revivals of near-extinct or embalmed local vernaculars, often in postcolonial reaction to the architectural globalization that has blotted out so many local traditions. Opposing such reactionary paths, Critical Regionalism, as the laudable new tendencies have been called, is double-coded and doubly informed in method. It distills local typologies, materials, forms, ornament, and other traits and infuses their re-creation with the spirit, iconography, and methods of various aspects of modernity, and vice versa. It makes possible the creation of world-class architectures that breathe the free air of the continuing international modern movement yet recapture and reanimate the spirit of a particular place, time, and memory. India, East Asia, the Islamic Middle East, Africa, Latin America, and other regions all have seen examples of this doubly ambitious idea. A notable example is the Supreme Court in Mexico City built in 1987–92 by Teodoro González de León (figs. 14-42, 14-43). The huge structure achieves a monumentality of civic function and appearance rare among public works of the twentieth century in any style. The powerful facade combines the deep-framed shape of Le Corbusier's High Court in Chandigarh, India, and the geometric-iconic abstraction of Aldo Rossi with indigenous, although extinct, pre-Columbian monumental typologies: the stepped platform, the portico, and the hypostyle hall. The last of these informs the structural scheme of the vast interior, where the numerous courtrooms are disposed on a long central axis forming a gigantic pergola. In plan the whole distinctly suggests the head, body, and legs of a human figure as depicted in pre-Columbian art.

Japan is exceptionally rich in Critical Regionalism, with numerous world-class architects advancing personal interpretations of Japanese traditions and international Modernism. Moreover, because of a singular situation involving high land values, management style, and cultural priorities, architectural originality has been granted unusual license and support in Japan, where unique buildings—ones that would seem bizarre in any other country—are plentiful. Contemporary Japanese architecture, in fact, is so diverse as to be unclassifiable. Nevertheless, examples of the work of two major figures suggest its uniquely expressive and sophisticated Critical Regionalism—which in this case could also fairly be called regionalist Critical Modernism.

The Fujisawa Municipal Gymnasium complex, built in Tokyo by Fumihoko Maki in 1984–1990, is a consummate exercise in expressive roof design (fig. 14-44). Both of Maki's roofs embody metaphorical shapes. The "cloud" building (Maki's term) is suggestive of a moored blimp, while the thrusting silhouette of its larger companion resembles Japanese temple roofs, medieval armor, and space technology. Critical to their visual success are Maki's sophisticated systems of interlaced girders that support the roofs (in spans up to 263 feet). The finely crafted stainless steel outer envelopes (only 0.5 millimeter thick) are typical of the high level of detailing, materials, and craftsmanship of the best of contemporary Japanese architecture.

If Maki's work stresses the High-Tech component of Modernism, Tadao Ando is perhaps the most brilliant of Japanese architects in fusing indigenous traditions and concerns with the reinforced concrete culture of Le Corbusier and Louis Kahn. In Ando's hands, however, the weighty massiveness of the medium tends to be undermined, as shuttering patterns, reveals, lighting, and other factors subtly produce an illusion

14-42   Teodoro González de León. Supreme Court. Mexico City. 1987–92

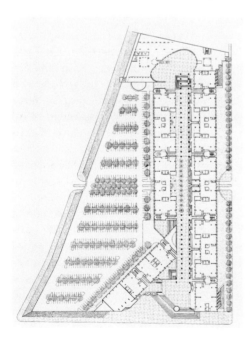

14-43
Teodoro González
de León. Plan,
Supreme Court

are the primary forms which light reveals to advantage . . . the most beautiful forms." At Minani-Kawachi a Zen-like architectural garden is suggested by the parallel-textured planes of the gentle steps of the Museum "roof." The play of light and shadow over exquisitely shaped geometric solids provide Modernist counterparts to a Zen garden's artful scattering of exquisite rocks. Ando's platform also conjures an aura of ancient ritual, and indeed it was intended as an open-air theater for drama festivals set against the surrounding hills. It also provides views over the adjacent tombs and tumuli of the ancient Kofan culture. As Ando wrote, "Architecture delivers place's memory to the present, and transmits it to the future."

Ando's museum is representative of the way the type became the central focus of architectural ambition and imagination in this period. Many museums exhibited the art of a particular time or place, their contents displayed as object-repositories of collective memories. Museum architectures could be poetically made to converge and resonate with these themes. This possibility is richly demonstrated in three extremely diverse, prominent European examples.

The Museum of Roman Art in Mérida, Spain, is one of the most widely admired buildings of this period. Built in 1980–86 by the Spanish architect Rafael Moneo, the museum adjoins the remains of the theater and amphitheater of the ancient Roman city to form a unified archaeological complex (fig. 14-46). Unlike the more typical museums of antiquities that are built on any available site to make a space where various archaeological objects are brought together, Moneo's structure roots down sev-

of almost membrane-thin panels, paradoxically mimicking the traditional Japanese vernacular. In his Historical Museum in Minami-Kawachi (near Osaka) of 1990–94 (fig. 14-45), Ando translates the more sculptural side of Kahn and Le Corbusier as he realizes the latter's doctrine that "architecture is the masterly, correct, and magnificent play of masses brought together in the light . . . Cubes, cones, cylinders, and pyramids

14-44　Fumihoko Maki. Fujisawa Municipal Gymnasium. Tokyo. 1984–90

eral meters below grade to real, intact remains of the Roman layer of the city that is the principal "object" on display (color-plate 90; figs. 14-47–14-49). The museum is built into an excavation that was dug and shaped for it, and whose perimeter corresponds to the four walls of Moneo's building, which thus looks down archaeologically into the earth at ancient Mérida (not unlike one of those glass-bottomed tourist boats designed for seeing aquatic life in the tropics). What makes this experience

14-45　Tadao Ando. Chikatsu-Asuka Historical Museum, air view. Minami-Kawachi, Japan. 1990–94

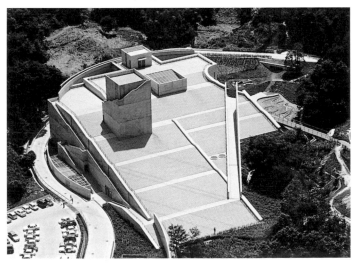

acutely effective and moving to the visitor are the particular forms, spaces, and materials that give the museum shape and resonance. The rectangular volume of the museum is subdivided into an undercroft at excavation level and a lofty skylighted space above. Through the entirety run ten intermediate cross walls, which are built, much like ancient Roman construction, of massive unreinforced concrete using Roman-style flat bricks for formwork that becomes permanent facing. These walls are not continuous, however. At the bottom in the undercroft they open into ranks of arches and piers, which rest directly on the exca-vated Roman layer, breaking step to avoid important features of the antiquities. Because the orientation of the museum was rotated a few degrees from the plan of the Roman city, the walls and columns of the excavated ancient houses and paleo-Christian church run at a slant to the museum arcades, separat-ing display from container, and indicating that the ancient buried city extends subterraneously beyond the museum in all directions. This lower level recalls such utilitarian ancient Roman works as the Porticus Aemilia (fig. 3-20), but it also brings to mind the crypt of a medieval church, where sacred remains and relics are displayed. Analogously, in the upper zone of the museum every cross wall is opened in the same relative place by an enormous arch, forming the museum "nave" (color-plate 90). This might be called the upper church, complete with gallery levels for additional display. The entirety thereby recalls not a generic medievalism but specifically the First Romanesque to which Spain contributed strongly. Moneo's building is thus

Modernisms: Renewal and Hyper-Diversity in Recent Decades　｜　577 formally, spatially, and materially an ancient warehouse, a medieval Spanish church, an excavated city (with an excavated paleo-Christian church on the spot), and also a brilliantly composed, superbly lit, and carefully crafted modern building that recalls specific layers of time and memories of place, reconstituted and brought before our eyes seemingly for all time.

The Musée d'Orsay in Paris, by Italian architect Gae Aulenti, completed in 1986, is one of the more distinguished of the numerous, often banal "grands projets" built under the long tenure of French President François Mitterrand. Other works of this ambitious enterprise, meant to rival monuments built under the French kings and the Napoleons, included the Parc de la Villette studied earlier, the Cité de la Musique (by Portzamparc), the Institut du Monde Arabe (by Jean Nouvel), the mammoth new Bastille Opera (Garnier's now devoted to dance), the Grand Bibliothèque de France (the technologically dysfunctional, grandiose new national library), and the Grand Louvre (expanding and reconfiguring the great museum into airportlike dimensions and tone). The Orsay project transformed the then unused train station built in 1898–1900 by Victor Laloux into a new museum to house the late-nineteenth-century French art previously held by the Louvre and other state collections (fig. 14-50). To thereby reunite art and architecture of the period when Paris was at its height of urban and cultural splendor and fame was a compelling idea, but one that posed a considerable architectural challenge. Few building types are more antithetical to the goals of a museum than a train station, particularly one dominated by the gigantic central hall of the Orsay, over 140 meters long and rising 35 meters to its iron, glass, and stucco-paneled vault. Yet Aulenti managed to avoid destroying the majestic original space or needlessly compromising the display of art objects. Her brilliant stroke—combining the *architecture parlante* method and the palimpsest theme—was to restore the lost trains, the old focus of the station, in architectural form. The twin rows of massive Egypto-industrial stone structures alongside the central entrance promenade look like nothing so much as two trains waiting to carry the museum visitor back into the world of nineteenth-century art. They are positioned where trains would have been and in fact appear in early photographs of the station (fig. 14-51).

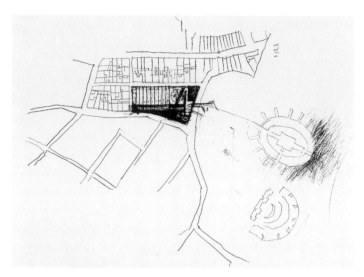

14-46   **Rafael Moneo. Museum of Roman Art, site plan. Mérida, Spain**

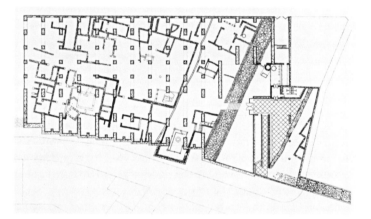

14-47   **Rafael Moneo. Basement plan, Museum of Roman Art**

14-48   **Rafael Moneo. Isometric, Museum of Roman Art**

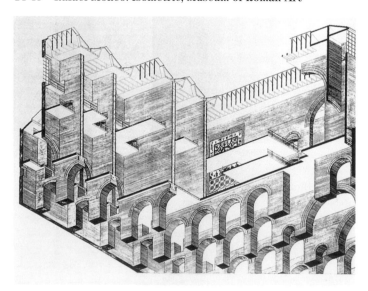

14-49   **Museum of Roman Art. Interior view with Roman columns, basement level. Mérida, Spain. 1980–86**

14-50   Gae Aulenti. Musée d'Orsay. Interior after remodeling. Paris. 1986

14-51   Musée d'Orsay. Interior before remodeling. Paris

They approximate the scale of trains, and remarkably, they conform to a generalized abstraction of the train image even in numerous suggestive details. They serve as time machines, a magical architectural medium between the present (the transformed Orsay station) and the past (nineteenth-century art). The terraced concourse seems a train platform populated with current time-travelers meeting sculpted visitors from the nineteenth century, while through the "train" doors one enters the painting collections, with the avant-garde and academic art on the left and right respectively, antithetical aesthetic worlds here mediated by Aulenti's architectural ingenuity. Paradoxically, by making the

building more completely a functioning train station, Aulenti made it more successful as a museum, in the act vindicating Ando's statement that "architecture delivers place's memory to the present, and transmits it to the future." Not to be neglected in accounting for her success, however, was the architectural magnificence of the original building.

Among the many powerful works of this period dedicated to place, time, and memory, the most radical is Daniel Libeskind's Jewish Museum in Berlin, designed and built in 1989–98 (colorplate 91; figs. 14-52–14-55). Although meant to exhibit relevant Jewish historical objects large and small, the architecture itself—still empty at the turn of the millennium—will endure as the main visual event and signifier to a degree beyond the autonomous architectural power of, for example, the museums of Wright and Gehry. The gleaming zinc-covered, zigzagging building, with its painfully slashed-in fenestration and spooky concrete labyrinthine spaces, shares the language of Deconstructivism—the colliding, oblique, and fragmented, bent and broken, cut and slashed prisms, bars, and shards of form seen in Zaha Hadid, Coop Himmelblau, and others. But the museum is not just playing the Deconstructivist game of challenging basic architectural concepts; if anything it extends to the maximum Deconstructivism's disquieting and tormented, psychologically engaged dark side. Assuredly it is like no other building that the visitor will have experienced; like the Sphinx, it asks troubling, dangerous, and even unanswerable questions. Its experience is disturbing; its apocalyptic subject is infinitely more so. Not explicitly a Holocaust

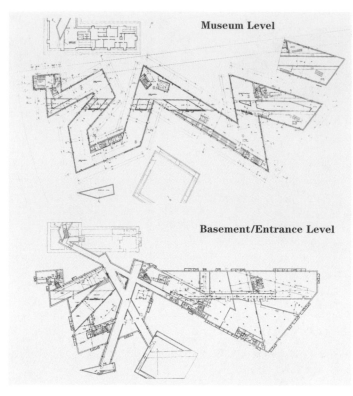

Museum Level

Basement/Entrance Level

14-52 Daniel Libeskind. Plans, Jewish Museum. Berlin

14-53 Daniel Libeskind. Jewish Museum. Berlin. 1989–98

memorial, the museum is dedicated to the history of the Jews of Berlin—a centuries-long history violently interrupted by the Nazis—or to the history of Berlin seen through its Jewish population. This role, in conjunction with its extraordinary form, make it the most eloquent and compelling of such memorials.

Libeskind's building communicates in a complex multileveled discourse. Its very existence as a building about Jews by a Jewish architect resonates doubly. The celebrated avant-garde culture of pre-Hitler Berlin in literature, music, theater, film, fashion, and all the visual arts would never have happened without a massive Jewish contribution. By his very act of inserting a building at the cutting-edge of world architecture into the still-devastated fabric of Berlin, Libeskind, an American Jew born in Poland, in effect restores the active Jewish presence in the city. Yet Libeskind's intentions go deeper. His idea was that the museum architecturally represent the effort to rescue the Jewish memory virtually obliterated by the Holocaust, to give form to the invisible Berlin. Recognizing that to give form to such an absence was immensely challenging, his underlying idea was "to erect the museum about an empty space that extends through the entire building." As Libeskind explains, two powerful forms organize the building: "One is a straight line, but broken into many fragments; the other is a tortuous line, but continuing infinitely. These two lines develop architecturally and programmatically through a limited but definite dialogue. They also fall apart, become disengaged, and are seen as separated. In this way they expose a void that runs through the museum and through Architecture—a discontinuous void." The plan of the building makes clear how the erratic zigzagging path of the museum is repeatedly traversed by a 13-foot-wide linear volume. At each intersection an "impenetrable void," rising 90 feet through the entire structure, is formed. None of the six voids thereby produced, which have skylights but no windows, may be entered. Three are glimpsed by the visitor through narrow slits in bridges that cross them erratically at the three levels of the museum. The other three voids, however, are completely sealed, invisible, purely symbolic spaces: the knowledge of their unseen presence makes all the more poignant the absence of Berlin's exterminated Jewish community, which they represent, uncanny spaces inhabited only by the lost echoes of a distant age.

Although the voids, which come and go irregularly as one winds through the tortuous narrow paths of the museum spaces, are the symbolic heart of this apocalyptic shrine, numerous architectural factors contribute powerfully to a psychologically intense, chilling atmosphere. These include the entrance, which is not at street level but through a basement maze from the adjoining Baroque building that serves the pre-1870 history of Berlin Jews; the dramatically lit, steep, tilted main stairway crisscrossed by ominous oblique girders; the agitated fenestration slashes and their sunlight patterns; the mysterious amplification of sounds by the hushed narrow gray concrete corridor-spaces; and the supplementary, detached Holocaust Void and Garden of Exile, the latter containing forty-nine square piers all filled with Berlin earth but one, packed with earth from Jerusalem.

The building resonates with the fury of the Holocaust and even more, the fierceness of the reactions to it. Frank Gehry has said of Libeskind, "You feel his anger about the Holocaust in this

14-55 Daniel Libeskind. Main stairway, Jewish Museum. Berlin. 1989–98

14-54 Daniel Libeskind. Interior (void with bridges), Jewish Museum. Berlin. 1989–98

building." Indeed one senses this emotion in the psychological atmosphere, the furious slashing-mutilation of the walls, and the startling broken and tormented plan that literally makes the entire building an apocalyptic sign. Libeskind has said that the zigzag form represents a dismembered Star of David, but if so it might similarly suggest a broken swastika. Virtually all commentators, however, see it as a lightning bolt, which raises horrific, paradoxically entangled possibilities of signification: the thunderbolt is of course the agent of divine wrath, yet in this context one must remember that it was also the infamous symbol of the dreaded Nazi SS, a hubristic emblem that glittered darkly on the uniforms of the master agents of genocide (and as late as 2000 was a sign that, for example, neo-Nazi skinheads shaved as patterns on their heads). Thereby the angry building—an architectural Götterdammerung—would represent the destruction of Berlin's Jews, but also the destruction of Nazi Berlin; signify the delirium of human folly and evil, the righteous anger of the architect as representative of the great court of humanity—and perhaps the ultimate retribution of a disillusioned God. Yet the building finally rises above anger and revenge: its unrelenting if discontinuous axial line of voids, while providing the enduring remembrance of a broken people, also witnesses their survival and rebirth, and that of a new Berlin, still troubled but struggling free of its tragic past. If at Bilbao Gehry set a new architectural level of aesthetic freedom and pleasure, in Berlin Libeskind revisited the limits of architecture's ability to produce meaning and redefined its status as a public art in the deepest sense.

George
Howe and
William
Lescaze.
Philadelphia
Savings
Fund
Society
Building.
1931–32

Glossary

Abacus: At the top of a capital, a thick rectangular slab of stone that serves as the flat, broad surface on which the architrave rests.

Acanthus: A plant of the Mediterranean region, whose serrated leaves were copied in stone to ornament Corinthian and Composite capitals; used also to decorate moldings and friezes.

Acropolis: The upper citadel of a Greek city, usually the site on which important temples were erected.

Acroteria: Sculptured figures or ornaments placed above the pediment of an ancient temple.

Aedicule: A framing motif consisting of an entablature and pediment supported by two columns or pilasters.

Agora: An open space or marketplace that was the center of public life in cities of ancient Greece.

Aisle: A passage or corridor parallel to the nave of a church or an ancient basilica and separated from it by columns or piers.

Altar: A tablelike structure for the celebration of the Sacraments in a Christian building; for sacrifice or offerings in antiquity.

Ambo: In early medieval churches, a raised stand from which the Gospels and Epistles were read, and from which sermons were sometimes delivered.

Ambulatory: A semicircular or polygonal passageway around the apse of a church.

Amphiprostyle: A Classical temple type with a portico at both its front and rear.

Amphitheater: An oval or circular building for contests and spectacles, its central arena surrounded by rising tiers of seats and a network of corridors and stairs.

Anta: In Classical temples, the pilasterlike projecting end of a portico wall often framing columns, which are then said to be in antis.

Antefix: An ornament, generally of terra-cotta and in the form of a palmette, placed at the edge of the roof of an ancient building to mask the ends of the roof tiles.

Apse: A semicircular, polygonal, or rectangular extension at the end of a Roman basilica or a Christian church.

Arcade: A series of arches supported on piers or columns. A "blind" arcade is a row of arches applied to the wall as an ornamental feature.

Arch: A structural device, curved in shape, to span an opening by means of wedge-shaped bricks or stones (voussoirs) that support each other by exerting mutual pressure and that are buttressed at the sides.

Architrave: A square beam that is the lowest of the three horizontal components of a Classical entablature.

Archivolt: A molded band carried around an arch.

Arcuated: Any form of construction using arches.

Arena: The open area or place of action in an amphitheater.

Ashlar: Building stone that has been squared and finished, and the masonry constructed of such blocks.

Atrium: 1. The open court in the center of a Roman house. 2. The open court, often surrounded by columns or arcades, in front of a church.

Axonometric Projection: A method of drawing that represents a building three-dimensionally, with the vertical lines drawn vertically and the horizontals represented at unequal angles to the base (cf. Isometric Projection).

Baldacchino (Baldachin): A fixed canopy over an altar or throne, projecting from a wall, suspended from above, or supported by columns or other vertical elements; also known as a ciborium.

Baptistery: In Christian architecture, a separate building, or part of a church, used for the sacramental ceremony of reception into Christianity.

Barrel Vault: A half-cylindrical vault, semicircular or pointed in cross section; also called tunnel vault.

Basilica: 1. In ancient Roman architecture, a large rectangular building used as a tribunal or for other public purposes and generally arranged with nave, aisles, and one or more apses. 2. In Christian architecture, a longitudinal church of related form.

Bay: A vertical compartment of a building in which several such compartments are repeated; each bay might be defined by columns, piers, windows, or vaulting units.

Bifora: A window or gallery space divided by a colonnette into two arches (trifora: divided into three arches).

Boss: Sculpted ornament of joints, found primarily in vaults.

Gloucester Cathedral.
14th century

Buttress: A projecting mass of masonry serving to provide additional strength for the wall as it resists the lateral thrust exerted by an arch or vault. Flying Buttress: in a church, a buttress in the form of an arch, or set of arches, that carries the thrust of a nave vault over the side aisle roofs down to a massive external pier.

Caldarium: The hot room in a Roman bath.

Cantilever: A self-supporting extended horizontal projection from a vertical support.

Capital: The uppermost part of a column, usually shaped to articulate the joint with the lintel or arch supported; in Classical types, comprising an abacus, echinus, and other carved detail.

Cartouche: An ornamental tablet with the edges formed like a curled piece of paper; generally used for inscriptions.

Caryatid: A sculpted female figure used as a support in place of a column or pier.

Catacomb: An underground cemetery, much used by early Christians, consisting of passages with niches for burial and small chambers for services.

Cavetto: A concave molding generally found on cornices and generally quarter-round in section.

Cella: The body and main sanctuary of a Classical temple, as distinct from its portico and other external parts; sometimes used synonymously with naos, the principal room of a temple where the cult statue is housed.

Centering: Temporary wooden framework used to hold construction material in place until a vault or arch is self-sustaining.

Chancel: The eastern portion of a church set apart for the clergy, and often separated from the main body of the church by a screen, rail, or steps. The term is also used to describe the entire east end of a church beyond the crossing.

Chevet: A French term used to describe the developed east end of a church, usually a French Gothic cathedral, with its apse, ambulatory, and radiating chapels.

Chevron: Zigzag ornament prevalent in Anglo-Norman Romanesque architecture.

**Bristol Cathedral.
12th century**

Choir: The part of a church, generally located toward or in the apse, reserved for clergy and singers.

Ciborium: See Baldacchino.

Circus: In ancient Rome, an oblong space for horse and chariot races, often arranged with tiers of seats on three sides. In England, an open space circular or semicircular in shape surrounded by buildings.

Clerestory: A part of a building that rises above adjoining rooftops and is pierced by window openings to admit light to the interior.

Cloister: An open square court surrounded by a covered ambulatory, often arcaded. It is generally attached to a church or monastery and is distinguished from a secular courtyard by its function as a place of seclusion and repose.

Cloister Vault: A dome that rises directly from a square or polygonal base, its curved surface divided into sections by groins or ribs.

Coffering: Recessed panels, square or polygonal, that ornament a vault, ceiling, or the underside (soffit) of an arch.

Colonnette: A small or greatly attenuated, slender column.

Colossal Order: Columns or pilasters that rise through several stories; also called a giant order.

Column: A vertical, usually cylindrical, support, commonly consisting of a base, shaft, and capital; in Classical architecture, its parts are governed by proportional rules.

Composite Order: One of the five Classical orders; favored in late Roman architecture. On the capital, large conjoined Ionic volutes are combined with the acanthus leaves of the Corinthian order.

Compound Pier: A pier with columns, shafts, and pilasters attached, sometimes in clusters, to its faces.

Concrete: Artificial stone formed by mixing cement, sand, and gravel with water. Used most effectively by the ancient Romans and later revived in the sixteenth century.

Console: A bracket or projecting support, usually scroll-shaped.

Corbel: A masonry block projecting from a wall to support a superincumbent element.

Corbeled Arch: Masonry constructed over a wall opening by a series of courses projecting from each side and stepped progressively further forward until they meet at midpoint; not a true arch.

Corinthian Order: The most richly embellished of the three orders (Doric, Ionic, and Corinthian) developed by the Greeks, with a tall capital composed of a bell-shaped core (kalathos) enveloped by layers of acanthus leaves terminating in corner volutes, surmounted by a concave-sided abacus.

Cornice: The uppermost, projecting portion of an entablature; also the crowning horizontal molding of a building or wall.

Corona: The projecting part of a Classical cornice.

Corps de Logis: In French architecture, the term for the main building as distinguished from the wings and pavilions.

Cortile: The Italian term for courtyard, the enclosed space within a building, commonly surrounded by a covered ambulatory defined by columns or piers.

Crocket: In Gothic architecture, an ornamental hooklike spur of stone projecting from the sloping sides of a spire, pinnacle, or gable; also used in Gothic capitals in place of leaves and volutes.

Cromlech: A prehistoric monument composed of a circle of huge stones (megaliths).

Crossing: The area where the nave and transept intersect in a cruciform church, frequently surmounted by a tower or dome.

Crypt: A vaulted space beneath the pavement of a church, often housing relics or tombs.

Cryptoporticus: In ancient Roman architecture, a covered passage or gallery defined not by columns but by walls with window openings for light and air; the term also refers to a subterranean passage.

Curtain Wall: In modern architecture, a non-load-bearing wall (often constructed of materials such as glass, steel, or aluminum) that is hung in front of the building's structural frame.

Cyclopean Wall: Constructed without mortar of irregular stones so huge it was later believed to be the work of a mythical race of giants called Cyclopes.

Cyma Recta: A double-curved molding, concave in the upper part and convex below.

Cyma Reversa: A double-curved molding, convex in the upper part and concave below.

Cymatium: In a Classical entablature, the name given to the molding that is the top member of each subdivision.

Dado: The intermediate portion of a pedestal, between its base and cornice.

Decorated Style: In English Gothic architecture, the second of three phases (Early English, Decorated, and Perpendicular). It flourished from the late thirteenth century through the first third of the fourteenth and was characterized by a profusion of rich curvilinear ornament, by multiple ribs and liernes, by ornate moldings, and by the double S-curve (ogee).

Dentil: A small toothlike block used in series in the corona of a Classical cornice.

Diaphragm Arch: A transverse arch across the nave of a church partitioning the roof into sections.

Dipteral: Referring to a temple surrounded by a double range of columns.

Distyle in Antis: In a Classical temple referring to a portico with two columns between piers (antae) projecting from the cella walls.

Dolmen: A prehistoric monument composed of two large stones placed upright with a covering stone slab, forming a chamber.

Dome: A curved vault that is erected on a circular base and that is semicircular, pointed, or bulbous in section. If raised over a square or polygonal base transitional squinches or pendentives must be inserted at the corners of the base to transform it into a near circle.

Domical Vault: A rib or groin vault whose center rises dome-like above its peripheral levels.

Doric Order: The column and entablature developed on mainland Greece; the fluted columnar shaft is without a base; its capital is an abacus above a simple cushionlike molding (echinus). The entablature has a plain architrave, a frieze composed of metopes and triglyphs, and a cornice with projecting blocks (mutules). In Roman Doric, the column is slimmer than the Greek prototype, is unfluted, and stands on a low base; the capital is smaller.

Dormer Window: A vertical window with its own gable pierced through a sloping roof.

Drum: 1. The cylindrical or polygonal wall supporting a dome. 2. One of the cylindrical sections comprising the shaft of a column.

Dry Masonry: Masonry laid without mortar.

Duomo: The Italian term for a cathedral.

Dwarf Gallery: In Romanseque architecture, a wall passage on the exterior face of a building screened by a small-scale colonnade.

Echinus: A convex, cushionlike molding between the shaft and the abacus in the Doric or Tuscan order; in an Ionic capital, found beneath the volutes, generally in decorated form.

Egg and Dart: A decorative molding alternating egg-shaped and dartlike forms.

Elevation: An architectural drawing made as if projecting on a vertical plane to show any one side, exterior or interior, of a building; also used to describe the vertical plane of a building.

Engaged Column: A column attached to or appearing to be partly embedded within a wall.

Entablature: The upper part of a Classical order comprising architrave, frieze, and cornice.

Entasis: The slight swelling of the vertical profile of a Classical column as it tapers toward the top to counteract the illusion of concavity that accompanies straight-sided columns.

Exedra: A semicircular recess or niche; a large apse.

Extrados: The upper surface of an arch or vault.

Facade: The principal exterior face of a building, usually the front.

Fan Vault: In English Gothic architecture, a vault of conoidal form, wherein the ribs have spread out from the springing point in a way that suggests the appearance of an open fan.

Fascia: In the architrave of an Ionic entablature, a horizontal band often used in a series of two or three, each projecting slightly beyond the one below.

Finial: A knoblike decorative ornament, often foliate in design, at the top of a gable, pinnacle, or spire.

Flamboyant Style: A late phase of French Gothic architecture characterized by flamelike tracery patterns.

Fluting: The shallow concave channels cut vertically into the shaft of a column or pilaster. In Doric columns, they meet in a sharp edge (arris); in Ionic, Corinthian, and Composite columns, they are separated by a narrow strip.

Foliated: Ornamented with leaflike patterns.

Frieze: A horizontal band, sometimes painted or decorated with sculpture or moldings. It may run along the upper portion of a wall just beneath a cornice or it may be that part of a Classical entablature that lies between the architrave and cornice. A Doric frieze is composed of alternating triglyphs and metopes; an Ionic frieze often has continuous relief sculpture.

Gable: A triangular element. It may be the end of a pitched roof framed by the sloping sides. It also refers to the top of a Gothic panel, or to the triangular area above the portals of a Gothic building.

Gallery: An upper story projecting from the interior wall of a building, or placed above the aisles of a church. It may function as a corridor or as an area for assembly or seating.

Groin: The sharp, curved edge formed at the intersection of vaulting webs.

Groin Vault: A vault formed when two barrel vaults of identical size intersect at right angles (also called a cross vault).

Guttae: Beneath each triglyph in a Doric entablature, small conical projections that may represent the wooden pegs used in the timber prototypes of the Greek temple.

Hall Church: A church in which the nave and aisles are the same height, giving the building the appearance of a great hall.

Heroa: Monuments, often funerary and central in plan, erected to commemorate important Roman personages.

Hexastyle: Having six columns across the front.

Hypocaust: An underground vaulted chamber of brick containing the central heating system—usually earthen pipes through which hot air was forced—for ancient Roman houses and bathing establishments.

Hypostyle: A structure—usually a large hall—in which the roof is supported by many rows of columns. The term is frequently applied to ancient Egyptian temples.

Impost: In a pier, the projecting molding at the springing of an arch. A rectangular impost block transmits the weight of an arch to a supporting member; it may appear between the capital of a column and the springing of the arch.

In Antis: The term used to describe columns placed between the ends of two walls, commonly projecting from the ends of the cella of a small Greek temple.

Intercolumniation: The space between adjacent columns in a colonnade, frequently determined by some multiple of the diameter of the column itself.

Intrados: The undersurface (as opposed to extrados) of an arch (or vault); also called a soffit.

Ionic Order: One of the five Classical orders, the Ionic is characterized by a scroll-shaped (voluted) capital element, the presence of dentils in the cornice, and a frieze that might contain continuous relief ornament.

Isometric Projection: A method of drawing in which a building is represented three-dimensionally, with the horizontals drawn at an equal angle to the base of the drawing while the vertical lines remain vertical (cf. Axonometric Projection).

Keystone: The central voussoir at the top of a completed arch.

Lancet Window: A tall, slender window with a sharply pointed arch (like a lance), common in early Gothic architecture.

Lantern: A cylindrical or polygonal structure that crowns a dome, its base usually open to allow light to enter the area below.

Florence Cathedral. 15th century

Lierne: In Gothic rib vaulting, a minor rib inserted between two major ribs springing from the wall.

Loggia: An arcade supported by piers or columns, open on one side at least; either part of a building (as a porch) or a separate structure.

Lunette: A semicircular wall area, or opening, above a door or window; when above the portal of a church, often called a tympanum.

Machicolation: A defensive construction projecting from the exterior wall of a medieval building or tower and supported by corbels, with openings in the floor between the corbels through which missiles or hot liquids could be dropped on besiegers.

Mansard Roof: Named after the seventeenth-century French architect François Mansart, who often used the shape, a roof with a double slope all around, the lower portion longer and steeper than the upper.

Martyrium: A structure, often of central plan, erected on a site sacred to Christianity, symbolizing an act of martyrdom or marking the grave of a martyr who died for the faith.

Mastaba: Derived from the Arabic word meaning "bench," mastaba refers to a type of Egyptian tomb, rectangular in shape and formed with sloping sides and a flat top, with a passage leading to an underground burial chamber.

Megaron: The principal hall of an Aegean dwelling, oblong in shape and sometimes subdivided into a larger and smaller section by a range of columns; thought to be the ancestor of the Greek temple plan.

Melon Dome: A dome subdivided into individual concave webs; sometimes called an umbrella dome.

Metope: In the frieze of a Doric order, the rectangular area between triglyphs; often left plain but sometimes decorated with relief ornament.

Mihrab: A niche hollowed out of that wall in a mosque oriented toward Mecca.

Minaret: A tall, slender tower with projecting balconies, close to a mosque, used by the muezzin to call the faithful to prayer.

Module: A unit of measurement used to regulate proportions in architectural design; in Classical architecture, commonly half the diameter of a column just above its base.

Molding: A sculpted, ornamental band, carved with a distinctive profile or pattern; highly developed in Classical architecture.

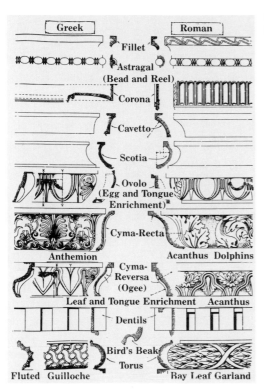

Greek and Roman moldings

Mortar: Lime cement laid between courses of masonry to even out irregularities in blocks (or bricks) and to gain greater adhesion.

Mortise and Tenon: A method of wood joining whereby a board formed with a projecting tongue (tenon) is fitted into a board with a hole (mortise) of corresponding shape.

Mullion: A slender upright dividing an opening, usually a window, into two or more sections.

Mutule: In the entablature of the Doric order, a rectangular slab projecting from the lower surface of the corona molding of the cornice, and above each triglyph.

Naos: The principal enclosed area of a Greek temple, containing the cult statue of god or goddess.

Narthex: A colonnaded porch in front of the facade of a church, in early Christian architecture often serving as the fourth side of an atrium; also a transverse vestibule preceding the church nave and aisles.

Nave: The central, longitudinal space of a basilican church, separated from the aisles or from side chapels, and extending from the main entrance to the transept or to the apse.

Necking: A narrow ringlike molding between the bottom of a capital and the top of the shaft of a column.

Niche: A concave recess in a wall, often used to house statuary.

Octastyle: A Classical temple type with eight columns at the ends; or an eight-columned portico.

Oculus: A round window.

Ogee: An S-curved line. An ogee arch, common in English Decorated and Flamboyant Gothic architecture, is a pointed arch formed with an ogee curve on each side.

Opisthodomos: The room at the rear of a Greek temple, behind the naos.

Opus Incertum: A Roman method of walling made by facing concrete with stones of irregular shape.

Opus Recticulatum: A Roman method of walling made by facing concrete with pyramidal stones or bricks set on their corners to form a diagonal, reticulated pattern of lozenges on the surface.

Order: A system for the forms and relationship of elements in the column and entablature of Classical architecture according to one of five modes: Doric, Ionic, Corinthian (developed by the Greeks), and Tuscan and Composite (developed by the Romans).

Oriel: A bay window projecting from the wall.

Palladian Motif: A triple opening formed by a central semicircular arch springing from the entablature of narrower flanking square-headed bays, used by architect Andrea Palladio. Also known as a Serliana because it was first illustrated in the architectural treatise of 1537 by Sebastiano Serlio.

Parapet: A low wall for protection at the edge of a balcony, terrace, roof, bridge, etc.

Pedestal: A supporting substructure for a column or a statue.

Pediment: A triangular space formed by the raking cornices (sloping sides) and horizontal cornice of a gabled temple; also used above a door or window. If the apex or base is split, the pediment is described as broken.

Pendentive: An inverted, concave, triangular piece of masonry serving as the transition from a square support system to the circular base of a dome.

Peripteral: Pertaining to a building surrounded by a row of columns on all sides.

Peristyle: A continuous colonnade around a courtyard or around the exterior of a building.

Perpendicular Style: In English Gothic architecture, the third and last phase. It ran from the mid-fourteenth through the sixteenth centuries, emphasizing vertical and horizontal lines and repetitive paneling, and it used fan vaults.

Piano Nobile: The principal reception and living area in an Italian palace, the first floor above the ground floor.

Piazza: The Italian term for a city square.

Pier: A massive vertical support often rectangular in plan and therefore differing from a column, sometimes having its own capital and base. When combined with pilasters, columns, or shafts, it is called a compound pier. Its proportions are far more variable than a Classical column. Pier is also the term used for the solid mass between windows, doors, and arches.

Pilaster: A column in flattened, rectangular shape, projecting slightly from the face of the wall.

Pilier Cantonné: In medieval architecture, the combination of a simple monocylindrical support and engaged colonnettes rising from floor to vault.

Pillar: A pier.

Pilotis: A French term for stilts used to lift a structure above the ground, freeing the space at ground level for uses other than support.

Plinth: A generally square block forming the bottommost element of a column base; or the projecting lowest portion of a wall.

Podium: A massive platform on which an Etruscan, Roman, or other ancient building was sometimes placed.

Portcullis: A heavy timber or iron grate that can be lowered to prevent access to a gateway or passage.

Portico: An open, colonnaded, roofed space serving as a porch before the entrance to a building.

Post and Lintel: A system of construction in which two or more uprights support a horizontal beam; also called trabeated.

Pronaos: The porch in front of the cella of a Greek or Roman temple formed by the projection of the side walls and a range of columns between the projections.

Propylaeum: A monumental entrance gateway to a temple precinct, as on the Acropolis in Athens.

Proscenium: The stage of an ancient Greek or Roman theater.

Prostyle: A Classical temple having columns across the front, set in a line forward of the side walls of the cella.

Pylon: In ancient Egyptian architecture, the sloping, tower-like walls flanking the entrance to a temple.

Qiblah: The wall oriented to Mecca in a mosque, containing the mihrab niche.

Quoin: Large stone or block laid at the corner of a building (or at an opening) used either for reinforcement of the angle or for ornament.

Reinforced Concrete: Concrete that is strengthened by steel rods and mesh implanted inside before the concrete hardens.

Respond: A support element corresponding to an arch or particular vault rib, generally in the form of a pilaster, half-column, or colonnette, as part of a large pier or bonded with the wall.

Revetment: The facing of a surface, usually a wall, with stone for ornamentation or protection.

Rib: A slender, projecting arched member of a vault, used to facilitate its construction, reinforce its structure, or articulate its form in varying ways in Roman, Byzantine, Islamic, Gothic, and Baroque architecture.

Rose Window: A large, circular window with tracery arranged like the spokes of a wheel or other radial patterns, commonly found in Gothic facades.

Rubble Masonry: Walling with coarse stones irregular in size and shape imbedded in thick mortar and not placed in regular courses.

Rustication: Masonry with massive, strongly textured or rough-hewn blocks and sharply sunk joints, distinguished from smooth ashlar.

Scotia: A concave molding used as the intermediate part of a base.

Serliana: See Palladian Motif.

Shaft: The cylindrical body of a column between capital and base.

Spandrel: The triangular area between adjoining arches, or the triangular area next to a single arch.

Spire: A tall pointed termination of a tower or roof.

Splay: The widening of windows, doorways, and other openings by slanting the sides.

Springing: The point from which an arch or vault springs or rises from its supports.

Squinch: A small arch, or sometimes a lintel, thrown across the angle of a square or polygon to make them more nearly round and thus able to receive the circular base of a dome or drum.

Stoa: 1. In Greek architecture, a long narrow building with an open colonnade in place of one of the long walls. 2. A detached colonnade or portico.

Stringcourse: A continuous, projecting horizontal course of masonry, usually molded, running along the surface of a wall, to mark an architectural subdivision.

Stylobate: The continuous platform of masonry on which a colonnade rests; the uppermost level of the stepped base (crepidoma) of a Greek temple.

Tablinum: In ancient Roman houses, a room or recess at the far end of the atrium, used for keeping family records.

Tambour: Relating to something of a cylindrical, or drum, shape, such as the base of a dome, or the core of the Corinthian or Composite capital.

Thermae: Roman bathing establishments usually of great size and consisting of bathing rooms of varied heat intensity and facilities for exercise and relaxation.

Tholos: In Greek architecture, a circular building; also in Mycenaean architecture, a circular tomb of beehive shape.

Thrust: The outward force exerted by an arch or vault.

Tierceron: In Gothic vaulting, a secondary or intermediate rib springing between the main diagonal and transverse ribs.

Torus: A large convex molding found principally at the base of a column.

Trabeated: An architectural system using a horizontal beam over supports, as opposed to an arched or arcuated system; synonymous with post and lintel.

Tracery: Ornamental intersecting stonework in Gothic win-

Amiens
Cathedral.
15th century

dows, panels, and screens of Gothic buildings; also used on the surface of late Gothic vaults. Varied techniques and patterns are given names such as plate tracery (built up in coursed layers like the framing walls), bar tracery (constructed of complex fragments of the total pattern), flowing tracery (seemingly freehand, curvilinear design, though compass-drawn), etc.

Transept: In a basilican church, the arm that crosses the nave at right angles, usually separating it from the apse; twin transept arms may also project from the nave without interrupting it.

Triconch Plan: Of trefoil or cloverleaf shape.

Triforium: An arcaded wall passage in a Gothic nave wall, between the clerestory and the main arcade in a three-story elevation; in a four-story elevation, it appears between the gallery and the clerestory.

Triglyph: In a Doric frieze, the projecting block marked by vertical grooves (glyphs) between the rectangular areas known as metopes.

Tufa: A soft, porous building stone.

Tumulus: A mound of earth surmounting ancient tombs.

Tuscan Doric Order: Developed by the Romans from the Greek Doric, it stands on a base, has an unfluted shaft, and its capital is a reductive version of the prototype.

Prehistoric tomb, Orkney Islands. c. 3200 B.C.

Vault: An arched ceiling or roof made of stone, brick, or concrete (cf. barrel vault, groin vault, fan vault).

Volute: Ornament in the form of a spiral scroll, and the principal feature of the Ionic capital.

Voussoir: A wedge-shaped stone used in the construction of an arch or vault.

Westwork: In a Carolingian or Romanesque church, the towerlike west end, often containing an entrance vestibule surmounted by a large room open to the nave.

Richard
Rogers
and Renzo
Piano.
Centre
Pompidou.
Paris. 1976

Bibliography

This bibliography is neither a list of works consulted nor a definitive syllabus of basic architectural writings; it is intended as a guide to further reading. It is restricted to English titles (with a few exceptions); foreign publications would vastly expand the relevant material, particularly in the ancient and medieval fields. Bibliographic references to both foreign-language and specialized literature will be found in the works listed.

GENERAL

Ackerman, J. S. *The Villa: Form and Ideology of Country Houses*. Princeton: Princeton University Press, 1990.

"Architectural History 1999/2000: A Special Issue of JSAH." *Journal of the Society of Architectural Historians* 58 (September, 1999), 278–513.

Davey, N. *A History of Building Materials*. London: Phoenix House, 1961.

Fleming, J., H. Honour, and N. Pevsner. *The Penguin Dictionary of Architecture and Landscape Architecture*. 5th ed. Baltimore: Penguin, 1998.

Fletcher, B. *A History of Architecture*, 20th ed., rev. Oxford and Boston: Architectural Press, 1996.

Girouard, M. *Cities & People: A Social and Architectural History*. New Haven: Yale University Press, 1985.

Kostof, S. *The City Assembled: The Elements of Urban Form Through History*. Boston: Little, Brown, 1992.

———. *A History of Architecture*. 2nd ed. New York: Oxford University Press, 1995.

———, ed. *The Architect: Chapters in the History of the Profession*. New York: Oxford University Press, 1977 and 1986.

Krinsky, C. H. *Synagogues of Europe: Architecture, History and Meaning*. New York: Architectural History Foundation; Cambridge: MIT Press, 1985.

Mainstone, R. *Developments in Structural Form*. 2nd ed. Cambridge: MIT Press, 1998.

Mark, R., ed. *Architectural Technology up to the Scientific Revolution: The Art and Structure of Large-Scale Buildings*. Cambridge: MIT Press, 1993.

Oliver, P. *Encyclopedia of Vernacular Architecture of the World*. 3 vols. Cambridge and New York: Cambridge University Press, 1997.

Pevsner, N. *A History of Building Types*. Princeton: Princeton University Press, 1976.

———. *An Outline of European Architecture*. 7th ed. Harmondsworth: Penguin, 1974.

Placzek, A. K., ed. *Macmillan Encyclopedia of Architects*. 4 vols. New York: Free Press, 1982.

Rudofsky, B. *Architecture without Architects: A Short Introduction to Non-Pedigreed Architecture*. New York: Museum of Modern Art, 1964; London: Academy Editions, 1973; Albuquerque: University of New Mexico Press, 1987.

Salvadori, M. *Why Buildings Stand Up: The Strength of Architecture*. New York and London: W.W. Norton and Company, 1980.

Trachtenberg, M. "Some Observations on Recent Architectural History." *Art Bulletin* (June 1988), 208–41.

Upton, D. *Architecture in the United States*. New York: Oxford University Press, 1998.

Watkin, D. *The Rise of Architectural History*. London: Architectural Press, 1980.

ARCHITECTURAL THEORY

Agrest, D. *Architecture From Without: Theoretical Framings for Critical Practice*. Cambridge: MIT Press, 1991.

Boren, I. and J. Rendell. *Intersections: Architectural Histories and Critical Theories*. London and New York: E&FN Spon, 2000.

Choay, F. *The Rule and the Model: On the Theory of Architecture and Urbanism*. Cambridge: MIT Press, 1997.

Conrads, U. *Programs and Manifestoes on 20th-Century Architecture*. Cambridge: MIT Press, 1970.

Hays, K. M., ed. *Architectural Theory Since 1968*. Cambridge: MIT Press, 1998.

Hunt, J. Dixon. *Greater Perfections: The Practice of Garden Theory*. Philadelphia: University of Pennsylvania Press, 2000.

Kruft, H.-W. *A History of Architectural Theory from Vitruvius to the Present*. Trans. by R. Taylor. London: Zwemmer; New York: Princeton Architectural Press, 1994.

Nesbitt, K., ed. *Theorizing a New Agenda for Architecture: An Anthology of Architectural Theory 1965–1995*. New York: Princeton Architectural Press, 1996.

Tafuri, M. *Theories and History of Architecture*. New York: Harper and Row, 1980.

PART ONE: THE ANCIENT WORLD
Architecture Before Greece
General

Badawy, A. *Architecture in Ancient Egypt and the Near East*. Cambridge, Mass.: MIT Press, 1966.

Lloyd, S., H. W. Müller, and R. Martin. *Ancient Architecture: Mesopotamia, Egypt, Crete, Greece*. New York: Harry N. Abrams, 1974.

Prehistory

Bradley, R. *The Significance of Monuments: On the Shaping of Human Experience in Neolithic and Bronze Age Europe*. London and New York: Routledge, 1998.

Burl, A. *The Stone Circles of the British Isles*. New Haven: Yale University Press, 1976.

Daniel, G. *The Megalith Builders of Western Europe*. London: Hutchinson, 1963.

Giedion, S. *The Eternal Present: The Beginnings of Architecture*. Vol. II. New York: Pantheon, 1962–63.

Hodder, I. *The Domestication of Europe: Structure and Contingency in Neolithic Societies*. Cambridge and Oxford: Oxford University Press, 1998.

Mellaart, J. *Catal Hüyük: A Neolithic Town in Anatolia*. New York: McGraw-Hill, 1967.

———. *Earliest Civilizations of the Near East*. New York: McGraw-Hill, 1965.

Morgan, W. N. *Prehistoric Architecture in Micronesia*. London: Kegan Paul, 1989.

Egypt

Arnold, D. *Building in Egypt: Pharaonic Stone Masonry*. New York and Oxford: Oxford University Press, 1991.

———. *Temples of the Last Pharaohs*. New York: Oxford University Press, 1999.

Badawy, A. *A History of Egyptian Architecture*. 3 vols. Berkeley: University of California Press, 1966; Reprinted, London: Histories and Mysteries of Man, 1990.

Edwards, I. E. S. *The Pyramids of Egypt*. New and revised ed. Harmondsworth and London: Yale University Press, 1993.

Friedman, F. D. "Notions of Cosmos in the Step Pyramid Complex." In P. D. Manuelian, ed. *Studies in Honor of William Kelly Simpson*. Boston: Museum of Fine Arts, 1996, 337–51.

Lacovara, P. *The New Kingdom Royal City*. New York: Columbia University Press, 1997.

O'Connor, D. B. "The Social and Economic Organization of Ancient Egyptian Temples." In J. Sasson, ed. *Civilizations of the Ancient Near East*. Vol. I. New York: Scribners, 1995, 319–30.

———. "The Status of Early Egyptian Temples: An Alternative Theory." In B. Adams and R. Friedman, eds. *The Followers of Horus: Studies in Memory of Michael Allen Hoffman*. Oxford: Oxbow Books, 1992, 83–98.

Reeves, N. and R. H. Wilkinson. *The Complete Valley of the Kings: Tombs and Treasures of Egypt's Great Pharaohs*. London: Thames and Hudson, 1996.

Stierlin, H. *The Pharaoh's Master-Builders*. Paris: Tenrail, 1995.

Wilkinson, R. H. *The Complete Temples of Ancient Egypt*. New York: Thames and Hudson, 2000.

Ancient Near East

Crawford, H. *Sumer and the Sumerians*. New York and Cambridge: Cambridge University Press, 1991.

Curtis, J. E. *Ancient Persia*. 2nd ed. London: British Museum, 2000.

Downey, S. B. *Mesopotamian Religious Architecture: Alexander Through the Parthians*. Princeton: Princeton University Press, 1988.

Frankfort, H. *The Art and Architecture of the Ancient Orient*. 5th ed. New Haven and London: Yale University Press, 1996.

Giedion, S. *The Eternal Present: The Beginnings of Architecture*. Vol. II. New York: Pantheon, 1962–63.

Kubba, S. A. A. *Mesopotamian Architecture and Town Planning*. Oxford: B.A.R., 1987.

Kuhrt, A. *The Ancient Near East, ca. 3000–300 B.C.* London and New York: Routledge, 1995.

Loud, G. *Khorsabad*. 2 vols. Chicago: University of Chicago Press, 1938.

Mathews, R. *The Early Prehistory of Mesopotamia, 500,000 to 4,500 B.C.* Turnhout: Brepolis, 2000.

Mieroop, M. van de. *The Ancient Mesopotamian City*. Oxford and New York: Oxford University Press, 1997.

Sasson, J. M., ed. *Civilizations of the Ancient Near East*. 4 vols. New York: Scribners, 1995.

Van Beek, G. W. *Arches and Vaults in the Ancient Near East*. New York: Scientific American, Inc., 1987.

Wilber, D. *Persepolis*. New York: Crowell, 1969.

Crete and Mycenae

Dickinson, O. *The Aegean Bronze Age*. Cambridge and New York: Cambridge University Press, 1994.

Evans, A. J. *The Palace of Minos at Knossos*. 4 vols. London: Macmillan, 1921–35.

Galaty, M. L. and W. A. Parkinson, eds. *Rethinking Mycenaean Palaces: New Interpretations of an Old Idea*. Los Angeles: University of California Press, 1999.

Graham, J. W. *The Palaces of Crete*. Revised ed. Princeton: Princeton University Press, 1987.

Hitchcock, L. *Minoan Architecture: A Contextual Analysis*. Jonsered: P. Åströms förlag, 2000.

Mylonas, G. E. *Ancient Mycena*. Princeton: Princeton University Press, 1957.

Rutkowski, B. *The Cult Palaces of the Aegean*. New Haven: Yale University Press, 1986.

Werner, K. *The Megaron During the Aegean and Anatolian Bronze Age: A Study of Occurence, Shape, Architectural Adaptation, and Function*. Jonsered: P. Åströms förlag, 1993.

Willetts, R. F. *The Civilization of Ancient Crete*. Berkeley: University of California Press, 1978.

Greek Architecture

Anderson, W. J. *The Architecture of Ancient Greece*. 3rd ed. Revised and rewritten by W. B. Dinsmoor. New York: Norton, 1975.

Ashmole, B. *Architect and Sculptor in Classical Greece*. New York: New York University Press, 1972.

Bervé, H., G. Gruben, and M. Hirmer. *Greek Temples, Theatres, and Shrines*. Trans. by R. Waterhouse. London: Thames and Hudson, 1963.

Biers, W. R. *The Archaeology of Greece: An Introduction*. 2nd ed. Ithaca, N.Y.: Cornell University Press, 1996.

Carpenter, R. *The Architects of the Parthenon*. Harmondsworth and Baltimore: Penguin, 1970.

Coulton, J. J. *Ancient Greek Architects at Work*. Ithaca, N.Y.: Cornell University Press, 1977.

Fyfe, T. *Hellenistic Architecture*. Cambridge: Cambridge University Press, 1936.

Hasselberger, L., ed. *Appearance and Essence: Refinements of Classical Architecture: Curvature*. Philadelphia: The University Museum of the University of Pennsylvania, 1999.

Hölscher, T. "The City of Athens: Space, Symbol and Structure." In A. Molho, et al., eds. *City States in Classical Antiquity and Medieval Italy*. Stuttgart: F. Steiner; Ann Arbor: University of Michigan Press, 1991.

Hurwit, J. M. *The Athenian Acropolis: History, Mythology and Archaeology from the Neolithic Era to the Present*. Cambridge and New York: Cambridge University Press, 1999.

Lawrence, A. W. *Greek Architecture*. Harmondsworth and Baltimore: Penguin, 1996.

Nevett, L. C. *House and Society in the Ancient Greek World*. Cambridge and New York: Cambridge University Press, 1999.

Nielsen, I. *Hellenistic Palaces: Tradition and Renewal*. Aarhus University Press, 1994.

Owens, E. J. *The City in the Greek and Roman World*. London and New York: Routledge, 1991.

Rhodes, R. *Architecture and Meaning on the Athenian Acropolis*. Cambridge and New York: Cambridge University Press, 1995.

Rykwert, J. *The Dancing Column: On Order and Architecture*. Cambridge: MIT Press, 1996.

Scranton, R. "Group Design in Greek Architecture." *Art Bulletin* 31 (1949), 247–68.

Travlos, J. *Pictorial Dictionary of Ancient Athens*. New York: Praeger, 1971.

Vermeule, E. *Greece in the Bronze Age*. Chicago: University of Chicago Press, 1964.

Wycherley, R. E. *How the Greeks Built Cities*. 3rd ed. London: Macmillan, 1976.

Roman Architecture

Bianchi Bandinelli, R. *Rome, the Late Empire*. Trans. by P. Green. New York: Braziller, 1971.

Boethius, A. *The Golden House of Nero* (Jerome Lectures, ser. V). Ann Arbor: University of Michigan Press, 1960.

Boethius, A. and J. B. Ward-Perkins. *Etruscan and Roman Architecture*. Baltimore: Penguin, 1970.

Brilliant, R. *Roman Art from the Republic to Constantine*. London: Phaidon, 1974.

Brown, F. *Roman Architecture*. New York: Braziller, 1965.

Clark, J. R. *The Houses of Roman Italy, 100 B.C.–A.D. 250: Ritual, Space and Decoration*. Berkeley: University of California Press, 1991.

Davies, P. J. *Death and the Emperor: Roman Imperial Funerary Monuments from Augustus to Marcus Aurelius*. Cambridge and New York: Cambridge University Press, 2000.

Favro, D. *The Urban Image of Augustan Rome*. New York: Cambridge University Press, 1990.

MacDonald, W. *The Architecture of the Roman Empire*. rev. ed. New Haven: Yale University Press, vol. I, 1982; vol. II, 1986.

MacDonald, W. and Pinto, J. *Hadrian's Villa and Its Legacy*. New Haven: Yale University Press, 1995.

Nash, E. *Pictorial Dictionary of Ancient Rome*. 2 vols. 2nd rev. ed. New York: Praeger, 1968.

Pallottino, M. *The Etruscans*. Harmondsworth: Penguin, 1955.

Richardson, L. *A New Topographical Dictionary of Ancient Rome*. London and Baltimore: Johns Hopkins University Press, 1992.

———. *Pompeii: An Architectural History*. Baltimore: Johns Hopkins University Press, 1988.

Sprenger, M. *The Etruscans: Their History, Art and Architecture*. Trans. by R. E. Wolf. New York: Harry N. Abrams, 1983.

Vitruvius Pollio. *Vitruvius: Ten Books on Architecture*. Trans. by I. D. Rowland. New York: Cambridge University Press, 1999.

Ward-Perkins, J. B. *Cities of Ancient Greece and Italy: Planning in Classical Antiquity*. New York: Braziller, 1974.

———. *Roman Architecture*. New York: Harry N. Abrams, 1988.

Welch, K. *The Roman Amphitheatre: From Its Origins to the Colosseum*. New York: Cambridge University Press, 2001.

Wilson Jones, M. *Principles of Roman Architecture*. New Haven: Yale University Press, 2000.

Yegul, F. *Baths and Bathing in Classical Antiquity*. Cambridge: MIT Press, 1992.

Zanker, P. *Pompeii: Public and Private Life*. Trans. by D. L. Schneider. Cambridge: Harvard University Press, 1998.

PART TWO: THE MIDDLE AGES
Early Christian and Byzantine Architecture

Demus, O. *The Church of San Marco in Venice: History, Architecture and Sculpture*. Dumbarton Oaks Studies, 6. Washington, D.C.: Trustees of Harvard University, 1960.

Krautheimer, R. *Early Christian and Byzantine Architecture*. Harmondsworth and Baltimore: Penguin, 1986.

———. *Rome: Profile of a City, 312–1308*. 2nd ed. Princeton: Princeton University Press, 2000.

———. *Three Christian Capitals: Topography and Politics*. Berkeley, Los Angeles, and London: University of California Press, 1983.

Mainstone, R. *Hagia Sophia: Architecture, Structure and Liturgy of Justinian's Great Church*. London: Thames and Hudson, 1988.

Mango, C. *Byzantine Architecture*. New York: Harry N. Abrams, 1985.

Mathews, T. F. *The Byzantine Churches of Istanbul: A Photographic Survey*. University Park and London: Pennsylvania State University Press, 1976.

———. *Byzantium: From Antiquity to the Renaissance*. New York: Harry N. Abrams, 1998.

———. *Early Churches of Constantinople: Architecture and Liturgy*. University Park: Pennsylvania State University Press, 1971.

Ousterhout, R. *Master Builders of Byzantium*. Princeton: Princeton University Press, 1999.

Von Simson, O. G. *Sacred Fortress: Byzantine Art and Statecraft in Ravenna*. Chicago: University of Chicago Press, 1948.

Pre-Romanesque and Romanesque Architecture

Ambrosini, A., ed. *The Cathedral of Pisa*. Modena: Panini, 1995.

Archer, L. *Architecture in Britain and Ireland, 600–1500*. London: Havill Publications, 1993.

Barral i Alteix, X. *The Romanesque: Towns, Cathedrals and Monasteries*. Cologne and New York: Taschen, 1998.

Bond, F. *An Introduction to English Church Architecture from the Eleventh to the Sixteenth Century*. London and New York: H. Milford, 1913.

Braunfels, W. *Monasteries of Western Europe*. Trans. by A. Laing. Princeton: Princeton University Press, 1973.

Clapham, A. W. *English Romanesque Architecture before the Conquest*. Oxford: Clarendon Press, 1930.

Conant, K. J. *Carolingian and Romanesque Architecture: 800–1200*. Baltimore: Penguin, 1987.

Crossley, P. "Medieval Architecture and Meaning: The Limits of Iconography." *Burlington Magazine* 130 (1988), 116–21.

Evans, J. *The Romanesque Architecture of the Order of Cluny*. Cambridge: Cambridge University Press, 1938.

Fergusson, P. *Architecture of Solitude: Cistercian Abbeys in 12th-Century England*. Princeton: Princeton University Press, 1984.

Fernie, E. *The Architecture of Norman England*. Oxford and New York: Oxford University Press, 2000.

Focillon, H. *The Art of the West in the Middle Ages: Romanesque Art*. Trans. by D. King. New York: Phaidon, 1963.

Gall, E. *Cathedrals and Abbey Churches of the Rhine*. London: Thames and Hudson, 1963.

Horn, W. "Romanesque Churches in Florence." *Art Bulletin* 25 (1943), 112–131.

Horn, W. and E. Born. *The Plan of St. Gall*. Berkeley: University of California Press, 1979.

Krautheimer, R. "The Carolingian Revival of Early Christian Architecture." *Art Bulletin* 24 (1942), 1–38.

———. "Introduction to an 'Iconography of Medieval Architecture.'" *Journal of the Warburg and Courtauld Institutes* 5 (1942), 1–33.

Kubach, H. E. *Romanesque Architecture*. New York: Electa/Rizzoli, 1988.

Paolucci, A., ed. *The Baptistery of San Giovanni Florence*. Modena: Panini, 1994.

Porter, A. K. *Lombard Architecture*. 4 vols. New Haven: Yale University Press, 1915–17.

Reilly, L. A. *An Architectural History of Peterborough Cathedral*. Oxford and New York: Oxford University Press, 1997.

Rivoira, G. T. *Lombardic Architecture: Its Origin, Development, and Derivatives*. Trans. by G. McN. Rushforth. 2 vols. London: W. Heinemann, 1910; 2nd ed., Oxford: Clarendon Press, 1933.

Shearer, C. *The Renaissance of Architecture in Southern Italy*. Cambridge: W. Heffer, 1935.

Stoddard, W. *Monastery and Cathedral in France*. Middletown: Wesleyan University Press, 1966.

Tobin, S. *The Cistercians: Monks and Architecture of Europe*. London: Herbert Press, 1995.

Waldeiere Bizzarro, T. *Romanesque Architectural Criticism*. Cambridge and New York: Cambridge University Press, 1992.

Whitehill, M. W. *Spanish Romanesque Architecture of the Eleventh Century*. London: Oxford University Press, 1941; reprinted, 1968.

Islam and the West

Asher, C. B. *Architecture of Mughal India*. Cambridge and New York: Cambridge University Press, 1992.

Behrens-Abouseif, D. *Islamic Architecture in Cairo: An Introduction*. 2nd ed. Cairo: American University in Cairo Press, 1992.

Blair, S. S. and J. M. Bloom. *The Art and Architecture of Islam 1250–1800*. New Haven and London: Yale University Press, 1995.

Ettinghausen, R. and O. Grabar. *The Art and Architecture of Islam, 650–1250*. Harmondsworth: Penguin Books, 1987.

Flood, F. B. *The Great Mosque of Damascus: Studies on the Makings of an Umayyad Visual Culture*. Leiden and Boston: Brill, 2001.

Frishman, M. and H.-U. Kahn. *The Mosque: History, Architectural Development and Regional Diversity*. London: Thames and Hudson, 1994.

Goodwin, G. *A History of Ottoman Architecture*. London: Thames and Hudson, 1987.

Grabar, O. *The Alhambra*. 2nd ed., rev. Sebastopoli: Solipsist Press, 1992.

———. *The Formation of Islamic Art*. New Haven and London: Yale University Press, 1973.

———. *The Shape of the Holy: Early Islamic Jerusalem*. Princeton: Princeton University Press, 1996.

Hoag, J. D. *Islamic Architecture* (History of World Architecture, Pier Luigi Nervi, ed.) New York: Harry N. Abrams, 1977; London: Faber and Faber, 1988.

Howard, D. *Venice and the East: The Impact of the Islamic World on Venetian Architecture 1100–1500*. New Haven: Yale University Press, 2000.

Koch, E. *Mughal Architecture: An Outline of History and Development*. Munich: Prestel, 1991.

Lehrman, J. *Earthly Paradise: Garden and Courtyard in Islam*. London: Thames and Hudson, 1980.

Michell, G. and S. Martinelli. *The Royal Palaces of India*. London: Thames and Hudson, 1994.

Necipoglu, G. *Architecture, Ceremonial and Power: The Topkapi Palace in the Fifteenth and Sixteenth Centuries*. New York and Cambridge: MIT Press, 1991.

———. *The Topkapi Scroll: Geometry and Ornament in Islamic Architecture*. Santa Monica: Getty Center for the History of Art and the Humanities, 1995.

Ruggles, D. F. *Gardens, Landscape, and Vision in the Palaces of Islamic Spain*. University Park: Pennsylvania State University Press, 2000.

Sevcenko, M., ed. *Theories and Principles of Design in the Architecture of Islamic Societies*. Cambridge: The Aga Khan Program for Islamic Architecture, 1988.

Tadgell, C. *The History of Architecture in India: From the Dawn of Civilization to the End of the Raj*. London: Phaidon, 1994.

Gothic Architecture

Brush, K., P. Draper, and V. Raguin, eds. *Artistic Integration in Gothic Buildings*. Buffalo and Toronto: University of Toronto Press, 1995.

Erlande-Brandenberg, A. *The Cathedral: The Social and Architectural Dynamics of Construction*. Trans. by Martin Thom. Cambridge: Cambridge University Press, 1994.

Fitchen, J. *The Construction of Gothic Cathedrals: A Study of Medieval Vault Erection*. Chicago: Chicago University Press, 1981 (orig. 1961).

Frankl, P. *Gothic Architecture*. New edition. Edited by P. Crossley. New Haven: Yale University Press, 2001 (orig. 1962).

———. *The Gothic: Literary Sources and Interpretations through Eight Centuries*. Princeton: Princeton University Press, 1960.

Grodecki, L. *Gothic Architecture*. Trans. by I. M. Paris. New York: Harry N. Abrams, 1977.

Harvey, J. *The Mediaeval Architect*. London: Wayland, 1972.

Kraus, H. *Gold Was the Mortar: The Economics of Cathedral Building*. London and Boston: Routledge & Kegan Paul, 1979.

Leedy, W. *Fan Vaulting: A Study of Form, Technology and Meaning*. Santa Monica: Arts + Architecture Press, 1980.

Mark, R. *Experiments in Gothic Structure*. Cambridge: MIT Press, 1982.

Panofsky, E. *Gothic Architecture and Scholasticism*. Latrobe: Archabbey Press, 1950.

Recht, R., ed. *Les Bâtisseurs des cathédrales gothiques*. Strasbourg: Editions les Musées de la Ville de Strasbourg, 1989.

Von Simson, O. *The Gothic Cathedral: Origins of Gothic Architecture and the Medieval Concept of Order*. London: Pantheon Books, 1956.

Ward, C. *Medieval Church Vaulting*. Princeton: Princeton University Press, 1915.

Wilson, C. *The Gothic Cathedral: The Architecture of the Great Church, 1130–1530*. London: Thames & Hudson, 1990.

Gothic in France

Abou-el-Haj, B. "The Urban Setting for Late Medieval Church Building: Reims and Its Cathedral Between 1210 and 1240." *Art History* 11 (1988), 17–41.

Adams, H. *Mont-Saint-Michel and Chartres*. Boston and New York: Houghton Mifflin Co., 1904.

Bony, J. *French Gothic Architecture of the Twelfth and Thirteenth Centuries*. Berkeley: University of California Press, 1983.

Branner, R. *Saint Louis and the Court Style in Gothic Architecture*. London: Zwemmer, 1965.

Crosby, S. McK. *The Royal Abbey of Saint-Denis from Its Beginnings to the Death of Suger, 475–1151*. New Haven: Yale University Press, 1987.

Davis, M. T. "Splendor and Peril: The Cathedral of Paris, 1290–1350." *Art Bulletin* 80 (1998), 34–66.

James, J. *The Contractors of Chartres*. Wyong: Mandorla; London: Croom Helm, 1981.

Kidson, P. "Panofsky, Suger, and St-Denis." *Journal of the Warburg and Cortauld Institutes* 50 (1987), 1–17.

Kimpel, D. and R. Suckale. *L'Architecture gothique en France, 1130–1270*. Trans. by F. Neu. Paris: Flammarion, 1990.

Murray, S. *Notre-Dame, Cathedral of Amiens: The Power of Change in Gothic*. Cambridge: Cambridge University Press, 1996.

Neagley, L. E. *Disciplined Exuberance: The Parish Church of Saint-Maclou and Late Gothic Architecture in Rouen*. University Park: University of Pennsylvania Press, 1998.

Panofsky, E. *Suger, Abbot of Saint-Denis, 1081–1151*. 2nd ed. Princeton: Princeton University Press, 1979.

Sanfaçon, R. *L'architecture flamboyante en France*. Quebec: Les Presses de l'Université Laval, 1971.

Stoddard, W. *Monastery and Cathedral in France*. Middletown: Wesleyan University Press, 1966.

Trachtenberg, M. "Suger's Miracles, Branner's Bourges: Reflections on 'Gothic Architecture' as Medieval Modernism." *Gesta* 39/2 (Feb. 2001), 183–205.

Gothic Outside of France

Ackerman, J. S. "*Ars sine scientia nihil est*: Gothic Theory of Architecture at the Cathedral of Milan." *Art Bulletin* 31 (1949), 84–111.

Bond, F. *An Introduction to English Church Architecture from the Eleventh to the Sixteenth Century*. London and New York: H. Milford, 1913.

Bony, J. *The English Decorated Style*. Oxford: Phaidon Press, 1979.

Coldstream, N. *The Decorated Style: Architecture and Ornament 1240–1360*. Toronto: University of Toronto Press, 1994.

Crossley, P. *Gothic Architecture in the Reign of Kasimir the Great: Church Architecture in Lesser Poland, 1320–1380*. Krakow: Ministerstwo Kultury i Sztuki Zatz Muzeowii Ochrony Zahytkow, 1985.

Emery, A. *Greater Medieval Houses of England and Wales, 1300–1500*. 2 vols. Cambridge and New York: Cambridge University Press, 2000.

Friedman, D. *Florentine New Towns: Urban Design in the Late Middle Ages*. New York: Architectural History Foundation; Cambridge: MIT Press, 1988.

Harvey, J. H. *The Cathedrals of Spain*. London: Batsford, 1957.

Norman, D., ed. *Siena, Florence and Padua: Art, Society and Religion 1280–1400*. 2 vols. New Haven and London: Yale University Press, 1995.

Nussbaum, N. *German Gothic Church Architecture*. 2nd rev. ed. Trans. by S. Kleager. New Haven: Yale University Press, 2000.

Reilly, L. *An Architectural History of Peterborough Cathedral*. Oxford: Clarendon Press, 1997.

Trachtenberg, M. *The Campanile of Florence Cathedral, "Giotto's Tower."* New York: New York University Press, 1971.

———. *Dominion of the Eye: Urbanism, Art and Power in Early Modern Florence*. Cambridge: Cambridge University Press, 1997.

———. "Gothic/Italian 'Gothic': Towards a Redefinition." *Journal of the Society of Architectural Historians* 50 (1991), 22–37.

White, J. *Art and Architecture in Italy, 1250–1400*. Harmondsworth: Penguin, 1993.

Yarza, J. *Arte y arquitectura en España, 500–1250*. 7th ed. Madrid: Cátedra, 1994.

PART THREE: THE RENAISSANCE AND BAROQUE
The Renaissance

Benevolo, L. *The Architecture of the Renaissance*. 2 vols. Trans. by J. Landry. Boulder: Westview, 1978.

Burckhardt, J. *The Civilization of the Renaissance in Italy*. 3rd ed. Oxford: Phaidon, 1995 (orig. 1890).

Guillaume, J., ed. *Les chantiers de la Renaissance*. Paris: Picard, 1991.

———, ed. *L'emploi des ordres dans l'architecture de la Renaissance*. Paris: Picard, 1992.

———, ed. *Les traités d'architecture de la Renaissance*. Paris: Picard, 1988.

Kaufman, T. da Costa. *Court, Cloister and City: The Art and Culture of Central Europe 1450–1800*. Chicago: University of Chicago Press, 1995.

La maison de ville à la Renaissance: Recherches sur l'habitat urbain en Europe aux XIVe et XVe siècles. Paris: Picard, 1983.

Onians, J. *Bearers of Meaning: The Classical Orders in Antiquity, the Middle Ages and the Renaissance*. Princeton: Princeton University Press, 1988.

Panofsky, E. *Renaissance and Renascences in Western Art*. New York: Harper & Row, 1972 (orig. 1960).

Scott, G. *The Architecture of Humanism*. Gloucester: P. Smith, 1965.

Thompson, D. *Renaissance Architecture: Cities, Patrons, Luxury*. Manchester: Manchester University Press; New York: St. Martin's Press, 1993.

Italy

Ackerman, J. S. "Architectural Practice in the Italian Renaissance." *Journal of the Society of Architectural Historians* 13 (1954), 3–11.

———. *The Architecture of Michelangelo*. 2nd ed. Chicago: Harmondsworth, 1986.

———. *Palladio*. 2nd ed. New York and London: Penguin, 1991.

Alberti, L. B. (Leon Battista). *On the Art of Building in Ten Books*. Trans. by J. Rykwert, N. Leach, and R. Tavernor. Cambridge: MIT Press, 1988.

Boucher, B. *Andrea Palladio: The Architect and His Time*. New York: Abbeville Press, 1998.

Burns, H. "Quattrocento Architecture and the Antique. Some Problems." In R. R. Bolger, ed. *Classical Influence on European Culture*. London: University Press, 1971.

Burroughs, C. *From Signs to Design: Environmental Process and Reform in Early Renaissance Rome*. Cambridge: MIT Press, 1990.

Coffin, D. *The Villa in the Life of Renaissance Rome*. Princeton: Princeton University Press, 1979.

Filarete, A. (Antonio di Pietro Averlino). *Filarete's Treatise on Architecture*. Trans. by J. R. Spencer. New Haven: Yale University Press, 1965.

Fiore, E. P., ed. *Storia dell'architettura italiana: il Quattrocento*. Milan: Electa, 1998.

Friedman, D. "Palaces and the Street in Late-Medieval and Renaissance Italy." In *Urban Landscapes: International Perspectives*. Edited by J. W. R. Whitehead and P. J. Larkham. London and New York: Routledge, 1992.

Goldthwaite, R. *The Building of Renaissance Florence: An Economic and Social History*. Baltimore and London: Johns Hopkins University Press, 1980.

Hart, V. and P. Hicks, eds. *Paper Palaces: The Rise of the Renaissance Architectural Treatise*. New Haven: Yale University Press, 1998.

Heydenreich, L. *Architecture in Italy 1400–1500*. Revised by P. Davies. New Haven and London: Yale University Press, 1996.

Howard, D. *The Architectural History of Venice*. New York: Holmes and Meier, 1981.

———. *Venice and the East: The Impact of the Islamic World on Venetian Architecture 1100–1500*. New Haven: Yale University Press, 2000.

Hyman, I. "The Venice Connection: Questions About Brunelleschi and the East." In *Florence and Venice Comparisons and Relations*. vol. I. Florence: La Nuova Italia, 1979, 193–208.

———, ed. *Brunelleschi in Perspective*. Upper Saddle River, N.J.: Prentice Hall, 1974.

Kent, F. W. "Palaces, Politics and Society in Fifteenth-Century Florence." *I Tatti Studies* 2 (1987), 41–70.

Klotz, H. *Fillipo Brunelleschi: The Early Works and the Medieval Tradition*. New York: Rizzoli; London: Academy Editions, 1990.

Lazzaro, C. *The Italian Renaissance Garden: From the Conventions of Planting, Design and Ornament to the Grand Gardens of Sixteenth Century Central Italy*. New Haven: Yale University Press, 1990.

Lotz, W. *Architecture in Italy 1500–1600*. Revised by D. Howard. New Haven and London: Yale University Press, 1995.

———. *Studies in Italian Renaissance Architecture*. Cambridge: MIT Press, 1977.

Mack, C. R. *Pienza: The Creation of a Renaissance City*. Ithaca, N.Y.: Cornell University Press 1987.

Millon, H. A. and V. M. Lampugnani, eds. *The Renaissance from Brunelleschi to Michelangelo: The Representation of Architecture*. New York: Rizzoli, 1994.

Palladio, A. (Andrea). *The Four Books on Architecture*. Trans. by R. Tavernor and R. Schofield. Cambridge: MIT Press, 1997.

Payne, A. *The Architectural Treatise in the Italian Renaissance: Architectural Invention, Ornament and Literary Culture*. New York: Cambridge University Press, 1999.

Payne, A., A. Kuttner, and R. Smick, eds. *Antiquity and Its Interpreters*. Cambridge and New York: Cambridge University Press, 2000.

Pepper, S. and N. Adams. *Firearms and Fortifications: Military Architecture and Siege Warfare in Sixteenth-Century Siena*. Chicago: University of Chicago Press, 1986.

Rosenberg, C. M. *The Este Monuments and Urban Development in Renaissance Ferrara*. Cambridge: Cambridge University Press, 1998.

Saalman, H. *Filippo Brunelleschi: The Buildings*. London: A. Zwemmer, 1993.

Serlio, S. *Sebastiano Serlio on Architecture: Books I–V of "Tutte l'opere d'architettura e prospetiva."* Trans. and ed. by V. Hart and P. Hicks. New Haven: Yale University Press, 1996.

Smith, C. *Architecture in the Culture of Early Humanism: Ethics, Aesthetics and Eloquence, 1400–1470*. New York: Oxford University Press, 1992.

Tavernor, R. *On Alberti and the Art of Building*. New Haven and London: Yale University Press, 1998.

Trachtenberg, M. "Michelozzo and the Pazzi Chapel." *Casabella* 642 (Feb. 1997), 56–75.

———. "The Old Sacristy as Model in Early Renaissance Church Architecture." In *L'Eglise dans l'architecture de la Renaissance*. Edited by J. Guillaume. Paris: Picard, 1996, 9–39.

———. Review essay on Howard Saalman, *Filippo Brunelleschi: The Cupola of Santa Maria del Fiore*. *Journal of the Society of Architectural Historians* 42 (1983), 292–97.

———. "Why the Pazzi Chapel is Not by Brunelleschi." *Casabella* 635 (June 1996), 58–77.

Wallace, W. E. *Michelangelo at San Lorenzo: The Genius as Entrepreneur*. New York: Cambridge University Press, 1994.

Westfall, C. W. *In this Most Perfect Paradise: Alberti, Nicholas V and the Invention of Conscious Urban Planning in Rome, 1447–55*. University Park: Pennsylvania State University Press, 1974.

Wittkower, R. *Architectural Principles in the Age of Humanism*. 4th rev. ed. London: Academy Editions and New York: St. Martin's Press, 1988.

Renaissance Outside of Italy

Babelon, J.-P. *Châteaux de France au siècle de la Renaissance*. Paris: Flammarion and Picard, 1989.

Blunt, A. *Art and Architecture in France, 1500–1700*. 5th ed. Revised by R. Beresford. New Haven: Yale University Press, 1999.

———. *Philibert de l'Orme*. London: A. Zwemmer, 1958.

Hitchcock, H.-R. *German Renaissance Architecture*. Princeton: Princeton University Press, 1981.

Kubler, G. *Building the Escorial*. Princeton: Princeton University Press, 1981.

Sankovitch, A.-M. "A Reconsideration of French Renaissance Church Architecture." In *L'Eglise dans l'architecture de la Renaissance*. Edited by J. Guillaume. Paris: Picard, 1996, 161–80.

Thompson, D. *Renaissance Paris: Architecture and Growth, 1475–1600*. Berkeley: University of California Press, 1984.

Thurley, S. *The Royal Palaces of Tudor England: Architecture and Court Life, 1460–1547*. New Haven: Yale University Press, 1993.

The Baroque

Blunt, A., ed. *Baroque and Rococo Architecture and Decoration*. Hertfordshire: Wordsworth Editions, 1988.

Hempel, E. *Baroque Art and Architecture in Central Europe*. Harmondsworth: Penguin, 1965.

Kaufman, T. da Costa. *Court, Cloister and City: The Art and Culture of Central Europe 1450–1800*. Chicago: University of Chicago Press, 1995.

Millon, H. A., ed. *The Triumph of the Baroque: Architecture in Europe 1600–1750*. New York: Rizzoli, 1999.

Norberg-Schultz, O. *Baroque Architecture*. Milan: Electa; New York: Rizzoli, 1986 (orig. 1971).

Baroque in Italy

Blunt, A. *Neapolitan Baroque and Rococo Architecture*. London: A. Zwemmer, 1975.

Connors, J. *Borromini and the Roman Oratory: Style and Society*. New York: Architectural History Foundation and Cambridge: MIT Press, 1980.

Elwin, C. "Optics and Mathematics in the Domed Churches of Guarino Guarini." *Journal of the Society of Architectural Historians* 50 (1991), 384–401.

Hopkins, A. *Santa Maria della Salute: Architecture and Ceremony in Baroque Venice*. New York: Cambridge University Press, 2000.

Krautheimer, R. *The Rome of Alexander VII, 1655–1677*. Princeton: Princeton University Press, 1985.

Marder, T. A. *Bernini and the Art of Architecture*. New York: Abbeville Press, 1998.

———. *Bernini's Scala Regia at the Vatican Palace*. Cambridge and New York: Cambridge University Press, 1997.

Meek, H. *Guarino Guarini and His Architecture*. New Haven and London: Yale University Press, 1988.

Pinto, J. *The Trevi Fountain*. New Haven: Yale University Press, 1986.

Pollak, M. *Turin, 1564–1680: Urban Design, Military Culture and the Creation of the Absolutist Capital*. Chicago: University of Chicago Press, 1991.

Pommer, R. *Eighteenth-Century Architecture in Piedmont: The Open Structures of Juvarra, Alfieri and Vittone*. New York: New York University Press, 1967.

Smith, G. *Architectural Diplomacy: Rome and Paris in the Late Baroque*. Cambridge: MIT Press, 1993.

Varriano, J. *Italian Baroque and Rococo Architecture*. New York: Oxford University Press, 1986.

Waddy, P. *Seventeenth Century Roman Palaces: Use and the Art of the Plan*. New York: The Architectural History Foundation, 1990.

Wittkower, R. *Art and Architecture in Italy, 1600–1750*. 6th ed., rev. Harmondsworth: Penguin, 1999.

The Seventeenth Century in France

Ballon, H. *Louis Le Vau: Mazarin's College, Colbert's Revenge*. Princeton: Princeton University Press, 1999.

———. *The Paris of Henri IV: Architecture and Urbanism*. Cambridge and London: MIT Press, 1991.

Berger, R. *The Palace of the Sun: The Louvre of Louis XIV*. University Park: Pennsylvania State University, 1993.

———. *A Royal Passion: Louis XIV as Patron of Architecture*. Cambridge and New York: Cambridge University Press, 1994.

Blunt, A. *Art and Architecture in France, 1500–1700*. 5th ed., rev. Harmondsworth: Penguin, 1999.

———. *François Mansart and the Origins of French Classical Architecture*. New York: Somerset, 1980.

Kalnein Wend, G. von. *Architecture in France in the Eighteenth Century*. New Haven: Yale University Press, 1995.

Mariage, T. *The World of André Le Nôtre*. Philadelphia: University of Pennsylvania Press, 1999.

Mukerji, C. *Territorial Ambitions and the Gardens of Versailles*. Cambridge and New York: Cambridge University Press, 1997.

Scott, K. *The Rococo Interior: Decoration and Social Spaces in Early Eighteenth-Century Paris*. New Haven and London: Yale University Press, 1995.

Walton, G. *Louis XIV's Versailles*. Chicago: University of Chicago Press, 1986.

Baroque and Rococo in Germany and Austria

Aurenhammer, H. *J. B. Fischer von Erlach*. Cambridge: Harvard University Press, 1973.

Fischer von Erlach, J. B. *Entwurf einer historischen Architektur*. Vienna, 1721.

Harries, K. *The Bavarian Rococo Church: Between Faith and Aestheticism*. New Haven: Yale University Press, 1983.

Hitchcock, H.-R. *German Rococo: The Zimmermann Brothers*. London: Allen Lane, 1968.

———. *Rococo Architecture in Southern Germany*. London: Phaidon, 1969.

Klingensmith, S. J. *The Utility of Splendor, Ceremony, Social Life and Architecture at the Court of Bavaria, 1600–1800*. Chicago: University of Chicago Press, 1993.

Otto, C. *Space into Light: The Churches of Balthasar Neumann*. New York: Architectural History Foundation, 1979.

Baroque and Rococo in Spain, Portugal, and the Americas

Bottineau, Y. *Living Architecture: Iberian-American Baroque*. Trans. by K. M. Leake. London: Macdonald & Co., 1971.

Kubler, G. *Art and Architecture in Spain and Portugal and Their American Dominions, 1500–1800*. Harmondsworth: Penguin, 1969 (orig. 1959).

Lees-Milne, J. *Baroque in Spain and Portugal and Its Antecedents*. London, 1960.

Levenson, J. A., ed. *The Age of the Baroque in Portugal*. Washington: National Gallery of Art; New Haven: Yale University Press, 1993.

Sebastian, S. *El barroco iberoamericano: mensaje iconografico*. Madrid: Ediciones Encuentro, 1990.

The Seventeenth Century in England

Bold, J. *John Webb: Architectural Theory and Practice in the Seventeenth Century*. Oxford and New York: Clarendon Press, 1989.

Cooper, N. *Houses of the Gentry, 1480–1680*. New Haven and London: Yale University Press, 1999.

Hunt, J. D. *Garden and Grove: The Italian Renaissance Garden in the English Imagination, 1600–1750*. Philadelphia: University of Pennsylvania Press, 1996.

Mowl, T. *Architecture without Kings: The Rise of Puritan Classicism under Cromwell*. Manchester: Manchester University Press; New York: St. Martin's Press, 1995.

Soo, L. M. *Wren's "Tracts" on Architecture and Other Writings*. Cambridge: Cambridge University Press, 1998.

Summerson, J. N. *Architecture in Britain 1530 to 1830*. 9th ed., rev. New Haven: Yale University Press, 1993.

———. *Inigo Jones*. Harmondsworth: Penguin, 1966; New Haven: Yale University Press, 2000.

Whinney, M. D. *Christopher Wren*. New York: Thames and Hudson, 1998 (orig. 1971).

PART FOUR: THE MODERN WORLD

The Eighteenth Century

Clark, K. *The Gothic Revival: An Essay in the History of Taste*. 3rd ed. London: Constable, 1995 (orig. 1950).

Germann, G. *Gothic Revival in Europe and Britain: Sources, Influences and Ideas*. Trans. by G. Onn. London: Lund Humphries, 1972.

Honour, H. *Neo-Classicism*. Revised ed. Harmondsworth and Baltimore: Penguin, 1991.

Macaulay, J. *The Gothic Revival, 1745–1845*. Glasgow and London: Blackie, 1975.

Middleton, R. and D. Watkin. *Neoclassical and 19th Century Architecture*. Revised ed. New York: Harry N. Abrams, 1987.

Kaufmann, E. *Architecture in the Age of Reason*. Cambridge: Harvard University Press, 1955.

Piranesi, G. B. *Giovanni Battista Piranesi: The Complete Etchings*. Edited by J. Wilton-Ely. San Francisco: Alan Wofsy, 1994.

Rykwert, J. *The First Moderns: The Architects of the Eighteenth Century*. Cambridge: MIT Press, 1980.

Summerson, J. N. *The Architecture of the Eighteenth Century*. London: Thames and Hudson, 1986.

Vidler, A. *The Writing of the Walls: Architectural Theory in the Late Enlightenment*. Princeton: Princeton Architectural Press, 1987.

Wilton-Ely, J. *The Mind and Art of G. B. Piranesi*. London: Thames and Hudson, 1978.

The Eighteenth Century in England

Darley, G. *John Soane: An Accidental Romantic*. New Haven and London: Yale University Press, 1999.

Girouard, M. *Life in the English Country House: A Social and Architectural History*. New Haven: Yale University Press, 1978.

Harris, J. *The Palladian Revival: Lord Burlington, His Villa and Garden at Chiswick*. New Haven: Yale University Press, 1994.

Hunt, J. D. and P. Willis, eds. *Genius of the Place: The English Landscape Garden 1620–1820*. Cambridge, Mass. and London: MIT Press, 1988 (orig. 1975).

Stillman, D. *English Neoclassical Architecture*. London: Sotheby's Publications, 1988.

Summerson, J. *Architecture in Britain, 1530–1830*. Harmondsworth: Penguin, 1970.

The Eighteenth Century in France

Braham, A. *The Architecture of the French Enlightenment*. Berkeley and Los Angeles: University of California Press, 1980.

Cleary, R. *The Place Royal and Urban Design in the Ancien Régime*. Cambridge and New York: Cambridge University Press, 1999.

Durand, J.-N.-L. (Jean-Nicolas-Louis). *Praecis of the Lectures on Architecture with Graphic Portion of the Lectures on Architecture (1802–5 and 1821)*. Trans. by D. Britt. Los Angeles: Getty Research Institute, 2000.

Etlin, R. A. *The Architecture of Death: The Transformation of the Cemetery in Eighteenth-Century Paris*. Cambridge: MIT Press, 1984.

Harouel, J.-L. *L'Embellissement des villes: L'Urbanisme français au XVIIIe siècle*. Paris: Picard, 1993.

Hautecoeur, L. *Histoire de l'architecture classique en France*. 7 vols. Paris: A. Picard, 1943–57.

Herrmann, W. *Laugier and Eighteenth-Century French Theory*. London: A. Zwemmer, 1985 (orig. 1962).

Kalnein, W. G. *Architecture in France in the Eighteenth Century*. Trans. by D. Brill. New Haven: Yale University Press, 1995.

Ledoux, C.-N. *L'Architecture considérée sous le rapport de l'art, des moeurs et de la législation*. Paris: Editions du Demi-circle, 1991 (orig. pub. by the author, 1804).

Rosenblum, R. *Transformations in Late Eighteenth-Century Art*. Princeton: Princeton University Press, 1967.

Vidler, A. *Claude-Nicolas Ledoux: Architecture and Social Reform at the End of the Ancien Régime*. Cambridge: MIT Press, 1990.

The Nineteenth Century

Benjamin, W. *The Arcades Project*. Trans. by H. Eiland and K. McLaughlin. Cambridge: Belknap Press, 1999.

Bergdoll, B. *European Architecture, 1750–1890*. Oxford: Oxford University Press, 2000.

Collins, P. *Changing Ideals in Modern Architecture*. London: Faber and Faber, 1988 (orig. 1965).

Condit, C. *American Building Art: The Nineteenth Century*. New York: Oxford University Press, 1960.

Foucault, M. *Discipline and Punish: The Birth of the Prison*. Trans. by A. Sheridan. New York: Vintage Books, 1979.

Hitchcock, H. R. *Architecture: Nineteenth and Twentieth Centuries*. 4th ed. Harmondsworth and Baltimore: Penguin, 1987.

Ladd, B. *Urban Planning and Civic Order in Germany, 1860–1914*. Cambridge: MIT Press, 1990.

Meeks, C. L. V. *Italian Architecture 1750–1914*. New Haven: Yale University Press, 1966.

Middleton, R. and D. Watkin. *Neoclassical and 19th Century Architecture*. New York: Harry N. Abrams, 1987.

Mignot, C. *Architecture of the Nineteenth Century in Europe*. New York: Rizzoli, 1984.

Mumford, L. *The Brown Decades: A Study of the Arts in America*. 3rd ed. New York: Dover Publications, 1971.

Pevsner, N. *Some Architectural Writers of the 19th Century*. Oxford: Clarendon Press, 1972.

International Neoclassicism

Ayres, J. *Building the Georgian City*. New Haven and London: Yale University Press, 1998.

Bergdoll, B. *Karl Frederick Schinkel: An Architecture for Prussia*. New York: Rizzoli, 1994.

Cook, J. M. *The Greek Revival: Neo-Classical Attitudes in British Architecture, 1760–1870*. Revised ed. London: John Murray, 1995.

Kennedy, R. G. *Greek Revival America*. New York: Stewart, Tabori & Chang, 1989.

The École des Beaux-Arts

Drexler, A., et al, eds. *The Architecture of the École des Beaux-Arts*. London: Thames and Hudson, 1978.

Lemoine, B. *Architecture in France 1800–1900*. New York: Harry N. Abrams, 1998.

Loyer, F. *Paris Nineteenth Century: Architecture and Urbanism*. Trans. by C. L. Clark. New York: Abbeville Press, 1988.

Pinkney, D. H. *Napoleon III and the Rebuilding of Paris*. Princeton: Princeton University Press, 1958.

Van Zanten, D. *Building Paris: Architectural Institutions and the Transformation of the French Capital, 1830–1870*. Cambridge and New York: Cambridge University Press, 1994.

———. *Designing Paris: The Architecture of Duban, Labrouste, Duc, and Vaudoyer*. Cambridge: MIT Press, 1987.

Victorian Gothic

Girouard, M. *Sweetness and Light: The "Queen Anne" Movement, 1860–1900*. New York: Oxford University Press, 1977.

Greitt, C. M. *Early Victorian*. New York: Abbeville, 1995.

Hersey, G. L. *High Victorian Gothic*. Baltimore: Johns Hopkins University Press, 1972.

Hitchcock, H. R. *Early Victorian Architecture in Britain*. 2 vols. New Haven: Yale University Press, 1954; reprint, New York: Da Capo Press, 1972.

Jones, O. *The Grammar of Ornament*. London: Studio Editions, 1986 (orig. 1856).

Lang, M. H. *Designing Utopia: John Ruskin's Urban Vision for Britain and America*. Montreal: Black Rose Press, 1998.

Muthesius, S. *The High Victorian Movement in Architecture, 1850–70*. London: Routledge & Kegan Paul, 1972.

Pugin, A. W. N. *Contrasts; or, A Parallel between the Noble Edifices of the Fourteenth and Fifteenth Centuries, and Similar Buildings of the Present Day*. London: by the author, 1836.

———. *The True Principles of Pointed or Christian Architecture*. London: J. Weale, 1841.

Ruskin, J. *Selected Writings*. Edited by P. Davis. London: J. M. Dent; Rutland: C. E. Tuttle, 1995.

———. *The Seven Lamps of Architecture*. New York: Dover Publishing, 1989 (orig. 1849).

Summerson, J. *Victorian Architecture: Four Studies in Evaluation*. New York: Columbia University Press, 1970.

The Architecture of Technology

Bracegirdle, B., ed. *The Archaeology of the Industrial Revolution*. London: Heinemann Educational, 1973.

Gideon, S. *Mechanization Takes Command: A Contribution to Anonymous History*. New York: Norton, 1969 (orig. 1948).

Loyer, F. *Architecture of the Industrial Age*. New York: Rizzoli, 1983.

Meeks, C. L. V. *The Railroad Station: An Architectural History*. New Haven: Yale University Press, 1956.

Mumford, L. *Technics and Civilization*. New York: Harcourt, Brace, and World, 1962.

Petroski, H. *Engineers of Dreams: Building the Great Bridge*. New York: Knopf, 1995.

Schivelbusch, W. *The Railway Journey: The Industrialization and Perception of Time and Space in the Nineteenth Century*. New York: Berg, 1986.

Trachtenberg, M. *The Statue of Liberty*. New York and London: Viking Penguin, 1966.

Modern Architecture

Banham, R. *Architecture of the Well-Tempered Environment*. Chicago: Chicago University Press, 1969. 2nd ed., 1984.

———. *A Concrete Atlantis: U.S. Industrial Building and European Modern Architecture, 1900–1925*. Cambridge: MIT Press, 1986.

———. *Theory and Design in the First Machine Age*. 2nd ed. Cambridge: MIT Press, 1980 (orig. 1960).

Benevolo, L. *History of Modern Architecture*. Vol. 2. Trans. by H. J. Landry. Cambridge: MIT Press, 1971.

Colomina, B. *Privacy and Publicity: Modern Architecture as Mass Media*. Cambridge: MIT Press, 1996.

Condit, C. *American Building Art: The Twentieth Century*. New York: Oxford University Press, 1961.

Curtis, W. J. R. *Modern Architecture since 1900*. Oxford: Phaidon, 1982 and 1996.

Etlin, R. A. *Modernism in Italian Architecture, 1890–1940*. Cambridge: MIT Press, 1991.

Ferguson, R., ed. *At the End of the Century: One Hundred Years of Architecture*. Los Angeles: Museum of Contemporary Art; New York: Harry N. Abrams, 1998.

Frampton, K. *Modern Architecture: A Critical History*. New York: Oxford University Press, 1980 and 1992.

———. *Studies in Tectonic Culture: The Poetics of Construction in Nineteenth and Twentieth Century Architecture*. Cambridge: MIT Press, 1995.

Friedman, A. *Women and the Making of the Modern House: A Social and Architectural History*. New York: Harry N. Abrams, 1999.

Giedion, S. *Space, Time and Architecture*. Cambridge: Harvard University Press, 1967 (orig. 1941).

Hall, P. *Cities of Tomorrow: An Intellectual History of Urban Planning and Design in the Twentieth Century*. Oxford: Blackwell, 1996 (orig. 1988).

Jordy, W. H. *Progressive and Academic Ideals at the Turn of the Twentieth Century*. Garden City, N.Y.: Doubleday, 1972.

Ockman, J., ed. *Architecture Culture, 1943–1968: A Documentary Anthology*. New York: Rizzoli, 1993.

Pevsner, N. *Pioneers of Modern Design: From William Morris to Walter Gropius*. 4th ed. London and New York: Penguin Books, 1991 (orig. 1936).

Scheer, T., J. P. Kleihues, and P. Kahlfeldt, eds. *City of Architecture of the City: Berlin 1900–2000*. Berlin: Nicolai, 2000.

Tafuri, M. *The Sphere and the Labryinth: Avant-Gardes and Architecture from Piranesi to the 1970s*. Trans. by P. d'Acierno and R. Connolly. Cambridge: MIT Press, 1987.

Tafuri, M. and Dal Co, F. *Modern Architecture*. New York: Rizzoli, 1986 (orig. 1976).

Tournikiotis, P. *The Historiography of Modern Architecture*. Cambridge: MIT Press, 1999.

Troy, N. *Modernism and the Decorative Arts in France: Art Nouveau to Le Corbusier*. New Haven: Yale University Press, 1991.

Wojtowicz, R. *Lewis Mumford and American Modernism: Eutopian Theories for Architecture and Urban Planning*. Cambridge and New York: Cambridge University Press, 1998.

Ninteenth-Century Forerunners

Fitch, J. M. *American Building: The Historical Forces That Shaped It*. Vol. I. 2nd ed., rev. and enl. New York: Schocken Books, 1966.

Hearn, M. F., ed. *The Architectural Theory of Viollet-le-Duc: Readings and Commentary*. Cambridge: MIT Press, 1990.

Hitchcock, H. R. *The Architecture of H. H. Richardson and His Times*. New York: Museum of Modern Art, 1936; 2nd ed. Hamden, Conn.: Archon Books, 1961; 3rd ed. London and New York: Penguin, 1995.

McKim, Mead, and White, architects. *A Monograph of the Work of McKim, Mead and White*. 4 vols. New York: 1915–25; reprint, New York: Arno Press, 1977.

Parry, L. *William Morris*. New York: Harry N. Abrams, 1997.

Sankovitch, A.-M. "Structure/Ornament and the Modern Figuration of Architecture." *Art Bulletin* 80 (1998), 687–717.

Scully, V. *The Shingle and the Stick Style*. New Haven: Yale University Press, 1971.

Semper, G. *The Four Elements of Architecture and Other Writings*. Trans. by H. F. Mallgrave and W. Herrmann. Cambridge and New York: Cambridge University Press, 1989.

Viollet-le-Duc, E.-E. *Dictionnaire raisonné de l'architecture française du XIe au XVIe siècle*. 10 vols. Paris: B. Bance, 1858–68.

———. *Discourses on Architecture*. Trans. by B. Bucknall. New York: Grove Press, 1959.

Early Modernism

Blau, E. *The Architecture of Red Vienna, 1919–1934*. Cambridge: MIT Press, 1999.

Brooks, H. A. *The Prairie School*. Toronto: University of Toronto Press, 1972.

Brumfield, W. C. *A History of Russian Architecture*. Cambridge and New York: Cambridge University Press, 1997.

Collins, G. R. *Antonio Gaudí*. New York: Braziller, 1960.

Condit, C. *The Chicago School of Architecture*. Chicago: University of Chicago Press, 1964.

Dal Co, F. *Figures of Architecture and Thought: German Architectural Culture 1880–1920*. New York: Rizzoli, 1990.

De Wit, W., ed. *The Amsterdam School: Dutch Expressionistic Architecture 1915–30*. New York: Cooper-Hewitt Museum, 1983; Cambridge: MIT Press, 1983.

Drexler, A. *Transformations in Modern Architecture*. New York: Museum of Modern Art, 1979.

Kahn-Magomedov, S. O. *Pioneers of Soviet Architecture: The Search for New Solutions in the 1920s and 1930s*. Trans. by A. Lieven. New York: Rizzoli, 1987.

Landau, S. and C. W. Condit. *The Rise of the New York Skyscraper, 1865–1913*. New Haven: Yale University Press, 1996.

Lane, B. Miller. *National Romanticism and Modern Architecture in Germany and the Scandinavian Countries*. Cambridge and New York: Cambridge University Press, 2000.

Meyer, E. da Costa. *The Work of Antonio Sant'Elia: Retreat into the Future*. New Haven: Yale University Press, 1995.

Morrison, H. *Louis Sullivan*. New York: Peter Smith, 1952.

Pehnt, W. *Expressionist Architecture*. Trans. by J. A. Underwood. London: Thames & Hudson, 1973.

Schwartz, F. J. *The Werkbund: Design Theory and Mass Culture before the First World War*. New Haven and London: Yale University Press, 1996.

Selz, P. and M. Constantine. *Art Nouveau* (Rev. ed.). New York: Braziller, 1974.

Solomonson, K. *The Chicago Tribune Tower Competition: Skyscraper Design and Cultural Change in the 1920s*. Cambridge and New York: Cambridge University Press, 2001.

Stern, R. A. M., G. Gilmartin, and J. Montague Massengale. *New York 1900: Metropolitan Architecture and Urbanism 1890–1915*. New York: Rizzoli, 1983.

Stieber, N. *Housing Design and Society in Amsterdam: Reconfiguring Urban Order and Identity, 1900–1920*. Chicago: University of Chicago Press, 1998.

High Modernism

Bayer, H. et al. *Bauhaus, 1919–1928*. 3rd ed. Boston: Branford, 1959.

Boesiger, W., ed. *Le Corbusier and Pierre Jeanneret: Oeuvre complète*. 7 vols. Zurich: H. Girsberger, 1935–65.

Cohen, J.-L. *Le Corbusier and the Mystique of the USSR: Theories and Projects for Moscow, 1928–1936*. Princeton: Princeton University Press, 1992.

———. *Mies van der Rohe*. Trans. by M. Rosengarten. London and New York: E&FN Spon, 1996.

———. *Scenes of the World to Come: European Architecture and the American Challenge, 1893–1960*. Exhib. cat. Montréal: Canadian Center for Architecture; Paris: Flammarion, 1993.

Collins, P. *Concrete, the Vision of a New Architecture*. New York: Horizon, 1959.

Franciscono, M. *Walter Gropius and the Creation of the Bauhaus in Weimar*. Urbana: University of Illinois Press, 1971.

Gutheim, F., ed. *Frank Lloyd Wright on Architecture: Selected Writings, 1894–1940*. New York: Duell, Sloan, and Pierce, 1941.

Hitchcock, H. R. *In the Nature of Materials: the Buildings of Frank Lloyd Wright, 1887–1941*. New York: Duell, Sloan and Pierce, 1942.

Hitchcock, H. R. and P. Johnson. *The International Style: Architecture Since 1922*. 2nd ed. New York: Norton, 1966 (orig. 1932).

Hyman, I. *Marcel Breuer Architect: The Career and the Buildings*. New York: Harry N. Abrams, 2001.

Kuper, M. and I. van Zijl, eds. *Gerrit Th. Rietveld, 1888–1964: The Complete Works*. Utrecht: Centraal Musen; New York: Princeton Architectural Press, 1992.

Le Corbusier (Charles Edouard Jeanneret). *Towards a New Architecture*. Trans. by F. Etchells. London: Architectural Press, 1952.

Levine, N. *The Architecture of Frank Lloyd Wright*. Princeton: Princeton University Press, 1996.

Longstreth, R. W. *The Drive-In, Supermarket, and the Transformation of Commercial Space in Los Angeles, 1914–1941*. Cambridge: MIT Press, 1999.

Mumford, E. *The CIAM Discourse on Urbanism 1928–1960*. Cambridge: MIT Press, 2000.

Nerdinger, W., ed. *The Walter Gropius Archive: An Illustrated Catalogue of the Drawings, Prints and Photographs in the Walter Gropius Archive at the Busch-Reisinger Museum, Harvard University*. 5 vols. New York, Cambridge and London: Garland Publishing Inc. and Harvard University Museums, 1990.

Pommer, R. and C. F. Otto. *Weissenhof 1927 and the Modern Movement in Architecture*. Chicago: University of Chicago Press, 1991.

Schultze, F. *Mies van der Rohe: A Critical Biography*. Chicago and London: University of Chicago Press, 1985.

Scully, V. *Frank Lloyd Wright*. New York: Braziller, 1960.

Wigley, M. *White Walls, Designer Dresses: The Fashions of Modern Architecture*. Cambridge: MIT Press, 1995.

Wingler, H. M. *The Bauhaus*. Cambridge: MIT Press, 1993.

Late Modernism

Drexler, A. et al., eds. *Five Architects: Eisenman, Graves, Gwathmey, Hejduk, Meier*. New York: Oxford University Press, 1972; rev. ed. 1975.

Global Architecture. I–XXXII. Tokyo: A. D. A. Edita, 1970–74.

Hines, T. S. *Richard Neutra and the Search for Modern Architecture: A Bibliography and History*. Berkeley: University of California Press, 1994.

Hitchcock, H. R. and E. Danz. *The Architecture of Skidmore, Owings and Merrill, 1950–62*. Trans. by A. Pehnt. New York: Praeger, 1963.

Roca, M. A., ed. *The Architecture of Latin America*. London: Academy Editions, 1995.

Stern, R. A. M., T. Mellins, and D. Fishman. *New York 1960: Architecture and Urbanism between the Second World War and the Bicentennial*. New York: Monacelli Press, 1995 and 1997.

Tafuri, M. *History of Italian Architecture, 1944–1985*. Trans. by J. Levine. Cambridge: MIT Press, 1989.

Second Modernism to Post-Modernism
Traditionalist Modern (Art Deco)

Krinsky, C. H. *Rockefeller Center*. New York: Oxford University Press, 1978.

Robinson, C. and R. H. Bletter. *Skyscraper Style: Art Deco New York*. New York: Oxford University Press, 1975.

Stern, R. A. M., G. Gilmartin, and T. Mellins. *New York 1930: Architecture and Urbanism between the Two World Wars*. New York: Rizzoli, 1987.

Counter-Modernism

Aalto, A. (Alvar). *Complete Works*. Co-editor Karl Fleig. Zurich: Girsberger, 1963.

Brownlee, D. B. and D. G. DeLong. *Louis I. Kahn: In the Realm of Architecture*. Exhib. cat. Los Angeles: Museum of Contemporary Art. Los Angeles and New York: Rizzoli, 1991.

Ronner, H. *Louis I. Kahn: Complete Works, 1935–74*. Boulder, CO: Westview Press, 1977.

Scully, V. *Louis Kahn*. New York: Braziller, 1962.

Tyng, A. *Beginnings: Louis I. Kahn's Philosophy of Architecture*. New York: Wiley, 1984.

Post-Modernism

Allen, G. *Charles Moore*. New York: Watson-Guptill, 1980.

Colquhoun, A. *Modernity and the Classical Tradition: Architectural Essays 1980–1987*. Cambridge: MIT Press, 1989.

Frampton, K. *A New Wave of Japanese Architecture*. Catalogue to IAUS. New York: Institute for Architecture and Urban Studies, 1978.

Girouard, M. *Big Jim: The Life and Work of James Stirling*. London: Chatto & Windus, 1998.

Jencks, C. *The Language of Post-Modern Architecture*. Revised and enlarged edition. New York: Rizzoli, 1981 and 1991.

———, ed. *Post-Modern Classicism*. London: Architectural Design, 1980.

Klotz, H. *The History of Postmodern Architecture*. Trans. by R. Donnell. Cambridge: MIT Press, 1989.

Museum of Modern Art. *Buildings for Best Products*. New York: 1979.

Papadakis. A., ed. *Post-Modernism on Trial*. London: Academy Editions, 1990.

Pommer, R. "Some Architectural Ideologies after the Fall." *Art Journal* 50 (Fall/Winter 1980), 353–61.

Portoghesi, P. *Postmodern: The Architecture of the Post Industrial Society*. Milan: Electa; New York: Rizzoli, 1982.

Portoghesi, P. et al. *The Presence of the Past: First International Exhibition of Architecture—Venice Biennale 1980*. Venice: Edizione "La Biennale di Venezia," 1980; London: Academy Editions, 1980.

Venturi, R. *Complexity and Contradiction in Architecture*. New York: Museum of Modern Art, 1966.

Venturi, R., D. Scott Brown, and S. Izenour. *Learning from Las Vegas*. Cambridge: MIT Press, 1972; rev. ed. 1977.

Wheeler, K. et al., eds. *Michael Graves: Buildings and Projects, 1966–1981*. New York: Rizzoli, 1982.

Modernisms: Renewal and Hyper-diversity in Recent Decades

James-Chakraborty, K. *German Architecture for a Mass Audience*. London and New York: E&FN Spon, 2000.

Lampugnani, V. M., ed. *Berlin Tomorrow: International Architectural Visions*. London: Academy Editions; New York: St. Martin's Press, 1991. (Architectural Design Profile 92).

Lillyman, W. J., M. F. Moriarty, and D. J. Neuman, eds. *Critical Architecture and Contemporary Culture*. New York: Oxford University Press, 1994.

Read, A., ed. *Architecturally Speaking: Practices of Art, Architecture and the Everyday*. London and New York: E&FN Spon, 2000.

Sorkin, M. *Exquisite Corpse: Writing on Buildings*. London and New York: Verso, 1991.

Steele, J. *Architecture Today*. London: Phaidon, 1997.

Vidler, A. *The Architectural Uncanny: Essays in the Modern Unhomely*. Cambridge: MIT Press, 1992.

Neomodernist Extremes: High-Tech

Banham, R. *Megastructure: Urban Futures of the Recent Past*. London: Thames and Hudson, 1976.

Buchanan, P. *Renzo Piano Building Workshop: Buildings and Projects, 1971–1989*. New York: Rizzoli International, 1989.

Davies, C. *High-Tech Architecture*. London: Thames and Hudson, 1988.

McKean, J. *Pioneering British High Tech by Stirling and Gowan, Foster Associates and Richard Rogers Partnership*. London: Phaidon Press, 1999.

Morgan, C. L. *Jean Nouvel: The Elements of Architecture*. New York: Universe, 1998.

Powell, K. *Richard Rogers: Complete Works*. London: Phaidon Press, 1999.

Quantrill, M. *The Norman Foster Studio: Consistency through Diversity*. London and New York: E&FN Spon, 2000.

Riley, T. *Light Construction*. New York: Museum of Modern Art and Harry N. Abrams, 1995.

Neomodernist Oppositions: Around Deconstructivism

Bedard, J.-F., ed. *Cities of Artificial Excavation: The Works of Peter Eisenman, 1978–1988*. Montreal: Canadian Center for Architecture; New York: Rizzoli International, 1994.

Betsky, A. *Violated Perfection: Architecture and the Fragmentation of the Modern*. New York: Rizzoli, 1990.

Dal Co, F. *Frank O. Gehry: The Complete Works*. New York: Monacelli Press, 1998.

Davidson, C. *Anytime*. Cambridge and London: MIT Press, 1999.

Friedman, M., ed. *Gehry Talks*. New York: Rizzoli, 1999.

Guisberg, J. and G. Bradbent, eds. *Deconstruction: A Student Guide*. London: Academy Editions, 1991.

Hadid, Z. *Zaha Hadid: The Complete Buildings and Projects*. New York: Rizzoli, 1998.

Hays, K. M., ed. *Hejduk's Chronotope*. New York: Princeton Architectural Press, 1996.

Hejduk, J. (John). *Mask of Medusa: Works, 1947–1983*. Edited by K. Shkapich. New York: Rizzoli, 1985.

Isozaki, A. *Arata Isozaki: Four Decades of Architecture*. Revised ed. New York: Universe, 1998.

Johnson, P. and M. Wigley. *Deconstructivist Architecture*. New York: Museum of Modern Art, 1988.

Kipnis, J. and T. Lesser, eds. *Chora L. Works: Jacques Derrida and Peter Eisenman*. New York: Monacelli Press, 1997.

Koolhaas, R. (Rem). *Delirious New York: A Retrospective Manifesto for Manhattan*. New ed. New York: Monticelli Press, 1994 (orig. 1978).

Lucan, J., ed. *OMA-Rem Koolhaas: Architecture 1970–1990*. New York: Princeton Architectural Press, 1991.

Monroe, A., ed. *Maki, Isozaki: New Public Architecture: Recent Projects by Fumihiko Maki and Arata Isozaki*. New York: Japan Society, 1985.

Noever, P., ed. *Architecture in Transition: Between Deconstruction and New Modernism*. Munich: Prestel, 1991.

Norris, C. and A. Benjamin. *What Is Deconstruction?* London: Academy Editions, 1988.

Papadakis, A., C. Cooke, and A. Benjamin, eds. *Deconstruction: Omnibus Volume*. New York: Rizzoli, 1989.

Tschumi, B. (Bernard). *The Manhattan Transcripts*. 2nd ed. London: Academy Editions; New York: St. Martin's Press, 1994.

Wigley, M. *The Architecture of Deconstruction: Derrida's Haunt*. Cambridge: MIT Press, 1993.

Woods, L. (Lebbeus). *OneFiveFour*. New York: Princeton Architectural Press, 1989.

Alternative Strategies: Place, Time, and Memory

Aulenti, G. *Gae Aulenti*. New York: Rizzoli, 1997.

Brooke, S. *Seaside*. Gretna: Pelican Publishing Co., 1995.

Dal Co, F. *Tadao Ando: Complete Works*. London: Phaidon, 1995.

Frampton, K., P. Saliga, and M. Thorne, eds. *Building in a New Spain: Contemporary Spanish Architecture*. Barcelona: Editorial Gustavo Gili; Chicago: Art Institute of Chicago, 1992.

Gonzalez, T. de Leon. *Gonzalez de Leon: Architecture as Art*. Milan: Arca, 1998.

Krieger, A. and W. Lennertz, eds. *Andres Duany and Elizabeth Plater-Zyberk: Towns and Town-Making Principles*. New York: Rizzoli, 1991.

Krinsky, C. H. *Contemporary Native American Architecture: Cultural Regeneration and Creativity*. New York: Oxford University Press, 1996.

Libeskind, D. *Daniel Libeskind: Radix-Matrix: Architecture and Writings*. Trans. by P. Green. New rev. ed. Munich and New York: Prestel, 1992.

———. *The Space of Encounter*. New York: Universe, 2000.

Maki, F. *Fumihiko Maki: Buildings and Projects*. New York: Princeton Architectural Press, 1997.

Mohney, D. and K. Easterling, eds. *Seaside: Making a Town in America*. New York: Princeton Architectural Press, 1991.

Moneo, J. R. *Rafael Moneo, 1990–2000*. Madrid: El Croquis, 2000.

Portzamparc, C. de. *Christian de Portzamparc (interview)*. Edited by Y. Futagawa. Tokyo: A.D.A. Edita, 1995.

Schneider, B. *Daniel Libeskind: Jewish Museum Berlin: Between the Lines*. Munich and New York: Prestel, 1999.

Trachtenberg, M. "The Lithic Trains of Gae Aulenti." *Art in America* 76 (Jan. 1988), 104–7.

Young, J. E. *At Memory's Edge: After-Images of the Holocaust in Contemporary Art and Architecture*. New Haven: Yale University Press, 2000.

Acknowledgments

The authors acknowledge their indebtedness to the many people who have helped them in the process of completing the first and second editions of this book. For reading portions of the manuscript and making valuable comments, and for other assistance they are grateful to Rosemarie H. Bletter, Beverly L. Brown, Jean-Louis Cohen, Ogden Goelet, Donald P. Hansen, Joel Herschman, Beth L. Holman, Eugene J. Johnson, Carol H. Krinsky, Sarah B. Landau, Ralph Lieberman, Robert Mark, Thomas Mathews, James R. McCredie, Peter Menz, Victoria Newhouse, Alina Payne, the late Richard Pommer, Christopher Riopelle, Anne-Marie Sankovitch, Priscilla P. Soucek, Suzanne Stephens, Edward Sullivan, and Guy Walton. A special debt of gratitude for photographic and technical assistance is owed to Philip Evola, and for judgment and guidance to Jerome E. Hyman. The authors are also grateful to Theresa Flanigan, who insightfully researched the expanded bibliography in the second edition.

The authors are appreciative of a dedicated team at Harry N. Abrams, who saw the first edition through many stages of editing and production. They wish to specially acknowledge Nora Beeson for editing a manuscript of such large proportions, John K. Crowley for assembling the corpus of photographs, and Judith Michael, the talented designer of the book, as well as Barbara Lyons, Ivan Stoler, and Anne Levy. In preparing the second edition, the authors are again indebted to the Abrams staff, in particular the editor Holly Jennings, the project manager Katherine Rangoon Doyle, again Judith Michael and John Crowley, and, for her sage consultation as director of textbook publishing, Julia Moore. For their continuing support of the project, they thank Paul Gottlieb and Margaret Kaplan.

Index

Architecture: 6-2, 6-3, 6-5; Hoeber, F., *Peter Behrens,* 1913: 12-61; Hoyle, F. *On Stonehenge,* 1977: 1-9; © Hursley, Timothy: 14-11, 14-12; Institute of Fine Arts, N.Y., courtesy of: 11-27; Istituto di Etrus. e Antichita Ital.: 3-2; Isituto Geog. Mil., Florence: 7-90; *Jahrbuch d. Dtsch. Werkbundes,* 1915: 12-44; Jencks, C., *Architecture Today,* 1982: 13-22; Jencks, C., *Post Mod. Class.,* Arch. Design, 3/80: 13-29; Johnson/Burgee Arch., courtesy of: 13-30; Josse: 9-47; Karo, G., *Führer durch Tiryns,* 1934: 1-63; Kempf, T., *Neue Ausgrabungen in Dtsch.:* 4-25; Kersting, A. F.: 3-89, 6-13, 7-43, 7-58, 7-61, 9-10, 9-73, 9-74, 9-75, 9-79, 10-10, 10-13,10-24, 11-46, 11-64, 12-46; Kidder-Smith, G. E.: 1-36, 3-44, 4-28, 6-10, 6-12, 9-23, 12-58, 13-5,13-21; Kleinschmidt, *Die Basil. S. Fran. in Assisi:* 7-68; Koldeney, R. and Puchstein, O., *Die griechischen Tempel:* 2-8; Krautheimer, R., *Early Christian and Byzantine Architecture,* 1965: 4-2, 4-7, 4-13, 4-15, 4-47; Krischen, F., *Die griechische Stadt,* 1938: 2-22; Krischen, F.: 2-41, 2-52; Kunst Museum, Basel: 12-66; Ladafalch, J. P., *La Geo. et Les Orig. du Prem. Art Rom.,* 1935: 5-24; Laev: 4-1; La France, R.: 13-20; Lambot, Ian: 14-1, 14-2; Lampl, P.: 4-5, 4-6, 4-20, 4-47; Landesmuseum, Trier: 3-61, 3-62; Lauer J. P.: 1-12; Lauer, J. P., *Fouilles a Saqqarah:* 1-17; Lawrence, A. W., *Greek Architecture,* 1957: 2-34, 2-59; Le Corbusier, *Vers une Architecture.:* 12-2; Le Corbusier, *Oeuvre Complète:* 12-74, 12-75, 12-80, 12-97; Ledoux, C.-N., *L'Architecture Considérée sous le Rapport de l'Art, des Moeurs et de la Législation,* 1804: 10-37, 10-38, 10-42; Lescaze, W.: p. 582; Letrauoilly, *Les Edifices:* 8-52*; Lib. of the Roy. Inst. of Brit. Arch.:* 11-84; Libeskind, Daniel, courtesy of: 14-52; Lloyd, S. Muller, H. W., and Martin, R., *Ancient Architecture: Mesopotamia, Egypt, Crete, Greece,* 1972: 1-38; Lotz, Hilda: 8-18; Luckhaus Studio, Los Angeles: 12-86; MacDonald, W., *Perspecta, IV,* 1954: 4-31; Mack, R., *Experiments In Gothic Structure,* 1982: 7-25, 7-59, 7-63; Mainfrankisches Museum, Würzburg: 9-61; Mainstone, R., *Developments in Structural Form,* 1975: 3-14, 11-52, 11-62; Makinen, E.: 13-8; Mango, C., *Byzantine Architecture,* Electa Ed., Milan, 1974: 4-39, 4-40, 4-43; Martinelli, A.: 13-35; Mary Evans Pict. Lib.: 11-48; MAS, Barcelona: 6-1, 6-9, 7-64, 8-93, 9-71, 12-35, 12-36; Masser, Phyllis Dearborn: 8-72, 8-74; Mates, R.: 12-89; Maucher, J. P.: 13-33; McCormick, T. J.: 11-19; McGrath, N.: 13-1, 13-25; *McGraw-Hill Encyclopedia of World Art,* 1961: 1-21; McKenna, R.: 8-56; McPeak, E.: 10-17; Met. Museum of Art, N.Y.: 1-37, 10-7, 10-8, 12-31; Met. Mus. of Art *Bulletin,* sp. 1973: 1-39; Meyers, M., *Global Architecture, Louis I. Kahn:* 13-17, 13-18; Michalowski, K., *Art of Ancient Egypt:* 1-15, 1-33; Middleton, R. and Watkin, D., *Neo-Classical and 19th Century Architecture,* 1977: 10-3, 10-34, 10-43, 11-50; Mies van der Rohe Archive, MoMA: 12-45; Millon, H. and Frazer, A., *Key Monuments in the History of Architecture:* 2-28, 2-29, 2-56, 3-64, 3-74, 3-84, 4-29, 4-35, 4-37, 5-15, 5-35; Ministry of Works, London: 1-10; *Mittelaterische Stadt. in der Toskana:* 7-89; Moncalvo, R., Turin: 9-34, 9-35, 9-36, 9-38; Moneo, Rafael, courtesy of: 14-46, 14-47, 14-48;

Muller, K., *Tiryns:* 1-62; Musée du Louvre: 1-44; Museo Civico, Como: 12-52; Museum of Brit. Transport, London: 11-68; Museum of Finnish Arch.: 13-6, 13-7, 13-10; Museum of Modern Art, N.Y.: 12-24, 12-39, 12-63, 12-72, 12-83; Museum of the City of N.Y.: 12-15, 13-2; National Gallery of Art, London: 10-18; National Gallery of Art, Wash., Kress Coll.: 8-24; Nat. Buildings Record, London: 9-82, 11-18, 11-40; Nat. Monuments Record, London: 11-44, 11-47, 11-74; Newberry, S. W.: 11-45; Nationalmuseum, Stockholm: 10-40; National Trust, London: 10-19 Oriental Inst., Univ. of Chicago: 1-48, 1-49, 1-53; OMA/Rem Koolhaas: 14-27, 14-28; Perrot and Chipiez, *History of Art in Persia,* 1892: 1-55; Pevsner, N., *An Outline of European Architecture,* 1943: 5-5, 5-6, 5-8, 5-11, 5-19, 5-37, 7-21, 7-33, 7-44, 7-81; Photo "Rex": 7-62; Phyllis Lambert Collection: 8-39; Piano, Renzo, courtesy of: 14-10; Pierrain-Carnavalet, Paris: 10-30; Powell, J.: 4-41, 4-42; © Poulet, Claude/Getty Images: 14-5; Pugin, *The Present State of Ecclesiastical Architecture in England,* 1843: 11-43; *Quaderni dell'Istituto di Storia dell'Arch.:* 9-37; Radio City Music Hall: 13-4; Railway Museum, England: 11-67; Rave, P., *Karl Friedrich Schinkel,* 1941: 11-5, 11-6; Reinharde Goutard and Co.: 11-56; Renfrew, Collin, *Scientific Am.,* Nov. 1983: p. 589; Renger-Patzch, A.: 12-62; © Richter, Ralph/architektur-photo/Esto: 14-35; © Richters, Christian/Esto: 14-38; Rimmel, E., *Recollections of the Paris Exhibition of 1867,*1868: 11-85; Robb and Garrison, *History of Western Art:* 3-10, 3-11; Richard Rogers Partnership, courtesy of: 14-6; Rossi, Paolo, A.: 8-2; Roubier, Jean: 5-29, 5-35, 5-36, 7-1, 8-91; Royal Commission on Anc. Monuments, Scotland: 11-16, 11-17; Royal Pavilion Art Gall. and Mus.: 12-7; Sammlung Architektonischer Entwürfe-Leo von Klenze, 1830: 11-7; Sankovitch, A. M.: 10-35, 10-36, 12-34; Scala/Art Resource, N.Y.: 8-27; Schaeffer, J. H.: 11-24; Schaubild, V. J.: 2-36; Schede, M.: 2-20; Schmidt-Glassner, Helga: 5-13, 5-18, 8-88, 9-56, 9-58, 11-34; Schulz, B. and Winnefeld, H., *Baalbek,* I: 3-43; Science Museum, London: 11-60, 11-65; *Scientific Am.,* Nov., 1981: 4-26; *Scientific Am.,* April, 1964: 1-3, 1-4; *Scientific Am.,* May, 1969: 1-2; Seagrams, courtesy of: 12-96; Sekler, E., *Josef Hoffmann, The Architectural Work,* 1985: 12-48; Service Photographiques, Musées Nat., Paris: 8-58; Sheldon, G. W., *Artistic Country Seats,* v. 1, 1886–87: 12-9, 12-11; © Shinkenchiku-sha: 14-8, 14-44, 14-45; Sir John Soane's Museum, London: 10-57, 10-59, 10-60, 10-61, 10-62, 10-63, 10-64; SITE: 13-37; Smith, Edwin: 9-80, 10-20, 10-21, 11-14, 11-51; Smith, Malcolm: 13-12; Smith W. S., *The Art and Architecture of Ancient Egypt,* 1958: 1-27, 1-41; Solomon R. Guggenheim Museum: 12-90; Soprintendenza Art. e Storici di Firenze: 1-29; Staatliche Bildstelle: 3-55, 11-4; Staatliche Museen Zu Berlin: 1-56, 2-54; Staatliches Museum, Schwerin: 9-7; Stadtarchiv Stuttgart: 12-84; Stettler, *Jahrbuch des Röm. German. Zentral-Museums Mainz,* IV, 1956: 4-24; Stierlin, H., Geneva: 1-18; Stoedtner, Franz, Düsseldorf: 12-33, 12-49, 12-57, 12-60; Ezra Stoller/Esto: 12-107, 12-110, 12-111, 13-16; Stratton, A., *Life . . . Wren:* 10-27; Tafuri, M. and

Dal Co, F., *Modern Architecture:* 12-76, 12-101; © Wim Swann: 9-70; Thames and Hudson: 8-53; Thomas Air Views, 13-3; Thomas Jefferson Mem. Found.: 11-21; Thudichum, F.: 9-59; Time, P., *Tell el Amarna vor der Dtsch. Aus. im Jahre 1911:* 1-41; Tourino Club Italiano, Milan: 1-8, 3-28, 3-29, 3-64; Trachtenberg, Marvin: 1-65, 1-66, 2-1, 2-6, 2-7, 2-8, 2-10, 2-18b, 2-27, 2-32, 2-33, 2-38, 2-45, 2-48, 2-51, 2-57, 2-58, 3-9, 3-17, 3-27, 3-38, 3-39, 3-40, 3-53, 3-54, 3-59, 3-65, 3-69, 3-70, 3-86, 4-9, 4-11, 4-17, 4-19, 4-30, 4-32, 4-34, 4-44, 4-48, 5-7, 5-27, 5-28, 5-34, 5-39, 5-41, 5-42, 5-43, 5-44, 5-45, 5-46, 5-48, 5-51, 5-55, 5-57, 5-58, 5-59, 5-60, 6-4, 6-15, 7-2, 7-3, 7-4, 7-9, 7-10, 7-12, 7-13, 7-14, 7-15, 7-16, 7-17, 7-18, 7-27, 7-28, 7-29, 7-30, 7-36, 7-37, 7-38, 7-39, 7-42, 7-45, 7-47, 7-48, 7-49, 7-50, 7-51, 7-52, 7-53, 7-54, 7-55, 7-56, 7-57, 7-60, 7-66, 7-77, 7-69, 7-70, 7-71, 7-72, 7-73, 7-76, 7-79, 7-83, 7-86, 7-87, 7-88, 7-91, 7-93, 7-94, 7-95, 7-96, 7-98, 8-3, 8-4, 8-5, 8-8, 8-9, 8-10, 8-14, 8-15, 8-16, 8-17, 8-19, 8-21, 8-23, 8-25, 8-26, 8-28, 8-31, 8-32, 8-33, 8-34, 8-36, 8-37, 8-44, 8-46, 8-48, 8-49, 8-50, 8-51, 8-63, 8-65, 8-66, 8-68, 8-69, 8-70, 8-71, 8-76, 8-79, 8-83, 8-87, 8-90, 9-2, 9-3, 9-5, 9-6, 9-13, 9-16, 9-17, 9-18, 9-25, 9-26, 9-30, 9-31, 9-32, 9-33, 9-40, 9-51, 9-57, 9-63, 9-66, 9-67, 9-72, 9-78, 10-28, 10-48, 11-1, 11-11, 11-12, 11-13, 11-25, 11-38, 11-39, 11-49, 11-53, 11-57, 11-73, 11-78, 11-79, 11-80, 11-81, 12-1, 12-23, 12-27, 12-38, 12-50, 12-77, 12-78, 12-79, 12-85, 12-91, 12-92, 12-94, 12-95, 12-100, 12-102, 12-103, 12-106, 13-15, 13-31, 13-32, 14-26, pp. 49–52, 372–73, 583–86, 588, 590, and endpapers; Tschumi, Bernard, courtesy of: 14-24, 14-25; Uffizi, Florence: 8-42; Underwood, Austin: 1-1; Univ. of Virginia: 11-23; V. Aragozzini Foto.: Milan, 8-35; Van Milligen, A., *Byzantine Churches in Constantinople,* 1912: 4-33; Venturi, R. D., *Complexity and Contradiction in Architecture,* 1966: 13-19; Vertut, Jean: 1-25; Verzone, P., *Arte del Primo Milleno:* 1-31, 4-14; Viñoly, Rafael, courtesy of: 14-13; Viollet, Roger, Paris: 1-34, 8-84, 11-28, 11-75; Viollet, Roger/Getty Images: 14-51; Viollet-le-Duc, E.-E., *Dictionnaire Raisoné de l'Architecture Française du XIè au XVIè siècle:* 7-26, 7-28, 7-29, 7-30, 7-31, 7-32, 7-33, 7-34, 7-35, 7-40; Viollet-le-Duc, E.-E., *Discourses on Architecture,* 1959: 12-3, 12-4; Viollet-le-Duc, E.-E. (Prop. KG VI): 7-84; Virginia State Capitol: 11-22; *Vitruvius Brit.,* v. 4, 1767: 10-2; von Gerkan, A., *Das Theater in Priene,* 1921: 2-61, 2-63; von Gerkan, A., *Das Theater in Priene,* 1921, photo Eric Pollitzer: 2-63; von Matt, Leonard: 3-1, 3-8, 3-48, 4-12, 8-62, 8-64, 9-1, 9-8; von Simson, O., *The Gothic Cathedral, Origins of Gothic Architecture and the Medieval Concept of Order,* 1956: 7-11; Ward-Perkins, J. B., *Roman Arch.,* 1974: 3-32, 3-47; Webb, G. *Architecture in Britain, the Middle Ages:* 7-46; Werlman, Hans, Hectic Pictures: 14-29; Wiegrand, T. and Schrader, H., 1904: 2-19; Woldbye, C., Museum of Decorative Art, Copenhagen: 11-20; Wyss, Kurt, Basel: 13-13; Yan Reportage Photographique, Toulouse: 5-31, 8-94; Zimmerman, W., *Das Münster zu Essen,* 1956: 5-14; Text © Zugmann, Gerald: 14-14, 14-15; Text from *Complexity and Contradiction in Architecture* by R. D. Venturi, © Museum of Modern Art, 1966: p. 535.